DATE DUE

~~DE 16 '01~~			
~~6 '08~~			
NO - 6 '09			

DEMCO 38-296

The Stop-Motion Filmography

The Stop-Motion Filmography

A Critical Guide to 297 Features Using Puppet Animation

NEIL PETTIGREW

WITH A FOREWORD BY
Ray Harryhausen

McFarland & Company, Inc., Publishers
Jefferson, North Carolina, and London

Frontispiece: *King Kong* (1933), conceived by Merian C. Cooper and brought to life by Willis O'Brien, is still the yardstick against which all stop-motion characters must be measured.

British Library Cataloguing-in-Publication data are available

Library of Congress Cataloguing-in-Publication Data

Pettigrew, Neil, 1956–
The stop-motion filmography : a critical guide to 297 features using puppet animation / Neil Pettigrew ; with a foreword by Ray Harryhausen.
p.   cm.
Includes bibliographical references and index.
ISBN 0-7864-0446-9
Arrestox B library binding
Alkaline paper : 50# Finch Opaque and 60# Sterling Litho Gloss ∞
1. Animation (Cinematography)
2. Puppet films — History and criticism.
I. Title.
TR897.5.P495   1999   791.43'3 — dc21   98-49799 CIP

Manufactured in the United States of America

McFarland & Company, Inc., Publishers
Box 611, Jefferson, North Carolina 28640

For Lamphun, my wife

Contents

Acknowledgments   viii

Foreword (by Ray Harryhausen)   1

Preface   3

Introduction   7

The Stop-Motion Filmography   29

*[There are two 16-page color sections,
containing 51 photographs in chronological order;
the first is between pages 200 and 201
and the second, between pages 488 and 489]*

Appendix A: Artists' Filmographies   791

Appendix B: Stop-Motion Effects Academy Awards and Nominations   801

Appendix C: Stop-Motion Top Ten Lists   805

Appendix D: Stop-Motion Memorabilia Price Guide   811

Glossary   815

Bibliography   823

Index   825

Acknowledgments

This book has been many years in the making. It began in 1969, when I was 13 years old. I had persuaded my father to take me to see *The Valley of Gwangi* at the Classic Cinema in Brixton, South London. Afterwards, I returned home to write three frantic foolscap pages of critique about what I then considered — and still do consider — the finest film experience of all time. That critique has been rewritten many times since then, eventually reaching the form it takes in this volume, but some of the ideas and turns of phrase penned back in 1969 can still be found lurking among the allegedly more mature prose.

Of course, in 1969 I had no idea that I would eventually write a book about stop-motion animation. I simply continued to watch all the films, and as a personal *aide mémoire*, I scribbled notes about the animation scenes. Over the years, the scribbled notes became more and more detailed. I continued to seek out films containing stop-motion, even though the task of tracking many of them down became more and more like detective work. By the late 1980s I realized I had the makings of a book.

Then the hard work began. The daunting task of transforming my notes into a comprehensive and accurate work of reference required the assistance of a number of people. Some helped in small ways, others in more significant ways, but all helped gladly and graciously. Some supplied extra information and reference material, some looked over the early drafts of chapters and made corrections and suggestions, and some helped out with illustrations. Others did some much-needed proofreading or assisted with computer problems.

Those who helped out include David Allen Productions, Steven Archer, Yancy Calzada, Randy Cook, Jim Danforth, Randy Dutra, Chris Endicott, Raj Gohil, Mike Hankin, Ray Harryhausen, Tim O'Sullivan, Rowland Pettigrew, the Tippett Studio, Harry Walton and the late Gene Warren. To all of you, and anyone else I should have mentioned, my thanks.

Foreword

Since the advent of computer generated imagery as a filmmaking medium, the critics and media have declared that so-called puppet animation is dead. But puppet animation — of which stop-motion animation is one kind — is *not* dead. Three-dimensional animated figures are alive and well. The announcement of their demise is definitely premature.

Granted, computer animation has had a tremendous impact on the public. Advertising companies constantly bombard our TV airways with some of the most amazing visual images ever seen. So amazing, in fact, that they make one forget the product that is being put on the market. Every news program seems to have an introduction that includes computer generated imagery. The use of CGI is so common that the public will eventually take it for granted.

Aardman Studios and Nick Park have contributed enormously to a revival of interest in claymation through their short films *Creature Comforts* and *Wallace and Gromit.* The *Thunderbirds* television programs have restimulated interest in the long forgotten string puppet. Jim Henson was responsible for giving new life to the age-old hand puppet, the use of which dates back to ancient Greece.

As I see it, the computer is another tool, a glorious one I know, but only a tool. There is room for every technique, known and unknown, whose final aim is to entertain.

I followed in the footsteps of Willis O'Brien in making the animated figurine a *star* in feature motion pictures, where the live-action characters interact with the stop-motion figures in a most intimate way.

Stop-motion photography will always be remembered as a twentieth century art form. Its achievement is the creation of an illusion of artificial life, acting and reacting in a world of its own fantasy and imagination.

Ray Harryhausen
Fall 1998

Preface

This book is an alphabetical survey of full-length films that have featured stop-motion photography combined with live action. Each film is assessed with regard both to its dramatic and technical qualities and to its contributions to the medium of stop-motion. It is not intended to be a practical guide to animation. Other books and journals have examined, for example, the different methods of model construction, the processes involved in optically compositing two pieces of film, the special customized cameras used, and so on. All these subjects will be discussed in the course of the text, but not as separate topics.

The Stop-Motion Filmography grew out of this author's desire to know more about the specific content of stop-motion films. Often a fabulous special effects scene comes and goes in a couple of minutes, almost too fast for viewers to take in all of the shots that make up the sequence; we are too caught up in the drama of the action to strip it down to its components. This, of course, is the director's intention. But that sequence is a labor of love on the part of its creator(s), representing weeks or perhaps months of effort. It *deserves* to be analyzed more closely.

For example, almost any publica-tion on the subject of stop-motion hails the allosaurus scene in Ray Harry-hausen's *One Million Years B.C.* as a clas-sic — yet, as far as this author is aware, no one has actually documented in de-tail *why* it so good. It is an elaborate four-minute sequence containing 42 skillfully edited cuts. The clever way that Harryhausen controls the pace and stage-manages the choreography of his puppet and the actors shows him at the height of his powers. By examining in-dividual shots in detail, as will be done in this book, it is possible to see *exactly* why he is a first-rate artist.

How should a stop-motion sequence be analyzed? There are six chief areas for criticism:

(1) How does the model rate for design, level of detail and mobility?

(2) How realistic is the animation, i.e., is the choreography correct and imaginative?

(3) To what extent does the puppet interact with its live-action environ-ment?

(4) What is the quality of the tech-niques used to composite different pieces of film into one shot?

(5) How well directed is the sequence?

6) How well integrated is the sequence into the film as a whole?

The director of a scene not involving special effects has to consider lighting, camera movement, the positions of his actors and the choreography of their actions. The designer of an animation scene has to consider all this and more. He has to imbue his lifeless puppet with credible movement, combine it with the live-action photography and synchronize moments of interaction between puppet and actors. Each shot can be a complex tableau of ingredients, and the result is a dynamic image whose total effect is, in varying degrees, greater than the sum of its parts.

Fan publications devoted to the subject (all defunct today), such as the four issues of the legendary *FXRH* magazine (the title is a kind of acronym for "Effects by Ray Harryhausen"), *Close-Up* or *Cinemagic*, contained the kind of in-depth coverage that more mainstream books and magazines lacked. These publications interviewed animators, assessed the quality of model construction, reproduced series of individual frame enlargements, pored over the aesthetics of animation choreography in particular scenes, and gauged the success of individual moments where a model has been combined with live-action footage.

But these magazines, because of their intermittent publication schedules, lacked the space to take the analysis even further. *The Stop-Motion Filmography* attempts to give an in-depth analysis of *every* puppet animation sequence in *every* film that has featured the process

in combination with live-action footage. Every time one of Harryhausen's monsters enters the frame, it is an image to treasure. These are fantastic tableaux to relish, as well as technical achievements whose camera trickery deserves to be understood in full.

In the past, scholars of animation had to catch their favorite films in erratic television screenings or re-release matinees in remote cinemas. There we would sit, glued to TV or movie screens, trying to commit every sequence to memory. But since the early 1980s, the common availability of the video recorder has allowed the luxury of watching these films whenever we wish and as often as we wish. Not only that, but we can freeze any image that is particularly appealing, and watch in slow motion any sequence whose complexity of design and choreography does not give up its secrets at normal projection speed. Could any monster lover ask more?

In the pages that follow, virtually every puppet animation shot that has appeared in a feature film is itemized, dissected and assessed. Readers may find their enjoyment of both text and film increased by reading these discussions in conjunction with watching the films on video. Where the author has made a "best guess" at explaining a shot, readers may wish to determine whether that guess agrees with their own interpretation.

This book is for anyone who has ever wondered how many stop-motion shots there are in *King Kong*, or where the matte lines are hidden in *The 7th Voyage of Sinbad*. All the spears, ropes and rocks that start out as props in actors' hands and then miraculously switch to miniature versions when they make contact with a stop-motion puppet are singled out for praise or otherwise. Whenever an animator has taken pains to improve a shot by having a puppet throw a shadow in a live-action area, or by having a partial miniature set merge with the live-action image, or by introducing painted or miniature props to enhance an illusion, or employs any of the other tricks that make a shot more dramatic and plausible — all these moments are assessed.

While this kind of analysis may increase appreciation of the skills involved, readers may fear that it will reduce the spontaneous enjoyment of the films. But it need not: Analysis and enjoyment are separate processes that should be carried out on separate occasions. In some cases, watching sequences out of context may actually be a good thing. For example, *Sinbad and the Eye of the Tiger* is on the whole an inadequately scripted film, and the finale, an appearance by a sabertooth tiger, upsets the pace and seems gratuitous. However, watching the finale as a self-contained episode reveals it to be a dynamic and beautifully crafted action sequence.

There need be no conflict between spontaneity and in-depth study. On one occasion, this author will watch a stop-motion sequence and consciously analyze how each shot was created. But on another occasion, he will watch the same sequence and suppress this analytical side. A striking image or sequence still fills him with a sense of wonder, and no matter how many times he watches *The Valley of Gwangi* he is always enthralled and on the edge of his seat.

Notes on the Format of This Book

Films are listed in alphabetical sequence. Foreign language films are listed under their country-of-origin titles where known, with English translations and alternate titles provided as cross references.

Each entry begins with the cast and credits for that film. Where someone has contributed to a stop-motion sequence but has not received a screen credit, this is noted.

Each film is awarded a double rating. The first rating assesses the film as a whole; the second rating assesses the quality of the stop-motion content. This distinction is necessary because often a poor film will contain superior stop-motion effects or, conversely, a good film may contain inferior animation. A one- to four-star rating system is used; one star signifies "poor" and four stars signify "excellent." Where the stop-motion content is very brief or purely functional, it will generally not be awarded more than a "☆☆½" rating. For example, *Indiana Jones and the Temple of Doom* contains a few seconds of technically first-rate animation composites, but since they are barely noticed by audiences and do not constitute an application of stop-motion for significant dramatic purposes, a higher rating is not appropriate.

This book does not discuss puppet animation feature films that have no live-action content and never attempt to convince that their puppets are living characters. Consequently, Michael Myerberg's *Hansel and Gretel* (1954), Jiří Trnka's *A Midsummer Night's Dream* (1959), *Mad*

Monster Party? (1967), *Dougal and the Blue Cat* (1972), Will Vinton's *Comet Quest* (1986) and others are excluded. Such films operate on a different dramatic level and evoke quite different reactions from an audience.

The Animal World (1956), on the other hand, *does* intend us to perceive its animated dinosaurs as living creatures and so is included, despite the fact that its stop-motion sequence features no live action.

The Daydreamer (1966) is included because, although its puppets are never more than puppets, they are featured in some composite shots in which they interact with live actors, a juxtaposition that immediately gives them a greater degree of plausibility and drama.

Films in which inanimate objects are made to move (such as a rope in *The Invisible Man Returns* [1940] and the spacecraft in *Earth vs. the Flying Saucers* [1956]) are included because we are meant to perceive that these moving objects are part of the live-action drama.

There are only two exceptions to the exclusion criteria. The short films of Willis O'Brien contain no live action but are included because they are crucial in tracing the early development of the man who is regarded as the founding father of stop-motion. The 1993 all-puppet film *The Nightmare Before Christmas* is also included because at the time of its release it seemed to herald a renaissance of interest in the process, and because it featured work by a number of artists who have made significant contributions to other films discussed in the book.

Abbreviations used in film credits are as follows: **Prod:** producer; **D:** director; **Scr:** screenplay; **Ph:** director of photography; **Art:** art director or production designer; **Mus:** music.

The author welcomes information regarding any films that may have been omitted in this book; such information should be sent care of the publisher.

Introduction

The essence of the cinema's appeal is that it is a world of illusions, and some of the grandest illusions of all have been created by a special effects process known as stop-motion photography.

In *King Kong* (1933), a giant ape fends off fighter biplanes from the dizzying summit of the Empire State Building. In *Jason and the Argonauts* (1963), set in mythological Greece, the title characters are attacked by a clattering horde of sword-wielding skeletons. In *The Valley of Gwangi* (1969), a posse of cowboys in turn-of-the-century Mexico tries to lasso a vicious prehistoric allosaurus. And in *The Empire Strikes Back* (1981), the second part of George Lucas' *Star Wars* trilogy, a division of elephantine mechanical giants on hundred-foot legs stomps across a snow-covered planet, firing cannons at a rebel outpost.

These surreal images tap the same area of our subconscious that fairy tales touched when we were children, startling us, exciting a sense of wonder and making our imaginations soar. This is the cinema doing what it does best, depicting a make-believe world that causes a mental double-take: We know these things cannot be real, and yet there they are, up on the screen.

Most people are surprised to discover that these dynamic creations are puppets that in real life have never moved, and that few of them are over two feet tall. For some people, this is not only a surprise but a disappointment: Surely these giant beasts cannot be mere doll-sized mannequins? But almost without exception, any initial disappointment develops into fascination as one learns more about how these images have been crafted, how the puppets have been made to move and how ingenious processes can transform toy-sized puppets into seemingly gigantic creations with such charismatic grandeur, interacting with living actors. For many, learning to appreciate the skill that goes into such sequences becomes part of the thrill of watching them. So powerful are the best of these sequences that understanding the reality of their construction does not spoil the dramatic impact of the finished illusion, and they can be enjoyed over and over again.

How *do* these puppets move? Every strip of film is made up of individual pictures, or frames. Each second of screen time is made up of 24 separate frames. In stop-motion filming, miniature puppets are minutely and precisely repositioned and rephotographed 24 times for every second of film that is to appear on the screen. When this series of static images is projected at normal speed, the puppets take on lives of their own. Stop-motion is the ultimate illusion: Life has been created where there is none.

Stop-motion photography (also known as stop-frame, stop-action, dimensional animation and puppet animation) has provided some of the fantasy genre's most unforgettable sequences, yet surprisingly it is a specialist art practiced by only a very few individuals and in very few films. By 1977, the cinema had been around for over 80 years but there had been fewer than 50 feature films that made significant use of puppet animation. Of these, 21 had been the work of just two men, the gurus of stop-motion, Willis H. O'Brien and Ray Harryhausen.

The reason for this scarcity is that stop-motion is a time-consuming process, which makes it unpopular with film producers. Investors who put up the funds for films want to see as quick a return as possible on their money. Stop-motion filming, requiring that models be moved one frame at a time and painstakingly synchronized with live-action footage, can tie up investors' money for several years before a finished product emerges. For example, production began on *Mighty Joe Young* in late 1946, but the film was not released until July 1949. The four-minute skeleton sequence in *Jason and the Argonauts* took Ray Harryhausen four and a half months to complete and was only one of many effects scenes in the film.

It is not only producers who are averse to using stop-motion. Many directors distrust the process because they feel it forces them to relinquish control of certain scenes to stop-motion anima-

tors, who add their creations during post-production. As a result, some directors choose less convincing methods of depicting fantasy characters because they can have them on the studio set, under their control, rather than relying on somebody else's special effects trickery.

In 1977, the huge commercial success of *Star Wars* ushered in a new era of fantasy filmmaking, rivaling the "Golden Age" of 1923 to 1936 and giving rise to a special effects renaissance. Stop-motion, along with a whole range of other advanced effects (special make-up effects, mechanical creations, optical processes, and puppetry of all kinds), was suddenly in demand.

The *Star Wars* boom also had an impact on the amounts of money that film producers were willing to spend on special effects sequences. Whereas prior to 1977 most fantasy films were low-budget affairs, fantasy filmmaking today is a multimillion-dollar business. Filmmakers at last have the luxury of being able to afford the quality special effects their films deserve. For example, *Terminator 2* (1991) cost approximately $100 million.

The cinema has come a long way from the genre movies of the 1950s when all it took was a catchy exploitation title like *Attack of the 50 Foot Woman* to attract audiences. Today's sophisticated moviegoers have higher standards and are more aware of the nature of special effects. Since 1977, they have been treated to a series of blockbuster fantasy movies with breathtaking special effects. Many of these have included stop-motion sequences, ranging from substantial episodes (such as the Scout Walker scene in *Return of the Jedi* [1983]) to features with a few barely noticeable animation shots (such as those in *Indiana Jones and the Temple of Doom* [1984]). Other big-budget fantasy films that have benefited, in varying degrees, from the use of stop-motion puppetry include *Robo-Cop* (1987), *Who Framed Roger Rabbit?* (1988), *Honey, I Shrunk the Kids* (1989), *Terminator 2* (1991), *Jurassic Park* (1993) and *James and the Giant Peach* (1996).

The last two decades have also seen stop-motion utilized successfully by the makers of many low-budget horror films. The process has been used to depict all manner of demonic creatures, eye-boggling monster transformations and gruesome zombie decompositions. Such films include *The Evil Dead* (1983*), House 2* (1986), *Hardcover* (1988) and *Braindead* (1992).

There is much current discussion of whether stop-motion photography is being made redundant by the rapidly developing medium of computer generated imagery (CGI). Certainly, it is now possible to achieve images with CGI that previously could be achieved only by stop-motion. Even so, stop-motion remains a highly popular process and continues to be used every year in a variety of film productions.

The Beginnings

The art of stop-motion is almost as old as the cinema. Its roots can be traced to the moment when one of the pioneers of the motion picture industry accidentally discovered trick photography. In 1896, Frenchman Georges Méliès was filming a street scene when his camera jammed, then restarted. When he later projected the footage, he was astonished to see a bus transform suddenly into a hearse.

Méliès had discovered time-lapse photography, and with it the motion picture's ability not only to deceive the eye of the audience but also to distract its perception of the passage of time. He went on to produce dozens of very popular short films of a whimsical, fantastic nature and single-handedly invented most of the trick devices still with us today: superimposition, dissolves, fades, wipes and so on. *The Haunted Castle* (1896 — considered to be the first horror film), *The Man with the Rubber Head* (1901), *A Trip to the Moon* (1902), *The Merry Frolics of Satan* (1906) and many others are regarded as classics of the early days of film fantasy. Working in his Paris studio, Méliès turned out films as fast as he could to satisfy his audiences' craving for fantasy. Consequently, he did not have the inclination to spend time developing stop-motion, and he is not regarded as a pioneer of the process. But he did use it on occasion, such as in *Cinderella* (1899), when he made a pumpkin transform into a coach.

Two years before *Cinderella*, the American company Vitagraph produced another early example of stop-motion in *Humpty Dumpty Circus*, which featured animated wooden toy animals. The same company's *A Visit to the Spiritualist* (1897) also used stop-motion. In 1906, Edwin S. Porter, best remembered for *The Great Train Robbery* (1903), produced a short film called *The Dream of a Rarebit Fiend* in which the title character's cheese-induced dream includes the sight of his bed dancing and leaping around his bedroom by means of crude stop-motion. The following year, Porter filmed *The Teddy Bears*, in which seven puppet bears were animated. Also in 1907, J. Stuart Blackton produced *The Haunted Hotel*, in which stop-motion was used to depict objects moving through ghostly intervention. Another film by Blackton, *Princess Nicotine* (1909), featured stop-motion cigarettes, matches and a pipe climbing into a box. In 1912, Edward Rogers made the first puppet film in color, *War in Toyland*.

In Russia in 1909, Władisław Starevicz used puppet animation in *Beyond the River Nyemen*, and he continued to make short films using the process right up until his death in 1965, when he was working on the unfinished *Like Dog and Cat*. His most famous films include *Mest's Kinematograficeskogo Operatora* (1912) with a cast of stop-motion insects, *In the Claws of the Spider* (1920) and *The Mascot* (1933). His elaborate films are uniquely surreal, featuring bizarre puppet characters often making dramatic movements in ways that still look remarkable today.

These films are interesting historically when tracing the development of stop-motion, but they fall outside the specific subject of this book. In these early films, the puppets are always merely puppets: We are not asked to perceive them as living beings. They are dolls or objects made to move by cinema trickery. This kind of filmmaking is a whole separate genre and has been the subject of several books. Today it remains a popular medium, most commonly used in children's television programs, countless commercials and short films. But because it never attempts to be realistic, it evokes a response altogether different

from our response to animation that perpetuates the illusion of life. It may be just as imaginative or technically skillful, but is less interesting dramatically because we are not asked to suspend our disbelief.

Willis O'Brien

In 1913, Willis H. O'Brien began exploring the potential of stop-motion for more dramatic ends. Fashioning cloth and rubber over simple-jointed wooden skeletons, he experimented with the possibilities of the medium, filming between 1914 and 1917 a series of five-minute comic films with prehistoric settings. Even today those films retain much of their charm, though, sadly, more than half are now lost. (As a general rule, *The Stop-Motion Filmography* does not include analysis of short films. However, an exception is made in the case of those by O'Brien, in the interest of painting a complete picture of his career.)

Public response to these was sufficient to get O'Brien the financial backing for a more ambitious project called *The Ghost of Slumber Mountain* (1919). This introduced live actors into his animated prehistoric tableaux, the camera cutting from models to actors to suggest simultaneity. *The Lost World* (1925) took this process one stage further, amazing contemporary audiences by combining models and actors in the same shot by means of some pioneering static matte and traveling matte processes. (See the glossary near the end of this book for an explanation of these and other technical terms.)

Willis O'Brien (right) on the set of *The Son of Kong* (1933).

In 1930, O'Brien began work at RKO Studios on his first sound feature, an elaborate prehistoric saga called *Creation*. But producer Merian C. Cooper canceled the production after only two sequences had been filmed, having decided that O'Brien's talents would be better served by a project of his own devising. He was quite right: *King Kong* (1933) remains today one of the most enthralling flights of fantasy ever put on film, and O'Brien's unrivaled effects sequences are still often used as a yardstick for other stop-motion efforts. The jungle sequences on Skull Island have a lush visual style that remains uniquely O'Brien's, while the finale of Kong fighting for his life atop the Empire State Building is one of cinema's most en-during images. Above all, he invested his steel and rubber puppet with a level of personality that made Kong one of the great tragic figures of the twentieth century.

RKO rushed out an acceptable sequel, *The Son of Kong* (1933), but O'Brien, dissatisfied with the results and suffering intense personal tragedy (his estranged wife had shot and killed his two sons), asked to have his name removed from the credits. Despite the enormous success of *King Kong*, it was 16 years before O'Brien would see his stop-motion effects up on the screen again. Various projects, most significantly *War Eagles* (about a lost tribe of Vikings who ride on the backs of giant prehistoric eagles) and *Gwangi* (about cowboys who capture an

Ray Harryhausen surrounded by some of his models from *Clash of the Titans* (1981).

allosaurus in a hidden valley and bring it back to civilization), were begun but never completed. At least when *Mighty Joe Young* (1949) eventually came to the screen, O'Brien had the satisfaction of receiving an Oscar for his work.

O'Brien subsequently worked on a number of films generally unworthy of his enormous talent, including *The Animal World* (1956), *The Black Scorpion* (1957) and *Behemoth the Sea Monster* (1959). Many other projects that he hoped to film were destined never to get past the storyboard stage. He died in 1962 while working on the designs for a minor effects sequence in Stanley Kramer's *It's a Mad Mad Mad Mad World*.

Ray Harryhausen

The creatures in Ray Harryhausen's films strut and stomp around the screen with a melodramatic force and sheer presence that no one else has matched.

It all started in 1933 when, at age 13, he saw *King Kong*. It had such a profound effect on him that he set out to understand and emulate the processes that had created the dinosaurs in O'Brien's magical fantasy world. Like O'Brien before him and other stop-motion artists after, he began shooting amateur films at home, teaching himself the techniques of the trade and using whatever materials were at hand. In 1938, he met O'Brien

Harryhausen (center) in the company of author Ray Bradbury (left) and cameraman Wilkie Cooper, afer receiving his Oscar on July 3, 1992. (Photograph by Arnold Kunert.)

on the set of *War Eagles* and showed him some of his models and drawings. In the early 1940s, they briefly worked together on the animation in George Pal's musical short films (called *Puppetoons*).

During the war years, Harryhausen worked for Frank Capra's film unit, helping to make propaganda films. He followed this work with a series of short fairy tales, his parents helping with the construction of armatures (the steel skeletons inside the puppets), sets and costumes.

His first feature film work came when he assisted O'Brien on *Mighty Joe Young*—in fact, 85 percent of the animation is Harryhausen's. In the 1950s he embarked on a solo career, demonstrating in a series of black-and-white sci-

ence fiction films that he was able to create spectacular effects on very limited budgets. The highly successful *Beast from 20,000 Fathoms* (1953) was followed by *It Came from Beneath the Sea* (1955), *Earth vs. the Flying Saucers* (1956) and *20 Million Miles to Earth* (1957). In 1956, he teamed with O'Brien again to create a brief but impressive prehistoric episode for Irwin Allen's documentary of animal life on earth, *The Animal World*. The classic fantasy *The 7th Voyage of Sinbad*, which has hardly dated since its release in 1958, forced him to stretch his talents further, the color photography making the composite designs that much more difficult to accomplish correctly.

Throughout the 1960s, Harryhausen

Ray Harryhausen and author Neil Pettigrew at Harryhausen's home in 1993.

maintained a successful partnership with producer Charles Schneer that had begun with *It Came from Beneath the Sea*. Together they produced a series of larger-budgeted fantasies that firmly established Harryhausen as leader of the field of special effects — not just as a model animator but as an all-around master of effects photography. These films were simple adventure stories, colorfully told with excitement and charm and often based on novels by classic authors: *The 3 Worlds of Gulliver* (1960) from Jonathan Swift, *Mysterious Island* (1961) from Jules Verne and *First Men in the Moon* (1964) from H.G. Wells.

Artistic success, however, was not always matched by commercial success.

Jason and the Argonauts (1963), which is Harryhausen's own favorite among his work and is often cited as containing his best work, merely broke even at the box office. *First Men in the Moon*, a delightful science fiction romp set in Victorian times, actually lost money. One can only assume that these disappointments were the result of inadequate and misleading publicity, because *Jason and the Argonauts*, a saga set in ancient Greece and boasting a dazzling array of special effects, is one of the finest fantasy films ever made.

Harryhausen broke away from Schneer to make *One Million Years B.C.* (1966) for Hammer Films in England. This lively prehistoric yarn is most memorable

Jim Danforth animates angels for a scene eventually dropped from *God's Army* (1995).

for a breathtaking battle between an allosaurus and a band of cavemen. Hammer's astute publicity department turned this one into a huge box office hit. He reteamed with Schneer for *The Valley of Gwangi* in 1969, taking as his inspiration O'Brien's old storyline about the discovery of fantastic creatures in a hidden valley where time has stood still. In this author's opinion, *Gwangi* is Harryhausen's finest work, a beautifully realized combination of the Western and prehistoric genres containing many extraordinarily evocative fantasy images and some of Harryhausen's most dynamic action sequences. Harryhausen blames this film's financial failure on the fact that it was released at the height of the "permissive era" when the public had

no interest in a conventional dinosaur story.

His films became more and more elaborate — so elaborate that there was now a wait of at least three years between releases. In the 1970s he returned to Arabian Nights territory, first with *The Golden Voyage of Sinbad* (1973) and then *Sinbad and the Eye of the Tiger* (1977). Both are full of impressive stop-motion sequences, but many critics were by now starting to complain that Harryhausen's storylines were lacking invention, serving merely as vehicles for the effects. This was certainly true of his last film, *Clash of the Titans* (1981), where an all-star cast and an astonishing amount of animation (he called in Jim Danforth and Steve Archer to assist) could not compensate

15

for a very stodgy script that never manages to grab one's attention.

Now retired, Harryhausen spends much of his time giving talks on his career at film societies and conventions in America and Europe, always finding an appreciative audience. Remarkably, not one of his films after *Mighty Joe Young* received an Academy Award for its special effects, nor even a nomination. But in 1992 he was awarded a special Academy Award recognizing a lifetime achievement in special effects. He insists that his retirement is permanent, but he has a legion of fans who cling to the hope that one day he will be tempted back to his animation table.

Other Stop-Motion Animators from the Earlier Era

For over sixty years — from *The Dinosaur and the Missing Link* (1914) to *Sinbad and the Eye of the Tiger* (1977) — the stop-motion genre was dominated by O'Brien and Harryhausen. Others had worked sporadically with the process, but only these two had consistently proved able to exploit the medium's potential, exercising creative control over their work and making commercially successful films.

Prominent among the ranks of other animators is Jim Danforth. He has produced outstanding stop-motion sequences in a number of films, including *Jack the Giant Killer* (1962), *The Wonderful World of the Brothers Grimm* (1962), *7 Faces of Dr. Lao* (1964) and his masterpiece, *When Dinosaurs Ruled the Earth* (1970). Always

trying to stretch the medium to new levels of realism and imagination, he received Academy Award nominations for these last two.

In the late 1970s, he began work on a film called *Timegate,* an ambitious project of his own devising that might have established him as an *auteur* of the same stature as Harryhausen. With almost full creative control over the production, Danforth would have fully exploited the potential of stop-motion as a medium for fashioning fantasy images. A trailer reel featuring a stop-motion tyrannosaurus was filmed, but for various reasons the project was shelved.

Danforth's later work includes assisting Harryhausen with the animation for *Clash of the Titans* (1981), for which he contributed some marvelous shots of the winged horse Pegasus in flight. He still contributes occasional animation to films, including sequences featuring the memorable hair-monsters in John Carpenter's compendium horror film *Body Bags* (1993) and some marvelous animation of an amiable dragon in *Dragonworld* (1994). He has also produced fine matte paintings for a number of films and is regarded as one of the best matte artists in the business.

Hungarian George Pal began his career in the 1930s making short puppet animation films in Hungary, Germany, France and Holland. In 1939, he emigrated to the United States, where he was soon filming a series of comic animation shorts called *The Puppetoons.* Subsequently, he produced or directed a number of full-length fantasy films, many of which have come to be regarded as classics, including *The War of the Worlds* (1953) and *The Time Machine* (1960). Although most of Pal's productions include brief stop-motion episodes, in the main his films are not remembered specifically for their stop-motion content but as inventive and highly palatable science fiction and "family" entertainment.

For the stop-motion episodes in his feature films, Pal relinquished much of the creative control—and all of the actual animation—to others. These sequences are the work of Gene Warren and Wah Chang, who, along with administrative partner Tim Barr, worked together as a company called Project Unlimited. Their output includes stop-motion episodes in *Tom Thumb* (1958), *The Time Machine* (1960), *The Wonderful World of the Brothers Grimm* (1962) and *The Power* (1968). Warren and Chang's early work includes performing animation for some of Pal's *Puppetoons* in the 1940s. Project Unlimited also supplied special effects on a budget for many other films of the period, frequently requiring extensive miniature work and often making use of stop-motion puppetry.

Warren and Chang hold a special place in the history of stop-motion. Their work has a colorful, whimsical nature that is irresistible and includes several classic sequences. But their puppet animation sequences often have a gaudy, playful look that suggests they were less interested in using stop-motion for realistic, dramatic effects.

In Czechoslovakia in the 1950s and 1960s, Karel Zeman created unique fantasy films featuring stop-motion in a style recalling the whimsical trickery of Georges Méliès. His work is full of marvelous imagery and offbeat moments of stop-motion, but his handful of films—including *Journey to the Beginning of*

Gene Warren in 1992.

Time (1954), *The Invention of Destruction* (1958) and *On the Comet* (1970)— never saw significant theatrical release in the United States and Britain, and even today remain obscure. They are ripe for rediscovery.

Later Stop-Motion Animators

In the last two decades of the twentieth century, the exclusivity enjoyed for so long by O'Brien and Harryhausen gave way to an explosion of stop-motion talent. The boom in fantasy filmmaking meant that suddenly, a whole generation

Gene Warren and Wah Chang on the set of *The Time Machine* (1960).

of O'Brien and Harryhausen fans found that their misspent childhoods, whiled away in dabbling with amateur stop-motion 8mm movies in their garages, had given them skills in demand by professional filmmakers. In the period 1925 to 1977, there had been approximately 50 films that contained stop-motion photography — an average of one a year. From 1977 through 1996, an average of eight such films appeared in the theaters every year. Some of these, such as *Howard the Duck* (1986), *The Golden Child* (1986) and *RoboCop 2* (1991), contain major stop-motion episodes that successfully exploit the potential of puppet animation. In others, the stop-motion content is extremely small, perhaps only one or two shots, with stop-motion artists having little creative control. Either way, it is clear that these have been boom years for puppet animation in terms of the sheer quantity of sequences that have featured the process. Today, the number of films featuring stop-motion stands at around 300.

David Allen has the longest track record of the current generation of animators. Early work includes contributions to *Equinox* (1968), *When Dinosaurs Ruled the Earth* (1970) and *Flesh Gordon* (1974). In 1978 he became involved with Charles Band, a producer with a liking for stop-motion and a commitment to making inventive low-budget fantasy films. Allen has subsequently worked on a host of films for Band, most notably *Laserblast* (1978), *Robot Jox* (1989) and *Bride of Re-Animator* (1990). Their relationship recalls the teamwork of Schneer and Harryhausen, albeit on a scale less grand. Away from Band, Allen has created remarkable puppet sequences for *Caveman* (1981), *Q the Winged Serpent* (1982) and major productions such as **batteries not included* (1987) and *Honey, I Shrunk the Kids* (1989). Ironically, the Oscar nomination he received for his work on *Young Sherlock Holmes* (1985) was for a puppet sequence that was achieved not with stop-motion but with string marionettes and rod puppets. Allen has the distinction of having contributed stop-motion sequences (many of them admittedly minor) to more films than any other person.

In 1978, Allen began work on *The Primevals,* a project written and directed by himself. This film is to tell the story of a group of explorers in the Himalayas who encounter a Yeti and some alien lizard-men. The production has been canceled and revived a dozen times since, but at the time of this writing it is all set for a 1999 release. By all accounts it will be well worth the wait — a film with a stop-motion artist in creative control, demonstrating the full potential of stop-motion as a medium for fantasy effects.

Doug Beswick did some superb animation for *Planet of Dinosaurs* (1979) and subsequently worked on stop-motion effects in sequences for *The Empire Strikes Back* (1980), *The Terminator* (1984), *The Evil Dead II* (1987), *Nightmare on Elm Street Part III* (1987), *Beetlejuice* (1988) and others. He has also spent time creating mechanical (that is, not stop-motion) puppet sequences, most memorably a vicious tyrannosaurus in *My Science Project* (1985).

Phil Tippett and Jon Berg produced a tiny but unforgettable sequence in *Star Wars* featuring a game of chess in which the pieces were miniature alien creatures. From such small acorns, mighty oak trees grow: Tippett has gone on to raise stop-motion effects to new heights of realism, helping to invent the go-motion process (a means of reducing the strobing effect of animation) and producing astonishing animation sequences in *Dragonslayer* (1982), *Return of the Jedi* (1983), *Ewoks — The Battle for Endor* (1985), *RoboCop 2* (1991) and others. For *Jurassic Park* (1993), he acted as "Dinosaur Supervisor," inventing choreography and supplying stop-motion footage on which subsequent computer generated imagery and full-size model movement were based. If anyone can claim to be Harryhausen's successor, then Tippett, initially working for George Lucas' Industrial Light and Magic effects group and now heading his own company, must be the number one contender. In the late 1990s, he has moved further away from conventional stop-motion and applies his talents to the development of CGI creatures.

The design of Tippett's puppet characters is always striking and original, and frequently sparked by a hint of the

Introduction

Steven Archer with the large Kraken model used for close shots in *Clash of the Titans* (1981). (Photograph by Simon Selby.)

absurd — for example, the mutant newt in *Piranha* (1978), the elephant-like tadpole monsters in *Ewoks — The Battle for Endor* or the four-legged Garthok in *Coneheads* (1993*)*. Once seen, they are never forgotten.

Randall William Cook has supplied impressive stop-motion for a number of films. He handled some of the animation in *Caveman*, also helped Allen on *Laserblast* and *Q the Winged Serpent,* and animated one of the monster manifestations of John Carpenter's *The Thing* (1982) (although most of his work on the latter ended up on the cutting room floor). Over the years, he has developed a distinctive style of animation, with

puppets making fast, dramatic moves, combined with live-action by means of inventive rotoscope matting. His style is most apparent in sequences with the unforgettable Terror Dogs in *Ghostbusters* (1984), the majestic Demon Lord in *The Gate* (1987) and the disturbingly credible Jackal Boy in *Hardcover* (1988).

Others who have made significant contributions to stop-motion sequences during the post–*Star Wars* boom include Pete Kleinow, Harry Walton, Steven Archer, Tom St. Amand, Dennis Muren, Ernest Farino, Laine Liska, James Aupperle and Randal Dutra. With the move away from the Harryhausen one-man-show style of moviemaking, some of

20

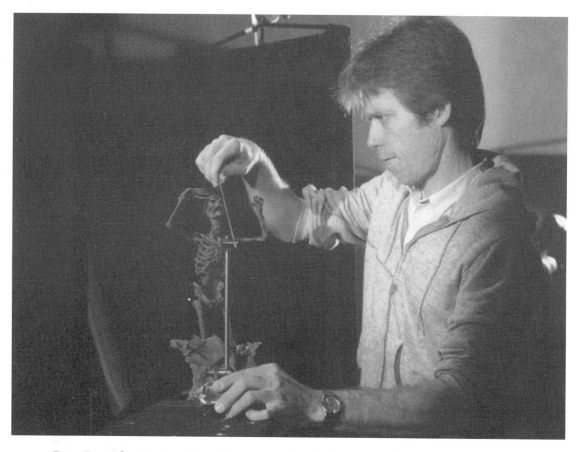

Doug Beswick animates the Freddy skeleton from *Nightmare on Elm Street III* (1987).

these artists may do less hands-on animation and tend to specialize in one area. For example, St. Amand is recognized as one of the industry's best armature makers, Aupperle specializes in lighting and photographing animation set-ups, and Muren designs and supervises sequences.

Between them, these artists have created a rich gallery of unforgettable fantasy creatures. The achievements of each of them is discussed in detail as each film is examined in the main section of this book. There are filmographies for each animator at the back of the book.

Stop-Motion Compared to Other Techniques

In the pursuit of quicker profits or greater realism, many techniques other than stop-motion have been used, with varying degrees of success, to animate creatures in fantasy films. In pre–*Star Wars* days, such attempts were often comically obvious and rarely successful.

Live lizards have had frills and spikes attached to them, been magnified by split-screen photography, and been tormented cruelly until they performed like the dinosaurs they were meant to be (*Journey to the Center of the Earth* [1959], the re-make of *The Lost World* [1960], and others). In such films, the results are invariably artificial and allow almost no interaction between the "dinosaur" and the live actors.

Actors have donned unlikely monster suits and wobbled awkwardly about miniature sets in slow-motion to suggest great size (*Godzilla* [1954], *Gorgo* [1961], and others). Children under the age of eight might be taken in, but nobody else. In *One Million B.C.* (1940), Victor Mature wrestled with an inanimate four-foot-long mock-up of a triceratops; he deserved an Oscar for keeping a straight face.

Other films have used half-size or even full-size mechanical props to represent giant creatures. While these are often elaborate and ingeniously built, their repertoire of movement is always restricted by their own cumbersome nature (the dragon in *Der Nibelungen* [1923-24], the clumsy 40-foot ape in the remake of *King Kong* [1976]). In the 1950s and 1960s, there was a glut of low-budget science fiction films featuring special effects that were done on the cheap: The "cucumber monster" of *It Conquered the World* (1956) and the "walking carpet" of *The Creeping Terror* (1964) are memorable only because they were so ridiculous. A series of films made in the 1970s by Amicus Studios based on books by Edgar Rice Burroughs featured many elaborate mechanical mock-ups of dinosaurs and other creatures. Most of them were poor, though a pair of styracosaurs in *The Land That Time Forgot* (1975) and a stegosaurus in *The People That Time Forgot* (1977) looked impressive; nevertheless, even they were unable to do much other than growl and sway about.

In post–*Star Wars* days, however, many brilliantly successful monster sequences have been achieved by means other than stop-motion. There have been major advances in rod puppetry, cable control, radio control, prosthetics, special make up effects, computer generated imagery and other techniques.

The terrifyingly believable title creature of *Alien* (1979), built by Carlo Rambaldi, was effective because it was only partly seen, except for a disappointing final shot in which it was revealed to be of vaguely humanoid shape after all. Rick Baker astonished everyone with his amazing man-to-werewolf transformations in *An American Werewolf in London* (1981), where the camera lingered on the sight of bones rearranging, a snout forming and hair growing. *The Thing* was an alien able to take on the shape of humans: make up wizard Rob Bottin showed the creature in the act of transforming, a dizzying array of swirling tentacles, ravenous mouths and disfigured limbs. Frank Oz and Jim Henson extended the skills they had honed in television's *The Muppets* to produce puppets of a more believable nature in *The Dark Crystal* (1983) and *Labyrinth* (1986), both films containing impressive menageries of grotesque beasts. *Return of the Jedi* (1983) included a huge slug-like creature called Jabba the Hutt, a credible mountain of wobbling flesh and lascivious expressions, brought to life by concealed operators.

The best non–stop-motion dinosaur for many years was the tyrannosaurus created by Doug Beswick for *My Science Project* (1985). But its movements were still very limited, and one couldn't help thinking that the half-million dollars spent on this scene could have been better spent on a ten-minute stop-motion episode.

Stan Winston took the possibilities of full-size mechanical dinosaurs to even greater heights in Steven Spielberg's *Jurassic Park*, building highly realistic models with an impressive range of movement. These were used for partial shots of the dinosaurs. Whenever a creature had to be seen in full, Spielberg used computer generated imagery (CGI). This, the newest of the alternative techniques to stop-motion, has only recently reached a level of sophistication that enables it to create convincing flesh-and-blood characters. For a long time, computer graphics always looked artificial, and it seemed that they would never be an acceptable substitute for other processes.

Early films using computer imagery — such as *Tron* (1982) and *The Last Starfighter* (1984) — were intriguing experiments, but their computer generated environments and spaceships simply did not look real enough. *The Abyss* (1990) took the medium one stage further with an impressive wormlike creature made to look as though it were composed entirely of water; this creature interacted convincingly with live actors. Dennis Muren, who supervised this scene, stretched the technology further in *Terminator 2* (1991), depicting a cyborg made of liquid steel who was able to transform from flesh to steel at will. These were marvelous images, but whether computer graphics were suitable for human and animal characters remained to be seen.

In *Death Becomes Her* (1992), Ken Ralston proved that *just maybe* they were. He used computer imagery to replicate human flesh, showing Meryl Streep's head twisting 180 degrees around on her neck: Her head and body were two separate pieces of film, and computer software did the rest. But in 1993 it was Muren again who astonished all longtime dinosaur lovers and stop-motion purists in *Jurassic Park*, putting on the screen a series of full-view shots of prehistoric animals stomping around with unprecedented realism. He and his team of computer artists demonstrated unequivocally that computer imagery *was* capable of depicting believable flesh-and-blood characters. After nearly a century of filmmaking, it was clear that there was an acceptable alternative to stop-motion animation.

If such sights as these can now be achieved with cable operated models, rod puppets and computer graphics, is there still a place for stop-motion filming? What can this laborious, intricate process offer today's filmmakers, who have so many alternative methods at their disposal? What are the merits of stop-motion over other methods, and what are its drawbacks? In particular, how can it compete with the kind of imagery seen in *Jurassic Park*?

In fact, stop-motion compares favorably with CGI in several respects. First, the cost of CGI is prohibitive and beyond the reach of most filmmakers. Only filmmakers with the clout of Spielberg or James Cameron (the director of both *Terminator* films) can even consider using them on the scale seen in *Jurassic Park*. Second, computer imagery is not currently flexible enough to allow significant interaction between live actors and the computer image; *Jurassic Park* contains few moments where the dinosaurs make physical contact with human characters. Third, is it truly practical, at the current level of technology, to realize with computer imagery a scene of the complexity of, for example, the Kong-tyrannosaurus fight in *King Kong*? Or could a computer generated horde of skeletons have an intimate swordfight with living actors as in *Jason and the Argonauts*? Perhaps it could be done, but it would require so much input from a legion of computer programmers that it would be impractical.

Then there is the simple question of character. The computer generated dragon in *Dragonheart* (1996) was a convincing flesh-and-blood being and technically astonishing, but it had considerably less dramatic presence than any of Ray Harryhausen's creations. It demonstrated that any such character, whether created by CGI or stop-motion, is only as good as the scriptwriter who devises the situations within which the creature performs and the special effects artists who give it life.

CGI has yet to produce an *auteur* of the likes of O'Brien or Harryhausen. And because these complex CGI creations are the product of a team of people, perhaps it never will. In five or ten years, when the cost of computer imagery has come down and the software is even more powerful, then perhaps a CGI *auteur* will emerge and it will be possible to say that stop-motion has become redundant. Until then, stop-motion remains the ideal medium for depicting full-view fantasy creatures interacting with human characters.

Robo-Motion

The early 1980s saw a series of science fiction thrillers whose shadowy, downbeat milieux took some of their inspiration from the *film noir* thrillers of the 1940s. Set in futuristic environments populated by all manner of SF gadgetry, weaponry and androids, this gloomy *tech noir* world was seen in films such as *Blade Runner* (1982) and *The Terminator* (1984).

Stop-motion filming was quick to exploit the potential of this subgenre and created a subgenre of its own —*robo-motion*. This was an application of puppet animation that hitherto had been largely neglected: the depiction of mechanical and robotic characters. Harryhausen had hinted at the possibilities of this subgenre when he animated the giant bronze statue Talos in *Jason and the Argonauts* and the Minoton, a golden automoton with a mechanical heart, in *Sinbad and the Eye of the Tiger*. But these were both essentially humanoid creations.

The Empire Strikes Back (1980) was the first film to show what *could* be done. Its house-high armored tanks stomped around on four mechanical legs in a way that cleverly suggested these creations were at once mechanical and animal. The follow-up film, *Return of the Jedi* (1983), contained an equally eye-popping sequence in which two-legged Scout Walkers, lesser cousins of the previous film's vehicles, strutted around a forest setting.

Other films that delivered inventive robo-motion spectacles include *The Terminator*, the climax of which featured a pursuit by a relentless android stripped of its synthetic flesh, revealing the steel endoskeleton beneath; *RoboCop* (1987), with its bungling mechanical law enforcer ED-209; *Robot Jox* (1989), set in a future where wars between people have been replaced by wars between giant humanoid robots; *RoboCop 2* (1991), in which a demonic seven-foot robot caused mayhem in Detroit; and *Naked Robot 4½* (1993, also known as *Invader*), which played its stop-motion title character for laughs.

Stop-motion is an ideal medium for the depiction of such mechanical beings because the illusion of life is not required. Any strobing or stiffness of gesture actually adds to the effectiveness of such puppets. The skill of animators like Phil Tippett, who worked on several of the robo-motion sequences mentioned above, is to add touches of personality to lifeless steel beings and turn them into dramatic, exciting characters.

The Appeal of Stop-Motion

Anyone who has ever tried his or her hand at puppet animation, however rudimentary, knows the thrill of seeing something inanimate move and take on a life of its own. At age 16, this author experimented with some inflexible plastic farmyard animals and an 8mm home movie camera. The camera had no single-frame advance; all the author could do was hit the exposure button very quickly and hope for the best. The results were so unimpressive that he never experimented again. Yet he can still remember the magical sight of a stiff-legged pig gliding around a toy filling station.

Stop-motion is not the only process suitable for depicting fantasy creatures. In *Cinemagic* #27, Jim Danforth said, "If the film is good, no one is going to care if it is stop-motion or Go-Motion, live-action or animation. What *counts* is the effect of what is on the screen and if the audience is being entertained; if people are enjoying themselves, they won't care how you did it." He is absolutely right, and what's more, the audience should be unable to tell which process is being used.

But while they may not consciously care whether they are watching stop-motion or some other process, they do know when they are being shortchanged and not seeing a fully realized sequence. This is where stop-motion has distinct advantages over other methods.

For one thing, once a model has been built, the animator has total freedom in deciding what he wants the character to do and total control over how it performs. He is not restricted by rods and cables that have to be hidden from view and need to be very complicated even to perform a simple gesture like opening and closing a hand. A puppet on an animation table can be entirely freestanding (except for any tie-downs that are necessary in its feet to keep it steady). Creatures portrayed with other techniques almost always have to be kept partly out of the frame to hide the means of operation.

Think of the dynamic scene in *The Valley of Gwangi* where an allosaurus is lassoed. This scene is full of striking long shots of the dinosaur seen in full view, surrounded on all sides by cowboys on horseback. Other techniques might have been able to portray this scene, but they would have required serious

25

compromises, probably including the loss of the long shots, which would have produced a much weaker sequence.

Stop-motion puppets are capable of a whole range of intricate movements and gestures. Consider, for example, the fight between King Kong and the tyrannosaurus. The two puppets leap about with great vigor, Kong lashing out with his fists, the dinosaur's tail swishing about wildly, the two creatures biting each other savagely and locking in close combat, Kong trying to pull the tyrannosaur's jaws apart. No mechanical puppet, man in a costume or cable-controlled creation has yet been invented that can perform such elaborate choreography so convincingly.

The most commonly heard criticism leveled at stop-motion photography is that it is "jerky." This "jerkiness"—or strobing—is caused by the absence of a blur on the film, because the puppet is stationary during each exposure (see the entry for "strobing" in the glossary). It is true that jerky animation can be very distracting, but smoothness is not necessarily crucial to the success of a scene.

For example, in *King Kong* there are many examples of scenes where the animation is crude or hurried, yet the film is put together with such a sure control of pace (and the audience is so wrapped up in the story) that this is hardly noticed. Likewise, the animation composites during the edge-of-the-seat climax of *The Terminator* are imperfect (the background image looks too much like a rear projection) yet they are dramatically successful because the whole sequence is so well-constructed. In other words, when people complain that a particular piece of animation is jerky, often they are re-ally indicating that the scene as a whole was deficient, because otherwise they wouldn't have even noticed the quality of the stop-motion.

Different people respond to stop-motion sequences differently. What one viewer sees as fluidly animated and dramatic, another may dismiss as jerky and unconvincing. This may be because the two viewers respond differently to the pace and drama of a sequence; on the other hand, there may be a precise physiological explanation. It is quite possible that stop-motion *does* look more jerky to some people than to others, perhaps because their persistence of vision is not as prolonged. Just as not all people perceive colors in the same way, or respond to music in the same way, or like or dislike the same foods, so it may reasonably be assumed that those mechanics in the eye that govern persistence of vision do not function exactly the same in all people. For people with reasonably long persistence of vision, each of the 24 frames that make up one second of film will dissolve happily into the next image. But someone with a shorter persistence will tend to see each image more distinctly—even if the difference is minimal—and so be more aware of strobing.

This strobing may actually be at the heart of stop-motion's special fascination. Animation effects, however fluid and however cleverly combined with live action, never look 100 percent convincing. There is always something artificial about the moving image, even if we register that artificiality only subconsciously. This applies even to the ultrarealistic gomotion composites of a sequence such as those featuring the two-legged Scout Walkers in *Return of the Jedi*. A special kind of magic is created because our response is jarred; we know that there is something not quite right about what is up on the screen, and yet we cannot pinpoint exactly what it is. This conflict creates a thrill, making these images at once real and surreal.

Several writers have tried to explain this effect. David Robinson, in a review of *The Valley of Gwangi* (*Financial Times*, October 17, 1969), wrote fondly of "the dream-like stop-action imperfection" of the process. Animator David Allen said in an interview with Paul Mandell (*Starlog* #21), "I also remember being aware of the mechanical aspects of Kong's appearance and movement. Instead of a turn-off, it was a turn-on. I'm sure anyone interested in stop-motion knows exactly what I'm talking about — that different kind of kinesis, that whole different *élan*." Neil Norman (in *Evening Standard* magazine, Summer 1993) wrote of Harryhausen's sequences that "the jerkiness of stop-frame animation didn't seem to matter, but rather added to the impact of these giant creatures. The process enhanced the mythical, not-quite-live quality."

This goes part of the way toward explaining why O'Brien's Kong, even in its most unconvincing scenes, is a more exciting character than Rick Baker's realistic man-in-an-ape-costume in the best scenes of the generally lifeless 1976 *King Kong* remake. O'Brien's film is of course the more skillfully directed of the two, but the difference goes deeper, and owes a lot to the charm and artifice of the medium of stop-motion itself. And it explains why a die-hard stop-motion fan finds it far more enjoyable to watch inferior animation in poor films like *The Beast of Hollow Mountain* or *Equinox* than to watch, for example, a lively and witty film like *Alligator*, which uses a real alligator and a mechanical one with very convincing results.

A stop-motion puppet is the on-screen expression of an artist. The look of a model and the way it moves are an extension of the animator himself, whose own personality diffuses through the fingers that manipulate the puppet, shaping the personality of his creation. In this way, it is a noble art indeed.

Is it possible to feel affection for a technical process? In the case of stop-motion animation, it seems that yes, it is. Because stop-motion is more than just a technical process. It is the means whereby, over the last hundred years, a thousand and one dreams have been made real, put on the screen and into the hearts of countless wonder-stricken audiences.

If, as a result of computer generated imagery, stop-motion animation were truly to arrive at the end of its useful life, then the cinema would lose a part of its soul. The special magic that characterizes stop-motion is missing from the photo-realistic sequences created by today's CGI. Fortunately, stop-motion fans — especially those who have gone on to become filmmakers — have done their part to ensure that stop-motion will always hold a cherished place in cinema history.

The Stop-Motion Filmography

The Abyss

1990. 20th Century–Fox. D-Scr: James Cameron. Ph: Mikael Salomon. Mus: Alan Silvestri. Art: Leslie Dilley. Visual Effects Supervisor: John Bruno. DreamQuest Images Visual Effects Supervisor: Hoyt Yeatman. Industrial Light and Magic Visual Effects Supervisor: Dennis Muren (Pseudopod Sequence). Fantasy II Film Effects Supervisor: Gene Warren, Jr. (Spire Rising Sequence). NTI Beings Created by Steve Johnson. Optical Consultant/Title Design: Ernest D. Farino. Conceptual Designer: Ron Cobb. Conceptual Artist: Jean "Moebius" Giraud. Sculptor: Screaming Mad George. Stop-Motion Animation (uncredited): Yancy Calzada.

Cast: Ed Harris, Mary Elizabeth Mastrantonio, Michael Biehn, Leo Burmester, Todd Graff, George Robert Klek.

Rating: ☆☆☆   Stop-Motion: ☆☆

The Abyss is another high-drama, edge-of-the-seat fantasy-thriller from James Cameron, whose earlier directing credits include *The Terminator* and *Aliens*. This time he achieves what many would have thought impossible: a convincing special effects extravaganza set underwater. Cameron does what Ridley Scott did with *Alien*: He takes old science fiction plots (this time *The Atomic Submarine*) and shows just how they should have been made.

Cameron stages his riveting thriller sequences with sure control. A nuclear submarine encounters a mysterious lifeform, crashes into a rock-face, fills with water and sinks. A storm uproots a crane on an oil rig and sends it hurtling down towards a team of divers in a craft on the sea-bed. Two small exploratory craft have an underwater dogfight, ramming into each other, the one eventually pushing the other down into a deep abyss.

A host of special effects studios was recruited to handle the various sequences. Dennis Muren at ILM supervised a wonderful sequence in which an alien lifeform comes aboard the submarine and investigates the crew. This shimmering, watery serpent is a computer generated creation, impeccably matted into the live-action. Gene Warren, Jr., at Fantasy II Film Effects created the climactic sequence

29

in which an alien craft rises to the surface of the sea.

DreamQuest Images were responsible for many of the scenes involving underwater vehicles. One of the underwater craft has a long grabber arm used for fixing and cutting cables. It twists and turns, extends on a jointed arm and ends in a vicious-looking pincer which opens and closes. These were actions beyond the capability of a mechanical device, and stop-motion was selected as the most appropriate means of achieving these shots. In four cuts, the stop-motion arm (animated by Yancy Calzada) reaches out for a cable and, later, moves in to attack Ed Harris. The arm is composited with a miniature sub, which moves through a murky simulation of water, lit up by halon lamps on the model.

The Addams Family

1992. D: Barry Sonnenfeld. Scr: Caroline Thompson, Larry Wilson. Based on characters created by Charles Addams. Ph: Owen Roizman. Mus: Marc Shaiman. Art: Richard MacDonald. Visual Effects Supervisor: Alan Munro. Optical Composites: VCE/Peter Kuran. Photographic Effects: Paul Gentry, Bill Conner, Gary George. Directors of Visual Effects Photography: Chris Nibley, Bill Pope, Bert Dunk, Jim Auperrel (sic). Stop-Motion Animation (uncredited): Doug Beswick.

Cast: Anjelica Huston, Raul Julia, Christopher Lloyd, Dan Hedaya, Elizabeth Wilson, Judith Malina.

Rating: ☆☆½   Stop-Motion: ☆☆½

This amiable romp has enthusiastic performances (Christopher Lloyd is marvelous as Uncle Fester) and plenty of good gags and one-liners. Where it fails is that it sticks so closely to the format of the 1960s television series that it seems like a half-hour idea stretched out to 90 minutes. Pace and audience interest suffer accordingly.

A variety of visual effects — supervised by Alan Munro — add sparkle when the plot sags. Especially impressive are the blue-screen effects used to place Thing — a disembodied hand — in amongst the actors. Most of these shots use an actor's real hand, but one cut features a stop-motion Thing animated by Doug Beswick.

In this cut, Thing hops like a frog across three lily leaves on a pond, finally leaping straight at the camera. Beswick animates this so smoothly that there is no contention between it and the live-action Thing. The puppet, which appears to be a separate blue-screen element, interacts convincingly with its environment: The leaves react when they are landed on and the puppet casts a reflection in the water.

In another sequence, Fester opens a book from which emanates a mini-tornado. Characters in the room are blown around in a circle and then out through a window. Two of these shots also employ Beswick's stop-motion skills, because to have done the shots live-action would have required expensive overhead wire-rigging. In the first cut, puppets of a woman riding a toy horse and a man being bitten on the backside by a polar bear rug smash through the window (blue-screened into the studio set). The second cut is an exterior long shot, with the puppets flying toward and over the camera.

These are accomplished effects, but their brevity makes them a poor showcase for Beswick's considerable talents.

The Adventures of Baron Munchausen

1989. D: Terry Gilliam. Scr: Charles McKeown, Terry Gilliam. Ph: Giuseppe Rotunno. Art: Dante Ferretti. Mus: Richard Kamen. Special Effects: Richard Conway. Optical Effects: Peerless Camera Co. Stop-Motion (uncredited): Steve Archer.

Cast: John Neville, Eric Idle, Sarah Polley, Oliver Reed, Charles McKeown, Jonathan Pryce, Robin Williams, Peter Jeffrey, Sting.

Rating: ☆☆☆　　Stop-Motion: ☆☆

This $40 million production — boasting an endless succession of elaborate sets, all credibly musty and full of impressive detail, and lavish miniature effects — was directed by Terry Gilliam, a genuine talent trying hard to break new ground in the fantasy genre. This is an improvement on his *Brazil* which, while visually dazzling, never let its plot get into gear; but it falls short of the impact of *Time Bandits* (smaller budget, more enthusiasm), which had an engagingly surreal plot and some fabulous fantasy sequences. At the end of the day, Gilliam's *Munchausen* is only slightly better than the 1943 German version, which cost a fraction of his budget.

John Neville's title character and his likable cohorts romp happily from one unlikely adventure to the next, but there is always an impression that Gilliam is trying so hard to impress, that his ideas get in the way of his story-telling. Sequences with Robin Williams on the Moon, Oliver Reed inside a volcano and Munchausen inside a giant whale (a reasonably creepy mechanical puppet) are amusing and always look good, but are forgettable because they lack dramatic force.

Steve Archer, uncredited, supplied a deft two-second stop-motion set-up shot against a blue screen. The Baron, holding onto a cannonball and hurtling through the air towards the Sultan's camp, jumps onto a ball fired in the other direction and miraculously reappears at his starting point. The puppet turns in mid-air and its coattails flap realistically in the wind. This is purely functional stop-motion: It depicts an action that could not be depicted any other way and it is over so quickly that few people would even be aware that it was not a live-action shot.

Archer worked for a week on the film. Initial tests to do the shot with a rear-screen proved unsatisfactory and it was decided to switch to doing the animation in front of a blue screen. Archer spent one day at the animation table executing two different cuts of this 40–frame shot. As it turned out, the shot with which he was least happy was the one that was selected for inclusion in the film.

The Adventures of Buckaroo Banzai Across the 8th Dimension

1984. Sherwood. D: W. D. Richter. Scr: Earl Mac Rauch. Ph: Fred J. Koenekamp. Art: J. Michael Riva. Mus: Michael Boddicker. Special Visual Effects Supervisor: Michael Fink. Matte Paintings: Dream Quest Images. Matte Artist: Rocco Gioffre. Stop-Motion Animation: Rick Heinrichs. Effects Photography (8th dimension sequence): William L. Hayward.

Cast: Peter Weller, John Lithgow, Ellen Barkin, Jeff Goldblum, Christopher Lloyd, Lewis Smith.

Rating: ☆☆½   Stop-Motion: ☆☆

In this tongue-in-cheek science fiction adventure, intrepid hero Buckaroo Banzai (Peter Weller) saves the earth from evil aliens, the Red Lectroids of Planet 10. He invents the Oscillation Overthruster, fits it to a car and drives through a mountain, thereby passing into the 8th dimension. In so doing, he accidentally unleashes the aliens.

As he passes into the 8th dimension, various objects rush past. Among them is one of the Red Lectroids, a humanoid creature depicted by means of a stop-motion puppet animated by Rick Heinrichs.

The Adventures of Pinocchio

1996. Kushner-Locke. D: Steve Barron. Scr: Sherry Mills, Steve Barron, Tom Benedek, Barry Berman. Based on the novel by Carlo Collodi. Ph: Juan Riuz Anchia. Art: Allan Cameron. Mus: Rachel Portman. Pinocchio Animatronics: Jim Henson's Creature Shop. Visual Effects Supervisor: Angus Bickerton. Stop-Motion Supervisor: Leigh Took. Stop-Motion Animation: Philip Dale. Stop-Motion Photography: Neil Culley. Stop-Frame Armatures: Ben Hall.

Cast: Martin Landau, Jonathan Taylor Thomas, Rob Schneider, Bebe Neuwirth, Dawn French, Griff Rhys Jones, John Sessions, Genevieve Bujold.

Rating: ☆☆½   Stop-Motion: ☆☆

Martin Landau plays Gepetto the wood-carver in this engaging live-action retelling of the old story. The tone is light, the pace is brisk and the cinematography is always attractive.

Most shots of Pinocchio use an animatronic puppet built and operated by Jim Henson's Creature Shop. Several shots of the puppet, where it is required to be seen in full, are achieved with a rod puppet blue-screened into the live action. Other full-view shots of the puppet, where it is required to perform more intricate action, use a stop-motion puppet.

The stop-motion effects, animated by Philip Dale and supervised by Leigh Took, include shots of Pinocchio climbing out of the window of Gepetto's house, then walking along the rooftop. Others include full-view shots of the puppet walking through a forest, running across a bridge and walking through a crowded fairground. The animation in these brief shots is always smooth enough to convince and the puppet is flawlessly combined with the live-action plate.

The film also includes some impressive matte paintings, a computer generated cricket and an impressive giant whale. One shot in particular, an aerial shot of Pinocchio in a tiny rowboat with the huge dark shape of the whale passing underneath, is a breathtaking edge-of-the-seat image.

After Midnight

1989. MGM/High Bar. D-Scr: Ken and Jim Wheat. Ph: Phedon Papamichael. Art: Paul Chadwick. Mus: Marc Donahue. Stop-Motion Animation: Doug Beswick Productions. Stop-Motion Puppet Construction: Yancy Calzada. Effects Cameraman: James Aupperle. Visual Effects: VCE/Peter Kuran.

Cast: Ramy Zeda, Jillian McWhirter, Pamela Segall, Marg Helgenberger, Mark McClure, Judie Aronson.

Rating: ☆☆   Stop-Motion: ☆☆

This routine compendium horror film, comprised of three tales, takes its inspiration from the British classic *Dead of Night* (1945). Both films end with the central character waking from a bad dream, then starting to relive everything that has gone before. If only some of the style and imagination had been copied as well.

In "The Old Dark House," a girl plays a trick on her boyfriend by luring him to a spooky old house and scaring the living daylights out of him; believing her to be a murderer, he beheads her. In "A Night on the Town," four girls are pursued by four savage dogs. In "Allison's Story," a telephone receptionist in an apartment block is stalked by a maniac. All three tales are presented with polish and some atmosphere, but offer nothing new to the genre.

At the climax, one of the characters in the linking passages gets burned to death as he is killing someone with an axe. But his skeleton lives on. Fleeing from him, a girl finds herself running through all the locations from the three tales (a device which is another steal from *Dead of Night*). Cowering behind a door, the girl looks up to see the skeleton smash its way through the door, growling, "You're next!" It is not seen again. Although a stunning image, the moment is contrived and cursory, and has little dramatic impact.

The skeleton is seen in two medium shots (shot from the waist up) which use a mechanical prop. Two shots filmed at Doug Beswick's studio use a stop-motion puppet to enable the figure to smash through the door, complex choreography which was beyond the capabilities of a mechanical creation. The animation is very smooth and includes the convincing frame-by-frame manipulation of pieces of falling wood as the door is broken. As the puppet steps through the door, its shoulder knocks another loose piece of wood, which also falls to the floor convincingly. When viewed out of context, it's a good little effect.

Filmed entirely in miniature, the two cuts were lit and shot by James Aupperle. The puppet was constructed by Yancy Calzada and may well have been built over the same armature featured in *Nightmare on Elm Street Part III*.

Alice

1988. GB/Switzerland/W. Germany. D-Scr-Design: Ján Švankmajer. Inspired by Lewis Carroll's *Alice in Wonderland*. Ph: Svatopluk Maly. Art: Eva Švankmajerova, Jiří Blaha. Animation: Bedrich Glaser.
Cast: Kristyna Kohoutova.

Rating: ☆☆☆   Stop-Motion: ☆☆½

Czech animator Jan Švankmajer's version of Lewis Carroll's story is full of startling and humorous surreal imagery and inventive animation trickery. But it doesn't stand up as a dramatic whole and tends to drag towards the end. Švankmajer would have done better to dispense with a narrative thread, rather than constrain himself by choosing a well-known story, because he doesn't have the skill to sustain audience interest on that level.

But such a criticism is almost irrelevant. The appeal of the film lies in its bizarre, often gruesome set-pieces. A stuffed white rabbit pulls its nailed-down paws free, breaks out of its cage and spends much of the rest of the film eating the sawdust that spills from its ripped side. Alice (an actress, not a puppet) is attacked by a skeleton horde (does this mean Švankmajer is a Harryhausen fan?) consisting of impossible combinations of parts of skeletons: a sheep's head on top of two tiny bird's legs, a part-living, part-skeletal crocodile, feathered chickens with bare skulls, etc. A squawking bed (yes, a bed) with wings and claws even joins in the attack. Later, snake skulls hatch from eggs and a bewigged frog-footman hops around, catching insects with his disgustingly huge and human-like tongue.

Such fabulous nightmare imagery is, however, let down by later more conventional episodes featuring the Mad Hatter's tea party and the Queen of

Hearts. The film needed something *really* weird to end on but doesn't deliver.

Švankmajer, who designed, scripted and directed, left the hands-on animation to Bedrich Glaser. They try some remarkably daring animation shots, notably the depiction of models in water, normally a taboo for stop-frame practitioners. A rat seems to swim through Alice's pool of tears, either by means of a static material which looks very much like water, or by allowing the ripples to settle in between each frame of animation! Later, a puppet of Alice is carried down river, limbs flailing as it floats. The model has again actually been animated in water, with the effect that the river seems to hurtle past her with breakneck speed.

Of course, Švankmajer is concerned with surrealism, not realism, and is not worried if clouds zoom past at impossible speeds or if parts of a miniature set move as if of their own accord — i.e., they were accidentally knocked by Glaser. Consequently, the animation itself is less than smooth, with Glaser shooting on twos or even greater frame increments. This is at the core of why *Alice* is less interesting than more conventional stop-motion films. Here, we are never asked to see the models as anything more than models — there is no illusion to make us think, even for a moment, that these creations are real and are interacting with real characters. We are often startled by what we see, but our sense of wonder is never excited.

Alice in Wonderland

1951. GB. Punch Films. Prod: Lou Bunin. Director of Live Action: Dallas Bower. Scr: Henry Myers, Albert Lewin, Edward Eliscu. Based on the story by Lewis Carroll. Ph: Gerald Gibbs, Claude Renoir. Mus: Sol Kaplan. Production Design: Bernice Polifka. Art/Special Effects: Irving Block. Art/Special Effects Assistant: Lloyd Knechtel. Puppet Animators: William King, Ben Radin, Oscar Fessler. Model Engineer: R. Bernstein. Model Makers: H. Silversher, Lilian Davis.

Cast: Carol Marsh, Stephen Murray, Ernest Milton, Pamela Brown, Felix Aylmer. Additional Puppet Voices: Peter Bull, Claude Hulbert.

Rating: ☆☆☆   Stop-Motion: ☆☆☆

In the late 1940s, Lou Bunin, who had filmed the puppet sequence in MGM's *The Ziegfeld Follies* (1946), traveled to Europe to make a feature-length version of Lewis Carroll's *Alice in Wonderland*. All the stop-motion was done in a studio in France. The actors used in the production were English. Carol Marsh, who had made a name for herself three years earlier in *Brighton Rock* and who would later be menaced in Hammer's *Dracula* (1958), played Alice. One of the scripters was Albert Lewin, who earlier had written and directed MGM's *The Picture of Dorian Gray* (1945).

The film sticks closely to Carroll's original and the designs of the puppet characters are based on drawings by

Tenniel that appeared in early editions of the book. Bunin even includes a 15-minute live-action prologue showing us Carroll's life at Oxford University and introducing the characters who later find their way into Alice's dream.

Walt Disney was producing his cartoon version of the story at the same time and tried to persuade Bunin to delay his production for three years. When Bunin refused and released his version first, Disney took him to court, but the case was thrown out on the grounds that the book was in the public domain. As it turned out, Disney's version is the superior one. Bunin's film contains several delightful scenes, intriguing puppets and much impressive animation, but on the whole lacks the charm and energy of Disney's production. Some of the musical numbers, written by Sol Kaplan, are dull and slow the pace of the film.

For the numerous composite shots in the film, Bunin utilized two MGM technicians, Irving Block and Lloyd Knechtel. Block would later contribute special effects to many low-budget fantasy films during the 1950s, including *Behemoth the Sea Monster* (1959), which contained stop-motion by Willis O'Brien.

The composites in *Alice* are rudimentary. Split-screen mattes follow the straight edge of a tree, a door or some other object. Alice typically stands on one side of the screen while the puppets perform on the other side. Occasionally, the matte is improved by being a double split-screen. For example, during the Mad Hatter's tea party, Alice walks behind the chair on which the Hatter sits and emerges on the other side. A straight-edged matte line follows the outline of

both sides of the Hatter's chair, which extends beyond the top of the frame. The most successful static matte design in the film depicts Alice dancing at the foot of the mushroom on which a puppet caterpillar sits. Care has been taken to match the red of the live-action studio floor with the red of the animation table, and the matte line follows not just the edge of a tree but also a plant in the foreground, thereby helping to disguise it. Most mattes, however, are far more obvious.

Traveling matte is used in a few shots (when Alice walks in front of a puppet, or when a cloud of red chili powder blows through the kitchen of the Duchess). These shots, however, always look like less-than-perfect process shots. On another occasion, traveling matte is used more successfully. Alice cries a flood of tears and an animated rat almost drowns in it. Bunin places his puppet in the live-action water by having the composited image of the rat cut off below the waist, thereby suggesting the point of contact with the water.

Alice is later chased by a crowd of strange beasts, including birds with outrageously enlarged beaks, rodents, an ape and some strange lizard-like creatures. These puppets, forever rushing around and all talking at the same time, are animated by Bunin and his team with extraordinary smoothness of movement. These intricate sequences must have taken months to film.

The film retains much of the nightmare quality of Carroll's story. For example, Alice encounters a 12-foot-high dog (another stop-motion puppet) which chases her through a forest of black and white shapes that has all the starkness of an old German expressionistic silent movie. The bell around the dog's neck booms out with deafening loudness.

Bunin enjoys filling his sets with puppet characters. The Queen of Hearts' croquet game is crowded with courtiers and the two-dimensional soldiers which make up a deck of cards. The final court-room sequence — in which Alice is ac-cused of stealing the tarts — is packed with birds, courtiers and other charac-ters. In another sequence, Bunin clev-erly achieves the impression of great ac-tivity when in reality only two puppets were animated. A lobster dance seems to involve two rows of lobster-puppets re-ceding far into the background. In fact, Bunin used mirrors that faced each other to create the desired effect.

Unfortunately, many of Bunin's se-quences — including the Mad Hatter's tea party, the Mock Turtle bewailing his lot, and the croquet game — simply lack the vitality and entertainment qualities needed for such set-pieces. They always look intriguing but come across as life-less and humorless. As such, the film is a mixed bag of sequences, some excel-lent, some disappointing.

Bunin continued for many years to make short stop-motion films as well as hundreds of animated television com-mercials. A major animated feature ver-sion of *The Ring of the Nibelungen* — with its gnomes, heroes and dragons — was begun but never finished.

The Alien Factor

1979. Cinemagic Visual Effects. D-Scr: Donald Dohler. Ph: Britt McDonough. Mus: Kenneth Walker. Title Sequence and Additional Photographic Effects: Ernest Farino.

Cast: Don Leifert, Tom Griffith, Rich-ard Dyszel, Mary Mertens, Richard Gei-witz, George Stover.

Rating: ☆☆   Stop-Motion: ☆☆

This is a film that was put together by a bunch of enthusiastic amateurs with very little money. Director and stop-motion fan Don Dohler knows that a scene must consist of long shots, medium shots and closeups but forgets that a little style and invention help as well. Acting is excruciatingly bad, hardly surprising as the cast is made up mainly of friends and relatives. The plot is es-sentially promising (three alien creatures intended for a zoo crash-land on Earth; a fourth alien comes after them), but doesn't stand a chance in these circum-stances. But Dohler and his team (in-cluding John Dods) should be admired for trying; and any filmmaker who de-cides to include a stop-motion alien can't be all bad.

The other aliens are men in inter-esting but lifeless costumes that recall the bad-old-days of 1950s monster movies. The last alien to appear is the stop-mo-tion Leemoid, built and animated by Ernest Farino and featuring in a scene that runs just over two minutes and con-tains 13 stop-motion cuts. The design is inventive: a 20-foot long slug-like creature with a long tail, two clawed arms and a large head that sports a crest of spines, savage teeth and two large dark eyes.

Dramatically the scene fails to deliver because it is poorly conceived. The monster just walks into the shot, battles Zacherey (the fourth alien) in a forest, then expires for no apparent reason. The poor standard of the special effects means that the scene is not even much fun for stop-motion fans. Eleven of the cuts have been achieved by filming the puppet against a black background and merely superimposing it over the live-action, with the result that it is transparent and always looks like part of another film. If the monster was intended to be a transparent creature of energy (or whatever), then why are there two shots using a rear-screen in which the puppet is solid?

None of the shots use mattes of any kind. Interaction is implied in several cuts by having the actor react to imaginary blows as the Leemoid slaps him around or butts him with its head, but the impression of contact is never really successful. Farino rotoscoped key frames from the live action and used these as a guide when animating his puppet so as to align puppet and actor.

Filming of the live-action was not properly pre-planned, with the result that in two cuts there is a camera pan which is not matched by movement of the camera that filmed the puppet. Just as bad is another cut in which light has got onto the animation table with the result that this too gets superimposed onto the background image. The monster looks quite good in long shots where it sits on the ground, aggressively growling and swaying its head; it looks even better in the two cuts that go to the trouble of using a rear screen. In the first of these it crawls across the frame, and in the other it blinks, shakes it head and collapses. The background image in these two shots always looks washed out, but they are more successful simply because the model is more of a solid presence.

In one clumsy shot, Zacherey swings at the Leemoid with a stick, the monster backs out of the shot for a few seconds, then reappears; this was done to conceal the fact that during those few seconds, there was camera movement in the live-action footage.

Android

1982. New World/Android Productions. D: Aaron Lipstadt. **Scr:** James Reigle, Don Opper. **Ph:** Tim Suhrstedt. **Special Effects:** New World Effects (Bill Conway, Jay Roth, Julia Gibson), Steven B. Caldwell.

Cast: Don Opper, Klaus Kinski, Brie Howard, Norbert Weisser, Crofton Hardester, Kendra Kirchner.

Rating: ☆☆½   Stop-Motion: ☆☆

This sporadically enjoyable science fiction drama set on an orbiting space station has a good no-nonsense performance by Klaus Kinski as an obsessed scientist (ultimately revealed to be an android), but it lacks cohesion and drive. It never seems quite sure how to balance its comic elements (such as ingenue android Max [Don Opper] packing a spare hand and eye in his suitcase) with nastier moments such as a vicious rape. More importantly, Opper never manages to look like anything other than an actor pretending to be a robot.

The opening credits sequence contains a few moments of stop-motion by New World Effects (who did all the film's effects, including some accomplished spaceship shots). Max is constructing a metal mannequin, about 14 inches high. He seats his toy on the edge of a table in a dejected position, then a second mannequin walks into the shot and puts its arms around the first one. It's a basic piece of animation, adequately smooth and not requiring composite photography. Its dramatic function is to plant the seed of the plot's main theme, the android's search for affection. Quite why two such dolls should be able to move of their own accord is not explained — are they meant to be mini-robots?

The Animal World

1956. Windsor/Warner Bros. Prod-D-Scr: Irwin Allen. Ph: Harold Wellman. Art: Bert Tuttle. Mus: Paul Sawtell. Supervising Animator: Willis H. O'Brien. Animation: Ray Harryhausen. Special Effects: Arthur S. Rhoades.

Narration: Theodor Von Eltz, John Storm.

Rating: ☆☆½   Stop-Motion: ☆☆☆

This history of animal life on Earth is unique among stop-motion feature films in that it is a documentary. As such, it cannot be judged in the same way as, say, *Jason and the Argonauts* where dramatic qualities, dialogue, the scriptwriter's imagination, pacing and so on are all considerations. As well as this, the animation sequences by O'Brien and Harryhausen are only a small part of the whole, a self-contained segment whose merits are independent of the qualities of the rest of the film.

Although it contains more on-screen animation than other atypical Harryhausen films like *The Three Worlds of Gulliver* or *First Men in the Moon*, *The Animal World* is his most atypical film. Recognizing this, S. S. Wilson excluded it from his definitive filmography of stop-motion (in *Puppets and People*), because "the animation is not combined with live action." This is true, but there is one brief — and laughable — scene where a human puppet is introduced into the prehistoric setting.

The absence of any significant live action, which could have created a wider mass audience appeal (or at least generated more interest from animation fans), goes part of the way to explaining why the film is almost impossible to track down today. But the main reason for its obscurity is that television companies do not consider a 30-year-old wildlife documentary to be of any interest to a public who already get a steady diet of similar material from recent television productions. And theatrical retrospectives of Harryhausen's career always opt for the more obvious choices for screening. Quite probably, the film has not been shown at all (certainly in Britain) since its original (and very restricted) release in 1956. Even Harryhausen himself had not seen the film again after its release, and in November 1988 this author had the pleasure of watching it with him for the first time since 1956 and hearing his recollections.

The wildlife sequences stand up remarkably well today, containing many episodes which still have the power to fascinate — and, admittedly, quite a few that don't. The tone of the narration is generally preferable to that of Disney's wildlife films (like *The Living Desert*) which were far too quaint and comical. On occasion, this does resort to a similar style, but is still palatable. However, David Attenborough would probably not have approved of the shot, repeated at various unexpected moments, of a grinning chimpanzee with a human laugh dubbed over it. Additionally, the script has a tendency to indulge in Biblical musings which today seem very naive.

The Animal World is another stop-motion feature that has been largely ignored by film historians. Even fan publications tend to rush over it. *FXRH* magazine barely mentions it except to say that clips from it were used later in *Trog* (1970); the scene in which a baby brontosaurus hatches from an egg garnered quite a few votes in the magazine's "favorite effect" survey. Don Shay's in-depth O'Brien biography in *Cinefex* #7

awards the film only one brief paragraph. Harryhausen's own *Film Fantasy Scrapbook* devotes only three pages to the film, most of which are illustrations. The best accounts are in Donald F. Glut's *Dinosaur Scrapbook* (he at least has seen the film and gives a scene-by-scene account of it) and Jeff Rovin's *From the Land Beyond Beyond*, although the latter refers to "the 20–minute prehistoric episode" which conflicts with the nine-minute sequence in the print on which this critique is based.

Cinefantastique (vol. 11, no. 4) further confuses the question of the running time by referring to "the film's opening 15–minute segment": the segment is neither 15 minutes nor is it an opening scene (it is preceded by numerous sequences showing more primitive forms of life). It is well-known that several gruesome shots of a ceratosaurus tearing a chunk out of a stegosaurus were removed because of adverse audience reaction, but have other sequences been lost as well?

Harryhausen told this author that he thought there had been other sequences, missing from this print, but he was unable to recall anything specific, so even his memory fails to provide the definitive reference source. However, he did say that the shot of the brontosaurus laying an egg was not the one originally filmed. The model was animated in a squatting position but this made it look more like it was constipated than laying eggs, so the sequence was refilmed. The pressbook for the film, which lists the running time as 82 minutes, contains three shots of a fight between the triceratops and the tyrannosaurus which did not feature in this print. Were they merely staged for the stills or did Harryhausen actually film this sequence? He vaguely remembered the encounter being longer, but again was unable to recall specific details.

So—what are the merits of this unusual stop-motion exercise? Time and budgetary restrictions prevented O'Brien (who left all the animation to Harryhausen) from designing the sequence with the same kind of lavish detail as he was able to give to *King Kong*: There are no glass shots and dense miniature jungles here. Instead, this is table-top animation enacted on a series of adequate but unexceptional miniature sets and disguised by colorful but unexciting background and foreground paintings.

Shortcuts have also been taken with the building of the puppets, which were cast from molds rather than being built up in layers (which give a more realistic appearance). Both ceratosaurs were taken from the same mold and given minor paintwork differences. One of the ceratosaur models doubled (without its horn) as both the allosaurus and tyrannosaurus. To speed up filming, several mechanical puppets were constructed for some of the closeup shots and, although they mesh well in appearance with the armatured puppets, they lack the liveliness that animation could have given them. But in view of the fact that producer Irwin Allen only allowed between six and eight weeks for the entire sequence to be completed, it's not surprising that there are shortcomings. Fortunately, the dedication of O'Brien and Harryhausen ensures that this series of prehistoric episodes has a vitality that transcends the budgetary problems.

The first stop-motion scene theorizes what might have happened if man and dinosaur had co-existed: a brontosaurus picks up a screaming caveman in its mouth. This might have been effective were it not for the fact that the human puppet is completely immobile except for a stiff arm which waves up and down: a far cry from the fluid "human" animation seen in O'Brien and Harryhausen's other films. (*Cinefantastique* has a still showing the caveman running past the dinosaur; it may be a shot that was posed just for the press still, because it does not appear in this print.)

Several cuts (both stop-motion and "live" closeups) show the brontosaurus plodding around and munching on the leaves of a tree. An allosaurus then strides into the scene, does a lot of growling (assisted again by closeups of its mechanical counterpart) and walks off. Unfortunately, the anticipated battle never materializes. Presumably to keep the animation simple, the two models are never seen in the same shot. In a brief and rather unlikely shot, the brontosaurus, still standing up, lays an egg which drops to the ground and rolls a few inches. The next cut betrays that, as mentioned earlier, this sequence was refilmed, because there is a batch of about ten eggs seen on the ground, even though we have only seen one being laid. Subsequently, the brontosaurus also walks off.

In a charming (but never cute) episode consisting of only two animation cuts, a baby dinosaur hatches from one of the eggs, makes a few gurgling noises and takes a timid step halfway out of the shell. Jim Danforth was influenced by this scene when executing his similar sequence in *When Dinosaurs Ruled the Earth*.

Next, a stegosaurus wanders across a plateau. In some shots, the cliff-edge is a foreground painting and in other shots it is a miniature model photographed from below to give an impression of great height. This low-key opening develops into an excellent protracted battle between first the stegosaurus and one ceratosaurus and then later between the ceratosaurus and a second rival ceratosaurus.

The first ceratosaurus leaps into the frame from the right (probably not an aerial-braced shot because part of the tail is always off-screen, providing a means of support), circles around the stegosaurus then bites one of the plates on its back. Both models' tails are constantly swishing to and fro, and at one point the stegosaurus swipes its attacker with its spiked tail. Eventually the stegosaurus collapses.

The second ceratosaurus now leaps into the frame, seemingly appearing from over our heads; it's a great dramatic device and one which Harryhausen admits to having used before and since, in his unfinished *Evolution* documentary and also in the phororhacos scene in *Mysterious Island*. The second carnivore charges into the first, forcing it to the ground. But it gets up again and there is a lot of biting, roaring and tail-swishing. Some shots, seen from two different camera angles, reveal how O'Brien optimized animation time by having more than one camera running concurrently; it is actually the same piece of animation seen twice. As ever aware of the importance of varying his perspectives, O'Brien closes the scene with another set-up in which the two dinosaurs lock in battle again and topple over the edge of the cliff.

A triceratops strides into another miniature set-up, combined with some closeups of a mechanical puppet. Presumably to suggest it is some kind of predecessor to the rhinoceros, O'Brien then has the beast ram a tree trunk and uproot it. When it hears the growling of some off-screen carnivore, it backs away nervously and, in a character-building touch, scrapes the ground with one foot.

A tyrannosaurus walks into the shot and is all set to engage in battle when it is suddenly interrupted by a volcanic eruption (live footage intercut with the animation). All scenes from now on are bathed in a red light to suggest the flames and heat. A shot of a miniature exploding volcano looks like it may have been taken from another film. Both animals stride off together in a series of cuts, the tyrannosaurus nearly tripping over the triceratops as it tries to escape the volcano.

In a fine scene that upset contemporary reviewers as too explicit, the triceratops stumbles into some lava and slowly sinks, screaming in pain as it goes under. A static matte cutting through the lava seems to have been used to create the illusion that the model is surrounded by lava.

The stegosaurus and brontosaurus are seen again (in one cut each) as they attempt to flee from the volcano. Miniature floors crack and pull apart, effectively suggesting the force of an earthquake. There is a memorable final sequence in which the tyrannosaurus is thrown about on a cracking floor, eventually falling into a fissure. This device recalls a more ambitious scene O'Brien did in *The Son of Kong*, when a miniature jungle set is moved about to depict the island being ripped apart by an earthquake.

There is no more animation in the film. The pterodactyl shown in a frequently published press still is in the film merely a static model briefly seen perched on a rock, its wings flapping in a breeze.

In interviews, Irwin Allen looked back on these memorable scenes and lavished praise on O'Brien and Harryhausen. These remarks may seem a little hypocritical to some, however, because four years later he went on to make his forgettable version of *The Lost World* entirely without animation; he was more interested in getting a quick return on his investment than he was in creating superior, albeit time-consuming, special effects.

The Animal World is one of O'Brien and Harryhausen's less interesting films because of the brevity of the animation sequence and because the budget forced the sets and models to have an artificiality which the dynamic animation never quite manages to transcend. But it is still essential viewing for animation fans and deserves to be rescued from its present obscurity. And last, but not necessarily least, its publicity posters boast a fabulous full-color painting (by an unknown artist) which is one of the best of its kind amongst stop-motion films.

Army of Darkness

1993. Renaissance. D: Sam Raimi. Scr: Sam Raimi, Ivan Raimi. Ph: Bill Pope. Mus: Joe DoLuca. Special Makeup Effects: Kurtzman, Nicotero and Berger, Inc., Tony Gardner. Special Visual Effects: Introvision International. Visual Effects Director: William Mesa. Book of the Dead Animation/Design: Tom Sullivan. Stop-Motion Supervisor: Pete Kleinow.

Cast: Bruce Campbell, Embeth Davidtz, Marcus Gilbert, Ian Abercrombie, Richard Grove, Michael Earl Reid.

Rating: ☆☆☆   Stop-Motion: ☆☆☆

Having already remade *The Evil Dead* once, Sam Raimi made sure that the third installment was a totally original film, with only stylistic similarities to its predecessors. *Army of Darkness* (wittily subtitled *The Medieval Dead* in publicity material) is a sword-and-sorcery romp set in the fourteenth century.

Only Raimi's distinctive camera tricks, a couple of stiff-necked zombies and Bruce Campbell link it to the earlier films. But even Campbell's character Ash has changed — instead of the wild-eyed ingenue of Parts I and II, he is now a wise-cracking, sub-Schwarzenegger macho-figure.

On the one hand, this all makes for an inventive, stylish and frequently amusing splatter-show. But on the other hand, a bigger budget has robbed Raimi of some of his frenzied spontaneity: This doesn't grab you by the scruff of the neck like *The Evil Dead* did. In the first film, style triumphed over an almost non-existent plot. *Army of Darkness* is lumbered with a conventional quest plot (Ash must retrieve an unholy book, the Necronomicon) which tends to make the film a series of special effects set-pieces rather than a satisfying whole.

There are several standout sequences and the climax — in which a castle is attacked by an army of skeletons — is marvelous.

In a creepy old windmill, shards from a shattered mirror each spawn a foot-high simulacrum of Ash. They attack Ash (involving some stunning Introvision front-projection composite shots) and one disappears down his throat. It starts to grow within him: First an obscenely blinking eye appears on his shoulder, then a second head and an arm. Eventually an identical twin splits away from him. In one shot, one of the two heads slaps the other — an effect achieved using a stop-motion puppet animated by Pete Kleinow, who also supervised the film's later stop-motion sequences.

Ash arrives at the cemetery where the Necronomicon is located and reaches for the book, but it develops a hole in its cover which sucks him in. When he climbs back out again, his face has become distorted by the suction into an impossibly long shape — this is a superb prosthetic make-up by Tony Gardner.

Ash forgets to say the magic words "Klaatu Barata Nikto" — yes, the same words that stopped Gort the robot in *The Day the Earth Stood Still* — and as a result unleashes the Army of Darkness. This long sequence begins relatively modestly with an attack by the Deadite harpy which was seen at the end of *The Evil Dead II*. The harpy flies into the castle, picks up the heroine (Embeth Davidtz) and carries her off to Ash's evil twin.

This sequence uses a good mechanical harpy-puppet as well as stop-motion

in three shots. The composites in this sequence — presumably rear-screen setups — are excellent. The first shot is a long shot of the creature flying high above the castle battlements. A puppet of the heroine is used in a shot in which the harpy picks her up from the castle grounds. The animation and lighting in this shot are extremely good, helping it to cut in smoothly with the live-action cuts. In the last stop-motion cut, the creature flies up over the battlements and away. In all these shots, the animation of the flapping wings is very smooth and probably aided by some motion-control blurs on the wings.

Back in the cemetery, the evil Ash summons up the dead — an army of hundreds of living skeletons. This is *almost* the sequence that Harryhausen wanted to make when he filmed his skeleton battle in *Jason and the Argonauts*: he has often stated that his one regret was that the scene could not have been shot at night. Raimi has his skeleton army charging across a field, battering down a door — some even ride on horseback. He tries to outdo Harryhausen and he might have succeeded, but where he fails is that he never quite settles on a unifying tone for the sequence and so doesn't adequately engage the audience. Sometimes he tries to be scary, sometimes jokey, sometimes theatrical (evil Ash spouts Shakespeare at one point) and sometimes spectacular. Harryhausen generated a quirky style and maintained it throughout his sequence: He knew his limits and as a result his scene never ceases to enthrall.

Raimi is too ambitious. He combines several techniques for bringing his skeletons to life and they never quite mesh into a happy whole. Some are full-scale props wheeled in on carts (not convincing); others are elaborate rod-operated props; others are thin actors seen in shadowy long shots. Among this wealth of skeletoria are approximately 25 stop-motion shots. All are animated very realistically and often combined with the live-action in impressive Introvision or rear-projection composites. Others cut in less well with the live-action and further upset the overall tone of the scene. But the sequence's faults are readily forgiven; this is a magnificent fantasy episode by any standards.

The first stop-motion cuts take place in the cemetery. In two astonishing long shots, about 20 skeletons are climbing out of their graves and digging up the graves of other skeletons. The evil Ash stands in the foreground giving orders — marvelous composites using Introvision techniques, whereby the actors were filmed in front of a large screen onto which the pre-shot animation footage was front-projected. In these cuts, six of the skeletons were stop-motion puppets animated in the conventional manner. The rest were rigged to stepper motors programmed to move during camera exposure. Les Paul Robley assisted Kleinow in the animation in these shots.

In a closer cut, a stop-motion skeleton pulls one of his fellows up out of a grave. Prop skeletons pass by in the foreground to give the shots extra depth and activity.

At the base of the castle, four skeletons use a huge stone as a battering ram. In two medium shots using rear projections, they rush at the door, stone held aloft. A superb long shot looks down at the skeletons running at the door. Two

more impressive long shots show the skeletons running over the drawbridge into the castle, combined by means of static matte with live actors who are also running over the bridge.

One skeleton tries to climb over the battlements but finds itself on the receiving end of a soldier's boot. Its head goes flying and the decapitated body briefly turns round to "watch" where its head is spinning. This grimly humorous moment is of course an affectionate nod towards a shot in Harryhausen's sequence. This is another excellent Introvision composite with the soldier a foreground element. This time the animation was shot after the live action, allowing the skeleton's backwards fall to be aligned with the soldier's boot.

The evil Ash gets set on fire, leaving only a living skeleton. He climbs over the battlements to face the "real" Ash. The animation here is again good but the lighting on the puppet fails to match up with the shadowy texture of the live action. The two engage in a brief sword-fight that recreates some of the thrilling choreography of *The 7th Voyage of Sinbad* and *Jason and the Argonauts*. More live-action shots using a rod-operated prop skeleton feature in the fight than stop-motion cuts.

Ash kicks his evil counterpart over the castle wall and (in a fine stop-motion cut) the skeleton hurtles to the ground, with blur again added to the image to soften it. It lands on a catapult — a consummate bit of animation as the puppet comes to a halt — and stands imposingly. Ash cuts the restraint on the catapult and the skeleton goes flying into the air, a superb stop-motion cut with the flailing puppet cartwheeling through the air. In mid-flight, the evil Ash finally explodes, becoming a ball of flame.

The early part of the film includes some stop-motion by Tom Sullivan, who did the marvelous zombie meltdown effects in the first film. A narrator explains the origins of the Necronomicon, which is seen on a table with its pages turning magically and lettering appearing frame-by-frame on the leaves.

Around the World Under the Sea

1966. MGM/Ivan Tors. D: Andrew Marton. Scr: Arthur Weiss, Art Arthur. Ph: Clifford Poland. Art: Preston Rountree, Mel Bledsoe. Mus: Harry Sukman. Special Effects: Project Unlimited, Inc. Stop-Motion (uncredited): Gene Warren.

Cast: Lloyd Bridges, Shirley Eaton, Brian Kelly, David McCallum, Keenan Wynn, Marshall Thompson, Gary Merrill.

Rating: ☆☆   Stop-Motion: ☆☆

This uninventive and overlong (nearly two hours) underwater adventure has a group of scientists in a nuclear-powered submarine planting earthquake-warning devices on the sea bed. The dialogue gives rise to several unintended laughs as the script struggles to create some human drama.

Gene Warren at Project Unlimited supplied the accomplished miniature shots of the sub (mostly shot dry-for-wet with a live-action miniature), including a sequence in which the vessel becomes trapped near an underwater volcano. A giant moray eel threatens the vessel at one point, in scenes that combine shots of a live eel, a miniature eel and a credible full-size prop of the head.

In a letter to the author, Warren explained his contribution to the film. "Four different effects methods were used to accomplish all the action: (i) A live eel was photographed in a tank containing the miniature submarine. Much footage was shot from which the necessary sections were edited to accomplish our action needs; (ii) A full-sized mechanized eel head (some 16 to 18 feet in diameter and 15 feet long) was sent to Florida to be photographed underwater with the actors in the action scenes; (iii) A miniature eel was photographed dry (using bee smoke to simulate water) to work stop-frame with the miniature submarine. This footage was then intercut with another rubberized puppet eel to accomplish the scene in which the eel was blown up in front of the miniature submarine; (iv) The miniature submarine was suspended on a wire-rig and photographed stop-frame in a dry atmosphere which simulated the water effect and matched the actual underwater scenes."

The Arrival

1996. Live Entertainment/Steelwork/ Thomas G. Smith. D-Scr: David Twohy. Ph: Hiro Narita. Art: Michael Novotny. Mus: Arthur Kempel. Special Makeup Designed and Created by Todd Masters. Visual Effects Producer: Charles I. Finance. Conversion Center Miniature: 4-Word Productions (Visual Effects Supervisor: Robert Skotak. Consulting Ph: Dennis Skotak). Planecorp Miniature: Hunter/Gratzner Industries. Digital Visual Effects and Alien Animation: Pacific Data Images. Imploder Effects Animation: Available Light Ltd. Arctic Pullback Effect: Dreamquest Images. Leaping Alien Effect: David Allen Productions.

Cast: Charlie Sheen, Lindsay Crouse, Teri Polo, Richard Schiff, Leon Rippy, Tony T. Johnson.

Rating: ☆☆☆   Stop-Motion: ☆½

Taut direction and a no-nonsense screenplay — both by David Twohy — ensure that this tense SF thriller keeps the audience watching right to the end. The plot is nothing new — aliens are hiding out on earth and plan to alter the planet's climate so as to make it inhabitable. Yet Twohy manages to make it all seem fresh, throws in plenty of twists and turns and additionally embellishes the film with numerous marvelous special effects that make the movie look very classy indeed. Only a half-baked ending, in which nothing is properly resolved, spoils the show.

The film opens with a stunning effect by Dreamquest Images, a dizzying aerial pull-back from Lindsay Crouse in a meadow, revealing that the meadow is surrounded by ice and snow and is in fact in the Arctic. This continuous shot concludes with a view of Earth from space.

Charlie Sheen, playing a hot-tempered NASA scientist scanning the airwaves for alien messages, tracks a signal to central Mexico and stumbles into the aliens' Earth base. In a superb ten-minute sequence, Sheen explores the base and comes face to face with some eye-boggling alien technology. The sequence is cleverly designed so that Sheen seems to be a helpless pawn among unfamiliar surroundings, at one point finding himself standing on a floor that rises up beneath him (he's on top of an elevator). On another occasion he falls over a balcony and tumbling down to a lower level; in another scene, he finds to his horror that he is standing in the path of a hurtling missile. Throughout this sequence, the miniature work by Robert and Dennis Skotak is outstanding and generates a real impression of alien power.

In an early scene, Sheen chases a man down a blind alley. In a remarkable effect, the man rearranges his legs so that they bend forwards at the knee, not backwards, crouches down, then leaps up onto a nearby roof and escapes. Originally, the shot of the legs rearranging was achieved with a stop-motion puppet animated by David Allen. But the shot was subsequently redone with footage of the live actor enhanced by computer generated legs.

Inside the base, Sheen sees the aliens in their real form, without their human disguises. Vaguely humanoid, they have goat legs, a mottled, squid-like skin and mysterious fleshy flaps at the backs of their heads which wriggle unpleasantly.

These memorable creatures have the "look" of stop-motion (particularly the goat legs and "arms-back" pose), but in fact all their shots are done with CGI.

At the climax, one of the aliens, in human form, is frozen solid by a fire extinguisher. Sheen breaks off his hand with an axe and it shatters when it hits the floor. The pieces of the hand, along with a number of other items, are then sucked into a mysterious device called the Imploder. A quick shot of the pieces of the hand moving across the floor towards the Imploder is a David Allen stop-motion effect.

Atlantis the Lost Continent

1961. MGM/Galaxy. Prod-D: George Pal. Scr: Daniel Mainwaring. Based on the play *Atlanta* by Sir Gerald Hargreaves. Ph: Harold E. Wellman. Art: George W. Davis, William Ferrari. Mus: Russell Garcia. Special Effects: A. Arnold Gillespie, Lee LeBlanc, Robert R. Hoag. Animation: Project Unlimited (Gene Warren, Wah Chang, Jim Danforth, Tom Holland).

Cast: Anthony Hall, Joyce Taylor, John Dall, Bill Smith, Edward Platt, Frank De Kova.

Rating: ☆☆   Stop-Motion: N/A.

For his next film after *The Time Machine*, MGM only allowed George Pal a small budget and forced him to work from a script that wasn't ready. The result is one of Pal's weakest productions. Its plot seems strangely unimaginative and Pal's direction is lackluster. Many of the ideas give the impression of having been stolen from other films: An Atlantean submarine resembles the one in *20,000 Leagues Under the Sea*, a risible duel between slaves in an arena imitates *Spartacus*, and the House of Pain, in which a surgeon transforms men into half-animals, is an idea lifted from *Island of Lost Souls*.

On the other hand, the film does contain one sequence which may well have provided some of the inspiration for *Jason and the Argonauts*: Neptune rises from the sea looking almost identical to *Jason*'s Triton.

The love interest (Anthony Hall and Joyce Taylor) is corny and poorly acted. The plot drags itself through all the usual "lost civilization" clichés, never adding anything new of its own. The highlight is the climactic sinking of the continent which, although always obviously executed with miniatures, is elaborate and exciting.

The film originally contained sequences featuring Atlantean soldiers wearing winged harnesses that enable them to fly. Project Unlimited handled these scenes, combining live-action shots of stuntmen hung on wires with shots of miniature puppets. In the bulk of the flying scenes, the soldiers were marionettes operated by invisible wires. And in a few shots, as Project Unlimited's Gene Warren explained to the author, "the flying Atlanteans were wire-armatured puppets hung on wire rigs and photographed stop-frame."

However, the negative reaction of preview audiences to these flying scenes was such that Pal decided to cut them all from the release print. Pal blamed the scenes' failure on the restrictive budget.

The film also features an impressive giant crystal which fires a destructive ray. "The shot of the 'power beam' coming from the Crystal," Warren also disclosed, "was done with a stop-frame miniature with an optical overlay of the actual beam."

Babes in Toyland (Re-release title: *March of the Wooden Soldiers*)

1934. Hal Roach/MGM. D: Gus Meins, Charles Rogers. Scr: Frank Butler, Nick Grinde. Ph: Francis Corby, Art Lloyd. Art: William Cameron Menzies. Mus: Harry Jackson.

Cast: Stan Laurel, Oliver Hardy, Charlotte Henry, Felix Knight, Henry Kleinbach (Henry Brandon), Johnny Downs.

Rating: ☆☆½   Stop-Motion: ☆☆½

Despite the success of *King Kong* and *The Son of Kong* (both 1933*)*, it would be many years before Hollywood made substantial use of stop-motion again. But the process did rear its head on a smaller scale in some unlikely places. One of these was this 1934 Laurel and Hardy feature, the climax of which features an army of man-sized wooden soldiers coming to life.

As a vehicle for the comedians, the film is a major disappointment—their talents were far better suited to the surreal mood of their shorts. There are few funny moments and the flimsy plot is constantly interrupted by weak musical numbers. But Henry Brandon makes a good Caligari-like villain and an army of Bogeymen—fanged, shaggy creatures who live in subterranean caves—put in a memorably tacky appearance near the end.

Who animated the wooden soldiers and designed the sequence is unknown, but it's skillfully done. Thought has gone into editing the sequence for maximum effect, conveying an impression of the vast numbers of these mechanical toys. There are only 11 animation cuts. Midway through the sequence, animation is abandoned in favor of live-action extras in costumes. Although this allows interaction between the soldiers and the Bogeymen, the sense of them being stiff, mindless automatons is lost.

There are about a hundred soldier puppets, although probably no more than 30 of them are ever animated in one shot. The animation is smooth enough and does not require much skill—only the puppets' legs and arms ever need to be adjusted.

One cut is a dramatic low-angle shot looking up at the advancing puppets. Two others, equally effective, tilt the

49

camera at an angle as the soldiers stomp past. The sequence includes two composite shots. In the first, Stan and Ollie stand in front of a full-scale rear projection, swinging open some doors to let the soldiers march out. The other is a seamless matte shot, with Stan and Ollie standing on one side of the frame as the puppets march out on the other side.

Babes in Toyland

1961. Disney. D: Jack Donohue. Scr: Ward Kimball, Joe Rinaldi, Lowell S. Hawley. Based on the Operetta by Victor Herbert and Glen McDonough. Ph: Edward Colman. Art: Carroll Clark, Marvin Aubrey Davis. Mus: George Bruns. Special Effects: Eustace Lycett, Robert A. Mattey. Toy Sequence: Bill Justice, Xavier Atencio. Matte Artist: Jim Fetherolf.

Cast: Ray Bolger, Tommy Sands, Annette, Ed Wynn, Tommy Kirk, Kevin Corcoran.

Rating: ☆½   Stop-Motion: ☆½

This wretched film is a depressing example of just how bad Disney's live-action productions could be. The songs are dull, the situations are contrived and the comedy is embarrassingly unfunny. Ray Bolger, as the dastardly villain, and Ed Wynn, as a dotty old toymaker, are wasted in poorly conceived roles. Young lovers Annette and Tommy Sands will make you reach for the sick-bag.

The climax is very much a poor imitation of the sequence in *Tom Thumb* where Russ Tamblyn dances with the living toys. In *Babes in Toyland*, Tom (Sands) brings an army of toy soldiers to life and they attack Bolger. This long scene is devised with little imagination or excitement, even though a lot of effort has clearly gone into it. Complementing a lot of shots using mechanical toys are approximately 20 stop-motion shots executed by Bill Justice and Xavier Atencio.

In these, groups of soldiers step out of their boxes and move into formation, marching across the floor and through a door. In some of these shots, Sands is a foreground traveling matte element. Much of the animation has been done by shooting on twos and it looks hurried. A series of replacement legs was used to depict the toys walking.

In an interview in *Filmfax* magazine (issue #24), Justice described doing the animation as "extremely tedious." His tedium is contagious — this is animation without feeling.

Justice and Atencio had a second stab at animating toy soldiers in *Mary Poppins* three years later. In the same year as *Babes in Toyland*, Justice and Atencio worked with T. Hee on a puppet animation sequence for the opening credits of Disney's *The Parent Trap*. This was conventional "puppets as puppets" animation, with two Cupid-like characters flying around the screen and trying to bring pairs of puppet-lovers together. No composites with live-action are included.

Baby Snakes

1980. D: Frank Zappa. Clay Animation: Bruce Bickford.

Cast: Frank Zappa, Joey Psychotic, Ron Delsener, Donna U. Wanna.

Rating: N/A.   Stop-Motion: N/A.

This offbeat musical combines concert footage of Frank Zappa with clay animation sequences by Bruce Bickford.

Baron Munchausen see *Baron Prášil*

Baron Prášil (a.k.a. *Baron Munchausen*)

1961. Czechoslovakia. Studio Gottwaldow. D: Karel Zeman. Scr: Karel Zeman, Joseph Kainar. Based on the novel by Gottfried Burger. Art: Karel Zeman, Zdeněk Rozkopal. Ph: Jiří Tarantik. Mus: Zdeněk Liska.

Cast: Milos Kopecky, Jána Brejchova, Rudolf Jelínek, Ján Werich, Rudolf Hrusínsky, Karel Höger.

Rating: ☆☆☆   Stop-Motion: ☆☆☆

Of the three sound versions of the exploits of the famous liar Baron Munchausen (the other two being the 1943 German film and Terry Gilliam's 1989 version), this is the most agreeable, but it suffers from the same basic flaw: There is no real plot as the Baron drifts from one adventure to another. Zeman imposes a vague structure by emphasizing the Baron's unrequited love for the heroine and by having an underlying theme about the importance of fantasy in life (presumably a reference to the oppressive Czech government). These help hold the film together, but it lacks the simple charm of the narrative of *Vynález Zkázy*, his previous film. Even so, it is a film full of fabulous images, deft moments of gentle humor and a uniquely fascinating style of special effects.

Unlike *Vynález Zkázy*, this has the attraction of color. It was shot in black-and-white but carefully tinted by Zeman, using a variety of pastel blues, yellows and reds and sometimes using full color to highlight key images, such as the blood that flows from a harpooned whale. The visual style is characteristically Zeman: sets that are often merely two-dimensional cut-outs, detailed like etchings; a sunset inspired by Gustav Doré's drawings; the expressionistically bleak corridors of a castle dungeon; a general impression of ingenious artifice as live actors perform in blatantly unreal surroundings.

Comic flourishes are many. A commentary, given by the captain of the

51

vessel inside the whale that has swallowed them, announces when they are swimming through the Red Sea, the Yellow Sea and the Black Sea. Each shot is tinted the appropriate color, making the commentary redundant. ("A profound knowledge!" mocks Munchausen. "What would we do without our admiral?") There is gentle slapstick in the cabin scenes where Munchausen tries to close a window and gets his foot stuck through it. The scene in which two fleets of Turkish ships accidentally destroy each other is engagingly unlikely, and includes an absurd shot in which a ship's figurehead is seen puffing away on a pipe: this surreal kind of two-dimensional animation makes one sure that Gilliam, in his early days on television, must have been influenced by Zeman. A typically playful Zeman-esque comic image arises during the climactic battle: A general commands his troops like an orchestra conductor, waving a baton in time to the upbeat musical score.

As in *Vynález Zkázy* there is a wealth of stop-motion, explaining the three-year gap between the making of the two films. Sometimes the process is used for purely functional or economic reasons, such as when puppet humans are seen in long shots in miniature sets. This avoids building huge studio sets or relying on a lot of process photography. But on other occasions it is used to create fantasy imagery which cannot be created any other way—for example when the Baron is surrounded by giant sea creatures or carried off by a huge bird.

The opening sequence is superb. Footsteps in the sand lead to a frog sitting atop a broken jug. From here we pan up through a variety of forms of flight, all achieved through stop-motion. First is a multitude of butterflies, then the camera continues to pan up and up, revealing a man on an early flying machine, then a flock of geese, a biplane, more birds, some jet planes and finally a rocket in space heading for the Moon. (Did Kubrick see this film before thinking up that key shot in *2001: A Space Odyssey* when the camera cuts from a bone thrown in the air to a spaceship, suggesting—like Zeman's film—the advance of man's progress?)

Closing in on the surface of the Moon, the camera reveals another set of footprints being followed by an astronaut (sometimes seen in stop-motion long shots) who is astounded to discover a glove lying in the Moon dust. As well as Gilliam and Kubrick, can it be that Harryhausen saw Zeman's film, incorporating this concept into *First Men in the Moon*, on which he was working at the time *Baron Munchausen* was released?

Munchausen takes the astronaut back to Earth in a wooden sailing ship pulled by seven stop-motion flying horses, one of which (with typical Zeman absurdity) is merely a wooden toy. It's a complex piece of animation, embellished by static mattes which place the actors on the deck of the miniature ship. In one attractive shot, the background is a picturesque Doré-style sunset. Back on Earth, they visit the palace of a Turkish sultan, depicted almost entirely by elaborate two-dimensional etchings into which the actors are matted. In one scene, a bunch of grapes held by the sultan is animated so that its movements match those of a belly-dancer. Whenever an actor gets too close to the sultan on his throne, mechanical spears thrust out toward him, and in one shot the camera pulls back to reveal they are operated by a network of stop-motion cogs beneath the throne, animated puppets of the humans in the top of the frame. A fire is started in the palace and red smoke billows around the yellow-tinted palace, a poetic visual image enhanced by stop-motion bats that flutter everywhere.

Munchausen, the astronaut and a princess whom they have rescued from the sultan are pursued for three days. This sequence includes a striking panoramic long shot of the actors riding on horseback through a stylized matte painting of some mountains, animated vultures swooping around above them. Later there is a beautiful shot that Willis O'Brien would have appreciated: a partially collapsed bridge over a deep ravine. The ravine and a range of mountains in the background are both paintings. The live actors jump over the ravine, but when one of their pursuers does the same, the bridge gives way and there is an accomplished switch to a stop-motion puppet of rider and horse as they plummet into the ravine, followed by a swarm of vultures. Another fine matte shot depicts the riders arriving at the top of a painted cliff, a ship sailing on the sea below. When they jump into the water, there are more clever switches from live actors to puppet horse-and-riders.

Adrift at sea with the princess at night, Munchausen finds himself surrounded by a variety of giant sea-beasts. A huge serpent with a snaking neck glides past, a flying dragon swoops overhead, an enormous six-legged spider walks across the surface of the water and a vicious-looking flying fish passes overhead. These are all brief moments of stop-motion, haunting images in flawless composites where the nonchalant Baron calmly looks on, puffing unconcerned on his pipe.

The three characters are swallowed by a whale, the inside of which is an almost cartoon-style drawing of its cavernous rib cage. The whale swims to the North Pole and there is another scenic fantasy panorama depicting painted icebergs, a stop-motion whale swimming across the surface of the water and animated sea birds swooping across the foreground by means of traveling matte.

Back on dry land, the cast comes to the edge of another deep gorge. This is an impressive matte shot, mostly painting and with an animated bird sitting on the sleeping form of a man halfway up the other side of the gorge. Totally gratuitously, an enormous stop-motion bird about 20 feet high now makes an appearance and menaces Munchausen (shades of Harryhausen again, this time *Mysterious Island*, also released in 1961). The Baron calmly tries to discourage the savage creature with a wave of his hand, but it picks him up and flies off out to sea. The animation of these shots is very smooth, with the wings rising and lowering slowly rather than strobing jerkily. The Baron sits calmly on the bird's claws, then gets dropped into the sea.

A long sequence follows that recalls the underwater passages of *Vynález Zkázy*, shot through a distortion glass to give the illusion of water. Munchausen rides on a stop-motion "sea-horse"—a fictitious creature with a horse's head and four webbed feet. Just how Zeman has combined the live-action Baron with his puppet is not clear, but it is a seamless effect (and preempts a similar effect in

Caveman [1981] when Ringo Starr rode on the back of a dinosaur). Perhaps the square outline of his saddle is the location of a matte line. Various other stop-motion sea creatures swim around in a vaguely menacing manner; a mermaid, when spurned by Munchausen, transforms into a shark.

During the battle scenes at the end of the film, there are various minor bits of animation. One is a cut in which the Baron jumps on a cannonball and is carried over to the enemy's side so he can spy on them; he then jumps onto a cannonball fired the other way, which takes him back to where he started. Filmed in long shot, this is almost identical to the stop-motion cut which Steven Archer did in Gilliam's version of the film, another indication that Gilliam was influenced by Zeman. The film closes back on the Moon, including a few more long shots of animated puppets walking about on the surface, and some poetic musings about the importance of fantasy in life.

Basket Case

1981. Basket Case Company. D-Scr: Frank Henenlotter. Ph: Bruce Torbet. Art: Frederick Loren. Mus: Gus Russo. Special Makeup Effects: Kevin Haney, John Caglione, Jr.

Cast: Kevin Van Hentenryck, Terri Susan Smith, Beverly Bonner, Robert Vogel, Diana Browne, Lloyd Pace.

Rating: ☆☆☆   Stop-Motion: ☆☆

This is one of the classic horror movies of the 1980s thanks to its wonderfully demented subject matter (Duane and his deformed Siamese twin Belial enact a bloody revenge on the surgeons who separated them) and the deft touches of humor and pathos instilled by director Henenlotter. It's a fine example of how imagination and good story-telling techniques can triumph over a minuscule budget — the sleazy location filming, mediocre acting and sometimes shoddy lighting add to the sense of fun rather than working against it. All the characters — Duane, his girlfriend, the hotel clerk and even the horrible twin himself ("He looks like a squashed octopus") — are very likable, and this, combined with the outrageous comic-strip approach of the splatter scenes, takes the edge off the nastiness.

Delightful moments include Belial — who is merely a head and two arms — munching noisily on a hamburger and a touching shot of his deformed hand reaching imploringly from the sack in which he has been discarded after the operation. The bewildered hotelier, who herds his sensation-seeking guests around like cattle, supplies welcome comic relief during some of the gruesome scenes. Several scenes have an engaging perversity which registers high on the sickometer: Belial in his basket fondling a pair of stolen panties, hiding in a lavatory bowl, and making love (after a fashion) to a naked girl. (This last scene suffers a major cut in the British video print.) A deft moment of comic splatter has the twins' father cut in two by a buzzsaw: All we see are his two legs falling over in opposite directions.

Belial himself is an ingenious blend of makeup and puppetry, a great screen monster, and it matters not a whit that he is not 100 percent convincing all the time — after all, the film never pretends to be anything other than artifice. On occasion he is just a lifeless rubbery prop. In four stop-motion cuts of him shuffling madly around his hotel room, the animation is extremely crude. Henenlotter is quoted in an interview in *Fangoria* #16: "I did the stop-motion scenes myself, and at first I cared very much about moving it very slowly and precisely ... then I started kicking it with my foot. ...Ray Harryhausen can certainly sleep tonight." Other shots are more successful, such as a closeup of him screaming in anguish as he tele-pathically experiences Duane kissing a girl.

Three of the stop-motion cuts occur in one scene when Belial goes berserk. He drops to the floor, shuffles around awkwardly on his knobbly, legless body, picks up a chair, throws it, pulls out a drawer and tips over a television. In a later scene, he jumps to the floor and crawls around. Both scenes are intercut with shots of the live-action puppet. Both scenes usually evoke squeals of amused delight from audiences who, although they are not fooled for a moment into thinking they are watching anything other than a bad special effect, still respond to the magic of stop-motion.

Henenlotter's contagious enthusiasm and assured direction and writing also characterized his next film, *Brain Damage* (1987), which also featured some enjoyably crude stop-motion. A sequel to *Basket Case* (*Basket Case II* [1990]) was less inventive and contained no stop-motion.

---

batteries not included

1987. Amblin Entertainment. D: Matthew Robbins. Scr: Brad Bird, Matthew Robbins, Brent Maddock, S.S. Wilson. Story: Mick Garris. Ph: John McPherson. Art: Ted Haworth. Mus: James Horner. Visual Effects: Industrial Light and Magic. Visual Effects Supervisor: Bruce Nicholson. Rod Puppet/Stop-Motion Supervisor: David Allen. Model Construction: Greg Jein. Go-Motion Animator: Tom St. Amand. Spaceship Design: Ralph McQuar-rie. Matte Painting Supervisor: Chris Evans.

Cast: Hume Cronyn, Jessica Tandy, Frank McRae, Elizabeth Peña, Michael Carmine, Dennis Boutsikaris.

Rating: ☆☆☆   Stop-Motion: ☆☆☆

This engaging modern-day fairy tale, conceived originally by executive producer Steven Spielberg, concerns the rag-bag inhabitants of a crumbling New York tenement. Destined for demolition, the building is saved in the nick of time by tiny metallic visitors from outer space, who befriend the occupants and restore the tenement to its former glory.

Matthew Robbins, who had directed *Dragonslayer* (1981), enlisted Industrial Light and Magic to handle the numerous effects shots of the various craft flying around the rooms and corridors of the tenement. Additionally, the script called for the two parent craft to procreate and produce three metallic offspring that would strut around on bird-like legs in a number of semi-comic episodes. This is robo-motion — but for a young audience.

Under the overall supervision of ILM veteran Bruce Nicholson, the final film is a consummate blending of a variety of effects techniques. On-set live action props (supported on wire rigs and operated by radio-control) are intercut with models shot with a motion-control process in front of a blue screen. Other shots requiring more intricate movement feature rod puppetry and stop-motion animation by David Allen or go-motion animation by Tom St. Amand. In keeping with ILM's high-quality effects history, all those involved were brought onto the project early on, unlike many other films where effects artists have been recruited late in the schedule, resulting in poorly executed sequences. In *batteries not included*, all the disparate elements mesh together beautifully.

Of course, the fact that these are metallic creations made the job a lot easier. Matching up different model versions of living creatures is much trickier.

David Allen's excellent rod puppetry sequences, like those featuring the living cakes in *Young Sherlock Holmes*, were only possible because the subjects did not have to be particularly expressive or fluid.

Several models were built of each of the five principal craft, their level of detail depending on the functions required of them. They were in part designed by Ralph McQuarrie, the dramatic pre-production artist of the *Star Wars* films. Greg Jein, part of the effects crew of *Close Encounters of the Third Kind* (1977), was one of the model builders, so it is no surprise that the impressively detailed spaceships have much in common with Spielberg's alien visitors.

The film's first 30 minutes, establishing the dire predicament of the tenement-dwellers, are full of likable sentimentality. Then Hume Cronyn begs, "Please...help us, somebody"— and the film enters a magical world with a sense of charm that recalls *Peter Pan*. James Horner's score catches the right balance of the playful and the creepy.

Two 12–inch-diameter spacecraft enter through an open window and glide gracefully around one of the apartments. One crashlands in the kitchen and, with the help of a couple of stop-motion shots by Allen, recharges itself by extending a plug and inserting it into a wall socket.

The two craft hide in a rooftop hut, emerging briefly to make a lightning-fast repair job on Cronyn's smashed watch. This sequence was achieved with go-motion animation of tiny watch-pieces animated by St. Amand, with blue-screen elements of the two craft whizzing about in a flurry of activity.

"Welcome to America!" offers

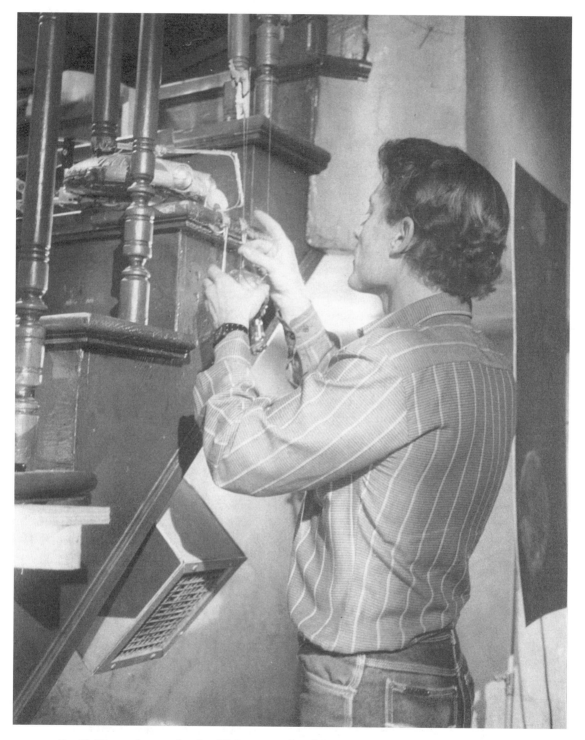

David Allen animates the tiny "living spaceships" for *batteries not included (1989).

Cronyn, arms outstretched in a gentle parody of the science fiction clichés of films like *The War of the Worlds*. In superb displays of composite and on-set photography, the two craft speed around the tenement, dynamically tilting and rotating, dodging people, dislodging crockery and giving an aerial display above the rooftops.

As a prelude to procreation, the "father" craft feeds metallic food to the mother-to-be. Allen stop-motioned an impressive cut in which the father cuts small pieces out of a Pepsi can and feeds them to his mate. Tiny robotic arms extend out of its underside, one holding a welding torch that cuts away at the can. The sparks from the torch were added later as a separate element. The pieces are placed onto an animated conveyor belt that leads into the other saucer.

Shortly afterwards, the mother-saucer produces three offspring. "Machines that reproduce themselves!" gasps one of the amazed on-lookers. "Living hardware!" These tennis ball–sized creations on bird-like legs suggest miniature distant cousins of the Scout Walkers of *Return of the Jedi*, or ED-209 of *RoboCop*. Many of the shots of the "babies" look like stop-motion but in fact were achieved with Allen's rod puppet techniques, shot in front of a blue screen.

These include fabulous little moments such as two of the babies first stepping into view, closely watched by the incredulous actors; one of them strutting across the grill in a diner and getting a slice of cheese thrown on top of it; the same saucer, now stuck inside a burger bun, stepping blindly along the top of the diner's counter and toppling off the edge; and a swordfight with paintbrushes between two of the saucers. These shots are all excellent composites, enhanced by carefully added shadows and reflections.

One of the three offspring finds its way into a plumbing system and emerges from a toilet bowl. Allen used stop-motion to show the saucer clambering up onto the toilet seat, matting puppet and seat onto footage of the toilet bowl and live-action set. Two shots of one of the parent craft producing a robotic arm and flicking on some electric switches look like stop-motion shots but again may have been done with rod puppets.

The most elaborate stop- and go-motion sequence occurs when the mother saucer teaches two of her offspring to fly by pushing them off the edge of a staircase. The first one plummets straight down, starts to fly only in the nick of time, then lands gracefully on a step only to topple over backwards. These shots were animated by St. Amand, whose go-motion blurs make the model's movements very convincing. The second saucer is pushed over the edge but has second thoughts and, in best cartoon fashion, extends two metallic arms and latches back onto the step. The mother saucer produces a little buzz-saw and cuts away the edge of the step (the sawdust is a separate superimposed element), causing her unwilling sibling to fall. The saucer deploys a metallic parachute-like contraption before finally getting the hang of flying.

Allen supplied two of the shots that make up this moment (the saucer hanging from the stair-edge and the mother producing the saw), with St. Amand handling the rest. Allen's cuts were animated on the live-action set; St. Amand shot his cuts against a blue screen. During the shot in which the second saucer starts to drop, Allen introduced an effective blur into the image by supporting his puppet on wires and lowering it slightly during the long camera exposure.

Later shots of the three offspring, including a sequence out on the street where they mistake a car hubcap for one of their parents, are done by rod puppetry. The final stop-motion shot, animated by Allen, is a touching shot of one of the offspring standing amidst the burnt-out ruins of the building, replacing one dislodged mosaic tile — a valiant but futile attempt to repair the damage. This shot had to be done with stop-mo-

tion because of the intricate arm and hand movements required in the placing of the tile.

The film ends with a stunning matte painting — by ILM regular artist Chris Evans — of the now-restored tenement standing between two halves of an enormous high-rise office-block, having resisted the plans of the property developer who tried to demolish it.

Allen also shot three stop-motion sequences which were not included in the final version of the film. These showed the parent craft repairing a torn photograph and two of the offspring chasing each other and playing with a set of keys.

Script collaborator S.S. Wilson is author of the 1980 book *Puppets and People*, an excellent survey of stop-motion in feature films.

The Bear

1988. Price Entertainment. D: Jean-Jacques Annaud. Scr: Gerard Brach. Based on *The Grizzly King* by James Oliver Curwood. Ph: Philippe Rouselot. Art: Toni Ludi. Mus: Philippe Sarde. Animation: Bretislav Pojar, Studio Kratky Film (Prague), Ceskoslovensky Filmexport. Animatronic Bears: Jim Henson's Creature Shop.

Cast: Bart, Youk, Jack Wallace, Tcheky Karyo, Andre Lacombe.

Rating: ☆☆☆   Stop-Motion: ☆☆

This engaging tale of a bear cub contains some marvelous footage of bears in the wild and makes full use of the spectacularly mountainous British

Columbia locations. Surprisingly, it utilizes stop-motion in two scenes showing the cub's dreams, the intention being to contrast the "unreality" of these sequences with the extreme naturalness of the rest of the film.

The first follows the cub's encounter with a frog. In his dream, he sees a frog-like creature with tentacle-like legs that snake above its head. A dozen frogs criss-cross each other and a fanged creature that looks like a cross between a bat and a frog swoops straight at the camera. The three quick stop-motion cuts form a dreamy, half-perceived montage.

In the second dream sequence, also featuring three stop-motion cuts, the cub licks his mouth, nuzzles his parent, then does a cartwheel and walks off. A fully armatured puppet of the cub and a miniature cave set were built for these shots which, although animated without great smoothness, achieve their purpose of suggesting the world of dreams.

Later, the cub eats some mushrooms and hallucinates a floating mushroom which changes color and transforms into a butterfly. These shots may also be puppet animation or perhaps cel animation, blue-screened into the live-action surroundings.

The Beast from 20,000 Fathoms

1953. Warner Bros. D: Eugene Lourie. Scr: Louis Morheim, Fred Freiberger. Based on a *Saturday Evening Post* story by Ray Bradbury. Ph: Jack Russell. Mus: David Buttolph. Art: Hal Waller. Technical Effects Created by Ray Harryhausen. Miniatures (uncredited): George Lofgren.

Cast: Paul Christian, Paula Raymond, Cecil Kellaway, Kenneth Tobey, Donald Woods, Lee Van Cleef, King Donovan.

Rating: ☆☆☆   Stop-Motion: ☆☆☆

Willis O'Brien was briefly considered for the task of producing the special effects of this fore-runner of all the 1950s monster-on-the loose films. *Mighty Joe Young* had won him an Oscar but its huge production costs also gave him a reputation for being expensive. Consequently, Ray Harryhausen landed his first solo feature film work. This was to be low-budget filmmaking: the $210,000 budget was small by contemporary standards, and Harryhausen's $6,000 share was less than generous considering that he toiled for between six and seven months on his post-production animation. But in so doing, he demonstrated an impressive ability to produce spectacular effects at reasonable cost — a talent that would serve him well and make him bankable throughout the rest of his career.

The Beast from 20,000 Fathoms remains one of the most watchable films of the science fiction boom of the 1950s. Its producers (Hal Chester and Jack Dietz) saw it essentially as a means of cashing in on the trend started by money-spinners like *The Thing* (1951), but fortunately they chose a director with a more sensitive outlook. Russian set designer Eugene Lourie shows a real interest in his subject, making the most of a script (by Fred Frieberger and Louis Morheim) that invents genre clichés rather than blindly following existing ones.

Lourie maintains the plot's sense of progression as the monster (a fictitious prehistoric "rhedosaurus") leaves the North Pole after its 150-million-year slumber has been disturbed by atomic bomb tests, moves south along the Canadian coast, into the streets of New York, and finally succumbs in the bizarre location of the Coney Island roller coaster park. Lourie keeps the live-action sequences low-key and credible, extracting likable performances from his cast, especially Cecil Kellaway as amiable old Dr. Thurgood Elson, "the foremost paleontologist in the world." Typical of the director's knack with character is a scene in which two lighthouse-keepers are chatting and singing just before they are killed by the Beast — it's nothing special, but just enough to give the scene a potent touch of pathos.

Lourie, who also designed all the sets, had a distinct and moody visual style, most evident in the early scenes during a blizzard at the North Pole, in the almost dream-like encounters with the Beast at sea, in the lighthouse and underwater, and in the haunting shots of the deserted streets of New York, patrolled by lines of soldiers succumbing one by one to a deadly bacterium.

Realizing that the budget would not stretch to glass shots and extensive miniature sets, Harryhausen knew he had to come up with a cheaper way of combining animation and live action. His innovation is a milestone in the development of stop-motion films and over the years has come to be known as "the reality sandwich." In essence, his technique was to drop his animation puppet into the middle of previously shot live-action footage. This compares with O'Brien's more elaborate shots that often involved having his puppet interact with detailed miniature sets, enhanced by glass paintings and with previously-shot live-action footage inserted in a tiny area of the set by means of miniature rear projection.

The reality sandwich is a rear-projection static matte composite, explained in a diagram in the Glossary in this book. The beauty of the reality sandwich is that it can deceive the eye into seeing objects (buildings, cars, people, etc.) in front of the puppet when in fact they are part of the rear projection. The effect is to create a believable illusion that the puppet really is in among all the live action.

In *Beast*, Harryhausen also achieved some of his composites by means of a prototype front-projection system. Front-projection systems today project the live-action footage onto a screen through a translucent mirror positioned at a 45–degree angle to the camera. The camera, aimed through the mirror, is therefore able to re-film exactly the pre-shot footage, incorporating the animation puppet at the same time. Harryhausen had no such translucent mirror. His front-projection set-ups are a combination of front- and rear-projection, with the foreground section of the split-screen initially matted out, then added during a second pass of the camera by front-projecting the image onto a carefully shaped piece of white card. This creates the illusion that some parts of the live-action image are in front of the puppet while others are behind it. The advantage of front-projection over rear-projection is that the image picked up by the camera is much brighter, because it has not been projected through a screen which robs it of some of its clarity. Throughout his career, however, Harryhausen's preferred composite method was rear-projection —*Beast* is a rare instance of him using front-projection.

There are 84 animation cuts in

Skull of the Rhedosaurus

This skull, seen here in a display at London's Museum of the Moving Image, is all that remains of Harryhausen's rhedosaurus from *The Beast from 20,000 Fathoms* (1953).

Beast, constituting less than five minutes of on-screen footage. Lourie and Harryhausen cleverly make it seem like much more, using brief snippets in several short scenes and saving the more elaborate stuff for the climax.

The rhedosaurus was sculpted by Harryhausen, who built the armature from parts machined by his father. Its meticulously detailed scaly hide was fashioned from casts taken of actual alligator skins. Harryhausen claims that a fictitious creature was invented because real dinosaurs were too small. Somehow this doesn't ring true; an animation puppet can be made to look any size an animator chooses to make it. Is the real reason that he didn't feel confident enough in his animation to have a swift-moving biped as the star? Or is it because

a biped would look unnatural walking around on the bottom of the sea? Whatever the reason, he chose a slow-moving quadruped with the vicious head of a carnivore. But the proportion of its front legs to its hind legs never looks quite right: it suggests a dog more than a reptile, and in some shots looks awkward.

Other miniatures were built by George Lofgren, who had worked with Harryhausen on *Mighty Joe Young* and would build models and miniatures in Harryhausen's three subsequent black-and-white pictures and *The 7th Voyage of Sinbad*.

The rhedosaurus is one of the classic monsters of the 1950s despite the fact that Harryhausen never really tries to imbue it with any personality. It has a brief moment of playfulness when it tramples on a car then brushes it aside, and we cannot help but feel sorry for it at the climax. But otherwise it is very much a conventional adversary. The poignancy of the short story on which the film is based ("The Foghorn" by Ray Bradbury) has been omitted: Originally the beast was attracted to the lighthouse because its foghorn makes a sound like a rhedosaurus calling out. In the film, this becomes merely another bit of wanton destruction.

The opening 15 minutes combine a documentary-style narrative with *Boys Own* thrills as "Operation X" gets underway, an atomic bomb test that causes a great upheaval in the Arctic (courtesy of stock footage of an explosion and studio shots of icebergs crashing into the sea, good effects done not by Harryhausen but by Lourie's unit). There are three stop-motion cuts during this sequence, all brief glimpses of the beast partly obscured by a superimposed blizzard. In the first, it walks behind two huge ice-blocks, barely seen. The blocks look like miniatures, or perhaps just cutouts, placed in front of the puppet.

In another quick cut, allowing a better look at its canine-like fangs and the spines running down its back, one of the scientists turns round and sees the monster standing above him growling. In this shot, the ice in the lower part of the shot suggests split-screen was used, the matte line heavily disguised by the blizzard. A later low-angle shot looks up at the monster on top of a wall of ice, the matte line following the ridge. When it turns to walk away, its tail sends the ice crashing down onto the scientist below — not animated ice but miniature ice done in a cut-away.

The night-time attack on the ship at sea is a shadowy sequence that demonstrates that Harryhausen was confident of being able to create the illusion of his puppet in contact with water, a perennial headache in effects shots. There are five animation cuts and also one closeup of a seven-inch hand-puppet built by Harryhausen and shot through a distortion glass to suggest it is seen through the water-soaked window of the ship's bridge. Two cuts are silhouettes of the beast's head and neck rising up in front of a static photo of the ship. Three long-shots show it attacking the ship, pushing down one side of the miniature craft then the other, biting into it and chewing on some broken timber. Film of crashing waves, shot previously at night, is superimposed around the area where puppet and model ship are matted into the live-action sea plate.

Of course, it's not entirely convincing, but it's a good little sequence: Harryhausen improved on it in a very similar moment in his next film, *It Came from Beneath the Sea.*

The attack on the lighthouse is a stylish, low-key affair. There are five animation cuts and the seven-inch head makes its second and last appearance. The lighthouse is a miniature; the sea behind it is a rear-projection; and the rocks in the lower foreground are all a front-projection, added during a second pass of the film through the camera. In silhouette, the monster clambers out of the sea and roars up at the beacon at the top of the lighthouse. In a closer shot, the puppet is still a silhouette but parts of it gleam wet in the glow from the beacon. Its tail swishing, it rears up and pushes on the lighthouse, sending it crashing down. Credible animation of lots of wire-supported pieces of falling masonry enhance this shot. A final extreme long-shot has the growling rhedosaurus standing among the ruins.

After an unpleasant stock-footage fight between a shark and an octopus, the beast is discovered in the rocky depths of Hudson Bay. Prof. Elson is lowered in a bathysphere (a miniature) among the rocky pillars of a studio set shot through murky glass by Harryhausen to create an effective illusion of being underwater. Featuring six stop-motion cuts (all very smoothly animated), this is a classic sequence mixing humor with terror to blackly memorable effect.

Three long shots have the beast walking slowly through the miniature set and another is a rear-screen shot of it passing in front of the battling shark

***The Beast from 20,000 Fathoms*:** Harryhausen's rhedosaurus, about to demolish an intricately detailed miniature building.

and octopus. But the highlights are two closeups of the great reptilian head coming straight at the camera, jaws open. Harryhausen cleverly has the head initially in shadow, then moving into bright light, making it a realistic shock effect. The script has the excited professor giving a mumbo-jumbo scientific commentary as all this is happening, totally oblivious to the danger: "The dorsal fin is singular, not bilateral, and the clavicle suspension appears to be cantileveric. But the most astonishing thing about it is that…"—and the radio link goes dead.

Eventually the rhedosaurus surfaces at the docks of New York city and enacts the kind of urban terror not seen in cinemas since *King Kong* in 1933. Lourie controls the crowd scenes surprisingly well, considering the low budget, and Harryhausen has created some startling composites of the beast in the city streets that have become classic images.

In a terrific static matte shot, the huge head of the beast rises up out of the river behind a group of dock workers, a bridge spanning the river in the background. This shot was the first composite Harryhausen filmed, to prove to himself that his reality sandwich would work—and it does, brilliantly, perfectly suggesting that the extras in the lower foreground are in front of the puppet, even though they are part of the rear-projection. In the next stop-motion cut, the rear part of this matte has been re-placed by a convincing miniature set containing freight boxes that get crushed by the beast as it clambers up onto the dock. Two medium shots have the beast walking past a rear-projection of a bridge. In a classic long shot, the rhedo-saurus appears on a busy street from be-hind a building on the right and lifts one of its forelegs in the air in a semi-threat-ening pose—one of the few moments where Harryhausen indulges in a bit of worthwhile animal behavior.

In an effective series of medium shots, the camera dollies backwards as the rhedosaurus stomps towards us. As it advances, it walks in and out of shad-ows thrown by the buildings—an all-important trick that helps to make the shots that much more believable. In one of these cuts, its tongue shoots out like a snake's (but probably not like a dino-saur's).

A brave but foolhardy policeman faces off against the monster, firing his gun at it. The huge head swoops down and picks him up in its teeth, the head of the puppet aligned so as to obscure the crane that is actually lifting the actor in the rear-projection. Some deliciously gruesome shots (probably inspired by Harryhausen having seen the uncut ver-sion of *King Kong*) have the beast with a puppet-human struggling in its mouth, legs kicking. The policeman is clearly seen being gulped down into the huge mouth. (A much-published press shot of three policemen standing in front of a full-scale rear-projection of the beast does not appear in the film.)

A miniature car gets realistically crumpled under the beast's foot and then brushed aside in a non-matte shot that simply has car and puppet in front of the rear-screen, in which panicking extras run past. In another enduring image, the beast walks into a street full of abandoned cars, the matte line fol-lowing the car roofs. Several extras run past in the foreground and their heads clearly pass in front of the monster's legs. This, of course, is impossible to do with a conventional static matte set-up, so Harryhausen must have placed a sheet of glass in front of the puppet and painted each of the heads on it frame by frame as they move across the image. In the background, it also looks as though he has animated (very crudely) a puppet or a cut-out trying to get out of one of the cars; only registered by us sublimi-nally, this effect is over in a fraction of a second.

The rhedosaurus picks up a minia-ture car, shakes it from side to side, then drops it. Again it rears up on one of its forelegs. In long shot again, the beast growls at the extras who are running straight at the camera.

A series of seven shots, done in a miniature set with no mattes, depicts the rhedosaurus demolishing a building. It walks into a street with several aban-doned miniature cars and knocks over a lamp post. It recoils in pain when shot by a policeman, rears up and smashes into the side of a miniature building, its head poking through the other side of the wall in a cloud of superimposed dust and lots of convincingly animated falling debris. After another dollying medium shot and two long shots, an impressively designed composite has extras running down into a subway, with the camera looking up out of the subway entrance as the beast, in a full-scale rear-projection, walks straight at us, slowly blocking out all the light. Harryhausen would use this claustrophobic design again (and to even better effect) in *The Valley of Gwangi* many years later.

By nightfall, the army has been mobilized. Five aerial shots look down from a rooftop at the rhedosaurus standing in a shadowy miniature street. In a clever touch, Harryhausen has his puppet lit up by searchlights, which are animated frame by frame so as to move across the model. In a full-scale rear projection, the beast advances on soldiers who are sheltered in the foreground by a wall of sandbags. An atmospheric long shot uses a split screen, with soldiers in the lower foreground and the beast in the background, behind a miniature wall and barricade. In another full-scale rear-projection set-up, soldiers run past the growling beast.

Five stop-motion cuts feature in the well-staged scene where the beast touches some electric cables, the model lit up dramatically behind superimposed showers of sparks. Struck by a missile fired from a bazooka, the beast roars in pain and walks around in a confused circle.

The novel idea of having the rhedosaurus make its last stand in a Coney Island rollercoaster was Harryhausen's, and it still looks spectacular today. The only disappointment is that the beast is dispatched a little too easily — the well-aimed missile (fired by a young Lee Van Cleef) for once succeeds the first time.

There are 20 stop-motion cuts, with Harryhausen combining live-action rollercoaster, animated puppet and miniature burning rollercoaster brilliantly.

An establishing long shot has the growling rhedosaurus standing in the middle of the miniature rollercoaster, matted into the live-action amusement park. An excellent extreme long shot adds the extra element of the soldiers in the lower foreground, while the distant monster chews on some timber it has bitten off. Medium shots of the monster (without mattes) and another long shot keep the action flowing as Van Cleef and Paul Christian prepare to fire the deadly missile into an open wound in the creature's neck. In one of these shots, it lunges at part of the rollercoaster and bites off a piece.

The bizarre sight of the two men in white protective costumes riding in the rollercoaster car adds another twist to what is already a visually striking sequence. An exciting long shot shows the beast rearing up as the two men stand at the top of the rollercoaster on the right. One half of this matte shot jiggles for a second because of a slip in the registration. In closeup, the camera tilts down from the beast's head to reveal the wound in its neck, blood (animated gelatin) oozing out. Van Cleef fires his missile and the preceding long-shot set-up is used again, with the dinosaur recoiling and screaming as the actors look on.

In a series of medium shots (not using mattes), the screaming dinosaur thrashes about, knocking into the sides of the roller coaster and sending the car crashing out of control, starting a fire. In subsequent shots, the puppet is lit by

The Beast from 20,000 Fathoms is trapped by fire inside a roller coaster. (National Film Archive, London.)

flickering light simulating the glow from the flames, reminding us that Harryhausen was adept at this trick long before the Medusa sequence in *Clash of the Titans*. Flames in the rear projection combine with superimposed flames and smoke to suggest that the puppet really is surrounded on all sides by fire. In a clever long shot, the puppet walks in a circle and its tail throws up a shower of burning wood into the air. The wood is a separate element that was shot previously at night and then superimposed.

The rhedosaurus knocks into the rollercoaster with its head, causing the burning miniature to topple over. This is achieved by having a vertical matte line down the side of the woodwork. Keen-eyed viewers will notice that the puppet's head briefly passes behind the woodwork and disappears, although it should still be visible through the scaffolding. The dying dinosaur walks out of the rollercoaster onto a miniature foreground, twice walks around in a dazed circle and then collapses. Finally it rears up onto its hind legs, lets out an almighty roar and slumps down dead. Beautifully animated, such agonizingly drawn-out death throes would become a Harryhausen trademark.

Although no masterpiece, *The Beast from 20,000 Fathoms* is one of Harryhausen's most durable films, not hampered by the artificial dialogue and acting that have marred later films. Lourie's direction and the special effects single it out from the countless imitations that it spawned, marking it as a landmark film both technically and in its subject matter. It was crying out to be remade by somebody like Joe Dante or John Landis during the monster revival of the 1980s (which included remakes of *The Thing* and *The Blob*) but, unfortunately it never happened.

The Beast of Hollow Mountain

1956. United Artists/Nassour. D: Edward Nassour, Ismael Rodríguez. Scr: Robert Hill (with Ismael Rodríguez and Carlos Orellana, uncredited). Additional Dialogue: Jack DeWitt. From an idea by Willis O'Brien. Ph: Jorge Stahl, Jr. Mus: Raul Lavista. Photographic Effects: Jack Rabin, Louis DeWitt. (Uncredited Model Construction: Henry Lion.)

Cast: Guy Madison, Patricia Medina, Eduardo Noriega, Carlos Rivas, Mario Navarro, Julio Villareal.

Rating: ☆☆½   Stop-Motion: ☆☆½

As low-budget monster-on-the-loose pictures go, this is well-staged and a lot of fun, but it is difficult to watch it without thinking how much better it might have been had Willis O'Brien been allowed to handle the special effects. He wrote the original story and sold it to producer Edward Nassour, getting a promise that he would be hired to do the effects. But Nassour reneged on his promise, barred O'Brien from the studio set, made drastic revisions to the story and gave the effects contract to Jack Rabin and Louis DeWitt.

Rabin and DeWitt brought in the animation sequences cheaper and quicker than O'Brien would have done, but they also missed the fantasy atmosphere and grander designs that Obie would have given the film. Adding insult to injury, Nassour boasted that he was some kind of special effects wizard. The press ads announced: "Regiscope [from 'register' and 'scope'] is the trademark for the new animation-in-depth screen process by which inanimate objects are made to move realistically and which producer-director Edward Nassour developed after 18 years of experimentation." He claimed that his new process was the result of "the expenditure of several hundred thousand dollars" and involved "the wizardry of electronics," controlling the movements of his models electronically. *Beast of Hollow Mountain* features no such electronic puppetry — this was merely the same kind of hyperbolic producer-speak that was heard 20 years later from Dino De Laurentiis when he was making his version of *King Kong*. Some literature suggests that Nassour even executed the puppet animation himself, but this seems highly unlikely.

However, *Beast* was not entirely without innovation. It was the first feature film to shoot stop-motion in CinemaScope. But Nassour's commercially sound idea to film in color must have given Rabin and DeWitt nightmares. Like previous films of this type, it would rely heavily on rear projection, but the problems of creating the illusion that puppet and background footage are part of the same image are multiplied when filming in color and require careful testing to ensure color matching. In many shots, Rabin and DeWitt fail to match the two elements, with the rear image looking faded and grainy while the foreground puppet is brightly lit and in sharp focus. This same problem made Harryhausen reluctant to film in color for *The 7th Voyage of Sinbad* (1958), and it may well be that his apprehension was caused by seeing Nassour's film. There are certainly dramatic similarities between the two films that suggest that Harryhausen had seen this picture.

Beast's most significant innovation is its use of replacement animation, a technique seen previously only in shorts such as George Pal's *Puppetoons* series. Replacement animation differs from conventional animation in that instead of one model being minutely moved one frame at a time, a whole series of separate models, each one slightly different from the preceding one, is constructed. For each frame of film, a puppet is removed from the animation table and replaced by the next puppet in the sequence.

In *Beast* this technique is used to great effect when the tyrannosaurus is shown walking or running, actions which are sufficiently cyclical and predictable to lend themselves to this method. More intricate actions and closeups were animated with conventional stop-motion. The intercutting in *Beast* between the two styles is the film's downfall: The stop-motion cuts often look hurried and seem even more artificial when compared to the extremely smooth replacement animation passages.

The replacement puppets, sculpted by Henry Lion (although some sources claim it was Walter Lyons), are actually better models than the stop-motion version which never quite manages to convince that it is anything other than a puppet. Its two arms project out in an effeminate pose that would horrify a paleontologist. This is a great shame because it was built up over the armature originally used by Marcel Delgado's fine Gwangi model in O'Brien's unfinished film of 1941.

The direction by Nassour and Ismael Rodríguez, the script by Robert Hill and Carlos Orellana, and the acting by leads Guy Madison and Patricia Medina (menaced the year before by the *Phantom of the Rue Morgue*) never rise above the routine. The first 50 minutes are conventional Western antics, enlivened by an entertaining fistfight in the street, a Mexican wedding attended by locals in exotic costumes and a well-staged cattle stampede through the town. A couple of scenes introduce us to a dangerous swamp and Hollow Mountain, from which a giant monster is said to emerge in times of drought.

The first animation sequence begins less-than-spectacularly with some live-action shots of the tyrannosaurus' feet — a man in a shoddy dinosaur costume — as it sneaks up on two cattlemen. The animated puppet is first seen in a long shot of it standing on a miniature set with a rear-projection of trees and sky behind. Two closeups show off its canine fangs and absurdly long tongue as it curls one of its lips up in an unlikely snarl that recalls O'Brien's brontosaurus in *The Lost World*.

After another long-shot and two medium shots, the Beast stomps into another miniature set and picks up an animated bull in its jaws. The bull does not require much animation but the stride of the Beast is extremely fluid, thanks to the replacement animation. The sequence ends with a conventional displacement animation medium shot of the Beast walking off with the bull in its mouth. No real interaction with the live action is attempted so far and the cutting from live action to miniature shots only heightens the artificiality of the animation set-ups.

Later on, little Panchito (Mario Navarro) wanders off into the creepy swamp in search of his missing father. The Beast is soon on his scent, seen in several medium shots against a rear projection of the forest, looking around hungrily, growling and flaring its cheeks. A bladder in the puppet's neck expands and contracts, a nice touch that suggests the dinosaur is breathing agitatedly. A shot from over the Beast's shoulder has the dinosaur looking down at Panchito in the rear screen. There are several live-action shots of the prop feet tentatively stepping in the mud of the swamp, and these weaken the scene's effectiveness. In another fine replacement animation long shot, the dinosaur walks down a slope,

followed by a stop-motion shot that suffers by comparison; in the latter shot, the puppet retreats warily from the edge of the swamp, which is shown to be behind and below the Beast by means of static matte.

From here on the film is one long, frantic animation sequence (interrupted only briefly by live-action shots) in which the tyrannosaurus relentlessly pursues most of the cast, kills the bad guy and eventually (and inventively) is lured to its death by Madison.

The first segment, in which the Beast menaces Panchito and heroine Medina in a cabin, is visually stylish and uses an impressive variety of composites. Panchito runs out of the swamps toward Medina, and several medium shots show the dinosaur looking at them (backed by a rear screen). A long shot of the puppet walking on a miniature floor towards the cabin uses the replacement models again, a very fluid cut in which the Beast's tail swishes from side to side and its feet curl down realistically each time it lifts one up to take a step.

Several medium shots of the displacement puppet give it a chance to snarl and breath, while two more replacement long shots show it walking around the cabin. Three long shots have the Beast start to demolish the roof of the miniature cabin, intercut with a shot of a lifeless prop arm trying to reach the actors, and a shot looking up from inside the cabin at the displacement puppet as it pulls away bits of the roof. The design of this sequence is very similar to the sequence in *The 7th Voyage of Sinbad* when the Cyclops tries to reach the sailors in his treasure chamber, another suggestion that Harryhausen had seen this film.

There is an attractive long shot from an unusual point of view when Madison looks down from a hill at the dinosaur in the miniature set. Only the model's cartoonish tongue, which seems to have grown even longer, spoils the shot.

Back in the cabin, Medina tries to fend off the monster with a stick but it snatches it away in its mouth, the broken pieces falling to the ground (probably supported by wire as they fall). A series of rear-screen shots has Madison in the background firing at the Beast. In a closeup, animated red blood trickles down its wounded snout and it rubs its wound with one of its claws. It's a nice touch, but O'Brien would have done it better, imbuing the model with more character.

Some rear-projection shots (without mattes) show the Beast turning its attention away from the cabin and toward Madison, and receiving another wound in its face. A number of smooth replacement shots of it slowly walking along include one especially good shot of it stomping across the frame, then turning away from the camera and walking behind a rock. The static matte really puts the model into the live-action setting and the slow, almost leisurely speed of the monster's gait (enforced by the predetermined series of replacement puppets) makes it seem (unintentionally) as though the dinosaur is so sure it will catch its prey that it has adopted a laid-back approach. Two further long shots are broken up by foreground miniature foliage but are ruined by another appearance of the absurd wagging tongue.

Bad guy Eduardo Noriega arrives and threatens to shoot Madison, only to be interrupted by the reappearance of the tyrannosaurus. Looking up from the actors' point of view, the dinosaur is seen standing at the top of a hill, the top of which provides the matte line. After some closeups of the dinosaur growling, there is a grainy rear-screen shot in which Noriega is thrown from his startled horse. Three memorable replacement long shots show the dinosaur running down the side of the hill, miniature or glass-painted foliage placed in front of the model to help merge it with the live-action screen.

Noriega dives into the swamp and the Beast tries to follow, snapping at him from the bank. The mixture of two long-shots (miniature foliage again disguising the matte line) and three closeups again serves to highlight the superiority of the model used for long-shots. Noriega runs into a dusty plain with the Beast in hot pursuit; two disappointing medium shots show the model "running" in front of a washed-out rear screen.

Madison comes to Noriega's rescue, pulling him up onto the back of his horse, but the persistent dinosaur is not to be outdone. In an ambitious and quite unforgettable composite, the Beast bounds across a miniature floor, matched to the terrain of the live-action plate in which Madison and Noriega speed away on the galloping horse. This is another extremely fluid replacement shot and prefigures the very similar moment in *The Empire Strikes Back* when the taun-taun gallops across the snow. It's a fine shot but the choreography of the Beast fails to convince 100 percent for the same reason as the taun-taun:

A publicity shot of *The Beast of Hollow Mountain* (1955).

Despite all its smoothness, the animation is simply too regular and cyclical, having none of the quirks and shifts of real movements.

Madison and Noriega come to the top of an embankment and force their horse to slide down it on the loose earth. There are two shots of the dinosaur hesitating at the top of the slope (and yes, that tongue seems to have grown even longer), then two successful shots of it sliding down, pushing miniature earth aside as it goes. This is one occasion when Rabin and DeWitt deserve praise for putting effort into devising interesting composites: It would have been all too easy to have the dinosaur simply walk down a solid hill.

At the bottom, another miniature floor is matched to the terrain in the live plate as the dinosaur gets back onto its feet (a well thought-out bit of animation — it could so easily have looked awkward). Determined as ever, the creature rushes off after the two men. A series of four quick rear-screen shots show the replacement puppet running across the frame; the background is different in each case.

The two men hide in a small cave (another precursor of a scene in *The 7th Voyage of Sinbad*) and a prop dinosaur hand is used in several cuts as the Beast tries to get at them. A few shots look out of the cave at the animation puppet. There are two good shots of the Beast holding, then discarding, a screaming puppet of Noriega, the animation of which is adequate for the few seconds it is on screen. Other cowboys arrive and there are two weak shots in which the puppet looks at a rider on a horse in a very washed-out rear screen.

The swamp finale suffers from contrast between the lighting of the model and the rear screen, but is lively stuff nonetheless. Madison lures the Beast over to the swamp in a series of cuts, some of which are replacement, some displacement. Two shots have Madison (off-screen) taunting it by waving a rope in front of it (an animated miniature).

Rabin and DeWitt allow their monster some characterization when a puzzled expression crosses its face as Madison throws the rope over a branch. Taunting it further, he throws a dagger, a miniature counterpart of which sticks in the Beast's snout until it brushes it away with a claw. In the next series of shots, the Beast stands on a grassy miniature bank matted into the edge of the swamp, trying to snatch at Madison as he swings on the rope just in front of him.

At last, the dinosaur can't resist reaching just a little too far and slides down into the swamp. As it tries to get up again, Madison swings over its head and lands on the solid ground on the other side. The closing effects shots look down at the model surrounded by glycerin in a miniature set, struggling helplessly and slowly being sucked down into the swamp — along with several fallen leaves which add a nice minor detail. Dramatically, it's a nifty climax but these last shots are let down, as elsewhere, by the fact that the displacement model always looks too "puppet-like."

Rabin and DeWitt have done their best with an inadequate budget. Several moments are truly inventive and their experimentation with replacement animation shows a real desire to achieve the best effects they could. It's difficult to say what they might have come up with if they had had the benefit of a generous budget and an interested director. They spent their whole careers (often teamed with Irving Block) creating effects on shoestring budgets, including dabbling with stop-motion on two more occasions, *Kronos* (1957) and *Monster from Green Hell* (1958). Both are less interesting than the ambitious *Beast*, which is their best work. But it is hampered by its inability to exploit the dramatic potential of its effects and is often clumsily directed by Nassour. It took Harryhausen to realize the full possibilities of O'Brien's vision of combining the Western and prehistoric genres when he made *The Valley of Gwangi* 13 years later.

Beetlejuice

1988. Geffen. D: Tim Burton. Scr: Michael McDowell, Warren Skaaren. Story: Michael McDowell, Larry Wilson. Ph: Thomas Ackerman. Art: Bo Welch. Mus: Danny Elfman. Visual Effects Supervisor: Alan Munro. Creatures and Makeup Effects: Robert Short. Visual Effects: VCE Inc/Peter Kuran. Snake Sequence: Ted Rae. Sandworm Sequence: Doug Beswick and (uncredited) Yancy Calzada. Stop-Motion Camera (uncredited): James Aupperle. Barbara/Adam Transformation: Tim Lawrence.

Cast: Michael Keaton, Alec Baldwin, Geena Davis, Jeffrey Jones, Catherine O'Hara, Sylvia Sidney.

Rating: ☆☆☆   Stop-Motion: ☆☆½

The 1980s produced any number of fantasy films like this: entertaining, generously budgeted, enthusiastically directed and full of impressive special effects. And at the end of the day forgettable because they added nothing new to the genre. *Beetlejuice* contains many images which very nearly touch that nightmare subconscious level in us, but is held back by its determination to be a wholesome middle–American light comedy; it even ends with a song-and-dance routine performed by ghosts. Imagine what David (*Eraserhead*) Lynch or Stuart (*Re-Animator*) Gordon might have done with this beyond-the-grave subject matter.

The film is an almost uninterrupted series of special effects: Its central couple (Alec Baldwin and Geena Davis) discover they have returned as ghosts after dying in a car crash and spend the rest of the film trying to scare off the new occupants of their home. Director Tim Burton (who had already directed *Pee-wee's Big Adventure* and would soon direct *Batman*) wanted the film to have a jokey visual style and wasn't too concerned with realism. Under the overall supervision of Alan Munro, the host of effects shots include a collection of grisly corpses in an after-life waiting room, a running headless body and a giant beetle (the latter sculpted by Laine Liska). Stop-motion and replacement animation provide some of the film's more outrageous sequences.

Whenever Baldwin or Davis leave

74

their house, they find themselves in a bizarre limbo-land, a desert planet with an unnaturally blue sky and strange rock formations jutting up from the sand. It is inhabited by sandworms, giant creatures that burrow through the sand and attack the couple. These sequences were realized through a combination of shots by Bob Short using a rod puppet sandworm and other shots using a three-foot-long stop-motion puppet built and animated by Doug Beswick and Yancy Calzada (the latter uncredited).

This surreal creature has the look of a cartoon character: a black-and-white-striped body, a shark's fin and a fang-filled mouth out of which emerges a second head. This second head has an equally vicious-looking set of teeth, big eyes like a duck and a tongue whose color pattern matches the striped body. Unfortunately, its weirdness is its downfall: It always looks like a creation of the special effects department and never convinces that it is a living creature. It appears in brief scenes at the beginning and end of the film but is never developed into the sinister threat it might have been. The animation is not as smooth as Beswick intended it to be because Alan Munro decided that the creature wasn't moving fast enough and skip-framed the footage that Beswick had shot, reducing the fluidity of the animation by half.

There are seven stop-motion cuts during the sandworm's first scene. After a long shot of the back of the rod puppet burrowing in the sand, the 50-foot creature rears up out of the foreground sand, its mouth opening to disgorge the second mouth. It snaps at Baldwin and Davis, lunging at them, but they escape back into the house just in the nick of time. The actors were placed into the desert landscape through a combination of blue-screen shots and shots of them in a forced-perspective studio set.

A second appearance of the sandworm was dropped from the film. Baldwin and Davis are hanging out of a window of their house as the monster snaps at them from below. Animated puppets of the actors were included in this sequence.

The sandworm makes a climactic appearance during the wedding of loathsome "bio-exorcist" Betelgeuse (Michael Keaton) to the daughter of the new owners of the house. The sandworm suddenly lunges through the ceiling, with Davis riding on its back, swallows Betelgeuse and crashes through the floorboards. There are three stop-motion cuts: a shot of the worm with an animated puppet of Davis on its back, a dramatic closeup of the creature lunging open-mouthed at the camera, and a final shot of it disappearing through the hole in the floor. As with many of the film's other gags, it doesn't work because it all happens in too much of a rush with little drama or rationale. Why, for example, is Davis riding on its back?

The film's best sequence features a giant rattlesnake with an absurd nightmare face that vaguely resembles Betelgeuse's. Technically impressive, it also whips up a minor chill. But ultimately this scene is also too short to realize its potential — it's really just a good quick scare.

There are about 15 stop-motion cuts in among a number of cuts using props of various kinds. The animation by Ted Rae (who had assisted David

Yancy Calzada animating the "statue garden" from *Beetlejuice* (1988).

Allen on *Dolls* and had his animation sequences dropped from the release print of *Jaws — the Revenge*) is excellent and the scaly hide of the creature is extremely realistic. Because the creature would never be seen in its entirety in any one shot, it was built as five different pieces, in three different scales.

In a creepy touch, the handrail of a banister transforms into the scaly hide of a snake. Suddenly the snake-creature appears, lunging at the actors gathered in the hall, tongue extended through needle-like teeth. Shots of the tail-rattle vibrating and the head and neck whipping around are effectively enhanced by blurs, achieved by moving the puppet during camera exposures. Successful composite shots have the snake pursuing the actors and, in one good moment of interaction, knocking over an actor with its tail. The composites were achieved not with rear projection but by the frontlight-backlight traveling matte process. An articulated head was built for shots in which the puppet is required to mouth a few lines of dialogue. Evil-looking cel-animated eyes were roto-scoped into shots of the non-animation puppets.

Two impressive replacement animation shots have Baldwin and Davis transform their faces into ghoulishly absurd proportions. Baldwin pulls out his nose and the top half of his head to a long point and pushes his hand up through his mouth, creating a comb-like crest on the top of his head. Davis stretches her mouth to crocodile-like proportions and pushes her eyes down so that they reappear resting on her tongue. Tim Lawrence took 20 weeks getting the shots to look just right, fashioning 30 heads for the first transformation and 25 for the second. The arms and hands which manipulate the heads were animated by conventional stop-motion methods.

A later replacement animation shot has a fireplace transformed into a warped expressionistic shape, a surround for the location of the wedding ceremony. This deft moment was done at Beswick's studio.

At another point in the film, Betelgeuse's magic causes two metal sculptures to come to life. One is a tree-like shape that overturns and walks on its branches like a deformed scorpion. The other is a wrinkled ball on a stalk that

shuffles along the floor like one of the flying brains from *Fiend Without a Face*. Again, these stop-motion creations are amusing throw-away gags and never amount to anything out of the ordinary.

Animated in a miniature replica of the living room set, these creations were animated by Yancy Calzada and lit and photographed by James Aupperle (both uncredited), again under Beswick's supervision. The animation in these five cuts is extremely smooth. The final cut is a composite with the two sculptures in the foreground, creeping up on two actors with their backs to the camera. Again, the means of combining the two images was a frontlight-backlight traveling matte.

As an entertaining diversion, *Beetlejuice* succeeds well enough, but its refusal to allow any of its effect setpieces to be anything more than quick comic moments makes it a disappointment.

Behemoth the Sea Monster (U.S.: *The Giant Behemoth*)

1959. D: Douglas Hickox, Eugene Lourie. Scr: Eugene Lourie. Story: Robert Abel, Allen Adler. Ph: Ken Hodges. Art: Harry White. Mus: Edwin Astley. Special Effects Designed and Created by Jack Rabin, Irving Block, Louis DeWitt, Willis O'Brien, Pete Peterson. Miniatures (uncredited): Phil Kellison.

Cast: Gene Evans, André Morell, Leigh Madison, Henry Vidon, Jack MacGowran, Maurice Kaufman, Leonard Sachs.

Rating: ☆☆½   Stop-Motion: ☆☆½

In *The Black Scorpion* in 1957, Willis O'Brien's usual striving after excellence was hampered by a B-picture budget, but in retrospect it must have seemed like a luxury compared to the paltry sum he was allowed on his next picture, *Behemoth the Sea Monster*. Producer David Diamond allocated around $20,000 for all the effects in the film but probably not more than half of this went to O'Brien. Despite O'Brien's track record, Diamond did not believe that he had the resources to produce all the effects the film required and consequently hired Jack Rabin's Studio Film Service (which included Irving Block and Louis De-Witt) to do all the non-animation effects sequences. Rabin in turn hired O'Brien on a sub-contract.

Diamond should have known better, of course: Rabin's studio-tank scenes are awful while O'Brien's sequences are the best thing about the film. One wonders what must have gone through O'Brien's mind at this stage in his career: He was working on a miserable film where his effects would have little chance to impress and also he had recently seen his protégé Ray Harryhausen enjoying great success with *20 Million Miles to Earth* and *The 7th Voyage of Sinbad*, both of which had comparatively large budgets.

Co-director/script-writer Eugene Lourie found himself under pressure from the producer to recreate the success he had six years earlier with *The Beast from 20,000 Fathoms*. The plot has so many similarities that it is almost a remake, but it is curiously missing all the qualities that made *Beast* such a good film. The earlier film had Lourie's sensitive direction, a brisk pace, likable characters, a trend-setting plot and a budget which, although limited, still allowed Harryhausen to achieve some spectacular sequences. *Behemoth*, however, struggles awkwardly through a dire hodgepodge of genre clichés and shows no evidence of Lourie's skill.

It has dull characters, in particular the two leads André Morell (normally excellent) and Gene Evans (the obligatory American actor dragged in to give the film commercial pull on both sides of the Atlantic). Even fine supporting players Maurice Kaufmann and Leonard Sachs are thrown away in inconsequential roles. Everybody looks thoroughly fed up with the perfunctory dialogue, but at least we are spared the usual trite love interest. The only remotely interesting character is a timid little museum employee (Jack MacGowran) who stares off dreamily into space when he hears about the dinosaur and babbles, "You know, all my life I've hoped this would happen. Ever since childhood, I've expected it..."

It's a film that only has interest for die-hard monster-on-the-loose fans and for people wanting to see what O'Brien was capable of in the twilight of his career. But it deserves a better treatment than most books of genre critique have given it.

There are several interesting effects sequences, most notably the well-staged scene when the behemoth wanders through some electricity pylons and some eerie shots at the climax when it is seen swimming underwater (an unusual sight in stop-motion filming). But there is a general level of crudity, enforced by the budget, which even O'Brien's talent cannot rise above. All his shots had to be achieved in a period of only six to eight weeks. The animation cuts are kept brief and, as in *The Black Scorpion*, are dimly lit so as to disguise the shortcomings of the miniature sets and to conceal where they meet a rear-projection screen. Many animation cuts are used more than once (again as in *The*

Black Scorpion) with shots being flopped or refilmed in closeup to make them look different.

The monster itself (a fictitious "paleosaurus" inspired by the rhedosaurus of *Beast*) has an impressively scaly skin texture (fashioned from casts of actual lizard skin) but its limbs look clumsy and it never achieves any sense of vitality or character. This is partly because O'Brien did not have the resources to design any elaborate sequences and also because Pete Peterson, who had assisted O'Brien on *Mighty Joe Young* and *The Black Scorpion*, was suffering from crippling arthritis to such an extent that he had to do all the animation while seated, working on miniature sets two feet off the ground. His animation is as smooth as ever but it must have been such an arduous task that he was prevented from giving his best.

Additionally, the impact of the animation effects is weakened by Rabin's sequences. A mechanical head was built for some closeups but its jaw mechanism was broken before filming and the budget didn't stretch to repairing it. Consequently it appears as a stiff, open-mouthed prop. Aerial glimpses of the behemoth swimming underwater are achieved by having a ridiculous and totally unconvincing white outline superimposed over footage of the sea. The monster's first big scene is its attack on the Woolwich ferry and this is so poorly staged by Rabin that it wouldn't fool an eight-year-old. The ferry bobs up and down in the studio tank like a bath toy, the prop head-and-neck clumsily nudges it around and half-asleep extras pretend to look terrified in poorly edited cut-away shots. O'Brien's subsequent animation scenes have little chance of recovering any dignity after this laughable opener.

The first animation sequence is preceded by one of the few live-action shots which suggest Lourie's talent: A man runs through a deserted dockyard, his footsteps echoing eerily. Then the camera cuts to two cranes in a miniature set, with the Thames and Tower Bridge in the background plate. To cut costs, this sequence used a photo blow-up for its background, rather than a rear projection. The convincing miniatures for this episode were built by Phil Kellison, who had worked with O'Brien on George Pal's *Puppetoons*.

The animated model climbs up onto the dockyard, the camera panning up as it does so, to emphasize its great size. It raises its head, roars at the sky, then bites into one of the cranes, tossing it aside. O'Brien has designed the set-up so that one of the cranes is in the foreground, giving the shot depth and allowing the behemoth to advance dramatically on the camera, walking into the second crane and knocking it over.

Later there is a street scene which begins with a shot which again seems to be modeled on a similar shot in *The Beast from 20,000 Fathoms*, the only difference being that the monster walks in from the left instead of the right. A Harryhausen-style reality sandwich has actors running in the lower half of the frame while the paleosaurus appears from behind a tall building in the background. As the monster twists its neck sinuously and growls, the camera zooms in on it, not to improve the shot but to disguise the fact that it will be used again later without the zoom.

D492-78

Behemoth the Sea Monster (1959) stomps through the streets of London. Animation by Pete Peterson; sequence designed by Willis O'Brien.

A closeup of the monster's foot stomping on a miniature car (which crumples convincingly) allows a good look at the surprisingly detailed, scaly skin texture of the model. However, it's not such a good shot that it needed to be shown twice more, but that's what we get. The second time it appears, we see it as it was actually filmed, not a closeup at all but a medium shot in which the monster's four legs stride across the frame as actors run past in the background plate. There are several closeups, shot slightly from below, of the monster licking its chops as it strides down the street. These are also copies of similar shots in *Beast*. Most of these shots are used more than once. Another brief cut shows the model's torso passing across the frame from left to right, emphasizing its great size. A second static matte allows the monster to walk behind a bus as actors flee in the foreground; the matte line follows the roof of the bus.

After the miniature car gets stomped on for the third time, the head and neck of the behemoth appear from behind the corner of a building. This is probably another of the photo cut-outs which

80

the film used to avoid designing time-consuming mattes; it's a very effective cost-cutting trick which is only possible in black-and-white films where color contrasts are not a problem. After a medium shot of the beast growling at the camera, a shot of its body passing across the frame is "enhanced" by some superimposed blurs, courtesy of Rabin, which are meant to suggest the radiation which the beast is unwittingly emitting. As a result, scar-faced extras run around and bump into one another.

Several repeat shots and radiation-glows later, there is a closeup of the monster growling at some soldiers who have fired on it, then a more dramatic composite in which it stomps into the shot from behind a building in a long shot, with extras running around in the lower half of the frame. In closeup, it knocks into the wall of a building which, in a live-action cut-away, falls on some more extras. After more repeated close-ups, the sequence closes with a shot in which the camera pans up from the monster's legs to its roaring head. This cut curiously jumps midway, presumably to hide some defect.

The encounter with the two electric pylons is an example of O'Brien making the most of his non-existent budget, but its choreography is disappointingly similar to the monster's attack on the dockyard cranes. It's filmed entirely in a miniature set and relies on very low lighting to hide any shortcomings. After stomping across the countryside in two very dark shots, the monster walks sluggishly into the set and recoils in pain when it touches the overhead wires, superimposed flashes of discharged electricity enhancing the effect. This image

is another direct steal from Harryhausen's film.

The behemoth bites into the first pylon and throws it aside, then walks straight at the camera, pulling down the second pylon with it. It walks right past the camera, which tilts down to show the monster's legs dragging the tangled remains of the pylon. This is a brief but impressively staged and animated passage, and it's the only moment when we feel any sympathy for the behemoth, who is too dumb to realize that electricity pylons are better left alone.

After several scrappy live-action scenes, there is more monster mayhem in central London. A matte or photo cut-out allows the behemoth to appear in front of Westminster Abbey, then there is an attractive matte shot in which the monster is seen walking on the far side of the Thames, the river flowing past below. Lourie then pinches yet another idea from *Beast* and has spotlights playing over the behemoth as it picks up a miniature car in its mouth. The imitation only serves to remind us how much better Harryhausen's version is.

There is a very smoothly animated closeup of the monster twisting its head from side to side, with the car in its jaws, like a cat playing with a mouse. When the monster throws the car into the river, it is supported on invisible wires for a few frames, a good effect that is spoiled by the subsequent shot in which the car hits the water: The scale of the water droplets makes it all too obvious that the car is only about three inches long. This sequence closes with a long shot of the behemoth rearing up on its hind legs.

The film's finale is an offbeat but

Behemoth the Sea Monster walks past Westminster Abbey. The building in the foreground may be a photo cut-out.

disappointingly anti-climactic underwater sequence. A two-man submarine armed with a radioactive torpedo is lowered into the water and manages to locate the paleosaurus. Nine animation cuts, plus a few shots of the live-action head nudging the sub, are all that is used to depict this encounter. Model animators traditionally avoid scenes that involve contact with water, but the problem is brilliantly overcome here by simply implying the presence of water. The behemoth is actually hanging in mid-air on wires throughout this sequence, but clever lighting and Peterson's credible animation suggest that it is totally submerged at all times. Its head snakes from left to right, its forelegs are held back against its sides and the rear legs kick to propel it along.

Eerie, low-key lighting on the model suggests the lights from the submarine penetrating the gloom. The behemoth swims across the frame in some shots, straight at the camera in others. In the final shot, an animated torpedo is fired into its open mouth, a superimposed explosion suggesting its less-than-spectacular demise. We have never been asked to feel any sympathy for the monster, but we end up feeling pretty sorry for it now because it gets such a low-key death scene.

The pressbook for the film boasted that it contained "some of the most thrilling and sensationally realistic scenes ever to be shown on the cinema screen," a blatant lie if ever there was one. In many respects "The Beast from 20,000 Dollars," as it might well be better called, is a good example of how *not* to make a monster movie. *Behemoth the Sea Monster* is a poor film, but O'Brien and Peterson have managed to make it look superior to many similar contemporary films whose cardboard, fake-looking monsters are only good for a few derisive laughs, despite having larger budgets.

The film's weak finale also represented a finale for O'Brien's career, a sad under-use of the talents of a man who was always capable of creating unforgettable flights of fantasy. He tried, unsuc-cessfully, to get producers interested in numerous other projects: *Umbah* (featuring a prehistoric lizard and various other giant animals), *Last of the Labyrinthodons* (mythological sea monsters), *The Last of the Oso Si-Papu* (a giant humanoid reptile), *Baboon* (a Yeti) and *The Elephant Rustlers* (elephants attacked by giant lizards). Irwin Allen hired O'Brien as technical advisor for his 1960 remake of *The Lost World* but very short-sightedly decided to use live lizards instead of animation; *The Animal World* in 1956 had taught Allen that stop-motion is a time-consuming process, and he was blind to its obvious merits over dressed-up iguanas and alligators. O'Brien took his ideas for *King Kong vs. Frankenstein* to an RKO producer only to find shortly after that it had been sold to Toho in Japan and transformed into *King Kong vs. Godzilla*, featuring a man in an unlikely monkey suit. His last work was for Stanley Kramer's *It's a Mad Mad Mad Mad World* in 1962, supervising a brief comic sequence that teamed him again with his old model-maker friend Marcel Delgado. Before the sequence was completed, however, O'Brien died from a heart attack on November 12, 1962.

Beware! The Blob
(a.k.a. *Son of Blob*)

1972. Jack H. Harris. D: Larry Hagman. Scr: Jack Woods, Anthony Harris. Story: Richard Clair, Jack H. Harris. Ph: Al Hamm. Mus: Mort Garson. Special Effects: Tim Barr. Additional Special Effects: Doug Beswick.

Cast: Robert Walker, Gwynne Gilford, Godfrey Cambridge, Carol Lynley, Shelley Berman, Burgess Meredith.

Rating: ☆☆½   Stop-Motion: ☆☆

This hilarious sequel to *The Blob* (1958) is dismissed by most critics as clumsy and ineffective. But it may be Jack H. Harris' finest hour: The deft but minor comic touches which he brought to the original *The Blob, Dinosaurus!* and other films are allowed freer rein here. For example, in one scene a hippy is having his hair washed in a hairdresser's sink only to have the Blob emerge through the plug-hole and messily devour him. In another scene, the Blob creeps up behind a man watching a TV showing of the original *The Blob* and consumes him. It's a film that is ripe for re-appraisal.

As in the first film, the Blob is depicted primarily by means of a live-action prop. Doug Beswick, who in later years would contribute to many memorable stop-motion sequences, worked on many of these shots and told this author that he also worked on "a stop-motion freezing effect when the Blob is frozen on the ice rink for the film's climax."

The Black Hole

1979. Walt Disney. D: Gary Nelson. Scr: Jeb Rosebrook, Gerry Day. Story: Jeb Rosebrook, Bob Barbash, Richard Landau. Ph: Frank Phillips. Art: Peter Ellenshaw. Mus: John Barry. Director of Miniature Photography: Art Cruickshank. Miniature Effects Created and Supervised by Peter Ellenshaw. Composite Optical Photography: Eustace Lycett. Matte Artist and Matte Effects: Harrison Ellenshaw. Miniature Mechanical Effects and Chief Modelmaker: Terry Saunders.

Cast: Maximilian Schell, Anthony Perkins, Robert Forster, Joseph Bottoms, Yvette Mimieux, Ernest Borgnine.

Rating: ☆☆   Stop-Motion: ☆☆½

The Disney Studio's attempt to cash in on the science fiction boom started by *Star Wars* was a dismal affair. The script is the chief culprit, coming across as lifeless padding leading up to a climactic trip into a black hole. And the climax itself is a hopelessly misjudged affair, struggling desperately to create an illusion of profundity: Heaven and Hell are encountered through the black hole. Gary Nelson's direction is lackluster, cast members mouth their lines indifferently, and John Barry's score, although initially effective, becomes dreary through repetition.

The film's only merits lie in its hardware. The least impressive component of these are the many unlikely robots, designed to appeal to the least demanding of children, and with "invisible" wires that are frequently conspicuous.

Other effects are in a different class altogether, including some marvelous matte paintings, beautiful spaceship models and a majestic depiction of the black hole itself. In one superb sequence, a meteor crashes into one of the spacecraft and rolls along its interior, nearly flattening the actors who stand in the foreground.

The imaginatively designed spaceships include miniatures of the *Cygnus* (a block-long craft that is lit up like a Christmas tree), the *Palomino* (a cylindrical deep space research vessel) and a slender, intricately detailed probe ship. In many shots, the movements of these models required that they be suspended on wires and stop-framed in front of blue screens for later compositing with the space backgrounds.

The Black Scorpion

1957. Warner Bros. D: Edward Ludwig. Scr: David Duncan, Robert Blees. Story: Paul Yawitz. Ph: Lionel Lindon. Art: Edward Fitzgerald. Mus: Paul Sawtell. Supervisor of Special Effects: Willis O'Brien. Animation: Pete Peterson. Additional Effects (uncredited): Wah Chang.

Cast: Richard Denning, Mara Corday, Carlos Rivas, Mario Navarro, Carlos Muzquiz, Pascual Peña.

Rating: ☆☆½   Stop-Motion: ☆☆☆

After the commercial failure of *Mighty Joe Young* in 1949, which failed to get anywhere near recouping its $2.5 million costs, Willis O'Brien found it progressively more difficult to realize his projects on the screen.

Several months preproduction work on *The Valley of Mist*, the highlight of which was to be a battle between a bull and a tyrannosaurus, were abandoned because producer Jesse L. Lasky could not raise the funds for what was intended to be a multi-million dollar color film. Merian Cooper hired O'Brien with the idea of remaking *King Kong* in Cinerama, but this too fell by the wayside. O'Brien also came up with a proposed series of short stories for television, *The Westernettes*, one of which featured a 30-foot lizard, but this project also collapsed. He wrote an original story for *The Beast of Hollow Mountain* and received a screen credit for it, but the producers, wishing to avoid the time-consuming costs of O'Brien's animation techniques, hired Jack Rabin and Louis DeWitt to do the special effects. Working for a few weeks in 1956 with Ray Harryhausen on the prehistoric sequence of Irwin Allen's *The Animal World* must have been a relief from all this frustration, although a far cry from the grander visions that he really wanted to be working on.

Eventually O'Brien had no choice but to accept the inevitable and work on the kind of low-budget exploitation productions which he had always tried to avoid. The first of these was *The Black Scorpion* in 1957.

Some sources (e.g., Don Shay's authoritative O'Brien biography in *Cinefex* #7) say he was approached by producers Frank Melford and Jack Dietz who, in the wake of successful films like *Them!* and *Tarantula*, were looking to make yet another giant-bug-on-the-loose picture.

(Dietz had first-hand experience of the profitability of such films — he was one of the producers of *The Beast from 20,000 Fathoms*.) Another suggestion, documented in *Filmfax #5*, is that O'Brien, with Pete Peterson acting as assistant, had put together a test reel in which a giant scorpion emerges from under a bridge, smashes a truck, picks a man off a telephone pole and stings him to death. They showed this reel to Dietz and Melford, who were so impressed that a screenplay was written around this sequence. Phil Hardy (in *The Encyclopedia of Science Fiction Movies*) puts forward another intriguing explanation, claiming that the special effects scenes "were created by Willis O'Brien ... in 1953, for a film about prehistoric life that was never finished."

Whatever the film's genesis, the end result was that O'Brien and Peterson (the latter did most of the actual animation) created the best giant-bug effects of the entire 1950s cycle, depicting a horde of loathsome crawling monstrosities with unnerving realism. Unfortunately, they had no chance of making the film the classic it might have been because they were battling against a meager budget, an uninspired script (by David [*The Time Machine*] Duncan and Robert Blees) and a mediocre director (Edward Ludwig). Ludwig had earlier helmed more prestigious productions like the two John Wayne vehicles *Wake of the Red Witch* and *Big Jim McLain*, but presumably on this occasion felt he was just doing a job of work. The script lumbers from genre cliché to genre cliché (theorizing scientists, a stale love interest, the military is brought in, etc.) and its only real claim to novelty, the fact that

it is set in Mexico, is actually a result of economics — actors and crew were much cheaper south of the border.

The effects sequences try hard to transcend all these problems, but even they suffer due to external circumstances. Several animation shots are repeated to save costs while at the climax a number of traveling mattes of the scorpion were left unfinished when the budget ran out, leaving just a featureless black silhouette among shots of fleeing extras. Additionally, some short-sighted individual, probably one of the producers, decided that (for closeups of the scorpions) a full-size mechanical prop should be used. This absurdly grotesque, constantly drooling creation, looking nothing like any scorpion that ever lived nor even the animated models that it is supposed to resemble, is seen in a handful of shots that are repeated *ad infinitum* during all the animation passages, considerably weakening their impact.

Thirty minutes of standard build-up precede our first sight of the scorpions. Like so many contemporary SF films, this kicks off with an overloaded narration by a radium-voiced commentator, here backed by library footage of volcanic explosions. Male lead Richard Denning plays a geologist who discovers more than he bargained for: a crushed car, a body frozen in fear, an empty gun, an abandoned baby and some ominous mouthings from the local priest about a "demon bull."

A credible miniature of the smoking volcano is matted into several long shots in scenes set in a town and a farm. A more extensive miniature set, including the rocky terrain at the foot of the volcano, allows a model car to drive across one shot: this kind of elaborate set-up is an O'Brien hallmark, distinguishing his films from the "reality sandwich" of Harryhausen's designs.

The first appearance of a scorpion is the alleged test-reel referred to above, and is a deft balance of horror and eeriness, as well as demonstrating O'Brien's inventive design. He varies the angle from which the action is perceived as much as his budget will allow, using a number of different miniature sets and keeping the flow of the action fluid. Like all the effects sequences, the lighting is kept very dark, partly to create mood and partly to help the miniature sets blend with the live action.

Three telephone engineers are fixing a fallen line when an enormous scorpion suddenly scurries down an embankment, snaps up one of the men and carries him off. This is shot in an entirely miniature set and there is a hungry purpose about the swiftness with which the scorpion rushes in and grabs its screaming prey (an animated human puppet). Peterson's animation of the scorpion is extremely fluid at the same time as catching exactly the characteristic jerkiness of movement which makes arachnids such unsettling creatures.

A second engineer then watches amazed as the massive pincers of the scorpion slowly emerge from under a bridge (another miniature set) and the creature scampers up another embankment with disturbing swiftness. It looks even more repellent in a medium-shot aerial view in which it runs across the frame, its eight legs working furiously as it pursues its prey. The engineer jumps into his lorry but the scorpion rushes after him. One cut is designed so that the scorpion is heading directly towards the camera; a second is shot from behind, the scorpion approaching a model of the lorry in a miniature set, backed by a live-action plate of distant mountains. The scorpion's movements are very realistic at this point and it picks up the lorry, smashes it into the ground, then turns and advances on the third engineer (who is still at the top of a telephone pole). In another extensive miniature terrain, the scorpion pulls the screaming man (another puppet) off the pole, then can be seen clearly stabbing him with its sting. Like all the other animation sequences, this is badly marred by an overuse of shots of the live-action prop.

The next effects sequence is a bit of a mess: There are about ten shots of the prop head and only two animation cuts. A scorpion arrives at the farm, appearing behind a wall; O'Brien angles this cut from below so as to enhance the impression of size. The monster crashes straight through the wall (an intricate and totally convincing bit of animation), then marches straight at the camera.

Three brief unfinished traveling mattes show the black outline of the scorpion advancing on some panicking townsfolk. Then a series of rear-projection shots depict it again coming straight at the camera. Unfortunately, all of these cuts are too brief and always spoiled by shots of the prop head.

However, O'Brien now pulls out all the stops with a superb 14–minute sequence that is the core of the film. Set entirely within a dark and shadowy fissure created by the volcanic explosions, it is the last opportunity O'Brien would have of fashioning a bizarre fantasy world populated with screeching birds and strange monsters. It may even be a conscious attempt by O'Brien to recreate *King Kong*'s spider-pit sequence: It must have been a great disappointment to him when that entire episode, with its elaborate miniature set and several animated creatures, was dropped from the film. Most shots in this sequence are done entirely in miniature sets, enhanced occasionally by either full-scale rear projections with actors in front of the pre-filmed animation, or (less frequently) rear projections of live action with the model in the foreground. This could never be mistaken for one of Harryhausen's films.

Denning and Carlos Rivas, wearing protective clothing, are lowered into the fissure by a crane. Long shots of the miniature set include a mock-up of the cage containing two human puppets making tiny movements. On the way down they pass one of the scorpions lurking on a ledge in the opposite wall, its pincers swaying menacingly. A bird caws loudly and is briefly glimpsed flying across the set; it's a typical flourish by O'Brien, adding significantly to the atmosphere.

A giant worm with vicious-looking pincers slithers across the cave floor, shuffling along like a caterpillar. When it rears up and threatens the actors in a rear projection, they startle it by taking a flash photograph and it retreats. Giving an idea of the level of dramatic inventiveness of the dialogue, Denning radios back to the surface: "I just saw a worm 30 feet long." They explore further into the crevasse and see a horde of scorpions scurrying out of a hole in a rock (the "horde" is actually three models animated in a cut that is repeated several times). Two of them attack Denning and Rivas, who are standing on a ledge in a miniature rear projection. The animation is again impressively fluid here, a complex whirl of shifting legs and claws reaching out.

A brief fight ensues between the worm and one of the scorpions, a gruesome set-piece that emphasizes the unpleasantness of this subterranean world. The worm rises up threateningly only to have its head grabbed by the scorpion's claws, then flaps about desperately. The two creatures separate, the worm rears up again, towering over its adversary, and they lock in battle again. But, in a sequence involving a full-scale rear projection with the two actors in the foreground looking at the action, a second scorpion joins in the struggle and stings the worm. The two scorpions drag the worm's corpse off into another full-scale rear-projection, and one of them tears a chunk out of it.

But suddenly an enormous scorpion, twice the size of those seen so far, appears over the top of a mound, obviously intending to make a meal of the worm. The two smaller scorpions run off, but one of them can't resist coming back for another bite (a deft demonstration of O'Brien's understanding of animal behavior) and pays horribly for its determination. The giant scorpion grabs it, turns it over (its legs kicking helplessly in mid-air), then stings it in its only weak spot — its throat. As if this wasn't grisly enough, the giant scorpion then reveals that it's not averse to a bit of cannibalism and bites into the smaller scorpion.

But this gruesomely realistic display of arachnoid hunger is not over yet. A little boy, Juanito, has stowed away in the cage and now wanders around the cave in search of his two friends. A flat, meter-square rock on the ground starts to tap up and down ominously and the boy can't resist lifting it up to see what is beneath it. In a great nightmare effect, he is suddenly confronted by a spider bigger than he is.

This repulsive creepy-crawly was originally built for *King Kong*, apparently one of the many incidental creatures in the cut spider-pit sequence. It's a bulbous, warty-looking thing that scampers about with alarming speed and emits a bizarre bird-like chirp. It chases Juanito across the cave floor and, in a particularly unsettling rear projection, seems to be almost upon him. Fortunately, our two heroes arrive in the nick of time and fire at the creature. It charges at them but goes down under the hail of bullets, its legs crumpling underneath it with a well-observed recreation of spider anatomy. The animation is first-rate and this nasty little episode "out-spiders" its stop-motion cousins in *Planet of Dinosaurs* and *Krull*; but we will probably never know how it compares with the enormous hairy monster in *King Kong*'s cut scene.

O'Brien's ability to imbue his models with touches of realistic animal behavior ("character" would be too strong a word in the case of these creatures) is seen again when a scorpion scampers over to the empty cage and, acting on brute instinct, starts to sting it repeatedly in a frenzied attack. With the cage destroyed, Denning and the others only just make it out of the fissure with

their lives, pulled up on a cable (as animated puppets again) while the scorpion reaches up below them, snapping at them with its pincers.

This whole episode is an unforgettable stop-motion set-piece (with shots of the prop head mercifully kept to a minimum) and a real arachnophobic's nightmare. But dramatically it is stilted, never having the pace and purpose of *King Kong*'s encounters. Without a Merian Cooper behind him, O'Brien's genius is unable to achieve its cinematic potential.

The nocturnal attack on the express train, however, is a fluidly cinematic sequence, both exciting and horrifying, and singled out by many critics as the high point of the film. Its success is due in part to the fact that it takes its stylistic inspiration from *King Kong*'s similar scene: The point-of-view of many shots and the sequence in which they are edited are almost identical. The effect of the tight budget is evident is this sequence — many of the animation shots are repeats of shots we have seen earlier — but fortunately the pace of the action makes these shortcuts barely noticeable.

A convincing miniature train rushes through the night, intercut with scenes of the scorpions emerging from the fissure (the same piece of film that was used earlier in the cave sequence). One of them climbs up onto the track and then heads directly at the train (the shot of it crossing the frame from right to left is another repeat). One effective moment has it advancing on the camera, shot from a low angle to emphasize its great size. Even more impressive is the shot, from the engineer's point-of-view,

The Black Scorpion (1957) reaches for a miniature helicopter. Animation by Willis O'Brien and Pete Peterson.

of the creature lit up by the headlights. The scorpion grabs the front of the train in one of its pincers and throws it off the track. O'Brien's attention to minor detail extended in this scene to placing small, movable silhouettes of the passengers in the windows of the train carriages, adding a subliminal effect to the realism of the moment.

Backed by the sound of the screaming, panicking passengers, the scorpions crawl all over the wreckage. A running puppet human is seamlessly inserted into a live-action shot of people fleeing and it gets snatched up by one of the scorpions. The scorpion waves its screaming prey high in the air, only to have it snatched away by another scorpion. Another human puppet is picked up as three of the scorpions fight amongst themselves in a memorable long shot: this vision of crawling, loathsome horror is a highpoint in the stop-motion genre.

The giant scorpion suddenly strides into the shot, picks up one of the other creatures, raises it above its head for a second, then dashes it into the ground upside-down, stinging it in the throat. This last action is another shot borrowed

WARNER BROS. present

"THE BLACK SCORPION" (X)

starring

RICHARD DENNING · MARA CORDAY
CARLOS RIVAS · MARIO NAVARRO

A dramatic moment from O'Brien's elaborately staged finale for *The Black Scorpion.*

from the earlier sequence, and it gets used for a third time when the giant scorpion grabs another of the smaller ones and kills that too.

A clumsy live-action scene now has us believe that the giant scorpion has killed all the others, thereby leading us economically into the finale in which the monster inevitably causes havoc in Mexico City and then, lured into a stadium, is destroyed by the military. It's a frenetic closing sequence featuring a surprising amount of animation as well as many convincing miniatures of tanks and helicopters. Apart from live-action

cut-aways, O'Brien has designed it to be shot entirely in miniature, thereby dispensing with mattes and rear projection. The constantly active scorpion, always scurrying about, turning, reaching out for its attackers, destroys everything it can grab. The soundtrack is a barrage of shell-fire and animal roars. But this scene is an example of a director and special effects man failing to put their heads together and make the most of the moment: The fast-paced animation shots are intercut with shots of the actors standing around disinterestedly and with too many shots of the drooling prop, sometimes the same shot repeated several times.

Leading up to this climax are scenes showing the people of Mexico City panicking, and again shots are repeated to cut costs. Included in this sequence are eight unsatisfactory cuts in which a silhouette of the scorpion looms over the crowds: These are more unfinished traveling mattes and there is no attempt at any interaction.

The scorpion climbs over the wall of the miniature stadium and walks down into the arena, unaffected by the superimposed flashes of shell-fire that bombard it. A miniature tank rolls up to the scorpion but is snatched up and smashed into the ground. It reaches up for, but misses, a miniature helicopter that flies overhead while other tanks continue to shower it with shell-fire. A second tank gets the same treatment as the first, then Denning fires his "600K volts" missile at the scorpion, failing to hit it in its weak spot, the throat.

Several more tanks advance on the creature which this time manages to grab a helicopter, brings it down and stings it as though it were alive. When a second helicopter is also brought down, it looks as though the same piece of film is used, but disguised by having been rephotographed closer up. Another tank gets stomped, but then Denning has another go, firing on the monster as it reaches up for a third helicopter. The animated missile flies realistically through the air on the end of a cable and sinks into the scorpion's underside. Still bombarded by explosions, it thrashes about on the end of the cable, twisting, circling, then collapsing for a moment before raising itself up again. It thrashes

about some more, then collapses again, its legs writhing desperately as it tries to get up again. It summons the strength to raise its pincers high in the air one last time, then finally lies dead.

Compared with the resolutions of other 1950s monster movies like *Them!* and *Tarantula*, neither of which used stop-motion, this is among the most elaborate and technically impressive. But it lacks dramatic punch: we feel none of the sympathy we felt for Kong. The lazy script simply lets us sit back and watch the scorpion get destroyed, never attempting to introduce any suspense or human involvement. It's a shame that the efforts of O'Brien and Peterson get such shoddy treatment at the hands of a disinterested director and scriptwriter.

The Black Scorpion demonstrates that O'Brien's kind of effects could function well in a low-budget environment and also that effects are only as good as the film that contains them. O'Brien's inventive imagination and technical genius were fighting against all the odds and at the end of the day, they lose out against a weak director and a crippling budget. But there is no denying that he created a handful of unforgettable sequences and somehow managed to put on screen more than double the amount of animation that there is in films of a comparable budget such as *The Beast from 20,000 Fathoms*. We can only fantasize what the film might have been like if he had been given the kind of budget he was used to working with.

The film was marketed with all the crass exploitative glee that is typical of 1950s horror films, including a superbly bad poster. Not only did the illustrator manage to paint a closeup of a scorpion even dafter than the prop used in the film (including a set of fangs and two big red eyes) but the blurb-writer went totally out of control and is worth quoting:

> Every horror you've seen on the screen grows pale beside the horror of the Black Scorpion ... Black — so you can't see him until he's ready to get you! ... Bloodless — That's why he wants yours! ... SHOWN UNCUT! Every terror *exactly* as filmed! ... We urge you not panic or bolt from your seats! ... NOTE: The management reserves the right to put up the lights any time the audience becomes too emotionally disturbed!

Black Sunday

1977. Paramount. D: John Frankenheimer. Scr: Ernest Lehman, Ivan Moffat, Kenneth Ross. Ph: John A. Alonzo. Mus: John Williams. Special Visual Effects (uncredited): Gene Warren (Excelsior! A.M.P.). Stop-Motion Animation (uncredited): Harry Walton.

Cast: Robert Shaw, Bruce Dern, Marthe Keller, Fritz Weaver, Steven Keats, Bekim Fehmiu.

Rating: ☆☆½   Stop-Motion: ☆☆½

This effective thriller concerns a terrorist group who hijack a Goodyear blimp and plan to send it crashing into a Superbowl game.

Gene Warren, who had formed Excelsior! Animated Moving Pictures after dissolving Project Unlimited, was contracted to handle the special effects shots in the film's climax. In a letter to the author, he described his contribution to the film: "The entire sequence with the dirigible entering the stadium, dipping down toward the ground and then finally leaving the stadium, was accomplished stop-frame with a miniature dirigible which was approximately three feet across." For this sequence, hyped by Paramount as "one of filmdom's greatest engineering feats," Warren took live-action footage of a football game and optically combined it with his stop-motion footage.

The actual frame-by-frame animation of the model airship was executed by Harry Walton.

Blackbeard's Ghost

1968. Walt Disney. D: Robert Stevenson. Scr: Bill Walsh, Don DaGradi; based on the book by Ben Stahl. Ph: Edward Colman. Mus: Robert E. Brunner. Art: Carroll Clark, John B. Mansbridge. Matte Artist: Peter Ellenshaw. Special Effects: Eustace Lycett, Robert A. Mattey.

Cast: Dean Jones, Peter Ustinov,

Suzanne Pleshette, Elsa Lanchester, Joby Baker, Elliott Reid.

Rating: ☆☆½   Stop-Motion: ☆½

This 1968 live-action comedy from Disney has a pirate ghost (Peter Ustinov, overacting behind a Cockney accent) summoned to the present day where he causes all kinds of mischief. There are a few laughs — mainly the result of Dean Jones being the only person able to see the ghost — but the script is generally short on inventiveness and the film is far too long at 107 minutes.

There are plenty of physical effects but few visual ones. Peter Ellenshaw supplied a series of good matte paintings of a coastal village at night.

Near the end of the film, Blackbeard helps Jones win at roulette and one shot employs stop-motion. Unseen by the croupier, Blackbeard moves all the chips on the table onto the winning number. The shot was filmed one frame at a time by Disney's regular effects men, Eustace Lycett and Robert A. Mattey.

Bláznova Kronika (*Insane Chronicle*); (a.k.a. *A Jester's Tale* and *Dua mosketyri* [*Two Musketeers*])

1964. Czech. Barrandov. D: Karel Zeman. Scr: Karel Zeman, Pavel Juracek. Ph: Václav Hunka. Art: Zdeněk Rozkopal. Mus: Ján Novák.
   Cast: Petr Kostka, Miroslav Holub, Emilia Vasaryova, Karel Effa, Edouard Kohout, Vladímir Mensik.

Rating: ☆☆½   Stop-Motion: ☆☆

Karel Zeman's fourth full-length film, set in a world of feuding musketeers during the Thirty Years' War, is characterized by the same gently mocking tone and charmingly ironic observations that are found in much of his other work. Here the target is the vagaries of war, with his central characters swapping sides every so often, whenever the situation suggests that would be the safest course of action.

Zeman's playful use of visual tricks makes the film a delight to watch, creating the impression that one is flicking through the surreal world of a children's book. The face of the god of war — actually an animated cut-out — blows clouds about, controlling the direction that a war is taking. Hanging paintings, carefully aligned with the live action, enhance shots of the inside of palaces and add bizarre detail to landscapes. In a sequence recalling some of the best images of *Invention of Destruction*, a deep ravine is crossed by a narrow log bridge. Most of the image in this sequence is actually a painting.

Although there is much animation of two-dimensional cut-outs, the amount of puppet stop-motion is negligible, featuring in only a handful of quick shots. Flags that flutter in the breeze, a cluster of arrows that fly through the air and some eggs laid by the image of a bird on a flag—all these are quick stop-motion effects. In brief shots of a miniature palace, animated puppets of three soldiers blow a trumpet fanfare and a woman empties a chamber pot out of a window. Later, a blast of lightning strikes a tree and a large branch tumbles to the ground—actually a smoothly animated miniature. When the log that crosses the ravine is picked up by a character and thrown into the ravine, that too is a quick stop-motion effect. Other than this, there is no stop-motion in the film. Perhaps Zeman was constrained by time and so unable to fill the film with the kind of delightful stop-motion figures that normally populate his movies.

Insane Chronicle, although diverting, is a lesser Zeman film. Its level of wit and imagination never matches that of his better films, and its camera trickery likewise never manages to achieve the same kind of unforgettable fantasy images that fill his other films.

The Blob

1988. Tri-Star. D: Chuck Russell. Scr: Chuck Russell, Frank Darabont. Ph: Mark Irwin. Art: Craig Stearns. Mus: Michael Hoenig. Makeup Effects Designed and Created by Tony Gardner. Creature Effects Designed and Created by Lyle Conway. Special Visual Effects: Dream Quest Images. Visual Effects Supervisor: Hoyt Yeatman. Stop-Motion Animator: Mark Sullivan. Additional Creature Effects Design and Supervision: Stuart Ziff. Miniature Construction: Greg Jein, Inc.

Cast: Kevin Dillon, Shawnee Smith, Donovan Leitch, Jeffrey DeMunn, Candy Clark, Joe Seneca.

Rating: ☆☆☆   Stop-Motion: ☆☆

This remake of the fondly remembered 1958 SF movie has a bigger budget than the original but is let down by a plot full of tiresome, predictable clichés. Practically the only effective plot device occurs when the character whom we expect to be the film's hero is killed early on by the Blob—and even that is an idea stolen from *Psycho*. Chuck Russell, who had earlier directed *Nightmare on Elm Street Part III*, again demonstrates that he knows how to put a film together professionally but little more: The film only comes to life during the special effects scenes. The film is a treat for monster-lovers but short on drama and excitement.

The work of Lyle Conway (monster effects) and Tony Gardner (makeup effects) and the rest of the team is excellent stuff and full of startling images. But comparisons with the remake of *The Thing* highlight how effects-maestro Rob Bottin had a more inventive vision of the potential of his effects, and that director John Carpenter knew how to make the most of them. Russell never makes his Blob as special as it ought to be.

However, some of the unforgettable

sights include the semi-transparent Blob slithering animatedly over a man's screaming face; a very messy death for a victim in a phone booth engulfed by the Blob; a man looking up at a ceiling and seeing the Blob hanging from it, a writhing victim squirming in its folds, tendrils reaching down to grab him; a necking scene in a car where the girl's face collapses inwards and slimy tentacles whip out to snare the boyfriend; and a victim pulled head-first into a waste-disposal unit (very messy).

Mark Sullivan, working for Dream Quest Images, contributed some stop-motion, allowing the Blob to perform more intricate action. In one shot, a huge tentacle slams down on a man and then retracts, revealing a flattened corpse spread over its underside. This humorous moment recalls the deadly tentacles of Harryhausen's octopus in *It Came from Beneath the Sea*. It's a smoothly animated composite. The live-action footage has been stopped for enough time to allow the actor to walk out of the frame, his disappearance obscured by the position of the puppet tentacle.

Another quick shot looks like it may also use stop-motion: Two victims are caught in the Blob's tentacles, their legs kicking frantically. But it may be that tiny mechanical mannequins were used.

Bloodlust—Subspecies III

1994. Full Moon Entertainment. D-Scr: Ted Nicolaou. Original Idea: Charles Band. Ph: Vlad Paunescu. Mus: Richard Kosinski, Michael Portis. Art: Radu Corciova. Special Makeup Effects Supervisor: Michael S. Deak. Animation: David Allen Productions, David Allen, Chris Endicott, Joseph Grossberg, Brett White, Wendy Grossberg.

Cast: Anders Hove, Denice Duff, Kevin Blair, Melanie Shatner, Pamela Gordon, Ion Haiduc.

Rating: ☆☆½   Stop-Motion: ☆☆

The third entry in the straight-to-video *Subspecies* series is almost indistinguishable from the second and adds nothing new, making it a rather unnecessary affair. Anders Hove is again magnificently revolting as the vampire, Ion Haiduc is an amiably incompetent cop, and director/writer Ted Nicolaou again makes creepy use of his Rumanian settings ("Filmed on location in Transylvania"), piling on the shadows. Essentially plotless, the script does contain a couple of good ideas: a creepy sequence in which the vampire lies down next to his bride in a dusty and claustrophobic crypt, and a novel device in which the bride is hidden in a military body bag to hide her from the sun's rays.

The second film began with a quick stop-motion sequence and this film ends with one. The vampire has been killed, impaled on the spiky branches of a tree, and his flaming blood drips onto the ground below. The pools of blood transform into the subspecies minions (red, foot-tall, humanoid beings with tiny, devil-like horns), who surround the bloodstone as it emits a glow suggesting that the series may not be over yet.

Eye-catching in its own right, the sequence seems out of place in a conventional vampire movie and seems like an afterthought. With regard to 1979's *Laserblast*, David Allen complained that his animation sequences were not properly integrated with the rest of the film. Fifteen years later, his complaint is still falling on deaf ears.

There are four stop-motion cuts, all shot in a miniature set without the complexities of combining them with live action. In the first, flames in a pool of blood go out, then the pool spreads over the ground, slowly forming into one of the subspecies. This appears to have been achieved by filming a wax model of the creature as it melted, then reversing the footage. Just before the prostrate creature starts to move, a dissolve allows the wax model to be replaced by the animation model. The minion, at first lying on its side and sleeping, slowly gets up and an orange glow appears in its eyes. The animation camera tilts up a frame at a time as the puppet stands up.

In the second cut, the minion looks back at a second minion who is beginning to revive, then adopts the arms-back pose and walks out of the frame. The third cut is a closer shot of the second minion, who sits up as his eyes light up. In the final cut, the first minion walks up to the bloodstone, next to which a third minion is already standing. Both puppets take a step backwards as the bloodstone starts to glow.

Bloodstone—Subspecies II

1993. Full Moon Entertainment. D-Scr: Ted Nicolaou. **Original Idea:** Charles Band. **Ph:** Vlad Paunescu. **Art:** Radu Corciova. **Mus:** Richard Kosinski, Michael Portis, John Zeretke. **Special Makeup Effects:** Alchemy FX. **Animation:** David Allen. **Special Effects Crew:** Mark Rappaport, Chris Endicott, Allan Barlow, Joseph Grossberg, Kevin O'Hara.

Cast: Anders Hove, Denice Duff, Kevin Blair, Melanie Shatner, Michael Denish, Pamela Gordon.

Rating: ☆☆½   Stop-Motion: ☆☆

Like its predecessor, *Subspecies*, this has magnificent location camerawork that harks back to the stylish chillers of the 1930s. Its repellent central character, a vampire with unkempt shoulder-length hair and impossibly long fingers, prowls the streets of Bucharest throwing huge shadows onto walls recalling the visual delights of similar devices in *Nosferatu* (1922) and *Dr. Jekyll and Mr. Hyde* (1931). This film has a feel for lighting and pace which is a refreshing change from the bland style of so many post–1940s fantasy films.

Unfortunately, the film is weak in the scripting area, failing to fashion a plot that grabs the interest. Instead, it drifts from sequence to sequence without any clear purpose, apart from a vague plot in which the vampire tries to acquire the title artifact. The climax in particular is weak, with the vampire all too easily dispatched. In a final twist that leaves the way open for *Bloodlust — Subspecies III*, the heroine is suddenly snatched and carried away by the vampire's mother, an old crone even more repellent than her son. Although disappointing, the script is considerably more engaging than that of the dreary first film.

The foot-tall minions — the Subspecies — are seen only very briefly at the beginning of the film, replacing the decapitated vampire's head. The vampire, beheaded at the end of the first film, lies prostrate on his castle floor. Four of his minions approach him, push his head back onto his body and remove the spear in his heart. As well as some impressive splatter effects, used to show the vampire's neck vertebrae reaching out for the head and then retracting, this sequence features three stop-motion cuts of the minions.

Two of the minions clamber onto the corpse, a shot apparently achieved by having a matte line follow the outline of the immobile corpse. Protruding from the corpse's chest is a bloody spear, which is a miniature prop. Two other minions stand on either side of the decapitated head. One pulls and the other pushes, and the animation effectively conveys an impression of the great weight they are moving. The head may also be part of the miniature set-up. However, the smooth way that its hair ruffles and its mouth opens and closes suggest it is part of the live-action plate. If so, then it is combined with the puppets impeccably. The puppets throw shadows onto the floor, suggesting they are not blue-screen elements and so perhaps making it more likely that the head also is part of the animation set-up.

The last of the three stop-motion cuts returns to the minions on the corpse's chest. They take hold of the spear, pull it out and toss it aside.

The three cuts are smoothly and realistically animated, with the creatures making many minor gestures which really bring them to life. Yet again, Allen has supplied some little moments of magic while at the same time being deprived of an opportunity to shine.

Body Bags

1993. Showtime Networks. D: John Carpenter ("The Gas Station," "Hair"), Tobe Hooper ("Eye"). Scr: Billy Brown, Dan Angel. Ph: Gary Kibbe. Art: Daniel A. Lomino. Mus: John Carpenter, Jim Lang. Coroner's Makeup: Rick Baker, Cinnovation Inc. Hair Creature Stop-Motion: Effects Associates. Hair Creature Digital Animation: Garden of Allah, Michael Hoover.

Cast: Robert Carradine, Alex Datcher, Wes Craven, David Naughton, Sam Raimi,

Stacy Keach, David Warner, Deborah Harry, Mark Hamill, Twiggy, John Agar, Roger Corman, John Carpenter, Tobe Hooper.

Rating: ☆☆½   Stop-Motion: ☆☆½

This diverting compendium of three horror tales brings together two of the genre's major directors — John Carpenter and Tobe Hooper — and features various other genre names in cameo roles. Carpenter himself, underneath a Rick Baker corpse makeup, even acts as host, introducing each tale from a body-filled morgue.

The first tale ("The Gas Station") is a polished but routine throwback to the women-in-peril films of the early 1980s: lots of quick shocks and messy splatter but little imagination and nothing new to offer. The third tale ("Eye") is an enjoyable variation on the old *Hands of Orlac* story, with Mark Hamill receiving a transplanted eye from an executed murderer and finding that he is becoming possessed by the murderer's personality.

Best of all is the comic relief second tale ("Hair") in which balding Stacy Keach receives a hair-restoring potion from David Warner. He wakes up the next morning with 18-inch-long hair and a nasty skin condition. It turns out that this is not hair at all, but tiny, snake-like aliens who want to feed on human brains.

Jim Danforth, who worked with Carpenter previously on *The Thing* and *They Live*, was called in to handle the ten closeup shots of the unusual aliens. Eight of these are stop-motion effects and the other two are computer animation shots, also supervised by Danforth.

In some shots he gives them a cobra-like ferocity and in others a surreal, snake-like charm that makes them delightfully offbeat characters.

In the first cut, a hairdresser has snipped off some of Keach's hair. Unseen among the fallen strands, two caterpillar-like creatures — not yet seen in any detail — inch along the floor. Shadows have been added to the live-action element to enhance the composite. In a similar shot later on, two hair-creatures inch along Keach's bedside table as he sleeps.

Keach starts to get a tickle in his throat and examines his mouth in the mirror. In an extraordinary shot of the interior of his mouth, a hair rises up from the back of his throat and curls over as if having a mind of its own. It looks as though the image of the mouth is a rear-projection against which Danforth has animated the hair.

Next morning, Keach cuts a hair that is growing from his mouth and hears it scream. Holding it between finger and thumb, he examines it closely with a magnifying glass. He is astonished to see that it has a mouth and a scaly body and that it hisses and snakes about as he holds it. It lunges for his finger and bites it. The animation of this quick movement is enhanced by a blur (possibly achieved through multiple exposure); and the finger and thumb are miniature props.

Keach drops the creature in the sink where it rears up at him in cobra-fashion, lunges forward again, then slithers down the drain. Danforth's animation, as in previous cuts, is extremely fluid.

Another hair-monster is seen in an

One of the hair-monsters animated by Jim Danforth for *Body Bags* (1993). The finger and thumb are also models.

extreme closeup of the side of Keach's face, wriggling out of a hole in his skin, its eyes glowing yellow. It hisses and slithers across his neck. This cut appears to use a miniature recreation of the side of Keach's scarred face.

Chief alien David Warner cuts open one arm of the now semi-comatose Keach. Four hair-monsters emerge from the gash and snake about in the air, recalling the many snake-like heads of Harryhausen's Hydra. The puppets appear to have been combined with the arm by means of a static matte running along the scar.

Warner explains that the eye is one means of access into the brain. In an extreme closeup of his eye, two hair-monsters emerge from the corner of the eye and writhe around. Again, this is probably a rear-projection set-up. The same set-up is used when Warner holds his finger near his eye so that the creatures can wriggle onto it and snake about in a very lively manner. The finger looks like it may be a photo cut-out, held in front of the rear projection.

This bizarre, inventive tale is full of unusual images, and features a refreshingly original use of stop-motion.

Brain Damage

1987. Brain Damage Company. D-Scr: Frank Henenlotter. Ph: Bruce Torbet. Art: Charles Bennett. Mus: Gus Russo, Clutch Reiser. Supervisor of Visual Effects: Al Magliochetti. Special Makeup Effects: Gabe Bartalos. "Elmer" Created by Gabe Bartalos, David Kindlon. Optical Services: Peter Kuran, Visual Concepts Engineering.

Cast: Rick Herbst, Gordon MacDonald, Jennifer Lowry, Theo Barnes, Lucille Saint-Peter, Vicki Darnell.

Rating: ☆☆☆   Stop-Motion: ☆☆

Fans of *Basket Case* (1981) had to wait six long years for Frank Henenlotter's follow-up, but it was worth the wait. *Brain Damage* is characterized by the same excess of gore and deft balance of black humor and it likewise revels in its demented subject matter. In addition, it has an appealing visual style in which colors are highlighted and distorted to give everything the look of a comic book. Henenlotter's confident, enthusiastic direction ensures that the best splatter moments are unforgettable and "offend tastefully."

Elmer is a foot-long, turd-like parasite who injects his guardians with a hallucinatory, highly addictive drug in exchange for them bringing him a regular supply of brains to eat. An elderly couple bring home a plate of brains to feed to Elmer and end up lying on the floor frothing at the mouth when they find him gone. New guardian Brian wakes up in blood-stained sheets, goes to the bathroom and is horrified to see Elmer suddenly appear on his shoulder: "Hi there...!"

Rivaling *Re-Animator*'s "giving head" scene for enjoyable bad taste is a fellatio scene in which Elmer pops out of Brian's trousers, into a girl's mouth, then ducks back in again with her bloody brains hanging from his teeth. Best of all is the scene where Brian goes cold turkey and hallucinates that he is pulling his own brains out through his ear, a superb splatter effect that goes on and on, like a magician pulling colored scarves from a hat.

In an absurd subway sequence, Brian is talking to his girlfriend and, in the best pantomime tradition, every time she looks away Elmer pops out of his mouth. In the enjoyably over-the-top finale, the old couple both have their brains eaten by Elmer — his technique is to burrow straight into the skull. Elmer expires dramatically after being forced to administer an overdose of his drug-juice to Brian. Brian, seen in the haunting closing shot, loses a chunk out of his cranium, a beam like a searchlight pouring out of his totally zonked brain.

Like *Basket Case*, this uses stop-motion in a few full-view shots of the monster. Technically it's slightly less crude than in the first film but is still at the level where its jerkiness amuses rather than convinces. This is quite appropriate for such an absurd monster because the film's connections with realism are distant, to say the least.

In the only substantial animated shot the puppet is standing on the head of a night watchman he has killed, pulling out pieces of brain and chewing messily on them. The man's head is a convincing prop. Another shot shows Elmer slithering across a shower room floor. Two other shots are very quick animated cuts of Elmer launching himself straight at the camera, fang-filled mouth open, as he attacks victims. It's a pity that nothing more ambitious was attempted: In all other shots, Elmer is a cable-operated puppet.

Henenlotter's next film, *Basket Case II* (1990), maintained the level of bad taste but was considerably less inventive and contained no stop-motion.

Brain Donors

1992. Paramount. D: Dennis Dugan. Clay-Mation Sequence: Will Vinton Productions. Animation Supervisors: Mark Gustasson, Skeets McGrew.

Cast: John Turturro.

Rating: ☆☆   Stop-Motion: ☆☆

This 1992 science-fiction comedy concerns the exploits of three characters whose antics recall the Marx Brothers.

During the opening and closing credits, the three characters are represented by clay-mation puppets seen in sequences produced by Will Vinton Productions.

Braindead (U.S.: Dead Alive)

1992. New Zealand. Wingnut Films. D: Peter Jackson. Scr: Stephen Sinclair, Frances Walsh, Peter Jackson. Ph: Murray Milne. Art: Kevin Leonard-Jones. Mus: Peter Dasent. Prosthetics Design: Bob McCarron. Creature and Gore Effects: Richard Taylor. Stop-Motion Animation: Peter Jackson, Richard Taylor.

Cast: Timothy Balme, Diana Penalver, Elizabeth Moody, Ian Watkin, Forry Ackerman.

Rating: ☆☆☆   Stop-Motion: ☆☆½

The film that out-splatters them all. This relentless blood-and-guts banquet relives the delirious excesses of 1980s movies like *The Evil Dead* and *The Terminator* — and goes way beyond them. Eyeballs, ears, arms, legs, heads, entrails and various unidentified writhing messes explode across the screen in equal combinations of realism and wit, making this a movie to treasure.

Peter Jackson's sure direction borrows much of its frenetic style from Raimi's films, but he is a better storyteller than Raimi and depicts characters who have charm and engage our interest. Who could resist overweight sleazeball Uncle Les, who makes an entrance with the line, "I've got a urinary infection"? Or the wide-eyed bewilderment of hero Timothy Balme, who combines

Bruce Campbell's double-takes from *The Evil Dead* with the mother-dominated whimperings of Anthony Perkins from *Psycho*? Jackson keeps the pace brisk, his dialogue avoids clichés and the splatter gags are inventive and outrageous.

Some of the wackiest moments include: a dinner party in which Mum's ear drops off into a bowl of custard and she spoons it up and chews on it; the half-digested leg of a dog being pulled out of Mum's mouth; a kung fu vicar who pounds a gang of punks to pieces with an absurd barrage of kicks and punches; a slapstick sequence in which Balme takes a baby zombie for a pram ride in a park and nearly batters it to death in front of horrified mothers; a demonic shot of Uncle Les wielding two meat cleavers at high speed and carving up a horde of attacking zombies; a half-eaten man whose legs are just bloody bones; a man who has all the skin on his head pulled away from the skull, like a glove being peeled off, revealing a fleshy, still-living deaths-head underneath; and the *way*-over-the-top climax in which Balme carves his way through a room full of zombies by holding up an electric lawnmower in front of him.

Braindead has something for everyone. Forry Ackerman makes a cameo appearance during one splatter scene, looking repulsed by what he sees yet unable to resist taking a photo. Jackson is a fan of the old stop-motion classics: On Balme's bedroom wall hangs an original Australian daybill poster for *The Beast from 20,000 Fathoms*, and the film's first scene takes place on Skull Island, no less, where an unseen creature is captured and taken back to "civilization."

The creature turns out to be a Rat Monkey, a creature spawned (we are told) when rats from passing slave ships bred with the local monkeys. Caged up in Wellington Zoo, this rodent-faced simian attacks and eats another monkey and then takes a bite out of Balme's mother—thereby turning her into a zombie.

For this sequence, Jackson and Richard Taylor built and animated a stop-motion puppet, seen in 16 cuts. The animation is sometimes hurried and the spindly-limbed creature is only barely believable, but this never matters: With Jackson, we always know we are only watching a movie. The Rat Monkey trots around its cage, chews on the hairy arm of the other monkey and in a few shots lunges at the camera. There are no composite shots. It meets a gory demise in live-action shots when Mum stamps on its head with her high-heeled shoes and squeezes its brains out.

Bride of Re-Animator (a.k.a. *Re-Animator 2*)

1990. Wildstreet. Prod-D: Brian Yuzna. Scr: Woody Keith, Rick Fry. Adapted from H. P. Lovecraft's "Herbert West" by Keith, Fry and Yuzna. Ph: Rick Fichter. Art: Philip J. C. Duffin. Mus: Richard Band. Crypt Sequence and Special

Makeup Effects: Screaming Mad George. Bride and Special Makeup Effects: K.N.B. EFX Group. Dr. Hill's Head and Bat-wing Effects: John Carl Buechler (Magical Media Industries Inc). Finger Creature and Dog Effects: Anthony Doublin. Stop-motion Animation and Miniatures: David Allen Productions. Supervisor: David Allen. Camera: Paul Gentry. Miniatures: Dennis Gordon. Assistant: Harvey Mayo.

Cast: Jeffrey Combs, Bruce Abbott, Claude Earl Jones, Fabiana Udenio, David Gale, Kathleen Kinmont.

Rating: ☆☆½   Stop-Motion: ☆☆½

David Allen has the distinction of having contributed stop-motion sequences to more feature films than anyone else in the history of the cinema. But after nearly 30 years working with the process, he has still not had the chance to produce work that would elevate him to the same status as Harryhausen. All too often, as here, he has been confined to creating brief sequences which, however excellent, are only a small aspect of a much larger whole. His Finger Creature in this film is one of the more memorable effects in an effects-heavy film, something that audiences will remember long after they have forgotten all the blood and guts. But is it also another example of Allen being deprived of the wider creative control that he deserves.

Bride of Re-Animator is a disappointing sequel to a modern classic. The taut pace, impressive characterization, deft black humor and ingeniously constructed plot of the original are all lacking here. Brian Yuzna demonstrates, as he did in *Society*, that although he loves the horror genre, he is an unremarkable director. The frantic climax of the original was superbly controlled by Stuart Gordon, but Yuzna makes the sequel's climax a bit of a mess. The bride, fashioned from bits and pieces of corpses, starts to come apart at the seams, while a horde of re-animated maniacs runs riot in the basement laboratory, and a collection of scuttling re-animated rejects is discovered in the adjoining crypt. It's all visually fascinating but of negligible dramatic impact. The disembodied head of Dr. Hill reappears to get revenge on Herbert West but lacks the manic intensity of the first film. At the climax, an inventive flourish has it flying around on bat wings that have been grafted onto it, but in Yuzna's hands this is merely another trick effect, not the nightmarish sight it should have been.

Some moments approach the gruesome hysteria of Gordon's film. A detective gets his hand chopped off by a machete, swings the heroine Fabiana Udenio's pet dog around and pulls off one of its legs, then later gropes Udenio's breasts with the bloody stump of his arm. But other sequences are contrived padding, such as the attack by the reanimated "patients" in a clinic or the graveyard sequence in which the same zombies chase Udenio. Jeffrey Combs lacks the likable qualities he had previously while his assistant Bruce Abbott is two-dimensional and merely gets in the way of the action, constantly expressing revulsion at Combs' experiments, then being persuaded to cooperate.

Allen's sequence occurs early on, designed as a humorous and low-key taster of what is to come. Bizarre and amusing, it is one of the few occasions where Yuzna shines. Originally Yuzna wanted Jim Danforth to do the animation, but he was unavailable. Anthony Doublin was overall supervisor of the sequence.

West sticks three severed fingers and a thumb together and plants an eyeball on top of them, then treats the result with some of his glowing reagent in a surgical tray. The creature comes to life and (in a beautifully smooth stop-motion cut) holds the thumb up a like a tail behind it, swivels its eye around and takes a few steps on its three "legs." Equally good is a long shot in which the creature jumps out of the tray (suspended in mid-air for a few frames) and scampers across the table, unseen by the two scientists who are talking in the well-matched rear screen. The whole of the table is a miniature and so a matte is unnecessary.

Upstairs in the living room, the scientists are being interviewed by the detective when the Finger Creature (this time a live-action prop) suddenly dashes across the floor past his feet. The humor in this and the rest of the scene is generated by the fact that Combs and Abbott are desperately trying to prevent the detective from noticing the creature, giving rise to pantomime-style gags as the detective always seems to be looking the wrong way when it appears.

It walks along the back of the sofa the detective is sitting on, and there is a close shot of the stop-motion model. The live-action prop jumps down onto the seat but the detective unknowingly slams down a book on top of it. The scene ends after the detective has left: Combs picks up the book only to find a flattened mess on the sofa, the eyeball squished to a pulp.

Cabin Boy

1994. Touchstone/Novi Pictures. D-Scr: Adam Resnick. Story: Chris Elliott, Adam Resnick. Ph: Steve Yaconelli. Mus: Steve Bartek. Art: Steven Legler. Special Makeup Effects: Tony Gardner, Alterian Studios. Visual Effects Supervisor: Michael Lessa. Visual Effects: Buena Vista Visual Effects. Matte Artists: Harrison Ellenshaw, Paul Lasaine. Stop-Motion Visual Effects: Doug Beswick Productions. Stop-Motion Animation Supervisor: Doug Beswick. Stop-Motion Puppet Construction: Yancy Calzada. Visual Effects Director of Photography: Paul Gentry.

Cast: Chris Elliott, Ritch Brinkley, Brian Doyle-Murray, James Gammon, Ricki Lake, Russ Tamblyn, Ann Magnuson.

Rating: ☆☆　　Stop-Motion: ☆☆½.

Star Chris Elliott, playing a spoiled rich-kid who finds himself at sea on "The Filthy Whore" with a bunch of gruff old sea dogs, is poorly served by a script seriously short on witty dialogue. The concept of making an affectionate spoof of Harryhausen's *Sinbad* films is an excellent one but this effort never decides what tone it is aiming for and so falls flat most of the time.

For example, Russ Tamblyn makes a few appearances as a sharkman (upper half man with the dorsal fin and tail of a shark) but does very little: Is he meant to be comic and, if so, why are there no gags? Also featured are a six-armed woman (only seen seated), her giant husband (a live actor) who wades into the water after our heroes' ship, a figurehead that comes to life (but never detaches itself from the ship) and other Harryhausen references. None are funny or spectacular.

However, Harryhausen fans will warm to a sequence in which the ship's crew are attacked by an iceberg monster. Eighteen stop-motion shots were supplied by Doug Beswick Productions. The bulk of the animation was done by Beswick himself, with Yancy Calzada animating four or five closeups. The puppet was sculpted by Calzada.

Initially this nine-foot-high creature is a costumed actor breaking out of a prop iceberg, In the rest of the sequence, as it climbs aboard the ship, menaces the crew and is eventually melted by their coffee machine, it is a stop-motion puppet. It's a witty sequence and technically impressive but is over too quickly — there were gags aplenty just waiting to be milked, but presumably the budget ruled them out.

Composite shots with the monster standing on the ship — probably rear-screen set-ups — are very well done. Miniature rigging and barrels in the foreground help to create the illusion that the puppet is in the same environment as the actors.

There is some effective interaction when the creature playfully pokes one of the crewmen with its finger. Shots in which one crewman lunges at the monster with a harpoon and another strikes it with an oar include moments when the props pass in front of the puppet, probably by means of partial miniatures suspended on wires.

The creature is given some rudimentary personality. In several closeups, it growls like a lion, and in another a puzzled expression passes across its face when Elliott stamps on its toe. In one successful gag, the creature's right hand is melted away and it holds up the stump, looking at it with a pained expression.

Two very accomplished long shots depict a crewman spraying the creature with coffee. Although the sprayed liquid ends at the point where the puppet is positioned in front of it, this is not noticed because the coloring of the white spray blends in with the white of the puppet, and because the eye is distracted by steam which is superimposed over the puppet as it starts to melt.

After a final medium shot of the iceberg monster growling, a live-action shot shows it hitting the deck and shattering into pieces.

Three long shots of the sharkman swimming underwater, his tail swishing from side to side and his arms pulling through the water, are achieved with a stop-motion puppet of the character.

In a nod to Willis O'Brien, shots of the crew in rowboats approaching a beach are designed in the manner of similar shots in *King Kong*, using a combination of miniatures and painted vistas to create a picturesque fantasy milieu.

Captain America

1989. 21st Century/Menahem-Golan. D: Albert Pyun. Scr: Stephen Tolkin. Story: Stephen Tolkin, Lawrence J. Block. Based on characters created by Joe Simon and Jack Kirby. Ph: Philip Alan Waters. Art: Douglas Leonard. Mus: Barry Goldberg. Special Makeup Effects: Greg Cannom. Special Visual Effects: Fantasy II Film Effects. Visual Effects Supervisor: Gene Warren, Jr. Visual Effects Assistant: Christopher Warren. Stop-Motion Animation (uncredited): Justin Kohn.

Cast: Matt Salinger, Ronny Cox, Ned Beatty, Darren McGavin, Michael Nouri, Scott Paulin, Bill Mumy.

Rating: ☆☆½   Stop-Motion: ☆☆½

Unlike DC Comics' Superman and Batman, Marvel Comics' characters (Spiderman, the Incredible Hulk, etc.) have always transferred awkwardly to cinema and television formats. *Captain America*, here a theatrical pilot for a television series that was never made, is no exception. But it is an admirably straight-faced attempt to handle a difficult character and avoids the silliness that has plagued many other comic book adaptions.

The plot follows the comics faithfully. During World War II, polio-stricken Steve Rogers (Matt Salinger) volunteers for a military experiment and is turned by the super-soldier serum into Captain America. Strapped to a missile by the evil Red Skull (Scott Paulin in effectively grisly Greg Cannom makeup), he becomes frozen in ice when the missile crashes in the Arctic. Revived decades later, he becomes a champion for the forces of good.

The script tries to cram too much into the running time with the effect that Albert Pyun's direction never decides what kind of pace it is aiming for and so generates none. Scenes that should be powerful rush by, missing their potential. There is the impression that some scenes may have been cut in an attempt to quicken the pace.

Gene Warren, Jr., supervised two sequences that make brief use of stop-motion. In the first, the Nazis are experimenting with their own version of the super-soldier serum and try it out on a rat. The result is a red, hairless creature, seen skulking in its cage with its back to the camera and then turning to reveal a hideous face, a fang-filled red skull that lets out a growl.

This is a realistically fleshy model and it is cleverly animated (by Justin Kohn) in the first of the two cuts so that it shivers in a very rodent-like manner. Apart from this, the model is not required to do much — it sways from side to side and its tail swishes, but that is all. This is intended just as a quick shock effect, suggesting the fate that will befall the boy who later becomes the Red Skull.

Later, a young boy is standing outside the White House at night and is astonished to see a missile, with Captain America strapped to it, fly over his head. A couple of shots in this sequence use a miniature that was stop-framed by Warren.

Caravan of Courage—
An Ewok Adventure
see *The Ewok Adventure*

Caveman

1981. United Artists/Turman-Foster. D: Carl Gottlieb. Scr: Rudy DeLuca, Carl Gottlieb. Ph: Alan Hume. Art: Philip M. Jefferies. Mus: Lalo Schifrin. Special Visual Effects: Effects Associates Inc. Visual Effects Supervisors: Jim Danforth (uncredited) and David Allen. Visual Effects Crew: Jim Aupperle, Randall William Cook, Spencer Gill, Peter Kleinow, David Stipes, Laine Liska. Model Construction (uncredited): Roger Dicken. Additional Armature Construction (uncredited): Ernest Farino. Matte Artists: Dan Curry, Rocco Gioffre, Jena Holman. Illustrator/Sketch Artist: Michael Ploog. Abominable Snowman Created by Chris Walas. Special Effects: Roy Arbogast.

Cast: Ringo Starr, Barbara Bach, Dennis Quaid, Shelley Long, John Matuszak, Jack Gilford.

Rating: ☆☆☆   Stop-Motion: ☆☆☆½

Caveman is a rare and wonderful example of stop-motion breaking away from the self-inflicted confines of the genre and trying something different. The animated models may be dinosaurs once again but this time they are used for comic effect and given distinct and endearing personalities. The grandeur of O'Brien's visions and the energy of Harryhausen's battles are consciously avoided, replaced by a charm and freshness which make this a unique production and one of the great stop-motion films.

However, a jaded public in 1981, caught between big-budget science fiction spectaculars and the gung-ho violence of films like *Rocky*, had no time for yet another tame prehistoric opus. The movie did poor box office business. In England, it got a miserable theatrical release that lasted all of one week before disappearing altogether.

The schoolboy humor is not to everyone's liking: the opening title is "One Zillion B.C.—October 9th"; cavemen discover fire and set light to their farts; someone is thrown into some brontosaurus dung; gay cavemen, etc. Carl Gottlieb directs with a light-enough touch to make most of the comedy irresistible. It hardly matters that his cast always looks uncomfortable with the grunt-and-groan dialogue; at least they're all enjoying themselves. Ringo Starr is amiable as the bumbling, hard-done-by Atouk, veteran comic actor Jack Gilford supplies many laughs as blind Gog, and the supporting cast includes enthusiastic performances from Shelley Long and Dennis Quaid, before either had achieved star status. Lalo Schifrin's bone-tapping score adds a lively charm to many scenes.

The effects crew assembled for the film is impressive. Roy Arbogast (*Jaws, Close Encounters of the Third Kind*, etc.) did the mechanical effects (e.g., a prop of a dinosaur tail, a fried pterodactyl egg). Chris Walas (*Gremlins, The Fly*, etc.) built the fabulous snow-beast costume. Roger Dicken (*The Land That Time Forgot, Alien*'s "chest-burster") built the "howling lizard" puppet and a miniature puppet of Ringo.

The stop-motion crew reads like a Who's Who of latter-day practitioners: Jim Danforth (uncredited because he left the project mid way), David Allen, Pete Kleinow, Randy Cook, James Aupperle, Laine Liska and Ernie Farino are among those who contributed. With all this talent on hand, it's not surprising that the film looks a lot classier than most, containing some ambitious composite photography, beautifully designed models and high-quality animation that is always imaginatively choreographed. Some animation sequences, particularly those with the tyrannosaurus, were shot outdoors in direct sunlight and this makes the composite shots aesthetically very attractive, avoiding the artificial studio lighting which so often betrays model scenes in other films. There are 107 stop-motion cuts in the film.

In a letter to the author, Danforth explained why his company, Effects Associates, received a screen credit while he himself did not. "While I certainly left the project (about two-thirds of the way), my credit was always to be 'Effects Associates, Inc.' This is because the Directors Guild *again* prohibited my 'Visual Effects Directed by': credit. My deal

memo on *When Dinosaurs Ruled the Earth* specified my credit as 'Visual Effects Designed and Directed by Jim Danforth.' Warners was forced by the DGA to change it, which is why some reviewers lump all of us — Roger [Dicken], Brian [Johncock] and me — into the same category. The same rules applied by the time of *Caveman*, except moreso. The DGA now prohibits co-direction credits (except for partners), so even though my deal was to co-direct the sequences with Carl, I couldn't get that credit."

The film plunges almost immediately into the first animation sequence. There is plenty of amiable slapstick as a group of cavemen are attacked by a dinosaur. They squabble over who is going to hide in which tree and Quaid gets thrown through the air by the dinosaur's tail.

The design of this model was the result of a misunderstanding between Danforth and Gottlieb. Gottlieb either didn't know the name for a triceratops or else, as Danforth put it, "was trying to write from a caveman's perspective." He asked for a "horned lizard"—and that is just what he got. Danforth's inventive design ensures that despite its horn and great size, the creature is a personable buffoon. This fictitious chameleon-like beast has spines on its back and popping-out eyes that swivel independently of each other with all the abandon of a cartoon character. The warty, wrinkled hide and moist, red mouth are impressively lifelike.

The sequence begins with Ringo trying to catch a small lizard for breakfast only to find that a much larger lizard has similar designs on him. The first shot is an ambitious pull-back from Ringo revealing the dinosaur behind him, sitting on a miniature rock, its eyes rotating comically. Its tongue licks its lips in anticipation. Unfortunately, the shift in focus in the rear plate wasn't matched in the miniature set and the live element "jumps" briefly. In the next shot, a vaguely horizontal matte along the ground allows the dinosaur to step down from the rock and pursue Ringo across the frame.

In a good example of how a "reality sandwich" can distort perspective, Ringo runs towards the camera as the dinosaur stomps in from the left behind him — even though the model is, of course, in front of the rear-projected screen. In the next static matte set-up, some cavemen in the foreground look back at the dinosaur, which gives a growl and a toss of its head. In two medium shots, not using mattes, it strides across the frame. A floor inlay is seamlessly blended with the sandy ground in shots of two cavemen throwing rocks at the beast.

Wire-braced miniature rocks bounce off the model realistically. Just what happened to the real rocks thrown by the actors is a mystifying piece of sleight-of-hand which may have required another matte. A comical "plopping" sound matches shots of the dinosaur catching two of the rocks in its mouth. In closeup it munches on the rocks, its eyes rotating wildly, then sticks its tongue out in disgust.

Moments later, Quaid jumps on its tail (Arbogast's prop), biting it to hold on! Kleinow, who animated these scenes, has the model scrape the ground with one of its front legs, giving it a gesture

like an angry bull. The dinosaur looks back over its shoulder with a puzzled expression on its face, then, in a shot that employs a full miniature foreground (i.e., there is no matte), it walks in a circle trying to catch up with the caveman (now a puppet built by Cook) on its tail. A miniature tree in the foreground lends depth and breaks up the shot.

The dinosaur circles again, swishes its tail and the Quaid-puppet somersaults over its head, supported by a wire that was later painted out by Kleinow.

In another static matte design, it walks up to a tree in which several cavemen are hiding. A traveling matte allows a change of perspective, looking down at the beast from the cavemen's point of view. There is no spill but the miniature element looks faded compared to the live-action footage. There is a perfectly executed moment of implied interaction when the beast rears up and apparently places its front legs on the tree. Kleinow pasted some card onto the back of the rear screen to create the model's shadow on the live-action tree.

The tree is pulled down by some off-screen wires, then the dinosaur walks behind the tree, the trunk of which disguises the location of the matte line. It looks as though a miniature branch has also been placed in the shot, because the model walks behind it — it's a satisfying example of how attention to minor details such as this can improve the credibility of a shot, even if it is only registered subconsciously by most people.

In the next two cuts, the dinosaur bites the leg of a live-action caveman and pulls him off to the left. In the second of these cuts, a miniature foot in the model's mouth is exactly synchronized with the real foot which it obscures — a fabulous moment of interaction which recalls the shot in *The 7th Voyage of Sinbad* when the Cyclops picks up one of the sailors by his boot. Finally, in a long shot reusing a static matte seen earlier, the dinosaur drags the flailing miniature human along the ground, drops it briefly in order to get a better "bite," picks up the limp corpse and walks off.

It's a fine scene, smoothly animated by Kleinow, full of deft touches of characterization and utilizing a great variety of technical tricks to vary the perspectives so as to keep the pace lively and allow lots of interaction between miniature and real elements.

The next effects shot, an amusing throw-away gag, is the first of three appearances by Roger Dicken's "howling lizard," which as well as howling like a wolf also does passable imitations of an owl hooting and a cock crowing. In the first two cuts, it is seen in long shot through an attractive Danforth glass painting of a miniature rock and some trees with the Moon up in the night sky. In the third cut, it is seen in a daytime glass painting of the same location. The model, never seen in closeup, looks very realistic and is very smoothly animated as it makes slight movements of its legs and head. There were originally to be more brief shots of dinosaurs. Cook began work on a triceratops and a brachiosaurus model, but they were scrapped to save resources.

Before the next animation sequence, there is another brief yet beautifully executed throw-away gag. Above a landscape painting, the Sun sinks and the Moon rises all in the space of about

four seconds, accompanied by a suitably absurd sound effect.

The decrepit, overweight tyrannosaurus, designed and built by Danforth, is one of the finest models ever to grace an animation film, up there with *Son of Kong*'s styracosaurus, Gwangi and the Cyclops (to name but a few). Danforth's great achievement (even though the actual animation was done by others) is that while the model and its gestures are obviously too absurd to ever convince us that it is real, at the same it is a living, breathing entity full of personality and sculpted with such attention to detail (lifelike skin texture, missing teeth, paunch, endearingly useless arms, etc.) that it *does* become a living creature. The tyrannosaurus is much more than a conventional stop-motion adversary that appears in one scene, is defeated and never seen again. This creature appears in three scenes, and is thwarted again and again in his less-than-ferocious attempts to make a meal of Ringo and his troupe.

His first scene begins with deft understatement. Blind Gog bumps into something large and unidentified (a prop of the dinosaur's underbelly). The camera cuts to a striking composite showing the tyrannosaurus towering over the bemused actor, who tentatively head-butts the obstacle. A shadow has been introduced beneath the model to help mesh the two elements. A fluidly animated closeup (animated by Cook) of the dinosaur with a puzzled expression on its face allows a lingering look at the amount of detail in this beady-eyed, wizened yet fleshy creation.

In two more closeups, the tyrannosaurus has a "dirty old man" expression on its face, its tongue hanging out, as Gog inadvertently investigates a certain part of its anatomy. Then it screams in pain when the old man decides to belt it with his walking stick. The next composite is beautifully convincing. Gog is blue-screened in front of the model, which in turn is combined with the background (in this instance not a rear projection but a photo blow-up) by means of a floor inlay. Gog ducks as the huge tail swishes over his head and the pained dinosaur walks away behind him. The lighting is especially well-matched in this shot.

In another attractive long shot, the dinosaur walks from behind some rocks, turns and sees three cavemen on a rock in the lower right corner of the screen. Some dust is thrown into the air in the rear plate to reinforce the impression that the model is interacting with its environment as it walks. A real bird fortuitously flies past in the background plate, accidentally lending extra credibility to the shot. The clever trick in this set-up is that the lower foreground is miniature, allowing the model to move from behind the rocks to a position in front of the rocks, a device that really helps to make us believe that this is only one piece of film.

In some medium shots, the model stomps across the frame, passing behind a miniature tree which adds depth to the image. In a fine touch of slapstick, the dinosaur walks towards the camera, licks its lips and wrings its hands together in anticipation of a meal.

Dinosaurs like this seem to have a liking for impaling themselves on sharp objects (see *One Million Years B.C.* and *Planet of Dinosaurs*) and this one is no

exception, happily throwing itself onto Ringo's sharpened tree trunk. Even when studied in slow motion and freeze-frame, this skillful moment of interaction refuses to give up the secret of where the real tree trunk ends and the miniature one begins. It's as good a moment of cinema magic as the matching of real and miniature rope in the tug-of-war scene in *Mighty Joe Young*.

There is a droll closeup of the dinosaur's realistically fleshy mouth as it belches (originally intended to be a scream but changed on Gottlieb's suggestion) and a shot of Ringo dangling from the tree trunk, one end of which is clearly sticking in the model. Again, it is impossible to detect where the prop becomes a miniature. This deliciously low-key sequence ends with the poor old dinosaur deciding to retire, hurt and hobbling away.

The outcome of the next stop-motion scene (again animated by Kleinow) is equally restrained: Ringo discourages the horned lizard from attacking by lobbing a melon onto its horn. It begins with a conventional static matte set-up showing the dinosaur munching on the fruit, with the extra detail of animated pieces of fruit dripping to the ground as it chomps. In closeup, the model stares with absurdly swiveling eyes at Shelley Long.

Another matte shot shows Ringo throwing a melon up into the air, the film cutting just before the moment of contact to a shot of a miniature of the fruit landing on the model's horn. Several blurred dinosaur's-eye-view shots suggest the lizard's disorientation, then the first matte set-up is used again when it scrapes its head on the ground trying, unsuccessfully, to dislodge the melon, eventually walking off. The background plate looks a little faded in some of these cuts but it's a minor complaint.

The tyrannosaurus reappears early next morning in a sequence made visually very appealing because it is set in dense jungle lit by sunlight. Ringo is relieving himself against a tree and turns to see the dinosaur walking through the undergrowth. In this static matte shot, several devices (most only registered subliminally by an audience) are used to add to its realism. A miniature tree blends with the foliage in the background plate; shadows from the foliage above fall on this tree and on the puppet; and there are several miniature trees in the foreground, or trees which are part of the live-action plate with mattes having been carefully drawn around their outline.

In closeup, the tyrannosaur growls, then advances on Ringo. In long shot, it walks directly toward the camera, an extensive and perfectly matched floor inlay allowing it to throw shadows on the ground and miniature shrubs. The next shot seems to be something of an affectionate nod to a Fay Wray/tyrannosaurus composite in *King Kong* — a caveman lies beside a fallen tree trunk with the dinosaur advancing in the background. The live-action element is blue-screened, allowing the caveman's hand to pass in front of the model's foot.

An unusual perspective from the caveman's point of view looks up at the dinosaur towering above him. When the tyrannosaurus strides across the frame in a dynamic medium shot, shadows are thrown onto its back to reinforce the impression that it is surrounded by trees.

An ambitious matte follows the outline of several irregular bushes on one side of the frame, permitting the model to step out of the undergrowth. Like most of the composites, this shot was almost certainly designed by Danforth, who did similarly successful mattes around bushes in *When Dinosaurs Ruled the Earth*. As originally conceived, however, such a matte would not have been necessary. Danforth: "I designed the shot so that the T. Rex could enter from behind a miniature tree, camera left. Dave Allen (on location while I was trouble-shooting in L.A.) ignored my instruction and made this shot much more difficult."

When Ringo calls out, the dinosaur emits a puzzled growl and puts on an amusing anthropomorphic expression which seems to say, "Who said that?" It stomps across a miniature floor towards Ringo, who climbs up a tree. The dinosaur has stepped on the campfire and smoke from its burning foot is superimposed over the model as it looks up at Ringo. Its eyes are full of life and look around quizzically as its brain slowly perceives the pain. Eventually it growls in pain and walks off again, shaking its visibly blackened foot as it hobbles away. A matte line down the side of a tree allows the puppet to walk behind that part of the live-action set. It's another delightfully low-key conclusion to a flawlessly executed sequence.

The pterodactyl appears briefly in about a dozen cuts, some animated by Allen and others by Kleinow. *Caveman*'s convincing flying reptile (sculpted and painted by Cook) glides and circles on the air currents with barely a flap of its mottled wings. However, the animators avoid any involved contact with the live

Caveman's narcotized tyrannosaurus, in a comic scene animated by Randall W. Cook.

action: The dramatic punch of this scene is not the usual sight of an actor being carried off in a pair of huge claws, but instead a pterodactyl egg getting fried on a geyser.

In the first cut, the camera tilts up to follow the model swooping overhead, thereby requiring an extra pass of the camera over a rear-screen composite. A smaller model turns in the distance and heads back towards the cavemen who have stolen its egg. In a beautiful long shot executed by Allen, the small model is way off in the distance and flying directly toward the actors in the foreground. Danforth decided to use a front-light-backlight traveling matte technique for this shot, thereby making the pterodactyl really seem like it is right in the shot, and not just a model hanging in front of a rear projection.

A shot looking over the creature's shoulder at the men below and a closeup of it screeching as it descends allow closer looks at the model's detail. Finally, a low-angle shot filmed from the foot of a cliff sees the creature fly over the cliff and disappear. The edge of the cliff provides an invisible matte line.

The scene on the rocky path, with the tyrannosaurus again pursuing Ringo and his motley group, is the highpoint of the film. Successful slapstick humor and some extremely fluid animation are combined in a breathtaking fantasy setting created by some fine matte paintings (by Rocco Gioffre) and two superior miniature sets.

The sequence begins with a composite of the actors walking along a path and a painting of a cliff edge occupying the lower left corner of the screen to create the illusion of great height. The di-

nosaur appears from behind a bend in the path (the cliff face disguising the matte line) and follows unnoticed behind the unwary group.—a broad comic device lifted straight out of pantomime.

The creature licks its lips, then (in a very striking long-shot) walks slowly behind the actors. The head-on viewpoint enhances the humor of the scene because it is the kind of flatly designed shot which directors would normally avoid. A matte painting of the cliff face, dropping away below, occupies the lower third of the screen.

A low-angle shot looks back over the still-unsuspecting Ringo's shoulder at the dinosaur behind him (which of course is actually in the foreground of a rear-projection set-up). When it growls at the cavemen, part of a real rock is matted in front of the model to break up the depth of the shot. The next shot sees the model in an extensive and impressively detailed miniature set: It's impossible to detect the point where the real and the false cliff face combine, even when logic indicates its probable location.

Ringo thrusts a branch laden with drugged fruit into the dinosaur's mouth. This clever composite (animated by Kleinow) was achieved by having Ringo mime the action. In reality he isn't holding anything—a miniature branch and two tiny puppet hands are carefully aligned with the actor's hands. A closeup of the model chomping on the leaves is followed by another shot of the miniature composite. This time the dinosaur sways drunkenly, falls onto a rock, gets up, collapses onto another rock, then teeters on the edge of the cliff with absurdly exaggerated gestures which defy the laws of gravity in the best traditions of cartoons. Eventually he topples over, and the sequence closes with the bizarre and unforgettable sight of the grinning tyrannosaurus lying propped up against a rock in a most un-dinosaur-like pose. It puts its tiny hands up to his mouth as if to say "What a predicament," and hiccups.

It's a classic sequence, again demonstrating the limitless (and all-too-rarely-tapped) potential of stop-motion. Like all the effects sequences, this cuts rapidly from one imaginative set-up to another, enlivening the pace and adding to the credibility. (Relying on one main composite perspective has weakened many inferior animation sequences in other films.)

The amusing slapstick of the live-action episode involving Chris Walas' shaggy snow-beast is followed by the film's final stop-motion sequence, a re-appearance by the horned lizard. As an example of the use of stop-motion for dramatic effect, it's less interesting than the preceding tyrannosaurus scene, with the puppet relegated to a supporting role (literally) when Ringo rides it into the camp for a final showdown with John Matuszak. Technically, however, it contains some of the film's most ambitious and successful effects, most astonishingly the shots (devised again by Danforth) of the live-action Ringo seemingly astride the puppet dinosaur.

Two brief animation cuts act as build-up to the final battle — one closeup and one full-view static matte of the lizard munching on some drugged fruit which Ringo has laid as bait. The first shot of the dinosaur striding into the frame with Ringo on its back invariably invokes gasps of delight from audiences — and gasps of amazement from viewers with some appreciation of effects processes.

First, Ringo was filmed riding on a cart whose height corresponded to the height of the imagined dinosaur. Then the same live-action location was filmed without Ringo and the cart. The two pieces of film were combined with a horizontal split screen across the center of the shot through Ringo's waist, creating a shot with Ringo's upper half seemingly suspended in mid-air. This footage was then used as a rear projection in front of which the dinosaur, complete with a puppet replica of Ringo's legs on its back, was animated and matched to the actor's upper half. Close scrutiny reveals that Allen's animation does not tie in with the live-action precisely, but is near enough to create a very satisfying illusion. It's one of the most daringly intimate moments of interaction between a puppet and live actor put on film.

A static matte set-up animated by Cook has a live caveman rush at the dinosaur, now with a full puppet likeness of Ringo on its back. The puppet Ringo swipes at the actor with a stick and the moment of contact is successfully implied when the actor tumbles to the ground. The dinosaur trots around with a convincingly lizard-like gait and two more cavemen charge at it, getting swatted by the prop tail.

The film's last animation cut includes another of those impressive subliminal details which do so much to enhance a shot. Matuszak, in the rear projection, runs at Ringo riding the puppet dinosaur and for a few brief frames actually appears to pass in front of the models. Cook achieved this by animating a puppet replica of Matuszak placed directly in front of the image of the actor, thereby obscuring him. Even in slow motion and freeze-frame, it's impossible to detect the moment of substitution — it's a perfect illusion. Unfortunately, the horned lizard is deprived of a farewell scene, and is conspicuously absent from the remaining live-action finale.

The inventiveness and technical wizardry of *Caveman* is another painful reminder of how the enormous potential of Danforth and Allen may never be realized in a big-budget, serious fantasy. Danforth came close in *When Dinosaurs Ruled the Earth*, and Allen keeps coming up with marvelous short sequences (such as in **batteries not included, Honey, I Shrunk the Kids* and *Doctor Mordrid*). Both are capable of creating fantasy classics of real stature, and it is a depressing indictment of the commercial shortsightedness of film producers that probably neither ever will.

Cestě do provĕku (US: *Journey to the Beginning of Time; a.k.a. Journey into Prehistory*)

1954. Czechoslovakia. Studio Gottwaldov. D: Karel Zeman. Scr: Karel Zeman, J. A. Novotný. Art: Karel Zeman, Zdenĕk Rozkopal, Ivo Mrdzek. Ph: Václav Pazdernik, Antonín Horak. Mus: E.F. Burian.

Cast: Vladimír Bejval, Petr Hermann, Zdenĕk Hustak, Josef Lukas.

American version: New Trends Associates. Prod-D-Scr: William Cayton. Additional dialogue: Fred Ladd.

Rating: ☆☆☆   Stop-Motion: ☆☆☆

In an alternative reality, where Karel Zeman left his native Czechoslovakia and emigrated to the United States, one can well imagine that his career might resemble that of Hungarian émigré George Pal. Their styles of filmmaking, rooted in fantasy and appealing to the child in us, have much in common. But in many respects we can be thankful that this never happened. Zeman's films have a charm and visual approach that are uniquely his own and would have been corrupted by the impositions of mainstream Hollywood filmmaking. Western plot clichés, trite love interests and star casts have no place in the world of Zeman. To anyone with even a passing interest in puppet animation, six of his feature films are essential viewing, containing many beautifully realized sequences that are as memorable in their own way as the best work of O'Brien and Harryhausen.

His early career also has parallels with Pal's. In 1944, he began making short animated films of a whimsical

117

nature. His first was *A Christmas Dream,* followed by *The Sluggard* (1946). *Inspiration* (1949) is a color short in which the characters were fashioned from glass and manipulated by heating them with a torch in between frames to make them malleable. His first feature-length film was *Cestě do prověku*, released in Czechoslovakia in 1954 but quite probably begun by Zeman two or three years earlier.

It was not picked up for screening in the West until 1960 when it was bought by producer William Cayton, retitled *Journey to the Beginning of Time* and shown on television by a company called Radio and Television Packagers. A few years later it was also shown on British television. Not only was it broken down into a series of five-minute episodes, but a whole new prologue and ending were filmed by Cayton, replacing the original sections. In 1966, Cayton trimmed this 100-minute version down to 93 minutes and released it as a feature. Video recordings of this version do circulate today but they tend to be of poor quality with much of the color washed out. The original Czech production is available from the Czech Film Archive. Readers are strongly advised to obtain a copy of this version, the sharp picture quality and lush colors of which make Zeman's prehistoric panorama a real treat for the eyes.

On a dramatic level, *Journey to the Beginning of Time* is less interesting than Zeman's later films. Its plot is a simple progression through a series of set-piece encounters with prehistoric creatures, as a group of four boys travel down a mysterious river that takes them back further and further into time. As a children's adventure it is adequate but the ironies and gentle humor of his other films are less in evidence here. The narrative (at least in the Americanized version) is done in a sometimes-labored semi-educational style with one of the boys identifying each of the creatures and giving a brief account of the period in which they lived and the kind of lives they led.

But visually the film is frequently stunning. It was the first full-length film to feature stop-motion photography in color — even though this seems to have largely faded from most prints in circulation today. Zeman fills his film with panoramic paintings of mountain ranges and ice floes, miniature jungle sets and tank-created cloudy skylines lit up by flashes of lightning, all matted into shots of the four boys drifting along the river. One very effective extreme long shot depicts the boys in the middle of an icescape, where foreground and background are paintings and the boys themselves are tiny cut-out figures moving slightly. More often these panoramas are simple split-screen mattes with the bank of the river forming the horizontal matte line, the live-action element on one side of it, a painting or miniature set on the other.

The puppets — there must be around 50 of them — are all highly detailed and believable. The only one that disappoints is a ceratosaurus near the end of the film, with bulky arms and legs that look more human than reptilian. Others, including a pair of woolly rhinoceros, a phororhacos and a stegosaurus, are impressive.

Journey to the Beginning of Time is the closest any film has come to exploiting the possibilities of the age of early mammals with all its fabulous beasts. O'Brien animated giant prehistoric birds and a two-horned arsinoitherium (although the latter was later dropped from *King Kong*) and Harryhausen has given us an eohippus and a saber-tooth tiger, but no one has ever really exploited this area. Zeman not only gives us a savage battle between two woolly rhinoceros and an encounter with a hungry phororhacos, but also populates his adventure with mammoth, prehistoric gazelles, a herd of prehistoric giraffes, an elephant-like deinotherium, a six-horned uintatherium, giant browsing indricotherium and other eye-boggling creatures.

Little has been written in western publications about the films of Karel Zeman, and that which does exist is unkind about *Journey to the Beginning of Time*. For example, Paul Mandell (in *Cinemagic* 29) is generally full of praise for Zeman, but he called the stop-motion in this film "tacky" and says it "left much to be desired." Roy Kinnard (in *Beasts and Behemoths*) writes about the film in some depth, admiring its general qualities but stating that Zeman's "techniques for combining his models with live actors are rudimentary." He says that all suggestions of simultaneity are achieved with the camera making "a fast, violent pan" across live-action footage, dissolving into a pan across a miniature set. He concedes that "there are a few stationary mattes combining actors and puppets, but for the most part the models and live actors do not interact."

In fact, only a few shots use the "swish pan" technique while stationary mattes are used in many shots. Kinnard makes no mention of the effective composites during the scene where the boys are attacked by pteranodons, nor of the excellent mechanical prop creatures that allow actors and dinosaurs to appear together in non-composite shots. He also fails to mention dynamic animation effects such as the superb tracking shots of the phororhacos sprinting through undergrowth. Of course, Zeman's composite shots are often basic, but Kinnard is unfair.

Inexplicably, Kinnard goes as far as to say, "A good pictorialist director would have been able to work wonders with this material, but Karel Zeman certainly did well enough." *Journey to the Beginning of Time* is not Zeman's most "pictorial" film, but he had one of the most impressive visual sensibilities of any fantasy director. One only has to look at *Vynález Zkázy* (*The Invention of Destruction*; US title: *The Fabulous World of Jules Verne*) or *Baron Prášil* (*Baron Munchausen*) for evidence.

Phil Hardy, in his *Encyclopedia of Science Fiction Movies*, is generally complimentary about Zeman's "marvelously inventive" style, but his review of *Journey to the Beginning of Time* has no specific criticism of any of the content. He also makes a curious reference to Zeman's "electronically controlled puppets animated with stop-frame techniques and multiple exposures, anticipating methods developed later by Harryhausen and the *Star Wars* (1977) type of special effects." He may be right about the multiple exposures (some of the pteranodon shots look like they may been done this way) but I think he is confusing the mechanical prop creatures (which may have been electronically operated) with the conventional stop-motion puppets, incorrectly implying that

Zeman developed a kind of prototype go-motion.

The animation by Zeman and his crew is often breathtaking. Prehistoric giraffes gallop fluidly alongside the river, a flock of pteranodons swoop and glide smoothly overhead, and a phororhacos dashes through a blur of miniature vegetation. Many other occasions are less ambitious, with puppets merely browsing among trees, their legs not moving, but even these sequences are realized with polish. As with all of Zeman's five live-action features, there is an astonishing amount of animation: *Journey to the Beginning of Time* has 118 cuts. Zeman's films are real labors of love, all taking several years to complete.

The first creature the boys encounter is a woolly mammoth, standing on the edge of the river bank as they drift past. A full-size model is used in shots from behind, allowing the boys to appear in the same shot. For three frontal shots in which the mammoth curls its trunk around some vegetation and then raises its head and roars, a puppet is animated in a miniature set. In three more stop-motion cuts, the mammoth slowly strides out of the frame, attractively shot in silhouette in the twilight gloom. One of these shots is a matte, with the boys in their boat in the lower half of the frame.

Later, one of the boys walks through some reeds, disturbing some ducks that fly off. About a dozen of these puppets are animated in one shot — it's a brief but realistic effect, but one is tempted to wonder why Zeman didn't take the easy option in this instance and use film of live ducks.

The boy pushes aside some under-growth and spots two bison walking through the forest. These are highly realistic stop-motion puppets, surrounded by dense and convincing miniature foliage. One interesting aspect of this shot is the fact that the puppets — and some of those which are seen subsequently — only walk in one plane across the frame. This indicates that in order to save time, Zeman may have constructed only one side of the puppet.

However, the puppets encountered next *are* fully-finished creations. Two woolly rhinoceros are discovered on the riverbank, engaged in a spirited battle. These impressive puppets really seem to smack into each with great force, and there are some dramatic low-angle close shots to emphasize their bulk. The only composite in this sequence has the boys watching from the opposite bank in the lower portion of the shot. The bigger rhino shoves the other one down the bank and into the river, at which point Zeman cuts to a prop-rhino in the water.

There are several shots of animated flamingoes, the live-action river matted in below. Three prehistoric gazelles bound across a picturesque miniature set, painted mountains forming a backdrop. In the same shot, an animated vulture wheels overhead, then two more gazelles leap by. The gait of these puppets is remarkably believable, requiring intricate wire-supported animation for much of their running cycle.

A deinotherium (an elephant from the Pleistocene period with short, downward-pointing tusks growing out of its lower lip) is seen in two long shots and one medium shot, chomping on some bushes but otherwise not moving.

In three cleverly designed shots, a

saber-toothed tiger strides through bushes in another set, the camera getting progressively closer with each shot, panning across the undergrowth as it does so. In other cuts, a vulture perched in a tree caws loudly and two more circle on the air currents.

In three marvelous shots, a herd of galloping giraffes pass the boys. These may be animation puppets, but it is hard to be sure. Zeman may even have taken actual footage of live giraffes and manipulated it to suit his needs. Certainly the running cycle is surprisingly fluid — it may be that Zeman used replacement animation to achieve this effect. In one of these cuts, nine animals are seen simultaneously, so if these *are* puppets, it must have been a Herculean task of animation. One shot is a striking pan and another is a composite, with the boys rowing their boat in the river below. It's an unforgettable moment.

Another animated vulture croaks down from a tree, and at night the boys are menaced by some crocodiles, convincing mechanical props half-submerged in the water.

The river takes the boys back into the Tertiary period. In a series of 12 stop-motion shots, a variety of animals are seen browsing in miniature sets, this time with no composites. A herd of antelope, a giraffe, two indricotheres (18–foot-high, long-necked relatives of the rhinoceros) and a uintatherium (a large quadruped with six stumpy horns on its hairy head) are all fine models, although not required to do much. In the last of these shots, the camera tilts up from the uintatherium to another circling vulture.

A herd of silhouetted prehistoric horses gallop across the horizon, another impressive demonstration of Zeman's consummate animation and pictorial skills.

One of the film's highlights is a brief but exciting engagement with a phororhacos, a giant flightless bird. This striking puppet has black and white markings on its body and a vicious-looking beaked head, and it screeches with hungry ferocity. Zeman puts all his energies into making it as purposeful a creature as possible. There are 14 stop-motion cuts including two composites.

One of the boys discovers it feeding on some small creature in a clearing. In a creepy closeup, its beady eyes stare hungrily at the intruder. Several superb tracking shots follow the bird as it races after the boy through tall grass, which pass in a blur in both foreground and background, giving the shots a real sense of pace. Again, the gait of the creature is surprisingly realistic, its head and body bobbing up and down. It may well be that Zeman kept his puppet and camera stationary, using long exposures that allowed him to move the grass past the camera while the shutter was open, thereby creating the blur. Several shots depict the creature standing wide-legged on the river bank, trying to reach the boys in their boat below, snapping at them and screeching. Is it possible that Harryhausen saw this on television in 1960, before making his similar (but much more elaborate) sequence in *Mysterious Island*, which was released the following year?

The river now takes the boys back to the Mesozoic era. Nineteen animation cuts, including three composites, feature in an excellent sequence in which they are attacked by pteranodons. It begins with a clever pan up from the boys to a shot of several of the creatures gliding overhead. One of these cuts has four puppets animated in the same frame. Their wing movements are slightly faster than a glide, allowing very smooth though not completely successful animation. One of the pteranondons sees the boys, turns, swoops and caws loudly. One dramatic cut has a pteranodon flying straight at the camera. In one shot the creature swoops low over the boat, and in another it knocks one of the boys into the water; these may be composites or it may be that Zeman used miniature animated puppets of the boys. The sequence ends picturesquely with a shot of three pteranodons flying away from the camera into the distance.

A series of panoramas of Mesozoic life begins with four shots of a styracosaurus walking ponderously through some trees and munching on leaves. It's a good model but not in the same class as Delgado's magnificent puppet in *The Son of Kong*. In the last of these shots, the camera pans across to two small bipedal dinosaurs bounding over the landscape. Several shots show a stegosaurus, including two composites with the boys in their boat matted in. This time the live-action element occupies the top half of the shots, with the stegosaurus walking along the near side of the river. A lingering close shot of the stegosaurus walking past allows a good look at the impressive detail of the puppet: its beaked head, the huge plates on its back, the knobbly hide and the four-spiked tail. Delgado would approve of this craftmanship. A slow tracking shot, following the plodding dinosaur, has impeccably smooth animation.

Large mechanical props are used to depict two duck-billed dinosaurs and a brontosaurus, all partly submerged in water. These are restricted in what they can do, but they stoop, turn and feed realistically enough and are superior to those in many Hollywood films.

The film's most ambitious animation, containing 30 stop-motion cuts, is the battle between the stegosaurus and a ceratosaurus (a horned bipedal carnivore). This is a competently staged episode but lacks the necessary impact, suggesting that Zeman's forte is not in action sequences but is more tuned to the picturesque and the whimsical. Zeman has certainly seen Disney's *Fantasia*, because some of the choreography (for example, of the two beasts warily circling each other) is lifted directly from that film. Some composite shots are included, as ever simple mattes with the boys watching the action from the near side of the river. Long shots show the two beasts engaging, and in closer shots the stegosaur's spiked tail smashes into the ceratosaur's chest, animated blood oozing out. In closeups, the ceratosaur roars in pain. Eventually, the wounded ceratosaur walks off. The stegosaur walks off in the other direction but, fatally bitten in the neck, slumps down dead.

The next morning, the boys cross the river and examine the slain stegosaur, clambering all over a full-size prop. Interestingly, a 1980 documentary about Zeman shows how a small painting of a stegosaur was placed near the camera and lined up with the boys, who were actually just climbing on a platform concealed by the painting. Very clever, but in fact this technique is not used in the

Cestě do prověku (1954): A confrontation between two of Karel Zeman's dinosaurs. (National Film Archive, London.)

film and was created solely for the documentary. The film uses only a full-size prop.

Back still further in the Cambrian period, Zeman makes good use of miniature swamps, successfully blending them with a studio swamp set that compares favorably with those of Skull Island. Several cuts show a foot-long dragonfly buzzing through the trees, its wings flapping at high speed. This may be a stop-motion puppet, but is more likely to be a mechanical creation supported on wires. Several amphibious creatures (all props) slither through the swamp water and a cute meter-long eryops (a hand puppet) snaps viciously with its wide mouth at one of the boys, looking like a prototype for Kermit the Frog.

In the Pre-Cambrian period, one extreme long shot of the boys walking through a rocky landscape looks as though it was achieved by animating tiny puppets, surrounded by paintings and a miniature set. This is a technique which Zeman would exploit more fully in extreme long shots in later films. The boys finally arrive at a sea — the source of all life — and the film ends with some unnecessary biblical musings, thanks to

Cayton's reshot epilogue. It is unlikely that these would have been part of Zeman's original.

Each of Zeman's films is unique. *Journey to the Beginning of Time* overcomes its plot crudities and the lack of invention in its composite shots by portraying a rich and endlessly changing panorama of prehistoric scenes. Like all of his work, it is a difficult film to track down, but once seen it offers up all kind of unforgettable rewards.

A Chinese Ghost Story

1987. Cinema City. D: Ching Siu Tung. Scr: Yuen Kai Chi. Mus: Romeo Díaz, James Wong. Ph: Poon Heng Seng, Sander Lee, Tom Lau, Wong Wing Hang.

Cast: Leslie Cheung, Wang Tsu Hsien, Wu Ma.

Rating: ☆☆☆   Stop-Motion: ☆☆½

The horror boom in America sparked a similar trend in the Far East. One of the most memorable of these East Asian fantasy films was Ching Siu Tung's *A Chinese Ghost Story*, which managed to be chilling, poetic, touching, spectacular and funny all at the same time.

Set in long-ago China, it tells the tale of a young student who falls in love with a beautiful girl only to find that she is a ghost. This leads him into a series of encounters with the family of spirits which the girl must obey and a swordsman who wants to destroy them all. Around this simple plot, the director has fashioned a film with a style and elegance not seen since the Golden Age of horror films in the 1930s, and at the same time distinctly Chinese. Eerie, luminescent lighting, imaginative camerawork, mustily credible sets and a haunting score combine to create a fantasy world not far removed from the world of dreams.

The hero is a gauche, likable character who never really understands what is going on. His love for the ghost-heroine is depicted with engaging simplicity. In one unforgettable scene, he is hidden by the girl in her bath barrel when the troupe of guardian spirits calls on her. To give him air, she pretends to wash her hair and leans into the barrel, giving him a long kiss — a long cut filmed with a sensual languor that is both erotic and comic.

Ching has seen *The Evil Dead*. In the act of seducing a lover, the girl-spirit rings the tiny bells on her anklet, and an unseen demon is summoned, seen in point-of-view shots hurtling through the woods at ground level. One of the witches, a tree-demon, can make branches become weapons that ensnare victims. Some of Ching's splatter effects are at least as outrageous as those of Sam Raimi. Monstrous tongues have featured in horror films before, but this one outdoes them all: a 200–foot monster that sprouts from a witch's mouth, surrounds a house, rips through floorboards and wraps itself around its prey like an octopus' tentacle. Ching skillfully blends cartoon-style farce with chills in a sequence in which the hero tries to flee from the tongue by climbing a ladder,

A Chinese Ghost Story

but as fast as he is climbing up, the tongue is pulling the ladder back down.

During the early part of the film, the hero beds down in a room in an old temple. He pricks his finger on a window-catch and this has the effect of bringing to life some shriveled corpses lying in the loft. These scrawny beings are realized by means of some stop-motion which relies for effect more on sinister atmosphere than the kind of dynamic spectacle that is usually associated with the process.

These skeletal beings — too thin to have been actors in costumes — are too brittle-boned to stand upright and drag themselves around the shadowy room with their hands, accompanied by the gruesome sound of crunching bone. Ching gives these nightmarish sequences a comic tone — the hero is always just out of the corpses' reach and, like in a pantomime scene, he remains unaware that they are even in the room with him.

There are 11 stop-motion shots and at least double that number featuring live-action mechanical corpses or, later, very thin actors dressed up. These latter shots are less spooky than the stop-motion shots but allow closer interaction on the set between corpses and the actor. The animation appears to have been shot in an extensive miniature set of the loft.

While the hero sits up at night writing by candlelight, the corpses awaken above him. They sit up stiffly, then shuffle across the floor of the upstairs room. Light from below seeps through the wooden slats and lights up parts of the puppets. One of them peers down through a gap in the wood. They drag themselves towards a hole in the floor. Investigating the noises, the hero places a ladder against the hole and begins to climb up as the corpses get nearer and nearer. In the only composite shot — using an invisible static matte — the actor is seen in the lower part of the frame at the top of the ladder, while the corpses are crawling around the floor above him. At the last moment, he is distracted by the sound of his lover playing a lute and leaves the room.

Later, the corpses start to climb down the ladder into the room. One of these shots is a bizarre medium shot of an upside-down corpse coming down the ladder. It pauses, opens its ragged mouth wide, then its head spins slowly round on its neck in a complete circle.

The hero walks back into the room, the force of the door hurling the ladder across the room and onto the floor, where all the corpses crash through the rotten floorboards into the basement below. Suspicious but still unaware of the corpses, the hero continues his writing. Down below, in the final stop-motion shot, the four corpses recover from their fall, writhing about on the basement floor, their long arms snaking through the air. Eventually, the hero goes down into the basement where he is nearly grabbed by the live-action corpses. When he throws open some dusty old windows, all the corpses melt down into a sticky goo.

A sequel, *A Chinese Ghost Story 2*, was released in 1990. It was equally inventive and atmospheric, but lacked the original's charm. It contained no stop-motion.

Clash of the Titans

1981. MGM. Prod: Charles H. Schneer, Ray Harryhausen. D: Desmond Davis. Scr: Beverley Cross. Ph: Ted Moore. Mus: Laurence Rosenthal. Art: Frank White. Creator of Special Visual Effects: Ray Harryhausen. Assistants to Ray Harryhausen: Jim Danforth, Steven Archer. Model Makers: Janet Stevens, Colin Chilvers and (uncredited) Lyle Conway. Special Opticals: Frank Van Der Veer, Ray Field.

Cast: Harry Hamlin, Judy Bowker, Burgess Meredith, Sian Phillips, Flora Robson, Freda Jackson, Laurence Olivier, Claire Bloom, Maggie Smith, Ursula Andress, Jack Gwillim, Neil McCarthy, Donald Huston.

Rating: ☆☆½   Stop-Motion: ☆☆☆

Harryhausen's last film was his most expensive, costing a hefty $16 million — 80 times the budget of his first solo venture, *The Beast from 20,000 Fathoms*. MGM marketed it aggressively and it made a substantial profit. But it is also one of his least interesting films, laboring under a stodgy script by Beverley Cross, who simply does not know how to engage an audience's interest.

A small fortune was spent on the actors who play the Gods of Olympus (including Laurence Olivier as Zeus) but they are always defeated by Cross' wordy, humorless dialogue. Director Desmond Davis holds everything together with polish but, like so many other directors of Harryhausen pictures, seems unable to inject the project with much energy. The 116-minute running time (longer than any previous Harryhausen film) frequently drags. Harryhausen fans were hoping for a film that would compare with his previous Ancient Greece tale,

Jason and the Argonauts, but many were sorely disappointed.

There is spectacle and action a-plenty but for the most part it is mechanical and ponderous. Harry Hamlin and Judy Bowker, as the young lovers Perseus and Andromeda, try hard but are ultimately forgettable. Even Burgess Meredith, as the poet Ammon, is little better. The score by Lawrence Rosenthal has some effective themes but is too imitative of the John Williams *Star Wars* style. Rosenthal has a distinctive theme for each of the film's major characters and replays it *ad nauseam* each time they appear. Much of the film's publicity was deceptively slanted to suggest the film was another *Star Wars* kind of film and one character, Bubo the mechanical owl, is clearly designed to cash in on the craze for cute robots inspired by R2D2 in the George Lucas space adventure. Harryhausen hotly refutes this on the grounds that Bubo is actually part of the Greek legends, which may be so — but the owl's personality (forever getting into trouble, falling over, bleeping and whirring) is a blatant steal.

Like *The Golden Voyage of Sinbad*, the film tries to create a unifying visual style. This is a commendable desire but works against *Clash of the Titans*. Most of the outdoor scenes are shot day-for-night and have clouds of machine-smoke wafting through them. This creates an eerie and naturalistic look but it also makes many scenes visually uninteresting. The bright sunshine and Technicolor look of *Jason* may not have looked true to life but are preferable to the dull, overcast settings of *Clash*.

Production design by Frank White is likewise dreary. He makes the halls of Olympus look like cheap sets from an amateur theatrical production. The swamp-lair of the villain Calibos should have been something special but instead is forgettable.

Fortunately, Harryhausen works his magic and comes up with some magnificent episodes. The destruction by flood of the city of Argos, the capture of the winged stallion Pegasus, Perseus wrestling with Calibos in the swamps, and the climactic encounter with the snake-tailed Medusa — these are all examples of Harryhausen at the height of his powers, technically and dramatically.

But he, too, is guilty of some misjudgments. The increased budget tempted him to produce an overdose of stop-motion effects: There are a staggering 364 cuts. Some sequences are merely routine, making one wish that he had omitted these and instead spent more time developing a few key scenes. The pace suffers half way through when three extremely dramatic stop-motion episodes follow one another in rapid succession. A battle with Dioskilos (a two-headed dog) leads straight into the encounter with Medusa, which is followed by an appearance by three giant scorpions. The impact of each scene is weakened by the proximity of the other two, as the audience is bombarded with monstrous characters. As a self-contained episode, each is superb, but in terms of dramatic context, Harryhausen's time would have been better spent concentrating on either Dioskilos or the scorpions, but not both.

The Kraken, a giant sea beast that appears at the beginning of the film and again at the climax, is a major disappointment. It never convinces that it is more than a rubber puppet. On its face are stiff, whiskery growths, and its eyes are curiously lifeless. Instead of being jointed normally, its four arms move like tentacles, making the creature look even more unlikely. The script is never sure what to do with this behemoth, and during the climax, in which it comes to claim Andromeda as a sacrifice, it merely stands around looking evil until Perseus destroys it.

Other stop-motion characters, however, look marvelous. Pegasus is one of the most elegantly realistic puppets ever seen in a film, benefiting from an authentic white fur covering and wings with actual feathers. The giant vulture, which carries Andromeda off in a cage to Calibos' lair, also has an impressive covering of feathers, a gnarled beak, beady red eyes and a pink head and neck that are believably wrinkled.

Calibos is one of Harryhausen's most ambitious creations. Punished by Zeus, Calibos has been transformed into a nightmarish creature who is only part-human, with one goat-leg, two horns and a long reptilian tail. He is a stop-motion puppet in some shots and actor Neil McCarthy in others. Harryhausen invites difficulties by cutting from one to the other, but he brings it off perfectly.

Calibos demonstrates Harryhausen's ever-growing confidence in his animation. His earliest humanoid creations (the Ymir and the Cyclops) are characterized by their bizarre posture and gait — bestial legs and an "arms back" pose — which means that audi-

127

ences do not expect them to have the natural pose and movements of a man. Later humanoid puppets — such as Talos and the skeletons in *Jason* — are anatomically more accurate but avoid having to create the illusion of fluid, natural movements because they are not flesh-and-blood creations. The troglodyte in *Sinbad and the Eye of the Tiger* was a leap forward since it was an entirely humanoid figure and also a living being — albeit characterized by a stiff, lumbering gait. Calibos (built over the Trog armature) takes the progression a step further. Some remarkable animation and careful attention to lighting and editing insure that few viewers are aware that the camera is cutting from live actor (primarily closeups of McCarthy's expressive, heavily made up face) to puppet. In some of the most perfect rear-screen composites of Harryhausen's career, he has the puppet Calibos wrestling with the live-action Perseus, the two actually seeming to make close physical contact.

Calibos, cracking a whip and sporting a vicious trident in place of one hand that Perseus has cut off, is a visually marvelous character. His unrequited love for Andromeda makes him a tragic figure. But Harryhausen seems to back away from elevating him to the status of a major character. He showed the same curious restraint with the Centaur in *The Golden Voyage of Sinbad*, where the creature's affection for Margiana could have lead to some King Kong–Ann Darrow pathos. The death of Calibos, slain by Perseus' sword, is not the climax of the film: It happens almost as a throwaway scene, as if Harryhausen were getting it out of the way so that he can move

on to the reappearance of the Kraken. This is a scripting flaw; the scenes should have happened in reverse order, the film ending with a climactic struggle between Perseus and Calibos, with Andromeda the prize, in the best Errol Flynn–Basil Rathbone fashion.

There is so much animation in the film that Harryhausen called in some assistants for the first and only time in his career. Jim Danforth, who had just left *Caveman*, and newcomer Steven Archer were recruited to handle many scenes. The breakdown of who did what is as follows. Harryhausen animated all the shots in the Medusa and scorpions sequences. He also animated all shots of Calibos except a few which were done by Archer. He animated all the shots of the vulture on the ground, leaving the flying shots to Archer. Archer also animated all shots of Bubo, except about four or five which were done by Harryhausen. For the Kraken, Harryhausen and Archer each did approximately half of the animation, with Danforth doing one shot. Archer did a few shots of Dioskilos but the bulk of this sequence was animated by Danforth. Danforth handled all the blue-screen shots of Pegasus in flight while Harryhausen animated shots of this puppet on the ground. Close shots of the horse's animated wings in front of a rear-projection were shared by Danforth and Archer.

The film also contains a wealth of non-animation effects. The flooding of a miniature of the city of Argos, Perseus wearing a helmet that turns him invisible, the face of the goddess Thetis (Maggie Smith) coming to life on a statue, a miniature of the walled city of Joppa, and a miniature of the ruins of a domed

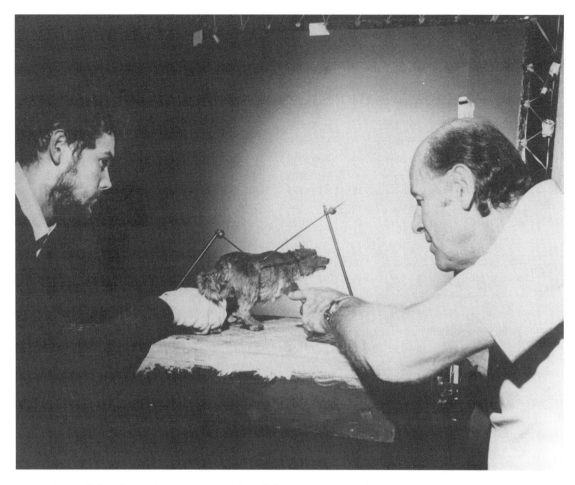

Clash of the Titans (1981): Steve Archer (left) animates Dioskilos, the two-headed dog, under Ray Harryhausen's supervision.

temple high on a hill are only some of the film's impressive effects.

The quality of the animation is generally excellent. Process and optical work includes some superb static and traveling mattes but (as ever) one or two substandard ones sneak through. A long shot of the city of Joppa includes a huge carved elephant with a conspicuous blue shimmer around it where the two parts of a matte have not been correctly aligned. Close shots of Perseus riding Pegasus employ traveling matte that is not up to the intricacies of the actor's hair and the horse's feathers, with the result that the sequences are significantly weakened.

The film begins with a good moody sequence (filmed in Cornwall) in which Danae and her baby Perseus are cast adrift in a casket at sea by Acrisius (Donald Houston). The credits are backed by stunning aerial footage over some Spanish mountains. This sequence is spoiled by the presence of a seagull soaring overhead, added to the footage by some

129

inferior traveling matte work. The seagull arrives at Olympus, a detailed miniature which unfortunately *looks* like a miniature, thanks to the poorly detailed rocks and the scale of the "clouds" around it. Still, it's better than the interior, which always looks like a film set, with Olivier looking very fake on his throne, backed by an unlikely blue glow. Angered by Acrisius' action, Zeus wants revenge: "Destroy Argos! Let loose the last of the Titans! Let loose the Kraken!"

An intricate miniature of Argos is much better, matted into a live-action seascape and backed by a painting of mountains and sky. Beneath the sea, Poseidon (Jack Gwillim) releases the Kraken. Gwillim is seen as a tiny figure, blue-screened into a miniature set with a huge steel gate that bars the entrance to a cave. A prop of the Kraken's tail is effectively used in one low-angle live-action shot showing it swim out from the cave.

Three quick shots — including one animation cut — give us teasing glimpses of the Kraken, which will be seen more fully at the film's climax. In the first shot, the head and torso of the growling beast rise up out of the water. Frothing water has been superimposed onto the foreground. For this live-action shot, the largest of three Kraken puppets was used, this one a four-foot-high creation. The Kraken submerges, frothing water again in the foreground and a rear projection of Argos behind it. In a shot animated by Archer, the huge tail snakes across the screen, the animation giving it more movement than could have been achieved with a live-action prop.

Harryhausen intended that the Kraken rise "in an explosion of churn-ing foam like a sea-to-land missile" but the reality is less dramatic. These three shots all look like effects composites; he is being too ambitious in trying to show such intimate contact with water.

Nevertheless, the ensuing tidal wave and destruction of Argos is marvelous. Shooting at 96 frames per second and using a five-foot high miniature set, Harryhausen demolishes columns, statues and buildings in a superb display of non-animation trickery. First-rate traveling mattes place tiny extras into the sets, deluged by the frothing water. The mattes are cleverly designed so that the extras seem to disappear as the water swamps them. Under Harryhausen's supervision, rotoscope mattes were drawn frame-by-frame by Roy Field's optical department over the footage of the actors so that they were progressively obscured as the water element surrounds them. This is probably the only occasion in a Harryhausen film where rotoscope matting has been used.

With the seemingly effortless precision born of years of experience, Harryhausen executes a series of non-animation effects before introducing his first full-blown stop-motion scene. Zeus takes a clay figurine of Calibos and its shadow transforms, by means of cel animation, into a horned, goat-legged creature. The giant hand of the goddess Thetis (Maggie Smith) deposits the sleeping Perseus in an amphitheatre in Joppa. Perseus discovers a helmet that turns him invisible and the poet Ammon is astonished to see footsteps appearing on the ground. And the city of Joppa is depicted in long shot by means of a striking static matte that combines huge statues and the walls of the city with a bustling crowd below. The statues and walls are miniatures, not a painted area — there are no matte paintings at all in *Clash*.

In a restrained and haunting sequence featuring 13 stop-motion cuts, the spirit of the sleeping Andromeda is carried off in a cage by a giant vulture. The vulture is one example of the way Harryhausen has gone to great lengths in this film to avoid criticism that his creations tend to appear once, engage in a battle and are defeated. The vulture is used here as an instrument of another individual (Calibos) rather than as an adversary in its own right and (like the Kraken, Pegasus, Calibos and Bubo) is a recurring character, appearing significantly in two later scenes.

Long shots looking out from Andromeda's bedroom show the vulture landing on the balcony outside, which is a miniature area perfectly matted into the live-action surroundings. The creature perches on a balustrade, screeches and flaps its wings in a way that credibly suggests its great bulk. Low-angle medium shots of the squawking bird allow a good look at the wealth of detail in its wrinkled and fleshy head and neck. It is easy to believe that this is a living creature.

The vulture waits patiently as Andromeda's spirit walks towards the cage. But Harryhausen doesn't let his creation merely sit idly by. Cawing gently, it shuffles along the balustrade. Its beady eyes blink as they watch Andromeda. In another rear projection, this time from behind the puppet, the bird starts to get agitated as she enters the cage. Once Andromeda is in the cage, the vulture spreads its wings. Seen in long shot again

from inside the bedroom, the bird flaps its huge wings, flies onto the top of the cage, grabs it in its claws, squawks and takes to the air. The attractive final shot uses the same static matte set-up and a smaller nine-inch puppet (with rubber wings rather than feathers) which flies off into the distance with the cage hanging under it. The wings flap up and down gracefully with none of the strobing that has impaired other flying sequences. This shot, and all subsequent shots of the nine-inch puppet, were animated by Archer.

Perseus has witnessed Andromeda's abduction and determines that when the vulture carries her off the following night, he will follow it. At Ammon's suggestion, the two decide to enlist the help of the flying stallion, Pegasus. The scene in which Pegasus flies down to drink at a moonlit pool and is captured and broken in by Perseus is one of the film's highlights. The model is beautiful and the magnificent animation (primarily by Danforth) makes it one of the most convincingly "alive" stop-motion characters ever. There are some exceptional composites and the sequence has a hushed, almost breathless tone that imparts a magical, "fairy tale" quality. There are 39 stop-motion cuts.

The opening shot is a stunner. In long shot, the distant puppet flies down behind a tree (which is part of the live-action area and the branches of which have been carefully matted around), its wings flapping smoothly, its four legs galloping on air. Its tail is made up of white wires animated so as to swish convincingly. This is a great improvement on the Centaur's muscular tail in *Golden Voyage of Sinbad*, although in some cuts

Puppets of Perseus and Pegasus from *Clash of the Titans*, as they were displayed at London's Museum of the Moving Image.

the tail remains static when the animator hopes the audience's eyes will be elsewhere.

In a closer rear-projection shot, Pegasus comes in for a landing, his rear legs hitting the ground first. Perseus and Ammon are hiding in the lower foreground behind a tree. The same set-up is used to show Pegasus walking in a circle, snorting, his wings still raised. The animation shots are intercut with shots of the head and legs of a live-action horse. The invisible Perseus throws a rope, which seems to extend from nowhere and wrap around the horse's neck. Ammon looks on as Pegasus flaps his wings anxiously, his front legs rear-

ing up. These are all flawless rear-screen composites, the puppet looking like it really is part of the live-action surroundings.

In the same set-up, Perseus' helmet is knocked off and he becomes visible, struggling at the end of the rope. This composite required another pass of the camera but its lighting and contrast are still perfectly balanced. There is a matte down the middle of the shot where the miniature rope is lined up with the live-action rope. In a series of shots using the same long-shot design, Perseus continues to restrain the whinnying Pegasus, eventually approaching him and mounting him. The moment when Perseus

132

actually leaps onto the horse is done in a close live-action cut.

Two more long shots using the same design have a puppet of Perseus astride Pegasus, who rears up in anticipation of taking to the air. The animation is convincing because the puppets are far off and because Perseus is partly obscured by the horse's wings. The opening long-shot design is used again to show Pegasus leaving the ground and flying behind a foreground tree.

The long sequence of cuts in which Pegasus tries to throw Perseus, eventually being subdued by the rider, contains some shots that are excellent and others that are disappointing. There are three basic designs. Extreme long shots have the two puppets blue-screened in front of a sky background. Medium shots are done one of two ways. In one, Perseus is blue-screened in front of film of animated wings, which in turn have been animated in front of a rear projection of the sky. In the other, the animated wings are shot in front of rear-projected footage of Perseus on a partly seen mock-up of the horse. The long shots are the most successful. The medium shots always look like effects shots because the traveling matte is unable to handle the intricacies of Perseus' hair blowing in the wind.

For the long shots, the Pegasus puppet was attached on its far side to a blue rod that allowed it to move in several directions, including up and down. Danforth's animation of the beast bucking and bending is very fluid. This is a complex bit of animation: as well as the kicking legs and the head, he also has to animate the wings, the swishing tail and the Perseus-puppet.

In one dynamic long-shot, horse and rider turn in the distance, backed by some very photogenic clouds. Eventually Pegasus is calmed and (in an attractive design) Perseus brings him in to land. The static matte designs seen earlier are used again, with Ammon looking on as Pegasus trots around in a circle, Perseus (live action again) having dismounted. Harryhausen cuts away to avoid showing Perseus actually dismounting — wisely so, since this might have betrayed the puppet Perseus. Pegasus folds his wings down by his side as the two men stand beside him. The closing shot in this fine scene is a romantic silhouette of all three characters, with Perseus petting Pegasus on the nose. This is a rear-projection composite, with the puppet aligned with footage in which Hamlin mimes the action.

The following night, Perseus is ready to follow the vulture and hides in Andromeda's bedroom. This long sequence, involving a stunning aerial chase and an encounter between Perseus and Calibos, contains 35 stop-motion cuts.

The first three cuts, in which the squawking vulture picks up the cage carrying Andromeda and flies off, use three rear-screen designs seen earlier. In a very striking long shot, the far off vulture (the nine-inch puppet) flies left to right above a nighttime composite of the walls of Joppa. In the same shot, Perseus enters from the left riding on Pegasus, all three puppets seeming tiny.

Animated against rear-projected footage shot from a helicopter, the vulture flies away from the camera, the wings flapping gracefully as though it is riding the air currents. The pursuit over some very dramatic craggy peaks combines long shots of the Perseus puppet and Pegasus blue-screened against the sky, long shots of the vulture and medium shots of Perseus with animated wings in the foreground. When the vulture flies low over the swamps near Calibos' lair, one can't help wishing that Harryhausen had had the time and budget that would have allowed him to introduce some O'Brien-style glass shots. In long shot, Perseus and Pegasus fly down through some clouds. This effect was probably achieved with some soft-focus rotoscope matting.

In a skillful rear-screen composite, the vulture deposits the cage on a muddy mound surrounded by an alligator-infested swamp. There is a puppet Andromeda inside the cage but because it is so far off and barely seen, Harryhausen doesn't need to give it any movement. The next two cuts use the same set-up, with the vulture alighting on a foreground log and looking on as Andromeda steps out of the cage.

The build-up to our first sight of Calibos effectively dispenses with a musical score, using instead the ominous sounds of frogs croaking. In two medium shots, the wizened vulture caws gently. Andromeda walks through the foggy swamp when suddenly a swarthy goat-leg steps into the foreground. The camera tilts up, revealing Calibos with his back to us, his dinosaur-like tail swishing to and fro. The miniature floor on which the puppet stands blends in perfectly with the dark background, withstanding even the tilt-up which might have given it away.

The camera dollies as it looks over Calibos' shoulder, following him as he walks behind Andromeda. The character limps because although one leg is goat-like, the other has been left in its human form. Why Harryhausen chose to animate this particular shot is a mystery: The puppet's tail and goat-leg are below the frame, so he could have used McCarthy. Perhaps he deliberately chooses to use McCarthy only for closeups, since long shots of the actor might have contrasted too noticeably with the puppet.

In a seamlessly matched static matte composite, Calibos sits on his throne, the live-action Andromeda standing to one side. The throne is an ornately carved miniature. The foreground steps leading down from the throne are part of the live-action plate. Calibos stands up, swishes his tail and cracks his whip (which momentarily disappears below the matte line — although this is only noticeable when watching in slow-motion on video). In a very fluidly animated cut, Calibos — now seated again — beckons Andromeda to him, and she kneels beside his throne.

The invisible Perseus looks on as Calibos bemoans his fate and recounts his twisted plans for revenge. If he cannot have Andromeda, then he will insure that no one else can. As Perseus leaves, he is unaware that Calibos has spotted his footsteps in the mud.

Perseus wades knee-deep through the swamp looking for Pegasus. Suddenly, Calibos appears and locks an arm around Perseus' neck. This audacious composite is brilliantly successful for a number of reasons. The alignment of puppet arm and the image of Perseus in the rear projection is done with rock-steady precision. Both characters are kept partly in shadow so as to disguise contrasts. The point at which Calibos makes contact with the water is obscured by a convenient rock in the rear projection. Harryhausen could not use McCarthy for this shot because he wanted to show Calibos' tail snaking high in the air.

Three more shots use this set-up as the two struggle. In another superb example of alignment, Calibos' other hand appears to have grabbed Perseus' arm. The two characters really do seem to be making physical contact. Enormous care has gone into this sequence: Medium-shots of McCarthy and Hamlin are intercut with the composite shots, but they never conflict, always seeming like part of the same scene.

In a different perspective of the struggle, Harryhausen takes his magic one step further — the Calibos puppet is clearly seen standing in the water as he batters at Perseus with his fist. The horizontal matte line goes through the water and, cleverly, the ripples caused by the actor seem to be caused by the puppet. It is one of the finest composites in Harryhausen's career. The scene ends abruptly as Perseus raises his sword and slashes down.

Back in Joppa, Andromeda stands in the temple of Thetis before a crowd and recites the riddle that Calibos has given to her. Any man who can solve the riddle can have her hand in marriage, but those who fail to solve it are burned at the stake. Long shots of the interior of the temple are skillful mattes, with the upper parts of the huge pillars and the statue of Thetis a miniature matched to the live action below.

At night the temple is deserted — except for Calibos, who comes to pray

to the goddess. In two outstanding extreme long shots (animated by Archer), the puppet (a second, smaller version) kneels at the foot of the huge statue, his tail swishing behind him. Part of the floor is miniature (the puppet throws a shadow onto it) but where it meets the live-action set is undetectable. These two high-angle shots, looking down at the tiny, bizarre creature groveling before the statue, are haunting fantasy images and among the most memorable in the film. Calibos reveals the stump where his left hand has been cut off by Perseus and pleads for Thetis to help him get revenge.

The next day, the statue of Thetis cracks apart (filmed in miniature at 96 frames per second). The enormous head comes to rest in front of Perseus and the face of Maggie Smith is superimposed over it as she speaks. This is a good bit of basic camera trickery, infinitely preferable to the unlikely figurehead that came to life in *Jason and the Argonauts.*

That night, Calibos and his swamp cronies capture Pegasus. This brief and subdued sequence, containing 12 stop-motion cuts, is a satisfying example of how Harryhausen is taking pains to make his special effects further the plot, rather than allowing the plot to serve the effects, as is more often the case. It is full of flawless composites, but one can't help wishing that Harryhausen had staged it in broad daylight. The shadowy lighting hides all the matte lines, but it also makes the scene less visually appealing.

The camera pans across from the live-action Pegasus (head and neck only) to a dark tree from behind which emerges Calibos, holding his whip. In this shot, animated by Archer, the invisible matte line follows the outline of the tree. In medium shot, Calibos lashes out with his whip, one of the few shots in the film in which the animation looks hurried. In long shot, both puppets are seen in full in a clearing, Calibos' whip wrapped around the stallion's neck. Pegasus rears up on his hind legs and (in a beautifully lit medium shot) extends his wings, which catch the moonlight.

Harryhausen moves his animation camera nearer to the same rear-screen set-up in the next shot, which has Calibos still restraining Pegasus with his whip, while the swamp men run up in the background. The matte line runs along the ground. In medium shot, a realistically animated net lands on top of Pegasus, who struggles under its weight. In long shot again, Calibos looks on as Pegasus is brought down, his wings tangled in the netting. A closer shot of Pegasus on the ground, surrounded by the men and struggling under the net, is a superb composite. Calibos' tail swishes excitedly. In two final medium shots (animated by Archer), Calibos raises a large shell to his mouth and blows on it like a horn, declaring his triumph.

The next morning, Perseus, Andromeda, Ammon and several soldiers set off in search of a means to defeat the Kraken. As they ride off across a desert, Calibos is revealed hiding behind a tree, watching them go. The puppet's feet are below the frame, so no matte is required. The rear screen looks particularly grainy because it contrasts with the bright daylight shots immediately preceding it. This shot was animated by Archer.

Zeus, wishing to aid his son Perseus, orders that the wise owl Bubo be sent to guide him. But Athene instead instructs Hephaestus to fashion a bronze mechanical owl. The character of Bubo, always bleeping, spluttering and falling over, is designed to add some comic relief; although he may amuse young children, he adds little to the film. It's another example of how the script adds more and more fantastic elements without developing each properly.

Three armatured Bubo puppets were built, one full size (that is, about 15 inches tall), another four inches tall, and a third only one inch tall, used for extreme long shots. Most of the shots of Bubo were animated — very smoothly — by Archer, who successfully imbues the character with lots of touches of personality. One wonders if Harryhausen left these sequences for Archer to do because he himself was not particularly inspired by the creature and preferred to work with the more original flesh-and-blood creations. In this first encounter with the owl, there are 16 stop-motion cuts.

Far off in the distant sky, Perseus and his group see the tiny Bubo flapping towards them. As the owl gets nearer, the mechanical clunk of its wings can be heard. It heads for a gnarled tree stump that appears to be a prop placed in the desert location. In closer shots, Bubo flaps noisily straight at the camera, then hovers above one of the tree's branches. Bubo lands on the branch but fails to grasp it properly, spinning downwards and hanging upside down. The branch snaps and breaks off; part of the branch is miniature and matched to the live-action tree, then animated frame-by-frame as it falls.

Bubo hits the ground head first, topples over onto his back, then rocks from side to side very credibly before coming to rest. In the same static matte set-up, the owl bleeps desperately and kicks his legs. Perseus picks up a mechanical prop version of the owl, finds he can communicate with it, then places him back on the branch. Hamlin mimes the action, and the puppet owl is carefully aligned in front of the rear screen so that it seems he is being held up.

Bubo's head spins around excitedly and he bleeps and clicks before taking to the air again. In long shot again, he flies upwards, animated against a rear projection of the sky, intending to lead Perseus to the Stygian witches who can help him in his quest. In the final long shot, the one-inch puppet flies above the galloping horses, traveling from the foreground into the background, probably moving about four feet into the rear-screen set-up.

Bubo is seen again shortly afterwards as Perseus and his group pass through some rocky terrain at the foot of the cliff where the witches' temple is perched. This short sequence has eight stop-motion cuts. The first cut, in which Bubo flies away from the camera into a rocky pass, looks too much like a process shot because of the way the rear image is locked off. A static matte of Bubo flying out from behind a rocky pillar is much better, with the character pausing and dipping in flight. Bubo flies between some rocky outcrops (another good static matte), circles, then settles on a rock in a closer shot that uses a matte where the puppet's feet meet the ground.

Archer pulls off some deft animation in two shots that play up the owl's less-than-perfect mechanics. Bubo blinks but his eyes are out of synch, then he extends one wing tentatively, then the other, before taking to the air again. In long shot, he hovers above Perseus and the soldiers who are climbing up the cliff face.

The domed ruins of the witches' temple are another of the film's fine fantasy images. The miniature ruins are matted into the top of the shot, with the soldiers approaching from below. One wishes that Harryhausen had included more shots like this.

The three cackling witches (Flora Robson, Anna Manahan and Freda Jackson) have no eyes and see with the aid of a crystal ball that they share. The amusing black humor of the sequence is the closest the script comes to genuine light relief, but it is clear that Cross is not comfortable with the style. Perseus commands Bubo to steal the witches' "eye," only promising to return it if they will reveal the secret of how the Kraken may be defeated. There are ten stop-motion cuts.

In a shot with rock-solid registration, Bubo takes off from the arm of one of the soldiers in the rear projection. In three more rear-projection shots, the wire-supported puppet flies around the inside of the temple, eventually snatching the eye from the hand of one of the witches and dropping it in Perseus' hand. The eye appears to be part of the live action and supported on an invisible wire. Bubo lands on a miniature rock and is seen in some cutaway shots as the witches reveal the secret of how to defeat the Kraken. "A titan against a titan!" they crow, telling Perseus to go in search of Medusa. Bubo blinks and rocks from side to side, full of activity, finally flying back up through a hole in the roof (a static matte).

137

Perseus and his men arrive at the banks of the River Styx. The far off Island of the Dead is a miniature matted into the shot. Superimposed fog once again makes the setting unnecessarily gloomy. Charon, the ferryman, turns out to be a living skeleton, but he's a poor relation to the skeletons of *7th Voyage* and *Jason*. This one is a live-action character whose only moving part is a hand that clutches at the coin which Perseus offers.

The ruins of the Temple of Aphrodite are a good location, but again the scene is weakened by the machine-fog that drifts through it, making a potentially striking setting merely dreary. Walking warily through the ruins, Perseus and two soldiers are set upon by Dioskilos, the two-headed dog that guards the ruins. This savage battle is excitingly staged and one of the few occasions in the film where Harryhausen indulges in a good old gratuitous setpiece, where the monster comes on, fights and is destroyed. It has no plot function — it merely delays the confrontation with Medusa. The excellent model has two very vicious heads and a convincing fur covering. There are 30 stop-motion cuts in the sequence, most of them animated by Danforth. The scene as filmed is shorter than originally planned, which may explain why Dioskilos is a disappointingly characterless adversary.

The first four cuts were animated by Archer, shadowy shots of a dark shape with two glowing eyes, hiding in a doorway. Then, in a dynamic action, the wire-supported dog leaps out from behind a pillar (a matted area) and knocks the two soldiers over, the contact suggested by alignment of puppet and actors. The puppet, well-matched with its rear-projected surroundings, lands on the ground and turns, ready to attack. The area of miniature floor on which the snarling dog stands is undetectably matted into the live-action area.

In closeup, the two animated heads of the dog snap at Perseus, who hides behind his shield. In an excellent static matte composite, Dioskilos rears up and pushes down on Perseus' shield, forcing him back. The same set-up is used in another excellent shot in which the two soldiers run in to help Perseus, and one of their swords (probably painted on glass) momentarily passes in front of the puppet. In the same shot, Dioskilos rears up on his hind legs and chases the soldiers out of the frame.

The soldiers run into a new static matte set-up, an area surrounded by pillars. In another dynamic moment, Dioskilos immediately leaps into the frame after them, crossing the equivalent of about four meters, then turns to face the men. This set-up, used in several shots, has the actors in shadow and the puppet in direct sunlight, which has the unfortunate effect of emphasizing the fact that they are pieces of film that have been shot separately. Several closeups show the two heads snapping viciously at the camera, and in some of them an animated miniature sword passes across the shot, adding subliminally registered impact.

The dog's heads lunge very quickly in and out of a closeup of a soldier protecting himself with his shield. There is a lot of dramatic camera-shake in this shot and it may be that the animation camera was tilted in small increments, one frame at a time. A long shot plays up the presence of the two heads, with one head barking at one soldier and the other head snapping in the other direction at the second soldier. In the same shot, Dioskilos bounds after one soldier, running into the shadowed area and behind a matted pillar.

In another forceful static matte design, the dog leaps after the soldier who has run between the pillars. The soldier falls backwards onto a stone platform and Diskilos goes for his throat. The matte line follows the edge of the platform, below which steps run down the near side, and very successfully makes puppet and actor appear to be part of one image. The live-action image of the soldier recoiling appears to have been slowed down so as to allow time for the animation choreography to match up with it.

In an extreme closeup with camera shake, Dioskilos' heads snap at the shield of the fallen soldier. Perseus runs into the static matte set-up and, as Dioskilos continues goring the soldier, he slashes at one of the dog's hind legs. A glass-painted sword passes in front of the puppet for a few frames.

In a slightly different perspective of the same set-up, Perseus stabs one of the heads, which squeals, drops and hangs limply while the other continues snapping and barking. This grimly humorous moment was conceived by Danforth. Dioskilos lunges at Perseus, who stabs at its other head. Again, a painted sword appears in front of the puppet for a few frames. Perseus continues slashing at the animal, eventually forcing it back.

Dioskilos is forced up onto his hind legs then topples backwards over the edge of the steps and falls out of the frame. Danforth animates this shot very ably — it could have looked awkward. The two final stop-motion cuts use yet another static matte set-up, with the dying dog on the ground at the foot of the steps. Perseus comes up behind it and delivers the death blow with his sword — recalling the design of the final shots in the Allosaurus sequence in *One Million Years B.C.* Dioskilos tries to rear up again, squeals and expires.

The audience is allowed only a few seconds to get its breath before Perseus and the two soldiers enter Medusa's temple. The temple is unlike anything we have seen before in a Harryhausen picture. This shadowy, low-ceilinged chamber has no windows and its only light comes from burning braziers that throw a flickering orange glow onto the walls and the many columns. It's the perfect location for the loathsome, crawling horror of Medusa.

Although this scene is a self-contained set-piece, it doesn't appear at all gratuitous since this is the goal of Perseus' quest: he must decapitate the Gorgon and use her head to turn the Kraken to stone. The scene is a good example of Harryhausen being in full directorial control. He milks the eeriness of the scene for all it's worth, carefully building tension and controlling pace so that it can hold its own dramatically. This is the antithesis of the conventional Harryhausen battle scene: here he is more interested in mood and suspense.

The six-minute sequence contains fifty-three stop-motion cuts, all executed by Harryhausen except for one that was done by Archer. Medusa is another of the film's excellent models, with a rattlesnake's tail and a woman's upper half, albeit green and covered in reptilian scales. In her hair are twelve small snakes that were also painstakingly animated by Harryhausen, as well as one more coiled around her wrist. Over her shoulder she carries a bow and a quiver full of arrows. Adding to the nightmarish look of the scene, Harryhausen keeps his creation partly hidden by shadows in many shots, and when she is seen more clearly, she is bathed in the flickering light from the braziers. The animation table must have been surrounded by lamps that would be turned on and off for a few frames to simulate the effect.

One of the sequence's greatest achievements is that this doesn't look like composite photography. There are no matte lines to be spotted here. Yet in almost every shot, the puppet has been matted into a full-size set of the chamber. Only a portion of the steps and one pillar were constructed in miniature.

Rosenthal's score is effectively creepy in this sequence, especially during the early shots when our sense of anticipation is highest. In the first three animation cuts, Medusa is seen only in part and as shadows: her raised tail on a wall, her snake-head on a column. In these shots, the wall and columns must be part of the miniature set, placed in front of the rear-projected chamber with its flaming braziers.

In a stunning long shot, backed by an unsettling musical theme, Medusa drags herself along with her arms at the top of a flight of steps, lit up by a brazier on the left in the rear projection. The idea that she should drag herself along, rather than shuffling on her snake's tail, is a chilling one, and was suggested to

Harryhausen by Archer. It is impossible to detect what part, if any, is a miniature set in this fine composite.

Since Perseus cannot look at Medusa directly, for fear of being turned to stone, he uses his shield as a mirror. In two shots, a composite of Medusa shuffling past the brazier, looking around and snarling, has been matted into the center of the shield. It looks like the footage of Perseus holding the shield has been freeze-framed, allowing a steady matte to follow the outline of his arm.

Many medium shots and long shots do not use mattes, with the bottom of the puppet below the foot of the frame. Others are long-shot static mattes, such as a shot of Medusa rearing up at the top of the steps, her raised tail swishing behind her as she reaches over her back for her bow.

Another rear-screen set-up looks over Medusa's shoulder into the chamber as she loads an arrow and fires it at one of the soldiers. The miniature sword is removed at the last moment (just before the arrow leaves the bow), replaced by a live-action sword with which the puppet has been carefully aligned. The camera zooms in from a medium shot to a closeup of Medusa's face. Her eyes light up and the snakes in her hair continue to writhe. An extreme closeup gives us a good look at her scaly green skin and jagged teeth. The fallen soldier looks up and is turned to stone. The glow in the Gorgon's eyes goes out.

In long shot again, Medusa loads another arrow and shoots it at Perseus, whose shield is struck. This very quick action is consummately animated by Harryhausen. In closeup, the Gorgon looks around hungrily, then drags her-self down the steps. Presumably, part of the steps are miniature but this is ob-scured by shadows. In two medium shots, she loads another arrow and fires it at a torch that Perseus has thrown as a distraction.

In a new long-shot static matte de-sign, Medusa, now standing upright and shuffling along on her tail, passes behind a statue, which is probably a foreground miniature. In a shadowy and very creepy closeup, her eyes look this way and that as she seeks out her prey. In two panning medium shots, she reaches for another arrow and slithers behind one of the pil-lars. The pillar is probably another miniature.

In a series of shots, she turns at the sound of Perseus' shield being thrown to the ground, hisses and shoots another arrow. A shot of just her tail shows it flicking and unfurling. One medium-shot of her crossing the frame is so deliberately shadowy that practically no detail on the puppet can be made out.

Another closeup looks like it may be a repeat of a cut used earlier. Another arrow is drawn and (in a new static matte set-up) Medusa stands in the background as Perseus hides behind a pillar in the foreground. It's a textbook example of how the "reality sandwich" fools the eye into thinking that a fore-ground puppet is actually far off and be-hind live-action figures. Medusa shuffles slowly into the foreground in a series of medium shots and closeups in which the camera dollies backwards. Heightening the tension, there is a shot of the rat-tlesnake tail flicking in the air, suggest-ing the Gorgon is ready to strike.

Another shot of the bulky tail shows how it moves along in sidewinder fashion.

Continuing to build the tension, there are two more closeups and a long shot of Medusa now level with the con-cealed Perseus. Suddenly, Perseus steps forward and cuts off the Gorgon's head with his sword. This carefully aligned animation requires that the head is sup-ported on wires for most of the shot. A scream rings out.

In another ingenious touch, one of Medusa's hands scrapes its fingernails noisily down the side of one of the pil-lars (a miniature). In long shot, the headless body slumps down, the tail snaking about behind it. She continues to struggle pathetically, her arms reach-ing out, her tail writhing desperately. It's a fitting image that this abhorrent crea-ture doesn't die straight away.

Red goo oozes out of the open neck of the prostrate Gorgon, a gruesome effect achieved with a matte line down the edge of the now-stationary puppet. In a new and final long-shot static matte set-up, Perseus stands on the right hold-ing Medusa's head while on the left the tail of the Gorgon, lying in a pool of red ooze, makes a last shudder.

There is little chance to unwind after this climactic encounter. The plot lunges straight into a nighttime battle with three giant scorpions and a final confrontation with Calibos. Out of con-text, these are fine scenes but — without any down-to-earth build-up preceding them — their impact is reduced: The jaded audience feels as though it has suffered a surfeit of fantasy.

The three models, each 18 inches long, are crafted with all the attention to detail and accuracy that one has come to expect of Harryhausen's designs. All the animation in this scene was done by Harryhausen. He had hoped that the scene could take place in bright daylight but the weather was against him on the day of live-action shooting, with the result that this is another of several scenes that are characterized by a flat visual tone. A few shots are marred by the lighting contrast between the studio-lit puppet and the live-action rear image.

The five-minute sequence contains 44 animation cuts, a total that includes three cutaways to reaction shots of Bubo, 19 shots of Calibos and 22 of the battling scorpions. There are several superb flourishes but on the whole this gratuitous set-piece, which could have rivaled the skeleton battle in *Jason*, lacks the dynamic pacing and choreography of that earlier sequence. For most of the scene there is no score and one can't help thinking how much Bernard Herrmann (who died in 1975) would have improved the level of excitement.

Perseus and his men sleep out at night, the head of Medusa hanging in a basket from a tree. Calibos appears and walks up to the bag. In this shot, the puppet's shirt is animated so that it appears to blow in the wind, a clever touch subliminally registered by viewers. Harryhausen could have saved himself some work by making this a medium shot and using McCarthy, but he wanted to show the character's tail snaking behind him.

Archer animated the next shot, in which Calibos stabs the Gorgon's head with the trident that now replaces his missing hand. In a long cut, three scorpions grow out of the blood which drips on the stony ground and grow in size. Presumably, in this static matte set-up,

Harryhausen gradually brought each puppet nearer to the camera as he animated them, giving the impression that they were getting larger (as he had done with the wasp in *Sinbad and the Eye of the Tiger*). Each one now the size of a horse, the scorpions wave their claws in the air threateningly. Looking on, Bubo's eyes pop open. He flaps his wings excitedly and his head spins round.

In long shot, Calibos steps across a miniature stony floor that is meticulously matched to the ground in the live-action plate. He cracks his whip and the prop Bubo falls off his perch into the river, waking Perseus and his men.

The three scorpions face the camera, their claws clacking and their stingers held aloft. They stand on a miniature floor, again carefully blended with the ground in the rear image. In a static matte design, one scorpion runs at Perseus and its claw knocks his sword flying, the contact effectively mimed by Hamlin. In the same cut, the other two scorpions run in from the left as the other soldiers run in from the right. In another long-shot static matte design, Perseus retreats as one of the scorpions advances on him.

Meanwhile, Calibos causes more confusion, cracking his whip and making the horses panic and flee. Harryhausen executes this tricky action convincingly, and as ever has the character's tail snaking from side to side, to remind us that this is no man in a costume.

One scorpion lunges and snaps at the camera, allowing a close look at the wealth of detail on it, especially the tiny bumps all over it. In a new long-shot static matte, Perseus faces off against the retreating scorpion, while in another shot the two soldiers battle the other two creatures. There is lots of implied physical contact as sword meets pincer and a shadow appears to have been rear-projected under one scorpion.

Perseus continues fending off his scorpion, narrowly avoiding getting injured by the stinger. The puppet stands on a well-matched floor inlay that allows it to throw a shadow. In a dynamic close shot, the scorpion snaps its claws at the camera. The soldiers, in medium shots, hack and duck as the other two scorpions attack them.

In a live-action cut, Calibos' whip pulls one of the soldiers to the ground. In a chilling shot, one scorpion scuttles noisily over to the fallen man. Standing on a miniature floor, the creature drives its stinger into the soldier's chest. The miniature floor on this occasion is not so carefully matched to the live action, but the suggestion of physical contact of man and stinger is very convincing.

In a medium shot with no matte, the other soldier slashes at a scorpion and chops off one of its claws, which is wire-supported briefly as it falls. This is a macabre little touch that recalls the beheading of a skeleton in *Jason*. The soldier then plunges his sword down through the creature's head, forcing it into the ground. This is an enjoyably gruesome moment, with the scorpion letting out a scream and kicking its spindly legs desperately. Harryhausen's animation makes you believe you are watching a living creature in its death throes.

While Perseus battles on against his scorpion in two long-shot static matte shots, Calibos intervenes again. In a live-action cut, he cracks his whip, then is

seen in a long-shot static matte pulling on the whip which is now around the neck of the second soldier. In a superb moment of intimate physical contact, Calibos wraps one arm around the soldier's neck, then sticks his three-pronged blade into his back. Puppet and actor really seem to be in the same shot. In long shot, Calibos steps back, his tail swishing, and watches the soldier fall to the ground. Pleased with his work, he turns to face Perseus.

In two long shots, Perseus reaches up, grabs the scorpion's sting and cuts it off with his sword. In a new rear-screen set-up, he cuts off part of one claw (wire-supported for a few frames), then drives his sword down into the scorpion's head, just as the soldier had done earlier. At this point in the sequence, it is clear that either some animation was planned but never filmed, or else that the sequence wasn't properly thought through in pre-production, because we never find out what happened to the third scorpion. This may have been omitted to improve the pace but it makes the sequence seem confused and unfinished.

With the scorpions dispatched, the scene is set for a duel between Calibos and Perseus. In two medium shots, Calibos cracks his whip and sends Perseus' sword flying. Perseus dives to the ground to retrieve it and in two long-shot static matte set-ups, Calibos cracks his whip at the prostrate hero.

With careful precision, Calibos' whip is lined up with the rear image of Perseus so that it seems to be wrapped around his neck. Standing on a miniature rocky floor, Calibos pulls on the whip as Perseus resists, trying to reach his sword. Perseus manages to reach his sword and, to Calibos' surprise, hurls it straight at him. In a fine medium shot, the wire-supported miniature sword flies through the air and embeds itself in Calibos' stomach. There is a look of shock on the villain's face as he slumps forward, growling in pain.

Calibos, now on his knees on an expertly matched floor inlay, clutches his stomach, reels backwards, roars in pain, then slumps forward onto the ground, his tail snaking behind him. In his final shot, he lies on the ground, one arm and a leg making slight movements before he expires. Harryhausen animates his death scene with entertaining melodramatic finesse, but one wishes that the confrontation were not over so soon.

Those wishing that we had seen the last of Bubo now have their hopes dashed. He emerges from the river into which he had fallen and is seen in six animation cuts. The remote-controlled model is used for the shot in which he is actually in contact with water. The subsequent static matte shots were all animated by Archer, who conceived the humorous gestures of the character. The bleeping owl walks up to the prostrate Perseus and shakes his wings dry. Gurgling and flapping his wings, he receives instructions from Perseus to rescue Pegasus. Finally, he flexes each wing tentatively, checking that they still function.

The freeing of Pegasus is another scene that is only dramatically half-realized. Not enough has been made of the fact that Pegasus has been captured and so his release is less than thrilling. The idea that the tiny Bubo should be able to terrify the vulture into such a panic that it accidentally sets light to the swampmen's lair is somewhat far-fetched. And

the sequence concludes without explaining what becomes of the vulture — are we meant to assume that it perished in the flames? There is a lot going on in these 23 animation cuts, but the audience's involvement is not engaged: it's another example of how more is less.

In a long shot of the swamp lair, the vulture is perched on a branch, shifting this way and that and cawing gently. The branch is part of the live-action and the puppet is carefully lined up with it. The small model of Bubo flies in from behind a tree, down the side of which runs a matte line. Archer animates the noisily clanking wings with convincing briskness.

The vulture model looks especially good in a shadowy medium shot in which its wrinkled face is lit up by the burning braziers. In a series of six rear-screen shots, Bubo flies around the lair, harassing the swamp-men. Avoiding the locked-off look of many such shots, Harryhausen had the camera pan across several of the live-action cuts. Bubo swoops this way and that, flying straight at the camera in one cut. In a reaction shot, the vulture actually seems to look startled, jerking its neck up.

In the same long-shot set-up that opened the sequence, Bubo flies over the head of the vulture, which ducks, screeches and flaps its wings agitatedly. Bubo continues harassing the vulture in several more cuts until the giant bird steps down off the branch onto a miniature floor (avoiding the need for a matte in this shot). Its wings spread, the vulture turns to avoid Bubo and knocks over one of the braziers — which is pulled over by unseen wires on the live-action set. Strutting around in a panic, the vulture only manages to spread the fire further.

In an extreme long shot, the tiny Bubo model flies around the lair, heading for the cage that contains the live-action Pegasus. In a shot deftly animated by Archer, the owl flies down to the catch on the cage and releases it — the animation is timed to coincide with the catch being pulled by a wire on the live-action set.

In a beautiful long shot — one of the best in the film — the Pegasus puppet trots out of the cage, spreads its wings and neighs, relishing its freedom. The wings are picturesquely lit by the orange-green glow from the flames. In the final animation cut in the sequence, Bubo flaps through the smoke and flames, wheezing as he escapes.

At last, the pace settles down for a while as we return to Joppa to witness Andromeda being prepared for the sacrifice to the Kraken. An excellent matte shot depicts a train of soldiers leading her below the walls and towers of the city.

The finale, involving no fewer than four of the stop-motion characters, brings the plot full circle, as Poseidon once more releases the Kraken. Unfortunately, this long sequence (there are 69 animation cuts) simply isn't exciting. There is plenty going on but this is "action by numbers." The Kraken menaces Andromeda; Perseus, riding Pegasus, defends her; both Pegasus and Bubo are injured by the Kraken; and finally Perseus uses the Gorgon's head to destroy the sea beast. It could have been gripping stuff but is poorly directed and poorly paced. Cassiopeia, Ammon and a crowd of extras look on disinterestedly,

unable to contribute anything to the sequence.

A major reason for the scene's failure is the fact that the Kraken never looks like anything more than a rubber puppet. The sharpness of the studio lighting on the model contrasts with the more natural graininess of the live-action elements. The skyline behind the puppet is an unlikely orange color and conflicts with the blue sky that backs shots of Perseus riding Pegasus, further highlighting the fakery of the episode.

Seen in extreme long-shot, the Perseus puppet rides Pegasus through the air, blue-screened against a deep blue sky. A closer shot of Perseus in front of the animated wings again suffers from traces of blue spill, spoiling the effect.

Andromeda is manacled to a huge rock on the shore. Parts of this rock and another rocky pillar to the right are miniatures in a studio tank, meticulously matted in. One enormous reptilian hand reaches up from the far side of the rocks and grips them. This is followed by a second hand and then, with grim humor, a third and fourth. (Video viewers will not see the last hand.) The animation of the hands is less smooth than one has come to expect of Harryhausen. A huge splash of water is thrown up, a superimposed element that has been carefully matted so that it matches up with the outline of the rocks. The head and shoulders of the growling Kraken rise up behind the rocks.

There is another close shot of Perseus riding the prop horse, again spoiled by blue spill. In closeup, the Kraken opens its mouth and roars — but this angry gesture fails to divert attention away from the fact that this is an

145

unconvincing puppet, with lifeless eyes. In several long shots using the matte design with the miniature rocks, the growling Kraken surveys the scene.

In extreme long shot, Bubo flaps across a cliff face. This is probably a blue-screen shot and is not marred by spill. In a shot animated by Danforth, the owl flies past a closeup of the Kraken, who roars at the creature. The force of the roar sends Bubo hurtling out of control and crashing into one of the cliffs. These shots use the large four-foot-high model of the Kraken (built only from the waist up) and Bubo is a separate blue-screen element. The shot of Bubo landing on the cliff face is probably a static matte design, rather than making use of a miniature rock face. In closeup, the Kraken looks down at the off-screen Bubo.

In the long-shot set-up again, the Kraken turns towards Andromeda and heads in her direction, causing another fountain of superimposed spray to be thrown up. The creature's animated tail rises up and follows behind it. The Kraken rises up near the rock to which Andromeda is manacled. Its arms grab the rocky pillars on either side of her. Intended to suggest an octopus' tentacles, these elbow-less limbs only serve to make the creature look even less believable. A forceful closeup of the four-foot model tilts up from the Kraken's stomach, glistening with gel, to its face.

In a long series of shots — a combination of medium shots, long shots and extreme long shots — the Kraken looks down at Andromeda, lowering itself into the water to get a closer view. It's almost as if Harryhausen isn't sure what to do with the character. At last, an animated hand reaches out, passing in front of a rear projection of the terrified Andromeda.

Perseus gets ever nearer, sometimes seen in extreme long shots as a puppet on Pegasus and sometimes (in closer shots) blue-screened in front of the animated wings. In one of these, he starts untying the sack containing Medusa's head. In one impressive extreme long shot, the two puppets fly over the heads of a group of soldiers standing on top of a cliff. The animation of horse and rider is first class, as usual. The camera pans left to right, following them.

Perseus and Pegasus, presumably a separate blue-screen element, fly into the set-up in which the Kraken is looking down at Andromeda. The sea creature looks up at the intruders. In one medium shot of Perseus, he flies past the huge head of the Kraken, a shot that effectively gives an impression of the creature's size. One of the Kraken's claws reaches out and swipes at Pegasus, causing horse and rider to tumble into the sea. This convincingly animated cut required careful timing since Pegasus is a blue-screen element, and therefore it was not possible for Danforth to align the puppet and the Kraken's claw simply by looking through the camera (as would be done in a rear-screen shot).

Stop-motion artists usually try to avoid showing puppets in contact with water but Harryhausen carries it off beautifully in a shot where Pegasus hits the surface of the sea. A horizontal matte line runs across the water and a fountain of spray is superimposed to hide the actual impact.

In several closeups, the Kraken growls some more (why doesn't he get

The Kraken comes to claim Andromeda in *Clash of the Titans.*

on with it?) while Bubo revives on the cliff face, his head spinning around and doing a kind of double-take when he sees what's going on. Bubo takes to the air and there is a dramatic shot of the tiny owl flying past the Kraken's stomach, superimposed spray churning below. The shot appears to be made up of four elements: the rear-projected backdrop, the spray and the two puppets, animated separately.

In two consummate moments of interaction, the owl picks up the sack from the water (actually suspended on wires), then drops it into Perseus' hands. The Kraken looks on and in one cut his lip curls into a sneer. Hamlin mimes the action of holding the Gorgon's head out in front of him, with the puppet head added in a rear-screen set-up. Its snake-hairs writhe and its eyes light up with an eerie energy.

In a low-angle medium shot, the growling Kraken draws back. Perseus continues to hold the Gorgon's head out in front of him. The Kraken starts to stiffen, backed by the sound of bones crunching. In long shot, the now-immobile Kraken changes to a stony gray color, an effect achieved by slowly dissolving to a gray plaster-of-Paris model.

Cracks start to appear on the Kraken's body. Archer achieved this by slowly revealing cracks in the plaster model that had been made earlier and obscured by painting over them. In a closer shot, cracks snake across the creature's head. In successful live-action

147

shots, the brittle puppet's arms break away then the whole thing falls into pieces. The Kraken's demise recalls the destruction of the bronze statue Talos in *Jason*, but that sequence is by far the better conceived of the two. Talos' death had a quality of tragic grandeur that is absent here.

The glow in Medusa's eyes goes out and Perseus throws the head far out into the sea. Where it lands, the sea starts to churn and Pegasus suddenly flies out of the water and up into the sky. This exciting static matte uses the same design seen earlier when the stallion fell into the sea. In extreme long shot, the neighing beast flies around in a large circle.

Perseus frees Andromeda, looked on by Bubo, who coos as the pair start to get romantic. In three magnificent extreme long shots, Pegasus comes in for a landing at the top of one of the pinnacles of rock, his wings held up and back to maintain balance. In the lower part of these impressive composites, the crowd cheers him. He trots around in a circle, neighs and rears up, looking splendid. Bubo, in his final shot, gets over-excited by all this and falls off his perch on the cliff face (this is an all-miniature set-up). The camera tilts down with the puppet as it bounces off the rocks and falls onto its side. For the benefit of those who may have missed it, this is a comic moment. The film's final stop-motion shot is another long-shot composite of Pegasus standing atop the pinnacle with the cheering crowd below.

After the box office success of *Clash of the Titans*, Harryhausen was all set to make a follow-up film. Cross wrote a script called *Force of the Trojans*. Its stop-motion characters were to include the Furies (a swarm of night creatures), the Sphinx ("a triple mutation from Phrygia"), Scylla ("Terror of the Sea") and the Four Horsemen of the Inferno. But Cross' writing here has the same lifelessness that marred *Clash*, so perhaps it is no great loss that the film was never made. Harryhausen, 61 at the time of the release of *Clash*, decided to call it a day, explaining that life was too short to spend years locked away in darkened animation studios. There was also a suspicion among fans that he felt that his style of filmmaking had had its day, superseded by the computer-aided wizardry of ILM and other effects companies that had sprung up since *Star Wars* in 1977.

Clash of the Titans has many magical moments but it is a disappointing farewell film from the man who has put some of the most exhilarating fantasy images of all time on the screen.

Class of 1999

1989. Original Pictures. Prod-D: Mark L. Lester. Scr: C. Courtney Joyner. Story: Mark L. Lester. Ph: Mark Irwin. Art: Steven Legler. Mus: Michael Hoenig. Visual Effects Supervisor: Eric Allard. Special Effects Makeup: Rick Stratton.

Cast: Bradley Gregg, Traci Lin, Malcolm McDowell, Stacy Keach, Patrick Kilpatrick, Pam Grier.

Rating: ☆☆½   Stop-Motion: ☆☆

This is a potentially interesting combination of *The Terminator* and *If* (it's even got Malcolm McDowell, presumably fallen on hard times) but forgets to add anything imaginative of its own. Violence in high schools has got so bad in 1999 that three android teachers are called in to restore discipline. But they get out of hand and start to kill the students.

In one of the best scenes, one of the androids grabs an unruly teenager, throws him over his lap and spanks him with a chilling robotic rhythm; it's both funny and scary. Stacy Keach, with white hair and matching contact lenses, is enjoyably mad as the androids' designer. McDowell lends a bit of class as the principal but for him it's just a job. Still, he meets a good grisly death when one of the androids shoves his fingers through his throat (recalling the hand-in-the-face effect at the end of *The Thing*).

There are some good special make-ups at the climax when all three androids peel off the skin on their forearms to reveal a variety of nasty weapons. But the film's real claim to fame is the splatter finale in which the last-remaining android gets his comeuppance. Hopelessly imitative of *The Terminator* (even down to individual shots, such as closeups of the mechanical feet dragging along the floor), it is nevertheless extremely well-done as the fine mechanical dummy, half its synthetic flesh stripped away by fire, gets speared by a fork-lift truck, then decapitated in exquisitely slow closeup, green blood oozing everywhere. The rod- and hydraulic-controlled puppets are by necessity only partially seen.

A half-hearted attempt is made to improve things with the inclusion of one stop-motion cut, all of four seconds long, a full-view shot of the android walking towards the camera in front of a very grainy rear screen. Smooth animation and a good model, but not stop-motion's finest hour. Eric Allard was in charge of visual effects, and may have been responsible for the stop-motion; Christine Z. Chang is credited as "Animator" but this seems to refer to the computer graphics during the android's-eye-view sequences. Fun but forgettable.

Class of Nuke 'Em High Part II: Subhumanoid Meltdown

1991. Troma/Pink Flower. D: Eric Louzil. Scr: Lloyd Kaufman, Eric Louzil, Carl Morano, Marcus Roling, Jeffrey W. Sass, Matt Unger. Original Story: Lloyd Kaufman. Ph: Ron Chapman. Art: James Claytor. Mus: Bob Mithoff. Special Creature Construction and Animation: Brett Piper, Alex Pirnie.

Cast: Brick Bronsky, Lisa Gaye, Leesa Rowland, Michael Kurtz, Scott Resnick, Shelby Shepard.

Rating: ☆☆½   Stop-Motion: ☆☆

This sequel from Troma maintains that company's policy of releasing outrageously artless low-budget films with great schlock titles. On this occasion, the plot concerns Tromaville College, which just happens to share the site of a nuclear power plant. This creates an opportunity to combine an endless stream of semi-naked college girls with a storyline about a mad scientist creating a race of "subhumanoids." Irresistibly sick moments alternate with scenes of mind-numbing crudity—there's something for everyone.

One of the film's highlights has a squirrel eat some radioactive waste and grow to Godzilla-proportions. This is depicted in deliberately unconvincing fashion with a man in a squirrel costume, stomping on immobile toy humans.

Some of the scientist's failed experiments in "combining human chromosomes with those of other life-forms" are kept in cells in a basement. These five bizarre creatures are stop-motion models built and animated by Brett Piper, previously responsible for the stop-motion effects in *Mysterious Planet*, and whose later credits include Troma's *A Nymphoid Barbarian in Dinosaur Hell*.

Although seen only briefly and never in composite shots combined with live action, these creatures lend the film some memorably weird moments.

The first creature glimpsed is part-man, part-lizard, a bulky reptile sprouting vaguely human limbs. "Here I combined a common lizard with a member of a hair group for men," the scientist tells us, drawing attention to an obvious toupee on the creature's head. Spines adorn its back and tail. Its long tongue licks the face and it roars bestially. This engagingly bizarre animal is seen in only two cuts.

The next display is part-man, part-fly, a green-colored monstrosity with one huge insect eye and one nightmare human eye. Seen in two cuts in its cell, it snacks on a human limb.

The third mutant is part-man, part-dolphin, another odd beast with human arms, a dorsal fin and a long, protruding lower jaw. This model is seen in four cuts. It takes one step across the floor, then spews some liquid from its mouth because it is starting to undergo a "subhumanoid meltdown." As it spews, the model is held in a stationary position.

Slightly more ambitious are two shots involving a flying subhumanoid. This is a human baby with a fish's tail and insect wings. It flies down a dark corridor, laughing insanely. The puppet was not wire-supported during animation; instead, it was animated on a tabletop which was then obscured by a static matte.

The fifth and final subhumanoid features in something approximating a proper sequence. The creature, a pale brown, long-armed, leather-winged humanoid with a vicious set of fangs, is depicted in 11 stop-motion cuts, lurking in its cell, then breaking out and pulling the head off a victim.

The beast is seen through the bars (also miniature) of its cage, growling. It then pulls the bars apart and steps through them. It turns to face its intended victim but is never seen in the same shot as the actor, and the moment in which it rips off the man's head is only implied, not seen. There is a brief live-action shot of the victim's neck being stretched impossibly. The beast holds the man's head in its claws while the head screams, "Don't eat me!" In two lingering medium shots, the subhumanoid is seen feasting on its meal, tearing a fleshy chunk out with its teeth.

Piper's animation is always confident and these are enjoyable vignettes, but Harryhausen set-pieces they aren't.

Cocoon

1985. 20th Century–Fox. D: Ron Howard. Scr: Tom Benedek. Story: David Saperstein. Ph: Don Peterman. Art: Jack T. Collis. Mus: James Horner. Conceptual Artist: Ralph McQuarrie. Special Alien Creatures: Greg Cannom. Special Creature Consultant: Rick Baker. Visual Effects: ILM. Visual Effects Supervisor: Ken Ralston. Matte Painting Supervisor: Chris Evans. Stop-Motion Supervisor: David Sosalla. Stop-Motion Technicians: Tom St. Amand, Margot Phillips, Anthony Laudati, Sean Casey.

Cast: Don Ameche, Wilford Brimley, Hume Cronyn, Jack Gilford, Steve Guttenberg, Jessica Tandy.

Rating: ☆☆☆   Stop-Motion: ☆☆½

This is a delightful example of mainstream Hollywood dabbling in the fantasy genre and almost getting it right for once. The core of the movie is the youthful regeneration which its main characters undergo, while the science fiction cause behind it is almost irrelevant. Toward the end of the film, however, everything has to be forced towards a tidy conclusion and the SF elements are pushed to the fore, tending to weaken what has gone before because they are really little more than another *Close Encounters* imitation: Everybody stands around looking amazed as a spaceship hovers over them in best *Close Encounters* fashion. The aliens even look like relatives of Spielberg's skinny, featureless beings.

There are many memorable comic scenes as Don Ameche and his pals go out on the town to enjoy their newfound vigor, and the sentimental scenes (of which there are many) avoid being sloppy. James Horner supplies a powerful emotional score — he is much better suited to this style than action pictures like *Willow*.

There is a generous helping of special effects supervised by Ken Ralston, including a *2001*-style shot of the Earth, the Moon and the Sun; the glowing spaceship appearing above the ocean, sucking a boat up into its interior in a swirling green vortex; and the eerie aliens themselves, brightly glowing, vaguely humanoid forms that float around the live actors by means of some excellent matte work.

A couple of enjoyably creepy moments show the aliens peeling away their fleshy human disguises to reveal their real form beneath. When one of the co-coons is cracked open, we see the dying form of a wizened alien, a credible cable-controlled puppet with a pathetically forlorn expression on its face — not very dissimilar to the alien in *Earth vs. the Flying Saucers*.

The climax features another example of ILM's application of "functional" stop-motion, like the flying bicycles in *E.T.— The Extra-terrestrial* and the run-away mine carts in *Indiana Jones and the Temple of Doom*. It is used because it is the most cost-effective way of achieving certain dramatic shots in a sequence. Unlike other stop-motion sequences, such as any by Harryhausen or the taun-taun shots in *The Empire Strikes Back*, these do not ask us to suspend disbelief, knowing that such creatures can *only* exist as special effects. Instead, we are expected to be fooled *completely* into thinking we are watching live action. In *Cocoon*, this is entirely successful.

At the climax, a boat floats up into the spaceship. Five long shots use a miniature boat with tiny animated pup-pets of the actors on board. This was a practical way to shoot the sequence (in-tercut with close shots of the actors) be-cause it avoided the expense of hoisting a full-size boat up with a crane on a blue-screen stage, and also because the puppets are only required to make the slightest movements. They seem ex-tremely realistic, partly because they are not required to do anything elaborate. A puppet may sway from side to side, or its arm makes a slight movement — but that is all. One of these shots is such an extreme long shot that the puppets were probably not animated at all.

Cocoon won another Oscar for ILM: The 1985 Academy Award for Special Vi-sual Effects went to the team of Ken Ral-ston, Ralph McQuarrie, Scott Farrar (vi-sual effects cameraman) and David Berry (optical supervisor).

Coneheads

1993. Paramount. D: Steve Barron. Scr: Tom Davis, Dan Aykroyd, Bonnie Turner, Terry Turner. Ph: Francis Keny. Art: Gregg Fonseca. Mus: David Newman. Conehead Makeup: David B. Miller. Visual Effects Supervisor: John Scheele. Monster Garthok Created by Phil Tippett, Randal M. Dutra, Peter Konig, Julie Tippett, Mar-tin Rosenberg, Bart Trickel, Sheila Duig-nan, Teresa O'Shaughnessy, Adam Valdez, Suzanne Niki Yoshii, Steve Reding, Douglas Epps, Rebecca Schiros.

Cast: Dan Aykroyd, Jane Curtin, Michael McKean, Laraine Newman, Jason Alexander, Lisa Jane Persky.

Rating: ☆☆½   Stop-Motion: ☆☆½

This is a likable comedy about two cone-headed aliens (Dan Aykroyd and Jane Curtin) who find themselves stranded on Earth and do their best to blend in with society. The gags come thick and fast, with most of them hitting the mark: Aykroyd getting a dentist to cap his pointed teeth, the

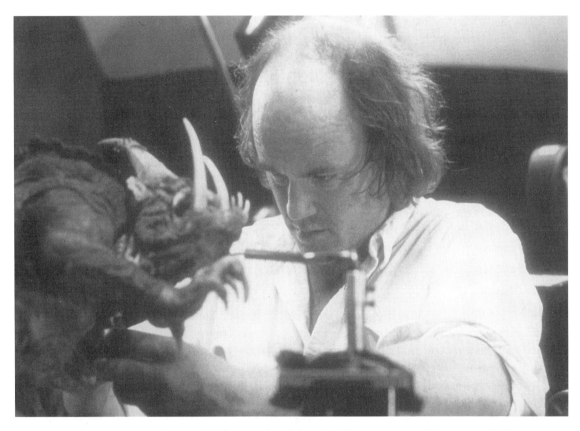

Phil Tippett animates the Garthok for *Coneheads* (1993). (Photo courtesy of Tippett Studio.)

daughter eating a sandwich at high speed, etc.

The aliens are eventually taken back to their own planet. There, Aykroyd is found guilty of a misdemeanor and sentenced to face the Garthok. This fantastic monster inhabits a labyrinth of carved stone pillars, surrounded by an auditorium in which the Coneheads gather for the spectacle of seeing one of their kind ripped to pieces.

The Tippett Studio handled the effects for this four-minute set-piece, with Phil Tippett and Randal Dutra sharing animation duties. Animation and composites are of the usual high standard associated with these artists.

There are only 18 animation cuts — presumably the post-production schedule didn't allow time for more. This is a shame because the Garthok is a fabulous puppet and deserved to be showcased in a no-holds-barred Harryhausen-style sequence. The setting is imaginative and the sequence had the potential to be something unforgettable. Instead, it comes across as just another of the film's gags, albeit an extended one.

The elephant-sized Garthok is an ugly, reptilian quadruped with an erect torso and two clawed hands on the ends of muscular arms. Two huge, upward-pointing tusks adorn a cavernous mouth rimmed with two rows of vicious fangs.

Its small eyes have a lively, watery appearance which gives it a suggestion of intelligence. The highly detailed body is realistically adorned with warts, bumps and fleshy folds of skin.

The first shot of the Garthok may not be stop-motion at all. The creature, some distance away and partly obscured by a fallen pillar in the foreground, stomps noisily towards the camera. Since the puppet's feet are hidden, it may be that it was rod-operated for this cut. In two closeups, the Garthok roars loudly, swaying its head from side to side dynamically. It lunges straight at the camera and devours (off-screen) one of the felons who preceded Aykroyd.

Aykroyd walks nervously into the labyrinth and behind one of the pillars. As he does so, the Garthok walks into the foreground from behind a pillar. This is probably a rear-projection set-up using a miniature foreground pillar. In this cut, animated by Dutra, the creature screams and lunges forwards slightly. In closeup, Aykroyd thrusts a spear into the creature's left eye.

In a complex long shot, the Garthok clasps its hands to its face, with Aykroyd a blue-screened foreground element and the spectators a background element in a rear-projection screen. Two foreground pillars look like they are also part of the blue-screened full-size set. In another closeup, the pained creature holds its head in its hands.

Aykroyd converts his spear into a golf club (a skill he has picked up on Earth), singing discordantly as he does so. In a deft medium shot (apparently another rear-screen set-up), the Garthok reacts to the sound quizzically. The next shot (Aykroyd in the foreground, the Garthok striding across the middle-distance and the spectators in the background) is a textbook example of using the "reality sandwich" to create the illusion that a foreground puppet is behind a rear-projected image.

In three fluidly animated medium shots, the Garthok prepares to strike, opening its huge mouth, screaming and walking towards the camera. Aykroyd swings his club and sends a rock hurtling towards the beast. In a dynamic perspective, the camera follows the rock's trajectory, zooming in on the puppet's open mouth. In a medium shot, the Garthok suddenly clutches its neck and makes some pained choking noises — the rock has lodged in its throat.

The animation camera has been manipulated again in the next cut so as to simulate the shaky look of a hand-held camera. The shot moves in close on the Garthok, which is now gulping desperately and pulling at the collar round its neck.

Dutra animated the two final shots, rear-screen composites allowing clear sight of the Garthok in full. Aykroyd, in the live-action plate, has looped his club around the creature's collar, gives it a pull and flips the Garthok over onto its back. This is a superb piece of animation by Dutra, with the limbs flailing realistically as the puppet recoils from the impact. It's a complex bit of choreography which could have looked awkward. The suffocating Garthok makes a final attempt to get up but expires.

The giant robot from *Crash and Burn* (1990), animated by David Allen.

Crash and Burn

1990. Full Moon Productions. D: Charles Band. Scr: J. S. Cardone. Ph: Mac Ahlberg. Art: Kathleen Coates. Mus: Richard Band. Special Makeup Effects: Greg Cannom. Effects Director: David Allen. DV-8 Design: Steve Burg.

Cast: Paul Ganus, Megan Ward, Ralph Waite, Bill Moseley, Eva Larue, Jack Mcgee.

Rating: ☆☆½   Stop-Motion: ☆☆½

Charles Band was back in the director's chair for this follow-up to *Robot Jox* and demonstrated that he can make a modest little SF thriller very watchable. It's an enormous improvement on the dull original. Like many of his later productions, the film was made for a straight-to-video release and had no theatrical distribution.

The year is 2030 and all that remains of the great days of the giant robot fighters is a junked DV-8 robot lying in the California desert. An assortment of characters in a nearby TV station discover they have been infiltrated by a cyborg from the Big Brother organization which runs the country and wants to close them down. From here on, the film becomes a second-rate *Terminator*, with the cyborg trying to bump off the cast before they can destroy him.

His rapidly deteriorating features are impressively handled by special makeup man Greg Cannom (e.g., he gets his face half blown off). At the end, he rips off one of his arms and both his legs, then slithers after the hero, an effect apparently achieved by employing a real-life limbless person.

At the climax, the heroine activates the robot, directs it to free the hero from under a collapsed pylon and instructs it to stomp on the cyborg. After all the preceding build-up, this is too brief and a bit of a disappointment, but is realized by David Allen with all his usual professionalism — the robot looks terrific. One story goes that these effects cuts were originally filmed for *Robot Jox* but not used, but this is hard to understand since this robot did not feature at all in the first film.

Midway through the film, there are two impressive effects shots with two characters seen in the same shot as the slumbering giant robot, one a static matte, the other a good traveling matte. Both effectively convey a sense of the great power of the robot. The climax contains only four stop-motion shots, intercut with a larger number of live-action shots of the prop model. The animation is extremely smooth as the robot slowly gets to its feet and then a takes a few steps, its metal claws opening and closing threateningly. Two medium shots of the robot advancing on the camera are also done with stop-motion. All other cuts — the robot's claw picking up the pylon, closeups of the glowing green-eyed head, the huge foot coming down on the cyborg and the full-view shots of the robot collapsing again when its power is depleted — are done live-action. It's a shame that such an impressive-looking creation could not have been put to more significant use.

The Crater Lake Monster

1977. Crown International. Prod-D: William R. Stromberg. Story and Scr: William R. Stromberg, Richard Cardella. Ph: Paul Gentry. Art: Roger Heisman. Special Mechanical Effects: Steve Neill. Stop-Motion Supervisor: David Allen. Stop-Motion Effects (uncredited): Randy Cook, Phil Tippett, Jon Berg, Jim Danforth.

Cast: Richard Cardella, Glenn Roberts, Mark Siegel, Bob Hyman, Richard Garrison, Kacey Cobb.

Rating: ☆☆   Stop-Motion: ☆☆½

Quite commendably, producer/director William R. Stromberg wanted to make "a neat little nostalgic kind of monster movie typical of the '50s" (as he is quoted in *Cinefantastique* volume 6, number 2). So successful was he that he even matched the appalling quality of most monster movies of that era. Is this

David Allen and *The Crater Lake Monster* (1977) (seen here with a miniature set for another production).

dreary, uninventive picture really the best that he and script writer Richard Cardella could come up with? The budget may well be minuscule (less than $200,000) but other filmmakers have proved that talent can overcome this hurdle. Direction is clumsy, the plot is predictable, all the old characters and clichés are wheeled out and the acting is stiff. An unnecessary subplot about a liquor store thief and a subsequent car chase are just padding. On a couple of occasions, the score tries to imitate Bernard Herrmann's great woodwind themes, but most of the time it sounds like someone borrowed a cassette of supermarket muzak. "Not worth your time," warns Leonard Maltin, and he is absolutely correct — unless you happen to be a dinosaur lover or stop-motion fan.

The film is only watchable as a showcase for the artistry of David Allen, who had already made a name for himself for his contributions to *When Dinosaurs Ruled the Earth, Equinox, Flesh*

157

Gordon and a Volkswagen TV commercial which recreated the climax of *King Kong*. Stromberg may not be a great director but at least he had the vision to see the potential of stop-motion as opposed to other special effects processes: "The guys in suits just don't make it," he said. As a result, Allen (credited as "Stop-motion Supervisor") had the chance to breathe life into a prehistoric plesiosaurus (or rather a fictitious close relative) and, although always held back by budgetary restrictions, produced a fine screen monster that compares favorably with some of Harryhausen's work. The plesiosaur is never given any characterization and many of its appearances are brief and only half-realized, but otherwise it is as good as the best of the 1950s monsters which inspired it.

There are 39 stop-motion cuts in the film but it seems like a lot more because they are intelligently used and intercut with many shots featuring the full-scale head built by Steve Neill (which suffers from being too static). Allen designed all the composites, was responsible for insuring that coloring and perspective were properly matched and did about 50 percent of the actual animation. Realizing that time was against him, he brought in assistant animators Randy Cook and Phil Tippett. Additionally, a few shots were animated by Jim Danforth, although what is said to be one of the best shots he did for the film (showing the plesiosaur being struck by a snow plow) disappeared mysteriously while the film was being edited.

The excellent plesiosaur model (only one was built) was a 15–inch puppet designed by Allen and Tippett over an armature constructed by John Berg. Cook, Tippett, Danforth and Berg did not receive screen credits for their work.

A meteorite crashes in a lake and the resultant rise in temperature causes a long-dormant prehistoric egg to hatch. The first sight of the full grown plesiosaur is a clumsy scene in which a backpacker is killed. Two medium shots of the growling beast's head and neck, animated against a rear screen of the forest, are intercut with lots of ineffectual shots of the screaming victim. Immediately afterwards, a bird-watcher is killed in a scene that relies entirely on the prop head. A stop-motion shot of the head and neck filmed against a rear screen of cows in a field suffers from graininess in the rear image. More effective is a quick long shot of the neck snaking across the foggy lake — the border of the lower half of the matte is kept slightly out of focus to suggest the irregularity of the water surface. Later on, a similar "soft-focus" matte shot shows the head and neck coming out of the lake at night.

A fisherman gets eaten by the prop head in a live-action scene that tries unsuccessfully to imitate the underwater suspense of *Jaws*. Even worse, we meet the film's two lovable rogues, Arnie and Mitch, who do a kind of Laurel and Hardy act throughout the rest of the film — except that they aren't funny. Much better is the attack by the plesiosaur on a girl and her boyfriend (spouting a laughably fake English accent). The composite work here (there are six stop-motion cuts) is excellent but unambitious. Two static matte set-ups are used, both following the gentle slope of ground by the lakeside and allowing

A static matte composite from *The Crater Lake Monster*. (National Film Archive, London.)

the model to be seen almost in full for the first time. It growls and rears up and there is a striking shot of the man setting fire to his boat with the plesiosaur growling in the background. The glow from the flames is convincingly matched on the puppet which, scared off by the fire, turns and walks back down into the lake, disappearing below the matte line.

Slightly more ambitious is the encounter between a policeman and the monster. Two rear-screen long shots show the plesiosaur's head and neck appearing from behind the brow of a hill,

with the policeman in the foreground. A small touch that adds much to the shot is a miniature rock that allows the puppet to cast a shadow. The monster recoils and growls when fired on, then there is a closer shot (another rear-screen matte) of it advancing on the policeman, and a closeup (with no matte) of it roaring. At last we get a full view of the model, a rear-projection shot of it approaching the car of the fleeing policeman, who almost gets stomped on but drives off just in time. The scene closes with two stop-motion shots looking over the plesiosaur's shoulder (do

159

plesiosaurs have shoulders?) at the car as it speeds off.

Although an enjoyable stop-motion exercise, the film's last scenes disappoint on a dramatic level because they don't have the necessary punch for a finale and the plesiosaur is defeated far too easily. Technically, the rear-projection composites are always well-matched and the animation smooth, but this monster deserved a more elaborate fate.

A mixture of closeups, medium shots and plesiosaur point-of-view shots depict the model advancing on a cafe. In long shot it walks behind a wall of hay bales, which conveniently provides a matte line and also removes the need to animate its flippers. It picks up one of the bales, its head snakes from side to side and it hurls the bale at an approaching police car (at which point we cut to a live-action bale striking the car).

There is another closeup of it with a second bale in its mouth, then an attractive series of six long shots with actors in the lower foreground and the monster in the background behind the hay bales, its tail occasionally swishing into view. In the last of these long shots, the plesiosaur has spotted the policeman running towards the snow plow and starts walking towards it, shadows on a floor inlay helping to mesh the two elements.

Two long shots depict the plesiosaur in the same shot as the plow. In the second of these it has a puppet Arnie in its mouth, then tosses the corpse aside. In this cut, the plesiosaur's head jumps slightly at one point, suggesting that Allen (or someone) may have accidentally knocked the model. A series of stop-motion cuts shows the live-action plow approaching the monster and there are several shots of the plow slashing into a prop of the monster's belly. There is an impressive bit of animation when the monster recoils in pain, its neck and tail swishing wildly. The last two cuts are full-view shots of the puppet, one in which it growls and collapses, and one non-animated composite shot of the puppet lying still on the ground. It's not a bad death scene but it certainly makes you appreciate the superiority of much of Harryhausen's work.

The film ends with all the cast feeling sorry for Arnie and his grieving friend Mitch — no one spares a thought for the plesiosaur. I would have thought that Stromberg, having stated his affection for the old monster movies, might have come up with a more sympathetic death scene for his memorable star critter.

Creation

1930/1931. RKO Radio. D-Scr: Willis O'Brien, Harry Hoyt. Adaptation and Dialogue: Beulah Marie Dix. Production Artists: Mario Larrinaga, Byron L. Crabbe, Ernest Smythe, Juan Larrinaga. Ph: Eddie Linden. Animation Supervision: Olga

A pre-production drawing by Byron Crabbe for *Creation* (1930–31). (National Film Archive, London.)

Celeste. Technical Staff: Marcel Delgado, E. B. Gibson, Orville Goldner, Carroll Shepphird, Fred Reefe.

Cast: Ralf Harolde, Snooky the Chimpanzee.

Rating: N/A.   Stop-Motion: ☆☆☆

Normally, an unfinished, unreleased film would not be included in this book. But *Creation* represents a milestone in O'Brien's career; also, its one surviving reel is freely available on video tape and film these days.

An amazing $120,000 was spent on *Creation* before Merian Cooper decided to scrap it (after a year's work) in favor of *King Kong*. Two test reels were shot, one of which, the destruction of a yacht at sea, no longer survives intact (some shots from it were used in *The Most Dangerous Game*). The other sequence, featuring Willis O'Brien's family of triceratops, is a fascinating demonstration of his unique vision and shows how far his techniques had advanced since *The Lost World*.

Marcel Delgado's models have far

more sculpted detail and realistic musculature than before. The clumsy static mattes of *The Lost World* are replaced in *Creation* by high-quality traveling matte, rear projection, miniature rear projection and multi-layered glass paintings. The jungle settings, including the silhouettes of foreground trees and vines and background paintings that seem to recede indefinitely, have a lush depth that is found only in the films of O'Brien.

The animation is extremely smooth in the opening shots of the mother triceratops and her two babies, making slight movements as they feed. In a deft moment of character animation, the two babies squabble over a morsel of food, each chewing on one end of it. Distracted by a live-action stork, one of the babies wanders into a second set, this one with a cave in the background and a live-action river matted into the lower foreground. Live-action birds fly across the shot, an image that would become an O'Brien hallmark.

The baby pokes its head inquisitively into a small cave, wagging its tail like an excited puppy. Presumably stung by a wasp, it suddenly withdraws and scratches its face with one of its front feet. When the baby steps into the center of another miniature set, there is a superb traveling matte of actor Ralf Harolde in the foreground walking right across the frame. After a closeup of a mechanical live-action eye (implying it is within the sight of Harolde's rifle), the baby is shot. It dies slowly and pathetically, stumbling, getting up, then falling down again. Harolde walks over to a good full-scale mock-up of the dead dinosaur.

The mother triceratops, half hidden behind jungle vegetation, looks up, roars, angrily uproots a tree, then strides out of the shot. In long shot, the triceratops advances straight at the camera. In a series of rear-projection shots, the dinosaur nearly catches up with the fleeing Harolde. Some of these use a prop head which bobs up and down acceptably to suggest the animal is running. Others are stop-motion shots looking from behind the puppet at Harolde in the rear-projected tracking shot. Finally, the triceratops catches up with Harolde, topples a tree onto him and gores him to death. These final shots are missing from many *Creation* prints because O'Brien used them in his *King Kong* test reel.

In an ideal world, it would have been marvelous if O'Brien had been allowed to finish *Creation*, then go on to *King Kong*. But there is little doubt that *Kong* is the much better film so, since the studio budget could only stretch to one of them being made, Cooper's choice was the correct one. Delgado made several other models for *Creation*. Some, like the two-horned mammal arsinoitherium, never made it to the screen. A superb styracosaurus model eventually turned up in *The Son of Kong*. Others — a brontosaurus, a stegosaurus and a tyrannosaurus — were all used in *King Kong*. The armature of a pair of wings for a dimorphodon served many years later as part of the skeleton of a dragon in *Q* (1982).

Cyborg

1990. Golan-Globus. D: Albert Pyun. Scr: Kitty Chalmers. Ph: Philip Alan Waters. Mus: Kevin Bassinson. Art: Douglas Leonard. Special Makeup Effects: Greg Cannom. Special Visual Effects: Fantasy II Film Effects. Visual Effects Supervisors: Gene Warren, Jr., Ernest Farino. Go-Motion Technician: Christopher Warren. Character Animator: Justin Kohn. Matte Artist: Ken Marschall.

Cast: Jean-Claude Van Damme, Deborah Richter, Vincent Klyn, Alex Daniels, Dayle Haddon, Blaise Loong.

Rating: ☆½   Stop-Motion: ☆☆½

Golan and Globus plumb new depths of tedium with this miserable action movie, of appeal only to those who enjoy watching wrestlers in *Mad Max*–style garb attacking each other interminably with knives. In a future where humanity has been almost wiped out by a plague, a female cyborg must reach the last scientists to give them data necessary to make a cure. This flimsy plot wears thin after ten minutes, not helped by the overuse of flashbacks, some used more than once. Van Damme is the good-guy fighter but lacks the charisma the role requires. Greg Cannom's company supplied splatter effects and some interesting shots of the cyborg's head and eyes being put together. Fantasy II Film Effects contributed some animation but if you blink, you'll miss it — it appears they were responsible only for two shots. In two closeups, the cyborg peels back her wig, revealing the metallic workings of the back of her head. This kind of shot — switching from an actor's head to a dummy head — has usually been achieved unsatisfactorily with a cut-away shot to another actor who is looking on. Here, Gene Warren, Jr., and Ernest Farino brilliantly pull the trick off in one shot, using a rotoscope matte that follows the edge of the actress' arm as it moves across the frame. In this way, the effects head replaces the live-action head in one fluid cut. Two small metallic rods which move at the back of the head are animated as the head tilts down. Farino, in a letter to the author, explained, "I designed the transition shot from the real actress to the full-scale go-motion robot head and composited the optical; Gene Warren, Jr., supervised the setups for Fantasy II."

Later shots of the head turning and blinking were also executed by Warren's outfit but since the only moving parts are the eyelids, they were achieved with motion-control moves rather than stop-motion. Fantasy II also executed two attractive matte paintings of cities in ruins.

Dark Continent: A Sherlock Holmes Adventure!

1994 (not yet completed). Story/Director of Special Visual Effects: Jim Danforth.

This is the second of two proposed Sherlock Holmes projects which have been devised by Jim Danforth and for which he has shot a promotional reel. The other is *West of Kashmir: A Sherlock Holmes Adventure!* "The idea," he explains, "derives from Sir Arthur Conan Doyle's oblique reference in 'The Adventures of the Sussex Vampire' to the unreported case of 'The Giant Rat of Sumatra.' I thought that pitting Holmes against giant or prehistoric creatures which were involved in a mystery was an exciting idea for a film."

In *Dark Continent*, Holmes travels to Africa and discovers the lost valley of Kor. Here he encounters H. Rider Haggard's Ayesha — She-Who-Must-Be-Obeyed — and a number of prehistoric creatures which are still living because, in ancient times, they stumbled into the immortalizing Eternal Flame of Kor. One of the animals he confronts is a two-horned rhinoceros-like arsinoitherium.

The promotional reel features a sequence in which a spinosaurus battles a giant snake.

Darkman

1990. Renaissance Pictures. D: Sam Raimi. Scr: Chuck Pfarrer, Sam Raimi, Ivan Raimi, Daniel Goldin, Joshua Goldin. Story: Sam Raimi. Ph: Bill Pope. Art: Randy Ser. Mus: Danny Elfman. Special Visual Effects: VCE; 4-Ward Productions (Visual Effects Supervisor: Robert Skotak. Cinematographer: Dennis Skotak); Introvision Systems International (Visual Effects Supervisor: William Mesa). "Strack City" Effects: Matte World (Supervisors of Special Visual Effects: Craig Barron, Michael Pangrazio). Burning Hand Animation: Chiodo Brothers Productions.

Cast: Liam Neeson, Frances McDormand, Colin Friels, Larry Drake, Nelson Mashita, Jessie Lawrence Ferguson.

Rating: ☆☆☆   Stop-Motion: ☆☆½

This engagingly offbeat melodrama is in many respects the kind of dark, brooding thriller that the disappointing *Batman* should have been. As with his earlier films (*The Evil Dead, Crimewave,* etc.), director Sam Raimi fills the plot with electrifying set-pieces and unexpected visual tricks. In particular, the early scenes in which Raimi establishes his ingredients (gangsters in the pay of a property tycoon, a dedicated scientist [Liam Neeson] searching for a stable synthetic flesh, his gruesome near-fatal beating by the gangsters) are directed with typical Raimi intensity. But once the Darkman starts to don his synthetic disguises and exact revenge, the plot is more conventional and doesn't hold the attention as fully. And (as ever) Raimi is occasionally guilty of being too self-indulgent. For example, the dizzying climax set atop the girders of a construction site is too self-consciously striving to be a show-stopper and so fails to be one. It is technically superb (with Introvision front-projection effects putting the actors into long shots of the miniature set) but sacrifices excitement for style.

The film has some fascinating special makeup effects. These include a painful moment when someone has two of their fingers bent backwards and a couple of shots of the Darkman's face (or one of his discarded masks) starting to bubble and decompose, using the kind of enjoyable bladder effects that were so popular in the early 1980s.

When Neeson is getting beaten up by the thugs, they force one of his hands onto an electrical device in his laboratory, causing the flesh to burn away. This gruesome two-second cut was animated by the Chiodo Brothers, whose earlier credits include sequences in *RoboCop* and *Pee-wee's Big Adventure*. It carries on the tradition of great "decomposition" shots enjoyed earlier in *Fiend Without a Face, The Evil Dead* and *The Hunger*.

In closeup, the hand (initially a convincing replica of Neeson's hand) turns red and blisters; the skin peels away and the bones start to show through. Superimposed sparks and smoke are carefully added to the shot.

The Day Time Ended

1979. Compass International/Manson International. D: John "Bud" Carlos. Scr: Wayne Schmidt, J. Larry Carroll, David Schmoeller. From a story by Steve Neill. Ph: John Morrill. Mus: Richard Band. Special Visual Effects: David Allen Productions. Special Visual Effects Supervisor: Paul W. Gentry. Stop-Motion Animation: Randy Cook, David Allen. Model Design and Construction: Lyle A. Conway. Armatures: Tom St. Amand. Model Design: Laine Liska. Cel Animation: Peter Kuran/VCE. Matte Paintings: Jim Danforth. Spaceship Models built by Dave Carson.

Cast: Chris Mitchum, Jim Davis, Dorothy Malone, Marcy Lafferty, Scott Kolden, Natasha Ryan.

Rating: ☆☆   Stop-Motion: ☆☆½

This is an inept attempt to cash in on the UFO boom inspired by *Close Encounters of the Third Kind*. Producer Charles Band deserves credit for having faith in an offbeat plot (something he would demonstrate often in the coming years), but the film falls apart under the constraints of a too-small budget and a hopeless script. The first 20 minutes engage audience interest as a series of bizarre, apparently unrelated events happen to a family. But then it transpires that they *are* unrelated, because the family's house is caught in a time warp, causing people and aliens to appear and disappear randomly. All sense of purpose is lost, and the plot drags itself to a feeble conclusion in which the family — in an undramatic, almost blasé manner — find that they will have to live out the rest of their lives in a city of the future.

The film is sparked by its wealth of special effects, even though many are often poorly integrated into the plot. Notable non-animation effects include a mysterious green-glowing pyramid, a cracked mirror that suddenly repairs itself, two attractive spacecraft with hollow, brightly-lit centers (designed and built by Dave Carson) and a lot of flashing blue cel animations that represent the time vortex. Striking matte paintings by Jim Danforth depict alien skyscapes, a desert full of vehicles dumped by the time warp and a final shot of the futuristic city.

Stop-motion sequences were shot at David Allen's studio under the supervision of Paul Gentry, with Randy Cook doing most of the animation and a few shots done by Allen. Of four puppets in the film, three were built by Lyle A. Conway, beautifully textured creations that deserve better scenes than they get here. Armatures were built by Tom St. Amand. Laine Liska produced some original designs for the creatures but these were not used and Conway came up with his own conceptions. The Troll Lady is an outlandish cross between a walrus and a gorilla, with facial whiskers and two beady, very lifelike eyes. The Wolf Lizard is a leaner, more ferocious biped with head frills like a styracosaurus and an "arms-back" pose in the Harryhausen style. The Gremlin is a hairless ten-inch-tall relation of *Close*

Encounters' aliens. A fourth animated model is a very sinister floating mechanical weapon with two spidery, armatured extensions that emit destructive rays. It appears in two scenes in about 15 stop-motion cuts (animated against rear screens). It's a unique stop-motion adversary but its role is limited and not helped by lifeless cutaway shots of actors trying to look horrified.

The Gremlin appears amid a glowing cloud of smoke at the door of a little girl's bedroom. The matte line all-too-conspicuously follows the base of the door. The playful creature leaps up onto a (presumably miniature) bedpost, then jumps over to a table where it delights the girl by dancing and spinning. When it detects the floating weapon approaching, it leaps back onto the bedpost and disappears. In its second and final scene, the Gremlin reappears in the parents' bedroom, floats over to the bed (along another distracting matte line) and attempts to get their attention by gesturing and squeaking. It is not seen again. Randy Cook's animation is very fluid and the Gremlin is a personable and unusual puppet character. It's a shame the script could not make better use of him.

The same can be said of the two grotesque battling aliens. The models look marvelous but are used in a drab, conventional scene with little sense of pace. Video viewers will be especially disappointed because the film, originally shot in Panavision, has been so clumsily panned and scanned that in two long animation cuts the puppets are almost entirely out of the frame. The Troll Lady emerges from the swirling vortex first, followed soon after by the Wolf Lizard.

The Day Time Ended (1979): The battle between the Troll Lady and the Wolf Lizard. Puppets designed by Lyle A. Conway.

In a lengthy but less than dynamic struggle — with one of the actors looking on indifferently — the Wolf Lizard emerges the victor. There is no attempt to suggest any contact with the live action during the battle.

Some enjoyable character animation enlivens two closeups of the wide-eyed Wolf Lizard, who is as startled as Dorothy Malone is when she opens her front door to be confronted by the growling creature. It tries to attack two characters who are hiding in a barn. Two clever miniature shots show its claws leaving scratch marks on the barn door. In an effective shock effect, a full-size prop of its head bursts through the bottom of the door. Two animated closeups of the head, poking through the door, allow a longer look at the impressive detail of the model. Taking a tip from *20 Million Miles to Earth*, Chris Mitchum imbeds a pitchfork in the alien's head. The interaction is suggested only in the editing. The creature withdraws and, after several cuts of it roaring in pain

Randall W. Cook animates the Wolf Lizard for *The Day Time Ended.*

and trying to remove the pitchfork, it eventually snaps off the handle before discarding the whole thing. It walks off in pursuit of a horse and is then surrounded by the blue vortex and disappears. The composites in this sequence are all excellent, with no distracting graininess, so it is a pity that the animation scenes are not stronger dramatically. Even so, they deserve better than the unfair remarks they received from Phil Hardy's *Encyclopedia of Science Fiction Movies*, which writes of "cardboard cutouts of prehistoric monsters … so crudely animated as to destroy any belief in the plot."

Little consideration was given to the effects shots during live-action filming and Allen was only called in at the last moment to save the film. Considering the meager effects budget, it's surprising that things turned out as well as they did: The blame for the film's shortcomings lies not with Allen but with the producer and script-writers. The special effects are the only interesting aspect of the film, yet no effects personnel are listed in the film's credits.

The Daydreamer

1966. Videocraft International/Embassy. D: Jules Bass. Prod-Scr: Arthur Rankin, Jr. From stories by Hans Christian Andersen: "The Little Mermaid," "The Emperor's New Clothes," "Thumbelina" and "The Garden of Paradise." Ph (live action): Daniel Cavelli. Ph ("Animagic Camera"): Tad Mochinaga. Mus: Maury Laws.

Cast: Jack Gilford, Ray Bolger, Paul O'Keefe, Margaret Hamilton. Voices: Tallulah Bankhead, Burl Ives, Victor Borge, Boris Karloff, Ed Wynn, Patty Duke, Hayley Mills, Terry-Thomas.

Rating: ☆☆   Stop-Motion: ☆☆

This 1966 part-animated children's film, telling the story of a young Hans Christian Andersen, is only of marginal interest here. It is included because it is a feature-length film containing stop-motion, because its puppets have distinct characters and because there are some composite shots in which puppets are combined with live actors. However, the animators never attempt to convince us that puppet characters are ever anything more than puppets, and so it falls outside the realms covered by this book. We are never asked for a moment to believe that what we are seeing is real: These are merely crude dolls made to move. The miniature sets in which they are animated are equally basic.

Arthur Rankin, Jr., may have been inspired to make the film because of the success of George Pal's *Tom Thumb* and *The Wonderful World of the Brothers Grimm*. The structure is very similar to that of the latter: A series of short tales is framed by the "true life" linking story of the author. However, all the freshness and inventiveness of Pal's touch are missing here. The songs are dire, the studio sets in the biographical sequences look fake, and the tales themselves are depicted with little flair and would only entertain a very undiscerning five-year-old. The cast includes two veterans from *The Wizard of Oz*: Margaret Hamilton as an ill-tempered woman and Ray Bolger as a dancing pie-man. Neither add anything to the film.

There are one or two good ideas. A giant frog nearly swallows up Hans and Thumbelina in one episode. Talullah Bankhead is the voice for the Sea Witch, a cackling crone with sea snakes in her hair (but alas no one bothered to animate the snakes). Terry-Thomas is the voice of one of the tailors in "The Emperor's New Clothes." Best of all, Boris Karloff provides the hypnotic voice for "The Rat" in the last episode. With all these fine actors available, it's a shame the film wasn't all done with live-action.

There are only four composite shots in the film, none of them well done. In one, a traveling matte puts two animated mice in the same shot as Jack Gilford and in the process they change from brown to a very clumsy purple. Gilford would be the subject of far more impressive composite photography years later in *Caveman*.

Dead Alive see *Braindead*

The Deadly Invention see *Vynález Zkázy*

Demonic Toys

1992. Full Moon Entertainment. D: Peter Manoogian. Scr: David S. Goyer. Original Idea: Charles Band. Ph: Adolfo Bartoli. Art: Billy Jett. Mus: Richard Band, Joker. Special Creature and Makeup Effects: Mechanical Media Industries Inc. Toy Soldier Design/Construction: Dennis Gordon, Mark Rappaport, Harvey Mayo. Stop-Motion Animation: David Allen, Chris Endicott, Yancy Calzada.

Cast: Tracy Scoggins, Bentley Mitchum, Daniel Cerny, Michael Russo, Barry Lynch, Ellen Dunning.

Rating: ☆☆   Stop-Motion: ☆☆

"Based on an original idea by Charles Band" say the opening credits, a line that has to be taken with a grain of salt since Charles Band has been remaking the same film about "tiny terrors" over and over again since *Ghoulies* back in 1984. But if there is an audience out there who make it pay, then is he wrong to do so? In any event, profits from production-line efforts like this help to pay for more risky ventures like *Doctor Mordrid*, *Prehysteria* and, one hopes, *The Hybrids* (a.k.a. *The Primevals*).

In *Demonic Toys*, a woman cop, a criminal and an assortment of other unlikable characters get trapped in a warehouse and are attacked by toys brought to life by a demon. The film lurches through a series of set-piece gore scenes in which victims get bits of their faces bitten off by a clown and a teddy bear, are shot by a toy robot or are stabbed by a cute dolly with an evil leer and a foul mouth. These effects are all realized with hand and rod puppets and are only moderately convincing.

Unlike the *Puppetmaster* series, stop-motion is confined to only one toy character, and an extremely forgettable one at that. Representing the forces of good, a toy soldier emerges from a box, helps the cop out of a sticky situation and at the climax reappears and shoots the demon in the face, just as the demon was about to commit an unspeakable act on his female victim. This characterless puppet proves the old adage that evil is more interesting than good, especially at the climax which is over far too abruptly and with little drama.

Once again David Allen and his colleagues were in charge of the stop-motion—13 shots in this case. The crew this time included Allen's long-time model-maker Dennis Gordon, Chris Endicott (who assisted Allen on *Doctor*

Mordrid) and Yancy Calzada (whose previous animation credits include *Beetlejuice*). The puppet is very smoothly animated and the sequence includes two good rear-screen shots. But the character's conception and its role in the film are so half-hearted that the stop-motion effects have negligible dramatic impact.

The soldier's first scene has a lot of potential, but it is never developed. A box is thrown open and two tiny, white-gloved hands reach up to grab the sides. The soldier climbs out of the box. In a skillful rear-projection shot, the puppet drops down from the table onto a miniature floor. The floor is impeccably matched to the live-action image. Multiple exposures for each frame give the impression of a blur on the puppet as it falls. The puppet walks off, unseen by the actor in the rear plate.

Later, the cop (Tracy Scoggins) is being menaced by the teddy bear, which has grown into a bear-sized monster. At the last moment, the toy soldier appears in a doorway and leads her to safety. This is seen in two cuts, one a long shot in which the puppet pushes the door open, the other a closer shot in which the puppet beckons the woman over.

In five animated cuts at the climax, the soldier appears, raises his bayonet-tipped rifle and fires at the demon. A superimposed flash is aligned with the end of the rifle. The puppet walks hurriedly across the frame and then, in a second rear-screen set-up, uses its sword to slash through the bindings holding the girl's wrists.

With the villain dispatched, the soldier appears in the film's closing shot, waving his hand at the (off-screen) heroine, walking slowly backwards and then fading away in a slow dissolve. Presumably this is meant to have some poignancy, but director Peter Manoogian botches it.

Yancy Calzada animated a shot in which some toy bricks spill out of a box onto the floor and spell some words. But the film's rushed schedule meant that he did not have the time to execute the shot properly: The hasty animation did not look credible and the shot was cut from the release print.

Destination Moon

1950. Eagle-Lion. Prod: George Pal. D: Irving Pichel. Scr: Robert Heinlein, Rip van Ronkel, James O'Hanlon. Based on the novel ***Rocketship Galileo*** by Robert Heinlein. Ph: Lionel Linden. Art: Ernest Fegte. Mus: Leith Stevens. Technical Advisor (Astronomical Art): Chesley Bonestell. Special Effects: Lee Zavitz. Animation Director: John S. Abbott. Animation: Fred Madison. Cartoon Sequence: Walter Lantz.

Cast: John Archer, Warner Anderson, Tom Powers, Dick Wesson, Erin O'Brien Moore, Ted Warde.

Rating: ☆☆☆   Stop-Motion: ☆☆½

Destination Moon

This landmark science fiction film leaves much to be desired on a dramatic level but is commendable for not pandering to Hollywood conventions. Its simple tale is well-told, dispensing with the normally obligatory love interest and also allowing only a minimum of comic relief to creep in (in the form of the spaceship's wise cracking radio operator). Many sequences seem simplistic today — for example, the lunar crash-landing — but generally the credible hardware and the documentary tone of the narrative mean that the film withstands the passage of time better than many contemporary SF films. Fortunately for producer George Pal, the film was a huge commercial success and boosted a career that was flagging after the failure of *The Great Rupert*.

Matte paintings by Chesley Bonestell include a disappointing 360-degree rendering of the Moon's surface and much better paintings of the distant Earth and a rocket on a launch pad. An extensive and convincing recreation of the lunar landscape was built inside the studio.

The film contains about ten stop-motion cuts, with animation by John S. Abbott and Fred Madison, who had worked together on *The Great Rupert* and on many of Pal's *Puppetoons*.

For a space-walk sequence, most shots are achieved with actors in spacesuits suspended on wires. But for about six extreme long shots of the characters floating around and walking on the spaceship, miniature puppets are used.

Pal chose to use stop-motion for purely economic reasons: To film the same shots live-action would have required either enormous studio sets or expensive traveling mattes. The puppets make slow and minor movements and as a result the animation is credible and cuts in smoothly with the live-action.

Four more stop-motion cuts enhance scenes once the spaceship has landed. In two of these, small puppets of the astronauts are animated so as to climb down the outside of the craft and walk across the ground beneath it. The third is more ambitious, a closer shot of two puppets descending the ship's steps. This shot is a very quick cut — less than two seconds — and may have been trimmed, perhaps because it was considered to be less convincing than the others. There is also a long shot of an animated spacesuit floating slowly to the Moon's surface, intended to suggest the low gravity. Again, these shots are done entirely in miniature and mesh well with the live action.

These shots are brief and functional rather than spectacular. They are all skillfully executed and very few viewers are aware that they are watching animation. The film is an example of how Pal, although he never entirely left his stop-motion origins behind him, also never felt inclined to explore the fuller possibilities of the technique.

Lee Zavitz, in charge of mechanical effects on *Destination Moon*, won the 1950 Academy Award for special effects.

The Diabolic Invention
see *Vynález Zkázy*

Diamonds Are Forever

1971. United Artists/EON. D: Guy Hamilton. Scr: Richard Maibaum, Tom Mankiewicz. Based on characters created by Ian Fleming. Ph: Ted Moore. Art: Ken Adams. Mus: John Barry. Visual Effects: Albert Whitlock, Wally Veevers. Stop-Motion Animation (uncredited): Jim Danforth.

Cast: Sean Connery, Jill St. John, Charles Gray, Lana Wood, Jimmy Dean, Bruce Cabot, Bernard Lee, Desmond Llewelyn, Laurence Naismith.

Rating: ☆☆½   Stop-Motion: ☆☆

The seventh James Bond film marked a return to the role by Sean Connery after a one-film break. The story, which had little to do with any Ian Fleming novel, concerned attempts by Charles Gray's Blofeld to hold the world for ransom with the aid of diamond-powered satellites which fire deadly laser beams at targets on Earth.

One very brief shot featured a miniature submarine that was stop-framed by Jim Danforth. The sequence begins with a shot of Blofeld's satellite gliding above an attractive painting of the Earth. Rather clumsily, the shot is frozen to allow the laser beam to be superimposed for a couple of seconds. In the sea below, Danforth's submarine, complete with a spinning propeller and dappled lighting effects to simulate the sunlight under water, begins to glow redder and redder and then explodes. This is followed by a shot of the surface of the water with the mushroom cloud from the explosion matted — less than cleanly — onto it. Only the shot of the submarine, not those of the satellite and the explosion, was supplied by Danforth.

Danforth, who was contracted to do the shot for visual effects supervisor Albert Whitlock, did not get a screen credit for this brief bit of work.

Diary of a Madman

1963. United Artists/Admiral Pictures. D: Reginald LeBorg. Prod-Scr: Robert E. Kent. Based on Stories by Guy De Maupassant. Ph: Ellis W. Carter. Mus: Richard La Salle. Art: Daniel Haller. Special Effects: Norman Breedlove.

Cast: Vincent Price, Nancy Kovack, Chris Warfield, Elaine Devry, Ian Wolfe, Stephen Roberts.

Rating: ☆☆   Stop-Motion: ☆☆

This potentially interesting chiller has Vincent Price as a French magistrate tormented by an invisible creature (the Horla) which takes possession of him and instructs him to murder. But it is let down by an insubstantial and slow-moving script (by Robert E. Kent) and direction (by Reginald LeBorg) that generate little mood and few thrills. In their hands, the Horla becomes a foolish gimmick that strains credibility.

Price acts with his usual likable polish but he was far better served by the series of Edgar Allan Poe films that were made by Roger Corman around the same time. He looks very striking in his red magistrate's gown in a couple of brief shots but LeBorg fails even to seize on this. Whenever the Horla possesses him, a blue light is shone over his eyes — a trick that looks as fake here as it has in every other film that used it.

Price sculpts a clay bust of smiling Nancy Kovack, but as he looks at it he is horrified to see its expression change to that of an evil frown, revealing Kovack's true character. For this five-second shot, the camera was locked off and the clay sculpture was manipulated one frame at a time. Although technically accomplished, the shot comes across as just another of the film's gimmicks and seems out of place.

The Dinosaur and the Missing Link: A Prehistoric Tragedy

1915. Edison Conquest. Prod: Herman Wobber. D-Scr-Ph-Stop-Motion Animation: Willis H. O'Brien.

This five-minute short, made in 1915 but not released until early 1917, is the earliest surviving example of the work of stop-motion genius Willis O'Brien, whose career spanned 47 years and ended while he was working on a film in 1962. It is a remarkable film, still entertaining today and featuring impressively smooth animation. As in O'Brien's other short films, all the characters are animated puppets and it has an engaging comic tone that demonstrates his innate and natural skills as a story teller. The running time passes all too quickly.

O'Brien wrote the story, built all the sets (consisting of real vegetation and rocks and also numerous miniature props), handled all the lighting and animation and built all the models. The early prototype models which he had created for an earlier one-minute test film had been clay fashioned over wooden skeletons, but here the mannikins are much more sophisticated, consisting of sheet rubber built around more durable metal skeletons. The proportions and musculature of all the human puppets are uncannily accurate: O'Brien never intends them to be seen as anything more than puppets but he shows an impressive understanding of gesture. If the viewer blurs his eyes a little, he can *almost* believe he is watching real actors.

A caption reads: "Mr. Rockface and his daughter Araminta in their country home"—and we cut to two cave people sitting in their cave. Two rival suitors fight outside and one of them is thrown into a cooking pot, from which clouds of steam arise up as he tries to clamber out. The steam is not superimposed — it may be a painting on glass placed in front of the model.

A Dinornis, a giant prehistoric flightless bird, is sitting in a most un-gainly posture when a hunter fires an arrow at it. The animated arrow, presumably suspended on invisible wires, flies through the air, misses the bird and strikes Mr. Rockface.

Wild Willie, an amusing precursor of the great apes of O'Brien's later career, climbs down from the trees, eats some wriggling snakes from the pot, then gets into a battle with a brontosaurus after mistaking its tail for another snake. Theophilus Ivoryhead, who has been canoeing on a lake, discovers the slain ape and when the others arrive he pretends that he has defeated it: "Yes, yes — a mere trifle!"

Dinosaurus!

1960. Universal/Fairview. Prod: Jack H. Harris. D: Irvin S. Yeaworth, Jr. Scr: Jean Yeaworth, Dan E. Weisburd. Ph: Stanley Cortez. Art: Jack Senter. Ronald Stein. Special Effects: Gene Warren, Wah Chang, Tim Barr (Project Unlimited). Stop-Motion Animation (uncredited): Don Sahlin, Tom Holland, Phil Kellison, Dave Pal. Model Construction (uncredited): Marcel Delgado, Victor Delgado.

Cast: Ward Ramsey, Kristina Hanson, Gregg Martell, Paul Lukather, Alan Roberts, Fred Engelberg.

Rating: ☆☆☆   Stop-Motion: ☆☆☆

Dinosaurus! is a much better film than you expect it to be. Plot synopses sound dire (Leonard Maltin's capsule comment: "Unintentionally amusing story of hazards faced by caveman and two prehistoric monsters who are accidentally unearthed on an isolated tropical island"). Stills give the impression that the special effects are going to be weak, depicting badly designed dinosaur models in unrealistic miniature settings, making one wonder if they really can be the work of 60-year-old Marcel Delgado. The reality is in fact an engaging fantasy with much simple appeal, crisply directed by Irvin S. Yeaworth, Jr. While always struggling with its low budget, it manages to come up with some impressive effects sequences. It's a refreshing change from the usual escaped-monster-finally-destroyed-by-the-military plots that plague the genre.

Jack H. Harris (who also wrote the original story) was one of those rare producers who actually liked stop-motion. Years later he took a semi-professional stop-motion film called *Equinox* and turned it into a feature for theatrical release. He also produced *The Legend of Hillbilly John* with its animated Ugly Bird monster in scenes designed by Gene Warren. In *Dinosaurus!* he allowed his effects crew enough control for them to make their limited sequences look a lot better than they otherwise might have. In particular, shadowy lighting is thoughtfully used at all times to hide the defects of Delgado's less-than-dynamic models, also making the dense foliage of the miniature jungles look a lot more convincing than it does in the brightly lit publicity stills.

A major weakness of the models is the exaggerated doll-like size of the eyes. However, a behind-the-scenes photo of Delgado working on the tyrannosaurus shows the puppet with smaller, more realistic eyes, and the model looks generally more convincing. Is this a prototype design and were changes made to the final armatured model so as to make it more appealing to the young audience at which the film is aimed? Whatever, Delgado (working alongside brother Victor) redeems himself with some superb mechanical dinosaur puppets that were used to augment the stop-motion sequences. Unlike most prop creations of this kind, these actually improve the film, as well as blending smoothly with the stop-motion puppets.

The special effects were handled by Project Unlimited, a company headed by partners Wah Chang, Gene Warren and Tim Barr. (Barr contributed no creative input to the company's work, instead handling the company's business and ad-ministrative needs.) Chang and Warren began their careers working on George Pal's *Puppetoons* short films and they continued to work together on films including *Monster from Green Hell*, *Tom Thumb* and *The Time Machine*, joined by Barr on the latter two films. In *Dinosaurus!* the Project Unlimited crew also counted (uncredited) Don Sahlin, Tom Holland, Phil Kellison and Dave Pal (the son of George) who did the actual hands-on animation. Sahlin's previous work featured in *Hansel and Gretel* (1954), *Tom Thumb* and *The Time Machine*. The quality of the animation is variable, sometimes hurried and jerky, impressive at other times.

The general design of the effects scenes is always hampered by the low budget but still memorable, containing many inventive low-key moments. Many of the set-ups are designed entirely in miniature with the puppets moving across extensive miniature sets, recalling the techniques of O'Brien. Some of the ideas may not earn marks for plausibility (frozen dinosaurs being winched out of the sea, a boy riding on the back of a brontosaurus, a tyrannosaurus picking up a woman in its front claws) but they make great cinema. These images look even more impressive in their original CinemaScope format: Viewers are recommended to see this, if possible, in a wide-screen format (as has been shown on British television) rather than in the more commonly broadcast panned-and-scanned version.

Yeaworth is a better director than many who have been the ruin of low-budget stop-motion films: One only has to think of some of Harryhausen's early features. In *Dinosaurus!* he keeps the pace brisk, maintains a childlike appeal and exploits the comic potential to the fullest on a couple of occasions. Hero and heroine (Ward Ramsey and Kristina Hanson) are dull but Yeaworth extracts an enjoyably slimy performance from villain Fred Engelberg, the island manager who wants to disrupt construction work at the harbor and who later wants to capture the revived caveman for his own financial gain. In one good scene, he feigns concern for a lost boy Julio (Alan Roberts), when we know he is only interested in capturing the caveman; and later on, he casually considers feeding Julio to the tyrannosaurus to create a diversion so that he can escape! But his worst crime, one of the most repellent in movie history, is when he callously crushes Julio's two toy dinosaurs underfoot. No wonder some publicity posters proclaimed that the film was "Not suitable for children."

Yeaworth's best bit of comedy is a long sequence in which the caveman breaks into a house and comes in contact with the accoutrements of twentieth-century living. Startled by a voice on a radio, he smashes it with an ax. His reflection in a mirror gets the same treatment. Tempting fruit in a bowl turns out to be wax and he spits it out in disgust. He even tries eating a book — after all, he hasn't eaten in a million years. He disappears around a corner for a few teasing seconds, then comes running out with a look of horror on his face — the sound of a toilet-flush behind him. In the bedroom, he finds a pretty pink dress to try on and in the kitchen he has problems coming to terms with the function of a chair, sliding out of it when he tries to copy Julio, and deciding that it is far

more comfortable to jump up onto it and squat down, a satisfied look on his face. Of course, this is all broad farce, but Yeaworth shows a well-balanced restraint throughout. Maltin's remark that the film is "unintentionally amusing" seems to miss the point entirely.

The film has a better-than-average score by Ronald Stein that includes many haunting woodwind themes, possibly inspired by Bernard Herrmann's earlier stop-motion scores. Stein was a prolific composer of B-movie scores, including many for fantasy and horror films such as *The She-Creature, Attack of the 50 Foot Woman* and *The Premature Burial.*

Fifteen minutes into the film, we get our first glimpse of the deep-frozen dinosaurs, discovered in suspended animation off the shore of a tropical island and hauled ashore by a crane. Rear-projection shots show the tyrannosaurus' head being pulled in (matched to the live-action line) and dragged along a miniature beach combined with the real one. A long shot of the beach at night shows the frozen tyrannosaurus model lying on its back, behind a live-action image of the sea.

The first stop-motion occurs 15 minutes later in a creepy low-key night scene in which the two beasts are revived by freak lightning. The lightning is cel animation superimposed over the two static puppets. The camera pans along the length of the brontosaurus, emphasizing its bulk; the eye of the manually operated puppet blinks open; the tail of the stop-motion puppet starts to writhe about; and the prop head and neck rolls over. Shortly afterwards, O'Leary (James Logan), a drunken Irishman standing guard over the dinosaurs, is attacked by the tyrannosaurus. There are two rear-screen stop-motion cuts of the beast, in one of which it picks O'Leary up off the ground in its teeth — the puppet's head obscures the point of contact and the wires which in the live plate are in reality lifting him up. The animation here is fluid, and augmented by a quick cut of the excellent manually operated model, which holds a motionless puppet of O'Leary in its arms.

Slightly more ambitious, but still modest measured by the Harryhausen yardstick, is the scene in which the tyrannosaurus attacks a bus. A long shot shows the dinosaur standing in the miniature jungle set, dappled by moonlight. It takes a couple of paces on its awkward oversized feet, then an animated bus (complete with headlights) drives into the shot. An effective bluescreen shot looks through the windscreen at the advancing puppet, then the prop head is used to show it peering in through the windows at the terrified passengers. In two more long shots, the stop-motion puppet stomps on the bus, which crumples very realistically. Once again the animation is smooth in this sequence, chiefly because the puppet makes small, slow movements — more dramatic action was outside the reach of the budget.

The next effects scene is a likable low-key moment in which Julio befriends the brontosaurus; it also makes use of extensive miniature sets in the old O'Brien style. Convincing and always full of dense vegetation, they nevertheless fail to come near to matching the quality of O'Brien's sets. There is a well-observed bit of child behavior in the moment when Julio, lost in the jungle,

suddenly hears the ground-shaking stomp of the approaching brontosaur: He stops dead and closes his eyes, hoping the danger will go away. Bluescreened behind him is the massive thigh of the animated monster walking past. (In fact, Delgado's model *was* massive and caused difficulties for the animators.) Two long shots of the miniature set show the dinosaur munching on some vegetation and a puppet Julio standing motionless in the foreground — nobody bothered to animate it. The manually operated head turns, looks down and continues to chew very realistically. In a rear-screen shot, a stop-motion closeup of the brontosaur's head examines Julio, its eyes watery, its mouth still chewing. Two medium shots show the stop-motion neck snaking around when it hears the growling of the off-screen tyrannosaur. An impressive bluescreen shot has the enormous bulk of the brontosaur walking behind Julio, then there are two long shots of it walking off into the trees, accompanied by the sound of more heavy footsteps.

The approach of the tyrannosaur is a series of shots using only the mechanical puppet, which looks particularly mean as it growls and dribbles saliva and looks better than a lot of mechanical puppets in larger-budgeted films. It's a highly detailed creation and looks convincing even in a medium shot (from the hips up) in which it walks through the miniature jungle.

Four long shots show Julio and the caveman riding on the back of the brontosaurus through the jungle. Constrained by the budget, the filmmakers made no attempt to show them climbing up onto it, and their miniature puppets sit motionless. There is more first-class use of the prop tyrannosaur head when it reacts to hearing the heroine scream: The head rises up through the trees and its neck muscles fold back realistically. Cliché fans will enjoy the moment when Kristina Hanson trips and falls, an accomplished blue-screen shot with the animated tyrannosaur stooping towards her in the background. Coming to her rescue, the caveman jumps off the brontosaur (a live-action cut), leaving it to stomp off through the jungle with Julio still on its back, a stop-motion cut in which a miniature tree is pushed aside by the dinosaur. A striking blue-screen shot (marred unfortunately by the paleness of the background image) has Hanson lying on the ground as the tyrannosaur looms over her, recalling the shot in *King Kong* in which Fay Wray lies by the toppled tree as the tyrannosaur and Kong fight it out behind her.

Cliché fans get a bonus in the next stop-motion cut, which has the tyrannosaur holding the heroine in his arms: We expect this sort of behavior from sex-starved hunch-backs, Black Lagoon Creatures, etc., but it's a first for dinosaurs. This shot is spoiled by the stiffly flailing arms of the puppet human. The caveman sinks his ax into the tyrannosaur's foot, a successful bit of implied interaction with the shadowy foot hiding the point of contact in the rear screen. The growling tyrannosaur stamps his foot, trying to dislodge the ax which he is unable to reach with his tiny arms, and finally walks off to the left. Altogether it's another deft little scene, flawed but fun.

The next sequence is the film's most elaborate piece of stop-motion, the in-evitable battle between the two dinosaurs. As well as shots of the prop heads and cut-aways to the live actors, there are 14 stop-motion cuts, full-length shots of the two growling beasts circling each other, their tales swishing, miniature trees getting knocked over and so on. The miniature foliage conveniently hides their legs for much of the time, reducing the complexity of the animation. One good cut has the brontosaur turn a full circle with the tyrannosaur following it hungrily. Animated blood is added to one gory moment in which the tyrannosaur bites the brontosaur's flank, and bone-crunching sound effects are added to a shot of the tyrannosaur biting its opponent's neck. The prop heads again perform extremely well, including one surprisingly chilling moment when Julio throws a rock to distract the tyrannosaur and it turns to look directly into the camera through its beady reptilian eyes. The poorly executed live-action cut-aways include such gems of dialogue as "Leave my friend alone, you bad old tyrannosaurus" and (from Ramsey) "Talk about ring-side seats." The animation is dynamic if not always smooth, and the scene's entertainment factor rates as equivalent to a lesser Harryhausen battle.

Most of the cast take refuge in the entrance to an old mine, and there are five animated long shots of the tyrannosaur trying to force its way into the small entrance. In these shots, the animation of the swishing tail is distractingly jerky, and emphasized by more shots of the prop head which only serve to make the animation look even less realistic by comparison. The prop head gets a petrol bomb in its mouth and it thrashes about

The tyrannosarus battles a miniature earth-digger in *Dinosaurus!*

wildly, knocking into the cave and nearly demolishing it; Engelberg and the cave-man both perish in the collapse. The stop-motion puppet turns and walks away, its awkward gait the result of some inferior animation.

The brontosaur, which we had thought slain in the battle, is now shown reviving — its animated head starts to raise itself up. Two shots show it stepping into quicksand in a miniature set. The gelatin used to simulate the quicksand reacts realistically to the puppet's tread. The hungry tyrannosaur walks into the scene and watches helplessly as the brontosaur sinks deeper. This could have been a striking tableau but it is marred by the hurried animation of the tyrannosaur, and dramatically it is a redundant piece of action.

The film has a satisfying climax which begins with all the islanders taking shelter in a fortress to protect themselves from the approaching tyrannosaur, and ends with a battle between the dinosaur and a mechanical digger. Like all the effects sequences it requires a fair amount of suspension of disbelief, but nonetheless is impressively staged (and certainly more exciting than the very similar climax to *The Crater Lake Monster*, in which a plesiosaur is killed by a snow plow). The tyrannosaur's approach is mainly shown via shots of the mechanical head moving through the jungle, but does include two rear-screen long shots, both brief and unremarkable, of the puppet standing in front of actors lined up on the fortress walls. When Ramsey sets light to a trail of gasoline, there is an effective shot of the prop head screaming in agony among the flames.

The fight with the digger (with a motionless puppet of Ramsey inside) again makes much use of the prop head and also contains ten good animation cuts. This sequence was animated by Phil Kellison and Dave Pal. The prop head again demonstrates surprising versatility, recoiling realistically when it is struck by the digger. The animation consists of a miniature cliff top set on which the dinosaur and the digger-model interact. In a series of long shots, the tyrannosaur circles round the digger, growls at it, the digger starts to turn away from the dinosaur, then the arm of the digger swings straight into the tyran-

nosaur's mouth. The dinosaur looks like it is going to force the digger off the edge of the cliff but instead releases it. Ramsey then swings the digger's arm and knocks the dinosaur over the cliff, its tiny arms clutching at air as it goes over. The sequence suffers from the absence of a shot showing the dinosaur falling into the sea, instead cutting to waves breaking on the rocks below and an underwater shot of the prop model.

Dinosaurus! is the kind of film with which it is easy to find fault, but if you are in the right mood it can be a lot of fun. Chang and Warren did their best on a meager budget and came up with some novel ideas, the design of which is always impressive even if the execution often leaves something to be desired. This inventiveness makes it a mystery why the film is generally neglected even by stop-motion fans. For example, even S.S. Wilson only finds time for one reference to it in *Puppets and People*, referring to its "lackluster sequences." The Project Unlimited team continued to produce excellent stop-motion effects in later years, chiefly for the films of George Pal, including *The Wonderful World of the Brothers Grimm*, *7 Faces of Dr. Lao* and *The Power*.

Doctor Mordrid

1992. Full Moon Pictures. D: Albert Band, Charles Band. Scr: C. Courtney Joyner. Original Idea: Charles Band. Ph: Adolfo Bartoli. Art: Milo. Mus: Richard Band. Special Visual Effects: David Allen Productions. Animation: David Allen, Chris Endicott, Randall Cook. Model Construction: Dennis Gordon, Harvey Mayo, Doug Beswick, Yancy Calzada, Brian Prosser, Jean Horihata. Special Effects Crew: Mark Rappaport, Steven Barr, Kirk Skodis. Special Photographic Effects: Motion Opticals Inc.

Cast: Jeffrey Combs, Yvette Nipar, Jay

Dr. Mordrid

Acovone, Keith Coulouris, Ritch Brinkley, Brian Thompson.

Rating: ☆☆½   Stop-Motion: ☆☆½

Once again, Charles Band dares to be different. And once again, a good plot idea is let down by a weak screenplay and indifferent direction. In this one, Dr. Mordrid (Jeffrey Combs), a modern-day practitioner of the occult, must prevent a rival magician from unleashing a horde of demons and destroying the world. Unfortunately, the budget isn't up to such an undertaking and Combs (so memorable in *Re-Animator*) is just not *occult* enough in the title role. Even as a low-budget production, this ought to have been fun, but it moves along in a stubbornly humorless way, with little style or invention.

Band once again called in David Allen to provide the film with some superior special effects. And special they are indeed, with Allen putting on screen a sequence that has long been the dream of many a stop-motion fan: Museum fossils of two prehistoric creatures come to life and battle it out. This time there are 18 stop-motion cuts, still a very small number but considerably more than Allen has been allowed to contribute to most Band productions. Four of these cuts are quick shots of the demons trying to escape from a tower in which they are held captive. The other 14, mostly animated by Allen himself in rear-projection set-ups, feature the fossil creatures—a tyrannosaurus and a mastodon.

Assisting Allen with the animation were long-time colleague Randall Cook and newcomer Chris Endicott. Among those responsible for the construction of the models were veteran Doug Beswick, Yancy Calzada and Allen's regular staffer, Dennis Gordon. The skeleton puppets both look superb, with the tyrannosaurus in particular having a meanness and grandeur in its intricately detailed skull.

The museum sequence is a surreal treat and its carefully balanced lighting insures that there are no grainy rear screens or mismatched stock contrasts to impair the finished image. Only the scene's brevity prevents it from realizing its potential: It could have been the most original, eerie stop-motion sequence in years.

Confronting Mordrid in a museum hall, Kabal sends a bolt of swirling energy (superimposed cel animation) at a tyrannosaurus skeleton. In an imposing low-angle shot (recalling a shot of Talos in *Jason and the Argonauts*), the dinosaur turns its head from side to side, accompanied by the sound of crunching bone. Two guards rush in, and in a marvelous composite they stare up at the tyrannosaurus which turns towards them. Deft lighting insures that this shot fools the eye completely into believing that the two actors are in foreground.

Despite budget restrictions, Allen remains aware of the need to maintain the dramatic flow of the scene and switches the perspective to a shot looking down from behind the tyrannosaurus. As the guards unload their guns at the skeleton, it roars and snaps its jaws at them.

In medium shot, the fossil fiend roars directly at the camera. A terrific long shot shows the creature with a puppet of one of the guards in its jaws. The animation of the guard puppet, its legs swinging, is just about good enough to convince that it is the real thing.

The next animation cut is another stunner, a long shot with the tyrannosaurus stomping across the museum floor towards the second guard. It walks behind a foreground statue, which is part of the live-action plate and has been matted around. The puppet's feet make contact with the floor, achieved by having a matte line running horizontally across the shot.

Mordrid replies by sending a bolt of eldritch energy at a fossil skeleton of a mastodon. This tusked behemoth stirs into life, growls and takes a step forward. In a long-shot static matte set-up, the mastodon strides over to the tyrannosaurus, which is looming over one of the guards in the background. Giving the shot some depth, the mastodon walks behind the foreground statue, while in the background the guard runs off. The two skeletons face off against each other apprehensively, then (in medium shot) they meet in battle.

In long shot (but with the puppets' feet just below the frame so as to avoid needing a matte), the tyrannosaurus bites into the mastodon's neck. In a dramatic low-angle shot they charge each other and the tyrannosaurus, struck by one of the mastodon's tusks, is toppled. Considering its bulk, the tyrannosaur puppet falls just a little too quickly.

Kabal meanwhile continues reciting spells that will summon his demons, but hasn't reckoned on being attacked by a mastodon. The quadruped stomps straight towards the camera and then, in a magnificent moment of gore, impales Kabal on one of its tusks. In long shot,

the mastodon raises its head into the air with its screaming victim — now a puppet — kicking helplessly. With a flash of magical sparks, Kabal disappears and the mastodon is left with just a blood-soaked tusk. It's a marvelous shot, an indulgent image of a monster doing what monsters do best. It's something which hasn't been done with such relish since *Planet of Dinosaurs* in 1979.

With Kabal defeated, the two skeletons fall to the ground, deprived of life again. This is an impressive bit of animation, both puppets sinking to the floor with a credible suggestion of collapsing bulk.

Interspersed with this episode are cuts of the demons, who are trying to push open a metal portal in a tower. There are four of these creatures and they are glimpsed only briefly. This is an intriguing fantasy concept but has negligible dramatic impact because the script and budget prevent the demons from ever doing much. One has horns, a beak and talons on the end of long arms. A second looks like it escaped from a zombie movie. The two background puppets are barely seen, but one is a wolf-like biped that began life as one of the werewolf puppets from *The Howling*.

In the first of four animation cuts by Endicott, the hand of one of the demons pokes out from the opening doorway. The portal is pushed up, revealing the demons behind a swirl of superimposed flashes of magical energy. A closer shot allows a better look at these beings, which are backed by a fiery furnace suggesting they are coming up from Hell. In their final shot, Kabal has been defeated and the portal starts to close again, forcing the puppets to retreat back into the tower.

Dr. Mordrid features some of the most ambitious stop-motion seen in a Charles Band film since *Laserblast*, but is yet another example of Allen being held back from demonstrating his true potential in fully realized sequences.

Dollman vs. Demonic Toys

1993. Full Moon. D: Charles Band. Stop-Motion Animation: David Allen.

Cast: Tim Thomerson, Tracy Scoggins, Melissa Behr, Phil Brock.

Rating: ☆☆   Stop-Motion: ☆☆

In the 1940s, Universal Studios used to get more mileage out of their monster characters — Dracula, Frankenstein's Monster and the Wolf Man — by having them meet each other in films like *Frankenstein Meets the Wolf Man*. Here Full Moon tries the same gimmick, bringing together characters from not only *Dollman* and *Demonic Toys* but *Bad Channels* as well. The result is one of Full Moon's least memorable efforts.

In one brief sequence, the Dollman shoots and kills a giant spider. This stop-motion puppet, seen in three cuts, was animated by David Allen.

Dolls

1986. Empire. D: Stuart Gordon. Scr: Ed Naha. Ph: Mac Ahlberg. Art: Giovanni Natalucci. Mus: Richard Band. Special Makeup Effects: John Buechler and MMI, Inc. Doll Effects: John and Vivian Brunner, Giancarlo Del Brocco, David Allen. Assistants to David Allen: Dennis Gordon, Paul Gentry, Linda Duron, Donna Littleford, Ted Rae. Conceptual Artwork: Neal Adams, Nancy Nimoy. Additional Stop-Motion Animation (uncredited): Laine Liska.

Cast: Stephen Lee, Guy Rolfe, Hilary Mason, Ian Patrick Williams, Carolyn Purdy-Gordon, Cassie Stuart.

Rating: ☆☆☆   Stop-Motion: ☆☆½

Whatever his limitations, Charles Band always deserves recognition for being brave enough to constantly come up with fresh ideas for genre films where most producers prefer to clone successful money-spinners. On the face of it, this sounds like a potentially dull failure — living dolls attack people in a spooky old house — but while it quite probably was a commercial failure (it never had a theatrical release in this country), dull it certainly isn't.

In fact, this is one of Band's most satisfying movies and recalls not only the

One of the deadly miniature characters of *Dolls* (1987).

liveliest B-movies of the 1950s but also possesses that unsettling quality of all the old fairy tales. Almost certainly this is due to the sure hand of director Stuart Gordon, who was responsible for the delirious delights of *Re-Animator* and would go on to direct *From Beyond*. The short running time (74 minutes) helps to keep the pace brisk, avoiding the padding that mars so many chillers. Gordon is probably responsible for introducing the nifty humorous tone which keeps everything afloat. There is also another good score from Richard Band.

The horror set-pieces are all deftly realized, the balance between fear and the absurd always judged right. The opener has a little girl fantasizing that a giant teddy bear transforms into a monster (created by John Buechler) and gores her nasty parents. One great splatter moment is the discovery of a girl who has been partially transformed into a doll — her eyes drop out into a pool of blood on the floor.

But the best scenes involve the murderous dolls, expertly depicted by a combination of string puppets, hand puppets, mechanical props and 20 stop-motion cuts. These were mostly animated by David Allen, with Laine Liska executing the rest. No complex interaction is attempted (moments of physical contact are done with hand- and rod-operated puppets), but the stop-motion cuts add enormously to the overall credibility of the dolls. Stop-motion is the perfect medium for these creatures: Both on-screen and in reality, they are puppets brought artificially to life and their stiffly jointed movements enhance this impression. In many of these shots, Allen uses the multiple exposure technique to introduce a kind of blur into the image.

The murder of the little girl's mother is outrageously gruesome and contains nine stop-motion shots among all the live-action shots. The latter include a doll biting a chunk out of the woman's arm, another doll bashing her with a hammer and two dolls sawing through her leg! Allen's shots allow two puppets to be seen standing on the bed, one of them raising and lowering a knife. In a rear-projection shot, the woman falls to the floor and two puppets, seen in full, walk towards her. Another puppet jumps off a table, brandishing a knife, the image softened by multiple exposure blurs.

Out in the corridor, a group of about eight puppets gathers, blocking the woman's escape. In a chilling shot, four of the puppets advance towards the camera, their doll faces cold and expressionless. It is a rare moment in which stop-motion is used to create real fear, rather than the more usual monster thrills. The woman leaps over the dolls

and crashes through a window, falling to her death. Allen includes an effective cut in which he suspends his animation camera above the cackling puppets, tracking over them to give the woman's point of view as she leaps.

Later, another character, Ralph, and the little girl find themselves shut in a basement room crammed with dolls. It begins with a memorable animated shot in which about 40 dolls sitting on shelves all turn their heads to look menacingly at Ralph. In several stop-motion cuts, the dolls walk to the edge of the shelves and leap off. Two lengthy medium shots show four dolls conferring with each other before they eventually allow Ralph to escape.

The final stop-motion cuts feature a Mr. Punch puppet, a scary character which in the hands of another director might merely have seemed silly. It dodges this way and that as a character throws objects at it, then retaliates by throwing a knife. After much mayhem, the character is himself transformed into a Mr. Punch doll: In a process shot, the animated puppet, its legs and arms kicking, slowly shrinks from human- down to doll-size, matted onto the live-action floor.

At one point, several dolls are smashed to pieces, revealing that underneath they are strange, gray, wrinkled creatures. But unfortunately Allen did not get the chance to animate them without their doll disguises — this could have given rise to some really bizarre images.

Dolls is a very engaging, original effort and a good example of how stop-motion was used innovatively by the horror genre in the 1980s.

Dragonheart

1996. Universal. D: Rob Cohen. Scr: Charles Edward Pogue. Story: Patrick Read Johnson, Charles Edward Pogue. Ph: David Eggby. Art: Benjamin Fernandez. Mus: Randy Edelman. Visual Effects Supervisor: Scott Squires. Special Visual Effects/ Animation: Industrial Light and Magic. Dragon Designs: Phil Tippett. Dragon Animatics: Tippett Studio. Matte Paintings: Illusion Arts (Syd Dutton, Bill Taylor).

Cast: Dennis Quaid, Sean Connery (voice), David Thewlis, Pete Postlethwaite, Dina Meyer, Julie Christie, John Gielgud (voice, uncredited).

Rating: ☆☆½   Stop-Motion: N/A.

This is a major disappointment. It was an opportunity to learn from the mistakes of *Dragonslayer* and put a full-blooded sword-and-sorcery tale on the screen. Instead it's the usual watered-down, cliché-filled hokum, aimed at undemanding kids.

Even more disappointing is the dragon itself which (although technically astonishing) has little dramatic impact on account of having been given the power of speech (Sean Connery's voice) and reduced to muttering smart-ass one-liners. Harryhausen's Cyclops had more sense of presence in its little finger than Draco has in all his high-profile, center-stage sequences. Draco could have been the most unforgettable fantasy creature ever put on film, but the movie demonstrates that it doesn't matter how clever the technology is, a character is only as good as the scriptwriter who conceives it. *Dragonslayer* is the weaker movie but Vermithrax Perjorative was a more

memorable character than Draco, whose personality seems intended to suggest an affectionate but slightly grumpy dog.

The composite photography in *Dragonheart* is always superb and the CGI dragon interacts in a totally credible fashion with the live action. There are 22 minutes of CGI in *Dragonheart*, much of it far more complicated than anything attempted in *Jurassic Park*. One especially impressive sequence has Draco splashing through a lake while villagers rush past him in the foreground — more scenes like this and fewer conversations between Dennis Quaid and Draco would have made this seem a much better movie.

No stop-motion animation is seen in the film but for some shots, as with *Jurassic Park* and *Tremors II — Aftershocks*, DIDs (Direct Input Devices) were animated in the traditional stop-motion manner in order to feed the creature's choreography into the computer. The DID shots were executed at the Tippett Studio, with Phil Tippett supervising.

For the key scene of Draco and Quaid in battle, the Tippett Studio also shot video animatics, animating two-dimensional representations of the characters in computer generated sets. As with the animatics which Tippett shot for *Jurassic Park* (which featured conventional stop-motion puppets), these were used by the film's director as a guide during live-action filming, helping him to visualize the sequence in detail.

Draco was designed by Phil Tippett, Doug Henderson and Peter Konig.

Dragonslayer

1981. Paramount/Disney. D: Matthew Robbins. Scr: Hal Barwood, Matthew Robbins. Ph: Derek Vanlint. Art: Elliot Scott. Mus: Alex North. Dragon Design, Graphics and Titles: David Bunnett. Supervisor of Mechanical Effects: Brian Johnson. Photographic Effects: Industrial Light and Magic, Inc. Supervisor of Special Visual Effects: Dennis Muren. Dragon Supervisors: Phil Tippett, Ken Ralston. Dragon Movers: Tom St. Amand, Stuart Ziff, Gary Leo. Closeup Dragon: Chris Walas. Dragon Set Design: Dave Carson. Dragon Consultant: Jon Berg. Matte Artists: Chris Evans, Mike Pangrazio.

Cast: Peter MacNicol, Caitlin Clarke, Ralph Richardson, John Hallam, Peter Eyre, Albert Salmi.

Rating: ☆☆½   Stop-Motion: ☆☆☆½

This is enjoyable sword-and-sorcery hokum and impressively recreates the look of Britain in the Dark Ages, but its uninspired screenplay makes it another of the great missed opportunities of big-budget fantasy filmmaking that followed in the wake of *Star Wars*. It promised to be the kind of saga that fantasy fans had been waiting years for, tapping a genre relatively unexplored by the cinema. But the tired storyline (by Hal Barwood and director Matthew Robbins) whips up little excitement and relies too heavily on *Star Wars* clichés (such as Ralph Richardson in an Obi Wan Kenobi role). Alex North's fine score lends atmosphere and Richardson is good in a gently comic role as the old magician, but the rest of the cast is lackluster. It's not that the film is bad — it's just that it should have been so much better.

Ultimately, the film's success lies almost solely in the scenes with the dragon — the rest is soon forgotten. Verminthrax Perjorative — which translates from the Latin as "the evil worm of Thrace" — is the aging but majestic dragon whom Peter MacNicol sets out to destroy, and is one of the most dazzling creations of the cinema. Designed by David Bunnett and brought to life by technicians at the Disney studios and the effects wizards of ILM (principally Dennis Muren, Phil Tippett and Ken Ralston), he is not only one of the most magnificent-looking puppets in the genre but also breaks new ground in fluidity of movement. The computerized motion-control system that was used to add blurs to the taun-taun in *The Empire Strikes Back* is here developed to such an extent that the characteristic strobing of stop-motion is almost entirely eliminated, resulting in it being dubbed the "go-motion" system.

Essentially the "dragon-mover" was a computer-controlled device with rods attached to the four limbs of the puppet. These were programmed to recreate certain moves during the exposure of a frame of film, creating a blur. Conventional stop-motion techniques were used for less conspicuous movements such as the jaw opening, the fingers curling or the wings making slight turns. The original plan was to animate the puppet in miniature cave sets built by Dave Carson, with shadows and rocks concealing the go-motion rods, and the neck and head animated with normal hands-on stop-motion. However, the "look" of the neck and head animation clashed with that of the go-motion limbs, and the team decided to add another rod to the head. This could not be concealed easily and so all the shots had to be filmed with a blue-screen, the head-and-neck pylon being obscured by rotoscope mattes hand-drawn frame-by-frame. Some shots required up to two weeks to program the computer to reproduce certain movements realistically.

Two smaller dragon models were built for use in the flying sequences, which were largely under the control of Ralston with Tom St. Amand doing about half of the animation. One of them contained a tiny motor which could take the wings through a flap cycle frame-by-frame, with the wing tips and other parts of the model animated by hand.

The Disney Studios created all the full-scale props of the dragon (the head and neck, a claw, the tail), which are used to great effect throughout the film. Because Tippett and Jon Berg were closely involved in their production, they are possibly the best such props ever seen, perfectly matching the miniature puppets and outclassing all those clumsy props which have weakened so many of Harryhausen's sequences. The head and neck prop, however, proved unwieldy and Chris Walas (an expert monster maker whose work has been seen in *Gremlins*, *The Fly* and many other films) was called in to produce an elaborate hand puppet.

The net result of all the input from this huge team is a creature superior to all the dragons that have gone before in film history, including the full-scale monster in Fritz Lang's *Der Nibelungen*, Harryhausen's puppet in *The 7th Voyage of Sinbad* and Jim Danforth's semi-comic beast in *The Wonderful World of the Brothers Grimm*. The design avoids similarities with dinosaur physiognomy, going instead for a slender lizard-like body with leathery bat wings. The evil-looking head has bony ridges over the eyes which extend back and grow into horns. Graceful and imposing in flight, on the ground it looks frightening yet awkward, very much like a bat crawling. When it opens its huge mouth to unleash a burst of flame, its jaws open like the reticulated mouth of a snake, emphasizing that this is a *hungry* monster.

The dragon's first appearance, in which it comes to claim a sacrificial virgin, is deliberately teasing, refusing to show us the creature in full. Shadows, sound effects, its fiery breath and glimpses of the full-scale claw and tail make this a restrained but powerful scene. Also done live-action are two scenes which feature the dragon's three offspring, an inventive twist reinforcing the impression that this is not just a fantasy creature but a living animal. These puppets, built by Ralston, Walas and Carson, avoid the cuteness that usually characterizes animal young, and have ugly, crumpled faces and spidery limbs. They are discovered by Galen (MacNicol) in the act of messily devouring the princess and he kills all three, decapitating one of them. These are good scenes but would have benefitted by being fleshed out by a few stop- or go-motion cuts.

The animation puppet is first seen in a short sequence in which it swoops low over a village, setting fire to it. After four cuts of it gliding over the burning live-action set, an impressive long shot shows it flying off towards the Moon, its wings flapping gracefully as it rides the air currents. Ralston filmed these shots using a Dystraflex camera in a manner similar to the way spaceships in the *Star Wars* films were made to fly. The dragon model was held stationary in front of a blue screen while the camera tracked in and out and tilted, giving the impression of flight. Because the scenes were shot one frame at a time, Ralston was able to animate the puppet by hand. The main benefit of this technique is that the camera moves at the precise moment of exposure, creating a blur on the film.

The film's highlight is the long sequence in which Galen confronts the dragon in the caverns. It is put together dramatically by Robbins, making full use of the shadowy tunnels and burning lake, and even giving the dragon an unforgettable moment of pathos when it discovers its slaughtered young. It makes a superb entrance, rising up out of the lake behind Galen, its huge horned head dwarfing the actor. (This cut uses a full-scale head sculpted from styrofoam by Derek Howarth.) A couple of shots looking over the dragon's head down at Galen use the Disney head.

The first go-motion shot is magnificent, looking up at the dragon rearing up, its wings half spread, its neck and chest swelling in preparation for a blast of flame. Galen seems to cower for an age before the endless torrent of fire behind his heat-proof shield made of dragon's scales. The flame is a superimposed element carefully matted around the outline of the puppet's mouth, making it seem that it really is emanating

from the dragon. Two fine go-motion cuts show the dragon tilting its head back and discharging the last of the flame at the cave roof, its relatively tiny fingers opening and closing in a subliminal minor touch.

The Walas closeup head snakes round after the fleeing Galen, then there is a nightmarish cut of the go-motion puppet hauling itself up over a rock, first its claws then its head and body coming into view. A superb composite has Galen fleeing left out of the shot as the dragon on the right takes a few ungainly bat-like steps after him. In a side view of it walking through a tunnel, its wings furl up realistically as it moves forward. Walas' closeup head discovers the dead babies and there is a breathtaking extreme closeup, its dull eyes suggesting a hidden pain. A deafening scream rings out through an empty chamber which is soon filled by the dragon walking with speed straight at the camera — this is a marvelously smooth yet complex bit of animation.

In another full shot of the dragon, the camera tilts up to reveal Galen standing over it on a ledge, spear held ready to strike. This clever shot was achieved using an O'Brien-style miniature rear projection, the live-action element of Galen projected onto a piece of white card placed in the set. Galen jumps onto the dragon's neck and plunges his spear into the back of its head. The go-motion dragon thrashes about, a miniature puppet of Galen on its back. As Verminthrax tries to dislodge Galen, shots of the Walas head and the full-scale head are all seamlessly intercut with the go-motion puppet. Another go-motion cut shows it about to unleash a blast of fire, but Galen pierces its chest with his spear before it can do so. Go-motion blurs significantly enhance a shot of Galen hanging onto the spear, swinging about under the dragon's neck as it snakes its head around. In another fine animation shot the dragon's tiny claw tries to pull out the broken half of the spear still stuck in its chest. A final go-motion shot of the dragon about to let out another blast of fire ends the sequence — curiously abruptly in fact, as Galen is next found semi-unconscious outside the cave, with no explanation of how he escaped the encounter.

Verminthrax has of course survived this battle and he is soon seen again, this time in three eerie night time shots of him in flight, the eclipsed sun giving off a murky blue haze. In the first, a gnarled miniature tree in the foreground adds depth to the image. His wings making only slight flapping motions, he glides through marvelous matte paintings of mountains (by Mike Pangrazio and Christopher Evans). In one dramatic cut, he swoops straight at the camera, then off into the distance and behind a painted pillar of rock, a shot enhanced by a camera pan. A beautiful long shot of him perched on the rock, grunting gently, his wings half spread behind him for balance, is the only shot in the film that was done entirely with conventional stop-motion (by Ralston). If you look closely, you can see the dark matte line where it follows the outline of the rock. After a closeup of the Walas head, its nostrils flaring as it sniffs for its prey, the go-motion puppet swoops straight down off the rock, then up and away.

The climax sees the revival of Ulrich the magician (who had been slain at the start of the film) and a final battle between him and Verminthrax. Ulrich conjures up some stormy weather and eventually the dragon arrives, gliding in from an extreme long shot, swooping behind Galen and Valeria, over Ulrich's head, then off into the distance. He turns in mid-air, hovering for a few moments and growling. The model looks superb in a dramatic shot where it is struck by a cel-animated bolt of lightning from Ulrich's magic staff. The model recoils, lit up by the blast, and plummets downwards, his neck and head hanging limply; then he revives and flies up again. He swoops straight at Ulrich, knocking him to the ground, the physical contact implied by careful alignment of puppet and actor.

Verminthrax again looks majestic in a closer shot in which he rears up over Ulrich, wings spread behind to keep himself steady, and is lit up by the orange glow of a fiery burst of dragon's breath. Then he turns and drops away, swooping down from the top of the rock. A series of high-altitude shots, backed only by the sound of whooshing air currents, show him gliding through the clouds, in one cut actually disappearing into a cloud (possibly using a soft-focus matte around the edge of the cloud) and in another dynamic cut falling away from the camera. Shots of him soaring at low speed over the mountaintops are seen from the dragon's point of view. He grabs Ulrich (the full-size claw is used here) and carries him off. Galen chooses this moment to smash the amulet, causing Ulrich to explode, taking the dragon with him. A final animation shot shows Verminthrax reacting to the explosion, then he falls in a cloud of smoke and flame.

The sequence is exciting and tech-

191

nically outstanding but is let down by the fact that the actors have been filmed against a blue screen; although there is no spill, these always look like effects shots. More crucially, it comes as something of a disappointment after the superb sequence in the cave — there is never a real sense of confrontation. Verminthrax swoops around the sky, picks up Ulrich in one of its claws and then explodes: It is too abrupt an end for such a magnificent creature and needed more scenes of the beast on the ground or perhaps clinging to the side of the mountain doing battle with Galen. The absence of shots like these highlights where go-motion loses out against conventional stop-motion: A stop-motion puppet can be made to do just about anything in any environment by means of static matte photography but this go-motion puppet is restricted by the dictates of the dragon-mover device.

The film represents an enormous advance in stop-motion artistry, so much so that many people afterwards proclaimed that conventional hands-on animation had had its day. However, the go-motion shots are all supplemented by manual animation of parts of the model not attached to the dragon mover — go-motion has to be seen as just another tool of the stop-motion artist. At present, it is difficult to imagine a go-motion device so sophisticated that it can control all parts of an animation model. Additionally, go-motion enforces the shooting of most scenes with a blue screen, thereby minimizing the amount of physical contact that can be suggested between puppet and actors. And it means that much of the model must be concealed from view to avoid extensive hand-drawn mattes to obscure the go-motion rods: ILM's dragon could not parade around on a beach in broad daylight like Harryhausen's did in *The 7th Voyage of Sinbad*.

Dragonslayer was not the money-spinner that Paramount/Disney hoped for and the executives must have questioned whether all the money that went into the development of the dragon-mover was well-spent. Although the film failed essentially because its script was not good enough, it was seen by many producers as another example of how films with stop-motion monsters just aren't commercial prospects. It reinforced the feelings many felt after being disappointed by the taun-taun in *The Empire Strikes Back*. Robbins and Barwood deserve credit for daring to experiment with a new genre and for giving Tippett and his colleagues an opportunity to stretch the field of stop-motion effects further, but they also warrant criticism for producing a film that may well have done the genre more harm than good. If it had been a box office hit, it would have spawned follow-ups and imitations. Instead, ILM and others have largely retreated to the safety of using stop-motion only for the depiction of mechanical creations such as the Scout Walkers in *Return of the Jedi*.

The special visual effects in *Dragonslayer* received an Academy Award nomination. Dennis Muren and Stuart Ziff received a Technical Achievement Citation from the Academy for their work on the go-motion process.

Dragonworld

1994. Moonbeam Entertainment. D: Ted Nicolaou. Scr: Suzanne Glazener Naha, Ted Nicolaou. Original Idea: Charles Band. Ph: Alan Trow. Art: Ian Watson. Mus: Richard Band. Creature Effects: Mark Rappaport. Dimensional Animation Effects: David Allen Productions. Visual Effects Supervisor: Chris Endicott. Stop-Motion Animation: Jim Danforth (uncredited), Paul Jessel, Joel Fletcher, Harry Walton. Animation Assistant: Yan Guo. Armatures: Jeff Taylor. Digital Blue Screen Composite Plate Supervisor: Paul Gentry. Digital Animation Supervisor: Randall William Cook. Dragon Design: Andrea Von Sholly.

Cast: Sam Mackenzie, Brittney Powell, John Galvin, Lila Kaye, John Woodvine, Andrew Keir.

Rating: ☆☆½   Stop-Motion: ☆☆☆

Dragonworld probably contains more stop-motion animation than any other Charles Band film and is also the first film for many years to have a stop-motion character in a central role. This fits the classic monster movie scenario: a monster — in this case a dragon — is discovered in a remote land (the wilds of Scotland), then captured and put on display in the "civilized" world, only to wreak havoc on its surroundings. The only difference is the tone: This is a children's film and the dragon is a gentle creature who never means any harm to anyone. Naturally there is a happy ending, with the dragon returned to the wild and reunited with his human friends.

The engaging first half-hour has John, a young, orphaned American boy, taken to meet his Scottish grandfather (Andrew Keir giving an effectively restrained performance). He finds that his attempts to play the bagpipes summon a baby dragon from a hole in the ground and they become good friends. The script then switches to 15 years later, when both John and the dragon have grown up. The appealing tone of these scenes takes a plunge when some Americans arrive on the scene and try to film and exploit the dragon. These characters may well be essential to ensure box office pull, but they also signal the beginning of mediocrity: The film is forgettable from here on.

Most shots of the dragon are achieved with on-set props and puppets created by Mark Rappaport. These are all acceptable although never quite convince that they are flesh and blood. Sprinkled among them are 47 excellent stop-motion cuts, filmed at David Allen's studio with Chris Endicott acting as supervisor. The highpoints of these cuts are some superb composites showing the dragon in a courtyard confronting attackers. These and the other stop-motion shots are all animated with remarkable fluidity. The bulk of the animation was split between Jim Danforth, Paul Jessel and Joel Fletcher, with Harry Walton animating one shot. Additionally, Randall Cook supplied seven superb shots that use computer generated images of the dragon.

The animation models — one for the baby dragon and one when it is older — are more lifelike than the on-set props. The dragon, named Yowler by John (Sam Mackenzie), is a 20-foot-high winged creature who physically has more in common with Disney's *Pete's*

Paul Jessel animates Yowler the friendly dragon in front of a rear-screen for *Dragonworld* (1994). (Photograph by Chris Endicott.)

Dragon than more serious forebears such as those in *The 7th Voyage Of Sinbad* or *Dragonslayer*. He walks on two legs and his hide is an interesting dappled mixture of pink, gray and orange.

Early scenes with the baby dragon use a mechanical prop for most shots, including full-view shots in which the creature stands stationary. However, one excellent stop-motion cut is featured during a scene in which John chases Yowler through a forest. In a locked-off long shot, the dragon runs right to left across the frame, pursued by the boy. This static matte (using either front- or rear-projection) has the puppet come from behind the trunk of a tree which

apparently has also been matted around. A grassy mound in the lower foreground, probably also miniature, helps give some depth to the shot. A slight graininess in the live-action plate is not significant enough to distract. The animation of the running beast is superb.

Fifteen years later, John plays his bagpipes out in the hills to attract Yowler. In two long shots, Yowler appears from behind the brow of a hill. This static matte set-up seems to follow the outline of a bush, although this may be a carefully matched miniature. In rear-projection shots viewed from behind the puppet, the dragon's head and neck are animated as he looks down at

194

characters in the background plate. Another long shot shows Yowler walking across the grassy hill; the matte line runs through the grass, allowing the puppet to seem to make contact with the ground.

A poignant nighttime long shot has Yowler standing outside the castle where John lives, his ears pricking up at the sound of music and letting out a long, lonely roar. Attractive low-key lighting enhances this back-projection composite.

Later, Yowler is summoned again by the bagpipes and fed some drugged cheese. In four long-shot stop-motion cuts, he appears from behind the brow of the hill and, in the last of the shots, slumps to the ground. This last shot, with John standing to the right of the image, is extremely well animated — it's an action that could easily have looked awkward.

Unscrupulous businessman John Woodvine has Yowler carried off to "Dragonworld," a medieval theme park where he is displayed in the enclosed courtyard of a mock village. He is billed as "The Eighth Wonder of the World" — haven't we heard that somewhere before?

Woodvine takes John through a high-security steel door to visit Yowler. In an attractive long shot, the dragon sits lethargically in the courtyard, surrounded by the high walls of the mock village. He growls gently, his tail swishes to and fro and his head sways dejectedly. Two shots look from behind the puppet at the actors approaching in the background plate. Yowler perks up at the sight of John.

A superb composite depicts Yowler standing on the right of the shot with the actors on the left. An area of miniature floor, onto which the puppet is able to cast a shadow, is matched exactly to the real ground. The dragon reacts angrily at the sight of Woodvine. After John leaves, Yowler is seen on his own again, looking miserable, lying down and curling up his tail and neck around himself.

The paying public arrives and lines the tops of the walls looking down into the courtyard. In medium shot, the dejected dragon sprawls on the ground, making slight movements with his head.

In long shot, two extras dressed as medieval knights and armed with lances approach the disinterested Yowler. This is another very good composite, using a perfectly matched floor inlay. Another striking composite set-up has one of the knights prod Yowler with his lance, which for a moment seems to pass in front of the puppet, possibly by means of a wire-supported partial miniature. In this cut, Yowler gets up slowly and growls gently. Another impeccably matched floor inlay is featured.

In closeup, the dragon looks straight at the camera as he investigates the crowd. This shot could not be done with the mechanical head and neck because the shot is angled so that the camera looks down the length of the creature's body.

In another great long shot, Yowler stomps across the courtyard, pursued by one of the knights. The puppet passes behind a wall in the lower foreground (which may a miniature) and behind one of the buildings (part of the live-action plate). In medium shot, the dragon growls at some of the spectators — halfheartedly because he is being forced to do it.

Dragonworld: One of 26 scenes animated by Jim Danforth at Effects Associates for David Allen/Charles Band.

A superb extreme long shot looks down into the courtyard from one the rooftops. A knight stands on either side of the puppet and the spectators look down from above. The floor inlay is again impeccable.

Later, John tries to reach Yowler, a sequence that uses four composite set-ups. John calls out through some cage bars and the dragon walks over to him — another excellent composite. Three knights force Yowler backwards and two beautiful long shots look down into the courtyard at Yowler confronting the knights. The shadow of his head and neck falls on an area of exactly matched miniature floor. A low-angle shot looks up at Yowler as the knights poke their lances at him.

The dragon's mouth starts to smoke and Yowler looks just as surprised as anyone. The prop head is used in some of the shots where smoke or flame emerge from his mouth. In a superb stop-motion long-shot, Yowler grabs his throat, growls with astonishment, then unleashes a blast of carefully superimposed flame. He then clamps his mouth shut with one hand and shoves his head into a nearby water trough. A static matte appears to follow the outline of the trough (or it may be part of the miniature set). Either way, some water splashes up at the moment of contact.

In a different aerial-view set-up looking down in to the courtyard, the three knights, plus three security guards, stand in the lower foreground confronting Yowler, who stands on an area of miniature floor. The dragon starts to spread his wings aggressively.

The guards fire tranquilizer darts and in medium shot an animated dart pierces Yowler's neck. In a stop-motion cut, he goes cross-eyed then (in long-shot) he crumples and falls to the ground. This awkward bit of animation is very well choreographed and uses double or triple exposure of some frames to create a blur plus a controlled camera shake at the end of the shot to suggest the impact.

That night, Yowler is seen lying motionless in the courtyard. John and his friend Beth decide to free him. In two long-shot composites, they run up to him and try to wake him. In static matte composites, Yowler gets up, watched by the two actors. They climb onto a prop of the dragon's back as Woodvine and his cronies try to prevent them escaping.

The next seven shots of the dragon are exquisite computer generated images created by Randall Cook, who is credited as "Digital Animation Supervisor." A low-angle long shot looks up at Yowler, who faces the camera, as he rears up and stretches his wings. John and Beth are mounted on the dragon's back and a spotlight moves across the puppet. Two more shots use this same striking set-up, with Yowler starting to flap his wings

slowly, then faster, creating a loud whooshing sound effect. His chest rises and falls with the effort — a good touch.

Because these are CGI shots and not conventional stop-motion, the movement of the wings is beautifully smooth with no evidence of any artificially created blur. In skillfully choreographed moves, the dragon slowly lifts off the ground, sinks back down a couple of times, then rises up again, his legs dangling beneath him. The camera tilts up with the rising figure.

In a magnificent long shot, Yowler rises higher, then flies away from the camera getting smaller and smaller. Again the choreography of the wings and legs is very convincingly executed. A very elegant all-CGI long shot shows Yowler in flight, backed by a panorama of stars. Cook has included billowing hair on the two human characters, blowing in the wind convincingly. The camera pans with the figure as it flies left to right across the shot and straight into a brightly glowing full moon. The dragon's wings flap up and down very smoothly and slowly, as though he were gliding on air currents.

Next morning, Yowler comes in for a landing on a grassy bank in the grounds of John's castle. In this, the final CGI shot, the choreography of the dragon landing is again very carefully thought out, and the human figures on its back make slight movements to enhance the credibility of the shot. A rear-projected shadow is added beneath the dragon.

In another composite, John orders Yowler to return to the hole in the ground from which he came. Just then, helicopters arrive to recapture the dragon and Yowler turns to look at them. The next shot uses the same set-up, with the dejected Yowler turning and walking away. In a clever static matte long shot, Yowler walks into a mist — a cloud that is part manufactured on location and part a miniature solid cloud animated so as to "blow" past the puppet.

Yowler reappears at the end of the film, prompted by the birth of a son to John and Beth. In the castle grounds, Yowler's head appears from behind the brow of a hill and he walks towards John, his feet appearing to make contact with the grass in shots recalling earlier ones. He is welcomed by John and, in a final static matte long shot, lets out a contented growl, looked on by John, Beth and others.

Dragonworld contains a wealth of stop-motion expertise. The film's release caused many stop-motion enthusiasts to wonder if Charles Band was on the verge of letting Allen and his team put the same amount of effort into an adult fantasy. Or would he continue to deny the process the kind of opportunities that it was now so ready to exploit?

Dreamscape

1984. Zupnik-Curtis. D: Joseph Ruben. Scr: David Loughery, Chuck Russell, Joseph Ruben. Story: David Loughery. Ph: Brian Tufano. Art: Jeff Staggs. Mus: Maurice Jarre. Special Makeup: Craig Reardon, Greg Cannom. Special Visual Effects: Peter Kuran. Stop-Motion Visual Effects Supervisor: James Aupperle. Stop-Motion Crew: Stephen Czerkas, Ernest D. Farino, Peter Kozachik, Linda Obalil. Matte Paintings: Dreamquest Images. Matte Artist: Rocco Gioffre. Dream Tunnel Effects: Dennis Pies.

Cast: Dennis Quaid, Max Von Sydow, Christopher Plummer, Eddie Albert, Kate Capshaw, David Patrick Kelly, George Wendt.

Rating: ☆☆☆   Stop-Motion: ☆☆½

Dreamscape is filled with an eye-catching range of effects (optical, mechanical, makeup, animation) and has an engagingly unpretentious approach to its subject matter. We are spared the heavy seriousness that marred other 1980s effects-oriented fantasy-thrillers like *Altered States* and *Brainstorm*. But it is let down by Joseph Ruben's direction, which never quite shifts into high gear, by its conventional conspiracy-against-the-president plot and by a few non-fantasy scenes which seem like padding. The latter are self-contained episodes which, although they may be entertaining out of context, here only weaken the film's otherwise considerable impact. Specifically, these are a comic sequence in which a husband dreams that his wife is committing adultery with everyone he knows — simultaneously; a soft-porn dream sequence featuring Dennis Quaid and Kate Capshaw in a railway carriage; and an unnecessarily protracted chase in which Quaid is pursued by government agents.

These flaws are readily forgiven,

however, because it is exciting that a film like this gets made at all: Essentially it's a schlock B-picture, dressed up in an enthusiastic display of cinema trickery. Peter Kuran was in charge of the generally high-standard optical effects. A powerful sequence has the president's wife running in slow motion towards the camera only to be engulfed by the mushrooming cloud of a nuclear explosion. A little trace of blue spill mars this forceful shot. A tense scene on a swinging girder on a building site makes clever use of fast-motion clouds and has a flawless traveling matte of Quaid falling from the top of a skyscraper. The tunnel of lights which heralds the passage into the dream world is a striking effect, but repetitive and unambitious. The matte paintings and miniature sets that depict a post-holocaust New York are impressive, and include one attractive shot in which a tram carrying the president (Eddie Albert) rumbles through the devastation in long shot.

The Snakeman is a great screen monster. In common with many post–*Star Wars* films that feature stop-motion, the cuts animated by James Aupperle and his team, including Stephen Czerkas (who built the model) and Ernest Farino (who machined the armatures), only make up part of the overall effect. There are only 11 stop-motion cuts and they are brief and shadowy, interspersed with cuts using various full-scale props, including Craig Reardon's articulated version.

In the first of two scenes featuring the Snakeman, Quaid enters the nightmare of a small boy who is cowering in a dark room. After the obligatory hand-through-the-window shock effect, the

Snakeman (David Patrick Kelly in a costume) leaps through the window. The first animation cut is a long shot of just the shadow of the Snakeman as he rips up the boy's father. Down in the basement, the Snakeman rears up as he walks through a doorway (in a rear screen), the camera panning up to emphasize the gesture. Quaid grabs the Snakeman and stop-motion is used in a shot of just their legs, the reptilian tail swishing down.

A puppet likeness of Quaid is used in a quick long shot of the Snakeman grappling with him. The head of the Quaid puppet is turned away from the camera to avoid spoiling the illusion. This shot and several subsequent ones use an extensive miniature set of the basement and its overhead pipes. Shadowy lighting ensures that it never conflicts with the studio set.

There are several live-action shots of the boy attacking the Snakeman with an ax, Quaid holding onto the struggling monster and Reardon's prop head lunging at the camera. After another low stop-motion shot of the tail, this time slithering around the legs of the puppet Quaid, there is a shot of the boy, brandishing his ax, blue-screened in front of the Quaid puppet and the Snakeman (who are still locked together). The full-scale puppet gets beheaded in a live-action cut, complete with a fountain of fake blood.

It's an exciting, eerie scene benefiting from carefully lit rear-screen composites and also from imaginative art direction which suggests the distortion of dreams: the twisted angles of doors and windows, an endless staircase hanging in a void, and a shadowy basement where lights flash on and off without reason.

The climax is even more elaborate. After some fun splatter in which Kelly rips out a man's heart and an encounter with Reardon's radiation-poisoned subway riders, Kelly transforms into the Snakeman. This is achieved in closeup by means of replacement animation, a rarely used technique here involving 32 moldings (sculpted by Reardon) to create a breathtaking one-and-a-half-second cut. A slight dissolve (added by Kuran) was made from each frame into the next one, to soften the transitions.

The creature pursues Quaid and Albert through sets which look like something out of Dante's Inferno. In a striking full-view stop-motion cut, the Snakeman walks towards Quaid, adopting the classic "arms-back" pose that Harryhausen first utilized to simplify animation back in 1957 in *20 Million Miles To Earth*.

A blue-screen shot looking from behind the president at the advancing Snakeman is marred because the background element looks faded. But a rear-projection side-view of the puppet facing off against Albert is much better. The replacement animation used to transform the Snakeman back into Kelly (or almost) is even better than the earlier effect, and uses Reardon's 32 sculpted heads again. The scene ends with a gruesome splatter effect when Albert rams a steel pipe through the Snakeman's chest.

The film's final trick effect has Quaid pulling his face apart to reveal the Snakeman underneath and giving Christopher Plummer a fatal bite in the neck. This convincing splatter shot is a special makeup effect created by Greg Cannom.

The special effects make the film seem a lot better than it actually is, and the last 20 minutes in particular are a treat.

Drop Dead Fred

1990. Working Title. D: Ate de Jong. Scr: Carlos Davis, Anthony Fingleton. Suggested by a story by Elizabeth Livingston. Ph: Peter Deming. Art: Joseph T. Garrity. Mus: Randy Edelma. Special Photographic Effects: Paul Gentry. Visual Effects: VCE/Peter Kuran/Kevin Kutchaver. Stop-Motion Animator: Doug Beswick.

Cast: Rik Mayall, Phoebe Cates, Marsha Mason, Tim Matheson, Carrie Fisher, Brigitte Fonda.

Rating: ☆☆   Stop-Motion: ☆☆

In this wild comedy, Phoebe Cates finds that the imaginary friend she had as a child comes back to torment her in adulthood. The friend, called Drop Dead Fred, is played by British comic Rik Mayall, here sacrificing much of his usual wit and invention for the sake of mere lunacy.

A sequence in which a tree is seen to grow rapidly was achieved with a miniature tree and stop-motion animation by Doug Beswick.

Top: In a charming moment from *The Animal World* (1956), a baby dinosaur hatches from an egg. Sequence designed by Willis O'Brien. *Bottom:* A triceratops from *The Animal World*.

A

Top: In a grotesque scene from *The 7th Voyage of Sinbad* (1958), Ray Harryhausen's Cyclops roasts a victim on a spit. The man on the spit is a miniature puppet. **Bottom:** The Cyclops of *The 7th Voyage of Sinbad* uproots a tree and uses it to attack the sailors.

B

Top: The dragon from *The 7th Voyage of Sinbad*. ***Bottom:*** In *The 3 Worlds of Gulliver* (1960), Gulliver (Kerwin Mathews) confronts a giant crocodile: a dynamic example of Ray Harryhausen's stop-motion skills.

C

Top: Animated puppet-boy and brontosaurus from *Dinosaurus!* (1960). *Bottom:* Harryhausen's marvelously spirited phororhacos menaces Beth Rogan in *Mysterious Island* (1961).

D

Top: Miniaturized by an evil magician and disguised as a harmless toy, the horned giant, Cormoran, performs a quirky dance in *Jack the Giant Killer* (1962). Animation by Tom Holland. Holes in the tabletop, used to secure the puppet, are just visible in this shot. *Bottom:* Jason (Todd Armstrong) confronts the seven-headed Hydra in *Jason and the Argonauts* (1963).

E

F

Opposite: Harryhausen's fabulous moon-cow, attacked by Selenites, in *First Men in the Moon* (1964). *This page, top:* In this all-miniature shot from *Equinox* (1968/71), Taurus, a tusked Simian creature, is about to be speared by an animated puppet-human. Animation by David Allen. *Bottom:* A dramatic confrontation inside a cathedral in Harryhausen's *The Valley of Gwangi* (1969). In this frame enlargement, the matte line, which runs along the top of the balcony and through James Franciscus, is clearly available.

G

COLUMBIA FILMS présente
Une Production CHARLES H. SCHNEER
LE VOYAGE FANTASTIQUE DE SINBAD
FILME EN DYNARAMA
Effets spéciaux RAY HARRYHAUSEN
Réalisé par GORDON HESSLER
Distribué par WARNER-COLUMBIA FILM Visa ministériel N°. 6159

The Golden Voyage of Sinbad (1973): *Top:* Gryphon and Centaur do battle. This shot is a publicity paste-up and does not appear in the film. *Bottom:* The statue of Kali performs a sensuous dance. This frame enlargement reveals that part of the puppet's foot disappears below the matte line, and that the character's shadow ends abruptly where miniature floor and studio floor meet. These flaws go unnoticed during ordinary viewing.

H

Top: This is a striking image of the characters and puppets from ***The Golden Voyage of Sinbad***, but in fact it doesn't appear in the film; it's a publicity paste-up. ***Bottom:*** This French lobby card for ***Sinbad and the Eye of the Tiger*** (1977) allows a good look at Harryhausen's imposing giant walrus—tusks, whiskers, leathery hide and all. This frame enlargement was taken from a print before the addition of a superimposed snowstorm, which in the finished sequence partly obscures the model.

Clash of the Titans (1981). *Top:* Judy Bowker stands before the evil Calibos. In this example of Harryhausen's "reality sandwich" matting technique, the puppet Calibos on a miniature throne has been combined with previously shot live-action footage. *Bottom:* Perseus tries to tame Pegasus. Animation of horse and rider by Jim Danforth.

J

Top: Close-up of Medusa from *Clash of the Titans*. *Bottom:* David Allen animates the tyrannosaurus for *Caveman* (1981).

L   *Caveman* (1981): Ringo Starr—actually a stop-motion puppet—rides the horned lizard, a likeably buffoonish creature designed by Jim Danforth.

Caveman: The narcotized tyrannosaurus in a comic scene animated by Randall W. Cook.

M

Top: The magnificent Verminthrax Perjorative of ***Dragonslayer*** (1981), one wing damaged in battle. ***Bottom:*** The dragon of ***Q*** (1982), riddled by gunfire, swoops over Manhattan. Creature designed by Randall W. Cook.

Stop-motion puppet for *The Thing* (1982), sculpted by Randall William Cook.

O

P

The Terminator (1984). Animation by Pete Kleinow.

Dua mosketyr see *Bláznova kronika*

The Dungeonmaster
(Video Title: *Ragewar*)

1985. Empire. D: Rosemarie Turko, John Buechler, David Allen, Stephen Ford, Peter Manoogian, Ted Nicolaou, Charles Band. Scr: Allen Actor. Ph: Mac Ahlberg. Mus: Richard Band, Shirley Walker. Special Effects Makeup: John Buechler/Makeup and Mechanical Imageries. Stop-Motion: David Allen. Animation Assistant: Mark McGee. Optical Effects: Ernest D. Farino. Cel Animation Sequence: Disney Studios.

Cast: Jeffrey Byron, Richard Moll, Leslie Wing.

Rating: ☆☆½   Stop-Motion: ☆☆½

Like all of producer Charles Band's early pictures, *The Dungeonmaster* is a garbled and disappointing effort. The Devil's sidekick, Mestema (Richard Moll), transports computer whiz kid (Jeffrey Byron) and his girlfriend (Leslie Wing) off to another dimension. There they are confronted by seven challenges, each forming a self-contained episode with a different director. The odds might suggest that at least one of them has to be something special, yet none of the directors shows much creativity.

Band himself directed the forgettable "Heavy Metal," in which the lead singer of the rock group Wasp nearly slits Wing's throat. Special makeups man John Buechler helmed "Demons of the Dead," so it's no surprise to encounter two gruesome zombies and a clever articulated puppet called Ratspit lurking in a dark cave. Like the other episodes, brevity prevents this from developing into anything interesting. In "Ice Gallery," dummies of Jack the Ripper, a mummy and a werewolf come to life. In "Slasher," the heroine almost becomes the victim of a stalk 'n' slash maniac. "Desert Pursuit" is a low-budget, low-interest imitation of *Mad Max*. "Cave Beast" is marginally better than these yawn-inducing episodes and includes an impressive monster which turns out to be an angel in disguise.

David Allen was given the opportunity to direct, write and supply special effects for a tale called "The Stone Canyon Giant." This could have been a chance for stop-motion to really shine but Allen — held back by budget and time constraints — is unable to come up with anything better than a poor relation of Harryhausen's Talos sequence in *Jason and the Argonauts*. The action is ponderous and never amounts to much: Byron pursues two dwarves to the base of a huge statue, the statue comes to life, takes a few paces then gets destroyed by Byron's laser-fire. Allen has had to dispense with "luxuries" like characterization, plot twists and humor. Even so, this is still the film's strongest episode. It may have been a last-minute decision to show it first, since the credits still refer to it as the fourth sequence.

The sequence contains 12 animation cuts as well as five non-animated shots of the stationary puppet. The main long-shot set-up is an attractive static matte composite of the giant on its pedestal in front of a hill, backed by a deep blue sky. The eye-catching puppet, built such that the character appears to be made of bricks, is never really put through its paces — the animation is smooth enough but unambitious.

The first cut is a near-seamless matte of the seated statue. Only the slightly brighter lighting on the miniature gives it away. The next cut is more dynamic because the camera pans across the model and zooms in on the two dwarves. It seems that Allen shot this as a locked-off rear-screen set-up, then refilmed the composite footage, at which time he introduced the camera movement. Another matte set-up shows Byron running towards the statue, which occupies the upper left-hand corner of the frame.

When the statue gets to its feet in long shot, some grating sound effects are added, but the moment cannot compare to the creaking turn of Talos' head. In closeup, a jewel in the giant's head begins to glow, then a bolt of red light is fired from it. Making good use of the depth-deceiving potential of the "reality sandwich," the next shot has Byron, in the foreground, leaping back from a superimposed blast of light fired from the distant statue. In another convincing matte set-up, Byron runs across a clearing, pursued by the giant's two huge legs striding across the frame. Three more brief medium shots show the giant firing another blast of light, turning and walking into the frame.

When Byron fires back at the giant, two pieces of dislodged stone are credibly animated as they fall away from the puppet. After a final animated closeup, the puppet receives a direct hit in the jewel. In a striking long shot, the puppet starts to break into pieces amid a shower of superimposed sparks, watched by Byron (hiding behind some foreground rocks).

It's an enjoyable vignette but suffers because of the lack of interaction between puppet and actor and because the Stone Giant has no character. Compare this with Talos' impressive majesty.

The film has some other merits. There is a promising opening sequence in which Byron is just about to make love to his girlfriend when four mysterious aliens burst in through a steaming doorway and snatch her away, all in slow motion. And in an equally potent later scene (with a similar fairy tale–like lack of logic), Byron batters away at an invisible barrier, trying to reach Wing, who is bathing in a lake; as he does so, his flesh starts to rot away. Having decided to go for quantity not quality, Band even called in the Disney company to provide a half-heartedly brief battle between two cartoon dragons. On paper, all this variety reads like great entertainment, but the reality is considerably less interesting.

Dungeonmaster II see *Pulsepounders*

E.T. the Extra-Terrestrial

1982. Universal. D: Steven Spielberg. Scr: Melissa Mathison. Ph: Allan Daviau. Art: James D. Bissell. Mus: John Williams. E.T. Created by Carlo Rambaldi. Special Artistic Consultant: Craig Reardon. Visual Effects: Industrial Light and Magic. Visual Effects Supervisor: Dennis Muren. Effects Cameraman: Mike McAlister. Optical Photography Supervisor: Kenneth F. Smith. Go-Motion Figures: Tom St. Amand. Matte Artists: Michael Pangrazio, Chris Evans, Frank Ordaz.

Cast: Dee Wallace, Henry Thomas, Peter Coyote, Robert Macnaughton, Drew Barrymore, K. C. Martel.

Rating: ☆☆☆   Stop-Motion: ☆☆½

A curious lack of any big-budget imitations of *Close Encounters of the Third Kind* left the way open for Spielberg to film his own pseudo-sequels — first the "Special Edition" of *Close Encounters* and then *E.T. the Extra-Terrestrial. E.T.* is one of the finest children's films ever made but considerably inferior to his best film, *Jaws*. The plot inadequacies and sentimentality (which could be forgiven in the cause of a willing suspension of disbelief in *Close Encounters*) are given free rein and are much harder to swallow.

For example, faceless officialdom rather contritely becomes the villain of the piece, forcing a hasty retreat by the mother ship at the climax for dramatic rather than logical reasons. The extra presence of Elliot's friends during the cycle chase (one of the film's most exciting scenes) is entirely gratuitous. And the weepy finale is way over the top. Spielberg is aware of these shortcomings but has decided that the emotional impact makes them permissible. These and other manipulative devices mean that the film does not stand up to repeated viewing.

Spielberg's toy- and gadget-laden "middle America" irks after several films, as does his much-loved technique, also used in *Close Encounters*, of bathing just about every other scene in hazy light (for example, an outhouse where E.T. hides, car headlights lighting up a forest, the lights from the spaceship), giving the film a kind of fairy-tale warmth. But it's tempting to put the film down simply because it has been so hugely successful. Despite the faults, this is still first-class escapist entertainment. Spielberg's enthusiasm for the medium is contagious and he extracts likable performances from his child actors. John Williams' fine score insures that a level of emotional excitement is maintained throughout.

Considering all the stop-motion expertise and go-motion technology at the disposal of ILM, it seems strange that Spielberg has chosen to go another route, depicting his title character primarily through the live-action mechanical creations of Carlo Rambaldi. It paid off in the amount of intimate interaction between E.T. and the cast, but the alien always looks awkward in shots of him walking (or, rather, struggling). A few intelligent stop-motion shots could have done a lot to make him a much more mobile character. But even though Spielberg grew up watching Harryhausen's films, he has no special fondness for stop-motion. He avoided using it to depict the aliens in *Close Encounters* and avoided it again when he made *Jurassic Park* (1993).

Stop-motion is used in 11 cuts in the film but for merely functional reasons and have nothing to do with bringing E.T. to life. Two sequences show actors riding flying bicycles. To avoid the high costs of location shooting and rigging actors and bicycles to cranes, Dennis Muren opted to shoot them in miniature with a blue-screen. Tom St. Amand and Mike Fulmer built miniature bikes and armatured puppets which precisely matched the actors. They were rigged up to a go-motion device which could turn the wheels and so set the legs in motion. Another go-motion rod was used to turn the head of each puppet. Any subtler movements — perhaps a rider tilting slightly, or an adjustment to his clothing — were animated in the conventional hands-on stop-motion manner. Although all five riders are seen simultaneously in the second flying sequence, each was filmed as a separate element and composited.

In the first sequence, E.T. suddenly causes Elliot to fly as he is cycling through a forest. In a superb long shot, he flies off the edge off a grassy bank, dips and goes behind what looks like a painted tree. A breathtaking aerial shot looks down at him flying over the treetops towards the camera, his shadow carefully added to the trees he passes over. The shot of him silhouetted against a huge Moon (actually a photo taken with a telephoto lens) has become the image for which the film is most remembered. In the last go-motion cut, he dips away from the camera into another part of the forest.

The seven cuts in the second sequence begin with the classic moment when all five riders, being pursued by governments agents, suddenly take to the air. The composite work is so good that this always looks like a live-action shot. Shadows of the riders have been added to the background plate, and one of them briefly passes behind the hood of a car — possibly achieved by having a blue-painted prop on the blue screen set that lined up with the car. A very evocative shot has all five riders flying away from the camera toward a setting Sun. They are also seen flying across the Sun — similar to the earlier shot with the Moon. Finally, a shot of them dipping down into the forest is enhanced by a camera pan.

The puppets' legs are always attached to the pedals, their arms are stationary and their heads make only minor movements, so it is no surprise that St. Amand and his crew fooled most audiences into thinking they were watching live actors. For this and all the other effects in the film, Dennis Muren, Carlo Rambaldi and Kenneth F. Smith received the 1982 Academy Award for Best Visual Effects.

Earth vs. the Flying Saucers

1956. Columbia. D: Fred F. Sears. Scr: George Worthing Yates, Raymond T. Marcus [Bernard Gordon]. Screen Story: Curt Siodmak. Suggested by the book *Flying Saucers from Outer Space* by Major Donald E. Keyhoe. Ph: Fred Jackman, Jr. Art: Paul Palmentola. Mus: Mischa Bakaleinikoff. Technical Effects: Ray Harryhausen.

Cast: Hugh Marlowe, Joan Taylor, Donald Curtis, Morris Ankrum, John Zaremba, Tom Browne Henry.

Rating: ☆☆½   Stop-Motion: ☆☆☆

Most reference material on Harryhausen's fourth feature film is contradictory, inaccurate or lacking in detail. Only Jeff Rovin in *From the Land Beyond Beyond* comes close to examining the film in any depth. Leonard Maltin curiously describes the film as "unremarkable" in one edition of his *TV Movies* guide, yet in another refers to the "superb special effects." Critical opinion runs to both extremes: John Baxter (in *Science Fiction in the Cinema*) found it "a tight and plausible little fantasy" while Steven H. Scheuer (in his *Movies on TV* guide) thought it was "as outrageous a plot as any inferior science fiction film has offered so far." Ted Newsom (in *Cinefantastique*) supplies a lot of fascinating behind-the-scenes facts but gives no critical appraisal other than to say that it was "a better picture than *It Came from Beneath the Sea*." The film is even excluded from S. S. Wilson's "bible" of stop-motion because it does not conform to his inclusion criteria: "no animated *characters* appear in the film."

The film is suffering from a bad case of critic-neglect. This is for the same reason that Wilson found for not covering it: The only animation in it is of the saucers — there are no dinosaurs, skeletons or dragons here. As if to compensate for this, Harryhausen goes to impressive lengths to imbue his mechanical models with as much dynamism as he can.

The saucers have a revolving inner section, a time-consuming animated feature surprising for such a low-budget film. This touch makes all the difference between a lifeless piece of metal and a vibrant, credible display of alien technology. Sometimes the saucers are seen alone and sometimes they fly past in formation. They raise and lower themselves on a central stem, allowing access to the entrance. On the ground, they generate a protective electrical force field that shimmers around the ship. In flight, they dip and swoop gracefully, getting perilously close to a car in one scene and hurtling directly at the camera in another. In battle, an animated ray gun emerges from the bottom of the saucer and twists in the direction of its target. When hit by the weapon that upsets their anti-gravitational means of flight, they tilt, wobble and finally descend out of control. By comparison, the aliens themselves — merely lumbering men in costumes — seem dull indeed.

Like many low-budget 1950s SF films, *Earth vs. the Flying Saucers* is initially a disappointment but improves with familiarity. On a first viewing, budget limitations and script deficiencies tend to obscure the film's many good points, which only really emerge later.

The plot progresses neatly via a series of isolated encounters with the saucers and aliens to a spectacular no-holds-barred destructive climax, which rates as one of the best of its kind and as good as that in *War of the Worlds*. Curt Siodmak's story contains enough twists to keep things interesting. Satellites launched into space are mysteriously shot down. The aliens make a failed attempt to communicate with scientist Hugh Marlowe. A hovering ball of light turns out to be the aliens' means of spying on the scientists. An alien machine robs a victim of his memory, and in the process makes his brain fully visible. And we are also treated to a fleeting glimpse of a sinister, atrophied alien face — designed by Harryhausen.

George Worthing Yates turns in a far better script than he supplied for *It Came from Beneath the Sea*. The dialogue in particular is a great improvement on the inane padding of the earlier film. Fred F. Sears directs crisply, making this the stand-out film in a grade-B career that included such triumphs of ineptitude as *The Giant Claw* and *The Night the World Exploded*. Mischa Bakaleinikoff's score is a lot livelier than the later one he did for *20 Million Miles to Earth*.

The film's budget was probably on a par with *It Came from Beneath the Sea*'s meager $150,000. As a result, it relies heavily on stock footage from a variety of sources, in fact employing more library shots than any other Harryhausen picture. Republic Pictures provided film

of explosions of miniature buildings and gas tanks, originally shot by the Lydecker brothers. Various military and civilian newsreels were plundered for shots of forest fires, floods, planes exploding in flight, battleships being destroyed, and missiles and rockets being launched. Even other contemporary SF movies were borrowed from: A cut of the destruction of Los Angeles City Hall was lifted from *War of the Worlds* and a shot of various world dignitaries gathered together was taken from *Day the Earth Stood Still*. Another brief shot, of a man running beside a wall during the climax, was pinched from Harryhausen's own *It Came from Beneath the Sea*. Always aware of ways of cutting costs, Harryhausen re-used a shot of the distant Earth, seen on the aliens' television monitor, in the opening sequence of *20 Million Miles to Earth*. All of this unrelated footage is skillfully meshed together and frequently used as background plates for shots of the saucers flying past or of their ray-gun blasts hitting targets. Had producer Charles Schneer decided to shoot in color, the film would probably never have been made, because color differences would have prohibited the use of library footage.

The script doesn't mess about, kicking off with the standard booming-voiced narration and a quick-fire series of pre-credits encounters between saucers and a military jet, a Kansas farmer (an elegant rear-screen composite with the actor looking up at the UFO passing overhead) and a civilian plane. In the latter, the saucer dips over and past the plane, then hurtles straight at the camera, demonstrating aerial acrobatics almost as impressive as ILM's *Millennium Falcon* seen many years later in *Star Wars.*

A short while later, Hugh Marlowe and Joan Taylor are driving through the desert in their car when a saucer, preceded by an ominous whirring sound, appears behind them. It flies over the car and hovers in front of them, as though peering in, and then flies behind them again, all the time tilting and swaying, giving an impression of aerodynamic grace. Both shots are achieved by having the car on a stage with the previously shot animation footage on a projection screen behind it. Marlowe gets out in time to see the saucer ascend directly above him and accelerate left out of the frame.

Two less satisfying effects occur in a night scene during which two of the aliens' spying devices are seen hovering in the sky (and the extent of the superimposed area is apparent because of a difference in "blackness"). One of the satellites is shown burning up in the Earth's atmosphere like a falling star, a rather sudden and poorly paced shot.

Four attractive composites show a saucer, accompanied as ever by a mechanical screeching sound, flying into Project Skyhook, the military base, as extras run about in various locations beneath it. A very potent shot depicts two actors in the control tower looking out through the windows at the saucer (in a full-scale rear projection) which seems to move in closer to get a better look at them.

The saucer's central stem descends and the saucer lands on an undetectable horizontal matte line. A shimmering force field of "solidified electricity" sur-

rounds the ship, making it impervious to gunfire. Harryhausen created this effect by re-filming the shot behind a distortion glass, then matting out the area that was not to be distorted, and combined the distorted area with the original film. In other words, these shots are made up of four elements, including the superimposed gunfire.

A prime example of the lengths to which Harryhausen will go to optimize an effect is the fact that all the time the saucer is on the ground, its middle section is still rotating, adding to the exciting visual impact. Various soldiers are destroyed by the aliens' (superimposed) ray-gun fire, dematerializing in an identical way to *Day the Earth Stood Still* and *War of the Worlds.* When the craft takes off again, its retracting stem is animated in mid-flight. Stock footage of burning buildings in the background plate depicts the carnage it has just caused.

Three different rear-projection designs are used for an eerie nighttime scene on a beach where one of the craft has landed. In all three, Harryhausen has added a shadow to the background plate to enhance the impression that the model is really "in" the shot. The first is a powerful high-angle shot in which the actors seem dwarfed by the craft. The second is shot from above and behind the saucer. The third is the only one that requires a matte, an eye-level set-up which allows the saucer to rise up on its stem (the middle section now starting to rotate) as the voice of one of the aliens invites Marlowe and his group inside. The effect is completed by a prop of the entrance which the actors walk through.

Before they know it, they have been whisked off up into space and are made to watch a TV monitor showing the aliens' presence on earth. Two saucers are seen flying over New York, three past the Eiffel tower and three over the Houses of Parliament. Another is seen dipping and turning as it destroys a battleship at sea.

Back on Earth, a spying device interrupts a scientific meeting, flies around the room, lunges directly at the camera and finally is shot down. Outside, a saucer is glimpsed flying behind some trees at night. Harryhausen presumably used miniature trees for this effect, but if so, then they blow in the wind very realistically. The saucer lands, a shadow once again added to the effect and the mid-section continuing to rotate. As some aliens emerge from the craft, there are several closer views of the model. When the de-stabilizer gun is fired at the saucer, it wobbles and sways above the aliens, who get back on board and take off. In the air, the stem retracts and the saucer becomes dangerously out of control, tilting in all directions before finally flying off.

Three impressive scenes of destruction follow (all making extensive use of library film). A saucer flies near a military plane, and there is a shot of it from the pilot's point of view looking out of the cockpit. The sinister ray gun emerges from the base of the saucer, twists in the direction of the plane, then sends out a (superimposed) blast. The saucer then seems to hover for a while, as though watching the flaming plane with relish.

Down below, a building is blasted and explodes. There are several shots of the saucer starting a forest fire and flying slowly through the burning trees, with flickering lighting falling on the ani-mated model to add to the realism. At a height of about 200 feet, the stem emerges and two corpses are ejected, small puppets which fall to the ground with the barest amount of animation. This dramatic sequence is spoiled by the inclusion of several shots of Marlowe and Taylor running through the burning forest — unfortunately these were achieved by having the actors running unrealistically on a treadmill in front of a rear screen. Finally there is an attractive long shot angled from above, employing a smaller model of the saucer, in which we look down at the saucer flying over the raging fire below.

The finale is 15 minutes of non-stop action. A saucer flies across the sky at speed and blows up two planes (actually real footage of a mid-air collision). Three missiles are fired at the saucer, explosions being convincingly superimposed on the model. Three saucers fly in formation over Washington and in a low-angle shot fly behind the City Hall; an intricate matte following the outline of several pillars enables the models to seem to pass behind the building. Struck by the de-stabilizing ray, one teeters and falls into the Potomac, a superimposed splash briefly suggesting its impact with the water. A barrage of shell-fire is superimposed over the shot of another saucer in flight.

There are two very attractive composites of the huge saucer half-submerged in the lake, water sizzling and steaming around it, a Jeep and live actors in the lower left foreground. Two bushes (presumably miniatures) on the lakeside in the lower right of the frame are actually in front of the model. It's a stunning image.

Another saucer blasts the corner of a building and several pieces of aerial-braced masonry come crashing down amid superimposed smoke. There are a number of shots from below of saucers flying over Washington buildings, and of gas tanks being destroyed and Jeeps vaporized. A saucer lands on the White House lawn, a shadow in the background plate again adding to the effect. When it takes off again, the de-stabilizing ray is aimed at it and, in a beautifully executed use of static matte, it crashes in a street full of cars, the impact being implied when it glides behind a building followed seconds later by an explosion.

In live-action shots, debris falls on running extras. Subsequently the grounded saucer is seen smoking in a debris-strewn miniature set. One of the miniature cars in this shot, a station wagon, crops up again later at the foot of the Capitol Building and has also been seen in other Harryhausen films.

Another saucer destroys the City Hall tower (a shot lifted from *War of the Worlds*), then glides out of control towards the huge window of a building. A dramatic shot from inside shows it coming straight at the camera and seeming to make contact with the window. By briefly cutting away to a shot of startled actors, Harryhausen wisely avoids the intricacies of actually showing all the smashing glass and debris. When he cuts back to the model, it is already tumbling through the wall (a deftly choreographed crash landing), eventually exploding in a cloud of smoke.

A fourth saucer flies past the Washington Monument and is bombarded with superimposed shell-fire. Wobbling out of control, it veers towards the Mon-

ument, seen in long shot with actors running across the foot of the frame. In one of Harryhausen's most exquisitely executed shots (and voted fifth favorite Harryhausen effect by readers of *FXRH* magazine), the saucer slices through the monument, momentarily bouncing on impact with the ground as the monument comes crashing down around it. Dozens of wires were required to support all the various pieces of falling debris painstakingly animated by Harryhausen. When one considers the time and effort which must have gone into this one shot, it becomes difficult to understand that Harryhausen was forced to do it this way because the cost of high-speed filming would apparently have been even higher.

A fifth saucer destroys more buildings (in library footage) and another Jeep, then fires on the pillars of the entrance to the City Hall. In three cuts, as many as ten separate pieces of aerially suspended debris fall to the ground; but on this occasion their rate of fall is slightly too slow to be convincing. The saucer disappears behind the building's roof (a convenient matte line), and is heard exploding off-screen.

Another saucer lands beside the Capitol Building and is briefly seen in a shot which must rank as the biggest blunder in all of Harryhausen's films: The bottom half of the matte has not been restored, leaving a large black area beneath the saucer.

A second saucer subsequently flies past the first one, using the same background film of the Capitol but with a miniature foreground (with our old friend the station wagon again). The first saucer takes off again but is hit by

209

Marlowe's ray. In another beautifully realized effect, it slides into the miniature pillars of the Capitol Building, bringing down more crashing debris around it.

In a spectacular final effect, the last saucer crashes into the Dome, a seamless matte joining the upper miniature portion with the real structure below. Bits of debris fall almost unnoticed from the side of the building, which is covered by superimposed smoke. The destruction ends with the deservedly famous shot of Marlowe and Taylor standing at the foot of the Capitol, the saucer and demolished Dome matted in behind them.

The film contains more intricate aerial-braced animation than any of Harryhausen's other films and is a testimony to his dedication. Not surprisingly, he is quoted in Brosnan's *Movie Magic* as saying, "It was something I would never do again." Fortunately for him, bigger budgets in his later films allowed him to rely more often on high-speed filming. *Earth vs. the Flying Saucers* is no classic — in dramatic terms it is every inch a dumb B-picture — but it is still fast-paced, enjoyable stuff. Although lacking any memorable animated characters, it is full of superb effects: brilliantly realized scenes of destruction, near-perfect animation, and several images of unforgettable visual impact.

The film received an homage (some would say "rip-off") in Tim Burton's *Mars Attacks!* (1996), in which the Earth is invaded by flying saucers. These computer generated saucers featured ray guns which emerged from the undercarriage of the craft in exactly the same way as those in Harryhausen's film.

Earth vs. the Flying Saucers was released on a double bill with another Fred F. Sears film, *The Werewolf*, and its substantial $1,250,000 gross enabled Schneer and Harryhausen to go into partnership again the following year to make *20 Million Miles to Earth* (after Harryhausen's brief teaming with Irwin Allen on *The Animal World*). Despite its many fine moments, however, *Earth vs. the Flying Saucers* rates low compared to his other films.

Ed Wood

1995. Touchstone. D: Tim Burton. Scr: Scott Alexander, Larry Karaszewski. Based on the book *Nightmare of Ecstasy* by Rudolph Grey. Ph: Stefan Czapsky. Art: Tom Duffield. Mus: Howard Shore. Bela Lugosi Makeup: Rick Baker. Visual Effects Photography: Alan Blaisdale. Special Visual Effects: Boyington Film Productions (Supervisor: Paul Boyington). Stop-Motion (uncredited): Kent Burton.

Cast: Johnny Depp, Martin Landau, Sarah Jessica Parker, Patricia Arquette, Jeffrey Jones, Bill Murray.

Rating: ☆☆☆   Stop-Motion: ☆☆

This is Tim Burton's best film, perhaps because he is forced to stay (more or less) within the bounds of real life (unlike the bizarre *Beetlejuice*) and because he does not have the luxury of a big budget which tempts him to become overblown (as in *Batman*). And one senses that in maverick director Wood, Burton saw something of a kindred spirit. Above all, this film is successful because of the affection with which Burton portrays Wood and Bela Lugosi, and it is as much a biography of the latter as it is of the title character. Wood and Lugosi are depicted as larger-than-life characters who are innately likable, and this is what gives the film its appeal.

In the opening credits, the camera prowls around a B-picture fake graveyard, past tombstones with the names of the cast inscribed on them, and down to the edge of a swamp. A giant octopus' tentacle snakes up out the water, waves in the air and then coils up. For this quick gag—a reference to Wood's *Bride of the Monster*—Burton once again used stop-motion. The smooth animation of this puppet is by Kent Burton.

The Empire Strikes Back

1980. Lucasfilm/20th Century–Fox. Exec Prod-Story: George Lucas. D: Irvin Kershner. Scr: Leigh Brackett, Lawrence Kasdan. Ph: Peter Suschitzky. Mus: John Williams. Special Visual Effects: Brian Johnson, Richard Edlund. Effects Director of Photography: Dennis Muren. Optical Photography Supervisor: Bruce Nicholson. Effects Cameramen: Ken Ralston, Jim Veilleux. Art Director — Visual Effects: Joe Johnston. Stop-Motion Animation: Jon Berg, Phil Tippett. Stop-Motion Technicians: Tom St. Amand, Doug Beswick. Matte Painting Supervisor: Harrison Ellenshaw. Matte Artists: Ralph McQuarrie, Michael Pangrazio. Model Makers: Michael Fulmer, Dave Carson and others. Animation and Rotoscope Supervisor: Peter Kuran.

Cast: Mark Hamill, Harrison Ford, Carrie Fisher, Billy Dee Williams, David Prowse, Anthony Daniels, Frank Oz, Kenny Baker, Alec Guinness, James Earl Jones (voice of Vader), Peter Mayhew.

Rating: ☆☆☆½   Stop-Motion: ☆☆☆½

Star Wars (1977) was a huge commercial success. A sequel was not only inevitable but also part of George Lucas' grand design. He had written a nine-part saga, split into three trilogies, of which *Star Wars* was the first part of the second trilogy. He now had the financial clout to make his follow-up a much more elaborate affair. The excellent special effects of the original could now be taken one stage further. Stop-motion photography, which had only been seen in the brief chess sequence in *Star Wars,* would make a major contribution in the sequel.

The Empire Strikes Back contains a whole range of dazzling special effects sequences produced at Lucas' Industrial Light and Magic workshops. The four individuals who headed up the project — Brian Johnson, Richard Edlund, Dennis Muren and Bruce Nicholson — received a joint Academy Award for special achievements in visual effects. Muren was responsible for the stop-motion sequences and designed all the composite set-ups. Phil Tippett and Jon Berg, who created the chess scene in *Star Wars*, were the natural choices for the role of animators. Doug Beswick, who had done fine animation for the ill-fated *Planet of Dinosaurs*, was enlisted to assist on animation and armature construction. Others brought onto the project were Tom St. Amand, Ken Ralston and Dave Carson, all of whom had been working on David Allen's aborted film *The Primevals*. Over the years to come, most of these names would figure large in the history of stop-motion feature films.

Almost all of the stop-motion occurs during the first half-hour of the film. And what a half-hour it is: a visually stunning, rapid-fire series of imaginative fantasy action sequences that grab your attention from the opening shots of the huge Star Destroyer sending out probe droids into space, right up until the moment when Luke Skywalker flies off in his X-Wing fighter in search of the Dagoba system. The quieter scenes that follow, in which Luke meets and is trained by the old Jedi master Yoda, are a welcome chance to let the adrenalin buzz subside.

There was a conscious decision made by all concerned to try to improve the look of stop-motion. Primarily this meant trying to introduce a blur to the finished image and also to keep the camera in motion, avoiding the locked-off look that previously characterized so many stop-motion sequences. Additionally, the process was used to propel the story along, rather than having self-contained stop-motion set-pieces for their own sake. All those involved were

long-time fans of O'Brien and Harryhausen but had a genuine desire to advance the art of stop-motion beyond their techniques, bringing it to a level acceptable to modern-day audiences hungry for hi-tech special effects.

The opening 12 shots are probably the most stunning start to any film — on a par with Kubrick's dramatic first shot of *2001: A Space Odyssey*. The grand movements in the shots and the superb sound effects are breathtaking — anyone who has only seen this film on television is only getting a fraction of the impact.

One of the Empire's huge Star Destroyers glides towards the camera, then unleashes a cluster of tiny probe spacecraft from its belly, each one soaring off in a different direction. The camera follows one probe as it roars towards a planet (a beautiful painting), down through its atmosphere, crashing into the snow below. A probe droid emerges from the snow, initially an eight-foot-high live-action prop and in the next cut a stop-motion puppet animated (in front of a bluescreen) by St. Amand. It hovers above the snow, spindly mechanical arms and legs unfurling beneath it.

The ninth shot of the film is a knockout, an aerial view of Luke (Mark Hamill) riding a taun-taun across a snowy plain. The taun-taun is a kind of cross between a llama and a dinosaur, a furry biped with a long tail. It was designed, sculpted and animated by Tippet. Its armature was built by Beswick and St. Amand. A full-scale taun-taun is seen in a few shots requiring intimate interaction, but it is the stop-motion puppet that steals the show. In this ninth shot, the camera zooms down and in onto the running animal and rider, starting from an extreme long shot. At first glance, this striking panorama suggests that we are seeing a puppet animated on a miniature set — in fact, the shot was done blue-screen. Not only that, but the camera remained stationary during this dynamic zoom, with the puppet being tilted up frame by frame, its moves carefully plotted to match the moves in the background live-action plate, which had been shot previously by helicopter. The lighting of the puppet is just right and the illusion is finished off with the taun-taun's shadow on the live-action snow, added optically as a separate element. It was probably the most difficult of all the taun-taun shots to get right.

In the next two shots, also stop-motion cuts but this time shot with a rear-projection screen, the camera is again moving, maintaining the vitality of the whole sequence so far. The taun-taun, neighing and screeching, runs behind a hill, the bags and packs beside Luke's saddle bobbing up and down realistically. In this cut, blur was added to the puppet movement by having a motion-control rod attached to its torso. This would actually move the puppet a fraction during the exposure of a frame, after all the other parts (head, legs, the Luke puppet, etc.) had been repositioned in the conventional hands-on manner. The rod was obscured by a white card which, by means of carefully diffused lighting, was made to blend in with the snow in the background.

In the next shot, Luke and the taun-taun walk up to the brow of a hill, the matte line following the outline of the hill. The twelfth shot, ending this un-

forgettable sequence, is a live-action closeup of Luke removing his goggles (establishing his identity), the head of the full-size taun-taun partly seen pulling on the reins.

In extreme long shot Han Solo (Harrison Ford) is seen riding another taun-taun, looking perfectly at home in a rear-projection set-up, the lighting again cleverly diffused so as to give the whole composite a grainy, outdoor feel. When he runs into a hangar, the composite includes a Ralph McQuarrie matte painting of the building's exterior. The blue screen shot inside the hangar, with the taun-taun sprinting down a runway surrounded by busy extras and spotlights, is another classic composite, a dim shadow under the puppet again adding to the credibility.

Later, Han goes out again to look for Luke, who has been abducted by a shaggy creature called a wampa. There is a superb rear-screen shot of the puppet Han on his taun-taun running towards the camera through a snowstorm. In-camera lighting effects on painted glass created the look of the storm, really making it seem as if the puppets are in amongst all the snow, in particular dense clouds around the taun-taun's feet. As it gets nearer, its tail swishes from side to side and its head rears up.

Another superb composite, again done rear-screen, shows Han walking away from the taun-taun on the right with its back to us; the taun-taun is growling gently, its tail swishing. Luke, nearly dead from the cold, sees a vision of Obi Wan Kenobi (Alec Guinness). As it fades away, he sees in its place Han galloping toward him on his taun-taun. This shot was done blue-screen with motion-control blurs on the puppet. Again, the image of the puppet is made clearer as it nears the camera, suggesting the snowstorm. (Another warning to television viewers watching a panned-and-scanned version: The animation in the preceding cut is totally lost off the edge of the screen. The cut before that, of Han dismounted, is missing entirely from some TV prints.) Luke's taun-taun has already been killed by the wampa. Now Han's beast dies, succumbing to the cold. Tippett's animation of the animal keeling over sideways, its saddlebags all flapping as it hits the ground, is excellent. Snow is superimposed over this shot.

There is no more taun-taun animation. Some sources state that there are 12 cuts but in fact there are nine. Shots of Han riding his taun-taun are known to have been dropped prior to release because they didn't cut well with the flow of the action — but have other cuts been made (with Lucas' approval) since the film's original theatrical release? This is quite possible in view of the fact that, amazingly, the taun-taun shots were poorly received by the public-at-large. Despite the fluid animation and the superb composites, audiences were alienated by something about these shots, leading many to dismiss this as old-fashioned "jerky" stop-motion once again. In fact, what spoils some of the shots is the fact that Tippett has been too ambitious in trying to depict the gait of a running animal. There is something not quite right about the bounding running cycle of this puppet, regardless of how smooth the animation is. Those who weren't willing to suspend disbelief in the interests of a superb fantasy image

felt cheated. The unfortunate impact of this was that the third installment in the saga, *Return of the Jedi*, featured no animation of fantasy creatures — stop-motion was reserved only for mechanical creations.

Animation of mechanical creations constitutes the remainder of this dramatic opening half-hour of *The Empire Strikes Back*. Evil Darth Vader sends five Imperial Walkers, hundred-foot-high armored tanks on bulky elephantine legs, to destroy the rebel outpost on the ice planet. The slow-moving walkers are natural subjects for stop-motion — and we do not have preconceived ideas of how they should move (as we did with the taun-tauns). Trudging heavily through the snow, most of the Walkers' movements are so slow that the animation can look extremely fluid, and even those moments where there is some strobing look perfectly acceptable because these are mechanical vehicles. In retrospect, it seems amazing that no one had previously thought of using stop-motion for hi-tech mechanical creations such as these; the closest things to them in earlier movies are the golem-robots in 1979's *Starcrash*. The Walkers, which could not have been depicted any other way, were so successful that they spawned a whole series of films featuring "robo-motion" mechanical puppets (*The Terminator, RoboCop, Robot Jox*, etc.).

The sequence is put together with rapid-fire editing. There appear to be 43 stop-motion cuts but is it difficult to be sure because there are so many quick cuts seen through the cockpits of the rebels' Speeders as they fly past Walkers, glimpsed so briefly that it is hard to tell if they are moving or not. Effects art designer Joe Johnston designed the impressive Walkers. St. Amand built three 18-inch puppets from construction designs by Berg. They were animated primarily by Tippett and Berg, with Beswick assisting on some shots.

A sizable miniature set was built and covered with fake snow. Trap doors were built into it to enable the animators access to the models. Exquisite background paintings by Ralph McQuarrie (the first shot of all the Walkers) and Mike Pangrazio (12 other paintings) helped bring the scene to life. Only a very few blue-screen shots were done — near the end of the sequence when there are long shots of soldiers in the lower foreground running from the Walkers. As with the taun-taun shots, a priority was to keep the camera moving to enhance excitement: There are lots of shaky point-of-view shots through Speeder cockpit windscreens, rapid pans following Speeders as they fly past Walkers and most dramatically, a Speeder point-of-view shot as it flies through the legs of one of the Walkers.

After lots of fine non–stop-motion effects shots of Star Destroyers, a huge cannon firing, and rebel transporters fleeing into space protected by little X-Wing fighters, our first sight of the Walkers sees them as tiny figures way off on the horizon. Photo cut-outs were used for extreme long shots like this. Next is a cleverly ominous shot seen through a soldier's electronic binoculars, a grainy, scratchy image which starts at the huge foot of one of the Walkers, then tilts up and pulls back to reveal this and two other Walkers in full. A classic closer shot shows all five Walkers plodding to-

ward the camera, red laser fire shooting out of the guns mounted on their slowly turning heads.

Equally good is a side view of three Walkers trudging across the shot. A sense of depth was ingeniously added to the set by hanging bridal veils at different distances from the camera, softening the focus. A blue-screened Speeder flits between the first and second Walker, then another Speeder flies between the second and third ones, again with optically added laser-fire issuing from speeders and Walkers. Closer shots of just the legs, bodies or feet really suggest the great bulk of these tanks. In particular, the feet have a very satisfying complexity, the toes opening and closing as the feet are raised, the lower legs expanding and shrinking like shock absorbers.

The magnificent sequence in which one of the Walkers is felled when a Speeder wraps a cable around its legs is breathlessly edited. The cable itself was cel animation done by Peter Kuran. Aerial shots of the Speeder circling the Walker are intercut with low-angle shots of the Walker's legs. After a fine stop-motion cut of the Walker struggling against the cable, a four-foot live-action model is intelligently used to depict it collapsing head-first into the snow.

ILM throw in another bit of magic at this point: In the background of a shot of a Walker firing its cannons, a two-legged mechanical Scout Walker struts past. Who cares that it's a totally unlikely and impractical vehicle? It's a bizarre throwaway moment that always draws a squeal of delight from audiences (unless you are watching the panned-and-scanned TV version in which the Scout Walker, in this shot and another later one, is barely noticeable). The puppet, dubbed a chicken-walker by the ILM crew because of its strutting walk, was built by Berg and St. Amand and animated against a blue-screen by St. Amand.

In a thrilling blue-screen point-of-view shot, Luke crashes his Speeder into the snow right into the path of one of the giant Walkers. Two imposing stop-motion cuts show the puppet's feet and legs inexorably approaching as Luke escapes in the nick of time. The Speeder is flattened by a full-scale foot.

Three unforgettable long-shots depict the Walkers advancing on rebel soldiers who are fleeing in the lower foreground. All have laser fire added as an extra element and again the lighting is perfectly calculated to blend the two principal elements. Two of these look like rear-screen shots. Smoke from an explosion crosses the matte line, helping to fool the eye into thinking this is one image. Another is done blue-screen, but one of the soldiers' heads moves past the feet of a Walker; presumably hand-drawn mattes were introduced frame-by-frame into the composite to match the movement of the extra's head.

Ralston animated the dramatic shot of Luke, a miniature puppet, pulling himself up on a rope under the belly of one of the walkers. He throws a bomb into the walker and it explodes in a series of live-action cuts using another four-foot model. Another fine stop-motion cut shows a Walker turning and firing at a Speeder which spins wildly and crashes. The Walker adopts a credibly ungainly pose with its legs spread as it turns.

The sequence ends with some superb blue-screen shots of Han Solo's *Millennium Falcon* taking off from the hangar and flying off above the snow, and of Luke's X-Wing fighter leaving the planet, backed by a beautiful painting of three tiny moons hanging in front of the great sphere.

After all this excitement, the rest of the film is a bit of a disappointment. But there is still much to enjoy, including an edge-of-the-seat chase through an asteroid field. There are three more stop-motion cuts in the film, all brief. Luke arrives on a swampy planet in the Dagoba system, full of snakes and half-seen monsters. Effectively conjuring up this unpleasant world are two panoramic matte paintings by Harrison Ellenshaw of vines hanging in the murk of the dense forest. In the first of these shots, two screeching stop-motion birds glide smoothly above Luke's crashed craft, and in the second, a bird flaps across the background, then swoops back the other way. These atmospheric fantasy images would have gladdened O'Brien's heart. The birds, animated against a blue screen by Ralston with motion-control blurs, were built by Tippett, who gave them vicious-looking alligator-like heads.

The film's other stop-motion cut, also animated by Ralston, is a long shot of a Luke puppet hanging from a radio mast underneath Bespin, the cloud city. Barely recognizable as stop-motion, this is a purely functional use of the process — the alternative, to shoot an actor in long shot against a blue screen, would have been more expensive.

The Empire Strikes Back is a landmark film in terms of its stop-motion. The Walker sequence demonstrated a completely novel application for the process and did it brilliantly. The superb taun-taun shots may not have been to everyone's liking but they are a classic example of stop-motion depicting a fantasy creature that could not be depicted any other way. And, more importantly, the use of a motion-control rig to introduce blurs to the image was the beginning of a technological revolution in puppet animation. It would be developed to a much more intricate level in *Dragonslayer* and dubbed "go-motion."

Equinox

1967. Tonylyn. Prod: Dennis Muren. D-Scr: Mark McGee. Ph: Mike Hoover. Special Effects: David Allen, Jim Danforth, Dennis Muren.

1971. (Extra footage shot for theatrical release.) Prod: Jack H. Harris. D-Scr: Jack Woods. Mus: John Caper.

Cast: Edward Connell, Barbara Hewitt, Frank Boers, Jr., Robin Christopher, Jack Woods, Fritz Leiber.

Rating: ☆☆   Stop-Motion: ☆☆½

Dennis Muren, David Allen and Jim Danforth have all come a long way since working on this clumsy low-budget fantasy. In 1967, Muren raised $8,000 to make a short 16mm film with a group of friends, all of whom had grown up watching the films of O'Brien and Harryhausen. In 1971, Jack Harris (who produced *Dinosaurus!* in 1960) picked the film up, blew it up to 35mm, shot extra sequences and gave it a theatrical release. Today, it's of interest only to stop-motion fans.

The opening credits —filmed against the cogs of a clock — and the title suggest this is going to be a time-warp tale. But neither have any connection with what follows, a tale of satanism told in flashback in which four kids are given a sinister book by an old hermit, and then have to defend themselves from a succession of monsters and a demon called Asmodeus (played by director Jack Woods) who try to retrieve the tome. The originality of this Lovecraftian plot is totally undermined by weak direction and dialogue. There are many unintentionally funny moments, most ludicrous of all when Woods attacks a woman and there is a closeup of his slobbering, rubber-lipped face; it looks as if he's intending to suck her to death.

The special effects are interesting for their own sake but their main failings are that they never generate much excitement, always look artificial and rarely integrate successfully with the live action. Much of this artificiality is caused by stock contrasts in composite shots and by animation which at times seems to have cut corners by "shooting on twos" (i.e., only 12 poses of the puppet per second instead of 24). For some of the stop-motion composites, Muren used a front-projection system that enabled "reality sandwich" shots to be achieved with only one pass of the camera.

Although he didn't do any of the animation, Jim Danforth did contribute two excellent matte paintings. One shows a distant castle perched on a cliff top. The other is a shot of some robed satanists approaching a glowing pit set in some red-tinted mountains. The latter is a beautiful and faultless composite, one of the few moments when the film conjures up a potent fantasy world.

There is plenty of animation — 67 cuts in three distinct sequences. There are three puppets — a tentacled cephalopod, a giant simian and a flying demon — and although their design is reasonable (and better than, say, those of *Jack the Giant Killer*), they never convince as anything other than models.

The first stop-motion sequence is a flashback within a flashback. As a result of Fritz Leiber meddling with things man was meant to leave alone, a nightmarish, enormous octopus-like creature has been summoned. The creature is never required to do much, but it does have a very realistic watery eye which makes it the most realistic of the puppets. In four cuts animated by Allen, it attacks Leiber's hut, a miniature set with a backdrop of "live" trees. The puppet's body doesn't move but its swirling tentacles emerge from behind the hut and break down the walls. The breaking planks are very plausibly animated. A miniature or painted tree in the foreground helps to give the shot some depth. This brief sequence is let down by its hurried animation and by a speeded-up live-action cutaway of Leiber running out his hut, a moment which is unintentionally comic.

The second stop-motion sequence is the longest of the three. It features some ambitious and memorable shots but is ultimately disappointing because of its flat pacing and, again, animation which is distractingly jerky. Jerky movements need not mar a scene if it is good in other respects (*King Kong* is the prime example), but it's difficult to ignore here because the scene has little else going for it. There are lots of different set-ups, some all miniature, some composites, and this gives the scene some vitality but the animation lacks the drama which the occasion requires. Taurus, the satanic tusked simian, is an imaginative model, part-hairy, part-scaled, and its growl sounds like a combination of a slowed-down lion's roar and a snake's hiss. It was not built specifically for *Equinox* but had been constructed in the early 1960s by Allen.

It appears in a shimmering ball of light in a cave mouth and chases an old hermit into an extensive miniature set in a forest. In two medium closeups and two long shots of the miniature set, Taurus picks up a puppet of the hermit, swings him into a tree, then smashes him into the ground. The timing of the hermit's flailing legs is not convincing.

In the next shot, Taurus chases two girls through the trees. A foreground miniature floor means there is no need for a matte. Rocks are thrown at the beast, bouncing off it very realistically. It may be that the rocks are part of the live-action plate and bounce off some object that is obscured by the puppet, and are animated only for a few frames in which they pass in front of the puppet. These shots are intercut with medium closeups and long shots of the snarling monster.

In one baffling shot, a character

Taurus, the tusked simian from *Equinox* (1971).

runs in front of the puppet. A slow-motion replay reveals that momentarily the puppet's head can be seen *through* the girl's leg. Muren and his team did not have access to blue-screen facilities and the girl is not an animated puppet, so one can only conclude that this is a rotoscoped matte.

The beast turns and is seen walking away in the distance, an attractive long shot that looks through a narrow gap in a cliff face. The rock face on the left is a miniature; a matte down a rock face in the live action on the opposite side creates the illusion that it ends abruptly to form the gap.

Taurus stands at the foot of the cliff growling up at an actor at the top. All but the top few feet of the cliff are miniature. The join is conspicuous if you are looking for it and the registration is a little shaky. Two cuts look down at Taurus, his lips pursing in anger, from the actor's point of view. In several cuts, Taurus tries to get at the actors through a gap in the rocks. Meanwhile, they look for something that can be used as a spear, hunting about in such a slow and disinterested way that the already-deficient pace nearly grinds to a halt altogether.

In two memorable shots, enjoyable in their own right but not meshing well with the live action, the monster's arm reaches through the gap for the book. In another striking cut, a puppet human runs at Taurus and spears it, his legs swinging forward with the impact as he is lifted off the ground. The miniature book, supported by wires and animated, flies through the air believably.

In a series of cuts, Taurus staggers around, removes the spear, collapses, gets up, then collapses again — all done in miniature without mattes. These death throes are clearly inspired by the dramatic demises of some of Harry-hausen's creations, but lack his theatrical grandeur. (Also, Taurus has never developed into a sympathetic character.) The animation in the two shots where he falls to the ground is stiff and not properly timed. There are several shots of the motionless corpse, two cuts of its arms briefly moving again and a final, optically enhanced shot of it surrounded by a yellow haze and disappearing.

Before the final stop-motion sequence, there is a dull live-action episode featuring an actor dressed as a neanderthal and enlarged by static matte photography.

Asmodeus transforms into a red, winged demon that seems to have taken its inspiration from the harpies of *Jason and the Argonauts*. Like Taurus, it is an expertly constructed model, especially its leathery wings and scaly talons, but its face is short on character.

A shot of Asmodeus standing at the top of a cliff and raising his arms is followed immediately by a cut of the model from a different angle. It's a clumsy transformation, with no attempt at using cel or replacement animation to depict a gradual change. A blur is effectively added to the first stop-motion cut, possibly by having the model pulled out of the frame in real time once it has taken to the air. A shot of it flying over the woods allows a good look at the detail of the wings. Two extreme long shots of the creature in flight are cel animations fluidly realized by Danforth.

A dramatic low-angle shot has the creature flying straight down at the camera, permitting a close look at its three-pronged tail, three-toed feet, two horns and devilish grin. In another shot, the harpy swoops down on the motionless puppet of a girl standing in a convincing miniature set. One very effective cut has the demon swoop into the frame from the right, scoop up an animated girl in its claws (from another miniature set, this one blending in well with the live-action backdrop), and then continue out of the left side of the frame. Because this is not a matte shot, the camera is free to pan right to left with the model, and it is this movement which gives the shot its dynamism.

The demon then swoops down at another character, who swipes at it with the book. The attempt at suggesting physical contact is impaired by the stock contrasts. The puppet lands on what is rather too obviously a miniature set and (in best Dracula fashion) cowers from a crucifix that is held up before it. In one cut, the character holding the crucifix is a puppet standing in the background.

The demon flies off and in one cut appears to glide behind some very convincing miniature trees. It flies down into a miniature set to attack the hero and heroine but neglects to notice that they are hiding behind a cross-shaped tombstone and so goes up in flames — happening very anti-climactically off-screen while the audience is forced to look at cut-aways of the actors' "horrified" faces. Dramatically this sequence is very mediocre, but the standard of animation is higher than in the other two episodes.

The film leaves a lot to be desired on all levels, but (of course) it was originally only conceived as an amateur project. Muren, Allen and McGee simply did not have the resources or experience that Harryhausen had, so making comparisons with his work is almost irrelevant. The film is a brave attempt to bring some offbeat special effects to the screen and the stop-motion episodes are always fun, even when they fail to convince.

In 1967, Danforth was already established. But *Equinox* was a significant training ground for Muren and Allen. Muren would later work for George Lucas' Industrial Light and Magic outfit and supervise the creation of some wonderful special effects sequences (often featuring stop-motion) for films including *Star Wars*, *The Empire Strikes Back*, *E.T. the Extraterrestrial*, *Terminator 2* and *Jurassic Park*. Allen would continue to develop his stop-motion skills and be kept busy adding his magic to a string of (mainly low-budget) films over the next two decades, including *Laserblast*, *The Crater Lake Monster*, **batteries not included* and many others.

Eraserhead

1976. D-Scr: David Lynch. Ph: Frederick Elmes, Herbert Cardwell. Art-Special Effects: David Lynch.

Cast: John Nance, Charlotte Stewart, Allen Joseph, Jeanne Bates, Judith Anna Roberts, Laurel Near.

Rating: ☆☆☆½ Stop-Motion: ☆☆

Shot by David Lynch while he was a student at film school, this surreal nightmare is one of the finest black comedies ever made. Uniquely, Lynch manages to be depressing and hilarious at the same time.

The location is a bleak, industrial landscape. The hum of machines provides constant background noise. Henry is invited to supper by his girlfriend Mary's family, only to be confronted with the fact that he has made her pregnant and has to marry her. But the baby is deformed — limbless and with a fish-like head. Mary moves into Henry's gloomy bed-sit but soon leaves him. Henry is left to look after the baby but accidentally kills it when it falls sick.

Lynch uses this simple plot as a springboard for revelling in the potential of the medium for its own sake, eschewing conventional rules of narrative and characterization. The pace is deliciously slow to exaggerate the bleakness of the environment: Elevator doors take forever to close, labored pauses punctuate the strained dialogue. Haunting, symbolic imagery is beautifully photographed in black-and-white, such as the opening and closing shots of the scarred signalman who pulls levers and seems to chart our course through this world. John Nance gives an immensely likable performance as the wide-eyed Henry, a shy and lost victim of circumstance.

The gurgling baby is a disturbingly lifelike creation. When it gets sick, Henry cuts the bandages around its torso, giving rise to one of the cinema's great sicko moments: He accidentally cuts through the baby's body as well. Horrified by what he has done and the sight of the baby's exposed internal organs, he decides to put it out of its misery and punctures one of its lungs with a pair of scissors. This is distressing splatter on a par with the most outrageous effects of *The Evil Dead* and the films of David Cronenberg.

The film is full of bizarre moments that seem to defy explanation. One of these is a short sequence that employs some basic stop-motion. One morning, Henry finds a strange maggot-like thing in his mailbox and puts it in a cabinet in his room. In the middle of the night, the cabinet doors open by themselves. The maggot-thing starts to wriggle about. Somehow, it wriggles onto a cratered landscape like the surface of the Moon, disappearing down holes and reappearing. It starts to enlarge and a huge mouth appears in one end of it. Seen in six stop-motion cuts, the maggot-thing is just a simple piece of plasticine.

Lynch's subsequent films include *The Elephant Man, Dune* and *Blue Velvet.*

The Evil Dead

1983. Renaissance Pictures. D-Scr: Sam Raimi. Ph: Tim Philo. Mus: Joe Loduca. Special Makeup Effects: Tom Sullivan. Photographic Special Effects: Bart Pierce.

Cast: Bruce Campbell, Ellen Sandweiss, Hal Delrich, Betsy Baker, Sarah York.

Rating: ☆☆☆   Stop-Motion: ☆☆☆

This is one of the great horror films of the 1980s and its climax uses stop-motion to novel and unforgettable effect. *The Evil Dead* grabs the splatter genre by the throat and takes it to new extremes of graphic gore, yet it is never repellent because Sam Raimi directs with great manic gusto and always plays up the ridiculous. He takes a conventional splatter premise (a group of kids stranded in a forest holiday cabin) but avoids the usual maniac-on-the-loose plot in favor of a full-blooded Grand Guignol style based on the supernatural and full of sensational, surreal images.

There is not much plot to speak of.

After a sinisterly foreboding opening 15 minutes, the film becomes a relentless series of technically astonishing exercises in showing characters being attacked, possessed by demons, disfigured or dismembered. The brilliantly sustained pace means that the film seems to end all too soon. The superb camerawork, always on the move, really throws the audience around by the scruff of its neck. An intelligently varied barrage of sound effects — heartbeats, clocks chiming, blood dripping, zombies screeching — makes dialogue almost redundant.

Frantic, wide-eyed Bruce Campbell as the only survivor gives one of the horror genre's best performances. He spends most of the film drenched by the gallons of fake blood that seem to pour out of everywhere and everyone. The stiff-necked, jerky movements of the possessed characters really do suggest re-animated corpses. Favorite moments include a possessed girl viciously calling out the value of playing cards she cannot see; dismembered arms and legs wriggling on the floor after an ax attack; a hole viciously gouged in someone's ankle with a pencil; Campbell wrestling with his decapitated girlfriend while her cackling head looks on; and a rape by trees — which sounds foolish on paper but in fact is very skillfully staged.

The climactic decomposition of the demons is a visual feast and uses a number of cleverly manipulative stops and starts to insure that the audience suffers as much as possible. Tom Sullivan and Bart Pierce spent three and a half months putting together a knockout sequence full of over-the-top sick moments whose lack of realism fits in perfectly with the style of what has gone before. Clay animation is used to show skin breaking up, pustules exploding, skin peeling away to reveal flesh and bone and so on. Two exposures per frame were taken to create greater fluidity of animation. Several shots use inventive in-camera mattes. There are 17 stop-motion cuts.

Campbell throws the skin-bound "Book of the Dead" into a fireplace, causing two demon-possessed characters to stop in their tracks. In two closeups, the skin of a blank-eyed, blue-faced girl-demon starts to peel away and her lips crack. It looks as though a matte follows the outline of her face, because her hair falls out in a live-action area of the same shot.

The live-action body and arm of another demon is combined by split-screen with a stop-motion hand and head. While the live-action body writhes convulsively, the hand and head break up, flesh seeming to crawl out of holes that appear in the skin. The flesh on the hand falls away, revealing the bone underneath. It's like watching time-lapse photography of a cut of meat rotting away. The hands of the girl-demon reach out in front of her, opening and closing as bits of them drop off (presumably wire-supported) and her blue face turns red as the flesh crawls its way to the surface.

The head of the zombie on the floor continues to decompose disgustingly. Part of its forehead is a live-action element matted into the rotting claymation head around it — this allows some live-action goo to bubble out of a hole in the front of the skull. There is a jerk in this shot where the registration wasn't held steady but few audiences notice this among all the mayhem. In three close-ups, an absurdly long tongue snakes out of the girl-demon's mouth and slurps around her cheek. By now all her hair and most of her features are gone, and her face is a mess of crawling maggots. These shots are matched by two animated shots of the book, an equally obscene tongue poking out of the face carved in its cover. Flames are superimposed.

After a teasing 25-second silence, everything erupts again into a frenzy of activity as live-action arms suddenly burst out of the stomachs of the two zombies. An ingenious long shot of the girl-demon has the now-shrunken animated head matted on top of a live-action prop body with several arms flailing wildly out from it. In closeup, her still-decaying head falls forward, then there are two magnificent cuts of the head falling straight down onto the camera, the face still writhing and falling apart, the camera moving backwards as though trying to get out of the way. It's a shocking image that has the distorted perspective of a nightmare. In the last stop-motion cut, the other zombie's head dissolves into a mushy gray goo, matted into some bubbling live-action pools of unpleasant-looking liquids.

The Evil Dead was a big commercial success and spawned two sequels and many imitations, yet its wonderful stop-motion sequence remains unique.

Evil Dead II

1987. D: Sam Raimi. Scr: Sam Raimi, Scott Spiegel. Ph: Peter Deming. Art: Philip Duffin, Randy Bennett. Mus: Joseph Lo Duca. Special Makeup Designed and Created by Mark Shostrom. Animated Dance Sequence and Tree Branch and Rotten Apple Head: Doug Beswick Productions Inc. (The Dance: Stop-Motion Animation: Doug Beswick. Effects Photography Supervisor: Jim Aupperle. Stop-Motion Armature: Yancy Calzada.) Animator: Tom Sullivan. Henrietta Transformations and Hand Animation: Rick Catizone, Anivision.

Cast: Bruce Campbell, Sarah Berry, Dan Hicks, Kassie Wesley, Theodore Raimi, Denise Bixler.

Rating: ☆☆½   Stop-Motion: ☆☆½

This has passages where it is as good as the original but the net impression is of an indulgent mess. The first film had a riveting economy of narrative, but the sequel is a collection of great moments, not a satisfying unit held together by a sense of style.

As before, the wildly active camera adds energy to even the most mundane sequences. For example, when Ash (Bruce Campbell again) falls down a flight of steps, the camera follows him down in three fast-moving cuts, making the audience feel that they are falling too. The film is full of imaginative, outrageous moments. A demon's eyeball pops out and flies into a girl's mouth. Another demon picks up a victim and smashes his head into a light bulb. And gallons of blood spurt from the walls and drench Ash.

Evil Dead II (1987), the "Dancing Corpse," seen here with animation gauges in the miniature set, was deftly animated by Doug Beswick.

This is all too over-the-top to be offensive and at its best the film is responsible for establishing a new genre: splatter-farce. Gore has been done tongue-in-cheek many times, but never like this. Much of the tone derives from Campbell's fine performance; he keeps a straight face even during absurd scenes such as when he tries to dislodge his girlfriend's decapitated head, which has sunk its teeth into his hand, by bashing it against walls and rushing out into the night with the head gurgling and giggling as he swings his arm about wildly. Or during an equally well-judged sequence when his hand becomes possessed and smashes all the kitchen crockery over his head. Sadly missing from the sequel is the famous wobbling zombie-strut which made the demons of the first film chilling as well as ludicrous; there are no scary moments in the sequel.

After Tom Sullivan's stop-motion *tour de force* in the first film, there were hopes that *Evil Dead II* would take the medium even further. In fact, these sequences are disappointing, especially so given that not only Sullivan but also Doug Beswick, James Aupperle and others worked on the film. Perhaps they were restrained by the low budget ($3 million), because in many instances the choreography of the animation is stilted with the effect that cuts to puppet shots are always conspicuous and conflict with the live action. Even more of a shame is the fact that all the models are exquisitely designed and detailed yet barely on the screen long enough to realize their potential (with the exception of Beswick's dancing corpse). Consequently, these scenes may have done more harm than good to the stop-motion medium, reinforcing the misguided belief held by some that it is an unconvincing process.

Sullivan animated the bizarre little demons seen in the prologue, including a bat-like creature and a spider-like creature, both with skull-heads, and a skin-bound copy of the Necronomicon with a monstrous face on the cover that comes to life and opens its huge mouth. All are glimpsed only fleetingly and never seen again.

Sullivan also animated the harpy-like Deadite in the final scene in which Ash finds himself transported back to the Middle Ages. It's a fine model with a vaguely human and very vicious, ancient-looking face. It swoops down to menace the knights in three stop-motion cuts and one live-action cut. In two side views, it flies across a very grainy rear projection of the knights, then flies straight at Ash in a long shot. In this cut Ash, aiming his rifle at the monster, is a blue-screen element, allowing the puppet's wings to pass behind the actor. The final shot is a live-action splatter effect in which the creature is shot in the head and explodes messily. The scene is too brief and gratuitous, gives the impression that Sullivan didn't have enough

time to test his set-ups and is a missed opportunity for such a mean-looking model.

Beswick is the most experienced animator of the team and his sequence (created with Aupperle's assistance) is the best. It is one of the few occasions when a stop-motion puppet has been genuinely creepy. There are ten stop-motion cuts, all done rear-screen and some make use of a miniature floor and tree which blend nicely with the forest in the rear plate. The puppet was sculpted and painted by Mark Trcic over an armature built by Yancy Calzada. It consists of a girl's decomposed body and a fresh, still rosy-looking head: The idea is that the previously buried body has started to rot while the head, chopped off by Ash, is still in reasonable condition. The sequence is Beswick's favorite among all his own stop-motion sequences.

The headless puppet performs a balletic dance, bends over, rejoins with its head, pirouettes, rolls its head down its arm and then back up onto its head again, pirouettes wildly again but this time leaves its head stationary (in best mock-*Exorcist* fashion), then finally skips over a branch in the rear screen and disappears into the night. It's an elegant sequence and Beswick's animation is always smooth but never convinces that this is more than a puppet: In trying to recreate actual human movement (as opposed to the usual subjects of stop-motion such as dinosaurs, aliens and so on), he has been too ambitious. The perspective is too obviously a locked-off tabletop set-up. The model seems to have been animated against a black background and merely superimposed.

If this was intended to make the corpse seem ghostly, then it didn't work — instead the effect just looks "unfinished."

Also, he is let down by the fact that the head not only fails to look sufficiently lifelike but also has blond hair whereas the actress to whom it is supposed to correspond had red hair — another instance of not having adequate resources to pre-test effects shots properly.

Beswick also handled two non-animation effects sequences, the "tree branch" which transforms into a huge hand and grabs Ash, and the "rotten apple head," the enormous face that appears in the hut's doorway at the climax only to get a chainsaw in its eye.

After Ash has chainsawed his hand off, it takes on a life of its own. Mark Shostrom designed several versions of it for different shots, including a radio-controlled one and a stop-motion one (animated by Rick Catizone) which scampers across the floor in one cut and drums its fingers impatiently in another.

Shostrom was in overall control of the memorable Henrietta-transformation scene, which includes four animation cuts. Henrietta, a disgusting, bloated corpse, shoots up through the cellar trap door, floats around the room, grabs her daughter by the hair, then gets beaten about by Ash, brandishing his chainsaw. Not to be subdued, she transforms into her true demonic form.

Through a combination of stop-motion and replacement animation, the puppet's neck grows longer and its head changes into a deformed, toothy, skull-like demon, screaming like an enraged chimpanzee as it sways from side to side.

This is a splendidly nightmarish closeup, animated again by Catizone, the camera tilting up as the neck extends. Intercut with closeup shots of a live-action head, it shouts out in a Popeye-like voice, "I'll swallow your soul! I'll swallow your soul!" Three rear-screen shots from behind the puppet (seen from the waist up) show the snake-like neck threatening Ash, and in one of them there is a moment of implied physical contact when Henrietta's head seems to knock into Ash.

The pace is pretty frantic at this point and the shots are very dark, but the graininess of the rear plate is still more conspicuous than it should be. There is no more stop-motion in this sequence but it continues in a similar manic splatter vein when Ash cuts off the demon's arms and heads with his chainsaw, then blows the still-living head apart with his rifle.

Stop-motion is used again in a brief and enjoyably sick cut to show worms wriggling about in the head of a demon that pokes up through a trap door. Also deserving mention is an attractive long shot, done entirely in miniature, showing Ash standing on one side of a ravine where demon forces have twisted the bridge into what resembles a skeletal hand. Ash is a smoothly animated puppet and the rest of the shot is a superior painting — it's the kind of fantasy image that recalls the milieu of *King Kong*.

Although ultimately disappointing, *Evil Dead II* is so full of eye-boggling effects that it has to be seen more than once.

The Ewok Adventure (Theatrical release title [Europe and Japan]: *Caravan of Courage—An Ewok Adventure*)

1984. Lucasfilm/ABC-TV. D-Ph: John Korty. Scr: Bob Carrau. Story: George Lucas. Art: Joe Johnston. Mus: Peter Bernstein. Visual Effects: Industrial Light and Magic. Visual Effects Supervisor: Michael Pangrazio. Post Production Effects Supervisor: Dennis Muren. Matte Painting Supervisors: Craig Barron, Chris Evans. Matte Artists: Frank Ordaz, Caroleen Green. Additional Matte Paintings: Effects Associates (Jim Danforth). ILM Creature Shop Supervisor: David Sosalla. Creature Supervisors: Phil Tippett, Jon Berg. Borra Puppet Sculptor (uncredited): Randal M. Dutra. Additional Special Effects: VCE.

Cast: Eric Walker, Aubree Miller, Warwick Davis, Fionulla Flanagan, Guy Boyd, Burl Ives (narration).

Rating: ☆☆½   Stop-Motion: ☆☆☆

This 1984 offshoot of the *Star Wars* saga is a TV movie aimed at children, but it still has much to recommend it, chiefly a brief but superb example of Phil Tippett and Jon Berg's animation skills and about two dozen excellent matte paintings by visual effects supervisor Michael Pangrazio and his team of artists. The paintings depict dramatic skylines, ravines, rolling hills, the tree houses of the Ewoks (three-foot-high teddy-bear–like creatures who were first encountered in *Return of the Jedi*) and the stone fortress of the Goraks. In the stop-motion episode, they form a picturesque backdrop of dense forest to a battle between a group of Ewoks and a Borra, a wart-hog the size of a dinosaur.

This ferocious model, designed by Tippett, has a slavering mouth full of huge teeth, a wet snout, claws like a bear, a leathery hide, knots of hair all along its spine and a swishing tail. Randal Dutra sculpted and fabricated the animation puppet and also sculpted a hand puppet used for some closeups. Shots of the animation puppet are intercut with shots of an impressive mechanical prop, used for closeups of the hog snarling or biting on a spear that has been thrust at it. This full-size prop was a team effort built by Tippett, Berg and Dutra. There are only nine stop-motion cuts, but it seems like a lot more because of all the live-action and prop cut-aways.

The hog is first seen in silhouette in an attractive miniature set, a five-second cut in which it howls like a wolf at the moon, its tail swishing gently behind it. This is followed by an attractive night-time long shot of the Ewok campsite, consisting of a painted setting, a live-action element of flickering flames and a flock of what appear to be stop-motion birds flying behind a foreground painted tree.

The hog later chases the two children

through the forest, a sequence achieved mainly with partial shots of the prop head and prop legs, but also using one fine stop-motion cut to depict the beast in full, running through the trees as the boy fires his laser at it, causing the model to light up momentarily in a flash of sparks.

The children take shelter overnight in a hollow tree trunk and are awakened next morning by the sound of the battle between the hog and the Ewoks. This is a real Harryhausen-style set-piece, the chief difference being that all the composites here are achieved by traveling matte instead of Harryhausen's favored static matte. In all the animation shots, the Ewoks are in the foreground, having been filmed standing on a studio stage decked out with bushes and rocks in front of a blue screen, reacting to an imagined adversary.

This means that the amount of interaction between the two elements is restricted. In one cut, the hog's paw seems to knock over an Ewok; a few seconds later, a second Ewok seems to slap the hog's face with his spear. Otherwise, all interaction is implied through the editing. For example, the moment when an Ewok jumps onto the hog's back (shades of *Mysterious Island* and *Golden Voyage of Sinbad*) consists of a shot showing the costumed actor swinging on a vine, then cuts to the hog with an animated miniature Ewok on its back. Another cut varies the perspective slightly by having the hog (on the left of frame) snapping at two Ewoks on the right, then charging at them. But basically it's the same design as in all the other six cuts that make up this sequence.

The final cut is filmed from a lower angle so as to heighten the impact of the action. An Ewok rushes straight at the camera, pursued by the hog, which, weakened by a poisoned dart in its side, crashes to the ground mere inches away from us. The last few seconds of this impressive moment seem to switch from stop-motion to live action: The hog's last movements as it hits the ground are blurred, suggesting that the puppet may have been manipulated by off-screen rods.

In all, this is an exciting sequence, animated with Tippett's usual excellence and ILM's customary high standard of matte work. On this occasion, the budget would not stretch to using the go-motion techniques that had been so successful in *The Empire Strikes Back*, *Dragonslayer* and *Return of the Jedi*. Even without it, the vicious dynamism of the hog again demonstrates the potential of stop-motion as a means of achieving fantasy effects.

Not everyone was impressed by this excellent sequence. For example, Bill Kelley in *Cinefantastique* (May 1985) wrote that the film's "effects shortcomings, particularly a jerky animation sequence of a monster chasing its tiny prey through the woods, should make moviegoers' jaws drop."

Later on in the film, we encounter a giant Gorak in his lair, a long-haired, long-snouted, pointy-eared creature (actually Jon Berg wearing a suit he built himself) filmed at high speed. It's a good makeup and, as these kind of sequences go, imaginatively handled. The creature is thought defeated when it falls into a ravine, but it climbs back out again, only to be sent hurtling to its death when it is forced back off the edge of the ravine. In both cuts in which the character falls away from the camera down into the ravine, it appears that a stop-motion puppet of the Gorak was used, making slight movements as it flails its arms and legs. These are very convincing effects and were presumably a cheaper option than using a stuntman and wire-rigging.

Ewoks—The Battle for Endor

1985. Lucasfilm/ABC Television. D: Jim and Ken Wheat. Teleplay: Ken and Jim Wheat. Story: George Lucas. Ph: Isidore Mankofsky. Art: Joe Johnston. Mus: Peter Bernstein. Special Visual Effects: Industrial Light and Magic. Visual Effects Supervisor: Michael McAlister. Stop-Motion Supervisor: Phil Tippett. Stop-Motion Animators: Tom St. Amand, Randy Dutra. Stop-Motion Photography: Harry Walton, Terry Chostner, Michael Owens, Patrick McArdle. Stop-Motion Miniatures: Tamia Marg, Sheila Duignan. Creature Designer: Jon Berg. Matte Painting Supervisors: Chris Evans, Craig Barron. Matte Artists: Michael Pangrazio, Lazarus, Caroleen Green, Sean Joyce. Additional Visual Effects: VCE/Peter Kuran.

Cast: Wilford Brimley, Warwick Davis, Aubree Miller, Sian Phillips, Paul Gleason, Carel Struycken.

Rating: ☆☆☆   Stop-Motion: ☆☆☆

The first Ewok telefilm was an adequate adventure fantasy aimed at children, and boasted one excellent stop-motion episode by Phil Tippett. This follow-up is an all-around better production: a simple plot told inventively, a small cast of likable characters and many deft touches of gentle humor. Most importantly, it has its finger on the pulse of what makes a good fantasy milieu. Add to that a number of discreet yet unforgettable stop-motion sequences by Tippett and his team, and you have a modest minor classic.

Most of the action takes place in a dense jungle, some on a perilous cliff face and the rest in an enjoyably dingy castle. Fine matte paintings by Chris Evans, Michael Pangrazio and others add to the fantasy atmosphere in the same way that they enhanced the look of the previous Ewok film: These are worlds that O'Brien would have approved of. Just one painting sneaked past ILM's usual criteria for excellence: The coloring of a painting that surrounds Cindle and Wicket on a cliff face is poorly matched.

The little heroine is as cute as she was in the first film (but never offensively so) and one of the creatures she befriends is an endearing three-foot-high white-furred thing called Teek who whizzes about at high speed. The lively baddies are Sian Phillips as a wicked witch and a gang of grisly-faced aliens with gravelly voices.

Tippett is "Stop-Motion Supervisor" of sequences involving a vicious giant bird and some elephant-like bipeds on which the aliens ride around. His

Above: A frame enlargement from ***Ewoks—the Battle for Endor*** (1985) shows one of the "Tadpoles from Hell" and a puppet soldier preparing for battle. The "Tadpole" was designed by Phil Tippett and sculpted by Randal Dutra. ***Below:*** Poster art of a "Tadpole."

output during this period constantly amazed both in quantity and quality. In *Battle for Endor*, the effects are not always flawless but when they are good they are magnificent. The bizarre models once again demonstrate the unlimited potential of stop-motion, perhaps best demonstrated in one particular composite (described later) which rates as one of the most beautiful in the genre.

The first animation cut occurs during the aliens' attack on the Ewok camp in the forest. Two growling cart-beasts, harnessed to wagons made from giant rib-bones, are being tended by one of the aliens as the battle rages. These fabulous models, dubbed the Tadpoles from Hell by the crew, are based on an early but unused design Tippett did for the taun-taun and were sculpted and painted by Randy Dutra. They have the rough hide of an elephant, two strong legs, tiny, use-less arms like a tyrannosaur, a muscular, newt-like tail for balancing and an enor-mous head with fish-lips and a savage set of teeth. In this thoughtfully designed composite, one model is in the fore-ground on the right and the other is in the middle distance on the left. In be-tween them, the live-action alien adjusts the covers of one of the wagons. Behind them is a background of trees, broken up by shafts of sunlight. It's an impec-cable composite, the ingenious but sub-tle perspective of puppet-actor-puppet succeeding in meshing the different ele-ments into one image.

The same set-up is later used again, but this time Tippett adds another di-mension by having a live actor (a travel-ing matte) cross the shot in the extreme foreground. In this cut, the foreground tadpole scratches its cheek and growls: Yes, this nice touch is Tippett's way of acknowledging his affection for O'Brien.

The next animation cut is another one to relish: A third tadpole, this one with a puppet rider on its back, is squat-ting forward on bent legs and slowly gets up. Having captured the Ewoks, the wagon train moves off and there is a shot of two tadpoles, animated riders on their backs, pulling the carts. The slow lum-bering way that they drag the carts be-hind them suggests that Tippett and an-imator Tom St. Amand have studied the movements of elephants.

John Ford seems to have inspired the next stop-motion cut, a beautiful long shot of the wagon train trudging through the forest, a red and yellow sun-set lighting up the sky behind the trees (actually a painting). A shot of three tad-poles pulling carts up a slight incline is timed so that only two models are ever in the frame at one time, presumably be-cause only two were constructed. In this rear-projection shot, the puppets are carefully aligned with the live-action carts.

Wicket and Cindle manage to drop out from the bottom of one of the carts onto the path but are nearly trampled by the tadpole walking behind them, a brief ground-level animation cut looking up at the advancing monster.

The little heroes escape from their captors and take refuge in a cave halfway up a cliff. Assembling a hang glider, Wicket inadvertently awakens the cave's occupant, a giant bird whose head looks like a cross between Godzilla and Rep-tilicus with big, yellow eyes, a savage beak and a nasty set of fangs. It was designed, sculpted and fabricated by Randy Dutra. Its expansive bat wings re-call the design of Vermithrax Perjorative.

Whereas the tadpoles had been in-cidental to the earlier scenes, the bird has a more dramatic role to play, in the best tradition of a Harryhausen battle. The plot could have merely had the charac-ters float out of the cave on the hang glider and crashland in the forest below without the interference of the bird, but instead gives us an entertaining and in-ventive episode.

After a shock closeup of the squawk-ing creature, a long shot shows it stomp-ing after the fleeing Wicket on long, thin legs, its long arms hanging down in front, its wings flapping slowly. A matte following a wall in the cave allows the bird to appear from around a corner. Two further closeups (animated by Dutra) of the bird snapping at Wicket are enhanced by a blurring of the head, achieved by means of a go-motion rod which moved the head slightly during the frame exposure.

In a rear-projection long shot, Wicket tries to fend off the bird using a long bone as a spear, but the bird snatches it away in its mouth — a textbook piece of interaction. Wicket throws a rock which is blue-screened over the puppet, recoiling to suggest the impact. Similarly, a burning torch thrown by Cindle is blue-screened against the puppet, which itself is blue-screened into the full-scale studio cave set. This impressive composite ends with the bird running from background to foreground.

A smaller model is used in the next three cuts as it is seen (from Wicket's point of view inside the cave) flying off with a miniature puppet of Cindle in its claws. The fluid animation of the wings and the general look of these shots again recall Tippett's work in *Dragonslayer*. In one of these shots, Wicket is on a miniature hang glider and flies behind the bird. In a very quick cut, the bird flies at the camera with the puppet Cindle in its claws. This suffers from a poor traveling matte but is followed by an attractive medium shot of the bird again flying straight at the camera with Wicket in hot pursuit in the background.

An aerial view looking down at the bird from Wicket's glider shows its astonishingly realistic detail: The wings pull and wrinkle, the skin on its back folds and wrinkles with each wing-flap and the head glances slowly from side to side. Wicket drops a miniature rock onto the bird's head and the prop claws release Cindle. In a long shot of both models, Wicket's glider ducks below the bird in pursuit of the falling Cindle, and the bird hovers momentarily before swooping down after them. In live-action shots, Wicket catches Cindle then crash-lands in the forest. There is an attractive composite looking up from ground level at the bird hovering, then flying off behind some (presumably miniature) trees, backed by a painting of a night sky. The episode closes with a beautiful long shot of the bird flying off into the distance, blue-screened against a matte painting of a moon hanging over a picturesque valley.

In the climax, Wicket and Cindle free the captured Ewoks from the castle and are pursued back into the forest by the aliens. Included in the scene of the aliens preparing for the pursuit is a fine shot in the castle forecourt of an animated soldier holding a tadpole on a leash. The anxious monster pulls the soldier to and fro while three blue-screened live-action soldiers cross the foreground. These traveling mattes are poor but not a problem because they are in the extreme foreground and the audience's eyes are focused on the tadpole in the background. For a brief second, a blue-screened tadpole also crosses the shot.

The next stop-motion shot, referred to earlier, is the best in the film. It's a panoramic view of a grassy plain sloping away into the distance, the backdrop a painting of snow-capped mountains. A scattered army of shouting aliens runs from the foreground to the background. In the middle distance stands one of the tadpoles, swaying from side to side and growling angrily, an animated rider on its back. This 100 percent–convincing composite appears to be a rear-projection static matte set-up, the matte line following a bump in the contours of the plain. The rider turns his mount and sets off in the direction of the army just as a second mounted tadpole stomps into the lower-right foreground, heightening the impression of great activity in the shot.

The animation shots in the forest, intercut with many live-action cuts of the soldiers and Ewoks, recall the complex set-ups that Tippett used to put his Scout-Walkers in a similar setting in *Return of the Jedi*. The first shot, another impeccable composite, has soldiers running at the camera through the trees with a tadpole walking between them, its mount urging it on. As it advances, it pushes two small trees aside, a design that is perhaps another nod to *King Kong*, recalling the moment when Kong first appears at the altar to which Fay Wray is tied and knocks two trees out of his way. A miniature shot (i.e., not using a matte) has a tadpole and its rider walk across the frame, the depth broken up by some miniature trees.

Some soldiers run through branches in the foreground as two growling tadpoles move around in the background. The foreground action in this excellent composite is dark and shadowy compared to the brighter miniature background, making this look almost as though the actors performed in front of a color rear screen. However, this is extremely unlikely. Rotoscope mattes were probably drawn around the actors to en-

able the puppets to seem to be behind them. There is certainly no blue spill anywhere to suggest this is a traveling matte.

The film's last animation cuts again feature the tadpoles. Two of the beasts have been tied up in the forest during the aliens' final battle with the Ewoks. As before, the tadpoles are not the center of the action but merely one entertaining element of a more involved episode. The main point of interest is whether or not our heroes will get their spaceship to take off before the aliens can catch them.

In a rear-projection shot, dappled sunlight from between the trees falls on the leathery hides of the two beasts as one of them idly chomps on a nearby branch. Teek hurries in between their legs (accurate full-scale props) and starts a fire. Rising smoke is superimposed over the next three stop-motion cuts in which one of the tadpoles, its foot burning, opens its huge red mouth and roars loudly. Its eyes nearly pop out of its head in best cartoon fashion and it runs off out of the frame.

In an attractive long shot, the two creatures gallop across the frame, the shot broken up by several miniature trees in the foreground. There is something absurd about these ungainly, unlikely two-legged animals scampering at high speed, yet at the same time the animators succeed in making them utterly convincing. Up until this shot, one might have thought that Tippett had learned from the poor audience reaction to the galloping taun-taun in *The Empire Strikes Back* and decided to keep his animals slow and ponderous, but this cut shows that he is still prepared to tackle difficult movements. Not just tackle them, but pull them off brilliantly. For this shot, one tadpole was animated by St. Amand and the other by Dutra, this being the only Tadpole animation that Dutra executed.

The final animation cut has the two beasts charging right at the camera (on a miniature floor matched to the rear-projected live forest) and there is a lot of blur and camera shake in the movement. This kind of movement is almost identical to the closing shot of the giant boar

episode in *Caravan of Courage* when the drugged monster crashed to the ground. They are both extremely dynamic shots, achieved by combining conventional animation with frames where the puppet has been moved by hand during the exposure to create a blur.

Once again, Tippett and his team have come up with some remarkable images, using stop-motion to portray thrilling fantasy creatures in a way that no other technical medium has yet matched.

Explorers

1985. Paramount/Edward S. Feldman. D: Joe Dante. Scr: Eric Luke. Ph: John Hora. Art: Robert E. Boyle. Mus: Jerry Goldsmith. Special Makeup Effects: Rob Bottin. Special Visual Effects: Industrial Light and Magic. Visual Effects Supervisor: Bruce Nicholson. Matte Painting Supervisor: Michael Pangrazio. Character Miniature Supervisor: Dave Sosalla. Character Miniature Crew: Charlie Bailey, Sean Casey, Robert Cooper, Anthony Laudati, Marghe McMahon, Margo Phillips.

Cast: Ethan Hawke, River Phoenix, Jason Presson, Amanda Peterson, Dick Miller, Robert Picardo.

Rating: ☆☆☆   Stop-Motion: ☆☆½

This lacks the sharpness of wit of Joe Dante's earlier fantasies *Piranha, The Howling* and *Gremlins*, where hackneyed plots were made to look fresh again. *Explorers* is offbeat and entertaining but is too self-indulgent for its own good. A group of three kids are transported to a spaceship occupied by two aliens who

have been brought up on an exclusive diet of American television. Everything they say or do is an impersonation of some screen personality or a rock 'n' roll song. Clips from television shows and movies are displayed on huge screens inside the spacecraft (among them *Earth vs. the Flying Saucers* and *20 Million Miles to Earth*). By trivializing everything to the point of becoming in-jokes, Dante loses audience involvement.

The aliens are the creations of Rob Bottin, credibly blubbery yet at the same time outlandish cartoon figures. Eventually they turn out to be only kids and are ticked off by their huge-bellied alien father. All are played by actors in elaborate costumes connected to wire systems that operate eyelids and other features.

Inside the spaceship, the boys are exploring a shadowy corridor when a huge mechanical spider-machine appears. This nightmarish creation chases them along the corridor, but when it catches up with them it is only interested in probing, photographing and decontaminating them. In shots where it must interact closely with the boys, the machine is depicted with full-scale mechanical devices. But in three long shots in which it is seen walking, stop-motion is used.

Animated smoothly by Anthony Laudati (a long-time stop-motion fan turned professional), the nine-inch puppet was shot in a miniature set of the tunnel. One especially striking cut of the robot has the two boys running from it into the foreground. They are bluescreen elements, seen in full by virtue of the fact that the blue-screen set on which they were filmed extended under their feet. Cel animated shadows have been added underneath them to enhance the composite.

For such a marvelous creation — reminiscent of the spider-machine in storyboards for the unfilmed sequence in *Mysterious Island*— it seems disappointing that it could not have been used in a more substantial scene. But how many times has that been said of stop-motion puppets?

Laudati also animated an earlier cut of one of the boys (River Phoenix) inside the floating bubble that serves as their means of transport. Hovering above a field, the sphere suddenly plunges down into the earth, with a puppet of the boy spinning inside it. This of course is "functional" animation and no one would know they were not watching an actor unless told so.

The Fabulous World of Jules Verne see Vynález Zkázy

Fantasia

1940. Walt Disney. D: Samuel Armstrong, James Algar, Bill Roberts, Paul Satterfield, Hamilton Luske, Jim Handley, Ford Beebe, T. Hee, Norman Ferguson, Wilfred Jackson. Production Supervisor: Ben Sharpsteen. Story Direction: Joe Grant, Dick Huemer.

With: Leopold Stokowski and the Philadelphia Orchestra. Narrator: Deems Taylor.

Rating: ☆☆☆☆   Stop-Motion: N/A.

Fantasia, Disney's masterpiece, contains one brief sequence which, like *Pinocchio* (1939), was achieved by having the artists trace their images over previously shot stop-motion footage.

Right at the end of "The Nutcracker Suite" sequence, a stream of large snowflakes glides down from the sky, drifts across the screen and is met by some fairies who float into the centers of some of the snowflakes, which then spin around them like skirts lifted by a breeze.

The flakes spin and turn with graceful ease, catching the light and shadows as they progress through this series of shots. In order to supply the artists with a guide to the complex choreography and lighting, these shots were first executed using metal models of the flakes, animated one frame at a time. The resultant stop-motion footage was then rotoscoped by the artists and combined with other drawn images and backgrounds. The result is a visually stunning sequence in which the snowflakes have a potent three-dimensional quality.

It may well be that other sequences in Disney films have also derived from stop-motion footage, but no further details have yet come to light.

The concept of basing a finished image on previously shot stop-motion footage surfaced again over 50 years later when *Jurassic Park* (1993) used stop-motion film of dinosaur models as a basis for much of its computer generated imagery.

Faust

1994. Czech Republic. Athanor. D-Scr: Ján Švankmajer. Ph: Svatopluk Maly. Animation: Bedřich Glaser.
Cast: Petr Čepek.

Rating: ☆☆½   Stop-Motion: ☆☆

Švankmajer's modern interpretation of Goethe's work is, like the director's *Alice* (1988), full of startling imagery. But it lacks the charm of the earlier film and is not populated by the grimly surreal stop-motion characters that made *Alice* so entertaining. Storytelling is not Švankmajer's strength and he is better suited to short subjects.

Compared to *Alice*, there is relatively little stop-motion. Instead, Švankmajer uses grotesque life-size string puppets (sometimes actors dressed up like string puppets) to represent Mephistopheles and other characters, interacting with his modern-day Faust, Petr Čepek. On this occasion, Švankmajer seems more interested in the general mood of his film, setting much of the action in an old run-down Czech house, a basement decked out like an alchemist's laboratory and a musty old theater.

As before, the stop-motion sequences are animated in part by Bedřich Glaser and again much of it looks jerky and hurried—Švankmajer is not interested in smooth, realistic movements but in jarring images. Furniture moves about a room of its own accord, fruit in a bowl suddenly decomposes when Faust looks at it, and some weird, bony creatures (in the style of some of *Alice*'s puppets) scuttle around the alchemist's laboratory. The most ambitious stop-motion episode is a battle between good and evil puppets, the protagonists all only six inches tall. Evil puppets clamber out of the head of a statue and attack the good puppets, beating them up, pulling them apart and (in one case) raping them. It's a diverting little vignette, but again the hurried animation is distracting.

Fiend

1980. D: David W. Renwick. Special Effects: Don Dohler.

Cast: Don Leifert, Richard Nelson, Elaine White, George Stover, Greg Dohler.

Rating: ☆☆   Stop-Motion: ☆☆

Sometimes fans make good movies. And sometimes they don't. Don Dohler, a longtime fan of stop-motion, deserves credit for achieving what most armchair critics (this author included) only theorize about, but he also deserves to be dragged over the coals for producing such a depressingly conventional movie.

Fiend is an ultra-cheap maniac-on-the-loose film almost entirely lacking in invention and with a pace that frequently threatens to grind to a halt altogether. There are two redeeming features. At the end, the maniac decomposes in an enjoyably gruesome set-piece. And at the start and finish of the film, the Fiend itself puts in an appearance: It is a bizarre stop-motion creation whose role in the plot is to re-animate the maniac's corpse.

The Fiend is a kind of cross between a meter-long orange wasp and an elephant with mandibles. It appears to have been simply superimposed over the live-action footage. It was probably created by Dohler in his spare time rather than being fashioned specifically for this film, since its limited movements here could easily have been achieved with a live-action prop. It floats around in an orange glow waving its long mandibles, but does little else. This is a shame because it's a nasty-looking creature and could have been used to generate a couple of good scares.

Not one of stop-motion's greatest moments.

Fiend Without a Face

1958. GB. Amalgamated. D: Arthur Crabtree. Scr: Herbert J. Leder. Based on the story "The Thought Monster" by Amelia Reynolds Long. Ph: Lionel Banes. Art: John Elphick. Mus: Buxton Orr. Special Effects: Baron Florenz von Nordhoff, Klaus-Ludwig Ruppel, Peter Nielsen.

Cast: Marshall Thompson, Terence

Kilburn, Kim Parker, Kynaston Reeves, Peter Madden, Michael Balfour.

Rating: ☆☆½   Stop-Motion: ☆☆☆

This British production is routine low-budget SF-horror, but its outrageous 15-minute finale is one of the classic special effects sequences of the 1950s.

A scientist (Kynaston Reeves) working at an atomic plant has inadvertently created "thought monsters" that suck out victims' brains and spinal columns, which they then use as their physical bodies. They are initially invisible and identified only by creepy slurping and shuffling sounds, but a surge in radiation from the plant causes them to become visible. Achieved by means of lively stop-motion, their night-time attack on a group of people stranded in a house is a *Grand Guignol* nightmare, a marvelous bit of high-energy splatter that prefigures the gruesome climax to *The Evil Dead* (1983).

Two Munich-based effects artists were recruited for the task: Baron Florenz von Nordhoff and Klaus-Ludwig Ruppel. Nordhoff designed and built the puppets, while Ruppel did most of the animation. These offbeat creatures are a perfect example of the limitless potential of stop-motion. Each is a human brain attached to a tail made up of vertebrae. On top of the "head" are two snaking antennae that look around hungrily for prey. The "tail" is used to push the creature along, shuffling like a caterpillar. Extending from the base of the brain are two long nerve-threads, used like arms to pull it along.

In some of the shots the animation is hurried, but in others Ruppel used a prototype go-motion system, connecting the puppets to a mechanism that was synchronized to the camera shutter and caused the puppet to make a slight movement while two frames of film were shot. As a result, some shots of the fiends flying through the air, rearing up on their tails or making other movements are extremely effective. Unlike today's go-motion sequences which attach the puppets to rods that are obscured by blue-screen mattes, Ruppel's puppets were attached to wires. These thin wires were rendered invisible because they were blurred during the two-frame exposure.

The stop-motion was shot in three weeks in Munich after the live-action photography was complete. In all, there are 80 stop-motion cuts, an astonishing amount of animation for a low-budget film. Interaction between puppets and actors is effectively suggested in a few rear-projection shots in which the brains launch themselves into the air and attack victims. Prop brains are used intelligently only in shots where they are required to do very little—when they are wrapped around a victim's neck, or at the climax when they fall out of trees. When the animated brains crawl over furniture in the house, mock-ups in the Munich studio match with the props in the live-action footage.

After several scenes featuring the creatures in their invisible state, one eventually materializes in two stop-motion cuts in the atomic plant control room. A dissolve is used to show the bizarre monster appearing, backed by a disgusting slurping noise and a pounding heartbeat. Several of the creatures are seen in some live-action shots of them in the trees surrounding the house in which all the characters are trapped. One of them shuffles down the side of a tree and crawls along the ground, a miniature set made of earth and long blades of grass. It rears up on its tail only to get shot, animated blood oozing from its wound.

Another drops down the chimney and its antennae wiggle threateningly at one of the actors. It leaps up at him (supported by wires), the camera cutting to a shot of the actor with a prop brain around his neck. Thrown to the floor, it makes a revolting gurgling noise when Marshall Thompson strikes it with an ax. The professor goes outside but three of the creatures fly at him, launching themselves from a miniature foreground floor. One is aligned so that it appears to land on his shoulder and gets knocked away by the professor. He falls to the ground and there is a gruesome shot of the creatures on his back, feeding on him noisily. A series of eight stop-motion cuts show the creatures in the bushes, crawling along the ground, getting shot by the soldiers in the house and oozing more dark blood.

Thompson runs to a hut containing some dynamite and is attacked by a brain. It shuffles along, rears up to "look" at him, then leaps (animated against a rear-screen) only to get shot in mid-air. On the ground, its tail and arms writhe desperately as blood oozes out.

An imaginatively conceived sequence has several of the creatures breaking the boards which have been hastily nailed up over one of the windows. One crawls along the ground and leaps up at the window; shot from inside, its antennae are seen wriggling obscenely through a gap in the boards. An-

other one reaches through and snatches away the hammer — a grimly humorous moment emphasizing that these are intelligent creatures.

The horrified group stare at the boards, now a seething mass of antennae and tails trying to reach through the gaps. A dynamic zoom-in shows the tail of one creature wrapped around a board, snapping it in two. In a fine shock effect, a brain flies through the hole. When it gets shot, its tail kicks up in the air and it twists over, oozing blood. Two more brains fly in, one landing on the floor, the other on a table, and they turn and stare at their intended victims. Both get shot but four more fly in. When one of these is shot, blood is splattered all over the wall behind it.

Another crawls up the side of an armchair and cocks its head interestedly at the heroine (Kim Parker) before also getting shot. Two more fly into the room and, in a clever moment enhancing the impression that actors and puppets are in the same location, one lands on the floor just as an actor has walked out of the frame. It gets shot but refuses to die straight away, crawling along with its two "arms" dragging limply by its side, before a second bullet finishes it off. Another brain crawls along, then launches itself at a rear-projection of the heroine (some superimposed smoke meshing the two elements). This brain also gets thrown to the floor and shot.

Back in the atomic plant, Thompson lights a fuse to destroy the radiation that is feeding the creatures. A brain crawls towards him, rears up and gets shot, its arms wriggling frantically. Half-dead, it crawls over to the fuse, intending to extinguish it, but expires just before it reaches it. The flame is a superimposed element.

In the house, another brain gets blasted and another flies in through the window. It lands on the armchair, sizes up the heroine and leaps up at her, at which point a prop brain is used again. However, the plant explodes and the brain now drops from her lifelessly. Several brains are seen dropping from the trees in live-action cuts. In six final stop-motion cuts, the fiends decompose by means of some splendidly messy replacement animation, reducing to gooey puddles, some of them in the house,

some outside on the ground. It's a great sicko ending to an unforgettable sequence.

A sure sign of the impact of Nordhoff and Ruppel's work is the fact that British censor John Trevelyan found the film "disgusting" and insisted on a number of cuts being made, and the film was banned outright in Ireland. *Fiend Without a Face* has a unique place among the science fiction films of its era — it's a shame that other producers didn't have the vision to see what stop-motion could contribute to otherwise ordinary films.

First Men in the Moon

1964. Columbia. D: Nathan Juran. Scr: Nigel Kneale, Jan Read. From the novel by H. G. Wells. Ph: Wilkie Cooper. Creator of Special Visual Effects: Ray Harryhausen. Mus: Laurie Johnson. Art: John Blezard. Technical Staff: Les Bowie, Kit West. Model Sculpture (uncredited): Arthur Hayward.

Cast: Edward Judd, Lionel Jeffries, Martha Hyer, Erik Chitty, Miles Malleson, Marne Maitland, Valentine Dyall, Peter Finch.

Rating: ☆☆☆   Stop-Motion: ☆☆½

This is one of Harryhausen's least typical films in that the story comes first and the animation is almost incidental: This is not a "stop-motion film." Instead of the episodic nature of the effects scenes in other films, here the animation is very low-key and complements the drive of the narrative rather than interrupting it. Partly as a result of originat-

ing from a strong literary source — the H. G. Wells novel — the script is one of the most coherent and satisfying of any Harryhausen film.

The first draft of the screenplay was by Nigel Kneale (his best work since *The Quatermass Experiment* in 1955) and was overhauled by Jan Read when Columbia bosses insisted that some love interest was included. Many story ideas also came from Harryhausen. Kneale conceived the ingenious prologue and epilogue, wherein a present-day expedition to the Moon discovers evidence that Man had reached there many years earlier (in Victorian times).

Nathan Juran, the only director with whom Harryhausen has worked three times, makes the quaint Victorian setting of the lengthy Earthbound section very agreeable. He keeps the pace ticking over very competently when the action shifts to the Moon and the grandeur of Harryhausen's designs takes over. Juran doesn't match the excitement and freshness he brought to *The 7th Voyage of Sinbad* but it's a vast improvement on his direction of *20 Million Miles to Earth*.

One of the reasons the film is still highly watchable today is Lionel Jeffries' Prof. Cavor, a fine comic performance of enthusiastic eccentricity. Cavor is the liveliest character in all Harryhausen's films and one of very few not immediately outclassed by the special effects. Edward Judd is likable as the "sensible" male lead but Martha Hyer is little more than a token female. (Compare her role with that of Sigourney Weaver in *Alien* [1979] to see how attitudes to women in SF changed in only 15 years.) The lively script and direction make their love scenes relatively painless. The film has an enjoyably "British" feel to it, with an amusing cameo by Miles Malleson as a doddery old clerk. There is an effective score — borrowing heavily from Bernard Herrmann — by Laurie Johnson, fresh from *Dr. Strangelove* and soon to compose the theme for TV's *The Avengers*.

There is comparatively little animation in the film. In the first 60 minutes, the only stop-motion to be found is a few shots of a miniature space shuttle in the prologue. There is no set-piece to compare with classic Harryhausen episodes like the skeleton battle of *Jason and the Argonauts* or the allosaurus attack in *One Million Years B.C.* There is an encounter with a giant Moon Cow but by comparison, this is undeveloped. Several semi-humanoid Selenites are animated but they are never required to do much more than stand around and look sinister. The film has none of the moments of interaction between puppet and actor which have become a trademark of some of Harryhausen's finest effects.

All this restraint was necessary because producer Charles Schneer had decided to shoot the film in Panavision. This wide-screen process prevented Harryhausen from using his traditional rear-projection methods, because the image is squeezed onto 35mm film and only reverts to its correct ratio when projected with an anamorphic lens. Consequently, all the animation had to be done in front of a blue screen, depriving Harryhausen of the ability to suggest puppet/actor interaction by lining his model up with a background image.

The irony today is that the film is rarely seen anywhere except on television where the impact of Panavision is totally lost. For example, a stunning moment when Judd swings precariously over a seemingly bottomless lunar pit was voted by readers of *FXRH* magazine as one of their favorite Harryhausen effects, yet on television it simply doesn't look special. But Schneer's choice was a good one — the lunar landscapes and subterranean world of the Selenites look magnificent when seen as originally intended. Occasionally, a CinemaScope print gets screened and a letter-box format print has recently been released on laserdisc, so all is not lost.

With less time needed on animation, Harryhausen was able to indulge other special effects skills. His fabulous lunar panoramas are realized in miniature settings (built by Les Bowie and his crew from Harryhausen's designs), matte paintings (also by Bowie) and full-scale sets. Some of Harryhausen's designs for long shots inside the Selenites' world are stunning. This film has more complete miniature sets than any other Harryhausen film and it highlights what a loss it is that he did not have the time or budget in other films to do similar things. Consider the Hyperborean shrine at the climax of *Sinbad and the Eye of the Tiger*, one of the most impressive settings of any fantasy film. The general standard of the traveling mattes, by means of which actors are dropped into the lunar sets, is very high, with only one or two exceptions. Several shots are very ambitious, consisting of up to four separate elements. The most convincing shots are extreme long shots where tiny actors are seen standing in seemingly enormous subterranean caverns.

There are five Selenite models — four scientists and the Grand Lunar. These bizarre creatures, sculpted (uncredited) by Arthur Hayward from Harryhausen's designs, exude otherworldly eeriness, which is more than can be said of the worker Selenites. These are realized by means of extras in costumes and, although Wilkie Cooper's camera sensibly keeps them in shadow most of the time, there are occasions where the lifelessness of their costumes is all too apparent. The stop-motion Moon Cow, a huge caterpillar-like monster, is a highly detailed, credible creation.

The lengthy prologue is very well done, employing realistic miniatures of a space capsule and mother ship which were based on NASA designs. Full-scale mock-ups of lunar 'scapes, built at Shepperton Studios, are also impressive. Harryhausen stop-frames the capsule as it descends to the Moon's surface and for once the "unnatural" look of animation — which is unable to obey the laws of gravity — is wholly appropriate because of course there is no gravity in space. On television, two composites of the capsule in space look very clumsy, with a pale area around the model revealing the extent of the matte. However, when seen at a cinema, the shot is flawless; presumably there is a slight color shift when film is transferred to television prints.

In 1899, Prof. Cavor has been experimenting with a paste that can block off the force of gravity. In a very convincing shot, the roof of his house explodes, sending a hail of glass and debris directly up into space. This was achieved with a matte combining the house in a live-action plate with a miniature roof which was filmed upside down to give the impression that the debris — actually falling downwards — has suddenly been released from the pull of gravity. The same technique is used ten minutes later when Cavor's space-sphere crashes up through the top of a miniature greenhouse.

The sphere hurtles away from the Earth, blue-screened against a superior matte painting of the great globe. It temporarily goes off course and has a close shave with the Sun (depicted rather disappointingly as just an expansive yellow light) and then is blue-screened again against two more good matte paintings as it rushes towards the Moon. The crash-landing is highly unlikely but is exciting because the quaintness of everything so far has created a "willing suspension of disbelief" in the audience.

Harryhausen's design of the sphere is absurdly impractical in light of what we know today and yet it *almost* looks like it might work.

Two magnificent wide-screen shots look out from the sphere at an expansive miniature lunarscape. These shots are made especially effective by the presence of Cavor's head on the far left of the frame — but this part of the image is missing from television prints. The shot is dramatic in a way that recalls the design of a shot in *Jason and the Argonauts*: Talos on a pedestal with Hercules looking up at it, his head down in one corner of the frame.

Bedford (Judd) and Cavor indulge in some entertaining antics on the full-scale Moon sets before discovering the huge crystalline dome that leads to the Selenites' subterranean world. The dome, sitting in a crater, is an impressive mechanical miniature with a partitioned roof that slides back to let in the Sun's rays. A series of matte shots show Bedford and Cavor falling down the side of the crater and crashing through the dome, with Bedford dangling on a rope over a dizzying painting of the lunar pit. A subsequent shot, when Bedford nearly falls into the pit a second time, suffers from matte spill around his outline as he clings to a rock-face. Two extremely attractive shots look up from the pit at the dome above, dust in the air caught in the sunlight that pours in. The two tiny actors occupy a small area of the lower right corner of the frame. A huge prism is used by the Moon people to harness the Sun's energy. It is seen in a flawless blue-screen shot enhanced by superimposed beams of green light.

The first encounter with the live-action Selenites is backed by the sinister sound of insect-like chirping. An impressive miniature set is combined with a full-scale set in shots that depict a rock bridge being lowered over a chasm above a river of hot, bubbling minerals.

The two astronauts escape back to the surface only to find that the sphere and Kate (Hyer) are missing. In another breathtaking panoramic shot, the camera looks from behind Bedford and Cavor (who are blue-screen elements) at a lunarscape painting in which the ground is cut by tracks where the Selenites have dragged the craft. Bedford and Cavor go off in pursuit, entering a doorway that leads into a network of caverns. In a series of shots, the actors are placed into Harryhausen's miniature cavern sets with seamless traveling mattes.

The Moon-bull is an omnivorous monster that decides to try to make a quick snack of Cavor. The hundred-foot-long creature has many wriggling legs, large, fiery red eyes and hungrily thrashing mandibles. It's a memorable beast and the setting is unusual (an expansive cavern full of weird vegetation and outcroppings of colored crystalline blocks), but this is not a great scene. Harryhausen does his best within the confines of filming in Panavision but can't overcome the fact that puppet and actor cannot interact intimately — the days of motion-control cameras were still more than a decade away when this was made.

In one shot, two of the creatures are seen together. The Moon-cow is alarmed by the arrival of the Moon-bull and scurries off down a tunnel. On television, you will see only one model at a time. Only one model was actually built, and duplicated by blue-screen matting. The bull pursues the two astronauts and growls like a dinosaur. It batters at some of the crystal blocks to get at its prey, the fragments being realistically animated as they fall to the ground. In one shot, it turns toward Bedford, who is standing on a ledge. Bedford throws his helmet but Harryhausen doesn't attempt to show it bouncing off the monster.

In one dynamic cut, Cavor, tiny and in the foreground, runs in front of the monster, a perspective that adds to the depth and credibility of the scene. Several closeups allow a good look at the ferocious head.

Cavor is dragged away by some live-action Selenites. Two striking long shots have a group of Selenites in the lower foreground blasting at the Moon-bull with superimposed laser-rays. The beast is slain and a complex long-shot composite shows the Moon-bull in the miniature set with live-action Selenites approaching from both sides and Bedford in the foreground, looking down at the scene from his ledge.

The first glimpse of one of the animated Selenites is a grotesque moment looking through a thick glass at the alien's distorted face. A dark outline around the model is the result of some spill from the blue screen.

Harryhausen now cuts to an even more bizarre shot looking over the shoulder of the animated Selenite into an X-ray machine in which Kate's skeleton walks around agitatedly, backed by the orange glow of the machine. This is a delightfully surreal moment, made even more so by the fact that the skeleton speaks with Kate's irate voice. The skeleton model is one of those seen in *Jason and the Argonauts*. The skeleton walks out of the X-ray and becomes Martha Hyer, in one fluid matte shot. This is a very brief moment — the skeleton is only seen for about five seconds — but is one of the best "throw-away" effects in Harryhausen's career.

Shots of Kate and Cavor are intercut with shots of the animated scientist Selenite, who stands in front of some colored crystals examining Kate's shoe, which she has thrown at it in anger. The Selenite has a simple conversation with Cavor, throughout which the model is more or less static, only making slight (but believable) movements with its arms and head.

The next scene returns to Bedford, still standing on the ledge and looking down at the Moon-bull. The monster has been stripped of its flesh by the Selenites and is now just a skeleton — in reality a foot-long model. A series of complex composites allow Bedford to walk in the foreground past the huge skeleton, which in turn is backed by a live-action element in which worker Selenites carry pieces of the beast up a rocky path in the cavern wall. In one cut, Bedford has walked behind the skeleton and is now part of the live-action set.

In a fabulous series of shots, Cavor and Kate are shown the scientific wonders of the Selenites' world, all achieved with perfect traveling mattes of the tiny actors dwarfed by their surroundings. First they are seen in front of a pair of colossal doors (an image which, it goes without saying, Harryhausen has borrowed from *King Kong*) which slide open to reveal some giant towers full of bubbling liquid, the means by which the Selenites manufacture oxygen. In an attractive long shot, they walk past these multi-colored cylinders. The next set-up is even more striking, when the pair come across an enormous crystalline structure that spins slowly, bathed in light which pours down from an overhead well that leads up to the surface.

They encounter a group of four scientist Selenites (although on television only three can be seen). The animated puppets stand in front of a stone table on which they have been attempting to duplicate Cavorite, the gravity-blocking paste. In all the cuts in this sequence, the puppets are in the foreground, matted against footage of the actors in the background. In one medium shot of one of the puppets, Harryhausen cheats by reusing a cut that he used earlier during the scene with the X-ray machine. Three of the Selenites walk off into an eerie device that cocoons them in a web-like substance, while the fourth walks off in the opposite direction.

An eclipse of the Sun is realistically depicted and there is an impressive low-angle shot of Bedford looking up at the well (a painting) as the light fades. Without the sun's rays, all the Selenites come to a halt.

The next two effects shots are superb. In the first, Bedford stands in the foreground matted against a cavernous miniature set, with Cavor far off in the distance walking up a flight of steps which have been seamlessly slotted into their miniature surroundings by means of a static matte. A superimposed beam of light gives the shot extra depth by passing behind a pillar of rock in the miniature set. In the foreground on the opposite side to Bedford are a group of live-action Selenites, barely noticed on

television prints, but important in lending the set-up an impression of busyness.

Equally sumptuous is the closer shot of Cavor walking up the steps which lead to the Grand Lunar himself. Jeffries is matted against a miniature set of the regal-looking steps, at the top of which is the crystal globe in which the Grand Lunar sits. Harryhausen's inspiration for this design may well be *Just Imagine* (1930), which he saw when young. In it, a flight of steps lead up to an alien leader, flanked on either side by partially concealed minions. Images from many films of the 1930s (including *She* and *The Last Days of Pompeii*) can be found throughout Harryhausen's work.

The shadowy Grand Lunar, partly obscured by the shifting refracted light of his globe and speaking in a voice that is sinister and threatening, is a very eerie presence. It's a pity that there is never a clearer look at this bizarre model with its enlarged head and long, spindly arms. As Cavor converses with the Grand Lunar, two animated Selenites stand to the right of the set-up, bearing spears. Their function is limited, however, to just standing around looking threatening. In a seamless composite, Cavor walks closer to the Grand Lunar, while three more animated Moon-men look on from the left. This is another set-up which looks magnificent when seen wide-screen.

The Grand Lunar makes it clear that he will not allow the Earthmen to leave the Moon. Bedford breaks in and tries to pull Cavor away. In one shot, he clouts one of the Selenites with the butt of his rifle. In this shot, the only moment of implied interaction in the whole film, the puppet is again in the foreground, blue-screened against the live-action footage of Bedford swinging his rifle. Contact is implied by having the puppet recoil from the imagined blow. Somehow, Harryhausen found a way to align his puppet with an image that he was unable to see while animating.

Bedford and Kate get into the sphere in the nick of time but Cavor chooses to stay behind. In a well-staged sequence, the sphere shoots up through the well that leads back to the surface, then hurtles away from a very realistic and attractive model of the revolving Moon. Back on Earth in the present day, some final miniature effects — seen on a television screen — depict the Selenites' world crumbling and collapsing. Poignantly, the whole civilization has been destroyed by coming into contact with germs carried by Cavor.

It is a mystery why this offbeat, stylish and very colorful fantasy lost money for Columbia. Like the commercially disappointing *Jason and the Argonauts* before it and *The Valley of Gwangi* some years later, either the publicity was misdirected or the film was released during a period when audiences' tastes were temporarily directed at some other passing fad. On a story and dramatic level, *First Men in the Moon* probably works best of all Harryhausen's films, has some stunning fantasy panoramas and withstands repeated viewings. Certainly, this writer has fond memories of seeing the film on its original release at the age of eight, totally engrossed in its lunar visions and bursting into tears at the end when Cavor decides to remain on the Moon.

Flesh Gordon

1974. Graffiti. Live-Action Directors: Michael Benveniste, Howard Ziehm. Special Effects Design and Direction: Howard Ziehm, Lynn Rogers, Walter R. Cichy. Scr: Michael Benveniste. Ph: Howard Ziehm. Art: Donald Harris. Mus: Ralph Ferraro. Special Effects Properties: Rick Baker, Tom Scherman. Special Visual Effects: David Allen, Mij Htrofnad (Jim Danforth). Special Miniature Construction: Greg Jein. Special Photographic Effects: Tom Scherman. Effects Technicians: Doug Beswick, Rick Baker, Greg Jein, Russ Turner, Craig Nueswanger. Uncredited Special Effects: Dennis Muren, Mike Hyatt, Bill Hedge, Mike Minor, Robert Maine, James Aupperle, Steven Czerkas, Laine Liska, George Barr, Joe Clark, Bob Costa, Joe Musso.

Cast: Jason Williams, Suzanne Fields, Joseph Hudgins, William Hunt, John Hoyt, Candy Samples.

Rating: ☆☆☆   Stop-Motion: ☆☆☆

Flesh Gordon is incompetently directed and cheaply put together, but succeeds because of its schoolboy sense of fun and some marvelous special effects. It was re-released in 1981 as *The Special Edition of Flesh Gordon*, cleverly parodying Spielberg's "Special Edition" re-release of *Close Encounters of the Third Kind* and also cashing in on the recent release of Dino De Laurentiis' *Flash Gordon*. *Flesh Gordon* proved to be the most enjoyable of the three, despite having a budget that was a fraction of the other two films.

The plot moves along briskly and enough of the gags work to allow one to ignore the sillier moments. Joseph Hudgins as Dr. Flexi Jerkoff is an enthusiastic, dotty scientist and William Hunt is crazily excellent as Emperor Wang, who unleashes his devilish sex ray on the inhabitants of Earth. The look and pace of the film recapture the essence of the old *Flash Gordon* serials of the 1930s, most deliberately in the unconvincing spacecraft that wobble across the frame on wires, spouting poorly scaled smoke.

The wealth of high-quality matte paintings, miniatures and stop-motion conceals the fact that the film's two-year production schedule was a constant battle between the effects crew and the producers. The net result was that producer Howard Ziehm not only omitted many of the effects personnel from the credits but also awarded himself the title of "Special Effects Designer and Director," despite having had nothing to do with the effects. The credits listed above are taken directly from the film. The many uncredited effects personnel have been appended. Working in various capacities was an army of effects personnel, including many stop-motion artists who would contribute much to the genre over the next decades—among them Jim Danforth, David Allen, Dennis Muren, Doug Beswick, James Aupperle, Steven Czerkas and Laine Liska.

The film contains three episodes making substantial use of stop-motion. They are all restricted by the budget and never attempt to be realistic but are nevertheless impressive.

In the first of these, Flesh (Jason Williams), Dale (Suzanne Fields) and Jerkoff have arrived on the planet Porno and are wandering around some shadowy caves. Suddenly they are confronted by a creature that Jerkoff identifies as a penisaurus. This outrageous seven-foot-high creature rears up from the ground and is a delightful parody of every movie brontosaurus that ever poked its head out of a lake. The scene lacks dramatic punch (it merely serves as a delaying gimmick) and the live-action plates always look very grainy, but it's still a lot of fun.

Animated by Bill Hedge and sculpted by Laine Liska, the beast has bulging veins running down its side, a spiky crest around its neck like a styracosaurus, and one giant eye that blinks with a horizontal motion and comic "pinging" sound effect. Because the puppet was just a "trunk" with no arms or legs, it was built over a wire armature rather than a more elaborate ball-and-socket skeleton. An earlier version of the penisaurus was designed by Steve Czerkas but never used.

There are 23 stop-motion cuts. Most of the long shots use front projection, enhanced by superimposed fog added by Ray Mercer's effects company. In all, three penisauri appear, seen in a variety of long-shot composites swaying threateningly in front of the three actors. In one shot, Jerkoff and Flesh are surrounded, with one creature on each side of the frame. In the only real attempt at interaction, one of the creatures sends Jerkoff flying—the actor merely leaps sideways to suggest the impact. Other

Flesh Gordon (1974): The sword-wielding Beetle Man, animated by Jim Danforth.

shots, in which a penisaurus nudges Dale suggestively, use a full-size prop. Several closeups allow a lingering look at the absurd puppets as they blink straight at the camera. The third penisaurus appears from the roof of the cave, lunging down and landing on Jerkoff. In the final three shots, Wang's henchmen fire their lasers at the creatures, which retreat into the floor of the cave.

The second stop-motion episode — a battle between Flesh and a Beetle Man — is more fully developed. The bizarre creature bursts through some doors into a chamber inside Wang's castle and engages Flesh in a full-fledged battle before succumbing to an arrow fired into its back by a mystery bowman.

The puppet began life as one of several Beetle Man models built and animated by Pete Peterson in the 1950s for an uncompleted project. George Barr designed a more elaborate look for the creature and Rick Baker (later to make a name for himself as a top special make-ups artist) sculpted the puppet's arms and legs, complete with vicious-looking pincers. Jim Danforth spent two months animating the sequence in rear-projection set-ups, in all contributing 23 cuts. He gives the creature an impressive liveliness, including several flourishes of character animation which make the monster at once chilling and amusing.

The sequence begins with a nod in *King Kong*'s direction as the wooden doors of the chamber start to buckle inwards under the weight of some unseen foe. In a flawless static matte composite, the doors open and the Beetle Man steps in, looking around and squawking noisily. Flaming braziers on the walls on either side of the puppet help to draw attention away from the location of the

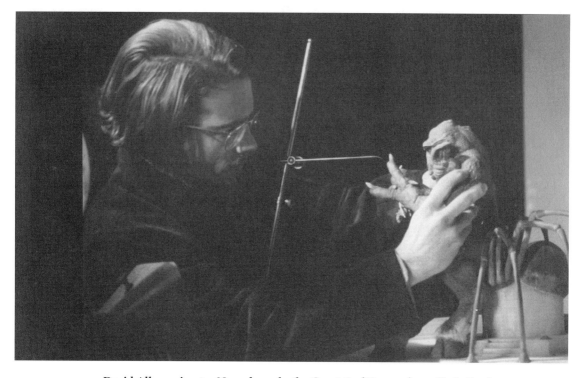

David Allen animates Nesuahyrrah, the Great God Porno, from *Flesh Gordon.*

matte. Three medium shots of the creature reveal the sharp teeth in its beak, the savage pincers and the wings on its back which open and close.

In long shot, the Beetle Man approaches Flesh, raising its pincers menacingly and clacking them together. It stands on an area of miniature floor seamlessly matted into the live action. In another set-up, it lunges at Flesh, landing on that part of the floor where Flesh had just been standing. This shot probably has a switch from live-action floor to miniature floor: The coloring is so perfectly matched that it's undetectable.

Flesh grabs a burning torch and smashes it down onto the Beetle Man. The flames actually seem to surround the puppet's head, suggesting that they were painted on glass for a few frames. Again, the illusion is impeccable. In long shot, the Beetle Man gets up and advances on Flesh again. It circles him, then smashes one of its pincers down on his shield, the impact suggested by careful alignment of puppet and rear image. An irregular matte line along the floor allows the full-view puppet to take several steps.

Flesh jumps up onto a ledge, swinging his sword at the creature below. In a convincing effect, the Beetle Man grabs Flesh's mace in its pincer (again achieved by careful alignment) and pulls the actor down off the ledge. In medium shot, the creature discards the mace and turns threateningly towards Jerkoff and Dale in the rear plate.

In long shot, Flesh swipes at the

Nesuahyrrah sits on a statue of a spider and, in best Kong fashion, contemplates his blond captive in *Flesh Gordon.*

creature with a sword. In an amusing medium shot, the Beetle Man squawks in pain and checks to see if its injured pincer is still working. In long shot, it starts to follow Flesh up a flight of steps, passing partly behind a pillar of rock which is part of the live-action plate. Flesh plants his sword in the Beetle Man's shoulder, only to see the creature pull it out and throw it aside.

A memorably creepy shot looks down the flight of steps at the Beetle Man crawling up them on all fours in pursuit of Flesh. In three final long shots, all using the set-up that mattes around the pillar of rock, the Beetle Man advances on Flesh and raises its pincers as if to deliver the killing blow. But at the last moment an arrow is fired into its back and

it topples over behind the pillar. As it falls, it desperately tries to reach behind its back to pull out the arrow.

The third and final stop-motion episode is an encounter with the Great God Porno. The character is actually unnamed in the film and was dubbed Nesuahyrrah (that's Harryhausen backwards) by the effects crew. The sequence successfully parodies the Empire State Building finale of *King Kong*. Wang brings the creature to life and commands it to destroy Flesh and his friends. The scene has many inventive comic touches and is always visually striking thanks to the splendid miniature sets built by Mike Minor and others.

This 40-foot monster has a permanently dour expression and is one of the few stop-motion characters in features films to have the power of speech: It is forever mumbling and muttering obscenities. Laine Liska did some of the sculpting for the puppet, which was built over parts of an armature from another unfinished Pete Peterson project, *The Las Vegas Monster*. David Allen assisted with the construction and also supplied between 15 and 20 animation cuts. James Aupperle animated five shots. Robert Maine spent nine months doing the bulk of the animation, finishing 60 cuts, even though many of these never made it into the final edit of the film. But it's still a long sequence, with 47 stop-motion cuts in the release print. Dennis Muren and Jim Danforth did the lighting set-ups for several shots. Many shots are not composites, but were done entirely in miniature making full use of the miniature sets.

The first shot is a stunner. An extreme long shot looks down into a huge darkened chamber, the statue of the Great God Porno standing motionless in it. In the center of the chamber is a sacrificial hole in the floor, in which a fire rages. To one side is Wang, bowing and scraping on the floor, lit by a shaft of sunlight pouring in through a hole in the ceiling. This combination of live action, painting and miniature is the best shot in the film.

The first bit of stop-motion is a shot of Porno's hand starting to move as it comes to life in response to Wang's plea. Flames are superimposed over this shot. In closeup, the creature's eyes light up, glowing red, and with some clever lip-synch it mutters, "Oh boy — I just love murder!" In a dramatic rear-screen shot, the monster's hairy goat-legs stride across the chamber, stepping over Wang.

A striking long shot outside the chamber has the puppet stepping out of the shadows of a tunnel into the daylight, emphasized by an upward camera tilt. The monster stomps around the side of a tower, a shot using a static matte around the outline of the full-scale tower. Only the lower part of the tower is actually on the stop-motion set, allowing the puppet to rest its arm on it as it looks at the actors fleeing in the rear projection. Another good matte shot looks out from a walkway on the tower, with the monster's huge head and arm appearing, trying to grab one of the running actors.

In full view, Porno stomps across another miniature set, the actors in the rear screen just ahead of his feet. Dale trips and is picked up by the monster who, in the first of many expressive closeups, sneers lasciviously and raises an eyebrow. Several shots make use of a rubbery full-scale prop hand holding Dale. In long shot, Porno strides off, carrying a kicking puppet of Dale in his hand. When he walks past a (miniature) mirror, he pauses to admire himself and lick down an eyebrow.

In an attractive long shot, he walks across an elaborate set containing miniature arches, towers and steps, heading straight towards the camera. After a medium shot looking from behind the puppet at a high tower, an extreme long shot shows a smaller five-inch version of the puppet (built by Steve Czerkas) approaching the tower and starting to climb. The animation looks hurried but this is still an impressive shot because of all the detail in the miniature set. The five-inch puppet climbs the tower (actually a painting) in best King Kong fashion, a cut animated by Aupperle.

The top of the tower is an unusual miniature, surrounded by great carved claws, its centerpiece a sculpture of a giant spider, and backed by a painting of far off mountains. Porno, still clutching the Dale puppet, reaches the roof and sits down on the spider-sculpting. In a design stolen unashamedly from O'Brien, the monster pulls off Dale's dress. The animated puppet is simply aligned with a rear projection of the actress held in the full-scale prop hand. Invisible wires pull the dress away, carefully positioned so that it looks as though the animated hand is pulling it. O'Brien would have approved of such a shot and who knows, he might have enjoyed the monster's dialogue as well: "I just want to look at your tits." In a series of closeups and long shots, he looks admiringly at his catch, playing with her, dangling her upside down and tweaking her playfully.

Flesh and Jerkoff attack the monster from their spaceship; two dramatic aerial shots home in on Porno at the top of his tower, a perspective directly modeled on the closing shots of *King Kong*. Porno growls at the craft circling in the rear projection, puts down the Dale puppet and gets up from his seat. He turns, his gaze following the path of the rear-projected craft. Shaking his fist, he exclaims, "Up yours, Gordon!" In a long shot, he is struck in the face with some superimposed laser-fire. This has been carefully added frame-by-frame so that it seems to "splash" around the puppet's head. In closeup, the puppet's face glows red from the impact, then he turns back to the

Dale puppet, struggling on the floor of the tower.

As he stoops to pick up Dale, Flesh scores a direct hit in the monster's rump: "My ass!" In longshot, he pats his wounded backside. In the background, a tiny model of Flesh, dangling on a rope ladder from his craft, hangs lifelessly in the background. The humor has sunk to such a low level by this stage that it hardly matters that this is a cheap effect that would look more at home in someone's home movie. A low-angle perspective looks up at Porno, still clutching his backside and now groaning, "The pain! The humiliation! The hemorrhoids!"

Flesh grabs Dale and starts carrying her back up the rope ladder. In three medium shots, Porno tears off one of the spider statue's legs (it had to be whittled away frame by frame during animation) and stomps straight at the camera, intending to use the leg as a weapon with which to strike Flesh. But in his anger he misjudges his momentum and, in a dramatic panning shot, strides to the edge of the tower and topples over. A static model is used in a long shot of Porno falling onto the balcony where Wang is standing.

The film also contains a number of excellent matte paintings, most done by Danforth. These include the main chamber of Wang's palace, with a curved ceiling, giant carvings of naked women adorning the walls and a huge hanging red jewel in the center of the room; a swan-like spacecraft that has crash-landed, surrounded by flames, with Flesh wandering away from the wreckage in the lower foreground; an attractive painting of the giant trees that conceal the rebels' hideout; and an aerial view looking down at one of the palace's towers, the ground far below. Another clever matte shot, also done by Danforth, has

Flesh, Dale and Jerkoff trapped in a room in whose floor a gradually enlarging hole appears.

Flesh Gordon 2—Flesh Gordon Meets the Cosmic Cheerleaders

1990. Filmvest. D: Howard T. Ziehm. Scr: Howard T. Ziehm, Doug Frisby. Ph: Danny Nowak. Art: Al Benjamin. Mus: Paul Zaza. Visual Effects Director: Thomas Hitchcock. Visual Effects: FX Center. Creature Effects: Jim Towler. Stop-Motion Animation and Design: Lauritz Larson. Assistant Animators: Don Bean, Brian Oshab, Michael Orlando. Matte Paintings: Robert Kayganich.

Cast: Vince Murdocco, Robyn Kelly, Tony Travis, William Dennis Hunt, Morgan Fox, Bruce Scott.

Rating: ☆☆½   Stop-Motion: ☆☆½

After 16 years, Howard Ziehm at last revived his over-sexed galactic hero, but in the interim Flesh had lost much of his mischievous sense of fun. Where the original was engagingly childish and smutty, the sequel is often merely crude and contrived. Many ideas are initially amusing but soon become tiresome: a spaceship powered by copulating chickens, farting asteroids that have to be stopped up, a cave full of Turd People, etc. This time round Emperor Wang (William Dennis Hunt) is a conventional foe, as forgettable as his pop-eyed assistant Master Bator (Bruce Scott). Ziehm's sequel just doesn't have the necessary pace or inventiveness.

There are two long sequences that feature stop-motion by Lauritz Larson. Larson's brief was clearly not to worry too much about realism: These two creatures never look like anything other than rubbery puppets and the animation is frequently jerky. There are one or two good composites and some clever moments of interaction, but otherwise this is very primitive stuff—basic tabletop animation in front of grainy front-projected live-action plates. In these hi-tech days of computerized go-motion and flawless blue-screen composites, the effects seem even more primitive by comparison, but in another sense it is a refreshing change to see old-style animation composites that are less than perfect.

Flesh (Vince Murdocco) crash-lands his phallic spaceship on a planet, disturbing an alien creature seen munching on a hamburger outside a McAliens fast food bar. This green, pop-eyed, scaly puppet looks something like a cruder, squatter version of Harry-hausen's elegant Ymir: It even has the double-jointed legs and arms-back pose. It attacks the spaceship, tearing down a miniature doorway that is matted into the live set, and peers inside. (This is the only matte shot in the sequence.) Seen with its back to the camera, it has grabbed one of the girls on the ship, the physical contact implied by having the puppet in front of the actress, partly obscuring her.

The creature throws a punch at Flesh, who ducks, but his second punch connects with Flesh's chin — an effective moment of alignment of puppet and rear image. In a closeup of its cartoonish face, the creature turns towards a second screaming girl. Flesh comes up behind it and plants a bucket on its head, requiring a clever switch from real to miniature bucket, with the actor dropping the real bucket into the area obscured by the puppet. Flesh kicks the creature on the chin, the puppet recoiling believably at the right moment to suggest the contact.

At this point, the film takes a leaf out of *Roger Rabbit*'s book: The action so far is revealed to be all done on a film set. The camera pulls back to show an irate director shouting at his cast. Meanwhile, the stop-motion alien drums his fingers impatiently and, as the director continues to rant, tweaks the breast of one of the actresses; again, this is a simple case of lining up the puppet's hand with the rear image. The director fires his entire cast and (in the scene's final stop-motion shot) the dejected monster is seen walking past the studio gates, carrying a placard that reads "Monster for Hire." This poorly designed shot looks exactly like what it is — a puppet in front of a rear-projection screen, not helped by the fact that the rear image wobbles and distorts.

The second stop-motion episode features the absurd Dickhead monster, a pink creature with two arms, two legs, a body like a scrotum, a huge face covered in makeup and an enormous penis growing out of the top of its head. It swings a handbag and talks in an over-the-top effeminate whine. It makes the penisaurus of the first film look positively restrained.

Flesh and Flexi crash-land among the Mammary Mountains and are startled to see the Dickhead emerge from behind a hill. Conventional but effective static mattes follow the slope of the hill. In another static matte set-up, the giggling Dickhead throws a bar of soap at the two travelers, in anticipation of the act it intends to perform on them. As Flesh bends over to pick up the soap, the Dickhead charges at him, penis-horn at the ready — an effective cut with the puppet running straight at the camera. Flesh sidesteps the oncoming creature, after which there are several reaction shots of the puppet as Flexi tries to communicate with it. In irritation, the Dickhead throws its handbag to the ground, exclaiming, "Your ass is mine, sugar britches!" This is followed by two more low-angle head-on shots as it charges at Flexi.

In an amusing moment, Flesh comes to the rescue and jumps onto the top of the Dickhead. This begins with a clever static matte set-up in which the live-action Flesh runs up a hill, then at the last moment is replaced by a puppet-replica which leaps onto the monster. This is dramatically more satisfying than similar moments in other films (including *Golden Voyage of Sinbad*) where the sequence simply cuts from a shot of the live actor to another shot of the two puppets already in contact. Closer shots of Flesh on top of the penis use a full-scale prop. The Dickhead waves its "horn" around in the air trying to throw Flesh. Flesh bites the edge of the glans (ouch!) and is thrown to the ground by the screaming creature. This is also achieved in one cut, with the Flesh puppet fluidly replaced by the live actor at a predetermined point.

Flesh and Flexi take shelter in a cave that is shaped exactly like — wait for it — the female sex organs. The Dickhead pursues them and, in a static matte set-up with the split following the outline of the cave, shoves his "horn" into the cave. After a few thrusts in and out, he deluges Flesh and Flexi with a slimy ejaculation, then sits back contentedly and belches,

as the two men are carried far down into the cave on a river of sperm.

On paper, the sequence appears outrageous and hilarious, but the reality is disappointing because Ziehm's direction is too clumsy. The rear screens are all conspicuously grainy, making one always far too aware that this is "a special effect." More realistic composites would have helped to increase the humor of the scene.

Other memorable non–stop-motion effects include a fine miniature of a floating "ice city" and some impressive shots of Emperor Wang's whale-shaped spaceship hovering above a miniature city and flying towards an attractive painting of a planet.

Flight of the Lost Balloon

1961. Allied Artists. D: Nathan Juran. Special Effects: Project Unlimited (Gene Warren, Wah Chang).

Cast: Marshall Thompson, Mala Powers, James Lanphier, Douglas Kennedy.

Rating: ☆½   Stop-Motion: ☆☆

In this low-budget adventure yarn, Marshall Thompson flies over Africa in

a hot-air balloon in search of a missing explorer.

Long shots of the balloon in flight were handled by Gene Warren and Wah Chang at Project Unlimited. "All of the balloon travel shots," explained Warren in a letter to the author, "were done with a hanging miniature balloon manipulated stop-frame against either a process screen or a plain sky backing."

Flight of the Navigator

1986. Disney/PSO. D: Randal Kleiser. Scr: Michael Burton, Matt MacManus. Story: Mark H. Baker. Ph: James Glennon. Art: William J. Creber. Mus: Alan Silvestri.

Max and the Creatures Puppeteered by Tony Urbano, Tim Blaney. Visual Effects Supervisor: Peter Donen. Additional Special Visual Effects: Fantasy II. (Uncredited

Fantasy II Visual Effects Supervisor: Gene Warren, Jr.)

Cast: Joey Cramer, Paul Mall, Veronica Cartwright, Cliff De Young, Sarah Jessica Parker, Matt Adler.

Rating: ☆☆½   Stop-Motion: ☆☆½

The very engaging first half of this children's SF adventure tells of a 12-year-old boy who is knocked unconscious and, on awakening, finds that eight years have passed. Meanwhile, a mysterious spacecraft has arrived on Earth and seems to be somehow linked to the boy's reappearance. But once the nasty NASA officials arrive and the boy boards the craft, the script degenerates badly, losing sight of its plot in favor of a cute robot character (voiced by Pee-wee Herman, credited as Paul Mall) and pop video–style flying sequences.

The spacecraft is a sleek, metallic shape which the NASA team are unable to open. However, when the boy approaches, a part of the hull seems to melt, forming a dark doorway and dripping a stream of metal which hardens into a flight of steps. This brief effect cleverly suggests the otherworldliness of the craft. It was achieved by Gene Warren, Jr., at Fantasy II Film Effects by means of replacement animation. A series of models of the doorway and the steps, in varying stages of solidity, were filmed in sequence, carefully lit and matched with the pre-shot footage of the spacecraft. Later, when the doorway closes, the same footage is used in reverse, giving the appearance that the metal is "melting upwards." There are similar replacement animation sequences depicting the stairs melting and reforming on two later occasions.

These striking effects predate the liquid steel images of *Terminator 2* (1991), which used computer imagery to create its effects.

Forbidden Planet

1956. MGM. D: Fred McLeod Wilcox. Scr: Cyril Hume. Story: Irving Block and Allen Adler. Ph: George Folsey. Art: Cedric Gibbons, Arthur Lonergan. Special Effects: A. Arnold Gillespie, Warren Newcombe, Irving G. Reis, Joshua Meador. Electronic Tonalities: Louis and Bebe Barron.

Cast: Walter Pidgeon, Anne Francis, Leslie Nielsen, Warren Stevens, Jack Kelly, Richard Anderson.

Rating: ☆☆☆   Stop-Motion: ☆☆½

Hailed as one of the great science fiction films, *Forbidden Planet* is hampered only by MGM's fear that straight SF would not find an audience: They tacked on some love interest (in Anne Francis) and some unnecessary humor (in the unlikely retorts made by Robby the Robot). Intended to give the film a broader appeal, these gimmicks inevitably only cheapen it.

Although Fred Wilcox's direction is mediocre, he keeps the pace brisk and his cast is lively and likable. Cyril Hume's script is well-conceived, albeit occasionally falling into the common SF pitfall of being overly ambitious — for example, the concept of the Id monster, a projection of Walter Pidgeon's mind, is never fully convincing.

The color CinemaScope photography and big-budget special effects set the film apart from most of its contemporaries. Many of the effects still look impressive even by today's high standards: a spaceship in flight, the expansive surface of a planet, the architecture of the Krel aliens and an attack by the Monster from the Id.

One striking shot of the spaceship in flight, passing an eclipse of a sun by the planet Altair-4, made use of stop-motion. A six-foot model of the ship was suspended on wires and moved one frame at a time across a painted backdrop of stars as lighting effects were gradually altered to create a corona effect around a hanging disc representing the planet. The red glow was also simulated on the miniature craft.

Freaked

1994. Tommy/20th Century–Fox. D: Tom Stern, Alex Winter. Scr: Tim Burns, Tom Stern, Alex Winter. Ph: Jamie Thompson. Art: Catherine Hardwicke. Mus: Kevin Kiner. Creature and Visual Effects Supervisor: Thomas C. Rainone. Preliminary Creature Designs: Screaming Mad George. Special Makeup Effects: Alterian Studios (Tony Gardner), Steve Johnson. Special Visual Effects: Fantasy II Film Effects. Visual Effects Supervisor: Gene Warren, Jr. Visual Effects: David Allen Productions. Stop-Motion Animation: David Allen. Puppeteers: Mark Rappaport, Chris Endicott, Joseph Grossberg, Angela Chao, Scott Woodard, Kevin O'Hara. Miniatures: Dennis Gordon, Ron Nelson. Clay Animation: Chiodo Brothers. Animation Director: Stephen Chiodo. Stop-Motion (uncredited): Kent Burton.

Cast: Alex Winter, Michael Stroyanov, Brooke Shields, William Sadler, Megan Ward, Mr. T, Randy Quaid, Morgan Fairchild.

Rating: ☆☆   Stop-Motion: ☆☆

This is a crazy, undisciplined comedy with some good ideas, a few good gags and some excellent makeup and visual effects, but it is defeated by uninspired direction and the absence of a decent script. Alex Winter and two friends pay a visit to a freak show and get turned into freaks themselves. They befriend the other freaks and eventually defeat the film's villains, the heartless business executives of EES (Everything Except Shoes).

The freaks encountered include Cowboy (a talking, walking cow), Sockhead (a man with a hand inside a sock instead of a head), Nosey (a man whose head is a huge nose), Frogman (a man in a frogman's diving gear) and Mr. T as a bearded lady. These are all tired and unfunny characters who make one yearn for the sensitivities of Tod Browning's *Freaks* all those years ago. One side of Alex Winter is transformed into a creature that looks like a Gremlin from Joe Dante's film.

Winter's two friends are merged by the mad freak show owner into one being with two arms, two legs and two heads. They are tied to an operating table, then a nasty green toxic chemical is smeared onto them (optically enhanced to give off a sinister glow). While the other characters look on, they turn into a big pink mass which goes through various stages before leaving them merged together. These stages include turning into the heads of a tyrannosaurus and the Cyclops from Harryhausen's *7th Voyage of Sinbad*. It's a witty moment, with an affectionate in-joke, but ultimately just a throw-away gag that raises a quick laugh, then is forgotten. The shot, lasting just under ten seconds, is a clay animation effect cleverly achieved by Stephen Chiodo.

At the climax, all the business executives get splattered by the same green toxic chemical. They melt down into a puddle of goo (a live-action effect) which then transforms into a giant shoe monster. This ten-foot long creature has three eyes down each side where the lace holes would be, a giant mouth (includ-

ing teeth and a fleshy tongue) around the top and long, spindly arms instead of laces. Its transformation complete, the shoe monster turns and walks off, using its long arms to drag itself along.

This is another quick gag which has little impact. Quite what the point of it is remains obscure. It's not particularly funny or scary. The two shoe monster cuts were created by David Allen, whose studio did its usual accomplished job. The first cut, in which the melted goo transforms into the monster, appears to have been achieved by melting a wax model, then projecting the footage in reverse. The smooth animation of the second cut, in which the monster walks off, includes some barely registered blurs which may have been achieved by double- or triple-exposure of each animation frame. The puppet sits on a miniature floor which is perfectly matched to the floor in a rear projection. An extra running off in the rear projection adds further plausibility to the shot.

Friday the Thirteenth Part VIII—Jason Takes Manhattan

1989. Paramount/Horror Inc. D-Scr: Rob Hedden. Ph: Bryan England. Art: David Fischer. Mus: Fred Mollin. Special Makeup Effects: Jamie Brown. Special Photographic Effects: Effects Associates, Jim Danforth.

Cast: Jensen Daggett, Scott Reeves, Barbara Bingham, Peter Mark Richman, Martin Cummins, Gordon Currie.

Rating: ☆½   Stop-Motion: ☆☆½

Those who enjoy watching the same film over and over again might enjoy this eighth entry in the *Friday the Thirteenth* series. Others will wonder how the producers had the nerve to make a film so devoid of inventiveness. This is production-line splatter, with kids getting dispatched in gruesome fashion every five minutes by hockey-masked Jason, a supernatural bogeyman with a penchant for putting sharp implements to unexpected use.

In this one, Jason is on board a ship sailing to New York. The ship is caught in a storm and for one nighttime long shot, Jim Danforth was called in to supply a quick stop-motion effect. Churn-ing waves in a studio tank are matted into the lower part of the frame. The ship, complete with numerous lights, is stop-framed moving slowly towards the camera. In the background, the cloudy night sky is lit by ominous bursts of lightning. Stop-motion was appropriate for this extremely good miniature shot because of the need to control the lighting in the shifting background frame-by-frame.

Fright Night Part II

1989. D: Tommy Lee Wallace. Scr: Tim Metcalfe, Miguel Tejada-Flores, Tommy Lee Wallace. Based on Characters Created by Tom Holland. Ph: Mark Irwin. Art: Dean Tschetter. Mus: Brad Fiedel. Special Makeup Effects: Makeup FX Unlimited (Bart J. Mixon), Greg Cannom. Special Visual Effects: Gene Warren, Jr., Fantasy II Film Effects. Stop-Motion Animation: Justin Kohn.

Cast: Roddy McDowall, William Ragsdale, Traci Lin, Julie Carmen.

Rating: ☆☆½   Stop-Motion: ☆☆½

This is cowardly filmmaking: It sticks strictly to the formula of the first film, including all the things that irked (a vampire attempting a trendy dance, the hero having a hard job convincing people that the vampires are real, etc.). There's always plenty going on in the effects department and Tommy Lee Wallace's direction keeps the pace brisk, but there is nothing new or stylish about this.

Nor is it saved by the kind of spectacular climax which made the original something special. This film's climax is very much a toned-down version of what we have seen before. A shaggy werewolf makes a number of interesting appearances, crawling up walls, and there is an explicitly sensual fanging by a vampire: In closeup, we see the girl's slender fang pierce her victim's neck wound and penetrate deeply, then she lasciviously licks the blood-stained tooth. Makeup effects are by Bart J. Mixon of Makeup FX Unlimited and Greg Cannom. One highlight has a vampire getting his stomach slashed open (a horde of maggots pours out.)

In the original film, Randy Cook was in charge of shots where the vampire transformed into a bat monster, effects that were achieved live-action with a rod puppet and a string marionette. For the sequel, Gene Warren, Jr., created a similar monster and included some brief bits of stop-motion. The animation itself was done by Justin Kohn. These cuts are very fluid and blurs on them suggest that double- or triple-exposure per frame was used, and or creating a blur by smearing grease onto a glass sheet between puppet and camera. Midway through the film, Julie Carmen falls down a deep stairwell and transforms into a small bat monster (as in the first film). Three very quick stop-motion cuts show it flying up to the ceiling and through a window. One cut allows a close look at the very evil-looking fanged face.

At the climax, she transforms (off-screen) into a person-sized bat monster, then, anti-climactically, reduces in size (again off-screen) to a bat-sized harpy.

Four or five stop-motion cuts show the creature flitting around a basement, including two chilling closeups of the savage head. One of these cuts is a rear-projection shot of it flapping at the hero and heroine. At least one cut seems to be done live-action, the bat monster a wire-supported prop that is flown around the set. The harpy is a splendidly unpleasant-looking fiend, and the stop-motion very accomplished (compare it with the hopeless bats that used to haunt the chillers of the 1930s, 1940s and 1950s), but it's probably on the screen for no more than ten seconds—hardly something to get excited about. Why wasn't it used more?

From Beyond

1986. Empire Pictures. D: Stuart Gordon. Scr: Dennis Paoli. Adapted by Brian Yuzna, Dennis Paoli, and Stuart Gordon from H. P. Lovecraft's "From Beyond." Ph: Mac Ahlberg. Mus: Richard Band. Art: Giovanni Natalucci. Special Effects Creatures and Transformations: MMI, Inc. (Design/Supervisor: John Buechler). Pretorius Creature and Body Prosthetics: Mark Shostrom Studio. (Design/Supervisor: Mark Shostrom.) Special Effects Makeup and Creatures: M.T.S.D. (Coordinator: John Naulin.) Physical and Photographic Effects: Doublin Effects. (Supervisor: Anthony Doublin.) Additional Special Effects Photography: Paul Gentry. Conceptual artist: Neal Adams.

Cast: Jeffrey Combs, Barbara Crampton, Ted Sorel, Ken Foree, Carolyn Purdy-Gordon, Bunny Summers.

Rating: ☆☆½   Stop-Motion: ☆☆

This was a great letdown after director Stuart Gordon's *Re-Animator* (1985), one of the most entertaining horror films of the 1980s. Dennis Paoli's script lacks the discipline of the earlier film, never adding much to the basic storyline of mad-scientist-invents-device-that-unleashes-monsters. The plot lacks excitement, the characters do not have the same eccentric enthusiasm as before and the special effects, although costing three times those in *The Re-Animator*, are less outrageous. Richard Band's score is occasionally effective but, lacking the Bernard Herrmann *Psycho* inspiration this time, doesn't generate the same energetic tension.

The film never properly conveys the impression that we are constantly surrounded by unseen monsters, visible only when the pineal gland is stimulated. Their presence is restricted to a few vicious eel-like creatures, a giant lamprey in the basement and the central creature that scientist Pretorius transforms into. But the film is still a lot of fun and even Lovecraft himself would have enjoyed it.

Monster and special makeup chores were shared among four special effects studios, helmed by John Buechler (a veteran of many other Charles Band productions), John Naulin, Mark Shostrom and Anthony Doublin. The cable-controlled mechanical creatures and the slimy prosthetics are always inventive but never entirely convincing, and are not depicted by Gordon with the same sure control and balance of tongue-in-cheek that he showed in *The Re-Animator*. This is simply over-the-top monster effects for the sake of it. The most memorable moments include Combs being swallowed alive by the giant lamprey, an excruciating moment when he has his pineal gland (a ten-inch-long, snake-like thing extending from his forehead) bitten off, the various appearances of the absurd Pretorius monster, and its huge and disgustingly rubbery hand that pursues the heroine.

Three shots of the Pretorius monster, a squat, bulky biped with enormous hands and a head on a low-slung stalk, were done with a kind of full-scale stop-motion, with various appendages moved around a frame at a time (although its legs remain in one position). A later shot of it flying straight at the camera (after it has sprouted wings) also looks like it was done by means of stop-motion although this is not successful because the model does not convey a sense of the great size of the monster, instead looking like a large bat. Paul Gentry, who worked with David Allen on many of his puppet sequences, was involved in the film and it may that he was responsible for this shot.

Frostbiter—Wrath of the Wendigo

1991. Troma/Excalibur. Prod-D-Scr: Tom Chaney. Ph: Tom Chaney, Gary Jones, Eric Pascarelli, David Thiry, Matt Sisson, Dave Moenkhaus. Art: Bill Siemers. Special Makeup and Mechanical Effects: Gary Jones. Effects Animation Supervisor and Miniature Photography: Tom Hitchcock. Wendigo Stop-Motion: David Hettmer.

Cast: Roy Asheton, Lori Baker, Patrick Butler, Devlin Burton, Tom Franks, Alan Madlane.

Rating: ☆☆   Stop-Motion: ☆☆

Working with a minuscule budget but heaps of enthusiasm, writer-director Tom Chaney tried to make his own version of *The Evil Dead*. Yes, we're in remote "log cabin territory" again. A supernatural circle of skulls has been disrupted by some drunken hunters, with the result that the Wendigo, a mythical destructive creature, is unleashed.

The Wendigo takes various forms

during its attack on the members of the cast. These are mostly mechanical puppets — a winged creature that attacks a plane, some dog-sized demons that emerge from a pot of chili — which are entertainingly vicious even if they fail to convince.

In one scene, a character called "The Guardian" is shot and his corpse decomposes at high speed, even while the skull continues to growl. Three eye-catchingly lurid stop-motion cuts — very much in the style of *The Evil Dead* — show the body's clothes and skin rotting and falling away

The film saves its most ambitious special effects for the climax, in which the Wendigo appears in its true form, attacks the cabin in which the surviving cast members are hiding, and is finally defeated when the circle of skulls is restored.

Thirty-five stop-motion cuts feature in this long nighttime sequence. The Wendigo is a 20-foot-tall, centaur-like creature. On its head are huge antler-like growths. Ribs show through the thin torsos of both its humanoid upper part and its horse's body. Its four legs look like oversized, fleshless bones. The creature is almost too weird to be effective. The animation by David Hettmer (who the same year supplied some good stop-motion for *Lunatics: A Love Story*) is never particularly fluid and the animal's gait always looks awkward. This is an intriguing sequence with one or two impressive moments but ultimately it must be looked on as another of the many low-budget efforts that serve to remind us just how good Harryhausen is.

In a series of medium and long shots, the growling Wendigo is shown smashing its fist into the roof of the cabin (which in these shots is a miniature). In two shots, the creature picks up a tree and uses this to pound the cabin. Shot by one of its intended victims, the Wendigo recoils and roars loudly before resuming its attack. It peels back the roof of the cabin, punches its fist through the ceiling and pulls out a screaming, kicking man. The animation of the puppet human is hurried and does not convince.

In long shot, the creature walks around the side of the cabin, still holding the kicking puppet. A series of low-angle long shots shows the creature swinging its victim into the cabin door, then putting the puppet human down and walking off.

A short while later, the creature reappears, pushing some trees aside in a striking shot that seems to deliberately recall Kong's entrance many years before. The Wendigo walks up to a miniature of a log cabin surrounded by a circle of skulls on poles, raises its arms and roars. A smoothly executed cut features a dramatic zoom-in onto the growling puppet. The creature smashes part of the cabin as the heroine (who is hoping to restore the circle of skulls) approaches.

The Wendigo unleashes a burst of magical energy (good cel-animated effects) at another character. The creature walks over to the man and, in one of the few attempts at composite photography, stands over the intended victim, who is part of a rear projection. The composite is largely successful because the subdued nighttime lighting helps to blend model and rear image. An area of snow in the lower foreground may be a miniature set or it may be part of a matte.

A rock, thrown by a third character, is an animated miniature for a few frames as it bounces off the monster. A second rock is thrown, caught by the Wendigo and casually discarded.

The heroine reinstates the missing skull and the Wendigo's fate is sealed. In medium shot, the creature turns abruptly, roars with rage and advances. It picks up one of the men and throws him to one side — but (again) the animation of the puppet human does not convince. The heroine sends some colorful blasts of magical energy at the beast, which in a series of shots recoils and falls back. In two final medium shots, the Wendigo grimaces in pain. Its last shot (done live-action) is a quick cut of the puppet exploding.

Galaxy of Terror

1981. New World. Prod: Roger Corman. D: B. D. Clark. Scr: Marc Siefler, B. D. Clark. Ph: Jacques Haitkin. Art: James Cameron, Robert Skotak. Mus: Barry Shrader. Special Visual Effects Supervisor: Tom Campbell. Visual Effects Photography: Dennis Skotak. Graphic Animation Design: Ernest D. Farino. Stop-Motion Animation/Model Shop Supervisor: Brian Chin. Second Unit Director: James Cameron. Optical Effects: Jack Rabin and Associates.

Cast: Edward Albert, Jr., Erin Moran, Ray Walston, Bernard Behrens, Zalman King, Robert Englund.

Rating: ☆☆   Stop-Motion: ☆☆

This SF chiller has a stylish look and some occasionally impressive visual effects but is devoid of anything resembling a script. A group of astronauts arrive on a planet to investigate the disappearance of some colleagues and discover a mysterious pyramid structure. Exploring the inside of the pyramid, they are picked off one by one in encounters with deadly creatures. Characterization is non-existent and dialogue is perfunctory.

Early on, one crew member explores a crashed spacecraft. Walking nervously through grimy corridors (blatantly inspired by the decor of *Alien*), the man is stalked and killed by a giant cockroach creature. Four quick cuts use stop-motion to depict this being, which unfortunately is never seen in full. Built and animated by Brian Chin, it seems to have spider-like legs and the outer shell of a crustacean. It skulks among the damaged corridors (which in these shots may be a miniature set) and in one cut its antenna wave in the air in best cockroach manner. The eventual attack is achieved with on-set props.

Ernest Farino designed and supervised various roto animation effects and titles. James Cameron, working as production designer and second unit director, survived the embarrassments of this film and went on to become one of the industry's hottest directors with *The Terminator* and *Aliens*.

The Gate

1986. Gate Film Productions. D: Tibor Takacs. Scr: Michael Nankin. Ph: Thomas Vamos. Art: William Beeton. Mus: Michael Hoenig, J. Peter Robinson. Special Makeup: Craig Reardon. Special Visual Effects Designed and Supervised by Randall William Cook. Randy Cook's Crew: Fumi Mashimo, Jim Aupperle, Michael F. Hoover. Visual Effects: Illusion Arts, Inc. Matte Photography: Bill Taylor. Matte Supervisor: Syd Dutton. Matte Artist: Mark Whitlock.

Cast: Stephen Dorff, Christa Denton, Louis Tripp, Kelly Rowan, Jennifer Irwin, Deborah Grover.

Rating: ☆☆☆   Stop-Motion: ☆☆☆

A low budget tale of a group of kids who discover a gateway to hell in their back garden, *The Gate* gave Randall William Cook an opportunity to display his talent for making effects look more "special" than they had for a long time. Making full use of a variety of techniques — blue screen, rotoscope matting, forced perspective and stop-motion — he created some startlingly off beat sights.

Although aimed at a mid-teen audience and slow to get going, *The Gate* is redeemed by a second half that is an endless delight. A horde of rat-faced, foot-high minions from Hell emerge from the hole in a garden and presage a climactic appearance by the enormous Demon Lord. Cook achieved almost all of the minion shots using actors in costumes and perspective distortion, yet at no point do these look like the awful "men-in-costume" sequences that have plagued so many monster films. In fact, on a first viewing, many of these shots look like stop-motion effects. This is partly due to the superior costumes that the extras wear and also partly due to the fact that many shots were filmed at 12 frames per second and then skip-framed to give their movements an unearthly quality. It's almost as if Cook were teasing us, making us think that we are watching complex, fluid stop-motion.

The forced perspective shots, all filmed in-camera, are impressive. Even when you know that the actors are in the foreground standing on a hanging set and the minions are below in the distance, it is difficult not be fooled by these flawlessly designed composites. In one shot, the camera tilts down a girl's body to reveal two minions standing at her feet. In another, minions tug at the leg of one of the boys. Foreground and background floors are so perfectly color-matched and aligned that the eye is completely deceived. For the latter shot, a 20-foot-long prop of the boy's leg was built.

In one of the film's most remarkable shots, two kids are cowering at the far end of a room from a zombie character. The zombie falls forward onto its face, then transforms into a dozen scurrying minions. Again, the kids are actually in the foreground, standing on a partial hanging set. Intricate rotoscope matting allows the astonishingly smooth transformation. (Rotoscope matting requires that a hand-drawn matte is individually applied to each frame of film.)

In one intriguing shot, a door is slammed on a minion whose arm gets shut in it. Stop-motion is utilized to show the dismembered arm drop to the floor and transform into a host of wriggling worm-like things which crawl back under the door. One closeup of a minion also appears to have been achieved with stop-motion, thereby allowing it to blink and snarl realistically.

There are 33 other stop-motion cuts, split into two episodes featuring the Demon Lord. This is the kind of full-blown stop-motion character which could not have been realized through any other medium. He's all on show, six arms and two snaking tentacles always moving, and his savage, fish-like head alert and watchful. Cook gives him a majestic aura befitting his origins. It's a beautifully detailed model and a classic monster. However, it's a shame that the character doesn't have more to do: It stands around looking menacing and eventually is killed but really doesn't do a lot else.

A gaping hole appears in the floorboards beneath the stairwell in the house. The first stop-motion cut is enjoyably theatrical. The horde of minions dance up and down excitedly around the top of the stairwell, anticipating the arrival of their master. The huge shadowy figure of the Demon Lord rises up behind them, his back to the camera. This impressive composite consists of three elements: a foreground live-action set, blue-screened minions and the puppet (animated in a miniature set of the stairwell and ceiling). The blue-screen element of the minions was processed by Illusion Arts: It actually consists of one piece of film that has been duplicated to make it appear that there were more minions.

The camera tracks in closer and the minions on the banister rail scatter, like a parting curtain. The monstrous Demon Lord is revealed nearly in full, growling gently, lit up by occasional flashes of lightning. As it breathes, its chest rises and falls.

In several medium shots and close-ups, it looks inquisitively at the small boy, Glen, cowering below it. A long-shot side view makes use of a partial miniature banister, with Glen on one side of it, the Demon Lord swaying gently on the other side. In a creepy shot looking over Glen's shoulder, the Demon Lord stoops towards the camera, casting a shadow on the miniature ceiling above, emitting exploratory growls as it decides what to do with the boy. The boy is either a traveling or rotoscoped matte element.

The level of anticipation rises and the boy starts to crawl away. In long shot, the Demon Lord suddenly lurches forward, one arm smashing through the miniature banister rail (parts of which are animated). The fluid, dynamic movement of the puppet employs multiple exposure and is the kind of gesture which over the next few years would become a Cook trademark. In long shot, the Demon Lord picks up Glen by his hand — the actor is actually supported by an invisible wire. In closeup, the creature blinks and reveals a row of small, pointed teeth.

The Demon Lord reaches for the boy's head with another claw, then, instead of killing him, drops him, turns and leaves, swooping out of the lower part of the frame. It's a deliciously low-key confrontation.

Opposite: The Demon Lord from *The Gate*.

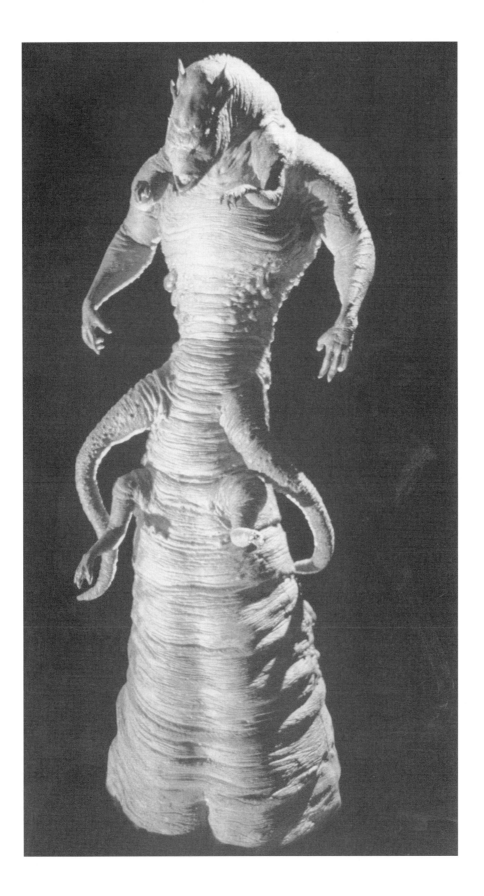

But the creature has abducted two of Glen's friends and, in the second part of the sequence, Glen decides to save them by summoning the demon back again. Presumably restrained by the budget, Cook stages this sequence in the stairwell instead of a new location.

In a quick long shot, the Demon Lord rises up in the stairwell again and, in medium shot, looks around hungrily, annoyed to have been called back. Glen is a foreground element, either a traveling or rotoscope matte. A low-angle shot looking up at the towering creature allows a clear look at the puppet's two snaking tentacles.

After a series of medium shots and long shots, Glen fires his toy rocket launch at the monster. The rocket, attached to a rod that is obscured by a matted-in trail of sparks and smoke, is animated as it heads towards its target. A close shot of the rocket entering the Demon Lord's chest was animated by Craig Reardon and Fumi Mashimo.

In long shot, the Demon Lord looks down at the point of impact and lunges at Glen (and the camera). He picks up the boy (this time an animated puppet) and swings him about by one of his legs. Lights and sparks start to appear in the creature's chest and he drops the Glen puppet. In a very low-angle shot, the creature's whole torso is lit up from inside. In a foreground roto-matte, Glen crawls away. Mouth agape, the creature lurches this way and that (very smoothly animated) and finally explodes. In a final animated cut outside the house, Glen is thrown through the front door by the force of the blast, cartwheeling through the air. For this shot, the Glen puppet was matted into the live-action set.

Craig Reardon provided the superior special makeups (a zombie, an eyeball blinking out of the palm of someone's hand, a face that collapses and releases several pints of goo) and Illusion Arts provided matte paintings and opticals, including a striking tornado effect.

Gate II

1990. D: Tibor Takacs. Scr: William Nankin. Ph: Bryan England. Art: William Beeton. Mus: George Blondheim. Special Makeup: Craig Reardon. Visual Effects: Ruckus Enterprises. Supervisor: Randall William Cook. Dimensional Animation: Randall William Cook, Steve Archer. Chief Technician: Fumi Mashimo. Matte Paintings: Rocco Gioffre.

Cast: Louis Tripp, Simon Reynolds, James Villemaire, Pamela Segall, Neil Munro, James Kidnie.

Rating: ☆☆½   Stop-motion: ☆☆☆

Director Tibor Takacs' admirable aim to make *Gate II* "a kind of fable, not without its Grimm aspects" (as he said in an interview with *Fangoria* magazine), rather than just another splatter movie, is an indication of the healthy freedom allowed fantasy movies these days: This kind of film couldn't have been made a decade and a half ago. There are plenty of inventive ideas and a full-blown Lovecraftian ending full of monsters set somewhere in Hell, but at the end of the day, this is really just another highschool romp full of stereotyped kids, never having the courage to break away entirely from the market-driven ingredients of nerds, punks, drugs, fast cars and all the trimmings.

As with the original, what sets this apart from other films is the superior special effects of Randall Cook. His inventively designed composites are always superb and frequently leave you (as before) totally baffled as to how particular shots were achieved. Sometimes the minion (there is only one in this sequel) is an actress in a costume, sometimes a remotely controlled puppet and sometimes a stop-motion puppet — and in many cuts it's impossible to tell which. The nine-foot-tall demon that James Villemaire transforms into is always a stop-motion puppet, but the animation by Cook and Steve Archer (each doing 50 percent of the work) and the flawless mattes are so good that you could be forgiven for thinking otherwise.

Near the start of the film, bespectacled nerd Terry (Louis Tripp) conducts an occult ritual and conjures up a foot-tall minion from Hell. At first it is seen standing at Villemaire's feet, shots using the costumed actress and achieved with the forced perspective technique that Cook used to such great effect in the first film. When Villemaire blasts it with his shotgun, the stop-motion puppet is filmed in front of the actors in a rear screen. In a cut animated by Archer, the puppet is blown back out of the frame by the gun shot. Blur on the image was created by actually moving the puppet backwards during the long ten-second exposures.

Terry picks up a limp prop of the minion, takes it home and pickles it, but during the night it heals itself and breaks out of the jar. Terry corners it in his bedroom, Cook again brilliantly using forced perspective to show the actress running around the actor's feet. In longshot, Terry swipes at the stop-motion minion (on this occasion a tiny three-inch puppet) with a hockey stick, sending it flying across the room, a high-speed cut with a lot of blur. Deftly animated against the rear screen, the minion smashes into a television set and falls to the floor. Giving it a bit of character, Cook next shows his puppet lying on its stomach on a miniature floor screaming up at the camera. This shot, and the preceding two, were animated by Archer.

Terry covers the minion with a bucket and gives a it a good bashing with the hockey stick. When he lifts up the bucket, the poor minion looks dazed and half-deafened, staggering about in a smooth bit of animation in front of a rear image of Terry. In the same cut, Terry grabs the puppet, a brain-teasingly clever shot which at first sight looks like it must either use a miniature of Terry's gloved hand (carefully positioned to obscure the real one), or else the remote-controlled puppet replaces the stop-motion one, requiring Terry to hold still for a second while the camera is stopped and the puppet brought in. In fact, the composite was achieved with rotoscoped mattes, black-painted onto glass and matching up with the outline of Terry's hand for each frame of film.

When Terry puts the minion into a bird cage, he is holding the extremely convincing remote-control puppet, which wriggles desperately. More superb forced-perspective shots show the minion in the cage, swinging on a perch, rattling the bars and eating some noodles. In many of these shots, Cook has skipped a few frames to give the minion's movements a slightly unnatural look — as he did in the original.

John and his punk partner Mo steal the minion and there is a well-staged scene where it escapes from its sack on the back seat of their car. Cook and Archer each did roughly half of the animation in this episode. There is an excellent rear-screen composite (complete with lots of blurs) when it rips its way out of the bag, steadies itself, then leaps up at Mo's neck. Cook probably created the blur by a multiple exposure technique: exposing the frame twice — or even three times — with the puppet in a slightly different position. An amazingly successful composite (animated by Archer) shows it standing on Mo's rising and falling chest. The remote control puppet is used in shots where it leaps up at John, grabs his hair, is pulled away by Mo and punched by John. One shot uses an animated mock-up of Mo's hand. In all, it's an impressive demonstration of matching different puppets in one sequence.

The punks tie up the minion and put it in the boot, terrifying it with some flames. Two shots (by Archer) of it gagged and helpless are enhanced by having superimposed flames in the foreground and a flickering orange glow on the puppet.

Bitten by the minion, John starts to undergo a gruesome transformation (courtesy of Craig Reardon's special makeups) and Terry, Mo and Liz (Pamela Segall) track him to a warehouse. Two shadowy closeups (by Archer) show John bemoaning his fate, now a gray, knobby humanoid stop-motion puppet with beady red eyes.

Mo falls to his death after a heart attack and the John-monster, seen in full for the first time, leaps down from some overhead pipes to claim the corpse. It's a nightmarish creation, half again as high as a man, with long slender arms and goat legs; no one could ever think this was an actor in a costume. The stop-motion puppet leaps down next to Liz and Terry, again with lots of blur — this time probably with triple-exposure. This is such a fast movement that the blur doesn't look naturalistic, but it is certainly better than no blur at all and is acceptable to most audiences. Standing over a very well-matched floor inlay, the monster picks up a puppet of Mo. The animation of the human puppet looks a bit hurried, like the animation of the boy puppet at the end of the first film. The monster howls deafeningly and climbs some steel pipes out of the shot, probably attached to a support obscured by a vertical matte running down the center of the shot. All shots in this sequence were animated by Cook.

Back at the house that provided the setting for the first film, Terry tries to conjure up the gate again. Inadvertently he stumbles upon the minion again, who bites his hand. This is another clever cut, initially using the stop-motion puppet which seems to have been replaced by the remote-control puppet as Terry tries to shake it off. He flings it across the room into a wall, the puppet's limbs flailing as it flies through the air; if this is a composite, then it's superb. In a more easily recognizable rear screen shot, the battered minion rubs its eyes only to get skewered by a barbecue fork when Liz sneaks up behind it. In two cuts (by Archer), the suggestion of contact between the squealing stop-motion puppet and the live-action fork is perfect. Liz picks up the minion, still wriggling on the end of the fork, and drops it into a large music box held open by Terry. The alignment of the puppet in front of the end of the fork is impeccable. This successful shot was complicated by the fact that Archer had to draw articulate mattes frame-by-frame around the box lid, which moves slightly as Terry holds it.

In the imaginative climax, Mo (also contaminated by the minion) has transformed into an ugly Reardon live-action monster. Terry wakes up in Hell and finds himself at the foot of some steps leading up to a sacrificial temple at the top of a precarious pillar high above an inhospitable rocky landscape. This is depicted by means of an effective matte paining by Rocco Gioffre, complete with greenish smoke billowing from two chimneys on either side of the tower. The gate, a glowing red pit down below, is a ten-foot miniature built by Archer. It's a bizarre setting and the composites during this sequence are excellent, really putting the John-demon in with the actors.

Several long shots show all the characters together: Mo on one side, Terry on the other, Liz lying on the altar and the smoothly animated John-demon standing between them, the matte line following the outline of the altar. Medium shots of the animation puppet and live-action cuts of the actors are intercut with these. In some of these shots, Archer made the puppet sway in a kind of slow figure-eight action rather than merely standing in the shot motionless.

In a superb composite, the John-demon leaps up into the air and over the altar, complete with blurs. What is particularly impressive about this shot is that the puppet is initially in front of the live-action altar but finishes up behind it. This was ingeniously achieved by introducing a second matte while the puppet was in mid-air, following the outline of the altar. There is a classic bit of interaction in two cuts (recalling a shot in *The 7th Voyage of Sinbad* where the Cyclops picks up a sailor by his boot) in which the John-demon picks up Terry by the hand, dangling him in mid-air: A miniature of the actor's hand is carefully positioned in front of his real hand. A complex long shot has the John-demon smashing a puppet of Terry into the ground, while Liz runs past in the foreground. The part of her arm which passes in front of the puppet may have been painted on glass, but is more likely another effective example of Cook's use of articulate mattes. Liz tries to throw the box of occult symbols into the pit (so as to close the gate) and there is a low-angle composite looking up from below the tower at Mo and the John-demon, the matte line conveniently following the edge of the tower floor.

The John-demon leaps back over the altar again and confronts Liz, looking splendidly imposing as he towers over her in two cuts. In a medium shot, he lashes out at her with his arm, which is blurred with multiple exposure. As she recoils from the blow, she staggers right in front of the puppet, suggesting that this must be a blue-screen shot; in fact, it's another impressive instance of rotoscope matting, the mattes painstakingly following Liz's moving outline. As he waits for Terry (now transformed into a live-action human-sized minion lookalike) to slay Liz with a sacrificial dagger, there are five medium shots of the animation puppet. It blinks and growls and its chest rises and falls — all very smooth. The breathing effect was achieved not by having a bladder inside the puppet but by moving a hidden screw in and out. Mo is on the left in some of these impeccable rear-screen composites.

The minion, held captive in the music box, chooses this moment to climb out, and the sound of the music brings Terry out of his demonic trance. Three quick cuts of the minion add to his character as he falls over and gets up again, the matte lines hidden by the shadow thrown by the box. In long shot, Terry hurls the dagger at the John-demon and gets him right between the eyes. A medium shot of the monster reacting is enhanced by lots of blur. In long shot, the monster takes a few steps backwards and topples over behind a pillar,

dead. (The vertical matte line follows the pillar.) There are two final animation shots of the minion, first standing by the music box looking up at the background action, then seen from behind as Terry walks over, picks him up and puts him back in the box. This looks like another deceptive switch from animation puppet to remote-control puppet.

The box is thrown into the pit, closing it and taking the demons with it. To keep his young audience happy, Takacs tacks on a happy ending in which all the cast revive, restored to their previous non-monstrous states — even a hamster that had been sacrificed early on. It's all gratuitous — especially as neither John nor Mo deserved a happy ending.

Cook has demonstrated again — as he did in *The Gate*, *Hardcover* and others — that he is capable of producing remarkable effects in unremarkable films. Not content merely to present stop-motion sequences in ways that we have come to expect, he stretches the medium a bit further, inventing new possibilities, new composite designs, new ways of improving the "look" of animation and seamlessly blending the animation cuts with other techniques such as forced perspective. The only problem with *Gate II* is that it doesn't allow him to indulge himself enough — what we need is a producer crazy enough to give him a budget to make a no-holds-barred stop-motion fantasy in the old Harryhausen vein.

The Ghost of Slumber Mountain

1919. World Film Corp. Prod: Herbert M. Dawley. D-Scr-Ph-Special Effects: Willis H. O'Brien.

Cast: Herbert M. Dawley, and (unconfirmed) Willis O'Brien.

Rating: ☆☆½   Stop-Motion: ☆☆½

Begun in 1918 with a budget of $3000 and a shooting period of three months, O'Brien's *Ghost of Slumber Mountain* represented a major advance in his art, both technically and dramatically. This critique is based on a print running 13 minutes, although some sources (e.g. Jeff Rovan) quote a longer running time of 16 minutes. The comical style of the short films is dropped in favor of a more exciting drama with live human characters interacting with the dinosaurs. The models are more believable, sculpted with more detail and more closely based on scientific reconstructions from fossils. The miniature sets in which the dinosaurs perform are much more elaborate, intercutting nicely with the location footage shot in some nearby forests.

Originally the film ran 45 minutes, but producer Herbert M. Dawley felt that audiences would not be able to sit through so much animation and trimmed it considerably, intending to use the cut footage in other productions. Some of the missing footage was apparently used in Dawley's 1920 release *Along the Moonbeam Trail*, but no prints of this survive. Even in the shortened form, *The Ghost of Slumber Mountain* was a huge commercial success, grossing $100,000.

In keeping with a plot structure which O'Brien would use again in *The Lost World* and *King Kong*, there is a relatively long buildup before we see our first dinosaur. Two children pester their Uncle Jack to tell them a story and he recounts a tale of a climbing expedition to Slumber Mountain where he discovered the cabin of an old hermit called Mad Dick. Inside the cabin, he finds a curious device like a pair of binoculars and is visited by the ghost of Mad Dick. (Unconfirmed rumor has it that this role was played by O'Brien himself, superimposed so as to look "spectral.") Mad Dick invites him outside and tells him to look through the device.

He is amazed to see a hundred-foot-long brontosaurus walking beside a lake and, in a second cut, stepping into the water. Water is something that cannot be manipulated one frame at a time and so requires that animators devise other means of showing it coming into contact with their puppets. In this instance, O'Brien achieves a convincing effect by animating gelatin around the puppet and including an impression of a white splash (possibly paper cut-outs) for a few frames.

In a second miniature set, Jack sees a diatryma, a huge flightless bird. O'Brien repeats a bit of characterization he first used in *Prehistoric Poultry* (1917) and has the bird scratch its ear. The bird walks across the set and picks up a wriggling snake in its beak.

For the first time, O'Brien moved his camera frame-by-frame in a panning shot which reveals an approaching triceratops — a clear indication that he was trying to improve the dynamism of his

273

set-pieces. A second triceratops arrives and they lock horns, circling each other until one runs off. (The triceratops models look remarkably similar to those in *The Lost World* — is it possible they were re-used?)

An allosaurus is now glimpsed standing among some miniature trees. It attacks the triceratops, defeats it and then, in an enjoyably gruesome shot, tears a chunk of flesh out of its prey, swallows it and licks its lips. The design of the allosaurus is impressive (moreso than Delgado's emaciated allosaurus in *The Lost World*) but its smooth skin lacks the detail necessary to make it seem really alive. The allosaurus now turns on Jack and a closeup again uses an animated camera, tilting up to the monster's head. Goldner and Turner state that one shot also uses a closeup of a full-scale allosaurus head. The allosaurus nearly catches up with Jack, courtesy of some unremarkable intercutting between the actor and medium shots of the puppet, at which point Jack wakes up — it was all a dream. Disappointed with this cop-out ending, the two children start attacking their uncle — and most audiences no doubt feel equally cheated at this point.

The film is a simple story engagingly told, but it is a shame that O'Brien's stop-motion scenes were not allowed to develop more: We can only surmise as to the content of the cut scenes. After the success of the film, O'Brien was depressed to find that Dawley was taking all the credit for the effects, had removed O'Brien's name from the release prints and was claiming to have devised all the animation techniques and built the models himself. As a result, the two parted company. Fortunately for O'Brien, he was soon contacted by producer Watterson R. Rothacker, a meeting which in 1925 would result in a real triumph of stop-motion photography — *The Lost World*.

There is an interesting footnote relating to the promotional material for *The Ghost of Slumber Mountain*. It is rare for cinema posters for a film of this vintage to survive but in the 1970s in Britain a cache of 12 original posters for the film were discovered when the walls of the basement of an old cinema were demolished. These three-sheets, six-sheets and a single one-sheet all have eye-popping dinosaur artwork rendered in vivid colors which, because the posters were shut away, have retained their brilliance. These beautiful lithographs are highly sought-after by collectors of stop-motion memorabilia.

Ghostbusters

1984. Columbia/Delphi. D: Ivan Reitman. Scr: Dan Aykroyd, Harold Ramis. Ph: Laszlo Kovacs. Art: John De Cuir. Mus: Elmer Bernstein. Visual Effects: Richard Edlund, Entertainment Effects Group. Visual Effects Supervisor: John Bruno. Chief Matte Artist: Matt Yuricich. Camera Operators: Jim Aupperle, John Lambert.

Dimensional Animation: Randall William Cook. Ghost Shop Advisor: Jon Berg. Armatures (uncredited): Doug Beswick.

Cast: Bill Murray, Dan Aykroyd, Sigourney Weaver, Harold Ramis, Rick Moranis, Annie Potts.

Rating: ☆☆☆   Stop-Motion: ☆☆☆

This big-budget fantasy kicks off with promising energy. A librarian, lost in a claustrophobic maze of book shelves where index cards fly out at her menacingly, is threatened by something unseen. Ray Parker, Jr.'s thumping theme music starts up and the Ghostbusters — a motley group of four would-be controllers of paranormal pests — are called in. They get howled at by the ghost of a lady librarian (a live-action puppet beautifully sculpted by Steve Johnson), then run screaming into the street, having failed to trap the specter.

But from here on the film loses much of its pace, becoming just a vehicle for its effects and gags. Bill Murray's smug remarks in desperate situations are too artificial and self-conscious to work. Rick Moranis' nerdish health fanatic, later transformed into the occult Keymaster, is another character that doesn't quite gel. Sigourney Weaver has little to do other than be on the receiving end of Murray's irksome chat-up lines.

Regardless of their individual merit, some of the effects set-pieces are digressions, making one wish that the plot would get down to the business of tackling the visitation by the demon Xuul. Chief culprits are the episodes with Onionhead (a floating green ghost) and the giant Mr. Stay-Puft, both of which are imaginatively filmed and technically flawless but leave one wishing that the $40 million budget had been spent on

something just a little less silly. Some of the quick "throwaway" effects, such as the arms that emerge from a chair to maul Weaver and the living dead cab driver, are fun but nothing that hasn't been seen before. Some eggs that smash themselves into a kitchen table kamikaze-style are a very poor relation of *Poltergeist*'s crawling steak.

The climax, like most of the film, is visually exciting, but Ivan Reitman (who had previously directed *Cannibal Girls* and *Meatballs*) doesn't make it as gripping as it should have been: The effects make everything else take a back seat. But Reitman holds everything together efficiently and a lot of the humor is successful. It is easy to be hard on the film simply because today's fantasy films are judged by much higher standards than those of 15 or more years ago.

Richard Edlund, having left ILM and set up his own company, was in charge of the effects and they look magnificent. Some of the best moments include the Ghostbusters firing their spook-trapping guns, sending out dazzling streaks of energy; the matte shots of a bizarre high-rise building overlooking Central Park; and the elemental forces surrounding the sky scraper as the magical forces build up.

Among the film's most memorable sights are the Terror Dogs, bulky, purple-hued quadrupeds with red-glowing eyes and horns. They are seen in 15 stop-motion cuts animated by Randy Cook and supplemented by a lot of full-scale puppetry. Live-action puppetry has come such a long way since the full-scale bust of Kong in 1933 that nowadays the stop-motion cuts are often, as here, fewer than the live-action ones.

Randall William Cook animates the Terror Dogs (which he also sculpted) for *Ghostbusters* (1984). He is working in front of a blue screen for later compositing with live-action footage.

This is one occasion when an all-out Harryhausen-style set-piece could really have worked, but unfortunately the dogs are never much more than a background menace. A fully-blown stop-motion battle between the Ghostbusters and the Terror Dogs could have been a real show-stopper, but it never happens.

The models look superb and Cook has them make dramatic, rapid movements in a way that would characterize all his stop-motion work from now on. He was assisted by Jim Aupperle, whose expertise in lighting stop-motion set-ups was particularly useful in shots where flashes of magical energy light up the puppets. Some shots employed a simple go-motion technique whereby part of a puppet was attached to a rod and synchronized to move during the camera exposure. The armatures were built by Doug Beswick.

In the first exciting animation scene, Moranis is pursued by one of the dogs, but the script has him faint before any confrontation occurs. After a shot of the full-scale puppet sitting on a bed in Moranis' apartment, Cook's puppet bursts through the door into a room full of partying guests. To create an impression of blur for this dynamic movement,

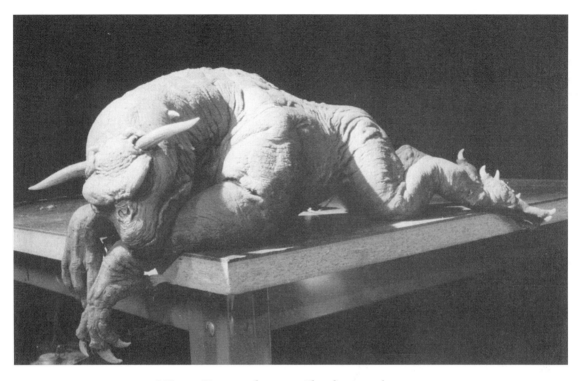

A Terror Dog rests between *Ghostbusters* takes.

Cook exposed the same frames of film more than once, with the puppet occupying a slightly different position each time. The second cut is cleverly timed so that the puppet seems to crash onto a buffet table, which collapses under its weight (actually pulled down by hidden wires). In the third cut, the dog chases Moranis out into the corridor, with a vertical matte line running down the edge of the doorway. Again, the puppet has a semi-transparent look to suggest a blur.

The fourth cut is an astonishing composite in which the puppet bounds out of the apartment entrance, running between two pedestrians. For this shot, Cook rotoscoped a matte frame-by-frame around the outline of the nearer pedestrian in the rear-projection image.

The final shot in this sequence has the dog run across a road, momentarily lit up by the glare from a car's headlamps, pass behind a lamp post, jump over a wall and disappear into some bushes in the live-action plate. The glare from the headlamps on the puppet, and the cel-animated shadow that follows beneath it, are tricks that are registered by us only subconsciously but which help to make the cut brilliantly convincing.

Near the climax, Weaver and Moranis, standing on pedestals on the roof of the apartment block, transform into a pair of Terror Dogs. This shot is superb, with the actors bathed in flashes of purple lightning and slowly dissolving into the puppet characters. In a closer shot, the eyes of one of the dogs glow menacingly red, the creature again lit up by

277

spectacular cel-animated lightning. The dogs leap off their pedestals one at a time, ambitious movements typical of Cook and carried off perfectly.

In two long shots, the dogs run up a flight of stairs that leads to a glowing yellow light, from which the demon Xuul will emerge. Cook takes this opportunity to put some character into the dogs, giving them a lolloping, almost puppy-like gait, dissipating their earlier ferocity. One of them hesitates at the top of the steps, like a playful dog momentarily forgetting its orders. Two stop-motion cuts have Xuul as the focal point in the center of the shot with the puppets sitting on either side of her, making minor and very fluid movements. Their "cuteness" is highlighted in a shot in which Xuul pats the full-scale puppet on the head.

The finale, in which the Ghost-busters are attacked by Mr. Staypuft and turn their "spook guns" on an interdimensional portal, includes two final stop-motion cuts. The actors stand in the foreground, aiming their guns up the flight of steps on which the two Terror Dogs still sit. One dog trots across the steps. Eventually both are engulfed by a fire ball, a clever composite in which actors, puppets and flames all mesh.

These are all fascinating shots and technically impressive, but, like the film as a whole, they lack real dramatic punch.

In the video version of the film, the viewer will see only one dog leap from the pedestals. He will see neither puppet in the two shots of them seated on either side of Xuul. A panned-and-scanned version seen on British television at least had the decency to pan from one leaping dog to the other. As ever, the best place to see the film is at the cinema.

Ghostbusters II

1989. Columbia. D: Ivan Reitman. Scr: Harold Ramis, Dan Aykroyd. Ph: Michael Chapman. Art: Bo Welch. Mus: Randy Edelman. Visual Effects: Industrial Light and Magic. Visual Effects Supervisor: Dennis Muren. Director of Effects Photography: Mark Vargo. Creature and Makeup Design: Tim Lawrence. Matte Painting Supervisor: Mark Sullivan. (Uncredited ILM effects: Stop-Motion puppet designed and built by Phil Tippett, Randy Dutra. Stop-Motion Animation: Harry Walton.) Additional Visual Effects: Apogee, VCE (Peter Kuran).

Cast: Bill Murray, Dan Aykroyd, Sigourney Weaver, Harold Ramis, Rick Moranis, Peter MacNicol.

Rating: ☆☆☆   Stop-Motion: ☆☆½

It's a pleasure to see cinema fantasy depicted with such enthusiasm, variety and technical excellence. The film delights in its own inventions, always aware of the comic angle yet never adopting the irritating smugness which ruined so many fantasy films of the period (Dino de Laurentiis being the chief perpetrator of such mistakes: *King Kong* (the remake), *Flash Gordon*, etc.). At last, in 1989, big budget mainstream films had reached a stage where no one felt embarrassed about liking monsters, ghosts and slimy monstrosities. It was hard work for the genre to reach this level of maturity and happily there is a receptive audience who will ensure that this new perception, which has its roots in the commercial success of *Star Wars*, will continue.

Having said all that, however, *Ghostbusters II* is a disappointment. It's merely very good when it should have been excellent. The fault is that it is too similar to the original in structure and content. A good finale could have made up for this, but the sequence in which the Statue of Liberty comes to life is a missed opportunity and inferior to the original's climax.

But all the five central characters are as likeable as before, with a bonus in Peter MacNicol's role as Sigourney Weaver's revoltingly wimpish museum boss. For the first two-thirds, the script is engaging and inventive. The Ghostbusters are introduced as has-beens: "Who you gonna call?" — "He-Man!" A malevolent river of pink slime runs through New York's sewers, a great surreal image. A sinister portrait in a museum seems to be half-alive. A courtroom scene ends in impressive chaos when some pink slime explodes and two flying ghosts go on the rampage. In a fast-paced montage of scenes, the Ghostbusters deal with various spooks and are hailed as heroes again. And Weaver and her baby get menaced by an amorphous pink blob that rises up out of her bath.

This is all fine stuff but towards the end the plot runs out of ideas. Humor, pace and inventiveness are replaced by a desire to have a spectacular but conventional ending.

This time round, the bulk of the effects shots were done by Industrial Light and Magic, with additional effects by Apogee and VCE. A long-shot of the museum covered in slime is good but a poor cousin to all the swirling occult energies that surrounded the apartment in the first film.

Missing is something to match the fabulous Terror Dogs: Stop-motion is conspicuous by its near-total absence. It is used in only one shot, when a huge ghost-monster with an enormous mouth and long arms floats through the Washington Square arch. The puppet is superimposed over live-action film of a crowd of extras running towards the camera in the lower foreground. This is a fine model and the animation is smooth — so why wasn't it used more? Why go to all the trouble of building the model if it is only going to be seen for a few seconds?

The model was designed and built by Phil Tippett and Randy Dutra. In view of their track record, why were they not asked to do more? One can only assume that they were busy with other projects. Harry Walton, who has done animation in *The Legend of Hillbilly John* (1973) and in other ILM projects including the harpy sequence in *Young Sherlock Holmes*, did the animation. For some reason, none of them received a screen credit.

The Statue of Liberty scenes were achieved using a man in a costume and high-speed filming. The results are satisfactory but lack excitement and grandeur. If anyone ever wondered why Harryhausen animated Talos instead of using a man in a suit, then here is your answer.

Ghoulies II

1987. Empire Pictures. Prod-D: Albert Band. Scr: Dennis Paoli. Story: Charlie Dolan. Ph: Sergio Salvati. Mus: Fuzzbee Morse. Ghoulies Creatures Created by John Buechler and MMI, Inc. Stop-Motion Sequences: David Allen Productions. Stop-Motion Assistants: Paul Gentry, Paul Jessel.

Cast: Damon Martin, Royal Dano, Phil Fondacaro, J. Downing, Kerry Remsen, Dale Wyatt.

Rating: ☆☆   Stop-Motion: ☆☆½

This is an unexciting follow-up to a reasonable original which itself was a rip-off of *Gremlins*. The plot drags as five two-foot-high, bestial Ghoulies hide in a fairground, attacking victims in a Chamber of Horrors. This time, executive producer Charles Band entrusts direction to another of the clan, his father Albert Band, who directs limply. Non-Ghoulie scenes are tiresome, but the puppet sequences are spirited and the only reason for watching.

John Buechler's mechanical and rod-operated puppet creations too often look like sophisticated Muppets. But there are five fine stop-motion cuts supplied by "David Allen Productions" which add significantly to the impression of the Ghoulies as living, walking beings. These cuts are all brief but it's an improvement on the first film, which had no stop-motion.

The first three cuts occur early on, nighttime shots depicting four of the creatures walking across a shadowy street. Two are extreme long shots and the third is a lingering closer look at the models as they walk towards the camera. One Ghoulie is an endearingly frog-like thing with a huge crocodilian mouth and tiny back legs. The others are bipeds, one with reptilian characteristics, one wolf-like (perhaps a modified puppet from *The Howling*?), the third bull-like. They are seamlessly placed into the rear-projected backgrounds.

Later on, the creatures break out of the Chamber of Horrors. Shot from behind, two of them scamper away from the camera along a miniature floor towards a rear projection of actors walking in the fairground. The other two Ghoulies leap down from above and behind the camera onto the miniature floor; it appears that they were lowered manually on wires while the camera shutter was open, so as to add a realistic blur to the image.

Seeing full-view shots of all these bizarre models is always more interesting than the partial shots of Buechler's puppets. It's a pity that Band did not allow Allen the resources to use his models in more scenes. The total amount of animation here probably amounts to less than 20 seconds.

The Giant Behemoth see *Behemoth the Sea Monster*

Gigantis the Fire Monster
see *Gojira no gyakushu*

God's Army (a.k.a. *Prophecy*)

1995. Neo Motion Pictures. D-Scr: Gregory Widen. Ph: Bruce Douglas Johnson, Richard Clabaugh. Art: Clark Hunter. Mus: David C. Williams. Cave Sequence Visual Effects Director: Bruce Douglas Johnson. Enemy Ghost Sequence: Todd Masters Company. Model Animation: Kent Burton. Beast Sculptor: Vince Nebla. Angel Effects and Mesa Mattes: Effects Associates Inc./Jim Danforth.

Cast: Christopher Walken, Elias Koteas, Virginia Madsen, Eric Stolz, Viggo Mortensen, Amanda Plummer.

Rating: ☆☆½   Stop-Motion: ☆☆½

In this offbeat fantasy-chiller, warring angels take human form on Earth, battle amongst themselves and plot to regain the position they once held in Heaven. Of course, this is far too ambitious a project, but Christopher Walken's powerful performance as the evil Gabriel — pallid-skinned, vicious and dangerous — just about manages to make everything seem plausible. Writer-director Gregory Widen is in sure control and insures that the film never topples into the absurd.

The film uses special effects sparsely and wisely, and not for their own sake. In one remarkable sequence, the walls of a cave dissolve to reveal a vision of a host of screaming angels impaled on spikes.

The soul of an evil cannibal has been hidden inside a young girl. At the climax, the girl disgorges the soul, which emerges from her throat by means of some grotesque bladder and prosthetic makeup effects.

The soul takes on the form of a scrawny, humanoid demon, surrounded by a supernatural glow. In two shots, the creature is a stop-motion puppet animated by Kent Burton. This is a quick, eye-catching effect and one wishes that more could have been seen of this eerie character.

The climax also features one marvelous shot, created by Jim Danforth, of some angels in flight. Dark, dramatic clouds scud past in the foreground and background, lit up by a flash of lightning. In the distance, the angels — smoothly animated stop-motion puppets — fly through the night sky.

Danforth also animated a second shot of the angels, but it was dropped from the film. In this shot, nearly a dozen of the angels flap and hover in the sky. Unfortunately, a communication breakdown between the filmmakers and the visual effects artists meant that Danforth was never told that the angels were meant to look evil. The shot was removed because the angels simply looked too angelic. Danforth tried to darken the shot by adding another layer of cloud, but it was still rejected.

Gojira no gyakushu
(U.S. title: *Gigantis the Fire Monster*;
a.k.a. *The Return of Godzilla*)

1955. Toho. D: Motoyoshi Oda. D (U.S. version): Hugo Grimaldi. Scr: Takeo Murata, Sugeaki Hidaka. Ph: Seichi Endo. Special Effects: Eiji Tsuburaya, Akira Watanabe, Hiroshi Mukoyama.

Cast: Hiroshi Koizumi, Setsuko Wakayama, Minoru Chiaki.

Rating: ☆☆   Stop-Motion: n/a

In this second film from the Toho studio, Godzilla (renamed Gigantis in the Americanized version) is found on a remote island battling Angorus (an armored quadruped that looks just as silly as Godzilla). It later stomps on Osaka and finally is defeated when fighter planes cause him to be crushed under an avalanche of snow (an entertainingly dumb climax).

There's lots of daft human interest in this one (heroic pilots and their anxious girlfriends) and it seems to consist mainly of stock footage of military film (including some shots of planes that are repeated *ad nauseam*) and library shots of volcanoes erupting, etc.

Its chief claim to fame is a three-second stop-motion cut borrowed from some as-yet-unidentified film. A group of scientists are watching various snippets of dinosaur footage (including *Unknown Island*), and one of them is a long-shot of two brontosaurs fighting, their long necks lunging at one another. A miniature shot, the background is a cliff face and there is miniature foliage in the foreground. The style is very much in the O'Brien–*Lost World* vein but this cut is not in any existing prints. Is it from an earlier O'Brien short, a missing scene from *The Lost World* or even the lost 1922 test reel which was made for *The Lost World*?

The Golden Child

1986. Feldman-Meeker/Eddie Murphy Productions/ILM. Dir: Michael Ritchie. Scr: Dennis Feldman. Ph: Donald E. Thorin. Art: J. Michael Riva. Mus: Michael Colombier. Demon Props: Chris Walas Inc. Visual Effects: Industrial Light and Magic. Visual Effects Supervisor: Ken Ralston. Demon Supervisor: Phil Tippett. Go-Motion Supervisor: Harry Walton. Go-Motion Animation: Tom St. Amand. Demon Designed and Sculpted by: Randy Dutra. Demon Fabrication: Tamia Marg, Sheila Duignan. Demon Armatures: Blair Clark, Conrad Bonderson. Supervising model-maker: Steve Gawley. Matte Dept Supervisor: Chris Evans. Matte Artists: Michael Pangrazio, Sean Joyce, Caroleen Green. Matte Photography: Wade Childress.

Cast: Eddie Murphy, Charles Dance, Charlotte Lewis, Victor Wong, Randall "Tex" Cobb, J. L. Reate.

Rating: ☆☆☆   Stop-Motion: ☆☆☆

This very engaging Eddie Murphy vehicle, enthusiastically directed by Michael Ritchie, contains some of the most impressive special effects sequences of 1986. Exotic Himalayan temples, a snake woman, a depiction of Hell and a climactic battle with a ghastly demon are some of the superior accomplishments of Industrial Light and Magic, done under the supervision of Ken Ralston.

The film kicks off with a very fluidly shot and edited prologue set in Tibet in which the Golden Child (young J. L. Reate giving the film's most likable performance) is kidnapped by Charles Dance. Shots of a Himalayan panorama and the inside of a temple are both terrific composites using glass paintings and miniatures. A later matte shot — the camera tilting up a mountain to another temple — is another stunner, complete with superimposed snow and tiny blowing flags added to the miniature temple.

A sequence in which the captive Golden Child causes a Pepsi can to come to life is a fabulously smooth bit of stop-motion, but doesn't sit happily with the tone off the rest of the film. Just why a Tibetan boy-priest should make the can do a Fred Astaire–style dance routine is never explained. The sequence was designed by Phil Tippett and animated by Tom St. Amand. A series of puppets was built (by St. Amand and Tamia Marg) to show the can transforming into a character with arms and legs. Lighting and photography were handled by Harry Walton. During some shots (especially

when the puppet spins around), St. Amand rotated the tie-downs slightly from below the animation table during shutter exposure, causing a very effective blur to appear on the finished film. There are eight stop-motion cuts, six of which are conventional tabletop animation. The other two are blue-screen composites.

The can is shown crumpling, uncrumpling, sprouting two-dimensional arms and stepping on a tiny chicken bone, sending it spinning into the air (supported on wires), then catching it and using it as a cane as it dances. A long shot, looking over the Golden Child's shoulder at the tiny can in the distance, is a sensational composite: Lighting and a sense of depth are precisely judged. Almost as good is a shot where the can goes down onto its knees in the classic Al Jolson pose, looks up at something, then gets flattened by Charles Dance's boot. The boot is a separate blue-screen element but the suggestion of contact is successfully conveyed. In the composite shots, cel-animated shadows were added, closely following the movements of the puppet. This brief scene demonstrates just how far composite photography had come in the decade following *Star Wars* — and also how quickly we grew to take it for granted.

The shock revelation of the snake-woman is a good creepy throwaway moment. Murphy throws aside a screen in a dark basement and she is seen in two quick cuts, cowering nervously, her long snake body writhing and making the sound of a rattlesnake.

It's a complex composite. Murphy is a foreground blue-screen element. The actress, suspended on a crane, was filmed as a separate blue-screen element and the go-motion tail was painstakingly matched to her movements. The movements were plotted frame-by-frame by Harry Walton. The end of the tail was a manually operated rod puppet. (The puppet only had one tail yet two can be clearly seen in these cuts, as if a decision was taken to put more writhing-movements into the shot. The second tail would have been added as a separate blue-screen element.) Articulate mattes, drawn frame-by-frame, were used to narrow the waist area of the snake body because Ritchie was worried that audiences might think this was merely an actress in a costume. A forked tongue darting out of her mouth was added as yet another element, but this is almost a case of ILM being *too* dedicated — it is doubtful whether anybody notices this. Perhaps it is registered by us unconsciously, but this author didn't notice it even when replaying the shots in slow motion.

There is no conventional stop-motion in this sequence yet it recalls the snake woman of *The 7th Voyage of Sinbad*. Similarities with Harryhausen don't end there: A later sequence, in which Murphy retrieves a sacred dagger, was to have featured a six-armed statue that comes to life, but the idea was dropped.

In a dark alley, Dance transforms into a rat. The shot has such a credibly fleshy and three-dimensional look to it that again we are reminded of how much special effects have advanced. This is light years ahead of the good old cel animation that turned John Carradine into a bat 40 years earlier.

A 60-second sequence in which Dance confers with the Devil in the caverns of Hell is breathtaking and deserves

to be seen on a cinema screen — it loses much on television. Defying gravity, the bricks of a wall fall away from the camera revealing the inferno of Hell behind. The camera dollies 360 degrees around the meditating Dance, then pulls back until he is merely a dot in the distance, the screen filled with a panorama of stalagmites, stalactites and bursts of flame (actually a 16-foot-deep miniature set). One of the bursts of flame obscures a switch from actor to photo cut-out, smoothly done so that this all seems to be one continuous shot.

Dance reverts to his true self, a scrawny, corpse-like but powerful winged demon. The protracted double-climax in which he and Murphy do battle is a stop- and go-motion classic. It has a fabulous puppet and some extremely smooth animation but its main contribution to the stop-motion genre is the fact that in many shots there is a lot of hand-held camera shake, adding to the drama and realism and avoiding the locked-off look of pre–ILM stop-motion. This was made possible by a motion-control system developed by Bill Trondeau that could store the details of any camera move onto floppy disk, whence the moves could be reproduced at any time on other pieces of film.

Phil Tippett was in charge of the demon sequences. He shared animation chores with Tom St. Amand and Harry Walton. Randy Dutra designed and sculpted three demon puppets — two 15-inch models and one 30-inch torso for closer shots. St. Amand designed the armature, which was machined by Blair Clark and Conrad Bonderson. Three go-motion mover systems were employed, including the one used in *Dragonslayer*.

The wonderfully evil-looking demon from *The Golden Child* (1986). The puppet, designed and sculpted by Randal Dutra, is here seen in front of a blue-screen prior to compositing with the live-action footage. Its legs and torso are connected to go-motion movers.

The rods, obscured by blue-painted paddles, were attached to the puppet's arms, feet and sometimes head in order to add realistic blurs to certain pre-programmed movements. Other appendages were animated with conventional hands-on stop-motion techniques.

The first of the two demon sequences features 22 stop-motion cuts and begins with Dance's transformation in front of Murphy. In two quick medium shots, his face begins to glow red, then breaks apart, made possible by matting out parts of his head. When a burst of flame recedes, it reveals the face of the black-eyed demon, a snarl on his lip. This moment needed a full-length shot of the demon and Murphy facing each other, but instead cuts to Murphy making his escape in a car with the Golden Child. In two quick full-view shots, the puppet smashes its way out of the burning house through the frame of a large window, straight at the camera. Window and puppet are separate blue-screen elements. The demon glides up towards the Sun, away from the camera.

Seen in long shot through the car's rear windscreen, the demon flies in pursuit, its wings making very smooth flapping movements. It flies down towards the camera, the car roof is peeled away (in live-action cuts), then it flies back up towards the Sun. What's missing here is a shot of the puppet on top of the car: It would have improved the scene, clarifying exactly what is going on. Murphy and the child take cover in the basement of a building and there is a very quick shot of the puppet flying past a water tower at the top of the building, causing it to collapse. The water tower is a miniature.

So far all the animation shots have been locked off, the sense of rapid pace and movement suggested in the editing. But the sequence from now on, inside the building, is full of dynamic camera shake, falling masonry and swirling clouds of dust. The camera tilts down as the demon flies out of the Sun and burrows straight into the ground, the animation synchronized so as to coincide with an explosion of earth being thrown up in the live-action plate. The cloud of earth is cleverly diffused around the image of the puppet.

Two impressive long shots, enhanced by camera shake and superimposed smoke, look down a tunnel at the demon standing on a pile of rubble at the far end behind an iron gate. He rips the door off its hinges as his wings start to unfurl on his back. In a tracking medium shot, the snarling monster advances through superimposed smoke, his slender, clawed arms reaching out menacingly. In three shaky long shots, he turns, grabs a piece of metal pipe from the wall and hurls it at Murphy. A live-action prop of the demon is used briefly and effectively in an over-the-shoulder shot. Pulling the building apart in his fury, the demon hurls two wooden beams at Murphy and the accomplished animation really gives a sense of the lunging creature unloading a great weight.

Two flawless composites look past Murphy at the demon walking behind him, turning and swiping him with one of his wings. The animation of the demon walking is astonishingly smooth, the composites are flawless, and the suggestion of contact between puppet and actor (achieved by means of articulate mattes drawn around the outline of the wing) is complete. In long shot, the demon looks down at the dagger dropped by Murphy, looks up as the ceiling starts to collapse and finally, in extreme long shot, gets buried under a ton of falling concrete, the live-action dust again somehow made to look as though it is surrounding the puppet.

The second appearance of the demon follows a few minutes later and although there are only 13 animation cuts this time, it is dramatically more successful because there is more of a sense of confrontation. In the first sequence, the demon was buried before he could do much. In a good shock effect, Murphy and the child are crossing a room when the demon suddenly bursts up through the floorboards. Blue-screened flying debris and swirling yellow cel-animation surround the puppet. A shaky closeup reveals that half of the demon's face has been bloodied in the tunnel collapse, and one of his horns is gone. Again pieces of blue-screened flying debris help bring the shot to life.

In two closeups, the demon draws the sacred dagger and raises it above his head ready to strike Murphy. But the knife is repelled by a medallion which Murphy is wearing and a fine long shot of the two characters shows the demon recoiling. His hand is on Murphy's shoulder behind the actor's head, a clever touch which helps to mesh the two elements. It's difficult to tell if articulate mattes were drawn around Murphy's outline or if he too is a blue-screen element, composited in front of the puppet.

The demon pushes Murphy to the ground, another effective moment of suggested interaction, with the puppet blue-screened in front of the actor miming the action. When the demon turns to retrieve the dagger, we get a good look at the knobby spines of his back, the bloody left arm, the scrawny tail and the wings that are half broken off. It's a shame that the deliberately hurried pace of the sequence didn't allow an opportunity to play up this idea of the demon being a physical mess — a couple of shots of him limping or nursing a wound could have added much to his character.

The blue-screened demon knocks over a table in the live-action film, stoops to pick up the dagger and turns and growls at Murphy. At the last moment, the Golden Child uses his telekinetic powers to send the dagger skimming across the floor, with the puppet watching it go. In a closeup with a lot of camera shake, the puppet turns back towards Murphy and in medium shot its vicious claws reach out for him. A cloud of swirling cel-animated eldritch energy surrounds him as he looks around at it anxiously (the cloud has been gener-

ated by the Golden Child, although the script is too rushed to make this clear). In a final explosive long shot, fragments of the demon fly at the camera, in a melee of yellow cloud and superimposed smoke.

Technically astonishing because of its level of heightened realism, the sequence disappoints because Ritchie has moved too far from the staginess of stop-motion of old. In his plan to keep everything moving and fast, he has lost some of the magic that these kind of fantasy images normally evoke. If ever a puppet demanded a few lingering, melodramatic shots, then Dutra's marvelous creation was it. Two long animation cuts were in fact cut out. One was a full-view shot of the demon's wings sprouting; the other showed him rearing up majestically behind a mound of earth, his wings unfolding. Presumably Ritchie felt that to dwell on his monster in such a way would be to the detriment of the pacing, but his decision also meant that the demon is stripped of all character. He could have been a truly terrifying, awe-inspiring fiend but instead becomes just another bogey man.

What was sorely needed was a little of the old Harryhausen theatricality. But, of course, Harryhausen enjoyed enormous creative freedom in his films, working with directors who understood that they were taking a back seat to the effects. If Tippett had directed *The Golden Child* and not merely been supervisor of the stop-motion sequences, then this would have been a *very* different film.

The Golden Key see *Zolotoi klyuchik*

The Golden Voyage of Sinbad

1973. Columbia. D: Gordon Hessler. Scr: Brian Clemens. Story: Brian Clemens and Ray Harryhausen. Additional Material: Beverly Cross. Ph: Ted Moore. Art: Fernando Gonzales. Mus: Miklos Rozsa. Creator of Special Visual Effects: Ray Harryhausen.

Cast: John Phillip Law, Caroline Munro, Tom Baker, Douglas Wilmer, Martin Shaw, Gregoire Aslan.

Rating: ☆☆☆   Stop-Motion: ☆☆☆

After the commercial and critical disappointment of *The Valley of Gwangi* (1969), Harryhausen's next film, made on a budget of $2 million, enjoyed a much more favorable reaction. Critics warmed to the lively swashbuckling ingredients, fans praised the special effects and the public turned out in number, making the film one of Columbia's big grossers for the year.

Alexander Stuart, writing in *Films and Filming* magazine, thought that "the film has much of what the Hollywood swashbucklers contained, and in some senses more. ... Technically far superior to the Hollywood creations of a couple of decades ago." Alex Noel Stuart, writing in the British press, was impressed by Harryhausen's effects: "The integration of his brilliantly made and animated monsters with the live action has a precision that is breathtaking. His fabrications at times really do look alive — particularly the homunculus and the ship's figurehead." Genre magazine *Castle of Frankenstein* enthused, "Harryhausen's talent comes thru better, greater than ever! ... RH's animation/spcl fx now look so much more natural that it's virtually impossible to see any traveling matte work." And, some years later, the film would be highly praised in Maltin's *TV Movies*: "Delightful ... Ray Harryhausen's finest 'Dynamation' effects ... Grand entertainment."

However, compared with Harryhausen's best work, *Golden Voyage* has some serious weaknesses. Gordon Hessler (who earlier directed a string of horror films including *Scream and Scream Again* and *Murders in the Rue Morgue*) is a routine talent, unable to enliven the non-effects passages. Scriptwriter Brian Clemens (best remembered for the TV series *The Avengers* and a number of Hammer horrors) wrote a satisfactory plot but his dialogue is clumsy, especially when it is trying to be spirited or witty (such as a feeble recurring joke about not forgetting to tie up one's camel).

The score by Miklos Rozsa, whose long list of credits includes memorable scores for *The Thief of Bagdad* (1940) and Hitchcock's *Spellbound* (1945), is occasionally effective (and much praised by Harryhausen), but is more often distractingly trite, employing corny Arabian Nights themes and working to the detriment of some scenes. (But it is superior to the scores of Roy Budd and Laurence Rosenthal in Harryhausen's two subsequent films.)

The plot is one of the stronger and more coherent of Harryhausen's films. For example, it is more rounded than the plots of *Mysterious Island* (which peters out amid a confusion of half-realized plot devices), *Jason and the Argonauts* (which degenerates into a series of set-pieces and has no conclusion), or *Clash of the Titans* (which is empty and hurried). Although S.S. Wilson (in *Puppets and People*) dismisses it as "clearly confused and episodic," it contains some thoughtful recurring images and themes (destiny, gold, the symbol of the eye, etc.) and culminates in a very classical restoration of order. Only the gratuitous appearance of a gryphon near the climax upsets this careful tone.

A distinct and satisfying visual style marks this as different to all Harryhausen's other films: This is the only one of his films to possess such a unifying quality. The color and lighting of most scenes is subdued and shadowy, with much of the action taking place either at night or in subterranean locations away from daylight. This is a brave variation on the bright colors and open spaces of other Arabian Nights movies. *Golden Voyage* includes a hidden underground chamber in the Vizier's palace, the Cave of the Oracle deep beneath the ruins of a temple, the subterranean tunnels of the lair of a race of Green Men and an attack at night by a ship's figurehead that comes to life. The somber hues of Harryhausen's models are deliberately in keeping with this eerie and original style. They are dark and sinister "children of the night."

Tom Baker, as the evil magician Koura, makes a lively, sneering villain (almost as good as Torin Thatcher in *The 7th Voyage of Sinbad*), but otherwise the cast is forgettable. John Phillip Law's Sinbad is far more credible than Patrick Wayne's attempt at the role four years later in *Sinbad and the Eye of the Tiger*. But Caroline Munro as heroine Margiana is even more of a token presence than is usual in these kind of films. Clemens' script never gives any of the other characters a chance.

Harryhausen spent a year in post-production on the special effects. Like all of his later films, it is remarkable for the sheer volume of effect shots, of which the stop-motion constitutes only a part. Unlike *The Valley of Gwangi*, this film uses extensive miniature sets to create a fantasy milieu, and in this respect is *Gwangi*'s superior. Actors and puppets are placed in among these sets by means of some superb traveling matte process shots, the quality of which is far in advance of most similar shots in earlier Harryhausen films. *Golden Voyage* is pleasing because of the *consistency* of the quality of the effects. Where other films have been let down by occasional glaring slips, this film maintains a high technical standard throughout, apart from one or two minor errors. Higher production values have allowed Harryhausen more time to perfect his composites.

The number of animation cuts is significantly less than in *Gwangi*, even though the running time is ten minutes longer (105 minutes). There are 253 cuts in *Golden Voyage* compared to *Gwangi*'s 335, a reduction of nearly 25 percent. Some of the cuts, however, are extremely long, such as in the scene where Kali, a six-armed statue brought to life, performs an elegant dance. As ever, Harryhausen's animation is extraordinary and the models are superb. His most visually dynamic character this time is the one-eyed centaur, a crop-haired brute with one golden earring, fangs, scaly torso and muscular horse's body.

Harryhausen's last films are often lumped together by fans and critics, who complain of the lack of invention and the staleness of the live action. One reason why *Golden Voyage* tends to get neglected is because there is no really outstanding animation sequence to rank with classics like the skeleton fights in *The 7th Voyage of Sinbad* and *Jason*, or the allosaurus battle in *One Million Years B.C.* The sword fight with Kali comes close but never achieves real dramatic punch because the character is never more than just an unfeeling statue. The hungry purpose and flourish of other animated villains are missing.

Nor are there any individual composites that leap out as being particularly ingenious. When one thinks of *Sinbad and the Eye of the Tiger*, the shot in which the animated baboon shakes hands with a live-action character always springs to mind. Or, in *Clash of the Titans*, who can forget seeing Perseus actually wrestling in close contact with the puppet Calibos? *Golden Voyage*, although it contains many wonderful composites, doesn't contain the kind of clever shots that are hailed by the fans as technical master strokes.

The story begins with an ominous, low-key prelude in which a strange, bat-like creature is seen flying above Sinbad's ship far out at sea. This tiny, purple-hued figure is a homunculus, created through alchemy by the wizard Koura. In a genre rather too fond of gigantism, the homunculus is a refreshingly unfearsome adversary. In its role as Koura's spy, it is more of a pest than a threat. Harryhausen gives it a high-pitched, squeaky cry which makes it almost endearing. The homunculus is more than just a monster that is met once and dispatched: It develops into a recurring figure crucial to the plot, acting as a telepathic messenger for Koura. And when it is caught and destroyed, Koura conjures up a second homunculus and sends that one off to do his bidding.

Twelve extreme long shots show the screeching creature up in the sky, an amulet glinting in its claws. These cuts are very smoothly animated by Harryhausen, with fluid wing movements unimpaired by strobing. He probably used a second, smaller model for this sequence of shots, which otherwise would have required a huge rear screen. A sailor shoots an arrow and the homunculus drops the amulet, which is animated as it falls. In two closer rear-screen shots using the larger model (it had a 16-inch wing-span), the creature harasses Sinbad and another sailor, trying to retrieve the amulet. Unlike the excellent long shots, these are impaired by grain contrast.

Sinbad retains the amulet and that night has a peculiar dream. The dream sequence includes four smooth cuts of the flapping, screeching homunculus, silhouetted against a night sky. The dream also introduces some of the images which will become significant later on: another amulet, a golden crown and a huge face carved into stone.

The next day, the ship arrives at the

port of Marabia and there are two establishing long shots which feature a miniature (or it may be a painting) of the walled city matted into the distance behind some trees. It's a quick but successful example of Harryhausen's mastery of more routine trickery.

Koura summons his homunculus to him. It is seen first in two long shots flying against a rear screen of the sky, then in two ambitious composites in which it sits on the magician's outstretched arm, its wings flapping to keep balance. There is a tiny amount of "drift" as Harryhausen tries to keep his puppet (hanging on wires) aligned with the actor's moving arm, but this is still an impressive effect.

In a secret basement, Sinbad is told the secret of the amulet by the golden-masked Grand Vizier of Marabia, unaware that they are being spied on by the homunculus. Harryhausen uses two different composite set-ups in a series of seven cuts showing the creature perched on a ledge above the two actors. Four of these are rear-screen static mattes, the camera looking up at the puppet from below, with the line of the ledge conveniently disguising the matte line. Three other rear-screen shots do not use a matte—the puppet and a miniature ledge are merely positioned in front of the background plate. The miniature ledge looks darker than the actual one, but this is a minor flaw. Flickering light from a fire in the chamber is duplicated on the puppet. Instead of merely having his puppet sit motionless, Harryhausen has it constantly making slight movements, crawling forward on its hands and knees, gently raising and lowering its wings and swishing its tail.

The elaborate second half of this sequence is delightfully bizarre and has a slightly comic tone far removed from the usual clichés in stop-motion confrontations. The homunculus gives its presence away and the vizier throws a book at it. It throws up its arms, topples over backwards and hits the ground, then limps off behind some vases which are placed into the foreground by another static matte set-up.

Adding a touch of likable sympathy, Harryhausen has his puppet squeak pathetically and drag its injured wing along the ground. As the vizier steps towards it, the poor creature backs into a wall and scurries behind a chest of drawers. This excellent composite, designed so that we are looking down at the homunculus, uses a partial miniature set. The creature runs, hops and stumbles across the floor, just evading Sinbad's clutching hand in the rear projection. A step in the floor disguises the matte line as Sinbad lunges straight at the puppet/camera. In the next cut, the homunculus, supported by wires, turns and leaps down off the step—in other words, the puppet crosses what was the matte line in the previous shot.

In the final shot in the sequence, Sinbad has grabbed the creature in both hands. In this clever composite, Harryhausen has freeze-framed the image of Sinbad's hands, allowing him to make a matte around their outline. The struggling puppet, seen from the waist up, is then dropped into the shot in the conventional "reality sandwich" manner. The shot gives us our best look at the homunculus' face so far—it's a shame the model wasn't detailed enough to allow for some lingering closeups. Finally, the

A ship's figurehead comes to life in *The Golden Voyage of Sinbad* (1973).

creature disappears in a puff of super-imposed smoke, leaving Sinbad with only a handful of ashes.

Fifteen minutes of slow live-action scenes follow, directed without energy by Hessler. Haroun (Kurt Christian), who supplies the film's weak comic relief, is recruited by Sinbad for his voyage, the ship sets off for the lost land of Lemuria, pursued by Koura's ship, and Sinbad gets romantic with Margiana. Koura decides to work his magic again, bringing to life the figurehead on Sinbad's ship one night, and instructs it to steal a chart.

This eerie, four-minute sequence, employing 42 animation cuts, is technically immaculate. The wooden automoton has the same kind of sinister, emotionless charisma as Talos in *Jason*.

The first effects cut is another enjoyable comic moment. As Haroun bemoans his lot to the figurehead, he briefly looks away and, in true pantomime fashion, it is at this moment that it lowers its outstretched arm — using the old trick of letting the audience in on something of which the character is unaware. This shot uses a different puppet than the one used in all subsequent shots. This one, only constructed from the knees up, is still connected to the masthead, and its moving arm is probably manipulated mechanically, rather than being animated one frame at a time.

Accompanied by cracking, splintering sound effects, the figurehead starts to tear itself away from the prow. First the head separates from its support, then the whole figure. These seamless static mattes blend in with the shadows on the boat. In two medium shots, the grotesque figurehead turns to look at a second sailor, who is grabbed around the throat by a prop hand. In three excellent long shots which matte around the entrance to the galley, the figurehead picks up the struggling sailor (now a smoothly animated puppet) and throws him overboard.

Other sailors rush onto the deck in a series of long shots using the same set-up described above. In one of these, the figurehead knocks some ropes off the roof of the galley, a consummate example of interaction through alignment of puppet and rear screen. In two medium shots, the figurehead is prodded by a miniature boat hook.

In another static matte set-up, the figurehead has stepped down (off-screen) onto a lower part of the deck. As it walks past the doorway leading into the galley, it turns, affording a good look at the wooden gash that runs all down its back. It walks behind some barrels that have been matted around and reaches stiffly for a sailor who ducks as he runs out of the doorway. With one heavy swipe of its arm, the wall of the galley is smashed — presumably pulled in by hidden wires in the live-action plate —

and the prop hand grabs the chart of Lemuria.

In one long and dramatic cut, the figurehead stomps over to the other side of the deck, passing behind some more foreground barrels. These have the look of a photo cut-out rather than a matted-in area: they are probably what was referred to in the publicity material as "a refinement of the process of metal cut-outs for perspective photography." One sailor runs at the figurehead and chops at it with an ax, For a few frames, a miniature ax is suspended in front of the rear image, allowing it to appear to pass in front of the puppet. When the sailor brings his ax down a second time, the miniature ax is left embedded in the automoton's chest. A second sailor swings at the figurehead with a boat hook — and again Harryhausen goes to the trouble of inserting a miniature hook for a few frames to enhance the illusion.

In three imposing medium shots, the figurehead looks down at the camera, the ax still grotesquely in its chest. The soundtrack jumps noticeably at this point, suggesting that some last-minute editing may have been done to shorten the scene. In a series of long shots (using the set-up already described) and medium shots, the figurehead fends off burning torches waved at it by some of the sailors. In the medium shots, the flames are superimposed.

In another set-up, the figurehead passes behind a mast and a barrel of apples. These are probably another "metallic cut-out" rather than a matte. The figurehead picks up a boat hook and lashes out at the sailors in three long shots.

In a series of medium shots and long shots, the figurehead backs the men up against the side of ship, trapping them. But then Koura telepathically calls out to it: "Return! Return!" In two medium shots, it looks up responsively and in a final long shot walks backwards into the right-hand side of the ship, smashing through the wood and falling into the sea. That part of the ship's side which the figurehead falls through appears to be a miniature, animated frame-by-frame as it splinters and perfectly matched to the real wood of the full-scale ship. A full-scale prop is used to show the figurehead hitting the water.

The next animation sequence is for many the highlight of the film. Koura creates a second homunculus — "Mandrake root and a few chemicals is all that is needed." This beautifully animated, restrained scene with its simple composite designs has enormous charm. Harryhausen imbues the pathetic, squeaking creature with a likably nervous personality, making it one of his finest bits of character animation. He chooses his favorite composite design for the fourth time in his career: The image of huge onlookers gazing at a tiny foreground figure on a raised platform has already appeared in *20 Million Miles to Earth, Three Worlds of Gulliver, Jason and the Argonauts* and *The Valley of Gwangi.*

Sixteen animation cuts in three setups make up the sequence. The first shots (non-mattes using a miniature floor) look down at the prostrate creature lying on a marble slab, making slight movements as the blood begins to course through its veins. Weakly, it raises one arm and partially unfurls a wing.

Then it raises its head, making a throaty bellow that sounds like it has just awoken from a long slumber. In a rear-screen static matte, the foreground creature backs away nervously on all fours when it sees Koura's face leering down at it.

The homunculus stands up and adopts the classic "arms back" pose of Harryhausen's bipeds. It unfurls its wings, squeaks apprehensively and hisses when Koura pokes at it playfully with some scissors. Its tail swishes smoothly from side to side behind it. The magician, delighted with his handiwork, makes chirruping noises as though he were trying to attract the attention of a kitten.

The sequence's third design is a side view with Koura on the left side of the frame facing the puppet on the right. The matte line follows the outline of Koura's arm — resting on the table — and allows the homunculus to walk over and jump up onto the arm. It's a very successful moment of interaction.

An adequate but rubbery prop of the homunculus is used in a long shot of Koura walking over to a window with the creature still on his arm. Another good matte is used to show the creature, still perched on Koura's arm, flapping its wings to maintain its balance. The matte around the actor's arm allows the far wing to pass behind it, considerably improving the illusion. In two aerial-braced shots, the creature flies off into the night, backed by a rear projection of the sea. The slow, natural rhythm of the wings means that there is no offensive strobing.

Sinbad and his group arrive at the shores of Lemuria. A very striking series of locked-off composites show the actors standing on the beach surrounded by cliff faces dotted with weird temples and with enormous carvings sculpted into them. The miniatures are perfectly color-matched with their live-action surroundings and there is absolutely no registration "jiggle." These marvelous images, inspired by a combination of Hindu and Khmer architecture, convey the impression that Lemuria is a magical, mystical land.

In a brief cut, the homunculus, in the foreground, spies on Sinbad's party in the distance. No matte is used, since the puppet's feet are below the edge of the frame. Unfortunately, Harryhausen pans across his rear screen, highlighting the grain in the image and making the shot look exactly like what it is: a puppet in front of a separate image.

Sinbad's group arrive at the Temple of the Oracle of All Knowledge. These temple ruins, situated in a lush jungle, are a magnificent fantasy setting, and give the impression that they have been lost for hundreds of years. The temple itself, with a huge face carved on each of its four sides, is a miniature, backed by a painting of trees and the sky. Prop trees, a full-scale carved image of the Buddha and the actors are placed into the foreground by means of some superb blue-screen matting. It's a seamless and evocative composite; it's a shame that the budget didn't stretch to more than one perspective of it.

Sinbad and his troupe enter the temple and descend into the cavern below. In two deft composites, the homunculus is shown to be following them. The camera looks up from within the cave at the men entering and zooms in on the feet of Sinbad, who is last in. As his feet step out the frame, the tiny homunculus crawls through the door-

way. The design of the shot, the camera movement and lighting perfectly matched on the puppet make these successful composites. Rozsa's slow score is ominously effective at this point.

The Oracle himself is a live-action creation, a huge goat-horned head that rises up out of a well in the floor amidst a whirl of superimposed flames. He tells Sinbad to travel north to a land with "a Goddess cast with many limbs." The scene is watched over by the homunculus, seen in three good static matte shots, perched high on a ledge.

Koura uses his alchemy to cause the temple to blow up, an extremely well-done miniature effect shot at 96 frames per second to create the illusion of bulk as the structure collapses.

Sinbad tries to escape from the cave by climbing a rope up to a hole in the roof. In a sequence containing ten stop-motion cuts, the homunculus makes its last appearance, launching itself into the air from its perch and harassing Sinbad as he clutches the rope. As ever, it is more of a nuisance than a danger and we can't help feeling some pity for it in its final shot — lying on the ground with an arrow through its body, wings twitching feebly.

The animation of the creature in flight is very smooth and the shadowy lighting on the puppet helps it to blend in with the rear-screen image. Some of these long shots probably use the smaller model that was seen in the film's opening scene. The arrow that finally kills the homunculus is wire-supported and animated frame by frame. The speed with which it crosses the frame is slightly too slow but doesn't spoil the effect. The final shot of the dying creature on the ground uses the rubber prop. A bit more pathos in its death scene would have been appropriate—after all, this is one of Harryhausen's most likable creations. Too bad Koura never gets around to fashioning a third one from his chemical jars.

Sinbad and his party escape from the cave and make their way to the Temple of the Green Men. This is another first-class fantasy setting. Pillars have been carved into a sheer rock face, surrounding the tunnel that leads into the temple. Carved into an adjoining rock face is an enormous statue of a seated god, holding a flaming dish in its lap. Only the scale of the flames gives away the true size of this excellent miniature. More superb traveling matte composites put the actors into this scene.

Inside the temple, Koura searches through the treasures belonging to the Green Men, looking in vain for the missing part of the amulet. To win their obedience, he gives them a demonstration of his powers, bringing to life a statue of their six-armed god Kali.

Kali's dance is one of the film's highpoints, with Harryhausen surprising critics who had pigeon-holed him as a creator only of monster battles. He imbues his puppet with graceful arm, leg and head movements, at the same time maintaining the impression that it is a metal statue. This sequence, which took him six weeks to film, not only required that he keep track of all the moving arms but also had the complication that all the movements had to be synchronized to the Indian sitar music that backs it. Fortunately, this is one of the few occasions when one of Harryhausen's full-scale props perfectly

matches the design and color of its miniature counterpart. The only disappointment in the 12 animation cuts in this sequence is the presence of a glaringly obvious floor inlay whose color does not match its live-action surroundings.

In concept, the scene has much in common with the dance performed by the four-armed snake-woman, also brought to life by a magician, in *The 7th Voyage of Sinbad*.

Koura throws a vial of yellow liquid at the statue and, in a medium shot, its head turns slowly with a dramatic squeal of metal that recalls Talos coming to life in *Jason*. To the amazement of the cowering Green Men, it waves its six arms up and down elegantly, then steps down off its pedestal with a heavy clank. Its head snakes from side to side in the fashion of an Indian dancer, and it begins to walk down the steps in front of it. These long shots are seamless static mattes, with the puppet and a miniature set of steps inserted into the live action, and Koura standing in the foreground.

"Dance! Dance for me!" calls the magician. Kali walks into another static matte set-up (with the poorly matched inlay) and in five long and very complicated cuts performs its slow and beautiful dance.

In a clever contrast, the dancer becomes a killing machine in the next stop-motion sequence. This superbly choreographed sword fight is Harryhausen at his fast-paced, dynamic best. Its 50 animation cuts contain some marvelous flourishes (such as the appearance of the five swords out of thin air), some fine instances of interaction and exact timing in matching the actors' gestures to the puppet's sword-arms. The actors, of course, had to be carefully rehearsed to convincingly battle with an absent opponent who would be added months later during post-production. However, this labor of love by Harryhausen is badly served by a half-hearted score by Rozsa which seriously undermines the pace of the visuals. As a result, it does not have the same impact as the skeleton fight in *Jason* (with its marvelous score by Herrmann) or the allosaurus fight in *One Million Years B.C.* (which achieved dramatic force with no score at all).

The first cut is a clever static matte long shot in which Koura throws his sword to Kali, who catches it. Either there was no live-action sword and Baker just mimed the action (with a wire-supported miniature sword added later during animation) or else there is a matte line running vertically down the center of the screen, allowing the real sword to disappear and be replaced at the crucial moment by a miniature. This matte line would be in addition to the floor inlay around the puppet's feet.

Swords appear in Kali's other hands, magicked from thin air. However, they don't merely appear: they *grow* upwards in the statue's hands. This enjoyable flourish may have been achieved by filming the shot in reverse, with part of each sword being whittled away frame by frame.

Each pair of swords is lowered purposefully in Sinbad's direction. A wicked leer crosses Koura's face, backed by an appropriately sneering musical note. In a series of long shots using one static matte set-up, intercut with medium shots, Sinbad faces off against the gently swaying statue, then engages the battle.

Another sailor rushes in, his sword is knocked away and he is slashed across the chest by one of Kali's swords — courtesy of a partial miniature sword used in a few frames.

In a slightly different set-up, Sinbad rolls across the floor beneath the statue's feet to retrieve the sword. This set-up is preferable to the previous one because it is not marred by an off-color floor inlay, using instead a simple linear matte line. The downside of this is that the puppet does not throw a shadow. Sinbad and Haroun battle the statue from opposite sides, while another sailor gets slashed by one of the ever-moving arms. Several medium shots highlight the busyness of the statue, with all six sword-arms slashing and striking.

In another, closer static matte set-up, Sinbad continues battling, then runs round behind Kali. The sequence's only use of traveling matte is an extreme long shot in which Haroun throws a flaming brazier at the statue. Haroun and the brazier are the blue-screen elements, added to a rear-screen composite of Kali and the other sailors. The brazier bounces off some object painted so as to match in with the blue-screen set and the resulting image carefully aligned with the position of the puppet. The illusion of contact is impeccable in this impressive shot.

Seven cuts use yet another static matte set-up depicting a flight of steps leading up to a raised platform. The bottom of the puppet's feet disappear below the matte line, but few people would notice this amid all the frenetic action. Sinbad is forced back up the steps by the relentless statue and there seems to be no way of stopping it.

The final 11 animation cuts take place up on the platform. Two different static matte designs and several medium shots have Haroun and Sinbad still battling against the unstoppable statue. But Kali is finally defeated when Haroun rushes at it from behind, knocks it over the edge and it shatters into pieces below. Harryhausen doesn't attempt any clever interaction at this moment, implying the contact merely through the editing: a shot of Haroun running across the frame cuts straight into a live-action shot of the statue falling.

Capturing Sinbad and his party, the Green Men intend to sacrifice Margiana to their "God of the Single Eye." The image of the rickety wooden crate holding Margiana being lowered into a forbidding pit is a fine fantasy image, but Harryhausen did it much better in a similar image in his next film, *Sinbad and the Eye of the Tiger*, when he had a baboon inside a cage raised up into a pillar of light.

One of the genre's most deliciously drawn-out buildups precedes our first sight of the centaur. At the bottom of the pit, Margiana apprehensively runs this way and that, knowing that something is about to emerge from a tunnel leading off to one side. The tunnel is a miniature matted faultlessly into the studio pit set. The eerie sound of echoing hooves and a shadow on the tunnel wall usher in this magnificent model. Half-stallion, a quarter human and a quarter monstrous, the centaur has a gray, leathery torso, a crop of spiky red hair and a single eye in the center of its forehead. On one wrist is a bracelet studded with metal spikes.

It is one of Harryhausen's most outlandish creations but unfortunately he doesn't develop it enough. The centaur had the potential to take on Kong-like sympathetic proportions, especially in view of its apparent fondness for Margiana. But Harryhausen is guilty of a serious miscalculation. Instead of spending time on scenes that would build up the personality of the centaur, he introduces another puppet character, the griffin, which gratuitously engages the centaur in a climactic battle. Some advance publicity referred to "the monstrous, sensual Centaur, raging with unearthly desires"—but this approach was dropped before the release.

The 12 stop-motion cuts of the centaur's first scene make use of three static matte set-ups as well as several medium shots. Still partly in shadow, the centaur has to stoop slightly as it emerges from the tunnel. In this set-up, a floor inlay is well matched to its surroundings. The other set-ups allow the creature to take several steps across the pit and get nearer to Margiana. Looking up at the shouting sailors above, the centaur growls angrily at them, making a sound that, perhaps deliberately, recalls the cries of Karloff's Frankenstein Monster.

In a deft touch, the centaur's hands clutch at the air as he reaches up ineffectually. It apprehensively stomps one of its forelegs on the ground and its tail is constantly swishing to and fro. Harryhausen makes matters easier for himself by giving the puppet a solid muscular tail rather than a hairy horse's tail. In the last three cuts, the centaur carries off a puppet of Margiana, whose arms hang down with credible limpness as the creature walks back into the tunnel.

Back at the top of the pit, the Grand Vizier removes his mask. His hideous, burnt face causes enough of a distraction for Sinbad and his party to break free and follow Margiana down into the pit. Three cuts show the centaur carrying Margiana through its underground lair (actually the Caves of Arta in Majorca). These are all long shots with the puppets successfully matted in between pillars of rock in the rear image. In the last of these cuts, the centaur puts its prize down and turns to investigate the sound of a rockslide — caused by Koura blasting his way into the tunnels.

The film's final setting is the chamber of the Fountain of Destiny, a pillar of magical bubbling water surrounded by a circle of Stonehenge-like slabs of stone. This is another impressive miniature creation, with the actors placed in the foreground by means of some more superb traveling matte photography. The scaled-up water for once does not look out of place: Projected at a slow speed, it has an unnaturalness which is suggestive of the magical qualities which the pool possesses.

Koura, rejuvenated by the pool, summons the centaur in order to defeat Sinbad. Surprisingly, Harryhausen again uses the device of having the centaur's arrival preceded by the teasing sound of hooves — dramatically unnecessary this time since we already know what the creature looks like. Another excellent floor inlay is used in a series of shots when the centaur emerges from a tunnel (probably the same miniature tunnel as before) into the cavern, this time brandishing a huge wooden club. In a wonderful medium shot backed by flickering light on the cave wall reflected up

from the rippling pool, the centaur growls and angrily grits its fangs, its hair bristling in the same way that Kong's fur bristled 40 years earlier.

Another set-up mattes around one of the fallen pillars. Sinbad jumps up onto it and ducks as the centaur swipes at him with the club. Closer shots of Sinbad engaging the centaur do not use a matte, but maintain the successful suggestion of co-existence of puppet and actor. The club shatters when the centaur smashes it onto the pillar, narrowly missing Sinbad, an effect achieved with a live-action prop. When the creature hurls the shattered remains of the club at Sinbad, the pace of the wire-supported miniature is a bit slow, but it's still a visually pleasing image.

The centaur is distracted by the sound of squawking coming from another tunnel. After four reaction shots of the centaur, looking across the cavern and angrily clenching its fists, the griffin steps out of the other tunnel. Half-lion, half-eagle, this is another beautifully detailed model, especially the fur on its body and the feathers on its wings.

But the film is dramatically weaker for its presence. Its gratuitous appearance upsets the pace, distracting from what should have been the real business of the climax. It has no character at all: It walks on, battles the centaur and gets killed. Out of context, the sequence is impressive, but Harryhausen fails to generate the kind of excitement that it needed. His masterful direction of the skeleton scene in *Jason* and the allosaurus battle in *One Million Years B.C.* is absent here. Part of the blame lies with Rozsa's score which during the centaur/griffin fight is feeble and recalls some inept B-picture.

The battle is a graphic display of bestial savagery and contains 27 animation cuts, including a number of ingenious touches.

In its first shot, the griffin steps out from a tunnel, its wings raised. The tunnel is another miniature, and a carefully matched floor inlay surrounds the puppet's feet. In a medium shot, the centaur rears up onto its hind legs. (Incidentally, a much-published still of the centaur, club in hand, facing the griffin, is a publicity pose and does not actually appear in the film. The same goes for a shot of Sinbad plunging his sword into the centaur's chest.)

In a classic melodramatic long shot, the two beasts face off against each other, circling warily. The puppets stand on an extensive miniature floor and the image is backed by the frothing fountain. Three shots use this attractive set-up, in the third of which the animals lock together, the centaur's arms closing around the griffin's head. A dramatic and shadowy medium shot has the centaur throttling the screeching griffin.

Another static matte set-up, used in two long shots, shows Koura standing in the foreground behind one of the pillars, looking out at the struggle. The centaur is gored by the griffin, is forced to the ground then gets up again. An effective medium shot pans left-to-right across the rear-projection, following the puppets as the centaur pushes the griffin across the cavern.

Constantly shifting the perspective from one static matte long shot to another and to medium shots, Harryhausen shows the griffin getting the bet-

ter of the centaur. The griffin lunges at the retreating centaur, bringing it down and goring it repeatedly. Then both animals are up again, tearing into each and wrestling closely. As ever, the sheer stamina of Harryhausen leaves you gaping.

In yet another static matte design, the griffin bites into the centaur's arm, the puppets standing on a well-matched floor inlay, and Koura looking on from the right. At this point, the script desperately tries to give the battle some dramatic context and has the Vizier mutter, "It is as the Oracle foretold — the forces of Good and Evil battling eternally."

Not wishing to see the centaur beaten, Koura steps out from behind the pillar and slashes one of the griffin's hind legs with his sword. For a couple of frames, a painted or miniature sword passes in front of the puppet, a very successful illusion of physical contact. The griffin partially collapses, vivid red blood glistening in its wound. The centaur seizes the advantage, strangling the griffin in three shots. The griffin's wings flap desperately and eventually it lies still.

A forceful low-angle medium shot looks up at the triumphant centaur who, in long shot, drops the corpse of its vanquished foe. The centaur gets up from its half-crouch and, in two more low-angle medium shots, turns to look around for the sailors.

The ensuing battle between the sailors and the centaur is a much more dramatic and integral sequence than the fight with the griffin. The plot, with all its references to the symbol of the one eye and the abduction of Margiana, has been building up to it. Harryhausen's control of pace picks up again here, making this an exciting episode.

The first of 16 puppet shots is a medium shot of the creature stomping towards the camera. A foolish point-of-view shot with a fuzzy outline is supposed to represent how the centaur sees things. An effective camera move enhances the next shot, tilting up as the puppet advances straight at the camera. Presumably, Harryhausen merely tilted his animation camera, careful not to tilt higher than the top of the rear screen.

Four static matte designs are used in long shots during the sequence, all very accomplished. In the first, the centaur strides left-to-right across the frame in front of four sailors retreating in the background. The second uses an impeccably balanced floor inlay, with the centaur standing on the right of the frame facing the sailors. The third design is first used in a dynamic shot in which the monster chases Haroun right-to-left across the frame towards the fountain. Harryhausen's animation of the centaur's gait is extremely realistic.

In a fabulous moment of high drama recalling the phororhacos scene in *Mysterious Island*, Sinbad leaps onto the centaur's back. Harryhausen achieves this smoothly by cutting from a live action shot of the actor leaping off one of the fallen pillars to a long shot (using the third matte set-up described above) of a Sinbad puppet already on the back of the centaur. The Sinbad puppet stabs at the monster, which roars and rears up onto its hind legs.

The fourth design is an effective change of perspective, showing the action from the far side of the pool, a matte line following the edge of the pool in the lower foreground. Sinbad continues stabbing at the centaur's back. Screaming, the beast is unable to shake off its attacker or reach behind to grab him. One quick cut employs a full-scale prop of the centaur's back and is successfully color-matched to the puppet.

The growling centaur stomps around in a circle. In a shot using the first matte design again, a sailor stabs at the creature with a spear only to have it grabbed by the centaur and find himself swatted away with a slap of its hand. The apparent switch from live to miniature spear is done with a favorite Harryhausen technique: In fact, there is no live-action spear. The actor pretends to be holding one and the miniature one is later lined up with his actions. Two tiny partial miniature hands are placed onto the sword so that it really looks as though the actor is grasping the spear. This subliminally registered but crucial trick was also seen in *The Valley of Gwangi* in the shots of Carlos wrestling with the grounded pterodactyl.

The centaur rears up and the puppet Sinbad falls backwards, cutting into a shot of the actor hitting the ground. A dagger left embedded between its shoulders, the screaming centaur tries desperately to reach back to pull out the blade but can't quite get at it. In medium shot, the howling creature makes wild, theatrical gestures in a long cut animated with enjoyable flourishes typical of Harryhausen. In long shot, the centaur finally collapses next to the corpse of the griffin and falls over onto its side, a classic image of Good and Evil together, backed photogenically by the churning fountain.

The film closes with an impressive

non-animation effects sequence in which the cackling Koura slowly becomes invisible and engages Sinbad in a swordfight. Finally, the disfigured Vizier is restored to his former self in a shot using a fairly basic series of dissolves.

The Golden Voyage of Sinbad is essentially a vehicle for Harryhausen's effects and its main flaw is that it lacks the feeling of excitement and grandeur

that its subject matter tries so hard to exude. But it is still a wonderful film, full of fresh fantasy images, shadowy monsters and technically superb animation effects. Forget that many of the live-action scenes are flat and watch Harryhausen's episodes out of context — and then appreciate the true genius of the man.

Goliath and the Dragon
(Italian title: *La Vendetta de ercole*)

1960. Italy/France (AIP). D: Vittorio Cottafavi. Scr: Mario Piccolo, Archibald Zounds, Jr. Ph: Mario Montuori. Art: Franco Lolli. Mus (US version): Les Baxter. Special Effects (uncredited): Project Unlimited (Gene Warren, Tim Barr, Wah Chang, Victor Delgado, Jim Danforth).

Cast: Mark Forest, Broderick Crawford, Eleonora Ruffo, Gaby André, Philippe Hersent, Sandro Maretti.

Rating: ☆☆½   Stop-Motion: ☆☆

This is thrown together without too much attention to dramatic coherence but is still occasionally spectacular and always a lot of fun. Bad guy Broderick Crawford, sporting a gruesome facial scar, generally gives Goliath (Mark Forest) a hard time. This includes dangling his girlfriend over a snakepit and nearly having Forest's brother's head crushed by an elephant.

The special effects are often laughable but get full marks for trying: a fire-breathing three-headed dog, a man-sized bat-creature, a centaur and a giant

bear. These are all extras in silly costumes. Better (but not much) is the dragon. Jim Danforth explained the genesis of these two scenes (in an article in *Cinemagic* #34): "It was originally intended as a very elaborate film, a sort of Hercules-styled Greek mythological adventure, but the plans went awry and they ended up purchasing an Italian strongman film and inserting the dragon sequence into it. So we at Project Unlimited built the dragon and animated about a half dozen scenes that they just cut into this other film. Strange sort of a mishmash, but AIP liked it." It seems that the stop-motion shots were intercut with shots from an existing dragon sequence (featuring a large mechanical prop head), rather than forming an entirely new sequence of their own tacked on gratuitously.

The dragon is first seen early on in two establishing shots. Two long shots, looking up at a ledge in a huge cave, reveal the stop-motion puppet, a slender, scaly creature in the conventional dragon mold. It rears up on its hind legs and roars. Neither human puppets nor actors in composites are included in these cuts, with the effect that we have no indication of the beast's size, considerably weakening the intended dramatic impact.

More successful are the seven stop-motion cuts that feature in Goliath's later battle, mainly achieved with shots of the prop head, a slack-jawed, unblinking creation that blows smoke through its nostrils. Once again, no interaction with the actors is attempted in the animated cuts. The dragon is shown rearing up on its hind legs, pushing a few animated rocks down onto the actors and throwing its head up in agony when Goliath pokes out the eye of the prop head with his sword. Half of the animation was done by Danforth and half by Victor Delgado, Marcel's brother and longtime partner. There is lots of unintentional humor in the shots featuring the prop head as Goliath biffs it with his sword, throws a rock at it and eventually takes a leaf of Kong's book when he rips its jaws apart. The stop-motion shots improve the sequence considerably — raising it from the level of awful to mediocre.

The Gorgon

1964. Hammer. D: Terence Fisher. Scr: John Gilling. Story: J. Llewellyn Devine. Ph: Michael Reed. Art: Bernard Robinson, Don Mingaye. Makeup: Roy Ashton. Special Effects: Syd Pearson. Mus: James Bernard.

Cast: Peter Cushing, Richard Pasco, Christopher Lee, Barbara Shelley, Michael Goodliffe, Patrick Troughton.

Rating: ☆☆   Stop-Motion: ☆½

This is shot in sumptuous Eastman Color but otherwise has little going for it. Even the reteaming of Hammer luminaries Christopher Lee and Peter Cushing is a letdown — they only have one brief scene together. John Gilling scripts this like he had just been turned to stone by his title character — nothing happens for 90 minutes. A few foolish people wander up to a spooky old castle (a typically poor Hammer matte painting), glimpse the wrinkly old Gorgon (complete with unconvincing rubber snakes in her hair) and turn to stone. Roy Ashton gives Michael Goodliffe a good stone-gray makeup for a scene in which he is gradually turning to stone, but this is the film's only novel idea. Terence Fisher directs on automatic.

In the climactic denouement, which the audience has seen coming a mile off, it is revealed that the Gorgon is actually Barbara Shelley. Her final shot, in which the face of the Gorgon transforms back into Shelley, features a special makeup effect which makes use of stop-motion.

A closeup of the decapitated head of the Gorgon was shot one frame at a time. A fabrication of the face of the monster was carved away little by little, as if peeling away from the face, and revealing Shelley's face (another fabrication) underneath. Finally, the image of the actress' face was dissolved into the shot, replacing the life mask. It's an ambitious effect and unfortunately not successful — this always looks like a special effect.

The Great Rupert

1950. Eagle-Lion. Prod: George Pal. D: Irving Pichel. Scr: Lazlo Vadnay. Story: Ted Allen. Ph: Lionel Lindon. Art: Ernest Fegté. Mus: Leith Stevens. Technical Supervisor: John Abbott. Stop-Motion Animation (uncredited): Fred Madison.

Cast: Jimmy Durante, Terry Moore, Tom Drake, Frank Orth, Sara Haden, Queenie Smith.

Rating: ☆☆½   Stop-Motion: ☆☆½

This amiable comedy was George Pal's first feature film. It tells the story of a down-on-their-luck vaudeville family who are amazed to find that when they pray every Thursday at three in the afternoon, $1,500 comes floating down through a hole in the skylight. To them, this is a miracle from Heaven. In fact, the money is being hidden in a joining wall each week by their neighbor. A squirrel that lives in the niche between them picks up what it considers litter and throws it into their house.

Jimmy Durante gives a likable performance as the kind-hearted father, always ready with a one-liner. Terry Moore — the star of *Mighty Joe Young* the year before — is the daughter. Irving Pichel, who co-directed *The Most Dangerous Game* (1932) and *She* (1935) and would direct Pal's next feature, *Destination Moon* — controls everything with a light touch which makes this a pleasant if unremarkable effort.

Rupert the squirrel is depicted in a combination of live-action shots and animated shots using a stop-motion puppet. The live-action shots use a partly trained squirrel seen in long shots of it running around and in shots in which actors hold the animal in their hands. The 39 animation shots were handled by John S. Abbott and Fred Madison, two of Pal's animators from his Puppetoon short films. Originally, Pal asked Ray Harryhausen to work on the film. But Harryhausen, having just completed *Mighty Joe Young*, was looking for more ambitious projects and had no desire to return to his $15-a-week Puppetoon days. A decade later, he would try his hand at animating a squirrel in *The Three Worlds of Gulliver* (1960).

In the stop-motion cuts, the animal makes intricate movements beyond the capabilities of a trained squirrel — catching a thrown walnut, throwing dollar bills around and even dancing and skipping. The animators make Rupert quite a personable little fellow, without ever overstepping the mark and making him comic or unbelievable.

A few very successful composite shots are included, but most of the stop-motion was done entirely on miniature sets, not requiring any mattes or extra camera passes. The standard of the animation is not exceptional but is generally smooth enough to have convinced many contemporary viewers that they were watching a live trained squirrel.

In the opening scene, Rupert, dressed in a kilt and tam-o'-shanter, is standing on a table and practicing his dance routine with his owner (Jimmy Conlin). Long shots in which Conlin dances around the table appear to be rear-screen set-ups, with the puppet and table placed in front of footage of the actor. These are very careful composites and do not look like effects shots. Closer shots look down at the puppet, dancing a Scottish jig which involves slow gestures with his arms and legs. In one cut, Rupert pulls out a rope and begins skipping in time to the music. When two other characters enter the room, Rupert removes his cap and bows.

Conlin is evicted from his apartment and decides to release Rupert in a nearby park. Two shots of Conlin's hand placing Rupert on the ground look as if a convincing prop hand was built, with the puppet making slight movements in its grip. In one shot looking down at the puppet on the ground, Rupert gestures with his arms, indicating that he wants his Scottish clothes to be removed. The puppet, its clothing removed, turns, looks up and then hops off reluctantly. It is not known what type of fur was used to cover the puppet, but the animators manage to avoid leaving ruffle marks on it that might have made it "bristle" in the way that King Kong's fur does.

Left to fend for himself, Rupert doesn't have much luck. In one cut, his head pokes through some miniature leaves and he spots a nut on the ground. But a second squirrel — also a stop-motion puppet — rushes in and snatches it up. Rupert walks over to another nut but an animated sparrow flits past and takes it. After a very realistic closeup of Rupert's face, nostrils and whiskers twitching, the live-action squirrel climbs up a tree, only to be scared off by an owl. The owl, seen briefly in one cut blinking and leaning forwards, is also a stop-motion puppet — and a very convincing one.

Rupert takes up residence within the walls of the apartment and is disturbed by the sound of a drill coming through the woodwork. In an animated closeup, the squirrel reacts to the sound of the drill. He watches the point of the drill coming through the wall and, curious, touches it. This gesture is a good idea and helps to make Rupert a likable character. He recoils as the drill (now an animated prop) breaks through the wall. The neighbor passes some dollar bills through the hole he has made but Rupert, who doesn't want these irritating bits of paper cluttering up his home, picks them up and throws them out through a hole in the opposite wall. In another nice touch, Rupert rubs his hands together, satisfied by a job well done.

In the apartment later, Durante is juggling with some walnuts. The live-action squirrel runs along a wooden beam above Durante. In a stop-motion cut, the puppet catches one of the walnuts (which are presumably wire-supported as they pass in front of the puppet) and runs off.

Week follows week and a series of four animation shots depict how Rupert

The Great Rupert (1950): Jimmy Durante poses with the squirrel puppet. (BFI Stills, Posters and Design.)

is performing his "miracle" each time Durante's wife says her prayer. In each, the squirrel picks up the bills as they come through the hole and throws them out. Each is shot from a different angle to give them some extra interest. In one of them, Rupert wakes up under a pile of bills and pushes his head up through them.

Later, Durante lights a cigarette and throws it up into the air, intending to catch it in his mouth. But Rupert catches the cigarette in mid-air (a similar shot to the walnut shot) and the live-action squirrel runs back into the wall. The cigarette sets the house on fire. In one clever shot, Rupert is seen surrounded by flames. The flames appear to be not a superimposed element but paper cut-outs skillfully manipulated during animation to look like flickering fire.

Rupert survives and is reunited with Conlin in the park. The stop-motion puppet pokes its head through a miniature bush; then, at the sound of Conlin playing the squeezebox, hops out into the foreground. This shot involves an extensive miniature set full of bushes and grass, which matches well with the location set. Finally, Conlin and Rupert find that their musical act brings them fame. Four stop-motion cuts are used to show Rupert, in his Scottish outfit, dancing on a table on a stage. Two of these are close all-miniature shots. The other two are impeccable composites — probably rear-screen set-ups again — with Conlin standing to one side.

In *The Great Rupert* Pal is not really interested in exploring the dramatic potential of stop-motion. Rather, he uses the process because it would have been impossible to make the film entirely with a live-action squirrel. He would use stop-motion many times in his career over the next 25 years, but usually in one-off, comic scenes. Despite his passionate enthusiasm for film fantasy, he was always reluctant to indulge puppet animation to the same extent as it was seen in the films of Ray Harryhausen. This is a shame because, with Pal's long history of working with the Puppetoons, he might have been the prime mover in advancing the process to new technical and dramatic levels.

Gremlins

1984. Amblin Entertainment. D: Joe Dante. Scr: Chris Columbus. Ph: John Hora. Art: James H. Spencer. Mus: Jerry Goldsmith. Gremlins Created by Chris Walas. Stop-Motion: Fantasy II Film Effects. Creature Crew: including Randy Dutra, Blair Clark, Anthony McVey, David Sosalla, Marghe McMahon, Tom St. Amand, Pete Kleinow. Creature Consultant: Jon Berg. Matte Paintings: Dream Quest Images. Matte Artist: Rocco Gioffre.

Cast: Zach Galligan, Phoebe Cates, Hoyt Axton, Polly Holliday, Dick Miller, Keye Luke.

Rating: ☆☆☆   Stop-Motion: ☆☆½

This extremely mischievous movie — about a swarm of 18-inch-high monsters that go on the rampage — was one of many likably indulgent fantasy films made in the 1980s. As with *Ghostbusters* and others, the filmmakers and audiences had started to realize that it was perfectly acceptable to like monsters after all.

Joe Dante (whose earlier credits include *Piranha* and *The Howling*) directs in hyperactive mode, throwing in so many in-jokes and gimmicks that the plot almost seems to get in the way. One gremlin wields a chainsaw (à la *Texas Chain Saw Massacre*) and another sits in a mock-up of George Pal's time machine. If nothing else, such moments at least induce a knowing smile. At times, Dante doesn't seem to care whether his movie is believable or not, yet he directs with enough assurance that we are kept wanting to know what is next going to happen to the characters caught up in this madness.

Produced by Steven Spielberg, the film had a budget of $11 million, approximately $1 million of which was spent on the effects required to bring the gremlins to life. In charge of creature effects was Chris Walas, whose credits include *Piranha, The Empire Strikes Back* (the shaggy cave creature) and *The Fly*. With a large crew of assistants, he populated the film with a menagerie of rod puppets and cable-controlled puppets with a staggering range of movements: cackling, smoking, riding a scooter, even break-dancing. In one memorable scene, he shows newly-born gremlins hatching out of gooey cocoons (of course, *Invasion of the Body Snatchers* is on a TV in the background) and at the climax, the chief gremlin, Stripe, decomposes unforgettably into a fleshy, wriggling skeleton.

But one shot was beyond even the capabilities of Walas' talents. For a long shot of a horde of gremlins walking along a street, Dante chose to go for stop-motion. It turned out to be one of the film's best moments, both because of its haunting, shadowy lighting and because the puppets, as they advance *en masse* towards the camera down a lonely street, are for once seen moving independently of any means of support hidden in floors, walls, trees, etc.

The street is a miniature surface matched to a surrounding live-action plate of the curb and houses. First Stripe emerges from the shadows, then he is followed by about 20 more gremlins, all cackling evilly, one or two leaping over others in the melee.

The shot was designed by Gene Warren, Jr., and Peter Kleinow at Fantasy II Film Effects. In a letter to the author, the shot was discussed by Leslie Huntley, the third of Fantasy II's three partners: "Peter did an amazing job on the gremlins shot. Gene and he set it up, did the lighting, figured out the split, etc., then Peter did all of the animation. Forty-six puppets, five days, one take. The shot was so well-received, everyone wanted more! Back to the set, turn on the lights, animate another 12 hours and the additional piece was jump-cut in."

Consider the mathematics of the effort required to produce this ten-second cut: approximately 240 frames of film, each requiring the manipulation of up to 46 puppets, each with four limbs and a head to animate...

Also on the long crew list are stop-motion luminaries Tom St. Amand, Randy Dutra and Jon Berg, although on this occasion none of them was involved with the film's one stop-motion shot.

Gremlins 2—The New Batch

1990. Amblin Entertainment. D: Joe Dante. Scr: Charli Haas. Ph: John Hora. Art: James Spencer. Mus: Jerry Goldsmith. Gremlin and Mogwai Effects Supervisor: Rick Baker. Stop-Motion Animation: Doug Beswick Productions (Doug Beswick, Yancy Calzada). Visual Effects Animation: VCE/Peter Kuran.

Cast: Zach Galligan, Phoebe Cates, John Glover, Robert Prosky, Robert Picardo, Christopher Lee, Dick Miller, Keye Luke, Tony Randall (voice).

Rating: ☆☆☆   Stop-Motion: ☆☆½

Chris Walas' superb live-action puppetry in the original film was supplemented by only one stop-motion cut. The sequel is slightly more ambitious, containing 12 cuts by Doug Beswick in two scenes. The live-action puppetry this time is by Rick Baker and is so good that it almost makes any use of stop-motion unnecessary; his puppets are so flexible and versatile that one wonders if the art can be taken much further. However, for elaborate actions by free-standing puppets, there was still no real substitute for stop-motion in 1990. So once again the process gets used as a "last resort" when no other technique is viable: Beswick must be disappointed that he was not asked to do more. His contributions are a bat-gremlin and a spider-gremlin, mutations that are the result of the creatures getting into a genetic research laboratory and drinking all the DNA concoctions. Armatures for both creatures were built by Yancy Calzada.

The bat-gremlin episode is brief but excitingly staged, uses several superior rear-screen composites and recalls (whether consciously or not) the harpy sequence of *Jason and the Argonauts*. The bulk of the excellent animation is by Beswick, with Calzada executing the final shots of the creature's demise.

On a table in the DNA laboratory, the gremlin sprouts wings, a clever shot which seems to have been achieved by blue-screening the gremlin's body in front of a pair of stop-motion wings. The wings had to be stop-motion rather than live action because of the intricate way they grow, unfurl and curl. In a static matte rear-projection shot, the stop-motion puppet, standing next to a live-action gremlin, takes to the air, its wings flapping very smoothly. The smoothness of the flapping motion is due to a go-motion device, built by Hal Miles, which was inserted into the puppet's wings, causing them to move slightly during the camera exposure.

The bat-gremlin flies over a group of four scientists, harassing them. In a marvelous seven-second cut outside the building, the stop-motion puppet swoops out of the window in the extreme distance, flies past another building (a shadow is momentarily superimposed onto the wall), flies into the foreground, then glides smoothly up and away behind another office block.

In the street below, tourist Dick Miller and his wife look up and are alarmed to see the bat-gremlin swooping down from the extreme distance into extreme closeup. In two rear-screen shots with lots of camera movement, the bat-gremlin attacks Miller. The way that its legs hang down recalls the harpies of *Jason*. Several cuts use a live-action puppet, always kept partly out of frame, but the two final cuts in the sequence are done with stop-motion. Miller coats the creature with concrete and in long shot it flaps stiffly up towards a cathedral spire. Finally it settles on the spire, turns a paler shade of gray and stiffens, becoming a stone gargoyle.

The spider-gremlin sequence had the potential to be genuinely scary but it may be that director Dante deliberately held back so as to insure an MPAA that would get him a younger audience. A girl wanders around the darkened corridors of her office and gets caught in a huge spiderweb. The suspense generated here is unfortunately dissipated by Dante, who cuts to other action elsewhere in the office. By the time we return to the girl the tension has all but gone.

Two stop-motion cuts are used in this sequence, unforgettable shots of the dog-sized spider coming around a corner towards the web. It's a very nasty-looking creature, a gremlin's head and torso bizarrely sprouting from the body and legs of a giant spider. The corridor is a miniature set, allowing the creature's feet to make contact with the floor and throw shadows on it. All subsequent cuts in the sequence use a live-action puppet seen in partial shots as it gets closer and closer to the victim, only to go up in flames when Gizmo fires a burning arrow at it. It's criminal that Beswick's beautiful model was not put to better advantage. Here, as in the bat-gremlin sequence, his animation is excellent; he deserved a bigger share of the action.

Gremlins 2 is at least as much fun as the original but is not a film for people who enjoy a good story. Plot is irrelevant as Dante flies through elaborate gags, in-jokes, pastiches of his and other people's films, and never lets the audience forget that what they are watching is mere artifice. Two gremlins have a good chuckle as they watch a TV re-run of *Beast from 20,000 Fathoms*. One sequence is a shot-by-shot reconstruction of Lon Chaney's unmasking in *Phantom of the Opera*, with gremlins playing both parts.

Most of the film is set in a skyscraper belonging to likably power-mad John Glover, and there are plenty of good gags sending up office life. Christopher Lee is boss of the top-floor genetics lab, running around mumbling, "The horror! The horror!" when things get out of hand. The absurd song-and-dance routine at the end, involving the elaborate puppetry of over a hundred gremlins, is skillfully handled by Dante so that we enjoy it rather than dismissing is as merely silly, which could so easily have been the case. Going one better than the original's food-blender episode, this one has a very messy scene where a gremlin gets shoved through a paper shredder.

The sheer scale of Baker's fabulous effects is staggering — he operated with a crew of 80 working under him. Careful lip-synch (voiced by Tony Randall) is used for a gremlin that drinks brain serum. Fetal gremlins move in membranous pouches on the bodies of other gremlins that have come into contact with water, and so reproduce. Near-perfect traveling mattes allow Gizmo to walk and dance in full view. The climax is a mass gremlin meltdown when they all get electrocuted.

Guyver: Dark Hero

1994. Biomorphs/LA Hero. Prod-D: Steve Wang. Scr: Nathan Long. Story: Steve Wang. Based on Characters Created by Yoshiki Takaya. Ph: Michael Wojciechowski. Art: George Peirson. Mus: Les Claypool III. Creature Shop Supervisors:

Steve Wang, Moto Hata. Flying Transformation FX Plates Photography: Ted Rae.

Cast: David Hayter, Kathy Christopherson, Bruno Giannotta, Christopher Michael, Stuart Weiss, Billi Lee.

Rating: ☆☆½   Stop-Motion: ☆☆

This fast-paced fantasy gets close to approaching minor classic in places, but is let down by Steve Wang's conventional direction. As producer, story writer and creature effects supervisor, Wang shows great talent, but he should have left the direction to someone else.

David Hayter transforms into the Guyver in order to do battle with the Solenoids, a race that has co-existed with humans but concealed their real forms: humanoid monsters with reptilian, crustacean and insectoid characteristics. These are all extremely good monster suits designed by Wang, but he is unable to do much with his creatures, apart from letting them indulge in fistfights and kung fu acrobatics which become repetitive after a while.

The film's highlights are sequences within an excavated spaceship, an eerie network of tunnels that recalls the biomechanical setting of *Alien*, and a beautifully staged flashback to the origins of the Solenoids, featuring a panoramic miniature of the world in volcanic turmoil and moody shots of a group of prehistoric Solenoids gathered around a fire.

For one shot, Ted Rae was called on to supply some stop-motion. Hayter, in human form, leaps off a cliff in extreme long shot, and as he falls he transforms into the Guyver. Fourteen tentacles emerge from his body and wrap around him, forming a metallic suit. This stunning shot, seen from below, used a puppet of the actor filmed on a tabletop, then blue-screened into the live-action plate so as to appear to be falling. It took ten hours to animate the two seconds of stop-motion that form part of this eight-second cut. The tentacles were actually animated "in reverse," progressively carving away pieces of the tentacles frame by frame.

Hayter does a similar transformation later on in the film, but this time the effect may have been achieved with computer animation, which is certainly used in an impressive morphing shot in which a character changes into a Solenoid in one continuous closeup.

Hardcover

1988. Trans World Entertainment. D: Tibor Takacs. Scr: David Chaskin. Ph: Bryan England. Mus: Michael Hoenig. Special Visual Effects Created by Randall William Cook. Special Effects by Ruckus Enterprises. Artistic Supervisor: Randall William Cook. First Effects Technician: Fumi Mashimo. Sculptor: Bill Bryan. High Speed Cinematography: Jim Aupperle. Special Thanks to Jim Danforth, Craig Reardon, Bill Taylor.

Cast: Jenny Wright, Clayton Rohner, Randall William Cook, Stephanie Hodge, Michelle Jordan, Vance Valencia.

Rating: ☆☆½   Stop-Motion: ☆☆☆

As a slasher movie, this is a "cut" above most, directed imaginatively by Tibor Takacs (under a shooting title of *I, Madman*) with an eye for eerie camerawork and an ability to whip up several mild scares. The inventive script has mad Malcolm going on a killing spree to replace the bits of his face that he cut off years earlier: nose, ears, lips, hair. He is brought back to life by the supernatural force that one of his books (hence the title) exerts on the heroine when she reads it. All well and good, but there's a bonus: Malcolm has combined his seed with the ovary of a jackal and produced the Jackal Boy.

Almost superfluous to the main action, this subplot allows Randall William Cook to indulge himself in an impressive stop-motion climax. It's an unforgettable episode: a bizarre model, surreal action, fast cutting, extremely smooth animation, lots of blur on the puppet and flawless composites unhampered by rear-projection grain. Technically it's as good as anything Phil Tippett and or ILM have come up with, but dramatically is let down by its brevity and by the way it seems tacked on to provide a convenient climax. Like so many stop-motion sequences, the best way to see it is out of context as a self-contained scene.

Cook (who also plays Malcolm) was in overall control, designed and sculpted the puppet and did all the animation. Jim Danforth provided the armature. The refusal to mention stop-motion in the credits suggests that Cook may have been consciously teasing his audience, refusing to let on how it was done. After watching these sequences, many viewers are quite baffled as to how the Jackal Boy was made to move; they have no idea it was stop-motion, so slick are the effects.

Cook also created Malcolm's grisly makeups, with an assist from Craig Reardon. Jim Aupperle shot some background plates and contributed the film's final haunting image, but was not involved with the animation.

The puppet makes a brief appearance at the start of the film (four quick cuts) in a passage that is eventually revealed to be an invention of the heroine's imagination as she reads one of Malcolm's novels. A hotel clerk is investigating complaints that a guest has an animal in his room. Looking around the darkened room with a torch, he is suddenly confronted by the growling Jackal Boy, only half-seen in the torchlight but clearly far from human: Beady eyes, sharp little fangs and skeletal limbs are glimpsed.

There is a significant blur on the second cut when the Jackal Boy lunges at the screaming clerk: Cook rewound each frame of film, then re-exposed it with the puppet in a slightly different position, creating the illusion of blur (a technique used earlier by Danforth in *When Dinosaurs Ruled the Earth*). A few seconds later, the heroine (in the adjoining bedroom) is startled to see the door collapse in a cloud of dust and the Jackal Boy leap into her room. This ambitious full-view shot is remarkable because the puppet's feet are standing in the live-action dust cloud. A soft-focus static matte was used to blur the point where dust and puppet meet.

The sequence closes with a very quick but effective cut in which the puppet advances straight at the camera from medium-shot to closeup, ending in an extreme closeup which seems to have been enhanced by the fact that a wide lens distorts the puppet's features. This has the dual advantage of blurring the image and adding to the nightmarish quality of the shot.

The Jackal Boy is not seen again until the last five minutes of the film, in a sequence full of startling images that were conceived by Cook. Hero and hero-ine (Clayton Rohner and Jenny Wright) are about to be finished off by Malcolm in a bookshop attic but Wright reads a passage from one of his books and causes the Jackal Boy to appear.

There is a rasping growl, then all heads turn to see the creature squatting on an overhead girder, its long tail swish-ing to and fro, arms held back in the classic pose of a Harryhausen puppet. This is a seamless rear-projection set-up with the live actors in the foreground, and is used in three cuts. In one, the ac-tors' arms pass in front of the model, achieved by having hand-drawn articu-late mattes (painted on glass) follow the movement of the arms frame-by-frame.

The third cut is a fluid piece of wire-supported animation as the Jackal Boy leaps down at Malcolm. There are approximately seven very rapid stop-motion cuts as Malcolm wrestles on the floor with his mutant son. Some are so quick that it is difficult to be sure that they are animation cuts and not shots using a prop. In some of these cuts, Cook used a stop-motion puppet of himself (built by Fumi Mashimi and sculpted by Cook). They roll one way, then the other, the puppet's scrawny arms surrounding Malcolm. In a series of medium shots, the Jackal Boy looks down at its father,

picks him up by the head and takes a bite out of his neck, then shakes him vio-lently from side to side. The cuts are blurred and rapid but never show any of the strobing which often impairs such actions.

A striking long shot shows the pup-pet standing up in the middle of the attic with no sign of a matte line or floor inlay. It picks up a puppet Malcolm and throws it at a far wall (the camera cuts to the live actor at the moment of impact). In three more rear-screen shots (from a different perspective), the puppet's feet are disguised in a convenient shadow where they meet the floor. The crea-ture turns slowly towards Wright and Rohner, cowering in the foreground, but then turns back to its hated father. Two medium shots show the puppet growling at out-of-frame Malcolm; in the second shot, it starts to walk towards its in-tended victim.

There is a very fine moment when Malcolm, in the foreground, grabs a fire extinguisher and swings it at the Jackal Boy. The extinguisher passes in front of the puppet, then smacks it full in the face; the illusion of contact is completely successful. The effect was achieved not with a painted or miniature prop but by Cook's favored method of rotoscoping mattes, drawn frame-by-frame so as to follow the outline of the extinguisher as it moves. It's impeccably done.

Filmed from behind, the recoiling creature falls back through a pane of glass, an ambitious shot requiring the animation of miniature shards of glass. Changing to a sideways perspective, Cook then shows the creature slamming onto the tabletop on the other side of the glass, its head and arms flailing around from the impact — another impressive bit of choreography.

The Jackal Boy is now allowed its only moment of pathos in two closeups which emphasize its human qualities. Its bestial features — green eyes, fangs, a wrinkled skin — are softened by the almost sad expression on its dazed face. It seems to realize that a large shard of glass is about to fall on it and tries to get up. But it's too slow, and lets out a scream as the glass cuts into it. A very gruesome shot shows the creature's lower half falling to the floor, the legs still kicking, animated blood trickling down the wall behind.

But it's not dead yet: Cook has kept one magnificently grotesque trick up his sleeve. Malcolm returns to the business of doing in his victims only to be interrupted by another growl. He turns and sees the top half of the Jackal Boy still alive and moving on the table. Croaking feebly, the puppet, which is now merely head, arms and torso, lifts itself up with its slender arms and jumps down, bounding across the floor towards Malcolm by using its hands as feet. Beautifully animated, this used 48 model poses to the second and had additional blurring added to it by Cook, who pulled the puppet slightly on invisible wires during the long frame exposures. This bizarre moment (comprising only four animation cuts) ends when the Jackal Boy leaps up at Malcolm and sends them both crashing through a window. They transform into the loose pages of Malcolm's novels and flutter away on the wind, a likably poetic end to a film that has always been a few steps outside reality.

Häxan (U.S. title: *Witchcraft Through the Ages*)

1921. Sweden. Svensk Filmindustri. D-Scr-Story: Benjamin Christensen. Ph: Johan Ankerstjerne. Art: Holst Jørgensen.

Cast: Maren Pedersen, Clara Pontoppidan, Elith Pio, Oscar Stribolt, Tora Teje, Benjamin Christensen.

Rating: ☆☆☆   Stop-Motion: ☆☆

This Swedish production, directed by Benjamin Christensen (who was Danish), is a visually remarkable and often horrific study of witchcraft from the Middle Ages through to the present day. The medieval section (which makes up the largest part of the film) is recreated with extraordinary detail, evoking a Chaucerian world of grubby costumes, musty old houses and larger-than-life characters. Elegant camerawork always makes the most of light and shadows, such as in the sequence in a dingy kitchen where firelight glows through a smoky haze.

Christensen deftly combines horror with comedy and fantasy. In one amusing episode, a wife administers a love potion to her obese husband, who chases her around their garden. To effect a curse, two old crones urinate into pots on the doorstep of their intended victim, turn three times and throw the pots at the door. The naked Devil (Christensen), a pointy-eared, horned figure with impossibly long talons, appears at a woman's window, tempting her away from her sleeping husband, and then seduces her. A sequence depicting torture instruments takes great delight in demonstrating how each should be applied.

Stop-motion is used briefly in one sequence. A woman falls to the floor dead and her spirit (a superimposed image) leaves her body and floats to Hell. Here, a shadowy black magic ritual is attended by beings that are part-human and part-animal, some wearing unsettlingly grotesque masks. As the woman looks at a wooden door, a creature on the other side starts to tear a hole in it with its hands. When the hole is big enough, the creature, a horned goat-like being with a mischievous aspect, steps through. This one shot, filmed entirely on a miniature set, uses a stop-motion puppet. Quite why Christensen should have gone to the trouble of building this puppet (presumably just a wire-jointed armature) for the sake of one shot, and what inspired him to use the process, will probably never be known. It may be that he had seen the animated Russian films of Władysław Starewicz and was trying to emulate their surreal images.

Hellbound: Hellraiser II

1988. New World/Cinemarque/Film Futures. D: Tony Randel. Scr: Peter Atkins. Story: Clive Barker. Ph: Robin Vidgeon. Art: Mike Buchanan. Mus: Christopher Young. Special Makeup Effects: Image Animation. Animation Sequences: Rory Fellowes, Karl Watkins.

Cast: Clare Higgins, Ashley Laurence, Ken Cranham, Imogen Boorman, Sean Chapman, William Hope, Doug Bradley.

Rating: ☆☆½   Stop-Motion: ☆☆☆

The original *Hellraiser* (1987) broke new ground in the horror genre and showed author Clive Barker at his best: full of wild imagination and fleshly depravity. But this sequel was merely an excuse for gratuitous gore and eye-catching splatter effects. Certainly there was no plot to speak of and characterization was nil. Some moments are unpleasantly nasty merely for the sake of it. For example, a madman who hallucinates that his body is crawling with maggots is given a cutthroat razor to play with by his doctor.

The film's highlights occur towards the end when Dr. Channard (Ken Cranham) is transformed into a Cenobite — one of a number of hideous, other-dimensional creatures that populate the film. The Channard-cenobite, who floats above the ground by means of a giant tentacle that has burrowed into his skull and holds him up, possesses murderous tentacles that emerge from the palms of his hands. These are depicted by means of stop-motion, allowing them to take on a life of their own, snaking and coiling with a vitality that would be denied mechanical contraptions. The extremely smooth and accomplished animation was done by Rory Fellowes and Karl Watkins, working for Bob Keen's Image Animation effects company.

These are bizarre sights — unpleasantly fleshy and slimy tentacles with blades at their tips doing nasty bits of splatter business. But the sequences suffer from the absence of any composite shots. There are no long shots of Channard with the tentacles snaking out of his hands. These were needed to visually clarify what is going on, but perhaps the filmmakers felt they lacked the budget to carry out such shots convincingly. All shots which feature the tentacles as well as Channard's hands use models of the actor's hands.

There is stop-motion in three sequences. In the first of these (containing ten animation cuts), the Channard-cenobite visits a patient in bed. In closeup, three tentacles snake out of a slit in one of his hands (a model). One has a knife at the end, another an eye. Another knife emerges messily through the eyeball. "I recommend amputation!" the doctor bellows. Knives appear at the ends of each tentacle and snake in the direction of the patient. Live-action cuts show the blades actually planting themselves into the patient's head.

There are eight animation cuts in the scene where Channard kills all the other Cenobites. First, he holds up his bloody palms and the snake-like tentacles emerge from them. A beautiful flower emerges from the tip of one. From another, a finger appears and beckons a victim to come forward. Behind these tentacles, others open and close their mouths hungrily. The other Cenobites cause hook-tipped chains to launch themselves at Channard. In response, two tentacles (tipped with knives) emerge from each of two model hands, then coil up. In live-action cuts they then whip out and cut through the chains holding the Cenobites. "I'm taking over this operation!" Channard boasts. In animation cuts, the tentacles shoot out of his palm, detach themselves and, in live-action cuts, spear the Cenobites.

The climactic scene in which Channard eventually gets his just deserts (he is messily beheaded) contains six animation cuts. The tentacles sprout scissors that snip hungrily at the air, then one produces a swirling cluster of blades like a Swiss Army knife gone berserk. A complicated cut shows three tentacles slithering back into the slits in each of his palms; a final animation cut has one tentacle lash out and slash the heroine's hand.

Hellbound is another example of the many films of the 1980s and 1990s that found a brief but highly original use of stop-motion, having realized that no rod puppets or mechanically operated prosthetics could match the versatility of the process.

Hellraiser III—Hell on Earth

1993. Fifth Avenue. D: Anthony Hickox. Scr: Peter Atkins. Original Story: Peter Atkins, Tony Randel. Based on Characters Created by Clive Barker. Ph: Gerry Lively. Art: Steve Hardie. Mus: Randy Miller. Special Effects and Special Makeup Effects Co-ordinator: Bob Keen. Special Visual Effects: Cinema Research Corp. Visual Effects Supervisor: Steve Rundell.

Cast: Terry Farrell, Doug Bradley, Kevin Bernhardt, Paula Marshall, Ken Carpenter, Ashley Laurence.

Rating: ☆☆   Stop-Motion: ☆½

Fond memories of the startling original are undermined even more by this feeble third entry in the series. Scriptwriter Peter Atkins is unable to devise a decent plot but tries to disguise this behind all manner of pretentious set-pieces and gory splatter-fests. Pinhead, trapped in a stone statue, wants to free himself and obtain the cube that acts as an interdimensional key. Atkins drags this out for 90 minutes, throwing in gratuitous Vietnam War and Second World War scenes in a vain attempt to spice things up. Anthony Hickox directs with the same lackluster style that he showed in *Waxwork, Sundown* and *Lost in Time*.

Plot loopholes are numerous and irritating; this is a screenplay that has not been properly thought through. How is it that Pinhead (Doug Bradley) is able to dispatch the entire clientele of a nightclub effortlessly yet struggles to retrieve the cube from lone heroine Terry Farrell? Once again, the Cenobites, so chilling in the first film, are reduced to comical bogey men. The weak "twist" ending is proof that Atkins had no idea how to resolve his film.

The eye-boggling stop-motion effects that featured in the second film are here reduced to four quick cuts, all of which look hurried and cut in awkwardly with the live-action effects. The statue of which Pinhead is still a part splits open to swallow a girl whole (after she has been stripped of her skin, naturally). The shot in which the hole seals up again uses replacement animation to show the gray stonework moving together like living flesh. In two other shots, the gray statue turns to flesh color and faces carved in it start to move. Later, a priest holds up a crucifix as defense against Pinhead but it melts in his hand. This shot appears to use a model crucifix, whittled away frame by frame, shot in front of a rear-projection of the priest and matted into a photo blow-up of his hand.

Herbie Rides Again

1974. Walt Disney. D: Robert Stevenson. Scr: Bill Walsh. Story: Gordon Buford. Ph: Frank Phillips. Art: John B. Mansbridge, Walter Tyler. Mus: George Bruns. Special Effects: Eustace Lycett, Art Cruickshank, Alan Maley, Danny Lee.

Cast: Helen Hayes, Ken Berry, Stefanie Powers, Keenan Wynn, Huntz Hall, John McIntire.

Rating: ☆☆   Stop-Motion: ☆☆

Walt Disney's amiable live-action comedy *The Love Bug* (1969), about a Volkswagen with a mind of its own, was followed by a series of increasingly lackluster sequels, the first of which was *Herbie Rides Again* in 1974.

Some of the shots in these films were filmed in miniature, allowing the driverless car to perform otherwise impossible actions, such as bouncing up in the air after impacting with another vehicle or making a cartoon-style leap into the air before accelerating.

Stop-motion is used not in a shot with the car, but in an extreme long shot in which Ken Berry is hanging beneath a window cleaning platform half way up a high-rise building. Presumably because no suitable location could be found, the building was constructed in miniature. As a result, the only feasible way to have the character dangling from the platform was to stop-frame a puppet. It's a brief cut and the animation of the kicking legs is very credible. The lower part of the shot is live action, with cars driving up to the base of an actual building which has been carefully aligned with the miniature top section.

Highway to Hell

1991. Hemdale. D: Ate De Jong. Scr: Brian Helgeland. Ph: Robin Vidgeon. Art: Phillip Dean Foreman. Mus: Hidden Faces. Special Makeup Effects Designed and Created by Steve Johnson. Special Visual Effects Designed and Created by Randall William Cook, Cinema Research Corporation. First Visual Effects Technician: Fumi Mashimo. Matte Paintings: Rocco Gioffre, Mark Sullivan. Special Thanks to David Allen, Illusion Arts, Jim Danforth.

Cast: Patrick Bergin, Adam Storke, Chad Lowe, Kristy Swanson, Pamela Gidley, C. J. Graham.

Rating: ☆☆½   Stop-Motion: ☆☆½

This fantasy-chiller veers wildly between inventive sequences (a diner crowded with living-dead cops, an attempted seduction by a hideous old succubus) and contrived padding (token appearances by a gang of bikers, a pointless and clumsy brothel scene). There is even a plot of sorts: A girl is abducted by Hell-cop, a bald-headed, scar-faced bogey man, and taken to Hell, from where her boyfriend must rescue her from the clutches of Satan himself (Patrick Bergin).

Steve Johnson, in charge of makeup effects, and Randy Cook, in charge of visual effects, supply all the bits of magic that make this look classier than many other films of a similar budget. Johnson's effects include the convincing full-body succubus costume and a pair of handcuffs that are just that — two disembodied hands on a chain that are used to inhibit captives. The fingers flex and unfurl in an extremely realistic manner.

Cook's effects include some accomplished sub–*Back to the Future* shots in which cars burst through a dimensional portal, an impressive matte shot of a highway disappearing into a vast mountain and an imposing miniature of Hell City — a jungle of impossibly high skyscrapers. Jim Danforth receives a screen credit — he loaned Cook a roto-stand used for some of the matte work.

One of the film's best sequences is a quick throwaway moment in which the hero (Adam Storke) has to get past the guardian of Hell City — Cerberus, a three-headed dog. This is played more for laughs than chills: Storke's pet dog distracts Cerberus by cocking its leg, allowing Storke to sneak past.

The realistically proportioned puppet stands on four scrawny legs and Cook really makes it seem alive. But it is let down by the design of its three heads which, although they have snarling jowls and vicious teeth, look too rubbery and lack the savagery which the character should possess. Perhaps this was part of a deliberate attempt to make this a jokey set-piece. The puppet was designed and sculpted by Cook. The armature was machined by Fumi Mashimo.

Cook's animation is exceptional and (as ever) he makes his puppet bound across the screen with the kind of dramatic choreography that is uniquely his own.

The first of 11 stop-motion cuts is a memorable long shot of Cerberus sitting outside his kennel. In the rear projection, smoke wafts up from his doggy bowl. When he senses Storke's approach, the three heads whip around one at a time. For this rapid action, as in subsequent shots, Cook uses multiple frame exposures (i.e., re-exposing the same frame of film with the puppet occupying a slightly altered position) to create the illusion of a blur.

In a cleverly timed shot, Storke runs towards the camera, then abruptly halts as Cerberus leaps in front of him. Multiple exposure again adds a blur to the image, this time with the added complication of having the puppet wire-supported during its leap. Shot from above and behind Storke, the next shot uses a rotoscoped matte around the actor's arm so that it seems to pass in front of the puppet's three snapping heads.

Cook keeps the puppet busy in several closeups. Cerberus growls and snaps at Storke as his heads bob up and down actively and his jowls sneer menacingly. In long shot again, the dog backs up and allows one of the dead to pass. One of the heads turns to watch Storke's dog while the other two continue to focus on Storke. At the sight of the dog cocking its legs, Cerberus lunges across the frame.

The two final shots shift the perspective so that the camera looks at Cerberus from behind Storke's dog. Cerberus leaps straight at the camera, a miniature chain around his neck aligned so that it appears to be attached to a concrete pillar that is part of the rear projection. Cook executes this ambitious bit of choreography perfectly. In the final stop-motion cut, Cerberus is up on his hind legs and straining on his leash, trying to get at the live-action dog, which sits calmly in the foreground.

An earlier shot, in which the succubus-demon falls through the floor into a seemingly bottomless pit, may be a blue-screen stop-motion effect. The figure falls such a great distance that it is unlikely that the shot could have been done live-action. If it is stop-motion, then Cook's animation of the flailing limbs is superb.

In the States, this had a brief theatrical release, but went straight to video in Britain.

Honey, I Shrunk the Kids

1989. Walt Disney/Silver Screen Partners III. D: Joe Johnston. Scr: Ed Naha, Tom Schulman. Story: Stuart Gordon, Brian Yuzna, Ed Naha. Ph: Hiro Narita. Art: Gregg Fonseca. Mus: James Horner. Practical Effects and Creature Mechanicals: Image Engineering, Inc. Mechanical Effects Coordinator: Peter Chesney. Visual Effects Photography: Rick Fichter. Visual Effects Coordinator: Michael Muscal. Creatures and Miniatures Supervisor: David Sosalla. Visual Effects Animation: Peter Kuran. Additional Ph: Paul W. Gentry, Michael Paul Lawler. Scorpion Sequence by Phil Tippett. Stop-Motion Animators: Harry Walton, Tom St. Amand. Design and Construction: Craig Davies. Armature Construction: Blair Clark. Bee Sequence Crew: Camera Operator: Jo Carson. Animator: Laine Liska. Stop-Motion Ant Crew: Stop-Motion Animator: David Allen. Construction: Dennis Gordon. Assistant to Animator: Brett White. Matte Painting and Additional Composites: Illusion Arts. Matte Artists: Syd Dutton, Mark Whitlock. Additional Stop-Motion Animation (uncredited): Randal M. Dutra.

Cast: Rick Moranis, Matt Frewer, Marcia Strassman, Kristine Sutherland, Thomas Brown, Jared Rushton.

Rating: ☆☆☆   Stop-Motion: ☆☆☆

This was the closest thing to a "stop-motion film" since Harryhausen retired after *Clash of the Titans* in 1981.

Not only do stop-motion puppets feature in three major sequences but there is even a battle between two of them — an ant and a scorpion — which recalls the heady days of dragons fighting with Cyclops, centaurs throttling gryphons, and all the rest. No one — other than Harryhausen — had attempted this kind of scene since David Allen and Randy Cook staged a battle between the Troll Lady and a Wolf Lizard in 1979's forgettable *The Day Time Ended*.

The abundance of animation was possible because the stop-motion scenes were shared out among a wealth of talent, including Phil Tippett, David Allen, Tom St. Amand, Laine Liska, Harry Walton and Randal Dutra. The exclusivity of Harryhausen's one-man-show style of filmmaking was, by 1989, a thing of the past, and it is a wonder that he managed to achieve so much working by himself. Even the combined team working on *Honey, I Shrunk the Kids* has produced considerably less screen-time of animation (74 cuts) than in most Harryhausen films. Even bearing in mind the fact that Tippett, Allen and all had much less time to create their effects than Harryhausen (who usually enjoyed a full year in post-production), one must still marvel at the stamina of stop-motion's elder statesman.

The success of the special effects of *Honey, I Shrunk the Kids* is due in part to the presence of several ex–ILM members on the crew. As well as Tippett, now operating his own company, the film has cameraman Rick Fichter (whose earlier credits include *Poltergeist* and *Ewoks: The Battle for Endor*), executive producer Thomas G. Smith (who worked on many ILM films and also wrote a book about the company, *Industrial Light and Magic — The Art of Special Effects*) and director Joe Johnston, who had been effects designer on several films including all three *Star Wars* films. Johnston directs with the skill of someone sympathetic to the requirements of a film heavy with effects sequences. He never allows effects to seem gratuitous or slow down the plot. Pace, characterization and an overall mood of gentle humor are maintained and it was a successful recipe: The film was one of the year's biggest earners.

Four kids get accidentally shrunk to a quarter-inch high by a device invented by mad scientist father Rick Moranis. They get swept into a garbage sack, dumped at the end of the garden and spend the rest of the film trying to get back to the house. The giant sets, crowded with blades of grass, are totally convincing, and there is a well-staged sequence in which the kids are rained on by water from a garden sprinkler.

Two of the kids climb the stalk of a weed in order to get their bearings. Close shots and medium shots are done with the live actors, either in the giant set or as blue-screen composites with the lawn stretching away behind. Two long shots looking up the stem at the sky use stop-motion puppets of the boys, clinging to the plant. As the stem sways, the legs of one of the boy puppets kick out realistically. The shots were not done live-action because the angle of the set-up would have meant that a large blue-screen would have to have been hung horizontally across the roof of the studio. Two huge red flowers in the lower foreground add color to these striking shots.

One boy falls onto a flower just as a swarm of bees is passing overhead. He is picked up by one of the bees, which thinks it is gathering pollen. The other boy goes to his friend's aid and jumps on the bee's back. The bee then flies off at great speed across the garden and through trees, giving the boys the roller coaster ride of a lifetime (and giving the film its most exhilarating sequence). Stop-motion bees and wasps have been seen before (in *Monster from Green Hell*, *Mysterious Island* and *Sinbad and the Eye of the Tiger*) but never have they had such cinematic energy.

Intercut with live-action shots of the actors riding a giant bee prop are 15 stop-motion cuts executed by Laine Liska. The intricately detailed puppet — 12 inches long — was designed and armatured by David Sosalla. It had mechanical wings that could beat up and down eight times during each four-second exposure of film, thereby creating a very credible blur on the film. Puppets of the two boys, carefully matched to their live-action counterparts, are animated making slight movements as the bee swoops and turns.

In a superb composite, one boy clings to a stem on the right of the shot while the bee, a blue-screen element, whizzes past him, flying straight at the camera with a dramatic sideways tilt and lots of motion-control blur. A shot of the boy lying in the flower, blue-screened in front of the bee, allows a closer look at the wealth of detail on the puppet, which is covered in tiny hairs. Blades of grass are animated so that they move out of the way when knocked by the insect.

Another shot looks down over the bee's back as it hovers over the screaming boy. Its antennae snake about in a lively way. A side view shows the bee right on top of the puppet boy, whose arms thrash about. A cloud of superimposed yellow pollen adds an important touch to the image. With both boys on board, the puppet hurtles straight at the camera through the blades of grass in a dynamic dolly shot. The shot is so quick that it is difficult to say if it required any stop-motion of the puppets.

In other shots, the puppet flies over the lawn at the camera, or up and away from the camera. The boy puppets are animated so that they are thrown to one side as the bee tilts, one puppet reaching out to hold onto the other. The subtle animation is so good that most viewers are unaware they are watching puppet likenesses of the boys.

The camera is always moving in these exciting shots. In one cut, the camera tilts down from a tree and dollies backwards as the bee flies towards it. The bee flies past a slatted fence and Liska ingeniously has a strobing light effect play on his puppet, suggesting the light coming through the gaps in the fence. This effect is only registered by viewers subconsciously but adds significantly to the energy of the shot. Even when replayed on video, it is only after a few plays that one realizes what is happening.

In a shot with a lot of successful blur on the puppet, the bee flies out of a pair of shorts hanging on a washing line. Dizzyingly, the puppet flies from closeup away from the camera straight at a character in the live-action plate. Flying over a fence — the camera dipping and rising with it — the bee heads for Moranis, the legs of the boy puppets kicking out. In the final stop-motion shot, the bee flies low through some blades of grass, heading straight at the camera again. Its legs furl and unfurl slightly as it flies. In a live-action cut, the boys are thrown off its back into the grass.

Later, the kids come across a giant cookie, seen in long shot in a fine matte painting. As they set about eating it, an ant appears, looking down at them from the top of the cookie. At first terrified, the kids eventually tame the ant and harness it so that it will carry them through the grass.

This character, seen in a combination of shots using a live-action mechanical creation and 13 stop-motion cuts executed by David Allen and his crew, reminds us just how effective 1954's *Them!* should have been. Ralph Ayers undeservedly received an Oscar nomination for the wobbly monster ants of that film. Allen got no mention at all at the 1990 ceremony, even though his creation is a superb example of stop-motion wizardry, making an impossible being believable and demonstrating flawlessly how to cut back and forth from a miniature puppet to a full-scale prop without making the differences seem obvious.

The script originally called for a swarm of ants and so eight puppets were built. Eventually, only one was required.

Allen's model is ten inches long and beautifully detailed, with two snaking antennae and a covering of tiny hairs. The timing and choreography of the six legs could have been awkward but Allen executes it realistically. In some shots, he added a blur to the leg movements by attaching them to a taut wire and vibrating them slightly during the frame exposure.

The first cut is a chilling shock effect, looking up at the ant on top of the cookie, its antennae snaking in the air and its mandibles opening and closing. A follow-up shot, looking down over the ant at the kids below, is done with the live-action prop since it doesn't require as much intricate movement of the head.

Two long shots have the kids in the foreground, peering through the grass at the ant which climbs down off the cookie and munches on a piece of it. The foreground is a blue-screen element; the ant is animated in a miniature set. Other long shots of the ant walking always use the stop-motion puppet. The mechanical prop is impressive but is only used for partial shots since it cannot walk convincingly.

The kids surround the ant and, in a striking long shot, the puppet on a miniature floor is flawlessly matched to the rear-screen footage of the actors on the giant set. Adding depth to the shot, one of the boys runs past in the foreground, a separate blue-screen element. In another excellent composite, the girl backs across the frame, luring the ant with a piece of the cookie. The ant's antennae wave in the air hungrily as it advances. This is another rear-screen composite. Rocks and earth have been matted into the lower foreground to hide the animation table.

In three superb composites, one of the boys rides on the back of the ant, which drags the other kids behind it in a makeshift cart. The design is essentially similar to a composite Allen employed in *Caveman*. The boy has been filmed riding on a prop, then his lower half has been matted out and replaced with the puppet ant which has puppet legs of the boy on it, carefully aligned to the live action. A harness on the ant puppet is aligned so that it seems to be pulling the cart, which is part of the rear image. Rocks and grass stems in the foreground appear to be blue-screen mattes. The camera tracks left to right as the ant walks, adding interest to the shots.

Later, the kids try to get rid of the ant, which has taken a liking to them and won't go. In long shot, one of the boys backs away from the ant, which in this set-up appears to be a blue-screen element. Unfortunately, the orange-hued lighting on the puppet doesn't mesh well with the live-action nighttime surroundings. It's the only disappointing shot in the sequence.

A long, elegant shot tilts down from a view of the back of the house, over the lawn, down through blades of grass and finally reveals the kids in the distance, the ant following them. This complex shot has a rotoscope matte following the edge of a blade of grass that bends right across the frame. This allows the switch from the live-action plate to the miniature set-up. The background image of the kids and the ant is a conventional rear-screen composite, with a matte line running along the ground.

323

The foreground blades of grass are blue-screened.

Allen's final contribution is an all-miniature shot of the ant surrounded by blades of grass, turning away as it finally leaves the kids.

That night, the kids come across a Lego brick in the grass and sleep inside it. But their rest is disturbed when a hungry scorpion arrives on the scene.

In the late 1980s, it was hard to say who was the busiest stop-motion animator, but if it wasn't Allen then it was certainly Phil Tippett. He supervised the scorpion scene, the film's most ambitious stop-motion episode (containing 43 animation cuts) and a dynamically staged *tour de force*. Although the scorpion has no personality, it is a vicious foe, generating some chilling moments and stomping through its scenes with remorseless power. Tippett adds some highly effective blur to many shots (not through a go-motion device but by actually moving parts of the puppet by hand for a few frames) and achieves some excellent composites. Although Tippett himself animated a few shots, he left most of the animation to Harry Walton and Tom St. Amand.

The magnificent scorpion puppet — more realistic than the animated scorpions of *The Black Scorpion* and *Clash of the Titans* — was designed and built by Craig Davies, who had earlier designed the ED-209 puppet in *RoboCop*. The complex armature was machined by Blair Clark from designs by St. Amand. For shots in which the scorpion battles with the ant, Tippett built a six-inch ant puppet rather than use Allen's model, since it had to be in scale with the scorpion.

In its opening shot, the fabulously nasty-looking arachnid scuttles across a miniature floor in the foreground, lifting its claws and stinger threateningly and advancing toward the unsuspecting kids in the Lego brick in the rear-projection. The kids wake up and all but one manage to jump from the brick and run into the grass. A shot of two of the kids in front of the huge scorpion suffers from very slight traces of blue spill. A shot of the kids running from the background to the foreground, with the scorpion in the middle distance, is a static matte design with a rear screen in the classic "reality sandwich" mold.

The scorpion tries to force one of its claws into a hole in the brick where the boy is cowering. Rather than use an unwieldy full-scale prop for these shots, Tippett chose to use his animation puppet, allowing greater control of movement. There is so much detail on the puppet that it can withstand such close scrutiny. Covered in tiny bumps and hairs, the puppet has a lifelike, slimy look to it.

Long shots of the scorpion poking its claw into the brick seamlessly combine a partial miniature brick with the giant brick built on the live-action set. The hole is miniature, allowing the claw to make contact with it and throw a shadow. Another shot looks out of the brick from the boy's point of view, the claw reaching in.

In a good rear-screen composite, the boy in the lower foreground waves a burning torch at the scorpion, which turns in his direction. After its claw is pulled out from the hole in the brick, the other boy appears, looking out from the hole. Presumably the rear-projected film is seen through the hole in the miniature brick. The boy jumps to the ground and the scorpion turns with unsettling speed to face him. Foreground rocks and earth — presumably miniature — hide the animation table.

In closeup, the scorpion advances towards the camera, mandibles snapping together viciously.

Meanwhile, the ant has made a reappearance, coming to the rescue of its friends. In an all-miniature tracking shot, the ant walks into the setting. Squeaking excitedly, it walks up behind the scorpion and bites one of its legs. In another consummate rear-projection set-up, the kids run toward the camera as the scorpion turns to face its attacker.

Many shots in the sequence are filmed entirely on the miniature set. In closeup, the ant rears up. Also in closeup, the scorpion, twice the size of its opponent, bears down. A dramatic shot through the legs of the scorpion sees the ant reacting as the arachnid advances toward it. In a very dynamic shot, the ant backs away as the scorpion's claws snap down at it and its stinger bears down. In a tracking shot, the advancing scorpion forces the ant to retreat across the miniature ground, smashing its sting down and barely missing the ant. Foreground rock and grass again add depth to the shot.

In a very fluidly animated cut, the ant, shot from behind, turns to face the scorpion. In closeup, the stinger is raised, then smashed into the ground again just as the ant moves out of the way. The squeaking ant tries to bite its foe again, but it is clearly outmatched. It retreats as first one, then the other claw swish across the screen in a blur and snap shut with a frightening clap.

A forceful low-angle shot looks up from under the ant at the scorpion bearing down, both claws swishing across the frame. With the camera looking down at both puppets, the ant is grabbed in one of the claws, accompanied by a crunching sound. The scorpion is now on top of the helplessly struggling ant. The stinger is raised again and a closeup of the ant emphasizes the fact that it is trapped. In closeup, the stinger lunges forward with a blur.

The ant, squealing desperately, is pierced by the sting, then is picked up and held aloft in the scorpion's claws. In a deft composite, the kids run into the left of the shot as the scorpion throws the ant across the frame, then turns to face the kids. The complex animation in this cut is carried off very credibly. The kids harass the scorpion with sticks and in a flawless blue-screen composite it lunges at them.

The ant, meanwhile, slumps half-dead to the ground in an all-miniature shot. One of the kids throws a stick and it pierces the head of the scorpion. There is a lot of blur in this shot as the creature reacts, presumably achieved by moving it by hand for a few frames — possible since part of the puppet is outside the frame and so can be manipulated unseen. A rock is thrown at the scorpion and bounces off it, probably a separate blue-screen element like the rocks that bounced off the Scout Walkers in *Return of the Jedi*. A second stick is thrown and pierces the underside of the scorpion. In this low-angle shot, one of the claws swishes across the frame with lots of blur.

The scorpion decides that it would prefer to live to fight another day. It retreats backwards across the miniature floor, into the grass. In a close shot, one of its claws pulls out one of the spears stuck in it. It retreats further into the miniature set, eventually disappearing behind some blades of grass.

The ant gets a tear jerker death scene, done entirely live-action with the mechanical prop.

Later, the kids are nearly sucked up into a rotary lawn mower. Extreme long shots of them flying through the air are clever blue-screen shots using puppets stop-motioned by Laine Liska. Stop-motion was the preferred medium for these shots since the speed and distance of the characters made live-action filming impractical.

A final stop-motion shot, executed by Randal Dutra working in Tippett's team, is a quick shot of one of the boys falling off the nose of a dog into his father's cereal bowl. The puppet's limbs flail about so realistically as it falls that it look totally realistic.

Harryhausen would have been impressed by these technically superb stop-motion sequences: fluid animation, successful composites and marvelously detailed puppets. But he might also have pined for some of the flamboyance of his own work. These scenes strive to be realistic and they succeed. There is no attempt to create a fantasy milieu nor, because this is a children's film, are the monsters made as frightening as they might have been.

In the sequel *Honey, I Blew Up the Kid* (1992), a baby is enlarged to gigantic proportions and goes on the rampage. Considering the success of the first film's stop-motion episodes, it seemed a short-sighted move on the producers' part that they chose not to use the process at all in the follow-up.

Hook

1991. Amblin Entertainment. D: Steven Spielberg. Scr: Jim V. Hart, Malia Scotch Marmo. Story: Jim V. Hart, Nick Castle. Based on the stageplay "Peter Pan" and stories by J. M. Barrie. Ph: Dean Cundey. Art: Norman Garwood. Mus: John Williams. Special Makeup: Greg Cannom. Special Visual Effects: Industrial Light and Magic. Visual Effects Supervisor: Eric Brevig. Matte Artist Supervisor: Mark Sullivan. Matte Artists: Yusei Uesugi, Rocco Gioffre, Chris Evans, Eric Chauvin. Motion/Wing Supervisors: Charlie Clavadetscher, Patrick T. Myers.

Cast: Dustin Hoffman, Robin Williams, Julia Roberts, Bob Hoskins, Maggie Smith, Glenn Close.

Rating: ☆☆☆   Stop-Motion: ☆☆½

Spielberg's updating of the old "Peter Pan" stage play has Robin Williams as a yuppie attorney who gets spirited away to Neverland and discovers that he is Pan, now grown up. Although marred by the usual overdose of Spielberg schmaltz, this has much going for it, including memorable character performances by Dustin Hoffman as Captain Hook and Bob Hoskins as Smee.

Industrial Light and Magic were recruited to execute numerous visual effects, including some striking matte paintings and the sequences in which Pan and other characters are made to fly.

Tinkerbell, who appears in over a hundred shots, was essentially actress Julia Roberts filmed in a flying harness in front of a blue screen. This image was enhanced with visual effects that made her glow and allowed her to sprinkle fairy dust.

The character's translucent wings were filmed as a separate element, actually a five-inch stop-motion model. The flapping motions were animated one frame at a time by effects cameraman Patrick Myers and the wings were attached to a go-motion rig which added blurs to any directional movement. The resultant footage was then painstakingly aligned with the previously shot footage of Roberts.

The Hounds of Zaroff see *The Most Dangerous Game*

House

1986. New World. D: Steve Miner. Scr: Ethan Wiley. Story: Fred Dekker. Ph: Mac Ahlberg. Art: Greg Fonseca. Mus: Harry Manfredini. Creature Designs: Kirk Thatcher, James Cummins. Creature Special Effects: Backwood Films. Special Visual Effects: Dream Quest. Stop-Motion (uncredited): Mark Sullivan.

Cast: William Katt, George Wendt, Richard Moll, Kay Lenz, Michael Ensign, Susan French.

Rating: ☆☆½   Stop-Motion: ☆☆½

It's baffling why insubstantial films like this and *Nightmare on Elm Street* became huge box office successes in America. It can only be their rapid-fire special effects, which are distinctly superior to their mundane surroundings: Dramatically, *House* is a mess, and director Steve Miner fails totally to get the right balance of humor and horror.

The first half is simply boring as William Katt moves into his dead aunt's house; it is played almost completely straight. When supernatural things start happening, Miner decides to go tongue-in-cheek and even throws in a pop soundtrack. He's a director who seems unsure of what he's trying to do (in his *Friday the 13th* stalk-and-slash films, he didn't *need* to know what he was doing), and he certainly doesn't know how to make the most of his excellent makeup artist James Cummins, allowing his creations to appear and disappear without exploiting their potential.

On the other hand, Miner is at least partly responsible for some very striking surreal images which recall the best moments of films such as *Phantasm* and *Eraserhead*. A little boy runs around, unaware that a demon's disembodied hand is gripping his back. A marlin mounted over a fireplace comes to life, slaps horribly against the wall trying to free itself and has to be shot. The best image in the film comes when Katt discovers that his bathroom cabinet leads Narnia-like to another world. There is a long shot from the other side which is completely black except for a small yellow rectangle in the top left which contains Katt's silhouette looking out. Because it is so suggestive of the Unknown, the shot has a threatening, dream-like force.

Cummins' designs are impressive, such as Vietnam vet zombie Big Ben or the amorphous War Demon that leaps out of a wardrobe. His most original creation is the revoltingly obese Witch with a hideous voice and ghastly face. Miner has no excuse for not making her a really terrifying adversary — unless, contrary to his claims, he deliberately toned his film down, to target a younger audience.

The best creation of all is the stop-motion Dingbat, animated by Mark Sullivan working for Dream Quest. This nightmare is a giant bat-like harpy with a fang-filled skull for a head, long, bony arms and leathery wings. As Katt lowers himself on a rope down into the darkness on the other side of his bathroom cabinet, the Dingbat flaps around him and steals his rifle. These seven shots have been filmed against a black background, eliminating problems with rear screens, and there are no composites.

The first cut looks up at Katt hanging on the rope and a half-seen shape flaps past above him. The creature is so quickly glimpsed that it's possible this shot was done live-action. One dynamic cut has the model fly off smoothly from grinning closeup into the extreme distance. A realistic model of Katt's hand is used in a cut when the Dingbat grabs his rifle. The jokey final cut has the Dingbat swivel the weapon like the Rifleman and fire at the rope, sending Katt plummeting into a lake far below. One shot of a disappointing mechanical Dingbat, built by Cummins, is included. Alas, the scene is over far too quickly for such a deliciously nasty creature.

Later, an impressive matte painting is used to show Katt hanging precariously from the top of a cliff face.

House II—The Second Story

1987. D-Scr: Ethan Wiley. Ph: Mac Ahlberg. Art: Greg Fonseca. Mus: Harry Manfredini. Makeup and Creature Effects Design: Chris Walas. Mechanical Effects: Image Engineering/Peter Chesney. Visual Effects: Dream Quest Images. Supervisors:

Hoyt Yeatman, Eric Brevig. Matte Paintings and Stop-Motion Flying Creatures: Mark Sullivan. Motion Control Supervisor: Michael Bigelow. Stop-Motion Unit: Design/Supervision: Phil Tippett. Stop-Motion Animation: Randal Michael Dutra, III. Model Construction: Tamia Marg. Camera: Sheila Duignan. Armatures: Jon Berg.

Cast: Arye Gross, Jonathan Stark, Royal Dano, Bill Maher, Lar Park Lincoln, John Ratzenberger.

Rating: ☆☆   Stop-Motion: ☆☆☆

This begins badly with a dull half-hour (duller even than in the first film) of horror set-pieces and kids partying in the worst traditions of teen movies. It then changes tack dramatically when one of the bedrooms in the house magically transforms into an entrance to a Mesozoic jungle. A dazzling fifteen-minute prehistoric sequence follows: One of the jungle's denizens—the dog-sized chick of a flying reptile—is brought back into the house, where it gets up to some amusing mischief. These scenes are an excellent showcase for the skills of stop-motion supervisor Phil Tippett, animator Randal Dutra (freelancing for Tippett), animator Mark Sullivan (working for Dream Quest Images), and some excellent on-set creature effects by Chris Walas.

Two kids enter the jungle in order to retrieve a glass skull that has magical powers. First, they see a brontosaurus in the distance, a beautiful model smoothly animated by Mark Sullivan in a lush jungle setting that recalls Willis O'Brien's Skull Island. The dinosaur features in only one cut, a long-shot split-screen composite with the actors walking through the jungle (actually a Los Angeles park) in the lower part of the frame.

The puppet stands in an extensive miniature set decked out with all kinds of vegetation and backed by a smoking volcano in a painted backdrop. Additional foliage and trees painted on glass by Sullivan help to mesh the two elements. Following in the tradition of other sauropod scenes (*One Million Years B.C.*, *Planet of Dinosaurs*), the puppet merely walks off, making one wish for something more elaborate.

Just as one of the kids is about to get clubbed by Arnold the Barbarian, a strange beast appears. Dubbed the Fishmonster by Tippett and his crew, this is some kind of giant prehistoric mammal with a whiskery face, a rough, leathery hide and a huge mouth full of rotting, yellow fangs. Never seen clearly, it features in only three quick and shadowy animation cuts, all animated by Randy Dutra. It rears up and lunges at the camera. In a final rear-projection shot of its head, it stoops down to pick up Arnold in its teeth (the interaction is not actually shown). It's an effective quick effect but one wonders why Tippett and his crew have gone to all the trouble of building this model to have it appear in a only few brief cuts.

One of the boys, Jesse, retrieves the skull, but a pterosaur swoops out of the night sky and seizes it in its claw. This creature, animated by Sullivan, is another fabulous model, boasting an unusual dappled appearance, a furry torso and a long beak full of teeth. It flies off into the distance above a lush miniature jungle set, its wings flapping smoothly and slowly. The camera pans with it and it briefly passes behind a miniature tree so as to give the shot some depth.

It flies over its nest at the top of a

stunted tree, drops the skull into it, then swoops down and away. The skull is animated realistically as it falls. As the puppet hovers over its nest, blurs are introduced into the wing movements, presumably by moving the puppet during the long frame exposures. (It is unlikely that go-motion rods would have been used, since this is not a big-budget film.)

Jesse climbs the tree; an extreme long shot looking up at his tiny figure near the top is an all-miniature effect, combining a puppet of the actor (animated by Sullivan) with a highly detailed painting of the tree draped in vines and other growths. To have filmed this shot live-action would have been uneconomical, requiring the construction of an enormous prop tree and having to shoot outdoors, with the risk that the lighting would not cut in with the other shots in the sequence.

Jesse finds the skull held in the beak of a chick (a lively Walas hand puppet) in the nest. When he tries to wrest it from the creature, the squawking parent reappears. In the first of three stop-motion cuts, the pterosaur swoops over the nest, then up and out of the frame. The reptile hovers over the nest, flapping and squawking, its long tail snaking behind it. Finally it swoops past again, knocking Jesse out of the nest, the interaction implied by careful alignment of puppet and rear projection. The puppet of Jesse is used again in a shot looking straight up as he falls, his arms and legs kicking out as he nears the camera.

These sequences get very close to recreating the feel of an O'Brien milieu in the style of *King Kong*, but unfortunately choose to end here. Only the

chick has a further role to play. In shots that sometimes use Walas' puppet and in others that are animated by Dutra and supervised by Tippett, the chick becomes one of the best realized characters of this kind seen for a long time, almost like a small and playful version of *Mysterious Island*'s vicious phororhacos. Squawking roguishly, it runs off with the skull, is chased around the house by Jesse and is finally placated into trading its catch for some raw steak.

Walas' puppet never clashes with Berg's model, which is seen in four cuts when the creature needs to be shown in full. When it runs up a flight of stairs, a static matte line follows the zigzag of the steps. When it jumps off a bed and onto a table to evade Jesse (in rear-projected footage), blur is added to the image, again probably by moving the puppet on wires while the camera shutter is open. Dutra's animation is particularly good in a shot in which it clambers awkwardly over a kitchen sink and falls in. The comic touch and pace are always judged right, indicating either that writer-director Ethan Wiley is attuned to the methods of his effects team, or perhaps that Tippett himself took over the directing reins for this passage.

Much of the credit for the success of this sequence goes to Dutra. He described his work on it in a letter to the author: "The young bird was a lively, mischievous character, and fun to animate because he had active scenes. My favorite was a shot where he is running on a counter in a kitchen and trips (there is interaction with the plate elements), and gathers himself up, somewhat disheveled, and is doing his best to balance himself. I had a great time coming up with those bits of business, and I think it shows in the animation."

There is one last stop-motion creation, a nightmarish zombie-horse seen in three cuts. This is another striking model with vestiges of flesh hanging to the skeleton visible beneath — Jon Berg and Tamia Marg have made it the complete opposite of the beautiful Pegasus model in *Clash of the Titans*. Again, this was animated by Dutra.

In two shots, Slim, a zombie-cowboy, stands next to his undead mount, and in the other it rears up on its hind legs. These are all rear-projection shots with the puppet's feet out of the frame so as to avoid having a matte. These are great images but again there is enormous unrealized potential here for a classic sequence. Unfortunately, there is no attempt to show the model interacting with the actor. The sequence needs an establishing shot of Slim astride the horse, but perhaps Tippett's team simply didn't have the time for a tricky composite like this. Apparently some stop-motion shots were cut out of this sequence before release.

The rest of the film improves slightly on the first half-hour (i.e., it achieves mediocrity) and includes an Indiana Jones–style raid on an Aztec sacrificial ritual. The film is full of fantasy ideas but lacks coherence and purpose, hoping to fool us into mistaking quantity for quality. All the same, it deserved better than the treatment it received from contemporary reviewers who, blinkered by insisting on labeling it a horror film, dismissed it as inferior because it wasn't frightening. They were simply unable to enjoy the imagery of its more imaginative passages, specifically the marvelous prehistoric sequence which alone makes the film essential viewing for stop-motion fans.

Howard the Duck (a.k.a. *Howard — A New Breed of Hero*)

1986. Lucasfilm. Dir: Willard Huyck. Scr: Willard Huyck, Gloria Katz. Based on the character "Howard the Duck" created by Steve Gerber. Art: Peter Jamison. Mus: John Barry. Ph: Richard H. Kline. Special Visual Effects: Industrial Light and Magic. Visual Effects Supervisor: Michael J. McAlister. Alien Monster designed by Phil Tippett. Stop-Motion Supervision: Phil Tippett, Harry Walton. Stop-Motion Photography: Terry Chostner, Patrick McArdle. Stop-Motion Animation: Tom St. Amand. Stop-Motion Construction: Randy Dutra, Tamia Marg, Sheila Duignan. Matte Painting Supervisor: Frank Ordaz.

Cast: Lea Thompson, Jeffrey Jones, Tim Robbins, Ed Gale, Chip Zein, Tim Rose.

Rating: ☆☆☆   Stop-Motion: ☆☆☆

Lucasfilm never quite worked out how to market a live-action film about a talking duck. As a result, the film was a commercial failure, which is a shame since this is a lively and original product with many good comic lines and some fine special effects from Industrial Light and Magic. The latter include an impressive sequence in which Howard first arrives on Earth from his dimension and a climax which is one of the best stop-motion episodes of the 1980s.

The stop-motion finale is a superb sequence supervised by Phil Tippett, another highpoint in a remarkable career. From the humble beginnings of his contributions to *The Crater Lake Monster, Star Wars* and *Piranha* he had progressed to the magnificent taun-taun and mechanical ATATs in *The Empire Strikes Back*, then to Verminthrax Perjorative in *Dragonslayer*, described by S.S. Wilson as "the first genuine advance in dimensional animation since the process was invented." From there on, he produced a series of sequences which demonstrated an imagination not confined by the usual genre clichés, and a dedicated striving to create special effects to the best of his ability. The Scout Walkers of *Return of the Jedi*, the giant boar of *Caravan of Courage*, the "elefish" of *Battle for Endor*, the prehistoric creatures of *House II*, the documentary realism of television's *Dinosaur!*—these are all stop-motion sequences to cherish.

Howard the Duck is predominantly a live-action feature. During the course of the film, villain Jeffrey Jones is slowly transforming into something inhuman, surpassing all expectations of monster-lovers at the climax when he reveals his final form as a scorpion-like alien the size of a dinosaur. This is an eye-boggling six-minute episode and a showcase for Tippett's genius. The sequence is staged very fluidly by Tippett and director Willard Huyck, keeping the pace fast,

maintaining the undercurrent of humor and using cut-aways to live actors as an integral part of the flow of the action, rather than the limp padding shots which mar so many stop-motion scenes.

The Darklord, designed by Tippett and built by a team including Randy Dutra, demonstrates again that stop-motion is *the* medium for these kind of effects, allowing a flexibility of movement and interaction denied other techniques. This bizarre creature is a 20-foot-high, gray, Lovecraftian monstrosity with an enormous head covered in spikes and pincers, and a gaping mouth full of vicious teeth, including some that move independently of the jaws. Its two huge front claws consist of four prongs that can be snapped together noisily and also open to allow a whiplash tentacle to shoot out.

Tippett imbues his creation with real character: This is an *angry* monster. It rushes around on its four spindly legs, roaring and growling, blasting at characters with energy bolts from its eyes and tail, and cursing them all in a deep, bestial voice. Working for ILM, the stop-motion supervision is by Tippett and Harry Walton. The fluid animation (there are 37 stop-motion cuts) is by Tom St. Amand.

This is a fully integrated scene. In several shots where miniature sets are matched with the real ones, the composites are so precise that one is never aware of any visual contention. Likewise, when live-action props are used to represent parts of the monster (its tail and one tentacle), these are so well-done that they never jar with the miniature puppet. The cel animation that is used to depict blasts of energy fired by the puppet (and by Howard's "neutron disintigrator" in the final showdown) is always superbly matched to the puppet and the live action.

The scene takes place inside an observatory-like laboratory that houses a giant space-laser (the device that accidentally brought Howard to Earth). Jennings (Jeffrey Jones) has started to transform into a Darklord (with the help of Tom Burman's special makeups), becoming more and more skull-like and growing spines on his back. Thinking him defeated, Howard looks up only to realize that the transformation is now complete. The full form of the Darklord is revealed tantalizingly through a series of shots, each of which shows us a little more.

The first stop-motion cut is a long shot of the Darklord ripping its way up through a steel walkway. Superimposed sparks fly everywhere and two long black claws wave threateningly in the air. In a second long shot, the Darklord (still only partially seen) smashes the steel platform with two blows from his left claw and two from the right. The claws can be heard snapping shut and the monster growls angrily. In the first closer look at this creature, we see that it out-aliens *Alien*: Two glowing red eyes stare out from a head which slowly rolls back, revealing a mass of spikes, then another face at the front of the head, containing a mass of teeth on all sides of the gaping mouth. On either side of the head is a series of little arm-like pincers, wriggling unpleasantly, and the inside of the mouth is red and fleshy and houses another set of internal teeth.

In another closeup the monster recoils from a shower of sparks, the suddenness of the movement enhanced by some go-motion blurring. Three medium shots teasingly show us a little more of this horror: Like the head, the torso also has a series of wriggling pincers on either side. This puppet is a candidate for having the most moving appendages of any stop-motion creation: So many claws, teeth and pincers are moving that one wonders how Amand avoided having a nervous breakdown trying to keep track of them all.

At last, in the eighth cut, we get a full view: The monster hops up onto its four thin, scorpion-like legs, its twin-pronged tail raised high behind it, its claws snapping noisily, its jaws and all its pincers moving furiously. A dramatic tracking medium shot follows the growling monster as it walks left, its beady eyes looking around anxiously. Howard is blue-screened in front of the advancing puppet in the next cut, and its head lunges at him (with a go-motion blur) as it roars, "Power!" Two blasts of blue cel-animated energy lash out from its eyes and floor the hero and heroine (Tim Robbins and Lea Thompson).

After another medium shot of the puppet, there is a close shot of one of its four-pronged claws opening up to reveal a fleshy hole inside. The Darklord points his claw at Howard and a 20-foot-long animated red tentacle whips out. The next two stop-motion cuts look like a conventional rear-projection set-up. The first is a long-shot side view of the Darklord pulling Howard toward it, snared in the tentacle, while Robbins and Thompson run past in the background. Again its body is a flurry of moving parts; it roars arrogantly, "There is no escape!" The second cut is a new perspective, looking down at the puppet from behind and above. Howard is wriggling about in the left background (it is impossible to spot where miniature and real tentacle merge) as the monster throws out a second tentacle towards Thompson and Robbins on the right. At this point, a credible prop tentacle is used to press a button that activates the laser-cannon.

After a medium shot of the tentacle retracting into the claw, another medium shot has the monster blasting Robbins and Thompson with some green cel-animated energy bolts. In a classic piece of blue-screen interaction, Howard, still snared in a tentacle, is dragged toward the growling monster in the background. There is a slight trace of blue spill when Howard's hand passes in front of the puppet, but this is the only flaw in an otherwise technically perfect sequence. A prop tentacle is used again and Howard slices through it with a buzzsaw. In two animated medium shots of the Darklord screaming at its wounded limb, its moving teeth and eyebrows lend vitality to its facial gestures.

There is another medium shot of the Darklord releasing a blast of green energy, then a closeup of it turning suddenly toward Howard (again with go-motion blur) and firing a bolt of blue energy at the duck. A brief comic moment, in which Howard drives over the Darklord's tail, keeps the tone of the scene in line with the rest of the film. In long shot, Howard drives the car holding the neutron disintegrator between the monster's legs. It's difficult to say whether this is a miniature car or if the puppet has been combined with the live-action car: As is so often the case these

days, composites are so flawless that one can only make a best guess — in this case, that it was a miniature car.

There is a closeup, with blur, of the monster looking down between its legs and making a puzzled grunt, then a shot of the car driving over the prop tail. The monster looks up again, screaming in pain. An impressive, complex long shot depicts the monster in full view in the background rather pathetically holding up its limp tail. In the lower left background are flickering images of Robbins and Thompson, held captive by the energy blasts; and driving in front of the puppet toward the camera is the live-action element of Howard in the car. Hand-drawn rotoscope mattes were used to put this latter element into the foreground.

In a closer full shot, the puppet looks at its limp tail, then walks straight at the camera, its claws outstretched menacingly, roaring, "Eat claw, duck!" In two cuts, one a long shot, the other a closeup of the tail, the monster raises its tail and points it at Robbins and Thompson. It starts to glow green, then a bolt of energy flies out. After another long shot of Howard driving at the Darklord, the monster is seen in a different long-shot perspective, looking particularly nasty.

It raises its glowing tail, poised to strike at Howard and, in an imaginative touch, drops down onto its front claws to get a better aim. In this shot, the monster's image is reflected in the floor beneath it. The floor appears to be part of the live-action plate, so just how this clever effect was achieved is a mystery.

It bellows, "Puny little duck!" then

Howard fires a blast of purple cel animation from the disintegrator, a shot combining the live-action Howard with the puppet. After a closeup of the roaring Darklord struck by the purple ray, it is last seen in a long cut from behind, a visually exciting shot of the puppet flailing wildly, the neutron gun's rays blasting holes right through it. A lot of swirling cel animation enlivens a shot of the static puppet as it finally explodes.

That is the end of the Darklord but there are two further stop-motion cuts as the laser cannon threatens to bring down more of these creatures from another dimension. Three of the growling monsters are seen scurrying down the swirling pink vortex created by the cannon, a complex blue-screen shot involving intricate animation (just count all those moving appendages) and the vortex itself is illuminated by flashes of lightning. At the last minute, Howard destroys the laser and in the final stop-motion cut the three monsters are thrown back up into the vortex again, disappearing at the far end.

The Howling

1980. Avco Embassy. D: Joe Dante. Scr: John Sayles, Terence H. Winkless. Based on the novel by Gary Brandner. Ph: John Hora. Mus: Pino Donaggio. Special Makeup Effects: Rob Bottin. Special Mechanical Effects: Doug Beswick. Stop-Motion Animation: David Allen. Stop-Motion Assistant (uncredited): Randy Cook. Puppet Construction (uncredited): Roger Dicken, Ernie Farino. Miniatures (uncredited): Dennis Gordon. Cel Animation: Peter Kuran.

Cast: Dee Wallace, Patrick Macnee, Dennis Dugan, Christopher Stone, Kevin McCarthy, John Carradine, Kenneth Tobey, Slim Pickens, Forrest J Ackerman, Dick Miller, Roger Corman.

Rating: ☆☆☆   Stop-Motion: ☆☆

The horror boom that began in the late 1970s with a revival of the vampire genre (in *Dracula, Love at First Bite* and *Nosferatu the Vampyre*) naturally turned to another classic theme in the early 1980s — the werewolf. First off the starting block was this highly entertaining romp from Joe Dante, who directs with the same confidence and sense of fun that he brought to *Piranha* (1978). *The Howling* is a film made by somebody who *loves* horror films: Most of the characters are named after directors of werewolf movies and the sequences in which man transforms into werewolf are the kind of spectacular show-stoppers that horror fans had waited years to see.

The plot (about a colony of werewolves trying to adjust to modern life) is sometimes clumsy. There are some colorless performances (especially Patrick Macnee) and a corny, tongue-in-cheek ending, but this is still one of best werewolf films ever made.

There are amusing cameos from Forrest J Ackerman, Dick Miller and Roger Corman, and a terrific perfor-

Two stop-motion werewolves trapped in a burning barn at the climax of *The Howling* (1980) — one of several shots animated by David Allen that were cut from the final print of the film.

mance from horror veteran John Carradine, sprouting fangs and bemoaning the fact that his kind are no longer allowed to go hunting humans like in the good old days. Just as bizarre is the sight of Slim Pickens with a mouthful of fangs. An interesting long shot shows two characters in silhouette transforming into wolves as they make love, using cel animation by Peter Kuran.

The film's real claim to fame are the special makeup effects of Rob Bottin (getting an assist from Doug Beswick with some of the mechanical devices; Randy Cook contributed the design for one of the female werewolf manifestations). Although Bottin admits that some of the tricks were learned from Rick Baker (who did his own amazing werewolf scenes in 1981's *An American Werewolf in London*), his werewolf transformations are a genuinely original contribution to the horror genre. Horror fans had been short-changed for too long with clumsy dissolves and cut-aways as actors had more fur applied to their faces: At last, here was the real thing. Hair grows out of skin, ears become pointed, fingernails lengthen, fangs sprout and a snout forms out of an actor's face — all right before our eyes and backed by the sickening sound of bones crunching and rearranging.

The climax in a burning barn was

intended to include full-view shots of the werewolves, done with stop-motion puppets because their narrow waists and wolf-like triple-jointed legs could not be simulated by dressing up actors in costumes. David Allen designed and animated, with assistance from Randy Cook, four cuts of three werewolf puppets, but three of them ended up on the cutting room floor. Poor planning and some last-minute reshoots meant that the stop-motion cuts did not mix comfortably with the live-action shots. *The Howling* is an all-too-common example of effects artists not being consulted closely enough or early enough during filming.

Roger Dicken sculpted and built the puppets according to Allen's designs, over armatures machined by Ernie Farino. A miniature set of the barn was built by Dennis Gordon.

The only cut that remains in the release print is a long shot of the werewolves surrounded by fog, standing in a road and making very slight movements. Trees in the background are a rear projection. The fog was added by a second pass of the camera. Originally a much longer cut, here it is just part of a two-second dissolve to a city skyline. Two other cuts showed the puppets in the burning barn, gasping for air and banging on the door. The fourth cut had a werewolf peeking out from behind a tree as Dee Wallace walks away.

The werewolves look great in their brief appearance — one can only speculate about the scenes Allen might have come up with had he been allowed freer rein. But even this one cut did not find favor with some. The Consumer Guide's *Best, Worst and Most Unusual Horror Films* reacted to the sight of the werewolves in this cut thus: "We see them for the buffoons they really are." A special effects shot that looks fine to some people sometimes has a totally different impact on others.

There were rumors that Allen's shots might surface in the sequel, but this did not materialize. They finally got a showing in the film's 1996 laser disc release, accompanied by an interview with Allen.

If nothing else, *The Howling* has the distinction of being the first film to demonstrate that stop-motion has a place in horror films. In the years to follow, a flood of horror films would use the process to provide memorable "quick scares."

The Hunger

1983. MGM/Richard Shepherd Company. D: Tony Scott. Scr: Ivan Davis, Michael Thomas. From the novel by Whitley Strieber. Ph: Stephen Goldblatt. Art: Brian Morris. Mus: Michel Rubini, Denny Jaeger. Makeup Illusions: Dick Smith, Carl Fullerton. Monkey Effects: David Allen, Roger Dicken and (uncredited) Dennis Gordon.

Cast: Catherine Deneuve, David Bowie, Susan Sarandon, Cliff de Young, Beth Ehlers, Dan Hedaya, Bessie Love, Bauhaus.

Rating: ☆☆☆   Stop-Motion: ☆☆½

Like his brother Ridley's *Blade Runner*, director Tony Scott's film is distinguished by its obsession with visual style. In *Blade Runner*, this got in the way of plot and dramatic interest; but in *The Hunger* the skillful lighting and camerawork enhance the themes of transience and immortality. It's an indulgence (lace curtains blowing in the wind, doves flying across a shot, etc.) but it works for many reasons, one of which is the fact that this is an ingenious variation on the vampire legend.

The immortality offered to the vampires by their seductress (Catherine Deneuve) lasts only 300 years, whereupon they age rapidly. She stores their decaying but still-living bodies in coffins in her attic. Makeup maestro Dick Smith was enlisted to create the superb sequences where David Bowie and Deneuve age at a rate of five years per minute. Deneuve's final moments make good use of an articulate wizened dummy.

Adding a modern-day pseudo-scientific twist is the presence of Susan Sarandon and her team of doctors, researching rapid aging and how it is linked to certain types of blood. One of their experiments causes a rhesus monkey to age rapidly, die and decompose on screen, an effect achieved by means of stop-motion filming executed by David Allen.

Assisted by Dennis Gordon (uncredited), Allen spent a grueling nine days on what was originally a single seven-second shot. Fur and skin were made to peel back from the body, and heat was applied to muscles (made from plastic urethane) to make them shrink. Bits of bones falling to the floor were supported on wires and animated frame-by-frame, then slowly disintegrated bit by bit. The bones of the skull were animated so as to fall apart. This kind of high-speed decay had been seen before in *The Time Machine* but Allen's version is much more intricate and realistic.

Scott took the shot and broke it down into ten quick cuts, intercutting it with shots of Bowie aging rapidly. Allen's lingering color sequence is reduced to fuzzy black-and-white shots seen on a monitor with lots of grain and video disturbance. Some sections are blown up into closeups. Stop-motion purists might complain but Scott's decision was the right one. We are not meant to enjoy this as an effects set-piece; its purpose is to set us thinking that this kind of decay is soon going to afflict Bowie.

Roger Dicken constructed mechanical apes that were intended to be used in a scene where they fight in the laboratory, but they never made it into the release print.

I'd Rather Be Rich

1964. Universal. D: Jack Smight. Scr: Oscar Brodney, Norman Krasna, Leo Townsend. Special Effects: Albert Whitlock. Stop-Motion Animation (uncredited): Jim Danforth.

Cast: Sandra Dee, Maurice Chevalier,

Andy Williams, Robert Goulet, Gene Raymond, Charles Ruggles, Hermione Gingold.

Rating: ☆☆½   Stop-Motion: ☆☆

This mildly entertaining remake of 1941's *It Started with Eve* featured Sandra Dee searching for a husband in order to please dying grandfather Maurice Chevalier.

One scene featured a pair of shoes that were made to move of their own accord by stop-motion. They were animated by Jim Danforth, on this occasion working for veteran special effects man Albert Whitlock.

Indiana Jones and the Last Crusade

1989. Lucasfilm. D: Steven Spielberg. Scr: Jeffrey Boam. Story: George Lucas, Menno Meyjes. Based on Characters Created by George Lucas, Philip Kaufman. Ph: Douglas Slocombe. Art: Eliott Scott. Mus: John Williams. Special Visual Effects: Industrial Light and Magic. Visual Effects Supervisor: Michael J. McAlister. Matte Painting Supervisor: Mark Sullivan. Matte Photography: Wade Childress, Harry Walton.

Cast: Harrison Ford, Sean Connery, Denholm Elliott, Alison Doody, John Rhys-Davies, Julian Glover, River Phoenix, Alexei Sayle.

Rating: ☆☆☆   Stop-Motion: ☆☆

The third chapter in George Lucas' *Indiana Jones* trilogy disappointingly plays it safe. Its story about a race against the Nazis to acquire a Biblical artifact is far too similar to the plot of the first film. Also disappointing is the fact that the fantasy elements are kept to a minimum, surfacing only at the climax, when the healing powers of the Last Supper chalice revive Jones, Sr. (Sean Connery), and when bad guy Julian Glover drinks from the wrong chalice. In the latter sequence, Glover undergoes some eye-boggling rapid-aging: His hair turns white and grows absurdly quickly, and his skin melts away from his shriveling face. Connery is excellent and the amiable father-and-son team is preferable to the sidekicks of the previous films. Otherwise, this is standard cliffhanger stuff.

There are two stand-out action sequences, one set in some rat-filled catacombs and another in which a plane crashes into a tunnel. The latter features a brief moment of stop-motion.

Indiana Jones (Harrison Ford) and his father are driving a car pursued by a Nazi plane. The car rounds a bend and enters a tunnel, but the plane is unable to pull up in time. It crashes into the mouth of the tunnel, the wings break off and the fuselage continues to skid along the inside of the tunnel, eventually exploding at the other end.

This spectacular sequence featured a model plane and a 200-foot-long miniature replica of the tunnel. In the opening shot of the sequence, the plane was shot as a separate motion-control blue-screen element and its aluminum foil wings were animated with traditional stop-motion methods so as to crumple and break away.

Indiana Jones and the Temple of Doom

1984. Lucasfilm. D: Steven Spielberg. Scr: Willard Huyck, Gloria Katz. Story: George Lucas. Ph: Douglas Slocombe. Art: Elliot Scott. Mus: John Williams. Visual Effects: Industrial Light & Magic. Visual Effects Supervisor: Dennis Muren. Chief Visual Effects Cameraman: Mike McAlister. Matte Painting Supervisor: Mike Pangrazio. Matte Artists: Chris Evans, Frank Ordaz, Caroleen Green. Stop-Motion Animation: Tom St. Amand. Effects Creative Consultant: Phil Tippett. Stop-Motion Technicians: David Sosalla, Randy Ottenberg, Sean Casey.

Cast: Harrison Ford, Kate Capshaw, Amrish Puri, Roshan Seth, Philip Stone, Ke Huy Quan.

Rating: ☆☆☆   Stop-Motion: ☆☆½

This second part of George Lucas' Indiana Jones trilogy is even faster-paced and more spectacular than the first. Like *Raiders of the Lost Ark*, it's a value-for-money film with the gags coming thick and fast and Spielberg always in sure control of the excitement and suspense. But the initially intriguing plot loses impetus after a while, giving way to the action set-pieces. The film is also marred by lazy characterization in Harrison Ford's smug title character and Kate Capshaw's smart-aleck heroine, and by some typical Spielberg schmaltz.

Some of the action scenes are terrific: a rickshaw caught up in a car chase, an edge-of-the-seat inflatable dinghy escape sequence, a banquet of snakes, eyeballs and chilled monkey brains, Ford and Capshaw negotiating a tunnel alive with insects and some elaborately staged thug sacrifices.

Like the one quick shot in *Raiders* that used stop-motion, the sequel uses the process for purely functional reasons when it would be too dangerous or too expensive to have stuntmen performing. These shots are so quick and executed so skillfully by the ILM crew that if we realize at all that these are effects shots, it is only on a subliminal level.

A superb chase in coal carts along rail tracks in a mineshaft is a genuine rollercoaster ride, supplemented by three stop-motion cuts animated by Tom St. Amand. The sequence's greatest achievement is the fact that it cuts repeatedly from miniature to live-action without ever giving the game away. It was shot by Mike McAlister, who built a camera small enough to be wheeled down the tunnels of the elaborate miniature sets. Highly detailed puppets of Ford, Capshaw, little Short Round (Ke Huy Quan) and several thugs were built by St. Amand and Phil Tippett.

All three stop-motion cuts have the puppets making slight movements as the mining carts hurtle out of control above a river of glowing lava. In two of them, the thugs are trying to pull Short Round out of his cart. In the third, the cart rushes around a bend on two wheels. Numerous non-animated miniature shots are included. Many shots have sparks superimposed onto the steel wheels. The sequence ends when the three characters emerge from the mouth of the tunnel and find themselves halfway up a huge cliff face, a breathtaking shot using a matte painting by Caroleen Green.

A short while later, the group is hanging from a broken vine bridge several hundred feet above a river infested with alligators. Seen in a dizzying view from above, Jones fights off three thugs who are also clinging to the vines and they go tumbling down into the river.

This fabulous two-second shot required seven passes through the optical printer. The actors were shot in a studio above mattresses for the stuntmen to fall onto. The river was a separate live-action element filmed in Montana. A slender strip of painted cliff merged the two live-action elements. Articulate mattes were drawn frame-by-frame to allow parts of the struggling actors to spread over into the painting and river. Tiny superimposed silhouettes of alligators were added to the river far below. And the three thugs transform seamlessly from actors into stop-motion puppets as they fall away from the camera. The stop-motion puppets were each filmed separately, tumbling head over heels in front of a blue screen.

In charge of all the effects was Dennis Muren, who received an Academy Award for his achievements.

Innerspace

1987. Guber-Peters. D: Joe Dante. Scr: Jeffrey Boam, Chip Proser. Story: Chip Proser. Ph: Andrew Laszlo. Art: James H. Spencer. Mus: Jerry Goldsmith. Special Makeup Effects: Rob Bottin. Special Visual Effects: Dennis Muren — Industrial Light and Magic. Visual Effects Cameramen: Peter Kozachik, Kim Marks, Harry Walton, Don Dow.

Cast: Dennis Quaid, Martin Short, Meg Ryan, Kevin McCarthy, Fiona Lewis, William Schallert.

Rating: ☆☆☆   Stop-Motion: ☆☆½

This is an SF screwball comedy, with the gags coming thick and fast and the special effects frequent and always top-class. Dennis Quaid is part of a miniaturization experiment and accidentally gets injected into the body of meek supermarket check-out clerk Martin Short. Can Quaid get out and revert to normal size before the bad guys get both of them? Joe Dante directs with pace and his usual contagious affection for fantasy filmmaking.

Dennis Muren at Industrial Light and Magic was in charge of the visual effects, primarily the impressive shots inside Short's body. Muren's world is nothing like the multicolored, brightly-lit world of *Fantastic Voyage*—this is the dark, fleshy world seen by miniature cameras in modern medical investigations. Muren deservedly won the 1987 Academy Award for visual effects.

In approximately 12 shots, stop-motion and or go-motion were employed to depict Quaid's pod and the pod of the bad guy who comes to get him. These intricately detailed miniatures were animated by Harry Walton and others against blue screens and then matted into shots of various parts of Short's body. The models make turns, float towards and away from the camera and sometimes hover and swivel. The extra element of a glow from their headlamps is carefully added to the image. In one shot, Quaid knocks the bad guy's pod flying and it cartwheels up and away. In another, the bad guy ejects from his pod, which floats down towards Short's stomach while the character flies upwards. These shots are all very smoothly animated and flawlessly combined with the miniature sets.

Insane Chronicle
see *Bláznova Kronika*

International House

1933. Paramount. D: Edward Sutherland. Scr: Francis Martin, Walter DeLeon. Story: Neil Brant, Louis E. Heifetz. Ph: Ernest Haller. Mus and Lyrics: Ralph Rainger, Leo Robin.

Cast: Peggy Hopkins Joyce, W. C. Fields, Rudy Vallee, Stuart Erwin, George Burns, Gracie Allen, Cab Calloway, Bela Lugosi, Franklin Pangborn, Lumsden Hare, Sterling Holloway.

Rating: ☆☆½   Stop-Motion: ☆☆

The best thing about this W. C. Fields vehicle is a comic performance by horror legend Bela Lugosi. Little did Lugosi know it but this 1933 Paramount film offered him the most substantial non-horror role he would ever get after *Dracula*. He plays a Russian general and ex-husband of Peggy Hopkins Joyce, whom he mistakenly believes is carrying on with Fields. The comedy revolves around his bumbling attempts to do away with Fields. He is one of a number of contemporary celebrities who enliven what is generally a very weak and unfunny Fields vehicle. Burns and Gracie Allen are embarrassing. Rudy Vallee sings a love song to his megaphone and

Cab Calloway sings "Reefer Man," a song that is usually cut from U.S. television screenings because it tells of a stoned double bass player.

The climax features an unusual application of stop-motion. Fields drives his car off the edge off a hotel roof and there is a long shot (lasting about four seconds) of a miniature car driving down the fire escape. At the time, Paramount's technical effects department was headed by Gordon Jennings and its process photography department was headed by Farciot Edouart. This convincing effect may well have been animated by Jennings, but the film's credits give nothing away.

There are also two striking shots of an elaborate miniature set of a Chinese town, aerial shots looking down at an autogyro (also miniature) flying over it.

The Invention of Destruction
see *Vynález Zkázy*

The Invisible Man Returns

1940. Universal. D: Joe May. Scr: Curt Siodmak, Lester Cole. Original Story: Joe May and Curt Siodmak. Ph: Milton Krasner. Art: Jack Otterson, Martin Obzina. Mus: Hans J. Salter. Special Effects: John P. Fulton.

Cast: Sir Cedric Hardwicke, Vincent Price, Nan Grey, John Sutton, Cecil Kellaway, Alan Napier.

Rating: ☆☆½   Stop-Motion: ☆☆

This was a brave attempt to recreate the thrills of *The Invisible Man* (1933), but director Joe May was no James Whale. The film does not have the excitement of the original nor do its many comic moments have quite the same bizarre force. A young Vincent Price, with his distinctive voice, was a good choice for the title role. But he is let down by a conventional plot in which he is wrongly convicted of a murder and must use his invisibility serum to bring the real culprit — Cedric Hardwicke — to justice.

The fascinating invisibility effects were the work of John P. Fulton. Fulton was Universal's regular special effects man; as well as supplying effects for *The Invisible Man*, he worked on many of the company's classic horror films, including *Frankenstein* (1931) and *Were Wolf of London* (1935). One of his Oscars was for his work in Cecil B. DeMille's *The Ten Commandments* (Paramount, 1956) in which he parted the Red Sea (one of many startling effects shots). For *The*

Invisible Man Returns, he received an Academy Award nomination.

His invisibility effects included relatively simple shots in which objects or clothes were wire-supported and more complex composite shots using a black-backing traveling matte process. *The Invisible Man Returns* contains all sorts of trickery, including an intriguing shot looking through the eye sockets of Price's bandaged face and seeing light through the bandages at the back; moments when he becomes partly visible as a result of someone blowing cigar smoke at him or when rain falls on him; and a fine effect at the end when the serum wears off and Price slowly materializes (first we see a series of veins and arteries, then muscles start to fade in and finally his flesh appears).

For one shot, some fairly basic stop-motion is used. The Invisible Man ties up a character's legs and the rope is animated as it seems to wrap itself around the stationary actor (only his legs are in the shot).

It see *Stephen King's It*

It Came from Beneath the Sea

1955. Columbia. Prod: Charles H. Schneer. D: Robert Gordon. Scr: George Worthing Yates, Hal Smith. Screen Story: George Worthing Yates. Ph: Henry Freulich. Mus: Mischa Bakaleinikoff. Art: Paul Palmentola. Technical Effects Created by Ray Harryhausen. Technical Assistant: George Lofgren.

Cast: Faith Domergue, Kenneth Tobey, Ian Keith, Donald Curtis, Dean Maddox, Jr., Harry Lauter.

Rating: ☆☆½   Stop-Motion: ☆☆☆

After the commercial success of *Beast from 20,000 Fathoms*, co-producer Jack Dietz set about preparing a similar follow-up. Ray Harryhausen wrote a screen treatment for him called *The Elementals*, and color test footage was shot (some of it in 3-D) of giant creatures that looked like a cross between a bat and a dinosaur. At the climax, the creatures were to attack Paris. But the project fell through and Harryhausen spent the following months working on two of his fairy tale shorts, *The Story of King Midas* and *The Tortoise and the Hare* (the latter was left uncompleted).

He was contacted in 1953 by Charles H. Schneer, a producer at Columbia, who wanted to make a film in the same mold as *Beast*. Instead of a dinosaur, the central monster would be a gigantic octopus, and Schneer had conceived of a spectacular set-piece in which the creature would tear down the Golden Gate Bridge in San Francisco.

Harryhausen rendered a series of sketches of the proposed film's dramatic high points, based on a treatment by George Worthing Yates.

The film struggles under a budget that was probably around $150,000 — at least $50,000 less than the budget on *Beast*. But Harryhausen's inventive animation sequences transform the film into something superior to nearly all the non-animation monster movies that proliferated in the 1950s. Some of his images — enormous tentacles waving in the air above city roofs, tentacles snaking hungrily through a street — have a surreal dynamism which they retain after several viewings. These are tentacles with attitude.

Harryhausen's main concession to the budget was to give his octopus only six tentacles in order to save time and money. Shots were designed so that only part of the creature was ever seen at one time, disguising the two absent limbs. Quite probably, no one would have been aware of this had Harryhausen himself not revealed it in interviews. Two other animation models were built for the film: a detailed two-and-a-half-foot long tentacle used in closeups, and a partial head used in an extreme closeup of the creature's eye opening.

Despite the budget, Harryhausen managed to put more animation into the film than there was in *Beast*: There are 135 cuts compared to *Beast*'s 84. But, of course, animating a tentacle is a lot less involved than bringing to life a snarling quadruped. Harryhausen, unable to use expensive traveling matte processes, fully exploited the possibilities of his front- and rear-projection reality sandwich techniques.

The film lacks a scene to match the dramatic force of *Beast*'s fairground climax but in some respects is technically more accomplished. Several of the static matte designs are more intricate than those in *Beast*. The numerous miniatures used — the Golden Gate Bridge, a sea freighter, a railway carriage, the Market Street tower and other buildings — are more detailed than before. Some of these were built by George Lofgren, who had earlier worked on *Mighty Joe Young*, although this time he received no screen credit.

Script and direction are the poorest of all Harryhausen's films. Director Robert Gordon has with good reason been excluded from most reference books and allows his cast to turn in wooden performances. The live-action sequences lack the polish that Eugene Lourie brought to *Beast*. More might have been expected from scriptwriter Yates, who had a hand in the classic *Them!*, George Pal's *Conquest of Space* and the later Schneer/Harryhausen collaboration *Earth vs. the Flying Saucers*. Too much time is wasted on a corny love triangle in which macho Kenneth Tobey tries to woo intelligent Faith Domergue ("She's one of a new breed of woman") away from dull scientist Donald Curtis.

At times, the live-action sequences plumb such depths of foolishness that one can only assume that Yates had his tongue firmly in his cheek. In one sequence, white-coated scientists Curtis and Domergue are trying hard to look industrious and intelligent but are revealed to be merely scooping goldfish out of a fish tank. In an absurd hospital scene, a terrified sailor is disturbed by the similarity between the doctor's stethoscope and his memory of the tentacles of the octopus. And in the most laughable scene, all the major characters and various somber officials are gathered around a table to discuss tactics, and one of them demonstrates the octopus' means of locomotion by blowing up a balloon and then letting it fly around the room.

Harryhausen's fine sequences make up for these deficiencies, but even he could not overcome the fact that it was almost impossible to put any characterization into his star performer. The monster is an enormous, horrifying, destructive force but never arouses any sympathy in us. Even at the climax, it is blown up abruptly and not allowed any of the pathos that usually accompanies a Harryhausen death scene.

Yet Harryhausen still manages to give his puppet some memorable touches of personality. When its tentacles are prowling around the San Francisco streets, he makes them act and react like independent beings. One rears up and recoils when a flame thrower is fired at it. Another bursts through a window and actually appears to look around the room. Harryhausen also overcomes the fact that his monster cannot roar or growl: to emphasize its destructive power, he gives it a kind of breathy rumble. And during the climactic attack on San Francisco Bay, enough excitement is generated (incorporating a high number of different locations and rear-projection set-ups) that the octopus' inherent lack of personality is not a handicap.

The film begins powerfully with three well-thought-out sequences but subsequently deteriorates to standard B-picture level. It starts, like so many 1950s

SF films, with a high-powered narrator proclaiming the perils of entering the atomic age, backed by stock footage of the launching of a submarine. "The mind of man had thought of everything — except that which was beyond his comprehension," booms the narrator, pouring out a stream of pseudo-scientific gobbledygook. This leads into an imaginative credits sequence in which the lettering seems to rise out of the waves of a turbulent sea. In case some of us still haven't got the message, a title card rolls up the screen, cautioning us about "the mysteries in the heavens, or in the seas below." Then there is a tense scene in which Tobey and his submarine crew are pursued and grabbed by some huge, unseen being which their radar is unable to identify. So far, so good — but from now on the film, has little to recommend it apart from its effects scenes.

Thirty minutes into the film the giant octopus is seen for the first time, attacking a ship. This two-minute sequence, containing 20 animation cuts, recalls the moody nighttime attack by the rhedosaurus on the fishing boat, but is more elaborate. It begins with a haunting nightmare image in which two sailors (standing in front of a full-scale rear projection) see a huge tentacle rise up out of the water, so massive that it continues to rise for several drawn-out seconds. The more detailed puppet tentacle was used for this shot, allowing an intimate look at its fleshy suckers, coated in glycerin to make them look wet and slimy. Other effects technicians might simply have used a static prop for this shot, but Harryhausen has his animated tentacle sway and unfurl before slipping back into the sea. The rear plate is a

It Came from Beneath the Sea (1955): Harryhausen's octopus attacks a ship. (National Film Archive, London.)

composite, with spray superimposed over the animation.

Animated against stock footage of the underside of a boat, the shadowy shape of the octopus swims under the craft. Another tentacle rises up by the side of the boat and the foreground sailors run around in panic. A series of shots look out from the ship's bridge at a tentacle outside the windows as the ship begins to rock violently from side to side. Several sailors leap overboard, the enormous tentacle behind them now much closer.

In long shot, the partially sub-merged octopus lunges towards the ship (a dramatic movement that might surprise mollusk experts), one tentacle snaking high in the air. Previously shot film of crashing surf is superimposed and obscures the matte line that crosses the background footage of a calm sea: not 100 percent realistic but preferable to the mis-scaled water droplets that ruin most effects scenes involving water. Several tentacles surround the miniature ship and in the final series of shots, all with superimposed spray, the craft is pulled under.

Later on (and again at night), our

heroes visit a beach to investigate some sucker imprints in the sand. Well — at least it makes a change from footprints. In six animation cuts, the octopus emerges from the sea and devours a policeman.

In an impressive long-shot static matte, a tentacle rises up behind a rocky promontory. The second shot, in which the creature has hauled its body up onto the rocks, uses the same design. In this way, Harryhausen can imply that the model is emerging from the sea without having to show it in contact with the water. (He would use the same trick years later in *Clash of the Titans*.) In long shot, a tentacle reaches across the beach. A rear-projected shadow of the advancing tentacle is added to a medium shot of the policeman looking up, standing in front of a rear screen. Backed by the victim's screams, the huge tentacle unfurls onto the beach: Physical contact with the actor is never attempted, but it is implied that the tentacle has snared him. Two final long shots show the octopus sprawled over the rocks, apparently replete after its snack, one tentacle rolling gently. Its body expands and dilates as it breathes, suggesting that there is a bladder inside the puppet. These shots use a different static matte design, the rear image having been shot from the other side of the promontory.

The monster next appears beneath the Golden Gate Bridge. The 25 animation cuts in this ingenious sequence include some unforgettable images. The scene is quite an achievement when one considers that the San Francisco authorities refused to give Schneer permission to film the bridge and so Harryhausen had to make do with newsreel footage

and also some shots that were taken surreptitiously from the back of a bread van.

First one tentacle, then a second, then a third, break the water and wrap around one of the support columns. Part of the column is miniature, carefully positioned so as to obscure the actual structure behind. Surf is again superimposed over the matte line where the puppet meets the water. This is a memorable composite, even though the surf is accidentally superimposed slightly higher than it should be — Harryhausen had neither the time nor the budget to correct such mistakes.

Several extreme long shots show the puppet with four tentacles lifted out of the water. The matte follows the outline of the overhead roadway, allowing one tentacle to rise up behind it. The lower foreground is also a matted area, so that buildings on the near side of the bay appear in front of the puppet. It wraps around the support pillars and in two low-angle composites a tentacle rises into the air.

Hoping to turn off the flow of electricity that has attracted the leviathan, Curtis runs onto the bridge. Amazed, he looks up to see one of the huge tentacles rising up (in a full-scale rear projection).

Seen in several long shots, the octopus has now pulled itself almost completely out of the water. In a classic miniature shot, a tentacle flattens a car on the bridge. The miniature car crumples realistically and the shot allows a close look at the wealth of detail on the two-and-a-half-foot puppet.

Accompanied by the sound of creaking metal, the octopus continues to squeeze the bridge. A piece of the miniature bridge breaks away and falls very smoothly — actually supported on an invisible wire and animated frame-by-frame. The bridge starts to crumple under the onslaught. Tobey drives onto the bridge to rescue Curtis and there is a breathtaking ten-second cut in which one of the tentacles seems to rise up forever behind him, recalling an earlier shot during the attack on the ship.

A tentacle pushes up through the roadway, animated bits of concrete falling away very realistically. In these three shots, Curtis stands in the foreground, reacting to the action in a rear projection. In long shots of the tentacles, more pieces of the bridge are ripped apart and fall. The electric current is turned off and, in two final long shots, the octopus slides down off the bridge into the water. Parts of the wrecked miniature bridge sway in the air precariously — animated, of course — in these impressive shots.

The monster now turns its attention to the Embarcadero docks. Five men sitting on the dockside are amazed to see a giant tentacle rise up on the far side of the loading piers. In these composites, the puppet looks faint compared to the live action, but these are still striking designs. The tentacle is also seen from the other side of the pier, spray superimposed where it meets the live-action water. Panicking extras in the foreground assist the illusion that the puppet is way off in the distance. In one shot, a crowd of extras rush out of the frame and the huge tentacle waves across the area they had just occupied — a clever way of emphasizing the illusion that puppet and actors are part of the same footage.

Using again the first two dockside composites, the tentacle is now seen clutching a rail-cart high in the air, then dropping the crushed wreckage. Another tentacle rises up beside the dock, this time in a closer shot in which Harryhausen has matted around the intricate edge of a horizontal railing so that part of his puppet can be seen behind it.

A series of cuts shows a tentacle waving in the air with a helicopter flying past in the rear projection. In shots from the pilot's point of view (looking out of the cockpit at a full-scale rear projection), the tentacle gets nearer and nearer to the camera until suddenly everything goes black. The sequence is successful without Harryhausen needing to show the actual impact.

In an extreme long-shot design that will be used again and again, the octopus sprawls across the dockside, half out of the water. One tentacle snakes into the air and another reaches across the roadway, searching the streets for prey. Part of the road and pier is a miniature set but it is not easy to spot exactly where it meets up with the rear-projected piers. The tiny cars that speed along the road look like they are animated. A building in the foreground may be a photo cutout or a front projection. The tentacles throw shadows onto the street, confirming that at least that part is a miniature.

A tentacle rises up beside the Market Street clock tower, which in this cut appears to be part of the live-action plate. Shots of extras panicking in the streets are intercut with a long sequence of events in which tentacles seem to be everywhere. In one effectively eye-deceiving cut, two tentacles rise up behind a dockside car park, with extras and cars in the foreground. The tentacles, which snake about behind an intricate matte along the irregular edge of a fence, really look like they are off in the distance. It may well be that Harryhausen used the larger puppet for this shot, animating it twice in two separate passes of the film through the camera. Four cuts using another static matte design show a tentacle rising up behind another dock-side building.

In an inventive little sequence, a tentacle pursues a crowd of people through an archway, bringing the arch crashing down on top of itself. The miniature floor along which the tentacle slithers blends imperceptibly with the live-action street where the extras are running. The first cut is seen from one side of the arch and the three subsequent cuts shoot from the other side as the tentacle wriggles through it, extras rushing along the right side of the frame. In these cuts, the arch is a miniature and pieces of animated debris fall very realistically onto the puppet. This image would recur years later in *Jason and the Argonauts* when the arm of the giant bronze statue Talos reaches through a natural rocky arch trying to snare the fleeing sailors. Is it an image from some old silent film that haunted the young Harryhausen, like so many other images that have roots in his childhood cinema-going?

In two stunning long shots, a tentacle rises up on either side of the clock tower. A miniature of the tower is used in shots where the tentacles wrap around it. The film's worst effect shot occurs at this point; mercifully, it is only on screen for about a second. Tobey and Curtis, out at sea in the submarine, look back through binoculars at the monster wrapped around the tower. To avoid having to build a smaller puppet for this extreme long shot, somebody decided it would be a good idea to flash up a painting of the octopus on the tower. To describe it as unconvincing would be generous.

In a series of shots, the tower is demolished. Harryhausen uses two different static matte designs with extras fleeing in the lower foreground. In one of these cuts, the hand of an extra crosses the matte line and disappears. Harryhausen was well aware of this blunder but clearly decided that it would not be noticed by audiences, because in the same cut he does take the trouble to correct a second mistake. The whole of an actor's head crosses the matte line, disappearing behind the miniature tower and for four or five frames Harryhausen appears to have painted a rough approximation of the actor's head onto glass. He gets away with this audacious trick because all eyes are focused on the action in the background. Bits of animated masonry fall away realistically from the tower, which eventually is pulled down completely by the mollusk.

One tentacle starts to crawl through the streets almost as though it has a mind of its own. Harryhausen uses four different composite designs, all effectively imparting a terrifying sense of the great bulk of the tentacle and playing up the surreal imagery of mundane city streets invaded by an impossible creature. Rear-projected shadows heighten the impact of these very successful shots. The tentacle unfurls from behind a corner building and flattens several people as they try to flee. Then it slides back along the street, the prey presumably flattened and attached to its suckers.

In another street scene, the tentacle, again acting like an independent being, rears up, passing partly behind a canopy that is part of the rear screen. In a closer shot, it rises up by the side of a building as extras run underneath it along the pavement. (Completists may wish to check out Sam Calvin's claim in *FXRH* #1 that this piece of footage was also used during the climax of *Earth vs. the Flying Saucers*— minus the tentacle, of course.) Harryhausen rear-projects a shadow of the tentacle into this set-up.

The tentacle smashes through an office window and, in another inventive instance of Harryhausen putting character into his puppet, seems to look around the room. This was achieved by filming actors in a mock-up of the room with the animation footage rear-projected into the area where the window should be. Bits of animated glass fall in the rear projection when the tentacle smashes through.

Soldiers have now arrived on the scene and use a flamethrower to force the creature back into the sea. In a long series of cuts — all of which make use of composite designs already used — the tentacle retreats back through the streets. The extreme long shot of the octopus sprawled over the dockside is also featured several times. The blast of flame from the flamethrower is superimposed so that it seems to pass partly in front of the puppet. The tentacle reacts believably, coiling and uncoiling, and the creature lets out a pained scream — another bit of artistic license. In one cut, the tentacle rears up aggressively but then is forced back farther by another blast of flame. In the final long shot of the dock area, the octopus waves one tentacle high in the air then slips out of sight into the water.

After these excellent sequences, the finale is a letdown. In their submarine, Tobey and Curtis approach the monster sitting on the bed of the bay and fire a high-voltage torpedo into it. The pace of this murky underwater passage is hampered by the fact that the water dictates that everything must happen slowly and in silence. (Harryhausen struggled with the same problem in *Mysterious Island*.) There is an attempt to make things more dramatic by having the torpedo initially fail to detonate, but eventually the creature explodes abruptly, with little drama and no pathos.

There are 14 animation cuts, some shot through a distortion glass to suggest the illusion of being underwater. The octopus is seen in full sitting on the bed of the bay, some of its tentacles unfurling, others already stretched out. In a closeup, the animated torpedo enters the octopus' side but does not detonate. In long shots, a miniature of the submarine drifts closer to the creature, is grabbed by two of the tentacles and pulled to the sea-floor.

Tobey and Curtis don wet suits and swim out to the octopus, hoping to trigger the torpedo's detonator. Shots of them swimming in front of the puppet appear to have been achieved by filming them separately in white suits swimming against a black background, then superimposing that footage onto close shots of the puppet. In most of these shots, the technique is successful but in one of Curtis swimming up to the octopus, the image of the actor is transparent. This shot uses an animated puppet of the side of the creature's face, with one eye blinking open. Curtis fires a harpoon into the creature's eye and in two long shots it lurches across the frame in pain, tentacles writhing frantically. The miniature submarine is released and sails away. In a long cut, consummately animated by Harryhausen, the tentacles continue to writhe desperately. A rear projection of rippling water is used to suggest the surface of the sea above. The glare of an explosion is superimposed over the final shot of the puppet. Harryhausen sensibly does not try to animate bits of octopus flying across the screen.

It Came from Beneath the Sea may not be the "tidal wave of terror" that its ad campaign promised, but it's still a very enjoyable monster-on-the-loose picture with lots of great effects scenes. And at least a few unintentionally funny live-action scenes relieve the mediocrity of the rest of the script. Harryhausen's achievements on such a small budget insured that the film was a commercial success and so it cemented a partnership between him and producer Schneer. They would go on to produce 12 more films together, many of which rank among the finest fantasy films of all time.

It's A Mad Mad Mad Mad World

1963. United Artists. Prod-D: Stanley Kramer. Story and Scr: William and Tania Rose. Ph: Ernest Laszlo. Art: Rudolph Sternad. Mus: Ernest Gold. Photographic Effects: Linwood G. Dunn, James B. Gordon, Film Effects of Hollywood (uncredited: Willis O'Brien, Jim Danforth, Marcel Delgado, Marcel Vercoutere).

Cast: Spencer Tracy, Milton Berle, Sid Caesar, Buddy Hackett, Ethel Merman, Mickey Rooney, Phil Silvers, Terry-Thomas, Jonathan Winters, Jimmy Durante, Eddie "Rochester" Anderson, Jim Backus, Peter Falk, Buster Keaton, the Three Stooges.

Rating: ☆☆½   Stop-Motion: ☆☆½

Stanley Kramer's epic comedy, trimmed from 186 to 154 minutes in most prints, is still far too long. There are lots of good gags as an assortment of comedians race each other for a buried treasure of $350,000, but the only consistently funny sections are those featuring Terry-Thomas as an English twit. However, the five-minute fire escape finale *is* funny and is the reason for its inclusion in this book. The special effects for this sequence were designed by Willis O'Brien, although he died before the finished film reached the screen.

A group of characters are clambering down a fire escape only to have it collapse under them. A fireman on a long ladder reaches them but they all climb on it at once, sending it out of control, swaying about madly and throwing the characters in all directions. Much of the footage designed and animated for this sequence never made it into the final cut but what remains is still remarkably well integrated, snaring the audience in its wild pace and never letting you sit back and groan, "It's a special effect." It's a final testimony to O'Brien's vision, even though it is small fry compared to his earlier work.

Realizing that stop-motion would be the best way to depict long shots of this action, special effects supervisor Linwood Dunn hired O'Brien. Marcel Delgado was brought in to build a whole series of human puppets. Jim Danforth was hired later to do some of the actual animation. He told the author: "Marcel Vercoutere was animating scenes when I arrived, but I took over. I believe his scene of the fire engine ladder being extended is in the film." There are two extreme long shots of the ladder extending, but these appear to use a manually operated miniature ladder combined with live-action footage of the actors clinging to the fire escape.

In a magazine interview, Danforth described the work that was done: "There were a lot of shots filmed but not used with animated figures of the 11 comedians they had on that ladder. One stop-motion shot that remains in the film is Sid Caesar being thrown through a boarded-up window. We did about 14 shots that way, together with miniatures worked mechanically and miniatures we rolled at high speed. There were three different sets of miniature people, each built to a different scale, with miniature settings to match" (*Lumiere* #25, July 1973).

According to Don Shay (*Cinefex* #7), 17 stop-motion cuts were filmed. But it seems that only the shot with a wire-supported Sid Caesar puppet made it into the release print. Even this shot has been cut down. It's a very quick shot and so smoothly animated that one is fooled into thinking this is live action.

Other effects shots in the sequence include long shots of a miniature ladder swaying about above the crowd, with tiny unmoving puppets clinging to it. Many shots are composites using a miniature of the building and painted backgrounds of other buildings or the sky. John Brosnan (in *Movie Magic*) states that 25 matte paintings were used in this one sequence. No more than six are seen in what remains.

Jack and the Beanstalk

1952. Warner Bros. D: Jean Yarbrough. Scr: Nat Curtis. Story: Pat Costello. Ph: George Robinson. Art: McClure Cooper. Mus: Heinz Roemheld. Special Effects: Carl Lee. Photographic Effects: J. R. Glass.

Cast: Bud Abbott, Lou Costello, Buddy Baer, Dorothy Ford, Barbara Brown, David Stollery.

This lesser Abbott and Costello vehicle begins in black and white with Costello reading the title story to a small child, then switches to "SuperCine-Color" when the fable itself begins, with Costello playing Jack and Abbott playing the village butcher boy.

The beanstalk that the two characters climb is seen in some shots as a full-scale prop. Two drawings — adequate but hardly realistic — are used for extreme long shots that include the sky above and the ground below. In two of these shots, very tiny figures of the actors can be seen clambering up the stalk. These shots appear to have been achieved by animating small puppets. However, the shots are extremely brief and the figures are far away, making it extremely difficult to be certain of the technique used.

Jack the Giant Killer

1962. United Artists/Zenith. D: Nathan Juran. Scr: Orville H. Hampton, Nathan Juran. Story: Orville H. Hampton. Ph: David S. Horsley. Art: Fernando Carrere. Mus: Paul Sawtell, Bert Shefter. Special Photographic Effects: Howard A. Anderson. Stop-Motion Sequences: Project Unlimited (Gene Warren, Wah Chang, Tim Barr). (Uncredited Effects: Stop-Motion Animation: Jim Danforth, Tom Holland, Dave Pal, Don Sahlin. Armatures: Marcel Delgado, Victor Delgado. Process Supervisor: Phil Kellison. Matte Artists: Bill Brace, Albert Whitlock. Creature Design: Louis MacManus.)

Cast: Kerwin Mathews, Judi Meredith, Torin Thatcher, Walter Burke, Roger Mobley, Don Beddoe, Anna Lee.

Rating: ☆☆½   Stop-Motion: ☆☆½

Over the years, producer Edward Small has come in for a hail of abuse for making this botched copy of *The 7th Voyage of Sinbad*. But was he really any more mercenary than any other producer, simply trying to cash in on a successful formula? Perhaps he deserves a bit of praise for at least attempting to put a spectacular fantasy on the screen — even if the result is seriously flawed.

To emulate *7th Voyage*, Small recruited Nathan Juran as director and Kerwin Mathews and Torin Thatcher as leading players. But all three lack the enthusiasm that they showed in Harryhausen's film. Small wanted his film, like *7th Voyage*, to be full of magic and monsters but the effects are a muddle of sequences produced by different companies and individuals, with no Harryhausen-style *auteur* at the helm. There are magical, dramatic moments beautifully executed, and there are bungled sequences that only make one appreciate all the more the artistry of Harryhausen.

In publicity material, Small boasted about his new special effects process Fantascope — "a revolutionary new system of trick photography." "At long last," the publicity claimed, "film process shots are treated in color. ... Developed secretly over the past two years by Small in conjunction with the Howard A. Anderson Company ... the Fantascope process contains innovations in color photography that impart depth dimensions to model animation. The system also features a matte process that integrates the use of stop-action puppets with live-

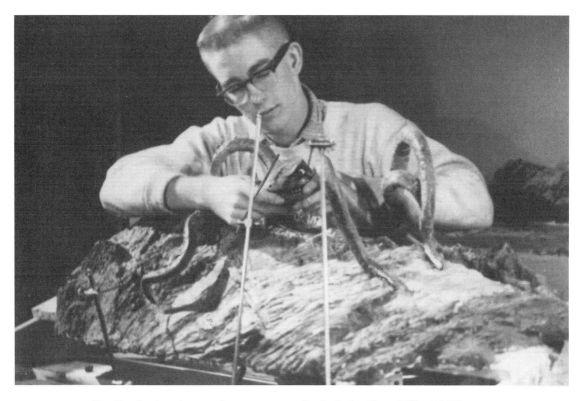

Jim Danforth animates the sea creature for *Jack the Giant Killer* (1962).

action, eliminating the necessity of using miniatures and thereby lending more realism to action scenes." Apparently, Small had managed to convince himself that Dynamation and *7th Voyage* had never happened.

The stop-motion sequences are *almost* wonderful. But all are let down by models which look foolish and synthetic. A horned giant called a Cormoran and a dragon-like harpy are acceptable, but a two-headed giant called Galligantua and a sea creature are poor. All the puppets have large, unconvincing eyes which make them look more like toys than living creatures. Wah Chang designed the sea creature and makes it look more like a child's plaything than a fearsome monster — one can only assume that he was

subconsciously recreating the surreal look of Pal's Puppetoons. Over the years, some fine models designed by Chang (including a dragon in *The Wonderful World of the Brothers Grimm* and the Loch Ness Monster in *The 7 Faces of Dr. Lao*) have had a similar playful appearance, but on those occasions it suited the tone of the films. Here, it undermines a potentially exciting sequence.

To handle the special effects, Small contracted Howard A. Anderson, who in turn subcontracted the stop-motion to Project Unlimited, the company run by Gene Warren, Wah Chang and Tim Barr. Anderson gave Phil Kellison — a veteran animator of many television commercials — overall responsibility for the stop-motion. The animation was exe-

355

The Cormoran of *Jack the Giant Killer.*

cuted by Jim Danforth, Dave Pal, Tom Holland and Don Sahlin. Danforth did approximately 50 percent of the animation. Sahlin did some test animation but then left the project — none of his work is in the final film. There are 179 stop-motion cuts in the film, although British readers may wish to note that several cuts have been made during the scene in which Jack battles the Cormoran. (These are during the sequences in which one character wields an axe, again when the Cormoran's hand is crushed by the stone wheel in a mill and again when the Cormoran is strangled with a rope, events apparently considered too horrific for young children. This cut version is the one that is still shown regularly on British television.)

Jack was Danforth's fourth feature film, and on all he was employed by Project Unlimited. The first three were *The Time Machine, Goliath and the Dragon* and *Master of the World* (for which he built human figures for long shots of an airship). One of his most important contributions to *Jack* was in explaining the application of static matte rear-projection set-ups to the other effects personnel, who previously had no understanding of Harryhausen's "reality sandwich" techniques and envisaged having to build a lot of foreground miniatures. Danforth had learned these tricks as a result of studying Harryhausen's films. Some sources state that he learned more about these techniques during a visit to Harryhausen on the set

356

of *7th Voyage of Sinbad*; however, Danforth wrote to this author, "Ray did not show me how he made splits when I visited *7th Voyage*. No matte set-ups were visible." Danforth in fact "had already done 'reality sandwich' mattes in 16mm after viewing *20 Million Miles to Earth*."

Armatures were machined not by Marcel Delgado (as stated in some sources) but by his brother Victor. At one point during early post-production, Anderson intended to use the original Kong armatures which he had found in an RKO prop room. But after stripping the puppets down, he found that the armatures were too worn to be usable, so Delgado built new ones.

The first stop-motion sequence is unforgettable because it is both charming and sinister. Plotting to abduct the Princess (Judi Meredith), the evil sorcerer Pendragon (Thatcher) has presented her with a gift, a ten-inch doll that performs a graceful dance on a table in front of her. These 12 cuts were animated by Tom Holland. The puppet's movements are a bit stiff but since it is meant to look like a mechanical toy, this actually improves the sequence. The doll is colorfully dressed in a pink-and-red jester's costume, yet its ugly face and the glowering presence of Pendragon make the simple dance seem loaded with evil possibilities.

Holland animated the puppet in three different set-ups. One is an all-miniature perspective looking down at the puppet on the table. The tabletop holes used to brace the puppet are briefly visible in one cut. A second perspective is a set-up looking from behind the doll at the Princess, who is dancing in the background. The third composite is

a side view of puppet and Princess dancing together. These last two were achieved not with rear projection but by a front-light/back-light system, thereby avoiding having to use a very large rear screen with all its grain problems.

Later that night, the Princess sleeps with the doll near her bedside. Pendragon appears at her window, casts a magic spell and brings the doll to life. This long sequence, featuring 30 stop-motion cuts animated by Pal, Danforth and Holland, is extremely well done, even if some of the animation is awkward. There are several bizarre images and some clever moments of interaction. Some grainy rear screens and the lifeless face of the puppet detract from the scene.

The drawbridge-like door of the box holding the doll opens and the puppet steps out. In closeup, the doll pulls off its jester's hood, revealing two horns on its head — a clever touch of macabre humor, something that is rarely found in stop-motion sequences. In four dramatic shots, the doll grows to gigantic proportions. Its clothes tear and fall away, supported on wires. A cel-animated shadow has been added to the composite, helping the two elements to engage. When it gets too big for the table, the giant steps down onto the floor. Presumably, the puppet was gradually moved closer to the animation camera to create the illusion of growth. In imaginative low-angle shots, the swelling giant pushes up into the ceiling, a miniature which splinters.

A huge hand reaches down towards the camera. In the following shot, in which the hand reaches for the Princess, it seems to be a blue-screened element, or it may be another front-light/back-light matte.

The King and his aides arrive in time to see the Cormoran walking off through a hole in the wall, the Princess in one of his hands. This long shot is a static matte, the matte line apparently following the edge of the smashed wall and the Princess a puppet in the Cormoran's hand. The flailing arms and legs of the puppet Princess in this and subsequent shots are not animated as fluidly as they should be, but most of these shots are quick ones so Danforth, who animated them, just about gets away with it.

Out in the courtyard, soldiers on horseback mill around under the monster's feet in a very well-balanced composite, the lighting on the puppet really making it look part of the live action. In medium shot, the Cormoran growls at soldiers on the battlements. In another excellent long shot, a rider is knocked from his horse and his sword passes in front of the giant's legs. This bit of trickery was the work of Danforth, who painted the sword on a series of sheets of glass placed between puppet and camera.

In two medium shots, a miniature spear pierces the Cormoran's shoulder and is extracted by the monster. In another long shot of the monster's legs in the courtyard, a soldier falls from his horse and falls clean past the giant's leg. This superb effect is another bit of glass-painted Danforth magic, and his painting is so carefully matched to the live-action soldier that there is no contention at all. It is such a good match that one is first led to believe that a matte must have been rotoscoped around the soldier

to allow him to pass in front of the puppet.

A different kind of interaction is attempted in a shot where the huge hand pulls a rider from his horse, the contact implied in the successful alignment of puppet and rear projection. In long shot, the Cormoran, still holding the Princess, stomps across the courtyard toward the portcullis. Another carefully matched static matte set-up has the creature standing before the huge door, soldiers surrounding his feet.

A miniature portcullis is animated falling in front of the creature, the camera looking from the outside through the doorway at the Cormoran. Likewise, a miniature drawbridge is pulled up, barring the giant's escape. In an excellent rear-screen shot, the giant rips the portcullis away from the doorway, with soldiers looking on from the battlements behind. In two stylishly shadowy low-angle all-miniature shots, the Cormoran, lit by torchlight, tries to barge through the drawbridge. In long shot, the miniature drawbridge falls and the giant steps through, the Princess puppet in his hand.

In a series of four all-miniature shots, the Cormoran stands by the moat as a hail of animated spears falls on him. He pulls up the drawbridge's chain, swings it around his head, then throws it at the battlements, knocking a dozen soldiers into the moat. The chain in flight is a cel animation. He rips up the drawbridge, then throws it to the ground. All these cuts are imaginatively lit by a flickering effect suggesting reflections from the water in the moat. The final animation cut in this sequence is a rear-screen long shot with the Cormoran standing by the moat, and the King and his aides standing in the doorway in the background.

The next morning, Jack (Mathews) is working on his farm when he is startled by the arrival of the Cormoran, who is trying to take the Princess to a boat on a nearby shore. This occasionally stunning sequence contains 25 stop-motion cuts and its bright daylight set-ups make a happy contrast to the shadowy nighttime settings of the previous scenes. Again, the quality of the composites varies throughout the scene.

In the opening set-up, the Cormoran steps over a miniature stone wall backed by grainy traveling matte footage of cliffs and the sea. Only the puppet's legs are seen, thereby increasing the impression of its great size. In the follow-up shot, the puppet is seen in full, stepping over the wall onto a miniature foreground and past a tree which is actually a glass painting by Bill Brace. In its hand, the Princess puppet struggles unconvincingly. In another front-light/back-light shot, the huge legs stride past Jack running for cover. In an interview in *SPFX* #3 (1995), Danforth explained why the animation in these cuts is less than smooth: "They thought the sequence was too fast, so they double-framed it optically. It's very jerky."

A striking long shot of the Cormoran standing over Jack has a miniature foreground impeccably matched to the live-action image. In an inventive perspective, the camera looks down at the Cormoran as he walks diagonally towards the camera, with Jack rear-projected behind him.

Another careful composite has the Cormoran standing on miniature terrain matched to a jetty in the live-action plate, with Pendragon's boat waiting in the water. In medium shot, the giant releases the Princess, now live-action again, and she runs away from him along the jetty. Pendragon's lackey, a demented dwarf, locks the Princess in a cabin, but Jack boards the boat and frees her. The dwarf calls to the Cormoran, who advances growling in a medium shot.

At this point, the flow of the action is interrupted by some messy editing or censorship. Suddenly we see that the cabin door has been smashed and the Princess is free. Was this done to improve the pace or has a censor removed some gruesome moment considered too scary for kids (which is certainly the case later on)?

In medium closeup, the Cormoran turns and growls, allowing a good look at the veins that run all over his arms and torso. This really isn't a bad puppet and it is only the eyes which let it down. (Like all the other puppets, it was sculpted by Chang.) Jack and the Princess run back to the farm, followed (in an imposing low-angle medium-shot) by the roaring Cormoran. The huge legs stride past the actors (another traveling matte set-up), the fur on the legs bristling where the animator has touched it, recalling *King Kong*.

Jack and the Princess cower under a hay cart, which is overturned by the monster. The cart in the live-action film was pulled over by hidden wires as the puppet was aligned with it. In a terrific long shot, the Cormoran stands by the overturned cart in the background while the couple run to the foreground. Jack runs in front of one of the puppet's legs, another uncannily realistic glass-painted effect by Danforth.

The couple hide in a mill. The Cormoran goes down on his knees to get at them, a series of four shots in which he punches at a plausible miniature of the mill. In one cut, he wipes his mouth with the back of his hand, a useful moment of character animation. Shots looking out through the door of the mill at the huge face peering in would be chilling were it not for the toy-like eyes of the puppet. The two-fingered hand reaches in through the smashed doorway. The stone wheel rolls over the giant's hand, crushing it. This shot is filmed entirely in the animation studio using a convincing miniature replica of the inside of the mill and the wheel. Outside, the giant retracts his damaged hand and roars. Reaching in blindly, the Cormoran pulls over the grindstone — a shot in which the puppet hand is aligned with the full-size wheel in the background plate.

Jack looks down at the giant from the mill's upper floor, and there are two unusual point-of-view animation shots with the puppet looking up, standing on a miniature set. Jack throws a rope, and the same overhead design is used in three shots in which an animated rope falls around the creature's head, then slowly tightens. Seen from behind and below in a rear-projection set-up, the Cormoran looks up at Jack in the mill. Jack throws a bucket of flour at the beast, who tries to brush the annoying powder away with his arms. In a medium shot, the giant rubs the flour out of his eyes.

In another shot from behind the model, Jack — a scythe in his hands — swings down toward the giant, lands on his torso and starts hacking at him. Neither the physical contact of Jack landing on the puppet nor the contact of scythe with the giant is depicted; both are merely suggested by the presence of the puppet with its back to the camera in front of the rear-projected actor. In medium-shot, the giant swipes at Jack with the back of his hand, knocking him away. In the last two animation cuts, the Cormoran falls backwards and crashes to the ground, his head bouncing up realistically as it hits, Jack looking on in the background.

It says a lot for the sense of wonder that stop-motion can evoke that the three passages with the Cormoran — despite the many flawed composites, the puppet's unlikely face and some lame live-action cut-aways — are still hugely enjoyable examples of the art.

Before the next stop-motion sequence, there are a number of interesting effects scenes. A detailed miniature of Pendragon's castle perches on a cliff, a dramatic skyline matted in behind it. Jack's ship is attacked by a horde of ghostly figures, extras in monstrous costumes printed in negative and matted in. One of these is a memorable character with a gaping reptilian maw out of which gushes an eldritch hurricane. Pendragon casts a spell that turns the Princess into an evil witch: When she stands by a mirror, her gaudy, evil appearance is revealed. An imp in a bottle is discovered and features in many artful composite shots. At Pendragon's castle, Jack is menaced by soldiers who sprout from the ground where the sorceror throws the broken teeth of a dragon's statue (prefigurings of *Jason and the Argonauts* here). Composite long shots of a temple on a hill with the castle behind use a very attractive glass painting. Some footage is missing from this middle part of the film: Jack and the others are suddenly Pendragon's prisoners, even though there is no scene showing them being taken captive.

Eventually, Jack and the others get free. However, as they run along a beach, Pendragon calls up another giant—a two-headed creature called Galligantua—to prevent them escaping. In response, the imp calls up a sea creature to battle it. This stop-motion sequence is the longest in the film, containing 60 animation cuts, and has an impressive variety of composite set-ups. It is also the weakest stop-motion episode, simply because the two models look so unlikely that it is hard to take them seriously. Anyone who has seen *7th Voyage* will also find it offensive how *Jack* has so obviously stolen the conception of this set-piece from the battle between the Cyclops and the dragon.

Galligantua is another creature of the furry-legged Cyclops school but its two faces — with tiny horns and fangs — are hopelessly lifeless. The sea creature has a foolish, smirking dragon's head, cartoon eyes and legs that bend like tentacles — it is as if Chang couldn't make up his mind what he wanted the beast to look like. Both puppets lack detail and always look like rubbery fakes. Harryhausen's Cyclops and dragon have nothing to worry about.

Although assisted by Pal and Holland, this scene was animated primarily by Danforth, who puts far more into the sequence than the puppets deserve. There are one or two fine moments where he really brings things to life: Gal-

ligantua smashing through a cave roof with an anchor to get at Jack and a dog leaping onto the giant's back.

In a magical swirl of red cel animation, Galligantua makes his appearance from behind some rocks on the beach. This long-shot static matte design is followed by another in which Danforth cleverly has the matte line divert from the top of the rock, thereby allowing the giant to actually step over it. This kind of thoughtful design helps to hide the location of matte lines, improving the composite.

Jack and the Princess are live-action elements running along the beach and Galligantua strides after them, reaching out with his clawed hands in a way that is modeled directly on the Cyclops. In a letter to the author, Danforth explained why he was not happy with this shot: "I had modeled the performance of Galligantua on Lon Chaney's "Hunchback" with flicking tongues. I also did a first version of the beach chase with the giant in a gorilla-like quadrupedal pose. This posture, plus the tongue action, gave a bestial effect unlike Ray's Cyclops. It was rejected, hence the terrible shot which is in the film."

Jack and the Princess take cover in some rocks and, in a series of shots, Galligantua peers in at them (just like the Cyclops), the live-action sea and beach projected behind the puppet. The giant picks up an anchor and starts to smash it down onto the miniature rocks, bits of which are animated realistically as they fall away. Several low-angle shots look up from Jack's point of view as the giant continues to smash away relentlessly.

In another long-shot static matte

Galligantua battles the sea creature in *Jack the Giant Killer.*

set-up, the sea creature appears. First its snaking tentacles writhe up from behind a rock, then its absurd head comes into view. The rear-projected sea jiggles about slightly, suggesting that the camera was not properly locked off during shooting of background plates. Galligantua, shot from behind, turns from the rocks he is smashing. In medium shot, the sea creature advances, "walking" on its tentacles.

The two creatures face each other in an impressive long shot. Rocks and the beach in the lower foreground look like they may be a photo cut-out. Galligantua strikes the sea creature with the anchor while Jack and the Princess run across in the background, cowering from the two beasts. They run back into the rocks and Galligantua makes a grab for them, while the sea creature, looking on, growls at him. The giant tries to reach through the crack in the rocks — again an image lifted from *7th Voyage.*

The sea creature resumes the struggle, striking Galligantua with one of its tentacles — an action which seems most unnatural. The giant grabs onto the miniature rocks behind, pulling a boulder loose. Between the rocks, Jack and the Princess look on from a rear projection. Galligantua swipes at the sea creature twice with the anchor and as he is

362

about to strike it a third time, a dog (actually a Viking transformed by sorcery) leaps onto the giant's back from another rock. This is a very deft effect, with Danforth switching smoothly from live dog to puppet dog in one cut. The puppet lands on the giant's back, animated realistically so as to recoil from the impact. In a series of long shots, Galligantua reaches over his back to get at the dog, while to one side the sea creature writhes weakly on the ground. Eventually, the puppet dog is grabbed and flung across the beach.

In closeup, the dying sea creature looks even less realistic than it did in long shot. Galligantua turns back to the crevice and his hand again reaches in, trying to grab Jack. From the top of the crevice, a chimpanzee (actually a boy, also transformed by sorcery) throws rocks at the giant. This is done in two imaginative shots looking down from above the puppet, with miniature rocks very plausibly animated as they fall on it.

In closeup again, the sea creature starts to revive. It gets to its feet, backed by a rear-projection of the sea.

Switching to yet another set-up, Danforth animates a side view of the giant growling at the chimpanzee on the rock. The giant reaches out directly towards the camera and then, in a side view again, reaches out for the chimp but misses. The sea creature lashes out and (in an all-miniature shot) one of its tentacles strikes Galligantua's head. In medium shot, one tentacle snakes around one of the giant's two necks. Switching perspective again, a low-angle shot looks up at the two creatures locked together, the sea creature biting into one

of Galligantua's heads and its limbs coiled around him. In closeups, a tentacle wraps tightly around one of Galligantua's necks. In another shot, a tentacle wraps around one of the giant's legs.

In long shot — another static matte design — Galligantua goes down under the onslaught, the sea creature still wrapped around him. Danforth executes this tricky bit of choreography very fluidly. In other shots using the same set-up, the giant tries to get up but is slapped back down by the sea beast. Galligantua hits the ground again and the sea creature lunges at him with its toothsome mouth agape. Galligantua sprawls on the beach, trying weakly to get up but eventually collapses — death throes which owe much to the death of the dragon in *7th Voyage*. The sea creature roars triumphantly.

Jack's battle with the harpy (actually Pendragon) is a briefer episode but more satisfying. Apart from its toy-like eyes, Chang's model is excellent, with a realistically scaly tail, feathered torso and lifelike, leathery wings. The scene is better paced than the battle on the beach and contains some even more accomplished animation trickery. Some of the composites are disappointing — grainy rear screens, for example — and once again the puppet never really convinces that it is a living creature. But on the whole this is an imaginative, visually striking sequence. There are 43 animation cuts all of which were done by Danforth, except two which Holland animated.

The opening shot is colorful but too obviously "a special effect." A traveling matte element of Pendragon, backed by a painting of his castle, floats towards the camera and as it does so it dissolves into the harpy, its wings flapping. In two extreme long shots, the harpy circles around the castle. This was apparently achieved by matting around the outline of the miniature castle. These elegant flying shots prefigure Danforth's animation of Pegasus the winged horse in *Clash of the Titans* (1981).

In a closer shot, the harpy swoops over the beach and picks up a rock. Suggesting the force of the wings, sand is blown about in the live-action plate: this is the kind of painstaking attention to detail that we take for granted in a Harryhausen film but which is all too rare here. Three low-angle long shots look up at the harpy hovering, clutching the rock which it is planning to drop on the boat. In the last of these, the creature swoops down towards the camera, releasing the rock, which is supported on wires and lowered one frame at a time with the puppet.

The creature flies up and away from the camera. Two attractive traveling matte shots look down at the harpy with the boat on the blue sea below. These shots require some suspension of disbelief on account of contrast differences, but they are still fine images. The harpy lands on the prow (a miniature) of the ship. In medium shots, Jack slashes at the creature with his sword and it growls back at him. One of its claws knocks Jack backwards; this was achieved by careful alignment of the puppet and a good mime by Mathews. In another shot using the same set-up, the harpy steps up onto the entrance to the galley, the contact again implied through alignment of images.

Two shots (animated by Holland) look up from the Princess' point of view at the harpy smashing its way into the galley. Jack slashes at the creature's foot with his sword. A closeup of the doll-eyed face harms what has so far been an impressive sequence. The harpy lunges at Jack, whose sword momentarily passes in front of the puppet by means of another deft series of miniature substitutions.

The harpy continues to smash its way into the galley. One effective shot uses a front-light/back-light matte to put the puppet in front of the cowering Princess. Jack climbs up onto the harpy's tail, walking along it — an interesting composite in which the puppet is positioned so as to obscure a platform in the traveling matte background on which Mathews is standing. Jack stands up on the creature's back, plunging his sword into it. Another miniature partial sword is used for this effect. The harpy's head turns round to face Jack, who strikes it with his sword. When Jack strikes the head again, Danforth has very skillfully inserted not only the miniature sword but also a miniature of part of Jack's arm, enhancing the shot immeasurably.

In an even more ambitious bit of trickery, Danforth makes a barely perceptible switch to a puppet Jack when the harpy's far wing is raised behind the actor: In one fluid cut, the wing is raised, the puppet Jack is animated in front of the image of the live-action Jack (now obscured by the wing), the wing is lowered and the puppet Jack is removed, revealing the live-action Jack again. This is an example of how Danforth is always aware of the need to make puppet and actor seem to exist in the same space.

The harpy flies off with Jack still on its back. In dramatic, picturesque long shots, the harpy and Jack, backed by the blue sea, are very convincingly animated in flight. The puppet Jack stands on the creature's back, brandishing a sword. In these shots, the puppet was not supported on wires but attached to a steel rod which extended from the back of the puppet and through a hole in the rear screen.

In closer shots, the harpy puppet is animated in front of the live-action Jack by means of traveling matte. One of these shots includes a devilishly clever moment when the harpy's tail snakes fully around the live-action Jack. This was achieved with an articulate rotoscoped matte, drawn around Jack's outline.

In very striking long shots, the puppet Jack dangles underneath the harpy, hanging on with one hand to its claw. One of these shots, however — an optical enlargement of the previous shot — is marred because the harpy puppet looks too red. A closer shot has the live-action Jack dangling underneath the harpy (i.e., hanging onto a rope that is obscured by the puppet). Danforth has the creature look down and growl at its "passenger."

The live-action Jack climbs back up the far side of the harpy. In closeup, the monster's head turns and growls. In a thrilling aerial shot, the camera pans across a rear projection of the sea and some cliffs, following the harpy's flight, with Jack still on its back, wielding his sword. In closer shot, the live-action Jack

slashes down again and, in closeup, the harpy rears up its head and screams.

Two more excellent aerial shots show the puppet Jack on the harpy's back. Jack cuts into its wing, which crumples up into its body. The next cut shifts the perspective, looking up from ground level at the harpy, which tilts to one side and starts to fall. Realistically animated, the puppet Jack jumps away from the beast and adopts a diving position in mid-air. In the final animation shot, the camera does a dramatic tilt down, following the two puppets as they hit the sea. The harpy hits the water upside down, while the puppet Jack dives in cleanly. An explosion in the rear-projected water is timed so that it seem to be a splash caused by the puppets, which are removed from the shot at the vital moment.

With the death of the harpy Pendragon, all the sorceror's spells are undone and his castle self-destructs. The explosions that rip through the miniature castle buildings are a good example of high-speed filming, convincingly staged and combined with blasts of cel-animated wisps of magical energy.

Jack the Giant Killer is hopelessly derivative but still enormous fun and intermittently impressive on a technical level. With better-designed models and with someone with a clearer vision at the helm, this could have compared favorably with Harryhausen's films. As is stands, however, it's the kind of film which reinforces the view of many producers that the stop-motion process is only appropriate in childish films with "jerky little monsters."

James and the Giant Peach

1996. Walt Disney. D: Henry Selick. Scr: Karey Kirkpatrick, Jonathan Roberts, Steve Bloom. Based on the Book by Roald Dahl. Ph: Peter Kozachik, Hiro Narita. Animation Supervisor: Paul Berry. Animators: Anthony Scott, Michael Belzer, Timothy Hittle, Trey Thomas, Justin Kohn, Christopher Gilligan, Richard C. Zimmerman, Steven A. Buckley, Guionne Leroy, Michael W. Johnson, Josephine T. Huang, Daniel K. Mason, Paul Berry, Kent Burton, Tom St. Amand, Webster Colcord, Chuck Duke. Armature Design and Supervision: Tom St. Amand. Computer Animated Water/Seagulls/Sharks: Sony Pictures Imageworks. CGI Animation Supervisor: Harry Walton.

Cast: Paul Terry, Joanna Lumley, Miriam Margolyes, Pete Postlethwaite, Steven Culp. Voices: Paul Terry, Simon Callow, Richard Dreyfuss, Jane Leeves, Miriam Margoyles, Susan Sarandon.

Rating: ☆☆½   Stop-Motion: ☆☆☆

A follow-up to *The Nightmare Before Christmas*, *James and the Giant Peach* (derived from a story by Roald Dahl) tells the charming story of a young orphan, living with two wicked aunts (Joanna Lumley and Miriam Margoyles), who discovers a fantasy world inside a giant peach which magically grows one day in his garden.

The early scenes with the aunts are live action, employing creepy, expressionistic sets to good effect. The middle section, in which James meets the bugs who live inside the peach and travels with them across the Atlantic to New York, consists of a series of elaborate stop-motion sequences. The finale in New York contains a confrontation between the bugs and the wicked sisters, and in some shots combines stop-motion and live action.

Like *Nightmare*, there is a huge amount of stop-motion in the film — 50 minutes of on-screen animation. The crew who created these sequences contains many of the same artists who worked on *Nightmare*. Paul Berry was in overall charge of the animation team. Harry Walton was one of the key animators and Tom St. Amand was again in charge of armature design and construction. Once again, the complex animation of a host of puppet characters is always impressively fluid, imaginative and thoughtfully lit. The bug characters — including a seductive female spider, an elderly glow worm, a melancholy earthworm and a feisty centipede — are brought vividly to life by smooth animation that is always full of character-giving touches.

The seamless composites in the finale include shots of the bugs atop the peach, surrounded by a crowd of extras in a street. In one impressive moment of interaction, the two aunts, suspended in a net of spider's web, are kicked by the grasshopper so that they spin around.

An earlier passage, in which the characters on the water-borne peach are attacked by a giant mechanical shark, features impressive computer generated imagery by Sony Imageworks.

Jason and the Argonauts

1963. Morningside/Columbia. D: Don Chaffey. Scr: Jan Read, Beverley Cross. Ph: Wilkie Cooper. Art: Geoffrey Drake. Mus: Bernard Herrmann. Associate Producer and Creator of Special Visual Effects: Ray Harryhausen. Model Sculpture (uncredited): Arthur Hayward.

Cast: Todd Armstrong, Nancy Kovack, Gary Raymond, Laurence Naismith, Niall MacGinnis, Michael Gwynn, Douglas Wilmer, Jack Gwillim, Honor Blackman, Patrick Troughton, Nigel Green, Andrew Faulds.

Rating: ☆☆☆   Stop-Motion: ☆☆☆☆

Jason is Harryhausen's best-known work and his own favorite among his films. Even the most cynical of audiences respond to the grandeur of the episode with Talos, the giant bronze statue that comes to life, and to the bizarre thrills of the battle with the seven sword-wielding skeletons.

Don Chaffey's efficient direction of the live-action passages makes it hard to believe he is the same director who was later responsible for the lifeless *One Million Years B.C.* (1966). The script by Jan Read and Beverley Cross enthusiastically conjures up a credible version of ancient Greece, with an essentially simple plot sparked by a variety of colorful characters and good dialogue. The credit for this must go more to Read than Cross. Read co-wrote the excellent script for Harryhausen's next picture, *First Men in the Moon*, whereas Cross was later responsible for the unimaginative treatments for *Sinbad and the Eye of the Tiger*, *Clash of the Titans* and the unfilmed *Force of the Trojans*. Cameraman Wilkie

Cooper really makes the most of the picturesque, rocky Italian locations, giving a vivid freshness to the outdoor scenes. Bernard Herrmann's magnificent score catches the right combination of the epic and the grotesque. It is at its most memorable during the skeleton battle where his ominous woodwind themes lead into high-speed staccato rhythms accompanying the fight itself.

It is more than half an hour before the first animation sequence but Chaffey insures that we do not get restless. These opening passages — Hermes' prophecy to Pelias, the storming of the temple, Jason rescuing the drowning Pelias, Jason's visit to the gods in Olympus and the selection of the Argonauts — still entertain after repeated viewing and have a liveliness and sense of grandeur missing from many much more lavish Hollywood epics.

They include a number of minor Harryhausen effects, all carried off flawlessly. Hera (Honor Blackman) appears as a cloud of smoke beside the river, with what looks like a miniature shrub placed in front of her to merge the composite. Hermes grows to a great height in front of Jason and disappears. Jason converses with the huge Olympians, merely a pawn-sized figure on a chessboard (depicted by means of excellent traveling mattes). Olympus is a fine miniature, matted around a central area in which the actors perform in long shots. And the disc thrown by Hercules and Hylas are stop-motion models shot against a rear projection — although just how Harryhausen got the water to splash is a

In this publicity shot from *Jason and the Argonauts* (1963), parts of the feet of the giant Talos disappear beneath the matte line. No such flaw occurs in shots actually seen in the film.

mystery. (It may be a superimposed third element.)

Chaffey, Read and Cross maintain this level of enthusiasm throughout the Talos episode, but thereafter the film starts to degenerate into little more than a series of effects set-pieces, and the film's sense of purpose is lost. In fact, the end of the film is quite unsatisfactory (and unclassical) because the conflict with King Pelias, whom Jason is prophesied to overthrow, is completely ignored. The story ends abruptly after Jason has seized the Golden Fleece while

Zeus announces from above, "We have not yet finished with Jason." It's a shame that the scripting excellence was not sustained to the end.

The encounter with Talos on the Isle of Bronze is a magnificent conception and makes good use of its beach and cliff locations. It is marred only by the inconsistent scale of the huge statue — too large when it picks the ship out of the water and too small when Jason struggles to loosen the plug in its heel. Otherwise this is a classic Harryhausen episode consisting of a series of unforgettable images and a novel conclusion. Talos, with his stiff, metallic movements and black, soulless eyes, is one of the screen's great bogey men. No man in a costume could have evoked the same presence.

Hercules (Nigel Green) and Hylas (John Cairney) stumble on the awesome Valley of Statues — the tiny actors walk across the bottom of an extreme long shot with four huge statues seamlessly matted into the landscape. Inside the base of Talos' statue they find a horde of treasure. A long shot of the interior uses a matte painting dripping with jewels. Outside again, Hercules hears an ominous creak of metal and looks up to see Talos' head turn towards him. This classic low-angle shot, with Hercules' head inserted in the lower right hand corner by means of traveling matte, is a genuinely haunting nightmare image. Brosnan (in *Movie Magic*) calls it "one of the great moments of cinema."

Six cuts show the great statue clambering off its pedestal and, in a deft touch, leaning back stiffly as though adjusting to its sudden consciousness. Three static-matte long shots show Talos emerging from behind a cliff, the sailors running about in the lower foreground. In one of these, Harryhausen has his creation swap his sword from one hand to the other, giving it an extra bit of vitality. In three more cuts, Talos stoops and his huge hand appears through a hole in the rocks, trying to reach the scattering sailors. Harryhausen adds an important touch to this static-matte set-up by superimposing a cloud of dust, thrown into the air when the statue drags his hand back again. When Talos gets up he walks past the hole in the cliff, a credi-

bly intricate matte which allows us to see his legs through the hole.

Varying the perspective to heighten the drama, Harryhausen cuts from an imposing low-angle shot looking up at the statue to a shot looking over Talos' shoulder at the Argonauts fleeing in their boat. When Talos turns and walks away, there is a slight jiggle in the lower half of the matte where the registration has not been held steady.

In a long sequence, Talos cuts off the sailors' escape route, stepping over the exit from the harbor and destroying their ship. He pivots stiffly, planting one foot on the other side of the channel (which may well have been put there by matte photography if it is not an actual location). Several very good traveling mattes allow the camera to look up at Talos from the sailors' point of view as the boat nearly drifts through his legs. Medium shots of Talos looking down at the Argonauts are intercut with several long shots of the tiny boat sailing below.

He swaps his sword hand again, stoops and picks up the boat, with Harryhausen effectively cutting between live-action shots of the actors being thrown about, a prop of the boat shaken from side to side in the air, and stop-motion long shots of Talos holding a miniature of the boat, tiny animated oars and the broken mast falling into the sea — probably suspended on wires for a few frames. After dropping the boat, Talos turns and walks away.

There is a pause in the action as the sailors swim to shore, then Talos reappears. A dramatic camera move pans from Jason and his men to the sight of Talos striding past some far-off rocks — it looks as though Harryhausen has moved his animation camera in closer and simply panned across the pre-shot background plate. After three cuts of Talos behind these rocks, a fourth has him step around the same rocks, cleverly helping to disguise the composite: The matte which initially follows the top of the rocks is replaced by a horizontal one along the beach.

A number of non-matte medium shots of the puppet (most dramatically a shot which tilts up from his waist to his head, and an impressive full-view low-angle view) are intercut with long shots of the Argonauts throwing rocks and spears. Talos swipes at them with his huge sword, which nearly fills the frame in one rear-screen shot as it swishes past the sailors. His enormous foot swings past Jason, who is waiting for an opportunity to get at the statue's weak spot, its heel. After a low-angle view looking up at Talos' back, Jason runs over to the heel. In some shots, a non-animated prop of the foot is used, matted onto the beach; closer shots, in which Jason actually releases the plug at the back of the heel, employ a full-scale prop. Several medium shots show Talos looking down with concern.

Steam and ichor, the statue's life-blood, escape from Talos' heel. Although it looks like a live-action fluid, the ichor was actually strips of cellophane that were turned on a wheel frame by frame to simulate a falling liquid; it is a totally convincing effect. Talos drops his sword, growls and clutches his throat as though suffocating — a characteristic moment of Harryhausen pathos. The puppet is motionless for a few seconds as Harryhausen adds a series of cracks to it, then it topples over, straight at the camera. A partial miniature floor is skillfully matted into the beach setting in the shot where Talos hits the ground, allowing the puppet to throw a shadow. The head and limbs are realistically animated as they break away. The satisfying narrative twist here is that Hylas is crushed under the statue as he tries to retrieve the very spear which Hercules had stolen from the treasure trove — the act which had incited Talos' revenge in the first place.

The conclusion to the Talos episode is one of many sequences in a Harryhausen film that reveals the identity of films that had a profound effect on him when he was young. In *The Last Days of Pompeii* (1935), with special effects by Willis O'Brien, the Colossus, a huge, helmeted, sword-bearing statue, cracks and collapses during the climactic volcanic eruption, falling on top of a fleeing extra.

The harpies episode is as bizarre a vignette as you could wish for and Harryhausen adds touches of grim humor to the antics of these pesky creatures which contrast neatly with the grandeur of the Talos encounter. The temple ruins provide another attractive location. Patrick Troughton gives a whole-hearted performance as the tormented blind hermit Phineas. Herrmann's light and quirky score adds its own bit of magic.

However, this is not a great animation scene. The first section, which takes place in daylight, suffers from graininess in the background plate and a poorly matched floor inlay. The two puppets are nightmarish creatures but have to be shot almost entirely in long shot because they are facially lifeless and would not stand up to closer scrutiny. And Harry-

Harryhausen's harpies torment Phineas the blind man (Patrick Troughton) in *Jason and the Argonauts.*

hausen has problems with the strobing of the wings in some shots, which is distracting. But these are complaints which only arise after repeated viewings: The first time around, the scene has enough shock impact to obscure the faults.

Many of the armature components of the harpies came from *Mysterious Island*'s phororhacos, which was stripped down and dismantled.

In the first animation cut, one of the noisily flapping harpies lands on a stone pedestal. A second harpy lands on the side of a ruined column (in three cuts). The creatures attack Phineas and there is lots of implied interaction in two long cuts as they teasingly snatch at him with their feet. One of them grabs his walking stick, a flawless effect in which the stick is pulled away by invisible wires. A floor inlay around a miniature of a stone table is poorly matched but does allow the puppets to throw shadows, an important ingredient in any composite. When one of the harpies pushes the table over, Harryhausen animates the dishes sliding to the edge but cuts away before the fruit actually falls to the ground, so as to avoid time-consuming wire-supported animation of miniature props.

One harpy unwinds a strip of cloth from Phineas' clothing — an effect again using an invisible wire and careful alignment of puppet and actor. It's an utterly convincing effect and one of the classic moments of interaction in Harryhausen's career. He adds an amusing bit of characterization to a shot of the two puppets on the ground, munching noisily on the fruit. In this cut, they hold their wings out behind them, making very smooth movements. When the Argonauts arrive on the scene, the harpies fly off, seen in a very good rear-screen composite way off in the distance. The harpies are so small in this shot that Harryhausen may have used two smaller models.

The second part of the harpies episode takes place at night and is even better than the first. The nighttime setting makes it more eerie and helps to mesh the composites — the harpies really look like they are in among the live-action footage. And there is the visually striking idea of a huge net dropped from the top of the ruins and a final comic role-reversal where the two harpies are held in a cage and forced to eat scraps thrown to them by Phineas.

The sequence opens with an attractive shot of the two harpies landing where the food table used to be and looking around for it. A terrific composite — quite chilling as well — shows them crawling up some stone steps into the temple. Miniature steps are seamlessly matted in among the real ones. Seen from inside the temple, the creatures emerge from behind one of the columns (providing a natural matte line) and take to the air.

An impressive long shot shows them flying behind two columns towards Phineas — the matte follows the outline of both columns. After a closer shot of the harpies harassing Phineas, the soldiers run into the temple and in a series of nine cuts wave their spears at the creatures flapping just out of reach. There are two low-angle shots of the harpies looking up at the net stretched over them. After the net is dropped, there are two fine shots, making a complex bit of animation look easy, with the harpies struggling underneath the net, their wings crumpling as they slowly fall to the ground. On the ground, they are surrounded by the Argonauts. This excellent composite really looks like one piece of film.

Later there are five cuts of the harpies in the cage. Three of them are static mattes with the Argonauts standing on the left. The other two are medium shots of the models behind the wooden bars (the closest we get to a good look at them). In one of them, a harpy catches some food tossed to it by Phineas. This closing moment catches the right tone of grim humor, and it makes a welcome change to have the creatures spared the normally obligatory death scene.

The live-action scene in which the sea god Triton saves Jason's ship from the Clashing Rocks is dramatically as effective as any of the animation scenes. But Harryhausen has problems with the beading of water droplets (which reveal the size of the studio tank) and a miniature mock-up of the Argo bobs along unconvincingly in some cuts. Addition-

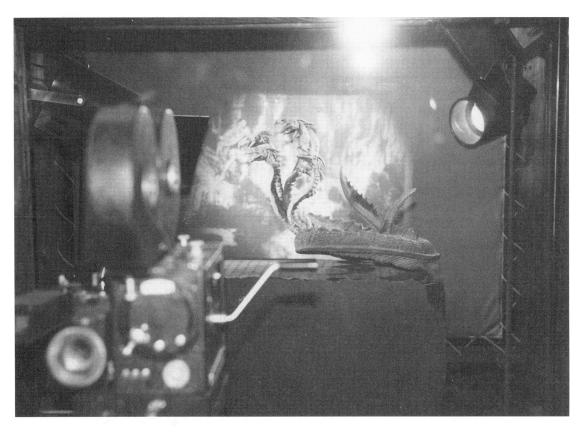

Harryhausen's Hydra puppet from *Jason and the Argonauts* in an exhibit at London's Museum of the Moving Image. The exhibit recreates the basic concept of a rear-projection set-up. The camera is in the foreground; the puppet is on an animation table (complete with holes to secure the model); and previously filmed footage of Jason (Todd Armstrong) has been projected from behind onto a translucent screen.

ally, some of the traveling mattes of the sailors looking out at Triton and the rocks are poor. Those who *want* to enjoy will engage a willing suspension of disbelief and respond to Herrmann's pounding score, the excellent miniature rocks that cascade into the sea and the silent grandeur of Triton. Others will probably sneer contemptuously.

Before the next stop-motion scene, there is a fight on board the Argo between Jason and Acastus (Gary Raymond), a dance in the court of King Aeetes on the island of Colchis and a scene in which Medea (Nancy Kovack) prays in the Temple of Hecate, enhanced by two reasonable matte paintings.

The seven-headed Hydra that guards the Golden Fleece is one of Harryhausen's finest models, taking full advantage of the unlimited potential of stop-motion: seven vicious, beaked heads on snake-like necks, a scaly, finned body and two tails, with the limp body of Acastus held in the coils in one of them. This is a nightmare creature that only stop-motion could bring to life. The setting is memorable: the fleece glimmering on a gnarled, lifeless tree beneath a cliff face, the rocks bathed in an eerie blue light, the ground shrouded in mist. Harryhausen's stamina seems to be limitless as he animates all the heads — apparently he did not chart the various directions of movement on paper but kept it all in his head.

It's a well-designed scene with some excellent composites but it's a shame that it was not developed beyond a simple battle with Jason and the Hydra's subsequent death — it's all over too quickly for such a magnificent model. Unfortunately, there are no closeups of the creature's heads — the model looks detailed enough to withstand closer scrutiny and the scene would have benefited. (The design of the heads — sloping back into horns — looks like it may have inspired the superb Verminthrax Perjorative in 1982's *Dragonslayer*.) Herrmann's score is curiously restrained and for once doesn't add much to the scene. A rubbery full-scale prop of the tail which ensnares Jason doesn't help, nor do live-action cut-away shots to Medea trying hard to look worried. But these are minor complaints.

The sequence kicks off with a good shock effect, a close shot of the seven heads lunging at the camera. In long shot, the creature slithers out of the cave on a well-matched floor inlay. The limp corpse of Acastus in one of the tails is a convincingly animated puppet. In a nice touch, the seven heads turn to look at their catch. Two dramatic dolly shots from behind the Hydra's heads move in on Jason in the rear screen. The static mattes of Jason in long shot, slashing at the seven heads snaking in and out, are excellent. Medium shots of the hissing heads are intercut with superior traveling matte composites of Jason standing in front of the puppet.

Particularly good is a static matte in which the creature slithers in front of Jason, a miniature branch in the lower foreground enforcing the illusion. In several cuts it looks as though Harryhausen has matted around the live-action tree and fleece, thereby allowing his puppet to slither behind them; if so, it's a very intricate matte and flawlessly executed. The animation of a puppet Jason held in the Hydra's tail in three long shots is remarkably credible. Another clever composite has the live-action Jason roll away from the tail along the ground.

The Hydra rears up over Jason, who stabs it twice in its chest. In a legendary moment of camera trickery, he leaves his sword embedded in the puppet. Just what happens to the live-action sword is open to speculation. A best guess is that there never was a live-action sword: Armstrong mimed the action and Harryhausen meticulously lined up a miniature with his hand. The Hydra writhes around, screaming in pain — but by Harryhausen standards, his death screams are restrained indeed. Six cuts show it dying, one head stubbornly taking longer than all the others to expire, and the tail giving a shuddery death rattle. Subsequently, the lifeless puppet is matted into several shots of Aeetes arriving on the scene and calling down fireballs to incinerate it: "Fetch me the Hydra's teeth!"

If the Hydra sequence gives the impression that it is over too quickly, then the climactic battle with the skeletons is quite the opposite. This four-and-a-half minute sequence is Harryhausen's masterpiece. The concept is startling, the rapid-fire editing and the enormous variety of rear-screen set-ups are breath-taking, and the animation is inspired. The pre-shot choreography of the live-actors fighting with thin air is skillfully controlled, and the interaction between puppets and actors is frequently so intimate that the illusion is totally successful. This sequence can be watched any number of times and it still amazes. Each time, it yields up new treasures, revealing the extent of Harryhausen's determination to go all out in this scene to do the best he knows how.

This closeup of one of the seven heads of the Hydra reveals the extraordinary detail of Harryhausen's sculpting. (Photo by John Coley.)

More crucial than the technical merits, the sequence is successful on a dramatic level as well: The balance of horror and black comedy is kept just right. Inventive touches such as the shot of the screaming skeletons charging, a skeleton getting beheaded, Jason punching another skeleton on the jaw when his sword seems to have no effect — all these insure that the audience is kept on the edge of their seats. Add to this Herrmann's adrenaline-buzzing score and you have the perfect animation scene.

Harryhausen took four and a half months to animate this episode. Sometimes he would average as few as 13 frames a day — just over half a second of film. Hardly surprising when you consider that in some cuts he was adjusting heads, arms and legs for all seven skeletons, plus any finger or jaw movements that were also required. Additionally, some composites required that the miniature swords of the skeletons were partially cut away or extended frame-by-frame to create the illusion that they were in contact with the Argonauts. One of the skeletons — but which one? — was the same model that had been used in *The 7th Voyage of Sinbad.*

The suspenseful build-up to the skeletons' appearance is brilliantly staged by Chaffey and Harryhausen. Aeetes, confronting Jason and his men among the ruins of a clifftop temple, scatters the teeth from the Hydra and calls on the "children" to appear. In a perfectly matched floor inlay, animated pieces of earth are pushed up by something below, then a sword emerges, and finally the first skeleton, pulling itself erect from a stooped position. It is joined by six others, intercut with shots of the astonished Argonauts.

For these shots, the skeleton puppets were concealed in a chamber beneath the miniature floor. One frame at a time, screws in hidden platforms beneath each skeleton were turned, raising them.

The army of living skeletons in *Jason and the Argonauts*.

Herrmann's score is effectively silent during the tense moment when all seven skeletons stand ready, swaying slightly. "Kill! Kill! Kill them all!" bellows Aeetes, and in a side view they march forward in unison. A beautifully designed "reality sandwich" shot has the three Argonauts retreating nervously in the left foreground, Aeetes and his men in the background and the seven skeletons walking forward in the middle distance. In another clever perspective, Harryhausen mattes around a pillar so that as the Argonauts retreat behind one pillar on the left, the skeletons can advance behind another pillar on the right.

With a terrifying scream, the skeletons charge, running at the camera in a superb medium shot. In a 1969 interview at Britain's National Film Theater, transcribed in *FXRH* #4, producer Charles Schneer mentioned that a shot of the skeletons charging was cut by the censor. "He felt that this was a bit too much for the younger audiences. And that came out, and it never went back, and we were satisfied that this was the only cut, even though it took two weeks of Ray's time." Is he referring to this cut — left in by the American censor — or was there a longer cut which we have never seen?

The Argonauts jump up onto a stone pedestal and there are three long-shot static mattes in which they are attacked by all seven skeletons. There is a dizzying amount of activity in these shots with skeletons brandishing their swords, getting knocked away and Jason jumping over the sword of a skeleton who swipes at him. In these cuts, the matte not only follows the line of the floor but also goes around the head of a fallen statue, supplying a crucial foreground element that breaks up the depth of the shot. In closer shots, the vertical walls of the pedestal are miniature, allowing the skeletons to throw shadows onto the set. A nightmarish medium shot from the Argonauts' point of view has two of the skeletons grinning up at the camera. The skeletons clamber up onto the pedestal and pursue the fleeing sailors.

One skeleton chases Phalerus (Andrew Faulds) to a low wall, the matte line following the outline of a fallen pillar in the foreground which the skeleton runs behind. In a closer shot, Phalerus swings his sword and it clearly passes in front of the skeleton's shield. Again, a partial miniature sword is wire-suspended for a few frames (or painted on glass) and matched to the live one.

In another part of the ruins, the third Argonaut, Castor (Fernando Poggi), trips one of the skeletons, sending it crashing to the ground. As it gets up again, a second skeleton runs into the shot and engages the argonaut in a sword fight. This is all superb high-speed animation, reinforcing the feeling that no

matter how many of the skeletons are knocked down, there are always others ready to rush in.

Meanwhile, Jason has jumped back onto the pedestal, battling two skeletons in a cut that uses the earlier set-up with the partial miniature pedestal. In a closer shot not requiring a matte, Jason kicks one of the skeletons in the head and sends it flying. As he does so, the other skeleton jumps onto the pedestal, only to get slashed by Jason's sword and fall out of the shot. At the same moment, a third skeleton jumps up onto the pedestal.

We now cut back to Phalerus who, in a simple yet brilliant bit of interaction, ducks as a skeleton charges him and throws it over his shoulder. At the same time, a second skeleton picks itself up from the ground on the right of the shot. In a well thought-out closer shot, this skeleton tentatively circles Phalerus and crosses swords with him. This action continues in a shot from behind Phalerus as the Argonaut leans back against the wall and lifts the skeleton with his boot and sends it somersaulting clean over his head — another classic moment of interaction achieved by careful alignment.

As this skeleton is getting up, the other runs in. Phalerus leaps into the air to avoid its sword. In yet another set-up of this sequence, Phalerus climbs over the wall only to see the skeleton also leap over it, joining his fallen comrade on the other side. Almost imperceptible, that part of the wall which the skeleton jumps over is a miniature, allowing it to throw a shadow. It crosses swords with Phalerus again and there is an unforgettable closeup of the sneering skeleton, after which Phalerus forces the skeleton away.

We now return to Castor in the same set-up as before, in a long sequence that ends with his death. A skeleton swings its shield and knocks the Argonaut's shield away — a superbly effective suggestion of physical contact. Castor then swipes at the skeleton with his sword and sends it reeling. This is all seen in three quick cuts, where one might have sufficed — the design indicates Harryhausen's determination to make this scene special.

The two skeletons chase Castor to the ruins of a wall, vertical matte lines allowing the puppets to seem to walk behind either end of the wall. It is a brilliant touch to have a skeleton adopt a threatening half-crouch and look hungrily along both sides of the wall for his intended victim — there seems to be no end to Harryhausen's inventiveness during this sequence. Castor is now up on the wall, clashing swords with the skeletons below, and there is another point-of-view shot of the two puppets. One skeleton is knocked down and gets up again in long shot as the other looks on.

Castor jumps from this wall to another, and one of the skeletons slashes at thin air as the Argonaut leaps over him. In the next cut, the other skeleton is up on the wall and jumps after Castor, a marvelously dynamic idea that required that the puppet be suspended on wires for a few frames. Castor is now at the top of another wall with a skeleton standing on each side of the steps leading down — a memorable design. The steps on the left are part miniature. He slashes one skeleton's arm and it clutches it as though wounded. The skeleton on the left side hacks Castor across his stomach and there is a delicious pause in the frantic pace as both skeletons watch the Argonaut fall forwards off the wall. Ingeniously, Harryhausen's animation suggests that the skeletons are *enjoying* seeing him die. This shot is an especially good composite because the actor seems to fall into the foreground past the skeletons, whose heads turn to look at him as he falls. It's a classic example of a static matte set-up fooling the eye into seeing an illusory depth.

Jason is still battling with other skeletons on the pedestal. In a long shot, he knocks one to the ground, then another, and fends off a third. In a closer shot, he beheads the second skeleton with his sword and its headless body struts around for a while, arms outstretched like a blind man. A shot of the skeleton hunting on the ground for its head was cut out after it induced chuckles from a preview audience — Harryhausen's fans would love to see this shot restored, but perhaps it was an instance of the comic aspects of the scene going too far. Even without this cut, this is still a great moment, always greeted with gasps of excited delight by audiences. (The cut leaves a slight jump in Herrmann's score.)

Phalerus battles on, kicking one skeleton away and crossing swords with another in a static matte set-up.

The next cut — with Jason engaging two skeletons on the ground in front of the pedestal — is one to treasure, containing not only the satisfying moment when he socks a skeleton in the jaw, but also two bafflingly good bits of camera trickery. Jason plunges his sword into the chest of a skeleton lying sprawled on the ground and leaves it there. The sword begins life as a prop in the actor's hand in the live-action footage but ends up a miniature in the puppet; just how and when the switch is made remains a mystery. It's a brilliant effect and a candidate for best-ever effect in a Harryhausen film.

Equally baffling is the quick moment when the second skeleton runs into the shot and its sword passes *behind* Jason. One way of achieving this would be to have hand-drawn mattes rotoscoped for each frame, their outline following Jason's moving body. But as far as is known, Harryhausen used this technique only once, during the flood sequence in *Clash of the Titans*. It seems more likely that he used a series of partial miniature swords, lining each up so that they ended where the actor's outline began in the rear screen. As the sword is lowered by the skeleton, more of it disappears behind the actor, then it reappears as the sword goes lower still. It is astonishing that Harryhausen should go to such lengths to improve the look of a shot; he could so easily have just had his puppet hold the sword clear of the actor's body.

In four dramatic long shots, Jason is chased to the edge of the cliff by three skeletons. The invisible matte line runs through the irregular rocky terrain. As in the whole of this scene, the electric variety of the choreography never lets up: Jason knocks the skeletons away with his sword, in a desperate bid throws his shield at them, then repulses another with his spear.

Phalerus' death scene also contains moments of dazzling interaction between puppet and actor. He is trapped against a wall by two skeletons. The sword of one of them passes behind the actor on two occasions and when Phalerus strikes at a skeleton's shield, a partial miniature sword is introduced to the shot so that it appears to be in front of the shield. In a celebrated effect, a skeleton plunges his sword deep into Phalerus' chest, the miniature sword being whittled away frame by frame to suggest it is piercing the actor. The puppet advances a step, really shoving the sword in, and a nightmarish medium shot of the grinning skeleton suggests that it is thoroughly enjoying itself. One skeleton runs out of the shot as Phalerus falls forward. Because the actor falls across the matte line, the second skeleton is able to seem to jump over his corpse as it follows its comrade.

There are four final stop-motion cuts at the clifftop. A medium shot of Jason forcing back three skeletons with his spear is followed by a long shot showing the puppets falling in a heap — a tricky bit of animation made to look easy. To his dismay, Jason sees three more skeletons running at him from the temple (one of them is supported on wires for a few frames as it leaps down from the stone pedestal). As a last gesture of defiance, Jason hurls his spear at the clattering horde, turns and jumps off the edge of the cliff. The relentless skeletons follow him and perish in the sea below. In this final cut, the cliff face is miniature, and the actor actually jumps onto a mattress hidden by an area of live-action sea matted into the right hand corner of the set-up.

Jason and the Argonauts is a milestone film and its skeleton scene ranks as one of the most exquisitely designed and executed sequences in any fantasy film. Yet the two years it took to make and the $3.5 million it cost failed to get the response it deserved at the box office. A flood of brainless Italian muscleman epics had just reached cinema screens at the same time as *Jason*'s release, and audiences just assumed that Harryhausen's film was one of them. It did much better business in Britain (which had less exposure to the Italian films), and became one of that country's big moneymakers of the year. On television and in revival cinemas all over the world, it is a perennial favorite, possessing a timeless appeal that delights young and old alike.

Jaws 3-D

1983. Alan Landsburg Productions. D: Joe Alves. Scr: Richard Matheson, Carl Gottlieb. Story: Guerdon Trueblood. Suggested by the Novel "Jaws" by Peter Benchley. Ph: James A. Contner. Filmed in Arrivision 3-D. Art: Woods Mackintosh. Mus: Alan Parker. "Jaws" Theme by John Williams. Special Visual Effects: Robert Blalack, Praxis Film Works, Private Stock Effects.

Cast: Dennis Quaid, Bess Armstrong, Simon MacCorkindale, Louis Gossett, Jr., John Putch, Lea Thompson.

Rating: ☆☆½   Stop-Motion: ☆☆

Steven Spielberg's original 1975 film was a classic thriller, but the series predictably weakened with each entry. The director of this third entry was Joe Alves, the mechanical effects supervisor of the first two films, and he is unable to generate the excitement and menace which are crucial. Characterization — so memorable in the original — is feebly stereotypic. Worst offenders are the British underwater photographer (Simon MacCorkindale) and his assistant. But the film does contain one memorable shark attack, in which MacCorkindale is swallowed whole. An unsettling shot from inside the shark's mouth shows MacCorkindale struggling to get out, only to be followed by the sound of teeth crunching against bone.

There is a lot of substandard bluescreen work, probably caused by the extra problems of shooting in 3-D. In one shot, a miniature mini-sub has been so carelessly composited with a model of the underwater theme park that it is possible to see clean through it. In a climactic shot of the giant shark swimming straight towards the camera and smashing through the glass window of the underwater control center, the shark miniature is held so immobile that it looks embarrassingly fake.

Most shots of the 30-foot shark use either live-action footage of a normal-sized shark or an unwieldy full-size prop. In an attempt to avoid this unwieldiness, one shot makes use of stop-motion. The shark has rammed its head into the control center and is trying to force itself further in to get at the people inside. In a long shot filmed entirely in miniature, an armatured puppet of the shark is stop-framed, its tail swishing from side to side, pulling back slightly from the miniature building and then ramming into it again. The shot cuts in well with the live-action film because of thoughtful lighting which has dappled shading (suggesting sunlight in the water) falling on the puppet.

A fourth film in the series, *Jaws—The Revenge*, featured stop-motion shark cuts animated by Ted Rae, but none were used in the final release of the film because they did not cut in well with the live-action shots.

A Jester's Tale see *Bláznova Kronika*

Joe's Apartment

1996. Geffen/MTV. D-Scr: John Payson. Based on the MTV short film "Joe's Apartment." Ph: Peter Deming. Art: Carol Spier. Mus: Carter Burwell. Visual Effects Producer: Michael Turoff. Visual Effects Supervisor: Randall Balsmeyer. Computer Generated Animation: Chris Wedge. Stop-Motion Animation: Fly/Films. Stop-Motion Supervisor: Peter Wallach. Stop-Motion Photography: Jamie Jacobson.

Cast: Jerry O'Connell, Megan Ward, Billy West, Reginald Hudlin, Jim Turner, Robert Vaughn.

Rating: ☆☆☆   Stop-Motion: ☆☆½

Joe's Apartment must have caused the marketing team a real headache: Just what kind of audience do you aim a comedy-romance-cum-monster-flick at? Joe (Jerry O'Connell) moves into a New York apartment only to find that he is sharing it with 40,000 intelligent, talking cockroaches. The roaches cause all kinds of disruption to Joe's life — especially in a hilarious sequence in which he invites a girlfriend back and tries to hide them from her. Eventually, the roaches prove to have hearts of gold and help Joe to thwart the plans of evil property developer Robert Vaughn and bring Joe and his girl together again. It's a likably unique production and deserves to be seen.

At one point, it was planned that the roaches would be depicted by means of stop-motion. However, the bulk of the shots were eventually done with computer generated imagery and only a few stop-motion shots remain in the film. In view of the complexity of many of the sequences and the number of insect characters in some shots (often hundreds), CGI was the sensible way to go, allowing the creation of sequences which would have been impossibly time-consuming to create with traditional puppet animation techniques.

Apparently, the only surviving footage of a stop-motion roach is a sequence in which a program called "Alternative Life with Charlie Roach" is showing on a television in Joe's apartment. It features a discussion between a rat, a pigeon, a squirrel and a roach, with all the characters sitting around a table. All are live animals with the exception of the roach, a stop-motion puppet, which is seen in several animated cuts, gesticulating, waving a pencil in the air and talking to the others.

Stop-motion also features in several cuts in which it was the simplest technique to achieve other images. For example, when the roaches infiltrate the City Hall and rearrange some files, stop-motion is used to depict books moving around on shelves, and drawers opening and closing. Later, the roaches transform a derelict plot of land into a beautiful garden, and stop-motion is the means whereby flowers stolen from a florist are seen to snake out of the doorway, turf is unrolled to form a lawn, and shrubs are made to look as if they are planting themselves.

Josh Kirby—Time Warrior!: Planet of the Dino-Knights (Chapter 1)

1995. Moonbeam. D: Ernest Farino. Scr: Ethan Reiff, Syrups Boris, Paul Calais. Ph: Christian Fugal. Stop-Motion Animation: Rob Maine.

Cast: Carbon Allured, Barrio Gingham, Derek Webster, Spencer Rochfort.

Rating: ☆☆   Stop-Motion: ☆☆

Josh Kirby was a series of six direct-to-video films that follow on from one another in the style of the old cliffhanger serials. In each, a different exotic location is explored by the central characters, a brilliant scientist, a female warrior and a furry alien creature.

Chapter 1, *Planet of the Dino-Knights,* is set in medieval England. It features a brief battle between two characters riding stop-motion dinosaurs, a tyrannosaurus (using the model from *Prehysteria!* with a new head fitted) and a triceratops. The riders are also stop-motion puppets. In the restrained encounter, the two adversaries approach each other and the riders strike each other with their lances.

Animation was executed by Robert Maine, who had worked on *Flesh Gordon.* On this occasion, his animation is rushed and unsatisfactory.

The battle begins in this chapter and concludes in the second episode in the series.

Josh Kirby—Time Warrior!: The Human Pets (Chapter 2)

1995. Moonbeam. D: Frank Arnold, Ernest Farino. Scr: Ethan Reiff, Syrups Boris, Paul Cassini. Ph: Christian Fugal. Stop-Motion Animation: Rob Maine.

Cast: Carbon Allured, Barrio Gingham, Derek Webster, Spencer Rochfort, John De Mita, Richard Lineback.

Rating: ☆☆   Stop-Motion: ☆☆

This second chapter in the six-part *Josh Kirby* series begins by concluding the stop-motion dinosaur battle begun in the first episode, then heads off for the year A.D. 7000

Journey into Prehistory
see *Cestě do provĕku*

Journey to the Beginning of Time
see *Cestě do provĕku*

Journey to the Seventh Planet

1961. Cinemagic/AIP. Prod-D-Story: Sidney Pink. Scr: Ib Melchior, Sidney Pink. Ph: Age Wiltrup. Mus: Ib Glindemann. Special Effects: Bent Barfod Films. Additional Special Effects (uncredited): Gene Warren, Wah Chang, Jim Danforth.

Cast: John Agar, Greta Thyssen, Ann Smyrner, Mimi Heinrich, Carl Ottosen, Ove Sprogoe.

Rating: ☆½   Stop-Motion: ☆☆

The year is 2001. John Agar leads a five-man United Nations exploratory mission to Uranus. There he must battle not only a giant spider, a giant rodent and a giant brain, but also the far worse terrors of a lousy script, weak direction and shoddy special effects. The team escape with their lives if not their dignity, but at least they can claim to have entertained a few undemanding kids on the way, and given the rest of us a few laughs.

Production and direction are by Sidney Pink, who co-scripted with Ib Melchior, the same team responsible for other low-budget delights such as *The Angry Red Planet* (1960) and *Reptilicus* (1962). The film was shot in Sweden, then more scenes were added when it was picked up for American release. What they *should* have done is cut scenes out. One only has to think of the awful dialogue in the sequences where the astronauts talk amongst themselves, or the insipid mediocrity of the encounters with various seductive girls whom the giant brain creates in their minds.

The special effects are credited to Bent Barfod Films, who presumably handled the Swedish end of things. Additional post-production effects scenes were added by Gene Warren, Wah Chang and Jim Danforth, all uncredited. Foremost among these is a modest episode in which three of the astronauts are attacked in a cave by a stop-motion monster. Dramatically the scene is weak, with poorly directed cut-away shots to the actors and negligible attempts to combine the puppet with the live action. It's over in a couple of minutes: The monster appears, the astronauts try to look terrified, they fire at it, then run away.

The animation (there are eight stop-motion cuts) is always competent and it's an intriguing-looking model, but it never convinces that it's not just a puppet; it's the kind of thing that would look happier in an animated television commercial. It was built over the armature used for the harpy in *Jack the Giant Killer*. It stands on two hairy legs, has long clawed arms, a long tail and a scaly chest. One large eye is in the middle of its snouted face. Just what it is meant to be is not clear until later on, when Agar announces, "It was of the rodent family"; another astronaut admits to having a phobia about rats which the giant brain seized upon. The miniature cave set is impressive and a lot better than the fake studio sets with which it fails to match up. A prop head of the monster is used for closeups: It looks good but its capacity for movement is limited and these cuts only slow down the pace of the scene.

The first stop-motion cut shows the monster rising up, a spiralling light effect superimposed over it to suggest the presence of the giant brain. Several full-view shots of the model show it walking across the cave and waving its long arms threateningly, emitting a combination of growls and squeaks. One cut (the only real bit of interaction) features a human puppet making slight movements as the monster walks toward it. Like any self-respecting Cyclops, it gets blinded after one of the astronauts fires at it: An animated closeup shows it recoiling in pain. The scene closes with two long shots of it waving its arms around blindly, as the astronauts run out of the cave.

For stop-motion completists only.

Jurassic Park

1993. Amblin/Universal. D: Steven Spielberg. Scr: Michael Crichton, Michael Koepp. Based on the Novel by Michael Crichton. Ph: Dean Cundey. Art: Rick Carter. Mus: John Williams. Full-Motion Dinosaurs and Special Visual Effects: Industrial Light and Magic. ILM Supervisor: Dennis Muren. ILM Lead Computer Graphics Supervisor: Stefen M. Fangmeier. ILM Matte Artists: Christopher Evans, Yusei Uesugi. Live-Action Dinosaurs: Stan Winston. Special Dinosaur Effects: Michael Lantieri. Dinosaur Supervisor: Phil Tippett. Tippett Studio: Production Supervisor: Jules Tippett. Computer Interface Engineer: Craig Hayes. Senior Animator: Randal M. Dutra. Animator: Tom St. Amand. Production Coordinator: Sheila Duignan.

Cast: Sam Neill, Laura Dern, Richard Attenborough, Jeff Goldblum, Bob Peck, Martin Ferrero.

Rating: ☆☆☆   Stop-Motion: N/A

This is one of the great stop-motion milestones, but no stop-motion is seen in the film.

The dinosaurs of *Jurassic Park*, depicted with a level of realism never before encountered, were achieved by a combination of full-scale mechanical props and computer generated imagery. Many of these dinosaur sequences were based on pre-shot stop-motion footage (called video animatics), which gave the prop controllers and computer animators specific choreography on which to base the movements of their creations. Additionally, much of the computer imagery was developed from elaborate armatures, known as Dinosaur Input Devices (or DIDs, and subsequently known as Direct Input Devices) which,

although not filmed, were animated like conventional stop-motion puppets and which at key points were rigged up with encoders connected to a computer. The encoders could record positions and movements, information which would subsequently be used by the computer to generate a moving image.

These are new applications of stop-motion and may well be the beginning of a new direction for the process. But the film's dinosaurs were not always going to be fashioned this way.

Like so many directors before him, Steven Spielberg wanted all his creatures to be full-size models on the set. Veteran makeup artist and mechanical creature specialist Stan Winston was recruited for the task. Soon, however, Spielberg realized that depicting creatures walking or making complex movements in full view was still beyond the capabilities of mechanical and animatronic technology. Winston said: "We never really got the coordination of a good, dynamic walk out of the raptors — or any dinosaur, for that matter" (*Cinefex* #55). So Spielberg called in Phil Tippett and his company to supply around 50 go-motion dinosaur shots to complement Winston's shots. A series of stop-motion tests, principally depicting dinosaurs running or walking, were made on 35mm film.

Meanwhile, Dennis Muren, in charge of special visual effects for the film, was working with his team at Industrial Light and Magic and investigating the possibility of taking conventional stop-motion footage and using computer technology to add a blur to the image, thereby eliminating strobing. Some successful tests were made and this technique proved to be cheaper than go-motion. However, as it turned out, there would be no need for this "digitally enhanced stop-motion." To date, no feature film has used this technique — it remains a useful tool for the animator and its potential is waiting to be explored.

The reason why this technique became redundant on *Jurassic Park* was that Muren's team of computer artists had been experimenting with generating computer graphics of the dinosaurs. Initially, it was felt that the technology had not come far enough to depict living, breathing creatures realistically. However, the CG images that his team produced surpassed everyone's expectations. Software packages were available which not only allowed figures to move plausibly, but also made them react to light and shadow, have their musculature expand and contract realistically beneath their exteriors, give them credibly watery eyes and simulate, for example, the effects of rain falling on their hides.

Spielberg's reaction to the CG tests was to abort his plans for go-motion scenes. Tippett was equally impressed: "At the showing, Phil groaned and pretty much declared himself extinct," said Spielberg in an interview in *The Making of "Jurassic Park"* by Don Shay and Jody Duncan. But it was not the end of the road for Tippett. His wealth of experience in bringing prehistoric creatures to life over the past two decades made him an invaluable asset. For example, one of his tasks was to teach the computer graphics artists about dinosaur choreography, to insure that their creations were vital and full of character. He also

made sure that the look and color of the CG dinosaurs always matched up with Winston's on-set puppets.

Tippett receives a screen credit as "Dinosaur Supervisor," a title which hardly does justice to his contribution. He devised and set up stop-motion tests of sequences involving two velociraptors — vicious eight-foot tall carnivorous bipeds — and a tyrannosaurus rex. Armatures for these were built by Tom St. Amand and Craig Hayes and the sculpting was based on models built by Winston's team. Puppet humans were included in some shots.

These animatic sequences, animated with traditional stop-motion methods by Randy Dutra, St. Amand and others, were subsequently used by Winston and his crew to give them an idea of how the dinosaurs should move and react. Additionally, Spielberg referred to them constantly while on the set. The two sequences — in which the tyrannosaurus attacks one of the park vehicles and the two raptors stalk two children in a kitchen — contained between 40 and 50 stop-motion cuts and were executed by four teams of animators over a period of four months. The action was based on storyboards that had already been drawn up, with Tippett and his crew adding several ideas of their own. For example, in the kitchen sequence, there is a shot in which the two raptors walk through the doorway and they are both framed in medium closeup, their heads snaking around searching for their prey: this is a repeat of one of Tippett's superb deinonychus shots in the television documentary *Dinosaur*.

Additionally, Tippett got together

with ILM to devise the DID, described by Muren as "a really good merging of two technologies — stop-motion and computer animation" (in *The Making of "Jurassic Park"*). Four DIDs were built — two raptors and two versions of the T. rex — by Tom St. Amand, Craig Hayes and Bart Trickel. Fifteen DID shots were executed by Tippett's studio, eight of which feature during the T. rex attack scene, the rest during the raptor kitchen scene.

Initiating CG imagery with stop-motion DIDs, rather than conceiving the images in the computer, has the benefit of avoiding the unreal look of pure computer imagery. The hands-on stop-motion element adds quirks, sudden changes of direction and touches of personality which prevent the finished image from looking too smooth and predictable. The DIDs only supply information about major movement — "minor" animation of finger and toes was added by the computer animators and supervised by Tippett.

Two of the dinosaur sequences — involving a sick triceratops and a venom-spitting dilophosaurus — were achieved entirely with Winston's full-size mechanical dinosaurs. Other scenes — an encounter with a gigantic browsing brachiosaurus, a stampede by a herd of ostrich-like Gallimimus, a climactic battle between the T. rex and the two raptors — are CG images created without the input of DIDs. In all, there are 52 CG shots. Some shots of the raptors were even achieved using a man in a dinosaur suit.

The net result of this merging of stop-motion, computer graphics and mechanical puppetry is the most astonishing dinosaur effects — perhaps the most astonishing effects of *any* kind — ever put on film. For once, nobody in the audience — not even those who stubbornly refuse to "suspend disbelief" — could groan about the effects not being polished enough for them.

The technical excellence of these scenes is matched by the edge-of-the-seat pace and drama which Spielberg gives them.

The T. rex attack on the two stranded cars is astonishing. The dinosaur looks magnificent and the composites are impossibly good. There is no contention at all between CGI shots (11 of them) and full-scale model shots. When the T. rex stoops down and gobbles up the slimy lawyer in one unbroken cut, one is amused, horrified and amazed all at the same time.

The herd of galloping Gallimimus is a show-stopper. Not since the films of Karel Zeman have we seen animated prehistoric beasts in such numbers, but even Zeman might be astounded by this sequence. Like a flock of birds, the herd (about 40 of them) all turn at once in the distance and head straight at the camera, rushing past the actors with dizzying blurs. When they leap over the dead tree under which the actors are cowering, the foot of one kicks off a piece of a branch (actually pulled off by an invisible wire) and the feeling of simultaneity of images is superb. This sequence ends with a magnificent shock effect when the tyrannosaurus suddenly appears and snatches up one of the herd — an image inspired by *The Valley of Gwangi*.

The scene in which the T. rex chases a Jeep is a stunner, the CG model looking to be right in with the live-action, running in a totally plausible manner, and smashing into an overhead branch that is part of the live-action set. This is a stand-out sequence that really gets the adrenaline pumping.

The velociraptors are magnificent. The sequence in the kitchen with the two children (including ten CG shots) is superb, both technically and in the way that the raptors are portrayed as thinking, agile predators, looking around warily, leaping onto tabletops, reacting to noises. The actors flee by crawling among the overhead cooling pipes and there is a terrific shock effect when a raptor leaps straight up at the camera, nearly grabbing the girl in its jaws. This effect is successful not because it shocks — quite the reverse: We expect the creature to leap up, yet the shot is executed with such dynamic force that the creature seems almost to leap out of the screen.

A sequence in which the actors flee by clambering down a fossil dinosaur takes composite photography to such a level that one is almost left thinking that *anything* is now possible. One of the raptors clings onto the swaying, collapsing fossil as the actors fall off one by one, and this never looks like a special effect.

In a sequence that looks so good that one's jaw hangs agape, the four actors (Neill, Dern and the kids) stand in a group with a raptor on either side, the two reptiles prowling purposefully and looking 100 percent real. A savior comes in the form of the T. rex, which suddenly appears and snaps up one of the raptors. The second raptor leaps across the hall and attacks the T. rex's flank with its vicious claws.

But the film is let down by a weak plot and insubstantial characterization — normally areas which Spielberg gets right. A group of characters arrives at Richard Attenborough's island, the dinosaurs get out, a few people get eaten, the survivors escape.

All the main characters have the potential to develop interestingly (in the way that the three male leads in *Jaws* make that Spielberg film so irresistible), but the script doesn't give them enough screen time. It was originally planned to give Attenborough a great death scene which could have made much of his character, but the desire for a sequel scotched that. Jeff Goldblum's "chaos mathematician" is an irrelevance; Laura Dern (Spielberg's obligatory tough blonde heroine) contributes little to the plot; Bob Peck's gamekeeper looks set to become important but gets killed off. Sam Neill's paleontologist is the closest the film comes to a sympathetic role — all dinosaur-lovers will identify with his open-mouthed wonder at seeing his first living dinosaur, subsequently going into shock, falling to his knees and gagging. But there is no human drama going on; these characters are just potential snacks for the dinosaurs.

This would not be a problem were it not for the fact that, as ever, Spielberg tries to make this an intensely "human" movie: People break into wide smiles or start weeping at all the right moments, backed by John Williams' overblown score (far too prominent this time), and Spielberg expects us all to laugh and cry along with them. But this time it doesn't work.

The film's greatest lapse is a subplot in which Wayne Knight tries to smuggle dinosaur embryos out of the park. This is a half thought out plot thread, and is merely an excuse to get all the park's security devices shut down.

While one is grateful to Spielberg for creating such wonderful dinosaurs, one can't help wondering why he didn't make a better film. One reason, perhaps, is that Spielberg consciously avoided making "a fantasy film" and always insisted that his dinosaurs be referred to as animals and not monsters. The film could have been full of images to give the film's setting much of the lushness and haunting beauty of O'Brien's Skull Island, but Spielberg avoids this approach. In fact, there is only one matte painting (by ILM regular artist Chris Evans) in the film, seen in a panoramic shot of a herd of browsing brachiosaurs at dusk.

What is the future for stop-motion after *Jurassic Park*? Many believe that the film has killed off any prospect of seeing conventional stop-motion again since it will now always be compared with Spielberg's effects. This author, however, believes that stop-motion will continue to be a favored tool for low-budget filming. More significantly, *Jurassic Park* heralds the beginning of a new age of using stop-motion in new ways: animatics, DIDs and digital blurring. Who knows what legions of monsters, aliens, robots and dinosaurs are waiting to prowl across cinema screens in years to come.

Sadly, *Jurassic Park* seemed as though it might be the end of the line for Phil Tippett. In an interview in *Cinefex* #55, he said: "When I saw the rough cut of the park tour sequence with the brachiosaur, I had tears in my eyes — because, for the first time, I could *see* a dinosaur. They were so grand and elegant and statuesque. The shots really conveyed the beauty in the beasts. And they fulfilled what, as a five-year-old child, I really wanted to see. So I guess that now *Jurassic Park* is over, I can get out of this business. I have fulfilled that five-year-old's directive — now I can move on to adolescence."

However, monster makers do not relinquish their vocations quite so easily. Tippett has since worked on *Dragonheart* (1996), in which he helped to create a magnificent CGI dragon, and is sure to be a prominent figure in many future fantasy films, whatever direction the genre and its technology take.

Killer Klowns from Outer Space

1987. Transworld/Chiodo Bros. D: Stephen Chiodo. Scr: Charles Chiodo, Stephen Chiodo. Ph: Alfred Taylor. Art: Charles Chiodo. Mus: John Massari. Matte Painting Visual Effects: Mark Sullivan. Special Visual Effects: Fantasy II Film Effects. Special Effects Supervisor: Gene Warren, Jr. Stop-Motion Animation: Justin Kohn.

Cast: Grant Cramer, Suzanne Snyder, John Allan Nelson, John Vernon, Michael Siegel, Royal Dano.

King Dong

Rating: ☆☆½   Stop-Motion: ☆☆.

The title is enough to put most people off, but this is a thoughtful and quite chilling horror-comedy. The plot is in the conventional 1950s aliens-from-outer-space mold, with the twist that the aliens just happen to look like clowns. The excellent clown makeups make these creatures grotesque and believable. In among all the clown gags—flowers that squirt water, custard pie fights, etc.—are several scenes that generate a real mood of terror. In one scene, a seven-foot-tall clown has killed a policeman and sits his corpse on his lap, operating him like a ventriloquist's dummy, his hand shoved deep inside the body. In another scene, popcorn thrown by the clowns grows into strange creatures (vicious clown heads on plant-like stalks) that wave about and bury their fangs into a victim.

Fantasy II Film Effects looked after various effects shots. One of these is an amusingly weird gag that required two brief stop-motion shots animated by Justin Kohn.

A motorist is being pursued at night by a clown who seems to be driving an invisible car, two headlights in his raised feet. The clown motors along suspended two feet above the ground, laughing insanely and trying to push the other car off the road. Two long shots were achieved by animating a puppet in front of a rear screen and pointing two beams of light below the puppet's feet to suggest the headlights. The puppet bobs up and down, realistically suggesting bumps in the road, and at one point bangs into the rear-projected car.

Later, a clown is amusing some pedestrians by projecting shadow shapes from his hands onto a wall. The gag is that these shapes—a rabbit, an elephant, a dancing girl, five men in a boat—are all impossibly realistic. Eventually the clown causes the shadow of a tyrannosaurus rex to appear and it promptly swallows up the group of people. The dinosaur is a cartoon animation but the previous shadows seem to have been created by stop-framing cut-outs and placing them behind a rear projection so as to create shadows.

King Dong (a.k.a. Lost on Adventure Island)

1984. MVC Video. D: Yancy Hendrieth. Special Effects: Keith Finkelstein, David Dane, L. B. Carvelo.

Cast: Crystal Holland, Chaz St. Peters, Dee Hendrieth.

This hardcore porn film sounds like it might be a lot of fun, but unfortunately finding a print of it is no easy task.

A spoof of *King Kong*, it tells the story of a woman shipwrecked on an island that is home to a giant female gorilla and an assortment of dinosaurs. The latter include stop-motion puppets of a brontosaurus, an allosaurus and even a replica of the 1933 Kong himself. Some good miniatures and matte paintings are also included. One sequence, featuring a shot of a man climbing a rope in order to escape the jaws of an allosaurus, would, in the words of John Thonen (writing in *Cinefantastique*, March 1988) "do even a Harryhausen or a Danforth proud."

King Kong

1933. RKO Radio. Prod-D: Merian C. Cooper, Ernest B. Schoedsack. Scr: James A. Creelman, Ruth Rose. Idea Conceived by Merian Cooper, Edgar Wallace. Chief Technician: Willis H. O'Brien. Technical Staff: E. B. Gibson, Marcel Delgado, Fred Reefe, Orville Goldner, Carroll Shepphird. Art Technicians: Mario Larrinaga, Byron L. Crabbe. Ph: Eddie Linden, Vernon Walker, J. O. Taylor. Mus: Max Steiner. Sound Effects: Murray Spivack. Settings: Carroll Clark, Al Herman. (Uncredited: Optical Photography: Linwood G. Dunn, William Ulm. Technical Artists: Juan Larrinaga, Zachary Hoag, Victor Delgado.)

Cast: Fay Wray, Robert Armstrong, Bruce Cabot, Frank Reicher, Sam Hardy, Noble Johnson, Victor Wong.

Rating: ☆☆☆☆   Stop-Motion: ☆☆☆☆

King Kong is a very special film. Its driving thrust came from two men who had the genius to put on film a kind of experience that no one else had managed to do. Producer-director Merian Cooper wanted to make the ultimate adventure film, reliving the excitement that he himself had felt on his trips to Africa and Asia years earlier. Willis O'Brien wanted to turn a fantasy world into reality, depicting a steaming jungle full of incredible beasts that one could actually believe were alive, and in particular one beast whom he imbued with such character that he became loved by generations and a tragic figure of mythical proportions.

What can anyone write about *King Kong* that hasn't already been written? The film has been dissected on every level by a multitude of critics and fans: as a simple adventure, as a fairy tale, as a Freudian exploration, as social comment (it was filmed during the Great Depression), as a technical marvel, as an example of "film grammar" (all the tricks of the director, writer, cameramen, composer, technicians, etc.) being used to full effect to achieve a happy whole. Of course, *King Kong* is all these. Perhaps the only dissection of *Kong* that is missing is the one that it rises above: a shot by shot account of all its effects sequences. *Kong* is put together with such a coherent force, such a calculated pace, keeping the audience on the edge of its seat throughout, that it almost seems an insult to attempt to break it down into its constituent parts. But it needs to be done: There is such a wealth of minor detail in *Kong*, so much that can be learned about O'Brien's technique, that it seems equally criminal just to watch the film and let all this grandeur rush by without indulging the luxury of going back and scrutinizing it in more detail. O'Brien created a world, chiefly on Skull Island but also in the New York scenes, quite unlike any other film: This movie *looks* better than almost any other film, of this period or any other.

Those wishing a detailed account of the film's background or for biographical details of Cooper, co-producer-director Ernest B. Schoedsack and others are referred to some of the excellent books and articles that have already been published, most notably *The Making of "King Kong"* by Goldner and Turner and Don Shay's O'Brien biography in issue #7 of *Cinefex* magazine. The following analysis is intended as a supplement to what has already been written, not as an alternative.

Statistics fans will want to know that the film contains 220 animation cuts, a figure which includes all the shots that were censored for the 1938 and 1952 re-releases. One hundred forty-two of these cuts feature during the Skull Island section, the remaining 78 in New York. Many of these are very long cuts, often employing a complex mixing of miniature rear projections, miniature sets and matted or superimposed elements. Many other animation cuts were filmed but discarded — the exact number is not known. These include the infamous missing "spider pit sequence" and an encounter with a family of horned triceratops.

Twenty minutes of live action lead up to the arrival of Carl Denham's ship "Venture" at Skull Island and another 20 before our first sight of Kong. Every scene is designed to increase our anticipation of what is to come, with Denham dropping larger and larger hints as the voyage nears its destination. Cooper and Schoedsack's direction of these passages has such single-minded purpose and sure control that even on repeated viewing they are extremely watchable. Melodramatic performances by the three lead actors somehow have avoided the ravages of becoming dated and possess a timeless enthusiasm. Robert Armstong gives his all in scenes where he films a test of Fay Wray on the deck of the ship and when he reveals the map of Skull Island to a disbelieving Captain Englehorn (Frank Reicher). When he talks heatedly about how film companies have insisted that his previous productions lacked love interest, this is clearly Cooper and Schoedsack speaking out about commercial response to their earlier films, *Grass* and *Chang*. Bruce Cabot is likable as a "real-men-don't-show-their-feelings" stereotype. Wray is irresistibly sensual as the wide-eyed and vulnerable heroine Ann Darrow, falling a little too eagerly into Cabot's arms, a sensuality that lends force to her abduction by Kong.

The fog bound scene of the arrival at Skull Island is extremely well-done, backed by the ominous sound of native drums in the distance. Long shots of the ship use a 12-foot miniature with carved wood figures on the deck. The next morning, the fog has cleared and there are two shots of Denham and Englehorn looking over the ship's rails at a full-scale rear projection of a beautiful painting (by Mario Larrinaga) of Skull Island, with Skull Mountain and the huge wall clearly visible. Superimposed live-action birds soar across the middle distance. Live-action film of waves breaking on a shore has been matted into the rear screen, adding realism to this fine fantasy image. A more detailed painting of the same view, with mountains in the background, is used in the closer shot of the oversized canoe landing on the beach, the live-action element perfectly matted into the lower portion of the frame.

Two long shots look through the native village at the huge wall in the background with Denham and his men in the lower foreground. These may use the full-scale set of the wall or they may be matte shots using the miniature wall — if so, then it's a seamless match. Back on the ship, a couple of quick effects shots have Denham and Englehorn looking out through a cabin to the village at night, a dark painting lit by tiny torch-lights.

The build-up to the natives' sacrificial offer of Ann to "Rama Kong" looks and sounds terrific thanks to the elaborate studio sets of the village and Max Steiner's thumping score. It's all done on a thrilling scale. The sight of the ant-like natives pushing the gigantic door closed and sliding across the wooden bolt is an unforgettable image lifted straight out of the world of dreams. Five very imposing shots show us the scene on the other side of the wall, looking up from a low angle at a miniature version of the wall, a row of natives standing along the top of it (by means of a split-screen matte) and Ann struggling to free herself from the altar in a miniature rear projection in the lower left foreground. Momentarily there is a lighting glitch in one of these shots when one of the altar pillars blacks out, but this is barely noticed in all the excitement. The gong behind the chief on top of the wall is struck to summon

Kong, and Steiner's almost playful stop-start theme teases us, heightening the sense of anticipation, interspersed with some off-screen growls.

After all this fabulous development, it's a disappointment to find that Kong's first appearance is one of the weaker animation scenes. The animation itself (six cuts) is insufficiently fluid and the sequence is marred by closeups of the unconvincing full-scale head. Close-ups of one of Marcel Delgado's 18-inch-high models would have been much more effective. In his first shots, Kong is half-seen behind a mixture of studio and miniature trees, with excellent traveling mattes of Ann making up the third element of the composite. Miniature trees are animated as Kong pushes them aside and the studio trees are pulled away by unseen wires. His lips curl to reveal fangs, his eyebrows lift and drop expressively and he beats his chest. With unexpected daintiness he "untwiddles" one of the clasps holding Ann (a clever bit of alignment considering that the animator was unable to see the altar, which was added later). Ann screams, faints and falls towards Kong behind the far side of the altar. Having her disappear for a moment allows O'Brien to switch to a puppet of Ann, which Kong picks up.

O'Brien now reuses the earlier split-screen perspective looking up at the miniature wall, but this time a long shot of the back of Kong replaces the rear projection of Ann. A foreground glass painting of some bushes gives the shot extra depth. The puppet Ann in Kong's hand waves its arms around and screams. Jack arrives at the great door and looks through a small opening at the bottom, in time to see Kong walking off, turning back to give a parting growl.

Denham and his men immediately set off in pursuit. A couple of shots of them walking through the jungle are enhanced by characteristically lush glass paintings. Paintings like these are used throughout the jungle passages and create a look that is unique to *King Kong*. They are at once skillfully realistic and yet suggestive of a fantasy world that can never really exist. Even the studio jungle used for closer shots of the actors is far denser and more credible than the usual kind of thing seen in other movies.

The encounter with the stegosaurus is a real show-stopper, yet is surprisingly achieved in only three animation cuts — and two of these are basically the same set-up, interrupted briefly by a live-action cut of the sailors. The camera looks over the shoulders of the men at a rear-screen image of a clearing in the jungle. This could have looked very clumsy, but O'Brien pulls it off because his miniature set in the rear projection, enhanced by multi-layered glass paintings of trees, seems to extend almost indefinitely into the distance, giving the shot a tremendous sense of depth. Far off is Delgado's magnificent stegosaurus model, a creation which looks better and better the nearer it gets to the camera.

Initially it walks left out of the shot then reappears several meters nearer. The dinosaur spots the sailors and charges straight at them/us. It is nearly on top of them/us when a gas bomb is thrown (possibly an in-camera explosion triggered off in front of the rear screen, rather than a separate element added later). It walks around in a circle, then collapses. O'Brien adds further

dynamism to this essentially straightforward perspective by having the camera track in with the men as they approach the fallen beast.

Denham shoots the stegosaurus in the head at close range, which causes it to get up and circle wildly. This allows a lingering look at the enormous detail which Delgado has put into the scaly hide of this puppet. It collapses again, it legs kicking in the air. The sequence closes with an unforgettable, protracted tracking shot in which Denham and his men walk past the corpse (another rear screen) of this huge brute, Steiner's weird theme suggesting the unworldliness of this image of man and dinosaur. Denham shoots the poor stegosaurus in the head again and its head hangs down limply. The men walk past the full length of the creature and its spiked tail makes three last snaking swishes in the air, terminating in a death shudder.

The sailors continue tracking Kong to the edge of a foggy lake, where they build a raft. An agile prop head-and-neck of the brontosaurus is used satisfactorily in about eight cuts showing it breaking the surface, diving again, coming up in a rear projection behind the men and picking up a couple of rather floppy puppets of sailors in its mouth. Three long shots have the stop-motion brontosaurus walking hurriedly through the swamp, intercut with shots of the men fleeing. One of these benefits from a foreground glass painting of a tree, but another has what is merely a superimposed tree trunk, through which the animation puppet can be clearly seen as it passes. A suggestion of interaction is implied in the third of these cuts: A sailor runs across the shot, followed swiftly by the dinosaur (probably a full-scale rear projection).

The highlight of this sequence is a series of long shots (using an extensive miniature set) in which one of the sailors is plucked out of a tree by the brontosaurus. Painted trees, a miniature trunk, some superimposed fog and an attractive background painting make this an image to treasure. In the first of these cuts, the sailors run across the lower right hand corner through some bushes; it's hard to tell if this is a miniature rear projection or a complex bit of animation involving several puppets. One of the sailors is lagging behind: A puppet of him runs into this miniature set pursued, in the same shot, by the brontosaurus. The animation of the sailor climbing the tree is extremely convincing. He thinks he is climbing to escape the reach of the dinosaur but at the top he is confronted by the huge tooth-filled head snapping at him: This is another fine nightmare image. Two cuts show the screaming, kicking man trying to fend off the huge head, which snakes this way and that; these may be either full-scale rear projections or traveling matte composites (the former is more likely). There are two more long shots of the miniature set, with the dinosaur harassing the sailor. In the second of these, it plucks the screaming man off the tree, shakes him and then puts him down on the ground with a view to making a snack of him.

The pace refuses to let up and Steiner insures that we stay on the edges of our seats as the men continue to run in terror through the jungle. The long sequence set atop the ravine is a hauntingly terrifying ordeal, very fluidly put together by Cooper, Schoedsack and O'Brien and one of the film's most unforgettable passages. Considering its muddled genesis and the number of pre-release cuts that it underwent, it is amazing that the end result is so effective.

The shooting script reveals that the sequence was to be preceded by an encounter between Kong and three triceratops, two of which he kills by hurling boulders at them. The third chases and kills one of the sailors. This footage was actually filmed although never completed.* In the original script, the sailors now start to follow Kong across the log that bridges the ravine, only to find they are trapped with Kong menacing them from one side and an arsinoitherium (a prehistoric two-horned mammal that had featured in another cut scene in which it attacks two men) from the other. But Cooper decided that he would rather have a styracosaurus chase the men onto the log and the arsinoitherium was dropped. Footage was filmed in which the styracosaur chases the men then tries to dislodge the log with its horn. This animation was cut and in the release version we are led to believe that the men are still running from the brontosaurus.

The scene underwent even more dramatic cuts than this: As originally

*An article in Film Weekly (April 21, 1933) on the sound effects of King Kong, apparently written before the film's release, refers to this scene and how the triceratops "bellows much like a bull, gores a man and tosses him into some long-forgotten bushes — to the accompaniment of a reversed and lengthened elephant roar lowered an octave."

King Kong (1933): This stunning shot of Kong and Fay Wray is a publicity creation that does not appear in the film. (National Film Archive, London.)

filmed, the sailors are shaken from the log and fall into the ravine where they are devoured by a monstrous spider, an octopus-like creature and a giant lizard. Depending on which story you believe, "the lost spider-pit sequence" was either removed because the Pennsylvanian Board of Censors considered it too horrific, or because Cooper felt it "stopped the show," diverting audience attention away from the attempt to rescue Fay Wray. It has become one of the great legends of the cinema — all that remain today are preproduction drawings by Mario Larrinaga and a few tantalizing stills.* One wonders what other undocumented footage has been cut from *King Kong*: The 14 reels of the pre-release version were trimmed to 11 reels to satisfy RKO bosses who felt the public would react badly to any film running over 100 minutes.

*The RKO props department was raided years later when the studio made a horror-comedy called You'll Find Out *(1940). In a shadowy basement can be seen what is almost certainly the giant spider, the octopus creature, one of the triceratops and also what looks like the lizard that climbs up the ravine.*

The legendary spider-pit scene from *King Kong* (1933).

The release version begins with a shot of Kong crossing the ravine, Ann in one of his paws. It's another richly evocative set-up, made up of background and foreground paintings of the lush jungle, the miniature log dripping with vines. In another miniature set-up, Kong arrives at a tree stump in a clearing, scaring off an animated bird that had been sitting there. A shot in which Kong places Ann into the crook of the tree makes ingenious use of traveling matte: The tree is a foreground live-action matte and the puppet Ann in Kong's paw is removed at the last second, replaced by the live-action Ann, who seems to fall out of the ape's hand into the tree. Nitpickers will notice that part of Kong's hand momentarily passes behind the tree, when logic dictates that it should pass in front of it. A beautiful shot of the sailors running across the log looks like it is entirely a series of paintings except for the actors. Kong is seen in yet another highly detailed miniature shot turning away from Ann in the direction of the ravine.

A stunning series of nine animation long shots, mixed with live-action cuts and shots of puppets of the men falling into the vine-strewn ravine, depicts Kong trying to shake the sailors from the log. These are Dunning traveling matte shots, the log and sailors a foreground element matched to the miniature footage behind. Kong's hands are never actually seen in contact with the log — they are always hidden by it. But the synchronization of the two elements is perfect, suggesting physical interaction. In some of these shots, the sailors are slightly transparent (a characteristic of the Dunning process) but this is barely noticed in all the excitement. O'Brien's animation of Kong is impressive: He picks up the log, puts it down again, lashes out with his arms, picks up the log again and, when the last sailor stubbornly refuses to drop, throws the whole log into the ravine. Characteristically introducing as much variety into the flow of the action as possible, O'Brien includes a fine animated medium shot of Kong and a side view of Kong watching the log fall away.

Jack has swung to safety on a vine into a cave just below Kong. An extensive miniature set of the side of the ravine, with Kong at the top of it, has Jack in a miniature rear projection, merged into it with the help of some surrounding vegetation painted on glass. Kong reaches down into the cave (the design of the shot allowing his hand to pass in front of Jack without requiring any mattes) and Jack stabs at the full-scale prop hand. This gives rise to our first glimpse of the likable side of Kong's nature: He looks at his injured finger with a puzzled expression on his face, Steiner's light-hearted theme emphasizing the humor of the moment.

The lower half of the same miniature set is used when the giant lizard crawls up out of the ravine in three stop-motion cuts. (In the original script, it was the spider. According to Goldner and Turner, this version was actually filmed but discarded.) Jack, in the miniature rear projection, cuts the vine supporting the creature (a nasty-looking beast with spikes along the back of its head and spine and two claws on each foot) and it falls out of the shot. The third of the cuts featuring the lizard includes a dynamic tilt, a dramatic camera trick denied shots involving static or traveling mattes: The camera tilts up from the lizard, over the miniature rear projection and up further to see Kong still trying to reach down to Jack.

Each effects scene is more spectacular than the last. There is no break in the action as Cooper hurls us straight into the battle with a tyrannosaurus, three-and-a-quarter minutes of breathless action. Delgado's model is superbly mean-looking, the miniature sets as ever are embellished atmospherically with glass paintings of trees and vines, the choreography of the animation (37 cuts by O'Brien and assistant Buzz Gibson) is exciting, and the pacing, with O'Brien constantly cutting from perspective to perspective, is designed to maximize audience involvement. For once, Steiner's score is not needed — instead there is a cacophonous onslaught of Kong's roars, the tyrannosaur's vicious hisses, the stomp of heavy footsteps and Ann's screaming.

The sequence opens with a superb traveling matte long shot of Ann sitting in the tree stump as the tyrannosaurus walks into the background, as yet unaware of her. It scratches its ear (a deft minor touch which contributes significantly to the impression that the tyrannosaur is a living creature), then advances on Ann. Two cuts show Kong, still at the ravine, hearing Ann's screams, and growling angrily at Jack because he has to leave him and protect his golden-haired prize.

The animation during the fight is brilliantly sustained: both animals snarling, the dinosaur's tail swishing, the ape's fists pounding, both animals biting each other. At one point, Kong throws the reptile over his shoulder, as another the tyrannosaur hops across the shot evasively, only to have Kong grab his leg, toppling him. In some of these shots, Ann and the tree are a foreground traveling matte; sometimes they are miniatures in the animation set. One magnificent effect has Kong walk backwards into the tree, sending it falling straight at the camera (which tilts with it), a dynamic design that O'Brien would repeat at the climax of *Mighty Joe Young*. Knocking Ann to the ground is an ingenious way of keeping the audience involved, insuring that this is not just a fight in a vacuum. It also allows another dramatic change of perspective: A split-screen matte follows the line of the fallen tree, Ann trapped below it, the two beasts continuing to fight in the top portion of the shot.

Kong leaps onto the dinosaur's back and tries to stretch its jaws apart. The two struggling models come right up to the camera in one cut, dwarfing Ann in the lower part of the screen. The beasts roll right over, Kong still trying to snap the tyrannosaur's jaws apart but failing to get a good hold. Eventually he succeeds, ripping the mouth apart with bloody explicitness, the jawbones crunching noisily, Ann looking on from below. There is some more O'Brien magic in the gruesomely comic moment when Kong tests the limp jaws of the tyrannosaur to check that it is dead, drops the head casually, then thumps his chest triumphantly.

He walks over to Ann, who is now a squirming animation puppet. The full-scale mechanical hand (also built by Delgado) lifts the fallen tree, then Kong picks up the puppet Ann and walks off. There is a shot of her in the full-scale hand cleverly matched to the puppet Kong in the foreground. Only the two closeups of the full-scale head, included at this point, mar this magnificent sequence.

A beautiful long shot, bristling with minor detail, has Jack (a live-action traveling matte) walking up to the slain tyrannosaur. Two animated birds flit across the mid-distance, another in the foreground. Way off in the background (this is a *very* deep animation table), Kong wanders off through the undergrowth. To allow Jack to walk right up to the dinosaur, he is now replaced by a puppet version, a none-too-smooth trick which is not helped by the fact that a miniature bush gets accidentally knocked out of position at this moment. But the next cut is superb: a closer shot of the live-action Jack walking in front of the huge head of the still-breathing tyrannosaur, animated blood (i.e., a glycerin that holds its position) dribbling from its jaws. O'Brien gives us a bonus in this shot: An animated vulture, which had been sitting on the great head, flaps off. The last effects shot of the sequence is a long shot of Kong walking through the jungle, Ann limp in his hand. He snaps a vine and grunts.

There is a brief live-action interlude now in which Denham, having managed to get back to the native village, fills Englehorn in on what has happened. Then we are back again with Kong, a wonderful composite showing the ape heading for his mountain lair. There is a glass-painted tree in the middle foreground, a live-action waterfall matted into the left corner of the background, painted rocks and a cliff face far off to the right, a traveling matte of Jack (still in pursuit) in the lower right foreground, and Kong himself in the center, walking behind the tree and down an incline, taking him out of the shot.

Kong's cavernous lair is a fabulous fantasy setting, a combination of background painting and miniature rocks, careful attention to lighting giving it that special O'Brien quality of looking very real at the same time as suggesting something out of a dream. Kong is seen standing in the entrance to the cave, a tiny animated puppet of Jack climbing over the rocks at the bottom of the shot. Small birds fly around and really help bring the image to life. The inside of the cave is a complex set-up including matted-in volcanic smoke wafting upwards in two places, live-action lava bubbling away in the foreground, live-action water in a pool matted into the center of the shot, Kong far off at the back of the shot, the puppet Jack following behind him. The whole panorama is bathed in light which pours down from an opening in the painted rock face.

The same set-up is used in the next cut, this time with Kong walking across the foreground. A half-seen shape is swimming around in the pool behind him. A closer shot of Kong shows him putting the live-action Ann onto a ledge. The elasmosaur makes for a good, slithery scare but its brief fight with Kong (five animation cuts) never impresses like the tyrannosaur battle: The beast is never a match for Kong, and O'Brien's

animation of its snake-like coiling motions never quite convinces.

The elasmosaur slithers up a rock towards a miniature rear projection of Ann. In long shot, Kong grabs it just as it is about to strike (with O'Brien adding superimposed smoke at this point to enhance the shot). Long shots of the fight use two different perspectives and contain miniature rear-projections of both Ann (on the left) and Jack (in the lower right). The elasmosaur wraps itself around Kong and there are two elegantly lit medium shots of the ape being throttled. Eventually Kong throws the beast over his head, smashing it twice into the ground. True to form, he examines its limp neck to check whether it is dead, then beats his chest in triumph. The sequence again demonstrates the flexibility of miniature rear projection: Once the stage is set up, the camera is free to move around the shot, in this case moving in for a closer view of Kong and Ann. Kong picks up the puppet Ann, Jack looking on from his rear-projection area.

Another beautiful interior long shot shows Kong high up on a path at the back of the cave, grunting gently and looking back down at the slain elasmosaur. He emerges on his "balcony," yet another breathtaking vista, the edge of the cliff dropping away abruptly and a background painting of the jungle seeming to extend indefinitely into the distance, the glimmering sea projected into it. Numerous animated birds flutter away when Kong arrives. He puts Ann down, requiring a clever switch from the animated puppet to the live-action Ann. She is contained in a miniature rear projection that is seamlessly matched to the miniature cave wall.

Kong beats his chest and looks out over Skull Island. When Ann faints (again), he picks her up (the puppet) and sits down. Perhaps deliberately, O'Brien has him sitting in a child-like pose rather than something more natural to a gorilla. The delicate scene in which Kong investigates his new bride was conceived and animated entirely by O'Brien, cleverly designed to transform the ape into a likable character. The ingenious principal composite is a side-view medium shot of Kong carefully matched to a miniature rear projection of Fay Wray in the full-scale hand, blending almost imperceptibly with the rock of the surrounding cliff face.

With his animated left hand, Kong pulls away two pieces of Ann's clothing (courtesy of some invisible wires) and sniffs one of them. O'Brien animates Kong's nostrils dilating. In two medium shots, Kong tickles Ann and then sniffs at the perfume on his fingers. Steiner's playfully "ticklish" music emphasizes the gentle absurdity of the scene. Much of this sequence was considered too risqué and the shots of Kong tickling Ann were censored shortly after the film's release. Fortunately this footage has been restored to most versions seen today.

Back in the cavern, Jack accidentally dislodges a rock, causing Kong to put down Ann and walk back in to investigate. Another exquisite miniature set-up is seen in two long shots of Kong looking down into the cavern from a ledge, the backdrop a painting of the opening that leads to the balcony. Back outside, the live-action Ann crawls behind a rock, is replaced by the puppet Ann (so as to interact with the miniature set) and crawls to the edge of the cliff

looking for a way to escape. O'Brien's animation of his human puppet is 100 percent convincing. Far off in the distance, a winged creature ominously flaps across the sky.

The pteranodon sequence is a thrilling episode and technically complex. The flying reptile had to be suspended on wires during animation. Additionally, puppets of Ann and Jack had to be animated in the background, and at other moments their rear projections had to be matched up with the miniature set. In all, O'Brien spent seven weeks designing and animating the eight miniature cuts in this sequence.

The pteranodon flies down into the shot and grabs the puppet Ann in its claws. Full-scale claws were constructed to allow closer shots of Ann being held. O'Brien makes the scene more difficult for himself, and more credible for his audience, by having the pteranodon snatch at Ann, drop her, then pick her up again. It is just about to fly off with her when Kong reappears and pulls it out of the sky. It drops the puppet Ann, then pecks at Kong with its savage beak. Kong retaliates by biting it in the head several times and nearly pulling one of its wings off.

Jack runs into the rear projection containing Ann. They are then replaced by their puppet counterparts which run behind the two fighting animals towards the edge of the ledge, hoping not be seen. The animation of the two human puppets is not as smooth as the earlier animation of Ann crawling but this is barely noticed as most of our attention is on Kong and the pteranodon. Stunt doubles climb over the side of the cliff and down a hanging vine, a shot which allows a longer look at the lush background vista. Kong finishes off the pteranodon and throws it over the edge, then looks around for Ann.

O'Brien now gives us another of the film's many haunting nightmare images: Four unforgettable long shots show Kong pulling up the vine as Ann and Jack are still climbing down it. In the last of these, Ann and Jack are animated puppets wriggling convincingly on the vine, just before they decide to drop into the river far below. Kong, looking angry, walks hurriedly back into the cavern.

A scene showing Kong climbing down the side of Skull Mountain and growling angrily was filmed but, like other moments, was removed by Cooper to improve pace. The sequence closes with another look at the fine composite of Kong's lair seen in the distance, this time with a traveling matte of Jack carrying Ann and running towards the camera.

The attack on the village is a brilliantly sustained action sequence, with Kong revealing an unexpected viciousness as he stamps on villagers or chews them to death. A series of seven stop-motion cuts of Kong hammering and pushing on the giant doors are intercut with live-action shots of actors on the other side straining to hold them back. Two of these cuts include glimpses of animated humans seen through the grilles at the bottom of each door, another example of O'Brien's endless attention to minor detail.

The sight of the doors finally bursting open to reveal the enraged Kong standing there, extras running around in the bottom of the shot, is one the cinema's never-to-be-forgotten images.

There is some spill on the traveling mattes of the actors but this is still an astonishing shot. Two long shots show Kong coming through the doors, natives and villagers running to and fro in the lower half of the screen. At first these look like conventional split-screen shots but in the second of these two shots Kong smashes down the small wall which had originally appeared to form the matte line, as villagers continue to run past. The structure of this composite remains a mystery. If it is a traveling matte, then it is one of the best in the film.

A low-angle shot has villagers run across the foreground with Kong in a full-scale rear projection. He picks up a miniature hut and throws it up into the air. In a simple but effective moment of interaction, it disappears out of the frame to be replaced by a full-size prop which smashes down onto the foreground actors. Then Kong walks straight at the camera until he nearly fills the shot, conveying a real sense of a great fury unleashed. Full-scale rear projection is used again when Kong, walking towards the camera, nearly stomps on a baby, snatched to safety at the last moment by a villager who runs across the foreground.

The sequence with the natives throwing spears at Kong from a wooden platform is another example of O'Brien packing everything into a shot for maximum dramatic impact. The trees in the background are a painting. The platform is a miniature. The natives standing on top of it are a miniature rear projection. Traveling mattes of actors in silhouette run across the foreground, giving the shot added depth. The actors pretend to

Another *King Kong* pose created for publicity stills. (Museum of Modern Art, New York.)

throw spears, their actions matched up to miniature wire-supported spears that fly across the shot and stick in Kong's side — he gives them a cursory look, then discards them.

Kong picks up a miniature tree and swipes at the platform. One man falls off and Kong picks up his puppet counterpart, its arms struggling wildly, and chews on it. A closeup of the mechanical head has the native trapped inside the jaws. In long shots again, he slowly pulls the man out, as though picking chicken meat off a drumstick. (These last two actions were cut from the film on its 1952 re-release on the grounds of being too horrific. They have now been restored.) Two more spears stick in his mouth but he removes them as easily as he would toothpicks. He smashes down with his fist into the platform (at which point the miniature rear projection of the villagers subtly disappears), gets another spear in his back, then stomps straight at the camera.

He walks into an extensive miniature set containing several huts, silhouettes of villagers running across the foreground. He crumples one of the huts with his hands, picks up a screaming villager and chews on him. Trying to flee, an animated villager dives out of the window of a hut on stilts and hits the ground head first! Kong walks over to him and tries to pick him up. The man crawls a few yards, then Kong picks him up, throws him to the ground and stomps on him, grinding him into the ground. A full-size prop of the foot grinds the man into the mud. In another long shot, another native (an animated puppet) can be seen at the window of the hut as Kong stomps on his friend. In a long cut, Kong reaches into the hut, pulls out the second native and likewise throws him to the ground and deliberately stomps on him. Kong shakes his fist angrily and walks on. The sequence with the second native was another victim of the 1952 censor's scissors.

Three long shots show Kong arriving at the beach, extras running around in foreground traveling mattes. A sand dune crosses the whole of this shot and O'Brien could have taken the easy option and used this for the location of the split screen, but instead he improves the shot by having the split lower down, thereby allowing Kong, now groggy from the gas bombs thrown at him, to step forward over the dune towards Denham's men. Kong clutches at his throat as the gas takes effect, rubbing his eyes several times before finally going down. The gas is a superimposed element: Close inspection reveals that the cut-off point of this doesn't match up with the outline of the dune where it is supposed to end.

The Skull Island section ends with an attractive close shot of Kong lying on the beach, his head and shoulders making slight movements as Denham, En-glehorn and the other sailors approach him in a rear projection. "We'll teach him fear," boasts Denham, thereby insuring that audience sympathy is ready to side with Kong during whatever is to follow.

The New York scenes make a sharp visual contrast with Skull Island: Lush tropical jungle is replaced by a concrete jungle. Characters and dialogue have a gritty realism that puts us firmly back in the real world. The miniature buildings and props constructed by O'Brien and his crew are so minutely detailed that it is often difficult to tell what is real and what is studio-fabricated. There are 78 stop-motion cuts in this segment of the film, culminating in the classic finale with Kong at the top of the Empire State Building, getting machine-gunned by fighter biplanes.

Steiner's jaunty theme heightens the sense of anticipation as the audience crowds into a Broadway theater where Denham is staging his show. Referring to his star attraction, Denham says, "We've knocked some of the fight out of him," suggesting that Kong has been drugged. Denham walks on stage and makes his speech: "Ladies and gentle-men, look at Kong — the Eighth Wonder of the World."

In long shot, the curtain rises, revealing Kong trussed up on a pedestal. Below him is Denham, with the audience in the lower foreground. Just how this stunning composite was achieved is not clear. Probably the entire top half of the frame is miniature, with the background to the stage carefully matched to the actual stage below. Or it may be that O'Brien animated his puppet in front of a rear projection of the stage, using the kind of static matte design that Ray Harryhausen would make his trademark years later. The rising curtain is animated frame by frame.

The full-scale head is used unnecessarily again for a closeup, weakening the moment. The long-shot set-up is used in a series of shots in which Kong looks down at Ann and Jack as they walk across the stage, and at a crowd of pressmen who gather at one corner of the stage. Kong rattles his chains, becoming agitated by the camera flashbulbs. "He thinks you're attacking the girl," warns Denham.

Several low-angle long shots look over the shoulders of the pressmen at a side view of Kong. It is difficult to say whether they are standing in front of a rear projection or are a traveling matte element. In these cuts, Kong bares his fangs, growls down at the pressmen, then rips first one then the other arm free. The audience starts to panic. In another side-view shot, Kong reaches down and frees one foot from the manacle binding it.

Ann and Jack run across the stage, away from the camera, and in a very dynamic moment Kong jumps from his (off-screen) pedestal, seeming to leap down from above and behind the camera. The puppet's feet land below the edge of the frame so no matte is required. O'Brien would use this simple but effective choreography again in *The Animal World* (1956).

Outside in the street, the theater's huge side doors buckle outwards as Kong smashes through them. Made of thin copper, the doors are animated so as to crumple realistically. Extras in the street flee in a rear projection. A building on the left side of the frame is a miniature, with the light from the doorway behind Kong causing him to throw a shadow onto the other building. Again, the puppet's feet are below the bottom of the frame, so no matte is required.

Kong walks toward another miniature building while extras in a traveling matte flee from him in the lower foreground. In an all-miniature shot, Kong reaches in through one the building's windows, pulls out a struggling animated man and puts him into his mouth. The full-scale head is used for a closeup of the victim in the ape's jaws. Then the animated Kong pulls out the screaming man and throws him to the ground. (The shot with the full-scale head was removed by the 1938 censor. In this instance, the moment is improved by the excision. It illustrates that O'Brien animated the sequence as one long cut, with the closeup being added later and splitting his shot into two cuts. After the closeup's removal, the shot flows as O'Brien intended it, in one uninterrupted stop-motion cut.)

In another traveling matte shot, extras run across the lower foreground as Kong demolishes a canopy over the building's entrance. Some superimposed smoke, emanating from vehicles that have crashed, adds depth to the shot. The miniature canopy that he throws up into the air and out of the frame becomes, in the same shot, a live-action prop that falls on the extras.

In three more all-miniature shots at the foot of the building, Kong looks up when he hears a girl scream, reminded of Ann. He starts to climb up the building, using the window ledges as foot-holds. A beautiful low-angle long shot depicts the full height of the (miniature) skyscraper, the night sky behind it, Kong climbing up it.

The next shot, in a bedroom interior, is a potent nightmare image. A girl sleeps in the bed as Kong's face appears at a window — actually a process screen set up behind the studio set. A series of shots show Kong clinging to the outside of the building, pulling out the girl. Extra horror is generated by the fact that Kong casually pulls her out upside down. (A shot so horrific, in fact, that this sequence was censored from most American prints, although it remained in European versions.) The full-size prop hand is used to good effect in a dizzying composite of the actress held high above the street. When he realizes that this brunette is not Ann, he drops the screaming girl, then starts climbing higher up the building.

Jack and Ann enter a room in the same building. "You're safe now, dear," he tells her. As he comforts her, Kong's massive face appears at the window. The open-mouthed creature, one of the animation puppets, has an expressive vitality that its full-scale counterpart can never match. An extreme closeup of Kong at the window is even better and makes one wish that all closeups had been done with Delgado's 18-inch-high puppets.

In two exterior long shots, Kong clings to the wall with one hand, shaking his fist at the crowd and sirens below. In the bedroom, Kong's face looks in as the prop hand reaches in through another window and knocks Jack to the floor. In a skillfully assembled series of cuts, Kong reaches in and pulls out a puppet Ann. The prop hand is used

again for close shots of the actress struggling. Kong climbs higher.

Kong arrives at the roof, another impressively detailed set with other miniature high-rise buildings in the background. In four cuts Kong climbs up over the edge and puts Ann down on the roof. In the first cut she is an animated puppet, in subsequent shots a live-action miniature rear-projection. As ever, the boundary of the projection screen is invisible. Ann crawls behind a tower on the roof and Kong reaches behind it, picking up the puppet Ann. In a long cut on another part of the roof set, Kong sits with his back to the camera, admiring the girl in his paw. Then he climbs over the side and descends.

The next sequence is a classic piece of monster-on-the-loose mayhem, yet it was filmed almost as an afterthought by Cooper. The original completed film ran 13 reels but Cooper, revealing a superstitious streak, decided to increase it to 14. It gave him the excuse he needed to film a scene that he had dreamed up in which Kong wrecks a train on an elevated railway line. Live-action cut-aways of extras being thrown around in the derailed carriages are energetically staged by Schoedsack. Steiner contributes another pulse-pounding theme, building tension as the train gets nearer and nearer.

The scene contains ten stop-motion cuts. Only three different set-ups are used, suggesting that O'Brien was not allowed as much time as he might have liked.

In a long-shot set-up that is used in seven of the ten cuts, Kong walks from behind a building into a street scene next to the elevated track. Extras in the lower foreground are a traveling matte element. The building on the right is a live-action area that has been matted in, with extras leaning out of the windows. In one hand he still carries Ann. He shakes his other arm angrily at the fleeing crowds. An animated miniature train speeds past behind him and after it has gone he smashes at the track with his fist, partly climbing up onto it, one leg swinging.

The next shot looks along the track, a deep miniature set with buildings on either side, all embellished with numerous minor details. Intercut with shots of strap-hanging commuters are shots of Kong demolishing the track, bits of it falling away (supported on wires and animated one frame at a time).

Two shots are seen from the engineer's point of view as he nears the hole in the track through which the head and one arm of Kong protrude. O'Brien dollied his animation camera one frame at a time towards the puppet and then used this footage in a full-scale rear projection in front of which the actor, in a mock-up of a train cab, looked out, amazed.

The carriage is derailed in front of Kong, animated convincingly as it runs off the track. A marvelous shot looks out from inside the carriage at Kong's huge face peering in at the panicking extras.

In the three final long shots, Kong pulls the carriage entirely off the rails, sending it crashing to the ground. Intercut with a montage of shots of the extras in disarray, he bashes at the carriage repeatedly with his fist, causing the sides to crumple. Finally he turns away as though having defeated a dinosaur on Skull Island, then begins to climb the building on the right. Of course, this building is part of the live-action, so the puppet actually appears to climb behind it, up the far wall.

Setting the climax at the top of the newly constructed Empire State Building was a stroke of genius by Cooper. This was the grand image that he had in his mind back in 1930 when he first conceived the film; everything else came to him later, after his encounter with O'Brien and the *Creation* footage.

The sequence begins with three extreme long shots in which Kong climbs the skyscraper. These are matte shots, with the puppet looking tiny against the building (which itself is a miniature). The animation (by Gibson) is extremely smooth in these shots, the puppet hanging down slightly and obeying the laws of gravity. For a long time it was believed that these shots used a man in costume, but this has since been denied by technicians who worked on the sequence. Intercut with these shots is film of fighter biplanes taking to the air.

Kong reaches the very top, another miniature set. The background panorama of New York is a multi-planed series of three paintings by Byron Crabbe, Larrinaga and his brother Juan Larrinaga. As such, it has more depth than if a photo blow-up had been used. The puppet Ann struggles in the ape's paw and in one shot the actress is clasped in the prop hand. Kong roars angrily at the sky, then puts Ann down on a ledge. At this point there is a seamless switch to the actress in a miniature rear projection, achieved boldly in one cut with the audience's eye directed at the area where the switch takes place. The puppet's hand is held so that most of it obscures the puppet Ann; the puppet Ann is removed; the first frame of the miniature live-action footage of Ann is projected and animation recommences. Again, it is impossible to detect the boundary of the miniature projected area.

Kong climbs to the apex of the dome and beats his chest. Always striving for maximum drama, Cooper and O'Brien stage a series of shots from the pilots' point of view. The animation camera, moving down a ramp one frame at a time and tilting from side to side, zooms in on the gesticulating ape. In some of these cuts, a miniature biplane, suspended on wires, is also animated as it closes in on Kong, firing its guns. There is no musical theme backing this part of the scene, which instead has an exciting combination of Kong's growls, the roar of the engines and the rat-a-tat of the machine-guns.

In medium shot, Kong looks up and growls in a subdued way that cleverly suggests that he may be resigned to his fate. In a different long shot perspective of the top of the tower, Kong reaches out for an animated plane that flies past. Another animated plane flies straight at the camera, with Kong in the foreground. In a very long cut, another miniature plane flies just out of Kong's reach (this time there is no camera movement), then Kong watches as a tiny animated plane flies past in the background. In the same cut, the plane comes in for another strafing run, but this time Kong grabs its wing and sends it crashing down behind the building. In a live-action traveling matte, the miniature plane falls down the side of the building in a cloud of smoke and flame.

In medium shot, Kong clutches at his chest which has been riddled with bullets. In long shots, he tries to reach for two more animated planes. In medium shot, he fingers the patch of blood that has appeared in his chest and a confused expression crosses his face. O'Brien succeeds in making Kong a truly pathetic character, although at the same time some of his gestures are too melodramatic. For example, in the next cut, a long shot, the now-weakened Kong actually wipes his brow as he makes a half-hearted attempt to grab another plane, then slumps down.

Kong receives another hail of bullets from one of the miniature planes, then slips down to the ledge where Ann is cowering. He clings on to the radio mast, barely able to prevent himself from falling. Steiner's tragic theme now starts as Kong reaches down for Ann. In another bewilderingly smooth switch, the live-action Ann is replaced by the puppet Ann in one fluid shot.

In a drawn-out long shot, he puts Ann down again, O'Brien deftly switching back to a miniature rear projection. The puppet's hand is aligned so that it seems that Kong strokes her gently with his fingers. Animated planes zoom in from behind the camera and shower Kong with more bullets and he grabs his wounded throat. In medium shot, the weary-eyed Kong slumps down, giving the planes a contemptuous sneer — O'Brien animates Kong's upper lip twisting into a snarl, recalling an expression made by his brontosaurus in *The Lost World*. In the film's final animation cut, a miniature plane makes another pass, filling Kong with bullets. The ape very nearly topples over backwards but grabs onto the mast. But Kong is finished: The mast slips through his fingers and he falls backwards.

A live-action extreme long shot has

Kong atop the Empire State Building: Another image fabricated by RKO's publicity department.

a puppet fall the full height of the building, bouncing off the side on the way down. One of the animation puppets is used in three shots in which the huge head and arm of Kong lie motionless in the foreground as a crowd gathers behind (in a rear-projection). "Well, Denham, the airplanes got him," observes a policeman. "Oh, no," Denham replies. "It wasn't the airplanes. It was Beauty killed the Beast."

Sixty years later, *King Kong*'s story devices have been turned into clichés by the dozens of films that have imitated it. But it remains a unique experience thanks to O'Brien's vision. David O. Selznick, head of RKO at the time, recommended to the Academy of Motion Picture Arts and Sciences that O'Brien be awarded an Oscar for his work. But the Academy had other ideas — they would not consider the field of special effects to be a category worthy of their interest until 1939.

King Kong vs. Godzilla
see *Kingu Kongu tai Gojira*

Kingu Kongu tai Gojira
(U.S. title: *King Kong vs. Godzilla*)

Japan. 1963. Toho. D: Inoshiro Honda. D (English version): Thomas Montgomery. Scr (English version): Paul Mason, Bruce Howard. Character and Name of "King Kong" by permission of RKO General. Mus: Peter Zinner. Director of Special Effects: Eiji Tsuburaya.

Cast: Michael Keith, Harry Holcombe, James Yagi, Tadao Takashima, Keji Sahaka, Ichiro Arishima.

Rating: ☆☆   Stop-Motion: ☆½

This risible film had its beginnings in a treatment written by Willis O'Brien in the early 1960s, "King Kong vs. Frankenstein." RKO, the studio that had made the original *King Kong*, expressed an interest in the project. Sadly, the course of action they took was to exclude O'Brien from any involvement in the film, and to sell the idea to Japan's Toho Studios, whose output included the successful *Godzilla* series. The result was a film featuring a man in a ragged ape costume battling a man in an unlikely dinosaur costume. We can only begin to imagine what O'Brien's reaction must have been.

There is an attempt to recreate the Skull Island sequences of the original film. Two Japanese representatives of a television company travel to a remote South Seas island, witness a sacrificial dance by the natives, explore the jungle, are attacked by a giant octopus, encounter Kong, subdue him (by means of some narcotic berries), then take him back to Japan. Events are depicted with a childlike glee which means that, while there is never any chance of mistaking this for serious filmmaking, there is a never a dull moment either.

In a long sequence, a giant octopus attacks the natives' village. A live octopus is used, presumably tormented cruelly to make it slither in all the required directions. The animal is combined with shots of the natives in a series of traveling matte composites which range from wretched to adequate.

In two quick shots, stop-motion is used to depict one of the tentacles snaring a man, then throwing him through the air. A puppet of one of the natives is utilized and traveling matte is used to combine the tentacle with the live-action footage. The animation of the tentacle is acceptable but nothing more.

Elaborate miniatures — mountains, tanks crossing a military base, helicopters, a whole town of buildings waiting to be stomped on by the monsters, etc.— are the impressive work of Toho regular effects man Eiji Tsuburaya.

Kronos

1957. Regal. Prod-D: Kurt Neumann. Scr: Lawrence Louis Goldman. Story: Irving Block. Ph: Karl Struss. Art: Theopold Holsopple. Mus: Paul Sawtell, Bert Shefter. Special Effects Designed and Created by Jack Rabin, Irving Block, Louis DeWitt, Menrad Von Mulldorfer, William Reinhold, Gene Warren and (uncredited) Wah Chang.

Cast: Jeff Morrow, Barbara Lawrence, John Emery, George O'Hanlon, Morris Ankrum, Kenneth Alton.

Rating: ☆☆   Stop-Motion: ☆½

Director Kurt Neumann generates some tension during the build-up to the first appearance by Kronos — a giant cubical robot from space — and there are moments when this looks like it might develop into superior SF. But once the robot has arrived and begins stomping around Mexico looking for energy sources, the film is destroyed by its inadequate special effects and by Neumann's inability to sustain any excitement or control action scenes. Crowds of disinterested extras run around looking in all the wrong directions during the scenes in which Kronos attacks power stations and cities.

Cursed as ever by a low budget (total cost: $160,000), Jack Rabin, Irving Block, Louis DeWitt, Gene Warren and the rest of the effects team do what they can. Early scenes show a hopelessly unconvincing flying saucer arriving on Earth.

The Kronos model was built by Wah Chang and animated by Gene Warren. In a letter to the author, Warren explained, "All the action scenes with Kronos were accomplished with stop-frame photography of the simple, very unsophisticated puppet (about ten inches in height) against process plates with foreground set pieces to allow the puppet to make actual contact with the ground." The robot looks imposing when stationary but its means of locomotion is poorly conceived and unlikely. Its four piston-like "legs" can only pump up and down, not forwards, so just how it is supposed to walk is not clear. Four or five animated long shots are used to depict the robot walking across miniature sets. Unfortunately, the shots only serve to weaken the impact of this automaton, making it look foolish.

Other silliness includes a scene where Kronos absorbs the explosion of an atomic bomb (stock footage of a mushroom cloud is followed by the same footage being projected in reverse) and a feverishly Freudian sequence in which shots of hero and heroine (Jeff Morrow and Barbara Lawrence) getting passionate on a beach are intercut with shots of scientist John Emery, possessed by an energy creature, sweating in his hospital bed, getting quite excited as the huge spaceship emerges from the sea behind the lovers.

If only Neumann could have brought the same camp intensity to the rest of the film. However, he demonstrated in *The Fly* the following year that he was a mediocre talent. The competent Cinemascope photography is by Karl Struss, who 25 years earlier had shot *Dr. Jekyll and Mr. Hyde* so magnificently.

Krull

1983. Columbia. D: Peter Yates. Scr: Stanford Scherman. Ph: Peter Suschitzky. Art: Stephen Grimes. Mus: James Horner. Visual Effects Supervisor: Derek Meddings. Special Makeup: Nick Maley. Animator: Steven Archer.

Cast: Ken Marshall, Lysette Anthony, Freddie Jones, Francisca Annis, Alun Armstrong, Bernard Bresslaw, Robbie Coltrane.

Rating: ☆☆☆   Stop-Motion: ☆☆½

When this $20 million fantasy was released, it was easy to dismiss it as just another *Star Wars* rip off: Freddie Jones' character is in the Obi Wan Kenobi mold, James Horner's score imitates John Williams' style, the opening shot has a huge spaceship flying overhead, etc. But in fact it is directed with enthusiasm by Peter Yates and much better than we were lead to believe by contemporary reviewers. Some of the devices don't work (such as Bernard Bresslaw in an unconvincing Cyclops mask), but there are many impressively staged set-pieces and the pace is brisk. In fact, Yates uses a fast-cutting technique also borrowed from George Lucas, although he isn't able to generate the same sense of excitement.

British special effects expert Derek Meddings (whose earlier credits include *Superman, Alien* and several James Bond films) supplied the excellent miniature effects. These include the fine opening shot with its massive, mountain-like spaceship passing a world with two suns, a beautiful fantasy image of a huge cavern with tiny figures crossing a rock bridge over a seemingly bottomless pit, and a stunning final sequence in which the Black Fortress (the mountain-like spaceship) is destroyed, collapsing upwards into the sky amid a shower of sparks, rocks and dust, as the actors look on from a lush meadow in the lower foreground. However, the Firemares — horses that take to the air, leaving a trail of flames from their hooves — are less successful because they are done live-action with blue-screen composites without any close shots of the horses in full. They are weak compared with the magnificent Pegasus in *Clash of the Titans* two years earlier. The villains are the Slayers, extras in costumes that are an imaginative combination of the reptilian and the bony, and looking especially sinister during an attack in a swamp.

Nick Maley's high-quality special makeups include the ground-burrowers that emerge from the helmets of stricken Slayers, Francesca Annis as an aged crone, and the costume for the chief Slayer, the Beast — an impressive humanoid monster but let down by being too easily defeated in a "love-conquers-all" ending in which the colorless hero and heroine get romantic.

The film's stand-out sequence has Jones visiting the "Widow of the Web" (Annis) in order to learn the location of the Black Fortress. She sits in a tiny chamber in the middle of a vast cavern, held in place by the web of a giant spider. For the task of animating the crystal spider, Meddings recruited Steven Archer, personally recommended to him by Ray Harryhausen, whom Archer had assisted on *Clash of the Titans*.

The Crystal Spider from *Krull* (1983), animated by Steve Archer.

Archer spent three months animating the 25 cuts in the sequence and pulls off a difficult bit of stop-motion impressively. Working in an extensive miniature set strewn with webbing made access to the puppet awkward. Additionally, the webbing had to be made to react to the spider's weight as it walked along it — springing up and down. Archer achieved this effect by having each of the relevant strands attached to a wire rig that could be drawn in or loosened frame-by-frame to move the webbing. The spider itself was supported by overhead wires since the webbing itself could not take its weight. Operating under these difficult conditions, Archer managed to film about three seconds of animation footage per day. The white spider, built from clear perspex by Medding's crew, has a three-foot leg span, a transparent body, two pairs of hungrily twitching mandibles and eight beady black eyes.

The ten-minute scene is delicately handled by Yates, who imbues it with

413

the mood and grotesquerie of a Grimm fairy tale. The setting is unusual and attractive, and Horner's restrained score adds to the tension. Archer's animation makes the spider unsettlingly believable, but the scene should have been scarier. Perhaps a shot of the creature devouring a victim could have added that extra punch needed.

Jones tentatively sets a foot on the webbing and the spider emerges from a crack in the rocks. Teasingly, only two of its legs are seen at first, then it sets off in pursuit of its prey. It emits a kind of shrill chirrup that adds to its presence. It inverts itself, busily spinning some webbing and dropping to a lower level of the web. In two cuts, it scurries straight at the camera.

The Widow (Annis) turns over an hourglass which has the effect of stopping the spider in its tracks and giving Jones valuable seconds in which to reach the chamber. In closeup, its mandibles open and close anxiously. This close shot allows a look at the detail on the puppet, in particular the eight eyes and the tiny hairs all over its legs and body. As the sand drains through the hourglass, the spider starts moving its legs in anticipation, springing up and down on the webbing. It advances and in a long tracking shot inverts itself again, dropping to another part of the web. It positions itself for the final strike, but Jones reaches the central chamber just in time.

After a long dialogue between Jones and Annis, Jones must attempt to get back across the web. Annis smashes the hour-glass and the camera creepily zooms in slowly on the spider, front legs and mandibles working busily. With renewed vigor it sets out across the web.

The only shot in which puppet and actor are seen together is an impressive extreme long shot with Jones a tiny figure dwarfed by the approaching arachnid. Archer achieved this with a variation on O'Brien's miniature rear-projection technique, front-projecting the footage of Jones into his animation set.

The spider nearly catches up with Jones, who escapes out of the cave mouth in the nick of time. In two shots looking into the chamber through the cave mouth, the spider walks straight at the camera but at the last minute turns and heads back to the chamber, where Annis is no longer protected by her hourglass. The haunting final shot shows the spider on top of the chamber, digging at it with its front legs as pieces of webbing fall away from it (animated one frame at a time). As originally filmed, this shot, which took Archer eight and a half days to animate, was 13 seconds long and showed bits of animated debris falling from the chamber. However, much of the shot was trimmed before the final release.

Archer also animated some other brief shots in which weapons are thrown, performing actions that would be hard to create with live-action props. One of these is the Glaive, a five-pointed star with a retractable blade at each point. It swoops across the screen during the opening moments, revealing the letters of the film's title. It is seen again later on in five more cuts when it is thrown by Marshall and cuts through a rock wall, and when it is used to attack the Beast, spinning and dipping through the air. Two axes were also animated as they cartwheel across the screen, pinning an actor beneath them. Most of these shots were animated against VistaVision rear projections, but another shot, in which the Cyclops' trident hurtles across the frame, appears to have been animated in front of a blue screen. They are all successful shots in that they do not look as though they have been stop-framed.

Additionally, Archer animated two shots in which a wall of ribs slowly closes around the heroine as she tries to escape from the Beast.

Laserblast

1978. Irwin Yablans. Prod: Charles Band. D: Michael Rae. Scr: Franne Schacht, Frank Ray Perilli. Ph: Terry Bowen. Mus: Joel Goldsmith, Richard Band. Special Effects Makeup and Props: Steve Neill. Animation: David Allen. Laser Effects: Paul Gentry. (Uncredited: Animation: Randy Cook. Armatures/Model Sculpting: Jon Berg. Spaceship Built by Greg Jein. Spaceship Interior Design: Dave Carson.)

Cast: Kim Milford, Cheryl Smith, Gianni Russo, Roddy McDowall, Keenan Wynn, Dennis Burkley.

Rating: ☆☆   Stop-Motion: ☆☆☆

Laserblast is an example of stop-motion being misapplied. David Allen's wonderful sequences featuring alien lizard men have been almost arbitrarily tacked onto a cheap and dull science fiction film. As a result, they look out of place and this tends to highlight their artificiality. As Allen himself said (in an interview in *Cinefantastique*, vol. 6, no. 4), "It's almost like cutting to puppet theater." Had Allen been brought in at the start of pre-production, this could have been a minor classic; as it stands, it is just a bad film with good stop-motion sequences.

Laserblast is one of the first films produced by Charles Band, who would make a career of bringing offbeat stories to the screen in low-budget films of variable quality. But his love for fantasy is never in doubt and he also seems to have a fondness for stop-motion, utilizing Allen's talents in a whole string of films.

Director Michael Rae is unable to imbue the action scenes with any excitement and the dialogue is feeble. Plot threads, such as the arrival of a sinister government agent, are poorly realized. Only the presence of Roddy McDowall and Keenan Wynn in minor roles lend the live-action passages any interest.

The lizard men are beautifully detailed puppets, co-designed by Allen and Jon Berg and built by Berg. All too rare in the world of stop-motion, they are also full of personality. Their bleating voices echo in an otherworldly way, the bottom eyelids in their turtle-like heads blink upwards, and they have long necks that twist about with an ungainly but credible vitality. Allen invests their actions with touches of humor which really bring them to life. Most of the animation was done by Randy Cook, with Allen supervising and animating a few shots himself.

The lizard men feature in 39 cuts in five brief sequences, the first of which is the most ambitious. A live-action green-skinned alien, running through a desert, looks up to see a spaceship fly overhead. This is a fine model built by Greg Jein, best known for his work on *Close Encounters of the Third Kind*, and (in two shots of it landing) it is stop-framed against a rear projection. A rear-projected shadow beneath it helps mesh the composite.

The aliens, who are benevolent beings in pursuit of the evil humanoid alien, emerge from their craft and one of them is first seen leaning on a partial prop of the spaceship, drumming his three fingers nervously and beckoning his colleague over. After some discussion in alien-speak, the two walk off, and are then seen in an attractive static matte set-up. The bottoms of their feet disappear behind the edge of the soft matte line (i.e., kept slightly out of focus so as to make it less obvious to the eye). A second static matte set-up has the live-action alien in the foreground and the two lizard men in the distance, successfully creating an illusion of depth. The evil alien fires at one of the lizard men (the laser-fire is superimposed), sending his gun flying. This is a quick and convincing moment of wire-supported animation. Allen adds some dynamism to a low-angle medium shot of the lizard men advancing on the camera, which tilts upwards as they get nearer.

The lizard men fire back, hitting the humanoid, and (in a deft medium shot) one alien nods to the other, an amusingly human gesture indicating that his

job is complete. Startled by an aircraft flying overhead, the two watch it pass, their necks twisting around with an almost comic elasticity — like a cartoon effect. One almost expects them to tie themselves in knots.

In the second stop-motion sequence, the two aliens, now in their spaceship, are berated by their irate commander, who appears on a monitor. Although this sequence has more animation cuts than the other passages — 13 — it is less interesting than the opening scene because there is no interaction with live actors. All the action takes place inside a miniature spaceship designed by Dave Carson.

Shots of the commander on a screen appear to be rear projections of previously shot animation footage. The commander, wagging an angry finger at his men for leaving a laser-gun behind, is very smoothly animated. In a likable medium shot, one alien turns to the other as though looking for moral support. In a close shot of one of the puppet's arms, it waves a hand over some controls and the ship sets a return course for Earth.

In the third sequence, the lizard men are seen again at the controls of their spaceship, this time in seven animation cuts. In the first shot, Allen again tries to avoid the "locked-off" look of animation. The camera pulls back from a shot of an exploding car, which is rear-projected onto a console at which the two lizard men are looking. The aliens talk among themselves in a series of medium and long shots. The earlier shot of a hand being passed over the controls is used again.

In the fourth scene, the lizard men

Laserblast's alien lizard men. The tabletop on which they stand is not seen in the finished film.

are back on Earth. In six cuts they discover a burnt-out car, evidence that someone has been using their laser-gun. Unfortunately, there are no mattes in these cuts and they all look rather too obviously like rear-screen set-ups. Making things worse, the background plates appear to have been shot at night, even though the scene occurs between two daytime live-action sequences.

As before, the animation is extremely fluid. In medium shot, the lizard men walk past a miniature tree, which helps a little to break up the "tabletop" look of these shots. In another good touch of character animation, one alien straightens his long-neck in a bird-like manner when he spots the car, then taps his colleague on the shoulder. Closeups allow a good look at the models' credibly watery eyes and unusual blinking action.

The final scene featuring stop-motion is the briefest and a big disappointment. There is a confrontation between the aliens and the human who has their gun, but it is over before it has barely started. Presumably, the budget simply ran out. In three matte shots, one alien is seen in extreme long shot on top of a roof, firing a gun at the actor in the street below. Once the actor is killed, the alien walks off towards the spaceship, which hovers in the sky above him (actually a photo cut-out).

How many times has the full potential of stop-motion been quashed by a restrictive budget? Allen's sequences in *Laserblast* are a visual delight and tease us with hints of what he might be capable of producing given a reasonable budget and schedule.

The Last Action Hero

1993. Columbia/Steve Roth/Oak. D: John McTiernan. Scr; Shane Black, David Arnott. Story: Zak Penn, Adam Leff. Ph: Dean Semler. Art: Eugenio Zanetti. Mus: Michael Kamen. Visual Effects Consultant: Richard Greenberg. Visual Effects Supervisor: John Sullivan. Visual Effects: RGA/LA, Sony Pictures Imageworks, Boss Film Studio, Fantasy II (Visual Effects Supervisor: Gene Warren, Jr.), VCE/Peter Kuran, Baer Animation Company, Industrial Light and Magic.

Cast: Arnold Schwarzenegger, Art Carney, Charles Dance, Anthony Quinn, Austin O'Brien, F. Murray Abraham, Sir Ian McKellen.

Rating: ☆☆½   Stop-Motion: ☆☆

On paper, *The Last Action Hero* probably looked like it was going to be an inventive and innovative fantasy. A young boy (Austin O'Brien) is given a magic cinema ticket which transports him into the movie world of his hero Jack Slater (Arnold Schwarzenegger), creating opportunities for thrill-a-minute action sequences, a host of affectionate in-jokes and a chance for Schwarzenegger to shine. The film is all of these, but unfortunately John McTiernan's direction never shifts into the kind of high gear that the story requires. Ultimately, this is just another action movie.

The film contains a wealth of elaborate special effects, including many shots that made use of digitally composited computer imagery. In amongst all of this state-of-the-art trickery, however, there was still room for a couple of good old-fashioned stop-motion shots, executed by the effects company R. Greenberg Associates (RGA/LA).

One of these is a very quick effect when the boy is watching a screening of the latest Jack Slater movie. The film-within-a-film includes a shot in its credits sequence where a steel wall explodes from within and peels back. The wall was made of lead foil and animated by Eoin Sprott. Explosions were later added to the effect.

In a gratuitous reference to *E.T.— The Extra-Terrestrial*, a later scene has the boy riding his bicycle at night and suddenly taking to the skies. In extreme long shot, he cycles past a huge image of a full moon, lands with a bump on a rooftop, pedals along it and then falls off the edge. This shot uses a little stop-motion puppet, seen in silhouette. It's a very accomplished effect, even though dramatically it adds nothing to the story.

The Legend of Hillbilly John

1973. Two's Company/Jack H. Harris Enterprises. D: John Newland. Scr: Melvin Levy. Based on the book *Who Fears the Devil?* by Manley Wade Wellman. Ph: Flemming Olsen. Mus: Roger Kellaway. Songs: Hoyt Axton, Hedge Capers, White Lightnin'. Special Effects Director: Gene Warren. (Uncredited Stop-Motion: Harry Walton.)

Cast: Hedge Capers, Severn Darden, Sharon Henesy, Denver Pyle, Percy Rodrigues, Alfred Ryder.

Rating: ☆☆½   Stop-Motion: ☆☆½

This is a low-budget 1973 production from Jack H. Harris' company, which also released other films containing stop-motion, including *Equinox* and *Dinosaurus!* Like *Equinox*, the only reason for watching it today is to catch the stop-motion sequences. These were created by Gene Warren, at the time operating as a company called Excelsior! A.M.P. after the dissolution of Project Unlimited.

Hillbilly John is a weird and simple tale of a boy who puts silver strings on his guitar and wanders off to confront the Devil. It attempts to create a kind of fairy tale atmosphere but all too often John Newland's direction lacks any style whatsoever and the pace is sometimes irritatingly slow. Scenes in which the hippie hero (Hedge Capers) wanders around the countryside playing his guitar are dated, to say the least.

S. S. Wilson (in *Puppets and People*) praised the film because it "avoided the effects-emphasis bias" found in most stop-motion features, containing only two brief animation scenes (probably no

more than 20 cuts in all). In fact, the effects scenes seem out of place in their gentle, hillbilly surroundings and come across as gratuitous set-pieces in just the same way as in so many other dramatically weak stop-motion films.

Ugly Bird, a giant, vicious-looking vulture, is never developed to the level of becoming a memorable stop-motion adversary. All the same, Warren's efforts here, using front rather than rear projection, are enjoyably offbeat and include one or two fine flourishes of technical ingenuity. Ugly Bird was built by Harry Walton, who also did about 85 percent of the animation, the remainder done by Warren. A decade later, Walton would make significant contributions to several films featuring stop-motion, including *Young Sherlock Holmes* (1986).

In a letter to the author, Warren described Ugly Bird as "a wire-armatured puppet, suspended on a fairly sophisticated stop-frame wire rig from which all the necessary scenes were accomplished."

Ugly Bird, "the projected soul-essence" of the film's villain (Alfred Ryder), is first seen as a silhouette in an attractive long shot, flying out of the sun. The animation of the wings on this smaller model is extremely fluid. Several closer shots of a larger, more detailed model, as it swoops down on Hedge Capers, show it to be an evil-looking, scrawny creature with a savage beak, claws and a green, scaly body.

In a deft moment of suggested interaction, it swoops low over the cowering actor, the force of its wings seeming to dislodge some gravel as it passes, its shadow falling on the ground below (probably achieved by having a piece of card, carefully cut to match the contours of the hill, behind the rear-projection screen).

Ugly Bird appears again later, once more flying out of the sun towards the camera in long shot. The larger model is used again as the creature swoops down directly at the camera, which retreats as the beast gets nearer — a dramatic move but one which highlights the graininess of the live-action plate.

The bird is next seen on the ground, with actors standing behind it, a shot probably achieved by aerially bracing the model in front of the background plate rather than using a static matte. Capers takes a swing at the beast with his guitar and a slow motion replay reveals that the

actor is in fact holding only the neck of a guitar and Warren has painted a dark shape onto glass in front of the model to suggest the contact. In slow-motion it looks clumsy (especially the sight of Capers subsequently holding onto the guitar neck) but at normal speed is effective and the interaction works.

Ugly Bird is then seen decomposing in a gruesome manner that predates the similar stop-motion effects of *The Hunger* and *The Evil Dead*. With the bird dead, his wizard master also decomposes in a bizarre shot employing a floor inlay in which a large area of miniature grass is matted into the background. The puppet of the actor is seen in long shot, slowly shriveling and shrinking as the live actors look on from either side. It's an original and effective use of stop-motion.

The Legend of the Phoenix
see *Peacock King*

Leonard Part VI

1987. D: Paul Weiland. Prod-Story: Bill Cosby. Special Visual Effects: Boss Films. Stop-Motion Animation: Pete Kleinow.

Cast: Bill Cosby, Tom Courtenay, Joe Don Baker, Moses Gunn, Pat Colbert, Gloria Foster.

Rating: ☆½   Stop-Motion: ☆☆

This weak comedy devised by Bill Cosby has government secret agents being bumped off by crazed animals. Ex-agent Cosby comes out of retirement to avenge his slain colleagues and eventually defeats the villain who has masterminded the whole affair.

In one sequence, Cosby rides on the back of an ostrich and the script called for the pair to leap off the top of a building. There was no way that a live ostrich could be persuaded to perform such a feat, so a special visual effect was called for. Working for Boss Films, Peter Kleinow executed this one shot as a stop-motion effect.

Lost Continent

1951. Lippert. D: Samuel Newfield. Scr: Richard Landau. Story: Carroll Young. Mus: Paul Dunlap. Ph: Jack Greenhalgh. Art: F. Paul Sylos. Special Effects: Augie Lohman. Opticals: Ray Mercer.

Cast: Cesar Romero, Hillary Brooke, Chick Chandler, John Hoyt, Acquanetta, Sid Melton, Whit Bissell.

Rating: ☆☆   Stop-Motion: ☆☆½

Considering the huge commercial success of RKO's *King Kong*, it is amazing that no other studio or independent producer attempted a similar kind of film until Robert Lippert made *Lost Continent* in 1951. Lippert's film is every inch a low-budget treatment of *The Lost World*. Its first 40 minutes, before the cast reach a dinosaur-infested mountain on a South Pacific island, is forgettable padding. A ponderous 20-minute middle section has the cast endlessly clambering over rocks. But the final half-hour, tinted an eerie green to suggest the dense jungle milieu, is an entertaining bid to recreate on a lesser scale the kind of thrills so spectacularly achieved by Willis O'Brien.

Lippert had scored a big success the year before with *Rocketship X-M*, cleverly beating *Destination Moon* to the box office. Director Samuel Newfield was a prolific B-picture man whose earlier credits include unremarkable horror films like *The Mad Monster* (1942) and *The Monster Maker* (1944). His direction of *Lost Continent* can most flatteringly be described as workmanlike. Cesar Romero is solid in the lead role. John Hoyt and Whit Bissell are two of the scientists along for the ride. Acquanetta makes a very brief appearance as a native girl.

Special effects are credited to Augie Lohman, although it is unclear whether he did the actual animation. Optical effects were handled by Ray Mercer, who many years later would supply some of the effects for *Flesh Gordon*. Design of the stop-motion sequences is clearly inspired by *The Lost World* and *King Kong*. Several of the set-ups, with puppets animated in miniature jungle sets, are unimaginative long shots with a design identical to the way that O'Brien had filmed his puppets 26 years earlier. Some individual shots are directly lifted out of *King Kong*: A brontosaurus chases a man up a tree and a triceratops charges directly at the camera, borrowing its choreography from the stegosaurus scene in O'Brien's film. The dense miniature jungles are a brave try at mimicking

A clumsy publicity paste-up of the triceratops from *Lost Continent* (1951). (National Film Archive, London.)

Skull Island on a low budget. There are no shots using glass paintings.

There are exactly 50 stop-motion cuts, a lot of animation for such a low-budget film. The animation is smooth enough — in fact, smoother than some of the animation in *King Kong* — but it lacks the presence which O'Brien would have given it. The models are satisfactory and certainly look a lot better in the film than they do in publicity paste-up stills where they appear fake and rubbery. But their eyes are lifeless and the two triceratops sport improbable collar

frills. Still, Roy Kinnard's comments (in *Beasts and Behemoths*) are quite unfair: "[T]he monsters ... are crudely, hastily animated, with the design of the models imparting unwanted cute, Disney-like qualities to the figures."

No ambitious composites are attempted. Several shots place the actors in the foreground by having them stand in front of full-size rear screens onto which is projected previously shot animation footage.

There are several effective moments during the stop-motion scenes — most notably the attack by the brontosaurus — but in general they lack pace and purpose. For example, when a pterodactyl flies overhead and gets shot, there is never any attempt to make anything dramatic out of the moment.

Our first sight of a dinosaur is a major disappointment. Not only is it a live lizard but (since this is not a composite shot) there is nothing in the frame to suggest the size of the animal. Consequently, it looks like the small lizard it is.

An encounter with a brontosaurus is much better, staged with thought given to rear-projection designs and generating some excitement. It contains 16 animation cuts, two of which are composites with the actors standing in front of a rear screen. In two extreme long shots, the dinosaur walks into an extensive miniature jungle set, enhanced by a painted backdrop. In closer shots it is seen munching on some trees. The miniature set extends back a long way and looks particularly effective in a composite in which the faroff dinosaur growls and turns towards the foreground actors, who flee as it starts to charge towards them. A low-angle medium shot looks up at the growling dinosaur as it advances.

One of the actors climbs a tree on the studio set as the dinosaur advances in a full-scale rear-projection. Another striking rear-screen shot is a high-angle perspective looking down from above the tree at the approaching brontosaur. In a series of seven cuts, all using the same perspective of a miniature set, the brontosaur, in medium shot, growls at the tree, butts it with his head, sends it crashing to the ground, recoils from some gunfire (with animated blood ooz-

ing from its head wound) and finally walks off. It's a shame that these last cuts could not have been enlivened by some more rear-screen shots.

Twenty stop-motion cuts depict an encounter with two triceratops. It's another enjoyable sequence and two rear-screen composites are present, but on the whole this is an undynamic series of events with little attempt at interaction. It also lacks O'Brien's vision and sense of excitement.

A triceratops is discovered feeding on some vegetation in another dense miniature jungle set, again with a painted backdrop of trees and mountains. It charges at the men, who are standing in the foreground in front of a rear screen. It is distracted by a second triceratops, seen feeding in another jungle set. In long shot, the two creatures lock horns, lifting each other's forelegs off the ground. They continue to battle in another rear-screen shot. The perspective of the miniature set is varied slightly as one of the dinosaurs bites the mouth of the other, animated blood pouring from its wound. The first creature spears the second one's chest with its horn, lifting it screaming off the ground, more blood oozing from the second wound. Lohman has tried to make this a realistic and gruesome battle but again it lacks the dramatic presence that O'Brien and Delgado could have created.

In three cuts (including two rear-screen shots), a pterodactyl flies over the heads of the group and lands on a distant rock in another miniature set. It folds its wings when it lands, only to get shot by one of the men and falls behind the rock. There are no close shots of the model. It looks acceptable in long shot but probably wouldn't have withstood closer scrutiny.

At the climax, the explorers come across the rocket they have been searching for, but are prevented from approaching it by several dinosaurs. Dramatically half-baked, this scene has five stop-motion cuts of the brontosaurus and two triceratops standing around aimlessly near the rocket in another miniature set. When the men fire their rifles, the creatures walk off.

More exciting is the scene (containing six animation cuts) where Sid Melton is gored to death by one of the triceratops. Hiding behind a fallen tree in the foreground, Melton fails to spot the dinosaur approaching him in the rear screen. The dinosaur runs at him and the physical contact is disappointingly implied by having it all take place out of sight behind the tree. In a final non-composite shot, the triceratops is seen chewing on the remains of its victim, then walks off when it is fired on, blood again oozing from its bullet wounds.

Although an interesting independent attempt to create stop-motion effects, *Lost Continent* ultimately only serves to emphasize the genius of O'Brien.

Lost in Time

1991. Electric. D-Scr: Anthony Hickox. Ph: Gerry Lively. Art: Steve Hardie. Mus: Steve Schiff. Special Makeup and Effects: Bob Keen (Image Animation).

Cast: Zach Galligan, Monika Schnarre, Martin Kemp, Bruce Campbell, John Ireland, David Carradine, Patrick Macnee.

Rating: ☆☆   Stop-Motion: ☆☆

Director Anthony Hickox repeats the lack of flair for comedy that he demonstrated in *Waxwork* (1988), to which this film is a sequel, and *Sundown* (1990). Zach Galligan and Monika Schnarre travel through time and have a series of encounters that are presumably intended as hilarious and affectionate homages to old horror films. Recreations include *Frankenstein*, *The Haunting*, *Nosferatu* and *Dr. Jekyll and Mr. Hyde*.

The overall impression is of a muddled film with good intentions but short on talent. Cameos by several likable actors and the makeup and other effects by Bob Keen help keep the film moving at a watchable pace.

Taking a page out of *The Evil Dead*, the Frankenstein monster pops out a victim's eyes, then squeezes his head so that his brain flies across the room into Galligan's hands. In the basement of a haunted house, Bruce Campbell has been crucified and all the flesh picked from his chest, revealing all his ribs. These and other splatter effects are fun, but Hickox presents them in much too flat a style.

Stop-motion is used in one brief sequence. Falling through the time tunnel, Galligan and Schnarre are attacked by a screeching harpy-creature. Shot against a black background, this memorable little creature is seen in five cuts. Its wings flap up and down slowly, avoiding strobing. One shot, in which it harasses Galligan, appears to be a rear-projection set-up. In another, it carries off Schnarre, the actress kicking and struggling below and just in front of the puppet. Just

how this was achieved is not clear. Could a full-scale mock-up have been used?

Like so many other stop-motion "scenes" since the 1980s, the moment is over before it has barely begun, making one question whether it was worth including at all. An almost identical sequence appeared in *House* (1986).

Lost on Adventure Island
see *King Dong*

The Lost World

1925. First National. D: Harry O. Hoyt. Additional D: William Dowling. Scr: Marion Fairfax. Based on the Novel by Sir Arthur Conan Doyle. Ph: Arthur Edeson. Art: Milton Menasco. Research and Technical Director: Willis H. O'Brien. Chief Technician: Fred W. Jackman. Technical Staff: Marcel Delgado, Homer Scott, J. Devereaux Jennings, Vernon L. Walker. Art Technician: Ralph Hammeras.

Cast: Bessie Love, Lloyd Hughes, Lewis Stone, Wallace Beery, Arthur Hoyt, Bull Montana.

Rating: ☆☆☆   Stop-Motion: ☆☆☆½

Today the dramatic weaknesses of this 1925 adaption of Arthur Conan Doyle's novel are all too obvious, but it was a milestone in the development of stop-motion photography. It was the first feature-length film to use the

process significantly and, above all, it demonstrated the potential of combining animation models with live-action drama to create a fantasy world that previously had only existed in audiences' imaginations.

For the first time, extinct dinosaurs were seen actually in the same shot as live actors, a breathtaking illusion appreciated by contemporary audiences who made the film the most successful production of 1925. We should try to imagine the impact the film must have had at the time. Most contemporary reviewers were clearly amazed by the spectacle of living, breathing dinosaurs. *The New York Times* declared, "Some of the scenes are as awesome as anything that has ever been shown." To get a feel for the film's effect on 1925 audiences, who better to quote than fantasy film historian Forry Ackerman, who saw the film on its original release? "I went, I saw and I was conquered by Sir Arthur Conan Doyle's dinosaurs. ... From the time the Missing Link appeared ... I held my breath. When they threw the flaming brand into the mouth of the angry Allosaurus, I was on the edge of my seat. I was thrilled by the Triceratops, staggered by the Stegosaurus. I had never imagined a bird could be as big as a Pterodactyl" (*Famous Monsters* #19).

Willis O'Brien's ambitious animation sequences, crude by today's standards, do contain a few moments that still take the breath away after more than 70 years and are as good as anything ever attempted in the stop-motion genre. His paintings of cliff faces and miniature jungles extending far into the distance look magnificent and are full of minor details of foliage and sparkling rivers. It was a distinctive visual style that he would perfect for *King Kong* eight years later.

A complete print of the film no longer survives. Walt Lee (in his *Reference Guide to Fantastic Films*) lists the length as 9700 feet, comprising ten reels. It is difficult to deduce exactly the running time of silent films from their length in feet because projection speeds varied greatly during the period, but *The Lost World* was a long picture for its day. Roy Kinnard (in *Beasts and Behemoths*) refers to a running time of 108 minutes. Goldner and Turner (in *The Making of King Kong*) say it was "about two hours." The current critique is based on a print that runs 70 minutes and is shorn of all the love interest in the opening live-action sequences, a subplot involving a half-caste girl and also several moments of animation. But at least this is ten minutes longer than the most commonly available print which is mentioned by Kinnard. Maltin's *TV Movies* also lists the running time as sixty minutes. The original film also contained red-tinted sequences during the volcanic explosion at the climax; tinted prints do still exist but this critique is based on the black-and-white version.

Existing prints of the nonrestored version have been taken from an abridged 16mm version created in 1930 by Kodascope for use in schools. A shot during the climax, in which the rampaging brontosaurus pokes its head through the window of a London club and destroys the building, was removed because it was considered too shocking for school audiences. But have other effects shots been removed? The film's trailer, held in the UCLA Film and Television Archive, was found to contain two animation shots that do not appear elsewhere. A recently examined roll of film held by the Library of Congress contains a clutch of previously unseen animation shots. Many of these are test shots but one or two are of such a quality that one wonders if they were part of the original release print. A closer look at these shots is given at the end of this chapter.

Adding further confusion are the various published stills from the film. The great majority are shots that never actually occur but were posed merely for the still. Among these are a shot of two allosaurs in battle with two triceratops; an allosaur attacking an anatosaur while two brontosaurs look on; two anatosaurs standing together in miniature foliage; and a triceratops confronting an agathaumus. Most special effects film rely on specially posed press stills to some extent but *The Lost World* is guilty of more "artistic license" than most.

The evolution of the film began in 1919 when producer Watterson R. Rothacker was so impressed with *The Ghost of Slumber Mountain* that he contacted O'Brien with a view to making a series of short films. Three or four of these were made but today they seem to be well and truly lost; not even their titles are known. Both men saw the potential for a longer, more ambitious project. They secured the rights to Conan Doyle's novel and struck a deal to co-produce the film with First National Pictures. Head of special effects there was Fred W. Jackman, a highly experienced technician who contributed much to the success of the matte work in the film. Ralph Hammeras, who had recently developed and patented the glass shot, was brought in to assist. Among his responsibilities was the construction of the elaborate miniature jungle sets in which O'Brien's dinosaurs would be filmed, including one massive set that measured 70 feet by 150 feet, used for long shots during the stampede at the climax.

O'Brien realized that his dinosaurs had to look more convincing than anything he had done before and enlisted the aid of a young Mexican artist, Marcel Delgado, to construct the models from his designs. Delgado proved to be enormously talented and worked with O'Brien again on *King Kong* and *The Son of Kong*. Over articulated steel skeletons he fashioned sponge rubber muscles which he covered in a skin of latex or rubber sheeting. External features such as horns, armor plates and warts were made separately, then attached to the model. For some models, a bladder was positioned inside the torso; it could be inflated and deflated frame-by-frame to create the illusion that the animal was breathing. Delgado fashioned about 50 of these models, averaging 18 inches in length, the amount of detail on them varying according to the prominence of their role in the film.

After two years of working behind locked doors, O'Brien and his team came up with a brief test reel which was shown by Conan Doyle in 1922 to the Society of American Magicians after a performance by Harry Houdini. In the reel, two tyrannosaurs attack a group of herbivorous dinosaurs, then each other. The victor is set upon by a triceratops, then flees and unsuccessfully attacks a stegosaurus. Conan Doyle, relishing the opportunity to astonish his audience, refused to answer any questions as to whether what he had shown was reality or trickery. The bewildered *New York Times* wrote, "If fakes, they were masterpieces." Like so much of O'Brien's early work, this footage is now lost.

Principal photography on *The Lost World* began in 1923 and a quality cast was assembled: Wallace Beery (as Professor Challenger), Bessie Love and Lewis Stone. But Harry Hoyt was a poor choice as director: He shows no concept of pace or excitement, presenting each scene in a flat, uncinematic way. Many of the animation scenes are spoiled by his stilted cut-aways to Love attempting to look terrified. On this level, the film compares unfavorably to other contemporary fantasies such as *The Thief of Bagdad* (1924) or *The Phantom of the Opera* (1925).

The conventional camerawork of the live-action scenes is by the otherwise-talented Arthur Edeson, who had already shot *The Thief of Bagdad* and would go on to shoot some of Universal's stylish horror films of the early 1930s. The camerawork in O'Brien's scenes is an advance on his previous short films: He uses closeups of his models to enhance the impact of a sequence, intercutting with medium shots, long shots and even, in a couple of unforgettable set-ups, extreme long shots. Also, he gives thought to the lighting, having some of the action occurring at night to create the chiaroscuro effects of which he was so fond.

In the print described here, there are 25 minutes of live action before Challenger's party arrives at the foot of the plateau. From then on, the animation is almost continuous apart from brief live-action passages required to propel the plot. This technique of having a long live-action build-up followed by a sudden jump into spectacular, unbroken fantasy sequences was employed again, but with greater dramatic impact, in *King Kong*.

The first process shot in *The Lost World* is a very picturesque panorama of a river winding its way to the foot of the plateau and (next to it) the pillar of rock which allows the party a means of getting onto the plateau. A mixture of miniature set and glass shot, this is one of several different perspectives of the plateau; the next shot is a closer look using a more detailed miniature of the plateau and pillar.

The sighting from below the plateau of the pteranodon is a restrained foretaste of the encounters that are to follow. In the first of three animation cuts, it glides through the air in long shot above the plateau, swoops toward the camera, then slowly back again. The animation of its wings making graceful flapping motions is very smooth. Several seconds of this cut were probably not animated as the model, supported by wires, glides with all parts of its body rigid. However, the position of the model jumps suddenly three times during this cut; presumably O'Brien accidentally knocked the wires out of position.

The pteranodon lands on the pillar and a larger model is used when it is shown in more closeup, framed by a dark matte suggesting Challenger's binoculars. As if wary of predators, it twists its crested head from side to side, then bites a piece out of the large boar it has in its claws A deft touch typical of O'Brien's attention to detail has the mouth of the boar vainly gulping for air. The pteranodon swallows the mouthful, then there is a final long shot of it gliding off to the left above the plateau, with only minimal wing movement.

In a third long-shot view of the plateau and pillar (another painting), Challenger is seen at the top of the pillar chopping at the one tree there. In some of these shots, O'Brien has skillfully inserted live-action footage of the tiny figure into his miniature panorama. In similar shots filmed from an even greater distance, it may be that O'Brien used tiny animated figures of Challenger and the rest of the cast. In another extreme long shot of the same scene (i.e., yet another glass-shot/miniature), the tree falls across the ravine that separates pillar and plateau.

The Lost World (1925): A publicity paste-up showing Professor Challenger (Wallace Beery) and a brontosaurus.

A brontosaurus, startled by the falling tree, snakes its long neck backwards, then chomps on some vegetation. In the lower third of the frame, a river flows past, the far bank forming the line of the matte. In another extreme long shot, the actors walk along the tree trunk bridging the ravine. Once again, they are so tiny that it is hard to tell if they are live actors in all the shots or if in the more extreme long shots they are puppets. Certainly the foliage blowing in the lower foreground is live action, adding to the depth and credibility of the shot.

After a shot of the brontosaurus walking slowly off to the left, the film gives us our first sight of live actors and animation model in one shot. In four cuts of the brontosaurus feeding, a small area in the bottom right corner of the frame has been matted out, allowing film of the actors to be inserted. Today it looks clumsy, the actors merely looking on as the dinosaur feeds and uproots a tree, intercut with shots of Love

429

The triceratops family of *The Lost World.*

looking scared, but 1925 audiences were staggered. This episode ends with another extreme long shot of the plateau, in which a tiny model of the brontosaurus nudges the fallen tree off the ravine, then walks away. Continuity between the long shots and the closer shots is lacking: It is left to our imaginations to interpret they are the same location.

O'Brien's love of the prehistoric milieu really takes off now in an impressive sequence of four encounters involving an allosaurus. An anatosaurus — a herbivorous biped — is feeding in a minia-ture set as the allosaurus walks in from the left. In a medium shot, the allosaurus growls, its rising and falling chest adding the extra touch of realism. The anatosaurus snaps back and the two animals circle each other tentatively before tearing into each other.

The animation is hurried and jerky and some have conjectured that it was executed not by O'Brien but by one the assistant animators who were revealed in footage found in the Library of Congress. There is a deft touch when the two beasts suddenly stop fighting and regard each other with frozen animal stares. The allosaurus bites the anatosaurus in the neck and it rolls down an embankment into a muddy lake. The water was actually a glycerin which held its position as O'Brien adjusted the position of his model between exposures. A final gruesome shot has the allosaurus chewing on a bit of flesh that it has ripped from its prey.

The next episode is more smoothly animated and contains many imaginative touches of animal characterization. The elaborate jungle set in which the triceratops is seen chomping on some leaves, uses miniature vegetation (some real, some cut from tin) and glass shots to create a realistic sense of depth, but again is something that O'Brien improved enormously when he designed the jungles of *Kong*.

A baby triceratops emerges from behind its mother and walks around to the front. The mother looks up apprehensively and gets the scent of the allosaurus, which is seen still feeding on its last victim. The mother triceratops nudges the baby with its head, sending it scurrying off to the right. After a cut of the allosaurus growling, the mother and baby walk into another jungle set where there are already two adult triceratops. The allosaurus lets out another growl and strides into the first jungle set. Clouds scud past in the background, presumably a realistic painting (or photo blow-up) moved across the set one frame at a time.

The two other adult triceratops walk off to the right and the baby hides in a dip in the foreground. The allosaurus swishes its tail apprehensively, then walks into the second jungle set,

immediately getting impaled on the triceratops' horn, which lifts it half off the ground. It looks down at its wound for several seconds as though trying to understand what has happened (a realistic bit of animal behavior), then decides on flight, walking away from the camera as the triceratops starts to make another lunge for it. The baby re-emerges, goes up to its mother and wags it tail as she licks its face.

The persistent allosaurus next attacks Challenger's party in a brief but unforgettably eerie nighttime sequence containing five animation cuts. Two glaring eyes stare out of the impenetrable dark of the jungle, then the allosaurus (in long shot) advances on the actors who are standing in the lower right corner of the frame (a split-screen almost identical to the earlier one with the brontosaurus). The dinosaur pushes trees aside in a way that is a clear precursor of Kong's entrance eight years later. The jungle back drop is enhanced by what looks like a glass painting of a tree above the actors, and actual grass planted in the miniature set by Hammeras.

In one closeup, the beast's lively tongue (and the saliva dripping between its jaws) make its intentions plain. In another closeup, after one of the actors has fired a rifle at it, animated blood oozes realistically from the wound on its snout. A burning torch is thrown and there is a closeup of the beast with the torch gripped in its mouth, swaying its head from side to side. It is impossible to animate flame, but it does not look like a superimposed element, nor is it a cutout, because the shape of the flames changes from frame to frame; just how

O'Brien achieved this shot is a mystery. In an attractive final long shot, the allosaur twists its head and throws the torch away (this time the flames *are* a cut-out), and runs off through the dense miniature jungle, first to the right, then zigzagging to the left, looking back with a farewell growl.

From here the film cuts straight to the allosaur's battle with an agathaumus, an ornately scaly, three-horned, frilled quadruped that Delgado based on a largely hypothetical museum painting. This short battle lasts 30 seconds and although the animation is smooth and dynamic, it is let down by the camerawork: All the action occurs in one long static cut, a shot of a miniature set with a flowing river and swaying foliage matted into the lower half. The allosaur slowly circles the agathaumus, then leaps onto its back, its tail swishing as the two animals continue to circle. The allosaur gets thrown off and then is impaled on the agathaumus' horn. It collapses, throws up its head in pain and then dies.

After a brief live-action interlude featuring Bull Montana's ape-like Missing Link, the agathaumus is seen again. This set-piece unimaginatively reuses the miniature set of the previous animation scene and the camerawork is again static, but the choreography of the animation is superb.

The agathaumus is feeding when a tyrannosaurus strides in from the right. In long shot the model looks impressive but it never gets the benefit of a closeup and must have been on a day's leave when all the press stills were taken because, strangely, no photos of it appear to have been published. It jumps onto the back of the agathaumus and bites into its neck behind the protective frill. The agathaumus goes down, gets up again. The tyrannosaur releases its grip, then bites into the same wound twice more, tearing a mouthful of flesh out of the still-struggling herbivore. Legs kicking desperately, the agathaumus eventually expires as the voracious tyrannosaur leaps onto its back again and tears another chunk out of its side. No one can say that O'Brien avoided the harsher side of animal behavior. Nor does the scene end there: O'Brien throws in another bit of magic, over in a few seconds, by having the tyrannosaur turn away from its prey and snatch a pteranodon from the sky, killing it swiftly in its jaws.

The pace slows down a bit after this extravaganza of carnivorous activity. Wallace Beery constructs a giant catapult to repel dinosaurs, a missing explorer's remains are found in a cave and Bessie Love decides to get married, but it's all pretty dull. Amongst all this live action is a low-key animation cut of another anatosaurus munching on some trees and a fine painting of the cliff face containing the tunnel opening that provides the means of escape.

A brontosaurus munches on some foliage in another miniature set. It strides slowly across the set from right to left while in the lower half of the shot, separated by a horizontal matte line which today looks painfully obvious, Challenger and one of his party look on ("A lovely specimen! We'll stalk it and observe its habits!"). This is the beginning of another impressive battle, this time set on a miniature clifftop and backed by a dramatic photo blow-up of a river winding its way between two ranges of distant mountains. In this scene, O'Brien is more aware of the importance of cutting to different perspectives of the action to heighten the drama.

After a matte shot of Challenger looking at the beast feeding, there is an extremely smoothly animated closeup of it plucking some leaves off a tree and dribbling at the mouth. The only disappointment here is that Delgado's model isn't lifelike enough to withstand a closeup. An allosaur walks in from the right and the two monsters stare each other out. A closeup of the allosaur growling makes good use of strands of saliva, but a closeup of the brontosaur, raising one of its lips into a snarl and revealing a row of teeth, is too exaggerated. The brontosaur lunges at its attacker only to get its long neck gripped in the allosaur's jaws. A long struggle follows.

A picturesque long shot from the foot of the miniature cliff includes two tiny animated models of the dinosaurs fighting at the top. Back in the main setup, the brontosaur takes a step backwards and finds itself half off the edge of the cliff. A shot of the miniature cliff has rocks and earth, dislodged by the battle, falling into the river below. The brontosaur goes over the edge, and as it does, O'Brien slips in another of his little touches of animal behavior: The hungry allosaur makes a grab for its prey even as it is disappearing over the edge, snapping its jaws in an instinctive last attempt to grab a meal.

There is a live-action shot of the small brontosaur model falling from the cliff top with a lot of earth and rocks. There is the inevitable problem with the scaling of water droplets when the model lands in the river. Back at the top, there is a lengthy cut of the allosaur looking perplexed, trying to figure out what happened to its intended dinner. The allosaur walks off, but its gait is very awkward, reminding us that armature design and animation choreography still had a long way to go in 1925. The episode closes with a composite shot of the brontosaur lying trapped in mud, the bank of the river providing a convenient matte line with the actors looking down at the model from the top of the frame and Challenger hatching plans to take the dinosaur back to London. This shot isn't animated, but the model is made to look alive by virtue of the internal bladder which makes it look like it is breathing.

O'Brien and Rothacker could have chosen the easy option and switched the action to London at this point, but they were determined to give the public the most spectacular film they knew how. The volcanic eruption and resultant chaos that climaxes the plateau sequence of the film remain stunning today and became genre clichés. The scenes of stampeding dinosaurs contain some of the most complex animation ever seen in a feature film, so complex, in fact, that O'Brien required assistant animators. (He is said to be solely responsible for the animation in all the other scenes, although this may not be so.) A brisk pace, a variety of miniature set-ups, several composites, an astonishing number of models, skillfully superimposed smoke and effective use of stock footage of flowing lava and forest fires combine to make this a climax to treasure.

The miniature of the smoking, flaming volcano is a convincing model, seen through foreground glass paintings of jungle vegetation. The first animated shots of the sequence use a composite of a miniature jungle set in the top two-thirds of the frame with Challenger looking on in the bottom portion. A stegosaurus walks onto the set in the middle distance, wandering about confusedly as five triceratops run across the foreground from right to left. Achieving realism when animating a running animal is notoriously difficult: O'Brien wisely conceals the legs of his triceratops behind miniature foliage. With Challenger still looking on, a brontosaurus stomps hurriedly in the same direction as the herd of triceratops. Superimposed smoke helps to mesh the two elements in this series of shots.

One of the film's best-remembered images follows, a simple yet beautiful long shot of a brachiosaurus (clearly differentiated from the brontosaur models by its steep chest) crossing a plain with a ravenous allosaur on its back the whole time. After lots of neck- and tail-swishing, the brachiosaur grips its attacker in its teeth and manages to throw it off. The allosaur, oblivious to the fact that it should be fleeing from the volcano, immediately tries to jump back onto the brachiosaur again. It's the kind of sequence that reminds us why stop-motion is such a special medium for producing elaborate, dynamic action.

In another long shot of this huge miniature table-top, the herd of five triceratops gallop across the picture. This time O'Brien's beasts are in full view and the animation of their running cycle is surprisingly well done. Super-imposed smoke really looks like it is a part of all these shots and not merely something that was added later. Equally complex is a closer shot of three bronto-

saurs milling around in a state of confusion. A small stegosaur wanders into the shot, gets pecked by one of the nervous sauropods and scurries off into the background.

Dawn the next day reveals one of the most fantastic sights ever seen on film. A darkened screen gets slowly brighter. Little by little we can make out the details of a fantastic panorama, alive with bestial activity. Distant mountains and clouds form a backdrop to Hammeras' expansive miniature set, enhanced by the presence of a river running through it and smoking geysers (presumably these are matted in, but it is hard to see where the split is). On the left side of the shot are two brontosaurs, in the foreground a stegosaur and on the right a group of five feeding allosaurs. It is impossible to take in all this activity on a single viewing.

O'Brien then cuts to a closer shot of the allosaurs tearing into the remains of their prey, a brontosaur standing in the background. His animation of the various heads looking around and raising and lowering as they feed is satisfyingly smooth. With such complex shots as these, it is not surprising that O'Brien took 14 months to complete all the animation. A good day's work on a straight-forward scene would produce only about 20 seconds of screen time, so one can imagine the input required to produce these two set-ups.

Challenger and his group escape from the plateau by climbing down a cliff face, seen in long shot in a beautifully detailed painting with a tiny, non-articulated human puppet clinging to a rope halfway down. Another of several germs of ideas that flowered in *King*

Allosaurus and brontosaurus in battle: a posed shot that did not actually appear in *The Lost World.*

Kong occurs when the Missing Link character starts pulling up the rope as one of the actors is climbing down it; Kong did exactly that when Fay Wray and Bruce Cabot were escaping from his mountain lair.

A series of seven animation cuts show the striking sight of the brontosaur trapped in mud at the foot of the cliff. The group discusses getting the monster back to London and good old Zambo (a white actor absurdly covered in black face paint) mutters warily, "Ah certainly hopes dat mud holds!" Four of the cuts

are done entirely in miniature, the dinosaur up to its middle in mud, lifting its long neck up with great difficulty and hopelessly trying to shift one of its rear legs. In the other three cuts, the model is in the lower half of the frame with a matte of the group of actors in the top half, the split conveniently (and by today's standards rather too obviously) following the brow of the pit. The long neck snakes about, a bladder gives the illusion of the animal breathing and the glycerin that stands in for the mud holds its position perfectly between frames,

435

creating an extremely fluid impression that it is responding to the brontosaur's movements.

The nighttime finale in London only lasts six minutes yet seems longer because O'Brien has put so much into it. The image of a monster rampaging in a city became a cinema cliché that O'Brien himself used again (to much greater effect) in *King Kong*. And near the end of his career, in *Behemoth the Sea Monster* (1959), he staged a very similar sequence when a dinosaur again causes havoc in London. In *The Lost World*, he combines crowds of fleeing extras, the destruction of buildings, elaborate miniature sets and cars, and also makes good use, for the first time in a stop-motion film, of the traveling matte process which had been patented in 1916. Dramatically the role of the brontosaurus is limited (it is reported escaped from its cage, causes havoc in some street scenes, then swims away down the river Thames) but O'Brien has included many good touches.

The composites in the first section are achieved by traveling matte. In a long shot looking down a crowded street, the brontosaurus appears from behind a building. The added flexibility of the traveling matte allows the model to walk down the street towards the panicking crowd. Superimposed London fog helps to blend the two elements. Goldner and Turner report that O'Brien is said to have used rear projection in only one shot in the film, and it may well be the next animation cut in which the brontosaur's head is seen snapping at some extras. (Like traveling matte, rear projection was a young process in 1925, the main hurdle in its development being the fact that the exposure of the camera and the timing of the projected frames in the rear plate had to be synchronized.) If this shot was in fact done with a split screen (quite likely, since model and actors are on opposite sides of the frame), then a later shot in which the model is seen in full and an extra runs behind it, would be the most likely candidate for the rear screen shot. A prop tail knocks over a group of people in another cut, then there is a closeup of the animated puppet snapping at the camera.

The brontosaur walks into a square in front of a large building and demolishes a miniature statue and a street lamp as it walks off to the right. An oft-published still of the model standing in front of a crowd of people gathered on the steps of a museum is a studio paste-up and does not appear in the film (despite an article in the May 1925 edition of Hugo Gernsback's *Science and Invention* which went to great lengths to explain this fictitious shot). A large prop foot is used to show a woman nearly being stomped on (premonitions of *King Kong* again).

A long shot shows the model rearing up on its hind legs in a miniature set. What appear to be two uncannily smoothly animated human puppets run past its feet. O'Brien's characteristic attention to small detail extends to having silhouettes of tiny people moving about in the lighted windows of the building. Another nice touch has a closeup of the brontosaur investigating a street lamp, recoiling when it gets its snout burned and then snapping angrily at it. In the original print, the brontosaur now pokes its head through a window of the building, but this print cuts to a long shot in which it rears up again as a miniature animated car drives past in the lower foreground. Then it crashes down into the building, demolishing it, surrounded by superimposed smoke. All of the collapsing masonry is animated.

The sequence on Tower Bridge uses a miniature of the bridge. In an extreme long shot, the dinosaur approaches the bridge from the right as animated model cars drive off to the left. Two closer shots show the brontosaur on the bridge, looking around and investigating a car. The creature is too heavy: There is a brief non-animated shot of the model rearing up and crashing down through the bridge into the river below. The cut is quick enough to prevent the stiffness of the model from looking awkward. The same applies to the two closing live-action shots of the beast swimming down the river. There is a satisfying poignancy about the unresolved escape of the brontosaur: *The Lost World* set many standards for monster-on-the-loose films, but the cliché of the arrival of the military wasn't one of them.

The film from the Library of Congress contains about 15 stop-motion cuts. Included among them are three frames where two assistant animators accidentally got caught on film. One of these is unidentified but the other appears to be J. L. Roop, who did animation for a short pastiche called *The Lost Whirl* in 1928.

Some closeups of the brontosaurus are very smoothly animated, and more credible than some of the closeups that appear in the film, where the animal's upper lip curls into an unlikely snarl. There are other takes of the scene in which the baby triceratops hides in a dip in the ground beneath its mother. Another triceratops is seen at the foot of a cliff in a miniature set that does not appear in the surviving print. An allosaurus hovers in the background of this cut.

In another shot, the monoclonius and a stegosaurus munch on some vegetation, a cut which allows a close look at the marvelous detail on Delgado's stegosaurus puppet, which is never featured prominently in the surviving print. Another shot is a classic bit of O'Brien magic, with the allosaurus scratching its ear at the cliff top, a bit of animal behavior which he had used before and would use again. In another cut, an anatosaur feeds on some vegetation while an allosaurus walks past in the extreme background. A medium shot of an anatosaur feeding is crudely animated and may well not be O'Brien's work.

Best of all is an extreme long-shot panorama which has two browsing brontosaurs in the foreground, a lake in the middle distance and a herd of browsing anatosaurs on the far side of the lake. As with some of the cuts in this reel, it is a mystery why such an attractive shot should have been left out of the release print.

Despite an enormous budget of allegedly $1 million, *The Lost World* was a great financial success and O'Brien and Hammeras began work on a follow-up film to be called *Atlantis*, set in an underwater kingdom and featuring giant sea beasts as well as prehistoric mammals in an ice age setting. However, three months of pre-production work amounted to nothing when a studio re-shuffle at First National put an end to the project. O'Brien then conceived the idea of filming Mary Shelley's *Franken-stein*, employing animation to show the model performing destructive feats that would have been impossible with a live actor. Despite initial interest by First National again, this project was also dropped. Hammeras moved over to Fox, where he was put in charge of the elaborate effects for the science fiction musical *Just Imagine* (1930). O'Brien assisted Hammeras for a while on this film, building some of the miniatures for a New York City of the future, but then felt the lure of things prehistoric again, re-teaming with director Harry Hoyt with a view to making a film very much in the same vein as *The Lost World* and to be entitled *Creation*.

In 1998 a restored version of *The Lost World* was put together by George Eastman House in New York, consisting of some new scenes in the Czech Film Archive, shots contained in the original trailer that for some reason were omitted from existing prints, and shots contained in the Library of Congress reel. The running time of this version (as timed by this author at a screening at London's National Film Theater) is 98 minutes. New shots include a moment when the pteranodon drops the boar before flying off; a shot of four brontosaurs feeding in an expansive miniature set; two triceratops feeding in the same set; many more animation shots during the volcano sequence; the legendary missing shot of the brontosaurus in London poking its head through a second-story window (which turns out to be rather a tame effect after all); and a closing shot of the brontosaurus swimming out to sea as a ship sails past in the other direction. Despite the fact that even this version does not represent a complete print, all admirers of O'Brien's work can rejoice that the film restorers have gone to such pains to repair a film that was long overdue for a reappraisal.

Lunatics—A Love Story

1991. Renaissance. D-Scr: Josh Becker. Ph: Jeffrey Dougherty. Art: Peter Gurski. Mus: Joseph LoDuca. Visual Effects Supervisor: Gary Jones. Stop-Motion Animation: Dave Hettmer. Assistant Animators: Bob Kayganich, Richard Ruby.

Cast: Theodore Raimi, Deborah Foreman, Bruce Campbell, George Aguilar, Brian McCree, Eddy Roumaya.

Rating: ☆☆½   Stop-Motion: ☆☆½

This likable comedy-fantasy-chiller is a simple story about a gauche loner (Theodore Raimi—brother of *The Evil Dead*'s Sam) who is just out of a mental hospital. He meets Deborah Foreman but the course of true love never did run smooth, and before the happy ending he experiences all manner of horrifying hallucinations.

These include Bruce Campbell coming through his apartment walls dressed as a surgeon and brandishing an oversized hypodermic. Out in the street, Raimi imagines an earthquake and watches as the road rips apart and swallows a car. Accomplished low-budget effects like these are the work of Gary Jones.

In the opening scene, we learn that Raimi has not left his apartment for six months. The camera finds him cowering under his bed, clutching his head in fear. An extreme closeup of his eye is followed by a shot of the top of his brain — actually a seven-foot-wide prop. Part of the flesh bursts open and a spider — a stop-motion puppet — crawls out. On the other side of the brain, a second spider crawls out from another hole. A third spider, larger than the other two, suddenly appears in closeup, looking directly at the camera, then joins its fellows, scampering across the brain. A huge hand holding a scalpel enters the scene, the spiders run off and Raimi emerges from his hallucination.

This is a delightfully offbeat moment, featuring very smooth animation. The brain, the hand and the scalpel are all miniatures.

In a stand-out hallucination sequence, Raimi imagines himself pursued by a giant spider — in reality a dust cart. This evil-looking creature is an excellent model and is very credibly animated by Dave Hettmer (who also supplied stop-motion for *Frostbiter — Wrath of the Wendigo*) in 15 stop-motion cuts.

Its entrance is especially chilling. Raimi leans against a wall and a spindly but huge spider leg silently lowers on either side of him. This live-action shot is followed by an animation shot in which the car-sized arachnid walks down the side of the building and onto the street. Several closeups allow a good look at its multiple pairs of eyes, twitching mandibles and hairy body.

Raimi runs down the street pursued by the spider. In these shots, the composite work is basic but effective, mainly relying on shots of the actor in front of a process screen onto which is projected (either rear or front) the pre-shot animation footage of the spider striding after him. The background image looks a bit faded but these are still effective images. One shot is a highly effective "reality sandwich" matte set-up, with Raimi running from background to foreground with the spider running behind him.

Shot by Foreman, the spider expires in a striking long shot with Raimi in the foreground. Its legs crumple, it tries to get up, then finally collapses — all consummately animated by Hettmer.

Lunatics' arachnids are a memorable addition to a long tradition of stop-motion spiders in films including *King Kong, The Black Scorpion, Planet of Dinosaurs* and *Krull.*

Mac and Me

1989. Vision International. D: Stewart Raffill. Scr: Stewart Raffill, Steve Feke. Ph: Nick McLean. Art: W. Stewart Campbell. Mus: Alan Silvestri. Alien Effects: Mark J. Becker. Special Visual Effects: Apogee (John Dykstra, Bob Sheperd, John

Swallow); Illusion Arts (Sid Dutton, Bill Taylor); CFI Optical Dept.

Cast: Christine Ebersole, Jonathan Ward, Tina Caspary, Lauren Stanley, Jade Calegory, Vinnie Torrente.

Rating: ☆☆   Stop-Motion: ☆☆

Shamelessly imitative of *E.T.*, this children's film would be just about watchable if it wasn't for one scene that sinks to a new low on the nausea scale: staff and customers in a McDonald's restaurant break out into a miserable musical number, with the title alien (the acronym stands for Mysterious Alien Creature) dancing on the counter dressed in a teddy bear outfit.

Mac and his family are depicted mainly by means of mechanical puppets and long shots of extremely thin actors in costumes. However, three interesting shots appear to make use of a kind of replacement animation. In two of these, the aliens are seen on their home planet encountering a probe from Earth. The probe extends a vacuum intended to collect samples to take home and accidentally sucks up Mac and his family. In these cuts, the aliens are puppets standing on a miniature rocky floor matched to a background painting of an otherworldly landscape. In the third cut, Mac, now on Earth, is sucked up into a domestic vacuum cleaner, despite clinging onto a curtain. In each of these shots, the characters change shape, twisting and narrowing as they disappear gradually into the vacuum. Suggesting that the aliens are not made of flesh and bone as we know it, these are quick but clever effects.

The pre-credits sequence on the alien planet is well done, using fine matte paintings of the alien world, a model of the probe craft and an expansive painting of the Earth seen from space.

Magic Island

1995. Moonbeam Entertainment. D: Sam Irvin. Scr: Neil Ruttenberg, Brent V. Friedman. Ph: James Lawrence Spencer. Art: John Zachary. Mus: Richard Band. Creature Effects: Mark Rappaport. Visual Effects: AlchemyFX. Visual Effects Supervisor: Joseph Grossberg. Stop-Motion Animation: Joel Fletcher.

Cast: Zachary Ty Bryan, Andrew Divoff, Edward Kerr, Lee Armstrong, French Stewart, Jessie-Ann Friend.

Rating: ☆½   Stop-Motion: ☆☆½

This direct-to-video release from Charles Band's Moonbeam company — which specializes in films for young children — tells the story of a boy who finds himself magically transported into the pages of a book full of tales of pirates, mermaids and monsters. The intended audience may enjoy it but adults will find it heavy-going and unimaginative.

Towards the end of the film there is an encounter with a 30-foot-tall statue that comes to life. This 3½-minute set-piece is a delightful throwback to the glorious days of the 1950s and 1960s, filmed Harryhausen-style with rear projection and static mattes. The sequence was supervised by Joseph Grossberg and the 23 animation cuts were executed by Joel Fletcher. For the first time on a Charles Band film, David Allen was not involved — presumably only because he was busy working on another of Band's films.

In a forest, the film's motley group of treasure-seekers discover a doorway to a hidden chamber. Surrounding the doorway is the statue of a seated giant. When the door is opened, the statue comes to life. It pursues the people who have disturbed it, uproots a tree which it uses as a weapon and is eventually defeated when a fallen tree is rigged up so as to strike the giant in the face, dazing it and causing it to fall to the ground and shatter.

The first shots are done all-miniature without the addition of a live-action element. The statue's head rocks from side to side as it awakens and its eyes glow red. The glow is possibly a superimposed effect that was added later. A dramatic low-angle shot looks up at the statue as it slowly separates itself from the doorway, sits back, looks down imposingly at the out-of-frame actors and frees its hands. The animation in this shot, as in most others in the sequence, is extremely smooth. Another shot shows one leg being pulled away from the doorway.

In a striking long shot, the statue stands up and looks around. Animated debris falls from it very realistically and a cloud of superimposed dust is thrown up in front of it. On the left and right of the statue, the actors back away. The nature of the composition of this rear-projection static matte is revealed to

keen-eyed viewers by a small area of a floor inlay around the statue's feet, its color not matching exactly with the surrounding ground.

In long shot again, the statue leans back angrily, growls and then stomps after the group on the right. In case anyone had not yet realized that Grossberg and Fletcher are big Harryhausen fans, they now have their statue do an impression of the Cyclops in *7th Voyage of Sinbad*. It kneels down and uproots a miniature tree behind which the actors are hiding. Still growling, the statue snaps the tree over one of its legs and holds one half of it like a club. This is all interesting choreography but the shots are designed unimaginatively, with an open sandy area extending fully across the foreground.

In medium shot, the statue swings the tree-club. A nervous pirate steps into a clearing to confront the giant. The matte line in this static matte composite invisibly follows the horizontal contours of the ground. The statue stomps into the shot with stiff strides which, although deliberately stiff to reinforce the idea that the figure is made of stone, are on this occasion just a little too stiff and awkward. The giant swings the tree and the pirate is knocked over backwards, the physical contact between actor and miniature implied through careful positioning of the model.

An effective low-angle shot from the pirate's point of view looks up at the statue. It slaps the tree-club into the palm of its other hand a couple of times, as if eagerly anticipating giving its foe a sound thrashing. Another good shot, this time looking down over the statue's shoulder at the prostrate pirate, helps to vary the perspective and keep the pace moving briskly.

Again in a low-angle perspective, the giant raises the club above its head, then brings it down. The stump hits the ground and topples over, its roots crumpling on impact. This latter image has an identical counterpart in *7th Voyage*—and, as in Harryhausen's shot, the sight of tree roots apparently moving of their own accord is unnatural and unconvincing. The pirate runs out of the shot and the statue follows him, its huge legs crossing the frame.

The pirate runs into the doorway just as one of the giant's feet steps in front of it. This is a dramatic image, enhanced by clouds of superimposed dust and by some camera shake to suggest the impact of the statue's weight.

The giant kneels down and tries to reach into the doorway — another image lifted directly from *7th Voyage*. The young boy runs into the shot from the foreground and briefly passes in front of the statue's leg. This subtlety, only registered subliminally by most viewers, makes this an especially impressive composite. It was probably achieved with rotoscope matting around the outline of the boy.

To distract the statue, the boy throws a rock at it. This is an animated miniature, possibly supported on a wire. It hits the statue on the side of the head — a convincing bit of animation. The statue rubs its head, puzzled by the distraction.

The next shot is the best in the sequence. In long shot, the statue gets up and strides towards the foreground with forceful purpose. Roto-matting is employed again to allow part of the boy's image to pass in front of the model. The very fluid animation and the startling way that the giant's image increases in size as it nears the camera make this a very dynamic image.

In medium shot, the growling giant strides across the frame in pursuit of the intruders who have awakened it, heavy footsteps reverberating on the soundtrack. The boy has rigged up a log on top of a rock and stands on it, calling the statue over. In a long shot using a static matte, the statue stomps in from the right and brings its foot down on the log just as the boy jumps off it. The log, a miniature, flies up into the air and strikes the statue in the face. The final stop-motion shot, very smoothly animated, has the statue swaying about in a daze, backed by the cartoon sound of chirping birds to suggest its dizziness.

Like Talos in *Jason and the Argonauts*, the statue topples over and smashes into pieces. Unlike *Jason*, this is done live action with a model rigged up so as to shatter on impact.

Although full of good touches, the episode lacks the magic touch which Harryhausen was able to bring to his sequences. Grossberg and Fletcher are happy merely to replicate old images instead of seizing the moment to invent some new devices.

The Magic Toyshop

1986. GB. Granada. D: David Wheatley. Scr: Angela Carter. Mus: Bill Connor. Art: Stephen Fineren. Special Effects: Aardman Anderson Lyons, Kirby's Flying Circus, Talbot and Talismen.

Cast: Tom Bell, Caroline Milmoe, Kilian McKenna, Patricia Kerrigan, Lorcan Cranitch, Gareth Bushill.

Rating: ☆☆½   Stop-Motion: ☆½

This British production is a tale of the sexual awakening of a 15-year-old girl (Caroline Milmoe) and how, when she and a brother and sister are orphaned, they are sent to stay with a tyrannical uncle (Tom Bell). The uncle is a toymaker ("I don't like children playing with my toys") and in his spare time stages shows featuring full-sized string puppets.

The film has some deft observations about growing up and includes many haunting moments of fantasy when the children are daydreaming, such as when the boy imagines his bedroom is a crow's nest at the top of a ship's mast. But toward the end, the film degenerates into less interesting gimmickry, becoming just a second-rate horror film. The family rebels against the uncle, he is attacked by his own mannequins which come to life, and is thrown on a bonfire.

Most of the shots of the moving mannequins are done live-action with string puppets and are effective. Some stop-motion shots are added, presumably to spice up the action, but their artificiality conflicts with the live-action shots and adds little. The seven cuts include shots of a puppet sitting up, one turning its head, another pedaling on a unicycle, the hat of another spinning on its head and the head of a sheep puppet revolving. In another cut, a dummy's hand opens and closes.

An earlier shot in the film makes good use of replacement animation. Bell is demonstrating to his nephew the pleasures of carving wood. "Wood's got life in it — not like plastic," he says, and a stem with three oak leaves on it grows out of a lump of wood. The wood appears to be held in a dummy hand, filmed against a rear projection of Bell's workshop. In another sequence, a seagull flies into the children's bedroom and it looks as though stop-motion was used to animate the model. However, this may be film of a string puppet that has been skip-framed to give it a dreamlike quality.

The Man Who Could Work Miracles

1937. London Films. Prod: Alexander Korda. D: Lothar Mendes. Scr: H. G. Wells. Ph: Harold Rosson. Art: Vincent Korda. Special Effects: Ned Mann and (uncredited) Laurence Butler. Mus: Mischa Polianski.

Cast: Roland Young, Ralph Richardson, Joan Gardner, Ernest Thesiger, George

Zucco, George Sanders, Torin Thatcher, Edward Chapman.

Rating: ☆☆☆   Stop-Motion: ☆☆

This enjoyable piece of whimsy, scripted by H. G. Wells, tells the story of naive, unimaginative Roland Young, who is given the power to work miracles. At first, he has to discover the extent of his powers, performing minor tricks like clearing the freckles from Joan Hickson's face and accidentally sending the local policeman to Hell when he tells him to go to blazes. The second half is less engaging and less cinematic, as Wells allows his script to dwell on the philosophical implications of his theme. By the end, it has become too much of a treatise and much of the initial charm and drama are lost. But this part of the film is sparked by marvelous eccentric performances by whiskey-sodden Ralph Richardson and idealistic Ernest Thesiger. Also interesting is the extent to which 1930s censorship allowed Young to express the fact that the miracle he would most like to perform is the procurement of sex — he makes some fairly explicit remarks (by contemporary standards) about how he is unable to influence a woman's mind.

The latter part of the film is also enlivened by some impressive special effects by Ned Mann, a Hollywood veteran whom producer Alexander Korda brought to Britain; his most famous work is in *Things to Come* (1936). A palace is created out of thin air and, when Young wishes that the world would stop, it does just that, with the result that there is no longer any gravity and everything spins out of control.

During the early section, Mann supplied some brief but smooth stop-motion effects when Young uses his telekinetic powers to wish that the shop in which he works would tidy itself up. There are no live-action composite shots.

"'Ere! Apple-pie order!" commands Young and, much to his astonishment, various animated items jump or climb into drawers and boxes. In seven stop-motion cuts, rolls of cloth fold themselves up and jump onto shelves, the sleeve of a suit adjusts its own price tag, drawers bang shut, untidy chairs line themselves up, gloves slide back into a box and a feather duster twirls along a counter, then hangs itself up on a wall.

The strong cast also included a young Torin Thatcher as one of the Gods who grant Young special powers. Many years later, Thatcher would become a favorite of stop-motion enthusiasts for his marvelous portrayal of the wicked magician Sokurah in *The 7th Voyage of Sinbad* (1958).

March of the Wooden Soldiers
see *Babes in Toyland* (1934)

Mary Poppins

1964. Disney. D: Robert Stevenson. Scr: Bill Walsh, Don Da Gradi. Based on the *Mary Poppins* Books by P. L. Travers. Ph: Edward Colman. Mus: Richard M. Sherman, Robert B. Sherman. Art: Carroll Clark, William Tuntke. Special Effects: Peter Ellenshaw, Eustace Lycett, Robert A. Mattey. Nursery Sequence Design: Bill Justice, Xavier Atencio.

Cast: Julie Andrews, Dick Van Dyke, David Tomlinson, Glynis Johns, Hermione Baddeley, Elsa Lanchester, Arthur Treacher, Reginald Owen, Ed Wynn, Jane Darwell.

Rating: ☆☆☆   Stop-Motion: ☆½

A film that it is hard not to like — no matter how much you try. For once, all the sickly ingredients of the "family musical" come together successfully, thanks to some fine performances, strong musical numbers, impressive dance routines and haunting special effects. This tale of a magical nanny (Julie Andrews) who comes to stay in an Edwardian household contains a number of unforgettable fantasy images: Mary Poppins sitting on a cloud high above London; a crowd of nannies being blown away down a street; Ed Wynn laughing himself up to the ceiling; merry-go-round horses bobbing up and down through a cartoon countryside; and Mary and her wards stepping gaily across the rooftops, backed by an impressive painting of London in a nighttime glow.

In one scene, Mary gives the two children a demonstration of how to tidy their nursery. Toys and clothes magically return to cupboards and drawers by means of some ingenious reverse-filming and wire supports. One shot uses some rudimentary stop-motion: Toy bricks form into a series of steps leading up to a box, and a group of toy soldiers marches up the steps and into the box.

Master of the World

1961. American-International Pictures. D: William Witney. Scr: Richard Matheson. Based on the Novels *Master of the World* and *Robur, the Conqueror* by Jules Verne. Ph: Gil Warrenton. Art: Harry Reif. Mus: Les Baxter. Special Effects: Tim Barr, Wah Chang, Gene Warren. Additional Special Effects (uncredited): Jim Danforth.

Cast: Vincent Price, Charles Bronson, Mary Webster, Henry Hull, Richard Harrison, Vito Scotti.

Rating: ☆☆½   Stop-Motion: ☆☆½

In this engaging adventure story based on novels by Jules Verne, Vincent Price gives an enjoyably hammy performance as Robur, a megalomaniac who builds an airship and uses it in his plans to put an end to war.

Most of the action takes place aboard the huge airship the *Albatross*. Only the rear deck of the Albatross was built full size. In all other shots, the craft was depicted by means of skillful miniature work by Gene Warren and Wah Chang of Project Unlimited.

Warren explained in a letter to the author, "All flying shots of the airship were accomplished stop-frame with a miniature airship which was approximately three feet in length. Some scenes were done against a process screen, others against plain blue skies and a few behind a moving glass with painted cloud formations on it which could be given internal movement, also by means of stop-frame."

Metalstorm: The Destruction of Jared Syn

1983. Empire Pictures. D: Charles Band. Scr: Alan J. Adler. Ph: Mac Ahlberg. Special Visual Effects: Frank Isaacs.

Cast: Jeffrey Byron, Tim Thomerson, Kelly Preston, Mike Preston, Richard Moll.

Rating: ☆☆   Stop-Motion: ☆☆

Filmed in 3-D, this SF-western directed by Charles Band has Jeffrey Byron on an interplanetary mission to retrieve a crystal from the bad-guy inhabitants of a desert landscape.

The climax contains a chase on sky-cycles through a narrow canyon. Some shots in this sequence feature a 22-inch model of a cycle with a rider mounted on it. The model was stop-framed in front of a blue screen and the head of the rider was animated to make it turn from side to side.

Metamorphosis: The Alien Factor

1990. D-Scr: Glen Takakjian. Stop-Motion Animation: Kent Burton, Dan Taylor. Animation Assistant: John Zdankiewicz. Exterior Spot Animation and Matte Paintings: Mark Sullivan.

Cast: George Gerrard, Tony Gigante, Allen Lewis Rickman, Tara Leigh, Katherine Romaine, Dianne Flaherty.

Rating: ☆☆   Stop-Motion: ☆☆

In this low-budget SF-horror yarn, genetic experiments in the Talos Research Laboratory (yes, producer Ted Bohus is a big stop-motion fan) go seriously wrong. George Gerrard gets bitten on the hand by one of the subjects and transforms into a giant fleshy mound, with a long plesiosaur-like neck and one bulky, elephantine leg.

In one ambitious sequence, the creature breaks out of the laboratory. Roaring loudly, it snatches up a scientist in its mouth, thrashing about violently. The monster is a cable-operated creation in many cuts, and in others a stop-motion puppet, slickly animated by Kent

Burton and Dan Taylor. In the stop-motion shots, the scientist is also an animated puppet.

The film's final shot features a second stop-motion creature breaking through a wall. This dog-sized amoeba-like being has big eyes, a big mouth and a tail. It was animated by Mark Sullivan, whose previous stop-motion credits include *House 2.*

Metropolis

1926. UFA. D: Fritz Lang. Scr: Thea von Harbou, Fritz Lang. Ph: Karl Freund, Günther Rittau. Special Effects: Eugen Schüfftan. Art: Otto Hunte, Erich Kellethut, Karl Vollbrecht.

Cast: Brigitte Helm, Alfred Abel, Gustav Fröhlich, Rudolf Klein-Rogge, Fritz Rasp, Theodor Loos.

Rating: ☆☆☆½   Stop-Motion: ☆☆½

Fritz Lang's futuristic German masterpiece is still visually stunning even 70 years after its production. Dazzling cityscapes with elevated freeways contrast with the intimidating machinery and drudgery of the subterranean world of the workers. The twisted, medieval house of the scientist Rotwang (Rudolf Klein-Rogge) contains an array of shimmering electrical equipment which he uses to create his female robot — the latter a sequence of great power and beauty. One sequence — in which Maria (Brigitte Helm) is pursued through shadowy caverns by Rotwang — is beautifully shot by Karl Freund as an arche-

typal horror sequence. Another sequence — the climax in which the underground world is flooded and destroyed — is a brilliantly staged *tour de force* combining striking set design with imaginative choreography of hordes of extras. The film is only let down by its plot, an essentially unappealing tale of a workers' revolt, smacking more of political treatise than cinematic drama.

The spectacular external shots of the city were achieved with vast, highly detailed miniature sets and include some shots that employ stop-motion. In these, planes or helicopters fly through the canyons formed by the skyscrapers, past elevated freeways and above cars traveling at ground level. The cars might have been filmed simply by pulling them on wires but, because the flying vehicles turn and dip in ways that would have been difficult to achieve realistically by suspending them on wires, Lang and his special effects man Eugen Schüfftan decided to use stop-motion.

Mighty Joe Young

1949. RKO. Prod: Merian C. Cooper, John Ford. D: Ernest B. Schoedsack. Scr: Ruth Rose. Story: Merian C. Cooper. Ph: J. Roy Hunt. Art: James Basevi. Mus: Roy Webb. Technical Creator: Willis O'Brien. First Technician: Ray Harryhausen. Second Technician: Pete Peterson. Technical Staff: Marcel Delgado, George Lofgren, Fitch Fulton. Photographic Effects: Harold Stine, Bert Willis. Optical Photography: Linwood G. Dunn.

Cast: Terry Moore, Ben Johnson, Robert Armstrong, Frank McHugh, Douglas Fowley, Nestor Paiva, Regis Toomey, Primo Carnera.

Rating: ☆☆☆½ Stop-Motion: ☆☆☆½

This is Willis O'Brien's last major animation film, and it earned him an Academy Award. It is a final display of the idiosyncratically complex variety of stop-motion choreography, rear projection and static matte techniques which he had been refining for 35 years. Sophisticated stop-motion trickery at this level would not be seen again until the late 1970s and afterwards, when advances in traveling matte and computer-controlled animation took the genre to new heights of realism. *Mighty Joe Young* contains an astonishing series of intricate rear-projection set-ups making use of glass paintings, extensive miniatures and optical enhancements. The design of some of these shots is so ingenious that, even after close study, it is not always possible to be entirely sure how the shot was constructed.

In years to come, Ray Harryhausen—one of O'Brien's assistants on *Joe*—would devise his own more economical "reality sandwich" matting techniques, a simplified version of O'Brien's style. His cost- and time-conscious techniques would give him a reputation for affordable special effects. O'Brien on the other hand became labeled as expensive and time-consuming and after *Joe* he found it increasingly difficult to convince producers to use his skills. All his work after *Joe* is minor compared to *The Lost World, King Kong* and *Mighty Joe Young.* Harryhausen's effects are frequently just as effective as O'Brien's, but O'Brien's visions have a more grandiose look and are often more aesthetically pleasing.

Joe is also the last film to feature extensive character animation of a central stop-motion protagonist. Other films have had animated stars with distinct personalities—*20 Million Miles to Earth* and *The Valley of Gwangi*—but not to the extent of the anthropomorphic Joe, a ten-foot gorilla captured in Africa and brought back to America and displayed in a Hollywood nightclub. Other stop-motion characters—such as the giant Porno in *Flesh Gordon* or the baboon in *Sinbad and the Eye of the Tiger*—have had strong personalities but they were not the stars of their films. Joe's personality and plight make him one of the cinema's most unforgettable tragic heroes. But his impact is weakened by a few "cute" comic touches which take him away from Kong's mythic stature and closer towards the humor of *The Son of Kong.*

The credibility of Joe's character is due in part to the fact that the animation is vastly superior to that of *Kong* (where the audience is so caught up in the gripping pace that some of the crude animation is hardly noticed). Scenes showing *Joe* moping in his basement prison contain some of the smoothest and most lifelike animation ever put on film, recent advances in go-motion and computer imagery notwithstanding. *Joe* features an enormous amount of animation (85 percent of it was done by Harryhausen) which, after the opening 20 minutes of live action, seems almost continuous. A roping scene in which cowboys capture Joe, a number of nightclub passages and the fiery climax at an orphanage are all superb. They may not have the grandeur and surreal impact of some of the genre's other great sequences — like *Kong*'s finale or the skeleton battle in *Jason and the Argonauts* — but they are still classic episodes.

Marcel Delgado, the great model maker from O'Brien's previous films, built several 16-inch-high models of Joe and a beautifully detailed four-inch model for extreme long shots. Also impressive are a number of subsidiary models, also built by Delgado, which add to the impact of several scenes: two horses, three lions and a variety of puppet humans. Some of the animation of these puppet humans in brief throw away moments (again mostly animated by Harryhausen) show a perfect understanding of anatomy and movement, pre-dating his much-praised puppet human animation in *20 Million Miles To Earth*.

The young Harryhausen had approached O'Brien many years earlier and shown him some experimental dinosaur footage he had shot after being so impressed by seeing *King Kong* at the age of 13. The two had even worked together on some of George Pal's *Puppetoon* short films. When O'Brien needed an assistant on *Mighty Joe Young*, Harryhausen was the obvious choice.

Ernest B. Schoedsack and Merian Cooper — the driving team behind *King Kong* — acted as director and producer respectively. Additionally, John Ford, known primarily for his westerns, served as associate producer. This combination should have made *Joe* a classic on a par with *Kong* and it's not easy to say why the magic is not quite there. All the fairy tale fantasy atmosphere and symbolism of *Kong* have been replaced with a more down-to-earth approach which it was felt was more in line with the tastes of postwar 1949 audiences. Comic elements are heightened to cater for jaded tastes of audiences whom the producers felt would no longer warm to a straight adventure story. The roping scene, for example, is punctuated with comic shots of Robert Armstrong and his uncooperative horse, seriously undermining the dramatic impact. There is even a happy ending, depriving Joe of the pathos a death scene to match *Kong*'s tearjerker climax.

Terry Moore makes a sweet heroine but cannot compare with Fay Wray's screaming *tour de force*. Armstrong's character — essentially Carl Denham but here called Max O'Hara — is reduced to an almost entirely comic figure, lacking the integrity and showmanship of the role in *Kong*. The score by Roy Webb is sometimes effective, but Webb is no Max Steiner.

Cooper had wanted to make the film in color. Some color tests of composites were done (not featuring

Mighty Joe Young (1949) investigates a lion cage. Much of the foliage is painted. Live-action rushing water is matted into the lower area of the frame. The lion is a miniature rear-projected image. Sequence designed by Willis O'Brien and animated by Ray Harryhausen. (National Film Archive, London.)

animation), but ultimately Cooper was unable to raise the extra finance and the idea was dropped.

The closest the film ever comes to recreating the fantasy milieu of *King Kong* is its opening composite shot. A painting of a small Africa village has a lake in the foreground, a range of mountains extending far off into the distance and a waterfall matted into the right-hand corner. Four birds — very probably animated puppets — fly across this panorama to give it some movement.

The camera tilts down into this shot, adding more movement.

The next trick shot some 15 minutes later has another matte painting, an establishing shot leading into the scenes with O'Hara and his men in the jungle. This painting of mountains and valleys is combined with live action at the bottom of the frame. The matte line is undetectable. O'Brien adds to the feeling of depth in the shot by including foreground trees, probably painted on glass, which cross over both elements.

A character walks in front of part of one of the trees, indicating another seamless matte line.

Joe's first appearance is a long series of events split into two sections — his destruction of a lion's cage in the camp and the subsequent attempt to rope him. These passages took one month to film in post-production.

Schoedsack skillfully uses the sound of off-screen growling and panic in the camp to build the tension before revealing his title character. Joe is eventually shown in a long shot beating his chest in an attractive composite. A river rushes past in the lower foreground and a painted jungle backdrop is enhanced by a middle-distance tree painted on glass. To one side is a cage containing a captured lion. The cage is a miniature and the lion is front projected into it with seamless precision. When Joe tips the cage up, the image of the lion is synchronized to tip over at the same rate. The timing is perfect and it's a bafflingly good effect. Did the front-projector also have to be tilted?

Joe beats on the overturned cage. The animation is choreographed so that puppet and live-action lion seem to react to each another. For example, Joe retracts his hand when the lion appears to bite it. In this shot, Joe's hand passes in front of the lion footage, which seems to give the lie to sources which claim that the lion footage is front-projected.

A credible look of pain crosses Joe's face and he follows this up with a characteristic primate gesture: He beats the ground with his fist. When Joe overturns the cage, it is skillfully animated so that its rate of fall is totally convincing. Joe rips off pieces of wood and discards

them, and again their trajectory is very convincingly animated. A puppet lion climbs out of the cage and, although its animation is hurried, this doesn't distract from the drama because it is such a quick moment.

Ingeniously, the puppet lion jumps behind the cage, allowing a switch to live-action footage of a real lion running off to the left in a miniature rear projection. Joe walks in front of this rear projection and throws a rock at the fleeing lion, then pursues it out of the frame. It is just possible to see reflections of the puppets in the background glass (on which the jungle foliage is painted).

O'Hara and his men decide to give chase. Joe is seen in three cuts walking away from his pursuers. In the first of these, he walks past a rear projection of a herd of stampeding elephants. No matte is involved. The two other shots, with Joe in front of a herd of zebra, include miniature grass and two trees, imperceptibly matched to the background. Another composite depicts the cowboys riding through the jungle: A matted painting of a rocky outcrop occupies the upper half of the frame and a glass painting of trees and shrubs occupies the lower foreground. This atmospheric throwaway shot helps enormously to create the impression of an extensive jungle setting, when in reality it barely existed at all.

The tremendous roping scene is brilliantly animated and uses all the tricks of the stop-motion trade. Even so, when Harryhausen worked his magic in his own roping scene in *The Valley of Gwangi* (1969), he managed to improve on this original, making a more protracted and dramatic sequence. But *Joe's* roping scene is still a classic and, unlike Harryhausen's episode, has the added charm of a low-key conclusion in which Jill (Joe's guardian) steps in and calms her pet.

The opening shot is an all-miniature set-up, with Joe swinging his arms aggressively at off-screen cowboys, backed by a painted rock face and distant mountains. In a rear-projection set-up, two live-action cowboys pass behind Joe while three animated cowboys ride in front. The latter is a labor-intensive extra, but essential to breaking up the table-top look of the shot and creating the impression that the ape is surrounded.

In a model example of implied interaction, Joe plucks a rider from his horse. This carefully timed shot is interesting because the nose of the horse (which rears up) momentarily disappears behind the painting which occupies the top half of the frame. The live-action footage has been edited so that the rider has time to get out of the shot, at which point O'Brien substitutes his puppet double. Joe picks up the flailing puppet and (in medium shot) angrily raises the man above his head. O'Brien then cuts to a live-action shot of a stunt man being hurled into a tree.

Three riders lasso Joe. During live-action filming, their target was actually a stake elevated by an off-screen bulldozer and ingeniously obscured by part of the miniature set which comes low enough to hide the platform. The riders on the left look like they may be a separate element, part of a matted area that obscures the bulldozer itself. The point at which the real ropes become miniature ropes is undetectable,

even when watched repeatedly in slow motion.

Wide-eyed Joe bites through one of the lassoes, an extremely fluidly animated medium shot. He pulls the rope from his neck and behind him are two animated riders. This is one of the few shots that were animated by O'Brien.

In another skillful interaction effect, Joe knocks over a horse with his arm. Even better, the next cut has him pulling on a rope that is held by a rear-projected rider. The puppet's arm obscures the point at which the live-action footage ends. Joe catches the rope thrown by another cowboy and pulls him from his horse. The fact that the rope can momentarily be seen emerging from Joe's other side reveals that in this shot the background plate extends right across the frame, and is not just a small area of the image as in previous shots.

In three rear-screen set-ups, Joe waves his fist at a fleeing horse in long shot, reaches for one of the cowboys in a medium shot, and in long shot again strides out of the frame. In another set-up, he actually lunges through the air at a rider and horse, bringing them down (i.e., the stunt rider makes his horse fall). Joe rolls over and the puppet suddenly jerks — as if Harryhausen had either accidentally knocked the puppet or else, being upside down, it fell out of position. Joe gets up again groggily.

As live-action cowboys gallop past behind the gorilla, he picks up a superbly animated puppet human, dangling him by his foot, then dropping him. When two more riders throw their ropes at Joe, there is no trace of where they extend beyond the puppet, suggesting that in fact there never were any real ropes: The actors mimed the action and miniature animated ropes were lined up with the image so that they extend all the way from the actors' hands to the puppet.

Another rider is pulled from his horse. This is followed by an extremely complicated set-up in which cowboy Gregg (Ben Johnson) beats Joe repeatedly with a branch. At the same time, Joe picks up another puppet human and an animated rider and horse run by in the foreground. It's a perfect example of the intricate lengths to which O'Brien would go to ensure maximum realism and drama.

Joe chases an animated puppet of Gregg behind a rock and is about to grab him when he is distracted by another miniature rider. In the next cut, Joe follows the animated rider, then turns and pulls a rear-projected rider from his horse. In a series of shots, he picks up two rocks and hurls them at Gregg, snarling.

The action cuts to a shot of O'Hara riding towards the scene, enhanced by a foreground painting of a strange-looking tree. This may have been added as an afterthought, because the registration of the background plate is not steady and jumps noticeably.

Joe now climbs the rock-face and in this shot eagle-eyed viewers will notice the puppet's reflection in the background glass. In two entirely miniature shots, Joe stands at the top of the cliff and beats his chest. He catches sight of O'Hara approaching and swings an arm down into the rear projected live-action part of the image, snatching O'Hara from his horse. In one shot, a full-scale prop hand is used. A switch is now made to a puppet of O'Hara, which Joe raises

over his head, with Jill and Gregg running into the lower part of the frame. Joe drops the live-action O'Hara. However, the rope which supported the stunt man is left in the shot, barely visible, even though Joe is supposed to have let go of it.

In a beautifully animated series of shots which really bring out Joe's personality, Jill talks to him, reprimanding him and gradually calming him down. All the while, the gorilla emits short, low growls which are more puzzled than aggressive. He makes a likable and very ape-like gesture, beating his hands on the ground. He picks up Jill from the base of the cliff, a convincing shot in which the actress clings to some support which is obscured by the puppet's hand. In the next cut, O'Brien has switched to a puppet version of Jill, which the ape lifts up and gently places down behind him. By having his puppet in front of the puppet of Jill, O'Brien is able to switch back to the live actress. The jungle background of the top area of these shots is painted and it appears that the actress has been combined with it by means of traveling matte. This composite footage was then used as the rear projection during animation.

Joe snarls and swipes at his attackers down below a couple more times, and finally Jill talks him into leaving, the pair walking away from the camera down an incline. This low-key resolution to a breathtaking action sequence makes for a very satisfying conclusion.

The pace calms down for a while and Joe's next scene is a much quieter episode, giving O'Brien and Harryhausen another opportunity to introduce some character animation. Gregg visits Jill in her homestead, a sequence that includes three scenic paintings, one of which is combined with what look like animated puppet birds. O'Hara joins the others to discuss his plans to take Joe to America and this delightful scene features a series of low-key shots of Joe interrupting the meeting.

All the animation cuts in this episode are backed by two very attractive paintings of trees, a lake and mountains. In long shot, Joe walks (with an impressively gorilla-like gait) up to the homestead and behind a carriage containing some chickens. The chickens are in a miniature rear-projected area within the miniature carriage. In closeup, Joe growls at the group of actors, a shot which uses a different model to the one seen in long shots; there are distinct facial differences.

Joe walks into a second miniature set-up and picks up a rock, intending to throw it at Jill's visitors. But Jill whistles "Beautiful Dreamer," Joe's favorite tune, and calms him down. He is finally placated altogether when she throws two bananas to him. In this engaging composite, the actors stand in the foreground, probably by means of traveling matte or possibly standing in front of an extremely large rear screen. Moore drops the real bananas just out of frame and when she lifts her empty hand again to mime the action of throwing them, they are replaced by wire-supported animated bananas. Just how O'Brien managed to synchronize the two actions is a mystery. Remember — he was not animating his puppet in front of previously shot footage of the actress.

The action now shifts to O'Hara's Hollywood nightclub, "The Golden Safari." Establishing long shots are composites in which a miniature exterior of the club is seamlessly matched to live-action footage of crowds entering. The miniature area at the top of the frame contains a huge neon sign and two giant carved lions. Interior shots of this vast club may also be part miniature, but if they are, O'Brien's composites are so good that it is impossible to be sure.

Joe's first public appearance and O'Hara's deliberately teasing introduction are the equal of the similar moment in *King Kong*. Roy Webb's score is at its most effective during this passage. The stage lights brighten to reveal Jill at a piano on a rotating platform, then the audience is astounded to watch her being lifted into the air, held aloft by a docile Joe. Long shots of Joe on the stage feature an animated puppet of Jill at her piano. Closer shots are composites with Joe meticulously matched to the speed of the rotating platform in the live-action plate. Other shots include closeups of Joe, with much character-building eye, eyebrow and lip movement. These shots were animated by Pete Peterson, who would assist O'Brien on several of his later projects. In these shots, Joe's fur bristles in the same curious way that Kong's did, and this may be because Peterson was not aware that he needed to touch it as little as possible, or it may be due to the ground-level lighting — aimed up at the puppet — which emphasizes all of the its features.

O'Hara stages a tug-of-war between Joe and a group of strongmen. It is one of the film's stand-out sequences, characterized by touches of gentle humor which, rather than cheapening Joe's stature (as had happened in *Son*

Of Kong), make him all the more likable.

In the first cut, Jill leads Joe onto the stage. This shot is composed of three elements. Jill is rear-projected; Joe stands on a miniature rocky platform; and in the lower right-hand corner, O'Hara, a separate rear-projected area, stands in front of a rock which blends imperceptibly with the miniature rock face above it. Only the very diligent would notice that when Joe reaches down to touch O'Hara's head playfully, the puppet's shadow comes to an end where the miniature rear-projected area begins.

Perhaps the most baffling ingredient in this sequence is how and where O'Brien switches from real to miniature rope during the tug-of-war. In the actors' hands it is clearly part of the live-action footage, and in Joe's hands it is clearly part of the miniature footage, but the point at which they "transform" is invisible. Logically, one might decide that the real rope ends at the point where Joe's hand obscures the rear projection. But this is not so, because in two of the cuts where Joe collects the slack on the rope, it passes in front of the puppet. At other moments, it is more apparent that a switch to a partial miniature has been made, but even these shots are so subtly matched that they are totally realistic.

In one irresistible moment, Joe temporarily forgets the tug-of-war and offers Jill the rope. The club's audience roars with laughter but cinema audiences are already feeling sorry for the ape, uprooted from his African home. Joe pulls all the strongmen one by one into the pool of water in the middle of the stage. Then he reaches down to help one of them (Primo Carnera) out of the water. In this cut, the rope from which the strongman dangles throws a shadow but Joe doesn't — a minor error only apparent after close scrutiny.

Joe and Carnera have a mock fist-fight, with the actor punching Joe and the ape replying with playfully restrained slaps. This is a classic piece of implied interaction and it may have inspired Jim Danforth in *When Dinosaurs Ruled the Earth* (1970) in a scene where an actress slaps one of the dinosaurs. Carnera walks behind Joe, allowing O'Brien to edit the live-action footage and substitute a puppet counterpart of the actor. Joe picks up the Carnera puppet and throws him into the audience. The animation of the puppet struggling in Joe's hands is very convincing, but it look stiff as it flies through the air. But most audiences are too caught up in the flow of the action to notice this giveaway. Finally, Joe takes Jill's hand and walks off.

These two spectacular nightclub scenes are rounded off poignantly with a brief scene in which Gregg leads Joe back into his cage. Here, Harryhausen's animation is uncannily smooth and full of character-giving flourishes. Joe looks longingly out of a window, sits dejectedly on the floor with sad, watery eyes (is this a trick of the light or have they been moistened with glycerin?) and absent-mindedly scrapes up some dust from the floor with his paw and stares it. In these cuts, Gregg stands in the foreground on the near side of the cage bars: The actor is actually standing in front of a full-scale rear projection. In the first of these shots, the cage door is part of the miniature set, allowing Joe to lean on it. In later cuts it is a prop in the foreground, with Gregg leaning on it.

After some live-action scenes, the same basement set-up is used again to show Joe looking even more miserable. Gregg again stands in the foreground. Joe knocks a bowl of fruit off a table and the fruit rolls onto the floor. The fruit may be part of a miniature rear-projected live-action area, or it may be animated, in which case it is astonishingly realistic. He looks out of his window but all his view affords him is the sight of a man in a dingy street emptying a garbage can. In several shots Joe makes slow and very convincing facial gestures.

The final night at the Golden Safari begins with a scene that has a haunting yet picturesque quality — the humiliation of Joe dressed as an organ grinder's monkey. Two initial long shots are done all-miniature with Joe walking on stage and a puppet Jill standing on the left. She only makes very slight movements and as a result is 100 percent convincing. This set-up is used again in the third cut when the audience starts throwing giant coins at the ape. The coins are cel animations added later.

Closer shots combine Joe with the live-action Jill. These shots appear to be the film's only instance of O'Brien using the kind of static matte design which Harryhausen would later make his trademark. The stage floor forms a horizontal matte line, with the live-action audience in the lower foreground and Jill standing behind the puppet.

Joe, with a hangdog expression, fends off the coins half-heartedly and then makes a pathetic gesture with a cup, holding it out to the audience, who are howling with laughter at him. In an angry gesture, he pulls off his cap and throws it to the ground. The final straw is when a drunk throws a bottle and it hits Joe on the side of the head. He rears up, growls at the audience, baring his fangs, and the curtain is brought down. The sequence contains some of the film's best animation, both in terms of fluidity and also in giving Joe realistic facial and body gestures which really bring out his dejectedness.

Caged up in his basement cell again, Joe is taunted by three drunks. These two scenes (interrupted by a live-action passage with Jill and Gregg in a restaurant) contain some of the film's best subdued character animation, something which is seen all too rarely in stop-motion films. This animation was the first that Harryhausen did for the film and it shows an assured understanding of gesture and movement. Many years later he created some similar sequences with a baboon in *Sinbad and the Eye of the Tiger* (1977).

The range of expressions which Harryhausen extracts from his puppet's face makes this the point in the film where it is hardest to believe we are looking at just a motionless, armatured model and not a living creature. The initial hangdog look, accompanied by gentle grunts, becomes a look of pain when one of the drunks burns Joe's hand with a cigarette lighter. Eventually, the look of pain transforms into snarling rage, with Joe baring his fangs again.

Twelve animation cuts make up these two scenes. Most have the three drunks standing in the foreground in front of a full-scale rear projection of Joe behind bars. Two of the shots add another perspective, side-view shots of

Joe in his cage with no live-action element. In these shots, O'Brien ingeniously got Harryhausen to add shadows of the three drunks on the cell wall, by animating off-screen puppet humans. One of the drunks hands Joe a liquor bottle, a trick done simply by having the actor walk in front of Joe's hand, obscuring it at the right moment. When the drunk burns Joe's finger with his cigarette lighter, he again walks in front of Joe's hand, although why this is so is not clear — surely contact could have been suggested on-screen, with flame lined up with the puppet's hand?

Joe drinks this liquor and polishes off a second bottle as well. Some sort of gel is animated running down his cheek as he spills some of the liquor. With a convincing swagger, he grabs the cage bars and pulls himself to his feet. After finishing off a third bottle, he lets out a belch: O'Brien and Harryhausen are able to make us laugh at this at the same time as being disgusted by the way the drunks are abusing Joe. He batters down the cage door, the bars of which are animated to show them twisting. In a miniature set of the area just outside the cage, he picks up the mangled door and hurls it after the fleeing drunks. The momentum of throwing the door causes him to reel drunkenly against a wall — another clever touch that adds plausibility. The last basement shot looks over Joe's shoulder as he walks towards the rear-projected drunks.

The action continues upstairs in the nightclub. Here, the animation is again extraordinarily good although the frantic pace enforces that some of it is not as smooth as during the slow basement scenes. But the dynamic choreography

and variety of composite set-ups mean that this is barely noticed.

Joe appears through a hole in one of the club's fake trees, battering away animated pieces of it as he pushes through. Two of these cuts are done in a miniature set and two have a live-action element of panicking extras matted into the lower half of the frame. These latter shots were achieved by front-projecting the live-action image, one of the very few instances of O'Brien or Harryhausen using this technique. Joe climbs the miniature tree and there is a dizzily effective aerial view of the audience with Joe on the tree in the foreground.

Nearing the platform at the top, the puppet grips two support poles which obscure their real counterparts in the rear plate. The miniature platform and swinging rope bridge so perfectly match the real ones that the eye is never aware of any contention, even when the camera cuts directly from shots of Joe shaking the miniature bridge to shots of the orchestra fleeing along the real one (shades of Kong rolling the log over the ravine, perhaps?).

Joe climbs onto the platform and batters at its roof. Overhead shots of his head coming through the roof and throwing away pieces of animated thatch must have been achieved with the model and miniature set in an almost horizontal position to give the impression that the background footage is actually down below. Reminding us that Joe is still intoxicated, there is a dizzying moment when he reels back, nearly falls, then pulls himself back just in the nick of time. Helping the two parts of the composite to mesh, Joe throws a piece of miniature roof up out of the frame and

457

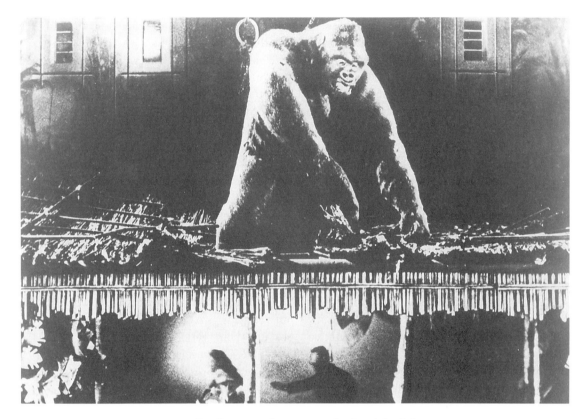

Joe Young on the rampage in the nightclub.

it comes crashing down, now part of the live-action set, onto the running extras, all in one cut. Joe throws more roofing and even a miniature double bass and piano, all matched by live-action cuts of the props landing among the terrified audience.

In another aerial shot, Joe grabs a hanging vine, gives it a couple of tentative tugs (a realistic touch) and swings over the audience. To add extra movement to shots of him swinging past rear-projected footage, the animation camera pans with the model. However, in this shot, the rear projection looks washed out, so it may be that the pan was added after the composite had been shot.

In a classic example of implied interaction, Joe, still swinging on the vine, grabs a man by his trousers, causing him to do a cartwheel. In reality, the extra is pulled over by a wire. Other cuts in this sequence feature a miniature rear projection of actors running in the lower half of the animation set, which consists of a low roof and a wall. This allows the puppet to swing over the live-action area and then land up on the roof. He belches (a distinctly un–Kong-like gesture) and throws some more ripped-up debris at the audience. He grabs another vine but misjudges his swing and spins around drunkenly on the spot.

Joe swings over to a roof above a glass-fronted cage containing live lions.

458

Instead of landing gently on the roof, he misjudges and crashes into it, bringing down a cascade of realistically animated bits of timber on his head, then falls to the floor. O'Brien's design, ever conscious of pace, adds to the excitement of this shot by having the camera zoom in on Joe as he gets to his feet.

The glass of the lions' cage is usefully concealed behind the fallen rubble, so that when Joe punches through it, the shattering is implied and not seen. On two subsequent occasions when animated glass is seen shattering on screen, the shots only get away with their obvious fakery by virtue of being very quick cuts. In both, miniature shards with dark outlines are inserted and moved about frame by frame.

Joe picks up a puppet lion and hurls it through another glass screen, an ambitious bit of animation which Harryhausen just about pulls off. The camera pans left, following Joe as he walks in front of another part of the lion enclosure. He pulls down a pole from the miniature set and throws it like a spear through some more glass. The camera pans left once again, but this time the lighting of the animation table is at fault: The light flickers, darkens and then settles down, as if a bulb faded and blew.

One piece of rear-projected footage of two live-action lions escaping from the cage is used twice, a trick revealed by the fact that a fallen piece of glass suddenly returns to its original position. Joe corners some of the lions (which are in another miniature rear projection), pulls down more of the miniature roofing and batters one of the puppet lions. Joe picks up a puppet lion

by its tail, swings it over his head, smashes it into the floor, batters it with his fist, picks it up and throws it across the club. This sequence of events is marvelously animated by Harryhausen.

The animation maintains its breakneck pace and complexity. One of the drunks — this time a puppet — is threatened by a lion, defends himself and then crawls away when Joe intercedes. The puppet drunk is very skillfully animated and this may be one of the two or three nightclub scenes which O'Brien himself animated. Joe beats this lion with his fists and throws it across the room. Two more puppet lions jump on his back, sending him rolling into yet another rear-projection set-up. As one of these lions bites his legs, a third jumps on him. In a dramatic medium shot, Joe growls in pain as he tries to pull the lion off, eventually throwing this one away as well.

The lions dispatched, Joe walks into another miniature set at the foot of one of the club's fake giant trees. Actors run past in the background and Joe reels drunkenly against a fence. He batters at the tree (a miniature) and in a marvelously animated cut leans into the tree, trying to push it over. The puppet really seems to be straining against the bulk of the tree (even though in this cut, the tree is now a full-size prop in the live-action). When the tree falls, it brings down most of the club with it and Joe is knocked on the head by various bits of wire-supported falling timber.

The police arrive on the scene. In two very realistic cuts, Jill stands in front of Joe, who is actually in a rear projection. The rubble in both the foreground and background elements really seems to blend them together. In these cuts, Joe still swaggers drunkenly.

This lengthy sequence ends where it began, with Jill leading Joe back into his cage, using the familiar full-scale rear projection seen before. In terms of the density of different composite designs per minute of screen time, this ranks as one of the most complex ever attempted in a stop-motion film.

The pace calms down for awhile as the authorities decide if Joe has to be put down. These live-action scenes are intercut with three animation cuts of Joe sitting in a prison cell awaiting execution. The design of these shots is identical to the earlier shots of Joe in the basement, with actors standing in front of a full-scale rear projection. Joe again looks miserable and utters low grunts. In the first of these cuts, Jill is aligned carefully so that she appears to be stroking Joe's head. The second and third cuts both use the same piece of animation footage of Joe getting to his feet. But they are separated by live-action scenes which prevent audiences from being aware that O'Brien has cut corners.

The pace quickens again when Jill, Gregg and O'Hara help Joe escape, and it doesn't let up for a minute until the film ends. With Jill standing in the foreground, Joe steps out of his cell onto an area of miniature floor. The animated cell door bounces realistically off a wall as it is pushed open. The next cut takes place outside the prison, this time with the puppet in the foreground and Jill in the rear screen. Joe climbs into a miniature truck, which dips with the gorilla's weight. A studio mock-up of the truck's rear doors is used in the next cut, placed in front of a rear projection of Joe inside

the miniature truck. This allows Gregg, in the foreground, to close the doors on Joe. The same set-up is used in an amusing scene in which a tramp looking for a ride opens the truck doors and is confronted by the huge ape.

Fleeing from the police, Joe is transferred to another truck. O'Brien depicts this in two different perspectives, as ever aware that relying too heavily on one set-up can "give the game away." The first of these cuts is shot from within the truck, with Joe climbing towards the camera and Jill standing in the rear projection. The second has Jill in the foreground pulling a canvas over the back of the truck, with Joe in the background.

Intercut with shots of a live-action truck, an animated truck bounces up and down credibly in front of a rear-film which gives the impression that the vehicle is moving left to right. In this same cut, Joe peeks out through the canvas and shakes a fist at a pursuing police car. In an all-miniature sequence, an animated truck trundles into a set of a muddy valley, its headlights throwing beams of light in front of it. The movement of the truck is a bit hurried but subsequent long shots of the puppet Jill urging Joe to push the truck out of the mud are much more successful. These shots, using the four-inch Joe model, were animated by Peterson.

A miniature police car (also animated) arrives on the same set and when it comes to a sudden halt in the mud, puppets inside the vehicle recoil realistically. The chase is eventually resumed and there are several shots of Joe hanging out of the back of the truck, growling and reaching for his pursuers. When the truck goes over a bump, Joe very nearly falls out — a deft bit of animation. He sits down on the back of the vehicle looking very self-satisfied, spits at the off-screen police car, wipes his mouth with the back of his hand and then drums his fingers on his knees, looking almost blasé about the whole business. This is one occasion where O'Brien has gone too far, making his ape far too human, and it usually elicits a groan from audiences.

Still fleeing from the police, Jill, Gregg, O'Hara and Joe pass a burning orphanage. These final scenes are genuinely exciting, full of suspense, and on occasion visually stunning. The episode is a marvelous triumph of melodramatic tragedy, with Joe nearly sacrificing himself to save a small girl trapped on the roof by the flames.

The sequence begins with some more all-miniature shots of the truck driving up the orphanage, which is a highly detailed five-foot-high fabrication seen on fire in a background plate. Shots in which Joe climbs out of the van, with children fleeing from the building in a rear projection, are enhanced by a simulation of flickering light from the flames on the puppet — a precursor of a similar effect in the Medusa sequence of Harryhausen's *Clash of the Titans* (1981).

Jill, who has run into the building, calls out to Joe and he reacts to her voice, climbing a miniature tree to reach her. The wall of the real orphanage is in a rear projection. In a striking extreme long shot, the small ape puppet, its arms flailing at the flames, climbs the tree with the burning miniature building in the background. This shot and a few others during this sequence were animated by

Delgado — the only known examples of him working in this capacity.

Joe climbs from the tree onto a corner of the miniature roof, smoke and flames filling the rear plate. In a very dynamic cut, Joe — wide-eyed with fear — walks directly toward the camera. A spectacular long shot, with a matte line running along the rooftop, shows Joe standing by a turret as half of the building collapses in a shower of flames. Hearing Jill's voice, Joe batters down the wall of the turret, revealing a miniature rear projection of Jill, Gregg and two children. A rear screen of the night sky forms the third element of this set-up.

In a superbly calculated moment of interaction, Joe's hand passes in front of the miniature rear projection and actually seems to pull Jill out of the live-action area and into the model set. This requires a switch to the puppet Jill and it is undetectable even in slow motion. Joe climbs back onto the tree with the puppet Jill clinging to his back. In a very fluidly animated shot, a branch gives way and the two fall several feet.

In a long shot looking up at the top of the building from ground level, Gregg is seen standing on a ledge with the two children. They are so tiny and far away that O'Brien is able simply to get away with superimposing animation footage of puppets of Gregg and the children onto the ledge, rather than devising a matte. The effect is successful because of the slight but realistic movements of the three models.

In animation shots, Jill falls from Joe's back, lands on a branch, climbs back onto the ape and is eventually set down on the ground. O'Brien falls back on superimposition again in a long shot

461

of Gregg climbing down a rope, but this time the technique is betrayed because the model looks transparent.

Joe climbs the tree again to rescue another little girl who has appeared on the roof. He snatches a puppet version of her from the ledge just as she is about to fall. In a series of shots, Joe is forced to climb higher up the tree because of flames burning it up from below. The flames are so skillfully superimposed onto the miniature trunk that only logic tells us that they cannot possibly be part of the same piece of film. Presumably the flames were shot against a black background burning an object which exactly matched the width of the miniature tree. One of these cuts is a beautiful long shot of Joe with the girl on his back, flames both in the foreground and consuming the building in the background.

When the flames lick at his foot, Joe kicks out in pain and climbs until there is no more tree to climb. A branch breaks and the pair fall to a lower part of the tree which has been left charred by the fire. These are deftly animated shots, but in one of them the wires supporting the models are momentarily but very clearly visible.

The fire finally gets the better of the tree. In a dramatic shot, Joe and the tree fall directly toward the camera; the ape has a look of horror on his face. The follow-up shot is even more exciting, a dizzying shot from behind Joe with the camera following the puppet as it hurtles towards the ground. These two cuts have a sense of dynamic movement which is all too rare in stop-motion films.

Flames are again very skillfully matched to the tree when it comes to rest and Joe crashes into the ground, cradling the girl with his hands to protect her. Seriously injured, he makes a few pathetic movements with his toes and hands as the girl crawls away from him in a rear projection. The building starts to collapse and falling masonry almost lands on the girl, but she is saved again when Joe crawls into the shot and covers her, taking the brunt of the masonry. In this cut, the girl is a very credibly animated puppet again. Feebly, Joe crawls a few more feet. In a shot of just his hand, he releases the girl, who is in the live-action rear screen. Finally, in long shot, Joe's prostrate body lies in the foreground making a few pained movements as Jill and O'Hara stand behind him.

In a closing sequence, we learn that Joe isn't dead after all. He is seen in a home movie that Jill and Gregg have sent from Africa to O'Hara in the States. This is another smoothly animated scene but in one shot Jill throws a banana to Joe; although he catches a miniature counterpart, the real banana can be seen continuing past the puppet. At the end, Joe gives a distinctly human wave, an unlikely gimmick which unfortunately reduces him to the semi-comic level of *Son of Kong*—a mistake after all the high drama of the preceding orphanage scenes. The final shot brings the film full circle, using the same composite of an African panorama that formed the opening shot.

Mighty Joe Young is frequently and unfairly dismissed as a second-rate *King Kong*, yet it is a thoroughly engaging story from start to finish. Schoedsack's direction lacks some of the control and pace of *Kong*, but the dramatic high points—the excitement of the roping

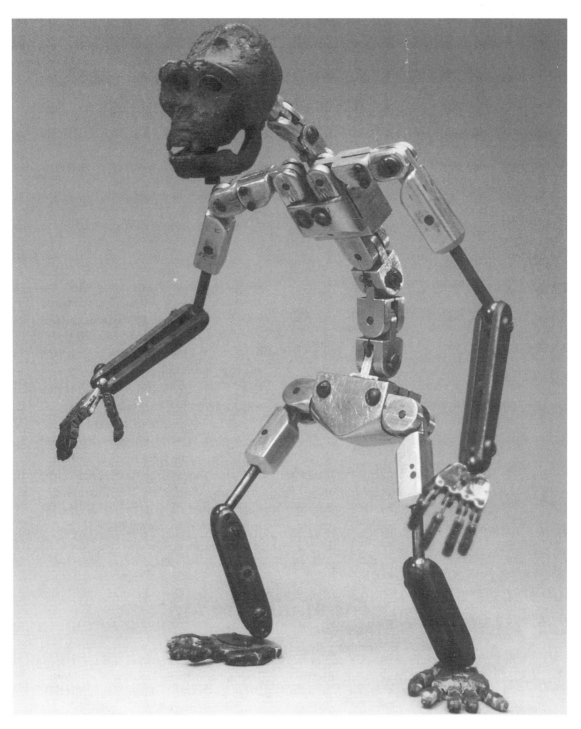

The Joe Young armature as it survives today, owned by Bob Burns. (Photograph courtesy Yancy Calzada.)

scene, the charm of the nightclub passages, the pathos of Joe in his cage, and the emotional pull of the orphanage sequence — earmark this as minor classic.

Joe falls short of being a great film, but it *is* a great animation film. O'Brien's technical genius is dazzling. He spared nothing in his design, and the variety of composites, constantly gripping the viewer's attention, never ceases to amaze. It is one of the great disappointments of the cinema that he was not allowed more opportunities to express his unique visions.

The Milpitas Monster

1976. Samuel Golden Ayer. D: Robert L. Burrill. Scr: David Boston. Story: Robert L. Burrill, David Kottas. Ph: Marilyn Odello, Scot A. Henderson, Mike Pearl, Mike Clausen, Andy Watts, Patricia Thorpe. Art: Duane D. Walz. Animation: Stephen C. Wathen. Mus: Robert R. Berry, Jr.

Cast: Doug Hagdohl, Duane Walz, Joseph House, Priscilla House, William Guest III, Michael W. Pegg.

Rating: ☆☆   Stop-Motion: ☆½

This low-budget semi-professional film tells the story of a 50-foot monster that grows out of the refuse dump of a town called Milpitas in the San Francisco Bay area. The monster — an actor in a costume — is vaguely humanoid in shape, has a pair of wings, long claws and wears a gas mask. It steals garbage cans, goes on a rampage and, in traditional King Kong fashion, climbs the broadcasting tower of a local television station. The tone is comic, spoofing the monster films of the 1950s.

A few stop-motion shots, animated by Stephen Wathen, are included. These include extreme long shots of the creature climbing a miniature replica of the tower and shots of the creature in flight. For the latter, the puppet was suspended from an overhead aerial brace.

The Monkey's Paw

1933. RKO. Prod: Merian C. Cooper. D: Wesley Ruggles. Additional Direction: Ernest B. Schoedsack. Scr: Graham John. From the Play by Louis N. Parker and the Story by W. W. Jacobs. Ph: Leo Tover. Art: Carroll Clark. Mus: Max Steiner. Photographic Effects: Lloyd Knechtel, Vernon L. Walker, Linwood Dunn. Effects Technicians: Harry Redmond, Jr., Marcel Delgado, Orville Goldner. Sound Recording: Murray Spivack.

Cast: Ivan Simpson, Louise Carter, C. Aubrey Smith, Bramwell Fletcher, Betty Lawford, Winter Hall.

Rating: N/A.   Stop-Motion: N/A.

No full prints of this film exist today and even the fragments that do remain seem to have dropped out of circulation entirely. Useful reference material on the film can be found in Walt Lee's *Reference Guide to Fantastic Films* (which contains the film's credits), *The RKO Story* and, primarily, George E. Turner's article in *American Cinematographer* (November 1985). It is of interest because of the involvement of many RKO employees who were concurrently working on *King Kong*.

The film is based on the classic short story by W. W. Jacobs in which a monkey's paw is said to give its owner three wishes, yet the wishes always bring tragedy. It was never intended as anything more than a B-picture, but the studio bosses were nevertheless horrified to find that director Wesley Ruggles had only managed to put together a half-hour film. So Merian C. Cooper supplied some story ideas that were fashioned into a prologue, to be directed by Ernest B. Schoedsack. (Cooper and Schoedsack were the producer-directors of *King Kong*.) The prologue, set in India, included glass paintings by the great matte artist of *King Kong*, Mario Larrinaga. The score was by Max Steiner and the sound effects were handled by Murray Spivack.

During one sequence in the Ruggles-directed section, Ivan Simpson makes a wish for £200. A sudden gust of wind blows up and the monkey's paw clenches its fist, then opens its fingers again. This moment was achieved with an armatured prop built by Marcel Delgado, the great puppet maker of *The Lost World* and *King Kong*. It was animated by Orville Goldner, who had worked on *Creation* and was currently working on *King Kong*, building miniatures and animating some of the birds that fly across O'Brien's panoramas. It seems that this brief moment was the only bit of stop-motion in the film.

Monster from Green Hell

1958. Gross-Krasne. D: Kenneth G. Crane. Scr: Louis Vittes, Endre Bohem. Ph: Ray Flin. Art: Ernst Fegté. Mus: Albert Glasser. Special Photographic Effects: Jack Rabin, Louis DeWitt, Gene Warren, Wah Chang (Warren and Chang uncredited).
Cast: Jim Davis, Robert E. Griffin, Joel Fluellen, Barbara Turner, Eduardo Ciannelli, Vladimir Sokoloff.

Rating: ☆☆½   Stop-Motion: ☆☆½

This is one of the stop-motion genre's most obscure and least-discussed films. It's obscure for a good reason — it's wretched. Produced by Al Zimbalist (famous for the notorious grade-Z film *Robot Monster* [1953]), it's one of those films that are so bad they're good. It has great low-budget charm and a brisk pace as it combines science fiction with a Tarzan setting and throws in monsters inspired by the giant ants of *Them!* (1954).

The 1940s–style narrative by the hard-nosed hero (Jim Davis, later famous in TV's *Dallas*) takes us from a space launch that goes wrong into darkest Africa where the rocket crashlands. There, Davis and his group are attacked by hundreds of angry natives (in footage pinched from *Stanley and Livingstone* [1939]) and discover a crevice full of giant wasps — ordinary wasps sent up in the rocket, but mutated by exposure to cosmic rays. In a desperate attempt to make the climax exciting, the final ten minutes (in which, to nobody's surprise, a volcano erupts) are tinted red. Direction and acting are appropriately bad throughout.

The sequences with the wasps were handled by Jack Rabin, Louis DeWitt, Gene Warren and Wah Chang, struggling as ever with a minuscule effects budget. Only Rabin and DeWitt get a screen credit and they presumably subcontracted the stop-motion work to Chang and Warren's Project Unlimited company. Absurd full-size mechanical props of the creatures, built by Chang, are intercut with 44 stop-motion cuts, using models that, because they are never required do much, were wire-jointed instead of having ball-and-socket armatures. All of the animation sequences had to be shot within three weeks, with the result that much of the animation is crude and several cuts are used more than once to cut costs. The few composites that the budget would allow are clumsy and obvious. The creatures lack any personality or presence but still look classier than many of the monsters that populated contemporary films without stop-motion.

Ten minutes into the film, one of the wasps is seen disturbing herds of African animals. Most of the shots use rear-projected stock footage of wildlife with the wasp very obviously a separate foreground element. Other shots show the wasp, its animated wings beating frantically, standing among some miniature foliage. A more ambitious shot is a static matte using a clip from *Stanley and Livingstone*, with the wasp matted into the background, coming over a hill. Some miniature foliage breaks up the matte line.

Our group hears the distant buzzing of the wasps and come across some huge three-toed footprints — more like those of a dinosaur than any wasp. "Typical wasp markings," remarks Davis, immediately losing all credibility. The suspense these moments might have generated is totally dissipated when the clumsy full-scale prop is wheeled out of the bushes and grabs an actor in its fake-looking pincers.

Much more impressive is a battle between one of the wasps and a giant snake, a sequence containing 13 stop-motion cuts. The snake is a convincing puppet and is animated smoothly by Warren. The snake uncoils, slithers towards the wasps and starts to curl around it. The wasp uses its claws to pull the snake away, brings it to the ground (a miniature floor) and pierces it with its mandibles. In a live-action cut, some nasty goo oozes out of the snake's wound in best early-splatter fashion. The open-mouthed snake writhes desperately and expires. This brief scene — probably animated by Warren — may not be one of stop-motion's finest battles but it's an enjoyable vignette.

At night, the camp is surrounded by wasps, mainly seen in shots using the full-scale props but also including two animated shots of a wasp among miniature foliage.

The group arrives at the foot of the volcano and discovers the lair of the wasps in a crevice. One shot, looking down onto the models, has three puppets walking across the shot. In other shots we see the Queen, which is supposedly larger than the other wasps, but since there is nothing else in the shot with which to make a comparison, the effect is lost. In several shots, grenades are thrown at the creatures, which are animated behind superimposed smoke. In one of the more dynamic set-ups, a wasp walks directly towards the camera, unperturbed by the grenades going off around it.

Traveling matte is used in three long shots in which a wasp hauls itself up out of the crevice. The actors flee in the lower foreground. These could have been dramatic shots but unfortunately the process work is unfinished and the wasp appears to be in negative.

In a sequence uncannily similar to a scene in Harryhausen's *Mysterious Island* (1961), the group seeks shelter in a cave and is trapped by a wasp. In matte shots looking out through the cave mouth, the wasp tries unsuccessfully to reach them. Two of these shots are effective because of the presence of the actors, matted into the lower foreground. In another shot, the laughable prop pincer makes an appearance, trying to grab Davis.

At the climax, the volcano erupts and destroys the wasps. This is very shoddily staged, using stock footage of lava which is carelessly superimposed over shots of the wasps. Not only that, but all these final stop-motion shots have been used before. One of them, in which three wasps walk towards the camera, is the same shot that appeared during the grenade sequence, except that previously it had been re-shot closer up so that only one puppet was visible.

The stop-motion cuts are occasionally effective but you can't make a silk purse out of a sow's ear — the monsters' fakery is always exposed by the low budget.

Moonwalker

1988. Lorimar. D: Colin Chilvers, Jerry Kramer. Scr: David Newman. Based on a Story by Michael Jackson. Ph: Tom Ackerman, Bob Collins, Fred Elmes, Crescenzo Notarile. Art: Michael Ploog, John Walker, Bryan Jones. Special Visual Effects: Dream Quest Images (supervisor Hoyt Yeatman). Robotic Effects: Rick Baker. "Speed Demon" Sequence by Will Vinton Productions.

Cast: Michael Jackson, Joe Pesci, Sean Lennon, Kellie Parker, Brandon Adams.

Rating: ☆☆½   Stop-Motion: ☆☆½

Pop superstar Michael Jackson is a genuine talent but an hour and a half of him in this format — a film split into seven different segments — neither does him justice nor holds the attention as a story. It is really a series of pop videos strung together and the one segment that does try to be more ambitious filmically ("Smooth Criminal," in which Jackson rescues some kids from a drug dealer) is all too pat because it forces all the plot elements into such a restricted running time.

"Speed Demon" is an entertaining excuse for Will Vinton to produce some more of his impressive Claymation effects (seen previously in *Return to Oz*) as Jackson is chased around a film studio and encounters all kinds of weird characters. These include animated cowboys, gangsters, a Statue of Liberty that comes to life, Jackson transforming into an animated rabbit, etc. The traveling matte and rear-screen composites are always good, including shadows added effectively to the live-action plate. A sequence in which Jackson skims along the surface of a river on a scooter is achieved by superimposing cel-animated spray; it looks good in this unreal environment but would be out of place if the sequence was striving for realism. In one se-

quence, Jackson and his animated rabbit counterpart do a dance routine — the composites are superb. All entertaining stuff, inventively designed by Vinton, but it never rises above the level of the kind of animation seen in many kids' television programs.

Snippets of animation are also seen in other segments: a slender female robot dancing, and Jackson dancing with a skeleton of the Elephant Man (complete with bony trunk).

The highlight of the film (not involving stop-motion) is the bizarre moment when Jackson transforms into a metal robot, bristling with guns, gadgets and sliding parts, a sequence devised by makeup maestro Rick Baker (who previously transformed Jackson into a werewolf in his "Thriller" video). Accomplished shots of a spaceship gliding overhead, its searchlights beaming out in all directions, look familiar for a good reason: They were done by DreamQuest Images, who did some very similar effects in *The Terminator*.

Morpheus Mike

1917. Edison Conquest. Prod: Herman Wobber. D-Scr-Ph-Special Effects: Willis H. O'Brien.

Rating: ☆☆½   Stop-Motion: ☆☆½

O'Brien's third all-animated short (made after *Birth of a Flivver*, which apparently has not survived) lives up to the promise of *The Dinosaur and the Missing*

Link. The animation is assured, the storyline is simply but inventively conceived and there is much humor. Morpheus was the god of sleep and dreams, and the bulk of the film takes place within a dream.

A goat swallows a woman's washing but Mike, a likable tramp, retrieves it: He actually pulls the line out of the

468

goat's mouth like a magician pulling out a string of handkerchieves. As a reward, she gives him some food, but when he looks away for a second, a dog steals it. The tramp lights up a pipe and O'Brien holds the puppet motionless for a few seconds and has actual smoke blowing out of its mouth.

Drifting off to sleep, Mike imagines he is in a prehistoric restaurant. Chisellings on a stone menu are translated by a caption as "tiger stew, ostrich egg and snake soup," all of which are served up by a prehistoric elephant. In a delightful moment, the ostrich egg hatches on his plate and a baby bird struts around the table. The soup is sprayed over Mike from the elephant's trunk, at which moment he wakes up to find the woman is pouring a bowl of water over him. Both of these last shots feature actual moving water — again the puppets remain motionless as O'Brien sprays the water over them.

Mosquito

1993. Acme Films Ltd./Excalibur MotionPictures. D: Gary Jones. Stop-Motion Animation: Paul Jessel. Animation Assistant: Yan Guo.

Cast: Gunnar Hansen.

Rating: ☆☆   Stop-Motion: ☆☆

It's low-budget SF-horror time again. A meteorite crashes on Earth and radiation from it causes some mosquitoes to mutate and grow to giant size.

Some shots of the mosquitoes use full-size on-set mechanical models. Additionally, there are five cuts of stop-motion mosquitoes animated by Paul Jessel.

The Most Dangerous Game
(GB: *The Hounds of Zaroff*)

1932. RKO-Radio. Prod: Merian C. Cooper, Ernest B. Schoedsack. D: Ernest B. Schoedsack, Irving Pichel. Scr: James A. Creelman. Based on the Short Story by Richard Connell. Ph: Henry Gerrard. Mus: Max Steiner. Art: Carroll Clark. Photographic Effects: Lloyd Knechtel, Vernon L. Walker. Optical Effects: Linwood Dunn. **Art Technicians: Mario Larrinaga, Byron L. Crabbe. Miniatures: Don Jahrous, Orville Goldner. Special Properties: Marcel Delgado, John Cerisoli.**

Cast: Joel McCrea, Fay Wray, Robert Armstrong, Leslie Banks, Hale Hamilton, Noble Johnson.

The Most Dangerous Game

Rating: ☆☆☆   Stop-Motion: ☆☆½

During the early months of the long 55 weeks that it took to make *King Kong* (1933), the same team made use of the studio jungle sets and available technical know-how to film a taut, exciting melodrama about a Russian aristocrat who hunts people for sport. *The Most Dangerous Game* has a great theatrical central performance by Leslie Banks as the psychopathic hunter, rapid-fire direction by Ernest B. Schoedsack which creates a relentless serial-style pace, several delightfully over-the-top Grand Guignol flourishes, a pulse-quickening score by Max Steiner and an imaginative jungle setting that uses glass paintings in a similarly impressive way as *King Kong*.

Banks had the potential to be a great horror actor but it was probably a label he tried to avoid. Whenever the hunting madness comes upon him, he strokes the scar on his forehead dreamily and leers at Fay Wray: "First the kill—then love! When you have known that, then you have known ecstasy!" One highlight is a scene in which he shows Joel McCrea his trophy room full of the heads of his human prey (some of which were fashioned by Marcel Delgado). Another is a dizzying crane shot that zooms in on Banks' face when he says suggestively that he will take good care of her brother (Robert Armstrong in a thankless role as a wisecracking drunk). Banks' demise is unforgettably melodramatic. Mortally wounded, he looks out of a castle window at the escaping lovers. "Impossible!" he gasps, and then falls to his death, to be devoured by his own ravenous hunting dogs.

In the early part of the film, a yacht is destroyed when it hits some reefs. This sequence apparently contains some shots that were originally part of the *Creation* footage.

The thrilling chase through the jungle includes head-on tracking shots of the actors pushing through the undergrowth, very similar to shots in *King Kong*. In fact, the jungle is very much a small-scale Skull Island. In one sequence, McCrea and Wray are pursued across the same log that was later shaken by Kong and thrown into a ravine. When *The Most Dangerous Game* was re-released in 1938, it was retitled *Skull Island*.

One long-shot composite shows McCrea walking toward Zaroff's castle. The castle is an evocative painting and in the foreground vines and trees have been painted on glass. In three other composite shots, another striking painting of the castle is used as a background to traveling mattes of the actors. In each of these three shots, stop-motion birds fly across the vista, adding an important bit of movement in the same way that they did in *King Kong*. The birds are little wooden models suspended on wires and have movable wings carved out of copper sheeting. In the last of the three shots, as many as ten birds fly in different directions through the air.

Who did this very smooth animation is not known. Probably, it was Orville Goldner, who built some of the miniatures for this film and also did some brief bits of animation for RKO's *The Monkey's Paw* (1933). Or could it have been O'Brien, taking time off *King Kong* to shoot these cuts uncredited? Even if he did not, they owe all their inspiration to his prehistoric visions.

Moving Violations

1985. Ufland-Roth/IPI. D: Neal Israel. Scr: Neal Israel, Pat Proft. Story: Paul and Sharon Boorstin. Ph: Robert Elswit. Mus: Ralph Burns. Art: Virginia Field. (Uncredited Stop-Motion Sequence: Fantasy II. Visual Effects Supervisor: Gene Warren, Jr. Stop-Motion Animation: Gene Warren, Jr., John Huneck.)

Cast: John Murray, Jennifer Tilly, James Keach, Brian Backer, Ned Eisenberg, Sally Kellerman.

Rating: ☆½   Stop-Motion: ☆☆

This feeble comedy attempts to emulate the style of the *Police Academy* series, with a group of traffic offenders assembled in a school to teach them the rules of the highway. The film has two or three laughs but these are all used up in the first ten minutes and the rest of the picture is an effort to watch. Smart-ass lead John Murray is so objectionable that one may find oneself starting to lose faith in human nature.

Midway through the film, Murray visits Jennifer Tilly at the NASA center where she works. They climb into a zero-gravity training chamber and make love. The camera pulls away from the couple to focus on their two discarded shirts, which float together, start groping each other and bump together rhythmically.

It's not a funny gag but it is an interesting application of stop-motion, and yet another occasion where it is featured in only one shot in a film. The 13-second cut was animated by Gene Warren, Jr., and John Huneck at Fantasy II Film Effects, although no screen credit is given.

Mysterious Island

1961. Columbia/Ameran. Prod: Charles Schneer. D: Cy Endfield. Scr: John Prebble, Daniel Ullman, Crane Wilbur. Based on the Novel by Jules Verne. Ph: Wilkie Cooper. Art: Bill Andrews. Mus: Bernard Herrmann. Special Visual Effects: Ray Harryhausen. Model Sculpture: Arthur Hayward (uncredited).

Cast: Michael Craig, Gary Merrill, Beth Rogan, Michael Callan, Joan Greenwood, Herbert Lom, Dan Jackson, Percy Herbert.

Rating: ☆☆☆   Stop-Motion: ☆☆☆

Harryhausen's ninth feature, full of spectacle and fantastic images, is a marvelous adventure film — despite the fact that its plot is a mess, going seriously off the rails halfway through.

Columbia had a script that was intended as a follow-up to Disney's successful *20,000 Leagues Under the Sea* (all of Jules Verne's works being by now in the public domain). This they presented to Schneer and Harryhausen, who now had to fashion it into a vehicle for their

471

Dynamation effects. Confusion resulted, with some plot ideas getting thrown out and others getting half-developed. The film's second half cannot make up its mind whether it is about a prehistoric island, genetically enlarged animals, a sunken city, a mad scientist or a band of pirates. One important theme — the cowardice of one of the central characters (Michael Callan) — gets lost en route and has no resolution.

Further weakening the plot is the fact that Harryhausen's four animation episodes are probably the most gratuitous of any in his films. All could be removed without harming the narrative. Giant creatures are encountered, battled and defeated, then the plot moves on.

Somehow, the film transcends all these weaknesses. This is in part because director Cy Endfield knows how to tell a good adventure yarn — two years later he would make the classic actioner *Zulu*. But more significantly it is due to the combination of Harryhausen's exhilarating sequences and Bernard Herrmann's score, which, although not as good as his work for *The 7th Voyage of Sinbad*, still insures that an atmosphere of anticipation and grotesquerie pervades every scene.

The four Dynamation sequences all exploit the dramatic possibilities of pitting humans against animals enlarged to dinosaur-size. Two of these scenes — battles with a crab and a bird — are real show-stoppers, guaranteed to leave even the most jaded jaws hanging open. Harryhausen animates these scenes with obvious relish, knowing that he was putting on screen the kind of startling images that at the time no one else was able to create.

All the models are superb. They were sculpted from Harryhausen's designs by Arthur Hayward, a skilled model maker working for the British Museum of Natural History. (After *Mysterious Island*, Hayward would sculpt the models for all Harryhausen's films up to and including *The Valley of Gwangi* [1969], although he never received a screen credit.) In particular, the multicolored feathered covering of the giant bird and the extreme detail on the bee — it is covered in hundreds of tiny hairs — make these puppets appear to be living, vital creatures. The crab was actually a real crab: It was dismantled by a museum worker (on this occasion not Hayward), the armature was inserted, and then it was reassembled.

The animation sequences in *Mysterious Island* are archetypal Dynamation episodes, yet there is not a large volume of animation in the film. It has 89 stop-motion cuts — only five more than the number in Harryhausen's first solo effort, *The Beast from 20,000 Fathoms*, and considerably less than in his previous major animation project, *The 7th Voyage of Sinbad*, which featured 232. Harryhausen's wizardry is to make us think we are seeing a lot more than we actually are.

In fact, we nearly *did* see more. Two further Dynamation sequences were conceived by Harryhausen but never filmed. A man-eating plant — with deadly tendrils that ensnare human prey — and a house-sized spider-like machine never got beyond the storyboard stage. The plant sequence was to have featured a character played by Nigel Green, whose name still features in the film's publicity material and is erroneously listed in many reference books.

Mysterious Island probably has the most matte paintings and miniatures of all his pictures up to this time. Hoping to give his uncharted island some of the fantasy atmosphere of O'Brien's Skull Island, Harryhausen includes painted panoramas of mountains, cliff faces and ravines. This is a welcome change from his more favored technique of dropping his puppets into a "reality sandwich," but the artist he chose to execute the paintings simply wasn't up to the job. Although the paintings look attractive in isolation, they cut in uncomfortably with the location photography (on the Spanish coast) and look glaringly fake.

There are six matte paintings. The first is a striking extreme long shot with two of the castaways walking along a beach behind which jungle foliage leads to jagged mountains and a huge volcano. This seamless composite is spoiled by the presence of a flock of live-action sea gulls which has been sloppily matted over the shot. Again, Harryhausen has tried to emulate O'Brien's Skull Island but failed.

The second painting features in a careful composite in which the castaways are building a hut in the lower foreground while behind them stretch mountains leading to the volcano. The third painting is another evocative extreme long shot with actors walking along a beach backed by jungle and mountains. The fourth painting is the best of the lot and an even more blatant borrowing from *King Kong*. The five castaways cross a fallen log that forms a bridge over a deep ravine, surrounded by lush foliage and with a waterfall cascading down a rock face in the distance.

The waterfall is not live-action film matted in but an artificially created ripple effect. The actors are the only live-action element in the shot, placed on the painted log by means of successful traveling matte.

The fifth painting depicts an imposing cliff face with two eye-like caves high in its sheer wall; behind it are more craggy peaks and a cloud-filled sky. Harryhausen might have gotten away with this one but when actors are combined with it by means of traveling matte, its fakery is highlighted. The final painting comes at the end of the film as the escaping group look back from their ship at the island. They are matted in front of an image of the distant volcano, glowing orange against a darkening sky and surrounded by mountains.

Harryhausen's use of miniatures is more successful. Very well-done are shots of a wind-swept hot air balloon flying low over a storm-tossed sea — actually a studio tank which for once actually looks like the real thing. A sculpted version of the cliff face with the eye-like caves is far more credible than the painting. A large cave containing a lake on which floats Captain Nemo's submarine, the *Nautilus*, is another impressive miniature. The volcano itself is only moderately convincing, but when it erupts at the climax, miniature rock faces and the walls of chasms crumble and collapse realistically.

The success of traveling matte composites (shot using the yellow sodium-lit process) is variable. The worst of them — the aforementioned shot of the sea gulls, and shots of the castaways in front of the animated crab — harm the film and should have been dropped.

473

Mysterious Island (1961): Harryhausen's crab on the attack.

Shots of the actors in a basket underneath the hot air balloon, backed by aerial footage, are better but still imperfect. Other traveling mattes are superb, most notably the early long shots of soldiers walking around the grounds of the Confederate prison beneath the balloon. In these excellent shots, everything — balloon, houses, etc. — is miniature except for the soldiers.

The giant crab is a classic monster and ideally suited to stop-motion. Its hurried, quirky movements and expressionless face make it easier for Harryhausen to convince us that this creature is alive than if it were a more humanoid character. If fact, many viewers are fooled into thinking they are watching an actual living crab. Herrmann's uptempo score complements the crunching and scraping sounds which the crab makes, really bringing the creature to life.

It's an unforgettable encounter, straight out of a nightmare. Its only failing is that Harryhausen doesn't have his puppet move around enough. The castaways battle it on the beach and force it over some rocks into a boiling geyser, but otherwise it never really scuttles about with sufficient purpose or variety. As ever, time and budget hold Harryhausen back.

The first of the scene's 22 animation cuts is a grimly humorous shock effect. Two of the castaways, Captain

Harding (Michael Craig) and Neb (Dan Jackson), are looking for food on a beach when the ground starts to move under their feet. In long shot, the giant crab gets up and they are thrown from its back. This clever static matte composite presumably required an additional matte to remove the platform in the live-action plate from which the actors fall. It is not simply obscured by the position of the puppet, since part of it would be visible through the crab's legs.

During the subsequent battle, several shots place the actors in the foreground by means of traveling matte. Unfortunately, these shots always look like effects shots because of film stock contrasts. A few shots feature closeups of what appears to be a live crab. Others feature full-scale partial props of the crab. Props of its legs look fine, but a mechanical claw simply is not up to the task and moves very stiffly.

Several stop-motion shots show the crab in long shot on the beach facing Harding, who threatens it with his spear. In these, the miniature floor on which the puppet stands is perfectly matched to the color of the rear plate. Neb is snatched by one of the claws and Harryhausen animates a puppet of the actor, its legs kicking very realistically. When Harding tries to spear the crab, his spear passes behind the puppet, so there is no need for painted or partial miniatures.

The other three castaways, Herbert (Michael Callan), Spillet (Gary Merrill) and Pencroft (Percy Herbert), rush to assist their colleagues and several dramatic shots show all four actors facing off against the crab, which still has Neb, screaming, in its claw. In one of these, Herbert runs under the crab in order to tie a rope to one of its legs. Harryhausen cuts from a long shot of Pencroft beginning to move under the puppet to a live-action shot of him with the prop legs.

Long shots of the men holding onto the rope with the crab trying to pull away from them are the kind of thrilling images for which Harryhausen is rightly famous. But he cheats a little in these composites, because close inspection reveals that the rope is not actually connected to anything and simply disappears behind the puppet (unlike *The Valley of Gwangi* in which he would combine live-action and partial miniature ropes in very elaborate composites).

In a new static matte set-up, the crab, still with the puppet Neb in its claw, scuttles sideways along a rocky part of the beach. The actors follow it up onto this raised area, crossing the invisible matte line as they do so.

In another set-up, the crab stands to the left of the frame on rocks that slope down behind it, while the actors face off against it on the other side of the shot. The whole of the sloping rock underneath puppet and actors may well have been matted in from an entirely different location, chosen because its incline serves the means of the crab's destruction — the actors use their spears to turn it over onto its back. Harryhausen's animation in the shot of it being flipped over is excellent — this could so easily have looked clumsy. The crab lies on its back, its eight legs kicking helplessly.

The group use their spears to lever the crab down the slope and into a pool of boiling water below. The contact between spears and puppet is implied by the positioning of the crab in front of the spears, which are actually pushing at nothing. One other rear-screen shot looks from behind the overturned crab at the four actors who are levering it.

A disappointing live-action shot closes the sequence, looking over the actors' shoulders at the crab sliding into the bubbling pool — the beading of the water droplets gives away the fact that this is a normal-sized crab.

Two more castaways are washed up on the island — Lady Mary Fairchild (Joan Greenwood) and her niece Elena (Beth Rogan). A safe shelter is discovered in a cave high in a cliff. This gives rise to an unintentionally amusing moment when Harding is exploring the cave. He encounters a normal-sized iguana lizard and looks absolutely terrified — and this is the man who has just battled a monster crab.

Some time later, Spillet is fishing in a river. Suddenly, the shadow of some tall creature passes over him and he runs back to the camp, looking over his shoulder in horror at whatever it is that is following him. When Spillet arrives at the goat corral, we see that the creature pursuing him is a ten-foot high bird that resembles a young chicken, with tiny wings and a savage beak.

This sequence — featuring 33 animation cuts — is the best in the film. Looking for a meal, the squawking, flapping bird struts around energetically, jumps over a fence, kicks Lady Mary over, and stomps around in a panic when Herbert leaps onto its back. Harryhausen's genius is that he makes it at once a dangerous and yet a slightly comic figure. It is the only stop-motion character in the film that possesses any personality, strutting and screeching

with enormous vitality. Unfortunately, no trace of this puppet survives today — its armature parts were recycled as part of the Harpies in *Jason and the Argonauts*.

Although it suits the plot that audiences take the creature to be a giant chicken, it is actually a prehistoric phororhacos. In an early draft of the script, the island was to be populated with primordial creatures, but by the time this angle had been discarded the model was already built. It's a classic example of how the script is a muddle — but needn't impair our enjoyment of this marvelous sequence.

The opening long shot is a stunner, with Spillet running from the foreground to the corral in the background as the phororhacos leaps down into the frame after him. The horizontal matte line is undetectable. There is great dynamism in the movement of the puppet, supported on wires as it jumps. The choreography of Spillet's movement — from foreground to background — gives the shot a feeling of depth, cleverly disguising the table-top nature of rear-projection set-ups.

In medium shot, the creature flaps its wing and screeches. Its feathers bristle where Harryhausen has touched them, recalling the fur on King Kong. In a striking long shot, Spillet and the two women stand cowering in the foreground as the phororhacos walks towards them. This shot is a textbook example of how the "reality sandwich" fools the eye into thinking a foreground puppet is in the background of a shot. (A studio paste-up artist used this set-up as the basis of a frequently published still in which Spillet's head is actually in front of

The phororhacos invades the castaways' camp in *Mysterious Island.*

the puppet's leg. No such shot appears the film.)

Spillet, Lady Mary and Elena run into the corral. In a classic shot, Spillet pulls the gate shut but the bird simply leaps over the fence (and Spillet) into the corral. It's another bit of tricky animation made to look easy by Harryhausen. That part of the fence in the foreground is a miniature, thereby allowing the puppet to appear behind it.

In another long-shot static matte set-up, the two women run to the other side of the corral, chased by the phororhacos. An alert, thinking predator, it watches Lady Mary as she runs off to one side, then turns its attention to Elena. The action that follows is thoughtfully directed by Harryhausen, intercutting long shots with closeups and medium shots of his creature.

A long shot has the bird towering over Elena. To emphasize the bird's size, Harryhausen keeps its head out of the top of the frame, as if it is too tall to fit into the shot. This closer shot of the puppet affords a good view of its credibly muscular thighs. Standing on a miniature floor, it lifts one claw in the air, bringing it down onto the fence next to where Elena is standing. Part of the fence is pulled away by an invisible wire to suggest that the puppet has knocked it away.

The other castaways arrive and Elena does the proper thing and faints.

Herbert (here an animated puppet) jumps on the back of the phororhacos.

The phororhacos places one claw on Elena and starts to bring its head down to feed. Its claw is carefully aligned with her image and really seems to be making contact with her.

In the same static matte set-up, Lady Mary thumps the far side of the bird's leg with a rifle butt. Reacting, it lifts its leg in pain. In the same set-up again, it raises a leg and knocks Lady Mary over, an effective moment of interaction with precise timing.

Spillet runs into the same set-up and hits the bird's leg with his spear. This time a partial miniature spear is used for a few frames, placed in front of the puppet's leg so that it seems he has struck its near side. Barely noticed in all the frenzy, this is exactly the kind of minor touch which helps to make the scene so plausible and vibrant. When Spillet hits the bird again, it squawks and leaps up into the air, turning as it does so to face him. It's a very dynamic — and very chicken-like — movement. It snaps its vicious beak at him with such force that the gesture sends Spillet toppling backwards.

Herbert runs towards the puppet. Harryhausen cuts from a live-action shot of him about to leap up, to a composite shot of a puppet Herbert flying through the air and landing on the back of the phororhacos. This is a great moment and more successful than a similar shot

478

which Harryhausen did years later in *Golden Voyage of Sinbad* (1973), which cut from a shot of Sinbad about to leap to a shot of his puppet counterpart on the back of the centaur, omitting the sight of him actually landing on the creature.

With Herbert clinging to its neck, the bird turns in a circle, trying to throw him off. Medium shots of the actor stabbing a full-scale prop neck are acceptable but this is a lazy prop — its white feathers do not match the red and gray feathers of Harryhausen's puppet.

Amid several closeups of the phororhacos screeching are three long shots (using the same static matte set-up used before) with the puppet Herbert holding onto its neck, and in two of these the creature makes a frantic hop into the air. Once again, Harryhausen suspended the puppet on taut wires for the ten or so frames while it leaves the ground.

The phororhacos struts into another static matte set-up. After a last closeup, there is the sound of a gunshot and the creature goes down. This is another clever shot, with well thought out animation of its legs crumpling under it, and a deft switch from the puppet Herbert to the actor. After the puppet hits the ground, the puppet Herbert is removed, while the rear-projected footage has been carefully edited so that the actor appears at this point, getting up and running away from the bird. The motionless corpse of the phororhacos is also seen in two static matte composites as the actors approach it.

Some time later, Herbert and Elena have their one and only romantic scene together. They discover a trickle of honey running down a rock face and decide to follow it back to its source. Having just encountered a giant crab and a giant bird, they might be expected to have more sense — but good sense is not one of the script's strong points.

Inside a cave opening, the couple discovers a huge honeycomb. Traveling matte composites of them dwarfed by the cave and honeycomb (all of which is an impressive miniature set) are very good. The cave set includes lots of realistically sculpted stalactites and rocks. As the couple are about to leave the cave, they hear a buzzing noise. In a memorably chilling animation shot, a giant bee flies down and lands on the lip of the cave opening. This exquisitely detailed puppet is totally believable. The strobing of wings which mars other animation puppets is not a problem here since even in real life, the rapidly beating wings of insects appear to strobe.

In this opening shot (the first of 19 animation cuts), and another which uses the same set-up, the area of the rock face beneath the cave is miniature, impeccably matched to the live-action footage. The advantage of this is that the puppet can throw a shadow, which helps to mesh the two elements.

Two successful traveling matte composites look out through the cave at Herbert and Elena retreating from the bee. The overhead part of the cave is part of the miniature set on which the bee has been animated, and behind the puppet is a rear projection of the sea. A similar perspective in which the bee walks into the cave mouth toward the camera has replaced the live-action area with a miniature cave floor. There is something unsettling about the site of this horse-sized monster, evoking all our natural

The giant bee returns to its lair in *Mysterious Island.*

nervousness in the presence of bees. Harryhausen has his creature walk in a very credible zigzagging direction on its spindly legs.

In long shot, the bee walks into the honeycomb set. Herbert and Elena climb into one of the sections of the honeycomb to escape it. A series of shots looks out from their hexagonal compartment at the face of the giant bee, which slowly seals them up by secreting a substance from its mouth and building a translucent wall across the aperture.

These shots allow several close looks at the highly detailed head of the puppet, with its long antennae, roughly textured eyes, moving mandibles and the hundreds of hairs. The bee, animated in front of a painting of stalactites, is combined with the live action by means of traveling matte. The shots in which it seals up the couple were animated in reverse order, with Harryhausen cutting away a small piece of the sheet one frame at a time. In the last of these shots, the bee is just a sinister shadow seen through covering.

Herbert and Elena escape by burning a hole in the other side of the honeycomb. The final two animation cuts are long shots of the cave, now with three bees walking around in it. Only one bee puppet was built, and animated in two extra passes of the camera in these all-miniature shots.

480

In the clutches of *Mysterious Island*'s nautiloid cephalopod.

Although always visually exciting, the bee episode never develops into a more satisfying dramatic scene. Perhaps it was kept short by the need to hasten the progress of the plot towards introducing Captain Nemo (Herbert Lom) and the *Nautilus*. A shot of a bee stinging someone to death would have been an unforgettable image but Harryhausen may have consciously avoided this because he knew he was aiming at a young audience — and had already suffered at the hands of the timorous British censor with *The 7th Voyage of Sinbad*.

Falling out of the back of the honeycomb, Elena and Herbert discover another huge cave. Moored on a lake is Captain Nemo's submarine, the *Nau-tilus*. This is another convincing miniature set and the two actors are placed in it by means of some more fine traveling mattes. Eventually Nemo makes his appearance and explains his experiments into enlarging animals to create a plentiful food supply for the world so as to eliminate the need for war. He also tells them that the volcano is due to erupt and they must flee the island as soon as possible.

He gives them underwater breathing apparatus and takes them on a subsea tour, showing them the ruins of a lost civilization. These are memorable fantasy images of gigantic Egyptian style statues and Roman style columned buildings. The actors are a traveling matte element and the trails of bubbles that come from their air tanks are a separate superimposed element. One of these composites is especially well-conceived, with two of the actors walking behind one of the statues. Unfortunately, the plot never makes anything of these images, which have negligible dramatic impact.

The same is true of an attack by a visiting pirate ship, which is destroyed by explosive charges placed on it by Nemo. It is all over very quickly and its only function really is to furnish the castaways with a means of escape — they decide to refloat the sunken ship by inserting the balloon and filling it with air. (Incidentally, one shot of the pirates jumping overboard was borrowed from *The 3 Worlds of Gulliver.*)

Just when the plot seems to have regained some impetus, as the castaways and Nemo try to refloat the ship, the script delivers a last and entirely gratuitous stop-motion episode. The group is working on the sea bed when they are attacked by a nautiloid cephalopod — a gigantic prehistoric octopus-like mollusc. The script, having dropped the prehistoric plot line, is happy to let audiences believe it is merely an enlarged modern-day octopus.

This is another excellent Hayward-sculpted model, with eyes full of evil intent and a huge, almost regal, spiraling shell on its back. Like its cousin in *It Came from Beneath the Sea,* the puppet has fewer than the normal number of tentacles (only six). The animation is very smooth, with Harryhausen making only very tiny adjustments to his puppet each frame in order to have the tentacles snake about very slowly in the water.

The animation was shot through a distortion glass to create the impression of filming underwater. Some of the live-action elements were actually shot underwater, while others were shot dry on a studio stage, then matted in front of the puppet. It's a striking scene, but Harryhausen is unable to make it exciting — because it is underwater, all the action takes place slowly. Part of the problem is that the scene is necessarily devoid of the grunts and screams that are usually trademarks of a Harryhausen battle. Herrmann's deliberately slow score for once doesn't add anything to the scene.

The first of 15 animation cuts is a creepy closeup of the monster's beady eye opening. In a rear-projection shot, one tentacle snakes across the foreground as the unsuspecting troupe of castaways walks by.

The camera is moved to good dramatic effect in a shot that begins with a close view of the great carapace, then slowly pulls back to reveal the creature in full, all its tentacles writhing. Pencroft is snared in a prop tentacle and in two marvelous long shots the mollusc holds a puppet version of the actor high off the sea bed. Its other tentacles all snake about menacingly. In these shots, the cephalopod sits on a miniature floor and no matte is needed.

A rear-screen set-up, again with the puppet on a miniature floor, has Harding trying to spear one of the tentacles. A convincing traveling matte set-up has foreground actors pretending to be underwater, while behind them the cephalopod continues to wave Pencroft about. This set-up is used in a second shot in which one of the live-action men is grabbed by a prop tentacle. The point at which the puppet tentacle becomes a prop tentacle is disguised by a large rock on the floor of the studio set.

After a medium shot of the creature's malevolent-looking head, with Pencroft still ensnared in a tentacle, Harding fires Nemo's "electric gun" at it. A blast of superimposed sparks hits the cephalod in an all-miniature shot. In a rear-projection set-up, a cloud of black ink — probably a cartoon animation — obscures the puppet and the actors behind it. In long shot, a second blast of electricity strikes the monster. Another cloud of black ink fills the screen as the puppet's tentacles all start to curl up defensively.

The episode has no proper resolution — we never learn what has happened to the cephalopod and have to presume that either it was killed or that it fled. Technically, there is little wrong with the scene, but it disappoints on a dramatic level.

Mysterious Island has flaws but it is still a magical movie. Over the years, only Harryhausen has been able to put giant creatures like these on the screen with such color and melodrama. It is interesting to compare his film with *Honey, I Shrunk the Kids* (1989), an entertaining later film with state-of-the-art special effects. It also features a menagerie of oversized animals (a bee, an ant and a scorpion) in exciting set-pieces, but they lack the sheer theatrical showmanship of Harryhausen's Dynamation classics.

Mysterious Planet

1982. Mysterious Planet Enterprises. Prod-D: Brett Piper. Very Freely Based on the Novel by Jules Verne. Ph: Nicholas Hackaby. Mus: Jefferson D. Rice.

Cast: Paula Taupier, Boydd Piper, Michael Quigley, Bruce Nadeau, George Seavey, Marilyn Mullen.

Rating: ☆½   Stop-Motion: ☆☆

Some fans of monster movies go on to make movies of their own. Obstacles like a non-existent budget are ignored: All that matters is to get some special effects up on the screen. Such is the case with Brett Piper's *Mysterious Planet*, which has a despicably trite screenplay, feeble acting, a soundtrack which is frequently inaudible and no-budget special effects. All of which adds up to a fun-filled 70 minutes which no fan of bad movies will want to miss. In a scene that puts *Plan 9 from Outer Space* to shame, Piper pans his camera across a woodland and manages to film one of his own crew, who is making a half-hearted attempt to hide behind a tree.

The not-very-special effects include some poorly lit spaceship sequences and a few reasonable matte paintings of alien landscapes and a cliff face shaped like a gruesome face. Piper's main achievement — other than getting the film produced at all — is that he has animated 64 stop-motion cuts, featuring a variety of alien creatures in sub–Harryhausen-style encounters with his group of ship-wrecked astronauts. The quality of the animation, models and composites is variable — never rising above the mediocre — but it is always fun to see how a Harryhausen fan attempts to emulate the kind of monster thrills that he grew up on as a child.

The first monster scene takes place on a beach and is directly inspired by the crab sequence in *Mysterious Island* — except that here the creature is a giant two-headed snail. A character discovers some slime on the beach. When he looks up, his acting deserves a prize for being the least convincing expression of terror ever attempted on screen.

Live-action shots using a prop snail head are intercut with 17 stop-motion cuts. In some of these, the animation is smooth enough, but it strobes badly in other cuts. The scene's main deficiency is that the snail never emits any character or sense of threat. The musical score sounds like a drunken orchestra tuning up.

In a static matte rear projection, the snail crawls from a behind a sloping hill. Medium shots of its two heads snaking slowly to and fro are intercut with full-view shots using a miniature replica of the beach. In these, the model is seen to have two front legs which it uses to pull itself along. One of the astronauts jumps onto the snail's shell, brandishes a spear at it, then falls backwards when it moves off. These cuts use a puppet human but are very poorly and abruptly staged. In extreme long shots, two animated human puppets face off against the snail. A final extreme long shot depicts the snail far out at sea, crashing surf attractively matted into the lower portion of the frame.

The group moves off through a forest. A stop-motion snake-like creature is seen in two cuts, hanging from a tree and blinking occasionally, but doing nothing else.

In a clearing, the group comes across an elephant-sized quadruped, its head sporting a crown of small bony ridges like the pachycephalosaurus "bonehead" dinosaurs. Bonehead is seen in four cuts, including two which are classic static mattes like something out of O'Brien's *The Lost World*, with the actors standing behind a rock in the lower right corner of the shot. The other two shots are all-miniature set-ups allowing a closer look at this intriguing model.

The astronauts have to cross from a cliff to a rocky pillar and string a rope between them, depicted in attractive long shots by means of a miniature set, with animated puppet humans standing on the cliff face or dangling from the rope (legs kicking unrealistically). The colors of the miniature set bear no relation to the live action, but by this stage it doesn't seem to matter.

A dragon appears from the sky, flapping above the girl on the rope. This scaly, bat-winged creature is a reasonable model but is badly served by this sequence. The wire-supported animation is fine. When the rope is bitten in half, it is animated so as to whip away realistically. But the rear projection in shots where the creature attacks two men is hopelessly washed-out. One of the men holds up a branch and the creature impales itself on it, a poorly directed sequence that is confusing. In the final shot, the slain puppet falls away from the camera down a ravine, and is animated far too stiffly to be at all convincing.

An astronaut is attacked by a plesiosaur-like creature that emerges from a lake. This model, seen in 12 stop-motion cuts, is considerably less detailed than the rest and the sequence switches from day to night and back again with a delirious disregard for continuity. A stiff prop head does not improve the scene. One good rear-projection set-up looks over the creature's shoulder at the actor in the background, but other shots are awkwardly animated as the beast walks through some trees, gets speared and expires. It's all badly paced, over too quickly and with negligible dramatic impact.

Inside a cave, a strange creature with one red eye and a long tail, wriggling on four tentacle-like legs, is briefly glimpsed in three stop-motion cuts.

In the final six animation cuts, Bonehead makes a reappearance. A close shot of the model as it chomps on some vegetation allows a good look at the warty detail of its skin. In a rare moment of interactive character animation, a girl in a washed-out rear projection slaps the creature on its nose and it recoils—a nice touch, albeit stolen from *When Dinosaurs Ruled the Earth*. In two shots in a miniature set, Bonehead has been harnessed up to some ropes in order to drag a spaceship out of some mud. The puppet takes a few stiff steps but nothing more. Again, this is a good idea whose potential is scotched by the low budget.

Na kometě
(U.S. title: *On the Comet*)

1970. Czech. Studio Barandov. D: Karel Zeman. Scr: Karel Zeman, Jan Prochazka. Based on the Novel *Hector Servadac* by Jules Verne. Ph: Rudolf Stahl. Special Effects: Karel Zeman, E. Pickhart. Art: Jiri Hlupy. Mus: Lubos Fiser.

Cast: Emil Horvath, Magda Vasarykova, Frantisek Filipovsky, V. Mensik, K. Effa, M. Nesvadba.

Rating: ☆☆½   Stop-Motion: ☆☆½

Karel Zeman's fourth foray into Jules Verne territory is again characterized by the director's delightfully quirky style, but this time lacks some of the charm and invention of earlier films. Simple yet deft satirical attacks on colonialism and the military are combined with lightweight, sometimes farcical humor, and the story is set in the kind of fantasy milieu that is uniquely Zeman's.

It is 1888 and the French, Spanish and British are all squabbling over Middle East countries. They are interrupted by the arrival of a passing planet whose gravitational force tears a chunk out of the Earth and sends it skyward, with all the story's characters still on it. In space, the warring factions learn to co-exist, but at the close of the film, when they return to Earth, they pick up their battles exactly where they left off, having learned nothing from their experience.

The film lacks the coherence of

Vynález Zkázy, Zeman's best film. Two prehistoric sections are poorly integrated with the narrative and seem out of place. The haunting visual style of other films — for example, the seascapes of *Baron Prášil*— is attempted only on a lesser scale here. It's as if Zeman has lost some of his imagination and sense of fun. But this is still an enchanting film, and quite unlike the work of any other filmmaker.

Zeman uses stop-motion like no one else. For example, he animates a top hat bobbing up and down on the breeze caused by an explosion. The film begins with shots of animated butterflies and birds, Zeman trademarks. But he doesn't expect to convince us his illusions are real; rather he wants us to delight in them. His paintings of cities, boats, a fortress on a hill and a cliff are all eye-catching but rarely realistic. A soldier hanging under his hot air balloon floats above a picturesque painting of an Arabian city, with stop-motion birds flitting around him. Casually he drops his cigar, starting a fire below. ("We helped spread our civilization," the narrator remarks dryly.)

Zeman combines his stylized etchings of landscapes, boats and buildings with matted areas containing live-action seas or actors. Two soldiers on top of a cliff are actually standing on flat ground; the cliff face is a painting. The effect is successful without needing to be totally convincing. When one soldier falls over the edge, he is replaced by a flailing stop-motion puppet at the point where he crosses the split.

Shots of the arrival of the planet are stunning: A huge ball covered in swirling blue gases looms over the horizon, and a real sea and live actors are matted into the lower part of the frame. Zeman doesn't have the resources to depict the ensuing upheaval as elaborately as he would like, settling for a lot of clouds of smoke in a red-tinted sequence. This includes a shot of a stop-motion puppet of a soldier in the army band, still playing his cymbals as he is sent hurtling through the air.

An encounter with a fly with a ten-inch wing-span (apparently a mechanical creation, not a stop-motion puppet) is the first indication that things on the fragmented world aren't as they were on Earth. Soon, the French fort is being attacked by dinosaurs. This is an ambitious sequence and impressively animated (in 24 stop-motion cuts) by Zeman and his team, but it lacks any interaction between puppets and actors. The dinosaurs never achieve any real dramatic presence: They arrive on the scene, look menacing and are eventually scared off.

As in *Cestě do prověku*, Zeman doesn't have merely one dinosaur in his panorama, but whole herds. In the striking opening shot of the sequence, a group of sauropods and tyrannosaurs plods slowly across a miniature set. In closer shots, a group of about ten bipeds and quadrupeds cross the frame. Some of the bipeds are fictitious creatures with long necks and spiny backs — a surprising move by Zeman since in *Cestě do prověku* he had striven for authenticity.

The French open fire with their cannons, which prove useless. In a low-angle shot, a tyrannosaurus is lit by a blast of gunfire and recoils. The bright light reveals that the model does not withstand close scrutiny — its eyes are too large and its upper claws are too human-like. In long shots, the dinosaur herd continues its march, large beasts in the foreground, small bipeds smoothly animated in the background. A typically moody Zeman skyline drifts past overhead. The cavalry is sent out and in three accomplished matte shots they first charge, then flee from two dinosaurs that tower over them.

A tyrannosaurus growls in closeup, then tramples on a tent in the marketplace. The crumpling canvas is animated extremely realistically. In an accomplished long shot, a distant group of bipeds advances on a crowd of extras in the market, matted into the lower portion of the frame. An even more striking long shot has two bipeds chasing an actor down a deserted street.

Zeman resolves the scene with a typically whimsical twist. A market trader, more worried about his pots and pans than the approaching dinosaurs, loads his wares into a cart. The horses bolt and run toward the dinosaurs, seen in a long-shot composite that uses the same matte used during the cavalry charge. The dinosaurs are startled by the sound of the clanking pots and pans and turn away, eventually walking off in a series of shots. One memorable medium shot has several fleeing beasts lit up by occasional flashes of lightning and a small bipedal dinosaur strutting along in the background. A dramatic low-angle shot of a dinosaur's legs running is weakened because the animation is just too smooth and cyclical to be realistic. In an impressive medium shot, ten dinosaurs plod heavily across the frame.

Later, the hero sets sail in search of his beloved. He sights what he at first as-sumes to be land but which turns out to be an enormous sea serpent. This potentially interesting encounter is depicted very flatly by Zeman, with the creature merely sitting in the water, then submerging when startled by the sound of the sailors banging pots and pans. Stop-motion is used to show the serpent making slight snaking movements through the water, its tail sinking out of sight behind superimposed water spray.

There is one more prehistoric sequence which, while entertaining in its own right, is wholly gratuitous and only serves to muddle the plot. Land is sighted again, seen initially in two attractive long shots of three pterodactyls gliding over an island backed by a yellow sky. It's an image that might have been designed by O'Brien. A dimetrodon — a bulky quadruped with a huge spiny sail on its back — plods across a miniature set while the ship — an animated painting — sails past in the background. In closeup, the dimetrodon growls, its neck and chest animated to suggest it is breathing. It's a fine model and it's a shame that Zeman did not make more use of it. In a striking panning shot, a pterodactyl glides down through the undergrowth, miniature foliage both behind and in front of the puppet. Seen in two shots, a styracosaurus stands growling in a miniature jungle set. This is another highly detailed but underused puppet.

Zeman cannot resist throwing in a moment of typically playful surrealism. Looking through his spy-glass, the hero declares, "We are witnessing the transmutation of the species!" An absurd fish-like creature trots along on erect hind legs, transforming in a series of four shots into a boar trotting on hind legs! A different puppet is used for each shot so that the change appears to be gradual. The creature is only ever seen from one angle so it may be that Zeman only sculpted one side of the puppets.

The sequence closes with a picturesque long shot of animated birds flying around an orange sky above a bay.

On the Comet is disappointing compared with Zeman's earlier films, but still contains more than enough wit, imagination and off beat stop-motion effects to reward the difficult search for a print of it.

Naked Gun 33⅓— The Final Insult

1994. Paramount. D: Peter Segal. Scr: Pat Proft, David Zucker, Robert LoCash. Based on the Television Series **Police Squad** created by Jim Abrahams, David Zucker, Jerry Zucker. Ph: Robert Stevens. Art: Lawrence G. Paull. Mus: Ira Newborn. Visual Effects Supervisor: Kimberly K. Nelson. Special Visual Effects: Illusion Arts Inc., Syd Dutton, Bill Taylor. Digital Animation: Fumi Mashimo. Stop-Motion Sequence (uncredited): Chiodo Brothers, Kent Burton.

Cast: Leslie Nielsen, Priscilla Presley, George Kennedy, O. J. Simpson, Fred Ward, Kathleen Freeman, Elliot Gould, Raquel Welch, Pia Zadora.

Rating: ☆☆½   Stop-Motion: ☆☆½

Like the two previous entries in the series, this piles the gags on thick and fast, with about one in three hitting the mark. Police officer Drebben (Leslie Nielsen) is brought out of retirement to foil a bombing plot which culminates in a slapstick recreation of the Oscar ceremony, with a number of stars making cameo appearances.

During the film's opening credit sequence, the camera follows a police car as it hurtles through all kinds of unlikely locations: down a bobsled run, soaring over Manhattan, and flying through *Star Wars'* Death Star canyon. At the end of the sequence, the car crashes into a mock-up of one of the dinosaur compounds of *Jurassic Park*. A Tyrannosaurus Rex, modeled after the one in Spielberg's film, steps on the car, walks into full view, turns to the camera, emits an absurdly high-pitched laugh, then stomps off.

This five-second cut features a beautifully detailed stop-motion model built by the Chiodo Brothers in a miniature setting complete with foreground and background foliage. The animation by Kent Burton is accomplished. The gag is a treat for stop-motion fans — who will also be infuriated by its brevity.

Top: The interior of a stop-motion puppet. This armature for a creature called the Oso Si-Papu was designed and built in 1986 by Steve Archer, using parts machined by Bill Hedge. It was intended to be used in a version of an old Willis O'Brien storyline, but the project was never completed. *Bottom:* The multi-limbed, multi-fanged Dark Lord of *Howard the Duck* (1986) is one of the most complex animation puppets ever made. Designed by Phil Tippett, this is a monster for connoisseurs.

AA

Opposite: One of the harpies of ***Young Sherlock Holmes*** (1986), animated by Harry Walton, visual effects supervised by Dennis Muren. ***Above:*** Randall William Cook sculpts the Demon Lord for ***The Gate*** (1987). Adding exceptionally small details helps to give the puppet a convincing sense of great size.

CC

Above: The Jackal Boy of *Hardcover* (1988). Sculpted and animated by Randall W. Cook. *Opposite: Honey I Shrunk the Kids* (1989). *Top:* Harry Walton animates the scorpion in front of a rear-screen. The instrument to the left of the puppet is a gauge used to mark its position prior to it being re-posed. This allows the animator to control the rate of movement of a character. *Bottom:* The scorpion puppet and rear-projected live-action footage.

EE

Top: A rare still of the tyrannosaurus from Jim Danforth's never-completed *Timegate* (1977–78). *Bottom:* Frame enlargement from another not-yet-completed Jim Danforth project, *West of Kashmir,* a project he devised in 1989. Seen here is an encounter with a giant Himalayan snow ape.

Top: Nancy Allen confronts *RoboCop 2* (1990), a terrifying evil robot. The armature for this puppet, built by Tom St. Amand, contained over seven hundred parts. *Bottom:* Randall W. Cook animates the John-Demon puppet for *Gate II* (1990). The puppet was designed by Cook and sculpted by Cook and William Bryan.

GG

Above: Three of the foot-tall minions of *Subspecies* (1991), animated by David Allen. *Opposite, top:* The fighting fossils of *Dr. Mordrid* (1992), animated by David Allen. *Bottom:* Randal M. Dutra animates the velociraptor D.I.D. (direct input device) for *Jurassic Park* (1993).

HH

II

JJ

Opposite: Two skeletons exhume one of their fellows in *Army of Darkness* (1993), animated by Peter Kleinow. *This page, top:* MRAS-2, the giant scorpionlike robot of *Robot Wars* (1993). *Bottom:* Joel Fletcher animating the minions for *Bloodlust—Subspecies III* (1994). (Photo by Brett White.)

KK

Above: Suteck, the ancient Egyptian warrior monster, animated by Joel Fletcher for *Puppetmaster V* (1994). *Opposite, top:* Suteck leaps onto Pinhead in *Puppetmaster V*, animated by Joel Fletcher and Paul Jessel. (Photo by Chris Endicott.) *Bottom:* Sherlock Holmes looks on as a spinosaurus battles a giant snake in *Dark Continent*. This is a frame enlargement from the promotional reel for this as-yet-uncompleted project, devised in 1994 by Jim Danforth.

MM

Opposite: The crazy shoe-creature from *Freaked* (1994), animated by David Allen. *This page, top: Ewoks— The Battle for Endor* (1995) featured this unforgettable panorama: stop-motion creature and rider combined seamlessly with live-action footage and a matte painting of distant mountains.

Bottom: David Allen animates a recreation of a scene from *King Kong* for an IMAX large-screen demonstration film, *Special Effects* (1996). *Next page:* The Yeti creature from *The Primevals*, a project David Allen has been developing for nearly 30 years.

PP

Naked Robot 4½

1993. 21st Century. D-Scr-Ph: Philip Cook. Mus: David Bartley. Special Visual Effects Created by Philip Cook, John R. Ellis. Stop-Motion Animation: Kent Burton. Big Harvey Design: John Poreda, Ken Walker, Mike Walker. Big Harvey Engineered and Built by Walkerworks Engineering. Painting/Finishing: Kent Burton. Matte Paintings: Philip Cook. Model Supervisor: Brad Ulvila.

Cast: Hans Bachmann, A. Thomas Smith, Rick Foucheux, John Cooke, Robert Biedermann, Ralph Bluemke.

Rating: ☆☆½   Stop-Motion: ☆☆½

Having shot this as a straight SF thriller, somebody clearly decided that it would fare better at the box office as a comedy. Its title became an imitation of *Naked Gun 2½*, and the title credit clumsily replaces the original working title (*Invader*) during the opening credits. The trailer took dialogue out of context to emphasize the comedy angle. A long stop-motion finale featuring a hundred-foot-high robot seems to change style midway, and its initially formidable puppet character is reduced to a comic level, bursting into song and muttering oaths in a way that recalls the giant Porno in *Flesh Gordon*.

Director-scripter-cameraman Philip Cook is in sure control as he tells his tale of mysterious goings-on at an Air Force base. Despite a lowish budget, he pulls off some effective edge-of-the-seat sequences. A fighter plane on a test flight goes out of control and crashes. Two cops are menaced by a hovering UFO which blasts them with laser fire. Lighting and photography are consistently thoughtful and excellent, making the film look stylish and a lot more expensive than it is.

Some software written for defense systems has developed a mind of its own and developed brainwashing powers. Having taken over the minds of all the personnel at the air base, it has instructed them to build a massive robot, HARV — Heavily Armored Rampaging Vaporizer. The software plans to make America great again — by wiping Russia and China off the face of the Earth. Having captured a photographer, a cop and a general, a brainwashed captain gives them a demonstration of Harvey in a subterranean installation.

This impressive robo-motion sequence features 31 stop-motion cuts animated by Kent Burton. Harvey is an imposing creation and the puppet is intricately embellished with mechanical minor details. In general design it resembles the spindly-limbed, slender-waisted RoboCop 2. Harvey's detachable head is the UFO that has appeared in earlier sequences. Only one shot combines puppet and live actors. The shadowy sequence is very dramatically lit, with blasts of flame illuminating the cavern.

In an imposing low-angle shot, the construction platforms on either side of the robot slide back to reveal Harvey. Blasts of flame rise up in the foreground (superimposed elements), lending the sight a satanic glow. The light of the flickering flames is successfully replicated on the puppet. The first animated cut is a closer shot of one arm, its vicious pincer-fingers opening and closing. In a low-angle long shot, the enormous robot steps out on chicken legs from between the platforms.

In a medium shot, Harvey stomps across the cavern and turns to face the camera. When one character calls him a white elephant, since the Cold War is over, Harvey reacts angrily, looking down at his (off-screen) accuser. In a series of medium shots, Harvey is lit up by a foreground burst of flame and raises his fist, smashing it down onto the platform where the actors had been standing. The impact is shown in a live-action miniature shot that cuts in well with the animation. In live-action miniature shots, Harvey's clawed hand tries to reach along a tunnel after the fleeing actors. In medium shot, the stop-motion puppet withdraws its hand from the tunnel and makes a disappointed grunt.

The actors run to a cathedral-sized cavern littered with military debris — old missiles, tanks and shells. This striking image is a combination miniature set and matte painting. Harvey smashes his way through the cavern wall and pokes his upper half through the hole he has created, glinting photogenically in the half-light. In the same set-up, he bashes a fist on the ground in anger.

In a stunning long shot, the group of actors is matted into the lower left corner of the frame as Harvey looks down at them from the side of the cavern. Unfortunately the live-action area jumps slightly but this is still a remarkable image. In medium shot again, Harvey realizes he cannot get at his prey this way and withdraws from the hole in the cavern wall.

In three cuts, he stomps angrily into another miniature set, smashes a steel pillar with one fist (with superimposed sparks aligned with the impact), then turns to face the camera. These full-view shots of the puppet are again lit by blasts of rising flame.

Harvey starts to go the same way as HAL, the robot in Kubrick's *2001: A Space Odyssey*. In a long shot lit up by more flame, he sings a verse from "As Time Goes By," then sits down and props his chin on one hand in a dejected manner. Back on his feet again, he takes up his plans for nuclear destruction again, baying "I'll light the world!" In medium shot, he plucks a missile from an overhead rail, passing it from one clawed hand to the other. "Lovely, lovely toy," he coos.

All the missile systems are ready and activated and, in two more striking long shots, the robot stands poised, laughing insanely. Meanwhile, his human opponents have loaded a 30mm bazooka and fire it at Harvey. In medium shot, the robot takes the missile on its shoulder amid a cloud of superimposed sparks. When the cloud clears, there is damage to the puppet's upper area but it is still active. In medium shot, it draws its head up angrily and in long shot throws the missile straight at the camera. For this shot, the missile is animated and wire-supported and its cartwheeling trajectory is exceptionally smoothly executed by Burton.

In a superb low-angle long shot, Harvey stomps towards the camera, stepping right over and behind it. "I'll grind your bones to make my bread!" he rants angrily. In other shots, he strides straight at the camera again and raises his fist, but a second missile is fired and this makes a direct hit on the UFO–head. The head is destroyed and, in a final long shot, Harvey steps backwards and then topples over.

For a low-budget first effort, this is an excellent sequence. Given more of a chance to shine in additional scenes, Harvey could have been one of the great robo-motion characters of the last two decades.

Harvey is also seen briefly in an earlier sequence as one character is being brainwashed. The victim's mind seems to travel down a glowing tunnel, at the end of which stands the robot. Harvey, silhouetted eerily by a bright light, stands among a pile of rubble and beckons with his clawed hands, calling "Come with me." It's an effectively chilling moment.

The miniature work is often superb. Fighter planes, helicopters, cars and an assortment of planes and other vehicles at the air base are all shot on miniature sets and look like the real thing. In one shot, a car races toward the camera, and behind it in the distance smoke rises from the wreckage of a plane in the air base. This is shot entirely in miniature, with the car a very smoothly animated stop-motion model. Other shots use stop-motion successfully to depict planes or buses moving through the air base, thereby avoiding having to composite live-action vehicles with miniature sets.

Necronomicon

1993. Necronomicon Films/Pioneer LDC Ozla. D. Brian Yuzna, Christophe Gans, Shusuke Kaneko. Scr: Brent V. Friedman, Christophe Gans, Kazunori Ito. Ph: Gerry Lively, Russ Brandt. Art: Anthony Tremblay. Mus: Joseph Do Luca, Daniel Licht. Special Mechanical and Makeup Effects: Thomas C. Rainone, John Buechler, John Foster, Screaming Mad George Inc., Steve Johnson's XFX Inc., Optic Nerve Studios, Tom Savini, Bart Mixon's Monster Fixins. Visual Effects Supervisor: Lee Scott. "Whispers" episode: Makeup, Mechanical and Stop-Motion Effects: Todd Masters Company. Creature Design and Animator: Todd Masters.

Cast: Jeffrey Combs, Bruce Payne, Belinda Bauer, David Warner, Bess Meyer, Signy Coleman.

Rating: ☆☆½   Stop-Motion: ☆½

This compendium horror movie, named after H. P. Lovecraft's fictitious work of ancient evil, makes a creditable attempt to suggest that author's world of demons from other dimensions. Its three tales, plus the linking story in which Jeffrey Combs, playing Lovecraft, reads from the eponymous book, are really an excuse to indulge in a cornucopia of slimy monsters and gruesome splatter effects. The third tale, "Whispers," features brief moments of stop-motion created by Todd Masters.

In this tale, a policewoman has been abducted and finds herself in a basement strewn with dismembered corpses. Clinging onto the walls are the strange bat-like creatures that have created all this carnage. These are depicted mainly by means of on-set mechanical and rod-operated puppets, but stop-motion is used in three shots where the action of one of the bat-demons could not be created any other way.

The first of these shots is very well done and shows a bat-demon detaching itself from the wall and taking to the air.

The other two shots, in which the creature is shown in flight, are both composite shots. They are less successful because the animation looks hurried and the lighting on the puppet conflicts with the lighting in the live-action set. But as quick effects within a busy sequence that is full of all kinds of other effects shots, they function adequately.

Nemesis

1992. Imperial Entertainment. D: Albert Pyun. Scr: Rebecca Charles. Ph: George Mooradian. Art: E. Colleen Saro. Mus: Michael Rubini. Effects Makeup: David P. Barton. Special Visual Effects: Fantasy II Film Effects. Special Visual Effects Supervisor: Gene Warren, Jr. Go-Motion Animation: Peter Kleinow. Motion Control: Christopher Warren. Sculptor: Dan Platt. Armatures: Scott Beverly.

Cast: Olivier Gruner, Tim Thomerson, Cary-Hiroyuki Tagawa, Merle Kennedy, Yuji Okumoto, Marjorie Monaghan.

Rating: ☆☆   Stop-Motion: ☆☆½

A soulless imitation of *The Terminator*, *Nemesis* put a lot of stuntmen and pyrotechnicians to work but has little to offer in terms of imagination or wit. It opens promisingly with a dynamically photographed action sequence in which part-cyborg cop Olivier Gruner is pursued by a gang of part-cyborg villains. Gruner's cynical narrative adds a touch of *film noir* style. But from there on, things go badly wrong, chiefly due to the near-complete absence of anything resembling a plot. In case anyone has missed the similarities with the Schwar-

zenegger film, *Nemesis* climaxes with a sequence in which cyborg Tim Thomerson is stripped of all clothing and flesh and engages the hero in a fight to the finish. But director Albert Pyun is no James Cameron and the scene lacks the unforgettable impact of the original. Its main failing is the fact that the script has forgotten to give the Thomerson character any personality and so his cyborg incarnation has negligible dramatic force.

Fantasy II Film Effects were recruited to produce this remarkable climax, with Gene Warren, Jr., supervising and Pete Kleinow doing the animation of the puppet cyborg. Where *The Terminator* relied mainly on shots of mechanical props, intercut with only a few stop-motion cuts (also by Kleinow), *Nemesis* chooses to shoot the sequence almost entirely in miniature and features a hefty 44 animation shots. These include many successful front-projection set-ups, some clever moments of implied physical interaction between puppet and actor, and some consummately executed moments of complex animation involving both the cyborg puppet and a puppet of Gruner, both hanging from the underside of a flying craft.

The animation is extremely fluid in many of these cuts, employing a go-motion device to add blurs to the finished image. However, the sequence as a whole sits unhappily in a film which up to this point has largely avoided visual effects. It comes across as something of a gratuitous afterthought and is more fully enjoyed as a self-contained set-piece, watched on its own.

In the first cut, Alex (Gruner) has fired a shot at Farnsworth (Thomerson) which blasts away his clothes and flesh, leaving just the metallic cyborg underneath. The cyborg pulls itself upright and looks around, accompanied by the sound of mechanical whirring. This long shot is bathed in a red light which is presumably meant to suggest the glow of the nearby volcano. It seems that the script at some point may have intended that the cyborg has its flesh burned away by a volcanic flare — there is no other explanation for the sudden red haze. This cut appears to have a painted backdrop, with foreground live-action flames adding some depth.

A few minutes later, Gruner and others take off in a small jet craft. As they take to the air, the cyborg runs at them and catches hold of the underside of the plane. Kleinow's animation of the running cyborg is excellent but this is a disappointing shot because the cyborg and the miniature plane — presumably both blue-screened elements — look semi-transparent. A follow-up shot of the cyborg hanging underneath the plane is much better — the puppet has been animated in a front-projection set-up and looks less like a separate image.

In closer shot, the cyborg swings its body and punches the underside of the plane — Kleinow makes the puppet do a well thought-out lunge. A similar shot, but closer still, allows a better look at the very evil-looking mechanical face.

In a shift of perspective, the next two animation cuts look down from inside a miniature of the plane at the floor as the cyborg rips its way in. A prop head is used effectively in some cuts.

In a series of shots, the cyborg attacks Gruner. Go-motion blurs enhance carefully aligned process shots in which the puppet lunges at the actor and strikes him, then is sent flying backwards when Alex returns a punch. Medium shots and long shots show the two facing off and the cyborg lunging forward again. Miniature steel struts in the lower foreground help to break up the table-top design of these shots. In another successful bit of implied interaction, the cyborg strikes Alex with the flat of its hand. Even better is a shot where the cyborg throws itself on top of Alex, who has fallen backwards onto the floor. Alex kicks the cyborg away and it crashes — with some go-motion blur — into the wall of the plane.

It stands upright again and advances. Alex strikes it twice and again the sense of physical contact is successfully achieved through careful alignment of images. As the cyborg falls backwards through the hole in the floor, it grabs Alex's arm, pulling him down. In gruesome live-action cuts using a prop head, Alex's forehead catches on the ripped steel and his scalp is pulled off.

Several long shots have the puppet

dangling from the miniature plane, pulling the puppet Alex partway through. The Alex puppet falls through the hole and flips over, hanging underneath the cyborg which holds him by his arm. In a dynamic shot, the plane flies straight at the camera with the two animated puppets hanging beneath it.

Varying the perspective again, some shots look down through the hole in the floor onto the two puppets. In a close shot of the puppets' arms, Alex manages to break free of the cyborg's grip and grasp its arm. Kleinow just about pulls off some ambitious animation as the Alex puppet climbs up over the cyborg (stepping on its head) and clambers back into the plane. The arms of the cyborg flail realistically, trying to grab Alex as he

climbs over it. In one shot, Kleinow very effectively animates Alex's trousers to give the impression that the material is flapping in the wind.

The two puppets continue struggling in a series of shots, including a stop-motion closeup of the cyborg's face as it gloats, "We own you. We paid for every part of you!" In response, Alex severs his own arm on the jagged steel. In the final two animation cuts, the cyborg falls away from the camera holding the severed arm, screaming and eventually bursting into a ball of flame as it descends towards the volcano below. This convincingly animated effect recalls Kleinow's final shot in *Army of Darkness*, in which the skeleton of the evil Ash cartwheeled through the air and exploded into flames.

Never Say Never Again

1983. Talia/PSO. D: Irvin Kershner. Scr: Lorenzo Semple, Jr. Story: Kevin McClory, Jack Whittingham, Ian Fleming. Ph: Douglas Slocombe. Art: Philip Harrison, Stephen Grimes. Mus: Michel Legrand. Optical Effects: Apogee. Supervisor of Special Visual Effects: David Dryer. Stop-Motion Animation: Harry Walton.

Cast: Sean Connery, Max Von Sydow, Klaus Maria Brandauer, Barbara Carrera, Kim Basinger, Edward Fox, Rowan Atkinson.

Rating: ☆½   Stop-Motion: ☆☆½

Sean Connery's return to the James Bond role after a 12–year absence heralded a return to the form of memorable

early Bond thrillers like *Dr. No* and *Thunderball*. Instead, this turned out to be as inconsequential as the latter-day Bonds, with glib dialogue and gratuitous foreign locations substituting for a decent plot. The most embarrassing moments in a generally misjudged film include Connery and Kim Basinger dancing a tango; Connery pretending to be a masseur and giving Basinger a rubdown (Was the script written by a 14-year-old?); and Rowan Atkinson appearing at odd moments in one of the least funny comic roles of all time.

Towards the end of the film, Connery and Basinger are pursued on horseback to the top of a tower. To escape, they leap off and plummet into the sea below. For an extreme long shot lasting one second, Harry Walton animated a puppet of the horse and two riders against a blue screen, making very slight but credible movements. The result is an immaculately convincing composite —

this does not look like an effects shot. It beats Harryhausen's falling horse in *The Valley of Gwangi* by a length.

This was Walton's first animation work in a feature film. He had previously assisted Gene Warren with the dinosaur animation of NBC-TV's *Land of the Lost* in the mid–1970s.

The NeverEnding Story

1984. Neue Constantin. D: Wolfgang Petersen. Scr: Wolfgang Petersen, Herman Weigel. Ph: Jost Vacano. Art: Rolf Zehetbauer. Mus: Klaus Doldinger, Giorgio Moroder. Supervisor of Special and Visual Effects: Brian Johnson.

Special Effects Makeup and Sculpture Supervisor: Colin Arthur. Matte Painting Supervisor: Michael Pangrazio. Matte Painters: Jim Danforth, Chris Evans, Caroleen Green, Frank Ordaz. Animator: Steve Archer.

The Luck Dragon from *The NeverEnding Story* (1984), animated by Steve Archer.

The NeverEnding Story

Cast: Barret Oliver, Noah Hathaway, Sydney Bromley, Patricia Hayes, Gerald McRaney, Tami Stronach.

Rating: ☆☆½   Stop-Motion: ☆☆½

This multi-million dollar children's epic, at the time the most expensive European-based film ever made, tries hard to involve its audience in a breathtaking fantasy saga. It almost succeeds, but director Wolfgang Petersen (who had made the highly acclaimed World War II film *Das Boot*) is no George Lucas. It all too soon becomes a series of set-pieces with little dramatic impetus. And, like many fantasy films, its plot aims to be too grand, concerning a quest to save the world of Fantasia from destruction. The human characters have little chance to develop among all this spectacle.

It's a fine children's film, but is afflicted with shallow dialogue and a hackneyed quest theme. Some of the set-pieces never really take off. For example, a meeting with a tiny elf couple (Sidney Bromley and Patricia Hayes) contains superb elf makeup, an intriguing crystalline telescope and a rickety chair-lift — all memorable images with great potential but let down by weak dialogue and lack of purpose. Gmork the Wolf could have been an imposing foe, but the script gives every impression that the character is only there because a film like this is supposed to have a dark and nasty villain — he doesn't actually do anything and is dispatched very easily when stabbed.

On the other hand, there is much to enjoy, including many first-class special effects. Michael Pangrazio, Jim Danforth and others provided some excellent matte paintings of fantasy landscapes, seamlessly matched to the live action. The tempestuous destruction caused by the Nothing — a mass of swirling clouds that devours everything in its path — is especially well-staged by Brian Johnson in one scene in which the ground shakes and trees and rocks are swept away. Johnson built a huge blue screen for the film and there are some superb traveling matte shots of actors looking up at giant creatures in the background. The film also contains many fantasy creatures realized by means of state-of-the-art animatronics, including an impressive giant Rock-biter and an enormous, wrinkled tortoise. But the facial gymnastics of the Gmork creature are overstated and too obviously trying to impress.

Unfortunately, the film chooses to over-indulge its animatronic creations and uses stop-motion only briefly — almost begrudgingly — in a few shots of a flying character, Falkor the Luck Dragon. This 40-foot-long white beast has shaggy fur and a puppy dog's head — an unlikely creation, to say the least, designed mainly to evoke sympathy from its young audience and never looking like anything other than a fluffy toy.

All close shots are done with a full-size animatronic puppet, but stop-motion is used in full-view long shots of the animal in flight. The animal dips and turns, its head and long tail undulating in a sleek rhythm as it flies — complex actions that were beyond the capabilities of a mechanical creation. Steven Archer animated seven cuts (in three different sequences) in front of a blue screen, all very fluid, and in each Falkor's ears flap believably in the wind. Two models were built (one three feet long, the other 18 inches long) and covered in rabbit fur. They were attached to go-motion rods to eliminate some of the strobing.

In one cut, the creature has rescued a young boy and Archer animated a small puppet of the boy hanging underneath the dragon.

In the lackluster climax, the young hero rides through a city on the back of the Luck Dragon. Although Archer animated one long shot, it was dropped for some reason, and the sequence is devoid of any full-view shots of Falkor and the boy, settling instead for traveling matte shots of just the animatronic head. Considering that the image of a boy riding the dragon was the mainstay of the film's publicity, it is a disappointment that Archer was not asked to do more, and that no other creatures were depicted with stop-motion. Potentially a chance for stop-motion to shine, *The Never-Ending Story* has to be filed in the "great missed opportunity" drawer.

After *Clash of the Titans* and *Krull*, this was a less than satisfying job for Archer.

The NeverEnding Story II
The Next Chapter

1991. Warner Bros. D: George Miller. Scr: Karin Howard. Based on the Novel *The NeverEnding Story* by Michael Ende. Ph: Dave Connell. Mus: Robert Folk, Giorgio Moroder. Art: Bob Laing, Gotz Weidner. Special Visual Effects: Derek Meddings, The Magic Camera Company, Cine Magic Berlin. Creature Special Effects Makeup: Colin Arthur. Creature Special Effects Animatronics: Giuseppe Tortora. Matte Painting Consultant: Albert Whitlock. Matte Paintings: Syd Dutton, Bill Taylor (Illusion Arts). Matte Paintings from *The NeverEnding Story*: Chris Evans, Jim Danforth.

Cast: Jonathan Brandis, Kenny Morrison, Clarissa Burt, John Wesley Shipp, Martin Umbach.

Rating: ☆☆½   Stop-Motion: ☆☆

In 1991, filmmakers were still churning out clones of *Star Wars* (1977). This filming-by-numbers effort even had the nerve to have a princess appear in a hologram-like vision and implore the hero, "You're my last hope." The script lacks invention, lurching from genre cliché to genre cliché. George Miller's direction is competent but humdrum. In short, the film has all the faults of the original and more.

Derek Meddings was in charge of special effects, but this time around they are not particularly special. The Silver City, surrounded by a sea of acid, is too obviously a miniature in a studio tank. The nine-foot-high bipedal crustacean baddies are a good idea but unremarkably realized with men in costumes. Had stop-motion been used to depict these creatures, they could have been memorable. As before, many fine matte paintings of alien landscapes lend much-needed sparkle to an otherwise studio-bound production. Albert Whitlock was

497

the matte painting consultant. Some paintings from the first film by Chris Evans and Jim Danforth get a re-exposure.

Falkor the Luck Dragon appears again but this time without the benefit of any stop-motion long shots of it in flight, which instead are achieved with a static model. Stop-motion does contribute something to the film, but on a small scale and with no attempt to exploit its potential. The snake-like logo on the front of the eponymous book is animated in two brief cuts where it uncoils and looks up at young Bastian, its eyes lit up with red-glowing cel animation.

Later, Bastian conjures up a huge green dragon which flies off over some mountains pursued by the boy on the Luck Dragon. This could have been an exciting scene had it been developed properly. Instead, the dragon merely gets blasted by one of the evil queen's laser-cannons before it has the chance to do much. The dragon begins life as a cel-animated green outline, then becomes an animatronic head and neck and subsequently is seen in six blue-screen stop-motion cuts when it takes to the air.

The first of these is an aerial shot looking down at the dragon flying (above a crowded room) as it expels two blasts of flame. Other shots look over Bastian's shoulder as he rides on Falkor, the blue-screened dragon flapping its wings in the distance against a background plate of mountains or flying through a miniature tunnel. Two side views allow a slightly closer look at the model as it soars past the side of a mountain, breathing fire as it goes. Other long shots use a static model presumably pulled on a wire. Just why the producers didn't feel it was worth making this creation a more interesting threat is a mystery.

The New Gulliver see Novyi Gulliver

Night Train to Terror

1986. Visto International. D: Jay Schlossberger-Cohen, John Carr, Tom McGowan, Greg Tallas, Philip Marshak. Scr: Philip Yordan. Ph: Susan Maljan, Frank Byers, Byron Wardlaw, Art Fitzsimmons, Bruce Markoe. Art: Ronald K. Crosby, Robert Chatterton. Mus: Ralph Ives. Special Visual Effects: William R. Stromberg and Associates. Effects Camera and Stop-Motion Animation: Anthony Doublin, William R. Stromberg. Puppet Construction and Matte Painting: Robert Stromberg. Joint Works and Puppet Armatures: Bill Hedge.

Cast: John Phillip Law, Cameron Mitchell, Charles Moll, J. Martin Sellers, Meridith Haze, Marc Lawrence.

Rating ☆☆   Stop-Motion: ☆☆

This low-budget horror film is a compendium of three tales and, like most compendium horror films, it is extremely forgettable. Its linking passages have God and Lucifer on a train discussing Good and Evil and introducing each story. Musical numbers also separate the tales, a desperate attempt to aim the film at a young audience. It began life as *Cataclysm*, made in 1980, then extra scenes were added for its theatrical release in 1986.

The first story tells of a series of killings in a hospital, with some explicit scalpel-attacks. The second and third stories are no better but are spiced up by some stop-motion sequences which are fun to see — even though always crude and unconvincing. The animation was shot by the Stromberg brothers and Anthony Doublin, with armatures built by Bill Hedge (who had done some of the animation for 1974's *Flesh Gordon*). Doublin would later supply stop-motion effects for *Sundown — The Vampire in Retreat* (1990).

The second tale concerns a group of thrill-seekers who devise ever-more deadly forms of Russian roulette. One of these involves the group attending a kind of seance at a spooky old mansion and being menaced by a foot-long black wasp. This could have been a chilling episode, as the wasp crawls out of a glass bottle, then hovers above the group before selecting a victim. The puppet, with six spindly legs, glowing yellow eyes and sinister mandibles, is not bad. But the animation fails to convince us that it is a living creature, especially in shots of it in flight. Some poor composites destroy any chance the sequence had of being effective. There are 18 stop-motion cuts

although it is possible that the first four — with the wasp inside the bottle raising and lowering its wings — were achieved with a mechanical version of the creature. It is hard to tell because the glass distorts the image.

The black insect steps out of the bottle onto a miniature table. When it takes to the air, its legs fold up slightly underneath it. A low-angle shot looks up at the puppet hovering overhead. The strobing of the wings does not offend the eye because this is the way we normally perceive insect's wings. The wasp lands on a prop of one of the actors' shoulders and in two closeups turns towards the camera, mandibles moving threateningly. It takes to the air again and lands on a convincing prop of an actor's hand.

The wasp flies up from the hand and out of the room. Two rear-screen shots show it flying past some trees, but the rear image looks so washed out that the shots are ruined. In slightly better rear-screen shots, the creature hovers over a man's face. When it stings his face, a prop head is used in a quick live-action closeup in which his cheek seems to explode with the force, splattering his girlfriend with blood.

The third tale has Cameron Mitchell on the trail of a demon in human guise. This is another botched story, but does have one amusing moment when the demon, stripping off to join an expectant girlfriend in bed, peels off a sock and reveals a cloven hoof.

There are three short stop-motion sequences, one featuring a bizarre spider-like creature, the other two showing the demon in his real form, a 20-foot-tall humanoid creature. The sequences are too brief to be effective and, as with the wasp scene, the budget didn't stretch to allowing for the kind of composites that make all the difference in animation scenes.

The spider-demon, seen in just seven stop-motion cuts, appears on a beach at night. Horse-sized, its upper part is a dark-skinned humanoid. It is another potentially terrifying creature that is not used to full effect. Breaking waves in the background are barely noticed because the rear projection is so dark.

Like a trap-door spider, the demon emerges from a covered hole in the beach — actually a miniature set. It grabs the kicking leg of a prostrate man, picks him up and disappears back down into the hole. The man is an animated puppet in these shots and the covering to the hole is also animated as it is replaced.

The giant demon himself is seen in nine animation cuts. Exploring a spooky old mansion, a man walks into a room shrouded in fog. In long shot, he is seen standing in front of the demon, which towers over him. For this cut, a puppet human was used and it is very crudely animated. The demon itself is a quite striking creation, with a very plausible muscular body and eyes glowing red (all the puppets in the film have glowing eyes for some reason). It has no nose and a fleshy, grill-like mouth. Its hands clench as it straightens itself, then it takes a step towards the man. In a low-angle shot, its foot comes straight down onto the camera.

Later, the demon in human guise transforms into his monstrous form. This is another half-realized moment and the puppet is seen in only three cuts. A superimposed ball of red energy obscures the actor, who is replaced by the puppet. The demon unleashes a ball of energy (another superimposed element, aligned with the puppet's movements), hurling it at an attacker.

The film closes with a stop-motion shot of the train traveling up into space, with a simulation of a smoke-cloud animated to look like it is coming from the engine.

Nightbreed

1990. Morgan Creek. D-Scr: Clive Barker. From His Novel *Cabal.* Ph: Robin Vidgeon. Art: Steve Hardie. Mus: Danny Elfman. Special Makeup and Visual Effects: Image Animation. Special Makeup Designers: Bob Keen, Geoff Portass. Animation Designer: Rory Fellowes. Animation Cameraman: Karl Watkins. Special Makeup (L.A.): Tony Gardner. Animated Optical Effects: VCE/Peter Kuran.

Cast: Craig Sheffer, Anne Bobby, David Cronenberg, Charles Haid, Hugh Quarshie, John Agar.

Rating: ☆☆½   Stop-Motion: ☆☆

Clive Barker is one of the best horror writers of recent years but he should let other people direct the films made from his books. In *Nightbreed*, he tries too hard to be faithful to *Cabal*, thereby missing the more cinematic potential arising from making prudent changes. The film also makes the curiously British mistake of taking itself too seriously (the plague of Hammer Films), with Barker trying to say something about the nature of evil and society but really having nothing new to say. His characters constantly mutter catchy lines of dialogue which are supposed to sound Very Significant but in fact just hide the fact that Barker is not very good at characterization.

But it seems a shame to criticize: It is a step forward that it is possible to make films like this at all. *Nightbreed* would have been unthinkable even as recently as ten years earlier. Even in 1990, the idea of setting most of the film in a subterranean world filled with sympathetic freaks and monsters was not quite acceptable, and the film never caught on at the box office. Midian is a fascinating world featuring some startling makeups by Image Animation and some impressive sets (e.g., the rope bridges strung across a cavernous chamber) but is let down by some weaker makeups (a silly porcupine woman and a poor man's rel-

ative of devil-horned Tim Curry in *Legend*) and a couple of unconvincing matte paintings of the cemetery above. Some of the best makeups include the fat man whose head hangs half way down his belly, the sludge-monster that writhes on the floor, and "the Tribes of the Moon," full-costume creatures that are released at the climax and go on the rampage.

Several stop-motion sequences of Midian monsters were animated by Rory Fellowes for Image Animation—including shots of a leopard-woman riding a dinosaur-like creature—but most of these were removed from the release print when producers tried to make the film look more like a conventional horror film. A few brief moments remain and they are good enough to make one wish to see more.

Down in Midian, a small dinosaur-like creature with a long neck, skinny limbs and a snaking tail, feeds on the bloody carcass of a rat—very smoothly animated in its one shot. In three quick process shots, a flying stingray-like creature with eyes on stalks and a cavernous mouth with savage teeth floats through the air and attacks one of the men who have invaded its world.

The Nightmare Before Christmas

1993. Touchstone. D: Henry Selick. Scr: Caroline Thompson. Based on a Story and Characters by Tim Burton. Ph: Pete Kozachik. Mus: Danny Elfman. Art: Deane Taylor. Animation Supervisor: Eric Leighton. Animators: Trey Thomas, Timothy Hittle, Michael Belzer, Anthony Scott, Owen Klatte, Angie Glocka, Justin Kohn, Eric Leighton, Paul Berry, Joel Fletcher, Kim Blanchette, Loyd Price, Richard C.

Zimmerman, Stephen A. Buckley. Visual Consultant: Rick Heinrichs. Camera Operators: Jim Aupperle, others. Armature Supervisor: Tom St. Amand. Sculptors: Norm DeCarlo, Shelley Daniels, Greg Dykstra, Randal M. Dutra. Mold Makers: Jon Berg, others. Additional Animation: Harry Walton, Paul W. Jessel, Michael W. Johnson, Ken Willard, Daniel Mason.

Cast (voices): Danny Elfman, Chris Sarandon, Catherine O'Hara, William Hickey, Glen Shadix, Paul Reubens.

Rating: ☆☆½   Stop-Motion: ☆☆☆

This full-length animated film does not really belong in this encyclopedia because there are no live-action characters in the film and because we are never expected to perceive the puppets as anything more than puppets. But it is being included for two reasons: Because significant use of stop-motion in a feature film is a rare thing indeed these days, and because *The Nightmare Before Christmas* contains more stop-motion than has been seen in a single film for many years. Additionally, the film employed the talents of a host of stop-motion artists, the work of many of whom is discussed elsewhere in this book. The film is included in the interests of detailing full accounts of their careers.

The Nightmare Before Christmas tells the story of the inhabitants of Halloweentown, in particular the long-legged, skull-headed Jack Skellington. He decides to kidnap Santa Claus and organize his own brand of Christmas, which involves distributing presents that include a shrunken head, a giant snake that devours a family's Christmas tree and other, similarly horrific gifts. But eventually he repents of his ways and Santa escapes and makes all well.

The film's failing is that its story never engages the interest and its characters never come to life. But it does create successfully a surreal fantasy world of dark and grimly humorous images and includes several brilliantly staged set-pieces. Above all, its puppet animation is beautifully choreographed and always fluid and credible. Lengthy animation shots of many seconds' duration are enhanced by imaginative lighting and by a restless camera which, because it is freed from the need to match up with any live-action footage, is able to move across the action dynamically.

The film was two years in production and contains 74 puppet characters, represented by nearly 300 puppets. One hundred forty of these were fully armatured (under the supervision of Tom St. Amand), with the remainder being either wire-armatured or wire and ball-and-socket combinations. Most of the wire armatures were built by Jon Berg. Randal Dutra was one of the key character sculptors for 14 of the major characters; he sculpted and helped design the series of interchangeable replacement heads that allow Jack to talk.

Among the rest of the crew, those who have made contributions to stop-motion sequences in other feature films include Eric Leighton, Justin Kohn, Rick Heinrichs, Jim Aupperle and Harry Walton.

Nightmare on Elm Street 3— Dream Warriors

1987. New Line. D: Chuck Russell. Scr: Wes Craven, Bruce Wagner, Chuck Russell, Frank Darabont. Story: Wes Craven, Bruce Wagner. Ph: Roy H. Wagner. Art: Mick Strawn, C.J. Strawn. Mus: Angelo Badala-menti. Mechanical Special Effects: Peter Chesney (Image Engineering). Krueger Makeup and Effects: Kevin Yagher. Special Makeup Effects Sequences: Greg Cannom, Mark Shostrom. Special Visual Effects: Dream Quest Images. Visual Effects Supervisor: Hoyt Yeatman. Stop-Motion Skeleton and Marionette Effects: Doug Beswick Productions. Stop-Motion Animation: Doug Beswick. Effects Photography Supervisor: Jim Aupperle. Stop-Motion Puppet Construction: Yancy Calzada. Marionette Construction: Mark Wilson.

Cast: Heather Langenkamp, Craig Wasson, Patricia Arquette, Robert Englund, John Saxon, Zsa Zsa Gabor.

Rating: ☆☆½ Stop-Motion: ☆☆☆

The 1980s were flooded by sequels to successful horror films: *Friday the 13th, Halloween, The Amityville Horror* and *The Howling* all prompted anywhere up to seven sequels. The best series by far was the *Nightmare on Elm Street* saga, not because the direction or plots were superior (although they were — slightly), but because they were filled with imaginatively surreal special effects set-pieces. The best of the series was *Dream Warriors*, which had some superb special makeup effects and also two sequences that used the stop-motion skills of Doug Beswick and Jim Aupperle.

By the mid–1980s, horror films had matured to the extent where they were able to dispense with a lot of the incompetent plot and characterization which weakens so many of them, instead getting on with the business of creating bizarre fantasy images. Freddy Krueger, the razor-fingered slasher around whom the Elm Street stories revolve, becomes almost gratuitous, merely a linking device to give all the effects scenes some kind of thematic common ground. As a consequence, he fails to be as creepy a menace as he ought to be, but it's a small price to pay. Discussing the film simply as a series of trick sequences is no disservice — it's the best way to enjoy the film.

On the whole, the ideas are original, although a few of them (like the other films in the series) borrow from sequences in other films. Tiny, writhing, screaming faces that grow out of Freddy's chest (an effect by Kevin Yagher) recall the faces on a mausoleum in *The Sword and the Sorceror*; makeup expert Greg Cannom worked on both films. Characters being pulled through mirrors is an idea lifted from *Orphee*. And the sequence in which a girl is unable to outrun Freddy because her feet are stuck in some kind of glue actually repeats a dream-like device from the first *Elm Street* film. Otherwise, *Dream Warriors* is full of innovative effects that are definitely the stuff of nightmares.

Tap faucets become gripping fingers on the ends of skeletal brass arms. Freddy's head and two mechanical arms

503

sprout from the top and sides of a television set to pull a girl's head into the screen and electrocute her. An enormous snake-like monster with Freddy's head almost swallows a girl whole, another amazing sight created by Yagher. A girl rips out a boy's tongue with her teeth, then spits out four other tongues that coil around his arms and legs and tie him to a bed — the floor beneath the bed disappears, revealing a fiery bottomless pit. A victim's arms and legs are cut open and his veins are pulled out and used to pull him along like a puppet on strings. There is an impressive shot looking up at a bell-tower with a gigantic Freddy manipulating the "strings" of his victim and trying to make him jump to his death.

A very nifty shock effect has Heather Langenkamp sit down in a chair and disappear into it, having been pulled into someone else's dream. A split screen unobtrusively follows the shape of the chair. This is that rare kind of inventive shock effect which momentarily throws us off-balance, unlike the all-too-common sudden face-at-the-window or thrusting arm.

The plot becomes too contrived at the end as five kids go into a dream to confront Freddy — a good idea but tritely realized as each kid has his or her own scene. One thinks he's a wizard-master from a Dungeons and Dragons game and gets menaced by a vicious-looking wheelchair. Another dreams she is a leather-clad punk and meets her death when Freddy's fingers turn into hypodermics and he gives her an overdose of heroin — her arms are covered in holes which pucker hungrily in anticipation of the drug.

Beswick, Aupperle and their team supplied 23 stop-motion cuts. Five are used to show a foot-high marionette of Freddy coming to life. The rest comprise a wonderful little scene where Freddy's charred and blackened skeleton comes to life and attacks Craig Wasson and John Saxon.

The marionette sequence begins when a featureless string puppet hanging on a wall transforms into a likeness of Freddy. It looks like clay animation was used to alter the appearance of the head and hand, although it could be a series of replacement puppets. Knives spring out of the tiny hand. The only composite shot in this sequence is a closeup of the puppet looking at the intended victim sleeping in bed in a rear projection. The puppet slashes its own strings and drops down, landing on the floor (a miniature set) on bendy legs that are deliberately unrealistic, and walks towards the bed. It's a quick and deliciously surreal moment, perfectly in keeping with the tone of the film.

The more-ambitious skeleton episode is a *tour de force*, albeit a minor sequence when compared with its screen forebears in *The 7th Voyage of Sinbad* and *Jason and the Argonauts*. Beswick and Aupperle are long-time Harryhausen fans and probably wanted to do a scene like this for years. The "arms back" pose and even some of the choreography seem to have been lifted, consciously or otherwise, from Harryhausen's sequences. Only the budget prevented this from being a classic scene: Some of the background plates look grainy compared with the animation puppet, and almost all shots are conventional rear-projection set-ups without static mattes which could have helped to mesh the two elements. But the animation is extremely smooth, there are lots of clever tricks of interaction and the skeleton is a terrifying adversary, especially in the unforgettable shots where it shovels earth into the grave that Wasson has fallen into—as nightmarish a role-reversal as anyone could hope for.

The scene is set in a creepy car salvage yard at night, where Wasson and Saxon have gone to give Freddy's remains a proper burial and so end his evil influence. After digging a grave, Wasson goes to pick up the sack containing Freddy's bones. Suddenly a (live-action) skeletal hand shoots out and grabs him. In a classic long shot, the skeleton rises up (out of a miniature sack at the foot of the shot) and swipes at Wasson, who falls backwards. In five medium shots (two from the front, three from behind), the skeleton advances on Wasson. The background shots were locked off during filming but in some of them the animation camera dollies forwards or backwards slightly to add movement. In the last of these, the skeleton swipes away a hubcap which Wasson holds up to protect himself.

It turns to give Saxon a nasty stare, then in long shot ducks as Saxon swings a metal pipe at it, the camera panning across the shot. In a convincing moment of alignment, it grabs Saxon's arm and with its other hand grabs him between the legs, lifts him (he is actually supported on unseen wires) and throws him backwards. He lands on the spiked wing of a car and dies.

With an open-mouthed snarl, the skeleton turns in medium shot toward Wasson again. In three cuts, it walks up to Wasson, slashes his chest, hits him on the head with a shovel, then spins around and hits him across the face, sending him falling into the grave. Two superb long shots, angled as if looking up from the grave, show the skeleton shoveling earth straight at the camera. These may be matte shots (with the matte line following the line of the ground) or it may be that the animated footage of the skeleton was used as a rear projection with a miniature mound of earth and live-action shovels full of dirt filmed in front of it. The animator could have been concealed below the table-top, throwing up handfuls of earth. The skeleton drops the shovel, then in a superb final shot raises its arms and roars triumphantly—a spine-chilling image backed by a jarring musical effect. Its job done, the skeleton collapses into a heap of lifeless bones, a tricky bit of animation made to look effortless.

Nightmare on Elm Street V— The Dream Child

1990. New Line. D: Stephen Hopkins. Scr: Leslie Bohem. Story: John Skipp, Craig Spector, Leslie Bohem. Ph: Peter Levy. Art: C. J. Strawn. Mus: Jay Ferguson. Visual Effects Supervisor: Alan Munro. Miniature Effects Photography: Jim Aupperle. Optical Effects: VCE/Peter Kuran. Freddy De-Merge Stop-Motion: Ted Rae. Diving Board and Phantom Prowler Sequence: Doug Beswick Productions. (Supervisor: Doug Beswick. Mark Cut-Out Animation: Larry Nikolai. Stop-Motion Animation: Yancy Calzada.)

Cast: Robert Englund, Lisa Wilcox, Kelly Jo Minter, Danny Hassel, Erika Anderson, Nick Mele.

Rating: ☆☆½   Stop-Motion: ☆☆

As in previous installments, a perfunctory plot is forced onto what is essentially just a series of effects set-pieces. The heroine is pregnant and Freddy wants to use the baby as a means of returning to life. To prevent this, a group of kids must free the soul of his mother—a nun who was raped by a hundred madmen, no less. Stephen Hopkins directs adequately but can't prevent the beginnings of tedium that creep in as nightmare follows nightmare without much dramatic impetus.

Many sequences are remarkable but even the best lack force because they are surrounded by so many other bizarre sights. Among the most striking are a scene in which the wires and cables of a motorbike burrow into the skin of the rider, eventually blowing away all the flesh from his skull; a trip into the heroine's womb where we meet the baby Freddy; and the sight of three heads on long stalks protruding from Freddy's stomach.

Some sequences include a few seconds of stop-motion. Doug Beswick's company, which had supplied effects for the third entry in the series, was contracted to do the work. This time, however, he does not get the chance to create anything as elaborate as that film's marvelous skeleton sequence — these are all minor effects. Jim Aupperle looked after the all-important aspects of getting correct light balances during rear-projection shooting. Yancy Calzada receives a credit for stop-motion but, although he did some stop-motion test shots, none of his work appears in the final film.

In one scene, Freddy makes a shock appearance in a kitchen refrigerator. Immediately beforehand, the contents of the fridge — cartons, bottles, a dish of sauce — all decompose and develop fungus, achieved in two quick animation shots making use of replacement animation.

Later, a girl is about to dive into a swimming pool when the board becomes covered with a brown fungus, splits into two giant hands of finger-like shards and curls up around her. The shot of the spreading fungus is a stop-motion cut. Most shots of the hands are done with full-scale props, but also included are two shots using miniature puppets animated by Beswick against a rear projection of the girl on the board. The whole sequence is a rather hurried and contrived attempt to come up with an original death scene.

In a more successful sequence, a character is transformed into a two-dimensional comic book figure during a battle with Freddy. Two full-length shots use a flat, paper-like puppet animated against a rear screen. Eventually, Freddy cuts him up into little pieces.

Near the end of film, Freddy "demerges" from the heroine's body, literally cutting his way out of her with the claws on his hands. This surreal scene is achieved mainly with special makeup prostethics but includes one long shot of the fully grown Freddy poking out of the girl, his legs protruding from her back, his head and arms emerging from her stomach. This is a very quick stop-motion cut — too quick to be effective really. One wonders if perhaps the director chose not to linger on this puppet because he knew that it would look fake.

In terms of its stop-motion, *The Dream Child* is a waste of the considerable talents of Beswick, Aupperle and crew.

1941

1979. Universal/Columbia. D: Steven Spielberg. Scr: Robert Zemeckis, Bob Gale. Story: Robert Zemeckis, Bob Gale and John Milius. Ph: William A. Fraker. Visual Effects Supervisor: Larry Robinson. Optical Consultant: L. B. Abbott. Matte Painting: Matthew Yuricich. Miniature Supervisor: Gregory Jein. Art: Dean Edward Mitzner. Mus: John Williams.

Cast: Dan Aykroyd, Ned Beatty, John Belushi, Lorraine Gary, Murray Hamilton, Christopher Lee, Tim Matheson, Toshiru Mifune, Warren Oates, Robert Stack, Nancy Allen, John Candy, Elisha Cook, Slim Pickens.

Rating: ☆☆½   Stop-Motion: ☆☆

Steven Spielberg's extravagant farce about Californians during World War II, paranoid about an attack by the Japanese, is the director's least commercially successful film — many people simply didn't find it funny. But it contains several brilliantly staged set-pieces, including some excellent comedy routines and one or two spectacular action sequences that feature superior miniature work.

The film includes a few seconds of stop-motion, barely noticed amongst all the destructive mayhem. In four or five shots, Ned Beatty looks out to sea from his clifftop home and sees a Japanese submarine in the extreme distance. A few crew members can be seen walking along the top of the sub. The sub is a miniature and the crewmen were small puppets made to move by a kind of prototype go-motion, their moving parts attached to rods that moved their limbs during single-frame exposures. The footage of the miniature sub was then combined with footage of an ocean sparkling in the moonlight and finally Beatty was blue-screened in the foreground of the image. It appears that only one go-motion shot of the sub was filmed, then re-used several times — composited with different elements whenever an extreme long shot of the sub was needed.

Ninja III—The Domination

1984. Cannon. D: Sam Firstenberg. Scr: James R. Silke. Ph: Hanania Baer. Art: Elliot Ellentuck. Mus: Udi Harpaz, Misha Segal. Matscene Effects: Effects Associates/Jim Danforth.

Cast: Sho Kosugi, Lucinda Dickey, Jordan Bennett, David Chung, Dale Ishimodo, James Hong.

Rating: ☆☆½   Stop-Motion: ☆☆

This Western-style martial arts programmer is conspicuously devoid of anything resembling a plot and is little more than a collection of fight scenes. What plot there is, takes a leaf out of the old werewolf movies: Heroine Lucinda Dickey is possessed by a black ninja's sword, causing her to commit murders which she cannot recall the next day. The pace is brisk, launching into a well-staged massacre on a golf course and indulging in lots of pseudo-supernatural trickery. The latter includes a Japanese-style exorcism and a climactic resurrection of a ninja in a Buddhist temple.

The resurrection requires that the evil spirit possessing Dickey leave her body and re-enter the evil ninja. The shadowy specter, bathed in an eerie blue glow, is seen in three quick cuts, emerging from the woman and floating through the air. Jim Danforth worked on this sequence and in a letter to the author described his contribution as "a brief glimpse of a stop-motion 'ghost' ninja seen enveloped in a cloud of 'ectoplasm.' In subsequent cuts, the ghost is cartoon animation done on paper."

Nosferatu, eine Symphonie des Grauens (U.S. title: *Nosferatu the Vampire*)

1922. Germany. Prana. D: F. W. Murnau. Scr: Henrik Galen; based on (uncredited) Bram Stoker's *Dracula*. Ph: Fritz Arno Wagner. Art: Albin Grau.

Cast: Max Schreck, Gustav von Wangenheim, Alexander Granach, Greta Schröder, Ruth Landschoff, John Gottowt.

Rating: ☆☆☆   Stop-Motion: ☆☆

A creepy, stylized version of Bram Stoker's *Dracula*, *Nosferatu* was directed in Germany by one of the cinema's pioneers, F. W. Murnau. Today, its story-telling appears occasionally heavy-handed and some of Murnau's camera tricks seem crude, but the film is still a feast for the eye, full of eerily atmospheric passages. Count Orlock, played by Max Schreck, remains the most loathsome and evil-looking vampire in the horror genre. The film has an engagingly artificial air which has been enhanced by the passing of time.

On several occasions, Murnau uses stop-motion (which he referred to as

508

"one stop one" filming) to enhance the otherworldliness of Orlock's actions. The coach which collects Hutter is intended to move through the forest like an apparition from Hell. In four shots, Murnau took a few frames of film, had Schreck and the coach advance a few feet, then took another few frames of film. In one of these shots, the actor playing Hutter had to stand motionless for several minutes by the path as the coach approaches.

Later, Hutter looks out his window and is astonished to see Orlock piling coffins onto a cart. Again, Murnau uses his "one stop one" technique to give these two shots a dreamlike quality.

After Orlock climbs into one of the coffins, Murnau animates the coffin lid (very crudely) so that it climbs up by itself onto the coffin and covers the vampire.

Stop-motion is used again in two brief shots. When the vampire's ship arrives in Bremen, a canvas covering the hold doorway pulls back unaided and the door then opens. Both actions are achieved with some very crude stop-motion. Finally, when Orlock is seen leaving his house in Bremen, the wooden door slides open at his command — another moment of crude stop-motion, with Schreck standing motionless for the duration of the effect.

Nosferatu the Vampire see *Nosferatu, eine Symphonie des Grauens*

Novyi Gulliver (U.S. title: *The New Gulliver*)

1935. MosFilm (U.S.S.R.). D: Alexander Ptushko. Scr: Bolotin, Grigori Roshal, Alexander Ptushko. Adapted from Jonathan Swift's *Gulliver's Travels*. Ph: Alex Renkov. Mus: Leo Schwartz. Animators: Sarah Mokil, Nicholas Renkov, Igor Shkarenkov.

Cast: V. Konstantinov, the Ptushko puppets.

Rating: ☆☆☆   Stop-Motion: ☆☆½

A boy named Petya is given a copy of Swift's *Gulliver's Travels* as a reward for making a yacht from an old wrecked boat. As he reads it out aloud to his friends, he falls asleep. In his dream, Petya has adventures with pirates, then is shipwrecked on an island inhabited by miniature people dressed in seventeenth century costumes. Petya is found on the shore by the Lilliputians who bind him down "as a precaution." Beneath the ground, the workers of Lilliput revolt against their oppressors. Petya comes to

The Russian crew of *Novyi Gulliver* (1935) surrounded by their puppets, including a larger-than-life puppet of Gulliver. (BFI Stills, Posters and Designs.)

their assistance. At the decisive moment, Petya awakes and the film ends with a "rousing song."

Topped and tailed by brief live-action sequences, the main bulk of *The New Gulliver*'s story occurs in the land of Lilliput and uses dozens of animated puppets combined with a child actor. According to Ptushko's article "The Coming of a New Gulliver" for *Sight and Sound* magazine, the animation — or "object Multiplication" as he called it — was achieved with small puppets "the size of a human palm," and made of rubber, metal, wood and cloth. In total, according to Ptushko, "60 settings and 3,000 dolls were required for this picture." The main doll characters — such as the Abbott, the Financier, the Dandy, the King, the Prime Minister and the Chief of Police — had "from two to three hundred interchangeable heads with various facial expressions."

"As a piece of sheer mechanics." wrote London's *The Observer*, "done with endless care and technical invention, the work is astonishing." On its original release, the film was "hailed as brilliant" by London's *Evening Standard* newspaper, which also recognized its story content as "broadly speaking, crude propaganda."

Swift's original story was an attack on hypocrisy in the form of (supposedly) a tale for children. Other cinematic interpretations of this classic story — for example, those by Max Fleischer, Ray Harryhausen and Peter Hunt — have, in the main, avoided the political elements and emphasized the fantasy. Ptushko emphasized the politics. In his adaptation, the petty-minded inhabitants of Lilliput are now "evil ministers with armaments blindly manufactured underground by downtrodden workers." Gulliver is no longer a kindly doctor, but a "Soviet Boy Scout" with Communist leanings who intends to save the workers.

Unfortunately, the propaganda in *The New Gulliver* is often as subtle as a sledgehammer and distracts from the charm of the film's puppet characters. If viewers can overlook the heavy-handedness of this approach, then the film is still well worth seeing today for its technical achievements. However, finding a print of this exceedingly rare film is no easy task.

There are numerous moments in the film that are memorable from a technical point of view. The scene showing the boy tied down surrounded by the Lilliputians used a full-size puppet of the boy. The boy character is unconscious for most of the "tied down" shots and so was not required to move. Also effective are the shots in which Gulliver is fed and scenes in which Gulliver is transported to the town. These highlight the elaborate miniatures and exquisitely made puppets. According to S. S. Wilson's *Puppets and People*, Ptushko used mechanically operated puppets and a live boy in some shots, and in others he combined the full-size boy puppet with the animated puppets of the Lilliputians.

The puppet designs in *The New Gulliver* are caricatures somewhat in the "Puppetoon" style. There is a very effective use of sound effects for the Lilliputians. The pitch of their voices is deliberately heightened so as to give them a shrill and "tiny" quality.

(This critique was written by Steven Archer.)

A Nymphoid Barbarian in Dinosaur Hell

1991. Troma/Chapter V Enterprises/ R.I.P. D-Scr: Brett Piper. Mus: The Astral Warriors. Special Effects: Cheap Tricks, Mark Frizzell.

Cast: Linda Corwin, Paul Guzzi, Alex Pirnie, Marc Deshales, K. Alan Hodder, Russ Greene.

Rating: ☆½   Stop-Motion: ☆☆☆

In these days of go-motion animation, computer generated imagery and motion-control composites, how marvelous to find that someone is still making films where the stop-motion puppets *look* like stop-motion puppets, where the camera is locked off during effects shots and where

511

you can still have fun trying to spot the matte lines.

In *A Nymphoid Barbarian in Dinosaur Hell*, writer-director-animator Brett Piper not only gives us five good old-fashioned, gratuitous stop-motion set-pieces but also takes a leaf out of films like *One Million Years B.C.* and *When Dinosaurs Ruled the Earth* and gives us a lousy plot as well. Or, more precisely, no plot at all, as characters wander around a post–Nuclear holocaust world with little purpose, occasionally getting kidnapped or bumping into dinosaur-like monsters that have mutated from present-day animals.

Although he filmed this on a non-existent budget (albeit considerably larger than that for his first film, 1982's *Mysterious Planet*), Piper has managed to get on screen 64 impressive animation cuts as well as a number of shots involving paintings or miniatures. The animation models are all carefully designed with wrinkled, warty hides and fleshy limbs. They are weird dinosaur-like mutations that have vestiges of giant beetles, bats, alligators and dogs. The animation is always smooth although the puppets are never required to do a great deal. Even the most elaborate stop-motion sequence — a fight between two creatures — never really allows the puppets to realize their potential. Moments of interaction between puppets and actors are kept to a minimum. Piper, although clearly a Harryhausen fan, doesn't seem to be interested in giving his puppet characters any touches of personality. This is a shame because, given the film's semi-comic tone, they might have taken on some of the style of the dinosaurs in *Caveman*.

Non-animation effects include a few quick shots of glass paintings and miniatures. A castle perched on a hill is seen in both a good painting and also, closer up, as a detailed miniature covered with menacing spikes and carved, monstrous faces. A glass shot of the heroine, Lia (Linda Corwin), walking toward another view of the castle betrays its origins because of greasy stains on the area of glass in front of the actress. A huge carved animal sits on a beach by means of another good matte and a great skull-shaped rock looks down over a live-action lake. These are all attractive fantasy images that suggest that, given a bigger budget, Piper could come up with something special.

Also on show is a leather-masked character who befriends Lia (and of course turns out to be hideously disfigured), a humanoid swamp monster that would look at home in any 1950s science fiction film and the "Tromasaurus," a 50–foot mutated worm that is actually a hand puppet combined with actors by means of some good static mattes.

The first stop-motion sequence features a giant mutant alligator. This fine model has a green, reptilian skin, a long snout and spines running down its back. Seen in only five animation cuts, the creature is not required to do much, but does have one glorious moment when it picks up a barbarian in its jaws.

Seen first as a full-scale prop, the head of the "alligatorsaurus" pokes out of a lake to grab an item of clothing that Lia is washing. The color match between prop and animation puppet is spot-on. When Lia runs off, it turns its attentions to another character. In medium shot (backed apparently by a photo blow-up of the lake scene), the stop-motion puppet swishes its head from side to side, the animated piece of cloth waving about believably. The creature growls gently and is seen in an imposing low-angle shot looking up from the victim's point of view. The head twists on the long neck, then looks down at the camera. The final shot is a long-shot static matte (the only true composite in the sequence) with the alligatorsaurus half submerged in the water. The lake is calm enough to allow the matte line to run through the water without being conspicuous. In the creature's mouth is a puppet of the screaming barbarian, his legs kicking realistically. Piper's resources did not stretch to showing his monster on dry land — the scene ends here.

After a tiresome encounter on a beach with the leather-clad villain and his lizard-faced henchmen (extras wearing very credible lizard masks), Lia is kidnapped and marched off. En route, the group encounters a creature that at first sight resembles a horned triceratops but shows signs of having mutated from a beetle. There are two horns on its head, the front one like a rhino's, the rear one like that of a horned beetle. Its rear end has a sectioned abdomen like an insect. Its body and legs are rough and bulky like a rhino.

The scene that follows is a low-budget copy of the battle between a triceratops and a ceratosaurus in Harryhausen's *One Million Years B.C.* Of the 27 animation cuts, only two use static matte, the rest being shot either entirely in miniature or combined with photo blow-ups of the surrounding

rocky landscape. Piper tries to keep the action lively by cutting to different perspectives of his battling puppets but the scene is weakened by another genre cliché — live-action cutaways of disinterested actors.

The opening shot is a striking static matte long shot with the actors at the foot of a cliff and the browsing beetlesaurus at the top. The matte line rather too obviously follows the line of the clifftop. A close all-miniature shot allows a better look at this unusual model.

A second dinosaur appears from behind another cliff. This squat quadruped with a mouthful of fangs is a mutated dog and in fact its design recalls Randall Cook's Terror Dogs in *Ghostbusters*. In a series of shots, the dogsaurus and the beetlesaurus growl and roar at each other. Then in a dynamic moment the dogsaurus launches itself across the divide between the two cliffs. Piper exploits the moment, including a dramatic shot that borrows its design from similar shots in *King Kong* and *The Animal World*. The dogsaurus jumps in from above and behind the camera, landing on the edge of the miniature cliff. Its tail swishing, the dogsaurus clambers up onto the top of the cliff.

In long shot, the dogsaurus bites the other creature in the neck and later bites its horn. The beetlesaurus never really retaliates, and merely stands there getting bitten. A long series of shots depicts the two beasts struggling together. Piper includes long shots, medium shots, closeups and also perspectives looking up from the foot of the cliff, with the models partly obscured by miniature cliffs. After all these miniature shots, a long-shot static matte (the same design as earlier) looks marvelous simply because it shows actors in the same shot as the monsters.

In miniature again, the beetlesaurus goes down and the dogsaurus bites its neck. In medium shots, the dogsaurus places a paw on top of its stricken foe, then tears two chunks of flesh out of its hide in very gruesome fashion.

The sequence seems to be over but, in a nice twist, Piper has the dogsaurus make another appearance a few moments later. The villain is berating one of his lizard-men for allowing Lia to escape when suddenly a huge set of jaws (a full-size prop) engulfs the henchman. In a splendid long shot, the dogsaurus sits on top of a cliff with a puppet of the screaming lizard-man kicking helplessly in its jaws. Unfortunately, there are no live actors in the lower part of this shot, which again seems to have been achieved with a photo blow-up.

The beetlesaurus is also seen again briefly in two composite shots in which the hero walks past its motionless corpse.

To escape from the lizard-men, Lia runs into a cave, only to run out again pursued by a giant batsaurus. This puppet takes its inspiration from Harryhausen's harpies in *Jason and the Argonauts* but unlike them has a large dog-like head full of teeth. Realized in 17 animation cuts, the sequence is more successful than the others because there is greater interaction between puppet and actors.

The screeching, flapping creature emerges from a skull-shaped cave, its long tail snaking beneath it. In a rear-projection shot, it hovers over one of the lizard-men and Piper moves his animation camera across the rear screen slightly in order to give the shot a bit of movement. The lizard-man waves a long stick at the creature and in another rear-screen shot Piper momentarily aligns a partial miniature stick with the live-action one, thereby allowing it to pass in front of the puppet. However, slow-motion scrutiny of this shot reveals that the two elements are in fact not properly aligned, although this is certainly not apparent at normal viewing speed.

The batsaurus flies down straight at the camera. Then in a memorable long-shot static matte (or possibly another photo blow-up), the hovering creature attempts to pick up a puppet of the lizard-man, prostrate on the ground and kicking defensively. In an attractive extreme long shot, the batsaurus hovers in the air, dangling the lizard-man upside down from one of its claws. In an inventive low-angle shot looking up at the puppet, the batsaurus releases the lizard-man and the animated puppet falls directly onto the camera.

The winged monster now harasses a second lizard-man, achieved in another rear-screen shot. In the final animation shot of the sequence, the batsaurus lands on a puppet of the lizard-man and starts eating him. This is another long-shot static matte but is unsatisfactory because the matte line too obviously follows a sloping rock.

Lia walks back into the cave and there is one shot of another bat-creature hanging from the roof. It spreads its wings and growls, but Lia manages to walk past it without disturbing it. Presumably this is also meant to be giant-size, but as it is not seen in composite with the actress this is never made clear.

Lia reaches the villain's castle, is caught again, and nearly thrown to a monster that lives in a pit in the cellars. This is another mean-looking model but is the least memorable on account of having little to do. Although it features in 15 animation cuts, there are only two set-ups. One is a static matte of the creature in its pit with the lizard-men looking down at it. The other is an all-miniature set-up of just the monster. There is some fun when two lizard-men throw a third into the pit and he gets eaten, but otherwise this is another case of unrealized potential.

This orange-hued quadruped has a large spike protruding from each side of its head and fangs. When the lizard-men at the top of the pit torment it with a long stick, Piper animates a miniature stick waving across his animation table. The monster bites the stick, then spits it out. Apparently just for the fun of it, two lizard-men throw one of their colleagues into the pit. In three slickly animated cuts, a puppet of the lizard-man struggles in the jaws of the monster. The lizard-men nearly throw Lia into the pit as well, but she is rescued in the nick of time.

A final effects sequence has the villain falling from a cliff to his death into a red river containing some live-action insect-like monstrosities.

Piper has proved not only that reasonable stop-motion effects can be achieved on a very low budget but also that they need not require years of post-production. In an interview in *Film Extremes* magazine (#1, 1992), Piper stated that each of the stop-motion sequences took only three to four days to film. Of course, he has kept composites and interaction to a minimum, but has still achieved impressive results. His film may be a minor work but it is always fun, and who knows what he could achieve with a larger budget.

Originally titled *Dark Fortress*, the film was bought up by the Troma company (notorious for low-budget schlock like *Toxic Avenger* and *Class of Nuke 'Em High*) who gave the film its wonderful release title and dubbed the giant worm hand-puppet the Tromasaurus. They also put together a tongue-in-cheek trailer whose booming narration is so deliberately overblown that it has to be quoted: "Way back beyond the future, in a land before time began, the day after has become the day before. The Tromaville of tomorrow has become a dinosaur hell! ... Deadly dinosaurs have arisen from nuclear holocaust ... and all of them are hot for *A Nymphoid Barbarian in Dinosaur Hell!* ... Yes! For the first time, the prehistoric meets the pre-pubescent. Not since Raquel Welch in *One Million Years B.C.* has one woman had to face such a fearsome collection of rabid reptiles! ... Only the Troma Team could bring you the incredible state-of-the-art special effects from internationally acclaimed effects wizards Brett Piper and Alex Pirnie. You'll swear you're watching the real thing ... You must see *A Nymphoid Barbarian in Dinosaur Hell!*"

Oblivion

1994. Full Moon. D: Sam Irvin. Scr: Peter David. Visual Effects Supervisor: Joseph Grossberg. Stop-Motion Animation: Joel Fletcher, Paul Jessel, David Allen. Model Sculpture: Laine Liska.

Cast: Richard Joseph Paul, Jackie Swanson, Andrew Divoff, Jimmie F. Skaggs, Julie Newmar, Meg Foster, Isaac Hayes, George Takei.

Rating: ☆☆½   Stop-Motion: ☆☆½

Another direct-to-video release from Charles Band's Full Moon company. Once again, the plot is enjoyably offbeat. This is a sci-fi comedy-Western, set in a lawless town on a distant planet, where the cowardly son of the local sheriff attempts to prove he's up to the job.

One sequence features an encounter with giant scorpion-like alien creatures. These impressive models were animated by Joel Fletcher and Paul Jessel, with David Allen additionally animating one or two shots. The puppets were sculpted by Laine Liska.

The creatures fight over their human prey; one notorious cut, in which two of the monsters pull a victim apart with their pincers and consume the remains, was considered so horrific that it had to be cut out from the release print.

On the Comet see *Na kometě*

One Million Years B.C.

1966. 20th Century–Fox/Hammer Films. D: Don Chaffey. Scr: Michael Carreras. Adapted from an Original Screenplay by Mickell Novak, George Baker and Joseph Frickert (for *One Million B.C.* [1940]). Ph: Wilkie Cooper. Special Visual Effects Created by Ray Harryhausen. Prologue Designed by Les Bowie. Art: Robert Jones. Mus: Mario Nascimbene.

Cast: Raquel Welch, John Richardson, Percy Herbert, Robert Brown, Martine Beswick, Jean Wladon.

Rating: ☆☆½   Stop-Motion: ☆☆☆½

In the mid-1960s England's Hammer Films, long famous for producing successful horror films, broadened its horizons and tried its hand at more spectacular action pictures. One of these, touted loudly (but falsely) as the company's one-hundredth film, was a remake of the 1940 prehistoric drama *One Million B.C.* The word "years" was added to give the title extra punch and distinguish it

Arthur Hayward sculpts the brontosaurus for *One Million Years B.C.* (1966). (Photo courtesy of Arthur Hayward.)

from the original. The film was brilliantly marketed: All publicity material emphasized the physical attractions of the recently discovered star Raquel Welch, with the result that it turned a healthy profit. But to dinosaur fans, she was just a distraction from the real interest — the superb special effects of Ray Harryhausen.

Caveman movies are generally renowned for their brainlessness and *One Million Years B.C.* is no exception. If the producers of Britain's *Carry On* comedy series had ever made *Carry On Caveman*, it would not have looked very dissimilar to this: There are moments when you half-expect Sid James or Hattie Jacques

Some of Ray Harryhausen's storyboard sketches for the allosaurus sequence of *One Million Years B.C.*

to appear clad in loincloths. Leonard Maltin's view is fairly typical of critical response: "Silly prehistoric saga which capitalized on Miss Welch's anatomy in its advertising; that remains its only real virtue."

Don Chaffey, who had directed *Jason and the Argonauts*, does his best with a seriously inadequate script by Michael Carreras. Carreras was normally a producer/director for Hammer and later managing director of the company; why he was allowed to have a go at scripting chores is a mystery. On the other hand, Carreras deserves full credit in his capacity as producer for his decision to utilize stop-motion rather than any other means of depicting the dinosaurs.

Harryhausen's regular cameraman Wilkie Cooper makes the most of the rugged landscapes of the Canary Islands where the film was shot, making the studio sets of Robert Jones look all the more unconvincing by comparison. This time, Harryhausen's regular composer Bernard Herrmann was not available, but Italian Mario Nascimbene is a competent replacement, his music lending a rough grandeur to the location scenes. The cast members never look like anything other than actors pretending to be

Harryhausen's storyboard sketches for the unfilmed brontosaurus sequence of *One Million Years B.C.*

cavemen, but they do a better job of it than the cast of Hammer's follow-up film *When Dinosaurs Ruled the Earth.*

The plot, such as it is, concerns two tribes of people, the Rock Tribe and the Shell Tribe. Tumak (John Richardson) is expelled from the Rock Tribe, meets up with Loana (Welch) of the Shell Tribe, takes her back to the Rock Tribe and encounters various dinosaurs and other dangers. A convenient earthquake provides a cataclysmic ending.

Harryhausen spent nine months working on the effects and his sequences give the film a stamp of quality that transcends all this mediocrity. The al-

losaurus episode alone is enough to make the film a stop-motion classic: It is four minutes of the most dynamically realized action ever put on film. The other animation scenes are not as memorable but all have qualities of their own, making this a film to relish.

It marks a departure in style for Harryhausen from the flamboyance of earlier fantasies like *Sinbad* and *Jason* or the monster-on-the-loose treatments of his 1950s films. *One Million Years B.C.* goes for greater realism: There are no elaborate costumes or fabled cities here. Harryhausen has dropped his beautifully detailed prehistoric creatures into the rugged, rocky terrain of the volcanic islands of Lanzarote and Tenerife, where they look perfectly at home.

The film begins with a prologue designed by Hammer's regular special effects man Les Bowie, a montage of swirling clouds and liquids representing the creation of the Earth. Harryhausen's first contribution is an impressive matte shot, used several times during the film, of a smoking volcano (part real, part miniature) combined with the stark Lanzarote landscape.

Most Harryhausen fans groan with disappointment at the appearance of the first dinosaur, because it is not a dinosaur at all. A real iguana lizard is combined by means of static mattes with shots of Tumak fleeing. To add insult to injury, some of these are not properly aligned and there is a dark line where the two halves of the shot meet. A few minutes later, Tumak comes face to face with a giant tarantula and this again is a live creature. Harryhausen has tried to wriggle off the hook by saying that it was a deliberate decision to have live animals as the first monsters encountered, as this would heighten the level of realism before his stop-motion models appeared. But the real reason must be that he was restricted by the budget.

This is made plainer by the fact that his first dinosaur, the brontosaurus, only appears in two cuts: An intended sequence in which the brontosaur attacks Tumak's camp was scrapped because it would have added another two-to-three months to the animation time. But the model had already been built so Harryhausen decided to use it briefly to pep up the long sequence in which Tumak crosses the wilderness after being ex-pelled from his tribe. The caveman hears a growl and the sound of heavy footsteps, looks up and sees the giant sauropod in the distance, then runs off when it turns and looks at him. Two rear-screen set-ups are used, the invisible matte line in both following the line of the rocks in front of the model. Built over the same basic armature that was used for the dragon in *The 7th Voyage of Sinbad*, it's an impressive model, wrinkles, warts and all, and it's a shame that it merely walks off.

Tumak arrives at the sea, collapses on the beach and is discovered by the blonde-haired women of the Shell tribe. But before he can be moved, an enormous turtle appears over the crest of the beach. Raquel Welch must have been swotting up on her prehistory textbooks because she cries out, "Archelon!" (In fact, the prehistoric turtle *Archelon Ischyros* of the cretaceous era grew to a size of four meters, considerably less than this giant.) Harryhausen's choice of an Archelon is an interesting shift from the kinds of dinosaur that normally inhabit genre movies, and it is another fine model. So good, in fact, that some critics were convinced he had used a live turtle; this may detract from appreciating his skills, but at the same time it is paying him the ultimate compliment.

Many viewers are disappointed by this scene because it never develops into a full-blown battle, with the turtle simply wandering off into the sea. It is skillfully designed as a low-key taster of the more frenetic action that follows later: this creature is simply trying to return to the sea, and the cave people are just a minor annoyance. Half of the shots during this sequence are of Loana comforting Tumak, with the battle almost relegated to a background role.

The sequence consists of 26 stop-motion cuts and is particularly notable for a number of floor inlays in which the color of the beach is perfectly matched to a partial miniature floor. Additionally they allow the model to cast a shadow, significantly enhancing the realism of the shot. As usual, Harryhausen uses long shots, medium shots, closeups and a variety of static matte set-ups to enliven the pace and vary the perspective.

Five cuts look up at the beast from the cave people's point of view as it comes over the hill, and in the last of these its beady eye stares down at Loana and Tumak. When it drags itself down the beach towards Loana and Tumak, Harryhausen breaks up what might have been a conspicuously even matte line by having his creature pass behind a small boulder. His animation of the shuffling flippers is just right, suggesting the enormous bulk of this beast.

Six traveling matte shots allow him to put first Loana and Tumak in front of the model and later several caveman as they attack it with spears. There is no spill at all in these shots (they appear to have used the sodium-backing process) but there is a difference in contrast between the two elements which prevents us from being fooled into seeing them as one shot.

Two superb long shots show the Shell people throwing rocks and spears at the turtle, some bouncing off it in a 100 percent believable way, the live-action props passing unseen behind the model as they are replaced by miniature foreground ones. In closeup, the turtle turns away, then four more long shots

show it walking in from behind a sand dune and being menaced by more Shell people. In one of these cuts, Harryhausen adds to the depth of the shot by having one of the men walk up onto the sand dune and attack the turtle from the other side. He stabs at its shell with his spear and for a few frames the spear passes in front of the model, a classic subliminal Harryhausen effect achieved either by painting it on glass or by suspending a partial miniature spear on wires. Two slightly closer long shots show cave people prodding it with spears in another rear-screen set-up; in the second of these there is the exquisite illusion of seeing a spear leave the hand of a caveman, stick in the turtle's neck then drop to the ground.

Two final cuts show the turtle sliding into the sea behind some rocks as the cave people shout and wave their spears after it. By matting around the rocks, Harryhausen wisely avoids having to show the model in contact with the water. There is a very slight jiggle in the registration of one of these cuts, but it's being picky to even mention this after such an excellent scene.

After much silliness involving the rock people catching a goat, Martine Beswick attempting to do a sensuous dance and Richardson learning how not to catch fish, we reach the film's highpoint.

The allosaurus sequence is successful because so much thought has been given to pace and choreography. Too often a technically brilliant stop-motion scene is spoiled because it has not been put together with enough attention to "cinema grammar," the editing tricks that make all the difference between a routine scene and a dramatically exciting one. The plot very slowly and deliberately creates a scene of picturesque tranquility at the lakeside camp of the Shell tribe, lulling us into a false sense of security, yet at the same time providing all the machinery necessary to the subsequent action — the people in the lake, the girl in the tree and the wooden shelter. The sudden arrival of the snarling allosaurus is actually quite startling after all this.

It's a superbly vital model complete with snapping jaws that have a trace of a ravenous sneer on them, and it is a smart touch to make it a juvenile animal "only" ten feet tall, thereby making the battle with the cavemen more even-sided.

Once again there are some impeccably matched miniature floors, such as in the opening two long shots in which the allosaurus strides up to the lake: The foreground is entirely miniature, blending imperceptibly with the lake in the rear screen. The next seven effects cuts use another rear-screen set-up as the dinosaur goes closer to the lake and picks a screaming man out of the water in its teeth (he was actually supported by invisible wires). The dinosaur drops him, picks him up again, shakes him around (by now the actor has been replaced by a smoothly animated puppet human), drops him on the ground, then bites into him with a sickening sound of crunching bone.

The hungry purpose of this creature is always emphasized by Harryhausen: Its tail is constantly swishing and in the last of these cuts it looks around eagerly when it hears the screams of the little girl trapped in the tree. A partial miniature floor is used in a series

of cuts where the allosaurus goes up to the tree — surely an affectionate nod to the scene in *King Kong* where Fay Wray is stuck in a tree while Kong battles the tyrannosaurus. After a closeup in which the allosaurus snaps at the girl causing her to fall, a clever long shot has Tumak run into the frame, then jump back realistically when the dinosaur lunges at him. Equally good is the shot in which Tumak stabs the creature with his spear and it lifts its leg in pain. Better still (and still using the same rear-screen set-up) is the shot in which Tumak slowly walks around the tree until he is behind the allosaurus, which all the time is following him with his gaze: This gives the scene real depth, avoiding the two-dimensional nature of some rear-screen confrontations. In one dramatic closeup, the allosaurus' neck muscles ripple with animal ferocity.

There is great dynamism in a medium shot in which the camera pans left to right, following Tumak as he retreats backwards from the snapping jaws of the dinosaur. Three long shots feature another flawlessly matched miniature floor as Tumak tries to fend off the beast with his spear and three of the Shell people run to the other side of the dinosaur so that it is surrounded. In one of these cuts, a spear is thrown, pierces the allosaur's neck, then drops to the ground. Harryhausen makes it all seem so effortless.

Likewise in the next shot: Harryhausen needed to have the wooden shelter collapse in order to provide Tumak with a sharpened pole with which to dispatch the dinosaur, but instead of merely having the beast knock into the shelter with his head, he has it bite the shelter,

This frame enlargement from *One Million Years B.C.* shows Harryhausen at his best. (National Film Archive, London.)

tear away some of the leaves in its mouth (miniature leaves which blend unnoticed with the leaves in the rear screen) and shake them around as though they were living prey. This mingling of the two elements, as well as the collapse of the shelter, really work to convince us that we are only watching one piece of film and not "a special effect."

Part of the puppet's foot briefly disappears below the matte line in these cuts but the action is so frenetic that no one would notice under normal viewing conditions. The collapsed shelter provides Harryhausen with a suitable object to hide the switch from actor to puppet when the allosaur picks up another of the Shell people in its mouth. Staying with the same rear-screen setup, three more cuts show Tumak spearing the dinosaur, which drops the screaming man as Tumak and another caveman force the dinosaur out of the frame with their spears.

A dramatically clever reversal of the earlier panning shot has the two cavemen stabbing at the retreating dinosaur, the camera again following left to right. In closeup, the dinosaur grabs one of the spears in its mouth and spits it out: Harryhausen doesn't miss an opportunity for emphasizing this creature's ferocity.

A series of four medium shots (i.e., no matte is required) show a caveman facing off against the allosaur, throwing a spear which lands in its neck (another astonishingly good switch from prop to miniature spear) only to be pulled out by the creature seconds later as it stomps across the frame. But by this time Tumak has grabbed one of the poles from the hut and there is a very dynamic traveling matte shot from behind him as the allosaur thunders down on him, filling the background.

The next long shot is a stunner: The allosaur is impaled on the pole in midair above Tumak, who is lying on the ground. It screams and kicks vainly, one of it legs passing behind the pole, thereby revealing that part of the pole is a miniature. In fact, carefully scrutiny reveals that Tumak's right arm is also a miniature, carefully aligned so as to obscure the real arm. The dinosaur topples over towards the camera, screaming as it hits the ground.

A closer shot has the pathetic beast thrashing wildly on the ground, its tail swishing and the pole rising and falling with its breathing. Tumak in the rear plate runs at it and thrusts his spear into the beast's neck. The screaming stops, the breathing becomes labored and eventually stops altogether as other cave people gather in the background. Two final composite shots show the motionless puppet with the cave people behind it.

Harryhausen's control over sound in this sequence is almost as remarkable as his animation. He demonstrates how exciting a sequence can be without any background music whatsoever. Instead he gives us a barrage of human and animal screams, the sound of the beast's jaws snapping together and the climactic climb-down at the end as the sound of dying breaths replaces the preceding cacophony.

The flow of the action is breathless. Forty-two stop-motion cuts rush past, enhanced by well thought out live-action cutaways. The pace, inventiveness of the choreography and the general level of excitement never let up: This is as good as it gets.

The allosaurus sequence begs the question: Why aren't all of Harryhausen's episodes so well designed? For example, the next stop-motion sequence in *One Million Years B.C.*, a battle between a triceratops and a ceratosaurus, is a major disappointment. Although the animation is as complex as in the allosaurus battle, the scene has little dramatic context, serving merely to delay Tumak and Loana. There is little interaction between puppets and actors, and the struggle between the dinosaurs is repetitious, lacking the careful pace of the allosaurus scene. The kind of clever devices that enlivened the allosaurus battle (the lake, the tree, the shelter and the pole) are absent, the fight being staged mainly as a conventional "table-top and rear-projection" scene. Contrast between the graininess of the live-action plate and the sharp studio-lit models is another detraction, though not a serious one. The faults constitute a curious lapse on Harryhausen's part: The fight itself is terrific, so why didn't he make more of it?

Harryhausen told this author that he was unhappy with the triceratops model. The plaster mold of the body was allowed to bake for too long and as a result it shrank more than intended. By comparison, the head, which was made from a separate mold, seems disproportionately large and makes the whole figure look somewhat "toy-like."

Tumak and Loana stumble on the bulky triceratops, munching (with a credible sideways action of its jaws) on some vegetation. Another very good floor inlay allows the model to throw a shadow. The cave people are in the foreground of the shot, lending an important sense of perspective-deceiving depth. The beast turns and growls when it hears them, lifting one of its forelegs in a semi-threatening gesture. It runs after them behind a hillock (no points for guessing where the matte line is) and in long shot is seen pursuing the actors. Its running cycle is a bit stiff but it's a brave try by Harryhausen.

The ceratosaurus, looking like a bigger version of the allosaurus with a horn on its head, suddenly appears at the top of another hill, the matte line following the brow of this hill, just obscuring the model's feet. The triceratops stops, growls and draws back. The ceratosaurus snarls down at the herbivore, with Tumak and Loana running across the lower foreground — another good example of suggestion of depth. Surprising everyone who thought they had identified the design of this composite, the ceratosaurus takes a step forward, stepping *over* the matte line and placing its foot lower down the hill. The expla-

nation is that Harrryhausen has again fooled the eye by making a small part of the hill a miniature, matching it perfectly to the real rocks around it, allowing his model to move onto it and significantly improving the "oneness" of the shot.

A dramatic impression of the biped's size is conveyed in a shot where just its feet and tail move across the frame as Tumak and Loana cower in a cave in the background. It's as if the dinosaur is too big to fit into the frame.

The battle is depicted in a variety of long shots and medium shots as well as in traveling matte designs looking out from the cave in which the cave people are hiding. The battle has great dynamism: The ceratosaurus bites into the triceratops' horns, tries to snap off its protective frill, bites into the fleshy part of its neck under the frill and even steps on the horns as it tries to get a better grip. For its part, the triceratops gores its attacker with its horn, lifting it off the ground and toppling it at one point, and later delivering a fatal wound with its horn, then stepping back almost triumphantly, its blood-soaked horns gleaming in the sun. Lots of tail-swishing, roaring and screaming add to the sense of animal fury.

Two cuts show the ceratosaurus' tail snapping down just in front of Tumak as he tries to sneak out of the cave. In the traveling matte shots, all using one design, contrast between the dark of the foreground live-action element and the brightness of the fight outside is not a flaw but is wholly appropriate to the location. The ceratosaurus gets a closeup when it screams out after being gored, then falls backwards, seen

The battle between the ceratosaurus and the triceratops in *One Million Years B.C.* (National Film Archive, London.)

finally in non-animated shots in which an internal bladder is used to suggest its dying gasps. The sound of its labored breathing lacks the impact it could have had, because it is too reminiscent of the death of the allosaurus.

Harryhausen has invested enormous time and effort into this sequence (constructing the puppets, animating them, designing the composites and the optical work) and, although the end results are not among his best work (dramatically rather than technically), the scene is still far superior to anything that anyone else was putting out at the time.

Hammer's usual clumsy attempt at titillation arises in the laughable wrestling match between Welch and Martine Beswick. Fortunately, it's not too long until we're back with the dinosaurs. An excellent matte painting (the only one in the film) is used in a long shot of a cliff face with cave people milling around on a plateau halfway up the face; then the action moves to a large lake for the film's final bit of stop-motion.

This scene is an improvement on the previous one: It involves five puppets, takes place in two locations, features much interaction between puppets and actors and has at least some dramatic context in the plot.

The puppets were built over the two harpy armatures from *Jason and the Argonauts*. The pterodactyl is a nightmarish, screeching monstrosity. It's a clever touch by Harryhausen to force us to feel sympathy for it when we realize it is a mother taking food to its two hungry offspring, both of whom get eaten when a rhamphorhynchus — another flying reptile — arrives on the scene and kills them and the mother. On the downside, there are again problems with stock contrasts, the rapid movement of the flying reptiles' wings causes a confusing strobing image that makes some shots look muddled, and Nascimbene's languorous score is inappropriate. If ever a quirky Herrmann theme was needed, it was here.

The script recreates on a lesser scale the slow build-up that led into the allosaurus sequence by having the cave people bathing in the lake. Suddenly there is a terrific squawking sound and a shadow falls over Loana, who looks up to see a pterodactyl swooping down at her. The aerial-braced puppet (the wires are always invisible in this scene) never throws a shadow on the ground but, in some long shots, the downbeat of its wings seems to blow up dust from the ground; this is almost certainly just a lucky quirk of the weather, because it is missing from other shots. There are several shots of the beast trying to snatch Tumak and Loana out of the water.

When some of the cavemen attack the hovering creature with spears, a partial miniature spear — so carefully aligned as to be barely noticed — enables physical contact to be suggested. Loana

falls behind a convenient rock, allowing Harryhausen to matte around it and so have his pterodactyl pick up a puppet version of her. There is good, dramatic camerawork in the panning shot that follows the pterodactyl as it flies left-to-right across the frame, then back again to the left and away, the Loana puppet kicking realistically all the while.

Tumak and another caveman follow the creature, and there is a striking long shot depicting a smaller model disappearing behind of a hill in the distance, the two men in the lower foreground. The creature's nest, on top of a jagged pillar of rock on a beach, is a real rock formation partly matted out and relocated. Shots of Loana held in convincing prop claws over the nest are made up of three elements: the two babies, bobbing up and down in anticipation of a meal, a rear projection of the sea, and a traveling matte of Loana. Unfortunately, the outlines of her flowing hair prove too delicate for the traveling matte process and spoil the shot. Harryhausen's pre-production drawings suggest he had planned a scene in which Loana gives food to the chicks in the nest, then is snatched up again by the mother. But this potentially memorable bit of character animation was scrapped.

The rhamphorhynchus (which in "real" prehistory was only a chicken-sized creature) now flies into the shot. It is distinguished from the other reptile by its darker coloring, tail and two rows of tiny teeth. The animation is extremely complex as Harryhausen has to keep track of the two battling adults, the two babies and the struggling Loana puppet all in the same composite. Closer shots of the two adults are weakened by the

The lively opera singer from *Oscar* (1991). Animation by David Allen, Randy Cook and Justin Kohn.

strobing of the wings. The rhampho-rhynchus bites the pterodactyl in the neck and the fight is soon over.

In long shot, the dying pterodactyl drops Loana (a realistic bit of "free fall" animation), then falls back and drops into the sea behind some matted-in rocks — again Harryhausen avoids having to show any contact with water. The sequence ends with a gruesome flourish as the rhamphorhynchus flies to the nest, lands next to the squawking babies and devours them. This is satisfactorily integrated into the plot by having Tumak arrive at this point and assume that it is Loana who is being eaten. The animation of the creature's wings is much smoother in these final cuts because it is making slower movements, holding its wings up to steady itself as it tears off and swallows bits of meat from its prey.

The finale in which the volcano erupts and an earthquake begins is a combination of good and bad shots, all the optical work again having been controlled by Harryhausen. There are some stunning traveling mattes of actors being crushed under a shower of rocks, some fine shots of crashing miniature rocks (recalling the Triton scene in *Jason and the Argonauts*) and some ingenious rear-projection shots in which miniature rocks fall away from background action. But there are also some inferior traveling mattes that suffer badly from spill and an unnecessary shot in which an iguana is brought back into service and shown falling into a fissure. Overall, the impression is that this is a good attempt at recreating the kind of drama that Disney did so well at the end of the prehistoric sequence of *Fantasia*.

As a dramatic whole, *One Million Years B.C.* does not rank very highly in relation to other Harryhausen films. *Mighty Joe Young* and *The Beast from 20,000 Fathoms*, for example, are much more entertaining films, held together by tight direction; *Jason and the Argonauts* is characterized by a visual freshness uncommon in motion pictures; *The 3 Worlds of Gulliver* and *First Men in the Moon* are both very strong on characterization and narrative; and *The Valley of Gwangi*, his next film, has a profound, almost mythical quality much like *King Kong*. But it represented a courageous and risky venture by Hammer, is a great improvement on the original 1940 version, and gave Harryhausen an opportunity to put on the screen a display of dinosaur thrills that had no precedent — including one sequence that is a classic of the stop-motion genre.

Oscar

1991. Touchstone/Silver Screen Partners IV. D: John Landis. Scr: Michael Barrie, Jim Mulholland. Based on the Play by Claude Magnier. Ph: Mac Ahlberg. Art: Bill Kenney. Mus: Elmer Bernstein. Animated Main Title: David Allen Productions. Stop-Motion (uncredited): David Allen, Randy Cook, Justin Kohn.

Cast: Sylvester Stallone, Ornella Muti, Don Ameche, Tim Curry, Vincent

Spano, Linda Gray, Yvonne De Carlo, Kirk Douglas.

Rating: ☆☆½   Stop-Motion: ☆☆½

This likable comedy was a change of pace for Sylvester Stallone. He gives a good comic performance as a gangster who tries to go straight and gets entangled in all manner of business and family misunderstandings. Also on hand are Kirk Douglas as Stallone's dying father and Tim Curry as an English upper-class twit who tries to give the gangster voice elocution. John Landis' direction is lively and the pace and gags are generally well-judged, apart from one or two lapses.

Presumably to emphasize the Italian connections, the opening credits are backed by a puppet character singing "Largo al Factotum" (a.k.a. "Figaro") from Rossini's opera *The Barber of Seville*. Ordinarily, a puppet sequence of this kind, unconnected with any live-action scenes and where the figure is only meant to be perceived as a puppet, would not be covered by this book. However, since the animators were David Allen, Randy Cook and Justin Kohn, it is appropriate to make an exception.

The puppet, a plump, mustachioed character, is very smoothly animated on a miniature stage, the curtains of which rise at the start of the credits. There is plenty of facial expression, raising of eyebrows, hand-gesturing and eye-blinking as the puppet sings. The lip-synch was presumably achieved with a series of replacement animation heads. Although mostly animated in long shot, the puppet is also seen closer in several medium shots, two overhead shots and one low-angle shot.

This was an unusual assignment for Allen and Cook, who are normally associated with monsters, demons and "tiny terrors." Cook told this author (in an August 1992 telephone conversation) that he enjoyed the opportunity to do some real character animation, putting touches of personality and gesture into the puppet. He animated 70 seconds of the sequence, which in total runs to two minutes, 56 seconds.

Peacock King (a.k.a. *The Legend of the Phoenix*)

Hong Kong. 1988. Golden Harvest. D: Nam Nai-Choi, Lan Nai Kai. Scr: Tang King-Sang, Izo Hashimoto. Mus: Micky Yoshino.
  Cast: Yuen Biao, Pauline Wong, Hiroshi Mikami, Narumi Yasuda, Ken Ogata.

Rating: ☆☆☆   Stop-Motion: ☆☆½

Peacock King is another entry in the ever-watchable series of gothic action-fantasies coming out of Hong Kong since the early 1980s. As ever, the pace is frantic, the plot is inexhaustibly inventive and the camerawork is superlative, bathing everything in thoughtful glowing lighting.

Unfortunately, the inventiveness is a few steps ahead of the budget with the result that some of the effects sequences are a bit muddled, but the eerie atmosphere and sheer enthusiasm of the direction (by Nam Nai-Choi) carry it through. It leaves most Hollywood actioners standing. The photography on occasion rises to a level of haunting poetry: red-robed warriors striding purposefully over gray rocks, their robes filling in the breeze; or the effects sequence in which Hell City rises up out of the ground, a huge rocky cliff face that contains a massive door looking like something out of *King Kong*. There is plenty of breathtakingly choreographed kung fu action, a battle with some dinosaurs (alas a live-action scene in which museum displays come to life), and an impressive live-action finale in which the giant Hell King climbs out of his underground lair (courtesy of low-angle high-speed filming).

The icing on the cake is two stop-motion sequences (in total containing about 40 animation cuts), one a jokey episode featuring a gang of miniature demons hiding in a hamburger box, the other a longer and creepier episode in which a bizarre monster attacks Peacock King and Lucky Fruit, the two heroes.

There are 16 stop-motion cuts in the first episode, a unique and amusing throwaway moment which doesn't really have much to do with the plot but is a lot of fun and even lets the animators imbue their models with a bit of character. Peacock King is walking along a Tokyo street and encounters a discarded hamburger box on the ground. Poking out of it is a writhing mass of tiny arms and legs. To the left of the box is what looks like a mock-up of Peacock King's foot. It moves slightly as the models wriggle; when the five little demons clamber out of the box, one of them tumbles over the foot.

The five demons are an unforgettable sight: yellow, pink, blue, some with tails, one with spikes all over its back, one with a great bulbous abdomen, one with tentacles and five eyes on stalks, one a lizard-like creature with two bodies. They make cute high-pitched squeaking noises. There is a great cut of them walking across the pavement, one of them bounding into the air. One clambers up the trouser leg (another prop?) of a passerby and peers out from under the cloth with a rodent face. The yellow one with the bulbous abdomen squeezes through a crack in the curbstone and another hides down a drain. A pink one with a wide-eyed stare can't catch up with the others and cowers pathetically when Peacock King summons a dog over: The demon chirps pathetically and shivers with fear as the dog bends down and eats it (the interaction being suggested by the editing). Smoothly animated and witty, the sequence recalls the tiny aliens of the chess scene in *Star Wars*.

The battle with Witch Raga is much more ambitious (taking much of its inspiration from Rob Bottin's bizarre special makeups in *The Thing*) and almost manages to be scary as well. It's an inventive use of stop-motion but the animators get carried away: Their model leaps all over the place at high speed in the best kung fu fashion, and the result is that many shots are spoiled by strobing because the action is just too fast.

531

The sequence has excellent shadowy photography, making the most of the cobwebby, rat-infested sewer in which the scene occurs. Flashing sparks of supernatural energy light up the model on several occasions and the miniature sets always match up with the live-action ones.

Peacock King and Lucky Fruit discover Witch Raga feeding messily on a live human and there is lots of leaping around as they try to rescue the Hell-virgin from the Witch's lair. Witch Raga's transformation into an outlandish monster has about a dozen stop-motion cuts and an equal number of live-action cuts of a mechanical version. Superimposed smoke and slight camera pans help put the model right into the setting. The witch raises her hands in the air, then there is a cut (rather too abruptly) to a shot in which she has already partly transformed into a pale, naked, skeletal creature. Backed by the sound of bones crunching, the torso twists around, the head contorts and the side splits open, sprouting long legs with claws. The end result, in long shot, is a nasty-looking quadruped with a human face that is actually one big mouth, opening top-to-bottom and full of outsized teeth.

Cackling evilly, it leaps up with an insect-like spring and turns to face Peacock King and Lucky Fruit. After a closeup of the hideous (live-action) head, the stop-motion puppet leaps up and hangs from an overhead pipe with its rear legs: This creature has a *very* odd physiognomy. The live-action model leaps down onto Peacock King and the head-mouth tries to bite him. When he kicks the monster away, three stop-motion cuts show it landing on an overhead pipe, then dropping down onto another pipe, lit up by flashes of blue light.

A dozen or so stop-motion cuts plus a number of shots of the live-action puppet (particularly when the retractable claws are throttling Lucky Fruit) feature in the last moments of this episode. One of the creature's arms is severed and stop-motion snake-like tendrils wriggle about before retreating into the bloody stump. The cackling puppet leaps up onto another pipe, does a cartwheel (this is far too jerky), then glides through the air (a more satisfying shot because the model is only making slight movements) and lands on the top of a pillar. It dodges a variety of weapons that are thrown at it, threateningly waves its retractable arms, then apparently perishes in an explosion caused by a bolt of energy hurled by Lucky Fruit, causing the sewer to collapse.

The sequence is remarkable for its offbeat creature and superior optical work, but is let down by the animation which, although dynamic, never convinces. The Raga-monster reappears later on, but this time the budget must have been pinching, because only the live-action model is used.

Peacock King II
(a.k.a. *Saga of the Phoenix*)

1990. D: Nam Nai Choi.
Cast: Yuen Biao, Gloria Yip Wong.

Rating: ☆☆½   Stop-Motion: ☆☆½

This lacks some of the visual elegance of the original but is still packed with inventive sequences, special effects set-pieces and dynamic martial arts battles.

Some of the effects scenes disappoint. Three carved stone lions come to life in a temple and are brought to life by that corniest of devices: two extras strapped together in a costume like a costume party horse. As in the first film, there is an evil witch of the Underworld and again she transforms at the climax into a monster. One stop-motion cut shows her in a skeletal form, with great bat-wings sprouting from her. All subsequent shots of this character use a mechanical prop or an actor in costume, and always look clumsy. It's as if the original intention was to shoot the whole sequence with stop-motion, but budget or time constraints forced a change of plan.

More successful is a two-foot-high gremlin-like creature who appears frequently. The rabbit-eared character has a high cute-factor, resembles Gizmo in *Gremlins* and seems designed to appeal to a young audience. Most shots of the gremlin use a hand- or rod-puppet, but stop-motion is also used in 29 cuts to show full-view shots of the character walking. Although the fluidity of the animation is sometimes mediocre, the shots nevertheless add much credibility and charm. Only two composite shots are attempted — most moments of interaction are achieved with the on-set puppets.

In its first stop-motion scene, the gremlin hops out of a sack and the wires supporting it during animation are clearly visible. Making cute gurgling noises, it waddles out of the room. Many of the subsequent shots show the gremlin scampering across floors, opening doors or even lowering a blind. In one deft shot, it gives a terrified look over its shoulder as it is pursued by a knife-wielding character whose cake it has just eaten. In another shot, it jumps off a window sill but its rate of descent is unrealistically slow.

The gremlin gets its revenge on its pursuer by sneaking up on him while he is asleep and shaving off one of his eyebrows. This stop-motion shot seems to use a background photo blow-up of the actor, onto which the hair must have been painted and removed frame by frame. In a half-hearted jokey moment, the gremlin swivels the razor like a pistol and holsters it.

The witch turns the gremlin into an evil being, causing it to grow fangs. It attempts to steal a girl's soul (achieved with some very good cel-animated magic effects), then, in five stop-motion shots, jumps onto a toilet bowl, pulls the chain, jumps in and is flushed back down to the underworld.

In the underworld, the witch sucks the girl's soul out of the gremlin and into herself, an effect again employing some superior cel animation. She discards the gremlin which, in a stop-motion cut, cartwheels through the air. In a successful composite that may be a rear-projection static matte set-up, the gremlin lands on the ground in front of her.

But the gremlin has failed to steal all of the girl's soul and is sent back to finish the job. Several stop-motion cuts show it walking back to her room. In its last scenes, it grows into a man-sized evil gremlin (shots which use an extra in a costume). By the end, however, all cuteness is restored.

Pee-wee's Big Adventure

1985. Aspen Film/Robert Shapiro. D: Tim Burton. Scr: Phil Hartman, Paul Reubens, Michael Varhol. Ph: Victor J. Kemper. Art: David L. Snyder. Mus: Danny Elfman. Special Visual Effects: Dream Quest Images. Animated Effects: Rich Heinrichs, John Scheele, Stephen Chiodo.

Cast: Pee-wee Herman [Paul Reubens], Elizabeth Daily, Mark Holton, Diane Salinger, Judd Owen, James Brolin, Morgan Fairchild.

Rating: ☆☆½   Stop-Motion: ☆☆½

An off-beat, occasionally surreal comedy, *Pee-wee's Big Adventure* has much charm but not enough inventiveness, and the initially likable Pee-wee becomes tiresome after a while. Kids will be entranced by the colorful world of fun that he lives in: This is reality seen through a child's eyes. Tim Burton's direction, as in *Beetlejuice* and *Batman*, is adequate but fails to rise to the occasion.

The highlight of the finale in the film studios is the chaos that Pee-wee wreaks when he stumbles onto a Toho set where Ghidrah is having a battle with Godzilla. Otherwise most of the set-pieces are forgettable.

One stand-out moment is a great absurd shock effect when ghostly Large Marge suddenly transforms into a pop-eyed ghoul. This is an excellent one-second replacement animation effect by Stephen Chiodo. "When they finally pulled the body from the twisted, burning wreck, it looked like this!" somebody exclaims. The eyes slowly expand to the size of tennis balls, the mouth enlarges, full of stumpy teeth, and a long stop-motion tongue snakes about. It took Chiodo 11 hours to animate this 36 frame cut (one and a half seconds of screen time).

Later, Pee-wee has a dream inspired by a dinosaur theme park. In four cuts animated by Rick Heinrichs, a rubbery tyrannosaurus walks into a shadowy miniature set and picks up Pee-wee's stolen bicycle in its mouth (lit up by a spotlight). A stationary puppet of Pee-wee stands to one side. The red dinosaur, its eyes glowing unnaturally in the dark, is never intended to be realistic and the animation is less than smooth. This is just a quick throwaway gag, not a developed set-piece.

Pinocchio

1939. Walt Disney. D: Ben Sharpsteen, Hamilton Luske. Sequence Directors: Bill Roberts, T. Hee, Norman Ferguson, Jack Kinney, Wilfred Jackson. Based on the Story by Collodi. Animation Direction: Fred Moore, Franklin Thomas, Milton Kahl, Vladimir Tytla, Ward Kimball, Arthur Babbitt, Eric Larson, Woolie Reitherman.

Rating: ☆☆☆☆   Stop-Motion: N/A.

It is reasonably well-documented that on occasion Disney animators have based their drawings on pre-shot live-action footage, and then either used this as a guide for their drawings or even traced around the outline of the live figures one frame at a time. Many of Snow White's movements in *Snow White and the Seven Dwarves* were achieved this way.

What is less well-known is that some shots were achieved by drawing over previously shot footage of stop-motion models. One example of this is a breathtaking early-morning shot in *Pinocchio* in which the camera slowly zooms in from an extreme long shot of a village, past a church bell tower (from which several doves fly out), down past several rooftops and walls (which seem to part as the camera glides between them), and eventually settles on the door of the house where Gepetto and Pinocchio live.

In order to insure that the artists were able to maintain the correct pace for the shot and to insure that the correct perspectives were maintained as the camera descended on the village, it was decided that the sequence would first be shot using models of all the buildings, animating them one frame at a time as they pull back to let the camera pass. The resultant footage was then rotoscoped — that is, the artists traced over the outlines of the models one frame at a time — to achieve the finished artwork. See also *Fantasia* (1940).

Piranha

1978. United Artists. D: Joe Dante. Scr: John Sayles. Story: Richard Robinson. John Sayles. Ph: Jamie Anderson. Art: Bill and Kerry Mellin. Mus: Pino Donaggio. Special Effects: John Berg. Creature Design and Animation: Phil Tippett. Special Makeup: Rob Bottin, Vincent Prentice. Special Properties: Rob Short, Chris Walas. Photographic Effects: Peter Kuran, Bill Hedge, Rick Taylor.

Cast: Bradford Dillman, Heather Menzies, Kevin McCarthy, Keenan Wynn, Dick Miller, Barbara Steele, Paul Bartel.

Rating: ☆☆☆   Stop-Motion: ☆☆½

This unashamed take-off of *Jaws* (1975) has a witty script by John Sayles and crisp direction by Joe Dante, the same team which in 1981 collaborated on

the droll werewolf spoof, *The Howling.*
Piranha plagiarizes gleefully and throws
in a number of genre in-jokes as well;
for example, in one scene, the 1950s sea-
monster movie *The Monster That Chal-*
lenged the World is showing on a television in the background. The balance of
the comic and the horrific is always kept
just at the right level. Dante demonstrates that he is able to control suspense
skillfully in scenes such as when a raft is
slowly pulled apart by the piranha or
when the killer fish attack a group of
children playing in a lake.

The film is let down by unappealing
performances by leads Bradford Dillman
and Heather Menzies. Horror queen
Barbara Steele has a small role and acts
appallingly. The cast also features Kevin
McCarthy as a misunderstood scientist
and Keenan Wynn, who gets both his
legs stripped of flesh by the mutant
fish.

Jon Berg was in overall control of
the special effects. The piranha, only
seen in fleeting but effective two-second
cuts, and the many splatter makeups are
the work of Rob Bottin, Chris Walas and
others. There were initial plans to film
the piranha using stop-motion but the
idea was rejected as being unfeasible.

The mutated piranha (the result of
scientific experiments) were intended to
be used as weapons in the Vietnam war.
Early in the film, another experimentally
bred creature makes an appearance. The
mutant newt, built and animated by Phil
Tippett, is a slimy yellow foot-tall monster, with the head of a mud-skipper, a
shark's dorsal fin, arms and legs like a
man and the tail of a newt. Although
seen only for a few seconds, it's a wonderful little character and animated with

many deft touches of timid personality
that really bring it to life.

The character is seen only briefly in
six quick animation cuts. All the cuts appear to be rear-projection set-ups and
include a number of clever flourishes.

The first two cuts take their design
from one of Harryhausen's favorite perspectives. The creature is standing in the
foreground on a laboratory table, with
two actors fighting behind it (and oblivious to it). The table-top is a miniature
and so the shot avoids the need for a
matte. Miniature test tubes and flasks in
the foreground enhance the look of the
shot. The creature lets out a little rasp,
then scuttles across the table, the gentle
sound of its footsteps adding an important but subliminal credibility to the
effect.

Later, the creature is on the floor
and Tippett keeps the puppet's feet just
below the bottom of the frame, thereby
again avoiding the need for mattes. A
simulated shadow passes across the
model to suggest the proximity of the
fighting actors. It runs off behind a
miniature stool leg, the rest of which is
part of the live-action plate. These two
shots allow a glimpse of the creature's
webbed hands.

The final pair of shots play up the
newt's nervousness. One bulging eye
peeps out from behind some furniture
(down which runs a vertical matte line),
blinks at the fight going on out-of-
frame, then its whole head hesitantly
appears. The creature lets out another
rasp, then apparently smiles! This final
closeup affords a good look at the highly
detailed, warty texture of the model's
skin.

The mutant newt has the distinction of being the stop-motion medium's most reserved monster — no one in the film even notices it. In the following years, this kind of brief appearance would become a common application for the process, with all manner of animated creations appearing in tantalizingly brief sequences.

Planet of Dinosaurs

1978. Cinema Dynamics. Prod-D: James K. Shea. Scr: Ralph Lucas. Story: James Aupperle. Ph: Henning Schellerup. Music and Special Sound Effects: Kelly Lammers, John O'Verlin. Special Visual Effects: Steve Czerkas, James Aupperle. Chief Stop-Motion Animator: Doug Beswick. Machinist: Victor Niblock. Matte Artist: Jim Danforth.

Cast: James Whitworth, Pamela Bottaro, Louie Lawless, Harvey Shain, Charlotte Speer, Chuck Pennington.

Rating: ☆½   Stop-Motion: ☆☆☆

Wouldbe stop-motion projects have always been notoriously prone to problems — witness the number of O'Brien scripts that were never realized and the aborted animated remake of *King Kong* — but *Planet of Dinosaurs* is probably the most unfortunate of all. After 15 months of dedicated post-production work, first-time filmmakers James Aupperle and Stephen Czerkas found themselves with a product that no distributor was interested in. It did eventually find a theatrical release in 1981 when it got an ignominious and immediately forgotten release as the bottom half of a double bill shown only at drive-ins.*

The blame lies mainly with Czerkas and Aupperle, acting in various production and storyline capacities. They are outstanding special effects artists but in the script and live-action areas they make all the same mistakes that have been made so many times before. As stop-motion enthusiasts, they should have known better and tried to avoid the usual dumbness of dinosaur movies. At the time, it seemed that the film could only promote the myth that all dinosaur movies are puerile and, in consequence, that stop-motion can't be treated seriously. In 1978, this seemed like a last gasp for dinosaur movies and for stop-motion effects (two genres heading rapidly toward extinction).

Despite a science fiction slant (the crew of a spaceship crashlands on a planet inhabited by dinosaurs), the plot is still a series of effects set-pieces linked clumsily by unimaginative live-action scenes. Direction and acting are miserable. The dialogue is frequently laughable. One character, trying to send an SOS, complains, "Maybe we're wasting our time. We could set out all the reflectors and something would just come along and

The film resurfaced on video entitled Planet of Dinasaurs *(sic). The careless misspelling seemed to add insult to injury for this unlucky picture. Large portions of the animation footage also turned up, without acknowledgment, in Fred Olen Ray's low-budget* The Phantom Empire *(1987) and* Wizards of the Demon Sword *(1991).*

eat them." Or later: "I was just wondering how many more things we're going to have to get used to—things like eating dinosaurs." The characters bicker pathetically with less dramatic interest than the grunting cavemen of *One Million Years B.C.* Were it not for the effects scenes, this would be a contender for inclusion in a *Fifty Worst Films* list. An offbeat electronic score gives the film an eerie quality reinforcing the "atmosphere" of science fiction but all too often is ill-equipped to give the passages the excitement and pace they need, instead weakening their impact.

On the other hand, the effects scenes are magnificent and make this a minor classic, the kind of film that has to be seen over and over again. Miracles have been achieved on a low budget: there are 14 distinct animation sequences as well as a number of non-animation process shots. Built by Czerkas, the stop-motion puppets all look marvelous and make the production look a lot more expensive than it is. Best of all is a mean-looking tyrannosaurus, the design of which recalls Delgado's dinosaur in *King Kong*.

Some of the animation sequences come over as too brief or are spoiled because of the lameness of the live action leading up to them, and so are best viewed out of context. None of the sequences attempts to match the theatrical "high drama" and complexity of Harryhausen's liveliest scenes, aiming instead for a more low-key and arguably more plausible style. Even the two longest passages—fights between two dinosaurs—are very one-sided and are finished quickly. This is an enjoyable change of style but also serves to make

one appreciate all the more the stamina and artistry of Harryhausen. Most of the animation—which is always confident and smooth—is by Doug Beswick, with some scenes animated by Czerkas and Aupperle.

Czerkas and Aupperle designed all the composites. Aupperle took charge of creating mattes, lighting animation set-ups and ensuring color matching. Rear projection is used in some shots and front projection in others. Some shots suffer from distracting graininess in the rear plate but others overcome this problem brilliantly, such as a night time attack by the tyrannosaurus or shots of the same creature outside its cave, which are filmed entirely in miniature. One technique used extensively and to good effect is having a miniature set occupy in full the lower portion of the frame, thereby allowing shots to be filmed in one pass of the film through the camera without any mattes. On each occasion, the miniature area is perfectly matched to the live-action environment, most successfully in the rear-projection set-up featuring a slain struthiomimus, where the color match is so good that the miniature ground blends imperceptibly with the real terrain. There are no traveling mattes.

Like most science fiction movies of the late 1970s, the first shot has a spacecraft fly past, a low-budget attempt to imitate the opening shot of *Star Wars*. A shuttle ejects from the main ship, which explodes. The model work here is good but nothing special. In one shot, the shuttle drifts towards the distant planet, which is a painting by Jim Danforth. Danforth, who was not involved in any of the animation, executed four paintings for the film. One of these (depicting two moons hanging in the sky above the planet's surface) is not seen, as it was part of footage that was dropped in an attempt to tighten the film's pace. His painting of the planet in this shot is striking but not nearly as good as a similar one he did for *The Thing* (1982).

The shuttle crashes in a lake. As the survivors swim to shore, the shuttle sinks slowly behind them. The shuttle model was animated one frame at a time and a wave effect was added to the image of the water with another pass of the film.

The stranded survivors encounter a brontosaurus chomping on some vegetation. This is a marvelous model with realistically muscular legs, but like its cousin in *One Million Years B.C.* it doesn't have a chance to do much. Unfortunately, the rear-projection set-up was so cramped that the animator — in this case Czerkas — was unable to manipulate his fully armatured puppet to any degree. In four long shots, it merely stands still on its four legs, never taking a step. A fifth shot is a closeup of its snaking neck and head. The miniature foreground, including plants, is realistic, and behind the model is a photo blow-up of sky and trees. The group of actors is huddled in the lower left corner of the frame, a design whose simplicity looks like it was lifted from one of O'Brien's composites in *The Lost World*. The composite was achieved not with a matte but by front-projecting the live-footage onto a dark area on the miniature set surrounded by miniature foliage.

As the group wanders, they encounter the gory, half-eaten remains of a large quadruped dinosaur. This is a de-

liberately low-key moment designed to heighten our anticipation for what is to follow. Again, the foreground is miniature with a photo blow-up behind.

Continuing their rather aimless wandering, the group passes three browsing stegosauri. These two short cuts maintain the low-key policy of suggesting a world full of dinosaurs and building to a more dramatic encounter. Once again, only the head and tail of the puppets move, while the legs remain stationary. On this occasion, a narrow floor inlay has been matted into the shot to allow the puppets to throw shadows. The three models, built by Czerkas over simple wire armatures, are realistically detailed and this is a fine "throwaway" image, but the graininess of the rear plate makes this look too much like "a special effect."

More ambitious is a fight between a tyrannosaurus and a stegosaurus. Both models are superb and there are numerous excellent touches. But the battle, animated by Beswick, lacks real energy and is weakened by live-action cutaways of disinterested actors.

A matte outline following the brow of a hill allows the stegosaur to lumber into the top of the screen, startling a girl in the lower foreground. In the next cut, the creature plods heavily into the frame from the right and the group flees. But they are confronted by the tyrannosaur which appears from between some rocks in the middle distance. The combination of somber lighting on the model and its exceptionally smooth movements make this an attractive shot. Keen-eyed viewers might spot that one character very briefly loses the top part of his head as he runs in front of the puppet's leg.

A shot of the stegosaur advancing across the frame uses a "soft" (out of focus) matte line at ground level which not only conceals the split but also has the unintentional benefit of suggesting that the creature's tail is stirring up dust. In closeup, the head of the tyrannosaur with its scaly hide and huge, fleshy mouth, looks chilling.

The battle is depicted in ten animation cuts, all of which use the same long-shot design (although in some Aupperle moves his camera in closer to give the sequence some variety). It is animated entirely in camera with an extensive miniature foreground and no mattes.

The two beasts square off tentatively in a way that suggests Beswick watched Disney's *Fantasia* (which features a battle between the same two species of dinosaur) before animating the battle. An actor leaps away from a carefully timed swish of the biped's tail in the sequence's only attempt at interaction. The tyrannosaur chews on one of the stegosaur's spinal plates, gets clubbed by its spiked tail and finally dispatches it in a splendidly grisly flourish, biting into its head to the sound of bones crunching sickeningly. In the two final cuts, the carnivore tears a chunk of flesh from the dead stegosaur and swallows it with a realistic scooping action.

A comparison with Harryhausen's fight between a triceratops and a ceratosaur in *One Million Years B.C.* shows that while Beswick's animation is smoother, his choreography is less elaborate and the earlier scene is the more exciting of the two, even though it tends to repeat itself.

Harvey, one of the group, discovers a clutch of eggs and so provokes an attack by a ceratopsian dinosaur. This is another excellent model with bumpy ridges running down its back and across the frill that protects its neck. However, its eyes are curiously lifeless. It resembles a styracosaurus but combines characteristics of other ceratopsians and was dubbed the Czerkasaurus on the set. Animated by Aupperle, the scene is rather hurried but boasts a superb conclusion.

The beast appears from behind a large rock, a vertical matte line following the edge of the rock. Seeing Harvey, it prepares to charge, scraping one of its front legs on the ground like a bull — a good touch which gives the puppet some character. Harvey fires a laser gun at it and a superimposed beam of laser hits the dinosaur, evoking a barrage of hisses and growls.

In two cuts, the quadruped runs after Harvey. Aupperle has the same problems making its gait look natural that Harryhausen had with his triceratops in *One Million Years B.C.* and that David Allen had with his chasmosaurus in *When Dinosaurs Ruled the Earth.* (Of the three, Allen's animation is the most plausible.) In closeup, the dinosaur's horn sinks into Harvey's chest, a deliciously gory shock effect. This was achieved with Aupperle animating against a very small rear screen and carving away more and more of the horn in each frame so that it seems to disappear into the actor's chest. Harryhausen performed a similar trick with a skeleton's sword in *Jason and the Argonauts.*

In a beautiful long shot, the beast stands on the edge of a cliff with a puppet of the screaming actor impaled on its horn. The flailing of the arms and legs of the puppet human is carefully animated to react as the dinosaur shakes its head up and down. Eventually, the victim is released and falls over the cliff. Animated as it falls, the puppet human was not supported on wires but attached to a rod which was later matted out in another camera pass. After a live-action shot of the gored victim, the episode closes with another attractive long shot, with the Czerkasaurus standing proudly — in best "Monarch of the Glen" style — on top of the miniature cliff, backed by the rich blues of a painted sky backdrop.

An encounter with a dog-sized spider is an even briefer scene but this time brevity suits the objective — to give a good, quick scare. The jarring musical score catches the right note. The spider, a stiff-legged, scurrying thing, is a perfect subject for stop-motion. This is a deftly executed vignette, infinitely preferable to the dull live-action spider of *One Million Years B.C.* Who knows how it might compare with *King Kong*'s spider sequence?

In a front-projection set-up, the spider scampers towards Pamela Bottaro. For this shot, a static matte allows the puppet to walk over rocks in the live-action plate. Additionally, Aupperle placed some actual rocks on his animation table so that the puppet could throw a shadow. In two cuts, the arachnid runs directly at the camera. One of these cuts uses a miniature foreground; the other is a closeup. When the spider runs up Bottaro's leg, the outline of her leg forms the unusual matte line. She swipes it away (possibly the puppet is wire-supported for a couple of frames) and the camera cuts to a believable full-scale

prop spider flying through the air. In a final animation shot, the thrashing spider has been impaled by a miniature spear.

In a tiresome sequence, the cast members attempt to enjoy some drinking and dancing but only succeed in looking foolish. The next day brings the liveliest stop-motion scene so far, an attack by a seven-foot-tall allosaurus. This episode was animated by Beswick and seems to take some of its inspiration from the classic allosaurus fight in *One Million Years B.C.* It's an accomplished sequence but lacks the pace and ferocity of Harryhausen's gem. The model is again highly detailed but this time its proportions don't quite convince.

The carnivore stomps in from the left of the frame to menace one of the women. This static matte design is followed by a closeup of the creature's gaping jaws. The woman throws superimposed sand into its face, giving rise to a memorable bit of character animation as the allosaurus uses its tiny arms to brush away the grit in its eye. It's a gesture which, probably deliberately, recalls the ear-scratching of *King Kong*'s tyrannosaurus and Gwangi.

The next shot is a superb example of how static matte can distort perspective and really put a model into a live-action setting. In long shot, the actress runs from the right background towards the camera while the blinded allosaurus stands in the left background, swishing its tail and rubbing its eyes. The puppet is of course in reality in the foreground on an animation table, but the choreography of the woman's run fools the eye into thinking otherwise.

The beast follows her into another

rocky setting and in closeup it snaps its jaws at her. In a rear-screen set-up it looms over the mini-skirted actress in such a way as to suggest that it is about to perform some perverse sexual act on her. Who knows whether or not this is what Aupperle and Czerkas intended? A second character, Chuck, throws a spear into its back and the puppet recoils credibly from the impact, screaming in pain.

In an eye-catching long shot, the allosaurus stands in the middle of the frame trying to shake off the spear, with Chuck standing on top of a rock to the left, the girl cowering on the right. In another rear-screen static mate set-up, Chuck holds up a knife in front of the beast. After a closeup, the dinosaur is hit by a blast of laser-fire. Finally, it decides that enough is enough and walks away from the scene.

But the sequence hasn't quite ended yet. After a live-action interval, the group members decide to hunt down and kill the allosaurus to prevent further attacks. In a medium shot, the dinosaur looks back over its shoulder at its pursuers. As it turns to continue its flight, the huge jaws of the tyrannosaurus suddenly loom down from nowhere and engulf the head of the allosaurus. This wonderful shock effect, over in a couple of seconds, again takes its inspiration from another film. This time the source is *The Valley of Gwangi*, in which the title character appears from behind a rock and snatches up an ornithomimus. Harryhausen's scene is the better conceived shot, a more elaborate composite with live actors in the foreground.

The complex animation of the two ostrich-like struthiomimids has to keep track not only of their claws, swishing necks and snaking tails but also the writhings of a tiny lizard which one of them is holding and intending to eat. The spindly limbed creatures and their bird-like chirruping give the scene a gentle comic tone which contrasts effectively with the preceding animation episodes. Once again the scene is a brief one — this time nine animation cuts. It is marred by grainy rear-screens but is fluidly animated and the unusual creatures make it irresistible.

The survivors spy on the two creatures and decide to kill one of them. An animated arrow pierces the side of one of the dinosaurs. It throws its neck around in pain then collapses, while the other creature runs out of the frame. Two dramatic shots looking down at the creature waving its fierce claws at the camera are filmed entirely in miniature and allow closer looks at the scaly detail on the puppet. A rear-screen set-up (mentioned earlier) has a flawlessly matched miniature foreground, used in a shot in which Chuck thrusts a spear into the creature. The implied interaction is achieved by having Chuck thrust his spear into the ground at a point obscured by the puppet. Blood appears on the puppet, enhancing what is a very good attempt at suggesting contact. The scene ends as the actors surround a convincing full-scale prop of the dead animal.

The attack at night by the tyrannosaurus has an eerie, nightmarish quality that is emphasized by the electronic score and the muted growls of the dinosaur. This is a very brief scene (only eight animation cuts) but extremely effective because of the shadowy lighting, superb model and excellent animation.

Planet of Dinosaurs (1979): The struthiomimus is killed.

Two characters are getting romantic when the huge dinosaur arrives at the stockade. In long shot, it tramples on the stakes that form a fence. The stakes and the rocks in the foreground are all miniature. In a dramatic long shot, the beast strides purposefully into the foreground, snarling straight at the camera. When it turns in the direction of one of the women, its tail knocks over a shelter that is part of the rear screen, a moment of interaction successfully implied by careful timing. Its huge head lowers into the frame to snatch up the woman in its jaws and in a final long shot the tyrannosaurus walks off with a puppet human

in its mouth. The arm of the puppet human is animated so that it appears to dangle limply.

The group decides to track and kill the tyrannosaurus. The next morning they seek its lair and en route they pass a coelophysis, seen only briefly in two cuts and reinforcing the impression that there are dinosaurs everywhere. This is another ostrich-like creature and it was built and animated by Aupperle a year earlier as a test. The beast is perched on a rock (presumably by means of a static matte) and, in a nice touch, it washes its face with its hands.

Attractive long shots of the cave

The tyrannosaurus makes a meal of the rhodosaurus (a tribute to *The Beast from 20,000 Fathoms*) in *Planet of Dinosaurs.*

entrance to the tyrannosaurus' lair are composites that impeccably match a fine Danforth glass painting with the live-action element. The humans decide that in order to confront the monster, they must lure it with some bait, so they set off to look for a more manageable dinosaur.

The polacanthus — a six-foot-long quadruped resembling a stegosaur but with spikes on its back instead of plates — is another impressive model. In seven animation cuts, three of the men surround the beast. The little creature doesn't stand much of a chance and Jim,

the group's leader, kills it by clubbing it on the head. Again, Beswick's animation is extremely fluid and realistic.

The scene uses only two set-ups. One is a simple rear-screen set-up, used in two cuts in which just the puppet's spiked tail is seen, waving threateningly at Chuck. The other is a static matte design with the matte invisibly following the sloping ground level and backed by the same striking rock formation that formed a backdrop to the fight between the stegosaurus and the tyrannosaurus.

In the long shots, the actors are positioned so that they really seem to

This shot of the majestic tyrannosaurus in *Planet of Dinosaurs* (1979) demonstrates how a static matte can be used to fool the eye into perceiving that a puppet that is animated in front of previously shot live-action footage is actually in the background.

surround the puppet on all sides, making this a very successful composite. The polacanthus initially digs at the ground with one of its front legs, searching for roots. The moment when Jim clubs the beast on the head is exceptionally well animated, the puppet's head jerking down from the impact. Jim is behind the dinosaur and the contact is suggested simply by alignment of the two images. The beast staggers about realistically for a while before going down on one knee, then keels over and expires after the obligatory final swish of its tail. When the men carry the corpse to the cave, another good full-size prop is used.

At the cave, the group is surprised when the tyrannosaurus emerges not from its lair but on the path behind them. The animation camera tilts up to give the shot extra punch. This could have been a fine shock effect but is weakened by the slow music and the dinosaur's restrained roar. Still, the visual impact of this superb model once again insures this is a scene to cherish. A spear is thrown and pierces the dinosaur's hide. The switch from real to miniature

545

spear is flawless, although the rear screen looks very washed out. A matte must have been used over some of the background area to obscure the real spear as it passes behind the model.

One of the group falls to the ground and in a forceful closeup the tyrannosaur's huge head moves down towards him, nearly filling the frame. A carefully matched miniature foreground again avoids the need for the matte in two long shots in which the dinosaur chews on the man (now a puppet) then walks off with his limp body in its jaws. The scene ends with an unforgettable shot, executed entirely in miniature, in which the tyrannosaur, its prey still in its mouth, walks back into its cave, looking back over its shoulder almost disdainfully as it disappears into the shadows.

Feature films with stop-motion are regularly criticized for the gratuitous nature of some of their effects scenes. Prize for the most gratuitous effects sequence of all goes to this film's next animation sequence, in which one of the group — the spaceship captain — runs off to find the tyrannosaurus "to give our friend some exercise." Out of context, this is a marvelous little episode (featuring five animation cuts) with the captain using a mirror to reflect sunlight onto the dinosaur, which reacts with a character-filled mixture of confusion and anger. But within the context of the plot, most viewers will condemn the scene as pointless padding and will probably feel that the captain deserves to get eaten for being so reckless.

In a long shot static matte, the captain crouches behind some rocks in the lower part of the screen as the tyrannosaur stomps in from the right. The captain aims a beam of sunlight at the puppet and this is animated frame-by-frame along with the puppet. It's a surreal sight, with the dinosaur shaking its head from side to side in discomfort. The beast pursues the captain into another long-shot static matte set-up (featuring that same rock formation for a third time — it certainly gets around). This is a well thought out design with the puppet walking into the area previously occupied by the actor before he ran off. This kind of choreography enhances the illusion that puppet and actor are inhabiting the same environment.

The action flows straight into the next animation scene as the captain finds his route blocked by another dinosaur. The film's final model is designed as a tribute to the fictitious rhedosaurus in Harryhausen's *Beast from 20,000 Fathoms*, although Czerkas' model is slightly more slender and lizard-like. The rhedosaurus' dramatic role is very limited: It serves only as another meal for the tyrannosaurus. The struggle between these two dinosaurs is abrupt and one-sided — a deliberately more true-to-life encounter than Harryhausen's drawn-out, theatrical confrontations.

In two static matte cuts, the captain runs underneath the rhedosaurus, which appears over the brow of a rock in the background. The beast's stare follows the captain as he runs past and it emits snakelike hisses and slurps as its tongue flicks out.

The tyrannosaurus strides into the same set-up, its foot seeming to make contact with the ground in the live-action plate. The tail of the puppet is out of the frame so this may have been achieved by simply supporting the puppet off-screen and aligning its foot with live-action ground. In six more animation cuts, the rhedosaurus is dispatched and carried back to the cave.

The tyrannosaurus bites into the rhedosaurus' neck, pulling it from the rock. When it drops the smaller reptile, the rate of fall is unrealistically slow. With characteristic savagery, the flesh eater bites into the rhedosaurus' head, accompanied by the usual bone-crunching sound effects. The victor walks off with its prey and the sequence ends with another all-miniature shot of the tyrannosaur walking into its lair. As before, the quality of detail on the miniature cave set and the eye-catching simulation of sunlight on the puppets and rocks, makes the shot look so good that it's tempting to wish that the film had dispensed with its live action altogether.

In the film's final stop-motion sequence, the tyrannosaur is lured out of its cave and killed. This is a more ambitious episode and contains 12 impressive animation cuts. Excitingly staged, the scene nevertheless disappoints because the tyrannosaur is killed too easily in view of all its earlier dramatic appearances. The scene steals the means of death from *One Million Years B.C.* by having the beast impaled on a wooden stake. It's a shame that Aupperle and Czerkas couldn't come up with something more original.

Outside the cave, the remaining five characters try to draw out the tyrannosaur by whooping and leaping up and down like children — not one of the script's more sensible ideas. The first four animated cuts use the miniature cave set. The first of these is a very striking tilt-up as the dinosaur stomps out of the shadowy cave and into the sunlight.

In medium shot, a spear pierces its neck but is later pulled out by one of the tiny arms.

The tyrannosaur strides after the fleeing group in a series of long shots and medium shots. One of the long shots uses the same set-up of the sloping path that was seen earlier when the dinosaur carried off one of the men in its jaws. Another marvelous long shot has all five actors run along a path (with painted or miniature rocks in the foreground to give the shot more depth), hotly pursued by the tyrannosaur. Only the puppet's lower half crosses the shot, cleverly emphasizing the impression of the creature's size by giving the impression that it is too large to fit into the frame. In this static matte set-up, the model's feet run across the same area of ground that the actors have run across, very effectively meshing the two elements.

The creature runs into another static matte set-up where a series of sharpened stakes (all miniature) has been set up. Unable to stop, the tyrannosaur is impaled on one of the stakes, and Beswick's animation conveys the impression of the beast's momentum being halted abruptly, one of its legs kicking forward as it is lifted off the ground. In two cuts, the creature raises it head and screams in pain. Beswick's animation is particularly good as it eventually crashes to the ground, including the animation of all the falling stakes.

The film closes with another Danforth glass painting, a faultlessly realistic landscape showing the lakeside huts that the survivors have built. Unable to resist one last act of screen pilfering, the film ends with a reprise of the cast, at the end of which is a repeat shot of the tyrannosaurus emerging from its cave. Yes — exactly the way that *Gwangi* concluded.

The effects scenes are a labor of love on the part of all concerned, which makes it all the more inexcusable that Aupperle and Czerkas did not seize the opportunity to show what can really be done with stop-motion. Surely between them they could have come up with a screenplay that did not insult the intelligence of an eight-year-old! Instead of demonstrating the potential of the genre, this film reinforced its image as a time-consuming and essentially childish medium.

Why have they given their puppets so little character? Again, they had the chance give them quirks of behavior which could have made each thoroughly memorable. There are several such touches, but they don't go far enough.

For example, the tyrannosaurus is an outstanding model and features in several good scenes but is almost entirely without character. Also, the decision to have a high number of brief animation scenes (rather than just four or five more elaborate ones) is questionable. While this does have the effect of creating the impression that the planet is literally crawling with dinosaurs, it also enforces a dramatic stiltedness of some sequences which deserve to be longer.

Faults aside, this is still one of the great dinosaur pictures. It's a thrill just to see such a variety of prehistoric creatures stomping, goring, biting and generally doing what dinosaurs do best. This is a spirited depiction of images that can only ever exist on the screen and proves that you can't beat a good dinosaur movie — or even a *bad* one for, that matter.

Poltergeist

1982. MGM. D: Tobe Hooper. Scr: Steven Spielberg, Michael Grais, Mark Victor. Story: Steven Spielberg. Ph: Matthew Leonetti. Art: James H. Spencer. Mus: Jerry Goldsmith. Special Effects Makeup: Craig Reardon. Special Visual Effects: Industrial Light and Magic. Visual Effects Supervisor: Richard Edlund. Effects Cameramen: Rick Fichter, Bill Neil. Stop-Motion (uncredited) Ken Ralston. Matte Painting Supervisor: Michael Pangrazio.

Cast: JoBeth Williams, Craig T. Nelson, Beatrice Straight, Dominique Dunne, Oliver Robens, Heather O'Rourke.

Rating: ✩✩✩½   Stop-Motion: ✩✩

In 1982, *Poltergeist* was a breath of fresh air amid all the stalk-and-slash horror pictures that were flooding the cinemas. It's a picture that the horror genre can be proud of, a full-blooded fantasy with well-rounded characters and a simple story imaginatively told with deft touches of humor, some unnerving horror set-pieces and a host of superb special effects.

Tobe Hooper, who directed the genuinely terrifying *Texas Chain Saw Massacre* (1974), leaves less of a stamp on the film than producer Steven Spielberg, who imprints his characteristic "sense of wonder" on the wonderfully restrained first half. Delightful minor effects during this part of the film include chairs moving on their own, a steak crawling across a kitchen surface and a ghostly presence emerging from a television set. A too-talky middle section, lumbered with the awkward character of a midget medium, harms the pace and the sense of purpose is never regained. Some supernatural nonsense concerning retrieving a tennis ball from "the other side" and less-than-convincing shock effects with a huge skull-face and bat-like goblin also mar the middle section.

It is a highly unlikely plot device that, after their house has been "cleaned," the troubled family should decide to spend a few more hours there, and so precipitate the climax. All the same, this is still probably the greatest "haunted house" movie ever made.

The superb finale includes a nail-biting scene in which JoBeth Williams finds herself in a muddy swimming pool full of corpses (beautiful special makeup creations by Craig Reardon) and a dazzling shot by Industrial Light and Magic in which the house literally implodes and disappears into a black hole (shot high-speed in miniature with the model being sucked into a vacuum).

The early part of the film includes an enchanting moment in which three psychic investigators open a bedroom door in the house and are confronted by the sight of a dozen objects flying round the room. Among all the lamps, books and records is a stop-motion puppet of an Incredible Hulk toy riding through the air on a horse. In one cut, it flies up close to the investigators, rears up then flies off.

Like each of the elements in the shot, the puppet was filmed separately against a blue screen by Rick Fichter using a motion-control camera. Ken Ralston (uncredited) animated the Hulk's head and arm and the horse's legs to enhance the impression that they really have come to life. Effects supervisor Richard Edlund described the nine cuts in this sequence as some of the hardest effects he has had to do, because of all the different blue-screen elements. Incidentally, a still that accompanies most articles on this film is a publicity paste-up of a situation that does not actually appear in the scene.

The Power

1968. MGM/Pal. Prod: George Pal. D: Byron Haskin. Scr: John Gay. Based on the Novel by Frank M. Robinson. Ph: Ellsworth Fredericks. Art: George W. Davis, Merrill Pye. Mus: Miklos Rosza. Visual Effects: Wah Chang, Gene Warren. Stop-Motion (uncredited): Dave Pal, Pete Kleinow.

Cast: George Hamilton, Suzanne Pleshette, Richard Carlson, Yvonne de Carlo, Gary Merrill, Arthur O'Connell, Michael Rennie, Aldo Ray.

Gene Warren works on one of the puppets from *The Power* (1968).

Rating: ☆☆½   Stop-Motion: ☆☆

As a result of the commercial failure of *The 7 Faces of Dr. Lao*, it was four years before George Pal brought his next feature to the screen. *The Power* is a less flamboyant affair, a serious science fiction treatment that concentrates more on its thriller elements than its fantasy trappings.

Tautly scripted by John Gay and well acted by a high-quality cast, it is badly let down by its failure to come to grips with its central plot device. A superhuman (Michael Rennie) assassinates members of a scientific project one by one as George Hamilton tries to identify and stop him. Unfortunately, the script never bothers to explain the exact nature of the superhuman's powers, why he has them, or even why, if he is so powerful, he should waste his time killing a handful of people. Effective sequences are offset by others that cause more laughter than suspense (a fight in a kitchen has both characters rolling around on the floor covered in food and drink from the fridge; some middle-aged groovers do some wild dancing at a party).

Along the way, the plot is spiced up by some special effects done under the

550

supervision of Wah Chang and Gene Warren. These are all competent effects but all have the same storybook colorfulness that characterizes effects shots in many of Pal's films, and look out of place in a film that is trying to be adult SF.

Hamilton, rejected by his colleagues because they suspect him of being the superhuman, walks past a toy shop. A wooden bird in the window turns and winks at him, a shot using stop-motion and (probably) replacement animation. A few moments later, a group of about 30 toy soldiers marches in formation, turns and fires guns at him. Animated by Dave Pal, these shots add nothing to the drama of the plot, and come across as mere gimmicky digressions. The script fails to explain the fact that Hamilton, who also has "The Power," has caused the toys to come to life.

At the climax, Rennie subjects Hamilton to a demonstration of "The Power." Hamilton hallucinates that his body is freezing and in one effective cut his face cracks opens. "All the scenes involving George Hamilton's head," Warren explained in a letter to the author, "were accomplished stop-frame on a wax model of Hamilton taken from a life mask." The cracking effect was achieved by painting cracks on the model frame by frame and by having pieces of it split away by means of stop-motion — recall-ing the demise of Talos in *Jason and the Argonauts*. Next, Hamilton imagines he is subjected to intense heat and in a five-second closeup the skin peels away from his face, revealing a skull cleaned by the flames. This shot recalls the Morlock deterioration near the end of *The Time Machine*. The sequence ends with three cuts in which a skeleton spins in space, slowly falling away from the camera, suggesting that Hamilton is nearing death. The skeleton was animated by Pete Kleinow, then combined with superimposed film of stars rushing towards the camera. It may well be the same model that was used at the end of *The Wonderful World Of The Brothers Grimm*.

Pal made only one more film, *Doc Savage, the Man of Bronze*, a forgettable superhero spoof released in 1975, and containing no stop-motion. He died in 1991. His career began with the stop-motion delights of his *Puppetoon* shorts and eight of his fourteen feature films contain stop-motion. In his films, it was usually present as a quick, playful effect, or, if used more elaborately, only in comic sequences such as those in *The Wonderful World of the Brothers Grimm* and *The Seven Faces of Dr. Lao*. It is a great shame that he never chose to exploit the medium more fully: Had he wished, he could have filmed major stop-motion sequences to rival those of O'Brien and Harryhausen.

Prehistoric Poultry: The Dinornis, or the Great Roaring Whiffenpoof

1917. Edison Conquest. D-Scr-Ph-Stop-Motion: Willis H. O'Brien.

Rating: ☆☆½   Stop-Motion: ☆☆½

This 1916 short (O'Brien's fifth) is the only surviving version of two which O'Brien made with the same title. The animation is slightly cruder than before, probably because O'Brien was now under contract to complete a series of films in a fixed time. The dinornis and some of the human mannikins reappear from previous shorts. It has a weaker storyline than the other three surviving shorts and there are fewer inventive humorous touches.

The dinornis is seen feeding, and the lumps of food cause its long neck to swell comically as it swallows. In a cave, an affectionate brontosaurus pokes its head in and licks a caveman. When the caveman lights up a pipe, O'Brien repeats a clever trick he used in *Morpheus Mike* and has smoke blowing out of the puppet's mouth. The "pesky dinornis" scratches its ear (a nice bit of animal behavior which would resurface with the tyrannosaur in *King Kong* many years later) and kicks the caveman. When the caveman climbs a small tree, the dinornis pulls it over and catapults the man into the air. The caveman cartwheels across the set; then the dinornis flies after him and gives him a final kick. Amusing stuff, but even for a five-minute short, the story needed to be developed more.

O'Brien continued to make short films for Edison but none of these survive. They were: *Curious Pets of Our Ancestors, In the Villain's Power, The Puzzling Billboard* (one of a series of shorts called *Sam Lloyd's Famous Puzzles*) and another series, *Mickey's Naughty Nightmares* (also known as *Nippy's Nightmares* and including one episode called *Mickey and His Goat*), in which for the first time live action footage was intercut with animation footage.

Prehysteria!

1993. Moonbeam Entertainment. D: Albert Band, Charles Band, Scr: Greg Suddeth, Mark Goldstein. Original Idea: Peter Von Sholly. Ph: Adolfo Bartoli. Art: Milo. Mus: Richard Band. Visual Effects: David Allen Productions. Visual Effects Supervisor: David Allen. Animation: David Allen, Chris Endicott. Puppet Effects Supervisor: Mark Rappaport. Dinosaurs Sculpted and Designed by Andrea Von Sholly.

Cast: Brett Cullen, Colleen Morris, Samantha Mills, Austin O'Brien, Stephen Lee, Tony Longo.

Rating: ☆☆½   Stop-Motion: ☆☆½

552

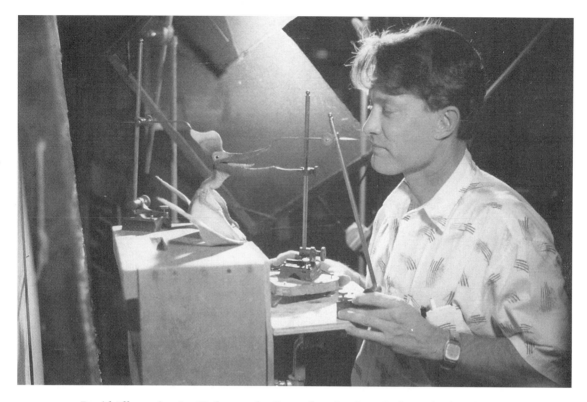

David Allen animates Madonna, the Quetzalcoatlus from *Prehysteria!* (1993).

Charles Band's *Prehysteria!* is very much a reworking of the Disney live action features of the 1950s and 1960s. Two kids find some unusual pets (in this case, miniature dinosaurs) and try to keep them a secret from Dad. The villains who want to get their hands on the dinosaurs are all excitable buffoons guaranteed not to scare a young audience. And everything ends happily ever after: The kids get to keep the dinosaurs, the villains are laughed out of town and Dad falls in love.

By Band standards, the film is well acted and the script is wittier than usual. The two children could easily have been obnoxious brats, but the film avoids this. Even the dinosaurs are presented in a restrained way that never descends to the merely cute. The only scene that oversteps good sense has the dinosaurs tapping their feet to some rock and roll.

Band's right hand man, David Allen, supervised the many dinosaur scenes, the majority of which were shot on-set using cable-controlled puppets that have an impressive array of gesture and movement. This is a great improvement on the rod puppetry seen in *Subspecies*. A brachiosaurus, for example, can rear up on its hind legs, and a tyrannosaurus can snap its jaws and lunge forward very effectively. The puppets, sculpted by Andrea Von Sholly, are all highly detailed and have excellent paint jobs. Although only used here for low-key dramatic impact, the puppets

Chris Endicott animates tyrannosaurus Elvis for *Prehysteria!*

are so good that they could easily stand up to a more demanding role as full-sized creatures in a more ambitious project.

The cable puppets perform so well that Allen needed to film only 19 stop-motion shots. Most of these feature a Quetzalcoatlus, a winged pterosaur puppet whose slender legs prevented the insertion of cables. Other stop-motion shots depict the other dinosaurs walking or running, actions that were beyond the capabilities of cable-controlled puppets. One of the puppets is a chasmosaurus, perhaps chosen deliberately by Allen to relive his first feature film

work in *When Dinosaurs Ruled the Earth.*

The first five stop-motion cuts feature the Quetzalcoatlus. Standing on a shelf with its yellow, leathery wings held down, the creature blinks and caws, its long tongue snaking out. On its head is a brightly colored crest. Later, it surprises the daughter (Samantha Mills) by flying out of a laundry basket and flapping past her head. In these two cuts, the puppet seems to have been combined with the live-action by means of front-light/back-light mattes. As Mills spins around, her hair passes in front of the puppet, an ambitious shot which may have used a series of intricate rotoscoped mattes. In fact, this is such a good composite that one suspects that it is actually an on-set effect, using a wire-supported marionette. However, the wings move up and down with such a credible action that this is unlikely. The pterosaur is later discovered sitting on a shelf in a toy cupboard and, in what looks like another front-light/back-light matte, it takes to the air.

The Quetzalcoatlus also features in several stop-motion closeups, animated by Chris Endicott, in which it is perched on Mills' shoulder. Endicott imbues it with touches of character: It sways its head from side to side, caws and blinks in a very lively way. Only the puppet's head appears in these rear-screen shots, so no matte is involved.

In another shot, the pterosaur flies around Dad (Brett Cullen) in the kitchen. This is a quick cut and it is difficult tell how it was achieved. If it is an on-set marionette, it is extremely convincing. If it is another rotoscope-matte, then it is flawless. The same applies to a shot in which the winged reptile flaps around Austin O'Brien's head in the living room, and other shots in which the creature flies around a greenhouse and out through a hole in the roof.

In one scene, the family is gathered around a table and the Quetzalcoatlus flies in through a doorway, lands on the table and folds its wings. These look like rear-projection shots, with a static matte line following the top of the table. Later,

Mills holds out her hand and the reptile flies down into it. This is a superb example of a puppet being carefully aligned with a part of a live-action image. When Mills' hand moves slightly during the shot, the puppet is also moved slightly so as to remain aligned.

Stop-motion shots of the other dinosaurs are few but effective. In a terrific long shot animated by Endicott, O'Brien is rooting around in a fridge while at his feet a foot-tall tyrannosaurus struts across the floor. In this matte shot, glass has been positioned below the puppet so that it makes a reflection which seems to be on the shiny kitchen tiles.

In a cable shot, the four dinosaurs look up at a closed door which is then rammed by the chasmosaurus. The door and floor all appear to be part of the animation set. Allen gets the animation of the running beast just right and conveys a real impression of impact as the puppet hits the door. The running cycle is also well-judged in a shot of the chasmosaurus chasing a rolling orange across the kitchen floor. This composite — with Dad looking on amazed in the background — seems to be another front-light/back-light matte.

At the end of the film, the four dinosaurs, which have been abducted by the villain, emerge from a box in which they have been held captive. The four puppets all walk directly towards the camera in a complicated and skillfully executed rod-puppet shot in which each character was filmed separately against a blue screen.

Prehysteria! 2

1994. Moonbeam. Prod-D: Albert Band. Scr: Brent Friedman, Michael Davis. Idea: Pete Von Sholly. Ph: James Lawrence Spencer. Art: Milo. Mus: Richard Band. Puppeteers: Mark Rappaport, Allen Barton. Special Visual Effects: David Allen, Chris Endicott, Brett White. Stop-Motion Animation: Yan Guo. Digital Effects Supervisor: Paul Gentry.

Cast: Kevin R. Connors, Jennifer Harte, Dean Scofield, Bettye Ackerman, Greg Lewis, Michael Hagiwara.

Rating: ☆   Stop-Motion: ☆½

This wretched sequel is a torture to watch. Even the young kids at whom it is aimed will tire quickly and switch channels. A rich kid, ignored by his father, obtains the miniature dinosaurs from the original film. The creatures cause mischief in the house. Eventually the boy and his father are brought closer together. The film treads in live-action Disney territory, but what is totally missing are the charm and liveliness of Disney's films.

Almost all shots of the dinosaurs use rod-controlled or cable-controlled puppets. In two traveling matte shots, Madonna the flying reptile glides across the frame. In these, the puppet is presumably rod-controlled and filmed against a blue screen.

There is only one stop-motion cut, animated by Yan Guo under David Allen's supervision. Madonna comes to rest on the edge of a crate, folds her wings and looks around.

Presumably the budget and shooting schedule prevented any more stop-motion cuts being included. And since they wouldn't have generated any more profit, why bother?

The Primevals

1968–1998. Darkzone/Empire/Full Moon. D: David Allen. Scr: David Allen, Randy Cook. Visual Effects Supervisor: David Allen.

Rating: N/A.   Stop-Motion: N/A.

This on-again, off-again project masterminded by David Allen has for nearly 30 years promised to give fantasy lovers and stop-motion enthusiasts a real treat. It has been announced in the press many times, only to be canceled shortly afterwards. It tells the tale of Himalayan explorers who stumble upon a lost crater and encounter a Yeti, alien reptile-men, a giant horned lizard, a spider monster and other fantastic creatures.

It began life in the late 1960s as a project called *Raiders of the Stone Ring*. Among those who worked on it during this early phase were Jim Danforth, Dennis Muren, Ken Ralston, Phil Tippett, Randy Cook and Tom St. Amand. Tippett built a Yeti puppet which over the years deteriorated so much that it had to be replaced by a new one constructed by Allen.

The alien lizard men as originally conceived by David Allen for *The Primevals*, an ongoing project since 1968.

Armatures were built by St. Amand, doing some of his first work in this field. Later, the puppet of a horned river lizard was constructed by Ron Lizorty.

The project went into limbo for some time and was revived in 1975–76. In 1978, producer Charles Band took an interest in the project and financed it. Among those who worked on it during this phase were Dave Carson and Jon Berg. Production was stopped and started many times during the 1980s.

Between 1993 and 1994 it was re-

vived again and all live-action footage was shot in Rumania, directed by Allen. The money dried up again and in 1995 the production once again shut down.

In 1996, Band raised further financing for the film and the stop-motion and other effects work was begun in earnest. All the animation is being done by Allen and Chris Endicott, and Allen has also sculpted all the models. As of March of 1997, about one sixth of the stop-motion has been completed.

Prophecy see *God's Army*

Pulsepounders (a.k.a. *Dungeonmaster II*)

1987. Empire Pictures. Prod-D: Charles Band. Stop-Motion Supervisors: David Allen, Justin Kohn. Stop-Motion Animation: Justin Kohn, Kim Blanchette.

Cast: Tom Thomerson, Jeffrey Combs Barbara Crampton, David Gale.

Rating: N/A. Stop Motion: N/A

Charles Band's Empire Pictures filmed this sequel anthology to three of their previous films, *Trancers*, *Re-Animator*, and 1983's *Dungeonmaster*, in 1987 but it became caught up in an ownership dispute when Empire went into dissolution. As a result it was never released, although there is talk that it may still surface one day.

One of its three episodes contains a sequence featuring stop-motion that was produced at David Allen's studio. Allen supervised the stop-motion effects but, busy working on other projects, he left the hands-on animation to Justin Kohn and Kim Blanchette. Kohn also sculpted the two stop-motion characters, a bipedal, long-tailed dragon-like creature and a humanoid stone giant with a face carved on both the front and back of its head.

In the film, the two creatures begin life as stone statues, are brought to life and engage in battle.

Puppetmaster

1989. Full Moon Productions. D: David Schmoeller. Scr: Joseph G. Collodi. Story: Charles Band, Kenneth J. Hall. Ph: Sergio Salvati. Mus: Richard Band. Puppet Sequences: David Allen Productions. Animation: David Allen, Justin Kohn.

Cast: Paul Le Mat, William Hickey, Irene Miracle, Jimmie F. Skaggs, Robin Frates, Matt Roe.

Rating: ☆☆½   Stop-Motion: ☆☆½

David Allen has carved himself a niche by putting "tiny terrors" on the screen: *Dolls*, *Ghoulies II*, *Young Sherlock Holmes* and the *Puppetmaster* series. But is this really what he wants to be doing? Think of the fabulous work he has done in *When Dinosaurs Ruled the Earth* and *Caveman*, and then think of the brief effects he has contributed to these later films. *Puppetmaster* is typical: There are only 11 stop-motion cuts in amongst all the live-action puppet cuts (which were also handled by Allen and his company).

These full-view animation cuts add significantly to the overall credibility of the puppets, but it's hard not to think that Allen's considerable talents are being underused. The mechanical aliens of *batteries not included* and the giant ant of *Honey, I Shrunk the Kids* gave him a better chance to show what he's capable of, but the classic David Allen film is still waiting to be made. (His dream project, *The Primevals*, is one of those on-again-off-again movies that seems doomed never to be made, although at the time of this writing, it seems to have been revived yet again and retitled *Hybrids*.) *Puppetmaster* was the first film from Band's Full Moon Productions, formed after Empire Pictures was liquidated. Its stated intention was to bring out low-budget horror and SF movies.

An irksome group of people with psychic powers gathers in an old hotel and are bumped off one by one by vicious little puppets. For Band, who co-wrote the story, this is a surprisingly uninventive plot and in many respects a retread of *Dolls* with the splatter level pumped up. An occasional moment of tongue-in-cheek brightens the gloom (such as Paul Le Mat throwing back his bedclothes and finding three decapitated heads grinning back at him; or one of the puppets tidying away three fingers that he has chopped off Jimmie Skaggs); otherwise, the puppets are the stars of the show and the only bit of originality.

There are five principal puppets (designed by Dennis Gordon) but only two of them feature in stop-motion cuts.

The other three are Leech Woman, who regurgitates leeches from her mouth and plants them on victims, Blade, who slashes his victims with a nasty array of weapons, and Jester, who has a head that swivels around in three rotating parts. The two puppets that make use of stop-motion are Tunneler, with a spinning drill on his head that he uses to cut into flesh, and Pinhead. Pinhead, with his two-inch head and full-size hands, is a bizarre creation and the best thing in the film. Allen seizes a couple of opportunities to add touches of characterization — as much as the budget will allow — but it would have been nice if he had gone further.

Most stop-motion films have the task of making an 18–inch puppet appear enormous, but here the models are their actual size in proportion to the actors, thereby precluding the need for elaborate optical or process work. One shot uses a rear-projection screen but otherwise all the animation appears to have been done on the live-action set and in-camera, with all interaction being done with the rod-puppets.

For some of the stop-motion cuts, Allen triple-exposed each frame, with the puppet in a slightly different position each time, so as to reduce strobing. For this, Allen used a specially customized camera that could rewind the film in sequence, leaving him free to concentrate on the animation itself.

The first stop-motion cut shows Pinhead climbing out a coffin and jumping to the floor; the shock effect of his weird appearance helps disguise the fact that the animation looks hurried. His attack with a firepoker on a woman is done entirely with partial shots of hand-operated puppets. The next stop-motion effect is a creepy "don't look under the bed" shot: Tunneler gets up from the shadows under the bed, his drill spinning with a high-pitched whine suggestive of imminent pain in a dentist's surgery, and runs at a girl looking under the bed.

Later on, Pinhead gets thrown across a room by someone and (in two endearing cuts) shakes his head, then struggles back to his feet. At the climax of the film, a handful of stop-motion cuts enhances the many rod-operated puppet shots. Skaggs falls back into an elevator and looks up to see Pinhead pulling the door shut, a realistic full-view shot of the puppet; likewise a shot of Pinhead advancing straight at the camera, his huge hands outstretched menacingly is also striking.

The puppets' killing of Skaggs is the gory climax. Tunneler runs across the elevator floor in a stop-motion cut, then drills into Skaggs' neck, giving rise to some very fleshy live-action splatter. Skaggs has pulled Pinhead's head off and there is a memorable shot of the puppet feeling blindly around the floor. Was this inspired by a shot filmed for *Jason and the Argonauts* (but taken out by Harryhausen) in which a decapitated skeleton searches for his skull? There is a stop-motion cut of Tunneler getting to his feet; another of Pinhead popping his head back on; and finally a rear-screen shot of the two puppets reaching up for Skaggs' feet as he hangs from the overhead trap door. This gruesome scene continues with lots of rod puppetry as the dolls get their revenge on Skaggs.

The script fails to come up with a decent ending and instead closes with a pathetic "twist" when a stuffed dog comes to life (not stop-motion), leaving half a dozen plot threads hanging. For David Allen fans only.

Puppetmaster II

1991. Full Moon Entertainment. D: David Allen. Scr: David Pabian. Story: Charles Band. Ph: Thomas F. Denove. Mus: Richard Band. Art: Kathleen Coates. Special Makeup: David Barton. Visual Effects: David Allen Productions. Puppet Supervisor: John Teska. FX Ph: Paul W. Gentry. Puppet Animators: Randy Cook, Justin Kohn, Yancy Calzada. Additional Creature Effects: Steve Neill.

Cast: Elizabeth MacLellan, Collin Bernsen, Steve Welles, Gregory Webb, Charlie Spradling, Jeff Weston.

Rating: ☆☆   Stop-Motion: ☆☆½

After decades of films in which special effects artists had been let down by directors who made the live-action scenes seem like merely padding, at last here was a film that promised to change all that. David Allen not only handled all the puppet effects in this 1990 sequel but was also the film's director. Yet the result was, if anything, slightly worse than the mediocre original. Even Allen

David Allen animates Blade leaping from the bed after slaying a victim in *Puppetmaster 2* (1991).

was not able to do much with a dull script and a restrictively low budget. The non-puppet scenes are bland and perfunctory, and the effects episodes not much better. Even at the short running time of 83 minutes, this direct-to-video effort lacks pace and purpose: Charles Band's sometimes fertile imagination dried up on this occasion (he wrote the story), leaving a producer only interested in making a quick profit.

In the original, Allen added a few likable character touches to Pinhead, a puppet with a tiny head and huge hands, but there is nothing like that here. Allen, who well knows the importance of imbuing stop-motion puppets with per-

sonality, was denied a budget that might have allowed such flourishes.

There are 12 stop-motion cuts, one more than in the first film. As before, they are always intercut with shots of the live-action rod puppets. Helping Justin Kohn, who did some of the original's animation, is Randall Cook, who had worked with Allen previously on several films (including *Laserblast, Caveman* and *Q*). Yancy Calzada, who receives a screen credit for his work on the rod-puppet shots, also did some of the stop-motion.

Pinhead, Tunneler, Jester and Blade all make a reappearance, and there are two new stop-motion puppets. One is

561

called Torch, dressed like a World War I German soldier, with a mouth full of nasty fangs and an arm that converts into a flame thrower. The other is a likable green demon seen in a flashback.

The attack on the first victim includes a stop-motion shot of Pinhead walking alongside her prostrate body—his baggy pullover bristling, like Kong's fur, where the animator has handled it. Later, Tunneler is glimpsed on a video monitor, a black-and-white cut in which the puppet walks through an open door. More ambitious are two cuts of the four puppets up in the Puppetmaster's attic, walking along the floor and into the box he keeps them in. In these rear-screen shots, the matte follows a line through the floor and up the side of the open box.

The best idea in the film is a half-realized flashback to the Puppetmaster in Egypt, displaying one of his creations—a little green demon with pointy ears, an earring and baggy trousers. Three stop-motion cuts smoothly animated by Yancy Calzada show this imaginative puppet making slight movements of head and hands, but it's a missed opportunity.

In another scene, a delighted little boy comes across Torch out in a forest, thinks him a great toy and then gets blasted by the puppet's flame thrower. The black humor of this moment should have been played up more. Some foreground miniature leaves and a well-matched miniature floor enhance two good stop-motion low-angle shots from behind Torch, looking up at the boy.

Blade makes bloody work of another victim in bed. In the first of two stop-motion cuts, he turns away from the corpse, brandishing a knife and a hook. In the best animation cut in the film, he leaps down off the bed and runs at the camera. The camera dollies with the puppet and some blur has been added to the animation. A real shadow thrown by the puppet onto the bed indicates that the bed is also part of the set-up in the animation studio.

The film's last animation cut is a shot of Pinhead attacking someone, flying through the air as he leaps down from a chandelier. Presumably the puppet was supported by wire for this shot.

The bizarre subject matter always makes the film watchable, but there is a shortage of energy and imagination.

Puppetmaster III—Toulon's Revenge

1991. Full Moon Entertainment. D: David DeCoteau. Scr: C. Courtney Joyner. Original Idea: Charles Band. Ph: Adolfo Bartoli. Mus: Richard Band. Art: Billy Jett. Special Makeup Effects: David Barton. Puppet Effects and Visual Effects: David Allen Productions. Stop-Motion Animation: David Allen, Chris Endicott. FX Photography: Paul W. Gentry. Sculptor: Dennis Gordon.

Cast: Guy Rolfe, Richard Lynch, Ian Abercrombie, Kristopher Logan, Aron Eisenberg, Walter Gotell.

Rating: ☆☆½   Stop-Motion: ☆☆½

The third entry in Charles Band's direct-to-video *Puppetmaster* series is marginally better than the other two by virtue of an offbeat plot set in Germany during World War II. German scientists, looking for a way to reanimate corpses that can be sent to the Russian front, try to wrest the Puppetmaster's secrets from him.

David DeCoteau, replacing David Allen in the director's chair, makes this more than just a killing-by-numbers splatter picture. This time Guy Rolfe (looking remarkably fit for his 76 years) plays the title character, reprising his similar role in Band's *Dolls*. As before, the film has a short running time: 78 minutes.

Most shots featuring the puppets are again achieved with rod- and hand-operated mannequins. There are ten stop-motion cuts, plus three (featuring the little green demon) that have been lifted from the second film. All the cuts are done entirely in miniature except for one cut that uses a rear projection. There are no mattes. A new doll-character is added: Six-Shooter, a cowboy with six arms, a gun in each hand and a demented chuckle. It's the closest the film gets to giving the puppets any character. The gentle touches of humor which Allen gave to the character of Pinhead (with the huge arms and tiny head) in the first film, are missing again.

The various puppets assemble for an injection of Rolfe's life-giving drug. In the first stop-motion cut, Pinhead and the Tunneler clamber up onto a table and walk towards the camera, which, to give the shot some extra dynamism, tilts up as they advance.

Leading up to the puppets' killing of a morgue attendant, Pinhead and Jester are seen leaping off a window sill onto the floor. These two cuts are extremely smooth—so smooth, in fact, that they may not be stop-motion at all, although the choreography has the "look" of stop-motion. After the murder, the two puppets are stop-framed as they walk out through a door.

Six-Shooter features in the next three stop-motion cuts. In the first, the laughing puppet rotates six pistols on a finger of each hand, in classic cowboy fashion. The next cut is the best in the film, with Six-Shooter climbing up the outside of a building using all his arms (suggesting a spider). The camera is angled so that it seems we are looking down at the puppet, with German soldiers walking in the street below in the rear screen. In a corridor inside the building, Six-Shooter confronts his intended victim, standing with all six hands ready to draw, the fingers twitching with anticipation.

In the remaining three stop-motion cuts, Pinhead throws a brick at a German, Tunneler runs at a victim (his drill-head spinning) and Six-Shooter (in a half-hearted jokey final shot) gives another demented chuckle as he holsters all his guns. As ever, the stop-motion cuts add significantly to the overall impact of the puppet sequences. But this is another disappointing underuse of Allen's talents.

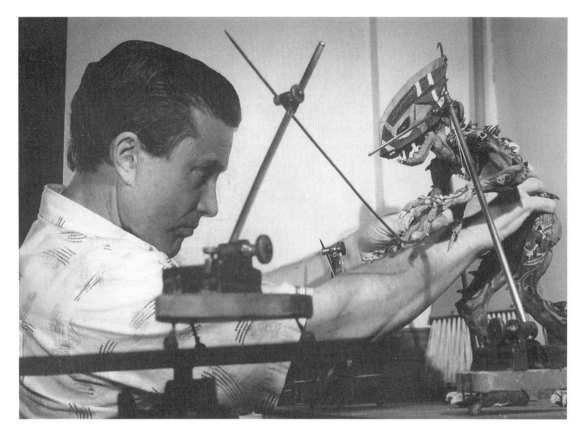

David Allen animates one of the evil Totem monsters for *Puppetmaster IV* (1994). (Photo by Chris Endicott.)

Puppetmaster IV

1994. Full Moon. D: Jeff Burr. Scr: Steven E. Carr, Jo Duffy, Todd Henschell, Keith Payson, Doug Aarniokoski. Original Story Idea: Charles Band. Ph: Adolfo Bartoli. Art: Milo. Mus: Richard Band. Special Makeup/Mechanical Effects: Alchemy FX. Puppet Effects Supervisors: David Allen, Chris Endicott. Stop-Motion Animation: David Allen, Randy Cook.

Cast: Gordon Currie, Chandra West, Ian Ogilvy, Nicholas Guest, Teresa Hill, Willard Pugh, Guy Rolfe.

Rating: ☆☆½   Stop-Motion: ☆☆½

After the video-rental success of the first three *Puppetmaster* films, producer Charles Band decided that the time was right to move back into theatrical releases. A full-length film was duly shot but, for various reasons, it was eventually decided that the movie would not get a cinema release after all. The film was re-edited into two separate movies and was released to video as *Puppetmaster IV* and *Puppetmaster V*.

In *Puppetmaster IV*, a group of four

tiny, evil aliens — called Totems — capture scientist Gordon Currie in the hope of preventing him from discovering the secret of life. The Totems are commanded by another new puppet character, Suteck, an ancient Egyptian warrior monster. But the puppets from the first three films come to the rescue, bring to life another new puppet, Decapitron, and battle the Totems.

The stop-motion sequences were supervised by David Allen and Chris Endicott with the animation itself executed by Allen and Randall Cook.

Puppetmaster V— The Final Chapter

1994. Full Moon. D: Jeff Burr. Scr: Steven E. Carr, Jo Duffy, Todd Henschell, Keith Payson, Doug Aarniokoski. Original Story Idea: Charles Band. Ph: Adolfo Bartoli. Art: Milo. Mus: Richard Band. Puppet Effects Supervisors: David Allen, Chris Endicott, Joseph Grossberg. Stop-Motion Animation: Joel Fletcher, Paul Jessel.

Cast: Gordon Currie, Chandra West, Jason Adams, Teresa Hill, Guy Rolfe, Ian Ogilvy.

Rating: ☆☆½   Stop-Motion: ☆☆½

In the fifth entry in Charles Band's *Puppetmaster* series, all the puppet characters from the previous films reappear. The evil Suteck wants to control the puppets created by the Puppetmaster (Guy Rolfe) and must do battle with Pinhead, Drillhead, Six-shooter, Decapitron and all the rest.

This time, visual effects supervisors were David Allen, Chris Endicott and Joseph Grossberg. Animation was handled by Joel Fletcher and Paul Jessel.

The Puppetoon Movie

1987. Leibovit Productions/Talking Rings Entertainment. Prod-Scr: Arnold Leibovit. Associate Prod: Fantasy II. New Animation Director and Ph: Gene Warren, Jr. Art: Gene Warren, Jr., Michael Minor. Mus: Buddy Baker. New Animation: Peter Kleinow. Arnie the Dinosaur Artistic Finishing: Charlie Chiodo, Steve Chiodo. Optical Duping: Harry Walton. Additional Graphics: Ernest D. Farino. Additional Puppet Characters Courtesy of David Allen Productions, Coast Special Effects, The Chiodo Brothers. Original Puppetoon Animators: John S. Abbott, Wah Ming Chang, Ray Harryhausen, Phil Kellison, Fred Madison, Willis O'Brien, Gene Warren and many others. Voice Director: Arnold Leibovit.

Voices: Dallas McKennon (Gumby), Paul Frees (Arnie the Dinosaur and Pilsbury Doughboy), Victor Jory (Tubby the Tuba), Art Clokey (Pokey), Dick Beals (Speedy Alka Seltzer).

Compilation film containing these Puppetoon shorts, made between 1937 and 1947: *Tubby the Tuba, John Henry and the Inky Poo, Tulips Shall Grow, Together in the Weather, Jasper in a Jam, Phillips Broadcast of 1938, The Sleeping Beauty, Phillips Cavalcade* and *Southsea Sweethearts*.

Rating: ☆☆½   Stop-Motion: ☆☆☆

The Puppetoon Movie is a compilation of nine of George Pal's Puppetoon shorts, fascinating to a historian of puppet animation, but a hopelessly uncommercial project. It's marvelous to see Pal's charming early work resurfacing but it's hard to imagine at what kind of audience this was aimed. These are short films and intended to be seen as such: an hour and a half of stylized animation is hard to take in one sitting. This is "puppets as puppets" filming—we are not asked to believe we are watching living creatures.

But it's great fun nonetheless. There are innumerable ingenious moments, the scope of Pal's imagination is always impressive and the humor of many sequences has remained undated (for example, the coy charm of *Together in the Weather* and the absurd antics of *South Sea Sweethearts*). Replacement animation allows Pal to create bizarre moving images which are denied the conventional stop-motion animator: puppets' limbs lengthen and shorten as they walk and arrows float out a bus window and transform into dancing girls. Addition-

ally there is much smooth animation in which the puppets have been moved frame by frame when it is easier to do so than build a series of models.

The powerful and moving *John Henry and the Inky Poo* was made by Pal in response to allegations of racism in his Jasper shorts. *Tulips Shall Grow* is a delightful allegory of the invasion of Holland featuring some very Flash Gordon–style planes and tanks: O'Brien and Harryhausen both worked on this one. Harryhausen also worked on another short included here, *The Sleeping Beauty*. Gene Warren, Sr. and Wah Chang are among the animators who worked on other Puppetoons featured here. Animator Harry Walton was responsible for re-framing the original shorts to conform to the film format ratio of 1 to 1.85.

For those who like their stop-motion more realistic, the eight-minute framing sequence created by Peter Kleinow and Gene Warren, Jr., is actually the most interesting part. After all, it does include a dinosaur in a very weird and inventive scene. Arnie the Dinosaur, looking remarkably like a reworking of Danforth's pot-bellied aging dinosaur in *Caveman*, can't bring himself to devour a deer, removes his false teeth (!) and says he blames it all on Pal: "I haven't been the same since I was a stand-in in one of George Pal's films."

He wanders around a film set (the camera making some subtle but imaginative pans as he does so), takes us, the deer and Gumby into a projection room (adorned with miniature posters of Pal's feature-length movies) and shows us a selection of Puppetoon films. The miniature sets (particularly the attractively lit forest) and the animation by Warren and

Kleinow are imaginative. In two of Arnie's opening shots, he shakes his head angrily from side to side and there is realistic blur on the image.

The models make a reappearance at the finale with a group of fantasy creatures (most conspicuously a Gremlin from Joe Dante's film), all paying their respects to Pal, to whom, they say, they owe it all. One of these is a recreation of Mighty Joe Young, although the puppet looks like a cross between Joe and King Kong: It may actually be David Allen's Kong model that he used in a Volkswagen television commercial.

Leibovit's film is a fine show of gratitude to a genuine artist who contributed enormously to film fantasy and inspired many others to do likewise. But there is one puzzle: Despite Arnie's claim, Pal never made a dinosaur picture, so just why is the character here?

Q (U.K. title: Q—The Winged Serpent)

1982. Larco. Prod-D-Scr: Larry Cohen. Ph: Fred Murphy. Mus: Robert O. Ragland. Special Visual Effects: David Allen, Randy Cook, Peter Kuran, Lost Arts. Additional Model-Makers: Roger Dicken, Dennis Gordon, Aiko, Deed Rossiter.

Cast: Michael Moriarty, Candy Clark, David Carradine, Richard Roundtree, James Dixon, Malachy McCourt, Bruce Carradine.

Rating: ☆☆☆   Stop-Motion: ☆☆½

It is a frequent complaint against stop-motion films that they almost invariably have weak plots and are little more than vehicles for their effects. Larry Cohen's *Q* goes to the other extreme: It is a successful character study of a small-time crook (Michael Moriarty) and his attempts to "be somebody," while the stop-motion element gives the impression of being a gimmick that was tacked on later.

Moriarty accidentally discovers the nest of a dragon in New York and uses this information to hold the police department for ransom — yet for plot purposes it could just as easily have been, say, a kidnapped businessman that he discovers. A third ingredient — Aztec cultists whose human sacrifices have summoned the dragon — is even less properly developed. Yet everything mixes together in a happy muddle, thanks to Cohen's tight script and enthusiastic direction. It recalls the B picture monster movies of the 1950s.

The reality behind the fine dragon shots of David Allen and Randall Cook is that they *were* tacked on later. Cohen, influenced by the success of *Alien* (1979), originally wanted to keep his monster more or less unseen, but Allen and Cook convinced him that this approach was not appropriate in this kind of monster-in-Manhattan movie — the audience would feel cheated. When he saw their dragon model and excellent animation effects, he was won over, and commissioned them to do more cuts than they first planned. But there was a problem — they were working with a very low budget and shaky background plates of New York that had been shot from a helicopter without any thought to future composite effects. Allen and Cook worked wonders in view of the situation — their 49 excellent stop-motion cuts may have been a salvage job, but this is still one of the memorable monster movies of the 1980s.

Quetzalcoatl, designed by Cook, is a pale-green, credibly scrawny-looking dragon with a vicious beaked head, long slender limbs and an interesting frayed look to its wings. Its wrinkled skin, beady eyes and fleshy red mouth are all convincing. Allen built the armature, using parts previously used in *The Howling, Caveman* and even a pair of wings originally machined by Marcel Delgado for a dimorphodon in the unfinished *Creation* (1930). A foot-long head-and-neck puppet used for closer shots made use of the old tyrannosaurus skull from *Caveman*.

Since most of the animation shots would show the puppet in flight, it was crucial to minimize the problems of strobing that normally afflict animated creatures making rapid movements (such as wing-flaps). Cook and Allen's solution was twofold: The dragon would flap its wings slowly almost as though gliding, and in many shots each frame of film would be rewound and re-exposed with the wings in a slightly different position, creating the illusion of a blur. Most of the full-view shots of the dragon in flight were achieved by having the model's far side attached by a rod to a glass screen mounted between

camera and rear projection. This avoided the need for a lot of time-consuming wire-supported animation or expensive blue-screen work.

At first, most of the animation cuts are very quick or the puppet is seen only in silhouette. In fact, the first shot of the dragon, in which it snatches a balloon out of the sky, is so quick and blurred that it may have been achieved by simply moving the static puppet across the shot. Three stop-motion cuts are used in the scene where a rooftop sunbather gets snatched up by the dragon. A closeup of the back of the dragon's head as it flies down to the roof is animated against a zoom-shot in the rear plate. A full-shot of it flying straight at the camera, claws outstretched, doesn't reveal much more of the monster's appearance — it's a very quick silhouette with a studio light behind the model standing in for the sun. This quick sequence ends with an extreme closeup of the dragon's mouth opening.

A similar quick closeup is used later when a construction worker gets attacked, accompanied by the sound of bone crunching. When Q flies off, an ingenious shot shows its shadow skimming over the buildings below. This cel animation by Peter Kuran exactly matches the shadow with the changing outlines of the buildings. Almost as good is a later Kuran shot in which the dragon's shadow passes over a bridge. In another very quick cut, the dragon flies right across the screen, and another construction worker is thrown up into the air — this is a dynamic shot with a lot of movement and blur on the puppet. Teasingly revealing a little more of the dragon's appearance, the next attack includes a closeup of the beady-eyed face.

More elaborate is the scene where a rooftop swimmer gets snatched out of his pool, making good use of a full-size claw. There is another full-view silhouette of the creature coming straight at the camera, then the best shot so far (this is 40 minutes into the film)—a brightly lit side-view of the dragon flying across a rear image of Manhattan buildings, squawking as it looks back over its shoulder.

The dragon is not seen again for another half-hour, although there are several point-of-view helicopter shots backed by the sound of heavy wings flapping. Most of this eminently watchable section concerns Moriarty's arrest and subsequent wheeling-and-dealing over the secret of the location of the nest.

The blood-streaked baby dragon (built by Steve Neill and operated as a hand puppet by Cook) that flops pathetically out of its shell after David Carradine pumps it full of bullets is totally convincing—but why did Carradine have to be as trigger-happy as his 1950s forebears? It would have been interesting to have some character animation of the dragon with its baby, but either the budget wouldn't stretch to it or else the filmmakers thought this would be too similar to 1981's *Dragonslayer*.

Another quick but effective stop-motion shot—with a fluid left-to-right pan—shows the dragon snatching a kite as it floats over Central Park. There are five longer animation cuts when Richard Roundtree becomes another rooftop victim. A full shot of Q flying past buildings in the rear screen keeps the model very near to the camera and slightly out of focus, thereby suggesting a blur. Once again we see the beast flying straight at the camera, but this is a more satisfying shot because the puppet is fully lit. It flies off with a tiny puppet of Roundtree in one of its claws but quickly drops him. The human puppet is probably wire-supported as it falls away from the dragon. Finally, there is an attractive shot of the dragon flying off, looking back over its shoulder, animated against a high-altitude shot of the city.

The finale is an impressive three-minute sequence that, on a smaller scale, deliberately recalls *King Kong*—except that here the roles are reversed: The flying creature tries to return to its nest at the top of the Chrysler Building, but concealed within are a dozen gunmen shooting out at it. Robert O. Ragland's score is inadequate and some rear-screen composites are deficient due to Cook and Allen not having been involved in the shooting of the background plates. But otherwise this sequence is an enjoyable minor classic, fast-paced and full of clever touches.

It begins with some establishing shots of the appropriately bird-like gargoyles of the Chrysler Building. An ambitious long shot (with the camera in motion) of the dragon appearing from behind the building was achieved by Kuran rotoscoping mattes over the moving outline of the tower. An effective aerial shot looks down very steeply at the building with the puppet seen from behind as it swoops down, neck and tail swishing energetically. Another shot of it flying toward the tower gives us a lingering look at its ribbed wings.

When Q flies closer to the tower, superimposed bursts of gunfire flash in

Quetzalcoatl, the impressively reptilian dragon designed by Randall Cook for *Q* (1982).

front of the model, enlivening the shot. In four quick cuts, the dragon, flying directly at the camera, swipes at a puppet gunman in a miniature window cleaner's basket and sends him flying. In a full shot of the puppet from behind, the wings rise and lower very smoothly, but from this angle the creature looks less anatomically plausible.

One superior moment has a policeman snatched from the very top of the tower and thrown to the ground. After a striking closeup pan across the larger puppet head, the dragon lands on the side of the tower. The open area inside

the tower is also matted around, allowing the dragon's head to be seen going right in and snatching a puppet human in its beak. The dragon twists its head to one side (with a lot of blur on the puppet human in its beak) and tosses its victim aside. The shot of the puppet human falling away from the camera, limbs flailing, is very good — the puppet was made to swing slightly on its wires during each exposure to create a blur.

Six more cuts show a marksman pulled from another basket. There is yet another shot of the dragon swooping at the camera (or is it the same bit of animation?), then it lands with a great thud on the side of the building. Two shots of the larger head grabbing the puppet human and tossing it aside use a partial miniature of the side of the building. This time a shot of the falling human puppet is less successful: The limb movements are *too* smooth and don't look like a person panicking.

A shot of the blood-streaked dragon flying away from the tower, screaming in pain, its wings, arms and legs all struggling desperately, is excellent. Three shots inside the tower were done with the actors in front of a blue screen. Carradine is congratulating everyone on having finished off the beast when suddenly its enormous blood-stained head appears through a hole in the wall behind him. It receives another hail of bullets and is seen through the hole in the tower flying away into the distance. Another rear-screen shot has the dragon flying straight at the camera, screaming again, its arms and legs in a panic of activity.

There are eight concluding stop-motion shots as Quetzalcoatl crashes into the pyramid-shaped roof of another building and then plummets to the ground. The pyramid part of the building is miniature, neatly matted in front of the top of the rear-projected tower. Squawking, the dragon crash-lands on the tower, wings held aloft as it struggles to maintain a hold.

A curious mistake: In closer shots, the beast's wing passes behind the outline of a skyscraper which should be way off in the background, but in the extreme long shot the wing correctly passes in front of it. It's a case of someone adding a matte where it wasn't needed. In one of these shots, Cook animated a bit of broken masonry falling across the matte line — a well-done "subliminal" effect that improves the shot. Eventually the creature falls backwards and there are two convincingly animated shots of it falling, wings held aloft (these look like they may have been shot blue-screen). There are no shots of it hitting the ground or even lying dead on the ground.

Allen and Cook never get the chance to show what they are really capable of, but they have nevertheless transformed a mediocre film into one that is a lot of fun and frequently impressive. Cohen doesn't invest the film with the level of excitement and sensitivity that he brought to his memorable 1974 baby-monster movie *It's Alive*, but comes close. Several splatter moments (a beheading, sacrificial victims having skin peeled off their faces) are more nasty than entertaining, but there are lively performances by Moriarty, Carradine and Roundtree. There are all too few monster-on-the-loose movies made these days so, although this one falls way short of its potential, it's still a film to treasure.

Q — The Winged Serpent see *Q*

Raiders of the Lost Ark

1981. Lucasfilm. D: Steven Spielberg. Scr: Lawrence Kasdan. Story: George Lucas, Philip Kaufman. Ph: Douglas Slocombe. Art: Norman Reynolds. Mus: John Williams. Special Visual Effects: ILM. Visual Effects Supervisor: Richard Edlund. Matte Painting Supervisor: Alan Maley. Matte Artist: Mike Pangrazio. Special Makeup Effects: Christopher Walas. Stop-Motion (uncredited): Tom St. Amand.

Cast: Harrison Ford, Karen Allen, Paul Freeman, Ronald Lacey, John Rhys-Davies, Denholm Elliott.

Rating: ☆☆☆   Stop-Motion: ☆☆½

George Lucas' thrill-a-minute adventure yarn, directed by Steven Spielberg, revitalized a whole genre in the same way that his *Star Wars* had revitalized science fiction in 1977. He took the format of the implausible, fast-paced serials of the 1930s and 1940s and gave them big-budget production values and impressive special effects. *Raiders* is primarily a showcase for some magnificent *physical* effects, such as Harrison Ford pursued by an enormous stone ball, or clinging to the undercarriage of a moving truck. But it also boasts a handful of unforgettable moments that required the *visual* effects skills of Industrial Light and Magic. One of these was a breathtaking two-second cut making use of stop-motion.

During a chase sequence, a Nazi staff car flies straight off the edge of a cliff and plummets hundreds of feet down. The sequence cuts from a shot of the live-action car going out of control to a superb matte painting by Alan Maley of the cliff dropping away. It was combined with live-action footage of other vehicles continuing on the precarious track and with three blue-screen elements (filmed separately) of a miniature car and puppets of two passengers who are thrown free, smoothly animated by Tom St. Amand. A camera tilt helps to convey the vertiginous feeling of the shot. In the cinema, the sheer scope of this shot always evokes gasps from audiences; on television, the impact is considerably weakened.

Other memorable effects shots (not featuring stop-motion) include a long-shot matte painting of a harbor area around a sea plane; a matte painting by Michael Pangrazio of an enormous warehouse filled with crates that seems to extend back infinitely into the background; and some horrifically graphic facial meltdowns (masterminded by Chris Walas) when the Nazi villains get their comeuppance.

The visual effects for *Raiders* were done under the supervision of Richard Edlund, who received an Oscar for his efforts.

Re-Animator 2 see *Bride of Re-Animator*

Return from Witch Mountain

1978. Walt Disney. D: John Hough. Scr: Malcolm Marmorstein. Based on Characters Created by Alexander Key. Ph: Frank Phillips. Art: John B. Mansbridge, Jack Senter. Mus: Lalo Schifrin. Special Effects: Eustace Lycett, Art Cruickshank, Danny Lee. Stop-Motion Animation: Joe Hale.

Cast: Bette Davis, Christopher Lee, Kim Richards, Ike Eisenmann, Jack Soo, Anthony James.

Rating: ☆☆   Stop-Motion: ☆☆

This sequel to *Escape to Witch Mountain* (1974) is, like so many of Disney's live-action features, a mediocre affair. Two children with alien powers (Kim Richards and Ike Eisenmann) are pursued by villains Bette Davis and Christopher Lee (neither is able to make anything of his/her role), who want to exploit their powers for their own selfish ends.

The shaky special effects include appearances by a flying saucer at the beginning and end of the film, floating over landscapes by means of some only-passable traveling matte composite photography. Most of the film's effects are physical, as objects levitate across the sets on invisible wires.

At the close, a beat-up old van is restored to a polished, undamaged state by the children's powers. This intriguing effect is accomplished in six stop-motion shots animated by Joe Hale, a Disney veteran who later received an Oscar nomination as part of the visual effects team that worked on Disney's *The Black Hole.* Crumpled metal straightens itself, smashed headlamp glass becomes whole, gashes in the bodywork heal up, the radiator grill untwists itself and dull paintwork takes on a gleam. Shot in miniature, all the cuts are filmed in closeup. The sequence suffers from the absence of any long-shot composites showing the actors looking at the van as it transforms itself.

The Return of Godzilla see *Gojira no gyakushu*

Return of the Jedi

1983. Lucasfilm. D: Richard Marquand. Scr: Lawrence Kasdan, George Lucas. Story: George Lucas. Ph: Alan Hume. Art: Norman Reynolds. Mus: John Williams. Visual Effects: Richard Edlund, Dennis Muren, Ken Ralston. Mechanical Effects Supervision: Kit West. Makeup and Creature Design: Phil Tippett, Stuart Freeborn. Key Sculptors: Dave Carson, Tony McVey, David Sosalla, Judy Elkins, Derek Howarth. Creature Technician: Randy Dutra. Creature Consultants: Jon Berg, Chris Walas. Special Effects Supervisor: Roy Arbogast. Optical Photography Supervisor: Bruce Nicholson. Art Director/Visual Effects: Joe Johnston. Stop-Motion Animator: Tom St. Amand. Matte Painting Supervisor: Michael Pangrazio. Matte Painting Artists: Chris Evans, Frank Ordaz.

Cast: Mark Hamill, Harrison Ford, Carrie Fisher, Billy Dee Williams, Anthony Daniels, Peter Mayhew, Ian McDiarmid, Frank Oz, James Earl Jones, David Prowse, Alec Guinness.

Rating: ☆☆☆½ Stop-Motion: ☆☆☆

The third installment of George Lucas' *Star Wars* saga was one of the most eagerly awaited films of all time. And inevitably it was a disappointment — albeit making a fortune at the box office. The weak plot offered little that wasn't a rerun of what had been seen before in the first two chapters, including the climactic destruction of another Death Star. The strong characterization and crisp dialogue of the first film were reduced to trite clichés, dragging out the theme of the Goodside versus the Darkside interminably. Harrison Ford's smugly impudent mannerisms had by now become more robotic than the droids, C3-PO and R2-D2.

Most importantly, in *Star Wars* Lucas conveyed an impression that he was gradually revealing to us, bit by bit, a whole new universe and a story of epic proportions, into whose complexities we find ourselves thrown randomly. But in *Jedi* everything is neatly mapped out, reduced to a conventional good-versus-evil plot. Disclosing that Darth Vader was Luke Skywalker's father in *The Empire Strikes Back* was a dramatically effective twist, but in *Jedi* Princess Leia turns out to be his sister, with the result that the whole story becomes fake and contrived; the epic sweep is completely gone. Of course, Lucas quite rightly knew he had to have a happy — and morally correct — ending because his enormously influential film would be seen by children throughout the world. But did he really have to go so far as to have almost his entire cast (including goodie-convert Darth Vader) all standing around smiling cheerfully like an escaped family from some Walt Disney live-action movie?

It doesn't matter how many times you see *Star Wars*: The sense of pace is always there, with every scene seeming to add something vital to the progression of the plot. *Jedi* tries to repeat the inventive cross-cutting technique, shifting between concurrent scenes, but much of it just seems like padding. Most of the scenes with Yoda, Obi Wan, Vader and the Emperor contribute nothing to the plot — except to slow it down.

Potentially interesting supporting characters like Lando Calrissian and Boba Fett, both of whom had been briefly introduced in *The Empire Strikes Back*, are shoved into two-dimensional background roles instead of fulfilling their earlier promise. Part of the problem lies with the fact that Lucas chose as director Richard Marquand, the man responsible for the abysmal horror film *The Legacy* (1978). Presumably no directors with vision were willing to take on a project in which they would have to take a back seat to the special effects.

And yet despite all these disappointments, *Return of the Jedi* is still one of the great fantasy films. Thanks to the creative input of George Lucas and the artists at Industrial Light and Magic, the film contains some unforgettable fantasy images and some of the most breathtaking action sequences ever put on celluloid. The film can only be enjoyed as a series of special effects set-pieces, and as such it is nearly 100 percent successful.

The supervising trio of Ken Ralston, Richard Edlund and Dennis Muren produced what may well be the finest display of "camera tricks" in the history of the cinema. Ralston was in charge of all the space sequences. Edlund handled a battle in a desert with levitating sailbarges, and the final attack on the Death Star. Muren handled Luke's encounter with the Rancor pit monster, a chase through a forest on hovering speeder bikes, and a battle between a horde of furry Ewoks and two-legged mechanical Scout Walkers. Eight million dollars — a quarter of the overall budget — was spent on the effects.

Stop-motion is used in many quick functional shots where it was necessary to have tiny figures make slight movements, to prevent them looking like miniatures. This is a continuation of an application seen before in ILM effects in *Raiders of the Lost Ark* and *E.T.— The Extraterrestrial*. A couple of moments make more elaborate use of stop-motion, but the process is really only taken full advantage of in the battle with the 20-foot-high Scout Walkers — dubbed chicken-walkers by the filmmakers because of their bird-like stride. Fans of *The Empire Strikes Back*, who had been hoping for a repeat appearance of the taun-tauns or something similar, were sorely disappointed to find that stop-motion was reserved for mechanical creations only.

In fact, all the flesh-and-blood creatures — the Rancor pit monster, the three-foot-high furry Ewoks, the slug-like Jabba the Hutt — are done live-action, either with actors in costumes or as rod-and-cable–controlled puppets. Lucas and his team felt that sophisticated contemporary audiences could no longer accept stop-motion as a realistic enough medium. They were strangely oblivious to the fact that audiences will accept anything that is intelligently staged, paced and edited; fluidity of puppet movement should not be the primary concern.

For example, the scene in which Luke battles the 20–foot-high Rancor monster suffers because there are no establishing long shots of the stand-alone monster facing off against Luke. Because the monster is rod-operated puppet, part of it is always kept off-camera to hide the means of locomotion. The puppet is a superbly wicked-looking monstrosity and its range of movement is impressive, but a sense that it is interacting with Luke is never properly conveyed. It was designed by Phil Tippett, who also manually operated it with help from Tom St. Amand and David Sosalla. The puppet was sculpted by Randal Dutra who, although he was not involved in any of *Jedi*'s stop-motion sequences, would in years to come make significant contributions to many puppet animation sequences.

The scene in the desert, when Luke is due to be fed to the Sarlacc monster in the pit, takes place on barges that levitate across the sand dunes. There are nine composite shots that feature miniature barges, blue-screened against a combination of actual desert and matte paintings. Full-scale barges, their means of support kept out-of-frame, also feature in several shots. The characters standing on the miniature barges are armatured puppets built by Dave Carson and David Sosalla. They were animated by Tom St. Amand and Ken Ralston so as to make slight swaying motions as the barges bank this way and that, thereby preventing them from looking like inflexible figurines.

In one shot of Jabba's sail-barge and a smaller skiff, a puppet soldier walks across the deck of the miniature barge, adding an important element of subliminally registered movement to the shot. Cel-animated shadows are skillfully added to the sand dunes as the vehicles fly over them. Every shot is a different perspective, with one of the skiffs flying across the screen, towards the camera or away and behind a live-action skiff. At the end of the sequence, Jabba's sail-barge explodes and there is an excellent composite (both technically and dra-matically) in which Luke and his friends escape on one of the skiffs, flying straight at the camera out of the flames. Again, the armatured puppets make subtle movements in this shot.

It's an exciting and offbeat sequence. It is only let down by the fact that ILM never quite overcomes the problem of blue-screening miniatures in front of a bright background — there is always a sensation that we are watching different pieces of film.

Luke travels to the Dagobah system and there is a beautiful shot of two stop-motion birds flying across a swampy live-action set. Their wings rise and fall extremely smoothly. The shot is similar to ones in *The Empire Strikes Back.*

The most exciting sequence is the chase through a forest on hovering speeder-bikes, with Luke and Leia pursued by a group of storm troopers. The sensation of speed and movement is brilliantly created by Muren and his team, making this a genuine edge-of-the-seat experience. If possible, see this on a cinema screen — not on a television set.

The characters race through the forest at terrifying speeds, avoiding trees and fallen trunks only at the last moment. Many shots are point-of-view shots; others are side views of the actors, or their miniature counterparts, blue-screened in front of the forest. In many of the shots, the camera is panning or tracking forward fast. The miniature bikes and puppets of the actors (built by St. Amand) on them were controlled by rods and strings and shot live at 48 frames per second. Stop-motion was not necessary because the puppets were mainly rigid: Arms and legs remain stationary and only the heads need to turn occasionally.

The tree houses of the Ewok village are depicted in a series of marvelous matte paintings, augmented by miniature rear projections of live-action Ewoks standing or dancing around fires. In one of these shots, an Ewok swings across on a vine; it may well be that it is a stop-motion puppet.

Elsewhere on the planet, Darth Vader's shuttle sets down on a landing deck in the forest, while a stop-motion AT-AT (probably one of the models used in *The Empire Strikes Back*) plods slowly alongside. It's a classic image, the camera tilting down as the graceful craft folds up its wings for landing, surrounded by an elegant painting of the forest. A second closer shot has the AT-AT walking directly towards the camera. Conventional stop-motion techniques, rather than go-motion, were used to animate it because of its slow movement, which allowed very small adjustments of the puppet for each frame.

After a vain attempt to shut down the force field that protects the Death Star, Han and Leia are led into the forest of the moon of Endor only to find themselves surrounded by storm-troopers and AT-STs — the two-legged Scout Walkers used by Vader's soldiers. One of these walkers was glimpsed briefly during the ice battle in *The Empire Strikes Back*. Here they take on a much more prominent role. Originally designed by Joe Johnston and Jon Berg, these fantastic mechanical walking tanks are just as unlikely as their four-legged counterparts — and just as eye-catching.

This long sequence, supervised by Muren, is brilliantly staged, containing many dramatic camera tilts and pans and many superb composites. This is one of the finest examples of composite photography ever seen in a stop-motion sequence and the high point of the robo-motion genre initiated by *The Empire Strikes Back*. The walkers really seem to be in among all the trees and the battling Ewoks. Glass trees and foliage are used in many cuts to enhance the illusion. Ingenious dappled lighting on the puppets carefully simulates the impression of sunlight piercing the trees. The puppets were animated by Tippett and St. Amand, with go-motion rods attached to the legs and rotating chassis. The pumping actions of the guns mounted on the walkers was achieved with conventional hands-on stop-motion. Altogether there are 29 animation cuts of the walkers. The puppets are separate blue-screen elements in almost all of them.

The first shot is a stunner, with the camera panning across a crowd of storm troopers. A full-scale live-action walker stands motionless on the left while an animated miniature one struts through some trees in the background. The matte around the outline of the trees is flawless. A second similar shot is equally eye-boggling, except that there is a trace of blue spill down the side of a tree trunk that the puppet walks behind.

There is a lot of frenetic activity in the third cut with storm troopers and Ewoks running in all directions and a walker strutting across the background. Careful roto-scoped mattes allow some of the soldiers' heads to pass in front of the walker's legs. In a dynamic shot of a walker moving away from the camera, two speeder-bikes whiz across the shot — each of these is a further blue-screen element.

Superimposed smoke wafts in front

of a walker as it clomps through some foliage, firing its cannons. The puppet's feet really seem to make contact with the foliage on the ground as it walks towards the camera, firing at Ewoks running straight at the camera. In a medium shot of a walker turning its chassis smoothly, a rock is thrown by an Ewok and bounces off its side; this is a separate blue-screen live-action element. Two close shots of a walker's legs show some Ewoks almost getting stomped on. A fabulous composite has the foot of a walker snared by a rope, dragging some Ewoks behind it. The point at which real rope becomes miniature is carefully obscured by a tree in the middle of the frame.

The Ewoks fire a catapult at a walker, seamlessly composited into the far distance. An extremely good medium shot, highlighting the animal character of these metallic creations, has a walker bombarded with (blue-screen) rocks, recoil, turn toward its attackers and fire its cannons, glare from the shots lighting up the model. It advances on them in another medium shot, firing its cannons as it goes.

After an impressive space sequence, we are back on the moon of Endor. A magnificent long shot has a walker strutting towards the camera from far off, firing its guns this way and that at fleeing Ewoks. A dramatic low-angle shot tilts up at an approaching walker as it fires on Ewoks in the foreground. Glass-painted foliage meshes the different elements. A walker struts behind a fallen tree as Chewbacca and some Ewoks walk in front of it, courtesy of some more flawless rotoscoped mattes. An Ewok swings on a vine over the top of a walker,

then there is a marvelous shot of two walkers together, one behind the other, lit up by their cannon fire. The nearer walker gets its top blasted off in a cloud of carefully superimposed smoke as the other walker continues to advance.

A shot of the lower half of a walker passing behind some ferns and a group of Ewoks is bafflingly well-done. The foreground elements (the ferns and Ewoks) look too complicated to have been rotoscoped mattes, yet they don't look like blue-screen elements either. After two more low-angle shots of a walker advancing, turning and firing its cannons, there is a long shot of it firing at fleeing characters, looking right at home among the burning foliage and smoke despite all the potential lighting problems. After a dynamic shot of an Ewok running straight at the camera, pursued by a walker, a live-action miniature walker is destroyed when it is crushed between two logs swung from the trees.

The best shot of the sequence is the moment when the Ewoks release a pile of logs from the top of an embankment, sending them rolling under the feet of a walker. The walker loses its footing, lurches one way and then the other, stepping awkwardly over them, then finally crashes to the ground. Tippett's animation is brilliant. The blue-screened walker is immaculately composited in among the logs and the impression of interaction between its feet and the live-action logs is perfect. Dust thrown up by the logs really seems to cloud around the puppet's feet. The live-action elements were filmed on a miniature set with a painted forest background. Tippett makes the puppet behave like a living creature, struggling to regain its footing. Seeing moments like this in 1983, it was tempting to say that the conventional static matte composites of traditional stop-motion photography had well and truly had their day.

A walker struts threateningly toward the camera, revealed at the last moment (in a live-action cut) to have Chewbacca at the controls. In the final animation shot, the walker commandeered by Han and Chewbacca walks into a long shot and turns to face the entrance to the bunker, as Han tries to convince the soldiers inside the bunker to open the doors.

There is no more stop-motion in the film, which climaxes with Richard Edlund's magnificent assault on the Death Star. It includes the breathtaking moment when the Millenium Falcon spaceship flies out from the central core of the Death Star, the flames from the explosion licking at it as it escapes in the nick of time. This is as accomplished a combination of blue-screen elements and motion-control miniatures as you are ever likely to see.

Quite deservedly, *Return of the Jedi* won the 1983 Academy Award for best visual effects.

Return to Oz

1985. Disney/Silver Screen Partners II. D: Walter Murch. Scr: Walter Murch, Gill Dennis. Based on the Books *The Land of Oz* and *Ozma of Oz* by L. Frank Baum. Ph: David Watkin. Art: Norman Reynolds. Mus: David Shire. Claymation: Will Vinton Productions. Illustrator/Storyboards: Mike Ploog. Creature Design: Lyle Conway. Model and Special Effects: Ian Wingrove. Visual Effects: Zoran Perisic.

Cast: Nicol Williamson, Jean Marsh, Piper Laurie, Matt Clark, Fairuza Balk, Emma Ridley.

Rating: ☆☆½   Stop-Motion: ☆☆½

No one ever expected *Return to Oz* to be a patch on the original, but it's a lot better than it might have been, passing 105 minutes quite agreeably. Fairuza Balk is likable as Dorothy but Nicol Williamson and Jean Marsh are not fleshed out enough to make scary villains. Walter Murch directs enthusiastically, but is let down by the bland photography and some dialogue which tries too hard to be glib. Fantasy characters this time include "the army of Oz" (a tin man), Jack Pumpkinhead and the Wheelers, the latter a bizarre group with wheels instead of hands and feet. These are all better than they sound on paper: Lyle Conway was creature design supervisor. There are many attractive, though not outstanding, matte paintings of landscapes, castles and cliffs.

The film's most innovative ingredient is the claymation animation of Will Vinton and his company, used in roughly 100 cuts to depict the stone

Gnome King (Williamson) and his rocky minions. Claymation differs from conventional stop-motion in that the models are malleable and so can alter their shape during animation. In *Return to Oz* this gives rise to some very fluid and bizarre images, even if the animation itself is not always smooth enough to convince.

Early on, there is a series of about ten cuts in which the Gnome King's minions spy on Dorothy, animated faces with shadowy stone eyes looking out from parts of boulders matted flawlessly into the live-action plate. When they return below to report to their king, animated closeups show their expressive rock faces shifting and reacting.

Split-screen work is generally very good — there are a number of shots of Dorothy and her troupe facing up to the Gnome King, who at this stage is just a giant, talking face in the rocks. When they are down in the caverns of his lair, he invites them to inspect his collection of ornaments, challenging them to pick out the one which is the transformed scarecrow. The entrance to the ornament chamber is a surreal concept that would have impressed M. C. Escher: A mass of claymation arms sprout out of the cave wall, crawling over each other in a snakelike manner as they dig away an opening, then dissolving back into the rock. This happens each time one of the characters passes through into the chamber and each time the cave wall closes up behind them.

Each character fails to select the right ornament, so the Gnome King slowly metamorphoses into something more and more human. He grows arms and a body and, in a deft moment recalling the figurehead in *Golden Voyage of Sinbad* detaching itself from the ship, separates himself from the rock face. At this stage, the animation puppet is replaced by Williamson in elaborate "rocky" makeup. One accomplished shot has the live-action Gnome King casually look over his shoulder to hold a conversation with an animated minion matted into the cave wall behind. Dorothy selects the correct ornament, causing the Gnome King to revert through all his stages of transformation. In one dramatic static matte, he is again a face in the cave wall, but manages to lift a giant stone hand to throw a magic spell at Jean Marsh, trapping her in a cage.

The climax is visually remarkable as the stop-motion Gnome King, one eye now turned to rock, transforms into a small mountain and calls on his gnome minions to come to his aid. His lair is being destroyed by earthquakes and the smoking air behind him (a rear projection) glows orange from the flames. In the lower foreground, Dorothy and her friends stand in the ruins looking up at the rock giant from their side of a matte. The Gnome King picks up a miniature of Gump, the living sofa(!), and drops it into his mouth, laughing wickedly.

In order to destroy the rest of Dorothy's troupe, he summons his minions, seen in about a dozen composite cuts emerging out of walls and floors and transforming into evil-looking gargoyles with fangs, claws and horns. One impressive tracking shot follows a wall as rock faces emerge from it, dissolve back into it, then reappear further along. Dorothy and the others run through all this chaos as the minions appear on all sides of them. Some of these shots are static mattes, others (where the actors need to be in front of the puppets) are traveling mattes. It's a dynamic piece of action even though there is minimal interaction between actors and models.

The Gnome King picks up a miniature of Jack Pumpkinhead and, in a memorably gruesome series of cuts, dangles him upside down over his huge mouth (which expands obscenely to receive the morsel). One shot looks down the gray rocky throat, at the far end of which is the red glow of the King's stomach-furnace. But Dorothy's pet chicken (a talking animatronic creature) has been hiding in Jack's empty pumpkin-head and chooses this moment to lay an egg which drops into the Gnome King's mouth. After a closeup of the giant's animated eye blinking, an expression of immense sadness crosses his face: "Don't you know that eggs are poison to gnomes?"

His face contorts, shifts and starts to harden. Jack is put down safely. The moaning minions writhe and dissolve back into the walls and ground (again many of these are rear-projection shots). The Gnome King, surrounded by flames (some rear-projected, some superimposed) continues to change. His remaining eye turns to rock, his face loses all its features, then he begins to crack and fall apart. Finally he is no more than a cluster of (wire-supported) rocks that tumble to the ground.

Will Vinton also made *Comet Quest* (also known as *The Adventures of Mark Twain by Huck Finn*), a children's feature filmed entirely in claymation with no live action. It is less interesting because we are never asked to believe that the characters are anything more than puppets.

RFD 10,000 B.C.: A Mannikin Comedy (a.k.a. *Rural Delivery, Ten Thousand B.C.*)

1917. Edison Conquest. D-Scr-Ph-Stop-Motion: Willis H. O'Brien.

Rating: ☆☆½   Stop-Motion: ☆☆½

This short film, O'Brien's fourth (and at just over ten minutes the longest of the series), features Henry Saurus, his mate Dinah and a rival suitor, Johnny Bearskin.

The brontosaurus model from previous O'Brien shorts reappears, this time pulling a postman's cart. A caption tells us that Bearskin is writing "a tender missive" to his love: The film cuts to a shot of him chiseling away at a piece of rock. The jealous postman switches it for another slab of rock, calling Dinah an "ugly old maid." Naturally she biffs Bearskin over the head for this insult, but he gets his revenge when he assaults the postman, who has been struggling under the weight of this morning's delivery: a dozen pieces of rock. O'Brien now introduces a surreal bit of humor when he has the postman cut in half and his top half hurled through the air, crashlanding in a tree. A caption tells us "Part II will follow shortly" and, sure enough, his legs come running along afterwards.

Consistently inventive, *RFD 10,000 B.C.* nevertheless doesn't quite have the charm of *The Dinosaur and the Missing Link.*

RoboCop

1988. Orion. D: Paul Verhoeven. Scr: Edward Neumeier, Michael Miner. Ph: Jost Vacano. Mus: Basil Poledouris. Art: William Sandell. RoboCop Design and Special Makeup Effects: Rob Bottin. Matte Artist: Rocco Gioffre. Special Photographic Effects: Peter Kuran, VCE. ED-209 Sequences: Phil Tippett. ED-209 Crew: ED-209 Designed and Created by Craig Davies, Peter Ronzani. Visual Effects: Harry Walton. Stop-Motion Animation: Randy Dutra. Armature Design: Tom St. Amand. ED-209 Effects Crew: Sheila Duignan, Tamia Marg, Blair Clark. 6000 SUX Commercial: The Chiodo Bros.

Cast: Peter Weller, Nancy Allen, Dan O'Herlihy, Ronny Cox, Kurtwood Smith, Miguel Ferrer.

Rating: ☆☆☆   Stop-Motion: ☆☆☆

An entertaining slice of hi-tech designer ultra-violence, *RoboCop* was the inevitable next step in the 1980s subgenre that began with *Blade Runner* and *The Terminator*. It's not as exciting as James Cameron's film because director Paul Verhoeven doesn't have the same masterly control of pacing, but was still the liveliest, most original fantasy film released for quite a while.

Unfortunately, its plot is mired in too many conventional devices, such as having the cyborg return to his home and brood over his lost human life, a gang of thugs, a shootout in a cocaine factory, a gratuitous scene in which a new weapon destroys cars and buildings, *ad nauseam*. It is never quite bold enough to tread in the totally new territory that the central subject matter deserves.

The film is constantly interrupted by television news broadcasts and commercials, a deft gimmick that enhances the atmosphere of hi-tech and adds touches of black humor. We are told that South Africa is about to detonate a nuclear weapon, and we are asked to buy a board-game called "Nuke 'Em!," demonstrated by a typical clean-cut family that delights in exploding a thermonuclear device on the living room table.

Another television commercial (for a car) features a comical stop-motion dinosaur with eyes that nearly pop out of its head cartoon-style. This smoothly animated figure is the work of the Chiodo brothers, who had earlier done special makeup effects in films like *The Sword and the Sorceror* (1982) and brief dinosaur animation in *Pee-wee's Big Adventure*

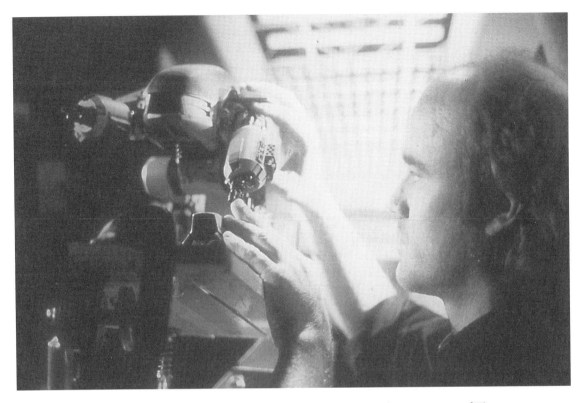

Phil Tippett animates the ED-209 puppet for *RoboCop* (1987). (Photo courtesy of Tippett Studio.)

(1985). There are seven animation cuts and the Chiodos have affectionately taken *The Beast from 20,000 Fathoms* as their inspiration. Two set-ups borrow their design directly from Harryhausen's film. One is a low-angle tracking shot of the orange-hued dinosaur walking straight at the camera. The other is a static matte rear-screen shot where the creature walks into a street from between two buildings.

A shot of villain Ronny Cox falling from the window of a high-rise building used a puppet realistically animated against a blue screen by Rocco Gioffre. It was not practical to use a stunt man for this shot because of the great distance from the camera which the character had to fall.

RoboCop himself, a one-time Detroit policeman who has been badly shot up and then rebuilt as part man and part machine, was designed by special makeup maestro Rob Bottin. His effects include the sight of RoboCop's fleshily convincing half-face when the metallic covering has been removed from the back of his head, revealing a maze of computer circuitry. He also created an entirely gratuitous and enjoyably sick toxic-waste makeup in a which a character's skin melts from his body and he is eventually splattered by a car, a revoltingly squishy effect in which the body visibly separates.

For many, however, the star of the film was neither RoboCop nor Bottin's

The Chiodo brothers, who supplied a stop-motion "television commercial" sequence for *RoboCop.* Left to right: Edward, Stephen and Charles.

effects, but a mechanical law enforcer called ED-209 seen in scenes supervised by Phil Tippett. This bulky, bipedal robot is another variation on the "mechanical animals" that Tippett animated in *The Empire Strikes Back* and *Return of the Jedi.* This time Tippett added character to the metal, making ED-209 a terrifying villain yet at the same time possessing many endearing quirks.

ED-209's stop-motion shots — about 50 cuts — were designed by Tippett with most of the hands-on animation being done by Randy Dutra, who previously worked with Tippett on several projects, including *The Golden Child* and the marvelous television production *Dinosaur!* Two 12–inch-high puppets of

ED-209 were built, allowing simultaneous filming of two set-ups. Armatures were designed by Tom St. Amand and built by Blair Clark. Stop-motion camerawork was handled by Harry Walton.

There are three scenes, all excellent examples of the kind of bizarre visual thrills which stop-motion is so well suited to create, and all featuring the customarily flawless composite work which has come to characterize Tippett's effects. A variety of perspectives and a lot of camera movement keep the editing fast and furious. Tippett used Vista Vision live-action plates and as a result the rear-screen images always look sharp and are not plagued by the graininess which mars many such sequences in other films. One wonders how many in the audience are fooled into believing they are watching an actual mechanical creation, not a stop-motion puppet.

ED-209's first scene contains 21 animation cuts. The robot is unveiled at a board room meeting only to malfunction and shoot one of the executives to pieces. The puppet is perfectly matched to a full-size prop as it struts around the room, but in one or two of the cuts the animation could have been smoother.

ED-209 exudes presence — all hydraulic whirrs and hisses — and when it walks, there is an impression of great weight. The horrific aspects of the scene are deftly balanced by comic touches (e.g., the victim being pushed aside by his self-preserving colleagues or the cartoonish sound effects when ED-209 finally seizes up), making this a rare example of stop-motion being used for black humor.

Go-motion blurs enhance the shots of the ED-209 striding into the board room, swaying from side to side. A closeup of its bulky three-toed feet shows they are at once animalistic and intricately mechanical. A shot of it from behind, stopping in front of all the seated executives, includes the effective minor detail of having screws on the backs of its "knees" tighten when it comes to a halt.

A "volunteer" is chosen to point a gun at ED-209, causing the robot to rise up threateningly, casings on the machine-gun arms sliding into position. Even after the volunteer obeys ED-209's command and drops his weapon, the robot takes a menacing step forward and lets out a lion-like roar: "You now have 15 seconds to comply."

There are two overhead rear-screen shots looking over ED-209's shoulder at the panicking executives. Blurs are present when it swivels left and right, keeping the victim in its line of fire. A bolder composite (the only static matte so far) is a full-view shot of ED-209, its feet believably planted on the floor as it blasts its victim in a hail of bullets. Bright flashes are superimposed over the pumping machine guns. Quick closeups of the guns firing look like they were done live-action.

Finally ED-209 shuts down, retracting back down to a non-threatening pose, accompanied by the semi-comic sounds of whirring mechanics gone wrong.

The second stop-motion sequence is the major one, a battle between RoboCop and ED-209. It contains 29 animation cuts. It begins in an office with a dramatic static matte composite of ED-209 walking into the room, at first in shadow but then, when the lights are turned on, in full view. Some excitingly staged tracking shots follow ED-209 as it strides over to RoboCop.

Two shots make use of a miniature floor strewn with broken glass, allowing more intimate contact between ED-209 and the set. In two quick shots, a puppet of RoboCop is used, one in which ED-209 delivers a crashing swipe and knocks him up into the air with a blow from one of its arms, and the other when RoboCop grabs ED-209's right machine-gun arm, twisting it around so that it blasts off its left arm. As if in shock, ED-209 jitters for a second — a clever little bit of subliminal characterization. Shots of ED-209 firing missiles at RoboCop use the stationary full-size prop.

After a shoot-out with *RoboCop* (Pete Weller), all that is left of law-enforcement agent ED-209 are its legs and smoking torso. ED-209 was designed by Craig Davies and animated by Phil Tippett.

A very dynamic tracking shot has ED-209 growling and striding purposefully after its fleeing foe. RoboCop ducks down a staircase and there is a static matte composite looking up the steps at ED-209 standing in the doorway at the top, RoboCop in the lower foreground. ED hesitates at the stairs, now a miniature replica of the actual stairs.

Dutra, in a letter to the author, said of this episode: "I worked out and animated the sequence with ED-209 trying to negotiate/consider the stairs before proceeding. And, of course, he falls, This fall was done live-action and overcranked, with a lead-weighted ED pup-

pet. I believe that this sequence was one that allowed the animator some real fun, pure character acting with a robot/creature that had no face as we know it. It all had to be communicated with carefully-timed pantomime."

It may be hard to believe that a sophisticated piece of equipment like this would be foiled by encountering something as commonplace as a flight of stairs but, regardless, there is a wonderful bit of characterization as it tries out the steps, toes retracting nervously like someone testing water in a swimming pool. In a stop-motion closeup, ED-209 looks down at this new challenge, before tumbling in the live-action shot described above.

The closing shots of this sequence (impressively animated by Harry Walton) are superb, with ED-209 lying on its back and screaming like a child, struggling to get up, its arms and legs going ten to the dozen. This is seen both from RoboCop's point of view in a static matte shot, and also from behind ED-209, looking down at RoboCop in the rear screen.

The robot's final appearance is near the end of the film when it guards the entrance to the Omnicorp building — the company that has built the robots. RoboCop, now grotesquely without mask, drives up to the entrance and the live-action ED-209 swivels in his direction: "You are illegally parked on private property." It struts over to the car, one ingenious composite matting along the line of the hood, allowing RoboCop in the foreground to fire his gun at ED-209.

The final composite not only looks great but also is another fine comic moment. RoboCop walks away nonchalantly as ED-209 steps menacingly into the shot, only to reveal that its top half has been blown completely away. Superimposed smoke is carefully aligned so that it seems to be pouring out of the puppet. In this shot, RoboCop is a stop-frame puppet, so realistically animated that it looks like a live-action element. ED-209 topples over (a credible bit of animation) and the toe on its left foot makes an endearing death twitch.

ED-209 is one of the best stop-motion adversaries of the 1980s, a clever demonstration of how to imbue even the most unlikely of puppets with touches of character and humor.

RoboCop 2

1990. Tobor. D: Irvin Kershner. Scr: Frank Miller, Walon Green. Story: Frank Miller. Ph: Mark Irwin. Art: Peter Jamison. Mus: Leonard Rosenman. RoboCop 2 Animation Sequences: Phil Tippett. RoboCop Designed and Created by Rob Bottin. Special Photographic Effects: Peter Kuran. Matte Paintings: Rocco Gioffre. Robot Monster Crew: FX Art Director: Craig Davies. FX Production Supervisor: Julie Roman Tippett. Visual Effects: Harry Walton, Rick Fichter-Kikugawa, Peter Kozachik. Stop-Motion Animators: Tom St. Amand, Eric Leighton, Randy Dutra, Pete Kleinow, Justin Kohn, Don Waller. FX Camera: Jim Aupperle, Paul W. Gentry. Model Makers: Jon Berg and others. Armature Machinists: Blair Clark, Chris Rand. RoboCop Stunt Suits: Chris Walas, Inc.

Cast: Peter Weller, Nancy Allen, Dan O'Herlihy, Belinda Bauer, Tom Noonan, Gabriel Damon.

Rating: ☆☆☆   Stop-Motion: ☆☆☆

Irvin Kershner, whose direction of *The Empire Strikes Back* was so memorably unremarkable, redeemed himself by making *RoboCop 2* actually better than the original. It is not without faults: The marketing men insisted on a major rewrite of Frank Miller's original script, so as to repeat many of the first film's ideas—drug trafficking, too much gunfire, cars exploding at the drop of a hat, three scenes where RoboCop prototypes malfunction and a disused industrial plant as the backdrop to a major shootout.

But the script is still full of good ideas and characters. Chief villain Cain (Tom Noonan) has Christ-like aspirations of drug-pedaling to the masses and enjoys forcing his teenage sidekick to watch a grisly scalpel killing. A female employee (Belinda Bauer) of OCP (the private corporation that runs the police force) has an obsession with creating RoboCop 2 with the brain of a murderer. And a likable, upright Detroit mayor (William Pugh) is desperate to prevent his city from being bought outright by OCP. Less interesting is the teenage villain who pedals the drug "nuke"—a novel idea, no doubt insuring a big under–15 audience, but unsatisfactory plot-wise.

Kershner's direction is always sure, generating suspense, excitement and/or humor in all the right amounts. He paints a skillfully depressing picture of a lawless Detroit, especially in the blackly humorous opening sequence in which a hit-and-run victim gets mugged then the mugger in turn gets mugged by two prostitutes.

RoboCop's first appearances are extremely well-done, breaking up a gang that has raided a gun shop, busting a nuke factory and dispatching a villain (holding a baby hostage) with an ingeniously ricocheted bullet. The editing is always fast and lively. Equally impressive are scenes where RoboCop is captured and dismembered, and where he has been turned into a "nice" robot,

proving totally ineffectual even when dealing with shoplifting kids. This latter sequence could have been ridiculous but Kershner maintains control.

Much fun again are the news bulletins and television commercials that remind us what a sick society this is. A nuclear reactor has leaked and destroyed the Amazon rain forests; a security company advertises a device that "deters" car thieves by pinning them to the seat and frying them with electricity; and an insurance company promotes itself with an ad in which someone down on his luck shoots himself.

Rob Bottin's creation looks even better than in the original, and this time includes a magnificent animatronic head and torso that wriggles on the ground and later is propped up in a lab, its eyes rolling in pain. Leonard Rosenman's score is adequate but it's a shame the film wasn't able to use the forceful themes of Basil Poledouris' score from the first film.

The star of the show is Phil Tippett who has taken the robo-motion genre one step further with his outstanding RoboCop 2 creation, featuring in more than 140 stop-motion cuts. Above all, he has demonstrated for the benefit of disbelievers the dynamic, dramatic potential of stop-motion. The fast editing, the constant varying of perspectives, the hyper-realism of the composites and the inventiveness of the animation choreography all make these sequences to treasure. Had RoboCop 2 been depicted by means of full-scale animatronic mechanisms, the character would not have had half the presence or versatility.

The only disappointment is that the five animation characters in *RoboCop 2* are all mechanical creations. There is no animation of flesh-and-blood characters (apart from a brief use of a puppet human), thereby confirming in some people's minds that stop-motion is only realistic when depicting robots and their ilk. What the stop-motion medium needs is a major, commercially successful film which features a flesh-and-blood creation depicted with the same dramatic intelligence as RoboCop 2.

Tippett assembled a sizable crew to handle the animation effects, including Pete Kleinow, Jim Aupperle, Tom St. Amand, Harry Walton, Randy Dutra and others. Eight effects units worked simultaneously in 16–hour stints over a period of four months to meet the tight deadline. Ten different models of RoboCop 2 were built as well as four of RoboCop 1, to be used in intimate combat shots. Thirty-five percent of Tippett's shots utilized go-motion, the rest being achieved with conventional stop-motion. Most of the composite set-ups employed rear projection.

The first stop-motion shot is a newsreel item recounting the malfunctioning of an ED-209 Combat Unit, a humorous throwaway gag and (sadly) the only appearance of this wonderful creation from the first film. The smoothly animated model (one of two that was used in the original) is seen in one cut floundering helplessly in a street, one foot trapped in a manhole. It tries to get up but fails pathetically. The miniature foreground blends in perfectly with the street in the rear screen and some miniature plastic traffic cones surround the puppet.

Later, OCP executives are shown a film of the company's two latest experi-ments in a "unique combination of software and organic systems." Both of these robots were designed by Craig Davies, who also designed RoboCop 2. The armatures for the two prototypes were designed by St. Amand and machined by Blair Clark. Again, these are amusing throwaway gags rather than extended dramatic sequences and less impressive than later scenes with RoboCop 2. The composites are designed as static head-on perspectives — the sort that a director would normally avoid, but appropriate here since this is meant to a be a company's demo film.

The central area of the floor and the sliding doors through which each robot walks are all matted into the front-projected live-action area, with OCP technicians standing on either side of the frame. The six cuts of the puppets and sliding doors were animated by Don Waller. There is a registration slip-up in the first shot — the lab doors slide open and the background image behind the doors (in which another technician is working) jumps slightly.

Robot number one, a sleek-looking cyborg topped by a bulky steel visor, walks through the doors, malfunctions and shoots the technicians on either side of it. In medium shot, its visor is raised, revealing a human face inside — actually an image projected onto a tiny screen inside the puppet. Superimposed gun flares are added as the puppet fires. Finally it shoots itself and goes limp, its head and arms hanging down lifelessly.

Robot number two, a slender-waisted female, is seen in only two cuts (one long shot and one medium shot). She steps out into the same set-up, then removes her helmet to reveal a screaming skull beneath and falls to the floor (out of frame) with a clank. The "Old Man"—OCP's boss—is not impressed.

Eventually OCP gets it right—by putting the brain of a murderer rather than a policeman into their next creation. RoboCop 2's first scene is an exciting five-minute episode containing 29 animation cuts. (There are 29 in the British video release but at least one shot has been censored.) In this scene, the puppet is deliberately kept in shadow most of the time, reserving a clearer view of it for the climax.

It's an impressive creation, seven feet tall, full of deadly gadgets and exuding a sense of menace. Working from Davies' design, St. Amand fashioned an armature consisting of over 700 parts. A mean-looking visored helmet tops a slender robotic figure with four powerful arms and strutting piston-like legs.

In its first scene, RoboCop 2 is sent to a disused factory to disrupt a deal between the mayor and the drug dealers. The sequence is full of rapid-fire animation cuts all fluidly combined with the live-action set—there are no matte lines, floor inlays or color mismatches here. To give the scene a realistic look, several shots were animated in a smoke-filled four-foot-by-four-foot room, an airtight chamber with the animators placing their hands in extended rubber gloves. Tiny halogen lamps were mounted on the puppet, allowing it to send shafts of light through the gloomy haze.

The scene kicks off with an ominously restrained shot of RoboCop 2's shadow falling on the steel shutter of the factory where the mayor and the drug dealers are gathered. At the edge of the frame, the robot's deadly metallic hand clenches into a fist. In two dramatic long shots, seen from within, RoboCop 2 lifts the shutter, then drops it behind it. The puppet is seen only briefly and in silhouette. The camera tilts up the full height of the shadowy robot, which sways slightly in anticipation of a confrontation. One of its arms is a rotating machine gun and (in a closeup shot) this arm is raised, fires and knocks out all the lights in the factory.

In medium shot, the puppet's four lamps come on and then it stomps across the frame. Its lumbering walk is accompanied by clanking sound effects which convey an impression of bulk. In medium shot, it turns and fires; then, in a striking long shot seen from behind and in shadow, aims a spotlight first at one victim and then another, shooting them both. The puppet probably obscures the actual spotlight which hangs down in the rear projection.

Two low-angle medium shots are enhanced by a miniature pulley hanging down in the foreground which helps to mesh puppet and rear projection. In a tracking shot, RoboCop 2 advances across the frame, pushing over a miniature steel fence and scrunching up a steel pipe in one of its claws. It strides over to a cowering girl—Cain's girlfriend before his brain was put into the robot. Its visor slides open and a monitor pivots out, powers up and displays a computer generated image of Cain's face.

Another arm unfurls and the steel claw is offered to the girl for her to caress. Then in five quick animated cuts, RoboCop 2 kills the girl. The monitor retracts, a three-pronged claw opens and reaches out (straight at the camera). In long shot, RoboCop 2 picks up a limp puppet of the girl by her head, accompanied by the noisy sound of her skull being crushed. The animation of her limp figure is very convincing. Seen through the robot's legs, the corpse is discarded in a crumpled heap and the killer strides off with an angry growl.

In a dynamic and chilling tracking shot, RoboCop 2 stomps purposefully and noisily across the factory (in medium shot), foreground props passing by in a blur. In two shots using traveling matte, a man in the lower foreground fires at the robot who swivels around, shoots him, then swivels back around again to aim a spotlight at another victim. Accurately coordinated lighting effects make these set-ups visually striking.

In a chilling static matte, Robocop 2 appears from behind some crates just as the mayor escapes down a refuse chute in the nick of time.

RoboCop 2's second and last scene is an elaborate 15–minute showdown with RoboCop 1, containing a staggering 104 stop-motion cuts. It begins in a lecture theater, spills out into the corridor, up an elevator shaft, onto the roof, crashes down beneath the street below and ends in the plaza outside the Civic Centrum. The pace is furious and it's a technically astonishing sequence.

The Old Man unveils RoboCop 2 at a press lunch. The robot emerges from beneath the floor, rising up in the middle of a model of OCP's vision of a new Detroit. In medium shot, the puppet adopts the classic arms-back pose of all stop-motion "humanoids." The Old Man, boasting that his company will rid the city of the menace of drugs, holds up a canister of "nuke," not realizing that the man whose brain has been placed into RoboCop 2 is an addict. The robot leans forward when it catches sight of the canister, its claws clenching and unclenching in anticipation. In long shot, it raises one of its arms and smashes a model tower block. In a dramatic medium shot, it stomps straight at the camera, the whirring and clanking sound effects enhancing the impression of its juggernaut-like massiveness. A fine long shot has the Old Man standing on the left with RoboCop 2 standing on the right, snatching at the canister. A miniature rope in the foreground, cordoning off the display platform, helps to mesh the two elements.

RoboCop 1 arrives on the scene and there is a very impressive extreme long shot looking over RoboCop 1's shoulder at RoboCop 2 far off on the platform. At the sound of RoboCop 1's voice, RoboCop 2 raises its shoulders, tenses and looks around. Presumably a rear-screen static matte, this is so seamless that it simply does not look like a composite shot.

RoboCop 2 raises his machine-gun arm and rotates it at high speed, preparing to fire, only to overhear the OCP technician say that its firepower capacity has been deactivated. RoboCop 2 turns and grabs the remote control unit from the technician, a shot involving an invisible switch from real to miniature unit. Using a pincer-like hand, RoboCop 2 activates itself by adjusting the controls, then smashes the unit. Extras scurry away in the background plate as the robot unleashes a round of machine-gun fire, a medium shot in which the magazine containing the bullets is animated as it snakes into the gun.

In an excellent series of eight shots, the two robots exchange gunfire. RoboCop 2 recoils from gun-shot, superimposed blasts of flame and smoke erupting off its steel chest. Striking a dramatic pose, RoboCop 2 turns suddenly and fires back at RoboCop 1, one arm held out behind it for balance like a swordsman. Out of RoboCop 2's shoulder a small firearm emerges, takes aim and launches a missile at RoboCop 1 in the rear projection, at the back of the lecture theater. Outraged by the conduct of his creations, the Old Man calls out, "Behave yourselves!", as though talking to two children.

The two cyborgs continue blasting at each other until RoboCop 1 gets a computer-aim on RoboCop 2's shoulder-weapon and destroys it in another shower of superimposed flame and sparks. In a series of three very forceful cuts, RoboCop 2 strides up the steps to his opponent. The first cut is from behind RoboCop 2, the edge of a row of seats forming a matte line. The second is a long tracking shot looking through RoboCop 2's legs. The third is from RoboCop 1's point of view as RoboCop 2 approaches him, superimposed sparks from ricocheting bullets lighting up the latter.

RoboCop 2 turns and one of his arms extends by about two meters, a metal club on the end of it smacking into RoboCop 1. In a live-action cut, RoboCop 1 crashes backwards through a wall.

In an impressive long shot, RoboCop 2 comes around the corner of a corridor (a miniature set) and walks towards the camera, gun firing. RoboCop 1 steps into an elevator while, in medium shot, the killer cyborg gets nearer. The next few cuts, taking place in the elevator shaft, are real thrill-a-minute excitement, brilliantly designed and animated.

Eric Leighton animated a creepy overhead shot showing RoboCop 2 entering the elevator behind RoboCop 1, somehow suggesting a huge spider about to descend on a helpless fly. A puppet of RoboCop 1 is used for the first time in this cut. RoboCop 1 shoots his gun through the elevator cable but grabs onto another cable, with the effect that he goes hurtling upwards.

The ensuing action (mostly animated by Leighton) occurs in five very quick cuts. RoboCop 2 looks up at the rapidly receding RoboCop 1, then looks down and, in a moment of gentle humor, realizes that it is plummeting downwards. The walls of the elevator hurtle past in a blur. The cyborg tries to grab the sides of the shaft, sparks flying off its hand. In long shot, it manages to bring itself to a halt, braced against the walls. For these shots, a 20–foot horizontal miniature elevator shaft was built, with trap doors every two feet to allow the animators access. A slit running along the set allowed a go-motion rod to be attached to the puppet.

A nightmarish shot looking down the shaft from RoboCop 1's point of view shows RoboCop 2 climbing up the shaft at high speed, using all its limbs and again suggesting a metallic spider. This one shot took Leighton 15 or 16 hours to film. RoboCop 2's momentum sends both robots crashing through a skylight at the top, the flailing arms of both puppets animated fluidly as they are wire-supported against a rear-projected night sky. In a dizzying long shot of the Detroit skyline (part miniature and part painting by Rocco Gioffre), RoboCop 2 manages to grab the edge of a building, with RoboCop 1 still clinging onto him. This shot is an ambitious but successful bit of animation, with the RoboCop 1 puppet swinging in an arc below the other robot.

A series of shots looks down from the roof at the two puppets dangling off the edge. "You're coming with me," drones RoboCop 1, trying to pull his assailant over with him. RoboCop 2 throws his arms out as he eventually falls backwards. The limbs of both puppets wave about realistically as they drop away from the camera down towards the street far below. Another shot looks up from ground level at the two rapidly approaching robots. The animation of puppets in free fall has always been difficult to get right: Tippett and his crew pull it off with near-perfection — although Tippett himself was disappointed with the shot.

The robots crash through the street into a basement and at first it seems that both have been destroyed by the impact. But RoboCop 1 crawls out of the debris and starts to walk away. The stop-motion hand of RoboCop 2 then emerges from the wreckage and grabs RoboCop 1's leg, a composite achieved by careful alignment of puppet and rear-projected image. RoboCop 2 gets up and in a stunning long shot towers over the RoboCop 1 puppet, which it knocks down with a swipe of one of its fists. In two startling medium shots, it picks up the RoboCop 1 puppet and walks along a corridor in the basement, slamming RoboCop 1 into the walls on either side as it goes. Again, the animation of this ambitious cut is excellent and the RoboCop 1 puppet perfectly compliments the live-action character. The nine cuts in the basement sequence make use of an extensive miniature set dressed out with gas pipes.

One of RoboCop 2's hands acts as a welding torch and is forced into RoboCop 1's face, but the latter pushes it away and into a ruptured gas pipe. After this quick bit of live action, a stop-motion cut has RoboCop 2 recoiling from the explosion.

RoboCop 1 climbs back up into the street. RoboCop 2 forces his way up through another part of the street amid superimposed and rear-projected flames and smoke. The orange light from the flames gives the relentless cyborg a demonic appearance. In two long shots, a policeman fires at the cyborg who, unperturbed, walks off. These cuts, animated by Harry Walton, use a miniature of the street, impeccably matched to the street in the rear projection. The lighting in these cuts, supervised (as elsewhere) by Jim Aupperle, brilliantly matches the glare and flames in the live and miniature areas of the composites.

RoboCop 2 fires randomly at the police who are surrounding it, killing officers and blowing up vehicles. Six medium shots, some angled from behind the puppet, some in front, depict the robot unleashing a tirade of firepower. In one dramatic low-angle long shot, RoboCop 2 stomps straight at the camera.

In two striking long shots, RoboCop 2 stands in the background, firing at a police officer crouching by his car in the foreground. These shots use a partial miniature floor matched to the rear-projected street. Superimposed sparks from ricocheting bullets light up the puppet in two more medium shots — these are the first shots in the film animated by Dutra. A series of eight more medium shots and closeups of RoboCop 2's gun-arm are enhanced by more convincingly superimposed smoke and bullet flares. The animated gun-arm is constantly re-positioning, swiveling and firing.

Cop Nancy Allen jumps into a riot-control vehicle and drives straight at RoboCop 2. Seen in long shot from her point of view, the cyborg (animated by Dutra) extends all its four arms, pre-paring for the impact. The actual colli-sion was shot live-action in miniature, using a three-foot mock-up of the car. In an excellent composite (animated by Dutra) using miniature car and minia-ture street, the seemingly unstoppable RoboCop 2 turns over the riot car and steps forward.

Allen gets the killer cyborg's atten-tion by holding up a canister of nuke. In two medium shots, RoboCop 2 looks around with a chillingly hungry purpose and there is a good melodramatic long shot of Allen facing the robot, nuke can-ister held aloft, the cyborg's fists clench-ing and unclenching anxiously.

She throws the canister up into the air and the robot, in a close shot of the stop-motion hand, catches it. In medium shot, its pincer hand opens the canister, consuming it by placing it on a live-action device that extends from its chest. In two medium shots looking up at the puppet, it waits for the nuke to take effect.

Fifteen superbly animated cuts make up the finale. In a clever compos-ite animated by Walton, RoboCop 1 jumps from the top of a truck onto RoboCop 2's back. In this very intimate piece of interaction, the live-action RoboCop 1 (in the rear projection) falls across the matte line and is replaced by his puppet counterpart as he connects with RoboCop 2, all in one uninter-rupted cut. This successful effect is more satisfying than a similar moment in the Centaur sequence in Harryhausen's *Golden Voyage of Sinbad*, where the mo-ment of contact was implied by the edit-ing and not actually seen; and is better than a fine shot in the Phororhacos se-quence in *Mysterious Island* which cut from a shot of the actor about to leap to a shot of an animated puppet human flying through the air and landing on the giant bird.

The cyborgs struggle together (an-imated by Dutra), RoboCop 2 trying to smash his opponent into a wall. As Dutra explained to the author, Robo-cop 2 "bashes Robo into a cement wall and 'grinds' him into it — that involved animating cracks in the wall and falling debris."

Both go down and in one dynamic cut (Dutra again) RoboCop 2 rolls right over as he tries to dislodge his attacker, landing in a shot that allows a close look at his bird-like, clawed feet as he up-rights himself. Lots of go-motion blur and camera shake add impact to these cuts.

In live-action cuts, RoboCop 1 pulls out RoboCop 2's brain and smashes it with his fist. In the final animation cuts (Dutra again), RoboCop 2 jerks spas-modically as bursts of discharging elec-tricity light up his body. Eventually he falls straight at the camera, dead.

Some have criticized the stop-motion sequences as being soulless slug-fests with little characterization or dra-matic context. This is true to an extent but there are numerous clever touches that demonstrate that Tippett and his crew have taken pains to add little touches of personality to RoboCop 2 (not to mention the brief glimpses of other robots). We may not get the pathos of Kong or the theatrical flourishes of Harryhausen's creations, but this is still a major work, full of imaginative situations and technical ingenuity.

RoboCop 3

1993. Orion. D: Fred Dekker. Scr: Frank Miller, Fred Dekker. Story: Frank Miller. Based on Characters Created by Edward Neumeier, Michael Miner. Ph: Gary B. Kibbe. Art: Hilda Stark. Mus: Basil Poledouris. RoboCop Designed and Created by Rob Bottin. Stop-Motion Animation Sequences by Phil Tippett. Tippett Company Crew: FX Camera: Peter Kozachik, Eric Swenson. FX Production Supervisor: Julie Roman Tippett. Camera Assistant: Sheila Duignan. Opticals: Harry Walton/Image FX. Armatures: Tom St. Amand, Blair Clark. Special Photographic Effects: VCE/ Peter Kuran. Matte Artists: Rocco Gioffre, Tim Cobb.

Cast: Robert Burke, Nancy Allen, Rip Torn, John Castle, Jill Hennessy, CCH Pounder.

Rating: ☆☆   Stop-motion: ☆☆½

Unfortunately, *RoboCop 3* is not a patch on its two excellent predecessors — the wit and invention are simply not there. Frank Miller was apparently given greater control over the script this time but in fact the weak plot could have done with a rewrite *à la RoboCop 2*. OCP and their heavies are trying to clear out a neighborhood to build Delta City but their fascist-style tactics turn RoboCop and the police force against them. The finale is a showdown pitching the local residents, the police and RoboCop against OCP henchman and a gang of splatterpunks (the latter being a particularly clumsy and unlikely gimmick).

The script lurches from one violent set-piece to another with little sense of purpose or human interest. When a bit of characterization does surface, it is usually just a retread of previous scenes in which RoboCop recalls his human life.

The budget was lower than the two previous films and the special effects quotient is down. However, Phil Tippett, having earned sufficient clout with *Jurassic Park* and various Oscars, now got a mention on the film's publicity: "Stop-Motion Animation Sequences Created by Phil Tippett," making him the only person to date to receive a specific stop-motion credit on a film's poster. The process features in two sequences.

The first, early on, is a welcome reappearance by dear old ED-209. But an unlikely plot device — a ten-year-old girl just happens to understand the robot's computer controls and at the last minute changes him from aggressive to friendly mode — destroys any chance of dramatic impact. There is little attempt to repeat the endearing character traits of earlier appearances. Fourteen stop-motion shots are combined with shots using the full-size prop.

In the animated shots, ED-209 rises up or hunkers down, positions his machine guns and takes a few steps. In two shots which help to give the figure some personality, ED-209 looks down at the girl beneath him as she tampers with his controls. In some shots, the girl is crouching beneath the full-size ED-209 prop, but in one very good composite, the puppet, animated on a foreground miniature floor, is aligned with the background image of the girl, conveying the successful impression that they are interacting. Another good composite is designed so that the camera looks through ED-209's legs as he stomps over to some cops in the background image before opening fire on them.

The climactic shootout features an appearance by RoboCop flying by means of a jet-powered back-pack. The distance of the character from the camera and the intricate nature of some of his midair turns made it impractical to do many shots live-action and so stop-motion — used in approximately 20 shots — was necessary. Many of these shots are successfully blue-screened into the live footage, but others are less finished and look like two separate pieces of film — a criticism that cannot normally be leveled at Tippett's sequences.

Some shots have the puppet flying through clouds of smoke or flame — these are clever effects that help the illusion that the figure is part of the live-action footage. In some shots, the puppet halts in midair and hovers. A glow from the backpack is flawlessly superimposed onto the stop-motion puppet. The animation is smooth enough and the choreography is well thought out, but the sequence lacks the dramatic punch that it needed.

Two quick stop-motion shots are used at the very end of the film when the top of the OCP building explodes. Robo-Cop, carrying two other characters, flies out of the building in the nick of time. The limbs and hair of the characters are animated so as to make slight movements. The stop-motion element, shot against a blue screen, is matted in front of the exploding miniature building.

Robot Jox

1989. Empire Pictures. D: Stuart Gordon. Scr: Joe Haldeman. Story: Stuart Gordon. Ph: Mac Ahlberg. Mus: Frederic Talgorn. Visual Effects Director: David Allen. Associate Effects Director: Paul Gentry. Conceptual Designers: Ron Cobb, Stephen Burg. Stop-Motion Animation: Paul Jessel, David Allen. Armatures: Localmotion Machine Works. Special Photographic Effects: VCE/Peter Kuran.

Cast: Gary Graham, Anne-Marie Johnson, Paul Koslo, Robert Sampson, Danny Kamekona.

Rating: ☆½   Stop-Motion: ☆☆½

It sounded like Charles Band had come up with another great idea, perhaps his best yet: a film about giant Transformer-style robots battling it out in the future, with Stuart *Re-Animator)* Gordon to direct, and with stop-motion wizard David Allen in charge of the effects. In fact, the end result is awful. The script is so mind-numbingly predictable that it's a wonder anyone had the nerve to film it: Is this really the original story that Gordon came up with? And even though the running time is only 80 minutes, why does the pace drag so? It's sacrilege to say it, but Japan's Toho Studios (who made the old *Godzilla* films, with men in monster costumes) could have done it better — or at least with a lot more enthusiasm.

There are three robot sequences, a brief one at the beginning and two lengthy battles, one ten minutes into the film, the other at the climax. In their own right, each is entertaining and technically impressive, but they are separated by tiresome live-action passages involving the hero Achilles, the villain Alexander, a female fighter Athena (specially bred in a test tube, no less), a Texan who turns out to be a spy and a Japanese scientist. Scriptwriter Joe Haldeman should quit now before he does any more damage. Perhaps the film's flaws can be blamed on the financial problems which almost caused it to go uncompleted, and which signaled the end of Band's Empire Pictures. Filming was completed in 1987 but *Robot Jox* had to wait two years before getting a release. Were significant changes made to the film in order to wrap it up as economically as possible? Still, kids no doubt love it and it probably did huge business in Japan.

As with many of his other later projects (like *batteries not included*), David Allen and his crew were responsible for more than just the animation shots. This means that there is a satisfying harmony between the live-action model work and the stop-motion cuts, with the different models always carefully matched. The stop-motion shots, using two-foot-high models, were filmed at Allen's Burbank studio. Live-action shots of five-foot-high cable-controlled models were shot out of doors in the Mojave Desert.

There are 45 stop-motion cuts which may sound like a high number (compared to many of Allen's films) but these are outnumbered by the live-action model shots. In the old days of Harryhausen and O'Brien, a sequence would be shot almost entirely with stop-motion, cutting to live-action "props" on only a very few occasions. Today the reverse seems more often to be true, with stop-motion only being used when there is no feasible alternative to creating a particular shot. Most of the stop-motion cuts in *Robot Jox* are functional ones and over in a second or two, or else they are ground-level shots looking up at just the models' legs, so as to increase the illusion of their enormous size. This is a shame, because when Allen is allowed to get into his stride with longer full-length shots of the robots stomping around and looking mean, the results are terrific. Even in a bad film, there is something magical about the idea of two giant robots slugging it out.

The film begins promisingly with a murky credit sequence that pans over a battlefield strewn with the remains of a robot battle; huge metal limbs and debris lie everywhere. A narrator informs

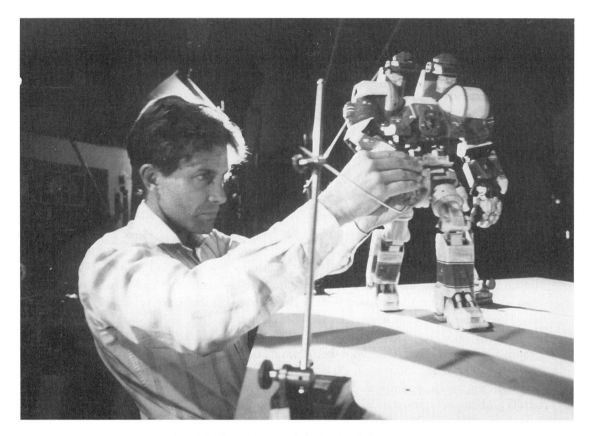

David Allen animates Achilles for *Robot Jox* (1989).

us that in this future time, territorial disputes are settled by having the greatest fighters from each country battle it out by operating giant robots in a huge arena somewhere in Death Valley. Russian fighter Alexander in his sinister black Alefsky-14 robot has defeated his American opponent, lying in a shattered cockpit on the ground, but flaunts the rules and moves in for the kill. Three stop-motion cuts are included (none of which is a composite). One is a medium shot of the robot rearing up, ready to attack. The second is a close shot of its arm, its three fingers opening up to allow a steel mace to retract. The third is a shot, watched on a monitor by the Americans,

of the robot raising its arms in triumph (after a live-action shot in which its huge boot has crushed the American fighter).

The first full battle sequence begins with Achilles getting aboard his robot, which looks very imposing as it stands stationary in the underground silo. Elevated to the surface, Achilles tests his control by stomping on the ground, thereby causing the robot to do likewise, and punching his hands together, an action which the robot does via stop-motion because its fingers have to move. This enormous red-and-white robot looks great in its first full-length shot, a stop-motion cut in which it pushes its elbows back in the best Harryhausen style and takes a few ground-shaking steps forward.

There is a stop-motion cut of the robot walking (watched on a monitor), then a striking low-angle composite of (blue-screened) workmen running for cover as the legs of the robot stride past in the background. A blue-screen shot looking through cheering crowds at the giant legs is followed by a well-designed cut looking out of Achilles' cockpit at Alexander's robot at the other end of the arena, taking a few stop-motion steps towards us. In a second cockpit shot, Achilles returns cannon fire at Alexander, who is now much nearer. There are many live-action cuts of arms, legs and boots in action, then two more stop-motion cuts: one of Alexander firing red laser-fire at Achilles and the other an imaginative long shot of both models seen from the crowd's point of view, Achilles reflecting Alexander's laser-fire with a mirror in one of his arms.

In another cockpit shot, Achilles gets the stop-motion Alexander in his sights. There is another low-angle shot (the perspective enhancing the impression of the great height of these robots) through Achilles' legs, with Alexander deflecting (optically added) laser-fire and responding with his own.

The referees' vehicle floats in and orders an end to long-range fighting, to be replaced by hand-to-hand combat. The two puppets square off in a "waist-high" stop-motion cut, their arms and fingers making slight movements, their bodies swaying apprehensively from side to side. Achilles fends off a live-action kick but goes down to a stop-motion two-fisted thump on his chest. A legs-only animation cut of Alexander stomp-

ing over to the prone Achilles is followed by a low-angle shot looking up at the black robot, which raises one of its ugly three-fingered claws, ready to strike a killing blow. But Achilles retaliates with a live-action welding torch, causing Alexander to teeter backwards several steps, arms flailing in a fine stop-motion cut.

He goes down and, being a sneaky villain, breaches the referees' rule, transforming his hand into a missile which he fires at Achilles. But the missile goes out of control, heading straight for the crowd. Heroically, Achilles gets up and there is a stop-motion cut of him stomping hurriedly (but very smoothly) over to the grandstand to intercept the missile. A composite from behind the blue-screened crowd shows the animated Achilles receiving the impact, a shower of sparks in the third element, a rear-screen. The sequence ends with a reasonable live-action shot of the model crashing into the grandstand.

It is best to ignore the dreary live-action passages in which Achilles, filled with remorse over the spectators he has killed, retires, then eventually changes his mind and returns to the game. Athena the "Tubie" makes sure that Achilles is out of action so that she can get a chance to operate the robot, but at the last moment the control room personnel realize she has taken his place and deactivate the silo elevator. Determined to fight, she makes the robot climb out of the silo, one of the huge boots accidentally kicking through the glass screen of the control room.

A memorable blue-screen shot has two workmen on a platform astonished by the appearance of an enormous hand rising up and clutching the edge of the silo: It's a startling image that recalls a shot in *It Came from Beneath the Sea* when Donald Curtis is confronted by a huge tentacle rising up beside the Golden Gate Bridge. So far, this is all good non-animation stuff. The first stop-motion in this sequence is in two shots watched on a monitor in the control room showing the robot taking a couple of heavy strides across the arena. Alexander transforms (alas off-screen) into a sinister four-legged spider-like robot and, in a low-angle stop-motion cut, launches himself at Athena. Stop-motion is used again to show him punching his prone opponent. She retaliates by firing a bolus out of one of her hands. In live action, it wraps around his right arm and severs it. There is a scary stop-motion full shot of Alexander punching his remaining arm straight at the camera, and three of him pile-driving Athena, who makes feeble gestures with her arms trying to fend him off.

To nobody's surprise, Achilles decides to come to her rescue and zips across the arena in a hover car courtesy of some good process shots. The referees try to come between Alexander and Athena (an attractive blue-screen shot) but get stomped on by his live-action boot. Achilles gets into the cockpit, takes control and several quick stop-motion cuts are used to show him tripping Alexander, then getting up. Alexander also gets up and starts to transform again. This sequence is all a little cluttered. Gratuitously (i.e., for the sake of another transformation), the two robots now head off up into space (backed by a fine series of paintings of the Earth), Achilles gets blasted in the foot and

crash lands back near the arena. The best stop-motion cut in the film follows, a full-shot of the four-legged Alexander robot walking over to Achilles. It's a bizarre image, the real stuff of fantasy films, and it's a shame there aren't more cuts like this in *Robot Jox*.

Achilles performs a lengthy live-action transformation into a tank-like vehicle, then there is a stop-motion cut of Alexander rearing up on his four legs and another one of his torso opening up and a deadly chainsaw emerging. After lots of live-action cuts, Achilles runs for the dismembered hand lying in the desert nearby. There are two significant stop-motion cuts of Alexander advancing on him, his one remaining hand opening and closing threateningly, and a good split-screen shot of Achilles sheltering in the hand with Alexander approaching in the background.

After three worm's-eye-view stop-motion cuts looking up at Alexander striding overhead and reaching down to grab Achilles, he is dispatched in a live-action explosion when the missile hand is fired straight at him. The film concludes with a half-baked finale in which the two fighters, now bereft of their robots, slug it out *mano a mano* and end up shaking hands and smiling at one another.

Robot Jox would seem like a good film if it could be trimmed to 30 minutes, leaving out all "human interest" passages. Allen's sequences, while always hampered by a medium budget and by their refusal to take full advantage of the stop-motion possibilities, are visually exciting, original and technically accomplished. One reason why many shots look good is because those not requiring composite photography were filmed outdoors in sunlight, shooting against a blue sky background. That must be a first in a genre normally associated with locked-off, darkened studio sets. *Robot Jox* is Allen's second contribution to "robo-motion" after *batteries not included* and the puppets lend themselves especially well to animation, comparing favorably to the more ambitious robot animation of Phil Tippett's ATVATs, Scout Walkers and ED-209 and to Doug Beswick's Terminator cyborg.

Robot Wars

1993. Full Moon Entertainment. D: Albert Band. Scr: Jackson Barr. Original Idea: Charles Band. Ph: Adolfo Bartoli. Mus: David Arkenstone. Art: Milo. Visual Effects: David Allen Productions. Effects Supervisor: David Allen. Stop-Motion Animation: David Allen, Paul Jessel, Chris Endicott and (uncredited) Jim Danforth. Model Shop Supervisor: Dennis Gordon. Armature Design: Yancy Calzada.

Cast: Don Michael Paul, Barbara Crampton, James Staley, Lisa Rinna, Danny Kamekoma, Yuji Okumoto.

Rating: ☆☆   Stop-Motion: ☆☆½

This is very much in the style of Charles Band's two previous giant robot pictures. On a dramatic level, it's better than the dismal *Robot Jox* but poor compared with the more satisfying *Crash and Burn*. The only witty moment in a generally humorless film is an in-joke in which a group of people walk past a cinema showing *Puppetmaster 54*. The plot is inconsequential, but at its core is a half-decent idea about the West operating "the last surviving mega-robot," only to have it hijacked by bad guys from the East. At the end, another giant robot, which has lain dormant for years, is revived and saves the day.

David Allen works his magic again, providing accomplished effects despite budget and time constraints. The real star of the film is MRAS-2, a giant walking robot designed like a scorpion, complete with six legs, two pincers and a stinger that shoots laser-fire. This creature stomps around the desert setting, controlled by two pilots in its cockpit, and carries groups of passengers in a compartment above its main body. Allen doesn't have the resources to give this monster some Talos-like grandeur but it's a pretty impressive beast nonetheless. Mega-1, the second robot, is of the humanoid variety, recalling the robots of the two earlier films.

In contrast to the two previous films, most of Allen's robot shots are achieved with stop-motion, using live-action puppet choreography only in closer shots. The film contains 33 stop-motion cuts, with Allen sharing the animation with Paul Jessel and Chris Endicott. Jim Danforth also animated a couple of shots that feature in the film's climax. Armatures were built by Yancy Calzada.

Most of the stop-motion cuts are brief — not more than two or three seconds — but in comparison to other Band productions, this film contains a lot. Unfortunately, only one composite is included, a stunning shot of actors in the lower foreground with Mega-1 striding behind them. More shots like this could have made *Robot Wars* something to remember.

The film has the rare distinction of being one of the few films to have stop-motion in its opening shot, a tilt-down from a blue sky to MRAS-2 walking across the desert, accompanied by appropriate whirring and clanking sounds. Many subsequent shots depict the puppet walking across the frame, backed by what is presumably a photo blow-up of sky and desert. One of these shots is made more visually interesting by the presence of two small towers in the foreground, presumably miniatures. In some of these shots, the head turns and simulated sunlight glints off glass in the cockpit — a clever little touch. In other shots, the puppet walks directly towards the camera.

In one shot, it recoils when hit by (superimposed) laser-fire, and in another it raises its stinger before unleashing a return blast. In other shots, MRAS-2 walks up to a control tower, a miniature which in some shots is animated so that it swivels around.

An attractive extreme long shot has MRAS-2 walking up to a pyramid-shaped building (also a miniature). This nighttime set-up has lights shining in the cockpit and the stinger of the model.

In closer shots, MRAS-2 unleashes laser-fire at the building.

In a live-action sequence, Mega-1 is reactivated and pushes its way up through a miniature street. In stop-motion shots, it stomps through the rubble and advances towards the camera. The ensuing battle between the two robots is occasionally visually exciting, but is far too brief to be properly dramatic.

Many close shots of the two robots in close combat striking each other are achieved live-action. About half of the shots during the fight are achieved with stop-motion.

In stop-motion long-shots, Mega-1 pulls the passenger compartment away from the top of the scorpion-robot, whose pincers open and close desperately.

After animated closeups of MRAS-2's tail turning, retracting and firing, MEGA-1 is struck by laser-fire and falls backwards. MRAS-2 attacks the fallen humanoid and the two robots strike one another. MEGA-1, upright again, grabs MRAS-2 by the tail. But the scorpion-robot's pincers encircle MEGA-1's hips, causing it to fall backwards. Animating a free-falling object is always difficult and this attempt is only partly convincing.

MRAS-2 clambers over its prostrate foe but MEGA-1 blasts it from below. In the final stop-motion cut, MRAS-2 is lit up by the blast, its limbs jerking outwards as its body lifts.

The Rocketeer

1991. Touchstone/Silver Screen Partners IV/Gordon. D: Joe Johnston. Scr: Danny Bilson, Paul De Meo. Story: Danny Bilson, Paul De Meo, William Dear. Based on the Graphic Novel *The Rocketeer* by Dave Stevens. Ph: Hiro Narita. Art: Jim Bissell. Mus: James Horner. Lothar Makeup: Rick Baker. Special Visual Effects: Industrial Light and Magic. Visual Effects Supervisor: Ken Ralston. Stop-Motion Animator: Tom St. Amand.

Cast: Bill Campbell, Alan Arkin, Jennifer Connelly, Paul Sorvino, Timothy Dalton, Terry O'Quinn.

Rating: ☆☆½   Stop-Motion: ☆☆½

The Rocketeer is an engaging attempt to match the thrills of the Indiana Jones series but lacks that series' wit, characterization and inventiveness. Set in Los Angeles in 1938, the story has Bill Campbell donning a jet-powered backpack designed by Howard Hughes to thwart a plot by Nazi spy Timothy Dalton, who masquerades as an Errol Flynn-type film actor. Unfortunately, there is not enough excitement and too many in-jokes: lookalikes of Clark Gable and W. C. Fields put in appearances and a scene on a film set recreates a climactic swordfight from *The Adventures of Robin Hood*.

The flying sequences are very well done, a combination of live-action cuts and miniature shots by ILM. Test shots with stunt men didn't convey the sense of great speed required by director Joe Johnston for certain sequences, and so it was decided to use a stop-motion puppet. Tom St. Amand built an 18–inch model and animated it in 21 stop-motion cuts showing the Rocketeer in extreme long shots.

The puppet was attached to a go-motion device which insured that blurs accompanied the puppet's rapid movements and so made the shots more realistic. Turns of the head and movement of the arms or legs were achieved with traditional hands-on stop-motion methods.

St. Amand's cuts include several during a scene in which the Rocketeer comes to the rescue of a pilot in an out-of-control biplane. This sequence includes a faultless stop-motion cut in which the Rocketeer puppet, carrying a puppet of the pilot, drops him onto a partially inflated parachute on the ground. A cel-animated shadow is added to the parachute to complete the effect.

Another ambitious cut shows the Rocketeer crash landing in a pond: The puppet is shown bouncing off the surface of the water, combined with live-action splashes in the live-action plate and matted-in splashes. Later shots include cuts of the Rocketeer taking off and landing, including one impressive shot in a nightclub in which he flies straight upwards and crashes through a skylight, sending a shower of glass crashing down.

At the climax, a huge zeppelin goes up in flames and the hero and heroine escape in the nick of time, clinging to a rope ladder hanging from a small plane. For this composite, a miniature plane is matted into the live-action footage, with tiny stop-motion puppets of the two actors making slight movements on the ladder beneath it.

All these cuts are impeccably executed by St. Amand, but once again he must have been disappointed to find that he was doing purely functional effects, allowing no creativity or character animation.

Rural Delivery, Ten Thousand B.C. see *RFD 10,000 B.C.: A Mannikin Comedy*

Santa Claus

1985. A Santa Claus Production. D: Jeannot Szwarc. Scr: David Newman. Story: David and Leslie Newman. Ph: Arthur Ibbetson. Art: Anthony Pratt. Mus: Henry Mancini. Director of Visual and Miniature Effects: Derek Meddings. Stop-Motion (uncredited): Pete Kleinow. Supervising Animatronic Designer: John Coppinger.

Cast: David Huddleston, Dudley Moore, John Lithgow, Burgess Meredith, Judy Cornwell, Jeffrey Kramer.

Rating: ☆☆   Stop-Motion: ☆☆½

Santa Claus is a dreary children's film from producers Alexander and Ilya (*Superman*) Salkind. Director Jeannot Szwarc cannot do much with a tired script by David Newman, and Dudley Moore is weak as an elf called Patch, constantly making unfunny jokes about "elf-confidence" and "elf portraits." A storyline in the second half, concerning John Lithgow as a slimy chairman of a toy company, improves things, but not much. Maybe young audiences warm to it, but there is precious little for adults to enjoy.

Sequences showing Santa (David Huddleston) and his reindeer in flight are extremely well done and the best thing in the film. A long episode in which he takes a boy for a ride over New York is especially impressive. Close shots of the reindeer employ some very good full-size animatronic puppets created by John Coppinger. There are about 40 long shots, including about 12 which make use of stop-motion by Pete Kleinow—shamefully uncredited. In extreme long shots, tiny non-animated puppets make slight movements, their feet partly disguised by cel animated sparks of magic dust.

Slightly closer shots, requiring more elaborate movement of the reindeer, fall back on stop-motion. These include shots of the reindeer coming in to land or taking off and, on one occasion, flying straight at the camera. They are very smoothly animated, mesh perfectly with the live-action cuts and were shot blue-screen, composited with aerial views of the North Pole, New York or a glistening matte painting of the sea at night. There is also a cut in which Patch and the boy are thrown out of their own futuristic sleigh, fall through the air and are caught by Santa in his sleigh; it looks like it uses tiny animated puppets of the actors.

Saturday the 14th

1981. New World. D-Scr: Howard R. Cohen. Story: Jeff Begun. Ph: Daniel Lacambre. Mus: Parmer Fuller. Creature Effects: Rick Stratton, Steve Neill. Stop-Motion Graphic Animation: Ernest D. Farino. Graphic Animation Photography: Mark Sawicki. Assistant Cameraman: Ted R. Rae. Stop-Motion Models: Brian Chin, Ron Lizorty. Opticals: Jack Rabin and Associates.

Cast: Richard Benjamin, Paula Prentiss, Severn Darden, Jeffrey Tambor, Kari Michaelsen, Kevin Brando.

Rating: ☆½   Stop-Motion: ☆☆½

Clumsily plotted and directed, the comedy-chiller *Saturday the 14th* is neither funny nor scary. Richard Benjamin and his family inherit an old mansion where they are beset by a series of extras in unlikely monster costumes. Shadowy lighting tries hard to disguise the cheapness of these sequences. The script never gives the cast much chance to make anything of their roles, although Benjamin is amiably bewildered on a few occasions and Severn Darden makes an offbeat Van Helsing, chewing his lines with relish: "I never drink... coffee."

Visual effects are modest: This is no *Poltergeist.* Accomplished stop-motion by Ernest Farino features in six cuts, but these are all very brief effects.

In the first stop-motion effect, one of the monsters peers in through a window, causing some flowers in a bowl to wilt and die suddenly. In a deft comedic touch, the last flower pirouettes before collapsing.

Two vampires are trying to gain possession of the house and in five stop-motion cuts they transform into bats and back again. These cuts are very smoothly animated by Farino, who avoids the strobing effect that frequently plagues flying creatures. They are a great improvement on the wire-supported bat props and cartoon bats which appeared in so many earlier vampire films.

In the first cut, the two characters are seated in a car. Surrounded by a cel-animated red glow, they transform into bats and fly off. The bats appear to have been animated in front of a rear screen. One of them passes behind the car frame, suggesting either that a partial miniature was lined up with it, or that a matte follows its outline. In other cuts, probably using rear projections again, the bats fly toward the house and in through a window. In the final cut, the bats transform back into the vampires and fly up a flight of stairs.

Saturday the 14th Strikes Back

1988. MGM/UA. Prod: Roger Corman. D-Scr: Howard R. Cohen.

Cast: Ray Walston, Avery Screiber, Patty McCormack, Juliana McNamara, Jason Presson, Leo Gordon.

Rating: ☆☆½   Stop-Motion: ☆☆

Marginally less interesting than its dull predecessor, this has a Los Angeles family attacked by a series of supernatural beings after a mysterious crack opens up underneath their house.

These beings include some vampires that transform into bats. As before, these are seen in a few shots that feature stop-motion puppets.

Screamers

1996. USA/Canada/Japan. D: Christian Duguay. Scr: Dan O'Bannon, Miguel Tejada-Flores. Based on the Short Story "Second Variety" by Philip K. Dick. Ph: Rodney Gibbons. Art: Perri Gorrara. Visual Effects Supervisor: Ernest D. Farino. Mechanical Screamers and Stop-Motion Sequence: The Chiodo Bros. Chiodo Crew: Edward Chiodo, Stephen Chiodo, Charles Chiodo. Stop-Motion Animator: Kent Burton.

Cast: Peter Weller, Roy Dupuis, Jennifer Rubin, Andy Lauer, Charles Powell, Ron White.

Rating: ☆☆   Stop-Motion: ☆☆½

The audience is screaming with frustration by the end of this turgid, medium-budget SF thriller, which is badly in need of a plot. Employees of a mining company on a distant planet cross overland to a rival company, discover everybody there is dead, battle with the title characters — and then the movie ends. At no point is audience interest engaged; there is no sense of plot progression, and the characters are dull.

However, there are some excellent special effects in among the tedium, executed by visual effects supervisor Ernest Farino. These include landscape matte paintings, some fine spaceship shots and a breathtaking opening scene in which the letters of the title split apart and become asteroids which fall into a planet's atmosphere and burn up.

Farino was also in charge of all shots featuring the Screamers. The Screamers are cat-sized bio-mechanical creations, originally designed to protect the mining colony but now out of control. These vicious-looking creatures resemble skeletal lobsters, with 32 spider-like legs, talons and long tails, and are equipped with deadly buzzsaws.

One brief sequence in which a Screamer is seen in full features some good stop-motion produced by the Chiodo brothers, Edward, Stephen and Charles. The hands-on animation was done by Kent Burton. Intercut with shots of an on-set mechanical Screamer (also built by the Chiodos), there are 18 smoothly animated stop-motion cuts which were shot in front of a blue screen. In this sequence, the composites are always impeccable.

In the stop-motion shots, the Screamer walks across a floor, jumps up onto a computer console, then begins to operate the equipment. It jumps back down to the floor and then leaps into the air (launching itself at an intended victim), only to get blasted by gunfire at the last moment. This brief sequence is one of the film's highlights and makes one wish that the Screamers had been featured more prominently.

The Secret Adventures of Tom Thumb

1993. Bolex Brothers/Lumen Films/ Manga. Conceived, Written, Edited and Directed by Dave Borthwick. Key Animators: Dave Borthwick, Frank Passingham, Lee Wilton. Mus: The Startled Insects, John Paul Jones.

Cast: Nick Upton, Deborah Collard, Frank Passingham, John Schofield.

Rating: ☆☆½   Stop-Motion: ☆☆½

Originally shot as a pilot film for a BBC television series, this 66-minute production received a theatrical release in both Britain and the United States.

Dave Borthwick's retelling of the Tom Thumb fairy tale is a grotesque and offbeat experience, and its bug-eyed, bald-headed title character looks a child of Chernobyl. Dialogue is almost entirely absent; Borthwick lets the visuals tell the story. Tom escapes from a secret laboratory, teams up with Jack the Giant Killer and, after a series of adventures, the pair eventually destroys the laboratory.

Both Tom and Jack are stop-motion puppets. Some human characters appear and these are combined with the puppets not by traditional matte techniques but by animating the actors, who were positioned motionless on the set as each frame of animation was exposed, then repositioned slightly for the next frame. This technique suits the film, whose intention is not to be realistic but to generate a surrealistic mood.

7 Faces of Dr. Lao

1964. MGM. Prod-D: George Pal. Scr: Charles Beaumont. Based on the Novel *The Circus of Dr. Lao* by Charles G. Finney. Ph: Robert Bronner. Art: George W. Davis, Gabriel Scognamillo. Mus: Leigh Harline.

Special Makeup: William Tuttle. Special Visual Effects: Wah Chang, Jim Danforth, Paul B. Byrd, Ralph Rodine, Robert R. Hoag (also Gene Warren, Pete Kleinow — uncredited).

7 Faces of Dr. Lao

Cast: Tony Randall, Barbara Eden, Arthur O'Connell, John Ericson, Noah Beery, Jr., Minerva Urecal, Royal Dano.

Rating: ☆☆☆   Stop-Motion: ☆☆☆

7 Faces of Dr. Lao is one of George Pal's lesser-seen films and yet his most engaging, possessing a simple charm not found elsewhere in his work. It is not a classic of the same proportions as his masterpiece *The War of the Worlds*, but it is hard to imagine a more pleasant way of passing 100 minutes.

Set in the old West, the film tells of the arrival of a mysterious Chinaman and his traveling circus. The townsfolk who visit his sideshows have their lives changed by their encounters and all their foibles and failings are exposed. Such a theme might sound like heavy going but in fact Pal directs with such a light, witty touch that the film is irresistible. There is a strong performance by Tony Randall (as not only Dr. Lao but also various characters in the circus), a jolly score, several impressive makeups by William Tuttle (he won the first-ever Academy Award for the field) and any number of offbeat circus set-pieces.

In addition, the film contains some haunting, almost playful fantasy images that have no equal. Sequences involving a giant serpent and a Gorgon are weird enough, but a final passage with the Loch Ness Monster is one of the most bizarre in the history of feature film stop-motion. "The film is so unique," boasted the publicity department, "that ordinary adjectives do not apply, and a word had to be invented — Fantodramystacom." It was a catch phrase which, not surprisingly, was never heard of again.

Heartless businessman Arthur O'Connell enters one sideshow and encounters a large serpent with a face uncannily like his own. The creature is realized mostly with a hand puppet, with stop-motion being used in three cuts when a complex facial gesture is required — for example, when it laughs, winks, or in the surreal moment when it catches a cigar in its mouth and has a pensive puff. Two of the shots were animated by Jim Danforth and the third by Dave Pal. The cigar shot has a cloud of smoke carefully superimposed so that it seems to come from the serpent's mouth. The animation could be smoother and the colors of the prop and the stop-motion puppet do not quite match, but this hardly matters in a scene whose impact derives from the exchange of quirky dialogue between the snake and O'Connell. It's like a mad scene out of *Alice In Wonderland*.

The Medusa sequence is impressive dramatically and technically. As in the rest of the film, the balance of humor and the bizarre is kept just right. There are several very evocative images, such as the sight of a yellow butterfly (a cel animation) fluttering around the snakes in the Gorgon's hair, a series of shock close-ups of Medusa with her green lips and eyes, and the moment when a victim turns to stone. The snakes themselves are disturbingly realistic but, contrary to some sources, are not made to move by stop-motion. They were sculpted by Wah Chang and controlled by magnets which enabled them to move in several different directions. Tuttle's makeup for Randall as Medusa is so good that it looks nothing like the actor, fooling most people into thinking they are seeing a woman.

Jim Danforth animating the Loch Ness Monster from *7 Faces of Dr. Lao* (1964).

Later, Merlin the magician (Randall again) performs a stage act which includes making flowering plants grow up the sides of the stage and along the curtain rail. These three shots were filmed in reverse with the plants cut away frame by frame.

The Loch Ness Monster sequence suffers from the usual curse of stop-motion: It is a gratuitous set-piece, an epilogue barely integrated with the flow of the action. But in all other respects, this is a scene to treasure, an exciting, witty episode that uniquely combines slapstick with the surreal imagery of dreams. Characters run about with unnatural choreography (Dr. Lao leaping wildly, two drunks taking long strides that get them nowhere) through a disorientating dust storm, the whole passage backed by eerie bagpipe music.

As with the film's other effects sequences, the Loch Ness Monster finale was created by Project Unlimited, the company headed by Gene Warren, Wah Chang and Tim Barr. Chang designed the creature and Jim Danforth was recruited to sculpt and animate it. Danforth also built armatured puppets of Randall and Royal Dano for shots where they interact with the monster. Pete Kleinow also did some of the animation. The sequence took three months to film and was rewarded with an Academy

Award nomination for special effects. (It lost out to *Mary Poppins.*)

The Loch Ness Monster is kept as a tadpole-sized pet by Dr. Lao in a goldfish bowl. In an earlier scene, he has warned that (out of water) it will grow into a giant creature. A drunk smashes the bowl and the squirming creature falls to the floor. In three astonishing cuts, it grows to dinosaur size.

Twenty slightly different puppets were built (some by Danforth) for this part-replacement, part-displacement effect. The first was a small fish-like model fashioned out of soft clay. The next six puppets were made of solid clay. The seventh was a wire-armatured puppet that was animated against a blue screen and combined with the live-action plate so as to look like a three-foot creature wriggling about. The squirming creature really seems to be underneath the startled drunks' feet. Six more clay models lead into a second wire-armatured model, which resembles a plesiosaur. This is followed by more clay models and eventually the full-grown creature, the only model to have a ball-and-socket armature. Additionally, the camera was tracked in during animation to give the impression that the puppet is increasing in size.

This final stage is a green dragon with flippers and a long swishing tail. Fleshy whiskers hang down from its jaws. One of the drunks throws his gun at the creature, which catches it in its mouth and swallows it with a comically noisy gulp. After a lingering closeup of the beast's red, gaping mouth, it picks up one of the drunks in its teeth. A close shot of the huge head surrounding the actor looks like a blue-screen shot.

In three superb, shadowy all-miniature shots—filmed from below to enhance the impression of the creature's size—Danforth animates a puppet of the drunk swinging about in the creature's jaws. The movement of the puppet man's arms and legs is uncannily well thought out. In the left foreground, one of the tent's support poles has a flaming torch in it, which is somehow in front of the puppet. The pole is a miniature and the flame is a separate element, but the composite is such a good one that everything looks like a part of the same shot. The flaming torch element was originally filmed for *Jack the Giant Killer*, and called back into service here. In one of these cuts, the drunk's hat is dislodged and although animated, it falls in an entirely convincing manner.

The monster pushes its way through the tent canvas and is seen in three close shots from outside. It tosses the drunk through the air, a quick but credible shot. The torn canvas is animated so as to look like it flaps in the wind, and crumples very realistically when the monster bites into it.

The monster walks hurriedly past Dr. Lao in a shot where only its body and flippers are in the frame, designed deliberately to suggest the creature is too big to fit in the shot. The puppet walks on a miniature floor; although this could have been filmed as a rear-screen set-up, traces of blue spill indicate that for some reason it was not done that way. The creature's flippers make a semi-comic slapping sound as it runs.

In long shot, one of the drunks runs from the background to the foreground, chased by the monster which appears in the distance. This clever front-light/

back-light traveling matte set-up totally fools the eye into seeing the composite as one piece of film, with the puppet a long way off. During animation, the puppet was supported on steel posts which were later painted out by hand. In a series of shots, the monster runs through some miniature trees, snapping its jaws at the drunks.

What follows is one of the most outlandish sights ever put on film. In a series of six shots (four shot from in front of the model, two from behind), the monster sprouts six more heads on long necks, each being one of Dr. Lao's many personae. This was filmed in reverse with parts of the rubber cut away frame by frame. It's an effect that always evinces a gasp from audiences. Some of the faces have animated beards which flap in the wind like the real thing. All the faces have been very carefully sculpted so as to match their live-action counterparts. After scaring the life out of the drunks, the heads retract back into the monster's body. The final shot in this sequence uses the same bit of animation in which the necks first appeared, but projected in the sequence it was shot. Because it had been shot in front of a blue screen, it was possible to combine it with two different pieces of live-action film for the two shots. (Incidentally, publicity artwork for the film depicts an inaccurate version of the seven-headed monster. In place of the monster's head, it has Dr. Lao's, and where Lao's head should be it has the head of the serpent — which doesn't appear on the stop-motion model.)

Dr. Lao arrives on the scene to retrieve his pet, carrying with him a rain-making machine which he hopes will cause the monster to shrink back to its former size. Flickering studio lighting on the puppet impairs two blue-screen shots looking down at it from behind. An all-miniature medium shot of the monster turning its head towards Dr. Lao is much better. In a traveling matte set-up, the huge jaws fill the screen and pick up Dr. Lao. To enhance the suggestion of physical contact, a shadow is thrown onto Randall and a matte has been drawn around the outline of the rain-making machine, behind which one of the jaws passes. However, the clever design of this shot is let down by contrast between the bright green puppet and a grainy optical dupe.

Five shots feature some very fluid animation of Lao dangling from the puppet's jaws in long shot. In the last of these, he is thrown through the air and lands with a thump on the muddy ground. This is a superb bit of interaction in which Danforth's animation is so well calculated that the Lao puppet really seems to hit and slightly sink into the ground in the live-action plate. All these shots include superimposed rain.

In closeup, the creature blinks, as if realizing what is about to happen to it. Drenched by the rain, it begins to shrink back to its original tadpole-size. Four cuts, animated by Pete Kleinow, make use of all the 20 puppets again. The model's flippers are just below the bottom of the frame, so no matte is required, yet once again the puppet seems to be right in with the live-action plate. As it shrinks, the monster yelps like a frightened puppy — another inventively eccentric touch.

The genesis of the one or two poor composites which mar this sequence was explained by Danforth in a letter to the author. "I fought hard to do these composites by rear projection and did a test to allow George Pal to decide which system to use — projection or matte. Bob Hoag at MGM opticals thought the projection shot was one of his opticals, and I thought it was pretty good — the color matching was better. Unfortunately Gene Warren went on vacation and only he and I knew of the agreement to let George Pal decide. Ralph Rodine refused to work with the projection and so all the money that could have gone to Project Unlimited went to the MGM optical department instead. That's why the colors don't match in the composites."

This ambitious scene is an engaging and unique experience. The history of stop-motion would be much poorer without it.

The 7th Voyage of Sinbad

1958. Columbia. Prod: Charles H. Schneer. D: Nathan Juran. Scr: Kenneth Kolb. Ph: Wilkie Cooper. Art: Gil Parrendo. Mus: Bernard Herrmann. Visual Effects Created by Ray Harryhausen. Technical Assistant: George Lofgren.

Cast: Kerwin Mathews, Kathryn Grant, Richard Eyer, Torin Thatcher, Alec Mango, Virgilio Teixetra.

Rating: ☆☆☆½   Stop-Motion: ☆☆☆½

Of all Harryhausen's films, *The 7th Voyage of Sinbad* has dated the least. Its Arabian Nights setting has a timelessness that is brought to life by Kenneth Kolb's economic screenplay and the enthusiastic performances of Kerwin Mathews as Sinbad and Torin Thatcher as the villainous magician. Bernard Herrmann's superb score perfectly complements the action, heightening the aura of fantasy and by turns offering magical, sinister or lyrical themes.

Harryhausen's stop-motion effects have a startling visual impact which they retain after several viewings. His creations — including a pair of giant, horned Cyclopses and a fire-breathing dragon — have enormous melodramatic appeal, imbuing the film with a sense of wonder that has rarely been matched.

Filmed on a budget of around $650,000, the film grossed a healthy $6,000,000 worldwide. The only country where business was disappointing was Great Britain, where the over-protective censor insisted that the film was given an "A" certificate (for those over 16 only) on the grounds that it might terrify younger children. In re-releases in the 1950s and early 1960s, the timid British censor went even further and removed one of the film's most talked-about sequences — a battle between Sinbad and a living skeleton.

The film represented a major advance for Harryhausen in that it was the first time his reality sandwich composites were in color. The contrast differences shown up by combining two or three generations of film in one shot

A posed shot of Harryhausen's magnificent Cyclops for *The 7th Voyage of Sinbad* (1958).

create far more complex problems in color filming than in black-and-white. Initially reluctant, Harryhausen was convinced by producer Schneer that color was essential if the film was to be a success. One problem he discovered was that if a scene was not completed by the end of a day and the film was left overnight in the camera, then there would be a shift in the color quality of the film stock. Another problem was that when cutting from a composite shot to a non-composite shot, the latter would always look brighter. Additionally, any lighting imbalance between a puppet and rear projection would be emphasized in

color filming. In some shots, Harryhausen experimented with disguising the grainy pattern of the rear screen by rotating it bit by bit as he animated in front of it.

Although Harryhausen brilliantly overcame most of these problems, there are many instances in *7th Voyage* where composites are unsatisfactory — for example, where rear screens look excessively grainy. But these are the exception rather than the rule and in any event the film's dramatic pacing almost always insures that such shots are not distracting.

In 232 stop-motion cuts, Harryhausen shows just why he was the master of his trade. His fabulous creations strut and stomp around the screen with theatrical flourish and imaginative choreography. In particular, he imbues the first Cyclops with such a degree of personality that he is as much a character as any of the live-action cast.

The film begins at night, with Sinbad's ship lost at sea. Through the fog, land is glimpsed — the craggy and forbidding peaks of an impressive Harryhausen miniature set. "May Allah grant we find food and water," Sinbad says hopefully. "And may Allah grant we find nothing more," retorts a wary sailor.

The next morning, Sinbad's ship anchors off the island. An effective static matte composite places a miniature of the ship next to a craggy peninsula. On the island, the sailors discover the huge print of a cloven hoof in the sand. Carved into a cliff is a huge face, the cave below forming its mouth. The cave mouth is part of the live-action set (filmed on a beach in Spain) but the face above it is another effective miniature, seamlessly matted in.

Still only a few minutes into the film, Harryhausen now lunges into a startling three-minute sequence that really grabs our attention. For sheer visual impact it has few equals. The horned Cyclops, with its hairy goat-legs, scaly torso and veins bulging on its arms, is an outstanding puppet. Harryhausen gives it an angry stare, clutching three-fingered hands and a purposeful gait. His animation, in 31 shots, is superb.

In long shot, the roaring creature stomps out of the cave, pursuing the magician Sokurah. The matte line runs down the wall of the cave and along the ground, leaving a small and impercep-

tible area of floor inlay on the beach onto which the puppet throws an all-important shadow. Two dramatic low-angle medium shots look up at the puppet from below, the carved stone face in the background. The shots emphasize the creature's height and allow a good look at the warts and veins that cover its body.

A second static matte set-up really seems to put the Cyclops in among some large rocks in the live-action plate, with the puppet running behind them as it chases Sinbad's men. In another striking long shot, Sinbad throws his spear and it sticks in the Cyclops' chest. The spear is part of the live action at the start of this shot but switches to miniature when it strikes the puppet. What happens to the live-action spear is not clear — it may be that Harryhausen matted out that area of the sky to one side of the puppet. In similar shots in other films, Harryhausen achieved the effect by having no live-action spear at all — the actor mimes the action and the animator lines up a miniature spear throughout the duration of the entire shot. But that is not the case here.

In medium shot, the Cyclops pulls out the spear and looks at it angrily. Its eye is always looking this way and that, and as it growls its mouth is forever opening and closing; this is a vital animal. In three closer long shots, the Cyclops is nearly upon Sinbad and his men. In these shots, a rear-projected shadow (i.e., a piece of carefully shaped card placed between projector and the back of the rear screen) follows the puppet's feet. The Cyclops stoops to pick up Sinbad but is distracted when another sailor throws a spear into its chest.

Reacting angrily, the Cyclops struts from behind a boulder into another static matte set-up, the spear still in its chest. Two subsequent shots use the same set-up, with the sailors all around the Cyclops' legs, slashing with their swords. A close shot of one of the creature's legs, with Sinbad slashing at it with his sword, looks like it was achieved by moving the animation camera very close to the puppet's leg and animating in front of a small rear screen. The same technique appears to have been used in a subsequent shot in which one of the Cyclops' hooves kicks a sailor away, the interaction being implied in the alignment of puppet with actor.

Meanwhile, Sokurah has been busy calling forth the genie of the lamp. A cloud of smoke pours out of the lamp and takes the shape of the genie (Richard Eyer). Harryhausen achieved this by matting around a previously filmed cloud of smoke so that it takes on a human shape, superimposing this onto the beach footage, and then dissolving in the film of Eyer.

The genie, instructed by Sokurah to protect him and Sinbad's men from the Cyclops, transforms into a fireball and floats across the beach in front of the monster. Following the fireball is a hazy, semi-invisible barrier, watched keenly by the Cyclops as it cuts him off from the men. The shot required four passes of the film through the camera: The animation footage of the Cyclops was added in the second pass, and the superimposed fireball and barrier are two separately added elements. Adding dynamism to the moment, Harryhausen makes the barrier a murky, constantly shifting thing.

In several shots, the Cyclops tries unsuccessfully to break through the barrier, smashing it with his fists and shoulders. The skilled animation in these cuts conveys a sense of the great force of the Cyclops' blows. The creature picks up a boulder and throws it high into the air, over the barrier. It is wire-supported for a few frames. In live-action cuts, Sinbad's group, fleeing in a row boat, are thrown into the water and the lamp starts to sink.

In a long-shot static matte set-up, the barrier recedes, watched by the growling Cyclops. The creature raises its head, roars and stomps towards the sailors in the water. In an attractive medium shot, it walks behind some miniature rocks, placing its hand on one of them as it passes and growling gently. In the background is the bright blue of a rear-projected sea.

In a series of marvelous long shots, the Cyclops is seen thigh-deep in water. Harryhausen gets away with the illusion by having a number of rocks scattered along the area of the matte line, thereby hiding the point at which puppet and water should come into contact. In a close shot of just the puppet's hand, the Cyclops retrieves the stolen lamp — this time a tiny miniature in the Cyclops' palm. Sinbad, Sokurah and the rest of the sailors are meanwhile escaping in their ship, and the Cyclops roars at them like an angry bull. It turns, walks back to shore and in a medium shot gives the invaders a final growl.

Back in Baghdad, an expansive long shot of the city looks so convincing that it may well be an actual location. If it is a matte shot and miniature, then it is superb.

***The 7th Voyage of Sinbad*: The evil magician Sokurah (Torin Thatcher) commands the Snake Woman to dance.**

Sokurah puts on an entertainment for the caliph, transforming the caliph's daughter's unsuspecting hand-maiden (Nana de Herrera) into a dancing snake woman. He promises her: "You will be the most exotic woman in all Bagdad." This brief sequence, containing eight stop-motion cuts, is characterized by a tone of black humor rare in the genre. Sokurah performs with all the relish and flare of a stage magician and the vain handmaiden is hypnotic, sinister and ridiculous, all at the same time. Herrmann's score is enjoyably exotic. Harryhausen's smooth animation makes the most of this offbeat puppet with its blue-hued skin, striped snake's tail and four writhing arms. Wisely, he keeps the puppet's face in shadow or turned away from the camera so that it will not clash with the appearance of the actress's face.

Sokurah places both the handmaiden and a snake into a giant urn. When he strikes it with an axe, it splits into three pieces which fall away and disappear. In this shot, the urn is a miniature filmed in front of Sokurah striking at thin air in the rear projection. The pieces are animated as they fall away. Accompanied by a trumpet blast, the snake woman is revealed, standing motionless, her tail coiled.

616

The snake woman performs her dance in front of rear projections of the amazed Caliph and his courtiers. In most of these shots, the puppet was animated on a square-edged red rug on the animation table; the rug is aligned so that it seems to be part of a circular rug in the rear projection. The advantage of this is that the puppet can throw a shadow on the floor. However, in one shot an oversight in live-action filming omitted the circular rug with the result that Harryhausen's miniature rug has nothing to match up with. Eagle-eyed viewers might wonder how a circular rug has transformed into a straight-edged one.

One medium shot with no matte is also included in the sequence. In the final long shot, the snake part of the creature starts to take over and the tail wraps around the woman's neck, strangling her. Sokurah throws a powder and the creature is transformed back into the handmaiden.

Plotting to return to the island of Colossa to retrieve the lamp, Sokurah shrinks Princess Parisa (Kathryn Grant) down to six-inch doll size. Harryhausen uses traveling matte to show her arm shrinking as she sleeps in bed. Later, when Sinbad stares down at the tiny Princess standing on a pillow, he uses a static matte which follows the square outline of the pillow, allowing him to insert film of Grant and a giant prop. A later traveling matte of the Princess walking on a table in Sinbad's cabin is less successful—the image of the actress looks washed out.

At this point, Harryhausen had planned another stop-motion episode, with Sinbad's crew attacked by harpy-like sirens, a scene depicted in one of the pre-production sketches he used to sell the film. But the budget prevented him from doing so. Instead there is a well-staged live-action scene featuring only the sound of the screaming sirens, with the tormented crewmen driven insane as their ship is nearly run aground on some rocks.

Later, the ship arrives back at Colossa. This time, Harryhausen's miniature of the mountainous island is seen in bright daylight, and it looks splendid. Below, live-action sea is matted in. The shot recreates some of the magic of the arrival at Skull Island, although it lacks the depth of O'Brien's glass shots and his animated birds.

Since leaving Colossa earlier, the script has been building expectations of another encounter with one of the Cyclops. On the island, the sailors assemble the giant crossbow which they have brought with them for the purpose of killing one of the creatures. This intimidating weapon is seen in full on the beach in one marvelous composite. Harryhausen built the crossbow in miniature and matted it into a live-action scene in which only one of the wheels was built full-size. To give the shot credibility, two sailors stand in front of the full-size wheel, which is carefully aligned with the two-foot miniature.

Sokurah leads Sinbad's troupe through the cave mouth and down some steps into the island's interior. He announces ominously, "This is the Valley of the Cyclops. Beyond it, in the center of the island, are the peaks where the great birds nest." Herrmann's baleful woodwind themes heighten the air of anticipation. Among some rocks, the sailors find the lair of a Cyclops, an enormous spiked club resting against a boulder and a skeleton hanging in a cage. Inside a stone shelter they find the Cyclops' treasure horde, including the magic lamp.

The ten-minute sequence that follows (containing *76* stop-motion cuts) is one of the most remarkable realizations of full-blooded fantasy ever seen on cinema screens. The second encounter with the Cyclops could not be farther from the much-maligned set-piece kind of episode for which Harryhausen's films are often criticized: It is an intricate little story in its own right. Harryhausen puts so many touches of personality into his puppet's actions that the Cyclops becomes at once likable and grotesque. Although he went on to make nine more films, Harryhausen never again indulged himself with a near-human character to such an extent.

As the sailors are ransacking the treasure horde, the stone roof is suddenly slid aside with a deafening sound of grinding rock. They look up to see the Cyclops staring down at them, a low-angle medium shot in which the growling creature looks extremely imposing. The roof and walls of the shelter are miniatures, allowing the Cyclops to rest his claws on them.

In the sequence of events that follows, the Cyclops reaches into the shelter, pulls out some of the sailors and drops them into a wooden cage. Medium shots looking up at the monster are intercut with long shots of it reaching into the shelter; the matte line follows the outline of the shelter, allowing the Cyclops' hand to reach behind the wall. In these long shots, the cage on the left of the Cyclops is also part of the live-action set except for those shots in which the puppet makes physical contact with it. In these, a miniature cage has been matted into the shot along with the Cyclops puppet, and it matches the full-size prop perfectly.

Also intercut in this sequence are several shots inside the shelter in which the Cyclops' huge hand reaches for the sailors. In one of these cuts, the puppet hand is carefully aligned with a rear projection of a sailor being hoisted on wires, so that it seems as though he is being picked up by his belt. In a later, similar shot, the animated hand reaches for Sinbad and knocks him over, then picks him up by his boot. This clever effect was achieved by placing a miniature boot in the Cyclops' hand and meticulously aligning this with the rear image of Mathews being hoisted on an invisible wire.

In long shots of the Cyclops holding the struggling sailors and dropping them into the cage, the animation of the puppet humans is always excellent, especially the shot in which a puppet of Sinbad dangles upside down. Two expressive closeups of the ferocious Cyclops are also included, and at one point the creature vents his fury by roaring powerfully at one of his captives.

With an almost disdainful swipe of the back of its hand, the Cyclops closes the lid of the cage. It picks up the cage and walks off. The three sailors inside the cage can be seen struggling — it can't have been an easy task for Harryhausen to manipulate his tiny puppets through the bars of his miniature.

In a series of long shots in another part of his lair, the Cyclops puts down the cage. Over to one side is a huge roasting spit (another miniature). The Cyclops reaches into the cage and pulls out his intended meal.

Maintaining the visual momentum, Harryhausen switches to another static matte set-up, viewing the spit from slightly below. This attractive reality sandwich shot has a row of boulders in front of the puppet — even though, of course, they are part of the rear projection. The Cyclops walks behind the boulders, clutching the sailor, who screams out breathlessly, as though his chest is being crushed. In a series of shots using the same set-up, the Cyclops ties the puppet-sailor onto the spit and, in a brilliant little bit of fairy tale grotesquerie, slides a wooden stool behind himself and sits down. Live-action flames in the rear projection seem to lick at the puppet human. Milking the black comedy of the moment, Harryhausen has his Cyclops turn the spit several times like a skilled chef. In one cut, a medium shot with a traveling matte of the live-actor on a spit in the foreground, the Cyclops even licks his lips.

With the aid of some more accomplished non-animation trickery, Sinbad pulls the tiny Princess from his pocket and she opens the latch on the cage. Meanwhile, Sokurah has arrived on the scene and is rifling through the Cyclops' treasure horde.

In a series of shots using composite set-ups already described, the Cyclops reacts to the metallic clanks coming from his cave, turns, roars and strides off. In two medium shots, the creature strides purposefully across the frame. In a new static matte long shot, Sokurah runs across a clearing, hotly pursued by the Cyclops. Rear-projected shadows add to the impact of this stunning shot, marred only by a grainy rear screen.

The next four shots — back in the area below the spit — also suffer from grain and this time are lacking any shadows beneath the puppet. But the hectic action keeps most viewers too busy to notice these flaws. The Cyclops stomps into the shot, nearly grabs Sinbad and then gets a spear in its back, thrown by one of the other sailors. Pulling the spear out, the Cyclops throws it to the ground angrily, turns to face the sailor who threw it and strides after him.

Harryhausen maintains the tone of inventive grotesquerie: The Cyclops uproots a tree and uses it as a weapon against the sailors who run around his feet like insects. But the creature doesn't simply wield the tree like a club — he uses it like a pestle, grinding victims into the ground. These eight shots are again marred by grain, but shadows thrown by the puppet onto a carefully matched floor inlay compensate for this and, as before, the pace of events is the most crucial factor. In one of these shots, the Cyclops throws the tree at a sailor. It is wire-supported for a few frames and, in the subsequent shot of it landing on the rear-projected victim, its roots are briefly animated to suggest the impact.

Meanwhile, Sokurah has taken cover in a niche between two boulders. The Cyclops turns his attention away from the sailors, determined to retrieve his lamp from the magician. In two long shots, Sinbad runs into the niche, with the Cyclops pursuing him. The matte line follows the outline of the two boulders forming the niche and also a smaller boulder in the middle distance. This allows the puppet to walk behind the smaller boulder, improving the credibility of the set-up. The Cyclops kneels down and tries to reach in between the rocks.

The subsequent action includes several shots from within the niche, looking out at the Cyclops. At least one source (Ted Newsom in *Cinefantastique* #4) cites these as traveling matte shots, with the actors and rock faces filmed in front of a blue screen. However, this does not appear to be the case. At no point do any part of the actors' bodies pass in front of the puppet, and there is no reason why Harryhausen might not have simply matted down either side of the boulders. In fact, in one of these cuts, the puppet's hand reaches in and passes in front of the rock face where Sokurah is standing, indicating that the rock face could not possibly be a separate blue-screen element. In this cut, the Cyclops' body is obscured by the rock on the right, suggesting that the matte line must begin by running down the right-hand rock face, then veers off to the right to allow the hand to reach in front of the rock. Harryhausen himself has said that there are only eight traveling matte shots in the film. Five of these involve the miniaturized Princess; another has Sinbad's hand placed next to the tiny Princess; the sailor on the spit is another; and the eighth is a set-up in the dragon's lair.

After a very smoothly animated extreme closeup of the monster — blinking and grinding its teeth — Sinbad thrusts a flaming torch into its one eye. The moment of contact is implied by the editing. With characteristically larger-than-life gestures, the Cyclops gets up, clutches its face, screams in pain and walks be-hind the two boulders. Still clutching its face with one hand, the creature drops to its knees again, one arm reaching out blindly, trying to catch its attackers. This splendid moment of Grand Guignol is always met by excited shrieks from audiences.

Sinbad runs from the niche and unties his half-cooked comrade on the spit. In long shot, he returns to the Cyclops, prodding him in the leg with the torch. The monster turns towards him, reaching out blindly. In two closer rear-projection shots of the creature just from the waist down, Sinbad again thrusts his torch into its leg.

Calling out, Sinbad lures the blind, pathetic Cyclops to follow him. A new static matte set-up is used in the next two cuts, long shots in which the sightless monster, arms reaching out warily, follows Sinbad across a sloping clearing.

The finale, in which the blind Cyclops topples over the edge of a cliff, uses a panoramic extreme long shot. For these three shots, Harryhausen built a small five-inch tall model of the Cyclops. The wire-supported puppet is a little stiff as it falls, but this is a good attempt at a notoriously difficult action. In one of the shots there is a brief registration slip-up, with the two halves of the matte coming out of alignment. A final non-animated composite shows the corpse of the Cyclops lying on its back in a river bed.

In order to restore the Princess to her normal size, Sinbad must obtain a piece of shell from the egg of a Roc, a giant bird. Less resourceful artists might now have staged a battle between the sailors and a full-grown Roc, but Harryhausen delays that confrontation. He injects another dose of charm and

The two-headed roc comes to avenge its slain chick in *The 7th Voyage of Sinbad.*

grotesquerie into his plot by showing us a chick hatching from an egg. This is a magical moment and a good example of the special attractions of stop-motion. The model, with two beaked heads, is utterly lifelike. Its furry down was the work of George Lofgren, who had crafted the fur on Mighty Joe Young and also worked uncredited on Harryhausen's four solo black-and-white films. There are nine animation cuts, all slightly impaired by grainy rear screens.

The sailors come across a ten-foot-high egg. The egg and the bundle of twigs on which it rests are miniature, matted into the rocky surroundings. Ominous chomping sounds emanate from the egg. The egg starts to crack and a hole appears at the top. Animated pieces of eggshell drop away convincingly. A beaked head pokes out of the hole and squawks. In the rear projection, the hungry sailors start to bash at the egg with their spears. One half of the egg cracks and falls aside. A beaked head appears, followed, seconds later, by another. Harryhausen deftly balances the humor and surprise of the moment.

621

Eyes blinking, the two heads look this way and that as the astonished sailors look on. The squawking bird takes a step and then sits down, still partly inside the egg. In long shots using a slightly different perspective, the baby Roc stands up, flaps its wings and screeches at the sailors, looking pathetically vulnerable to their spears.

It seems that some animation may have been cut out at this point. The soundtrack jumps and the film cuts from a shot of Sinbad and Sokurah to a composite shot of the chick lying on its back, the sailors sticking spears into it, its heads dropping limply as it expires. What is missing is a shot of the chick being wounded and turned over. Did Harryhausen remove it because, in view of the chick's "cuteness," the shot was too gruesome? Or was it that the animation was unconvincing and so was better omitted?

A weak live-action episode follows, with the Princess climbing into the genie's lamp and befriending him. Eyer's genie, forever longing to be like other boys, is a two-dimensional wimp.

The parent Roc arrives to avenge its slaughtered chick. This is another terrific model, a black-feathered fiend with a much deadlier demeanor than its offspring. Harryhausen carries off the aerial-braced animation consummately, with only a slight strobing effect on the wing movements. The scene is excitingly staged, with plenty of live-action events happening simultaneously (Sinbad tries to rub the genie's lamp as he fights the Roc; Sokurah spears a sailor then runs off with the Princess). Its only flaw is that is isn't developed into something more elaborate. There are 19 stop-motion cuts.

The two-headed bird flies above the heads of the sailors, who are roasting its chick over a fire. A great wind blows up in the live-action film, caused by giant wings that make thumping sound effects as they flap. After hovering for a while, the Roc lands on a boulder (courtesy of a static matte) and knocks a sailor off the edge of the mountain with its beak. All these shots use one long shot set-up.

In a series of much closer shots, the two heads of the Roc peck at the sailors who try to fight them off with swords. In one of these cuts, part of Sinbad's sword is painted on glass for a few frames so that it can appear to strike the front of one of the bird's beaks. Back with the original long-shot, the Roc takes to the air again, snatches up a puppet of Sinbad and flies off.

The two final shots in the sequence are done entirely in miniature. The Roc flies up to its nest at the top of a rocky pillar, an attractive miniature backed by a deep blue sky, which is probably a photo blow-up. The Sinbad puppet is dropped into the nest and the bird flies off.

The two Roc episodes constitute an enjoyable double vignette but they seem hurried and contribute little to the plot. The sailors get their piece of eggshell and Sinbad is separated from them long enough for Sokurah to kidnap the Princess, but the puppets do not function as characters in the way that the Cyclops did. In any event, there is a huge plot loophole here: Sokurah captures the Princess but carelessly leaves behind the lamp, which is supposedly his whole motivation for returning to Colossa.

In order to rescue the Princess, Sinbad must now walk to Sokurah's castle, built within a cave. But a gargantuan dragon guards the cave entrance, kept chained to the wall by the magician and used to prevent attacks by the Cyclopes. Built up over the armature of the rhedosaurus in *The Beast from 20,000 Fathoms*, this magnificent puppet exudes bulky menace. Its blue-green, warty hide is beautifully detailed. Two spiraling horns, a forked tongue and a spiny frill running down its back are complemented by a cold reptilian stare. In best guard dog fashion, it has a steel collar around its neck, attached to a rattling chain that leads through a hole in the cave wall. On the other side of this is a wooden cog that is wound and unwound to restrict the creature's movements so as to allow people to pass. These are unforgettable fairy tale concepts.

In this sequence there are 11 shots of the dragon standing in a convincing miniature cave set. In two of the shots, a superimposed blast of flame is matched to the open mouth of the puppet. The agitated creature walks in a circle, its tail swishing past the camera, then is slowly dragged toward the hole in the wall as Sinbad turns the cog-wheel. Three of the shots use traveling matte to place Sinbad in the foreground, nervously inching past the dragon. A minor complaint is the fact that the traveling matte shots conflict with the all-miniature shots in that they are more brightly lit. A bladder inside the puppet is inflated and deflated frame by frame to suggest that the monster is breathing.

Sinbad arrives at Sokurah's castle, another highly detailed miniature, matted into footage of some shadowy caves filmed in Mallorca. The inside of the magician's castle has a believable musty and medieval feel to it and the decor includes a skeleton hanging from the ceiling. This is, of course, an important establishing shot for the action that is to follow. First, however, Sokurah restores the Princess to her normal size, a sequence involving more accomplished static and traveling matte effects.

Sinbad refuses to hand over the lamp until he and the Princess are safely on board the ship. In response, the magician brings the skeleton to life and orders it to kill Sinbad. This two-minute, fifteen-second episode is classic Harryhausen, a set-piece with a superb setting and equally superb control over pacing. It is a genre archetype, demonstrating how stop-motion is the only medium that can breathe life into free-standing fantastic figures. Surprisingly, there are only four more stop-motion cuts in this sequence than there were in the scene with the adult Roc. The reason why Sinbad's battle with the skeleton is a much more successful scene is because Harryhausen spares no effort in making this as visually dramatic as possible. The battle with the Roc used only three set-ups whereas the skeleton fight uses 16 different composite set-ups (including nine distinct static matte designs) in 23 stop-motion cuts. By constantly shifting the point of view in this way, Harryhausen insures that viewers are caught up in the flow of the action. And, unlike the Roc sequence, the skeleton fight includes a high number of very effective instances of puppet and actor interacting.

The fight, spilling out from the magician's laboratory and onto a spiral staircase, is brilliantly choreographed.

Mathews is extremely good at feigning the sword-play, bringing his sword to an abrupt halt in midair at a point where the sword of the animated skeleton would be added months later in Harryhausen's animation studio.

In long shot, the skeleton, hanging in the foreground, drops to the ground as Sinbad, the Princess and Sokurah look on in the rear screen. Its feet fall just out of frame, so the shot did not require a matte. Ingeniously, Harryhausen has his creation come to life gradually, as though awakening from a deep sleep. With its back to the camera, it sways slightly from side to side, its arms hanging limply, its head down. In three medium shots, it slowly pulls itself upright, the grinning skull face looking straight ahead. As it takes its first few steps, its arms still hang loosely by its sides.

"Kill! Kill him!" commands Sokurah in an intense extreme closeup. When the skeleton reaches for a sword and a shield, Harryhausen could have made his job easier by having a miniature sword, shield and wall in the foreground. Instead, he chooses to make the shot look a lot better by introducing a matte line and putting part of the rear-projected image into the foreground. The matte line runs down the edge of a wall, allowing the skeleton to reach behind it and aiding the illusion that the puppet really is on the live-action set. The skeleton turns to face Sinbad, who jumps over a table and engages it in battle.

Herrmann's marvelous "clackety" score starts up at this moment, at once grotesque and exciting. In a clever and dynamic medium shot, the rear-projected Sinbad at first appears to be in the foreground with the puppet, sword raised aloft, looking back at him. But as they lock swords, Sinbad circles around behind the skeleton, the actor seemingly walking 270 degrees around the puppet. Making the illusion even more plausible, Sinbad's sword strikes the puppet's shield — actually painted on glass for a few frames so that it seems to be between shield and camera.

Sinbad runs behind a foreground table, immediately pursued by the skeleton, whose sword smashes several vials on it. This masterly bit of interaction required that a sword was held by an out-of-frame assistant and sliced into the vials. At the exact moment when this live action sword swings out of the frame, the skeleton runs in, rushing behind the table, whose edge forms a matte line. The combination of the smashed vials and the design of the matte really makes the puppet seem part of the live action. Harryhausen goes beyond even this: His puppet spins around as it runs past, owing to the momentum of the sword stroke. The cut continues as puppet and actor lock swords again, including two instances of a painted sword passing in front of the miniature sword.

In long shot, Sinbad and the skeleton face each other from opposite sides of a low table, swords clashing. Another partial painted sword enhances the impression of physical contact for a few frames. In medium shot, the skeleton lunges forward with his sword arm, his open mouth agape as though grinning wickedly. In the same cut, the skeleton's sword is knocked out of its hand, wire-supported for a few frames. Not to be bested, the skeleton hurls its shield at Sinbad — another dynamic moment, with Harryhausen demonstrating his understanding of human gesture.

The skeleton picks up his sword again and in a superb long shot battles Sinbad in a doorway, actor and puppet making seven or eight expertly timed thrusts and parries. The puppet is seen in full, its feet in contact with the floor. In an eye-catching medium shot, Sinbad dashes out through the doorway followed by the skeleton, thanks to a vertical matte line running down the edge of the door.

The two combatants run out into a shadowy area of the cave beneath a spiral staircase. The matte line follows a foreground rock, so that actor and puppet seem to emerge from behind it. The next cut, in which the skeleton forces Sinbad backwards onto the steps, is marred by the contrast between the brightly lit puppet and the grainy rear screen. Once again, however, the thrilling pace encourages a willing "suspension of disbelief."

The skeleton forces Sinbad up the steps, pushing him backwards and walking past him. The matte line follows the zigzag of the steps. In a medium shot, the skeleton forces his sword towards his opponent's throat, pushed back by Sinbad's sword — an effective bit of miming by Mathews. The skeleton runs up around the steps and out of view, the matte line running down the edge of the central pillar.

The image of a spiral staircase has been a creepy ingredient in many films but this one has a special nightmare quality — it leads to nowhere, terminat-

ing in midair. The skeleton looks almost startled when it realizes this. In the final long shots, with the puppet standing at the very edge fighting with Sinbad, the top of the steps are a miniature, but so carefully lit that it looks like part of the rear projection. A chilling medium shot has the grinning skeleton slashing its sword wildly. Sinbad knocks the skeleton's sword away again. When it looks around and realizes that it has nowhere left to run, Sinbad brings his sword down on its back, sending it crashing over the edge. The puppet's fall is very well executed, and as it falls it throws a shadow on the underside of the steps, confirming that they are a miniature prop. Finally, a live-action prop skeleton smashes on the rocks below.

After this magnificent episode, no one would have been surprised if Harryhausen had chosen to wind down his plot to a conclusion. But he still has several tricks up his sleeve.

Sinbad and the Princess flee from the castle and must cross a rocky bridge over a chasm full of bubbling lava. Trying to cut off their escape, Sokurah causes the bridge to explode and fall away. The pieces of the bridge are miniatures animated against a rear projection of the actors. Hoping to transform the genie into a normal boy, the Princess throws the lamp into the lava river, and in a brief effect Harryhausen uses static matte to show the prop lamp sinking into the live-action lava.*

Sinbad and the Princess have to pass the dragon again. In a series of seven shots, the great beast has its chain

---

*In Harryhausen's original storyboard sketches, Sinbad encounters giant rats as he tries to escape. He battles with one of the rodents on the rocky bridge, eventually making good his escape when the bridge is destroyed, preventing the rats from following.

wound tight again, so that the two may sneak past. It lifts up one foreleg, trying to loosen the annoying collar. Three of these shots are traveling mattes with the actors in the foreground.

The pair run out of the cave mouth into the sunlight and are immediately confronted by another of the island's fantastic denizens—a second Cyclops. Many viewers assumed this to be the same creature that Sinbad has presumed dead earlier, even though it is distinguished by having on its head not one but two horns, which curve forward unlike the backward-curving horn of the first Cyclops. Harryhausen should have emphasized the differences further, perhaps by having the puppet's goat-hair black or blond, unlike the brown hair of its fellow. The puppet uses the armature of the Ymir in *20 Million Miles to Earth*, stripped down and reassembled. Fourteen inches high (four inches shorter than the other Cyclops), the puppet's scale permits it to be seen in the same shots as the dragon. A planned battle between two Cyclopes was dropped because of cost.

In long shot, the bellowing Cyclops looks down at Sinbad and the Princess on the beach, then struts after them into the cave (the matte runs down the edge of the cave mouth). Inside the cave, a large area of the middle distance, surrounded on three sides by the rear-projected live-action cave, has been matted out so that the puppet can walk into it. The dragon is seen in three more traveling matte shots of Sinbad and the Princess creeping past it. Sinbad cuts a rope that releases the cog-wheel, allowing the dragon to pull back on the chain to its full extent, eventually snapping it.

The animated broken chain swings back realistically.

The Cyclops, standing in the shadowy matted area of the cave, growls apprehensively at the dragon. The dragon matches it with a mighty roar. The Cyclops half turns away, as though contemplating avoiding a fight. The dragon roars again, its huge mouth gaping wide. The Cyclops growls back again, then the dragon steps forward—in the process revealing that its gait is, not surprisingly, identical to that of the rhedosaurus.

The battle that follows contains more intricate, theatrically enjoyable animation but lacks the dramatic punch of earlier scenes. More than any other scene in the film, it comes across as very much a gratuitous set-piece. Unlike other sequences, only two set-ups are used: the shadowy matte design inside the cave and an unimaginative long shot composite on the beach outside. It also suffers because Herrmann's score at this point is uncharacteristically ponderous.

The dragon steps into the cave matte set-up, biting the Cyclops' arm. With its free hand, the Cyclops thumps the dragon in the head. The following three stop-motion shots (intercut with standard live-action cutaways of Sinbad and the Princess looking concerned) all take place in the same shadowy set-up. Its tail snaking about violently, the dragon is caught by the Cyclops in a stranglehold and forced to the ground. The Cyclops backs up, delivers another punch to its attacker's head, then gets bitten in the arm again. The two creatures edge backwards out of the right of the frame.

The fight continues out on the beach beneath precipitous cliff faces.

Nine stop-motion cuts, intercut with shots of Sinbad and the Princess looking on, all use the same long-shot design. A floor inlay, expertly matched to the sandy surroundings, allows both puppets to throw shadows. The Cyclops backs out of the cave followed by the dragon and immediately grabs it around the neck. Forcing the dragon to its knees, the Cyclops pounds at its head with its fists. The beasts separate and in an imaginative touch the Cyclops momentarily falls back against the dragon's body.

Seeming to have the upper hand, the Cyclops grips the squealing dragon around its head. In the rear projection, Sinbad and the Princess sneak behind the battling giants. The Cyclops delivers another powerful punch, the creatures separate then lock in combat again. The dragon bites the Cyclops' shoulder, eliciting a wide-mouthed roar. The dragon forces its opponent to the ground, places one foot on the Cyclops, clamps its mighty jaws around its neck and drags it along the beach. A second time, the dragon bites into the Cyclops' throat and the arms of the prostrate Cyclops flop down limply. The dragon walks around its slain foe, then stands on it — a credible bit of animal behavior suggesting it is protecting a meal from scavengers.

Sokurah runs into the same long-shot set-up and calls upon the dragon to help him pursue the sailors. "Follow!" he cries out and the dragon roars back at him. Apparently well-trained, the dragon turns, gives a snake-like hiss and walks after the magician.

In two spectacular static matte designs, the growling dragon follows Sokurah, who runs just a few feet ahead of it. The power of these shots comes from the proximity of tiny human and enormous dragon. In the second of these designs, the dragon comes from behind a matted rock face on the left. In the foreground, a sparkling blue lake looks like it may be a separate element. Another fabulous image follows, a long shot in which the dragon emerges from the cave with the carved face above it, Sokurah running just ahead of it.

Harryhausen animated a shot in which the dragon picks up one of Sinbad's men in its jaws and munches on him, but he subsequently cut this out of the release print, considering it to be unnecessarily gruesome.

He has saved one of his most fanciful conceptions until now. The great wooden crossbow has been assembled by Sinbad's men. On seeing the dragon, Sinbad calls them into action: "Pull for your lives!" he cries, urging them to haul back on the crossbow. The giant arrow is fired, hurtling straight into the dragon's chest. In long shot, the beast realistically recoils from the impact.

Two forceful shots of the impaled dragon rearing up are shot with the camera looking up at the creature, emphasizing its great size. Crashing back to the ground again in long shot, the dragon lands on the screaming magician, killing him. Harryhausen makes this tricky piece of animation look effortless; it's a haunting image that he would use again in *Jason and the Argonauts* in the shot where the giant statue Talos falls on one of the characters.

The mortally wounded dragon gets to its feet again, the arrow still embedded deep in its chest. Meanwhile, Sinbad, the Princess and the sailors have escaped to their ship and are setting sail.

In the dragon's protracted death scene, Harryhausen gives the monster some pathos — who could not feel some sorrow at the sight of such a majestic beast expiring painfully? But there are no comparisons with *King Kong*'s death scene since we have never been asked to perceive the creature as a sympathetic character.

In closeup, the monster screams pitifully. In medium shot, it crosses the frame in pursuit of the sailors who have harmed it. It comes from behind some rocks in an effective static matte set-up, fleeing sailors at its feet. In a final static matte design, seen from Sinbad's perspective on the retreating ship, the dragon walks to the edge of the beach, its legs starting to collapse beneath it. Some small rocks along the shore help to break up the matte line. The weakening beast tries to get to its feet again, only to collapse back down. In closeup, the dragon raises its head melodramatically, emitting a subdued scream as though expecting the end. In the final long shot, the head slumps down and the snaking tail at last lies still.

The 7th Voyage Of Sinbad did not even receive a nomination for 1958's Special Effects Academy Award, which was won by Tom Howard for *Tom Thumb*. Perhaps the Academy objected to the fact that much of the film was shot in Spain instead of Hollywood. Or perhaps they were simply unable to accept that a film about fantastic monsters could be worthy of their interest. Regardless, this flawed masterpiece has a pivotal position in film fantasy and remains a testament to the possibilities of stop-motion photography.

Sinbad and the Eye of the Tiger

1977. Columbia. Prod: Charles H. Schneer, Ray Harryhausen. D: Sam Wanamaker. Scr: Beverley Cross. Story: Beverley Cross and Ray Harryhausen. Ph: Ted Moore. Mus: Roy Budd. Art: Geoffrey Drake. Special Visual Effects Created by Ray Harryhausen. Stop-Motion Model Sculpture (uncredited): Tony McVey.

Cast: Patrick Wayne, Margaret Whiting, Patrick Troughton, Jane Seymour, Taryn Power, Kurt Christian, Peter Mayhew.

Rating: ☆☆☆   Stop-Motion: ☆☆☆½

Eye of the Tiger came in for a hail of adverse criticism, much of it justified, when it was released. But, like many films that disappoint on initial contact, it improves with repeated viewing and in retrospect is one of Harryhausen's more enjoyable and imaginative pictures.

It is a much better conceived film than effects vehicles like *Mysterious Island, Jason and the Argonauts, One Million Years B.C.* and *Clash of the Titans*, holding together satisfactorily as a dramatic entity and not marred by the erratic pacing that characterizes other Harryhausen films. Several of its animated characters are recurring figures crucial to the plot, not merely creatures to be met once and destroyed. *Eye of the Tiger* has a generous variety of unusual locations, including the startling carved rock faces of Melanthius' island (filmed in Jordan) and the polar regions surrounding Hyperborea. (This is more than can be said for Harryhausen's next film — *Clash of the Titans*— which was seriously lacking in exotic locales.)

The plentiful effects are superb, and although there is no one real showstopping sequence, this hardly matters because there is so much else to enjoy. The baboon — an ape whose anthropomorphic gestures often recall Harryhausen's animation of Mighty Joe Young — and the Troglodyte are two of the animator's most unforgettable characters. The Shrine of the Four Elements, with its huge, curving stairway, sizzling aurora borealis effects and crashing stalactites, is the most impressive location in a fantasy film since Skull Island.

But the film has some serious deficiencies. Director Sam Wanamaker has some enthusiasm for his subject but ultimately seems resigned to the fact that anything he can contribute must take a back seat to the effects scenes which Harryhausen directs. Despite a lively plot, Beverley Cross' script never comes to life and is littered with clumsy dialogue which defeats the lackluster cast. Only Patrick Troughton as bearded old magician Melanthius and Margaret Whiting as sorceress Zenobia put any sparkle into their roles. Patrick Wayne as Sinbad and heroines Jane Seymour and Taryn Power are all bland. Roy Budd's score is effective in the slower passages, including a playful theme during scenes with the baboon prince and a poundingly repetitive

motif suggesting the mindless power of the Minoton as he rows Zenobia's ship, but it is hopelessly inadequate at suggesting the bizarre and exciting tone of action scenes. His music actually works to the detriment of the battle with the three ghouls and the fight between Trog and the saber-tooth tiger, undermining the impact of what could have been classic episodes.

Frank Jackson in *Cinefantastique* #2 concludes that "the acting and writing [in Harryhausen's pictures] are going downhill" while Leonard Maltin really slams the film: "Dreary ... unusually hackneyed script ... disappointing Ray Harryhausen effects, and goes on forever." Roy Kinnard's *Beasts and Behemoths* gives a cursory account of the film and dismisses it as "a pretty turgid affair."

It *is* a long film. At a running time of 113 minutes, it was Harryhausen's longest film to date (eight minutes longer than *Golden Voyage of Sinbad*). Amazingly, a further 20 minutes were cut out to improve pace, including some animation shots. There is a huge amount of effects work in the film. Harryhausen spent 13 months on the animation sequences, compared to a mere four months which it took to shoot the live action. Altogether, including preproduction, it was three years from conception to release.

The general standard of the composite shots is extremely high. Of course, there are moments when a rear screen is too grainy, when a traveling matte looks too obvious or the color of a floor inlay is not perfectly matched. But these flaws are the exception and it seems like doing Harryhausen a disservice to have to

Sinbad and the Eye of the Tiger (1977): Three ghouls are conjured out of the flames to battle Sinbad.

point them out. For example, a series of traveling mattes depicts Sinbad's party walking around Melanthius' island and, although there is no spill, these always look like effects shots. Yet at the climax, when actors and puppets are placed into the miniature set by traveling matte, the results are superb. Many of the rear-screen plates were shot using a new higher-grade Eastman film stock with the result that some of the composites (most notably the first encounter with the Troglodyte in Hyperborea) are some of the most perfect ever put on film. Yet others, including some of the shots during the scenes with the ghouls and the

giant walrus, still suffer glaringly from the kind of generation differences that have always been the bugbear of this kind of filming.

The film opens with an effects shot, a brief nighttime view of a matte painting of the distant city of Charak, its towers glowing pink above the live-action sea below. Location shots (filmed in Spain) of the market at the foot of the city walls are backed by a detailed miniature of the city, the matte line seamlessly following the battlements along the top of the wall.

Evil witch Zenobia and her son Rafi (Kurt Christian) have lured Sinbad and

630

his men to their tent and she conjures up three other-worldly ghouls to attack him. This entertaining sequence recreates on a smaller scale the thrills of the skeleton battle in *Jason*, with three fabulous models, inventive choreography and a number of ingenious technical flourishes. But the pacing never grabs the attention the way that *Jason*'s scene does, and this is partly due to Budd's drab score. Part of the fight was cut out by Harryhausen because some of it was repetitive. This is unusual for him because he normally has one eye on the budget and has meticulously storyboarded every animation cut that he wants in the finished scene.

The sequence begins with a closeup of Zenobia's eyes transforming into cat's eyes, a disappointing "locked-off" effect that is used again at the climax when she transfers her spirit into the saber-tooth tiger. The ghouls rise one by one out of a fire in the tent and stand poised for battle, gently swaying. They are about five feet tall, with huge, colored, insect-like eyes and scrawny yet fleshy bodies, and they chirrup like beetles. The foreground floor is a miniature and the flames in which they are standing are part live-action in the rear screen and part a third element which has been superimposed after the animation has been added.

Two medium shots and two close-ups afford good looks at these fine models: Like all the models in the film, their paintwork is detailed and believable. In long shot, one ghoul scoops up some burning embers and throws them at Sinbad. Like later shots in which a ghoul brandishes a flaming torch, this effect was ingeniously achieved by having a

black-clad actor performing with flames against a black background, resulting in a strip of film with only the image of the flame. This is superimposed against the live-action Sinbad and then the puppets are synchronized with the resultant image by means of conventional rear-projection animation.

One of the ghouls has a sword, another an axe, and when they rush at Sinbad, the third ghoul stops to pick up a staff. During the battle, the puppets' feet sometimes disappear below a matte line but this is hardly noticed amid all the frenetic swordplay. In a nice minor detail, one of the ghouls drops its sword and picks it up again. Medium shots of the ghouls brandishing their weapons again recall similar shots of the skeletons in *Jason*. In one quick cut, Sinbad's hand and boot both pass in front of the puppet when he kicks it in the head; these must be painted on glass for a few frames.

There is a bafflingly good moment when one of the sailors, in long shot, thrusts his sword clean through the chest of one of the ghouls and it emerges from its back, now a miniature sword; presumably the positioning of the miniature sword obscures the end of the real sword in the rear plate. A humorous medium shot has the ghoul look down at its chest, realize that it is unhurt and then resume fighting.

A pan in the animation camera follows the green-eyed ghoul as it walks across the tent, its axe glinting in the firelight. In a classic moment of interaction, the ghoul swings its axe at Sinbad, who ducks, and one of the pillars supporting the tent is split in two (pulled by off-screen invisible wires) as the ghoul falls to his knees after the momentum of his spin. The red-eyed ghoul now threatens Sinbad with the burning torch. When Sinbad parries with his sword, part of it is painted on glass, allowing it to seem to be in front of the torch. The ghoul nearly topples over backwards and Sinbad kicks it, his boot again passing in front of the model.

Another ghoul whacks one of the sailors on the behind with its sword (the actor has to mime the impact), then is sent reeling when Sinbad kicks it across the tent (this interaction implied by the alignment of the puppet in front of the rear screen). When the three ghouls chase the sailors out of the tent, the ingenious matte follows not only the opening in the cloth but also a central pillar, so that the ghouls walk behind the pillar and then out into the night. This extra touch helps make them seem like part of the shot.

The contrast between different elements deteriorates outside, where Harryhausen has less control over lighting. In several shots the models are brightly lit and in sharp focus whereas the location-shot backgrounds are dark and fuzzy. A vertical matte allows the ghouls to be seen running out of the tent into the market. Grainy rear projections mar medium shots of them battling Sinbad, but long shots are much better, with the matte line in some following a pile of sacks in the foreground and in others some large barrels, making it seem like the models are right in the shots.

One ghoul swings its sword wildly and sends a small barrel in the rear plate flying. Several medium shots of the twittering creatures are intercut with the long shots. Two long shots of all three ghouls use a miniature foreground that is very well matched to the live ground. Two attractive long shots show Sinbad arriving at a pile of timber with the ghouls running into the shot after him from the left. Two closer shots, in which Sinbad kicks a barrel at them, use a well-integrated floor inlay, allowing the puppets to throw shadows on the ground.

The pile of timber is actually a miniature: When Sinbad cuts the rope holding the logs, he is in fact acting in front of a blue screen. The ghouls walk past the timber, only to be crushed by the falling logs, a tricky effect which could have looked awkward. Harryhausen carries off the animation expertly but ironically is badly let down again by a grainy rear screen which makes this shot look too much like "a special effect." Only two of the logs are animated; the rest are miniature logs in a rear projection.

The next morning, Sinbad and his men are loading their ship to sail in search of Melanthius, the Hermit of Casgar. In the background, a good miniature of the walled city (actually 18 inches long) is matted onto the horizon. Even better are shots of Zenobia's castle at night, a miniature backed by a painting of clouds, live-action sea and rocks below, a real moon and fog superimposed to lend an extra touch of eeriness.

The script has up until now teased us about the nature of the horrible fate that has befallen Prince Kassim. All is now revealed when a cage being loaded onto the ship is dropped and turns out to contain a live baboon. Four animation cuts, all using the same static matte set-up, show the baboon walking excitedly around its cage and screeching, then calming and sitting down after his sister Farah (Seymour) talks to him. It looks as if only the back of the cage existed on the live set, with the front and floor of the cage being a miniature that is aligned with it.

From this humble beginning, the baboon prince's character is developed until he becomes the film's most significant animated character. Many viewers and no doubt most children (the primary target audience) are fooled by Harryhausen's superb animation into believing that this is a real ape. In reality, baboons cannot be trained to cry, write and get angry on cue, so animation was the only viable alternative. Tony McVey's anatomically correct sculpting of the model is complemented by a realistic fur covering which at times experiences a ruffling effect during animation that recalls the bristling fur of Kong. The baboon is one of stop-motion's most memorable characters, on a par with the genre's other great apes Kong and Mighty Joe Young. He is a dynamic character, regressing slowly during the course of the picture into a more and more savage state, and this helps give the plot a sense of urgency: Sinbad has to find a way of transforming him back into the prince before it is too late.

After a potent live-action scene in which a mechanical heart is put into the chest of the dormant Minoton, causing its eyes to open and its fingers to flex, we are back on board Sinbad's ship. The baboon prince is below deck playing chess with Farah in a scene that finds Harryhausen putting more character into his animation than we have seen since *Mighty Joe Young*. In fact, some shots (after the baboon has climbed back into

his cage and looks out dejectedly) might well have been modeled on similar moments in that earlier film.

The baboon is sitting on a stool at one side of the chess table, scratching his thigh, gently swishing his tail and making contented growling noises. He moves a chess piece on the board, placing it amongst the live-action pieces in the rear screen. Some closeups reveal what a marvelously expressive model this is. When Hassan bursts in, the baboon jumps down to the floor and there are a couple of rear-screen shots looking over the puppet's shoulder at the cowering sailor. Shots of the baboon climbing back into his cage and pulling the door closed after him, with Farah standing to the side, are perfectly matched composites that look like one piece of film. When the baboon writes "I am Kassim" on the wall, Harryhausen has added a bit of each letter frame by frame. Budd's score catches the right tone in this sad but humorous scene.

The Minoton now gets his first major scene, rowing Zenobia's ship so that it rams a small boat and then gruesomely killing one of the survivors. The Minoton is a silent but sinister force, mindlessly powering his mistress' ship and obeying all her commands. He provides a well-judged contrast to the sympathetic animated characters of the Troglodyte and the baboon. Harryhausen's animation perfectly conveys a sense of mechanical threat, a feeling that could not have been achieved if a man in a costume had been used. Of course, economics dictate that a man in a costume (Peter Mayhew — Chewbacca in the *Star Wars* films) is used in many long shots and these are always perfectly

A delightfully surreal chess game between a baboon and a princess is a highlight of *Sinbad and the Eye of the Tiger.*

matched up with the closer stop-motion shots.

There are 12 animation cuts in this first scene, initially showing him at the rowing machine which powers three pairs of oars. In a long shot of the ship's deck (including a small floor inlay to allow him to throw a shadow), he walks over to the side of the ship. Several shots look up at him from the struggling soldier's point of view, including one in which he picks up a vicious-looking boat hook. He spears the soldier, then, in two cuts using the same long-shot static matte used before, he waves the impaled soldier high in the air and discards him over the other side of the ship. The animation of the squirming puppet soldier (the only puppet human in the film) is very fluid. Displaying an unexpected bit of character, the Minoton takes a step towards the edge of the boat to check that his victim is dead.

The middle section of the film is a race between Zenobia and Sinbad to the land of Hyperborea. The script cuts back and forth between the two parties and includes many quick cuts of the Minoton at the helm of the witch's ship. Some of these are in-camera medium shots looking from behind the puppet, with Zenobia and Rafi in the background.

Another is a static matte with Rafi standing in the foreground. Many are enhanced by superimposed fog during the night shots. One is a very attractive shot in bright daylight of the Minoton still pumping away mindlessly at the oar control. The lighting on the puppet matches nicely with the bright live-action image.

After a distracting series of traveling matte shots (mentioned earlier) in which Sinbad's party arrives at Melanthius's cave (the budget didn't stretch to taking the cast to Jordan), the baboon prince is introduced to the hermit. There are eight cuts of the baboon in his cage, with Harryhausen as ever keeping a careful eye on pacing and using three different (but similar) rear-screen perspectives. In deft moments of implied interaction, the baboon bites Melanthius' finger and then licks his daughter Dione's hand, all the time making little growls and squeaks. Once again the cage is part miniature and part live-action.

The scene in which the baboon is examined in Melanthius' laboratory is a pivotal sequence and one of the most delicate moments in Harryhausen's career. It makes you wish that he had done more scenes like it. There are 20 animation cuts and five different composite perspectives.

The baboon lies on his back on a table making slight, very smoothly animated movements as the hermit examines him. The matte line follows the edge of the table. Sinbad helps him into a sitting position, his hand obscured behind the puppet's back. This composite is spoiled because Melanthius' eye-line is incorrectly looking at an area behind the puppet. A closer shot has the baboon recoiling from some smelling salts. Other shots from a third perspective have a more ambitious matte line that follows the outline of some foreground vials, improving the sense of "being in there." In one of these cuts the puppet's hand momentarily disappears behind one of the vials when of course we should be able to see it through the glass.

A mirror is held up to the baboon (achieved by a split screen in which the matte line follows the outline of the mirror and the fingers that hold it up) and there are some marvelous closeups of the distressed ape, including an animated tear (made of gelatin) that trickles down one cheek. He puts his hands over his face to hide his despair but Melanthius, having now realized that the baboon really is Prince Kassim (because he did not attack his reflection as would a true baboon), offers his hand in friendship. In the next two cuts, one a long shot, one closer, puppet and actor actually shake hands — an intimate yet basically simple bit of interaction with Harryhausen carefully aligning the two images. Purists might complain of a little jiggle in the second of these shots, but in the first the illusion is superb, the two hands genuinely seeming to be making contact.

There are about a dozen animation cuts of the baboon during the scene in which Melanthius conducts a chemical experiment to demonstrate the powers discovered by the Arimaspi, the original inhabitants of Hyperborea. Dione hands the ape two bananas which he carefully peels and eats, shots requiring a switch from real to miniature bananas. As the ape looks out anxiously through the bars of his cage, waiting to hear if Melanthius will agree to go to Hyperborea, it looks as though Harryhausen has made his job easier by freeze-framing the rear image of the laboratory: There are no actors behind the puppet, so there was no need to advance the projector frame-by-frame.

The group sets sail for Hyperborea. After a couple of shots of the baboon in his cage on deck, and two more of the Minoton rowing Zenobia's ship in pursuit, there is an entertaining live-action effects passage in which the miniaturized Zenobia sneaks around the ship trying to discover Melanthius' destination. Some of the traveling mattes showing her running along the floor of his room are excellent, sometimes with the studio floor on which she is standing part of the matte, allowing her to throw a shadow. But later shots in which Melanthius tries to catch her are substandard: She is brightly lit while the background is grainy. Two of these shots have Zenobia clasped in a giant (but entirely static) hand — a throwback to *King Kong*. These shots are quite well done, with Melanthius' eyes correctly aligned with his catch.

Intercut with all this are scenes of Dione trying to help the baboon to read. One clever matte around a foreground barrel is let down again by a grainy rear image. There are two well-staged bits of interaction when he knocks a book to the floor (i.e., the actress simply drops it) and when she slaps his hand. And Harryhausen puts further deft touches of characterization into shots of him sitting down in his cage and looking miserable.

He starts to get restless when he smells the presence of Zenobia. There are two cuts of the tiny witch running

below the cage as Kassim looks down: These shots are made up of three elements. Kassim gets more and more agitated, pushes the door of his cage open, leaps out, strides past Dione and goes over to a pile of books behind which Zenobia is hiding. In the last of these cuts, a floor inlay is very well matched in, the puppet throwing an all-important shadow. But shots of Zenobia bluescreened in front of the baboon suffer from the same visual separation that spoiled similar shots with Melanthius.

Captured, she is placed in an upturned glass jar on the hermit's desk. This image of a tiny character being examined by giants is a recurring one in Harryhausen's films and has a direct parallel in *The 3 Worlds of Gulliver* where Kerwin Mathews is trapped in a similar situation. Likewise, the effect is intriguingly good because Zenobia walks behind reflected light on the glass; perhaps Harryhausen has introduced the glass into the shot by means of a static matte as he would one of his puppets. The glass is certainly not superimposed because Melanthius's hand distorts when it passes behind it. Perhaps just the area of reflected light is superimposed.

Harryhausen now indulges in another great set-piece: an attack by a giant hornet. Of course it's gratuitous; why Melanthius should be so stupid as to feed the hornet some of Zenobia's enlarging fluid is never explained. The scene's only function in the plot is as a distraction, so that Zenobia, transformed back into a seagull, can escape from Sinbad's ship. There are about 24 animation cuts in among a well-staged confusion of activity: the cowering Melanthius, Sinbad and his men rushing in and out,

Zenobia trying to escape and the screaming baboon. (In a couple of shots where the baboon is barely noticed in the background, an extra in an ape costume is used.) The buzzing, flapping insect is a natural for stop-motion photography. The strobing effect of its wings for once looks perfectly natural because this is how we see insect wings in real life.

The scene begins beautifully with the hornet growing in size on Melanthius' desk, the hermit cowering behind it and Zenobia looking on from her jar on the right. Harryhausen gradually brings the puppet nearer to his camera frame-by-frame to suggest the size increase (but was a smaller model used for the very first shots?). There is no real interaction during this sequence: most shots just show the hornet flying in front of a rear screen as actors react to it, or show the hornet flying straight at the camera. Recognizing this, Harryhausen tries to increase the sense of pace by introducing camera pans into five shots. It looks as though he has increased the size of the rear screen (or moved his camera closer) and simply panned across frame-by-frame following the puppet, rather than actually having a pan in the background footage. The scene ends when Sinbad throws his knife; a prop of the hornet is pinned against a beam in the ceiling. It's a fine little scene but never quite lives up to the promise of those great nightmarish opening shots of it enlarging.

Three fine daytime cuts show the baboon seated on deck playing chess with Melanthius. His savage nature is starting to take over and he knocks the chess pieces onto the floor (they are pulled over by an invisible wire).

There is a good live-action scare scene back on Zenobia's ship when she discovers that there was insufficient enlarging fluid left and one of her feet is still the webbed claw of a gull. "Not enough! Not enough!" she wails tormentedly, and has to limp through the rest of the film.

The icy wastes of the Arctic are extremely well done, one of the film's great unsung achievements. It is a combination of location photography in the Spanish Pyrenees, studio footage in a huge tank measuring 400 feet by 300 feet in Malta, a few matte paintings, stock footage of collapsing icebergs and avalanches, traveling mattes of the actors and superimposed snow. The studio tank was filled with imitation pillars of ice and a tunnel leading to the entrance to the Arimaspi shrine. The matte paintings include one looking out through the mouth of a painted cave and two of huge rocky fissures, all lending atmosphere to the overall effect.

The three-and-a-half-minute attack by the walrus ("Walrus giganticus — prehistoric!" yells Melanthius, making it up as he goes along) is another great showcase for Harryhausen's talents, featuring an enjoyably offbeat monster and an unusual setting. Initially the composites are fine but through the scene they get more careless, the rear projections clearly a generation out of step with the model.

The opening shot in which the beast breaks through the ice is a complex five-element composite. The model is animated against a rear-screen; then splashing water is superimposed over this image. The actors are a traveling matte in front of this. Finally, falling snow is superimposed.

The hornet from *Sinbad and the Eye of the Tiger*, as it was displayed at London's Museum of the Moving Image.

A quick cut of Sinbad running back to the camp has been speeded up — this sort of unconvincing attempt to quicken pace should have died out in the 1940s. The walrus has a realistic leathery hide, and closeups give us a good look at its whiskery face and massive tusks. It shuffles along credibly into a static matte set-up and there are two successful pieces of interaction when sailors throw lumps of ice at it. (The ice is switched for miniature props, animated bits of which fall to the ground when they break up.)

Another good composite is a long shot of the group of sailors on one side of the shot facing the walrus. In a closer shot, one of them is sent flying when the walrus butts him with a tusk and he disappears beneath the broken ice. Sinbad throws a spear straight into the walrus' chest; as so often in other films, Harryhausen makes this look so easy.

The walrus shuffles into the camp, knocking aside a box with his tusks. It's a well-synchronized effect but it is at this point that the rear screens start to look grainy. As the monster turns away, another spear is thrown into its hide. Three sailors throw a net over its head, a miniature net carefully aligned with the live-action one. There is lots of to-ing and fro-ing, then one sailor gets flattened by a puppet flipper. Having decided it is outnumbered, the walrus

COLUMBIA FILMS présente une
Production CHARLES H. SCHNEER
**SINBAD ET
L'ŒIL DU TIGRE**
Filmé en DYNARAMA
Distribué par WARNER-COLUMBIA FILMS

Visa Ministériel n° 7 391

Trog, the most vital and credible of all Harryhausen's humanoid creations, was a magnificent presence in *Sinbad and the Eye of the Tiger*.

heads back to the water, oblivious to the fact that it is dragging one of the sailors with it, caught in the netting. After a couple of close shots of the puppet walking away, the sailor is cut free at the last moment as the walrus slips back into the water, a shot using the same set-up as the sequence's opening shot.

Trekking through the mountains, Sinbad's party catches sight of the aurora borealis, swirling light effects that Harryhausen has added above a distant rock face, the top half of which has been removed by a matte. The traveling mattes of the actors in the snow settings are excellent.

About ten stop-motion cuts are used in a brief scene where Kassim steals meat being cooked by one of the sailors, emphasizing his increasing savagery. The ape walks out of his cage, a miniature which is well matched to the rocky terrain around it. The floor inlay that the puppet walks on as it approaches the sailor and snatches the meat looks like just one more of the many rocky patches that surround it. Back in his cage, the baboon chomps on his food, slumps against the door and wipes his mouth, another good example of Harryhausen's character animation.

The first encounter with the Troglodyte, or Trog as he is referred to, is a pivotal scene containing some of the film's smoothest animation and many fine composites done in bright daylight. It is a favorite Harryhausen sequence, and Budd's restrained score works to advantage here. This horned seven-foot neanderthal is actually a very gentle character and the tone of the scene is enjoyably low-key, the complete opposite of the kind of fight scenes which are Harryhausen's trademark. The model is superb, leathery and muscular, a furry cloth strapped around his torso and tiny hairs covering his back and arms. Like the Minoton, he exudes a presence which could not have been achieved by merely using a man in a costume.

Dione and Farah have been bathing in a pool and are disturbed by Trog's arrival. Three cuts look up from Dione's point of view at Trog standing on top of some rocks. The matte line, which follows the top of the rocks, can just be seen passing through her head when she looks up. Two cuts show him standing on some more rocks making gentle growling sounds, Dione running away in the foreground. "He's as frightened of us as we are of him," exclaims Melanthius.

An impeccable composite is used in a series of cuts in which Sinbad approaches Trog, who walks into the shot from behind a large boulder on the left, throwing his shadow onto a floor inlay. In a closer shot he thumps his club on the ground, then there is a marvelous series of shots which reveal how expressive the model is. He looks startled, then quizzical, and nervously peers down at the ground for a moment before looking back up again at these intruders.

As Dione approaches Trog, the baboon shrieks at him from a small rock on which he is sitting, causing Trog to look wide-eyed and baffled; presumably he has never seen a baboon before. After more good composites of Trog, the baboon and Dione together (using a smaller four-inch baboon model, in scale with the Trog puppet), the neanderthal takes two stiff steps towards the actors, walking into another great composite. Melanthius is in the foreground drawing in the sand, the rest of the actors are walking across the background and Trog is in the middle distance, the horizontal matte line seamlessly following a small rock and some shrubs.

Recognizing the shrine entrance that the hermit has drawn, Trog attempts to point them toward it — in another good touch he first points in the wrong direction before correcting himself and growling. Several cuts show him growling quietly as Kassim bobs up and down, excited at the prospect of reaching the shrine. A final clever bit of interaction has Dione stroking the baboon; the contact is not actually seen because her hand is at the back of his head.

The studio tank is used to good effect again in the scene where Zenobia and Rafi arrive at the tunnel which leads to the entrance to the shrine. The Minoton continues to pound away at the oars in three cuts as ice crashes down into the sea behind them. Icy mist is superimposed over these shots.

More fine rear-screen composites depict the group arriving at the entrance to the shrine. In three set-ups, Sinbad and his group are walking through some grassy slopes with Trog and the baboon-prince right in there with them. In one cut, the baboon turns and walks behind a bush, the invisible matte line deviously hidden in among the leaves. However, once they arrive at the doors of the shrine, the quality is very patchy: Traveling mattes of the actors walking in front of the doors (a miniature set) are poorly matched. The huge doors, complete with a great sliding bolt, are an obvious descendant of *King Kong*.

Shots of the party at the foot of the doors are a complex mix of traveling matte, rear screen and animation. In some of these, Trog and the baboon have been animated in front of a blue screen and then matted into the shot, but the coloring is wrong and they have a dark outline. The two puppets climb the miniature steps leading up to the doors and Trog drops his club. Again, in these shots the models look darker than the live actors (a separate traveling matte). Much more successful is a shot in which Trog walks up to Sinbad and crew, looking like a conventional rear-screen shot, only to have the puppet then walk behind the actors and approach the doors: The actors are in fact a traveling matte element. Also impressive are several extreme long shots of the doors being pulled open, revealing the pyramid-shaped Shrine of the Four Elements (a painting) in the background, the aurora borealis sparkling above it. The models are so tiny in these long shots that one wonders if Harryhausen had smaller puppets built.

Zenobia and Rafi now reach the underground entrance. A series of static mattes has the Minoton standing on the deck, but Harryhausen makes life easier for himself by having his puppet remain stationary in all but the last of these shots, when the creature grabs one of the spear-like boat hooks. In the tunnel there are two sinister low-angle medium shots of the Minoton striding along, lit by orange torchlight; and a long shot of him rounding a corner. They emerge from the tunnel and there is a spectacular view of the distant shrine, snow-capped mountains behind it, two huge (miniature) carved pillars flanking the tiny actors who are a traveling matte at the foot of the shot. Harryhausen introduces a static matte into the shot, allowing the Minoton to walk behind the actors. This is a fabulous panorama and it is not doing Harryhausen a disservice to say that once again he has taken his inspiration from a 1930s film; *She* (1935) contains an almost identical design, but Harryhausen has improved on it.

There is a quick cut of Trog and the baboon continuing to follow Sinbad's group, then an extreme long shot of Zenobia, Rafi and the Minoton at the foot of the shrine. This is another excellent, complex shot: The shrine on the right of the shot is presumably a miniature, the actors are traveling mattes and the Minoton has been added via an invisible static matte line. Trog and the baboon are seen in an unusual and effective composite, standing between a bush and a boulder, the matte line again hidden in the leaves (partly obscuring Trog) and along the ground.

Zenobia, Rafi and the Minoton have climbed to the first level of the stepped pyramid and are looking for an entrance. The Minoton at first stands motionless, the base of the step providing a convenient and invisible matte line. But then he pokes at one of the huge building blocks with his boat hook, trying to loosen it. When he starts to pull the block out, it is a miniature, another convenient matte line following the vertical edge of the adjacent block. The animation in this sequence is very smooth, particularly in closer side and rear views of the Minoton struggling with the great weight.

In one quick cut, the two blocks above this one are also miniature, animated for a brief second as they drop down behind the extracted block. When the Minoton realizes that he is going to fall back with the block, he attempts to take a quick glance over his shoulder, but it is too late to save himself. The long shot in which he actually falls back is done live-action, the puppet remaining static, falling rocks crashing down with him in the rear screen. "He's done his work," intones Zenobia, disappointing all those members of the audience who were hoping to see him engage in a climactic battle with Trog. Such a battle would have been much more satisfying than the gratuitous appearance of the saber-tooth tiger, especially since the Minoton has been a recurring character throughout the film and deserved some kind of dramatic final confrontation with the forces of good.

There are three good static matte composites showing Trog and the baboon standing among the rubble beneath the opening which the Minoton has made in the shrine, Sinbad and his group above them walking inside. The inside of the shrine is an unforgettable scene. The walls are lined with huge Egyptian-style statues, icy stalactites hang from the pyramid-shaped ceiling, and a huge, curving, stone staircase leads up to a pool of swirling water, down into which a massive column of blue shimmering light pours, topped by a cloud of steam. "Drawn down from the crown of Apollo itself!" exclaims Melanthius.

At one side of the top of the stairs is another smaller staircase leading up to a cage hung on chains which are designed to pull it into the tower of light. On a pedestal to one side of the stairs is the guardian of the shrine, a saber-toothed tiger encased in ice (which, incidentally, is another idea spawned by Harryhausen's childhood film-going — the same image occurs in *She*). Budd's score catches the right note with an otherworldly drone.

Four cuts show the baboon walking into the shrine courtesy of a static matte that cuts diagonally across the studio set. Outside, Trog drops his club and picks up the Minoton's boat hook, testing its weight appreciatively. The baboon starts to walk up the steps in the shrine, his paws seeming to make contact with the steps by virtue of a zigzagging matte line which follows each step. Zenobia and Rafi appear from behind the smaller flight of steps and there are two shots looking down from their point of view at Sinbad, Melanthius and the baboon, the matte line this time following the curve of one of the steps.

Attempting to stab Melanthius, Rafi leaps down, only to have his arm grabbed by the baboon (suggested by alignment of puppet and rear image). The two tumble down the steps, Rafi clasping a mock-up of the ape. At the bottom, the baboon gets to his feet but Rafi, in the rear projection, is dead, his neck broken. Subtly emphasizing the baboon's increasing savagery, Harryhausen has him sit down calmly, unconcerned by the vicious act he has just committed. A couple of shots show him recoiling nervously as everyone awaits Zeno-bia's reaction to her son's death.

The wonderful image of the tiny cage pulled up on steel chains to a great height is another idea that Harryhausen has extracted from a 1930s film, this time the creation scene in *Bride of Franken-stein* (1935). Because the shrine has been opened by the Minoton, the pillar of light is starting to break up and Melan-thius has to hurry the baboon into the cage. He is led up to the pool, his paws really seeming to pad on the steps as he walks up, by virtue of another zigzag-ging matte. Complex long shots of the miniature pool and pillar of light have Melanthius and Dione in one traveling matte element and the small baboon puppet in another. Even more successful are long shots of Melanthius guiding the baboon into the cage. Shots of the cage being raised into the blue light are ex-treme long-shots and so Harryhausen can get away with not animating the puppet inside. The cage disappears into the sparking, crackling pillar and then is brought down again, smoking, eventu-ally revealing the restored Prince Kassim inside. It's a magical sequence and Har-ryhausen pulls it off beautifully.

The battle with the saber-tooth tiger is an easy target for the criticism that it is gratuitous. Kassim has already been restored to human form and it seems a bit late in the day to introduce a new monster. Budd's half-hearted score would be much better suited to something like a sea voyage, not a life-or-death battle between two fantastic creatures. Another flaw is that while the model is superbly sculpted and has an-other excellent fur job, its unblinking eyes lack character and consequently

make the puppet seem more toy-like than terrifying. These are all major faults but despite them this is still a good se-quence, especially when watched out of context so that its place in the plot is ir-relevant. The matching of rear screens and puppets is always excellent, Harry-hausen's animation is as accomplished as ever and the choreography is full of in-ventive touches.

Zenobia transforms into a cloud of green smoke and drifts over to the frozen saber-tooth. Five cuts show the tiger on its pedestal as the ice melts and falls away. These cuts come in for a lot of criticism that the ice is not realistic enough, but at this late stage in the film a "willing suspension of disbelief" makes this readily ignored. The beast growls, there is a closeup, then it tenses to spring down to the floor. In a quick cut it leaps straight at the camera, then is suspended in the air for a few frames before it lands in a static matte set-up, the actors in the background having to stop suddenly and change direction. Several head-on shots show its ears pricking up as it prepares to attack, taking a few steps forward. A miniature foreground is used and is poorly matched to the background, but this is barely noticed as all eyes are on the tiger.

Trog now arrives on the scene and there are several reaction shots of both puppets. The two creatures face each other in a static matte set-up, a slightly paler floor inlay just visible but not dis-tracting. Trog pokes the tiger with his spear, the tiger brushes it aside and then, after some closeups of both models, the tiger knocks the spear out of Trog's hand and lunges at him, the two locking in a deadly embrace. They fall and Trog beats

COLUMBIA FILMS présente une
Production CHARLES H. SCHNEER
**SINBAD ET
L'ŒIL DU TIGRE**
Filmé en DYNARAMA
Distribué par WARNER-COLUMBIA FILMS

Visa Ministériel n° 7 391

This shot of the saber-tooth tiger from *Sinbad and the Eye of the Tiger* allows a close look at the puppet's realistic fur covering.

at the tiger's head with his fist. They roll over, the tiger now on top, but Trog pushes the cat away. The tiger bites him on the arm and they roll over again. An effective change of perspective in a couple of shots looks up at the battling models with the stalactite-encrusted roof of the shrine in the background.

The two creatures separate then lock together again, the animation camera panning across to add an extra bit of movement. Trog throws two punches which connect with the tiger's head, this time the background formed by the row of huge statues lining the shrine walls. After another series of closeups and medium shots, Trog tries to throttle his opponent from behind, then rams into it with his horn, piercing its shoulder. Nothing further is made of this gruesome wound — were some of the more graphic bits of the fight cut out to make it more palatable to a young audience?

Trog throws the tiger over his shoulder and then pounds it with his fist, recalling the choreography of the battle between Kong and the tyrannosaur. In long shots using the principal static matte set-up again, Trog picks up his spear and waves it wildly at the tiger. A matte around the staircase allows Trog to drive the tiger back behind it, lending depth to the shot. In another brutal sequence, the tiger bites into one of Trog's arms, then the other, with plenty of blood appearing on the puppet. Both puppets fall back onto the steps (using another static matte set-up) and the tiger bites Trog in the neck, causing him to scream desperately.

Sinbad runs into the shot and thrusts his sword into the tiger's leg, drawing blood. For a few frames his sword is painted on glass so that it can pass in front of the puppet. The tiger turns and, in three deft moments of alignment, swats Sinbad and two other sailors with his paw. Trog slumps forward and falls off the steps. The tiger climbs on top of him as though intending to make a meal of him but, again, the shot is not followed up.

Trog's death is disappointingly unsympathetic, lacking the melodrama that we usually associate with a Harryhausen death scene.* But there is little time to dwell on this as we now go straight into the final confrontation between Sinbad and the Zenobia-possessed tiger. There is a good series of cuts in which the tiger slowly walks around Sinbad, sizing him up and exuding ferocity. Sinbad backs up the steps with the tiger following him in the foreground. This time, however, the matte does not follow the outline of the steps — it is merely a lazy diagonal line, with the result that the animal's paws do not seem to make actual contact in the same way that the baboon's did in previous shots.

Some aerial long shots look down at both characters on the steps, the tiger knocking the spear out of Sinbad's hand. In these shots, the area of the steps im-

mediately under the puppet is miniature, matched passably to the studio set. A good composite looks over the tiger's shoulder as both it and Sinbad are distracted by a falling stalactite.

Sinbad regains his spear and the cat lunges at him, only to get impaled on the weapon. In a shot in which the impaled puppet falls across Sinbad, a miniature spear has replaced the actual one. Four shots show the mortally wounded tiger lying on its back at the foot of the steps, the spear in its stomach, its legs kicking, the bladder in the model's chest suggesting the labored breathing. The means of death recalls the climax of the allosaurus scene in *One Million Years B.C.*, and, like that film, this scene closes with a shot of Sinbad delivering the death blow. *Eye of the Tiger*'s final battle is enjoyably staged, but lacks the superb editing and direction that made the battle in *One Million Years B.C.* a classic.

It's been an almost continuous display of fantastic scenes and fabulous creatures. The sheer volume of animation in the film is staggering and one cannot but admire Harryhausen's stamina in performing all of it singlehandedly. Not only that, but the general standard of *all* the effects in the film — mattes, miniatures and opticals — is superb. Anyone unwilling to forgive the few shortcomings is being very hard indeed. On a dramatic level it is harder to forgive the failings, but it is still a lively and colorful adventure full of impressive locations and strikingly varied styles of animation scenes. In retrospect, it is one of Harryhausen's freshest and

*Harryhausen's pre-production sketches include four drawings of Trog battling a two-horned arsinoitherium, a prehistoric relative of the rhinoceros. So it may be that his death during the battle with the saber-tooth was not part of Harryhausen's original concept.

most ambitious productions. Little did we know in 1977 that Harryhausen would only make one more film, the disappointingly stodgy *Clash of the Titans*, compared to which *Sinbad and the Eye of the Tiger* would seem like a milestone of inventiveness indeed.

Slave Girls from Beyond Infinity

1987. D: Ken Dixon.
Cast: Cindy Berl, Elizabeth Cayton, Don Scribner, Brinke Stevens

Rating: ☆½   Stop-Motion: ☆½

This low-budget variation on "The Most Dangerous Game" has three female astronauts land on a planet only to find themselves pursued by a sadistic hunter and his robots.

Several shots of the spaceship in flight use a miniature model that was filmed one frame at a time.

Some Kind of a Nut

1969. United Artists/Mirisch. D-Scr: Garson Kanin. Ph: Burnett Guffey, Gerald Hirschfeld. Art: Al Brenner. Mus: Johnny Mandel. Optical Production Design: Jerome Rosenfeld/The Helix Group, Modern Film Effects. (Uncredited Stop-Motion: Project Unlimited. Supervisors: Gene Warren, Wah Chang. Animation: Phil Tippett.)
Cast: Dick Van Dyke, Angie Dickinson, Rosemary Forsyth, Zohra Lampert, Elliott Reid, Steve Roland.

Rating: ☆½   Stop-Motion: ☆☆

This is another film that only stop-motion completists will want to endure. Garson Kanin, who both wrote and directed this feeble comedy, must take full blame. There are precious few laughs during this half-baked story about a bank clerk (Dick Van Dyke) who rebels against company rules and grows a beard. In amongst all the contrived slapstick and Van Dyke's posturing, Kanin seems to think that he is making a sophisticated screwball comedy and that there are lessons for us to be learned here about man's individuality. Certainly there are lessons — about how not to write and direct a movie.

During the early part of the film, Van Dyke takes off with his girlfriend in a red, open-topped car and tours around the States. His arrival at each town is represented in an effects shot in which a miniature replica of the car crosses a map and then drives into a photo of a street scene. These five shots were done uncredited by Project Unlimited under the supervision of Gene Warren and Wah Chang. Front-light/back-light matting was used to show the car driving across the map. The car had to be animated because it turns in several directions in a way that would have been tricky to do mechanically. Inside the car are two human figures but neither moves. In the most ambitious shot, the car emerges from a behind a bus, down the side of which runs a matte line.

Warren explained to the author, "The car was a purchased scale model from a model store which matched the live-action car." He also described another effects shot: "The entire short sequence of the car racing up the freeway and jumping the gap was accomplished with stop-frame animation. The car was suspended on an overhead wire rig." However, it appears that this sequence does not appear in release prints of the film.

All the animation in these cuts was executed by 18-year-old Phil Tippett, getting his first work on a feature film. Who would have foreseen that the same man who animated these unremarkable shots would later help to bring to the screen such wonders as the Imperial Walkers of *The Empire Strikes Back* (1980), Verminthrax Perjorative in *Dragonslayer* (1981) and ED-209 in *RoboCop* (1987), and receive Academy Awards for his work on *Return of the Jedi* (1983) and *Jurassic Park* (1993)? But that was all still a long way off. Tippett had begun doing professional animation for television commercials at the age of 17, and continued to do this over the next few years as well as attending art school. After *Some Kind of a Nut*, he would have to wait seven years for his next feature film work—in *Star Wars* (1977).

Son of Blob see Beware the Blob!

The Son of Kong

1933. RKO Radio. Prod: Merian C. Cooper. D: Ernest B. Schoedsack. Story: Ruth Rose. Ph: Eddie Linden, Vernon L. Walker, J. O. Taylor. Mus: Max Steiner. Settings: Van Nest Polglase, Al Herman. Sound Effects: Murray Spivack. Chief Technician: Willis O'Brien. Technical Staff: E. E. Gibson, Marcel Delgado, Carroll Shepphird, Fred Reefe, W. G. White.

Art Technicians: Mario Larrinaga, Byron Crabbe. Cameramen: Bert Willis, Linwood Dunn, Clifford Stine, Felix Schoedsack.

Cast: Robert Armstrong, Helen Mack, Frank Reicher, John Marston, Victor Wong, Noble Johnson.

Rating: ☆☆½   Stop-Motion: ☆☆☆

The Son of Kong

The Son of Kong is so overshadowed by the original *King Kong* that it has been largely ignored by fans and critics. Even most of the specialist books written about stop-motion and its practitioners tend to allocate the film a mere fraction of the space they give to its famous predecessor. Stop-motion is a genre that normally attracts discussion of technical qualities, so it is alarming that the film's dramatic shortcomings have thoroughly discouraged so many from taking a closer look. (The best accounts of the film can be found in Goldner and Turner's *The Making of* King Kong and Paul Mandell's article in *Fangoria* #5.)

The film has many faults, chief among them being that it fails almost entirely to recreate the excitement and grandeur of *King Kong*. For example, in the original the careful live-action build-up that preceded Kong's first appearance was calculated to maximize audience anticipation. In the sequel, the first 35 minutes, concerning a disreputable sea captain, the murder of the heroine's father and a mutiny, are extraneous to the subsequent events on Skull Island. This is inexcusable since they occupy half of the running time. Even once on the island, scriptwriter Ruth Rose is unable to imbue the plot with much passion, stumbling through a series of gratuitous set-pieces. The storyline of the original had considerable impetus but the sequel, apart from a very lame search for some lost treasure, has little to unify it. Consequently, audience involvement — so crucial to *King Kong*— is lost.

The film was rushed out by RKO bosses, completed in October 1933 at a cost of $250,000 — roughly half of *King Kong*'s budget. Approximately $50,000 was spent on the effects. Willis O'Brien was unhappy about the whole concept of a hurried sequel and partway through production turned his back on it, leaving much of the animation to E.B. "Buzz" Gibson, one of his assistants on the first film. In particular, O'Brien objected to the way that Little Kong, a 12–foot high, white-furred version of Kong, was portrayed as a whimsical and occasionally outright comic character. It has been suggested that O'Brien's disagreement with the producers may have induced them to deliberately misprint his name on publicity material as Willis J. O'Brien. If so, then Marcel Delgado must also have upset them because his first name is misspelled in the credits as Marcell.

Three models of Little Kong were built by Delgado over King Kong armatures. The giant mechanical hand from the first film was re-furred and used in two crucial scenes. A beautifully detailed styracosaurus, originally used in a cut scene from *King Kong*, appears in one scene. Other models built specifically for the sequel are a cave bear, a dragon-like dinosaur and a sea serpent.

The special effects outclass the film that contains them but are nevertheless often misjudged or derivative of the first film. A number of matte paintings, glass shots and miniature sets go some way to recreating the magical qualities of *King Kong*, but Skull Island never has the lushness it had before. The budget forces too much of the action to take place in one miniature set and the pace suffers accordingly: A clearing at the foot of a huge carved temple serves as the location for the discovery of Little Kong in a quagmire, various scenes outside the entrance of the temple and a fight between the ape and a cave bear.

On the other hand, much of the animation is smoother than in the original (there are exactly 100 stop-motion cuts) and several composites are technically more accomplished. The "bristling fur" problem that plagued King Kong's animation is avoided here.

Robert Armstrong reprises his role of Carl Denham, fleeing from lawsuits resulting from the destruction caused by Kong, and ransacked with guilt: "Old Kong, I'm sure paying for what I did to you." His enthusiastic performance makes Denham an even more likable character than before. Helen Mack as Hilda, although not required to recreate Fay Wray's high-decibel impact, is also ingratiating. Frank Reicher (as Captain Englehorn), Victor Wong (as Charlie the cook) and Noble Johnson (as a native chief) all reappear to suggest continuity with the original. John Marston makes his villainous role enjoyably degenerate.

An evocative Mario Larrinaga matte painting is used to depict the arrival at Skull Island. The row boat containing the actors and the sea are live-action elements, backed by a long beach and (behind that) a panorama of cliffs and jungles. Strangely, Skull Mountain is nowhere to be seen. Forced by the natives to land elsewhere, the group rows beneath some towering cliffs, another impressive matte shot. A pillar of rock in the foreground is a separate painted element, allowing the boat to appear to enter a gap in the cliffs.

The first stop-motion sequence is, presumably deliberately, the complete antithesis of Kong's unforgettable entrance. There is no build-up: Denham and Hilda simply climb over a rock and come across the Son of Kong, trapped in a quagmire. "Well, if it isn't a little Kong!" remarks Denham, almost blasé. This long 30–second cut has the actors on a studio rock in front of a full-scale rear projection. Little Kong, seen from the waist up, is very fluidly animated and grunts gently at the sound of voices.

Little Kong is up to his waist in the mire, an effect achieved credibly by animating the puppet in glycerin which holds its position between frames. This miniature set-up is backed by a mixture of miniature and painted jungle foliage. The puppet's face is extremely expressive (more so than his father's), conveying the creature's distress. He blinks and squeaks forlornly.

He pushes this way and that in the mire until Denham and Hilda decide to help him. In another set-up, the actors are a miniature rear-projected element in the right middle distance with Little Kong in the mire in foreground. Rippling water in the lower foreground is a matted-in live-action element, an important extra ingredient characteristic of O'Brien's attention to detail. To aid the ape, Denham tries to push over a tree, which is actually part of the miniature set — Armstrong mimes the action, a clever bit of alignment.

An impressive extreme long shot shows the full miniature set for the first time. Little Kong is in the quagmire at the foot of the set, Hilda and Denham are rear-projected just behind him, and the temple entrance, with its huge carved idol, occupies the top half of the frame. Little Kong clambers out of the mire.

In medium shot the ape looks at an

The Son of Kong (1933): Denham (Robert Armstrong) helps to rescue Little Kong from a quagmire. (Frame enlargement.)

injured finger, growling like a puppy. Max Steiner supplies a sleazy trumpet motif at this point, playing up the comic angle. Again in extreme long shot, Denham and Hilda look on as the ape walks behind some miniature trees.

The other three members of the group encounter a styracosaurus, a fabulous Delgado creation, but unfortunately not made the most of in the brief eight cuts in which it is seen. The sequence is exciting but incomplete. In a stunning long shot, the dinosaur, a bulky quadruped with a horn and a protective frill of spikes around its neck, stands on one side of the frame while the three men, in a miniature rear projection, stand on the left. In the middle is a beautifully detailed miniature tree, twisted and gnarled. In the lower foreground, a matted-in live-action river flows by.

One of the men fires his rifle and the beast momentarily collapses, getting up again immediately. In the next shot it chases the group, its running cycle very convincingly animated. Two glass-painted trees in the foreground help add depth to the design of this shot. The men take cover in an opening in a rock face and the styracosaurus slams into it, nearly collapsing from the force of the impact. Again, this is a tricky bit of choreography pulled off extremely well. Several shots look over the shoulder of the beast as it tries to get into the crevasse, the actors cowering in the rear-projection between two miniature rocks. In long shot, the beast grabs the rifle in its beak and crushes it.

The action now cuts away from the styracosaurus, which unfortunately is not seen again. The next stop-motion sequence is a long battle (comprising 21 animation cuts) between Little Kong and a 15-foot high cave bear. No doubt intended to have the same impact as the Kong/tyrannosaurus fight, it lacks the ferocity and excitement of that classic episode. The barrage of bestial sound effects that enhanced that scene are absent from this imitation. The fight is too long and occasionally repeats itself, and the camera views it mainly from one angle in the already-familiar temple set. Still, the bear is a convincing model, even though its face lacks vitality. There are some good touches and the complex animation is very smooth, but it is too much of a gratuitous set-piece.

Denham and Hilda are returning from the jungle where they have caught a bird to eat. In a shot recalling *Kong*'s stegosaurus sequence, the bear runs at them through an extensive jungle set, the actors in the foreground in front of a rear screen. Denham shoots at it and it tumbles over, momentarily stunned. It picks itself up, growls and continues the chase.

It bounds into the temple set, with Denham and Hilda up on a ledge in a rear-projection. Hilda screams and Little Kong, in another jungle set, looks up and turns. The bear starts to climb up toward them, but the ape grabs one of its legs and pulls it down. The bear kicks Little Kong away, then in a long cut they lock in combat, rolling over together and throwing several punches. The bear gets the ape in a bear hug, lifts him, then throws him against a rock. In closeup, Little Kong rubs his head and blinks, silly cartoon gestures that are backed by a comical trumpet sound effect. This is the first of several such moments which cheapen his character.

In long shot again, Little Kong jumps onto the bear's back and in closer shots they land blows on each other. The bear gets on top of the ape and seems to have the upper hand, but Little Kong wriggles out of its grip. He bites the bear's leg but then gets swiped in the head by one of the bear's clawed paws. In extreme long-shot, the two beasts lock together again, then separate and face off. In medium shot, Little Kong grabs the bear in an arm-hold and punches his face repeatedly. He lands a final punch and the bear goes limp. The ape makes a very human gesture towards Denham and Hilda, waving his arm as if to say, "Well, that's that."

In medium shot looking down at Little Kong from Denham and Hilda's viewpoint on the ledge, the ape gestures towards the unconscious bear as though saying, "Look what I've done." But, in extreme long shot again, the bear revives and jumps on the ape. Little Kong goes down and bites the bear's leg. In a cheap gimmick, Little Kong crawls through the legs of the bear who seems not to notice — he carries on with the struggle on his own. The ape grabs a tree trunk and swipes at the bear five times, causing him to accept defeat and walk off.

Little Kong has got a splinter in one of his fingers and in medium shot nurses it, a hurt expression on his face. An extreme long shot view of the right-hand side of the miniature set has Denham and Hilda come running down the steps (in a miniature projection again) with the ape seated on the left. Denham winds a bandage around the injured finger in a series of medium shots which align the puppet with the mechanical prop hand in the rear screen. O'Brien adds character in these shots by having the ape scratch his side, chirrup gently, squeak when his finger is touched and scratch his head. Several closeups are also used in this sequence, making full use of the puppet's expressive face, lively eyes and flexible lips. Denham talks to the ape, apologizing for what he did to his father, and in a final closeup the ape licks his bandaged finger approvingly.

The sequence is a delight, maintains a deft balance of humor and danger, and is technically flawless, but steals its concept from *King Kong*. Compare it with the moment when Kong peels away Fay Wray's clothing and immediately one realizes which is the more resonant. *King Kong*'s scene comes across like a bizarre sexual fairy tale, but this scene never attempts anything on that level.

In the next set-up, O'Brien moves his animation camera into yet another part of the same miniature set. Standing on the ledge at the entrance to the temple, Denham and Hilda try to shake down some coconuts from a tree. In two cuts, Little Kong shakes the miniature tree, causing about a dozen miniature coconuts to come cascading down. Each of these must have been supported on an invisible wire and lowered frame by frame — the animation is extremely convincing. Some of the coconuts nearly fall on Hilda. Denham calls out, "Watch what you're doing, you big dummy!" and the ape backs away nervously. It's the kind of unfortunate remark which makes Little Kong seem weak and child-like, the complete opposite of his imposing father.

Night falls and in a beautiful long shot, Denham and Hilda are seen huddled near a camp fire halfway up a painted cliff face, backed by a picturesque night sky. A painted tree on a foreground glass sheet gives the shot depth.

The couple starts to get romantic and in three stop-motion cuts (two long shots, one medium shot) Little Kong stands guard over them, tactfully staying out of sight around the edge of a rock face. Of course, the idea that the ape could be tactful is another irritatingly anthropomorphic gimmick, but these are flawless composites, with the edge of the miniature rock face blending imperceptibly with the studio one.

The advent of morning is depicted by another fine composite blending of a panoramic painting and lush jungle set, with animated birds flitting through the trees. It's a shame that there are not more shots like this.

In a long cut (using the main miniature set again), Denham stands on the ledge while Little Kong snoozes below. He fires his rifle to alert the rest of his party and the startled ape stands bolt upright, raising both hands in the air.

He then rubs his eyes sleepily as Denham and Hilda talk about trying to get into the temple.

In a closer shot, Little Kong climbs up to the temple doorway, which is blocked by a wall of stones. He scratches his head thoughtfully, then pushes at the wall, sending it crashing down. The falling stones are live-action miniatures, rear-projected behind the ape (who is animated so as to suggest the physical contact).

Hilda and Denham enter the temple. Then, in a very attractive long shot, done entirely on the miniature set with no rear projections, Little Kong clambers after them. The exquisite detail of the rock faces and the surrounding foliage is evident in this cut, with Little Kong himself appearing to be bathed in bright sunlight. The extra lighting in this shot was possible because there was no requirement to light-balance the miniature set with any live-action projections.

The inside of the temple is another impressive miniature, built with all the attention to detail that is characteristic of O'Brien. At one end is a statue topped by a grotesque carved face with long fangs. Hilda and Denham cross the cave floor, backed by a full-scale rear projection of Little Kong walking behind them.

In another set-up, with Denham and Hilda in a miniature rear projection at the foot of the statue, the ape reaches for the diamond-encrusted necklace that sits on the idol. In three long cuts, Little Kong plays with Denham's rifle, accidentally firing off a shot, then snapping the weapon in two. In these cuts, the actors are in the foreground in front of the rear-projected animation footage.

Superimposed smoke is added at the moment when the gun goes off.

At this point, another of the island's monstrous denizens enters the temple. This long-necked quadruped looks more like a mythological dragon than any prehistoric creature, a result of O'Brien's instructing Delgado to come up with something no one had seen before. This is a shame because its unlikely, emaciated musculature weakens the already shaky credibility of the plot: It is not one of Delgado's best models. Its eyes are curiously white and lifeless. The eight animation cuts that make up the battle between Little Kong and the dragon are as accomplished as ever but can't overcome the impression that this is just another gratuitous set-piece.

The giant lizard is first seen walking along the ledge outside the temple entrance, an all-miniature shot. Two striking shots look out through the mouth of the cave at the approaching creature, which hisses and snarls as it gets nearer.

Denham and Hilda, standing in front of Little Kong in a rear screen, retreat nervously. In extreme long shot, the two beasts face one another, growling apprehensively. Denham and Hilda stand in a miniature rear projection occupying a tiny portion of the foot of the image (and not standing on top of the statue as depicted in a frequently published studio paste-up). This shot allows a particularly good look at the expansive cave set with its hanging stalactites. The two creatures engage, roll over, and the ape throws a lot of punches. At one point it is possible to see the reflection of the dragon on the rear-projection screen — a flaw that only sneaked into the release

A paste-up by RKO's publicity department for *The Son of Kong.* In the film, Denham (Robert Armstrong) and Hilda (Helen Mack) are actually positioned in the dark ground-level area between the puppets. (National Film Archive, London.)

print because of O'Brien's loss of interest in the project.

In an intricately animated closer shot, the long-tailed lizard coils around the ape, biting him. Little Kong takes a leaf out of his father's book and tries to force his opponent's jaws apart. In long shot, Little Kong grabs the lizard around its torso and holds it upside down, smashing it into the ground. The lizard's tail writhes constantly as the ape punches it in the face. In a closer shot, Little Kong punches the lizard's head repeatedly.

Then he picks up the limp head to check that it is dead, rubbing his hands with satisfaction. In a foolish touch, the ape holds his hands together like a boxing champ. The lizard momentarily revives and bites Little Kong, who delivers a final blow to its head.

In a medium shot that curiously doesn't appear to have any context in the plot, Little Kong scratches his head and holds out his paws with a shrug. It's another case of character animation being taken to extremes.

654

The five castaways gather at the entrance of the temple, seen in two attractive long shots with Little Kong standing in the doorway looking at them.

Suddenly (and all too conveniently), the island is ripped asunder by an earthquake. The ensuing cataclysm is marvelously staged by O'Brien and his crew, ending the film with a brilliant climax that almost makes up for earlier shortcomings. At last, scriptwriter Ruth Rose's imagination shifts into high gear and the film achieves a level of grandeur to match *King Kong*, elevating Little Kong to tragic status and ending the picture with a particularly haunting final shot. The miniature work showing the island being pulled this way and that, cliffs crumbling, rainswept jungles ripped apart by a storm and the churning seas, are all depicted superbly. O'Brien had hoped to include a dinosaur stampede at this point, but the budget precluded this.

Helstrom tries to steal the row boat and escape alone. But as he reaches the boat, a giant sea serpent (another departure from the prehistoric conception) rises up in a rear projection. This is a mechanical head-and-neck prop, which in a subsequent cut chews on a dummy of Helstrom. One stop-motion closeup of the creature is used, adding vitality which otherwise would be lacking: Its head draws back, the mouth opens and the eyes look around. The miniature rock faces and studio pool are successfully matched to the foreground live-action. This brief scene recalls the brontosaurus episode in *King Kong*, which was in every way a more dramatically satisfying sequence.

In an impressive extreme long shot, the inside of the temple starts to collapse. Little Kong and an animated puppet of Denham are rear-projected into a tiny area in the lower left corner of the shot as rocks fall all around them in the extensive miniature set. This shot is an interesting departure from other uses of miniature rear projection, where it is normally the live-action element that has to be projected. A closer shot of this action combines the live-action Denham with the puppet ape, as rocks cascade in front of them. This time the rocks are a separate element, probably superimposed film of falling rocks shot against a white background.

Another superb composite, used in two cuts, shows Little Kong helping the puppet Denham to climb up the temple wall as churning water in the foreground starts to rise beneath them.

Outside, Hilda, Englehorn and Charlie have made it into the row boat. The mechanical head-and-neck prop of the brontosaurus from the first film briefly rises up out of the frothing water.

Little Kong helps Denham out through a hole in the roof of the temple, a clever effect in which Denham starts off live-action, then switches to his puppet counterpart as he passes behind the ape. In the foreground, more superimposed rocks crash down. The next shot is a stunning image, looking down at Denham and Little Kong emerging from the opening. Denham is in the foreground, struggling over some rocks and battered by the rain. Immediately behind him is the huge head of the ape, looking up at the storm, responsive and growling with fear.

The island is sinking beneath the

waves and all that remains above water is a hillock of land on which Denham and Little Kong are standing. In the first of these impeccably realized composites, the ape and the puppet Denham are miniature, rear-projected into a small area of the hillock. The area they occupy is tiny, suggesting that the hillock must have been about a 20–foot long miniature. In a closer shot, the ape angrily waves his arm at the rising sea. One side of the hillock crumbles into the sea, leaving just a rounded dome with Little Kong and the puppet Denham at the foot of it.

O'Brien now switches to a miniature rock in scale with the puppets, allowing them to climb up it. The churning water at the base of the rock is a separate element, and O'Brien brilliantly overcomes the problem of making it appear to be in contact with the rock by having a soft (i.e., slightly out of focus) matte run along the base of it. Little Kong picks up the Denham puppet and climbs higher. They are spotted by the group in the boat, who start to row toward them.

The same composite is used in a series of cuts in which the rock slowly sinks lower and lower into the waves. A closer shot has the live-action Denham clutching at a rock with Little Kong in a rear projection, raging at the storm. A hole opens up in part of the miniature rock on which the puppet is standing and traps the ape's leg. Denham, backed by a rear projection of the ape's legs, tries to pull the rock away without success.

In closeup, the ape growls desper-

ately. In long shot, the two puppets stand on the tiny bit of remaining rock, Little Kong raising his arms frantically and growling pathetically. In vain, Denham continues trying to move the rock while in closeup Little Kong seems to have accepted his fate.

As the last bit of the rock disappears under the water, Little Kong picks up the Denham puppet. The ape slowly slips under the water, holding the Denham puppet aloft. The huge prop hand is used again for close shots of Denham being held above the waves. The final animation cut is a long shot of Little Kong's hand holding the Denham puppet, its legs kicking desperately. The row boat comes alongside and the prop hand delivers Denham into the boat in the nick of time. The last sight of Little Kong is an unforgettable image of the prop hand just above the waves, the bandage on one finger blowing in the wind.

The huge commercial success of *King Kong* should have ushered in a whole series of fantasy films utilizing stop-motion. Unfortunately, RKO was still too deeply mired in financial problems to consider undertaking similar high-investment projects, and other studios did not have the expertise. *The Son of Kong* proved to be the last such film for another 16 years, when O'Brien would reteam with Merian Cooper to make *Mighty Joe Young*. This scarcity makes it all the more surprising that *The Son of Kong*, a flawed film with great moments, has been so neglected over the years.

Spacehunter— Adventures in the Forbidden Zone

1983. Columbia. D: Lamont Johnson. Scr: David Preston, Edith Rey, Dan Goldberg, Len Blum. Story: Stewart Harding, Jean LaFleur. Ph: Frank Tidy. Art: Jackson De Govia. Mus: Elmer Bernstein. Special Makeup Effects: Thomas R. Burman. Special Visual Effects: Fantasy II Film Effects. Special Effects Supervisors: Gene Warren, Jr., Peter Kleinow. Effects Animation: Ernest D. Farino, Bret Mixon.

Cast: Peter Strauss, Molly Ringwald, Ernie Hudson, Andrea Marcovicci, Michael Ironside.

Rating: ☆☆½   Stop-Motion: ☆☆½

This SF adventure, originally shot in 3-D on a budget of $8 million, steals most of its ideas from *Star Wars* and *Mad Max*, but the director is no George Lucas or George Miller — excitement is conspicuous by its absence. Characterization is of the tedious smart-ass school and the score (by Elmer Bernstein) is yet another imitation of John Williams' *Star Wars* themes.

There are some good special makeups by Tom Burman, including a robot meltdown (an idea taken from *Alien*) and some blubbery aliens resembling grotesque Michelin men. Michael Ironside is barely recognizable as the splendid villain Overdog, a skullfaced biomechanical nasty with steel pincers on the ends of six-foot-long arms. Set design is also imaginative, although it always borrows heavily from *Mad Max* and *Alien*—bizarre, battered vehicles and the biomechanical lair of Overdog.

All of the film's space sequences are contained in the opening five minutes and the final half-minute, in excellent shots created by Fantasy II Film Effects, the company run by partners Gene Warren, Jr., Peter Kleinow and Leslie Huntley.

A starliner — an elegant and intricately detailed model — is cruising through a solar system when it is caught by sparking nebular gases and explodes. Just before it explodes, a space shuttle manages to escape and fly off to the nearest inhabitable planet. Gene Warren stop-framed a three-foot model of the shuttle in two shots, flying away from the exploding starliner and bluescreened against a background of stars. A one-inch model of the shuttle was animated in a subsequent shot in which it flies low over the planet's surface. For this shot, the planet's surface was a miniature and the background was a painting. Shots of the shuttle crash-landing were done live-action.

Peter Kleinow animated a four-foot-long model of the spaceship flown by the film's anti-hero, Wolff (Peter Strauss), hiding in an asteroid belt. The asteroids, which were made of foam and hung on wires, were moved a frame at a time as they glide slowly past the spaceship. The same spaceship model was animated in shots of it leaving the asteroid belt and in the closing shots of it flying away from the planet's surface and off into space.

The Spaceman and King Arthur

1979. Walt Disney. D: Russ Mayberry. Scr-Story: Don Tait. Based on Mark Twain's *A Connecticut Yankee in King Arthur's Court*. Ph: Paul Beeson. Art: Albert Witherick. Mus: Ron Goodwin. Special Photographic Effects: Cliff Culley.

Cast: Dennis Dugan, Jim Dale, Ron Moody, Kenneth More, John Le Mesurier, Rodney Bewes, Cyril Shaps.

Rating: ☆½   Stop-Motion: ☆☆

A limp and unfunny live-action effort from the Walt Disney studios, *The Spaceman and King Arthur* will only entertain undemanding children. Its uninspired screenplay has NASA scientist Dennis Dugan spinning out of control in a spaceship and accidentally returning to the time of King Arthur. The plot and the gags are all routine. A marvelous collection of British comic actors — including Jim Dale, Kenneth More, John Le Mesurier and Ron Moody — is almost entirely wasted.

There are numerous physical effects plus a few very modest visual effects, supplied by Cliff Culley. Some of the shots of the spaceship in flight are live-action effects using mechanical props. Approximately six shots of the spaceship use stop-motion to depict more elaborate movement such as spinning out of control or turning 180 degrees. In some of these shots, the ship flies past an attractive background painting of the Earth. These are competent effects but too brief to have much dramatic impact.

Star Trek III— The Search for Spock

1984. Paramount. D: Leonard Nimoy. Prod-Scr: Harve Bennett. Based on *Star Trek* created by Gene Roddenberry. Ph: Charles Correll. Art: John E. Chilberg II. Mus: James Horner. Special Makeup Appliances: The Burman Studio. Special Visual Effects: Industrial Light and Magic. Supervisor of Visual Effects: Kenneth Ralston. Creature Supervisor: David Sosalla. Matte Painting Supervisor: Michael Pangrazio. Matte Artists: Chris Evans, Frank Ordaz. Stop-Motion Animation (uncredited): Tom St. Amand.

Cast: William Shatner, Leonard Nimoy, DeForest Kelley, James Doohan, Walter Koenig, George Takei, Nichelle Nichols, Christopher Lloyd.

Rating: ☆☆☆   Stop-Motion: ☆☆½

Like all the films based on the *Star Trek* television series, this has outstanding special effects by Industrial Light and Magic. But it is badly let down by a weak plot: It becomes fairly obvious early on that Spock isn't dead and so any suspense is lost. Dialogue frequently indulges in overdoses of emotion — but then *Star Trek* wouldn't be *Star Trek* without the corny exchanges between Kirk (William

Shatner) and his crew. The sets on the Genesis planet (a jungle, a snowbound area, earthquake scenes) are curiously unconvincing and static — a trademark of the television series. But it's a surprise to find such fakery in a mega-budget feature film. Seven years after *Star Wars*, composers (in this case James Horner) are still borrowing heavily from John Williams' themes. And there is even a *Star Wars* cantina-scene imitation when Dr. McCoy tries to buy the services of an alien pilot.

ILM's special effects, supervised this time by Ken Ralston, include standout sequences when the *Enterprise* docks with a beautiful revolving space station, an extreme long shot of the *Enterprise* (now a half-destroyed wreck) falling out of control through the sky, and a breathtaking panorama of a Klingon ship coming in for a landing on the planet Vulcan, bathed in the orange glow of a setting sun. Most of these and other effects shots use stunning matte paintings by ILM's regular artists, including Michael Pangrazio, Chris Evans and Frank Ordaz, who over the years have

been responsible for creating some amazing sights.

One stop-motion shot was animated by Tom St. Amand, who did not receive a screen credit. During a climactic fistfight between Kirk and the Klingon captain (Christopher Lloyd — best known as Doc in the *Back to the Future* series), an earthquake has caused a great lake of bubbling lava to appear beneath them. The Klingon grips the edge of a rock face but Kirk kicks him down into the lava. In one impressive cut, the actor is replaced by a stop-motion puppet which flails its limbs very realistically as it falls away from the camera. It was impractical to shoot a live actor in front of a blue screen because of the great distance that the character has to fall away from the camera. (In any event such shots, where a stuntman is waving his arms about in a feigned panic, usually look fake.) St. Amand's subtle animation, however, is very convincing and doesn't look like animation. The switch from live actor to puppet ingeniously coincides with a flash of lighting, thereby distracting the eye at the crucial moment.

Star Wars

1977. Lucasfilm/Fox. D-Scr: George Lucas. Ph: Gilbert Taylor. Art: John Barry. Mus: John Williams. Special Photographic Effects Supervisor: John Dykstra. First Cameraman: Richard Edlund. Second Cameraman: Dennis Muren. Assistant Cameramen: Douglas Smith, Kenneth Ralston, David Robman. Matte Artist: P. S. Ellenshaw. Production Illustrator: Ralph McQuarrie. **Effects Illustration and Design: Joseph Johnston. Stop-Motion Animation: Jon Berg, Phil Tippett. Makeup Supervisor: Stuart Freeborn. Second Unit Makeup: Rick Baker, Doug Beswick.**

Cast: Mark Hamill, Harrison Ford, Carrie Fisher, Peter Cushing, Sir Alec Guinness, Anthony Daniels, Kenny Baker, Peter Mayhew, David Prowse.

Star Wars

Rating: ☆☆☆☆   Stop-Motion: ☆☆½

The renaissance which stop-motion has enjoyed over the last two decades is in part due to a very dull SF movie called *Futureworld*, released the year before *Star Wars*. *Futureworld* contained no stop-motion but did include a scene of a chess game played with holograms of miniature people, an idea which George Lucas had intended to use in *Star Wars*. Determined to avoid criticism that he lacked inventiveness, Lucas spiced up his chess game by playing it instead with holograms of miniature monsters.

He hired Phil Tippett and Jon Berg to think up alien creatures for a live-action sequence set in a rowdy bar. They made some small sculptures, intending them as merely design ideas for this scene. But they so impressed Lucas that the idea occurred to him to use them in a stop-motion sequence, to be supervised by Dennis Muren. With their long track record of doing stop-motion for commercials and having recently finished working on *The Crater Lake Monster*, Tippett and Berg were the obvious choice to do the scene.

It's an extremely brief moment, consisting of only four cuts, and most audiences barely remember it among all the other more spectacular effects that surround it. But it forms an important background element in a busy scene, part of Lucas' ingenious design throughout the film to give an impression of bustling activity and simultaneity of plot threads. As such, it set a precedent in the use of stop-motion: No longer would the process be associated with center-stage set-pieces but instead it could be incidental, functioning as just one of many effects techniques that contribute to an overall design. The main thrust of the scene is the fact that Obi Wan Kenobi (Sir Alec Guinness) has telepathically "felt" the faroff destruction of a planet and consequently prompts Luke Skywalker (Mark Hamill) to take up his training in the ways of "the Force" with greater urgency. The game of chess between R2-D2 (Kenny Baker) and Chewbacca (Peter Mayhew) is almost irrelevant.

Berg and Tippett built ten models but two of them were not used in the film after Lucas decided eight would be adequate. Seven of them have armatures; the eighth, a staff-wielding creature, is a static model. The design of all of them is inventive and outlandish — the kind of monsters that only stop-motion can bring to life. Berg and Tippett shared the animation duties, completing several more cuts than are in the finished film; again Lucas wanted to keep things brief and low-key. In all the cuts, the animation has been filmed against a black background and then merely superimposed over the live-action, its "see-through" quality giving the models the look of holograms. (Unfortunately, some viewers did not appreciate that they were meant to be holograms and assumed that these were inferior composites.)

In the first cut, a low, squat biped with four small horns on its head waggles its face at a taller reptilian creature, then squeaks and retreats a couple of squares on the board. Behind it is an animal with wiggling snail horns. The reptilian creature, a model built by Tippett several months before he was asked to work on the film, has a long, drooping neck and wears a ragged jacket and boots. Behind them, a long-armed insect-like creature with an elephant's trunk and huge hands makes threatening gestures at another chess piece.

The second cut is a closer look. A red centipede rears up on its back legs while a bulky, yellow brutish thing with a potato-face in its chest and carrying a club, takes two jumps to the center of the board. In the third cut, the big reptile walks over to potato-face, picks him up and slams him into the floor, then looks up triumphantly and lets out a squeak. The elaborate foreground action in the third cut hides the fact that, unlike the two previous cuts, there is very little movement in the background puppets.

The fourth cut is a non-animated long shot. In the foreground, Luke fends off a hovering training robot (inserted with traveling matte) with his light-saber (also added optically) while in the background Chewbacca, R2-D2 and C-3PO sit around the chess table, onto which is superimposed a small image of static chess pieces.

Amusing and bizarre, this brief sequence always evokes murmurs of delight from audiences. For a few seconds the enormous potential of stop-motion flickers across the screen, a potential that Berg and Tippett were to tap again and again over the coming years.

Starcrash

1979. Italy. Columbia/AIP/Film Enterprise. D: Lewis Coates [Luigi Cozzi]. Scr: Lewis Coates [Luigi Cozzi], Nat Wachsberger. Ph: Paul Beeson, Roberto D'Etorre. Art: Aurelio Crugnolla. Mus: John Barry. Special Effects Directors: Armando Valcauda, Germani Natali.

Cast: Marjoe Gortner, Caroline Munro, Christopher Plummer, David Hasselhoff, Robert Tessier, Joe Spinell.

Rating: ☆☆   Stop-Motion: ☆☆

Somebody must have leaked details of George Lucas' closely guarded script for his planned *The Empire Strikes Back* to the makers of this picture. There is an emperor who appears as a holographic image; an ice-planet; a floating city; a character in a helmet who looks remarkably like Boba Fett; a scene where the heroine is suspended upside down by troglodytes who resemble the snow creature of Hoth; and a scene where she is deep-frozen in ice (like Han Solo at the end of *Empire*). To add insult to injury, one of the characters unashamedly wields a light-saber. An explanatory narrative rolls up the screen at the start of the film, exactly as in *Star Wars*—except that here the words roll so fast you can barely read them.

Another more curious similarity with *Empire* is an abundance of stop-motion, almost as if the filmmakers had heard rumors that Lucas was going to use the process and so hoped to imitate this as well.

Replete with all of those commercially sound, if unethical, ideas, *Star-*

Starcrash (1979): The two mechanical sword-wielding golems in a rear-projection set-up.

crash beat *Empire* to the cinema by a year. But there is a big difference: *Starcrash* is an awful film. The brisk pace and wealth of special effects make it watchable, but director Luigo Cozzi lacks the ability to generate any sense of excitement, the script is lazy and occasionally incoherent, the dialogue brainless and the actors, especially Caroline Munro, are embarrassing. The two male leads are dull. Christopher Plummer is the token classical actor (another *Star Wars* ripoff)—he has our sympathies. John Barry's score must be his worst—it just drags along, slowing down the action. But the sets and costumes are colorful and a few moments playfully recall the old *Flash Gordon* serials. For example, soldiers are fired from one spaceship to another inside giant gold torpedoes.

The special effects were handled chiefly by Armando Valcauda, clearly struggling with a restrictive effects budget of $30,000. The many spaceship models that fly across the screen are imaginatively designed, effectively put into shots by static matte rather than any expensive motion control system. The battles in space are interesting but rarely convey much excitement; neither Cozzi nor the budget were up to that. Matte shots of alien landscapes with bizarre skylines are disappointing because the two halves of the matte frequently don't match.

The spirit of Harryhausen's Talos influences a scene from *Starcrash*.

Valcauda is a Harryhausen fan and doesn't try to hide the fact. Unfortunately the standard of the animation is also at fan-level and its main achievement is to remind us just how good Harryhausen is. A battle with two mechanical golems is occasionally impressive but suffers because there is not a single matte in the whole sequence. The escape from a giant female statue, however, is the sort of thing that gives a stop-motion a bad name. Two or three shots of a head in a glass bowl, with stop-motion tentacles waving in front of it, are more successful because they are less ambitious.

Valcauda also uses stop-motion effectively to depict the spaceship of the evil Count Zarth Arn (Joe Spinell). It is shaped like a huge upturned claw, closing into a fist when preparing for battle.

The battle with the giant statue is a hopeless imitation of the Talos sequence in *Jason and the Argonauts*. The poorly proportioned puppet is seen in 16 shots as it pursues Stella Star along a beach. Its movements seem clumsy and unlikely whereas Harryhausen's creation was imposing and gave a real sense of a statue come to life. There are several successful static mattes during the sequence, one including a background painting of a neighboring planet. The statue is blasted by laser-fire from a passing spaceship; when it falls to the ground (awkwardly), Valcauda tries to mimic the melodramatic flourishes of Harryhausen's death scenes. But here the results are ludicrous, especially as the statue was never a living thing. The episode is hurried and dramatically inept.

The two golems are intriguing creatures, barely more than ornate armatures, and (being mechanical) they lend themselves perfectly to stop-motion. Valcauda deserves credit (unless this idea was another steal from Lucas) of initiating the "robo-motion" genre which would become a mainstay of stop-motion from now on in films like *The Terminator, Return of the Jedi, Robot Jox* and many others. The animation is always smooth and the rear screens never grainy enough to distract, but in all the 34 animation cuts during the battle, plus a couple of earlier shots when the golems are first displayed by the Count, no matte shots are attempted. This always looks like a sequence where animation puppets have been simply placed in front of a rear screen, despite some clever moments of implied interaction during the swordfight.

In several cuts the two golems just stand threateningly in the foreground, heads turning slightly, fingers opening and closing, and making whirring, clicking sounds. In two shots, the golems advance in unison towards the actors, swords raised — this choreography is lifted directly from a similar shot in the skeleton sequence in *Jason and the Argonauts*. The actors perform their shadow-fighting well and the interaction is further pepped up by superimposed flashes from the light-saber. The moment when an actor pushes one of the golems over from behind is very successfully achieved by careful matching of puppet with the rear image. This is an exciting episode, but let down because the golems are defeated far too easily — they may be sophisticated mechanical robots but all they are armed with are good old swords.

Valcauda also animated sequences featuring a giant crab, a dinosaur-like creature and a swamp monster, but these were all dropped by Cozzi, who claimed they were simply too unconvincing.

The Empire Strikes Back used stop-motion inventively in sequences featuring the taun-tauns and the AT-ATs, serving to further the plot rather than just being present for its own sake. *Starcrash*, however, takes a leaf out of the most gratuitous moments from Harryhausen's films, presenting its stop-motion episodes as self-contained set-pieces. It is heartening and entertaining that a film like this — which is prepared to invest money in a time-consuming and often derided process — gets made at all, but *Starcrash* is an example of how *not* to use stop-motion in a feature film.

Starman

1984. Columbia. D: John Carpenter. Scr: Bruce A. Evans, Raynold Gideon. Ph: Donald M. Morgan. Art: Daniel Lomino. Mus: Jack Nitsche. Starman Transformation: Dick Smith, Stan Winston, Rick Baker. Special Visual Effects: Industrial Light and Magic. Supervisor of Special Effects: Bruce Nicholson. Matte Painting Supervisor: Michael Pangrazio. Matte Artists: Caroleen Green, Chris Evans, Frank Ordaz.

Cast: Jeff Bridges, Karen Allen, Charles Martin Smith, Richard Jaeckel, Robert Phalen, Tony Edwards.

Rating: ☆☆½   Stop-Motion: ☆☆½

Over the years, John Carpenter's films have become less and less interesting, treading in cliché territory and playing it safe. *Starman* is science fiction for Mills and Boon readers, slushy romance that has a few good tricks up its sleeve but ultimately goes nowhere.

E.T.'s alien-love theme and *Close Encounters*' "we-must-get-to-the-strange-rock-formation" plot device are shamelessly ripped off as heroine Karen Allen falls in love with alien Jeff Bridges, who has cloned himself into a replica of her dead husband (yes, *Invasion of the Body Snatchers* is also robbed), and helps him return to space. He restores a dead deer to life, discovers love ("Define love," he asks Allen, dragging out another hoary cliché) and makes Allen pregnant, even though doctors have told her she cannot have children. Presumably we are all meant to be sobbing into our tissues by this point.

ILM handled the special effects, including an impressive prologue in which *Voyager II* crashes through the rings of Saturn, and the climax in which a spaceship appears in the desert. Both sequences are technically flawless but by today's standards nothing to write home about. There is also an effective moment when Bridges examines a hair, his microscopic vision probing deeper and deeper until it reaches DNA level.

His rapid growth from baby to man is handled by the knockout combination of makeup wizards Dick Smith, Stan Winston and Rick Baker. However, the sequence only contains four effects cuts. The first cut, by Baker, is of an extremely lifelike monster baby. The second two, by Winston, are shots of his legs lengthening (in a similar manner to *An American Werewolf in London*).

The last shot in this sequence, by Smith, is a startling locked-off closeup; its flickering coloring indicates that it was achieved with fluid replacement animation as his face changes from a young boy into Jeff Bridges (the eyes blink, the cheeks swell out and the bones readjust). Smith built 104 replacement heads for this five-second cut which took three-and-a-half days to film. The shot included a slight turn of the head, but this was removed by Carpenter when he decided to trim the shot by one-and-three-quarter seconds.

665

Stephen King's It

1990. Konigsberg/Sanitsky Co. D: Tommy Lee Wallace. Teleplay: Lawrence D. Cohen, Tommy Lee Wallace. Ph: Richard Leiterman. Art: Douglas Higgins. Mus: Richard Bellis. Special Visual Effects Supervisor: Gene Warren, Jr., Fantasy II. Stop-Motion Animation (uncredited): Pete Kleinow. Special Effects Makeup: Bart J. Mixon.

Cast: Harry Anderson, Dennis Christopher, Richard Masur, Annette O'Toole, Tim Curry, Olivia Hussey.

Rating: ☆☆½   Stop-Motion: ☆☆½

Originally a made-for-TV multipart movie, *Stephen King's It* was released on video as a 180-minute feature. The first 70 minutes is a typically lazy King narrative: Each of seven characters gets a sinister phone call, leading into flashbacks of experiences each had when a child. Horror set-pieces are trundled out repetitively, the plot refusing to develop into anything. In retrospect, this proves to be the best part of the film, which degenerates into contrived sentimentality as the characters have a reunion and face up to the horror from their childhood.

This horror is Tim Curry in a clown makeup with fangs, giving rise to a few moderately good scares and eventually revealing his true form at the climax down in some shadowy caverns: a loathsome spider-crustacean that harks back to the fabulous monsters of 1950s SF films. This one looks like a cross between the creatures of *Them!* and *Attack of the Crab Monsters*. It's an enjoyable schlock ending to an overlong film which, in typical King fashion, takes itself far too seriously most of the time.

Gene Warren, Jr.'s Fantasy II supplied some interesting stop-motion effects, primarily long shots of It at the climax, but also in two quick effects early on.

During yet another variation on *Psycho*'s shower scene, Pennywise the clown appears by pulling himself up through the plug hole. Two puppet hands push the opening apart, crumpling the floor until it is wide enough for him to emerge. The miniature floor was adjusted frame by frame to give the impression that it was being pushed aside. It was shot in front of a rear projection of the live-action shower set, water spray superimposed over the foreground.

Less effective are two cuts later on when Pennywise is defeated by the children, starts to shrivel and disappears down a six-inch-wide drain. It's a bizarre idea and the animation is convincingly composited with the rear image of the children. But it is spoiled because the animation is unable to make the movement of the clown's baggy clothes look realistic; these shots look too much like a special effect.

At the climax, the main six characters go down into some subterranean caverns for a showdown with the monster. This splendid creature carries on in the great tradition of giant stop-motion spiders that have gone before: *King Kong*'s cut scene, *Planet of Dinosaurs*, *Krull* and *Gremlins 2*. An elaborate mechanical It is used for the close shots, but stop-motion is employed to great effect in eight long shots animated by Pete Kleinow. Eerily lit miniature caverns are seamlessly blended in with the rear projections of the actors, making for a very satisfying sequence.

The creature was designed by Joey Orosco, sculpted by Aaron Sims, and the armature was machined by Mike Joyce.

In the chilling first cut, six enormous spider legs scurry up over a rise. Later shots of the creature in full reveal it has two human-like arms hanging down at the front of its crustacean body. Two shots with actors in the foreground use impeccable rotoscoped mattes to allow the actors to pass in front of the monster. In another miniature set, a final quick stop-motion cut looks down at the spider-crab taking a few steps before the group rushes at it, tips it over and destroys it.

By Harryhausen standards it's a brief scene, but enjoyable nonetheless.

The Stolen Airship
see *Ukradená vzducholod*

The Stolen Dirigible
see *Ukradená vzducholod*

The Strangeness

1980. Stellarwind. D: David Michael Hillman. Ph: Kevin O'Brien, Stephen Greenfield. Mus: David Michael Hillman, Chris Huntley. Special Visual Effects: Mark Sawicki, Chris Huntley. Matte Artist/ Additional Animation/Title Design: Ernest Farino.

Cast: Dan Lunham, Terri Berland, Rolf Theison, Keith Hurt, Mark Sawicki, Chris Huntley.

Rating: ☆☆   Stop-Motion: ☆☆

This 1980 semi-professional effort is set entirely within a disused gold mine, its cast getting picked off one at a time by a slimy stop-motion monster. It had the potential to be a low-budget *Alien*, but the cast and director just aren't up to it. The eerie photography of the tunnels, lit by lanterns and flares, has a certain newsreel appeal, but after a while our straining eyes are yearning for some professional lighting.

Mark Sawicki, Chris Huntley and Ernie Farino contributed 21 animation cuts. The monster is a seven-foot tall, tentacled Lovecraftian blob, its mouth closely (and presumably deliberately) resembling the female sex organs. In one scene, a character gets ensnared in its tentacles and his head disappears into what can only be described as its labia. In *Alien*, this kind of sexual suggestiveness worked to great dramatic effect — but not here.

The pace of the film is far too slow, and it is only after half an hour that we get our first glimpse of the vaginasaurus, a quick cut of its tentacles reaching out in one of the tunnels. When one of the girls gets attacked, there is a quick shadowy closeup of the thing. Equally brief is the shot where a tentacle curls around another victim's leg (a miniature prop).

A good idea surfaces in the scene where one of the girls has lost her flashlight and so lights her way by repeatedly setting off the flash on her camera. The monster, tentacles waving menacingly, advances straight at us, seen for a second, then lost in the darkness, then seen again only closer as the flash goes off.

The only ambitious scene has Rolf Theison grabbed by the monster. A good slobbery closeup shows the monster discharging a milky fluid from its mouth all over its victim. This is followed by a series of stop-motion long shots of the puppet with its captured prey, intercut with feeble reaction shots of the actors. A human puppet is used in these shots, its legs kicking desperately as it gets sucked head-first into the monster's "mouth." The animation is crude but adequate.

Later, the monster returns to its lair, eventually getting blown up by the only two survivors. Three cuts, attractively bathed in the red glow from a flare, show the creature approaching from behind a rock, tentacles swirling. Advancing on the off-screen actors in three closer shots, the monster is coated in a generous helping of gelatin to make it look unpleasantly slimy. There are four closeups as it seems to sense the burning fuse that is going to destroy it, and finally a clumsy long shot of it on fire, flames superimposed unconvincingly over the model. The film ends with a matte shot of a painted hill on fire with the two survivors looking up at it from below in a very washed-out rear projection.

As ever, it's good to see animation fans having the determination to see a project through to the end and achieve some kind of commercial release, even when they are so mercilessly restricted by a negligible budget. The stop-motion creature is entertainingly bizarre even if the animation is merely competent, and it is never on screen long enough to make much of an impression. Watch out if this creature ever meets up with the penisaurus from *Flesh Gordon*.

The Stuff

1985. Larco. D-Scr: Larry Cohen. Ph: Paul Glickman. Mus: Anthony Guefen. Special Visual Effects: David Allen, David Stipes, Dream Quest Images, Jim Danforth—Effects Associates, Jim Doyle—Theatrical Engines, John Lambert, Paul Gentry. Mechanical Makeup Effects: Steve Neill, Rick Stratton, Ed French, Mike Maddi.

Cast: Michael Moriarty, Andrea Marcovicci, Garrett Morris, Paul Sorvino, Scott Bloom, Patrick O'Neal.

Rating: ☆☆½   Stop-Motion: ☆☆

As with *It's Alive* and *Q*, Larry Cohen really should have made *The Stuff* a minor classic. It's hard to say why the whole is less than the sum of its inventive and often excellent parts. *It's Alive* is still his best picture because its simple plot has a sense of dramatic progression which his other films lack. The central idea of *The Stuff* is a good one: An ice-cream-like food bubbles up from the center of the Earth and takes over the minds of the people who become addicted to it. But Cohen never makes the Stuff menacing enough, and it is never clear if it or the men who market it are the real villains. But all credit must go to Cohen for rustling up the financial backing to put such delightfully offbeat subject matter onto the screen; there's not much point moaning that he's no James Whale.

The characters are likable, the tone is playful and fast-paced, and Cohen even throws in some perceptive remarks about consumerism along the way. Michael Moriarty is excellent as a cocky industrial spy and Paul Sorvino provides over-the-top humor as a Rambo-style colonel. Reacting to a Stuff-ravaged victim, he exclaims, "I kinda like the sight of blood … but this is disgusting."

The Stuff itself is impressively depicted in a variety of effects shots, from the low-key sight of a dollop of it crawling across the inside of a fridge, to more spectacular set-pieces such as a character being thrown around a room by gallons of it, to the final miniature shots of the processing plant being blown up.

David Allen shot some stop-motion tests of a Stuff-creature walking on semi-fluid legs but Cohen rejected this concept in favor of something more amorphous. He also shot some stop-motion of "baby Stuff," but this was omitted from the final print, which was shorn of about 30 minutes to improve pace. The only stop-motion that remains in the film was described to the author in a letter from Allen: "The blob in the radio-control room at the film's end was a hand-operated rod puppet single-framed by puppeteers in front of a step-projected rear screen."

Other eye-catching shots include some that are live-action effects projected in reverse: the Stuff suddenly attaching itself to Moriarty's face and shots of it rippling inwards on the surface of the lake where it emerges. Other accomplished low-budget effects shots include matte shots of the Stuff flooding a chamber, bubbling up into strange shapes in a lake surrounded by live actors, and a Jim Danforth painting of a heap of Stuff cartons that get burned at the end of the film. Danforth was not asked to supply any stop-motion effects.

Enjoyably gross special makeup effects by Steve Neill and others include a dog puppet that vomits up the Stuff and a series of mechanical heads of Garrett Morris with mouths that stretch to impossible proportions as the Stuff disgorges itself.

The Stupids

1996. Savoy/New Line. D: John Landis. Scr: Brent Forrester. Based on Original Characters by James Marshall, Harry Allard. Ph: Manfred Guthe. Art: Phil Dagort. Mus: Christopher Stone. Visual Effects Supervisor: Walter Hart. Stop-Motion Animation: Chiodo Brothers (Charles Chiodo, Stephen Chiodo, Edward Chiodo). Animators: Kent Burton, Joel Fletcher, Don Waller.

Cast: Tom Arnold, Jessica Lundy, Bug Hall, Alex McKenna, Christopher Lee, David Cronenberg, Robert Wise, Norman Jewison.

Rating: ☆☆½   Stop-Motion: ☆☆½

John Landis intended this to be a children's film, but it was marketed as a comedy for adults — with the result that audiences stayed away in droves. It tells the story of extremely dimwitted suburbanite Stanley Stupid (Tom Arnold) who believes he is the victim of a conspiracy to steal his garbage. The offbeat style of humor is not to everyone's liking and few of the gags are successful.

The Stupids' household includes a dog and a cat, both of which are stop-motion characters produced at the Chiodo Brothers' studio and animated by Kent Burton, Joel Fletcher and Don Waller. Fletcher's previous credits include animation for *The Nightmare Before Christmas* and *Magic Island*. Burton had previously animated one of the title creatures in *Screamers* (again working for the Chiodo Brothers).

The two puppets are deliberately given the plastic appearance of toys, yet do not look out of place among the primary colors of the Stupid home. Neither puppet contributes much to the film, and they are seen in only two scenes each. In one, the cat looks on in despair as the Stupid kids inadvertently leave a note stating they have been kidnapped by the police. Later, the dog, standing by holding the car keys, watches in disbelief as Stanley attempts to get the car started. Both stop-motion characters are seen again at the end of the film — the cat soaking up the sun at a swimming pool, the dog looking on in horror as Stanley's barbecue gets out of control.

The puppets are animated extremely smoothly and are combined flawlessly with their live-action surroundings. However, the script serves them very badly: They could have been memorable comic characters but are given little chance to shine.

Subspecies

1991. Full Moon Entertainment. D: Ted Nicolaou. Scr: Jackson Barr, David Pabian. Original Idea: Charles Band. Ph: Vlad Paunescu. Art: Lucian Nicolaou. Special Makeup: Greg Cannom. Subspecies Puppets Created by David Allen Productions. Visual Effects Director: David Allen. Mechanical Supervisor: Mark A. Rappaport. Effects Crew: Anthony Allen Barlow, Steven Barr, Randy Cook, Bob Cooper, John Davis, Dennis Gordon, Louis Gutierrez, Mark Killingsworth, Shimpei Kitamura, Donna Littleford, Mark L. Sisson, Kirk Skodis.

Cast: Michael Watson, Laura Tate, Anders Hove, Michelle McBride, Irina Movila, Angus Scrimm.

Rating: ☆½   Stop-Motion: ☆☆½

Charles Band's seemingly endless ability to come up with fresh plot ideas dried up with this tiresomely routine vampire tale. Perhaps Band was just looking for an excuse to take a vacation in Eastern Europe — the film was shot in Rumania. Cliché piles upon cliché as a slobbering vampire terrifies a village, in particular three girls who are visiting from America. The pace is so draggy that, by comparison, some of the old Hammer horrors don't look so bad after all.

The only concessions to inventiveness are the demonic title creatures, horned, foot-high minions who serve the vampire. However, the script never quite decides what role they are to play and they are kept as half-realized background figures who perform menial tasks. As ever, Band enlisted David Allen to handle the "tiny terrors," on this occasion giving him a lot freer rein than in

other, similar projects such as *Ghoulies II* or the *Puppetmaster* series. Allen and his team supplied 15 stop-motion cuts, including several that are unmistakably the work of Randall Cook — stunning little shots in which the puppets make fast, dramatic movements. There are approximately the same number of shots using rod puppets shot blue-screen, when no intricate limb or facial gestures were required.

The rod-puppet shots (using skills which Allen honed on *Young Sherlock Holmes* and **batteries not included*) avoid time-consuming frame-by-frame animation but are always inferior to the stop-motion shots. When walking, the puppets' center of gravity is not correct — they look like they might tip over backwards. Additionally, the traveling mattes used to obscure the rods and place the creatures into the live-action footage have caused the models to look washed out, and their pale pink contrasts unhappily with the darker red of the stop-motion puppets. The rod-motion shots are unable to give the puppets any character.

By contrast, the stop-motion shots are full of movement and character, with the minions grimacing, reacting to each other, stooping, running and generally giving the impression that they are living creatures.

Unfortunately the minions' first scene is done entirely with rod puppets, a poor sequence from which they never quite regain any dignity. But their conception is original: The vampire snaps off the ends of his long, spidery fingers, throws them to the floor and they transform into the Subspecies.

Much better is a later sequence featuring eight stop-motion cuts in which a minion retrieves the Bloodstone (a mythical jewel containing the blood of saints) for its master. The first shot looks down at three minions which stand on a miniature floor, blinking as they look up at their (off-screen) master. In medium shot, one of the creatures blinks, nods its head in response to the vampire's command and then walks off. Its walk is enhanced by some blur on the image, probably achieved by double or triple exposing the film with the puppet in slightly different positions each time.

The minion approaches the entrance to the hole in the wall where the Bloodstone is hidden. This is carved like a skull and the minion slips through a gap between skull and wall — a static matte runs down the edge of the skull. In a moment of rare inventiveness, the minion drops down into a small chamber on the other side, where is housed a series of levers and cogs that open the hiding place. This is a dynamically animated shot, full of movement: The minion drops to the floor (with lots of blur on the image), turns and pushes the lever.

In an even more remarkable stop-motion shot, a minion runs from foreground to background and leaps up into the open chamber. This fast, extremely fluid choreography recalls similarly dynamic animation by Cook in *Ghostbusters*, *Hardcover* and *Gate II*. The minion stoops down, picks up the Bloodstone and hurries out of the frame — another example of realistic, confident animation.

The minion hands the Bloodstone down to the other two minions, who then walk off. The last stop-motion shot in this sequence looks down at two minions from the vampire's point of view, as they hold the Bloodstone up to him.

One quick stop-motion shot is used in a scene in which the three girls find themselves lost in some woods. Two minions are lurking in the trees — a highly detailed miniature set — and their eyes glow with magical energy. The puppets look around furtively, turning, crouching, always reacting and giving the impression of being living creatures. It's a shame more was not made of this potentially interesting sequence.

One stop-motion shot is used during a sequence in which the vampire has a long struggle with his virtuous brother. Two minions look on, their arms reaching out excitedly.

One of the girls is captured and chained up in a dungeon. "My little friends will keep you company," taunts the vampire, implying that the minions are going to commit some perverse act on the girl — but it's a theme that is not developed. Rod-puppet shots depict the minions walking across the dungeon floor and again their gait is stiff and unconvincing. A stop-motion medium shot has one minion turning to look at another. A magnificent second medium shot has one minion blink its yellow eyes and then snarl viciously, shaking its head from side to side. This dramatic action has lots of multiple-exposure blur on it.

Later, two stop-motion minions are seen on a ledge in the dungeon looking down at the girl (whose dress is now in tatters — what dastardly acts have they performed on her?). Their eyes glow yellow and they raise and lower their arms as they look on.

During the climax (a contrived swordfight between the two brothers), a minion runs across the floor and picks up the Bloodstone. This is an impressive stop-motion shot with the puppet moving at speed, stooping to pick up the jewel and then running off. Again, the animation is fluid and assured.

The final stop-motion occurs after the vampire has been beheaded. In a dismal twist ending, the eyes of the vampire open. In the foreground, minions walk into the shot (one from the left, one from the right), reacting to the presence of their revived master. The minion on the left is a pink, washed-out rod puppet and doesn't do much except stand there. The minion on the right is a stop-motion puppet and makes intricate gestures with its hand and head, turning and recoiling.

Subspecies had the chance to make its title characters something special, but (as ever) Band holds Allen back from really indulging himself. No doubt the producer has realized that even if he spent twice as much time and money on a movie, it would still only make the same profit.

Sundown—The Vampire in Retreat

1990. D: Anthony Hickox. Scr: John Burgess, Anthony Doublin. Story: John Burgess. Ph: Levie Isaacks. Art: David Brian Miller. Mus: Richard Stone. Special Makeup Effects: Tony Gardner, Larry Hamlin. Special Visual Effects: Anthony Doublin. Sculptor: Cary Howe. Crawling Bat Armature: Hal Miles. Go-Motion Programming and Animation Assistant: Steven Labed.

Cast: David Carradine, Morgan Brittany, Bruce Campbell, Jim Metzler, Maxwell Caulfield, M. Emmet Walsh, John Ireland.

Rating: ☆☆   Stop-Motion: ☆☆½

This is a botched attempt to film an imaginative variation on the vampire myth. All the world's vampires have assembled in an American town, drinking a blood substitute and wishing to live in harmony with mankind. But some of them want to revert to the old ways of hunting and the film ends with a Western-style shoot-out between the two factions. It sounds good on paper, but the direction, script and dialogue are awful — this is mindless filming by numbers, stealing cliché after cliché and failing to make anything of its new ideas. David Carradine (following in his father John's footsteps as Dracula), John Ireland and Bruce Campbell (struggling enthusiastically with the thankless role of a comic vampire hunter) all fail to save the show.

Doublin Effects, headed by Anthony Doublin, contributed some interesting stop-motion sequences, featuring smoothly animated bats that are a welcome advance on the limp props that usually populate vampire films (*Fright*

Night excepted). These mainly feature in a few quick shots of them flying through the night, but there is a more ambitious sequence in which one of the vampires pays a visit to Morgan Brittany.

It begins with an animation shot done in a shadowy miniature set of some bushes, with two bats hanging upside down and chatting amicably to each other. This is intended to be amusing but falls completely flat. There are 14 stop-motion cuts in Brittany's bedroom when the bat attacks her. Rear-screen shots of her fending off the flapping creature are very well matched and the bat looks especially creepy as it crawls along her bed. However, in closeups its bright yellow eyes look too toy-like and spoil the effect.

One of the shots of three bats in flight is an impressive and lengthy cut in which the puppets fly straight at the camera and then off towards the moon as the camera pans after them. Their wings swish down very smoothly as they half-glide through the air. Doublin used his own version of go-motion to achieve this remarkable fluidity. Again, the shot is meant to be humorous — one of the bats has a white beard corresponding to Ireland in his human form — but director Anthony Hickox (son of *The Giant Behemoth*'s co-director Douglas) has no idea how to generate a laugh. Another shot has the stop-motion Ireland-bat flapping in a cave as all his followers fly out, in the form of some cel animated shadows on the cave walls.

It's hard to tell from this minor effort if Doublin is capable of greater things.

Tales from the Darkside: The Movie

1990. Paramount. D: John Harrison. Scr: Michael McDowell ("Lot 249" and "Lover's Vow"), George Romero ("Cat from Hell"). "Lot 249" Inspired by a Story by Sir Arthur Conan Doyle. "Cat from Hell" Based on a Story by Stephen King. Ph: Robert Draper. Art: Ruth Ammon. Special Makeup Effects: K.N.B. Effects Group. Makeup Effects Consultant: Dick Smith. Stop-Motion Animation: Ted Rae.

Cast: Deborah Harry, Christian Slater, David Johansen, William Hickey, James Remar, Steve Buscemi.

Rating: ☆☆½   Stop-Motion: ☆☆

A compendium of three horror stories, *Tales from the Darkside: The Movie* is superior to many that have attempted the formula. "Lot 249" has a creepily credible mummy awakened from its sleep to enact some gruesome murders — including pulling a victim's brain out through his nose (just off-screen). "Cat from Hell" is an atmospheric vignette in which an assassin attempts to kill a murderous cat and fails. It includes the unforgettable site of the cat climbing down into his throat and later emerging from his corpse through the mouth. "Lover's Vow" includes some good old 1980s–style transformation effects when a woman changes on-screen into a monstrous gargoyle. All the tales are done with imagination and, thanks to the thoughtful photography, maintain the right mood of eeriness.

"Lover's Vow" contains one quick but effective stop-motion shot animated by Ted Rae. After the woman has transformed into the gargoyle, a shot looks down through a skylight as the creature takes to the air and flies straight up. Its wings flap smoothly, its tail swishes behind it and its head looks up as it rises. The foreground skylight is a miniature and it may be that the floor of the room below is also part of the miniature shot.

Tales from the Hood

1995. Undertakers, Inc./Savoy. D: Rusty Cundieff. Scr: Rusty Cundieff, Darin Scott. Stop-Motion Sequence Produced by the Chiodo Brothers. Stop-Motion Animation: Kent Burton.

Cast: Clarence Williams III, Wings Hauser, Corbin Bernsen, Anthony Griffith, Michael Massee, Tom Wright.

Rating: ☆☆☆   Stop-Motion: ☆☆½

This anthology horror film, executive-produced by Spike Lee, is set in an urban black neighborhood and combines social satire with macabre subject matter to great effect. Four short terror tales are framed by a linking story in which an insane mortuary attendant (Clarence Williams III) spins his yarns to three street punks.

In one of the tales, justice is meted out to a corrupt politician (Corbin Bernsen) in the form of some demonic voodoo dolls. Shots of the "killer dolls" were supervised by the Chiodo Brothers, Stephen, Edward and Charles. In some shots the dolls are on-set puppets and in others they are stop-motion models. All were designed and fabricated by the Chiodo Brothers. The animation itself was performed by Kent Burton.

Taste the Blood of Dracula

1969. Hammer. D: Peter Sasdy. Scr: John Elder [Anthony Hinds]. Based on the Character Created by Bram Stoker. Ph: Arthur Grant. Art: Scott MacGregor. Mus: James Bernard. Special Effects: Brian Johncock.

Cast: Christopher Lee, Geoffrey Keen, Gwen Watford, Linda Hayden, Peter Sallis, Ralph Bates, Roy Kinnear, Michael Ripper.

Rating: ☆☆   Stop-Motion: ☆☆

This was the fourth entry in the successful series made by Britain's Hammer Studios. Their first entry, *Dracula* (1958), was merely routine, and subsequent films just got worse and worse. Their chief crime was that they failed to exploit the presence of Christopher Lee as the blood-sucking Count, relegating him to a mere non-speaking background presence in most films.

Taste the Blood of Dracula is a lifeless bore, marred by all the usual trite Hammer dialogue and contrived plotting. A musty church set is impressive but the film is photographed unimaginatively by Arthur Grant, the lighting always uninterestingly bland. Roy Kinnear is enjoyably nervous during the prologue (in which Dracula is discovered in a forest, impaled on a spike) but unfortunately he has little else to do. Lee mutters the occasional monosyllable, but not much else. His dispatch is very weak: a hymn recited in Latin causes him to fall off a window ledge onto an altar. Bela Lugosi, despite all the criticism his performance attracts (in the 1931 version), at least made his Dracula a threat to be reckoned with.

A brief moment of stop-motion is used early on as Dracula is revived, when a layer of hardened dust slowly cracks to reveal the Count's face underneath.

Terminal Force

1995. Morphosis/Interlight/Osmosis. D: William Mesa. Scr: Nick Davis. Ph: Robert C. New. Art: Charles Wood. Mus: Christopher L. Stone. Visual Effects: Flash Film Works. Director of Special Visual Effects: William Mesa. Stop-Motion Animation: Peter Kleinow. Stop-Motion Camera Assistant: Chris Dawson. Stop-Motion Puppet: Ed Martinez.

Cast: Brigitte Nielsen, Richard Moll, John H. Brennan, Roger Aaron Brown, Fred Aparagus, Sam Raimi.

Rating: ☆☆   Stop-Motion: ☆☆

This straight-to-video sci-fi effort begins with an overhead spaceship shot in the style of *Star Wars* and subsequently proceeds to plagiarize just about every major sci-fi film of the last two decades (*The Empire Strikes Back*, *The Terminator* and *RoboCop* are among those that provide the inspiration). In every case, the original was better. *Terminal Force* doesn't have a single new idea; the filmmakers just throw together tried-and-true ingredients that they feel sure will generate a profit.

During the film's opening sequence — almost a remake of the first 15 minutes of *The Empire Strikes Back* — a rebel outpost is being attacked by interplanetary bad guys. A small boy walks along a corridor, transforms into a deadly metallic cyborg, fires at some of the rebels and is eventually deactivated by Brigitte Nielsen. This half-hearted attempt to mimic the robo-motion thrills of other films is brief and poorly realized. It features numerous medium shots of an on-set mechanical creation and four stop-motion shots animated by Pete Kleinow.

Kleinow's animation is always smooth, but the perfunctory nature of the scene allows him no opportunity to give the character any presence. The design of the cyborg is unimaginative and its legs are fashioned in a way that makes its gait seem awkward.

The boy's transformation appears to have been achieved by computer morphing — it's a good shock effect. The end of this shot uses the stop-motion puppet, standing on a miniature floor and making slight movements. In an impressive "reality sandwich" set-up, the cyborg walks into the corridor, turns and fires at an actor in the foreground. The matte line runs along the floor.

The cyborg enters a command chamber and fires at the characters in it. This appears to be another rear-projection set-up. Finally, Nielsen walks into the chamber and is struck by the cyborg (the contact implied by aligning the puppet carefully in front of the image of the actress). She grabs the cyborg (the mechanical prop) and deactivates it.

The Terminator

1984. Pacific Western. D: James Cameron. Scr: James Cameron, Gale Anne Hurd. Ph: Adam Greenberg. Art: George Costello. Mus: Brad Fiedel. Special Terminator Effects Created by Stan Winston. Special Visual Effects: Fantasy II Film Effects. Fantasy II: Special Effects Supervisor: Gene Warren, Jr.; Terminator Stop-Motion: Pete Kleinow; Stop-Motion Terminator Model: Doug Beswick; Matte Artist: Ken Marschall. Graphic Animation/Title Design/ Insert Special Effects: Ernest D. Farino.

Cast: Arnold Schwarzenegger, Michael Biehn, Linda Hamilton, Lance Henriksen, Paul Winfield, Rick Rossovich, Dick Miller.

Rating: ☆☆☆   Stop-Motion: ☆☆½

A superior sci-fi splatter thriller, directed with panache and imagination by James Cameron, *The Terminator* demonstrates just how to revitalize hoary old plot devices to keep the audience on the edge of their seats. This is *tech noir* territory — a dark world populated by sinister weapons, robotics and gadgets of all kinds. There is no shortage of mindless violence — shoot-outs, car chases, etc. — but Cameron weaves it all skillfully into a satisfying whole. And in the character of Arnold Schwarzenegger's Terminator — a po-faced cyborg-assassin from the future — he has created one of the most charismatic icons of the 1980s.

Cameron has a special knack with fantasy, and several haunting images have a visual resonance rarely found in this type of chase thriller. The naked Terminator, newly arrived in the present day, surveys a nighttime cityscape that conceals his prey. And in the future whence he has come, giant bulldozers crush mounds of human skulls.

The brief but impressive scenes set in 2029 are the work of Fantasy II Film

Effects, a company set up by Gene Warren, Jr. (after his father retired from special effects), with partners Pete Kleinow and Leslie Huntley. Bizarre machines of destruction blast away relentlessly at a future mankind. Dynamic superimposed laser fire and fine composites, putting the machines in the same shots as fleeing actors, really bring these miniature effects to life. One shot has a stop-framed spaceship fly overhead, bank to the left behind some miniature ruins, hover for a while, then shoot a blast of laser fire at the ground. Restricted by the low budget ($6 million), the filmmakers use the same cut later on when the hero Kyle Reese (Michael Biehn) is dreaming of his future world, but this time only the first few seconds of the cut are used.

Splatter makeup effects were supplied by Stan Winston, including the exposed mechanics of the cyborg's injured arm and a false head (only moderately convincing) which allows Schwarzenegger to remove a damaged eye, revealing an infra-red one. The cyborg's penultimate appearance, his eye gleaming horribly in a half-destroyed face, is a superb makeup, but even this is surpassed in the climax.

Kyle and the woman, Sarah Connor (Linda Hamilton), whom he has come to protect from the Terminator seem to have finally outwitted the cyborg, who is consumed in a fire when a gas tanker explodes. But suddenly his metallic endoskeleton, stripped of all flesh, rises from the flames and resumes the pursuit. What follows is one of the best thriller sequences of the decade.

Ten stop-motion cuts showing the cyborg in full, performing actions beyond the capability of a mechanical creation, complement the many live-action cuts by Stan Winston, whose intricate mechanical props are seen in partial shots of the robot's head, arms or legs. The two-foot-high stop-motion model, built by Doug Beswick, perfectly matches the live-action version and is confidently animated by Pete Kleinow. Some of the composites suffer from slightly grainy rear screens, but the sequence is so exciting and so well integrated into the plot and live action around it, that few but the most picky of viewers would even notice. In most of the shots, the animation camera moves slightly across the rear-screen set-up, adding a touch of dynamism in line with the hand-held feel of the live-action cuts. Stop-motion is a perfect medium for the depiction of this synthetic cyborg — it does not have to convince us that it is a living organism.

The first cut is a stomach-lurching shock effect, a satanic vision of the cyborg, now a steel skeleton, rising from the flaming debris left by the exploded truck. The foreground elements of Biehn, Hamilton and the flames were filmed in front of a full-size rear projection yet do not look like a different element: It's an impeccable composite, successful because the eye is drawn to the action in the rear projection rather than the foreground characters. Another quick cut gives a closer look at the steel skeleton, now standing erect and still bathed in flickering light from the flames (simulated by switching studio lights on and off during animation). The puppet starts to move forward, flames and smoke superimposed in front of it.

It's an ingenious extra twist to give

it a limp in one leg, making this nightmare creature all the more gruesome as it drags its lifeless limb along the ground. In two rear-screen medium shots, the cyborg strides along a corridor in pursuit of Biehn and Hamilton. In the second of these, Cameron has it increase its speed, adding significantly to the sense of pace: Even stripped of flesh, the cyborg retains its unnerving purposefulness.

An excellent shot — probably using a rotoscope matte — has Kyle and Sarah in the foreground slamming a door on the approaching cyborg; once again, this doesn't look like a composite. Live action is used to show the cyborg smashing its way through the door, then stop-motion again allows a fuller shot of the cyborg as it walks into the robotics plant. Two miniature pipes in the foreground help blend the puppet with the pipes and machinery in the rear screen.

It pursues the couple up a flight of steps in shots using Winston's mechanical prop-cyborg. Two dramatic stop-motion cuts show the full-view cyborg confronting Biehn on an elevated platform. A miniature platform and hand rail are carefully aligned in front of their real counterparts, helping create the illusion that the puppet is interacting with the same environment as the actor. There are two memorable bits of implied contact between actor and puppet: Biehn smacks the cyborg in the face with a piece of steel pipe, then in reply the puppet slaps him across the face with the back of its hand. Timing, sound effects and careful alignment create the impression of contact. To add a simulated blur to the puppet's slap, Kleinow smeared Vaseline onto a sheet of glass positioned between camera and puppet.

The final stop-motion cut is a shot from the foot of the steps looking up at the prostrate Kyle as the puppet advances on him in the background. Once again, partial miniature stair rails are carefully aligned to obscure their real counterparts. An ambitious static matte follows the outline of Kyle's shoulder, allowing the puppet to appear to be partly obscured by him, and so considerably improving impact of the shot.

The rest of the climax is done live-action, an agonizingly tense sequence in which the cyborg gets blown to pieces but still refuses to give up and die. Its upper half drags itself along the floor in pursuit of Hamilton, who eventually manages to trap it in a crusher and reduces it to scrap metal.

Terminator 2—Judgment Day

1991. Pacific Western/Lightstorm. Prod-D: James Cameron. Scr: James Cameron, William Wisher. Ph: Adam Greenberg. Art: Joseph Nemec III. Mus: Brad Fiedel. Special Makeup and Terminator Effects: Stan Winston. Computer Graphics Images: Industrial Light and Magic (Supervisor: Dennis Muren). Special Visual Effects: Fantasy II Film Effects (Supervisor: Gene Warren, Jr. Go-Animation: Pete Kleinow. Effects Photography: Paul Gentry, Michael Karp).

Terminator 2—Judgment Day

Cast: Arnold Schwarzenegger, Linda Hamilton, Robert Patrick, Edward Furlong, Earl Boen, Joe Morton.

Rating: ☆☆☆   Stop-Motion: ☆☆½

Terminator 2 is value-for-money fantasy entertainment with many outstanding moments, but it disappoints because it sticks too closely to the plot devices of the first film — similarities no doubt imposed by financially cautious executive producers rather than by director James Cameron.

The two characters from the future arrive in the present day, surrounded by swirls of crackling energy, in sequences identical to the first film. Arnold Schwarzenegger then proceeds to get the better of a gang of bikers (it was street punks in the first film), and from there on the film becomes a series of pursuits, just like the first film, ending in — no surprises here — an industrial plant where Arnie even gets partially crushed in a mangler at one point. Even specific moments are revived: "I'll be back" and "Get out!" are two lines pinched from the first film, the only twists being the choice of vehicles that get commandeered/smashed up. Affectionate nods are one thing, but lack of invention is quite another.

In all other respects, this is a must-see film, exciting, suspenseful and with superb special effects. Dennis Muren's team at Industrial Light and Magic produced the remarkable liquid steel sequences in which the T-1000 cyborg transforms smoothly and credibly right in front of our eyes by means of optically enhanced computer imagery, seamlessly combined with the live action. Some of the unforgettable images include an arm transforming into a huge blade and piercing a character's skull; the T-1000 Terminator emerging from its disguise as a tiled floor, rising up and transforming into a human being; the T-1000 passing through the steel bars of a security door; a little pool of liquid steel, temporarily separated from the rest, rolling over to the T-1000's boot and merging with it; the gaping bullet wounds that heal almost immediately; and the penultimate image of the T-1000, blown into an impossible shape by Schwarzenegger's gunfire, his head twisted round at the end of a sheet of twisted metal. Nobody will ever be able to get away with a dissolve or cut-away again, after these incredibly smooth transformations.

Fantasy II Film Effects, headed by Gene Warren, Jr., supplied many of the film's other effects, including the elaborate miniature work at the start of the film showing the tanks and airborne craft blasting away at the remaining humans in a future society ruled by destructive machines. Also included in this sequence is one "Go-Animation" shot (as it is referred to in the credits) by Pete Kleinow.

The original puppet of the Terminator endoskeleton, built by Doug Beswick for the first film, was overhauled for use in Kleinow's own version of go-motion. A go-motion rod was attached to the puppet's waist so that the most significant part of its forward movement would have a blur. The arms, head and the leg that was off the ground were animated with conventional hands-on stop-motion. Warren and Kleinow decided to use go-motion because the animation footage was going to be used as a background plate which would have two of Stan Winston's mechanical endoskeleton puppets in the foreground, and they felt that the two techniques in the same shot might highlight the strobing on the stop-motion puppet.

The puppet was animated not against a blue screen but on a miniature set strewn with rubble backed by a Vistavision rear plate. The same puppet was then animated against a second Vistavision plate which matched up to the first one, so that when combined into one shot, the result was a wide-screen image with two endoskeletons walking across it. Audience attention is primarily on the foreground live-action endoskeletons. The go-animation puppets are there to enhance the impression that a whole army of cyborgs is engaged in battle.

Later on, a tanker containing liquid nitrogen jack-knifes, turns on its side and slides out of control. Schwarzenegger's Terminator rides it like a surfer, then jumps to the ground and rolls directly toward the camera. This shot was achieved superbly by Fantasy II using a 13–foot-long version of the tanker in a miniature set. A radio-controlled puppet of the Terminator was used while he is riding the truck. This puppet was then converted for use as a go-motion puppet for the shot in which he leaps to the ground. This was animated by Kleinow, with the puppet supported on wires and combined with the miniature footage by means of front-light/back-light matting. A shadow was added separately to enhance the impression that the puppet is reacting with the set.

The endoskeleton shot took three months to complete and the tanker shot two months. Both are impressive, but it is a major disappointment that stop-motion wasn't used more. After the thrilling climax of the first film, many fans had been hoping to see a whole army of endoskeletons in battle with humans in scenes that would recall the skeleton horde of *Jason and the Argonauts*. When stop-motion enthusiasts discovered that the real star of the show was the CGI effects and that the quantity of puppet animation was negligible, many were beginning to suspect that the days of stop-motion set-pieces had gone forever.

Tetsuo: The Iron Man

1989. Japan. Kaijyu Theatre. D-Scr-Art-Special Effects: Shinya Tsukamoto. Ph: Shinya Tsukamoto, Kei Fujiwara. Mus: Chi Ishirawa.

Cast: Tomoroh Taguchi, Kei Fujiwara, Shinya Tsukamoto, Nobu Kanaoka, Naomasa Musaka, Renji Ishibashi.

Rating: ☆☆½   Stop-Motion: ☆☆½

Amid the squeaky-clean perfection of so many Industrial Light and Magic sequences, it was refreshing in 1989 to see something with some rough edges.

The plot of this sometimes-surreal black-and-white Japanese production, originally shot on 16mm, seems to concern a time in the future when people find themselves turning into bio-mechanical beings — why this should be is never explained. The hero looks into his shaving mirror and sees a tiny metal spike protruding from one cheek. Slowly, his hand, legs and the rest of him become a wild mess of cables, pipes and metal. Making love to his girlfriend, his penis becomes a massive spinning drill that would look at home digging the Channel tunnel. When she lovingly impales herself on it, the walls of the bedroom are rapidly splattered with blood.

The narrative of the rest of the film is intentionally obscure. The hero has a battle with another transformer and ends up merging with him, the result a ten-foot high metallic mass with two faces peering out. Full of bizarre images, credibly weird bio-mechanics and violent camerawork, this is gripping viewing, but would have benefited from a more approachable plot.

Stop-motion is used in about 40 cuts to show pieces of steel moving, cables coiling around and rigid characters moving at high speed along streets (the latter a kind of time-lapse photography). Unfortunately it's all a little crude and detracts from the force of an otherwise often stunning film.

Tetsuo II: Body Hammer

1992. Kaiju Theatre. D-Scr-Art: Shinya Tsukamoto. Ph: Shinya Tsukamoto, Fumikazu Oda, Katsunori Yokoyama. Special Makeup/Effects: Takashi Oda, Kan Takahama, Akira Fukaya. Mus: Chu Ishikawa.

Cast: Tomoroh Taguchi, Nobu Kanaoka, Shinya Tsukamoto, Keinosuke Tomioka, Sujin Kim, Min Tanaka.

Rating:☆☆½   Stop-Motion: ☆☆

This follow-up to *Tetsuo: The Iron Man* (1989) is less a sequel and more a bigger-budgeted remake. As before, the central character (Tomoroh Taguchi) is alarmed to find that his body is gradually transforming into a bio-mechanical monster. In the protracted climax, the hero has become a grotesque semi-steel conglomeration and battles with another character who has similarly transformed.

Shinya Tsukamoto's direction is again impressively frantic. The sparkling photography is irresistible, the editing is fast-paced and the soundtrack features a haunting rock score. Grotesque visuals abound during the transformation sequences. The script is more accessible than in the first film but towards the end deteriorates into a less-than-gripping slugfest between the two mechanoids.

As in the first film, Tsukamoto uses stop-motion in some of the more bizarre moments. In one cut, the barrel of a gun sprouts from the palm of Taguchi's hand. For this shot, the actor held his hand stationary while the gun — possibly a clay construction — was animated a frame at a time so as to appear to emerge from the flesh.

In another sequence, Taguchi is on all fours during a transformation when hundreds of tiny wires sprout from his body, and wriggle agitatedly until he is covered with steel. Once again, the actor held still while the wires were animated around him. Other pipes and devices — also animated — grow all over him. In one eerie cut, he lifts his head to howl like a wolf, surrounded by the writhing wires. In this cut, the actor has lifted his head frame-by-frame while the wires were animated around him.

Later, the villain's face begins to decompose and rust is applied to his face a frame at a time as he holds his head still in closeup. He is decapitated but,

when Taguchi approaches him, a pipe emerges from his forehead and penetrates Taguchi's head. This sequence features two quick stop-motion cuts in which the pipe is animated and the heads are mock-ups. Later, Taguchi's head spins around out of control, is surrounded by hundreds of wriggling stop-motion wires and transforms into a smooth, metallic ball.

The animation is never smooth in these shots — although less crude than that in the first film — but the images are so remarkable that one is never able to look away.

That Funny Feeling

1965. Universal. D: Richard Thorpe. Scr: David R. Schwartz. Special Effects: Project Unlimited (Gene Warren, Wah Chang). Stop-Motion Animation (uncredited): Jim Danforth.

Cast: Sandra Dee, Bobby Darin, Donald O'Connor, Nita Talbot, Larry Storch, Leo G. Carroll, Robert Strauss.

Rating: ☆☆   Stop-Motion: ☆☆

This comedy features Sandra Dee and Bobby Darin getting into various unfunny romantic entanglements — she's a housemaid and he is the apartment-owner she has never seen.

One sequence required the skills of Project Unlimited, the special effects company run by Gene Warren, Wah

Chang and Tim Barr. In a letter to the author, Warren described their work. "It was necessary to create a sequence of a car chase on a four-lane freeway, to be matted into a portion of a live-action scene. This was done with stop-motion action of miniature cars — all of which were scale-model cars bought from a model shop."

Jim Danforth, who executed the actual animation of the models, described this (also in a letter to the author) as a shot of a "stop-motion traffic jam of miniature cars on a Los Angeles freeway with an original-negative, latent image composite of real traffic going in the other direction."

They Live (1987): The eye-probe, animated by Jim Danforth.

They Live

1989. Alive Films. D: John Carpenter. Scr: Frank Armitage. Based on the Short Story "Eight O'Clock in the Morning" by Ray Nelson. Ph: Gary B. Kibbe. Art: William J. Durrell, Jr., Daniel Lomino. Mus: John Carpenter, Alan Howarth. Special Effects: Roy Arbogast. Special Photographic Effects: Effects Associates/Jim Danforth.

Cast: Roddy Piper, Keith David, Meg Foster, George "Buck" Flower, Peter Jason, Raymond St. Jacques.

Rating: ✩✩½   Stop-Motion: ✩✩

John Carpenter kept trying to recreate the thrills of his first three pictures (*Dark Star* [1974], *Assault on Precinct 13* [1976] and *Halloween* [1978]), but seemed to have run out of steam. He has a genuine interest in the genre, so it is a shame that he can't come up with anything better than *They Live*, a perfectly adequate SF-thriller.

The first half is intriguing as down-on-his-luck Roddy Piper finds a pair of sunglasses that reveal that all of society's better-off people are really skinless aliens. But then the plot degenerates into a half-hearted buddy movie with endless shootouts, ending with a very predictable climax when Piper destroys the aliens' transmission dish. Scenes showing the revealed aliens mingling with normal humans and shots of all the subliminal messages on billboards and in magazines ("Conform," "Obey," etc.) are fun, but these good ideas never lead to anything.

They Live features one of the rare moments of stop-motion done by Jim Danforth since *Clash of the Titans*—albeit just one quick cut—plus two non-animation effects cuts. Piper looks up at one point to see a small disk flying overhead. It pauses, opens up and a stalk snakes out; from the end of this stalk, an eye on a secondary stalk emerges. Piper immediately destroys it with his machine gun. This is a rear-screen shot with the model hanging on invisible wires, and it seems odd that it is used only in this one cut (although the disk is glimpsed again, but with no sign of the stalk).

Danforth's other contributions are two shots of aliens walking into a space-travel device. They are swallowed up by a pillar of light and whiz off into the stars in a background matte painting. Very competent—but, like the film as a whole, nothing special.

The Thing

1982. Universal. D: John Carpenter. Scr: Bill Lancaster. Based on the Story "Who Goes There?" by John W. Campbell, Jr. Ph: Dean Cundey. Art: John J. Lloyd. Mus: Ennio Morricone. Special Makeup Effects Created and Designed by Rob Bottin. Special Visual Effects (matte paintings): Albert Whitlock. Dimensional Animation Effects Created by Randall Cook. Crew: James Aupperle, James Belohovek, Ernest D. Farino, Carl Surges. Miniature Supervisor: Susan Turner. Main Title Sequence Visual Effects: Peter Kuran, Visual Concepts Engineering. Matte Artist (uncredited): Jim Danforth.

Cast: Kurt Russell, A. Wilford Brimley, T. K. Carter, David Clennon, Keith David, Richard Dysart.

Rating: ☆☆☆   Stop-Motion: ☆☆½

After proving himself a superior genre director with *Dark Star* (1974), *Assault on Precinct 13* (1976) and *Halloween* (1978), John Carpenter aimed to make *The Thing* the ultimate monster movie. He may well have succeeded—despite the fact that his plot lacks impetus and the characterization is stubbornly undeveloped. The special makeup effects of Rob Bottin, used to depict the title creature in various stages of transformation, are outlandish, imaginative, revolting and utterly convincing. They go way beyond anything the genre had seen before and the technical artistry leaves one breathless. Where *Alien* had cut away or hid its monster in shadow, Carpenter's creation is on full display and invites the audience to sit back and gasp.

At the finale, Carpenter had planned to use stop-motion in a number of long shots of the monster grown to a huge size. Five cuts were produced under the supervision of Randall Cook but ultimately they suffered the same fate as had befallen the animation cuts in the previous year's *The Howling*. The three most elaborate cuts were dropped by Carpenter because he felt they did not cut in well with the mechanical version of the monster. The two remaining cuts are quick shots of only a part of the monster or just its tentacles. In one of them, its tentacles burst up through some floorboards in a flurry of snow and debris. In the other, a tentacle grabs a detonator and pulls it down into the hole, while the main trunk of its body rises up out of another hole on the other side of the frame.

It was the old problem that has plagued stop-motion sequences time after time. Cook was not brought onto the project until its last months, was given only three and a half months to complete his shots, and was not given the opportunity to coordinate closely enough with the crew who were building the mechanical version. By all accounts, his animation was some of his best ever. The mechanical version is in fact very static and doesn't do a great deal other than just stand there and get blown up. By comparison, the animation puppet was *too* intricate and must have looked like a totally different creature.

The monster has a huge snake-like body sprouting tentacles and with a human torso rising out of its mid-section. It has one human arm and two long insect-like arms. Out of the side of the human face is a grotesque fanged mouth. The stomach opens up and a slimy half-formed dog emerges on the end of a long tentacle. The armature for this outrageous creation was built by Ernest Farino. The camerawork for the animation sequences, requiring careful attention to lighting so as to match the flickering orange light from a flare, was handled by James Aupperle. Susan Turner and James Belohovek built the detailed miniature set, corresponding to the cluttered basement in live-action cuts.

The three cuts that were dropped showed the monster rearing up toward the ceiling; the dog emerging from the stomach; and the dog crawling toward some dynamite just before it gets blown up. Some frames of the tentacles were double-exposed to create the illusion of a blur. With more foresight by Carpenter, Cook could have made the sequence a classic monster episode. As it stands, it is almost an anticlimax after all the magnificent Bottin scenes that have preceded it.

Although not stop-motion, Bottin's best effects deserve a mention. Most stunning is a long episode in which a character's chest forms into a huge mouth and bites off the hands of a doctor who is trying to administer artificial resuscitation. The doctor, possessed by the Thing, waves the stumps of his arms around while his head rises up on a fleshy stalk and clings to the ceiling with tiny insect-like claws. Meanwhile, the head of his patient detaches itself from the body, slides messily down onto the floor and drags itself under a table by pulling itself along with a huge tongue that shoots out of its mouth and wraps around a chair leg. As if this wasn't enough, the head now sprouts six spider-legs and two eyes on long stalks and scuttles out of the room. It is one of the most bizarre and technically brilliant moments in any horror film.

The film opens with a beautiful effects shot in which a spaceship (built by Susan Turner) flies out of control toward the Earth — a superb painting by Jim Danforth, who received no screen credit.

Three Ages

1923. Metro. D: Buster Keaton, Eddie Cline. Scr: Jean Havez, Joe Mitchell, Clyde Bruckman. Ph: William McGann, Elgin Lessley. Technical Director: Fred Gabourie. Stop-Motion (uncredited): Max Fleischer.

Cast: Buster Keaton, Wallace Beery, Margaret Leahy, Joe Roberts, Horace Morgan, Oliver Hardy.

Rating: ☆☆☆   Stop-Motion: ☆☆

Buster Keaton's first feature film, a burlesque on D. W. Griffith's *Intolerance*, consists of three episodes. One is set in the Stone Age, the second in Ancient Rome and the third in the present day.

Surprisingly, the first episode includes two stop-motion cuts showing Keaton in caveman garb riding on the back of a brontosaurus. What makes it surprising is the fact that at the time no one in American movies apart from O'Brien was using puppet animation; it seems odd that Max Fleischer, who did the animation, should leave these two cuts as an isolated effort and never have tried anything else. Fleischer, the creator of cartoon characters Betty Boop and Popeye, is known to have seen *The Ghost of Slumber Mountain* and even included clips from it in his film *Evolution*, also made in 1923. Perhaps he was inspired by O'Brien's work to experiment with the process, but ultimately abandoned it in favor of two-dimensional drawn animation.

Keaton is first seen on the back of a partial full-scale mock-up of the dinosaur — probably built by Keaton's regular physical effects man, Fred Gabourie. Both stop-motion cuts are long shots of a tiny puppet Keaton on top of the brontosaurus. Miniature rocks in the foreground and middle distance are backed by a painting of a mountain range. The dinosaur puppet has an impressively leathery hide but the animation of its walking cycle is stiff. With Keaton on its head, the dinosaur raises up its long neck, allowing the rider to scan the horizon. Then it lowers its head so that Keaton can dismount. As the puppet Keaton walks away (very jerkily), the dinosaur barks at him angrily.

It's a shame that Keaton chose not to develop the dinosaur idea: These two brief cuts, while crude, are very promising.

The 3 Worlds of Gulliver

1960. Columbia/Morningside. D: Jack Sher. Scr: Arthur Ross, Jack Sher. Based on the Novel *Gulliver's Travels* by Jonathan Swift. Ph: Wilkie Cooper. Art: Gil Parrendo, Derek Barrington. Mus: Bernard Herrmann. Special Visual Effects Created by Ray Harryhausen.

Cast: Kerwin Mathews, Jo Morrow, June Thorburn, Lee Patterson, Gregoire Aslan, Charles Lloyd Pack, Peter Bull.

Rating: ☆☆☆   Stop-Motion: ☆☆☆

Like *First Men in the Moon*, *3 Worlds of Gulliver* is often overlooked by critics and fans of Harryhausen simply because of its scarcity of animation sequences. *Jason*, *Gwangi* and the *Sinbad* films have all been done to death by the fan magazines but *Gulliver* remains relatively obscure despite the fact that it contains some of his most consistently excellent traveling matte work and also a gem of a stop-motion sequence in the fight with the crocodile. There is not a great deal of difference between the quality of the direction and script of this film and those of, say, *Jason* or *7th Voyage*, but because *Gulliver* contains no surreal fantasy images of comparable impact, it has been neglected.

The lively plot retains much of the satire of Swift's novel, while at the same time making it palatable to a young audience. Jack Sher may have been an odd choice as director, not having previously had any experience with this kind of film, but in fact he controls everything very deftly, keeping the pace brisk and extracting enthusiastic performances from eager-to-please Kerwin Mathews and also from a colorful cast of British character actors, notably Peter Bull as a crotchety Lilliputian, Gregoire Aslan as the childishly temperamental king of Brobdingnag and Charles Lloyd Pack as his chop-licking alchemist. On the whole, this film is better conceived and has a more engaging screenplay than most of Harryhausen's films, and much of the reason for this is because it is not constrained by gratuitous stop-motion sequences.

Gulliver is another of many Harryhausen films to benefit from photography by Wilkie Cooper and from a score by Bernard Herrmann. It is the second of four scores Herrmann wrote for Harryhausen and the composer's favorite among them. It is an effective combination of a classical style (to suggest the seventeenth-century setting) with his characteristically evocative woodwind themes (to emphasize the fantasy elements of the effects scenes), and is at its most idiosyncratic and sinister during the game of chess and during the scenes in Makovan's shadowy laboratory.

Harryhausen used all the tricks of his trade to depict the inhabitants of Lilliput and Brobdingnag in the same shot as Gulliver: static matte, traveling matte, perspective distortion using deep focus lenses, sound amplification, miniature sets, giant sets, high-speed filming and of course stop-motion. The publicity boasted: "*Gulliver* reportedly is the most complicated film ever made, using more than 200 trick photographic shots, the most ever attempted in a single film, making it one of the most remarkable of all time."

This was a bald lie—*King Kong* contained more than 200 trick shots. But *Gulliver* certainly contains more traveling matte effects than any other Harryhausen film and possibly more than had appeared in *any* film at the time. Realizing that the film would stand or fall depending of the quality of these shots, Harryhausen wisely chose to do the optical work in England where a sodium-backing process was available. This was not only a much simpler process than blue-screen filming, halving the number of steps needed to produce the final composite, but also did not suffer from the equivalent of "blue-spill" which has marred so many matte shots in other films. It was this process that prompted the use of the label "SuperDynamation" rather than the "Dynamation" tag of the previous film, *The 7th Voyage of Sinbad*. *Gulliver* would be unwatchable if it had been filmed using the old blue-screen techniques with all the problems they caused. Instead, it is one of the finest examples of traveling matte work of pre–*Star Wars* days.

Some of the most memorable traveling mattes in the film include the flawless shots of Gulliver tied down on the beach surrounded by Lilliputians; the Emperor walking past the prostrate Gulliver (a shot where Harryhausen seems to have consciously recalled the moment in *King Kong* where the sailors walk alongside the slain stegosaurus); the scene in which Gulliver clears a forest as Lilliputians wander around his feet at the bottom of the frame; Gulliver appearing behind the boat containing terrified sailors (filmed in front of a yellow screen); the shot on the beach where Gulliver meets his first Brobdingnagian—as he looks up at her, the camera also pans up, the timing of the two pieces of film having been meticulously matched; and the two occasions when Gulliver and Elizabeth (June Thorburn) are trapped under upturned glasses. In these shots, light reflected on the glass is actually in front of the matted-in actor and moves as the glass is moved, which suggests that it isn't superimposed—just how it was achieved is not clear. Perhaps the reflected light is an extra superimposed element.

Giantism/miniaturization is a recurring theme in Harryhausen's career. One of his favorite images, found in nearly every one of his films, is of someone or something on a table-top being looked down upon by huge figures in the background. There's plenty of scope for that image in this film, for example when the Lilliputians are delivering food to Gulliver or when Gulliver is being tested for being a witch in Makovan's laboratory, both shots achieved by customarily fine traveling mattes.

Perspective distortion, a time-saving device requiring no optical work (and a technique which years later was revived to great effect by Randall Cook in *The Gate*), is employed on several occasions, for example when Gulliver is kneeling on the beach and talking to the Lilliputian emperor on a stand. The depth of focus is so exactly calculated that even when you know how the shot was achieved, it's difficult to make the brain interpret the shot correctly.

Static matte, or split-screen, allows Gulliver to walk behind the castle (the careful matte line following the tiny battlements) and to sit within the walls of a miniature castle, conversing with the rulers of Lilliput. It also enables Glum-dalclitch to peer in at Gulliver and Elizabeth in her doll's house. It is used in the film's first effects scene when Gulliver appears from behind a rock to the horror of a group of Lilliputians in the lower foreground. Unfortunately, this shot is also the only slip-up in an otherwise technically near-flawless film: The tips of Mathews' fingers disappear briefly beneath the matte line. Harryhausen might argue that they are actually disappearing behind a separate rock but it's more likely a blunder which the restricted budget prevented from being refilmed.

Later there is an interesting shot in which Gulliver pulls out the bars of a prison cell from the walls of the miniature castle; an actor appears in the hole and drops into Gulliver's hands. This has the look of one of O'Brien's old miniature rear-projection set-ups but is far more likely to have been achieved by having a split-screen matte line follow the outline of Gulliver's hands and the hole in the castle wall.

The first of the film's two stop-motion sequences occurs when Gulliver and Elizabeth go for a walk in a forest outside the Brobdingnag palace. Sitting under a tree, Gulliver says contentedly, "I suppose I don't have a thing to worry about for the rest of my life." Suddenly, there is a high-pitched screech and Gulliver is dragged off by a giant squirrel, disappearing down a hole in the ground.

It's a startling shock effect. Harryhausen's animation in this brief scene is good enough to convince most audiences that they are watching a real squirrel. Its realistic fur, constantly twitching nose and the background noises of screeching and sniffing give the puppet a credible vitality.

The first cut is a static matte, with the squirrel pulling Gulliver out of the frame with his boot in its mouth. Mathews is actually pulled away by a rope obscured by the puppet, and a miniature boot in the puppet's mouth has been carefully aligned with the rear-projected image, in the same way that the actor was picked up by his boot by the Cyclops in *The 7th Voyage of Sinbad*.

The second cut is an extreme long shot showing the squirrel dragging a puppet Gulliver down into its lair. This shot, and a later one using the same set-up, appear to be traveling matte composites rather than rear-projection set-ups. Rear projection was not feasible because it would have required an enormous background, with consequent loss of image clarity.

The squirrel leaps up out of its lair and bounds over to Elizabeth, who runs behind a tree. This set-up, a close shot of the puppet in the foreground, does not use a matte — the puppet is standing on a miniature floor matched to the rear projection. Miniature acorns and grass are scattered over the floor.

The squirrel picks up one of the acorns in its mouth, runs back to its lair and drops the acorn (which in a live-action cut falls on Gulliver's head). In two final shots again using the miniature floor, the squirrel walks back toward Elizabeth but is distracted when it hears Glumdalclitch's voice, and runs off. In a live-action conclusion, Glumdalclitch rescues Gulliver from the squirrel's lair by lowering one of her pigtails and letting him climb up it.

The highlight for most people is the

battle with the crocodile. While not in the same class as the allosaurus fight in *One Million Years B.C.*, it is still very exciting and frequently ingenious, and the model is a fabulously vicious and realistic one. It is also a textbook example of two of Harryhausen's more subtle skills — the varying of perspectives to avoid the table-top look of animation set-pieces, and the use of intricate yet barely noticed moments of "actual" physical contact between puppet and actor, most of which are only registered by audiences subconsciously yet which cumulatively help enormously in creating the illusion that actor and puppet really are locked in mortal combat.

Harryhausen ingeniously builds up to the scene by preceding it ten minutes earlier with a teasing glimpse of the caged crocodile. The king of Brobdingnag shows off to Glumdalclitch his collection of miniature creatures (a static matte of live animals in cages), saving until last his favorite pet, the croc. It is seen in five cuts in its cage on a table, the matte line following the outline of the table and cage. Three cuts show it hissing and snapping savagely at the morsel of food which the king taunts it with, and in the last two it has calmed down, its tail swishing smoothly behind it.

Later convinced that Gulliver is a witch, the king sentences him to death by making him a meal for his pet and the fight begins. There are four more brief cuts of it in its cage, all vaguely similar — no one would have noticed if Harryhausen had used the same piece of animation more than once (as he did in *Mighty Joe Young*, *First Men in the Moon* and probably elsewhere), but instead he

painstakingly makes each one slightly different.

An actor in the rear projection pulls up the gate of the cage, the movement skillfully matched to the animated miniature gate rising, the roof of the cage conveniently disguising where one ends and the other begins. Presumably, Harryhausen must have filed down the bars of the miniature gate frame by frame as they "became" the live prop. The crocodile strides out onto the table and there is a menacing closeup of it.

Giving us a bird's-eye view of the action, Harryhausen cuts to a shot looking down at the actors crowding around the table (seen in its entirety by means of a static matte) on which the crocodile and an animated puppet of Gulliver are making slight but realistic movements. There are several cuts of the beast snapping at the ducking actor, interspersed with shots of the Brobdingnagians looking on with relish. In one amazing cut, the crocodile swipes at Gulliver with its tail, which actually strikes him on the chest, passing behind his right arm. For about 20 frames, Harryhausen must either have animated an aerial-braced miniature arm or have employed a series of glass paintings.

Gulliver picks up a brooch which the queen has thrown to him and bashes the reptile on the snout with it. Although it clearly passes in front of the model to suggest the impact, it neither looks painted nor is there any indication that a miniature brooch was carefully aligned over the real one — yet logic tells us that one of these techniques must have been used.

When the crocodile bites the shield, trying to wrest it from Gulliver, once again there is implied physical contact between the two elements, this time, close study reveals that glass paintings have been used to depict those parts of the shield which must pass in front of the puppet's mouth as he twists his head from side to side. Explaining it, however, doesn't make it any less impressive.

There are several cuts in which Gulliver swipes at the crocodile with a sword and in some of them the sword can be seen hitting the near-side of the puppet's snout. Once again, either a carefully aligned partial miniature has been aerial-braced or else glass paintings have been used. There is an effective change of perspective in the next stop-motion cut, a traveling matte depicting Gulliver looking up at the towering croc, the Brobdingnagians in the background in a third element.

Another bird's-eye view shot, this time with the positions of the two models swapped, shows the puppet Gulliver on its back, shuffling away from the monster. When Gulliver stabs the crocodile in the neck in another rear-projection set-up, Harryhausen once again chooses to make his job ten times more difficult than it need be for the sake of added realism. A partial miniature or glass-painted sword sinks into the puppet's neck for a few seconds. The animator could have gotten away without this and nobody would have complained, but the way he has chosen to do it is much more satisfying and credible. The screaming beast rolls over onto its back and in the final animation cut the rear-projected Gulliver finishes it off by stabbing it again in the neck (although this time no contact between the two elements is attempted).

It's a fine scene, technically flawless, and is a good example of how Harryhausen makes the most intricate and time-consuming effect look effortless. S. S. Wilson devotes a paragraph to it in his book *Puppets and People*, but otherwise it has been undeservedly ignored by most critics.

Ticks

1993. First Look/Ticks United. D: Tony Randel. Scr: Brent V. Friedman. Based on an Idea by Doug Beswick. Ph: Steve Grass. Art: Anthony Tremblay. Mus: Christopher L. Stone. Associate Producer/Special Visual Effects: Doug Beswick. Stop-Motion Animation (uncredited): Yancy Calzada.

Cast: Rosalind Allen, Ami Dolenz, Seth Green, Virginya Keehne, Ray Oriel, Alfonso Ribeiro.

Rating: ☆☆½   Stop-Motion: ☆☆½

Ticks is a good old-fashioned monsters-on-the-loose plot, directed crisply by Tony Randel and enlivened by creepily effective creature effects by Doug Beswick.

Deep in the forest, some locals have been using steroids to boost the growth of marijuana. Some has leaked out and transformed the tick population from tiny bugs into crab-sized nasties with a penchant for burrowing into human flesh. A group of vacationing kids are trapped by the ticks in a cabin. One of their group is infested by the bugs and transforms into a dog-sized tick.

Most of Beswick's effects use mechanical ticks which scamper across floors extremely realistically. Another is a fleshily gooey creation that gets autopsied by a vet. Before hatching, the ticks are seen as chrysalis forms clinging to trees and walls, dripping with a nauseous syrupy ooze when prodded. In one disturbingly realistic sequence, an infested dog — actually a superbly credible puppet — convulses sickeningly as the ticks burrow through its body. The boy-to-tick transformation is the kind of impressive set-piece which recalls sequences in films like *The Thing* and *The Fly* but which has been all too rare in the 1990s. It manages to be astonishing,

sickening and tongue-in-cheek with just the right balance of each.

Beswick achieves all these marvelous effects "live" but does resort to stop-motion for a couple of quick shots that were beyond the capabilities of mechanical puppets.

During the tense scene in which the dog is autopsied, a tick emerges messily from the corpse and scurries around the surgery. In one stop-motion cut, the tick drops from the top of a cupboard onto a ledge, bounces slightly from the impact, then runs along the ledge. In another stop-motion cut, the tick rears up on two of its legs, wriggles its mandibles in the air, then launches itself straight at the camera. These two cuts are very smoothly animated by Yancy Calzada and blend in nicely with shots of the mechanical props.

The Time Machine

1960. MGM/Galaxy Films. Prod-D: George Pal. Scr: David Duncan. Based on the Novel by H. G. Wells. Ph: Paul C. Vogel. Mus: Russel Garcia. Art: George W. Davis, William Ferrari. Makeup: William Tuttle. Special Photographic Effects: Gene Warren, Wah Chang and (uncredited) Tim Barr (Project Unlimited). Stop-Motion (uncredited): Jim Danforth, David Pal.

Cast: Rod Taylor, Alan Young, Yvette Mimieux, Sebastian Cabot, Tom Helmore, Whit Bissell.

Rating: ☆☆½   Stop-Motion: ☆☆½

The Time Machine won the 1960 Academy Award for special effects, is

highly regarded by George Pal fans and was his most commercially successful film. But its screenplay (by David Duncan, who had co-scripted *The Black Scorpion*) is routinely unimaginative, especially in the second half which degenerates to the level of a bad episode of *Star Trek* as blond-haired, uninteresting goodies (the Eloi) fight shaggy, cannibalistic and dramatically undeveloped baddies (the Morlocks). By comparison with *War of the Worlds* and *7 Faces of Dr. Lao*, it seems weak indeed.

The framing sections have a turn-of-the-century charm but are very static,

693

confined mainly to one room. Best of all are the middle 20 minutes when Rod Taylor travels to 1917 (where he finds his house boarded up and a war going on), then 1966 (where he nearly gets destroyed in a bomb blast) and finally 802,701. The sleigh-like time machine itself, designed by William Ferrari, is at once quaint and intriguingly believable.

The special effects of Project Unlimited are always imaginative but frequently fail to convince. The initial time-travel sequence, with sun and stars hurtling past a skylight and flowers unfurling and closing their petals, is a *tour de force*. It would almost be a credible depiction of time rushing past were it not cheapened by a series of shots that show a shop window dummy's clothes changing with the times — a cheap gimmick which points the whole thing up as a lie. Matte paintings of a street scene in 1917 and of lush landscapes of the future are mediocre. A painting of a ruined futuristic dome is only slightly better. The 1966 street that gets covered in lava from a volcanic eruption is a very obvious miniature. Equally disappointing is the miniature set used to show the destruction of the surface openings to the Morlocks' underground caverns. The sphinx-like miniature (built by Wah Chang) matted into shots of the Morlocks' world is another unconvincing effect.

Stop-motion is used in seven quick cuts. During the time-travel sequence, the flowers on a potted plant open as a snail races past on the floor. The shadow from a window frame moves across the shot, adding a clever subliminal touch to the image. In later shots, the flowers close up again, while outside a tree branch sprouts flowers, apples appear, grow to full size and ripen from green to red. The apples look like a replacement animation effect but were in fact depicted in a series of very convincing glass paintings.

Later on, a quick composite shot shows pieces of solid lava rolling away from Taylor in his machine as the mountain is eroded over a period of milennia. Taylor is a blue-screen element and the pieces of rock are animated.

The most elaborate stop-motion is in a gruesome three-cut sequence in which Taylor witnesses a Morlock decompose at high speed. This was animated by David Pal, who progressively altered and removed pieces of a clay and plaster model built by Chang over a real skeleton. It's a good, bizarre moment and, in the context of all the film's other special effects, adequately believable.

In the first cut, the face of the seated Morlock turns black, its white hair begins to fall out and one eye drops out of its socket. In the second cut, the skin blackens even more, disappears from the skeleton altogether and (an inventive macabre touch) the skull drops down onto the chest. In the last cut, a long shot, the skull rolls away from the body along the floor as the last items of clothing disappear to leave just a skeleton, which collapses in a heap.

Assisting with the special effects was Jim Danforth, getting his first work in a feature film. Although he did no puppet animation in this film (contrary to some sources which erroneously state that he animated the snail), he was involved in animation of a kind. In a letter to the author, he wrote, "I did not animate the snail in *The Time Machine*. I animated only mechanical camera moves such as the shot in which the time traveler looks up as he walks in the futuristic domed building and sees the cracked ceiling in a dolly shot, and I changed 4x5 glass slides—and animated lighting to simulate the passage of time in other shots." A humble beginning indeed for a man who would go on to produce some of the most remarkable stop-motion effects ever put on film and receive two Oscar nominations for his efforts. (Neither Danforth nor David Pal received a screen credit for their work.)

The Time Machine is good entertainment but not half the film it should have been. It certainly did not deserve to win that year's Oscar for special effects which, if there had been any justice, ought to have gone to Harryhausen for his immaculate work in *The 3 Worlds of Gulliver*.

Tom Thumb

1958. MGM. Prod-D: George Pal. Scr: Ladislas Fodor. From a Grimm Fairy Tale. Ph: Georges Perinal. Art: Elliot Scott. Mus: Douglas Gamley, Ken Jones. Photographic Effects: Tom Howard. Animators: Gene Warren, Wah Chang (also Don Sahlin, Herb Johnson, uncredited).

Cast: Russ Tamblyn, Alan Young, June Thorburn, Terry-Thomas, Peter Sellers, Bernard Miles, Jessie Matthews, Peter Butterworth, Peter Bull.

Rating: ☆☆☆   Stop-Motion: ☆☆½

George Pal's first two films (*The Great Rupert* and *Destination Moon*) both featured stop-motion but he abandoned the process in his next five productions. *When Worlds Collide* (1951), *The War of the Worlds* (1953), *Houdini* (1953), *The Naked Jungle* (1954) and *Conquest of Space* (1955) were all remarkable films and the first two of these received Oscars for their special effects. His next film contained a wealth of Puppetoon–style stop-motion characters, so much so that Pal felt for the first time that he should direct the film as well as produce it.

Tom Thumb is a frequently delightful children's film with many eye-catching special effects. Pal's direction is always lively and the photography has a clarity and colorfulness that one would expect from cameraman Georges Perinal, who had shot *Le Sang d'un Poète* and *The Thief of Bagdad*. Terry-Thomas and Peter Sellers make two memorably slimy comic villains, and at one point they engage in a hilarious pastiche of the classic Hollywood swordfight. But the film is marred by an overdose of sloppy sentimentality in passages featuring Tom's doting parents Bernard Miles and Jessie Matthews, and some sickly love scenes between young lovers Alan Young and June Thorburn.

Veteran effects man Tom Howard, who had already won an Oscar for his work on *Blithe Spirit* (1946), supervised

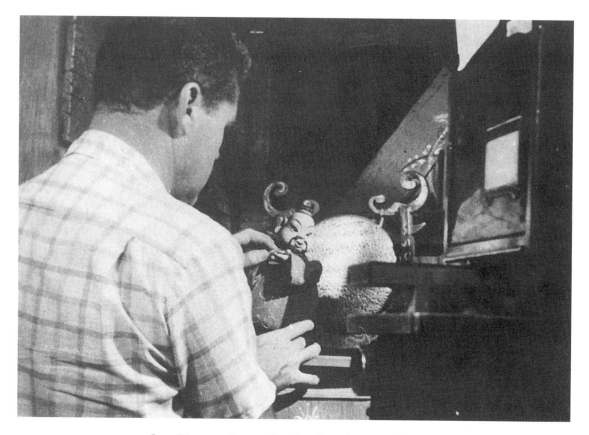

Gene Warren animates Con-Fu-Shun for *Tom Thumb* (1958).

the opticals required to place tiny Russ Tamblyn into live-action footage and also in pre-shot stop-motion footage. Some of his composites are excellent and for some shots he pioneered a process he called "automotion" — actually roto-scoped static mattes — whereby the matte line moves during the course of a shot. These allow actors to pass in front of Tamblyn, even though he is a separate traveling matte element. This is used to best effect during a sequence in which the tiny Tom dances among the feet of a crowd of reveling villagers, and in a couple of shots their legs pass in front of him. Howard also had cel-animated shadows added to some of his compos-

ites to enhance the illusion. In other shots, for example when an actor is hold-ing Tom in his hand, Howard has the actor keep his hand rigid and uses the outline of the hand as a cut-off point for a partial traveling matte image of Tom.

Although generally excellent, sev-eral of Howard's traveling mattes are shaky or look washed-out, and it seems extraordinary that he should win that year's Oscar for special effects. His achievements pale in comparison beside those of Harryhausen, whose *The 7th Voyage of Sinbad*, also released in 1958, did not even receive a nomination. Could it be that the Academy members who voted for Howard were (as is often the case) not fully informed about who had done what on the film and were really responding to the stop-motion sequences?

Pal had contacted two of the animators from his old Puppetoon days, Gene Warren and Wah Chang, and found that they had formed a company called Project Unlimited with a third partner, Tim Barr. Project Unlimited would supply special effects to a number of films over the coming years, with Warren and Chang supplying the creative input, and Barr acting in an organizational, scheduling role.

For *Tom Thumb*, they worked for five months animating the toys that come to life in Tom's bedroom. Assisting on the animation chores were Don Sahlin and Herb Johnson. These are charming sequences but the stop-motion puppets are never intended to be seen as anything more than toys and puppets. We are not asked to perceive then as real beings. As such, they lack the force of animation sequences in — for example — the films of O'Brien and Harryhausen, and are not the true subject of this book.

In a major musical routine, Tom dances with the toys in his bedroom. In some of these shots a split-screen matte allows Tom to be in the same shot as the puppets. In other shots, Tom is a traveling matte element, and in others the puppets are animated in front of a rear projection of Tom. In some shots, as many as a dozen moving puppets are animated together. One recurring character is a Chinese doll called Con-Fu-Shun, who has several conversations with Tom. The fluidly moving mouth and facial gestures of the puppet are the

work of Chang, who sculpted a series of replacement heads.

Tom paints a crude picture of himself and the two-dimensional image peels itself off the paper and dances alongside Tom. This is a clever episode, using a stop-motion puppet that is bluescreened into the shot and meticulously timed so as to match Tom's movements. It's a bizarre sight and a precursor of the two-dimensional figures that would appear years later in *Young Sherlock Holmes* (1986) and *Who Framed Roger Rabbit* (1988).

During the same dance routine, strange dancing devil characters emerge from the floor, dance alongside Tom and then sink back into the floor. These are traveling matte elements, and the surreal way that they slide through the floor recalls the weird, playful effects that Pal used to achieve in his Puppetoons.

In one shot during this sequence, Tom jumps onto a box out of which a Jack-in-the-box suddenly springs. This is a stop-motion puppet, yet Tom, who is not a traveling matte element, clearly passes in front of the puppet. It may be that this was another of Howard's "automotion" shots. However it was achieved, it's a magnificent composite.

The "Dancing Shoes" sequence is another musical number. It begins with a cobbler emptying a sack of shoes onto a table and they perform a little dance. It's a smoothly animated scene and includes one split-screen composite in which the villagers look down at the shoes.

Back in his room, Tom is too excited to sleep, so Con-Fu-Shun summons the Yawning Man. This amusing character — a yawning old man in a night shirt — is very smoothly animated by Warren and again makes use of

697

replacement heads sculpted by Chang. The Yawning Man's sleepy song usually has audiences yawning along with him. It's a fine piece of character animation and a stand-out sequence.

Pal's association with Project Unlimited would prove to be a happy one over the years, with Warren, Chang and their co-workers supplying effects to a number of his subsequent films.

Pal impressed MGM executives by producing *Tom Thumb* for less than a million dollars and it turned out to be one of the company's big earners for that year. As a result, he was given a contract that would allow him to create a whole series of colorful fantasies, including *The Time Machine* (1960), *The Wonderful World of the Brothers Grimm* (1962) and *7 Faces of Dr. Lao* (1964).

Topper

1937. Hal Roach. D: Norman Z. McLeod. Scr: Jack Jevne, Eric Hatch, Eddie Moran. Ph: Norbert Brodine. Art: Arthur I. Royce. Mus: Hoagy Carmichael. Special Effects: Roy Seawright.

Cast: Constance Bennett, Cary Grant, Roland Young, Billie Burke, Hedda Hopper, Alan Mowbray.

Rating: ☆☆☆   Stop-Motion: ☆½

Topper is an amiable comedy about two ghosts who are trapped on Earth until they perform a good deed, but the humor of carefree wealthy couple Cary Grant and Constance Bennett hasn't survived the passing of over 50 years too well. Fortunately, the film is still a delight due to Roland Young's magnificent performance as henpecked, well-meaning Cosmo Topper and the amusing invisibility gags. The best moments are still hilarious: a drunken Topper being carried through a busy hotel lobby by the two unseen ghosts; and his tie, handkerchief and hair rearranging themselves as he stands in court before a judge.

Roy Seawright was in charge of the lively special effects which, while always competent, lack the bizarre force which John Fulton (of the *Invisible Man* series) might have given them. Most are conventional: footprints appearing, cigarette smoke, indentations in chairs and beds, doors opening and closing, and empty clothes "walking."

In one scene, an onlooker is amazed to see a pen levitate and make an entry in a hotel register. This was achieved in some cuts with a pen hanging on invisible wires and in one close shot by means of some simple stop-motion. The pen was stuck into the register with a pin and, as Bennett's ghost writes the words "And me" after Young's entry (then crosses it out), the pen was moved frame-by-frame across the book and the letters added little by little.

Topper Takes a Trip

1939. Hal Roach/United Artists. D: Norman Z. McLeod. Scr: Eddie Moran, Jack Jevne, Corey Ford. Based on the Novel by Thorne Smith. Ph: Norbert Brodine. Art: Charles D. Hall. Mus: Edward Powell, Hugo Friedhofer. Special Effects: Roy Seawright.

Cast: Constance Bennett, Roland Young, Billie Burke, Alan Mowbray, Irving Pichel, Franklin Pangborn.

Rating: ☆☆ Stop-Motion: ☆☆

As with all three films in the series (*Topper Returns* followed in 1941), this has dated badly and its comedy seems hopelessly contrived, just a long series of stock comic situations as Roland Young gets led around by ghostly Constance Bennett and her equally ghostly dog. The rest of the cast spend most of their time doing double-takes and looking alternately baffled or angry as objects move of their own accord, with Young getting shoved around by unseen hands.

There are some successful gags: Topper on a dance floor with an invisible partner; the dog, only its front half visible, terrifying a maid. But more often than not a joke is dragged out until it dies, such as in a bar scene with a befuddled bartender.

Young is again on form as the henpecked banker but the rest of the cast are forgettable. Cary Grant appears in a long flashback to the original.

The special effects are the usual Roy Seawright stuff—i.e., nothing really imaginative. They are considerably less interesting than they might have been had Universal's John Fulton (responsible for *The Invisible Man* and its sequels) done them. Seawright uses stop-motion of a kind to depict a drink disappearing from a champagne glass floating above a bar. In between each frame of film, some of the liquid was drained off and the cherry moved, so as to suggest that Bennett is drinking it.

In 1939, "Special Effects" became a category in the Academy Awards ceremony. *Topper Takes a Trip* has the distinction of being the first film making use of stop-motion photography to receive a nomination. The winner in that first year was E. H. Hansen for 20th Century–Fox's *The Rains Came*.

Tremors II—Aftershocks

1996. Universal/Stampede. D: S. S. Wilson. Scr: Brent Maddock, S. S. Wilson. Ph: Virgil Harper. Art: Ivo Cristante. Mus: Jay Ferguson. Creature Effects Created and Designed by Alec Gillis and Tom Woodruff, Jr. Special Effects Designer: Peter Chesney. Matte Artist: Rocco Gioffre. CGI Creatures: Tippett Studio. Computer Graphics Supervisor: Phil Tippett. Art Director/Co-Supervisor: Craig Hayes. Animators: Tanya Spence, Peter Konig. Technical Director: Bart Trickel. Optical Effects Supervisor: Jim Aupperle.

Cast: Fred Ward, Christopher Gartin,

Troll

Helen Shaver, Michael Gross, Marcelo Tubert, Marco Hernando.

Rating: ☆☆½   Stop-Motion: N/A.

This doesn't quite match the charm and pace of the original *Tremors*, but is still a diverting piece of monster hokum. Director S. S. Wilson (author of the marvelous 1980 stop-motion study *Puppets and People*) is someone who knows what makes a monster movie tick. As before, a group of people in a remote area are menaced by the ground-burrowing graboids, 30–foot long worm-like creatures with huge mouths. The extra twist here is that one hour into the film the graboids transform into two-legged creatures the size of big dogs.

Most shots of the graboids and their two-legged successors are achieved with on-set mechanical puppets. Additionally there are 14 CGI cuts executed by the Tippett Studio. As with *Jurassic Park*, no stop-motion is seen on screen although the action in many of the CGI shots was achieved by stop-framing armatures whose joints were connected up to a computer — or Digital Input Devices, as they were called on *Jurassic Park*. The choreography thus fed into the computer was then given fleshly form by the imaging software.

In one impressive CGI long shot, four of the creatures stomp slowly between some wooden crates. In another, one creature recoils after having its tongue stabbed and falls over backwards. Attempting to reach a victim at the top of a tower, the smart creatures climb on top of each other; in two ambitious CGI shots, one creature is shown leaping into the air and landing on its fellows. Also very impressive is a cut in which eight of the creatures run into a warehouse, throwing up dust as they go. Other shots of the creatures running on their ostrich-like legs are eye-catching but the running cycle does not quite convince.

Troll

1986. Empire. D: John Carl Buechler. Scr: Ed Naha. Ph: Romano Albani. Mus: Richard Band. Art: Giovanni Natalucci. Troll Creatures Created by John Carl Buechler. Stop-Motion Visual Effects: James Aupperle. Stop-Motion Assistant: Gail Anderson. Miniature Supervisor: James Belohovek.

Cast: Noah Hathaway, Michael Moriarty, Shelley Hack, Jenny Beck, Sonny Bono, June Lockhart.

Rating: ☆☆½   Stop-Motion: ☆☆½

Troll is one of Charles Band's more rounded and entertaining films, even if it is unashamedly derivative of *Poltergeist* and his own *Ghoulies*. One feels that there is a great work in there somewhere, but it is crushed by the low budget and muddled script. A family moves into an apartment only to find that a Troll in the basement is slowly transforming the building into a medieval fantasy world full of forests, elves and other creatures. The Troll takes possession of the daughter (Jenny Beck), then proceeds to cause magical disruptions in each apartment one after another.

Special makeups man John Buechler directs this fantasy as well as supplying the creature effects. The central Troll character is a midget in a costume that works well, with a particularly credible face. Other creatures that appear among the foliage that springs up in each apartment are less convincing. They have that unblinking rubbery appearance that characterizes much of Buechler's work.

Brief but effective use is made of stop-motion on two occasions. The first begins when the Troll transforms Sonny Bono into a seed pod, an enjoyable series of gruesome special makeups including some good use of rippling bladders under artificial skin. The seed pod splits open and some snake-like plant tendrils burst out, growing rapidly and filling the room with greenery.

These four shots, intercut with reaction shots of the Troll, are very fluidly animated by James Aupperle and assistant Gail Anderson. By the end of the sequence, there are 40 to 50 vines; the

grueling animation sometimes only achieved one frame in 20 minutes. The great achievement of these shots is that they are filmed in a miniature replica (built by James Belohovek) of the studio apartment set — all the minor details, as well as coloring and lighting, are so perfectly matched that there is no contention at all.

Later, the tendrils grow to monstrous size and in five stop-motion cuts are seen bursting through the building's roof. These exterior shots have extras in the street looking up at the building, where a split screen along the top of the roof allows the tendrils to appear by means of a front-projection "reality sandwich." Aupperle adds some clever touches by animating bits of falling debris and by designing his split to allow one tentacle to snake over and down the building, rather than merely appearing above it. The giant tendrils snake in the air with a sense of power that recalls Harryhausen's octopus in *It Came from Beneath the Sea*. Much of their armatures came from parts of the Snakeman which Aupperle animated for *Dreamscape*.

---

20 Million Miles to Earth

1957. Columbia/Morningside. Prod: Charles H. Schneer. D: Nathan Juran. Scr: Bob Williams, Christopher Knopf. Story: Charlott Knight and (uncredited) Ray Harryhausen. Ph: Irving Lippman, Carlos Ventigmilia. Art: Cary Odell. Mus: Mischa Bakaleinikoff. Technical Effects Created by Ray Harryhausen. Technical Assistant (uncredited): George Lofgren.

Cast: William Hopper, Joan Taylor, Frank Puglia, Tito Vuolo, John Zaremba, Arthur Space.

Rating: ☆☆☆   Stop-Motion: ☆☆☆

Harryhausen's sixth feature represents a significant advance in his animation skills. In it, he brings to life a dynamic biped that has a distinct, vital personality and interacts intimately with human and other puppet characters. This was not true of *The Beast from 20,000 Fathoms, It Came from Beneath the Sea* or *Earth vs. the Flying Saucers.*

The screenplay was fashioned around a treatment called "The Giant Ymir" which Harryhausen wrote after the success of *The Beast from 20,000 Fathoms*. In Harryhausen's original story, the Ymir was the snow giant of Norse mythology, but the 1950s craving for science fiction films dictated that it become a Venusian creature brought back to Earth in a manned spaceship. The word "Ymir" is never mentioned in the film but fans and Harryhausen himself always refer to the creature by this name.

Director Nathan Juran, in the first of three associations with Harryhausen, controls the live action scenes competently but with less enthusiasm than he later put into *The 7th Voyage of Sinbad* and *First Men in the Moon*. On a dramatic level the film is an improvement on *It Came from Beneath the Sea* and *Earth vs. the Flying Saucers* but lacks the stylish charm of Lourie's *The Beast from 20,000 Fathoms*. Script and dialogue also fall into the "competent" category. The action begins compellingly with a series of well-conceived scenes involving the rescue of crewmen from a crashed spaceship and the retrieval of a sinister canister. But thereafter it is disappointingly content to follow all the usual monster-on-the-loose clichés. The score by Mischa Bakaleinikoff is mostly adequate and sometimes drab, failing to impart the sense of excitement that Harryhausen's sequences cry out for.

Producer Charles Schneer wanted to make the film in color. Certainly this would have made some scenes — the spaceship crashing into the sea, the Ymir trapped at the top of the Colosseum in Rome — more visually striking. But Harryhausen was determined to remain with black-and-white. This was not purely because of a reluctance to tackle the problems that color composite filming would create. He was excited about a new Kodak black-and-white high-grain film stock which would allow him to combine film of different generations with barely any tell-tale contrasts, enabling him to create more daring composites. Additionally, he wanted "to work with the black-and-white to get a mood, to make the picture more dynamic visually" (in an interview quoted in Rovin's *From the Land Beyond Beyond*). Encounters with the Ymir in a darkened caravan and in a shadowy barn achieve an eerie atmosphere because of their carefully lit camerawork, an effect that would have been lost had they been filmed in color.

Because the live-action characters are unremarkable and because the plot is standard hokum, most of the audience involvement is aimed at the Ymir itself. This was the last time until *The Valley of Gwangi* (1969) that Harryhausen would concentrate on one central animation character (in the style of *King Kong*) and he makes the hounded, pathetic Venusian one of his liveliest and most rounded creations. Yet he inexplicably seems to pull back from giving the character too much personality. Several times the script is on the verge of delving deeper into the Ymir's personality but then drops the idea. There are the beginnings of a Kong/Fay Wray relationship between the Ymir and heroine Joan Taylor but the idea is not developed. Early in the film, she looks down at the caged creature and says, "It's so ugly — and yet it seems so frightened," and it stares back up at her, making an other-worldly cawing sound. Later, when the creature reaches out to her through the bars of a cage, she exclaims, "It's claw was so strangely hot." Such moments toy with the possibility of some kind of beauty-and-the-beast theme but it is not taken any further.

The script stresses that the Ymir is only aggressive when provoked and a shot of it confronting a helpless lamb is followed by a sequence in which it eats some wheat, implying that it is not a meat-eater. Such ideas seem designed to direct sympathy towards the Ymir, so it is odd that they are glossed over so quickly.

Humanizing touches that really bring the puppet to life — such as when the tiny Ymir rubs its eyes in a dark caravan when the light is suddenly turned on — are few and far between. Consequently it is strange that a readers' poll in the Harryhausen fan magazine *FXRH* voted the Ymir as "favorite animated character" — Joe Young and Gwangi are both more spirited and realistic, and attract greater audience sympathy. But the Ymir is a superb creation nonetheless. This scaly, fork-tailed reptile is kept constantly on the move, either fleeing or pursuing. Dramatic momentum is generated by the fact that the Earth's atmosphere causes it to grow rapidly, from a few inches tall at the beginning to about 25 feet at the climax. Harryhausen's animation understands how

this affects his choreography: when small, the Ymir's stride is achieved in about ten or 12 frames; when at full height, this becomes 20 frames per stride, to convey the heavier, slower movement.

Two versions of the Ymir — one large, a smaller one for long shots — were built from Harryhausen's sketches by George Lofgren. The famous "arms back" pose of Harryhausen's humanoid creations makes its debut here. The pose saves Harryhausen the chore of having to animate the arms hanging freely (which would be more natural) and has the happy side effect of making the character look like it is always ready for a fight. The number of animation cuts — 198 — is well up on previous films.

The eye-catching opening scenes are staged with visual energy. By post–*Star Wars* standards they are modest, but their imagery still has a freshness that makes them irresistible. Fishermen in small boats off the coast of Sicily look up to see a sleek craft hurtling down from the sky. Harryhausen's wire-supported model flies towards the camera and skims above the surface of the sea, filmed against a rear projection and throwing a shadow onto the sea. The shadow, an important part of the effect, is created by placing a piece of card behind the screen and in front of the projector. Superimposed steam and splashing water and a static matte enable the craft to be seen partly submerged, its bottom half poking out of the sea. Shots of the tiny fishing craft dwarfed by the enormous spaceship are lasting fantasy images, consummately executed by Harryhausen.

Two of the fishermen climb through

703

a hole in the spaceship's side. The model is carefully aligned so that it obscures some kind of platform in the live-action plate, so that it seems the actors are stepping up into the model. Two crewmen are rescued in a tense sequence ably staged by Juran. In long shots, the craft slowly slides under the surface, the water bubbling and steaming around it as the fishermen look on.

The young boy Pepe discovers a canister washed up on the shore, and inside is a jelly-like eggsac containing a shadowy form. The revolting sliminess of this physical effect prefigures the Freudian excesses of *Alien* over 20 years later, and is an original and credible device which helps distinguish the life cycle of the Ymir from all the other inferior monster-on-the-loose films that proliferated at the time.

After a surprisingly well-scripted sequence in a hospital ward where Joan Taylor and William Hopper argue over the condition of the dying second crewman, Harryhausen unveils his first bit of animation magic. It turns out to be one of his finest — a restrained, touching sequence which elicits gasps of genuine wonderment.

The egg sac lies on a table in the darkened caravan of Dr. Leonardo (Frank Puglia). A tiny arm, with two fingers and a thumb on the hand, pushes its way through and clutches at the air. The table is a miniature. Bubbling liquids in test tubes ensure that the rear projection is not a totally lifeless image. In a second cut, a leg and an arm are clearly seen, the beast curling up into a fetal position.

The next cut is marvelous and an astonishing 37 seconds long. Taylor enters the caravan as the dark shape of the Ymir rises to its feet. Taylor turns on the light and the startled creature rubs its eyes, holding one arm up in front of its face. When Puglia walks in, the Ymir takes a nervous step backwards, caws like a bird, then struts over to the left of the table then back again, its forked tail swishing in the air.

The shot is designed so that the viewer is on the same level as the puppet, looking up at the seemingly enormous humans in the rear projection. It's a setup that would become a Harryhausen favorite, reappearing with slight variations in many of his later films, including *The 3 Worlds of Gulliver, Jason and the Argonauts, The Valley of Gwangi, The Golden Voyage of Sinbad* and *Sinbad and the Eye of the Tiger*. Its juxtaposition of the gigantic with the miniature evokes that sense of wonder which is one of the main attractions of stop-motion photography.

Three similar but shorter cuts are included, and in each the eye-lines of the two actors are perfectly matched up with the movements of the puppet, a crucial factor in the plausibility of the scene. One is a shot of the table from a slightly different angle, evidencing Harryhausen's directorial skills: He is aware that relying solely on one perspective deadens the audience's response to a scene. The subdued lighting, low-key action and extremely smooth animation make this a haunting episode.

Things are spoiled slightly when Puglia picks up a lifeless prop of the Ymir (also built by Lofgren) and carries it outside to a cage. Long shots of Taylor and Puglia looking at the Ymir in the cage are matte shots with miniature bars

Joan Taylor and Frank Puglia witness the birth of the Ymir, a bit of Harryhausen magic from *20 Million Miles to Earth* (1957).

carefully aligned with a partially built cage in the live-action plate. These totally convincing composites are typical of the results achievable with the high-grain film stock. In one of these cuts, the Ymir briefly scratches its ear, a barely noticed bit of magic which helps to bring the creature to life and is a trick Harryhausen learned from watching the tyrannosaurus in O'Brien's *King Kong*. Two other cuts are done entirely in miniature, the camera looking down through the bars of the cage at the puppet from the actors' point of view. The Ymir paces around the cage and caws, and we can't help but feel sympathy for the bewildered creature.

By next morning, the Ymir has grown to about four feet tall. In two impressive shots, the creature pulls the canvas cover into the miniature cage, roars angrily and starts to smash the bars. One wonders what material the canvas was made of, since it had to be animated one frame at a time — possibly copper sheeting.

In three long shots, the Ymir leaps to the ground (requiring that the puppet be wire-supported for a few frames), growls at the astonished Taylor and Puglia, and stomps this way and that before walking off, its tail swishing agitatedly. The miniature floor on which the puppet lands, imperceptibly matched to the live-action plate, extends right across the frame, so no matte is needed.

A series of 11 shots depicts the Ymir's progress through the countryside. These are disappointing because not one of them uses a matte, instead showing the puppet in medium shot standing in front of various rear projections — of the forest, looking down at a farm, scaring off some horses, confronting a solitary lamb. Harryhausen's animation is full of energetic touches but is let down by the unimaginative design of the shots.

Consequently, the next three shots are like a breath of fresh air, full-view shots of the Ymir walking through the doors of a barn and throwing a shadow onto a floor inlay. The invisible matte line follows the vertical edge of the door.

In the long series of events in the barn (consisting of 48 animation cuts), Harryhausen fully exploits the light-and-shadow potential of black-and-white photography. Unfortunately, this is the last time Harryhausen would be able to indulge himself like this, as all his subsequent films were in color. He occasionally attempted similar things in color sequences (such as when the eohippus is displayed on a dimly lit table in *The Valley of Gwangi*, when the homunculus spies on Sinbad in a dark dungeon in *The Golden Voyage of Sinbad*, or the torch-lit Medusa sequence in *Clash of the Titans*), but of course without the same chiaroscuro impact.

Five long shots show the Ymir inside the barn, throwing a shadow onto a miniature floor. The puppet really looks part of the live-action surroundings, and its presence is emphasized by the way it reacts to action in the rear plate: Horses rear up and bolt, and a squawking chicken rushes out through the door.

A partial miniature of the barn — walls, floor and a pile of sacks — was built for the next cuts. The Ymir walks up to the sacks and, exhibiting some

credible touches of animal behavior, looks around nervously, pushes one sack onto the floor (animated as it falls) and slashes open another one. In a series of medium shots, the Venusian chomps on the wheat, the movement of its jaws evidencing the intricate detail of the model.

At the sound of a barking dog, the Ymir recoils nervously. Harryhausen cuts from a shot of the live-action dog running at the camera to a shot, done entirely in miniature, of the two struggling animals obscured by the pile of sacks, their shadows thrown onto the wall behind. The head of a dog puppet is just glimpsed for a few frames but otherwise only its shadow is seen. Showing the battle only as a shadow fight is a clever idea which enhances the mood of the sequence. The Ymir pummels the dog with his fists until the animal is dead.

The farmer, Hopper and a group of soldiers arrive on the scene. "The creature has to be taken alive!" orders Hopper. The Ymir, now up in the hay loft, squeals and retreats into the shadows at the sound of the men. These long shots are static matte designs looking up at the creature from Hopper's point of view. Three more shots — not using a matte — look down over the Ymir's shoulder at the men below, the creature pacing to and fro, growling and waving an angry fist at them.

In a dynamic long shot, the Ymir jumps down from the loft in front of Hopper. The puppet is wire-supported during its leap and when it hits the ground, it squats down in a very credible bestial pose — Harryhausen's choreography is spot-on again. This same long-shot static matte is used in a series of shots in which Hopper (brandishing a pole) and the Ymir confront one another. The Ymir snatches at the pole, then Hopper walks around behind the creature which walks across to the other side of the frame. Hopper walks into the foreground, so that the two characters have now changed places—a simple yet effective way to enforce the impression that puppet and actor are part of the same piece of film.

Hopper tries to force the Ymir into a wooden cage. In a series of five medium shots, the Ymir retreats towards the cage, snatching at an animated pole that passes across the frame. Adding a subliminal bit of movement to the design, Harryhausen pans slightly across his rear plate, following the puppet. The last of these shots is a fine piece of interaction. The men try to push the cage door shut onto the Ymir, who pushes it back into them. There is a real suggestion of physical contact between puppet and rear-projected door, enhanced by the fact that Harryhausen has simulated shadows of the bars of the door on his puppet.

In medium shots, the Venusian backs into Hopper's pole, screams, then grabs the pole and throws it aside. The pole is part of the live-action at all times: The puppet is carefully aligned with the pole as Hopper throws it aside.

The Ymir only wants to get away. In long shot (a new static matte design), it walks through the barn, only to be attacked by the farmer, who lifts up a pitchfork in the rear projection. In two gruesome medium shots, the screaming animal has the pitchfork stuck in its back. It turns, the pitchfork drops out and the Ymir advances towards the camera. The Ymir jumps on the rear-projected farmer and brings him down. This quick shot is a magnificent example of intimate interaction, essentially a simple case of alignment, and totally convincing.

A series of full-view shots show the Ymir wrestling on the ground with the farmer. Harryhausen's animation is assured and spirited throughout this tussle. He uses a puppet of the farmer, and his animation of the man's flailing arms, kicking legs and twisting head is uncannily realistic. Hopper, in the background plate, hits the Ymir several times with a shovel; the implied point of contact is hidden on the far side of the puppet. Harryhausen imbues his puppet with animal vigor: It holds its swishing tail high as it grapples with its opponent, bites into his hand (accompanied by the sound of bones crunching), then bites into his shoulder, shaking its head from side to side as it tries to tear out a chunk.

In the same set-up, it turns towards Hopper and swats him with one arm, sending him toppling backwards (the contact is implied by the timing), then lunges at the farmer with renewed ferocity, biting into his arm. The soldiers start firing at the creature and it turns to face them. In a series of unsettling medium shots, the Ymir walks straight at the camera, eerily lit from below to give the creature a satanic look. Other medium shots look over the puppet's shoulder at the retreating men. The men flee through the barn door; when the Ymir reaches it, it pounds on it with its fist. Harryhausen keeps his animation camera moving slightly during these cuts, increasing the dramatic momentum.

The Ymir escapes (off-screen) by smashing through the wall of the barn. The tempo now settles down for a while into a live-action interlude in which Hopper and Taylor start to get romantic and the military discuss plans to capture the Ymir by dropping an electrified net onto it.

In two attractive long shots, the Ymir crouches beside a waterfall, scooping water into its mouth. Flowing water matted into the lower foreground insures that the puppet looks right in among the live-action plate. These are its last moments of peace: From here on, it is all "seek and destroy." When the Ymir hears the sound of barking dogs, it walks off. A miniature foreground tree enhances a medium-shot of the Ymir standing in front of another waterfall. The animation cuts in this sequence are intercut with shots of the live-action pursuers and their dogs.

A series of shots in an even more attractive set-up sees the fleeing Ymir walk towards a huge waterfall. Its tail swishes agitatedly and it throws a shadow onto some miniature rocks that occupy one side of the frame. It turns angrily to face its pursuers, cowering from the bullets fired at it then climbing up the miniature rock face.

The screeching creature reaches a clearing at the top of the rock face. In an eye-catching long shot, a soldier on one side of the frame blasts the Ymir with a flame thrower. The screaming beast, surrounded by plausibly superimposed flame, turns and walks away. In medium shot, the reptile roars with rage.

In a daring long shot, Harryhausen mattes around the irregular outline of a bush in the background plate in order to allow his puppet to walk behind it. When the Ymir walks away from the bush, the bush gets reduced to ashes by the flame thrower, while the puppet walks behind a rock face (another matted area).

The Ymir walks past some bubbling sulfur pits and growls up at a helicopter which flies overhead, carrying a net. These shots do not use a matte but merely place the puppet in front of the rear projection, keeping its feet below the edge of the frame. The next set-up is better, a long shot static matte design with the Ymir walking along some sloping ground to some shelter under a tree next to a large boulder. The boulder may be matted in — as ever, contrasts are so well matched that it's hard to tell.

Bags of sulfur — the Venusian's favorite food — are dropped nearby to tempt the creature into the open so that the net can be dropped. Seen in another attractive static matte set-up, the Ymir, between two foreground rocks, stands in the extreme distance, investigating a miniature sulfur sack. The puppet throws a shadow onto a seamless floor inlay.

Harryhausen varies the perspective again, to keep the sequence flowing. A low-angle shot looks up at the Ymir feeding, then growling at the helicopter overhead in the rear projection. In still another static matte set-up, the Ymir looks around nervously, scoops up a handful of sulfur powder and chomps noisily — actions which help to make it a sympathetic character. Behind it, the helicopter approaches through the trees.

Low-angle shots of the Ymir feeding are intercut with live-action cutaways and long shots of soldiers creeping up on the Venusian. In one low-angle shot, an animated net is dropped on the Ymir, who screams and struggles against the mesh. In a dramatic long shot, the Ymir grapples with the net as soldiers rush up to it. A miniature floor occupies the whole of the lower part of the frame, avoiding the need for a matte. Harryhausen intercuts shots of this set-up with low-angle shots of the struggling Ymir. His animation of the net is good but less convincing than a similar bit of animation during the harpy sequence in *Jason and the Argonauts* six years later. The net is electrified and superimposed sparks are added to a shot of the Ymir becoming rigid then shuddering from the shock — for once, "jerky animation" is appropriate. In the long-shot set-up, the creature slumps to the ground, and is seen as a static puppet in two more composites as the soldiers surround it.

Although captured and sedated, the Ymir is still growing. When next seen, it is about 20 feet tall and manacled to a huge platform inside a building in the Rome zoo. This is another eye-catching fantasy tableau, with the actors dwarfed by the huge, prostrate monster above them. A bladder inside the sleeping puppet is used to make its chest rise and fall. Closer shots have the actors standing in front of a full-scale rear-projection of the puppet.

The composite is more complicated than it at first looks — it is not a simple static matte with the matte line running along the horizontal edge of the platform. One of the puppet's hands hangs down slightly over the edge of the platform, below where one might have expected the matte line to be. The hand throws a shadow onto part of the platform, suggesting that perhaps part of the

platform is a miniature. If it is a miniature, then the point at which it becomes part of the live-action plate is undetectable. Perhaps it is more likely that the shadow is rear-projected, and that part of the platform is not miniature. Harryhausen baffles the viewer still more (and improves the shot) by having a technician wheel a piece of machinery between the Ymir's hanging hand and the platform — and the hand throws a shadow onto the piece of machinery as it passes.

The creature is being kept sedated by a current of 1800 volts flowing through it, but this gets disrupted when a piece of equipment is dropped accidentally into some cables. The Ymir's head arches back and it roars as it awakens. In long shot, actors run beneath the monster as it rouses itself. In one shot, Hopper stands in front of a full-scale rear projection of just the Ymir's tail and arm, with the puppet clenching its fist. In four long shots, with horrified actors looking on below, the Ymir snaps the manacle around its wrists and eventually the buckle around its waist. Still groggy, the Ymir leans back against a miniature replica of the platform — a credible bit of character animation — before steadying itself and walking off.

In three cuts of the exterior of the building — shot entirely in miniature — Harryhausen animates the wall being torn apart and the Ymir stepping through it. The creature rears back triumphantly, but when it is challenged by an angry elephant it retreats — again, Harryhausen is stressing that the Ymir is a victim rather than an aggressor.

The battle with the elephant, realized in 13 animation cuts, is very fluidly

COLUMBIA PICTURES presents
'20 MILLION MILES TO EARTH' ·X·
starring WILLIAM HOPPER · JOAN TAYLOR

This stunning frame enlargement from *20 Million Miles to Earth* formed one of the British set of eight stills used to promote the film in cinema lobbies.

animated and is as excitingly choreographed as any of the best of similar fights in Harryhausen's later pictures. It is a good example of how skillful a director he can be when in total control of pacing and editing. The sequence opens with several shots of a real elephant, thereby inviting problems when cutting to the model — but Harryhausen pulls it off perfectly. Animating a familiar creature means that any unrealistic gestures it makes will be all the more apparent to audiences, but Harryhausen has studied the movements of a living elephant and his animation is excellent — the bulk, stride and posture of his puppet look just right.

The live elephant charges, at which point Harryhausen cuts to a shot of his puppet elephant ramming the Ymir. In medium shot, the Ymir grabs the elephant around the head. The Ymir pushes the animal backwards along a miniature floor, which is seamlessly matched to the rear projection. The elephant is toppled and lands on top of its trainer and a photographer, who mime the action as the puppet is positioned so as to obscure them. The Ymir backs off and the elephant gets to its feet, a credible bit of animation that in someone else's hands might have looked awkward.

In a glorious long shot (see illustration), the two screaming beasts spill out through the pillared entrance of the zoo, battling their way right across the frame as extras rush about both behind them and to their left. An imperceptible area of floor inlay allows the puppets to throw shadows. This is Harryhausen using his "reality sandwich" to maximum advantage.

In two dramatic long shots in a street, with extras running past in the background, the Ymir pushes the elephant over onto a miniature car, which crumples under the impact. The elephant gets up, roars and pushes the Ymir out of the right side of the frame.

In another street scene, extras rush through an overhead viaduct while in the foreground on a miniature floor (there is no matte) the elephant knocks the Ymir to the ground. A frequently published still of this set-up includes a puppet man running across the foreground. This puppet does not appear in the sequence and was specially posed for the still.

In a striking perspective looking through the viaduct arch, the elephant lifts the Ymir off the ground. The matte line follows the curve of the arch. Three cuts in a final rear-screen set-up (again with a miniature floor and no matte) show the Ymir biting into the elephant's trunk, bringing the creature to the ground and pounding it with its fists. The Venusian bites into the elephant's neck (leaving a messy hole). The sequence ends with a few non-animated shots of the elephant puppet lying on a

carefully matched floor inlay, a bladder causing its chest to rise and fall slowly.

The Ymir continues its rampage, and in two unforgettable long shots demolishes a miniature lamp post with one hand while holding a screaming man in the other. These shots use an extensive miniature floor, matched to the rear projection with no matte. The legs and arms of the puppet man respond correctly as the Ymir swings it about, but the animation is just a little too smooth to be realistic. The Ymir drops the puppet man, which attempts to crawl away.

Hopper, in a car, rams the creature. Two shots look through the windshield of a studio mock-up of a car at a full-scale rear projection of the Ymir. In the second, Harryhausen has dollied his animation camera one frame at a time towards the puppet to create the impression that Hopper is driving straight at it. Hopper jumps free of the car as the Ymir gets up, the car and actor on a stage in front of a very large rear screen containing the animation footage. It's the kind of shot that in the 1950s could only be successful in black-and-white footage.

In a dramatic static matte design, Hopper hides in the foreground behind a pillar as the enormous legs and torso of the Ymir stomp past him. In still another striking static matte set-up, the bellowing Ymir strides along a street as extras flee from it, and shadows from nearby buildings are simulated on the puppet.

The Ymir disappears into the Tiber but Harryhausen doesn't attempt to depict this, nor even add the sound of an off-screen splash to suggest the image. This, and the absence of a shot earlier showing the Ymir breaking out of the barn, make Paul Jensen suspect (in

Phantasma #4) that "perhaps certain effects shots were planned but time ran out before the animation could be completed."

Grenades are thrown into the river and eventually the Ymir surfaces, now Kong-sized. Its enormous head and shoulders rise up behind a group of soldiers on a bridge, who are actually in front of another large rear screen. The puppet is coated with glycerin to create the illusion that it is wet from the river. In a sequence that some see as an unoriginal rehash of a scene in *It Came from Beneath the Sea*, the Ymir demolishes the bridge.

An extensive miniature bridge is matched up with the live-action bridge and (in five animation cuts) cracks appear in the concrete and the Venusian pushes up through it. The animation of the rending concrete and bricks is extremely convincing. Although this is only a brief sequence, Harryhausen sparks visual interest by cutting from long shots to closer shots and to a shot of the soldiers in front of a rear screen. In a dramatic long shot, the Ymir pushes a part of the street straight up toward the camera, blocking out the light. Finally, the puppet stands among the rubble it has created and walks off. The rubble appears to be all miniature, and no matte is needed.

The Ymir continues to create, as Harryhausen calls it (in *Film Fantasy Scrapbook*), "a mass of new ruins among the old." The reptile arrives at the ruined pillars of the Temple of Saturn, a striking setting seen in a sequence featuring nine animation cuts.

In a series of long shots, the Venusian walks behind the pillars, an elaborate static matte design wherein the matte line follows not only the outline of several pillars but also a foreground hillock. A group of soldiers, looking tiny in the lower foreground, fire their rifles at the Ymir and eagle-eyed viewers will notice that a cloud of smoke thrown up by the gunfire briefly disappears behind the puppet when it should pass in front of it.

A flame thrower is fired at the creature and a superimposed shower of flame, also matted behind the pillars, surrounds the puppet. When a soldier runs across the lower foreground, part of his helmet momentarily vanishes as it crosses the matte line.

Other cuts use a miniature replica of the temple pillars. Another blast of flame is matted behind them, then the screaming Ymir pushes through the pillars, bringing them down on top of the soldiers. Prohibited by the cost of high-speed filming of miniatures, Harryhausen again has to animate the falling masonry. A host of large and small chunks, supported on invisible wires, falls around the puppet in a surprisingly credible shot. Traveling matte is used to show large stones falling on the soldiers. It's the only occasion in the film when the process is used and is a fairly wretched effect. In the last shot of this sequence, the Ymir stands in an all-miniature set-up among the new ruins it has made, then stalks off.

The Ymir strides across an impressive long shot, a pile of matted-around ruins on each side of the frame. With perfect timing, soldiers run out of an area just as the Ymir steps into it. A rear-projected shadow under the puppet reinforces the "wholeness" of this clever composite.

Harryhausen stages his climax at the Colosseum, a photogenic setting for a sequence in the style of *King Kong*'s finale. Although not as spectacular as the fairground climax of *The Beast from 20,000 Fathoms*, Harryhausen insures that this is a fast-paced, exciting sequence by incorporating a large number of static matte set-ups of his creature in different parts of the Colosseum, and exploits to the full the possibilities of this curved structure in his composites. The means of the Ymir's destruction — a couple of direct hits by a bazooka — is too low-key an ending for a such a fabulous creature; something more inventive should have been dreamed up. A stronger score and some extra touches of pathos might have made this a classic episode. There are 30 animation cuts.

Three long shots have the Ymir standing in front of the Colosseum on a miniature floor (there is no matte), roaring at the army vehicles that arrive in live-action cut-away shots. Two composites have the Ymir standing on a floor inlay flawlessly matched to the curving side of the Colosseum, which the creature then climbs up. The Ymir is just on the far side of the building so Harryhausen does not need to show it in contact with the wall as it climbs. It's a striking sight to see this giant lizard, its long tail snaking down, scaling a world-famous ruin.

There is a tense live-action passage as the soldiers are deployed around the Colosseum, waiting for the Ymir to make a reappearance. Some stones are dropped on one group of soldiers who look up to see the growling Venusian above them on one of the building's many inner walls halfway to the top, a low-angle composite with the matte following the curve of the wall.

Hopper fires a bazooka at the creature. Harryhausen shows this from the point of view of both Hopper and the Ymir. In the first cut, the Ymir is way off in the background, matted into the shot, smoke and flame superimposed where the bazooka hits. The second cut looks from behind the Ymir at Hopper, and does not need a matte since only the puppet's torso and legs appear in the foreground of the frame.

Soldiers run from the foreground into the background of a striking long shot with the Ymir far off between two ruined walls. The beast roars out and begins scaling the wall on the right of the shot. A cloud of smoke is superimposed where some bazooka fire hits the wall just below the puppet.

A low-angle extreme long shot looks up at the tiny Ymir now at the very top of the Coliseum, a dramatic perspective following the line of sight of two soldiers in the lower foreground. Several shots look down over the Ymir's shoulder at the tanks and soldiers in the street far below. Some of these show the puppet in full, standing on a partial miniature of the top of the wall.

Another design, done entirely in miniature, looks up at the Ymir on the wall as he picks up a loose stone and throws it into the street below. When a shell is fired and hits the wall near the reptile's feet, pieces of loose masonry are animated as they drop away. Another cut using this set-up shows the Ymir clutching its throat after it has been hit, walking in a circle, its tail dangling over the edge of the wall.

Yet another set-up has a group of

713

Another unforgetable image from Harryhausen's *20 Million Miles to Earth*: The Ymir atop the wall of Rome's Colosseum.

soldiers running up a flight of steps in the foreground with the Ymir matted onto the top of the wall in the extreme distance. Still another depicts Hopper at the foot of the Colosseum with a bazooka aimed up at the Ymir, which again is in the extreme distance.

The Ymir clutches a wounded arm as it looks down at the soldiers below. Hopper fires the bazooka again and the Ymir clutches its stomach and collapses, one leg hanging over the side of the wall and kicking helplessly, its tail thrashing the air. In a low-angle perspective looking up from the point of view of two spectators, the wounded Ymir gets to its feet again.

Seen from above, the Venusian begins to slip off the edge of the wall, growling in rage and pain, barely clinging on with its claws. A dynamic all-miniature shot from below shows the Ymir clinging to the wall and swishing its tail about agitatedly. In the same set-up, a shell from a bazooka hits just to one side of the hounded creature, and a cloud of smoke and flare is superimposed. Another shell finds its target, exploding just above the Ymir. The creature falls backwards, taking a piece of the

714

wall with it. In an extreme long shot, the Ymir falls to the ground, still roaring. The rate of fall of the puppet is about as realistic as is possible with this technique—in other words, not totally convincing, but close. Several wire-supported rocks fall with the puppet.

Harryhausen avoids showing the actual impact and closes with four non-animated composite shots of the dead Ymir lying in front of a crowd. Fans of corny closing lines are not disappointed: One character turns to another and ponders, "Why is it always, always so costly for Man to move from the present to the future?"

Although the live-action scenes of *20 Million Miles to Earth* are frequently mediocre, Harryhausen's consistently inspired animation and composite design make this one of the archetypal monster films of the 1950s. He achieved miracles on a budget that was only slightly larger than those of previous films. The picture was a financial success and so allowed an even larger budget for his next film with Schneer, an Arabian Nights fantasy (*The 7th Voyage of Sinbad*) whose color photography would soak up all the extra dollars thrown at it and would also force Harryhausen to push his skills still further.

Twilight of the Dogs

1995 (not released). D: John Ellis. Scr: Tim Sullivan. Ph: Alicia Craft. Mus: David Bartley. Stop-Motion Animation: Kent Burton. Matte Paintings: Ron Miller. Special Effects Makeup: Tim Davis.

Cast: Tim Sullivan, Ralph Bluemke, Gage Sheridan, George Stover, Mike Evans, John Kessel.

Rating: N/A.   Stop-Motion: N/A.

In this 21st century tale, most of the earth's population has been wiped out by a plague, plunging the world into a new dark age. A group of disease-free survivors band together to destroy the plague-ridden humans and are helped by a half-human alien woman who carries a cure.

The film features some dog-sized black widow spiders which were animated by Kent Burton. Burton's other stop-motion credits include *Invader*, *Ed Wood* and dinosaur animation for the television series *Land of the Lost*.

At the time of this writing *Twilight of the Dogs* had not been released.

Twilight Zone—The Movie

1983. Warner Bros. Prologue and Segment 1: D-Scr: John Landis. Ph: Stevan Larner. Segment 2: Dir: Steven Spielberg. Scr: George Clayton Johnson, Richard Matheson, Josh Rogan. Story: George Clayton Johnson. Ph: Allen Daviau. Segment 3: D: Joe Dante. Scr: Richard Matheson. Story: Jerome Bixby. Ph: John Hora. Special Makeup Designed and Created by Rob Bottin. Matte Paintings: Dream Quest Images. Matte Artist: Rocco Gioffre. Segment 4: D: George Miller. Scr: Richard Matheson. Story: Richard Matheson. Ph: Allen Daviau. Special Makeup Created by Craig Reardon, Michael McCracken. Visual Effects: Peter Kuran/V.C.E.; Jim Danforth/Effects Associates; David Allen. Stop-Motion Assistant (uncredited): Dennis Gordon. Armature (uncredited): Jon Berg. Monster Conceptual Design: Ed Verraux. Art: James D. Bissell. Mus: Jerry Goldsmith.

Cast: Dan Aykroyd, Albert Brooks, Scatman Crothers, John Lithgow, Vic Morrow, Kathleen Quinlan, Kevin McCarthy, Dick Miller.

Rating: ☆☆½   Stop-Motion: ☆☆½

This was another Great Missed Opportunity in the decade of fantasy films that followed *Star Wars*. On paper it looked terrific: four genre directors with excellent track records combining to produce a nostalgic recreation of a classic television series. As it turned out, only two of the four episodes lived up to the promise.

John (*An American Werewolf in London*) Landis' episode opens powerfully with Vic Morrow unleashing a torrent of pent-up racial bigotry in a bar, but subsequently meanders hopelessly. Steven Spielberg's episode is the weakest, an unimaginative tale that sees him moving farther away from the skillful tension and excitement of his earlier work (*Duel, Jaws*) and deeper into the sentimentalities that characterized *E.T.: The Extra-Terrestrial.* Here he tries so hard to evoke the much-acclaimed Spielberg "sense of wonder" that he falls flat on his face. Joe (*Piranha, The Howling*) Dante's neat little horror story is far more satisfying and includes one genuinely scary shock moment when Rob Bottin's monstrous rabbit leaps out of Kevin McCarthy's top hat. Another bizarre Bottin special makeup is a girl with no mouth, staring blankly at a television screen.

George (*Mad Max*) Miller's episode, set on board an airplane in a violent storm, is easily the strongest and contains one stop-motion cut by David Allen (who in the credits suffers the infelicity of having his name misspelled Allan). John Lithgow gives a fine performance as a passenger with a phobia about flying who sees a hideous gremlin on the wing of the plane. Lithgow's growing hysteria is painfully credible and the balance of humor and horror is just right. Tension builds steadily, climaxing with the unforgettable sight of Lithgow hanging half out of the plane's window, being first menaced by the fiend and then playfully admonished by a wag of its finger before it flies off into the clouds.

For this final cut, Allen and Dennis Gordon (uncredited) animated a six-inch puppet which they built over an armature made years earlier by Jon Berg. Shot against a blue screen, the distant puppet spirals up and away, making very slight movements of its body. In all other shots, the gremlin is an actor in a costume and mask built by Craig Reardon and Michael McCracken.

A dramatic point-of-view shot, moving through some drifting clouds towards the runway, was done by Jim Danforth's Effects Associates company. In a letter to the author, Danforth described this shot as "a complex composite with many stop-motion elements — clouds, wing lighting, landing lights, camera tilts and dolly, etc."

Two Musketeers see *Bláznova Kronika*

2001: A Space Odyssey

1968. MGM. Prod-D: Stanley Kubrick. Scr: Stanley Kubrick, Arthur C. Clarke. Ph: Geoffrey Unsworth. Special Photographic Effects Designed and Directed by Stanley Kubrick. Special Effects: Wally Veevers, Douglas Trumbull, Con Pederson, Tom Howard. Art: Tony Masters, Harry Lange, Ernie Archer.

Cast: Keir Dullea, Gary Lockwood, William Sylvester, Daniel Richter, Leonard Rossiter, Douglas Rain (voice of HAL), Robery Beatty.

Rating: ☆☆☆☆   Stop-Motion: ☆☆½

Stanley Kubrick's science fiction masterpiece is one of the great cinema experiences. He combines an almost hypnotic display of admiration for the beauty of technology with an indulgent, half-understood mysticism in a way that leaves one in awe of his mastery of cinema technique. No subsequent film — not even the sequel *2010* (1984) — has even attempted to recreate this kind of impact.

His plot is essentially simple but he deliberately makes it obscure so as to heighten the sense of drama. A black monolith left on Earth by aliens imparts the necessary intelligence to neanderthal man to allow him to evolve into modern man. Thousands of years later, man has evolved sufficently to be able to travel to the moon. Here another monolith is discovered, and it guides man on his way to taking the next evolutionary step.

In Kubrick's space sequences, the craft move across the screen with a cold precision and lack of theatricality that would be soulless were it not for the fact that his choice of background music — Strauss' "The Blue Danube" — creates a juxtaposition which ingeniously imparts to every shot a grace and beauty which make them unforgettable.

In some of these shots, the models of the spaceships were shot one frame at a time as they were moved along tracks in the effects studio. Some of these models were huge — the revolving space station was nine feet across. The *Discovery* was 54 feet long. As a result, it was necessary to shoot four-second exposures for each frame in order to achieve the correct focus for such a depth of field.

The effects team, supervised by Wally Veevers, tried to avoid using traveling mattes because they felt they would not produce realistic composites.

Instead, many composites were achieved by means of rotoscope mattes, each matte painstakingly drawn by hand so as to conform to the outline of a spaceship and then repositioned one frame at a time as the model moved across a background image.

2001: A Space Odyssey won the 1968 Academy Award for Best Special Effects.

2010

1984. MGM. Prod-D-Scr: Peter Hyams. Based on the Novel by Arthur C. Clarke. Ph: Peter Hyams. Art: Albert Brenner. Mus: David Shire. Visual Effects Director: Richard Edlund. Chief Matte Artist: Matthew Yuricich. Stop-Motion: Randall William Cook.

Cast: Roy Scheider, John Lithgow, Helen Mirren, Bob Balaban, Keir Dullea, Douglas Rain.

Rating: ☆☆☆   Stop-Motion: ☆☆

In its own right, *2010* is an entertaining work with superb effects, but it is impossible to divorce it from the shadow of the original which was infinitely superior and did not need a sequel. Only the climax, in which "the Earth's landlord" turns one of the moons of Jupiter into a second sun in order to bring peace to the world, goes beyond the plot of the original. The bulk of the film, like the book, is merely concerned with getting to the *Discovery* (the spaceship abandoned at the end of Kubrick's film) and as such is really all padding and repetition.

Peter Hyams does not have Kubrick's visual or aural sense and goes for a more realistic approach, most apparent in the special effects which, while technically flawless, lack the poetry of Kubrick's shots. There are many stunning and complex composites depicting Jupiter, its moons and the two spacecraft, but they are presented in a matter-of-fact manner (accompanied by David Shire's unremarkable score) and are forgettable. Kubrick's images stay with you for years.

Randall William Cook animated two shots of a probe craft exiting from a spaceship and gliding over one of the moons. Its receptor panels swivel and move into position and gauges hanging below it unfurl. Later, some of the extreme long shots of the astronauts space-walking were also achieved by stop-motion (recalling the animation in *Destination Moon*). This is all competent blue-screen animation, but for Cook it was merely a job of work allowing little creative input.

2010 received an Academy Award nomination for its special visual effects.

The Two Year Holiday
see *Ukradená Vzducholod*

The Twonky

1953. Prod-D-Scr: Arch Oboler. Story: Henry Kuttner. Ph: Joseph Biroc. Mus: Jack Meakin. Stop-Motion: Gene Warren.

Cast: Hans Conried, Gloria Blondell, Trilby Conried, Billy Lynn, Janet Warren, Ed Max.

Rating: ☆☆   Stop-Motion: ☆☆

In Arch Oboler's satirical attack on the newly arrived medium of television, a creature from the future invades a television set and tries to take control of Hans Conried's life. The set walks about the house, performs all the household chores and hypnotizes anyone who tries to shut it down.

Gene Warren was recruited to execute some brief moments of stop-motion. He explained, "The only effect with which we were involved required rigging a TV set to be moved stop-frame as if it had a life of its own."

Ukradená Vzducholod
(*The Stolen Dirigible*) (a.k.a. *The Stolen Airship*; *The Two Year Holiday*)

1967. Czech. Barrandov/Gottwaldov. D: Karel Zeman. Scr: Karel Zeman, Radovan Kratky. Inspired by Characters Created by Jules Verne. Ph: Josef Novotny. Art: Jaroslav Krska. Mus: Jan Novak.

Cast: Michal Pospisil, Hanus Bor, Jan Cizek, Josef Stranik, Jan Malat, Cestmir Randa.

Rating: ☆☆½   Stop-Motion: ☆☆½

After the disappointing *Bláznova Kronika (Insane Chronicle)* in 1964,

Ukradená Vzducholod is something of a return to form for Karel Zeman, although still considerably less memorable than his three great works, *Journey to the Beginning of Time, The Invention of Destruction* and *Baron Munchausen*. Set in the nineteenth century, it tells the story of five boys who steal an airship while it is being displayed at a show. They drift over Europe, out over the Atlantic and crashland on an island

719

where they encounter Captain Nemo and his submarine, the *Nautilus*. In his usual unique style, Zeman combines deft moments of gentle, satirical humor with an inventive, distinctive fantasy milieu.

Ukradená Vzducholod contains much more stop-motion than *Bláznova Kronika*, but it is reserved chiefly for fleeting moments when it was not practical to shoot something live-action. Only on a couple of occasions does Zeman chose to use the process to create the kind of quirky fantasy images for which he is famous.

Zeman depicts a dozen different kinds of newly invented airships crossing the screen. For extreme long shots, he uses stop-motion miniatures. For example, on a platform hanging beneath one airship, a group of girls performs the can-can: These are live actors in close shots but stop-motion puppets in a couple of quick miniature shots. Another airship, with typical Zeman quirkiness, is powered by three rowers with oars shaped like large wings; again, stop-motion is used for a few extreme long shots.

Newly invented land-based vehicles also come in for the Zeman treatment. Best of all is a brief sequence in which the camera pulls back from a medium shot of a man driving a car to reveal that the vehicle moves by means of horses' legs. This is a clever matte shot and the legs are animated puppets.

Stop-motion is also used for a shot in which the airship crashlands. A tree demolished by the collision is a stop-motion element, and its branches are convincingly animated as they splinter and fall to the ground.

A stop-motion shark features prominently in one long sequence. A cannon falls from a clifftop into the sea and is swallowed by the shark. The weight of the cannon distorts the shark's body and causes the animal to sink to the sea bed. One of the boys dives into the sea and a stop-motion puppet of the boy swims up to the shark, props its huge red mouth open with a stick, then swims inside to retrieve something from its stomach. This entertaining sequence is one of the film's highlights and the closest in spirit that the film gets to *The Invention of Destruction*.

Scenes on the island also make extensive use of hanging paintings to create various panoramas of mountains and clifftops, all executed with Zeman's usual idiosyncratic and eye-catching panache. Adding life to these images, flocks of birds — sometimes live-action, sometimes stop-motion puppets — fly around in the foreground.

The Valley of Gwangi

1969. Warner Bros.–Seven Arts. D: James O'Connolly. Scr: William E. Bast. Based (uncredited) on an Original Concept by Willis O'Brien and Harold Lamb. Additional Material: Julian More. Art: Gil Parrondo. Ph: Erwin Hillier. Mus: Jerome

Moross. Model Sculpture (uncredited): Arthur Hayward. Associate Producer and Creator of Special Visual Effects: Ray Harryhausen.

Cast: James Franciscus, Gila Golan, Richard Carlson, Laurence Naismith, Freda Jackson.

Rating: ☆☆☆   Stop-Motion: ☆☆☆☆

This is Harryhausen's finest hour, a visually marvelous and frequently thrilling blend of the Western and prehistoric genres, full of fresh ideas and superb animation. Yet it was a commercial failure and was given short shrift by the critics.

Contemporary reviewers, caught up in the vogue for social comment and permissiveness, had no time for an old-fashioned monster picture and, curiously, were unimpressed by the special effects. Most found the plot too conventional to be effective; many started from the assumption that *any* film about dinosaurs must be awful. Most made glib remarks that had little do with the actual film. David Robinson in *The Financial Times*: "The fabulous beasts are in pretty color ... but they no longer cut any ice. Not that they could, really, with such a dreadful old script and unconvincing playing." Penelope Mortimer in *The Observer*: "Great lolloping Dynamated prehistoric dinosaurs jerk about the screen with considerably less effect than *King Kong* at the dawn of cinema time." (Since when was 1933 the dawn of the cinema?) Nina Hibbin in *The Morning Star*: "I don't know anybody who would claim *The Valley of Gwangi* as his own kind of nonsense... [The dinosaurs] look like papier-mache concoctions from the prop department." Jan Christie in *The Daily Express*: The

dinosaurs "appear to be made of rubber and move with a jerkiness that indicates they suffer from arthritis. These animals grind their teeth so loudly that they sometimes disturb your sleep." *The Monthly Film Bulletin* was less off-hand, but no less disapproving: "No one would expect the thin mock-up of a story to be anything but a mounting for Ray Harryhausen's celebrated special effects. Even the visual flights of fancy, however, here find the drag of a trite narrative too much of a burden."

Later reviewers have not been any kinder. John Brosnan, in his special effects book *Movie Magic*, found it "a very disappointing picture ... the only touch of real originality it contains is in having the dinosaur cornered inside a church." Roy Kinnard, a dinosaur fan and author of *Beasts and Behemoths* (a book devoted to dinosaurs in the cinema), was even less impressed: The film "lacks energy ... just a tired reworking of *King Kong* ... a mediocre picture." Animator David Allen disliked the film: "*Gwangi* is much overstuffed with cliché situations and characters... and I just do not see on what basis anyone could be passionate about this picture" (*Photon* magazine, 1972). No wonder Harryhausen seriously considered retiring as a result of this onslaught.

So what *are* the film's merits? Neither director James O'Connolly nor scriptwriter William E. Bast (with additional material by Julian More) are anything more than competent, but they supply a very solid base from which Harryhausen can work his genius, transforming the mediocre into something special. Willis O'Brien's prehistoric visions from his unfilmed *Gwangi* project of 1942 have inspired Harryhausen to transcend the usual limitations of the genre, exploiting the exciting combination of Western trappings with the breathtaking impact of his special effects, encouraging a complete and willing suspension of disbelief. Of course, the plot *is* a conventional reworking of *The Lost World* and is plagued by shallow characterization and trite love interest, but in fact the film is extremely palatable and withstands several viewings. It is enlivened by an unusual setting (Mexico) and period (1912) and by colorful ingredients such as the circus, the gypsy group and the cathedral finale. Characterization may not be the film's strong point but at least James Franciscus is enthusiastic and Gila Golan has far more spirit than the heroines of the Sinbad films. Richard Carlson never gets the chance to develop his role but Laurence Naismith's Prof. Bromley, full of breathless astonishment and dreaming of scientific fame, is immensely likable. Jerome Moross' rousing score, reworking his own theme for *The Big Country* and stealing unashamedly from Bernstein's theme for *The Magnificent Seven*, catches the right balance of excitement and grandeur, and for once Bernard Herrman is not missed.

But it is Harryhausen's film. The dramatic pacing, exceptional realism of the models, wealth of animation and imaginative composites combine to suggest a magical world of prehistoric thrills. More than this, his sequences possess a special resonance rarely found in animation films: He gives the film poetic qualities, creating images that linger after the film ends. The mixture of cowboys and dinosaurs creates a peculiarly satisfying harmony and Harryhausen

embellishes this with individual evocative moments that are touches of real genius. These include the moment when a tiny prehistoric horse rubs noses with a modern-day horse; Tuck (Franciscus) having a dream-like early morning encounter with Gwangi, a 20–foot-high allosaurus; Gwangi being towed in a wooden cart by a troupe of horses (a design that would look at home in a John Ford Western); and the significance of the final cathedral setting. In this film, Harryhausen reached his creative peak, demonstrating a fantasy sensibility keener than he had shown in other films.

The film's technical achievements have also been the subject of a lot of adverse criticism. Mike Natale, in the first issue of the Harryhausen fan magazine *FXRH*, wrote, "The technical quality of many of the photographic effects is low for a Harryhausen film." In particular, reviewers have complained about the graininess of some of the background plates used during rear-projection shots, making them too conscious of the fact that they are watching "a special effect," and distracting from the story. *The Hollywood Reporter* (April 24, 1969) thought the photography was "afflicted with undue grain by post-production process and re-filming work, which unnecessarily cues action intended to surprise."

In several shots, the contrast between the model and the live-action plate *is* too conspicuous, but this seems to have blinded many reviewers to the fact that in the vast majority of shots the composites are superb. As a result, there has been little in-depth analysis of the effects, which is remarkable considering the fact that *Gwangi* contains some of

The ornithomimus puppet from T*he Valley of Gwangi* (1969) as it was displayed at London's Museum of the Moving Image.

Harryhausen's most vital animation and inspired matte work. In any event, contrast problems in many scenes — for example, a couple of shots of the tiny eohippus in its pen, or medium shots of the ornithomimus running in front of a rear screen — are overcome by the sheer charm of much of Harryhausen's animation. His skill is to generate a sense of wonder evoked by the fantasy image, not dependent on its technical perfection.

Harryhausen spent a year and a half on the effects scenes. Nearly five months of this was spent animating the climactic episode in which cowboys attempt to lasso Gwangi. In all, there are 335 stop-motion cuts in the film; compare this with the 84 that were in *The Beast from 20,000 Fathoms.* Ambitious sequences like the lassoing and the battle between Gwangi and an elephant are carried off beautifully by Harryhausen. There are numerous moments of interaction between puppet and live action that are as good as anything in the genre: the lassoes around Gwangi's neck that extend from the cowboys' hands; the pteranodon snatching up young Lope from his mule; Gwangi biting a flagpole held out by Tuck, etc. In several "reality sandwich" shots, the puppet's feet partly disappear beneath the lower part of the matte, or a faint line can be seen running through actors who cross the matte line, but the sense of excitement of most scenes keeps these faults from being distracting.

There is only one matte painting in the film, a view of a huge stone arch formation, used in long shots of the Forbidden Valley. It's good enough to make you wish that Harryhausen had used more paintings, because in most other shots the valley looks disappointingly normal. Traveling matte is used sparingly but effectively: riders in front of Gwangi during the lassoing scene, panicking extras running in front of Gwangi as he escapes from the bull ring, and shots looking out at the allosaurus from the cathedral as Tuck tries to close the huge doors on it. The quality of these shots is excellent — although again Natale found them to be poor. Perhaps this is the result of the difference between seeing a film on the big screen and on television, where color and contrast can change.

More than any other of his creations, Harryhausen makes Gwangi seem to be *alive*. From his first imposing shock entrance to his final thrashing about amid the flames that destroy him, Gwangi is always *moving*, looking for prey, stalking victims, running this way and that. S.S. Wilson (in *Puppets and People*) put it well: "Harryhausen makes him so lively, so purposefully swift, so balefully attentive to every sound and movement around him, that he is a terrifying apparition indeed." On several occasions, Harryhausen makes his puppet look in one direction at a character, turn to look at another character and then perhaps turn back to the first again, implying that this is a thinking creature, making decisions during confrontations,

weighing pros and cons. Another clever device is to have many shots designed so that Gwangi is either stepping into a shot or stepping out of it, again creating impetus — much more than if Harryhausen had merely had his puppet standing in the middle of a shot, looking mean.

Consciously or otherwise, the plot emphasizes the impression that Gwangi is an unstoppable force of almost mythic proportions. The human characters are unable to subdue him (unlike in, say, *The Lost World* or *King Kong*) and it is his own actions — bringing down two tons of rock on his own head — which enable him to be brought back to civilization. At the climax, it is not the human characters who destroy him — Gwangi is destroyed by a fire which he himself has been instrumental in spreading. The scene where Gwangi tries to pound his way through a hole in a rock face and when he batters down a cage door effectively emphasize this impression of hungry relentlessness.

Harryhausen allows his creation two beautifully restrained moments when he is seen as something other than a nightmarish predator — a shot of him scratching his ear early one morning, unaware that he is being watched, and a sequence in which he is carried back to town in a wooden cart, half-dazed from concussion and emitting gentle, quizzical growls. He doesn't attract the same kind of sympathy that King Kong does, but he is a classic villain, a superbly crafted puppet and Harryhausen's best character.

The pteranodon and styracosaurus are more conventional prehistoric adversaries, but Harryhausen really shines

One of Harryhausen's pre-production drawings for *The Valley of Gwangi*.

in the sequences with the eohippus and the ornithomimus. Both are offbeat, unthreatening creatures, sensitively animated so as to give each a touch of gentle humor. These are the kind of puppet characters that only the medium of stop-motion can do justice to: The shots of the nervous eohippus clip-clopping around a table-top in a shadowy room, and of the scrawny ornithomimius perched on a rock, chewing on a meal, its long tail snaking behind it, are images that are never forgotten.

One of the film's strengths is the structure of the plot. The slow buildup to the arrival in the Forbidden Valley and Gwangi's appearance is ingeniously conceived. It deliberately recalls the structure of *King Kong* yet surprisingly it is the only time Harryhausen has used this technique. Its dramatic impact doesn't quite match that of *King Kong*'s buildup but is still full of clever hints designed to heighten the sense of anticipation. In the enjoyably teasing prologue, an unidentified creature squirms and squeals in a sack held by a dying escapee from the Forbidden Valley. A paleontologist (Naismith) is found in the desert searching for 50–million-year-old fossils. We learn that the harmless, diminutive El Diablo (the eohippus) may have relatives in the Valley. And a blind gypsy woman and her mute dwarf accomplice warn of "the law of Gwangi." As in *King Kong*, once the title character has been

725

encountered, the pace of the action is breathless, the effects scenes following one another almost without pause, other than a brief interlude after the creature has been taken back to civilization. The much-maligned set-piece nature of animation sequences in other Harryhausen films is successfully avoided here.

O'Brien's storyboard sketches for his unfilmed *Gwangi* are interesting evidence of the way that Harryhausen has both preserved and transformed his source. The encounter with the pteranodon is filmed almost exactly as O'Brien planned it. Bromley falling into a pit, the cowboys sheltering in an elevated cave, fending off a dinosaur that tries to enter the cave, and the climactic lassoing scene — all these keep very close to O'Brien's original images. One shot of Gwangi during the lassoing sequence, lying on his back with his tail in the air creating a photogenic "U" shape, has an exact parallel in Harryhausen's animation. Also in the storyboards is a sketch of a cowboy spearing the horned dinosaur as it battles Gwangi (exactly as in Harryhausen's film); and the idea of having Gwangi towed back to town in a wooden cart is O'Brien's.

More revealing are the ways that the two projects differ. O'Brien's story, set in a remote corner of the Grand Canyon rather than a Mexican valley, had no eohippus, beginning instead with a herd of miniature modern-day horses. The triceratops in O'Brien's sketches becomes a styracosaurus as a result of Harryhausen not wishing to repeat a creature from his previous film, *One Million Years B.C.* The semi-comic ornithomimus is entirely Harryhausen's idea, as is the superb shock first appearance of Gwangi. The dramatic moment when Carlos (Gustavo Rojo) is plucked from his horse by Gwangi is Harryhausen's invention. O'Brien had his wooden cart towed by a motorized truck, a much less attractive idea than Harryhausen's train of horses. Gwangi's battle with a circus elephant replaces O'Brien's intention of having the dinosaur attacked by lions (as in *Mighty Joe Young*). The visually striking image of the huge balloon over the draped cage concealing Gwangi is a Harryhausen creation. Most impressive of all is the inspired choice of a cathedral as the location for the film's final scenes, departing significantly from O'Brien's plot which had the dinosaur pushed over a cliff by a truck. Luis Bunuel alarmed audiences with his surreal image of sheep in a church in *The Exterminating Angel* in 1962, but Harryhausen goes one better, giving us the unforgettable sight of a ravenous dinosaur stomping on pews with scant respect for sanctuary.

Harryhausen's first effect is merely satisfactory. As part of her Wild West show, T.J. Breckenridge (Golan) jumps on horseback from a 20–foot-high platform into a tub of water. This is achieved in a quick long shot in which Harryhausen animates puppets of rider and horse falling, the matte line following the outline of the tub. The puppets appear to maintain the same posture during the shot, suggesting that they weren't armatured. As a quick shot, it's acceptable but even to untrained eyes looks too much like "a special effect."

It is 20 minutes before we meet the eohippus, Harryhausen's first bit of serious animation. Before this we meet Bromley, a paleontologist trying to prove his "theory of the humanoid," and who has found the 50–million-year-old fossil of a human tibia and, beside it, the footprint of an eohippus. Back in the bull ring that serves as the circus arena, little Lope (Curtis Arden) is nearly gored by a bull, in a live-action sequence that includes a silly point-of-view shot in which the camera has been strapped to a mock-up of the bull's head. We must assume that Harryhausen had nothing to do with this shot.

In one of the arena's shadowy back rooms, T.J. decides to reveal El Diablo to Tuck. Standing next to a small hut and fenced-off area on a table, she announces, "Meet El Diablo!" The miniature horse emerges from its hut, neighs and steps out, the clomp of its hooves resounding eerily in the quiet room. "Well, if that don't beat all!" exclaims Tuck. This magical moment consists of two non-composite shots looking down at the puppet in its miniature corral, and four rear-projection composites with puppet and miniature table in front of the actors. No matte was needed in these shots. The foreground fence is miniature, aligned with the rear part of the fence which is part of the rear plate.

The dawn horse walks across the enclosure and back again. Then, its tail swishing, it walks over to some sugar which T.J. has put down for it. It chews on the sugar and, in a nice character touch, its ears prick up and its head turns to follow Tuck and T.J. in turn as each walks out of the shot. The animation, including the swishing tail, is extremely smooth and believable and this excellent model has a very credible covering of shiny fur, light brown on its body and white on its legs. The eye-lines

of the actors are always correctly matched up with the position of the puppet. The fact that the eohippus is more brightly lit than its live-action surroundings does not spoil the composite but rather suggests that some kind of spotlight is aimed at the creature, adding to the theatrical charm of the scene. In this and the following two animation scenes, we can trace another of the many influences that early fantasy films had on Harryhausen: In Schoedsack's *Dr. Cyclops* (1940), a miniaturized horse is displayed on a table in the shadowy laboratory of the title character.

Shortly afterwards, Tuck shows El Diablo to Bromley, a scene made irresistible by Naismith's open-mouthed amazement. There are five animation shots in this episode, including three rear-screen cuts that use the same set-up as in the previous scene and two looking down at the miniature table. One of the better ideas of Bast's script surfaces here, with the two men dreaming egotistically of all the fame and/or money that the eohippus could bring them, both lost in their own musings while the little creature quizzically tilts its head from side to side and raises a foreleg. Again, no real interaction is attempted but the eye-lines are correct and this is enough to create the sense of simultaneity.

The same rear-screen set-up is used again in a later shot in which one of the gypsies steals El Diablo. Instead of attempting any complicated interaction or using a prop, Harryhausen wisely cuts away just as the gypsy's hand reaches out for the whinnying horse.

Bromley tempts Tuck into accompanying him into the Forbidden Valley:

"Just think what you and Miss Breckenridge could do with a dozen eohippi!" They catch up with the gypsies just as they are releasing El Diablo near the entrance to the valley.

In a clever static matte shot, the eohippus emerges from the sack held open by one of the gypsies. Harryhausen avoids having to animate the sack by having his matte line follow the vertical edge of the sack, which is held rigid by the actor. The matte line then runs along the ground, allowing the puppet to walk off. In two long shots, the creature walks away, turns and whinnies, then trots behind a little rock that Harryhausen introduces into his matte line to break up what would otherwise be an obvious split. "Fly, little one—fly home to your master!" the gypsy commands ominously.

The next animation shot is a brief teaser, a nighttime glimpse of a pteranodon flying off with Bromley's mule in its claws. The model, modified from one of those used in *One Million Years B.C.*, is a good one and the subdued lighting successfully suggests that the puppet is way off in the distance. Some strobing on the wing strokes impairs the shot. The rock face from behind which the pteranodon emerges may well be a foreground miniature rather than a matted area. It's a shame that the puppet isn't seen flying behind another rock face: It is unsatisfactory that we are meant to believe that the actors can no longer see the creature simply because it has flown out of the frame.

Tuck, T.J., the show's manager Champ (Carlson) and several of the cowboys try to recapture the eohippus in a marvelous little scene that catches the right balance of humor and excitement. Moross' score makes its first significant contribution to enlivening events, and from now on the pace of the film quickens, with the live-action taking a back seat. The 15 stop-motion cuts that make up this episode all use static mattes but unfortunately do not include any floor inlays that might have allowed the puppet to throw a shadow on the ground. However, the pace is quick enough to prevent most viewers from registering this.

The sequence begins with one of the film's classic images, as the eohippus rubs noses with a modern-day horse. Almost a throwaway moment, this cleverly understated picture of two creatures bridging a 50–million-year divide has a poetic force that is missing from Harryhausen's other films. Fortuitously, the live-action horse shakes its head just after the eohippus touches it, probably because it was irritated by a fly; the action helps to suggest the impression of physical contact. Two other shots use this same static matte set-up, with the eohippus reacting to the presence of the cowboys and then walking off left.

In two low-angle shots looking up from the eohippus' level, actors in the background advance toward the puppet, which whinnies and runs off to the right when two of them leap at it. It looks back at its would-be captors, then calmly trots away. Harryhausen makes the puppet's running cycle, which includes a few frames where it has to be aerially supported by wires, extremely credible. T.J. lassoes the eohippus and brings it down, a convincing bit of choreography made to look easy by Harryhausen. In this shot, he mattes around the outline of a bush, allowing the puppet to walk partially behind it before it is suddenly yanked back by the lasso. The eohippus pulls back on the rope, disappearing behind the bush, which provides a convenient live-action prop enabling Tuck to grab the concealed animal.

Thinking that Tuck wants the eohippus for his own selfish ends, T.J. yells, "Get your thieving hands off!" and, in a good little comic twist, Tuck does just that, letting the animal escape again. It runs out from the other side of the bush, into another rear-screen set-up and pauses near a cleft in a rock face that leads into the Forbidden Valley. When it walks into the opening, Harryhausen uses a vertical matte running down the edge of the cleft and throws a shadow onto his puppet to add to the illusion that it is really walking into the gap. It's a shame that El Diablo is not seen again after this shot — it has been one Harryhausen's most likable characters.

The cowboys ride through the opening in the cliff face and find themselves in the Forbidden Valley. Most of the subsequent live-action was shot among some unusual rock formations in Spain but one elaborate matte painting is used to set the scene, a long shot of a rocky arch stretching across the middle distance as the cowboys ride below it. This one shot does much to heighten the "fantastic" look of the Valley and it's disappointing that Harryhausen didn't use other paintings. He is well aware of the benefits of matte paintings, so it must have been the cost of commissioning matte artists which discouraged him.

The second encounter with the pterodactyl is the closest the film gets to the kind of self-contained set-piece for which the genre is so often criticized. Harryhausen softens this gratuitousness by having had the creature briefly appear earlier and also by having it provide a meal for Gwangi later on. It's an exciting sequence but let down technically because in some shots the pterodactyl looks exactly like what it is — a studio-lit puppet hanging in front of a grainy rear screen. Dramatically, the confrontation is muddled and so never has the impact it should have: The script never makes it clear that the pterodactyl, which has snatched Lope from his horse, is brought to the ground because its prey is too heavy. For example, Rovin in his synopsis says that the cowboys coax the creature to the ground. Harryhausen had to keep the episode low-key so as not to detract from the force of Gwangi's appearance, but this has resulted in a half-realized scene.

The episode contains 16 stop-motion cuts. The sudden appearance of this screeching purple creature above the heads of the group recalls the appearance of the pterodactyl in *One Million Years B.C.* Long shots of the flapping creature hovering above the actors are intercut with closer shots of just its claws trying to grab one of them. In a classic panning long shot, the pterodactyl snatches Lope from his horse, a superb effect requiring careful alignment of puppet and actor and the use of an off-screen crane to pull up the boy on invisible wires. The effect is a considerable improvement on the similar moment in *One Million Years B.C.*, where Harryhausen had Raquel Welch fall behind a convenient rock at the moment the creature picked her up.

After another striking long shot of Lope in the puppet's claws and a close

729

The Valley of Gwangi: The pterodactyl carries off young Lope (Curtis Arden). In this shot, Lope is a stop-motion puppet. A slight blur is apparent on the pterodactyl's wing. Harryhausen achieved this by gently flicking the wings so that their natural tension would cause them to vibrate during camera exposure.

shot of the actor clasped in credible prop claws, Harryhausen switches to a puppet of the boy for two panning long shots as the creature gains height — presumably too high for the shot to have been achieved using the crane. The animation of the puppet Lope is extremely good throughout the rest of this sequence. In another panning shot, the creature (its wings flapping desperately) slowly descends, brought down by Lope's weight. It makes an ungainly landing (convincingly animated) on top of the puppet Lope.

Five cuts of the creature sprawled on the ground use a horizontal matte line across the rear screen. As ever trying to avoid making his designs too obvious, Harryhausen mattes around a small rock, allowing the wing on the right of the screen to pass behind it. The huge wings flap up and down, preventing the puppet Lope from crawling away. Quite why the creature doesn't just fly off is a mystery — perhaps we are meant to think that it has been riddled with bullets. Carlos runs in from behind and jumps on the creature, twisting its neck with a grisly sound of crunching bone. In fact, the actor mimed the fight entirely and Harryhausen pulls off the illusion by adding two tiny puppet hands on the parts of the pterodactyl's head and neck where Carlos has grabbed it. Only registered subconsciously by audiences, this touch makes all the difference to the impression of contact. The prop of the pterodactyl used in closer shots is a good model but its color doesn't match the miniature puppet, spoiling the effect.

The ornithomimus is seen in only a few cuts yet Harryhausen manages to make it a vital, energetic creature and even imbues it with some personality, capitalizing on its semi-comic appearance; one character remarks, "It looks like a plucked ostrich!" Two models were built, one of them a smaller version used in the final long shot, and they are beautifully crafted. Because the puppet runs at a rapid pace, the animation is not smooth, but (as in some of *King Kong*) this doesn't matter because the episode is constructed so well on a *dramatic* level, and because Harryhausen has got the running cycle of the long-legged creature just right. Harryhausen cleverly plays on our expectations of another self-contained set-piece so as to make the sudden appearance of Gwangi, snapping up the ornithomimus in his huge jaws, a marvelous shock effect.

The little creature is seen feeding in two long shots, perched on top of a rock in the live-action plate. The cowboys decide to catch it for their show but when it sees them, it lets out a high-pitched squawk and walks down the far side of the rock. In a tracking medium shot (not using a matte), the ornithomimus runs left to right and looks back nervously over its shoulder; it looks as though Harryhausen has panned across his rear screen. In an attractive extreme long shot, it runs right across the set-up from behind a rock, pursued by the cowboys. After another tracking medium shot, the puppet runs up a slight incline in an extreme long shot with the cowboys riding behind.

Gwangi's unexpected appearance from behind a large rock, engulfing the other creature in his jaws, constitutes the only real shock effect in stop-motion filming. Perfectly timed, it's another example of how Harryhausen's imagination was at its most inventive in this film. The three cowboys in the foreground of this long shot are a crucial part of its success — like the presence of Hercules' head at the foot of the shot of Talos coming to life in *Jason and the Argonauts*. The squirming neck and tail of the tiny ornithomimus add a touch of horror to the image.

Five more shots use this effective rear-screen set-up, with Gwangi, half in shadow from the rock behind him, stooping to chew on the ornithomimus, reacting to the rifle shots fired by the cowboys, and then lunging forward into the sunlight. In one of the film's many enjoyable plot twists, the cowboys suddenly find they are no longer the hunters but the prey.

Emerging from behind a rock, Gwangi steps into a very attractive composite set-up, trees in the background. In another good rear-screen composite, he stands with his back to the camera, throwing his shadow onto a very well-matched area of miniature floor.

The horrified cowboys race back to where Bromley has been admiring the corpse of the pterodactyl. "It's hideous," squirms T.J., to which the enraptured professor retorts, "It's beautiful!" Reluctant to leave his treasure, he ignores Tuck's warning that a "hungry lizard" is approaching, only changing his mind when he sees the allosaurus: "Great Scott! I see what you mean, Mr. Kirby!"—and then runs for cover.

The cowboys find their retreat blocked by a styracosarus—a lumbering, horned quadruped with an array of bony spikes extending back from its head—that just happens to be wandering in their direction. The styracosaur model with its squat posture and warty hide is fine, but is let down by its rather lifeless face; it is less impressive than Delgado's magnificent styracosaurus in *Son of Kong*. In Harryhausen's pre-production sketch it looks far more imposing, but has lost something in its transition to a sculpted model.

Harryhausen's intention seems to have been to suggest that the Valley is full of prehistoric creatures, because the action has led directly from the pterodactyl to the ornithomimus to Gwangi and now to the styracosaurus. It's a good idea but unfortunately the effect of the styracosaur's appearance is to take the attention away from Gwangi, who at this point in the plot should be the center of attention. It would have been better to save the styracosaur for later.

There are two rear-screen shots (non-mattes) looking over the styracosaur's shoulder at the cowboys. Gwangi meanwhile is standing over the dead pterodactyl, stooping down and nudging it with his head. A slight slope in the ground improves the look of this static matte set-up. Five shots using this same set-up are backed by a truly alarming cacophony of animal noises from Gwangi—a disgusting, terrifying barrage of hisses, growls and slurps. Gwangi leans this way and that, his tail swishing, his posture making him appear alert, and he reacts quickly when he hears pebbles disturbed by Bromley, stomping over in his direction.

Gwangi snaps at Bromley, who is sheltering in the mouth of a cave partway up a cliff face. The puppet's feet are below the edge of the frame so no matte is needed. In four shots using the same static matte design, the styracosaurus walks in from the left, roaring and shaking its armored head threateningly. The confrontation between the two beasts includes two striking extreme long shots with the puppets facing each other from the extreme edges of the frame, Bromley just a tiny speck in the background cave. The small size of the puppets in relation to the live-action image suggests that Harryhausen used an unusually large rear screen for these shots. Gwangi looks at Bromley, then at the styracosaurus, sizing up the situation; then, still growling, both creatures start to back off. The styracosaurus retreats into another static matte set-up, walking behind a

The styracosaurus from *The Valley of Gwangi.*

jagged rock face that provides the matte line and throws a shadow which Harryhausen duplicates on the puppet.

Gwangi returns to the pterodactyl, picks it up in his teeth and walks off. The animation of the wings, hanging down limply, is very convincing. This climbdown by both dinosaurs is an unexpected but credible conclusion to the encounter, Harryhausen again teasing the audience, building up expectations of the more dynamic action that is to follow.

When night falls, Harryhausen allows his audience to unwind for a few minutes. T.J. and Tuck have a romantic scene and, in a comic moment, Bromley falls into a trap dug by the cowboys. But then Harryhausen launches into one of the longest and most exciting animation sequences ever filmed. From Gwangi's early morning appearance to the moment when he is knocked unconscious by falling rocks, there are nine and a half minutes of uninterrupted animation, consisting of exactly 100 stop-motion cuts — nearly a third of the animation in the film. The brilliantly staged lassoing sequence takes some of its inspiration from *Mighty Joe Young* but Harryhausen surpasses even that classic scene.

With a subtlety shown elsewhere in the film, Harryhausen begins this *tour de force* with one of his gentlest images. Collecting water from a stream early in the morning, Tuck catches sight of

733

A classic example of static matte rear-projection and a magic moment in *The Valley of Gwangi*: Tuck (James Franciscus) encounters Gwangi early one morning.

Gwangi in the distance. These two shots are the core of the film's visual poetry, exuding an intangible beauty that makes them the best moments in the film. The design of the static matte is simplicity itself, the line following the jagged edge of a hillside, and Harryhausen has got the quality of the print contrasts just right, suggesting that Gwangi is bathed in a hot morning haze. Giving the moment a special charm, the allosaurus is at first unaware that he is being watched and, in an endearing gesture intended as a tribute to O'Brien's tyrannosaurus in *King Kong*, scratches his ear several times.

Mike Natale was unimpressed with these shots, finding them "impaired with especially high grain." The rear screen *is* grainy, but because the lighting on the puppet carefully matches the quality of the light in the live action, the composite is successful, the puppet really seeming to be in the shot. A grainy rear screen is only a problem if it contrasts conspicuously with a puppet.

Gwangi pursues Tuck back to the cave. In a tracking medium shot, the snarling puppet's neck swells and its lip curls slightly, really making it seem like a living creature. Near-flawless long-shot composites have Gwangi snapping at the cowboys in their cave, his tail swishing, throwing a shadow onto a just-noticeable floor inlay. In two other static matte designs, looking out from the mouth of the cave, Gwangi's head and neck appear in the right foreground. In two medium shots, the cowboys try to fend off the allosaurus, who bites onto a blanket held by Carlos and pulls the actor off the ledge. It's another example of Harryhausen making tricky interaction look easy.

Tuck leaps to the ground and is immediately chased by Gwangi, whose gait has a hungry determination about it. In a series of static matte shots using a well-matched floor inlay, Gwangi tries to reach Tuck as he cowers halfway up a rock face behind a small pillar. Always aware of the visual flow of the action, Harryhausen includes a shot from Tuck's point of view, matting round the outline of the pillar with Gwangi behind it.

The film's first traveling matte is a long shot of two cowboys on horseback in the foreground, with Gwangi still menacing Tuck by the pillar in the background. This combination of static matte and traveling matte makes a dynamic composite, but perhaps in theatrical prints the color is different, because Natale describes this as "a terrible shot." In television prints, all the traveling mattes look good and there is no evidence of the "thick blue line" which Natale finds so offensive. It is interesting to note that Harryhausen chooses to use traveling matte for this shot rather than have animated riders in the foreground, which was how O'Brien achieved similar designs in *Mighty Joe Young*.

In long shot, a cowboy feigns the action of throwing a lasso and a carefully aligned miniature lasso lands on Gwangi's snout, only part-way over his head. In his first closeup, Gwangi struggles with the rope around his jaws. The highly detailed puppet head withstands such close scrutiny: Its lifelike eyes, scaly skin, rows of tiny teeth and the fleshy inside of its mouth are extremely realistic.

The action from now on is a breathless sequence of events as Tuck, T.J., Champ and another cowboy try to lasso Gwangi. Like the battle with the skeletons in *Jason and the Argonauts*, this is an occasion where Harryhausen has clearly decided that he is going to spare no effort in making the action as dramatic as possible. It is full of clever touches such as having Gwangi brought to the ground when his foot is lassoed, pulling off a lasso with his claw and knocking a rider off his horse with a swipe of his tail. Harryhausen cuts fluidly from long shot to medium shot to closeup, keeping the pace lively. The sequence uses several different static matte designs and some superb composites, principally the long shots of Gwangi caught in lassoes (which are part miniature and part live-action).

In one long shot, Gwangi's attentive eyes follow Tuck as he jumps on a horse and rides out of the frame, the dinosaur striding swiftly after him. When he is surrounded by three riders, Gwangi looks at each in turn, before chasing after the one he has decided on. In shots not using a rear screen, Gwangi's foot in closeup is caught in a miniature rope. The animation of the puppet falling to the ground and subsequently getting up is superb — these are the kind of moments which in the hands of a less skilled animator look clumsy.

The cowboys attempt to lasso Gwangi in *The Valley of Gwangi.*

Adding a further perspective to the flow of the action, several shots are low-angle medium shots looking up at the puppet with lassoes around its neck. But the sequence's most stunning design is the long shot set-up of Gwangi, now with four lassoes around his neck, two cowboys standing on each side of him, pulling on the ropes.

Harryhausen is modestly evasive when asked to explain the design of these complex shots, dismissing it merely as "hocus pocus." During live-action film-ing, the actors' lassoes were actually at-tached to a pole mounted on a Jeep. The Jeep was driven backwards and forwards slightly to create pull on the ropes which would later be matched by the puppet. A second piece of film was shot, with the camera locked in the same position as during filming of the Jeep, but this time with neither actors nor Jeep in the shot — in other words, just the empty lo-cation. The central area of this footage was then matted onto the central area of the previous footage, thereby blocking

Gwangi is captured with the lasso.

out the Jeep. In the resulting piece of film, the actors' lassoes suddenly end in mid-air. This footage was then used as the rear projection behind the Gwangi puppet, with partial miniature ropes carefully aligned so as to meet up with the live-action ones. Another matte line — a horizontal one — was introduced at the point where the puppet's feet meet the ground. This horizontal matte is discernible in the final composite but the vertical matte lines which allow the Jeep to be hidden are undetectable. No doubt they follow fault lines in the background rockface, but even knowing that does not make them any easier to locate.

"They've got him!" yells Lope. But at this point the styracosaurus reappears, and its presence spurs Gwangi into breaking free. Dramatically, it's a mistake on Harryhausen's part to have the styracosaur arrive before the audience has had a chance to unwind after the roping scene. The roping scene is so good that the subsequent action is anticlimactic — it would have been far better to have a lull in the pace, with Gwangi tied up for a while, and only later have the styracosaurus disrupt things.

The styracosaur plods toward the camera on a miniature floor in two shots, intercut with long shots of Gwangi still held by the four ropes. In long shot

737

static mattes, the horned dinosaur reaches the cave and rears up, trying to look into the cave. Meanwhile, Gwangi struggles with the ropes in closeups and, in a deft character touch, thumps his tail powerfully on the ground, responding to the presence of the other dinosaur.

Looking out from the cave mouth, the next shot has Carlos waving a burning torch at the beaked head of the styracosaurus, the matte line following the cave floor and going through the actor's waist. Back with the exterior long-shot design, Carlos throws the torch to the ground. A bush catches fire and the styracosaurus scrapes its foot along the ground in a bull-like manner, as though thinking of attacking the bush.

In a combination of long shot, low-angle closeup and medium shot, Gwangi continues to resist the ropes holding him, eventually biting through one of them. The styracosaurus starts to walk in his direction (along a miniature floor) and in two more medium shots Gwangi bites through two more of the ropes. The animation of the ropes dropping away is extremely convincing. The cowboys realize the situation is hopeless and retreat.

The battle between the two beasts, consisting of 14 long animation cuts, is staged with Harryhausen's usual enthusiasm and is more dynamic than the similar battle in *One Million Years BC*. But it is really best enjoyed out of context, where it does not suffer from immediately following the roping sequence. (Harryhausen made the same error later in *Clash of the Titans*, in which three extremely dramatic sequences followed one another rapidly: the encounters with the two-headed dog, Medusa and the three giant scorpions.)

The scene begins in the same area as the roping scene, moving into another static matte set-up when the styracosaurus pushes Gwangi back. The two beasts circle one another, then Gwangi jumps onto the quadruped's back, biting its horn. Gwangi is knocked away by the horn, then bites onto it again, causing a sickening sound like a tooth being extracted. In medium shots, Gwangi bites the styracosaurus' back; when he bites one of its rear legs, the animal is lifted up off the ground.

The styracosaurus gores Gwangi with its horn, making him topple over and scream horribly. When Gwangi gets up, the styracosaur maintains the advantage, lifting the screaming allosaurus into the air with its horn. Carlos intervenes at this point, hoping to give Gwangi the upper hand so that he can be later recaptured. He rides into a static matte long shot and plants a spear in the styracosaurus' hide. In this clever shot, Harryhausen aligns a partial miniature spear with the live-action one, which is actually embedded in some prop obscured by the styracosaur puppet.

Gwangi climbs onto the back of the weakened styracosaurus. In the second use of traveling matte, riders pass in front of the two dinosaurs. Gwangi now has the better of his opponent, biting into the styracosaur's back. In the most gruesome shot in all of Harryhausen's films, Gwangi bites a chunk of flesh out of the still-screaming styracosaurus, which is stained with blood. The cowboys, now thinking only of fleeing from the valley, ride past in the background. The ever-attentive Gwangi turns to follow them.

Gwangi's pursuit of Carlos includes

a number of elegant static matte designs. The first is an attractive long shot matting around three sides of a rock face, with Gwangi center stage. Another clever design looks along a tunnel-like rocky passage: Gwangi appears from the left and nearly catches up with Carlos, who gallops into the foreground. In the next shot, the matte line follows the outline of another rock face and even an irregular bush. All of these shots are designed so as to maximize the impression that Gwangi is interacting with his environment.

The next shot is a stunner, as Gwangi at last catches up with Carlos and snatches him off his horse with his teeth. Again, invisible wires hanging from an off-screen crane were used to pull a stunt man into the air. In a long-shot view of Gwangi from behind, the allosaurus chews on a kicking and screaming human puppet, very convincingly animated.

Gwangi continues after the other cowboys, who have now fled through the hole in the cliff face through which they first entered the valley. The opening is too small for Gwangi to pass, but he's not about to let a small thing like ten tons of rock get in his way. In six interesting static matte shots, he pounds away at the opening, just his head and the front half of his body emerging. Harryhausen mattes down the outline of the opening and, again aware of the importance of keeping the action visually alive, uses three different perspectives in these six shots, each one slightly nearer to the puppet. Eventually Gwangi brings rocks toppling down on top of himself and slides down an embankment toward the cowboys. These shots use a stiff prop of the puppet, and always bring groans of disappointment from audiences. It's the old problem of Harryhausen simply not having unlimited resources to achieve every effect as well as he would have liked. Because the prop shots were done in miniature, traveling matte is used in one shot when the cowboys walk past the unconscious dinosaur. Tuck ties a rope around the jaws of a prop head.

Unlike *King Kong*, which cut from the moment of its title character's capture to his being displayed back in the civilized world, *Gwangi* shows us the creature being transported, and it is one of the film's most deliciously restrained sequences. The subdued Gwangi is tied up in a makeshift wooden cart and towed back into town by a train of horses. Harryhausen uses four different perspectives of the creature during this brief moment. Extreme long shots of the troupe in silhouette (using a full-size cut-out of the dinosaur) are evocative images. Two medium shots of Gwangi in the cart, ropes around his neck tied to each corner of the cart, have him growling gently, as though puzzled by his predicament. Excellent long shots of the cart being pulled by a rider use a static matte and require that the turning wheels of the miniature cart are animated. Close scrutiny reveals that in fact there is nothing connecting rider and cart — the pole extending out of the front of the cart simply ends at the matte line. But, as with a stage magician's trick, audiences' eyes are elsewhere and it is a fabulous image. Four closer shots of rider and cart do not use a matte because the wheels are below the bottom of the frame.

When the troupe passes the gypsy woman, she warns of the dire consequences of capturing "the Evil One," Bromley scoffs at her: "Balderdash! He's no more evil than an alligator." But Gwangi looks back over his shoulder at her and gives her a knowing growl. And, later, Harryhausen deliberately stages his finale in a religious setting to reinforce the idea that Gwangi is indeed some kind of devil.

The final sections of the film are full of impressive images and plot twists. Scenes of crowds panicking when Gwangi escapes are very well handled by O'Connolly. The flow of the action shifts fluidly from bull ring to town streets to cathedral. Harryhausen's superb animation keeps the pace buzzing at a thrilling pace.

In the center of a bull ring, a huge gray balloon floats above the red drapes that conceal Gwangi in his cage. Harryhausen must have dreamed up this inspired image after the pre-production stage of the film, because the balloon is not featured in his sketch of the cage in the arena. These composites were achieved not with rear projection but with perspective photography, a miniature balloon being suspended in front of the camera at the time of live-action filming, carefully aligned so that it seemed be to attached to the cage.

Many viewers have been fooled into thinking that the performing elephant is a live creature. Animating an animal with which audiences are familiar is always more difficult because we have expectations of how it should move, but Harryhausen carries it off superbly. In four cuts, the animal does a headstand, a well-matched floor inlay allowing the puppet to throw a shadow.

Intercut with these shots, tension is teasingly built up by a series of eight shots of Gwangi in his cage. His satanic charisma is enhanced by having him bathed in a red glow from the drapes. His tail swishes to and fro gently and, in medium shot, he snaps at the dwarf who has been sent by the gypsy woman to free him.

The elephant, now matted into one of the entrances to the arena, trumpets nervously when it hears Gwangi's roar and rears up. Again, these shots are extremely convincing and also help to push the sense of anticipation up a few more notches.

The balloon starts to rise up, taking the curtain with it. At first just the tail and legs of the dinosaur are revealed. Then, in an unforgettable gruesome image, Gwangi is seen in full, the screaming dwarf in the beast's jaws, his legs kicking wildly. Again, Harryhausen uses several perspectives and milks the moment for all it is worth. The composites are superb, the dinosaur really seeming to be on the raised platform in front of the horrified onlookers, men below pulling on the ropes, trying to bring the balloon down again. Growling, Gwangi puts the dwarf puppet down and starts to knock against the bars of the cage.

The soundtrack jumps just before we first hear the off-screen dwarf's screams: Surely some animation has been removed. Harryhausen includes a still of the missing scene in later editions of his *Film Fantasy Scrapbook*, showing a close shot of the dwarf and Gwangi facing each other from either side of the cage bars. Was the moment removed because Harryhausen felt it weakened the shock impact of seeing Gwangi with the dwarf in his jaws, or because it was considered too horrific by a censor? Harryhausen has told this author that no animation is missing and that the still was merely a pose set up for publicity purposes — but that fails to explain the jump in the soundtrack.

How did Harryhausen manage to animate a puppet that was surrounded by a cage? He may have manipulated the puppet from below, reaching up into the cage; or it may be that the rear of the cage was part of the live-action set, allowing him to access the puppet from behind; or it may be that he removed and replaced the front part of the cage for each frame of film. The last of these is the most likely. Whichever way he did it, the animation is very dynamic, with Gwangi knocking at the cage and buckling it in six cuts.

In three very striking long shots, backed by a yellow drape behind the platform, Gwangi breaks out of the cage. Hoping to prevent catastrophe, Bromley runs into the arena, a tiny figure on the lower right, dwarfed by Gwangi. A fluidly animated miniature cage door falls toward the camera and onto Bromley, killing him. In a well-choreographed bit of wire-supported animation, Gwangi leaps to the ground.

The elephant has meanwhile been getting more and more agitated on the sidelines, in three shots using the same static matte composite as earlier. In long shots using an extremely good floor inlay, dinosaur and elephant confront one another, while extras flee from the arena in the background.

Harryhausen's stamina seems to know no bounds: He could simply have had Gwangi break out into the streets at this point, but instead he stages an impressive battle between the two creatures, containing 12 long animation cuts. Nobody would have blamed him if he had omitted it.

The elephant smacks Gwangi with its tusks. With a scream, Gwangi replies by trying to bite the elephant's back (in medium shot). Three imaginative aerial shots look down at the two puppets locked in combat. In these shots, the whole of the arena floor is miniature, the matte line following its curving edge. These are very plausible composites, with fleeing extras running across the background plate. In a close shot, Gwangi bites the elephant's trunk and in another shot bites the back of its neck.

In a different static matte set-up, an eye-level long shot using another good floor inlay, the elephant strikes Gwangi with its tusks, knocks him down and strikes him again. But he gets up, bites one of the elephant's rear legs and nearly pulls it down. Gwangi bites the elephant in the underside of its neck and, in three shots using yet another static matte design, the elephant is eventually defeated, with Gwangi roaring in triumph. These inventive shots look into the arena through one of the exit tunnels, with the puppets surrounded on three sides by a matte line. Good examples of the "reality sandwich" fooling the eye into seeing depth, these shots have extras running into the foreground along the tunnel.

In an attractive long shot using a static matte, Gwangi strides across the arena toward one of the exits, extras in the background plate still trying to flee. Traveling matte is used effectively again in two shots looking out into the arena

Gwangi breaks out of his cage, part of which falls on Professor Bromley (Laurence Naismith), in *The Valley of Gwangi.*

through the exit. The shadowy, nightmarish figure of the dinosaur nearly fills the opening, blocking out the light, with extras rushing across the foreground. In these shots, Gwangi has to stoop to get into the tunnel, the walls of which are miniature.

A touch of black humor makes the next shots unforgettable. Gwangi steps out into the street, a screaming victim in his jaws, and stands beneath a banner ironically proclaiming "Gwangi the Great." These three long shots (one of them slightly closer) all use static matte.

In the last of the three, Gwangi drops the puppet and walks off left, as ever full of purpose and energy. It's strange that there was no shot showing Gwangi pick up this victim, so it may be another case of a censor insisting on a cut.

After a series of well-staged shots of extras running in terror through the streets, a dramatic full-view shot has Gwangi stomp into a street and turn to face the camera. In two long shots, he strides through an archway into another street. The matte line follows the curve of the arch, with Gwangi ducking slightly as he passes under it. In several good long shots, all making effective use of static matte, the dinosaur pursues some fleeing extras and snaps at Tuck, who fires his rifle at him. In closeups, Gwangi turns this way and that and reacts to the rifle fire, growling.

Gwangi strides purposefully out of one set-up and into another, standing partly in shadow in the courtyard in front of the cathedral. The partial shadow helps the illusion that the puppet is part of the live-action. In a series of 13 long shots and closeups, Gwangi continues to roar at the extras, who are fleeing into the cathedral, and at Tuck, who is still firing at him.

Gwangi sets one foot on the steps leading into the cathedral and, in a clever touch, his eyes follow an extra who falls and tumbles down the steps. In images recalling *King Kong*, Tuck and several extras close the huge cathedral doors behind them. Traveling matte is used successfully in six cuts looking out through the doors at the dinosaur outside. These are intercut with long shots of Gwangi standing on the steps, backing up against the door and pushing against it. The door gives way and (in the last of the traveling matte shots) it bursts open. In an inspired and blackly humorous twist, the townsfolk, who had all run into the cathedral expecting sanctuary, now turn and flee out of the back entrance.

The concept of an allosaurus running wild in a cathedral is charged with symbolic resonance; it's the sort of startling image that only stop-motion could exploit fully. Again, Harryhausen is in full control, maximizing not only the visual impact but also making clever use of echoing sound effects. Wisely, he chooses to do without Moross' score, replacing it with an eerie series of reverberating footsteps and the gurgles and growls of his title creature. The static matte designs in this sequence are all first class, matting around several pillars to reinforce the illusion that his puppet is interacting with the live-action set.

In a side-view long shot, Gwangi stomps into the cathedral and walks behind one of the pillars. In a superbly creepy static matte, he strides behind a pillar that Tuck is hiding behind, then in closeup looks around hungrily. In two clever depth-deceiving composites, T.J. and Lope run toward the camera as Gwangi walks into the shot and occupies the area where they had been, then turns and starts to pursue them. In shots where Gwangi is nearer the camera, a well-matched miniature floor is matted in. In the same set-up, T.J. and Lope shelter in a low chamber to one side of the aisle, and Gwangi stoops down, snapping at them, peering in through the wooden supports.

In a different long-shot set-up seen from Tuck's point of view, Gwangi, partly obscured by a pillar, snaps and growls and T.J. and Lope. Tuck throws a chair at the dinosaur to distract him; when Gwangi lunges at him, the puppet's head and neck pass behind one of the pillars.

While Gwangi continues trying to get at T.J. and Lope, Tuck climbs to the top of the sanctuary, causing Gwangi to look up. Three shots, looking over Tuck's shoulder, use a static matte that follows the edge of the roof, above which Gwangi's head snaps at the cowboy as he waves a flagpole at him. Using the same set-up as before, a long shot of Gwangi next to the chamber has him grab the pole in his teeth and try to pull it from Tuck — a very effective moment of interaction.

Falling backwards, Tuck lands on a pipe organ, causing a series of discordant notes. Harryhausen seizes the moment and includes two bits of character animation, closeups of Gwangi looking around in puzzlement at the strange sounds.

Using the previous static matte design again, the next shot has Tuck throw the pole at Gwangi; it pierces the side of his head. Gwangi screams and spins around and, after a closeup, plucks the pole out with one of his claws. In an excellent long shot looking down the length of the cathedral, Tuck, T.J. and Lope run from the background to the foreground as Gwangi strides into the background from behind a pillar.

The fiery finale relies mainly on one static matte design, a long-shot of Gwangi standing among some pews, but intercuts it with many medium shots and closeups. Tuck throws a burning torch which lands in front of the dinosaur and sets fire to the pews. Superimposed foreground flames and flames in the rear projection combine to create a real impression that the puppet is surrounded by fire, even though in some shots the scale of the flames is disappointingly mismatched.

Gwangi's tail knocks over a burning brazier, an effect in which the live-action brazier was pulled over by an invisible wire. In several long shots and medium shots, Gwangi screams at the flames that are rapidly engulfing him. The flames spread and in closeup Gwangi throws his head back, scream-

ing, a huge circular stained glass window high in the cathedral wall behind. He collapses momentarily, then gets up again. In an unforgettable closeup he throws his head back and lets out a scream, and the circular window behind him shatters. Of course, it is the fire which has caused the window to break, but Harryhausen cleverly implies that it is the force of Gwangi's scream.

The remaining six animation shots are intercut with exterior matte shots of the cathedral burning, a crowd gathered below it. Again, these shots are weakened because the scale of the flames is poorly mismatched to the size of the building. Gwangi has a final screaming closeup, then collapses in long shot, now totally engulfed by flames. In his last two shots, animated falling masonry convincingly lands on top of the puppet. In his final shot, the puppet is stationary, barely visible among all the flames. Moross' score intensifies the melodrama of the moment. Outside, a tear trickles down Lope's cheek.

It's a superb climax to a superb film. *The Valley of Gwangi* is entirely successful within the confines of its objectives and cannot be dismissed as "just another *Lost World* story." In retrospect, it is a much better film than O'Brien's version would have been; above all, its central character is so vibrantly alive that it is almost impossible to believe that Gwangi is just a 12–inch-high puppet. Even harder to believe is the fact that the film was passed over by the Academy Award ceremony for that year — the special effects Oscar went to a very mediocre science fiction film called *Marooned*.

Variety Girl

1947. Paramount. D: George Marshall. Scr: Edmund Hartmann, Frank Tashlin, Robert Welch, Monte Brice. Screenplay for Puppetoon Sequence: Thornton Hee, William Cottrell. Mus: Joseph J. Lilley. Ph: Lionel Lindon, Stuart Thompson. Art: Hans Dreier, Robert Clatworthy. Special Photographic Effects: Gordon Jennings. Puppetoon Sequence in Technicolor Executed by George Pal. Animation (uncredited): Gene Warren and others.

Cast: Mary Hatcher, Olga San Juan, DeForest Kelley, Frank Ferguson, Bing Crosby, Bob Hope, Gary Cooper, Ray Milland, Alan Ladd, Barbara Stanwyck, Paulette Goddard, Dorothy Lamour, Sonny Tufts, William Holden, Joan Caulfield, Burt Lancaster, Lizabeth Scott, Gail Russell, Diana Lynn, Sterling Hayden, Robert Preston, Veronica Lake, William Bendix, Barry Fitzgerald, Cecil B. DeMille.

Rating: ☆☆½   Stop-Motion: ☆☆½

A flimsy plot about two girls looking for stardom is really just an excuse for Paramount to stage a few musical numbers and have all their contract players make cameo appearances. Not surprisingly, the film looks very dated today. Midway through, heroine Mary Hatcher gets a job on the crew supplying voices and sound effects for a George Pal Puppetoon entitled *Romeow and Julicat*.

The Puppetoons were short puppet films — each running about eight minutes — that proved extremely popular during the war years as part of support programs. Between 1941 and 1947, Pal, a Hungarian emigré, filmed 41 such shorts, earning six Academy Award nominations. Always whimsical and with a strong musical rather than spoken soundtrack, these intricately animated projects have retained much of their charm over the years. They favored replacement animation over conventional one-puppet stop-motion. (A whole series of static puppets would be sculpted, each one slightly different from the one before it. A frame of film would be shot of one puppet, which would then be replaced by the next puppet in the series and another frame taken, and so on. Eventually, a simulation of movement would be achieved.)

Among the animators who worked regularly on the Puppetoons were Wah Chang and Gene Warren, who would later contribute much to feature films using stop-motion. Willis O'Brien, at the time unable to bring any of his own projects to the screen, worked for Pal on one of the Puppetoons, probably *Hoola Boola* (1941). A young Ray Harryhausen, still many years away from a career in feature films, worked for Pal on 12 Puppetoons: *Western Daze* (1941*)*, *Hoola Boola* (1941), *Sleeping Beauty* (1941), *Dipsy Gypsy* (1941), *Gay Nighties* (1941), *Rhythm in the Ranks* (1941), *Gooseberry Pie* (1941), *Jasper and the Haunted House* (1942), *Jasper and the Watermelons* (1942*)*, *Jasper and the Choo-Choo* (1942*)*, *Tulips Shall Grow* (1942*)* and *The Sky Princess* (1942*)*. (Some sources include *Nuts and Bolts* [1942], although this may just be a working title for *Tulips Shall Grow*.)

Romeow and Julicat, filmed in 1947, proved to be Pal's final Puppetoon. It tells the story of two feuding families,

Gene Warren animates the "Romeow and Julicat" sequence of *Variety Girl* (1947).

one all cats, the other all dogs, and of a romance between a cat and a dog. Gene Warren, in a letter to the author, briefly described his work on the film: "This seven-minute sequence was accomplished stop-frame with a simple wire-armatured puppet and a series of wax replacement heads to simulate the dialogue."

The comedy in *Variety Girl*, however, comes less from Pal's Puppetoon than it does from the cutaways to the actors adding the sound effects. For example, to supply Julicat's laugh, two crew members hold Hatcher down while a third tickles her foot with a feather.

Arguably, the film is out of place in this encyclopedia, since the puppet characters are never intended to be seen as more than puppets and because there is no interaction with live actors. But Pal's Puppetoons occupy a special niche in animation history and so deserve a mention here. And there is interaction of a sort: In two composite shots, the live actors on the studio stage are seen standing next to a screen on which the Puppetoon is being projected. To prevent the color footage from looking washed out, it is not an actual projection but inserted into the black-and-white live-action footage by static matte.

La Vendetta de ercole
see *Goliath and the Dragon*

Vynález Zkázy
(U.S./European titles:
The Invention of Destruction;
The Fabulous World of Jules Verne;
The Diabolic Invention;
Weapons of Destruction;
The Deadly Invention)

1958. Czech. Studio Gottwaldow. D: Karel Zeman. Scr: Karel Zeman, Frantisek Hrubin. Based on the Novel *Faces aux Drapeaux* and others by Jules Verne. Ph: Jiří Tarantik. Art: Zdeněk Rozkopal, Karel Zeman. Mus: Zdeněk Liska. Special Effects: Karel Zeman, Jiří Tarantik.

Cast: Lubor Tokos, Arnost Navratil,

The giant octopus attacks: Karel Zeman's *Vynález Zkázy* (1958). (BFI Stills, Posters and Designs.)

Miroslav Holub, Jána Zatloukalova, Václav Kyzlink, František Slegr.

Rating: ☆☆☆   Stop-Motion: ☆☆☆

Karel Zeman's combination of a fresh imagination, deliberate artifice and an almost playful use of all manner of special effects techniques, makes him very much a latter-day George Méliès. His second feature film, an adaptation of various elements from Jules Verne books (including *For the Flag*, *20,000 Leagues Under The Sea* and *The Mysterious Island*), has a deliberately naive charm with all the appeal of a fairy tale.

The plot, concerning a professor kidnapped by pirates who want his invention, is nothing original, but Zeman films it with such visual flair and lightness of touch that it is irresistible. Underwater pedal-driven vehicles have bicycle bells on them; there is a clockwork repeating pistol; and two divers indulge in an underwater swordfight.

Zeman took his visual inspiration from engravings that illustrated an edition of Verne's works. Many sets and objects are merely two-dimensional drawings, such as animated boats that sail across live-action seas by means of

748

static matte, or the pipes and machinery of a laboratory which are painted on foreground glass. In another shot, a live actor is shamelessly matted into an animated drawing of a steam train. This fakery sits happily with the greater realism of other paintings such as the striking volcanic island, seemingly propped up by a massive rocky arch like a flying buttress; Willis O'Brien would have approved of this image, particularly the superimposed live-action birds and rolling waves matted in below.

Adding enormous vitality to this fantasy world is the extensive stop-motion content. It is easy to see why Zeman's films, like Harryhausen's, were separated by gaps of several years. Yet they are often overlooked or neglected. S.S. Wilson (in *Puppets and People*) excluded discussion of Zeman's films by saying, "His films form a class of their own, and deserve separate treatment." In fact, Zeman's films would have been right at home in Wilson's stop-motion "bible."

Vynález Zkázy contains much fine animation, always very smooth and often ingeniously combined with live action. What is most astonishing is the number of different animated puppets (human, animal and mechanical) that appear, many only fleetingly (the gulls that glide and circle in the foreground of many long shots; a flock of herons on the ground that look up at a passing airship). A complicated system of cogs and pistons in a laboratory are animated miniatures combined with the live-action by static mattes. Stop-motion is often used in long shots where it would have been too expensive to construct a live-action set, such as the deck of a boat where four puppet humans stand on the bridge, or a beautiful shot of a puppet human scaling a cliff face to reach the pirates' castle, a live-action lake matted in below and another rock face forming the background on a rear-projection screen. The icing on the cake of this shot is an animated eagle that flies in the foreground.

Prefiguring Harryhausen's Verne film *Mysterious Island*, there are several stop-motion sequences set underwater (i.e., filmed through a distortion glass). There is even a battle with a giant octopus, this one emerging from a deep crevasse in an attractive painting. Just as in Harryhausen's film, a human puppet gets caught in one of the tentacles, a convincingly lifelike effect. Long shots of actors on the lake bottom are achieved using realistically animated puppets. In one shot, five puppets are crossing the lake bottom while two more float by above them on small pedal vehicles; the propellers and the riders are animated. These shots are carefully intercut with shots of the actors.

Several scenes include elaborate animated fish swimming by, as well as some sea horses and a shark which later attacks one of the men, who responds by stabbing it as it lunges at him. When the hero's air supply runs out, he starts to hallucinate and sees two fish swim directly into one another and merge; their tails form a delicate butterfly.

Also underwater, a bizarre submarine comes to the hero's rescue, powered by four flipper-like paddles that move by stop-motion. In a long stop-motion cut, the pilot of this submarine climbs down a ladder, throws the unconscious hero over his shoulder and climbs back into his submarine as a puppet swordfish swims around them. The animation is extremely lifelike in this sequence, surprisingly so considering the fact that Zeman was not particularly interested in realism.

All these stop-motion cuts are brief but ingenious and represent a unique use of the medium in feature-length cinema. They are never set-pieces in the way that American films have used the process, rather a collection of moments which cumulatively create an entertaining impression of surreal activity. In-depth discussion of Zeman's artistry is rare, though no doubt is more available in Czechoslovakia with its long tradition of puppetry. He gets a brief mention in

Paul Rotha's *The Film Till Now* but it is an almost derogatory remark: "A long tradition of filmmaking exists in Czechoslovakia but, with rare exceptions, it has been a tradition of cultural and animated films." The "but" implies that the author doesn't consider such films to be worthy of his time.

In 1971, Denis Gifford wrote in *Science Fiction Film* that this had never been shown in Britain, so it is possible that its premiere here was not until 1990 when it was screened on Channel 4 television — 32 years after it was made. Happily, this was the original version with subtitles, and not the Americanized version available to television in the United States.

Weapons of Destruction
see *Vynález Zkázy*

West of Kashmir:
A Sherlock Holmes Adventure!

1989 (not yet completed). Story/Director of Special Visual Effects: Jim Danforth.

This is the first of two proposed Sherlock Holmes projects which have been devised by Jim Danforth and for which he has shot a promotional reel. The other is *Dark Continent: A Sherlock Holmes Adventure!* "The idea," he explains, "derives from Sir Arthur Conan Doyle's oblique reference in 'The Ad-

ventures of the Sussex Vampire' to the unreported case of 'The Giant Rat of Sumatra.' I thought that pitting Holmes against giant or prehistoric creatures which were involved in a mystery was an exciting idea for a film."

West of Kashmir, set in 1885, takes Holmes to the Indian Himalayas. "The mystery," Danforth writes, "centers around the legendary 'Eater-of-Men'—

Jim Danforth's Himalayan snow ape fights a tiger in this posed publicity still for *West of Kashmir.*

a creature which is believed by the mountain-dwelling people of India to be a 'Rakshasas,' or demon. It is actually an extremely rare Himalayan Snow Ape."

The film also features "many Satur-day matinee action sequences," including an ambush by turbanned Pathan warriors, a horseback chase, an avalanche, an escape in a hot air balloon and a sword-fight between Holmes and the villain.

When Dinosaurs Ruled the Earth

1971. Hammer. D-Scr: Val Guest. Treatment: J. G. Ballard. Ph: Dick Bush. Art: John Blezard. Mus: Mario Nascimbene. Special Visual Effects: Jim Danforth. Special Effects: Allan Bryce, Roger Dicken, Brian Johncock. Additional Stop-Motion (uncredited): David Allen.

Cast: Victoria Vetri, Robin Hawdon, Patrick Allen, Drewe Henley, Sean Caffrey, Imogen Hassall.

Rating: ☆☆   Stop-Motion: ☆☆☆½

Compared to Harryhausen's films, this is rarely screened, and over the years the critics and fan magazines have given it a fraction of the attention that is lavished on his pictures. Television channels consider it less of an audience-puller than the more familiar *One Million Years B.C.,* the film to which this was a follow-up. Yet in terms of plot and acting, the later film is the more competent (some would say the less inept), and Jim Danforth's magnificent special effects suggest that he is fully aware of the potential of film fantasy and has an imagination in tune with the grander visions of Willis O'Brien.

On the live-action side, the film makes the usual compromises with commercialism and mistakes. Twentieth-century actors fail almost entirely to look even remotely prehistoric, notably Robin Hawdon with his blow-dried hair and designer stubble, and Patrick Allen, whom it is difficult to take seriously in any role, let alone as the leader of a band of cavemen. The love triangle is as redundant and badly executed as in *One Million Years B.C.* and, as in that film, Hammer indulges in some half-baked titillation with a ridiculous wrestling bout between two women. The plot is no more intelligent than in the first film, but at least is framed by the novel concept of the birth of the moon, which provides a memorable climax. Otherwise, it consists of a rather muddled series of pursuits and escapes whose main purpose is to lead into the special effects set-pieces.

Val Guest's introduction to his screenplay suggests what the film *might* have been: "This screenplay has been written with the intention of shooting it in completely factual style … using a form of *cinema verite* … it will be an ex-

tension of the film treatment we used in *The Day the Earth Caught Fire.*" The latter film was a minor classic and Guest's finest hour, but he fails to come anywhere near recreating that style here, defeated partly by the cheap studio sets and awkward acting and also by the fact that his script simply isn't good enough.

Additionally, his first draft script reveals that he had little experience with effects films of this kind. The sheer volume and complexity of the dinosaur sequences which he describes make it a fascinating but totally unfilmable proposition. As well as the sequences which made it into the finished product, there is an elaborate prologue featuring brief glimpses of a dimetrodon, a pterodactyl and an unspecified dinosaur; a scene in which a band of cavemen steal eggs from a nest on a cliff face and are attacked by two pterodactyls; Sanna throwing food to a giant crab; two dinosaurs battling a triceratops at the top of a volcano crater; an army of giant red ants destroyed by flowing lava; a climactic battle on the beach between a horde of stranded sea monsters and several land dinosaurs (described casually by Guest as "the greatest battle of all"); and several throwaway shots of dinosaurs walking briefly into scenes. Danforth sensibly talked Hammer into dropping most of these ideas, yet still got the blame for taking too much time over the remaining effects sequences.

Hammer cheated the audience by including footage borrowed from elsewhere, including shots from the 1960 version of *The Lost World*, some film of hovering vultures and the later tidal wave shots (all of which were intended for wide-screen films and look doubly out of place here because the frame ratio has not been adjusted and the image looks "squeezed"). Also dragged into service are hoary old devices such as a man-eating plant and an attack by a lethargic boa constrictor. But on the whole the producers deserve credit for allowing Danforth as much freedom as they did; and his inventive contributions give the film a stamp of quality in the same way that Harryhausen's effects in the earlier film transcended their surroundings.

In terms of dynamically choreographed animation, there is no one scene which stands out in the way that Harryhausen's breathtaking allosaurus episode did in *One Million Years B.C.* But Danforth's effects are remarkable for a number of reasons, not the least of which is their refreshing divergence from the Harryhausen mold. His use of locations is more interesting than Harryhausen's in *One Million Years B.C.* (both were filmed in the Canary Islands) and this is complemented by several marvelous matte paintings which add immeasurably to the impression of a spectacular fantasy milieu and hark back to O'Brien's techniques in *King Kong*.

The matte paintings add much to the look of the film, yet it was not Danforth's first choice to utilize them. "The paintings were not used because I wanted to improve the visuals, but rather because the sets built by Hammer were not large enough to allow the dinosaurs to fit into the compositions; and because I was not allowed to use existing locations in the Canaries instead of sets for some sequences. Also, night scenes shot at noon had white skies which had to be obscured. This added

months to the schedule and caused me to send for David Allen so I could paint while he animated."

Additionally, Danforth showed a willingness to experiment beyond conventional static matte set-ups, introducing complex traveling matte elements into his composites to increase their realism: Fire and water were successfully matted into some shots as well as human characters. Various labor-intensive techniques were used to overcome the problems common in stop-motion films such as the strobing effect of animation and the graininess of background plates. He took the characterization of his models beyond anything Harryhausen had attempted at that time, and made the mother and baby dinosaur two of the most likable of all animated "monsters" in feature films. For reasons beyond his control, Danforth went over budget (and consequently discouraged Hammer from using stop-motion in their third prehistoric film, *Creatures the World Forgot*) but the abovementioned qualities are not solely the luxuries of overspending — they evidence a genuinely imaginative talent.

Hammer producers decided which dinosaurs they wanted in the film. It was producer Aida Young's misguided decision not to have an allosaurus or tyrannosaurus in the film because it was felt that their small arms made them look effeminate. Danforth designed all the models and he made a conscious effort to avoid the stereotypic look of stop-motion dinosaurs. The construction of all the models is first-class. The mother dinosaur and the rhamphorhynchus are particularly vital creatures. Jeff Rovin (in *From the Land Beyond Beyond*) considers

One of Jim Danforth's complex composite shots during the plesiosaur sequence of *When Dinosaurs Ruled the Earth* (1970).

that, with the exception of the mother and baby dinosaur, the monsters are "bland" and lack the "distinctive motion and presence of Harryhausen characters." This is unfair because Danforth did not try to compete with Harryhausen's dynamic, melodramatic choreography; he tried to create a style of his own.

The film contains 9 minutes, 50 seconds of animation (compare this with *The Valley of Gwangi*'s 18 minutes) in 112 cuts, about 17 of which were executed by David Allen. For Allen, this was a first assignment in a professional feature film.

The impressive plesiosaur model, designed by Danforth and sculpted by Roger Dicken (who later worked with Danforth on *Caveman*), features in the film's first animation sequence. This excitingly staged monster-on-the-loose set-piece boasts imaginative choreography, thoughtful lighting (the orange glow from the flames contrasts with the bland studio lighting of model scenes in many other films) and optical work of such complexity and variety that this passage alone ought to have won Danforth an Oscar. Danforth added many deft ideas that were not in the original script.

The opening long shot sets the scene beautifully, an atmospheric twilight composite of the captive plesiosaur on a beach. In this rear-screen static matte set-up, a smaller version of the model thrashes about on one side of the screen, and cave people mill around on the other side. All are bathed in firelight.

The next shot — a closer shot of the fluidly animated plesiosaur surrounded on all sides by cave people — is another stunner. This complex composite is made up of several different elements, all of which mesh happily into a whole. The basic design is a rear-projection static matte set-up. A group of cave people in the right foreground are actually part of the rear image. Two cavemen to the left are animated puppets, making slight but very credible movements. Another caveman is placed directly in front of the plesiosaur behind a large boulder, the outline of which forms part of the matte line. A flaming torch in this area throws flickering light and shadows onto the creature, an effect which was carefully simulated frame-by-frame on the animation table. The sea in the background is a separate matted area. Areas of the sky and the foreground sand are painted on glass. The puppet and the torch are seen reflected in a foreground pool of water, an effect achieved by positioning a horizontal sheet of glass between camera and the glass painting. The live actors hold onto a rope which extends around the puppet's neck. At one point, a caveman holding the rope is lifted up into the air by the struggling beast, an effect which enhances the illusion that actor and puppet are co-existing. This superb example of stop-motion sleight-of-hand was achieved by having the real rope disappear behind a painted area, at which point a miniature, animated rope was aligned with it.

Danforth commented on the use of puppet cavemen in this sequence: "The caveman puppets were used not for design reasons, but because Hammer wouldn't let me shoot stunt men in front of the real ocean, working with the full-size plesiosaur tail. (The tail was used in one very wide plate — but not used in the film because of bad lighting on location.)"

Later, similar shots of the captured plesiosaur add to the complexity by having two cavemen and a burning torch placed in front of the model by means of successful traveling matte. While all this is going on, two model cavemen are attempting to spear the creature and one of them is knocked over, adding to the general impression of activity and doubling the amount of animation required. When the foreground blue-screened actors pull on their rope, it is matched to the miniature rope, pulling the creature's head to the ground. These shots are intercut with closeups of the growling animal. The whole set-up is entirely convincing, its complexities the antithesis of Harryhausen's economy-conscious tendency toward simplicity.

In a much simpler rear-projection shot, the creature's head and neck pull on the ropes, sand in the miniature set blending perfectly with the location footage behind. When one of the ropes snaps, Danforth chooses to leave some of it dangling from the model's neck, a

The chasmosaur of *When Dinosaurs Ruled the Earth*, seen here on a miniature set with painted backdrop. After the animation by David Allen was completed on this shot, live-action cavemen were placed in the foreground by means of traveling matte.

minor detail requiring more painstaking animation but adding to the realism of the moment. Other traveling mattes are employed to show cavemen running toward the camera, the model behind them, and a boy looking up at the towering monster as its flipper snaps the last of the ropes. Another very attractive long shot shows the plesiosaur stamping along the beach, some cave people fleeing from it, and waves below it breaking in the foreground. There is a burning torch in front of the model — this last is a barely noticed detail (achieved either by projecting it onto glass or simply by superimposing it) which increases the shot's credibility.

In two static matte set-ups, live actors throw spears at the creature. The real spears disappear behind the model and are replaced undetectably by miniature ones which pierce its side. Two

30016-/05

Frame enlargement from the chasmosaur sequence of *When Dinosaurs Ruled the Earth*.

more static matte set-ups show the plesiosaur approaching a blazing mat and again careful attention to lighting has flickering flames reflected on the model. The flames were rear-projected onto glass during a second pass of the camera. Unfortunately, a reflection of the puppet's head and neck in the glass can clearly be seen to one side of it.

A stunning composite of blue-screened actors and flames in front of the screaming model has a minor flaw: Smoke in the foreground disappears abruptly near the top of the frame. The plesiosaur tips over one of the flaming mats with its head. The mat is a stop-framed miniature, yet it is animated so smoothly that it looks like part of the live-action plate. The flames on the mat are a double-exposure, shot at 48 frames per second and carefully synchronized with the moving mat. In another attractive composite, the creature walks between two huts, both in the live plate. When it stamps on one of them, the hut is flattened, an interaction which is suggested by having a series of animated mattes wipe it off.

757

Tara, a traveling matte element in front of the beast, throws a flaming torch at it, causing a pool of oil to ignite, and a great flash of light illuminates the model. Flames and smoke are superimposed; there is another caveman in the rear plate. Several dramatic closeups show the screaming animal engulfed in flames, recalling the fiery fates of the rhedosaurus and Gwangi. Here, however, the illusion is more successful because the model really seems to be surrounded on all sides by the flames, not merely standing between a rear screen and a superimposed element. The sequence closes with several composites of actors standing in front of the burning, shrieking creature, which walks in a circle before it finally keels over, its flipper giving a final wave.

The chasmosaur, with its highly detailed, scaly hide and majestic head armor, is a first-class model. Guest's original script featured a triceratops — it was Danforth who was responsible for this innovation. He said: "I didn't want to use a triceratops because of *One Million Years B.C.* I would have used a styracosaurus, but Ray was going to have one in *The Valley of Gwangi*." Its dramatic purpose, however, is limited (two brief scenes), making this the kind of gratuitous animation set-piece which plagues the genre: It is merely an episode that delays the plot. Far better to watch it out of context on video, and sit back and enjoy the variety and complexity of Danforth's composite designs, some deft moments of interaction and a series of fine glass paintings.

David Allen's animation (80 percent of the animation in this scene is his) is accomplished. His attempt at showing the model running is superior to Harryhausen's similar moment when the triceratops chases Raquel Welch in *One Million Years B.C.* But the beast never acquires the theatrical presence which Harryhausen would have given it.

The first sequence begins with a shock effect when the beast charges out of its cave, with two cavemen placed in the foreground by traveling matte. A static matte follows the brow of the embankment and the wall of the cave, allowing the model to run out from right to left and send an actor flying with one of its horns. In a second static matte, a long shot of the cave set, the beast turns the other way and shoves a second cavemen down the slope with its beak. It then retreats into the miniature cave.

The second of the two episodes begins with another superior traveling matte composite, this time with Tara cowering before the massive beast. A beautiful long shot of the cave set has the model in the center and actors running around it on all sides. Tara runs from the left of the screen, down below the model and up the embankment on the other side, an action designed to give the perspective vitality and enhance the illusion that the model really is surrounded. One frame of this cut — animated by Danforth — contains the classic animator's gaffe: He has forgotten to remove a surface gauge, positioned in front of the model's head. The top of the shot is a perfectly matched painting of the cave roof with sky and mountains in the distance.

A painting of a rock face and an orange-glowing twilight sky is the backdrop to another thoughtfully designed traveling matte composite of three cavemen standing in front of the approaching creature. Another imaginative perspective, this time from the right side of the cave, has two actors in a foreground traveling matte and the chasmosaur behind them, in front of two more actors in a rear projection beneath another sky-and-mountains painting.

The finale, in which Tara is chased by the dinosaur, features three more fine paintings which supplement the rocky location, most notably the superb final shot in which the chasmosaur falls over the edge of the cliff face, a river valley snaking away far below. This classic shot features a couple of minor touches which evidence Danforth's determination to make the most of every set-up: A couple of animated rocks tumble down with the model, and an animated puppet of Tara, barely noticed in the top left corner of the frame, looks down at the falling model. With all this effort gone into what is a very a brief sequence, it is no surprise at all to learn that it took Danforth 16 months to complete the film. (It was worth it, although Hammer didn't think so: The studio never used animation again.)

The series of stop-motion scenes featuring the mother and baby dinosaur (fictitious creatures referred to by Rovin in *From the Land Beyond Beyond* as Protosuchus for some reason) are unforgettable. They depart from the conventional set-piece approach which characterized the two previous sequences. Not only do the two creatures reappear in a succession of short scenes (instead of just appearing once and getting killed), they are imbued with a level of personality rare in stop-motion feature films. This is typical of Danforth's style — witness *The*

Wonderful World of the Brothers Grimm and *7 Faces of Dr. Lao*. Is it that Hammer allowed him greater freedom than they did Harryhausen, or is it that Harryhausen avoided giving his models too much pathos? After all, there is not the slightest hint of humor or charm in any of the dinosaurs in *One Million Years B.C.*, while in *Clash of the Titans*, where he appears to have had almost total control over a relatively lavish effects budget, the most personable creation he could come up with was the mechanical owl Bubo, whose animation he left to assistant Steven Archer. (Of course, Harryhausen *has* created sympathetic characters, such as the eohippus in *The Valley of Gwangi*, and the baboon and Troglodyte in *Sinbad and the Eye of the Tiger*, but in the main he does not seem interested in exploring these possibilities.)

In a letter to the author, Danforth explained the creatures' design: "At one point I was going to base the mother and baby on Neave Parker's reconstruction of acanthopolis. But I changed my mind (after armatures were started — necessitating remaking the rear legs) and went back to my earlier idea of a monitor-like shape."

Mario Nascimbene's score, which is merely adequate during the action scenes, catches the right balance of the bizarre and the playful during these remarkable scenes.

Having Sanna fall asleep in an empty shell next to a cluster of dinosaur eggs is a fine fairy tale idea. The camera pans left to a miniature egg which starts to rock. Cracks appear, pieces of the shell fall away and the baby quadruped tumbles out (a moment which Danforth admits was inspired by a shot in *The*

30016-91

When Dinosaurs Ruled the Earth: The mother dinosaur returns to find Sanna (Victoria Vetri) has been sleeping in one of her eggs.

Animal World). It squawks, clambers to its feet, gurgles and then sits down again, apparently quite pleased with itself. The animation is extremely smooth and the creature is endearing and 100 percent believable. Guest's script merely describes the action in this scene — it is Danforth who has added the touches of characterization. This delightful scene is one of very few in the genre that do not rely on a confrontation with a live actor for their impact: Victoria Vetri sleeps through the whole episode.

When the parent dinosaur appears the next morning and presents Sanna, whom it thinks is its offspring, with a stag for breakfast, this delicately restrained scene recalls the classic episode where Kong toys with Fay Wray in his mountain retreat. It features the film's most stunning composite, an image suggestive of all the fantastic visual splendor of which stop-motion composites are capable, yet so rarely achieve. The contrast between the cowering Sanna and the enormous yet gentle behemoth is awesome enough, but is complemented by striking background and foreground paintings of a verdant mountainside. This reinforces the "early morning" feel of the scene, giving it an irresistible freshness akin to the breathtaking moment in *Gwangi* when the title character, bathed in the haze of a rising sun, emerges from behind a hillock to startle James Franciscus. O'Brien would have approved of the three animated birds which squawk across the shot. In fact, the design of the shot in conception has much in common with Obie's techniques. Vetri is the only live element (a rear projection) in an otherwise entirely miniature set-up, recalling the miniature rear projections of *King Kong*, and totally the opposite of Harryhausen's "reality sandwich" where the only miniature element is the model itself.

Using paintings, however, was not Danforth's first choice. "I would have preferred to have used a location, as Harryhausen would have, because it would have saved *weeks*. Two other matte artists attempted the painting before I finally had to rework it. I prefer the 'O'Bie' approach but I wouldn't have chosen it for a low-budget picture for Hammer. They forced me into it because they couldn't grasp the fact that by saving on location expenses they were adding costs to the effects budget. Whether it was actually a net saving or a net expense is probably known only to Roy Skeggs [current owner of Hammer Films], but in any event, as you correctly say, I got the blame."

The animation of the dinosaur is fabulous — it doesn't matter how many times the scene is replayed, it's hard to believe that this is not a living, breath-

ing creature. The model, the only one in the film entirely designed and built by Danforth, is the best in the picture. The face, with its gentle dark eyes, is particularly mobile and expressive: It blinks, the tongue snakes out and Danforth has even animated folds of skin around the throat to create a sense of it breathing and swallowing. Arguably this is the most convincing piece of stop-motion ever filmed.

Also worth mentioning is the animation of the dead stag hanging limply from the dinosaur's mouth, and the realistic way it bounces slightly when it is dropped in front of Sanna. Danforth makes a difficult piece of interaction look all too easy when the dinosaur, in closeup, bites off a piece of the shell in which Sanna is sleeping, causing the egg to spin around. The background footage of Sanna spinning around was originally too smooth, so Danforth skipped some frames to make the movement suggest the sudden bite of the dinosaur.

Four animation cuts, all using static mattes and rear projection, show Sanna playing chase with the baby dinosaur. Danforth inbues the infant with puppyish charm as it looks around for Sanna (who is hiding behind a tree), calls out for her, then bounds after her with a lolloping gait. In one of these cuts, Danforth mattes around the irregular shape of a bush (disguised by keeping the matte line slightly out of focus), heightening the impression that the model is part of the scene. Danforth explained how this shot was more complex than originally designed: "Val [Guest], despite arguments from me *and* his continuity girl, reversed the direction of Sanna's look on a closeup. So I had to reverse the direction of the baby's entrance necessitating painting around a bush and a split which added two days to the shot. I try *never* to matte through bushes, but as in this example, sometimes people fail to follow instructions and ... up goes the cost."

In another of these cuts, Danforth has the puppet run behind some foreground rocks to give the shot added depth and interest. The animation of the creature running after Sanna could have looked awkward, but Danforth pulls it off brilliantly. It's a deceptively simple-looking bit of animal choreography.

Later there is some more enjoyable character animation when Sanna blows her flute at the baby and gives it orders. The animal sits obediently on the ground, growling gently and swishing its tail with a kittenish charm. Danforth depicts this engaging moment in five stop-motion cuts using two composite designs. One is an extreme long shot of Sanna and the puppet, which is standing in a carefully matched floor inlay. The other design is a closer long shot of just the puppet, again inserted into the live-action surroundings by means of a floor inlay.

The character is not seen again, but the mother reappears in the next scene, menacing Tara and another caveman before Sanna calls it off. The appearance lasts only a minute and features ten stop-motion cuts. These are a combination of closeups of the dinosaur roaring and long shots of it confronting the two cavemen. Again the animation is impressive, allowing some lingering looks at this highly detailed model.

One shot is a dynamic pan from left to right as the beast advances on the retreating cavemen. The look of this shot is enhanced by the fact that the puppet passes behind a large cactus plant, which is part of a glass painting occupying the whole of the lower foreground. An area of rocks in the upper part of this shot is also a painting, so skillfully executed by Danforth that even on close inspection it looks like part of the background plate. Another shot is a closer look at the beast as its great head and snapping jaws lunge at Tara. In one composite Tara cowers behind a boulder in the foreground, the outline of which provides the location of a matte line. The final stop-motion shot in this sequence is another example of Danforth's skill at depicting animal behavior: At the sound of Sanna's voice, the dinosaur doesn't turn and follow her straight away, but looks back several times at the fleeing cavemen, as if reluctant to give up the fight.

Before the mother dinosaur's next appearance, there is another self-contained set-piece, this time an encounter between Tara and a rhamphorhynchus, a flying reptile. So what if it is totally gratuitous?— sit back and enjoy an exciting sequence that shows the extent to which Danforth was trying to push the techniques of stop-motion beyond contemporary levels. In most of the flying shots, he tapped the puppet's wings, causing them to swing slightly on the wires during the long camera exposure, thereby suggesting a blur and eliminating much of the offensive strobing that has marred similar sequences (such as those in *One Million Years B.C.*). Some sources state that he exposed each frame twice, each time with the wings in a slightly different position, but this technique was not used on account of the expense.

Not everybody was so impressed with this brief scene (20 animation cuts in one minute, 50 seconds). Sam Calvin in *FXRH* #4 thought that "the blurred action ... made the creature appear to be a mechanically operated device. And this effect of a mechanical contraption worked against the 'realistic' and yet strangely unimpressive smoothness of the animated action."

The model is another first-class creation, with a particularly ferocious-looking head, but again Calvin was mysteriously unimpressed, opining, "The pterodactyl is unimpressive and somewhat cartoonish." Danforth has got the choreography of this swooping, flapping nightmare just right, the downbeat of its wings halting its forward progress at all the right moments, such as when it turns or hovers. The tail snakes about so fluidly that is hard to believe it is animated. In one shot, he pans left to right, following the direction of the model, to improve the flow of the action. Two convincing shots show the rhamphorhynchus holding a miniature puppet of Tara in its claws. In closer shots of Tara held in full-scale prop claws, Danforth adds a pair of animated wings to the composite — a design he would work with again in shots designed by Harryhausen of Perseus riding Pegasus in *Clash of the Titans.*

In an imaginative flourish, Tara slashes the creature's wing with his spear; it's a deceptively simple-looking piece of interaction. A shot of Tara running at the grounded reptile is one of the few traveling mattes in which "bleeding" is seen on the live-action outline. In a striking long shot, the creature falls from its clifftop nest — Danforth has got the rate of fall just right. The final rear-projection shot has the gasping, crushed creature lying on a miniature foreground. Tara is aligned in the background plate so that he seems to pull his spear out of the model.

A splendid little scene, on a dramatic level it is nevertheless a poor cousin to Harryhausen's multi-faceted sequence in *One Million Years B.C.* which involved two locations and four winged models, and which was more crucial to the plot.

Determined yet again to avoid conventional static matte set-ups, Danforth has the mother dinosaur reappear in a striking extreme long shot, walking behind Sanna. Shot from a high angle on a hillside, this required a substantial floor inlay to be matted into the surrounding sand and shrubs. On the cinema screen, the colors of the two elements seem poorly matched, but on video prints a color shift has occurred and the difference is much less noticeable. This perspective is used in four shots and, astonishingly, Danforth uses the same piece of film each time. Harryhausen has "cheated" in this way in some of his films, but never to this extent.

Danforth commented on these shots: "This scene is dreadful. It was one of the last two shots done at the end of the schedule. (The other was the just-hatched baby trying to get up.) My recollection is that it was originally supposed to be used only twice rather than the four cuts. I had set this shot up previously but had to strike it when Hammer moved me into a store room so they could rent my stage to another production to whom they had promised it."

The rest of this sequence includes a

Tara (Robin Hawdon) is attacked by the rhamphorhynchus in *When Dinosaurs Ruled the Earth.*

number of subliminal flourishes which make all the difference between a routine composite and a superior one. In a shot of Sanna walking toward the camera with the dinosaur following, the matte line at first seems to follow the obvious choice of the brow of a slight hill which runs across the frame. However, the model walks over the hill and takes two paces toward the camera down the near side of the slope, pushing aside a miniature rock as it does so; the matte line is slightly lower than the crest of the hill, Danforth imperceptibly having inserted an area of miniature ground into the terrain, adding considerably to the illusion.

In a static matte long shot of the dinosaur following Sanna, Tara leaps into the frame in the foreground and momentarily his spear passes in front of the model, painted on glass as a blur. This is not something that most people notice consciously but again it lends a lot of credibility. Just when it looks like the monster is going to make a meal of Tara,

764

The ferocious rhamphorhyncus designed and animated by Jim Danforth for *When Dinosaurs Ruled the Earth.*

Sanna walks up to it and slaps it with a spear four times. Two of the blows involve alignment of partial miniatures of her arm and the spear in front of the model, and the suggestion of contact is perfect. Tara looks on amazed, as well he might. The episode closes with another fine piece of character animation as the behemoth, looking cowed and ashamed, lowers its head.

Hammer originally planned to have numerous other dinosaurs appearing in quick "throwaway" scenes but Danforth convinced them that they did not have the resources to do them. However, a tylosaur, a prehistoric sea reptile, does appear in two quick animation cuts (or at least its head and neck do). This brevity partially explains how the usual problems with water composites are overcome: The shots don't have time to look unconvincing. Its appearance is very gratuitous — it serves merely to free Tara from a burning raft, then disappears without even attempting to eat him. (Very poor form for a dinosaur.)

Four elements make up the first shot. Behind a traveling matte of Tara, who is tied to a raft and surrounded by flames, the tylosaur rises up through a rear projection of a calm sea, splash and bubbles superimposed at the point where the matte line would be. In the second cut, a long shot, the tylosaur overturns the raft. Superimposed spray successfully disguises a switch from the real raft to a miniature which the puppet picks up in its teeth. The horizontal matte line is hidden by keeping it slightly out of focus, thereby softening the line.

"A shot was deleted (I don't know why)", Danforth recalled, "in which the tylosaur submerges with the raft in its mouth, unaware that Tara has been flung off. Also long shots of the burning raft from the previous sequence were deleted, leaving only the terrible full-size studio shots."

In these cuts, Danforth experimented with improving the graininess that often plagues rear-projection shots. Each frame of the rear footage was actually a blend of two consecutive frames, thereby "superimposing two patterns of grain structure and making them less visible" (S. S. Wilson in *Puppets and People*). The animation allows movement of the model's mouth and tongue, but this is a rare occasion where it might have been more cost-effective to use a hand puppet with cable-controlled facial details.

Danforth explained that the dinosaur *had* been conceived as a hand-puppet: "Roger originally built such a model to be worked by a scuba diver in the Shepperton tank. Aida, however, failed to budget for the studio electricians needed to light the tank for high-speed photography. Weeks were spent looking for other daylighted tanks or reservoirs for this and the climactic tidal wave miniatures (large miniature rafts with 18–inch tall human figures). No luck, so all was canceled and Roger remade the tylosaur, much smaller for animation."

After a lengthy live-action sequence in which Tara and Sanna are pursued by Patrick Allen and his cronies, the mother dinosaur makes her final appearance. This is another brief but impressive vignette, consisting of seven animation cuts in four composite set-ups.

In a surprisingly realistic static matte, the model stomps into the frame from behind some bushes (part real, part miniature) and walks behind a tree — actually, the real tree is behind the model in the background plate, but Danforth has painted a miniature trunk on glass which is placed in front of the puppet. An imaginative dolly shot shows the dinosaur advancing on the camera. Because there is no matte, Danforth was able to add a little camera shake into the shot to add to the effect.

In two long shots, the model walks into a clearing and, to the horror of all present, picks up a fluidly animated puppet of Sanna in its teeth. A non-matte rear-projection shot shows the model in the foreground growling at the actors; some miniature blades of grass in the foreground add depth to the perspective. Finally the model walks off with Sanna in its teeth. Danforth uses the same set-up as in the opening shot of this sequence but for some reason has left out the painted tree trunk, with the effect that the same tree is now behind the model, not in front of it. Danforth

Tara cowers before the mother dinosaur of *When Dinosaurs Ruled the Earth*.

explained, "The painted tree trunk only worked because the dinosaur's head was low as it charged into the clearing. Its position in the final scene placed the head high enough to intersect the moving palm fronds."

Strangely, this is the last we see of either the mother or baby dinosaur. Did the budget prevent Danforth from animating other planned scenes or did he consciously avoid the stop-motion cliché of having them both killed? He recalled: "No other final shots of the mother were planned, but I felt they were needed. Roger always wanted to have Sanna ride the dinosaur into the camp to rescue Tara instead of just running in."

The final stop-motion scenes, featuring the some crabs, are something of a missed opportunity: This could have been a scene comparable to the skeleton fight of *Jason and the Argonauts*. However, Danforth did not have the luxury of being able to lock himself away for four months to concentrate on one scene, like Harryhausen. Instead, Val Guest ingeniously designed the episode so that the crabs only constitute one ingredient of a fairly hectic climax, the main concerns of which are the receding tide and subsequent tidal wave. Eerie music lends everything a haunting quality which harks back to the bizarre climax of Danforth's Loch Ness Monster sequence in *7 Faces of Dr. Lao*.

By bathing the whole episode in moonlight, Danforth makes these clattering, scuttling creatures all the more chilling. In fact there was only one model, duplicated optically in one setup to suggest there are two. Allen built the model, taking a leaf out of Harryhausen's book by inserting a metal armature into a real crab as in *Mysterious Island*.

The first shot is a fine shock effect in which a crab emerges from some shadowy rocks, startles a group of four cavemen, and runs across the sand with impressively lifelike animation. The shadows completely disguise the floor inlay, making this an impeccable composite. The crab chases the cavemen along the beach, pulls one down and drags him along the ground. This composite is remarkable for two reasons. First, there is an astonishingly smooth switch from actor to miniature puppet. Second (and recalling a device in one of the plesiosaur set-ups), glass has been placed in the foreground to suggest a pool of water, and it reflects both the actors and the puppet, a skillful way of meshing different elements of the composite.

Next, two crabs surround three cavemen and again a foreground pool of water reflects both puppets and rear-projected actors. In a second cut using this set-up, one of the actors has been replaced by a puppet, allowing it to make physical contact as it struggles with the crab. These two cuts are broken up by a closeup of the model, its pincers snapping menacingly. Later, there are two more animation cuts when another crab (the same model, of course) scurries into the camp, walks across a well-matched miniature floor and pulls down the wooden frame that Tara had been tied to in the rear projection, accompanied by suitably unnerving clattering sound effects.

The crab scenes may be dramatically redundant, but they are far more effective than the less visually attractive, less imaginative scorpion fight in *Clash of the Titans*, which they resemble.

After a shoddy tidal wave sequence, comprising a variety of archive footage and obvious studio tank scenes, the film closes with two beautiful shots using matte paintings (one by Danforth, the other by Les Bowie) both containing live action elements and flowing water, depicting the "new world" bathed in moonlight after the tides have settled.

Like so many stop-motion films, *When Dinosaurs Ruled the Earth* is dramatically risible, but Danforth's work is so remarkable that this somehow doesn't matter. In retrospect, this film's effects are more innovative than Harryhausen's more conventional work in the sister film *One Million Years B.C.*, notably in four areas: puppet characterization, the use of matte paintings, the intricacy of composites and the use of techniques to reduce strobing. Consequently, it's no surprise that Danforth's Pegasus shots in *Clash of the Titans* are among that film's best moments, nor that his contributions to *Caveman* made that film one of the most enjoyable stop-motion films of the 1980s. By all accounts, his shelved *Timegate* project (about time-traveling dinosaur-hunters) would have been the first film

for many years to come anywhere near to matching the stature of *King Kong*.

The special effects of *When Dinosaurs Ruled the Earth* were nominated for an Academy Award but lost out to Disney's *Bedknobs and Broomsticks*.

Who Framed Roger Rabbit

1988. Touchstone/Steven Spielberg. D: Robert Zemeckis. Scr: Jeffrey Price, Peter Seaman. Based on the Story "Who Censored Roger Rabbit?" by Gary K. Wolf. Ph: Dean Cundey. Art: Elliot Scott, Roger Cain. Mus: Alan Silvestri. Director of Animation: Richard Williams. Mechanical Effects Supervisor: George Gibbs. Special Visual Effects: Industrial Light and Magic. Visual Effects Supervisor: Ken Ralston. Stop-Motion Animation: Tom St. Amand. Stop-Motion Camera: Harry Walton. Stop-Motion Armature: Blair Clark.

Cast: Bob Hoskins, Christopher Lloyd, Charles Fleischer, Joanna Cassidy, Stubby Kaye, Alan Tilvern.

Rating: ☆☆☆   Stop-Motion: ☆☆½

This is a technical masterpiece and one of the best feature-length cartoons of all time. The three-dimensional quality of the drawing, the spot-on synchronization between live actors and cartoon characters, the perfectly matched lighting, the ingenious devices used to make live-action props appear to be moved by non-existent drawings only added later in post-production, and the sheer volume of minor detail which brings every scene to life — all of this makes it astonishing that the film was made at all. Time and money on this scale have not been

invested in a cartoon for many years. Had this not been a huge commercial success, it could have marked the death knell for feature-length cartoon projects.

The dramatic qualities of the film are never exceptional, however, although the film is always a lot of fun, as private eye Bob Hoskins teams up with cartoon character Roger Rabbit to investigate a mystery. Various "real" cartoon characters make cameo appearances, including Dumbo, Yosemite Sam and — briefly seen sweeping litter — the brooms from *Fantasia*.

The deliriously grisly climax has the live-action villain (Christopher Lloyd) getting a cartoon-style comeuppance; it includes some puppet animation. Lloyd is run over by a steamroller, screaming in wild agony as he is ever-so-slowly crushed from the legs upwards. Then, in true cartoon fashion, he unpeels himself from the floor and, completely flattened, takes a few steps and re-inflates himself from a compressed-air bottle. Finally, he is destroyed in a graphic meltdown when he is sprayed by his own evil turpentine dip.

The initial shot of Lloyd scraping himself up from the floor was achieved

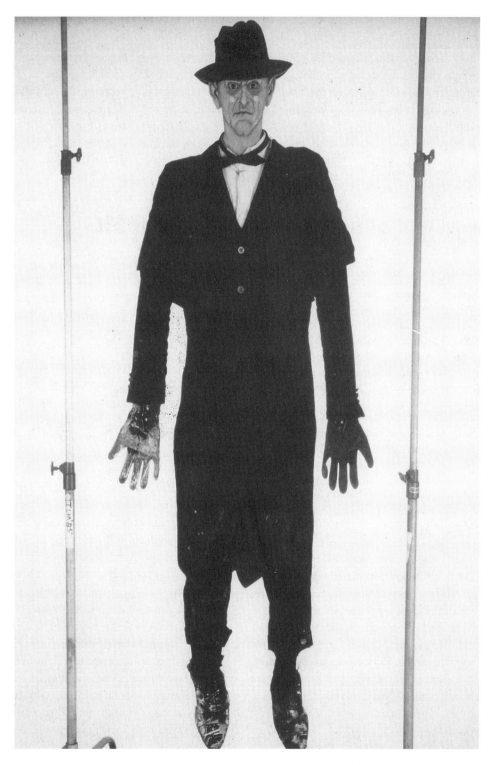

Who Framed Roger Rabbit (1988): The stop-motion puppet of Christopher Lloyd, animated by Tom St. Amand.

live-action with a puppet built by mechanical effects supervisor George Gibbs. This is followed by three stop-motion cuts in which he wobbles like a sawblade (complete with twanging sound effects) and walks over to the compressed-air bottle. Tom St. Amand animated this 18–inch puppet against a blue screen. The legs were attached to go-motion mover rods while the arms and head were made to move with conventional stop-motion. Shadows were later added to the live-action plate to complete the composite. It's a fine effect, although minor compared to the film's superb cel animation.

The Wicked Stepmother

1988. Larco Productions. D-Scr: Larry Cohen. Ph: Bryan England. Mus: Robert Folk. Special Effects: Hollywood Optical Systems. Stop-motion: Larry Arpin. Special Makeup: Mark William.

Cast: Bette Davis, Barbara Carrera, Colleen Camp, Lionel Stander, David Rasche, Tom Bosley.

Rating: ☆☆½   Stop-Motion: ☆½

The first 30 minutes of *The Wicked Stepmother* are excellent: a fine performance from Bette Davis as an eccentric stepmother and Larry Cohen in sure control of the comic and gruesome elements. Audiences may wonder if Davis died during the making of the picture or simply got fed up with the production. She is seen no more after this and the film deteriorates into an uninspired series of gags, only occasionally funny, as if Cohen has tried to salvage something of his project. Cohen, the skillful talent behind exploitation pictures like *It's Alive* (1974), *God Told Me To* (1977), *Q* (1981) and *The Stuff* (1985), seems to lose interest in his project.

The film is full of special effects but most are routine. At the climax, the witch — now in the persona of Barbara Carrera — is destroyed and a plant grows to monstrous proportions. This includes one clumsy stop-motion cut (by Larry Arpin) in which two huge tentacles burst out of the roof of the house and snake about in the air.

It's a shame that the sensitivity of the opening passages could not have been maintained.

Willow

1988. Lucasfilm. Executive Prod/Story: George Lucas. D: Ron Howard. Scr: Bob Dolman. Ph: Adrian Biddle. Art: Allan Cameron. Mus: James Horner. Visual Effects: Industrial Light and Magic — Dennis Muren, Michael McAlister, Phil

Tippett. Matte Artists: Chris Evans, Mike Pangrazio. Special Creature Supervision: David Allen. Visual Effects Cameramen: Kim Marks, Harry Walton. Visual Effects Art Director: Dave Carson. Stop-Motion Animator: Tom St. Amand. Stop-Motion Model-Makers: Blair Clark, Randy Dutra, Craig Davies, Sheila Duignan, Paula Lucchesi, Tamia Marg, John A. Reed III.

Cast: Val Kilmer, Joanne Whalley, Warwick Davis, Jean Marsh, Patricia Hayes, Billy Barty.

Rating: ☆☆☆   Stop-Motion: ☆☆☆

If *Willow* had been directed by George Lucas, it would probably have been a classic. But he merely supplied the story and acted as executive producer, entrusting the direction to competent but unremarkable Ron Howard. Howard did a good job with the gentle comedy *Cocoon*, but he is out of his depth here. Lucas, "the Great Regurgitator," borrows from a hundred different sources, never really adding much of his own, but this still passes a pleasant two hours; children lap it up. The problem is that it's all too *mechanical*— the plot devices are contrived and predictable, once again suggesting that Lucas is retreating to the safe ingredients of *Star Wars*. There is even the comic relief of a bumbling duo not unlike R2-D2 and C-3PO, except that here they are foot-tall brownies — and not even remotely funny. James Horner's cliché-ridden score borrows heavily from John Williams. It's sad to have to say it about a Lucas film, but this is fantasy without heart.

There are many fine matte paintings by ILM regulars Chris Evans and Michael Pangrazio— so good that on two occasions this author was fooled into thinking he was watching the real thing. The shot of the silhouetted actors walking past a mountain range at sunset and the stark interior of Queen Bavmorda's castle are exquisite examples of the technique. Another unforgettable matte painting, taking a leaf out of *King Kong*'s book, has Willow and his troupe crossing a log bridge over a leafy ravine. The film closes with a stunning matte shot of the Nelwyn village, pulling back seamlessly from a close shot of the actors to an extreme long shot of the hamlet surrounded by trees, backed by mountains, and with a live-action river shimmering alongside.

The blue-screen composite work with the tiny, forest-dwelling brownies was supervised by Michael McAlister and is superb. Especially good are shots of them surrounding their two captives, Gulliver–style, and the high-speed chase when two brownies are thrown around in the back of a cart, the camera moving all the time. These, and other brownie shots, are some of the best matched blue-screen composites ever seen.

Patricia Hayes' transformation from a goat to human form — via intermediate ostrich, turtle and tiger forms — was designed by Dennis Muren and David Allen. This astonishing six-second cut is so fluidly achieved that one is left gasping, "How did they do that?" In fact, it is a combination of rod puppetry and computer imagery. It's a great trick and in 1988 was a major leap forward for computer generated imagery, but really this is ILM showing off. It doesn't add anything to the drama of the story. In the hands of a really good director, it could be just as well served by an old-fashioned cloud of smoke and quick jump to the transformed actor.

Stop-motion features during two sequences. In both cases, Lucas and Howard have gone so far away from the style of the much-maligned Harryhausen set-piece that they have reached the other extreme. In both scenes, there is a wealth of activity going on and the stop-motion element is only one of many ingredients. The intention is to create an impression of a fast-paced simultaneity of action as many things happen at one time. Whether or not this succeeds with the majority of audiences is hard to say, but stop-motion fans and monster lovers feel disappointed because the animation characters never get the chance to develop.

The first of the sequences, in which a fire-breathing two-headed dragon emerges from a castle moat, was supervised by Phil Tippett. Tippett designed the creature while Tom St. Amand and Harry Walton did the animation. One full dragon model was built and another was just from the necks up for closer shots. Most of the shots were done bluescreen but some were done with rear projection. Go-motion rods were used for the most significant parts of the puppet moves (the heads and necks) with the rest (the mouths, eyes, and puppet humans) being moved by conventional stop-motion techniques.

Willow is trying to batter his way into the castle, Madmartigan (the obligatory Han Solo–style likable rogue) is fighting off Bavmorda's soldiers, trolls are crawling about the walls of the castle (by means of blue-screen composites) and the queen's daughter suddenly finds herself in love with Madmartigan. In the midst of all this, the dragon makes its appearance. Willow has pointed his

magic wand at one of the trolls who for some reason turns into a furball that sprouts two squirming stop-motion tentacles, and subsequently becomes a fleshy blob from which emerge two heads, in the best tradition of the chestburster scene in *Alien*. Willow kicks it into the moat, where it grows into the full-sized dragon. The lack of any rationale behind this is an example of Lucas wanting to have too much going on and not bothering too much with basic storytelling.

This monster is *weird* looking. On the top of each of its heads is an ugly, bony ridge. Its lipless, fang-filled mouth resembles a shark's. Under each head is a pouch like a turkey's wattle. It halfclambers out of the moat, leaving its rear end still submerged, so we never get any full shots of it walking about. It rises up behind Madmartigan in a series of shots that recall Verminthrax Perjorative rising out the lake behind Peter MacNicol in *Dragonslayer*. As it hauls its front legs out of the moat, the camera tilts up, Madmartigan is blue-screened in front of it and flames from a small fire are superimposed to add depth to the shot. It unleashes a blast of flame from one of its mouths. A closeup shows us the watery eyes blinking, the neck-pouch swelling and shrinking as it growls and breathes.

In a rear-screen long shot, the two heads turn to look at Willow up on the bridge over the moat. After a bluescreen shot of Willow in front of one of the heads, another rear-screen shot has a dramatic pan as one of the heads lunges after the running Willow and lets out a blast of flame. One of the heads swoops down open-mouthed and plucks a liveaction rider off his horse, a clever effect

The two-headed dragon from *Willow* (1988). Sequence and puppet designed by Phil Tippet; stop-motion animation by Tom St. Amand and Harry Walton.

achieved by having roto-mattes painstakingly drawn around the rider's arm and horse's head for each frame. The camera tilts up, revealing a kicking human puppet in the dragon's mouth; it is gulped down in the next cut. A soldier shoots an arrow at the beast and it growls back at him. A longer close shot of the puppet has another victim dangling from one of the mouths.

There are four animation cuts in a great little moment when a troll gets snatched up by the dragon. Its huge head lunges straight at the camera, mouth wide open. There is a sound of bones crunching as the troll is plucked from the bridge, followed by the gruesomely comic sight of the second head trying to bite the protruding legs of the troll from the mouth of the first head. However, this moment is marred by some confusion which is typical of the scene as a whole. The troll had been hanging precariously from the bridge with Willow hanging even more precariously from the troll's legs. At first it is assumed that it is Willow who is grabbed by the monster, but in fact he has swung out of reach. The logic of the moment is rushed for the sake of pace.

An impeccable long shot looks down at the monster breathing fire, half out of the moat, surrounded by running soldiers and fires burning everywhere.

Another shot is weak because it is "too busy": It has a blue-screened troll crawling along a wall, the monster breathing fire straight at the camera and Willow trying to bash down a door — all this simultaneity is designed deliberately, but it just doesn't come off. What looks like a cel-animated arrow flies past the two heads of the dragon, then Madmartigan is thrown through the air by a catapult, across a shot of the heads seen behind the bridge. This is probably a rear-screen shot with a matte following the outline of the bridge.

Madmartigan kicks a troll off the bridge and as it falls, its arm and leg pass in front of the dragon. This time, the best guess is that these elements were painted on glass, because the furry outline of the troll looks too fuzzy to have been done with rotoscope matting. Likewise, in a dramatic cut when the huge head of the monster rears up behind Madmartigan, his arm and sword look glass-painted as they pass in front of the puppet.

Madmartigan leaps onto the back of one of the heads, following in the tradition of stop-motion sequences in films like *Mysterious Island, Jack the Giant Killer, Golden Voyage of Sinbad* and *Dragonslayer*. A long shot of the model swaying this way and that trying to shake off its unwelcome rider is enhanced by a lot of go-motion blur. An interesting closer shot of Madmartigan sitting on the head seems to have been achieved by putting the actor on a support prop which is subsequently obscured when the dragon puppet is blue-screened in front of it.

Madmartigan plunges his sword clean through the top of the dragon's head and out through the lower side of its jaw. It is not made clear, but the idea is that the dragon is now unable to open its mouth. It thrashes its head from side to side and, after a quick closeup, explodes as a result of unwisely trying to breathe fire again. When the two heads fall to the ground, these look like live-action shots. A final animated long shot (using the same high-angle perspective seen earlier) shows the beast sprawled on the ground, the one remaining head making slight movements, surrounded again by running soldiers and fires. It's a good composite to end the scene on, but you can't help wishing there was more.

David Allen's later stop-motion episode, in which a metallic brazier comes to life, is little more than a minor distraction from the real action, the struggle between the queen and the sorceress. Although there are only six stop-motion cuts (all shot blue-screen), the original plan was to have other inanimate objects struck by random blasts of magical energy during the struggle, namely a chair and a stone gargoyle. In the interests of pace, these latter two were scrapped, but the net impression is that Willow's encounter with the brazier is an irrelevance, rather than part of a more elaborate, dramatically purposeful sequence.

Struck by a bolt of magic, the four-legged brazier leaps up into the air and down again, assisted by a little go-motion blur. Willow runs in front of it by means of a rotoscoped matte. It follows him around the altar in the center of the room and there is a tracking shot seen through the legs of the altar. Quite what is meant to be inside the brazier is never explained, but a wriggling worm-like tentacle hangs out of one side and the hands of a human skeleton half open the lid. This is another case of ideas only getting half-developed for the sake of pace. Far better to leave such distractions out altogether.

After an irritatingly long interruption showing Madmartigan's swordfight outside, we return to Willow and the brazier. In a shot backed by the two sorceresses fighting, Willow has a tug-of-war with the brazier, which has trapped his spear in its lid. There was no rear screen with which to line up the puppet, so Allen achieved the interaction by hav-

ing tracings of each live-action frame suspended between puppet and camera during the blue-screen animation. Willow swipes at the brazier's legs with his spear and flips it over, another shot using go-motion blurring. When he spears its "belly," it looks like a partial miniature or painted spear is placed in front of the puppet. He slides it out through a window, the matte line conveniently following the vertical side of the window. It's an enjoyable moment, smoothly animated by Allen, but is over far too quickly. It had the potential to be something special, weird yet light-hearted — but Lucas misses the opportunity.

Willy Wonka and the Chocolate Factory

1971. Wolper. D: Mel Stuart. Scr: Roald Dahl. Based on his Book *Charlie and the Chocolate Factory*. Ph: Arthur Ibbetson. Art: Harper Goff. Lyrics and Mus: Leslie Bricusse, Anthony Newley. Special Effects: Logan R. Frazee. Stop-Motion (uncredited): Jim Danforth. Wonkavator Assistants (uncredited): Dennis Muren, David Allen, Tom Scherman, Bill Taylor, Bill Hedge.

Cast: Gene Wilder, Jack Albertson, Peter Ostrum, Roy Kinnear, Michael Bollner, Tim Brook-Taylor.

Rating: ☆☆½   Stop-Motion: ☆☆

This engaging children's film benefits from a fine performance by Gene Wilder as the chocolate maker with a mischievous sparkle in his eye. But it is let down because the low-budget means that the sets and costumes

always look like studio fabrications. For example, the umpah-lumpahs are meant to come across like the munchkins in *The Wizard of Oz*, but they always look like what they are — midgets in unlikely costumes and wigs. What is missing is the sense of being in a fantasy world.

At the end of the film, Wonka takes to the skies in his Wonkavator, a diamond-shaped craft that bursts through the roof of his factory and disappears into the clouds. As originally filmed, some shots of the Wonkavator in flight were unsatisfactory and Jim Danforth was called in to redo two long shots.

He built and animated a ten-inch model, showing it tilting and drifting, its top section rotating, with tiny (but unmoving) puppets of the actors inside.

Both shots use traveling matte to place the model in front of footage of a town and the sky. In the second cut, the camera pulled back on a 40–foot dolly, giving the impression that the Wonkavator is soaring way off into the distance. As the end credits start to roll, the craft disappears into a cloud, probably achieved by moving it behind a soft-edged cut-out on the blue-screen set. For these shots, Danforth was assisted by Dennis Muren, David Allen, Bill Taylor, Bill Hedge and Tom Scherman.

Winterbeast

1992. D: Christopher Thies.
Cast: Tim R. Morgan, Mike Magri, Charles Majka.

Rating: ☆☆

This low-budget horror thriller, filmed on a semi-professional basis, features a stop-motion giant chicken, a dragon, killer totem poles, a mummy and a Bigfoot creature.

Witchcraft Through the Ages see Häxan

Witches' Brew

1979. A Joshua Lightman Production. D: Richard Shorr. D (additional sequences): Herbert L. Strock. Scr: Syd Dutton, Richard Shorr. Ph: Norman Gerard. Ph (additional sequences): Joao Fernandes. Art: Marie Kordus. Mus: John Parker. "Lucifer" Demon Created by David Allen. Additional Animation: Visual Concepts Engineering.
Cast: Richard Benjamin, Teri Garr, Lana Turner, James Winker, Kathryn Leigh Scott, Bill Sorrels.

Rating: ☆☆   Stop-Motion: ☆☆

This initially likable comedy about three wives who use occult powers to further their husbands' careers, runs out of ideas halfway through and becomes just a cheap and forgettable horror film. Despite the presence of Richard Benjamin, Teri Garr (who had recently found fame in *Close Encounters of the Third Kind*) and even Lana Turner (as an older witch), the film never found a distributor.

A brief stop-motion episode featuring a demon animated by David

Allen seems out of place in a film that relies more often on down-to-earth moments of supernatural bad luck such as Benjamin cutting himself shaving, stepping on a drawing pin or his car not starting. The Lucifer demon is kept mostly hidden in shadows apart from two quick live-action closeups of its horned head and glowing eyes. The idea is to make it a terrifying half-seen presence like the creature in *Curse of the Demon* (1958), but director Richard Shorr botches it.

There are only four very quick stop-motion cuts. The scene takes place at night and the dimly lit puppet is always carefully matched with the rear-projection plates. The armature included wings originally built by Marcel Delgado for a dimorphodon in the unfinished *Creation* (1930), and later brought into service again by Allen for the dragon in *Q* (1982).

In Cut 1, the six-foot-high Lucifer egg cracks open (an animated effect) revealing the crouching winged creature inside. Cut 2 is a long shot of Benjamin running underneath the flying puppet as it sends out bursts of cel-animated energy from its eyes. Cut 3 has the puppet flying straight at the camera, claws on its hind legs reaching out — the cut is so quick that you just get a quick impression of the claws and nothing else. In Cut 4 the puppet is barely glimpsed as Turner casts a spell, causing it to explode in a cloud of superimposed green flame and smoke.

A later effect in which Garr is surrounded by supernatural flames is convincingly handled by Peter Kuran.

Extra scenes added to pad the film to feature length were directed by Herbert L. Strock, famous for schlock trash like *I Was a Teenage Frankenstein* in the 1950s.

The Wonderful World of the Brothers Grimm

1962. MGM/Cinerama/George Pal. D: Henry Levin. D of Fairy Tales: George Pal. Scr: David P. Harmon, Charles Beaumont, William Roberts. Based on *The Brothers Grimm* by Hermann Gerstner. Ph: Paul C. Vogel. Art: George W. Davis, Edward Carfagno. Mus: Leigh Harline. Special Effects: Gene Warren, Wah Chang, Tim Barr, Robert A. Hoag. Stop-Motion Animation (uncredited): Jim Danforth, Dave Pal, Don Sahlin, Peter Von Elk, Tom Holland. Dragon-head Prop (uncredited): Marcel Delgado, Victor Delgado.

Cast: Laurence Harvey, Claire Bloom, Karl Boehm, Barbara Eden, Walter Slezak, Oscar Homolka, Ian Wolfe, Martita Hunt. "The Dancing Princess": Russ Tamblyn, Yvette Mimieux, Jim Backus, Beulah Bondi. "The Cobbler and the Elves": Laurence Harvey, George Pal's Puppetoons. "The Singing Bone": Terry-Thomas, Buddy Hackett, Otto Kruger.

Rating: ☆☆☆   Stop-Motion: ☆☆☆

An entertaining George Pal fantasy, *Brothers Grimm* was filmed in the three-camera Cinerama process originally invented by Fred Waller a decade earlier (at a time when filmmakers were putting money into gimmicks designed to woo audiences away from television).*

This may be part of the reason why it is so rarely seen today. The 145–degree image that audiences would have seen on Cinerama screens looks clumsy when transferred to a panned-and-scanned TV version, and the two vertical lines where the three elements meet is distractingly conspicuous. A CinemaScope version was released at the same time for screening at cinemas without the three projectors that were required for Cinerama, but even these prints are seldom shown at revival cinemas. In England, a CinemaScope print was last seen at the National Film Theatre in May 1983.

Pal himself directed the three fairy tales contained in the film but entrusted the framing sections (telling the story of Wilhelm and Jacob Grimm) to Henry Levin, who had earlier directed *Journey to the Center of the Earth* (with its live lizards intended to look like dinosaurs). Like that film, this has a large budget, colorful sets and a respectable cast and, also like that film, his sequences are conventional and dull. Laurence Harvey is enthusiastic as Wilhelm and Oscar Homolka is enjoyably over the top as the pompous duke who employs the brothers. A bonus is Otto Kruger as a king in the third fairy tale.

Pal's sequences, which comprise a total of only 35 minutes in a film over two hours long, are the best thing about the film — it's a shame he wasn't able to include the six tales that he originally planned. The first tale, "The Dancing Princess," is the least memorable of the three, essentially a musical episode with Russ Tamblyn; it is the other two that shine.

All three tales feature stop-motion produced by Project Unlimited, the company run by Gene Warren, Tim Barr and Wah Chang. The first tale has only one shot, animated by Jim Danforth (all of whose work in this film is uncredited), in which a flower is given a sleeping potion, curls its petals up into the shape of a face, yawns and falls asleep. Tom Holland attempted the animation for this shot several times but none of his versions was used and none of his animation is seen in the release print of the film.

"The Cobbler's Tale" features Laurence Harvey as the gray-haired old cobbler and "The Puppetoons" as the elves who repair all his shoes while he sleeps. The animation was shared by Pal's son Dave and Don Sahlin, with Danforth contributing two shots. While the animation is not particularly smooth, the elves, built by Chang, are full of character, and good use is made of replacement heads for dialogue and facial expressions. In some shots in which the elves leap about on a shelf and jump to the ground, the puppets were supported on wires. There is only one composite shot in the sequence, a skillful traveling matte long shot in which two elves knock Harvey on the head with a hammer when he wakes up. Unfortunately the backgrounds are always flickering because the set-ups were not lit with bulbs that burned at a steady rate. The series of

*CinemaScope and 3-D were two of the other gimmicks.

heads used for one of the elves is the same used in "The Yawning Man" sequence in *Tom Thumb*.

Far more interesting is "The Singing Bone" in which Terry-Thomas and Buddy Hackett battle a fire-breathing dragon. The stars have been funnier and here are only mildly amusing—it is the dragon that steals the show. Designed by Chang, the jewel-encrusted creature is never intended to be 100 percent believable (its fiery breath is some very basic cartoon animation) but Pal's and Chang's inventive ideas and Danforth's animation really bring it to life. Some of the gags are broad farce—the dragon licks its lips in anticipation of roasting Terry-Thomas, and its head spins around 360 degrees.

Three customized animation cameras were built, two of which were used by the Project Unlimited crew. The third went to the MGM crew that composed the titles. The dragon sequence is technically excellent apart from one poorly matched floor inlay and (in some shots) a conspicuous difference in the contrasts in two adjoining Cinerama elements. There are 53 animation cuts. A miniature cave set was built and matches happily with the full-scale studio sections. An article in *Cinemagic* #29 refers to a full-scale dragon head built by Victor and Marcel Delgado. However, there is no sign of this in the finished film and it may be that writer Paul Mandell is thinking of the prop head in *Goliath and the Dragon*. Jim Danforth said in a letter to the author, "I don't believe there was a dragon head prop by Marcel and Victor (or anyone else). I drew the blueprints for the plaster full-size dragon and I never drew the head."

The dragon is first seen in a shot with Terry-Thomas and Hackett walking down a path on one side of the shot, the dragon's head and neck snaking in on the other side. In this shot, the dragon is a traveling matte element. A closeup allows us a good look at its beady red eyes, forked tongue, big flared nostrils (all the better for breathing fire), two long fangs and "whiskers" that hang down from its chin. It catches a spear (thrown by Hackett) in its mouth, the switch from real to miniature spear conveniently done behind a rock pillar in front of the split. It chomps noisily on the spear and slurps up the last morsel with its tongue. When it swallows, a lump passes down its long neck, accompanied by a loud gulp.

An attractive long shot of the whole cave (a composite set-up used many times in the sequence) has Hackett trying to sneak along the ground beneath the dragon as it sends a blast of fire at Terry-Thomas high up on a ledge. The dragon rocks its head and lets out a rumbling laugh at the sight of the knight's singed helmet feathers.

In closeup it blinks and looks mildly concerned as Hackett stabs at a full-scale prop of its legs and belly. (The prop is too solid and motionless to convince.) In a daring but totally successful long shot, the dragon looks down at Hackett, who is now a miniature animated puppet in front of the dragon's leg. The animation of the puppet human is so successful in the latter part of the shot that this author was fooled into thinking that a switch had been made to the live actor. Danforth explained in a letter: "This is a puppet throughout this scene—there is no live Buddy Hackett.

A publicity paste-up still for *The Wonderful World of the Brothers Grimm* (1962). (National Film Archive, London.)

The first part of the scene was animated according to Gene Warren's instructions, while the part you thought was real was animated as I saw fit."

Two medium shots of the dragon rearing up are intercut with two cuts of an animated claw slamming down and nearly crushing Hackett. Little explosions of dust in the rear image help to suggest the physical contact. A dark area in the shape of a claw painted on glass is also animated to create a shadow. In a long shot, Hackett runs away, the bright orange of the floor inlay clashing distractingly with the dark brown of the rest of the set.

A broad gag in which Hackett runs around a pillar and comes face to face with the open-mouthed dragon is spoiled by the contrast differences in two of the Cinerama elements, one darker, one brighter. In closeup, the dragon hears Terry-Thomas and its ears prick up like a dog's. It sends a blast of flame at him, causing his suit of armor to fill with steam and his helmet to fly off, watched intently by the dragon. In two cuts it burns away a rock behind which Terry-Thomas is cowering, then licks its lips at the prospect of roasting his exposed rump.

In long shot, Hackett drops an animated miniature rock on the dragon's tail and it roars in pain like a puppy. Again like a puppy, it starts to chase its tail, and there is a shot from Hackett's point of view, looking down on the puppet as it circles. It falls onto its side, reaches for its tail and begins to lick it noisily. It looks up at Hackett (who is now swinging on a vine over the cave) and its head spins around 360 degrees with a painful creaking sound, suddenly

snapping back again — a daft but amusing gag. Another point-of-view shot looks directly down at the open-mouthed dragon looking up. Its head pops into the bottom of two shots, snapping at Hackett, then it chews on a vine that it has bitten off and spits it out, a look of comic disgust on its face.

In three superb cuts the Hackett puppet drops onto the dragon's neck, slides down onto its back, gets thrown off, then scampers under its stomach looking for somewhere to hide. Danforth's animation of the human puppet is totally convincing. The dragon looks under its stomach and decides to crush Hackett, who is seen struggling under the full-scale prop. In long shot, the puppet Hackett crawls out from under the dragon. In medium shot, the dragon rears back, then Hackett plunges his sword into the chest of the prop dragon, causing purple smoke to pour out.

In closeup the dragon roars in pain, then in long shot it lunges at Hackett. Its front legs crumple and it lets out two bursts of flame. In another long-shot perspective it tries to pull the sword out with one of its claws, making a ridiculous twanging sound. It keels over, gets up again, its tail swishing, then collapses. In two closeups seen through the mouth of a cave, its head crashes down and rolls over, followed by a final long shot in which the puppet rolls over and lies still, the sword in its chest giving off a self-satisfied sparkle. The sparkle "was an actual reflection done by angling the sword to catch a special light off the set," said Danforth.

"The Singing Bone" has one more stop-motion trick up its sleeve — an animated skeleton, no less. Terry-Thomas has slain Hackett but he magically revives at the end. A series of bones appears one by one, assembles into human form, makes a few slight movements, the skull spins around, and then it dissolves into the live-action Hackett.

Young Sherlock Holmes

1986. Amblin Entertainment. D: Barry Levinson. Scr: Chris Columbus. Suggested by Characters Created by Sir Arthur Conan Doyle. Ph: Stephen Goldblatt. Art: Norman Reynolds. Mus: Bruce Broughton. Special Effects: Kit West. Animatronics Supervisor: Stephen Norrington. Illustrator: Michael Ploog. Visual Effects: Industrial Light and Magic. Visual Effects Supervisor: Dennis Muren. Effects Art Director: Dave Carson. Pastry Sequence: Motion Supervisor — David Allen; Effects Cameraman — Scott Farrar. Glass Man Sequence: Pixar Computer Animation Group, a Division of Lucasfilm, Ltd. Matte Painting Supervisor: Chris Evans. Harpy Sequence: Effects Cameraman — Michael Owens; Go-Motion Animation — Harry Walton; Creature Fabrication — David Sosalla; Armatures — Tom St. Amand (uncredited).

Cast: Nicholas Rowe, Alex Cox, Sophie Ward, Anthony Higgins, Susan Fleetwood, Freddie Jones, Nigel Stock, Patrick Newell, Michael Hordern (voice only).

Rating: ☆☆☆   Stop-Motion: ☆☆☆

Young Sherlock Homes performed badly at the box office even though it is an enjoyable adventure story and full of marvelous special effects. Perhaps adults dismissed it as a children's film and kids were put off by the Victorian setting. Certainly, it should have been better than it is: Barry Levinson's direction and the cast are merely efficient, and the plot — concerning devil-worshippers in Wapping — is too conventionally devised. Fine supporting players like Freddie Jones and Nigel Stock add eccentricity but not much else.

The effects feature in several brief set-pieces that are intended merely as the momentary hallucinations induced in victims by a poisoned dart from a blowpipe. They are not meant to be major episodes but are still fabulous little set-pieces, packing in a wealth of impressive technical detail.

In the first of these, Patrick Newell (fondly remembered as Mother in the television series "The Avengers") imagines himself attacked by a roast pheasant on his dinner plate. This vicious animatronic creation is the work of Stephen Norrington. Norrington contributed another impressive moment near the end of the film when Sophie Ward imagines she sees a grinning corpse chiseling her name onto a tombstone.

Special visual effects for the other hallucination sequences were supervised by Dennis Muren at Industrial Light and Magic. In one scene, Nigel Stock browses in an antique shop and is attacked by two harpies — brass bookends that come to life. These lively creatures look like miniature cousins of Harryhausen's harpies in *Jason and the Argonauts*. It's an exciting sequence and technically superb but over far too quickly — it lasts less than a minute and a half. Levinson wants it to be just a good, quick scare — there is no time to linger over the puppets as one would in a Harryhausen encounter. Although all the composite shots are locked off (no camera moves), the sequence is very dynamic due to the excited movements of Stock and the puppets, and some daringly intimate interaction.

The sequence consists of nine animation cuts in among 23 live-action cuts. Muren designed the series of shots and recruited Harry Walton — whose earlier feature film credits included stop-motion for *The Legend of Hillbilly John* — to do the animation. Only one puppet was built, standing in for both creatures. The armature — eight inches high with a 15–inch wingspan — was designed and built by Tom St. Amand (uncredited) and the puppet was sculpted by David Sosalla. Footage of a man trying to shake off a parrot on his arm was examined so that the movement of the harpies' wings and the timing of the blurs would be as realistic as possible. The only flaw is the fact that the static models used in live-action shots are a darker color than the orange-hued animation puppets.

Like Verminthrax Perjorative in *Dragonslayer*, the harpy was first attached to a model-mover. This was placed in front of footage of Stock flailing his arms about. Aligned with the live-action film, the model was moved a frame at a time and each move was recorded by a computer connected to the model-mover. The moves could then be recreated later during filming in front of a blue screen, so that they could be prop-

erly composited with the live action. Only the main body moves of the puppet were controlled in this way by go-motion. Walton animated by hand the more intricate movements of head, mouth, wings, hands and tail. Hand-drawn rotoscoped mattes were used to blot out the rods supporting the puppet. For some shots, the wings were attached to a motor which moved them up and down during the frame exposure, introducing a blur to the image.

Stock's dotty professor examines one of the bronze sculptures in the antique shop and is alarmed to see its eyes suddenly glow a demonic red. In the first animation cut, the puppet leaps off its stand and flies directly at the camera into an extreme closeup. No blurring has been introduced in this shot — in fact, when freeze-framed it appears that the puppet has no wings at all. This is because in matting out a background rod, the rotoscope department also removed the ghostly image of the blur. The shot is not harmed because this is not apparent when viewed at normal speed.

A long shot of the shop shows the tiny model flying away from Stock and briefly flying behind a pillar in the room; the pillar is one of those touches that normally go unnoticed yet add immeasurably to the credibility of the composite. The second harpy leaps off another table and there is another long shot, this time with Stock being harassed (in the best tradition of *Jason and the Argonauts*) by both the creatures. The first one flies around on the left, then Stock rushes to the foreground as both harpies land on his shoulders, still flapping their wings.

Shouting with horror, he throws one to the ground, then the other; the suggestion of physical contact is fault-less. Not only do they initially seem to be sitting right on his shoulders but his hands appear to grab them, even when watched in slow motion. This is quite an achievement by Walton considering that the puppets were animated against a blue screen — i.e., he had no rear-screen image with which to align his puppets.

The next shot looks down at the harpies at Stock's feet. Cel-animated shadows on the floor add an important touch of realism. The creatures fly up again, one landing on Stock's forearm, the other on his shoulder. Trying to fend them off, one of his arms passes in front of the animated model on his shoulder; a matte must have been fashioned frame-by-frame to match the incre-ments in Stock's movement. The other harpy flies past Stock's face, then he runs to the door.

As he reaches for the handle, one of the harpies lands on his hand, and this time blurring of the wing movements is introduced, making a very fluid shot. The next composite is similar, except that the harpy is on the far side of Stock's moving hand, partly obscured by it; again a painstaking frame-by-frame matte has been produced. The last stop-motion shot has Stock reaching for a sword only to have a harpy land on his hand again. Wings flapping, it moves slightly up and down, reacting exactly to the movements of the live-action arm. The scene closes with some live-action shots of a prop harpy wriggling into Stock's overcoat, causing him to stab himself with the sword.

Muren also supervised a clever se-quence in which the two-dimensional image of a knight jumps down from a painting in a stained glass window and attacks another hallucinating victim. In this instance, the image was computer generated and seamlessly integrated into the live action.

Later, Watson (Alex Cox) halluci-nates that he is attacked by living cakes and pastries, and to supervise this semi-comic episode Muren recruited David Allen. Considering Allen's track record, it is intriguing to discover that the se-quence contains no stop-motion what-soever. Muren decided that the pastries could be brought to life by means of rod puppets and marionettes, so Allen was initially surprised that Muren chose him. Muren believed that Allen would bring touches of humor and character to the puppets, and in this he was proved right.

The "Pastry Sequence," devised by Muren, Levinson and producer Steven Spielberg and story-boarded by Dave Carson, is an even shorter episode than the "Harpy Sequence." Bizarre and mag-ical, it is characterized by the sort of sur-real comic style seen in many television commercials. Some shots feature more than a dozen moving puppets, some of which are separately filmed blue-screen elements, and others string puppets that have been shot on the live-action set. Some cuts requiring intricate interaction with the actor (such as shots of the cakes forcing themselves into Watson's mouth) make use of "live-action" props operated mechanically by one of Allen's puppeteers (who is kept just out of the frame). Cel-animated eyes have been matted into the faces of the pastries in some shots. Cel-animated shadows enhance other cuts.

The puppets were filmed and ma-nipulated at slow speed, so that when projected at normal speed they take on a curious vitality. This subconsciously registered artificiality of movement gives the puppets the look of stop-motion. On first seeing this sequence, many people (this author included) thought they were watching some of the most fluid and complex stop-motion shots ever put on film!

Young Sherlock Holmes also contains some superb matte paintings of nineteenth-century London. An extreme long shot of Nicholas Rowe (Holmes), Cox and Ward sliding down a giant wooden pyramid was achieved by stop-framing two-dimensional drawings of the actors down a sheet of glass placed in front of a Chris Evans matte painting.

Allen received an Academy Award nomination for his work — well-deserved but ironic considering that after nearly two decades of contributing stop-motion sequences to feature films, he should finally get recognition for a sequence that contained none.

The Ziegfeld Follies

1946. MGM. D: Vincente Minnelli, George Sidney, Lemuel Ayres. Ph: George Folsey, Charles Roshner. Art: Cedric Gibbons, Merrill Pye, Jack Martin Smith.

Cast: William Powell, Fred Astaire, Gene Kelly, Judy Garland, Fanny Brice, Lucille Ball, Lena Horne, Red Skelton, Esther Williams, Bunin's Puppets, Edward Arnold, Cyd Charisse, Hume Cronyn, Keenan Wynn.

Rating: ☆☆   Stop-Motion: ☆☆½

This MGM production was an excuse for the studio to showcase several of its stars in a series of musical and comedy sketches. Fred Astaire has a number of dance routines (including an unusual one in which he wears eyelid prosthetics to make him look Chinese), Judy Garland goes over the top in a semi-musical routine in which she undergoes an interview, Red Skelton and Keenan Wynn contribute weak comedy sketches, and a host of others perform the kind of dance routines which always leave this author cold.

At the start of the film, William Powell plays the late Ziegfeld in his Heavenly base, reminiscing over his early successes. First night at a Broadway show in 1907 is recreated through the puppetry of Lou Bunin in a charming sequence that lasts just over four minutes. One reason why it was decided to do this sequence with animation was that some of the stars depicted were no longer alive in 1946.

Russian emigré Bunin began making color stop-motion shorts in the late 1930s. His first was *Petroleum Pete and His Cousins*, commissioned by a petroleum company. *Bury the Axis* was made during World War II and contained puppet caricatures of Hitler, Mussolini and Hirohito. He provided a variety of special effects and animated inserts for various Hollywood studios during the 1940s.

His best remembered feature film work is *Alice in Wonderland*, released in 1951.

Bunin's set-ups in *The Ziegfeld Follies* are full of activity, featuring as many as 25 puppets in one shot. This is characteristic of his work and would be a feature of many of the sequences in *Alice in Wonderland*. In the opening shot, the camera pans over a street scene outside a theater, with stop-motion cars moving along the street and various characters walking on the sidewalk. The theater lobby is full of well-dressed characters milling around before the show. On the stage, a line of 12 chorus girls does a can-can routine; close shots of their legs kicking are very smoothly animated. Puppets of Marylin Miller, Fanny Brice, Eddie Cantor and Will Rogers appear in engaging cameos. Brief shots of puppets of members of the audience are also full of activity and character.

There is no attempt to combine any of the puppets with live-action footage.

Zolotoi Klyuchik
(a.k.a. *The Golden Key*)

1939. Soviet Union. D-Special Effects: Alexandr Ptushko. Based on the Story *Pinocchio* by Alexei Tolstoi. Mus: Lev Schwartz.

Rating: ☆☆☆   Stop-Motion: ☆☆½

Even in a faded old print (which is all that appears to be currently available) and in its original Russian language (which this author does not speak), the charm of Ptushko's second feature film shines through. This adaption of the Pinocchio story (with the characters given different names) combines live action, marionettes and stop-motion to great effect. The larger-than-life live-action characters include Karabas-Barabas (the villainous owner of a puppet theater), with a beard that hangs down to the ground. A couple of engaging musical numbers add to the film's magical appeal.

There is a lot of stop-motion in the film and some remarkable composites, but this is not a great stop-motion film. Ptushko does not imbue the puppets — including a rat, a cat, a fox and a turtle — with any special degree of character, an ingredient which should be essential in a film of this whimsical nature. The choreography is lively and makes use of some extensive miniature sets, but the animation lacks the fluidity that could have really brought the figures to life. These figures are never more than puppets that have been manipulated frame-by-frame. All the same, some intriguing effects are carried off brilliantly, including animated ripples in a pond and a puppet appearing to swim underwater.

Ptushko achieves some stunning composites in live-action shots using perspective distortion. For example, the puppet Buratino comes to life (played by an actress in a costume), jumps off a table and does a dance at the feet of the puppet maker, Papa Carlo. This seamless scene was achieved by having the actress (and the floor on which she dances) off in the distance and carefully aligned with the foreground set and actor so that they appear to be one image. By keeping both the near and far images in focus, the camera makes it seem that they are happening in one plane. The same principles were applied in a superb shot where Papa Carlo seems to stroke the head of Buratino (again played on this occasion by the actress). The alignment must have been rehearsed a dozen times or more before the actor's hand was able to give the impression of physical contact.

Other shots seem to defy explanation. A scene in which Buratino (the actress) stands below a storekeeper's stand, with two full-size actors in the foreground, would appear to be another perspective-distortion shot — except that one of the actors steps into the area occupied by the supposedly faroff puppet.

In another baffling shot, the Buratino actress hops down some steps, at the foot of which stands Karabas-Barabas' crony. Buratino actually walks in front of the crony. Almost certainly, Ptushko constructed a huge pair of false legs. Above these, and hanging in the upperforeground, is the actor with his legs tucked out of view, and aligned with the faroff prop legs. All well and good, until another actor then walks right across the shot, in front of both parts of the crony. It's as if Ptushko takes a perverse delight in confounding his viewers.

For closer shots of Buratino, Ptushko uses stop-motion. In the first such sequence, Buratino is accosted by a scrawny rat, an amusing episode but let down by animation that looks hurried. The only shot in this sequence where a puppet is combined with live-action is intriguingly not a composite at all. Papa Carlos offers some food to the puppet and it looks as if Ptushko has had the actor actually hold his hand steady in the frame while the puppet is being animated.

In a later composite, an animated cat and fox walk along the ground in front of a stallholder. This successful composite appears to be a conventional static matte, with the split following the outline of the stall.

Later, there is a long sequence, filmed entirely in miniature, in which the cat and fox lure Buratino away from the town and into a forest. One composite shot is included: The puppets are combined with live-action footage of a swan on a river.

Another sequence has Buratino trapped in a cave. A stop-motion spider puts in a brief appearance on a web but, alas, is not called on to do much. Later, the cat and the fox fight each other and fall into the pond. Animated ripples on the water look sufficiently convincing, as do ripples in a sequence where Buratino encounters a frog on a lily leaf. A turtle is also encountered: Ptushko has it seem to swim underwater by suspending it on wires and filming through gauze.

One of the film's best fantasy images occurs near the end when Papa Carlo, Buratino and their friends set out on a little boat on a river that flows beneath a huge vaulted cave. This shot is a combination of animation, miniature set and painting. The film ends with an unforgettable image when a huge sailing ship flies above a village. The shots are another seamless example of Ptushko's compositing techniques. The final stop-motion shots show the various puppets climbing a ladder up into the ship, which is going to take them away to safety.

Appendix A
Artists' Filmographies

The following are filmographies for artists who have contributed significantly to stop-motion sequences in feature films. Most of them have worked on special effects scenes not involving animation in other films, but those are not listed here.

An entry may not necessarily indicate that an artist has executed the animation for a sequence: He may have constructed the armatures, sculpted the models, designed the composites, and so forth. For specific details on each contribution, refer to the chapter for that film.

Sometimes, an artist known for animation work has contributed other kinds of effects to a film with stop-motion sequences. For example, Doug Beswick worked on *Star Wars* and *The Howling* but was not connected with the stop-motion sequences in these films. Consequently they are not listed in his filmography.

David Allen

Equinox (1968/1971)
When Dinosaurs Ruled the Earth (1970)
Willy Wonka and the Chocolate Factory (1971)

Flesh Gordon (1974)
The Crater Lake Monster (1977)
Laserblast (1978)
The Day Time Ended (1979)
Witches' Brew (1980)
Caveman (1981)
The Howling (1981)
Q (1982)
The Hunger (1983)
Twilight Zone — The Movie (1983)
The Dungeonmaster (Ragewar) (1985)
The Stuff (1985)
Ghoulies II (1987)
**batteries not included* (1987)
Dolls (1987)
Pulsepounders (Dungeonmaster II) (1987; not released)
The Puppetoon Movie (1987)
Willow (1988)
Honey, I Shrunk the Kids (1989)
Puppetmaster (1989)
Robot Jox (1989)
Bride of Re-Animator (1990)
Crash and Burn (1990)
Oscar (1991)
Puppetmaster II (1991)
Puppetmaster III (1991)
Subspecies (1991)
Demonic Toys (1992)

Doctor Mordrid (1992)
Bloodlust — Subspecies III (1993)
Bloodstone — Subspecies II (1993)
Dollman vs. Demonic Toys (1993)
Prehysteria (1993)
Dragonworld (1994)
Freaked (1994)
Oblivion (1994)
Prehysteria 2 (1994)
Robot Wars (1994)
The Arrival (1996)
Puppetmaster IV (1996)
Puppetmaster V (1996)
The Primevals (1999; tentative)

Steven Archer

Clash of the Titans (1981)
Krull (1983)
The NeverEnding Story (1984)
The Adventures of Baron Munchausen (1989)
The Gate II (1990)

James R. Aupperle

Flesh Gordon (1974)
Planet of Dinosaurs (1978)
Caveman (1981)
The Thing (1982)
Dreamscape (1984)
Ghostbusters (1984)
Troll (1985)
Evil Dead II (1987)
The Gate (1987)
Nightmare on Elm Street 3 (1987)
Beetlejuice (1988)
After Midnight (1989)
Nightmare on Elm Street 5 (1990)
RoboCop 2 (1990)

The Addams Family (1992)
The Nightmare Before Christmas (1993)
Tremors II — Aftershocks (1996)

Jon Berg

The Crater Lake Monster (1977)
Star Wars (1977)
Piranha (1978)
Laserblast (1979)
The Empire Strikes Back (1980)
Dragonslayer (1981)
Return of the Jedi (1983)
Twilight Zone — The Movie (1983)
The Ewok Adventure (Caravan of Courage) (1984)
Ghostbusters (1984)
Ewoks: The Battle for Endor (1985)
The Fly (1986)
House II (1986)
RoboCop 2 (1990)
The Nightmare Before Christmas (1993)
The Primevals (1999; tentative)

Doug Beswick

Beware! The Blob (Son of Blob) (1972)
Timegate (1977/78; uncompleted)
Planet of Dinosaurs (1978)
The Empire Strikes Back (1980)
Ghostbusters (1984)
The Terminator (1984)
Evil Dead II (1987)
Nightmare on Elm Street 3 (1987)
Beetlejuice (1988)
After Midnight (1989)
Drop Dead Fred (1990)
Gremlins 2 — The New Batch (1990)
Nightmare on Elm Street 5 (1990)
The Addams Family (1992)

Doctor Mordrid (1992)
Cabin Boy (1993)
Ticks (1993)

Irving Block

Alice in Wonderland (1951)
Kronos (1957)
The Giant Behemoth (1959)

Kent Burton

The Alien Factor (1979)
Pogo for President (1980; claymation)
Naked Robot 4½ (Invader) (1993)
Freaked (1994)
Naked Gun 33⅓ (1994)
Ed Wood (1995)
God's Army (The Prophecy) (1995)
Tales from the Hood (1995)
Screamers (1996)
The Stupids (1996)
Twilight of the Dogs (1995; not released)
James and the Giant Peach (1996)

Yancy Calzada

Evil Dead II (1987)
Nightmare on Elm Street 3 (1987)
Beetlejuice (1988)
The Abyss (1989)
After Midnight (1989)
Gremlins 2 — The New Batch (1990)
Nightmare on Elm Street 5 (1990)
Puppetmaster II (1991)
Demonic Toys (1992)

Doctor Mordrid (1992)
Ticks (1993)
Cabin Boy (1994)
Robot Wars (1994)

Wah Chang

Variety Girl (1947)
Monster from Green Hell (1958)
Tom Thumb (1958)
Dinosaurus! (1960)
Goliath and the Dragon (1960)
The Time Machine (1960)
Journey to the Seventh Planet (1961)
Atlantis the Lost Continent (1961; stop-
    motion cut)
Jack the Giant Killer (1962)
*The Wonderful World of the Brothers
    Grimm* (1963)
7 Faces of Dr. Lao (1964)
The Power (1968)
Some Kind of a Nut (1969)

The Chiodo Brothers (Edward, Charles and Stephen)

Pee-wee's Big Adventure (1985)
Killer Klowns from Outer Space (1987)
The Puppetoon Movie (1987)
RoboCop (1987)
Darkman (1990)
Freaked (1994)
Naked Gun 33⅓ (1994)
Tales from the Hood (1995)
Screamers (1996)
The Stupids (1996)

Randall William Cook

The Crater Lake Monster (1977)
The Day Time Ended (1979)
Laserblast (1979)
The Howling (1980)
Caveman (1981)
Q (1982)
The Thing (1982)
Ghostbusters (1984)
2010 (1984)
The Gate (1987)
Hardcover (1988)
Gate II (1990)
Highway to Hell (1991)
Oscar (1991)
Puppetmaster II (1991)
Subspecies (1991)
Doctor Mordrid (1992)
Dragonworld (1994)
Puppetmaster IV (1994)
The Primevals (1999; tentative)

Stephen Czerkas

Flesh Gordon (1974)
Planet of Dinosaurs (1978)
Dreamscape (1984)

Jim Danforth

Goliath and the Dragon (1960)
The Time Machine (1960)
Journey to the Seventh Planet (1961)
It's a Mad Mad Mad Mad World (1962)
Jack the Giant Killer (1962)
The Wonderful World of the Brothers Grimm (1962)

I'd Rather Be Rich (1964)
7 Faces of Dr. Lao (1964)
That Funny Feeling (1965)
When Dinosaurs Ruled the Earth (1970)
Diamonds Are Forever (1971)
Willy Wonka and the Chocolate Factory (1971)
Flesh Gordon (1974)
The Crater Lake Monster (1977)
Timegate (1977/78; uncompleted)
Caveman (1981)
Clash of the Titans (1981)
Twilight Zone — The Movie (1983)
Ninja III — The Domination (1984)
Hardcover (1988)
Friday the Thirteenth Part VIII (1989)
They Live (1989)
Body Bags (1993)
Robot Wars (1993)
Dragonworld (1994)
God's Army (The Prophecy) (1995)
West of Kashmir: A Sherlock Holmes Adventure! (uncompleted)
Dark Continent: A Sherlock Holmes Adventure! (uncompleted)
The Primevals (1999; tentative)

Marcel Delgado

The Lost World (1925)
Creation (1930)
The Most Dangerous Game (1932)
King Kong (1933)
The Monkey's Paw (1933)
The Son of Kong (1933)
Mighty Joe Young (1949)
Dinosaurus! (1960)
It's a Mad Mad Mad Mad World (1962)
Jack the Giant Killer (1962)
The Wonderful World of the Brothers Grimm (1962)

Victor Delgado

King Kong (1933)
Dinosaurus! (1960)
Goliath and the Dragon (1960)
Jack the Giant Killer (1962)
The Wonderful World of the Brothers Grimm (1962)

Louis DeWitt

The Beast of Hollow Mountain (1956)
Kronos (1957)
Monster from Green Hell (1958)
The Giant Behemoth (1959)

Roger Dicken

When Dinosaurs Ruled the Earth (1970)
The Howling (1980)
Caveman (1981)
Q (1982)
The Hunger (1983)

Randal M. Dutra

The Ewok Adventure (Caravan of Courage) (1984)
Ewoks: The Battle for Endor (1985)
The Golden Child (1986)
House II (1986)
Howard the Duck (1987)
RoboCop (1987)
Willow (1988)
Ghostbusters II (1989)
Honey, I Shrunk the Kids (1989)

RoboCop 2 (1990)
Coneheads (1993)
Jurassic Park (1993)
The Nightmare Before Christmas (1993)
The Lost World — Jurassic Park (1997)

Ernest D. Farino

The Alien Factor (1979)
The Howling (1980)
The Strangeness (1980)
Caveman (1981)
Galaxy of Terror (1981)
Saturday the 14th (1981)
Slapstick of Another Kind (1982; stop-motion cut)
The Thing (1982)
Dreamscape (1984)
The Dungeonmaster (Ragewar) (1985)
The Puppetoon Movie (1987)
Cyborg (1990)
Josh Kirby — Time Warrior: Chapter 1 — Planet of the Dino-Knights (1995)
Josh Kirby — Time Warrior: Chapter 2 — The Human Pets (1995)

Paul Gentry

The Day Time Ended (1979)
Dolls (1987)
Ghoulies II (1987)
Honey, I Shrunk the Kids (1989)
Robot Jox (1989)
Bride of Re-Animator (1990)
RoboCop 2 (1990)
Puppetmaster II (1991)
Puppetmaster III (1991)
Terminator 2 — Judgment Day (1991)
Cabin Boy (1994)

Dragonworld (1994)
Prehysteria! 2 (1994)

Dennis Gordon

The Howling (1980)
Q (1982)
The Hunger (1983)
Twilight Zone — The Movie (1983)
Dolls (1987)
Honey, I Shrunk the Kids (1989)
Puppetmaster (1989)
Bride of Re-Animator (1990)
Puppetmaster III (1991)
Subspecies (1991)
Demonic Toys (1992)
Doctor Mordrid (1992)
Freaked (1994)
Robot Wars (1994)

Ray Harryhausen

Mighty Joe Young (1949)
The Beast from 20,000 Fathoms (1953)
It Came from Beneath the Sea (1955)
The Animal World (1956)
Earth vs. the Flying Saucers (1956)
20 Million Miles to Earth (1957)
The 7th Voyage of Sinbad (1958)
The 3 Worlds of Gulliver (1960)
Mysterious Island (1961)
Jason and the Argonauts (1963)
First Men in the Moon (1964)
One Million Years B.C. (1966)
The Valley of Gwangi (1969)
The Golden Voyage of Sinbad (1973)
Sinbad and the Eye of the Tiger (1977)
Clash of the Titans (1981)

Arthur Hayward

Mysterious Island (1961)
Jason and the Argonauts (1963)
First Men in the Moon (1964)
One Million Years B.C. (1966)
The Valley of Gwangi (1969)

Tom Holland

Dinosaurus! (1960)
Jack the Giant Killer (1962)

Phil Kellison

The Giant Behemoth (1959)
Dinosaurus! (1960)
Jack the Giant Killer (1962)

Peter Kleinow

The Wonderful World of the Brothers Grimm (1962)
7 Faces of Dr. Lao (1964)
The Power (1968)
Caveman (1981)
Goliath Awaits (1981; TV movie)
Spacehunter: Adventures in the Forbidden Zone (1983)
Gremlins (1984)
The Terminator (1984)
Santa Claus (1985)
The Puppetoon Movie (1987)
Leonard Part VI (1987)
RoboCop 2 (1990)
Stephen King's It (1990)

Terminator 2 — Judgment Day (1991)
Nemesis (1992)
Army of Darkness (1993)
Terminal Force (1995)

Justin Kohn

Killer Klowns from Outer Space (1987)
Pulsepounders (Dungeonmaster II)
   (1987; not released)
Captain America (1989)
Fright Night Part II (1989)
Puppetmaster (1989)
Cyborg (1990)
RoboCop 2 (1990)
Oscar (1991)
Puppetmaster II (1991)
The Nightmare Before Christmas (1993)
James and the Giant Peach (1996)

Laine Liska

Flesh Gordon (1974)
The Day Time Ended (1979)
Caveman (1981)
Dolls (1987)
Honey, I Shrunk the Kids (1989)
Oblivion (1994)

George Lofgren

Mighty Joe Young (1949)
The Beast from 20,000 Fathoms (1953)
It Came from Beneath the Sea (1955)
Earth vs. the Flying Saucers (1956)
20 Million Miles to Earth (1957)
The 7th Voyage of Sinbad (1958)

Dennis Muren

Equinox (1968/1971)
Willy Wonka and the Chocolate Factory
   (1970)
Flesh Gordon (1974)
Star Wars (1977)
The Empire Strikes Back (1980)
Dragonslayer (1982)
E.T.— The Extraterrestrial (1982)
Return of the Jedi (1983)
The Ewok Adventure (Caravan of
   Courage) (1984)
Indiana Jones and the Temple of Doom
   (1984)
Young Sherlock Holmes (1986)
Innerspace (1987)
Willow (1988)
Jurassic Park (1993)
The Primevals (1999; tentative)

Willis O'Brien

The Dinosaur and the Missing Link
   (1915)
Birth of a Flivver (1916)
Curious Pets of Our Ancestors (1917)
In the Villain's Power (1917)
Mickey's Naughty Nightmares (1917;
   series)
Morpheus Mike (1917)
Prehistoric Poultry (1917)
The Puzzling Billboard (1917)
RFD 10,000 B.C. (1917)
The Ghost of Slumber Mountain (1919)
The Lost World (1925)
Creation (1930/31; uncompleted)
King Kong (1933)
The Son of Kong (1933)
Mighty Joe Young (1949)

The Animal World (1956)
The Black Scorpion (1957)
The Giant Behemoth (1959)
It's a Mad Mad Mad Mad World
 (1962)

Dave Pal

Dinosaurus! (1960)
The Time Machine (1960)
Jack the Giant Killer (1962)
The Wonderful World of the Brothers
 Grimm (1962)
The Power (1968)

Pete Peterson

Mighty Joe Young (1949)
The Black Scorpion (1957)
The Giant Behemoth (1959)

Alexandr Ptushko

Novyi Gulliver (The New Gulliver)
 (1935)
Zolotoi Klyuchik (The Golden Key)
 (1939)

Jack Rabin

The Beast of Hollow Mountain (1956)
Kronos (1957)
Monster from Green Hell (1958)
The Giant Behemoth (1959)

Ted Rae

Jaws 3-D (1983)
Saturday the 14th (1984)
Jaws — The Revenge (1986; stop-motion
 cut)
Dolls (1987)
Beetlejuice (1988)
Nightmare on Elm Street 5 (1990)
Tales from the Darkside (1990)
Guyver: Dark Hero (1994)

Ken Ralston

The Empire Strikes Back (1980)
Dragonslayer (1982)
Poltergeist (1982)
Return of the Jedi (1983)
The Golden Child (1986)
Who Framed Roger Rabbit (1988)
The Rocketeer (1991)
The Primevals (1999; tentative)

Don Sahlin

Tom Thumb (1958)
Dinosaurus! (1960)
Jack the Giant Killer (1962)
The Wonderful World of the Brothers
 Grimm (1962)

Tom St. Amand

Timegate (1977/78; uncompleted)
The Day Time Ended (1979)
The Empire Strikes Back (1980)
Raiders of the Lost Ark (1981)
Dragonslayer (1982)
E.T. — The Extraterrestrial (1982)

Return of the Jedi (1983)
Indiana Jones and the Temple of Doom
 (1984)
Star Trek III (1984)
Cocoon (1985)
Ewoks: The Battle for Endor (1985)
The Golden Child (1986)
Howard the Duck (1986)
Young Sherlock Holmes (1986)
batteries not included (1987)
RoboCop (1987)
Who Framed Roger Rabbit (1988)
Willow (1988)
Honey, I Shrunk the Kids (1989)
RoboCop 2 (1990)
The Rocketeer (1991)
Jurassic Park (1993)
The Nightmare Before Christmas
 (1993)
RoboCop 3 (1993)
James and the Giant Peach (1996)
The Primevals (1999; tentative)

David Sosalla

Return of the Jedi (1983)
*The Ewok Adventure (Caravan of
 Courage)* (1984)
Indiana Jones and the Temple of Doom
 (1984)
Cocoon (1985)
Young Sherlock Holmes (1986)
Honey, I Shrunk the Kids (1989)

Mark Sullivan

House (1986)
House II (1986)
The Blob (1988)
Metamorphosis: The Alien Factor (1990)

Tom Sullivan

The Evil Dead (1983)
Evil Dead 2 (1987)
Army of Darkness (1993)

Phil Tippett

Some Kind of a Nut (1969)
The Crater Lake Monster (1977)
Star Wars (1977)
Timegate (1977/78; uncompleted)
Piranha (1978)
The Empire Strikes Back (1980)
Dragonslayer (1982)
Return of the Jedi (1983)
Indiana Jones and the Temple of Doom
 (1984)
*The Ewok Adventure (Caravan of
 Courage)* (1984)
Ewoks: The Battle for Endor (1985)
The Golden Child (1986)
House II (1986)
Howard the Duck (1986)
RoboCop (1987)
Willow (1988)
Ghostbusters II (1989)
Honey, I Shrunk the Kids (1989)
RoboCop 2 (1990)
Coneheads (1993)
Jurassic Park (1993)
RoboCop 3 (1993)
Dragonheart (1996)
Tremors II — Aftershocks (1996)
The Primevals (1999; tentative)

Harry Walton

The Legend of Hillbilly John (1973)
Black Sunday (1977)

Laserblast (1978)
Never Say Never Again (1983)
Ewoks: The Battle for Endor (1985)
The Golden Child (1986)
Howard the Duck (1986)
Young Sherlock Holmes (1986)
Innerspace (1987)
The Puppetoon Movie (1987)
RoboCop (1987)
Who Framed Roger Rabbit (1988)
Willow (1988)
Ghostbusters II (1989)
Honey, I Shrunk the Kids (1989)
RoboCop 2 (1990)
The Nightmare Before Christmas (1993)
RoboCop 3 (1993)
Dragonworld (1994)
James and the Giant Peach (1996)

Gene Warren

Variety Girl (1947)
The Twonky (1953)
Kronos (1957)
Monster from Green Hell (1958)
Tom Thumb (1958)
Dinosaurus! (1960)
Goliath and the Dragon (1960)
The Time Machine (1960)
Atlantis the Lost Continent (1961; stop-motion cut)
Flight of the Lost Balloon (1961)
Journey to the Seventh Planet (1961)
Master of the World (1961)
Jack the Giant Killer (1962)
The Wonderful World of the Brothers Grimm (1962)
7 Faces of Dr. Lao (1964)
Around the World Under the Sea (1966)

The Power (1968)
Some Kind of a Nut (1969)
The Legend of Hillbilly John (1973)
Black Sunday (1977)

Gene Warren, Jr.

Goliath Awaits (1981; TV movie)
Spacehunter: Adventures in the Forbidden Zone (1983)
Gremlins (1984)
The Terminator (1984)
Moving Violations (1985)
Flight of the Navigator (1986)
Killer Klowns from Outer Space (1987)
The Puppetoon Movie (1987)
Captain America (1989)
Fright Night Part II (1989)
Cyborg (1990)
Stephen King's It (1990)
Terminator 2 — Judgment Day (1991)
Nemesis (1992)

Karel Zeman

Cestě do pravěku (Journey to the Beginning of Time) (1954)
Vynález Zkázy (The Invention of Destruction) (1958)
Baron Prášil (Baron Munchausen) (1961)
Bláznova Kronika (Chronicle of a Madman) (1964)
Ukradená Vzducholod (The Stolen Dirigible) (1966)
Na kometě (On the Comet) (1970)

Appendix B
Stop-Motion Effects Academy Awards and Nominations

The following is a list of all feature films containing stop-motion photography that have been nominated for or won an Academy Award for Special Effects.

Readers should bear in mind:

(1) The Academy did not introduce a category for special effects until 1939.

(2) Recognition by the Academy in the category of special effects was for years a notoriously unreliable indicator of quality. This was because since 1946 the Special Effects award was voted upon by the entire Academy membership and not by a committee of members with specialized knowledge. Not one of Ray Harryhausen's solo features received even a nomination. Jim Danforth resigned from the Academy over this issue in 1977 when he learned that the live-action remake of *King Kong* had been nominated for (and later won) a Special Achievement Award for Special Visual Effects.

(3) Where a film has been nominated only in a category other than Special Effects, it is not listed. For example, *The Wonderful World of the Brothers Grimm* (1962) won an award for Costume Design and was nominated for Cinematography, Art Direction and Musical Score. But it did not get a mention in the Special Effects category and so is omitted from this list.

(4) In some of these films, the award may not be specifically recognizing the stop-motion content of a film. For example, *Terminator 2 — Judgment Day* contains only two brief stop-motion shots among all its dazzling miniature effects and computer graphics. But the stop-motion effects are an essential part of the finished product, and so the award is listed here.

(5) In 1972, the category title was changed from "Special Visual Effects" to "Special Achievement Award for Visual

Effects" and would not necessarily be given every year. For example, no award was given for 1973, the year that Harryhausen's *Golden Voyage of Sinbad* was released. Since then, it has been both reinstated as a regular category and reverted to "Special Achievement Award" several times.

1939

Nomination: *Topper Takes a Trip*. Roy Seawright.

1940

Nomination: *The Invisible Man Returns*. John P. Fulton.

1943

Special Award to George Pal for the development of novel methods and techniques in the production of short subjects known as *Puppetoons*.

1949

Award: *Mighty Joe Young*. Willis H. O'Brien.

1950

Award: *Destination Moon*. Lee Zavitz.

1952

Honorary Award to Merian C. Cooper for his many innovations and contributions to the art of motion pictures.

1955

Nomination: *Forbidden Planet*. A. Arnold Gillespie, Irving Ries, Wesley C. Miller

1958

Award: *Tom Thumb*. Tom Howard.

1960

Award: *The Time Machine*. Gene Warren, Tim Barr.

1964

Award: *Mary Poppins*. Peter Ellenshaw, Hamilton Luske, Eustace Lycett.
Nomination: *7 Faces of Dr. Lao*. Jim Danforth.

1968

Award: *2001: A Space Odyssey*. Stanley Kubrick.

1971

Nomination: *When Dinosaurs Ruled the Earth*. Jim Danforth.

1977

Award: *Star Wars*. John Stears, John Dykstra, Richard Edlund, Grant McCune, Robert Blalack.

1979

Nomination: *The Black Hole*. Peter Ellenshaw, Art Cruickshank, Eustace Lycett, Danny Lee, Harrison Ellenshaw, Joe Hale.

1980

Award: *The Empire Strikes Back*. Brian Johnson, Richard Edlund, Dennis Muren, Bruce Nicholson.

1981

Award: *Raiders of the Lost Ark*. Richard Edlund, Kit West, Bruce Nicholson, Joe Johnston.
Nomination: *Dragonslayer*. Dennis Muren. Phil Tippett, Ken Ralston, Brian Johnson.
Technical Achievement Award (Citation): Dennis Muren and Stuart Ziff of Industrial Light and Magic,

Incorporated, for the development of a Motion Picture Figure Mover for animation photography.

1982

Award: *E.T.—The Extraterrestrial*. Carlo Rambaldi, Dennis Muren, Kenneth F. Smith
Nomination: *Poltergeist*. Richard Edlund, Michael Wood, Bruce Nicholson.

1983

Award: *Return of the Jedi*. Richard Edlund, Dennis Muren, Ken Ralston, Phil Tippett.

1984

Award: *Indiana Jones and the Temple of Doom*. Dennis Muren, Michael McAlister, Lorne Peterson, George Gibbs.
Nomination: *Ghostbusters*. Richard Edlund, John Bruno, Mark Vargo, Chuck Gasper.
Nomination: *2010*. Richard Edlund, Neil Krepela, George Jensen, Mark Stetson.

1985

Award: *Cocoon*. Ken Ralston, Ralph McQuarrie, Scott Farrar, David Berry.

Nomination: *Return to Oz.* Will Vinton, Ian Wingrove, Zoran Perisic, Michael Lloyd.

Nomination. *Young Sherlock Holmes.* Dennis Muren, Kit West, John Ellis, David Allen.

1987

Award: *Innerspace.* Dennis Muren.

1988

Award: *Who Framed Roger Rabbit.* Richard Williams.

1989

Award: *The Abyss.* John Bruno, Dennis Muren, Hoyt Yeatman, Dennis Skotak.

Nomination: *The Adventures of Baron Munchausen.* Richard Conway, Kent Houston.

1991

Award: *Terminator 2 — Judgment Day.* Dennis Muren, Stan Winston, Gene Warren, Jr., Robert Skotak.

Gordon E. Sawyer Award (instituted 1981 to honor lifetime achievements in scientific or technical fields): Ray Harryhausen.

1993

Award: *Jurassic Park.* Dennis Muren, Phil Tippett, Michael Lantieri, Stan Winston.

Appendix C
Stop-Motion
Top Ten Lists

Stop-motion animators and others associated with the medium were asked to supply lists of their ten favorite stop-motion sequences from feature films. Some included brief descriptions of each choice. Unless stated, the lists are not in any particular order.

David Allen*

1. *King Kong* (1933). Kong/tyrannosaurus fight.
2. *The 7th Voyage of Sinbad* (1957). The skeleton duel.
3. *Mighty Joe Young* (1949). Joe's scene with the caged lion.
4. *The Golden Voyage of Sinbad* (1973). The centaur versus the Gryphon.
5. *The Lucy Show* (television). Puppet introduction by Jim Danforth.
6. *RoboCop 2* (1991). RoboCop versus RoboCop 2.
7. *Dragonslayer* (1981). The dragon in its cave.

8. *20 Million Miles to Earth* (1957). The Ymir versus the elephant.
9. *Clash of the Titans* (1981). Medusa sequence.

*David Allen provided only nine choices.

Steven Archer

1. *King Kong* (1933). Kong / tyrannosaurus fight. Atmospheric jungle setting. Sixty years on, this work is still inspiring and hard to match. The best example of character animation and the best-staged animation fight ever.
2. *Mighty Joe Young* (1949). Nightclub rampage. Excellent, with "acting" and exciting action. The sequence equals the orphanage sequence in drama and staging.
3. *The 7th Voyage of Sinbad* (1958). Second Cyclops sequence. The first Cyclops is dynamic — a great entrance! — but it's the second one that makes it for me. Love that meal-time. Herrmann really matches Ray Harryhausen's dynamated moves brilliantly.

4. *Jason and the Argonauts* (1963). Talos sequence. A sequence which illustrates the meaning of the term "cinematic." The effect is doubled by Herrmann's majestic score. Exciting, frightening and thrilling. An inspiring movie and an even more inspiring sequence. My particular favorite of the maestro's work. Highly recommended!

5. *The Valley of Gwangi* (1969). Roping sequence. A very lively piece of animation and a well-staged sequence backed by Jerome Moross' exciting music. It excels more for staging than "acting" ability. The definitive roping sequence for my money and the best sequence in the film.

6. *Flesh Gordon* (1974). Beetleman sequence. A really nifty piece of work, this, with sharp "acting" ability and slick matte work, showing great sensitivity in character and staging.

7. *The Golden Voyage of Sinbad* (1973). Figurehead sequence. A superb example of the maestro's restraint and acting talent here. Wonderful show of controlled strength in movement.

8. *Hardcover* (1988). Last Jackal Boy sequence. A feel for sensitivity and vulnerability is displayed in movement and the model's design. Beautifully staged and animated. One of the most realistically animated characters I've ever seen.

9. *Clash of the Titans* (1981). Medusa sequence. An atmospheric sequence with great mood and tension. Great sense of presence in acting. The maestro's all-time best sequence!

10. *Jurassic Park* (1993). First Tyrannosaurus sequence. Astonishingly captures and makes believable the behavior and manner of what a real dinosaur might actually be like. Runs a very close equal with the velociraptor sequence. Astounding and incredibly realistic in movement and look. Greatly enhanced by the film's night time setting. A real tough act to follow!

Doug Beswick

In chronological order:

1. The tyrannosaurus fight from *King Kong*. Hard to beat for energy and excitement.

2. The roping sequence, *Mighty Joe Young*. A classic stop-motion scene that is not only technically marvelous, but contains some brilliant character animation.

3. The first Cyclops sequence on the beach, *The 7th Voyage of Sinbad*. Fantasy at its best!

4. The skeleton from *The 7th Voyage of Sinbad*. Outstanding choreography and animation.

5. The skeletons from *Jason and the Argonauts*. Once again Harryhausen's choreography and animation are outstanding.

6. The allosaurus, *One Million Years B.C.* Great model and animation.

7. The baby and mother dinosaur sequence, *When Dinosaurs Ruled the Earth*. Jim Danforth's puppets and animation are outstanding.

8. Kali sequence, *The Golden Voyage of Sinbad*. Again great choreography, and the animation is superb.

9. The raptor kitchen sequence, *Jurassic Park*. A technical masterpiece. The raptors are totally believable.

10. The Oogie Boogie Man sequence, *The Nightmare Before Christmas*. Wonderfully animated and directed.

Wah Chang*

1. *The Lost World* (1925)
2. *King Kong* (1933)
3. *The New Gulliver* (1935)
4. *The Emperor's Nightingale* (1949) (Jiří Trnka all-puppet film)
5. *A Midsummer Night's Dream* (1957) (Jiří Trnka all-puppet film)
6. *The 7th Voyage of Sinbad* (1958)

"...and many others of Ray Harryhausen's films, and finally George Lucas' *Star Wars*, etc."

*Wah Chang provided only six choices.

Jim Danforth

1. *King Kong* (1933). The fight in the grotto with the elasmosaurus because it is so moody, eerie and powerful.

2. *King Kong* (1933). The stegosaurus charge because of the daring, almost documentary, way in which the first set-up is staged and directed.

3. *The Son of Kong* (1933). The styracosaurus attack because I like the set-ups, the lighting and the power of the styrac hitting the cliff.

4. *20 Million Miles to Earth* (1957). The newly hatched Ymir on the table because I like the pantomime of the Ymir and the intensity of the actor's focus.

5. *The Black Scorpion* (1957). The underground sequence because it is so moody, eerie and creepy.

6. *The 7th Voyage of Sinbad* (1958). The Cyclops scenes in general, particularly those around the roasting spit because I like the absolutely startling "look" of the Cyclops. I also like the little touches, like the Cyclops pulling up a stool so he can sit down while he roasts Harufa.

7. *The 7th Voyage of Sinbad* (1958). Sinbad's duel with the skeleton, because I like the horrorific and startling conception as well as the flawless execution.

8. *The Valley of Gwangi* (1969). The eohippus scenes because I guess I'm just a sucker for cute, little furry animals.

9. *The Golden Voyage of Sinbad* (1973). The Kali sword fight because it's *swell*— real movie magic! (And that inscrutable Kali expression.) If we can stretch it also to include the Kali dance, the steps and poses are authentic as well as being kinetically interesting.

10. *Sinbad and the Eye of the Tiger* (1977). All the Trog "acting" sequences because I think they are the best and most subtle humanoid creature pantomime that I have seen. Underrated and under-appreciated. Take it from me, this is extremely skillful work requiring enormous understanding.

Danforth added, "If one is allowed to include short films, I would probably substitute Phil Tippett's original monoclonius and tyrannosaurus film (*Prehistoric Beast*) for no. 10, because I liked the naturalistic opening scenes of the monoclonius browsing.

"Are you including pure puppet films? If so, I would like to substitute the scenes of the artisans rehearsing and performing 'Pyramus and Thisbe' from Trnka's *A Midsummer Night's Dream*."

Dennis Muren*

1. *The 7th Voyage of Sinbad* (1958). First Cyclops scene on the beach.

2. *The 7th Voyage of Sinbad* (1958). Skeleton duel.

3. *20 Million Miles to Earth* (1957). Birth of the Ymir.

4. *King Kong* (1933). Kong/tyrannosaurus fight.

5. *Jason and the Argonauts* (1963). The skeleton fight.

6. *When Dinosaurs Ruled the Earth* (1970). Plesiosaur sequence.

7. *When Dinosaurs Ruled the Earth* (1970). Baby dinosaur scene.

8. *Mighty Joe Young* (1949). Joe's first scene with the caged lion.

Dennis Muran provided only eight choices.

Neil Pettigrew

In order of preference:

1. *The Valley of Gwangi* (1969). Cathedral sequence. As surreal a juxtaposition as you could hope for: a dinosaur in a place of worship. Great, echoing sound effects and some haunting images.

2. *The Lost World* (1925). Dinosaur stampede and the "morning after" panorama. Complex animation in huge and remarkable miniature sets, full of marvelously busy touches of animal behavior.

3. *Jason and the Argonauts* (1963). Skeleton fight. Harryhausen always gets the balance of the horrific and the absurd just right in this astonishing, exciting sequence that evidences his almost inhuman stamina at the animation table.

4. *King Kong* (1933). Kong investigating Fay Wray in his mountaintop lair. O'Brien makes this scene horrific,

comical and erotic all at once, and imbues Kong with irresistible touches of personality.

5. *Mysterious Island* (1961). Phororhacos sequence. Once again, Harryhausen creates a deft balance between the comic and the startling. His giant bird hops, squawks and flaps about with enormous vitality and character.

6. *The Son of Kong* (1933). The sinking island at the climax. A beautifully realized finale of truly tragic proportions. Underrated and often overlooked.

7. *Return of the Jedi* (1983). Ewoks versus the Scout Walkers. So far, the pinnacle of "robo-motion." Tippett imbues his unlikely two-legged vehicles with unforgettable touches of personality—sometimes imposing, sometimes comic. Some impeccable composite work.

8. *Ewoks—The Battle for Endor* (1985). Tippett's outlandish bipedal monsters—looking like a cross between a fish and an elephant—are never more than background figures but feature in some delightful scenes. They encapsulate the fantasy possibilities which stop-motion all too rarely exploits.

9. *One Million Years B.C.* (1966). The allosaurus fight. Harryhausen is in total control as director here, maintaining an electric pace through well-conceived choreography and dynamic editing.

10. *The 7th Voyage of Sinbad* (1958). The second Cyclops sequence. This long sequence is full of resonant fairy tale images such as the Cyclops pulling up a rickety wooden stool as he roasts a sailor on a spit, or blindly following Sinbad to the edge of a cliff, arms outstretched pathetically in front of him.

Phil Tippett

1. *King Kong* (1933). T-Rex fight.
2. *The 7th Voyage of Sinbad* (1958). Cyclops on beach.
3. *The 7th Voyage of Sinbad* (1958). Skeleton sword fight.
4. *When Dinosaurs Ruled the Earth* (1970). Mother dinosaur.
5. *The Golden Voyage of Sinbad* (1973). Wooden statue.
6. *Mysterious Island* (1961). Big Bird.
7. *Clash of the Titans* (1981). Medusa.
8. *The 7th Voyage of Sinbad* (1958). Dragon.
9. *20 Million Miles to Earth* (1957). Little Ymir.
10. *The Black Scorpion* (1957). Pit sequence.

Harry Walton

1. Roping sequence from *Mighty Joe Young*—a superb blend of animation and live action in a fast-paced action sequence.
2. Drunken cage sequence from *Mighty Joe Young*. A great acting performance from Joe Young via Ray Harryhausen in facial as well as body movement.

3. Skeleton fight sequence from *The 7th Voyage of Sinbad*—a superbly executed sequence of animation and live-action choreography.
4. Dragon in the cave sequence from *Dragonslayer*. If dragons were real, this is what one would look like. Excellent animation, model and lighting.
5. The sequence with the baby hatching from an egg and the mother dinosaur from *When Dinosaurs Ruled the Earth*. The performance between the mother and baby was so wonderful, I remember the audience's emotional responses.
6. The "Yawning Man" sequence from *Tom Thumb*. The performance did what it was intended to do—make you yawn!
7. The "Cobbler's Elves" sequence from *The Wonderful World of the Brothers Grimm*. Great fun, gags and antics in animation.
8. The eohippus in the corral in *The Valley of Gwangi*. Ray evoked a wonderful sense of mutual curiosity between El Diablo and the actors.
9. "Pepsi Man" sequence from *The Golden Child*. A stupendous performance from a most difficult subject.
10. The scorpion sequence from *Honey, I Shrunk the Kids*—great animation, if you don't mind me saying, by Phil Tippett, Tom St. Amand and Harry Walton, and live-action composting in true "Dynamation" fashion.

Appendix D
Stop-Motion Memorabilia Price Guide

The theatrical releases of all the films discussed in this book were accompanied by promotional material, including posters, lobby cards, stills, campaign books and other formats. Much of this is now sought after by stop-motion enthusiasts and is becoming increasingly rare. The following is a guide to the prices one should expect to pay (as of roughly January 1999). Values are based on prices realized in auctions and advertised by dealers, as well as the knowledge acquired by this author during thirty years of collecting.

The value of a piece may depend on several factors, including the popularity of a film, the scarcity of the item, the age and condition, and the appeal of the artwork. The prices listed are only a guide and should not be regarded as an indication of exact value. Actual sale prices are always a matter of negotiation between vendor and buyer.

Only titles regarded as "stop-motion films" are listed, i.e., those with a significant stop-motion content. This guide is only a selection. There is much more material available than is listed here.

When two or more copies of a piece have sold at significantly different prices, then a range of values is given. All prices are in U.S. dollars. For reasons of space, only items valued at $100 or more are included. All prices are derived from sales or advertisements since 1994.

All items are of U.S. origin except where stated otherwise.

The following terminology is used:

1-sheet	U.S. poster size 27" × 41"
3-sheet	U.S. poster size 41" × 81"
6-sheet	U.S. poster size 81" × 81"
Half-sheet	U.S. poster size 22" × 28"
Insert	U.S. poster size 14" × 36"
Lobby card	U.S. 11" × 14" card, usually in a set of eight, one of which is a title card

G.B. quad   British poster size 30" × 40"
Belgian   Belgian poster size 14" × 21"

A re-release of a film is indicated by the letter "R"; e.g., "R38" indicates a 1938 re-release.

The Animal World, 1-Sheet $100
The Animal World, 3-Sheet $150
The Animal World, G.B. Quad $100
The Animal World, Italian 55 × 79 $183
The Beast from 20,000 Fathoms, 1-Sheet $500–$1,200
The Beast from 20,000 Fathoms, 6-Sheet $1,300
The Beast from 20,000 Fathoms, Insert $475
The Beast from 20,000 Fathoms, Australian 3-Sheet $500
The Beast from 20,000 Fathoms, Belgian $100–$150
The Beast from 20,000 Fathoms, Lobby Card Set $150–$250
The Beast from 20,000 Fathoms, G.B. Quad $400–$600
The Beast of Hollow Mountain, 3-Sheet $175
The Beast of Hollow Mountain, Lobby Card Set $135
Behemoth the Sea Monster (*The Giant Behemoth*), G.B. Quad $200
Behemoth the Sea Monster, Insert $175
Behemoth the Sea Monster, Half-Sheet $175–$225
Behemoth the Sea Monster, 1-Sheet $115–$250
Behemoth the Sea Monster, 3-Sheet $450
Behemoth the Sea Monster, Lobby Card Set $150
Behemoth the Sea Monster, Italian 13 × 27 $100

Behemoth the Sea Monster, Italian 39 × 55 $150
Behemoth the Sea Monster, Italian 55 × 79 $145
The Black Scorpion, 1-Sheet $75–$150
The Black Scorpion, 3-Sheet $250
The Black Scorpion, Lobby Card Set $125
Dinosaurus!, 3-Sheet $125
Dinosaurus!, 6-Sheet $175
Dinosaurus!, French 47 × 63 $125
Earth vs. the Flying Saucers, Half-Sheet $300
Earth vs. the Flying Saucers, 1-Sheet $400–$700
Earth vs. the Flying Saucers, 3-Sheet $1200
Earth vs. the Flying Saucers, Lobby Card Set $300–$400
Earth vs. the Flying Saucers, U.S. Press Book $115
Earth vs. the Flying Saucers, Australian Daybill 13 × 30 $200
Earth vs. the Flying Saucers, French 47 × 63 $150
Earth vs. the Flying Saucers, Italian 55 × 79 $2,600
Earth vs. the Flying Saucers, G.B. Quad $340
Fiend Without a Face, 1-Sheet $125–$500
Fiend Without a Face, Lobby Card Set $100
First Men in the Moon, 1-Sheet $75–$100
First Men in the Moon, G.B. Quad $100–$125
First Men in the Moon, French 47 × 63 $75–$100
First Men in the Moon, Italian 55 × 79 $175
Ghost of Slumber Mountain, 1-Sheet $1,650–$5,000

Ghost of Slumber Mountain, 3-Sheet $2,500–$5,000

Ghost of Slumber Mountain, 6-Sheet $5,000

It Came from Beneath the Sea, 1-Sheet $250–$800

It Came from Beneath the Sea, 3-Sheet $300

It Came from Beneath the Sea, 6-Sheet $1,000

It Came from Beneath the Sea, Lobby Card Set $150–$300

It Came from Beneath the Sea, G.B. Quad $300

It Came from Beneath the Sea, Press Book $125

It Came from Beneath the Sea, Italian 39 × 55 $400–$600

Jack the Giant Killer, 1-Sheet $75–$100

Jason and the Argonauts, 1-Sheet $75–$200

Jason and the Argonauts, 3-Sheet $140–$275

Jason and the Argonauts, G.B. Quad $125

Jason and the Argonauts, French 47 × 63 $125–$175

King Kong, 1-Sheet $50,000–$90,000

King Kong, 3-Sheet Style A $45,000–$100,000

King Kong, 3-Sheet Style B $22,000–$42,500

King Kong, 6-Sheet $40,000–$50,000

King Kong, Title Lobby Card $4,000–$7,000

King Kong, Scene Lobby Cards $1,000–$4,000 (Each)

King Kong, Press Book $3,500–$4,200

King Kong, French 47 × 63 (Coudon Art) $6,000–$8,500

King Kong, French 47 × 63 (Peron Art) $4,000–$4,900

King Kong, French 63 × 94 $10,000–$12,000

King Kong, French 94 × 126 $4,500–$9,900

King Kong, Belgian 24 × 33 $1,400–$2,500

King Kong, Swedish 47 × 25 $9,000

King Kong, R38 1-Sheet $5,500

King Kong, R40s G.B. Quad $1,500–$3,000

King Kong, R42 1-Sheet $1,600–$1,800

King Kong, R42, Banner 24 × 82 $2,645

King Kong, R52 1-Sheet $300–$400

King Kong, R52 Lobby Card Set $225–$350

King Kong, R56 1-Sheet $500–$1,000

King Kong, R59 Belgian $500

King Kong R? Argentinian 1-Sheet $2,000–$2,200

The Lost Continent, 1-Sheet $125–$285

The Lost Continent, 3-Sheet $225

The Lost Continent, Italian 39 × 55 $250

The Lost World, 1-Sheet $20,000

The Lost World, Austrian 37 × 73 $4,300

The Lost World, Lobby Cards $500–$750 (Each)

Mighty Joe Young, Half-Sheet $500–$600

Mighty Joe Young, 1-Sheet $500–$1,000

Mighty Joe Young, Press Book $100–$150

Mighty Joe Young, Belgian $125–$500

Mighty Joe Young, Lobby Card Set $300

Mighty Joe Young, Italian 14 × 27 $125

Mighty Joe Young, R53 1-Sheet $125

Monster from Green Hell, Lobby Card Set $100–$175

Monster from Green Hell, G.B. Quad
$100–$125

The Mysterious Island, 1-Sheet $75–
$100

The Mysterious Island, 40 × 60 $100

The Mysterious Island, Lobby Card Set
$75–$100

The Mysterious Island, G.B. Quad
$75–$100

One Million Years B.C., G.B. Quad
$225

One Million Years B.C., 1-Sheet $35–
$125

One Million Years B.C., 40 × 60
$100–$175

One Million Years B.C., French 47 × 63
$125–$300

The 7th Voyage of Sinbad, Insert $95–
$150

The 7th Voyage of Sinbad, Half-Sheet
$100–$150

The 7th Voyage of Sinbad, 1-Sheet
$100–$250

The 7th Voyage of Sinbad, G.B. Quad
$250–$300

The 7th Voyage of Sinbad, French 47 ×
63    $150–$200

The 7th Voyage of Sinbad, Italian 27 ×
39    $250

The 7th Voyage of Sinbad, Italian 39 ×
55    $250–$300

The 7th Voyage of Sinbad, Lobby Card
Set $150–$200

The Son of Kong, 1-Sheet $16,000

The Son of Kong, Window Card 14 × 22
$5,000

The Son of Kong, Press Book $600

The 3 Worlds of Gulliver, G.B. Quad
$125

The 3 Worlds of Gulliver, 3-Sheet
$50–$200

The 3 Worlds of Gulliver, Italian 39 ×
55    $100

20 Million Miles to Earth, Insert
$175–$250

20 Million Miles to Earth, Half-Sheet
$125

20 Million Miles to Earth, 1-Sheet
$150–$350

20 Million Miles to Earth, 3-Sheet
$250–$400

20 Million Miles to Earth, Lobby Card
Set $100–$150

20 Million Miles to Earth, Italian 39 ×
55    $700

20 Million Miles to Earth, Italian 55 ×
79    $1,500

20 Million Miles to Earth, G.B. Quad
$300

The Valley of Gwangi, 1-Sheet
$65–$150

The Valley of Gwangi, 40 × 60 $100

The Valley of Gwangi, Italian 39 × 55
$250

When Dinosaurs Ruled the Earth, G.B.
Quad $120

When Dinosaurs Ruled the Earth,
French 47 × 63 $100

Glossary

aerial brace This has come to be the accepted term for any device that is used by an animator to support a puppet in mid air. A flying creature, an animal for part of its running cycle, a spear thrown through the air, pieces of falling debris that need to be in the same shot as the puppet—all are examples of occasions when something requiring animation is not in contact with the animation table. Usually the puppet or prop will be suspended on wires from an overhead brace, which is supported on a rail that allows it to travel horizontally in the direction of the desired movement.

armature The armature is the skeleton of a puppet. Its design is dependent on the role of the puppet. For a small model that is not required to perform complex movements, a simple wire armature may be adequate. A larger model that is to be the central figure in a sequence, and which must perform realistically even in closeup, may be as detailed as the skeleton of a living animal, consisting of an intricate arrangement of hand-machined steel plates and joints.

All stop-motion armatures must have the ability to retain any position that the animator imposes on them.

blue screen A screen in front of which actors or objects will be filmed as part of a process to composite their image with other footage. (See "Traveling matte" below.)

composite shot Any shot which is made up of different elements of film, combined by whatever means.

D.I.D. A D.I.D. (Direct Input Device) may be regarded as the bridge between conventional stop-motion and computer-generated imagery. A D.I.D. is a stop-motion armature that has been enhanced so that information about its position can be fed into a computer. Various points on the armature are equipped with encoders connected to the computer. Manipulating that information, the computer constructs an internal pictorial wire-frame figure which will later be fleshed out by software that gives it a realistic appearance.

The D.I.D. (originally known as the Dinosaur Input Device) was developed by Industrial Light and Magic and the Tippett Studio for *Jurassic Park*.

floor inlay Generally, a static matte rear-projection (see below) set-up is designed to obscure the animation table.

However, it may improve a shot if part of the table-top, surrounding the model's feet, is actually left in the final composite. One advantage of this is that the model can throw a shadow onto the miniature floor. Without this shadow, the shot might look fake — especially if the puppet is surrounded by actors who are all throwing shadows in the live-action footage. Another advantage is that a floor inlay allows the camera to look down at the puppet, varying the perspective from the more usual eye-level design.

The floor inlay is achieved by means of the matte/counter-matte process described below, except that the two mattes are designed not to match up exactly, leaving an area of the animation table in the finished shot. Care has to be taken that the coloring of the floor inlay matches up with the coloring of the surrounding area in the rear-projection.

front-light / back-light matte This is another method of matting around moving images. For each position of the puppet, two frames of film are exposed. In the first, the puppet is lit from the front against a completely black background. In the second, the puppet is in darkness against a bright background, so that the puppet appears as just a silhouette. These two sequences of frames now effectively constitute a matte and counter-matte which can be used to combine the animation footage with any other piece of film.

front projection This has the same purpose as static matte rear-projection, but the live-action footage is projected from in front of the animation table, not

behind it. The projector is positioned at right angles to the camera and the image is projected onto the rear screen via a semi-translucent mirror placed at a 45 degree angle. The camera shoots through the same mirror, thereby achieving alignment of camera and projector. Of course, this means that some of the projected image will fall on the animation puppet; this is corrected with additional lighting. One advantage of front projection is that the background image is sharper than it would be if projected from behind the rear screen.

generation A first-generation film print is footage that has been printed from the original negative. Hence the image contained in a rear-projection set-up is referred to as second generation footage, and so on.

glass painting *see* **matte painting**

go-motion photography Go-motion (also known as go-animation) is a method of introducing a blur into the filming of an animation model in order to increase the realism of a shot. A prototype was devised for use during some of the animation in *The Empire Strikes Back*, but it was more fully developed in 1980 by Dennis Muren, Stuart Ziff and Phil Tippett when working on *Dragonslayer*. Those parts of the model which are considered to require a blur (for example, the legs of a running animal) are attached to computer-controlled rods. (Those rods which are not obscured from the camera by the puppet may be concealed later by mattes individually hand-drawn onto each frame of film.) The computer is programmed to reproduce a certain movement, e.g., advance a leg through one pace in 20 small increments. The computer is synchronized with the camera: The frame exposure coincides with the precise moment that the computer causes the movement of the model. The model still has to be photographed frame-by-frame, because other parts of the model, such as its arms and face, may need to be animated in the conventional stop-motion manner. But now the most significant movement in the final image is softened by a blur.

grain Film emulsion contains grains of silver, or, if it is color film, images derived from grains of silver. Ordinarily unnoticed, grain can become conspicuous if an image is frozen for a number of frames or enlarged and combined with an image with a contrasting grain.

high-speed filming Certain kinds of live action are sometimes filmed at high speed, often 96 frames a second. When projected at normal speed, such action is slowed down to one-quarter of its actual speed. This is done to convey an impression that something is much larger than it really is. For example, a miniature model of an exploding volcano filmed at normal speed will always look like a miniature because all the bits of flying debris will be moving at a rate proper to small objects. By slowing down the film, they appear to have the velocity of much larger objects. Care has to be taken with lighting such sequences: Decreasing the shutter speed by one-fourth means that four times as much light is required during shooting.

interaction A catch-all word used to describe any moment when subjects in different elements of film appear to make physical contact. This may be merely implied through the editing of a sequence; it may be achieved by clever alignment of images on either side of a matte line; or it may be achieved by having partial replicas (actual or glass-painted) of articles in one element of the composite extending into another element. There are other techniques. The dramatic impact of animation sequences is often dependent on the variety and ingenuity of its moments of interaction.

matte A matte is something that obscures part of the image recorded by the camera, thereby preventing a section of the film from being exposed. It may be a piece of card positioned in front of the lens or an area of black painted on a sheet of glass, placed between camera and subject. Its function is to allow separate images to be combined on one strip of film. This is done by rewinding the film in the camera, then re-exposing it, this time with a counter-matte in position. (A counter-matte is a matte that obscures precisely that part of the film which was left unobscured during the first pass.) The subjects of the two exposures will now appear to be contemporaneous.

matte painting The matte referred to above may be a painting instead of merely a black card. If the edge of the painting is carefully aligned with the live action behind it, an impression is created that they are one image. Paintings such as these are commonly used to depict landscapes (jungles, cliff faces, mountains) or elaborate buildings when the locations chosen for filming do not meet all the script requirements. They may even save the expense of location filming altogether. The painting may be done on glass (**glass painting**), leaving a clear area through which the live action is to be seen.

miniature rear projection This use of rear projection, pioneered by Willis O'Brien, is a means of introducing a small area of live-action footage into film of a miniature set. A projector is concealed behind the miniature set, a small part of which is a translucent screen. As the puppet in the set is animated, so the film on the screen is advanced a frame at a time.

miniature set A set built in miniature to save on the cost of location shooting or constructing full-size sets. In stop-motion photography, it is built to the same scale as the animation puppet, giving the puppet a physical environment with which to interact.

optical printer A camera used to combine previously shot pieces of film with other footage.

rear projection Rear projection is a staple of all kinds of effects shots. Behind the principle subject of a shot is a large screen, onto which is projected footage that has been filmed earlier. The projector is positioned behind this screen, which is translucent to allow the image to be seen from the front. Often it is used to save the cost of location shooting: For example, an actor may be filmed in front of stock footage of a jungle.

In stop-motion photography, rear projection has an added benefit. The an-

imation puppet is placed in front of the rear screen and for each slight adjustment of its position, so the rear film is advanced one frame and photographed by the camera. With careful alignment of the two elements, an animator can suggest that the puppet is interacting with something in the background image. A disadvantage of this technique is that because the rear film is now a second generation image, it may lose some definition or contrast and appear "washed out" compared to the sharper foreground image. In black-and-white photography it was common to place actors in front of a full-size rear projection in sequences where they were required to pass in front of the animated puppet. In color photography this is impractical because grain and lighting make it all too obvious that these are two separate pieces of film; consequently, traveling matte is used (see below).

registration Registration is the positioning of film in the camera. For the purposes of rewinding a piece of film and re-exposing it, an animator has to be sure that the sprockets and sprocket holes will hold the film in exactly the same position as in the first pass. Otherwise, any slight variation will be magnified in a composite shot, preventing the two elements from matching up. Specially designed cameras are usually employed to insure stability.

replacement animation Replacement animation is one kind of puppet animation. Instead of one model being repositioned 24 times per second of footage, a series of slightly different models — commonly but not necessarily one per frame —

1. A simplified example of a static matte rear-projection set-up. The aim is to show a dinosaur walking between two hills. The two hills are contained in previously-shot footage projected onto a translucent screen from behind. A matte, painted on glass and matching the outline of the foreground hill, is placed between the camera and the animation puppet.

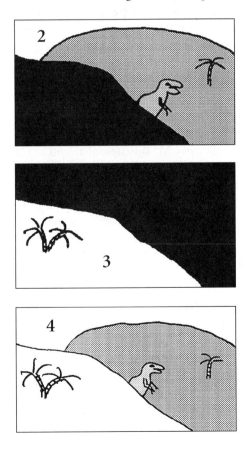

2. What the camera sees in the setup above (figure 1) during the first pass of the film through the camera. The black area is the matte. It blocks the light and causes that area of the film to remain unexposed. The rear-projected film is advanced one frame at a time as the puppet dinosaur is animated.

3. The film just recorded by the camera is rewound to the beginning of the shot, and the previously filmed live-action footage is rewound in the projector. The matte screen shown in figure 2 is replaced by a counter-matte (figure 3), which obscures everything except the previously unexposed area — the foreground hill. The model and animation table are removed. The rear-projected footage is now rerun, and the camera this time will see only the foreground hill, recording it on the previously unexposed area of the film.

4. The finished composite.

is used. Each is sculpted to represent one stage in a movement or gesture, most commonly a facial gesture (such as a smile or a yawn) or a movement whose repetitive nature lends itself to this technique (such as walking). A model is positioned, one frame of film is exposed, then the model is replaced by the next one in the sequence, and so on. Some very fluid effects have been achieved this way, but it is not suited to more intricate, varied actions. Its use in feature films has been infrequent — examples can be seen in *The Beast of Hollow Mountain* (1956), *Tom Thumb* (1958) and *Beetlejuice* (1988). To distinguish it from replacement animation, normal stop-motion animation is sometimes referred to as displacement animation.

rotoscope matte Like traveling matte (see below), rotoscope matting is a method of matting a moving image into a shot. It is cheaper than traveling matte but time-consuming. In stop-motion filming, it may be that part of an actor — his arm, for example — is required to pass in front of a puppet, yet the actor is part of a rear projection in front of which the puppet is animated. For each relevant frame, a matte and counter-matte are precisely hand-drawn around the outline of the moving arm, occupying a slightly different position in each frame. The shot therefore effectively consists of a series of static matte composites projected in sequence. A device called a rotoscope — a small lamp housing — is attached to the camera so that pre-shot film can be projected through the camera itself, blown up and traced.

static matte rear-projection This is a means of obscuring the table-top on which the puppet is standing and also of introducing something from the live-action footage into the foreground, giving the illusion that it is in front of the puppet. For example, the rear footage may be of two hills, one in front of the other, and the animator wishes his puppet to appear to be walking between them. (See diagram on previous page.) This technique is called a static matte because the element which now appears in the foreground is a stationary one. If the foreground element is required to move (for example, an actor running in front of a puppet), then a traveling matte or a rotoscoped matte may be used.

strobing In the context of stop-motion filming, this is the tendency of some puppet animation to look jerky. This is caused by the absence of any blur on the film. Normal "live-action" movements (e.g., a man running) record a blur on each frame of film because the subject is moving at the moment the camera shutter is opened. But because animation puppets are stationary during each exposure that makes up a shot, there is no blurring. Strobing is most apparent when models are required to make rapid actions, such as the flapping of wings, because the model has to make a significant movement in a very few frames. Animators have devised a number of ways of compensating for this lack of blur, or disguising it.

traveling matte This is a means of combining two images when one of those images is moving (people walking, rocks falling). It is unacceptable to do this with a rear projection in color photography because contrasts between the two films would be conspicuous. There are many different traveling matte processes and the most popular is the "blue-backing" one. The moving subject is filmed against a blue background in a studio: The blue area will not be registered by the film. From this footage, two new strips of film are printed, one in which the subject is matted out and surrounded by an entirely clear background, and another in which the background is matted out, leaving a clear area where the subject was. These allow the subject to be combined with any background image when run through the optical printer.

Traveling matte is commonly used in animation films when actors have to pass in front of puppets, or in extreme long shots of actors in miniature sets. A recurring flaw in blue-screen filming is that light from the rear screen reflects onto the actors, causing "blue spill"—a dark outline that spoils the finished composite. Sometimes this blue spill can be removed by carefully retouching each frame by hand.

Bibliography

The following is a list of books, magazines and fanzines containing information on films featuring stop-motion photography. Reference has been made to many of these in the text of *The Stop-Motion Filmography*.

Books

Archer, Steve. *Willis O'Brien, Special Effects Genius*. Jefferson, North Carolina: McFarland, 1993.

Boorman, John and Walter Donohue. *Projections 5: Film-makers on Film-making*. London: Faber & Faber, 1996.

Brosnan, John. *Movie Magic*. London: Macdonald, 1974.

Culhane, John. *Special Effects in the Movies: How They Do It*. New York: Ballantine, 1981.

Dohler, Don. *Film Magic: The Fantastic Guide to Special Effects Film-making*. Maryland: Cinema Enterprises, 1984.

Dunn, Linwood, and George E. Turner. *The ASC Treasury of Visual Effects*. American Society of Cinematographers, 1983.

Eisner, Lotte. *The Haunted Screen*. London: Thames and Hudson, 1969.

Fielding, Raymond. *The Technique of Special Effects Cinematography*. New York: Hastings House, 1968.

Giesen, Rolf. *Sagenhafte Welten: Der Trickspezialist Ray Harryhausen*. Frankfurt: Deutsches Filmmuseum, 1988.

Gifford, Denis. *Science Fiction Film*. London and New York: Studio Vista / Dutton, 1971.

Glut, Donald F. *The Dinosaur Scrapbook*. Secaucus, New Jersey: Citadel, 1980.

Goldner, Orville, and George E. Turner. *The Making of King Kong*. Cranbury, New Jersey: Barnes, 1975.

Halas, John, and Roger Manvell. *The Technique of Film Animation*. New York: Hastings House, 1968.

Hardy, Phil. *The Encyclopedia of Science Fiction Movies*. London: Aurum, 1984; revised ed., Octopus, 1986.

Harryhausen, Ray. *Film Fantasy Scrapbook*. New York: Barnes, 1st ed., 1972; 3rd ed., 1981; 4th ed., 1989.

Hickman, Gail Morgan. *The Films of George Pal*. Cranbury, New Jersey: Barnes, 1977.

Holman, L. Bruce. *Puppet Animation in the Cinema*. Cranbury, New Jersey: Barnes, 1975.

Hutchison, David. *Special Effects vol. 1*. New York: Starlog, 1979.

Jewell, Richard B., and Vernon Harbin. *The RKO Story*. London: Octopus, 1983.

Jones, Stephen. *The Illustrated Dinosaur Movie Guide*. London: Titan, 1983.

Kinnard, Roy. *Beasts and Behemoths*. Metuchen, New Jersey: Scarecrow, 1988.

Lee, Walt, and Bill Warren. *Reference Guide to Fantastic Films*. Los Angeles: Chelsea-Lee, Vol. 1, 1972; Vol. 2, 1973; Vol. 3, 1974.

Lord, Peter, and Brian Sibley. *Cracking Animation — The Aardman Book of 3-D Animation*. London: Thames and Hudson, 1998.

Maltin, Leonard. *TV Movies*. (1981–82 Edition.) New York: New American Library, 1980.

Pos, Jan. *Czech Animated Film 1934–1994*.

Prague: Ministry of Culture of Czech Republic, 1994.

Rovin, Jeff. *The Land from Beyond Beyond: The Films of Willis O'Brien and Ray Harryhausen.* New York: Berkley Windhover, 1977.

_____. *Movie Special Effects.* Cranbury, New Jersey: Barnes, 1977.

Schechter, Harold, and David Everitt. *Film Tricks: Special Effects in the Movies.* New York: Harlin Quist, 1980.

Shay, Don. *Making Ghostbusters.* New York: New York Zoetrope, 1985.

_____, and Jody Duncan. *The Making of Jurassic Park.* London: Boxtree, 1993.

Smith, Thomas G. *Industrial Light and Magic — The Art of Special Effects.* New York: Ballantine, 1986.

Vaz, Mark Cotta, and Patricia Rose Duignan. *Industrial Light and Magic — Into the Digital Realm.* London: Virgin, 1996.

Wilson, S. S. *Puppets and People.* New York: Barnes, 1980.

Magazines

The following magazines have included many issues with articles on stop-motion animation, and many of them were consulted in the course of compiling this book.

The Animation Journal. 1964 to 1966, issues 1 to 9. Publisher: Bill Schrock.

Animato! 1988 to present. Publisher: Patrick Duquette.

Animator. Publisher: David Jefferson.

Cinefantastique. 1970 to present. Publishers: Frederick S. Clarke.

Cinefex. 1980 to present. Publisher: Don Shay.

Cinemagic. 1979 to 1987, issues 1 to 37. O'Quinn Studios.

Close-Up: 1975 to 1976, issues 1 to 3. Publisher: David Prestone.

Famous Monsters of Filmland. 1958 to 1983, issues 1 to 191. Publisher: Warren Publishing; Forrest J Ackerman, editor.

Famous Monsters of Filmland. 1991 to present. Publisher: Dynacomm.

Fangoria. 1979 to present. Publisher: O'Quinn Studios.

Fantastic Films. 1978 to 1985, issues 1 to 46. Publisher: Blake Publishing.

FXRH. 1971 to 1976, issues 1 to 4. Publishers: Ernie Farino, Sam Calvin.

Monster World. 1964 to 1966, issues 1 to 10. Publisher: Warren Publishing.

Photon. 1963 to 1977, issues 1 to 27. Publisher: Mark Frank.

SPFX. 1977 to 1978 and 1995 to present. Publishers: Jay Duncan, Ted A. Bohus.

Starlog. 1976 to present. Publisher: Starlog Publications.

Stop-Motion Animation. 1980 to 1982. Publisher: Don Dohler.

Stop-Motion Monsters of Filmland. 1995 to 1998, issues 1 to 8. Publisher: Toshizi Motohashi, Studio 28.

Other Publications referred to in the text:

American Cinematographer. November 1985. Article by George E. Turner.

Daily Express. October 16, 1969. Review by Jan Christie.

Evening Standard. Summer 1993 magazine supplement to this British daily newspaper.

Film Extremes. #1, 1992.

Film Weekly. April 21, 1933.

The Financial Times. October 17, 1969. Review by David Robinson.

The Hollywood Reporter. April 24, 1969.

Lumiere. July 1973. Article ("Danforth's Dinosaurs") April 24, 1969 by Graham Shirley and Bill Taylor.

The Morning Star. October 18, 1969. Review by Nina Hibbin.

The Observer. 1969. Review by Penelope Mortimer.

Phantasma. Spring 1990. Article ("Ray Harryhausen — Cinemagician as Filmmaker") by Paul Jensen.

Rotha, Paul. *The Film Till Now.* Feltham, Middlesex: Hamlyn, 1967.

Index

Numbers in boldface indicate black & white photographs; color plates are indicated at the ends of entries in small caps: A–P are in the first color section, between pages 200 and 201, and AA–PP are in the second color section, between pages 488 and 489.

Aardman Studios 1
Abbott, Bruce 105
Abbott, Bud 353
Abbott, John S. 172, 304
The Abyss 23, 29, 793, 804
Ackerman, Forrest J 103, 335, 426
Acquanetta 421
Addams, Charles 30
The Addams Family 30, 792, 793
The Adventures of Baron Munchausen (1989) 31, 792, 804
The Adventures of Buckaroo Banzai Across the 8th Dimension 32
The Adventures of Mark Twain by Huck Finn see *Comet Quest*
The Adventures of Pinocchio 32
The Adventures of Robin Hood 603
After Midnight 33, 792, 793
Agar, John 383
Albert, Eddie 199
Alice 34, 237
Alice in Wonderland (1951) 35, 787, 793
Alien 22, 29, 109, 264, 311, 333, 412, 567, 657, 667, 685, 704, 773
The Alien Factor (1979) 37, 793, 795
Aliens 264
Allard, Eric 149
Allen, David 18–19, 26, 47–48, 55–59, **57**, 75, 97, 98, 103–105, 108–117, 155–156, 156–160, **157**, 165–167, 170–171, 181–184, 184, 184–186, 193–198, 201–202, 212, 217–221, 247–

254, **249**, 258–259, 262, 280, 320–326, 335–337, 337–338, 415–418, 441, 516, 528, 530, 540, 552–555, **553**, 556, 556–557, 558, 558–560, 560–562, **561**, 562–563, 564, **564**, 565, 567, 567–571, 597–601, **598**, 601–602, 669–670, 671–673, 716, 721, 753, 756, 758, 768, 772, 775, 776, 777, 778, 785–786, 791–792, 804, 805; PLATES G, K, HH, OO
Allen, Gracie 342
Allen, Irwin 13, 41, 83, 85, 210
Allen, Karen 665
Allen, Nancy 594
Allen, Patrick 752, 766
Alligator 26
Along the Moonbeam Trail 273
Altered States 198
Alves, Joe 380
Ameche, Don 151
American Cinematographer (magazine) 465
An American Werewolf in London 22, 336, 665, 716
Amicus 22
The Amityville Horror 503
Andersen, Hans Christian 169
Anderson, Gail 701
Anderson, Howard A. 354, 355, 357
Andrews, Julie 445
Android 38
The Angry Red Planet 384
The Animal World 6, 12, 13, 39–43, 83, 85, 210, 405, 513, 759, 796, 798, 812; PLATE A
Annette 50
Annis, Francesca 412, 413

Apogee 279
Arbogast, Roy 109, 110
Archer, Steven vii, 15, 20, **20**, 31–32, 54, 126–148, 268–272, 412–415, 495–497, 511, 759, 792, 805; PLATE AA
Arden, Curtis 727, 730
Armstrong, Robert 391–409, 449, 470, 649, 650
Armstrong, Todd **373**, **376**; PLATE E
Army of Darkness 43–46, 494, 797, 799; PLATES JJ, KK
Arnold, Tom 670
Around the World under the Sea 46, 800
Arpin, Larry 771
The Arrival 47, 792
Ashton, Roy 303
Aslan, Gregoire 688
Assault on Precinct 13 684, 685
Astaire, Fred 786
Atencio, Xavier 50
Atkins, Peter 317
Atkinson, Rowan 494
Atlantis 437
Atlantis the Lost Continent 48, 793, 800
The Atomic Submarine 29
Attack of the Crab Monsters 666
Attack of the 50 Foot Woman 8, 177
Attenborough, David 40
Attenborough, Richard 388
Aupperle, James 20, 21, 34, 77, 108–117, 198–200, 224–227, 247–254, 276, 312, 502, 503–505, 505–507, 537–548, 589, 593, 686, 701, 792

Index

The Avengers (television series) 242, 288, 783
Ayers, Ralph 322
Aykroyd, Dan 152–154

Babes in Toyland (1934) 49
Babes in Toyland (1961) 50
Baboon 83
Baby Snakes 51
Back to the Future 319, 659
Bad Channels 184
Bakaleinikoff, Mischa 206, 702
Baker, Kenny 660
Baker, Rick 22, 99, 249, 309, 336, 467, 665
Baker, Tom 289
Baldwin, Alec 74–77
Balk, Fairuza 579
Balme, Timothy 102–103
Band, Albert 280
Band, Charles 19, 155, 165, 170, 182, 184, 193, 201, 262, 280, 415, 440, 446, 516, 553, 557, 558, 561, 563, 564, 565, 596, 601, 671, 673, 700
Band, Richard 261
Bankhead, Talullah 169
Banks, Leslie 470
Barker, Clive 500–501
Baron Munchausen see *Baron Prášil*
Baron Prášil 51, 119, 486, 719, 800
Barr, George 249
Barr, Tim 17, 176, 355, 609, 683, 697, 779, 802
Barry, John 84, 662
Barwood, Hal 188
Basinger, Kim 494
Basket Case 54, 101
Basket Case II 55, 102
Bast, William E. 721
Batman (1989) 74, 164, 210, 534
*batteries not included 19, 55–59, **57**, 117, 221, 559, 597, 601, 671, 791, 799
Bauer, Belinda 588
Baxter, John 205
The Bear 59
The Beast from 20,000 Fathoms 13, 60–68, **62, 64, 67**, 78–81, 86, 92, 103, 126, 310, 344, 345, 472, 529, 544, 546, 583, 623, 701, 713, 723, 796, 797, 812
The Beast of Hollow Mountain 26, 68–74, **72**, 85, 795, 798, 812, 820
Beasts and Behemoths (book) 119, 422, 426, 629, 721
Beatty, Ned 507
Beck, Jenny 701
Bedknobs and Broomsticks 769
Beery, Wallace 427, 432

Beetlejuice 19, 74–77, **76**, 171, 210, 534, 792, 793, 798, 820
Behemoth the Sea Monster 12, 36, 77–83, **80, 82**, 436, 674, 793, 795, 796, 798, 812
Bell, Tom 443
Belohovek, James 686, 701
Benjamin, Richard 605, 777, 778
Bennett, Constance 698, 699
Berg, Jon 19, 158, 189, 211–217, 228–230, 308, 331, 415, 502, 536, 557, 660–661, 716, 792
Bergin, Patrick 318
Bernsen, Corbin 675
Bernstein, Elmer 657, 722
Berry, David 152, 803
Berry, Ken 318
Berry, Paul 366
Best, Worst and Most Unusual Horror Films (book) 337
Beswick, Doug 19, **21**, 22, 30–31, 33, 74–77, 84, 105–106, 182, 200, 211–217, 224–227, 248, 276, 309–310, 336, 503–505, 505–507, 537–548, 601, 678, 680, 692–693, 791, 792, 806
Beswick, Martine 521, 526
Beware! The Blob 83, 792
Beyond the River Nyemen 10
Bickford, Bruce 51
Biehn, Michael 678
The Big Country 722
Big Jim McLain 86
Birth of a Flivver 468, 797
Bissell, Whit 421
The Black Hole 84, 573, 803
The Black Scorpion 12, 77, 78, 79, 85–93, **90, 91**, 324, 439, 693, 798, 807, 809, 812
Black Sunday (1977) 93, 799, 800
Blackbeard's Ghost 93–94
Blackman, Honor 367
Blackton, J. Stuart 10
Blade Runner 24, 338, 582
Blalack, Robert 803
Blanchette, Kim 558
Bláznova Kronika 94–95, 719, 720, 800
Blees, Robert 86
Blithe Spirit 695
The Blob (1958) 68, 84
The Blob (1988) 95–96, 799
Block, Irving 36, 74, 77–83, 411, 793
Bloodlust—Subspecies III 96, 97, 792; PLATE KK
Bloodstone—Subspecies II 97, 792
Blue Velvet 222
Body Bags 16, 98–100, **100**, 794
Bohus, Ted 446
Bolger, Ray 50, 169
Bonderson, Conrad 284

Bonestell, Chesley 172
Bono, Sonny 701
Das Boot 496
Borthwick, Dave 607
Boss Films 421
Bottaro, Pamela 541
Bottin, Rob 22, 95, 235, 336, 531, 536, 583, 588, 685–686, 716
Bowie, David 338
Bowie, Les 242–243, 520
Bowker, Judy 126–148
Brace, Bill 359
Bradbury, Ray **13**, 62
Bradley, Doug 317
Brain Damage 55, 101–102
Brain Donors 102
Braindead 9, 102–103
Brainstorm 198
Brandon, Henry 49
Brazil 31
Bresslaw, Bernard 412
Brice, Fanny 787
Bride of Frankenstein 643
Bride of Re-Animator 19, 103–104, 791, 796
Bride of the Monster 211
Bridges, Jeff 665
Brighton Rock 35
Brittany, Morgan 674
Bromley, Sidney 496
Brosnan, John 210, 353, 369, 721
Browning, Tod 258
Bruno, Jon 29, 803, 804
Bryan, William 2–7
Budd, Roy 629, 643
Buechler, John Carl 185, 201, 262, 280, 701
Bull, Peter 688
Bunuel, Luis 726
Bunin, Lou 35–37, 786–787
Bunnett, David 188
Burman, Tom 333, 657
Burns, Bob 463
Burns, George 342
Burroughs, Edgar Rice 22
Burton, Kent 211, 281, 447, 488, 534, 606, 670, 675, 715, 793
Burton, Tim 74–77, 210, 489
Bury the Axis 786
Byron, Jeffrey 201, 446

Cabal (book) 501
Cabin Boy 105–106, 793, 795
Cabot, Bruce 392, 435
Caesar, Sid 353
Cairney, John 369
Callan, Michael 472, 475
Calloway, Cab 343
Calvin, Sam 351, 763
Calzada, Yancy vii, 29–30, 34, 74–77, **76**, 105–106, 171, 182,

226, 309, 463, 506, 561, 562, 601, 693, 793

Cameron, James 23, 29, 264, 492, 582, 677, 679–680

Campbell, Bill 603

Campbell, Bruce 43, 103, 222–227, 424, 438, 673

Cannibal Girls 275

Cannom, Greg 106, 156, 163, 260, 503

Cantor, Eddie 787

Capers, Hedge 419

Capra, Frank 13

Capshaw, Kate 198, 340

Captain America (1989) 107, 797, 800

Caravan of Courage — An Ewok Adventure see *The Ewok Adventure*

Cardella, Richard 157

Carlson, Richard 722, 728

Carmen, Julie 261

Carnera, Primo 455

Carpenter, John 16, 95, 99, 665, 684, 685–686

Carradine, David 569, 571, 673

Carradine, John 284, 336

Carrera, Barbara 771

Carreras, Michael 518

Carroll, Lewis 34, 35

Carry On (television series) 517

Carson, Dave 165, 188, 212, 557, 576, 785

Castle of Frankenstein (magazine) 288

Cataclysm 499

Cates, Phoebe 200

Catizone, Rick 226

Caveman 19, 20, 54, 108–117, **114**, 169, 322, 512, 558, 561, 566, 568, 754, 791, 792, 794, 795, 796, 797; PLATES K, L, M

Cayton, William 118

Cepek, Petr 237

Cestě do Pravěku 17, 117–124, **123**, 486, 719, 800

Chaffey, Don 367, 368, 375, 518

Chaney, Lon 310, 361

Chaney, Tom 262

Chang 392

Chang, Christine Z. 149

Chang, Wah 17, **18**, 48, 175–181, 256, 354–365, 384, 411, 446, 466, 549–551, 566, 608, 609, 647, 683, 694, 697–698, 745, 779, 780, 793

Chester, Hal E. 60

Chevalier, Maurice 339

Chin, Brian 264

A Chinese Ghost Story 124–125

Chinese Ghost Story 2 125

Chiodo, Stephen 259, 534, 793

Chiodo Brothers 165, 488, 582, 583, **584**, 606–607, 670, 675, 793

Christensen, Benjamin 314–315

Christian, Kurt 292, 630

Christian, Paul 66

Christie, Jan 721

A Christmas Dream 118

Cinderella (1899) 9

Cinefantastique (magazine) 40, 41, 156, 205, 229, 391, 415, 629

Cinefex (magazine) 40, 85, 353, 385, 392

Cinemagic (magazine) 4, 25, 119, 780

Clark, Blair 284, 324, 584, 589

Clash of the Titans 15, 16, 67, 126–148, **129**, **132**, **147**, 289, 290, 320, 324, 331, 348, 364, 367, 379, 412, 461, 497, 628, 629, 646, 685, 706, 738, 759, 763, 768, 792, 794, 796, 805, 806, 809; PLATES J, K

Class of 1999 148–149

Class of Nuke 'Em High 515

Class of Nuke 'Em High Part II: Subhumanoid Meltdown 149–151

Clemens, Brian 288, 289

Close Encounters of the Third Kind 56, 109, 151, 165, 203, 247, 416, 665, 777

Close-Up (magazine) 4

Cobb, Ron 29

Cocoon 151, 772, 799, 803

Cohen, Larry 567, 669, 771

Coley, John 375

Combs, Jeffrey 104–105, 182–183, 491

Comet Quest 6, 581

Conan Doyle, Arthur 164, 425, 426, 427, 750

Coneheads 20, 152–154, **153**, 795, 799

Conlin, Jimmy 305

Connery, Sean 173, 187, 339, 494

The Conquest of Space 345, 695

Conried, Hans 719

Conway, Lyle 95, 165, 167, 579

Conway, Richard 804

Cook, Philip 489

Cook, Randall William vii, 20, 108–117, 156–160, 165–167, **168**, 181–184, 193, 197, 260–261, 265–268, 268–272, 275–278, **276**, 311–314, 318–320, 320, 336–337, 415, 513, 528, 530, 556, 561, 565, 567–571, 671–673, 685–687, 689, 718, 794; PLATES M, N, O, CC, DD, GG

Cooper, Merian C. iv, 11, 85, 89, 160–162, 391–409, 449, 465, 656, 802

Cooper, Wilkie **13**, 243, 367, 518, 688

Coppinger, John 604

Corman, Roger 174, 335

Corwin, Linda 512

Cosby, Bill 420

Costello, Lou 353

Cox, Alex 785, 786

Cox, Ronnie 583

Cozzi, Luigi 662, 664

Crabbe, Byron 161, 407

Craig, Michael 475

Cranham, Ken 315

Crash and Burn 155–156, **155**, 601, 791

The Crater Lake Monster 156–160, **157**, **159**, 181, 221, 332, 660, 791, 792, 794, 799

Crawford, Broderick 302

Creation 11, 160–162, **161**, 407, 438, 465, 470, 568, 778, 794, 797

Creature Comforts 1

Creatures the World Forgot 753

The Creeping Terror 22

Crimewave 164

Cronenberg, David 222

Cronyn, Hume 56

Cross, Beverly 126, 127, 367, 368, 629

Crouse, Lindsay 47

Cruickshank, Art 803

Cullen, Brett 555

Culley, Cliff 658

Cummins, James 327

Curious Pets of our Ancestors 552, 797

Currie, Gordon 565

Curry, Tim 501, 530, 666

Curse of the Demon 778

Curtin, Jane 152

Curtis, Donald 344–352, 600

Cushing, Peter 303

Cyborg 163, 795, 797, 800

Czerkas, Stephen 199, 248, 537–548, 794

Dahl, Roald 366

The Daily Express (newspaper) 721

Dale, Jim 658

Dale, Philip 33

Dallas (television series) 466

Dalton, Timothy 603

Dance, Charles 283

Danforth, Jim vii, 15, **15**, 16, 25, 41, 48, 98–100, 105, 108–117, 126–148, 156–160, 164, 165, 173, 189, 193–198, 217–221, 247–254, 259–260, 281, 302–

303, 312, 319, 339, 352–353,
354–365, **355**, 384, 391, 455,
496, 498, 508, 538, 544, 547,
556, 566, 601, 607–612, **609**,
669–670, 683, 684–685, 687,
694–695, 717, 750–751, 751–
769, 776, 777, 779, 780, 782,
794, 802, 803, 805, 806, 807;
PLATES J, L, FF, LL
Dano, Royal 609
Dante, Joe 235–236, 258, 307–
308, 308–310, 335–337, 341,
535, 536, 566, 716
Darden, Severn 605
Darin, Bobby 683
*Dark Continent: A Sherlock
Holmes Adventure!* 164, 750,
794; PLATES LL, MM
The Dark Crystal 22
Dark Fortress 515
Dark Star 684, 685
Darkman 164–165, 793
David Allen Productions vii
Davies, Craig 324, 586, 589, 590
Davis, Bette 573, 771
Davis, Desmond 126
Davis, Geena 74–77
Davis, Jim 465–466
Dawley, Herbert M. 273
The Day the Earth Caught Fire
752
The Day the Earth Stood Still 44,
206, 207
The Day Time Ended 165–167,
167, 168, 320, 791, 794, 795,
797, 798
The Daydreamer 6, 169
Dead Alive see *Braindead*
The Deadly Invention see *Vynález
Zkázy*
Dead of Night (1945) 33
Death Becomes Her 23
De Couteau, David 563
Dee, Sandra 339, 683
De Herrera, Nana 616
De Laurentiis, Dino 68, 248, 278
Delgado, Marcel 69, 83, 122,
160–162, 175–181, 274, 303,
352–353, 357, 391–409, 423,
425–438, 449, 465, 470, 538,
568, 648, 650, 653, 732, 778,
780, 794
Delgado, Victor 176, 303, 357,
780, 795
DeMille, Cecil B. 343
Demonic Toys 170, 184, 791, 793,
796
Deneuve, Catherine 338
Denning, Richard 85–93
Dern, Laura 388
Destination Moon 171–172, 304,
421, 695, 718, 802

DeWitt, Louis 68–74, 78, 85,
411, 466, 795
The Diabolic Invention see
Vynález Zkázy
Diamond, David 77
Diamonds Are Forever 173, 794
Diary of a Madman 173–174
Dicken, Roger 109, 111, 337, 338,
754, 766, 795
Dickey, Lucinda 508
Dietz, Jack 59, 85, 86, 344
Dillman, Bradford 536
Dinosaur! (television special)
332, 386, 584
The Dinosaur and the Missing Link
16, 174–175, 468, 582, 797
Dinosaur Scrapbook (book) 40
Dinosaurus! 84, 175–181, **180**,
217, 419, 793, 794, 795, 796,
798, 800, 812; PLATE D
Dipsy Gypsy 745
Disney, Walt / Disney Studio 36,
40, 50, 84, 93, 122, 188, 193,
202, 236–237, 317–318, 471,
535, 540, 553, 556, 573, 574,
658, 769
Doc Savage, Man of Bronze 551
Dr. Jekyll and Mr. Hyde (1931)
97, 411, 424
Doctor Mordrid 117, 170, 181–184,
791, 793, 794, 796; PLATES HH,
II
Dr. No 494
Dr. Strangelove 242
Dods, John 37
Dohler, Don 37, 238
Dollman 184
Dollman vs. Demonic Toys 184,
792
Dolls 76, 184–186, **185**, 558, 559,
791, 795, 796, 797, 798
Domergue, Faith 345
Doré, Gustav 51
Doublin, Anthony 105, 262, 499,
673–674
Dougal and the Blue Cat 6
Douglas, Kirk 530
Dracula (book) 508
Dracula (1931) 342
Dracula (1958) 35, 676
Dracula (1979) 335
Dragonheart 24, 187, 389, 799
Dragonslayer 19, 56, 187,
188–192, 194, 216, 229, 233,
284, 332, 374, 569, 647, 773,
775, 784, 792, 797, 798, 799,
803, 805, 809, 816; PLATE N
Dragonworld 16, 193–198, **194**,
196, 792, 794, 796, 800
Dream of a Rarebit Fiend 9
DreamQuest Images 29, 30, 47,
96, 328, 468

Dreamscape 198–200, 701, 792,
794, 795
Drop Dead Fred 200, 792
Dua Mosketyri see *Bláznova
Kronika*
Duel 716
Dugan, Dennis 658
Duncan, David 86, 693
Duncan, Jody 386
The Dungeonmaster 201, 558,
791, 795
Dungeonmaster II see *Pulse-
pounders*
Dunn, Linwood 353
Dunning (matte process) 397,
398
Durante, Jimmy 304–307
Dutra, Randal vii, 20, 152–154,
228, 230–235, 279, 284, 285,
287, 308, 320–326, 328–331,
331–335, 386, 502, 576, 584,
586, 589, 594, 795; PLATES
HH, II
Dykstra, John 803

Earth vs. the Flying Saucers 6, 13,
152, 205–210, 235, 345, 351,
702, 796, 797, 812
Ed Wood 210–211, 715, 793
Edeson, Arthur 428
Edlund, Richard 211, 275–278,
549, 572, 575, 579, 803
Edouart, Farciot 343
Effects Associates 109, 717
Eisenman, Ike 573
The Elementals 344
The Elephant Man 222
The Elephant Rustlers 83
Ellenshaw, Harrison 216, 803
Ellenshaw, Peter 94, 802, 803
Elliott, Chris 105–106
Ellis, John 804
The Emperor's Nightingale 807
The Empire Strikes Back 7, 19,
24, 71, 152, 188, 192, 211–217,
221, 229, 234, 308, 332, 574–
577, 583, 587, 647, 661, 664,
676, 792, 797, 798, 799, 803,
816
*Encyclopedia of Science Fiction
Movies* (book) 86, 119, 168
Endfield, Cy 472
Endicott, Chris vii, 170, 181–184,
193, 194, **554**, 555, 557, 565,
601; PLATE LL
Engelberg, Fred 177
Equinox 19, 26, 157, 176, 217–
221, **219**, 419, 791, 797; PLATE G
Eraserhead 74, 221–222, 328
Escape from Witch Mountain 573
Escher, M. C. 580
E.T.— the Extraterrestrial 152,

203–204, 221, 418, 440, 575, 665, 716, 797, 799, 803
Evans, Chris 59, 190, 230, 389, 498, 659, 772, 786
Evans, Gene 78
The Evening Standard (newspaper) 510
The Evil Dead 9, 43, 102, 103, 124, 164, 165, 222–224, 239, 262, 263, 420, 424, 438, 799
Evil Dead II 19, 44, 224–227, **225**, 792, 793, 799
Evolution (1923) 687
The Ewok Adventure 228–320, 235, 332, 792, 795, 797, 799
Ewoks — The Battle for Endor 19, 20, 230–235, **231**, 321, 332, 792, 795, 799, 800, 808; PLATE OO
Excelsior! A.M.P. 93, 419
The Exorcist 226
Explorers 235–236
Eyer, Richard 615

The Fabulous World of Jules Verne see *Vynález Zkázy*
Famous Monsters of Filmland (magazine) 426
Fangoria (magazine) 55, 268
Fantasia 122, 236–237, 529, 540, 769
Fantastic Voyage 342
Fantasy II Film Effects 29, 163, 257, 308, 389–390, 471, 492, 657, 666, 677, 680–681
Farino, Ernest D. 20, 29, 37, 109, 163, 199, 264, 337, 605, 606, 668, 795
Farrar, Scott 152, 803
Farrell, Terry 317
Faulds, Andrew 377
Faust (1994) 237
Fellowes, Rory 316, 501
Ferrari, William 694
Fichter, Rick 321, 549
Field, Roy 130
Fields, Suzanne 248
Fields, W. C. 342
Fiend 238
Fiend Without a Face 77, 165, 238–241, 812
Film Fantasy Scrapbook (book) 40, 712, 740
The Film Till Now (book) 750
Film Weekly (magazine) 395
Filmfax (magazine) 50, 86
Films and Filming (magazine) 288
The Financial Times 721
First Men in the Moon 14, 39, 52, 241–247, 367, 529, 688, 691, 702, 796, 812; PLATE F

Flash Gordon (1936) 248, 662
Flash Gordon (1980) 248, 278
Fleischer, Max 511, 687
Fleming, Ian 173
Flesh Gordon 19, 157, 247–254, **249, 250, 251**, 382, 421, 448, 489, 499, 668, 791, 792, 794, 797, 806
Flesh Gordon 2 — Flesh Gordon Meets the Cosmic Cheerleaders 254–256
Fletcher, Joel 193, 441, 442, 516, 565, 670; PLATES KK, LL
Flight of the Lost Balloon 256, 800
Flight of the Navigator 256–257, 800
Flynn, Errol 127
The Fly (1958) 411
The Fly (1986) 109, 189, 308, 693, 792
"The Fog Horn" (short story) 62
For the Flag (book) 748
Forbidden Planet 257, 802
Force of the Trojans 148, 367
Ford, Harrison 213, 339, 340, 574
Ford, John 232, 449
Foreman, Deborah 438
Forrest, Mark 302
Francis, Anne 257
Franciscus, James 722, 761; PLATE G
Frankenstein (book) 438
Frankenstein 343, 424
Frankenstein Meets the Wolfman 184
Freaked 258, 792, 793, 796; PLATES NN, OO
Freaks 258
Freund, Karl 447
Friday the Thirteenth 327, 503
Friday the Thirteenth Part VIII — Jason Takes Manhattan 259–260, 794
Frieberger, Fred 59
Fright Night 674
Fright Night Part II 260–261, 797, 800
From Beyond 185, 261–262
From the Land Beyond Beyond (book) 40, 205, 702, 753, 759
Frostbiter — Wrath of the Wendigo 262–264, 439
Fulmer, Mike 204
Fulton, John P. 343, 698, 699, 802
Futureworld 660
FXRH (magazine) 4, 40, 242, 351, 376, 703, 722, 763

Gabourie, Fred 687
Galaxy of Terror 264, 795
Galligan, Zach 424
Gardner, Tony 44, 95

Garland, Judy 786
Garr, Teri 777
Gasper, Chuck 803
The Gate 20, 265–268, **267**, 689, 792, 794; PLATE CC
Gate II 268–272, 672, 792, 794; PLATE GG
Gay, John 550
Gay Nighties 745
Gentry, Paul 30, 262, 795
Gernsback, Hugo 436
Gerrard, George 446
Ghost of Slumber Mountain 11, 273–274, 427, 687, 797, 812, 813
Ghostbusters 20, 274–278, **276, 277**, 307, 513, 672, 792, 794, 803
Ghostbusters II 278–279, 795, 799, 800
Ghoulies 170, 700
Ghoulies II 280, 558, 671, 791, 795
The Giant Behemoth see *Behemoth the Sea Monster*
The Giant Claw 206
Gibbs, George 771, 803
Gibson, E. B. "Buzz" 398, 407, 648
Gifford, Dennis 750
Gigantis the Fire Monster see *Gojira no Gyakushu*
Gilford, Jack 108, 169
Gillespie, A. Arnold 802
Gilliam, Terry 31, 51, 54
Gioffre, Rocco 115, 271, 583, 593
Giraud, Jean "Moebius" 29
Glaser, Bedrich 34–35, 237–238
Glover, John 310
Glover, Julian 339
Glut, Don 40
God Told Me To 771
God's Army **15**, 281–282, 793, 794
Godzilla (1954) 22, 507
Gojira no Gyakushu 282
Golan, Gila 722
Golan-Globus 163
The Golden Child 17, 282–287, **285**, 584, 795, 798, 799, 800, 809
The Golden Key see *Zolotoi Klyuchik*
The Golden Voyage of Sinbad 15, 126, 127, 131, 229, 255, 288–302, **292**, 479, 580, 594, 629, 704, 706, 775, 796, 802, 806, 807, 809; PLATES H, I
Goldner, Orville 392, 398, 426, 436, 465, 470
Goliath and the Dragon 302–303, 356, 780, 793, 794, 795, 800
Goliath Awaits 796, 800

Goodliffe, Michael 303
Gooseberry Pie 745
Gordon, Dennis 170, 182, 337, 338, 559, 716, 796
Gordon, Robert 345
Gordon, Stuart 74, 104, 185, 261, 597
Gorgo 22
The Gorgon 303–304
Gottlieb, Carl 108–117
Grant, Arthur 676
Grant, Cary 698, 699
Grant, Kathryn 617
Grass 392
Gray, Charles 173
The Great Rupert 172, 304–307, **306**, 695
The Great Train Robbery (1903) 9
Green, Caroline 341
Green, Nigel 369, 472
Greenwood, Joan 476
Gremlins 109, 189, 235, 280, 307–308, 533, 796, 800
Gremlins 2 — The New Batch 308–310, 666, 792, 793
Griffith, D. W. 687
Grossberg, Joseph 441, 442, 565
Gruner, Olivier 492, 493
Guest, Val 752, 760, 767
Guinness, Sir Alec 213, 660
Gulliver's Travels (book) 509
Guo, Yan 556
Guyver: Dark Hero 310–311, 798
Gwangi 11, 721
Gwillim, Jack 130

Hackett, Buddy 780, 782, 783
Haggard, H. Rider 164
Haiduc, Ion 96
Haldeman, Joe 597
Hale, Joe 573, 803
Hall, Anthony 48
Halloween 503, 684, 685
Hamill, Mark 99, 212, 660
Hamilton, George 550
Hamilton, Linda 678–679
Hamilton, Margaret 169
Hamlin, Harry 126–148
Hammer Films 14, 303, 501, 516, 519, 520, 529, 671, 676, 752, 753, 755, 761
Hammeras, Ralph 427, 431, 437, 438
"The Hands of Orlac" (story) 99
Hankin, Mike vii
Hansel and Gretel (1954) 5, 176
Hansen, E. H. 699
Hanson, Kristina 177, 179
Hardcover 9, 20, 272, 311–314, 672, 794, 806; PLATE DD
Hardwicke, Cedric 343
Hardy, Phil 86, 119, 167

Harolde, Ralf 162
Harris, Ed 30
Harris, Jack H. 84, 175, 217, 419
Harryhausen, Ray vii, 1, 3, 4, 8, 12–16, **12, 13**, 17–20, 24, 34, 39–45, 52, 53, 55, 60–68, 69, 70, 74, 77, 79, 81, 85, 87, 88, 96, 100, 104, 106, 108, 117, 119, 121, 126–148, 151, 152, 153, 158, 160, 165, 176, 187, 189, 192, 200, 201, 204, 205–210, 212, 217, 220, 229, 232, 241–247, 251, 254, 259, 263, 272, 279, 284, 287, 288–302, 304, 320, 344–352, 354, 356, 361, 365, 367–380, 391, 405, 412, 440–442, 448–464, 467, 471–483, 495, 504, 511, 512, 513, 514, 516–529, 536, 538, 540, 542, 546, 551, 560, 566, 583, 594, 595, 597, 598, 612–628, 628–646, 663, 664, 667, 688–692, 695, 696, 697, 701, 701–715, 720–744, 745, 749, 751, 753, 755, 758, 759, 761, 763, 767, 768, 773, 783 , 796, 801, 802, 804, 805, 807, 808, 809; PLATES B, C, D, G, I, J
Harvey, Laurence 779
Hatcher, Mary 745, 747
The Haunted Castle 9
The Haunted Hotel 10
The Haunting 424
Hawdon, Robin 752, 764
Häxan 314–315
Hayes, Craig 386, 387
Hayes, Patricia 496, 772
Hayter, David 311
Hayward, Arthur 243, 472, **517**, 796
Hedge, Bill 248, 499, 777; PLATE AA
Heinrichs, Rick 32, 502, 534
Hellbound: Hellraiser II 315–316
Hellraiser 315
Hellraiser III — Hell on Earth 317
Helm, Brigitte 447
Henderson, Doug 187
Henenlotter, Frank 54–55, 101–102
Henson, Jim 1, 22, 33
Herbert, Percy 475
Herbie Rides Again 317–318
Herman, Pee-wee 534
Herrmann, Bernard 157, 177, 242, 261, 297, 367, 370, 373, 376, 378, 472–483, 518, 527, 612–628, 688, 722, 805, 806
Hessler, Gordon 288
Hettmer, David 263, 439
Hibbin, Nina 721
Hickox, Anthony 317, 424, 674

Hickox, Douglas 674
Hickson, Joan 444
Highway to Hell 318–320, 794
Hill, Robert 69
Hitchcock, Alfred 288
Hoag, Bob 612
Hoffman, Dustin 327
Holland, Tom 48, 176, 356, 357, 361, 364, 779, 796; PLATE E
The Hollywood Reporter (magazine) 722
Homolka, Oscar 779
Honey, I Blew Up the Kid 326
Honey, I Shrunk the Kids 9, 19, 117, 320–326, 483, 559, 791, 795, 796, 797, 799, 800, 809; PLATES DD, EE
Hook 326–327
Hoola Boola 745
Hooper, Tobe 99, 548
Hopkins, Stephen 506
Hopper, William 704–715
Horner, James 151, 412, 413, 659, 772
Hoskins, Bob 327, 769
Houdini 695
Houdini, Harry 427
The Hounds of Zaroff see *The Most Dangerous Game*
House 327–328, 425, 799
House 2 — The Second Story 9, 328–331, 332, 447, 792, 795, 799
Houston, Donald 129
Houston, Kent 804
Hove, Anders 96
Howard, Ron 772
Howard, Tom 628, 695–697, 802
Howard — A New Breed of Hero see *Howard the Duck*
Howard the Duck 18, 331–335, 795, 799, 800; PLATE AA
Howarth, Derek 190
The Howling 183, 235, 280, 307, 335–337, **336**, 503, 536, 568, 686, 716, 791, 794, 795, 796
Hoyt, Harry 427, 438
Hoyt, John 421
Huddlestone, David 604
Hudgins, Joseph 248
Hume, Cyril 257
Humpty Dumpty Circus 9
Huneck, John 471
The Hunger 165, 337–338, 420, 791, 795, 796
Hunt, Peter 511
Hunt, William 248, 254
Huntley, Chris 668, 678
Huntley, Leslie 308, 657
Huyck, Willard 332
Hyams, Peter 718

The Hybrids see *The Primevals*
Hyer, Martha 242

I, Madman see *Hardcover*
I Was a Teenage Frankenstein 778
I'd Rather Be Rich 338–339, 794
If 149
Illusion Arts 268
Image Animation 316, 501
In the Claws of the Spider 10
In the Villain's Power 552, 797
Indiana Jones and the Last Crusade 339–340
Indiana Jones and the Temple of Doom 5, 9, 152, 340–341, 797, 799, 803
Industrial Light and Magic 19, 29, 56, 148, 152, 188–192, 203–204, 211–217, 228–230, 230–235, 275, 279, 282–287, 312, 321, 332, 340, 342, 385–389, 549, 572, 575, 576, 603, 658, 665, 680, 681, 772, 783, 803, 815
Industrial Light and Magic — the Art of Special Effects (book) 321
Infested see *Ticks*
Innerspace 341–342, 797, 800, 804
Insane Chronicle see *Bláznova Kronika*
Inspiration 118
International House 342
Intolerance 687
Invader see *Naked Robot 4½*
Invasion of the Body Snatchers (1956) 308, 665
The Invention of Destruction see *Vynález Zkázy*
The Invisible Man 343, 698, 699
The Invisible Man Returns 6, 343–344, 802
Ireland, John 673
Ironside, Michael 657
Island of Lost Souls 48
It see *Stephen King's It*
It Came from Beneath the Sea 13, 14, 63, 96, 205, 206, 344–352, **347**, 482, 600, 701, 702, 712, 796, 797, 813
It Conquered the World 22
It Started With Eve 339
It's a Mad Mad Mad Mad World 12, 83, 352–353, 794, 798
It's Alive 571, 669, 771

Jack and the Beanstalk 353–354
Jack the Giant Killer 16, 218, 354–365, **355**, **356**, **362**, 384, 610, 775, 793, 794, 795, 796, 798, 800, 813; PLATE E

Jackman, Fred W. 427
Jackson, Dan 475
Jackson, Frank 629
Jackson, Freda 137
Jackson, Michael 467
Jackson, Peter 102
Jacobs, W. W. 465
Jacques, Hattie 517
James, Sid 517
James and the Giant Peach 9, 366, 793, 797, 799, 800
Jason and the Argonauts 7, 8, 14, 24, 39, 44, 45, 48, 126, 135, 143, 182, 201, 220, 242, 245, 247, 288, 292, 294, 296, 297, 299, 309, 350, 360, 367–380, **368**, **371**, **373**, **375**, **376**, 442, 449, 476, 504, 514, 519, 527, 529, 540, 551, 560, 627, 628, 631, 663, 664, 681, 688, 704, 709, 731, 735, 767, 783, 784, 796, 806, 808, 813; PLATE E
Jasper and the Choo-Choo 745
Jasper and the Haunted House 745
Jasper and the Watermelons 745
Jasper in a Jam 566
Jaws 109, 158, 535, 716
Jaws — the Revenge 76, 381, 798
Jaws 3-D 380–381, 798
Jeffries, Lionel 242–247
Jein, Greg 56, 416
Jennings, Gordon 343
Jensen, George 803
Jessel, Paul 193–198, 469, 516, 565, 601; PLATE LL
A Jester's Tale see *Bláznova Kronika*
Joe's Apartment 381–382
John Henry and the Inky Poo 566
Johncock, Brian see Johnson, Brian
Johnson, Ben 453
Johnson, Brian (previously Johncock, Brian) 109, 211, 803
Johnson, Herb 697
Johnson, Laurie 242
Johnson, Noble 649
Johnson, Steve 275, 318
Johnston, Joe 215, 321, 603, 803
Jones, Dean 94
Jones, Freddie 412, 413, 783
Jones, Gary 439
Jones, Jeffrey 332
Jones, Robert 518
Josh Kirby — Time Warrior: Planet of the Dino-Knights 382, 795
Josh Kirby — Time Warrior: The Human Pets 383, 795
Journey into Prehistory see *Cestě do Prověku*

Journey to the Beginning of Time see *Cestě do Prověku*
Journey to the Center of the Earth 22, 779
Journey to the Seventh Planet 383, 793, 794, 800
Joyce, Mike 667
Joyce, Peggy Hopkins 342
Judd, Edward 242–247
Juran, Nathan 241, 354, 702
Jurassic Park 9, 19, 23, 187, 204, 221, 237, 385–389, 488, 595, 647, 700, 795, 797, 799, 804, 806, 815; PLATE II
Just Imagine 438
Justice, Bill 50

Kanin, Garson 646
Kaplan, Sol 36
Karloff, Boris 169
Katt, William 328
Kaufmann, Maurice 78
Keach, Stacy 99, 149
Keaton, Buster 687
Keaton, Michael 74–77
Keen, Bob 316, 424
Keir, Andrew 193
Kellaway, Cecil 60
Kelley, Bill 229
Kellison, Phil 79, 176, 181, 355, 796
Kelly, David Patrick 199
Kent, Robert E. 174
Kershner, Irvin 587
Killer Klowns from Outer Space 389–390, 793, 797, 800
King, Stephen 666
King Dong 390–391
King Kong (1933) **ii**, iv, 4, 7, 11, 12, 24, 26, 49, 64, 85, 88, 89, 106, 113, 119, 158, 161, 162, 179, 218, 227, 234, 245, 249, 251, 253, 273, 330, 359, 390, 391–409, **396**, **397**, **403**, **409**, 410, 421, 426, 427, 431, 435, 436, 439, 448, 449, 450, 462, 465, 470, 473, 513, 522, 529, 531, 537, 538, 541, 552, 569, 628, 636, 641, 648, 652, 655, 656, 666, 688, 702, 705, 713, 721, 724, 725, 731, 734, 739, 743, 753, 761, 769, 772, 794, 795, 797, 801, 805, 806, 807, 808, 809, 813; PLATE OO
King Kong (1976) 22, 26, 68, 278
King Kong vs. Frankenstein 83
King Kong vs. Godzilla see *Kingu Kongu tai Gojira*
Kingu Kongu tai Gojira 83, 410
Kinnard, Roy 119, 422, 426, 629, 721
Kinnear, Roy 676

Kinski, Klaus 38
Kleinow, Pete 20, 44–45, 108–
117, 308, 421, 492–494, 551,
566, 589, 604, 609, 611, 657,
666, 677, 678–679, 680–681,
796; PLATES P, K
Klein-Rogge, Rudolf 447
Kneale, Nigel 241
Knechtel, Lloyd 36
Kohn, Justin 106, 260, 389–390,
502, 528, 530, 558, 561, 797
Kolb, Kenneth 612
Konig, Peter 187
Korda, Alexander 444
Kovack, Nancy 174, 373
Kramer, Stanley 83, 352
Krepela, Neil 803
Kronos 74, 411, 793, 795, 798, 800
Kruger, Otto 779
Krull 89, 412–415, **413**, 439, 497,
666, 792
Kubrick, Stanley 52, 212, 490,
717–718, 802
Kuran, Peter 30, 199, 215, 336,
568, 778

Labyrinth 22
Land of the Lost (1960s) (televi-
sion series) 495
Land of the Lost (1990s) (televi-
sion series) 715
The Land That Time Forgot 22,
109
Landau, Martin 32
Landis, John 530, 670, 716
Lang, Fritz 189, 447
Langenkamp, Heather 504
Lantieri, Michael 804
Larrinaga, Juan 407
Larrinaga, Mario 392, 396, 407,
465, 649
Larson, Lauritz 254
Laserblast 19, 20, 97, 221,
415–418, **417**, 561, 791, 792,
794, 800
The Las Vegas Monster 252
Lasky, Jesse L. 85
The Last Action Hero 418
Last Days of Pompeii (1935) 245,
370
Last of the Labyrinthodons 83
Last of the Oso Si-Papu 83
The Last Starfighter 23
Laudati, Anthony 236
Laurel and Hardy 49, 158
Law, John Phillip 289
Lawrence, Barbara 411
Lawrence, Tim 77
LeBorg, Reginald 174
Lebovit, Arnold 565–567
Lee, Christopher 303, 310, 573,
676

Lee, Danny 803
Lee, Spike 675
Lee, Walt 426, 465
The Legacy 575
The Legend of Hillbilly John 176,
279, 419–420, 784, 799, 800
Legend of the Phoenix see *Peacock
King*
Leiber, Fritz 218
Leighton, Eric 502, 592
Le Mat, Paul 559
Le Mesurier, John 658
Leonard Part VI 420, 796
Levin, Henry 779
Levinson, Barry 783, 785
Lewin, Albert 35
Like Dog and Cat 10
Lion, Henry 69
Lippert, Robert 421
Liska, Laine 20, 74, 109, 165,
185, 248, 320–326, 516, 797
Lithgow, John 604, 716
Lloyd, Christopher 30, 659, 769,
770
Lloyd, Michael 804
Lofgren, George 62, 345, 621,
703, 704, 797
Logan, James 177
Lohman, Augie 421
Lom, Herbert 481
Long, Shelley 108
The Lost Continent (1951)
421–424, **422**, 813
Lost in Time 317, 424–425
Lost on Adventure Island see
King Dong
The Lost Whirl 437
The Lost World (1925) 11, 70, 161,
273, 274, 282, 408, 421, 425–
428, **429**, **430**, **435**, 448, 465,
484, 539, 721, 724, 744, 794,
797, 807, 808, 813
The Lost World (1960) 22, 43, 83
The Lost World — Jurassic Park
795
Lourie, Eugene 59–68, 77–83,
345, 702
Love, Bessie 427
Love at First Bite 335
The Love Bug 318
Lovecraft, H. P. 262, 491
Lucas, George 7, 19, 126, 211–217,
339, 340, 412, 496, 572, 574,
575, 657, 660, 661, 664, 772,
773, 776, 807
Lucasfilm 331
The Lucy Show (television series)
805
Ludwig, Edward 86
Lugosi, Bela 211, 342, 676
Lumiere (magazine) 353
Lumley, Joanna 366

Lunatics, A Love Story 263, 438–
439
Luske, Hamilton 802
Lycett, Eustace 94, 802, 803
Lynch, David 74, 221–222
Lyons, Walter 69

Mac and Me 439
MacCorkindale, Simon 380
MacGowran, Jack 78
Mack, Helen 649
Mackenzie, Sam 193
Macnee, Patrick 335
MacNicol, Peter 188, 279, 773
Mad Max 163, 201, 657, 716
The Mad Monster 421
Mad Monster Party 6
Madison, Fred 172, 304
Madison, Guy 69–74
Magic Island 440–442, 670
The Magic Toyshop 443
The Magnificent Seven 722
Maine, Robert 252, 382
Makeup FX Unlimited 260
The Making of Jurassic Park
(book) 386
The Making of King Kong (book)
392, 426, 648
Maley, Nick 412
Mall, Paul 257
Malleson, Miles 242
Malone, Dorothy 167
Maltin, Leonard 157, 177, 205,
288, 426, 518, 629
Mandell, Paul 26, 119, 780
Manahan, Anna 137
*The Man Who Could Work
Miracles* 443–444
Man with the Rubber Head 9
Mann, Ned 444
March of the Wooden Soldiers see
Babes in Toyland
Marg, Tamia 283, 331
Margoyles, Miriam 366
Marlowe, Hugh 206–210
Marooned 744
Marquand, Richard 575
Mars Attacks 210
Marsh, Carol 35
Marsh, Jean 579
Marston, John 649
Marvel Comics 106
Mary Poppins 50, 445, 610, 802
Marx Brothers 102
The Mascot 10
Mashimo, Fumi 268, 313, 319
Master of the World 356, 445–
446, 800
Masters, Todd 491
Mathews, Kerwin 354–365,
612–628, 633, 688, 690;
PLATE C

Mattey, Robert A. 94
Matthews, Jessie 695
Mature, Victor 22
Matuszak, John 116
May, Joe 343
Mayall, Rik 200
Mayhew, Peter 633, 660
McAlister, Michael 340, 772, 803
McCarthy, Kevin 536, 716
McCarthy, Neil 127
McCracken, Michael 717
McCrea, Joel 470
McCune, Grant 803
McDowall, Roddy 415
McDowell, Malcolm 149
McQuarrie, Ralph 56, 152, 213, 215, 803
McTiernan, John 418
Meatballs 275
Meddings, Derek 412, 413, 497
Medina, Patricia 69
Melchior, Ib 384
Méliès, Georges 9, 17, 748
Melford, Jack 85
Melton, Sid 424
Menzies, Heather 536
Mercer, Ray 421
Meredith, Burgess 126–148
Meredith, Judie 357
Merrill, Gary 475
Merry Frolics of Satan 9
Mest's Kinematograficeskogo Operatora 10
Metalstorm: The Destruction of Jared Syn 446
Metamorphosis: The Alien Factor 446–447, 799
Metropolis 447
Mickey and his Goat 552
Mickey's Naughty Nightmares 552, 797
A Midsummer Night's Dream 5, 807
Mighty Joe Young 8, 12, 13, 16, 60, 62, 79, 85, 112, 304, 345, 399, 448–464, **450, 458, 463**, 529, 633, 656, 691, 726, 733, 735, 794, 796, 797, 798, 802, 805, 806, 808, 809, 813
Miles, Bernard 695
Miles, Hal 309
Miller, Dick 309, 335
Miller, Frank 587, 595
Miller, George 497, 657, 716
Miller, Marylin 787
Miller, Wesley C. 802
Mills, Samantha 554
Milmoe, Caroline 443
The Milpitas Monster 464
Miner, Steve 327
Minor, Mike 251

Mr. T 258
Mitchell, Cameron 499
Mitchum, Chris 167
Mixon, Bart J. 260
Moll, Richard 201
The Monkey's Paw 464–465, 470, 794
Monster from Green Hell 74, 176, 321, 465–467, 793, 795, 798, 800, 813, 814
The Monster Maker 421
The Monster That Challenged the World 536
Montana, Bull 432
Monthly Film Bulletin (magazine) 721
Moody, Ron 658
Moonwalker 467
Moore, Dudley 604
Moore, Terry 304, 449
Moranis, Rick 275, 321–326
More, Julian 721
More, Kenneth 658
Morell, Andre 78
Morheim, Louis 59
Moriarty, Michael 567, 571, 669
The Morning Star (newspaper) 721
Moross, Jerome 722, 728, 743, 806
Morpheus Mike 468–469, 552, 797
Morris, Garrett 670
Morrow, Jeff 411
Morrow, Vic 716
Mortimer, Penelope 721
Mosquito 469
The Most Dangerous Game 161, 304, 469–470, 794
Movie Magic (book) 210, 353, 369, 721
Movies on TV (book) 205
Moving Violations 471, 800
Munro, Alan 30, 74, 75
Munro, Caroline 289, 662
The Muppets 22
Murders in the Rue Morgue (1971) 288
Murdocco, Vince 254
Muren, Dennis 20, 21, 23, 29, 188–192, 204, 211–217, 217–221, 248, 341, 342, 385–389, 556, 575, 576, 577, 660, 680, 772, 777, 783–785, 797, 803, 804, 807, 816; PLATE CC
Murnau, F. W. 508–509
Murphy, Eddie 283
Murray, Bill 275
Murray, John 471
Museum of the Moving Image 62
My Science Project 19, 22
Myerberg, Michael 5

Myers, Patrick 327
Mysterious Island (book) 748
Mysterious Island 14, 53, 121, 229, 236, 299, 301, 321, 330, 351, 371, 467, 471–483, **474, 477, 478, 480, 481,** 484, 594, 628, 749, 768, 775, 796, 808, 809, 814; PLATE D
Mysterious Planet 151, 483–485, 512

Na kometě 17, 485–488, 800
Nai-Choi, Nam 531
Naismith, Laurence 722, 727, 742
Naked Gun 2½ 489
Naked Gun 33⅓ — The Final Insult 488, 793
The Naked Jungle 695
Naked Robot 4½ 25, 489–491, 715, 793
Nascimbene, Mario 518, 527, 759
Nassour, Edward 68–74
Natale, Mike 722, 724, 734
Naulin, John 262
Necronomicon 491–492
Neill, Sam 388
Neill, Steve 158, 569, 670
Neeson, Liam 164–165
Nelson, Gary 84
Nemesis 492–494, 797, 800
Neumann, Kurt 411
Never Say Never Again 494–495, 800
The NeverEnding Story 495–497, 792
NeverEnding Story II — The Next Chapter 497–498
Neville, John 31
The New Gulliver 498
Newell, Patrick 783
Newfield, Sam 421
Newland, John 419
Newman, David 604
Newsom, Ted 205
New York Times 425, 427
The Nibelungen 22, 189
Nicholson, Bruce 56, 211, 803
Nicolaou, Ted 96
Nielsen, Brigitte 676
Nielsen, Leslie 488
Nightbreed 500–501
The Nightmare Before Christmas 6, 366, 501–502, 670, 792, 795, 797, 799, 800, 806
Nightmare on Elm Street 327
Nightmare on Elm Street 3 — Dream Warriors 19, **21**, 33, 95, 503–505, 792, 793
Nightmare on Elm Street 5 — The Dream Child 505–507, 792, 795, 798
Night the World Exploded 206

Night Train to Terror 498–500
1941 507
Ninja III — The Domination 508, 794
Nippy's Nightmares 552
Noonan, Tom 588
Noriega, Eduardo 71–74
Norman, Neil 26
Norrington, Stephen 783
North, Alex 188
Nosferatu, eine Symphonie des Grauens 97, 424, 508–509
Nosferatu the Vampire see *Nosferatu, eine Symphonie des Grauens*
Nosferatu the Vampyre 335
Novyi Gulliver 509–511, **510**, 798, 807
Nuts and Bolts 745
A Nymphoid Barbarian in Dinosaur Hell 151, 511–515

Oblivion 516, 792, 797
Oboler, Arch 719
O'Brien, Austin 418, 555
O'Brien, Willis H. iv, 1, 3, 6, 8, 10–12, **11**, 13, 15–18, 24, 26, 36, 39–43, 53, 59, 60, 68, 69, 70, 74, 77–83, 85–93, 106, 108, 117, 119, 134, 160–162, 174–175, 176, 178, 190, 212, 216, 217, 230, 232, 253, 273–274, 282, 329, 330, 352–353, 370, 389, 391–409, 410, 414, 421–424, 425–438, 448–464, 468–469, 470, 472, 484, 487, 537, 539, 551, 566, 581–582, 597, 647–656, 690, 697, 705, 721, 726, 734, 735, 744, 745, 749, 752, 753, 761, 797–798, 802, 818; PLATES A, AA
The Observer (newspaper) 510, 721
O'Connell, Arthur 608
O'Connell, Jerry 381
O'Connolly, James 721, 740
Olivier, Laurence 126
On the Comet see *Na kometě*
One Million B.C. 22, 516
One Million Years B.C. 3, 14, 112, 139, 242, 290, 297, 299, 329, 367, 512, 513, 515, 516–529, **517, 518, 519, 523, 526,** 538, 539, 540, 541, 547, 628, 645, 691, 726, 728, 729, 738, 752, 753, 758, 762, 763, 768, 796, 806, 808, 814
Opper, Don 39
Ordaz, Frank 659
Orellana, Carlos 69
Orosco, Joey 667
Orphee 503

Oscar **528**, 529–530, 791, 794, 797
Oz, Frank 22

Pack, Charles Lloyd 688
Pal, Dave 176, 181, 356, 357, 361, 551, 608, 694, 695, 779, 798
Pal, George 13, 16–17, 48–49, 69, 79, 117, 169, 171–172, 176, 181, 304–307, 345, 355, 449, 549–551, 565–567, 607–612, 693, 695–697, 745–747, 778–783, 798, 802
Pangrazio, Mike 190, 215, 228, 230, 496, 572, 659, 772
Paoli, Dennis 261
The Parent Trap 50
Park, Nick 1
Parker, Neave 759
Parker, Ray, Jr. 275
Paulin, Scott 106
Peacock King 530–532
Peacock King II 533–534
Peck, Bob 388
Pee-wee's Big Adventure 74, 165, 534, 582, 793
The People That Time Forgot 22
Perinal, Georges 695
Perisic, Zoran 804
Perkins, Anthony 103
Peter Pan (stage play) 326
Peterson, Lorne 803
Peterson, Pete 77–83, 85–93, 249, 252, 454, 460, 798
Peterson, Wolfgang 496
Pete's Dragon 193
Petroleum Pete and His Cousins 786
Pettigrew, Neil 14, 808
Phantasm 328
The Phantom Empire 537
Phantom of the Opera (1925) 310, 427
Phantom of the Rue Morgue 69
Phillips Broadcast of 1938 566
Phillips Cavalcade 566
Phoenix, River 236
Pichel, Irving 304
Pickens, Slim 336
The Picture of Dorian Gray 35
Pidgeon, Walter 258
Pierce, Bart 223
Pink, Sidney 384
Pinocchio 236, 535
Piper, Brett 149–151, 483–485, 511–515
Piper, Roddy 684
Piranha 20, 235, 307, 308, 332, 335, 535–537, 716, 792, 799
Pirnie, Alex 515
Plan 9 from Outer Space 483
Planet of Dinosaurs 19, 89, 112,

182, 212, 329, 439, 537–548, 666, 792, 794
Poe, Edgar Allan 174
Poggi, Fernando 377
Pogo for President 793
Poledouris, Basil 588
Police Academy 471
Poltergeist 321, 548–549, 605, 700, 798, 803
Porter, Edwin S. 9, 10
Powell, William 786
The Power 17, 181, 549–551, **550**, 793, 796, 798, 800
Power, Taryn 629
Prehistoric Beast 807
Prehistoric Poultry 273, 552, 797
Prehysteria! 170, 382, 552–555, **553, 554,** 792
Prehysteria! 2 556, 792, 796
The Premature Burial 177
Price, Vincent 174, 343, 445
The Primevals 19, 170, 212, 556–557, **557,** 559, 792, 794, 797, 798, 799; PLATES OO, PP
Princess Nicotine 10
Project Unlimited 17, 46, 48, 93, 176, 181, 256, 302, 355, 356, 419, 446, 466, 609, 612, 647, 683, 694, 697, 779, 780
Prophecy see *God's Army*
Psycho 95, 261, 666
Ptushko, Alexander 509–511, 787–789, 798
Pugh, William 588
Puglia, Frank 704, 705
Pulsepounders 558, 791, 797
Puppetmaster 170, 558–560, 671, 791, 796, 797
Puppetmaster II 560–562, **561,** 791, 793, 794, 795, 796, 797
Puppetmaster III — Toulon's Revenge 562–563, 791, 793, 796
Puppetmaster IV 564–565, **564,** 792, 794
Puppetmaster V — The Final Chapter 565, 792; PLATES LL, MM
The Puppetoon Movie 565–567, 791, 793, 795, 796, 800
The Puppetoons 13, 16, 17, 69, 79, 172, 176, 304, 307, 355, 449, 551, 745–747, 802
Puppets and People (book) 39, 59, 181, 205, 289, 419, 511, 692, 700, 724, 749, 766
The Puzzling Billboard 552, 797
Pyun, Albert 106, 492

Q 19, 20, 162, 561, 567–571, **570,** 668, 771, 778, 791, 794, 795, 796; PLATE N
Q The Winged Serpent see *Q*

Quaid, Dennis 108–117, 187, 198–200, 341–342
Quan, Ke Huy 340
The Quatermass Experiment 241

R. Greenberg Associates (RGA) 418
Rabin, Jack 68–74, 77–83, 85, 411, 466, 798
Rae, Michael 415
Rae, Ted 75, 311, 381, 675, 798
Ragewar see *The Dungeonmaster*
Ragland, Robert O. 569
Raiders of the Lost Ark 340, 572, 575, 798, 803
Raiders of the Stone Ring 556
Raimi, Sam 43, 102, 124, 222–224, 438
Raimi, Theodore 438
The Rains Came 699
Ralston, Ken 23, 151, 188–192, 212, 216, 283, 549, 556, 575, 576, 798, 803
Rambaldi, Carlo 22, 203–204, 803
Ramsey, Ward 177, 181
Randall, Tony 310, 608, 609, 611
Randel, Tony 692
Rankin, Arthur, Jr. 169
Rappaport, Mark 193
Rathbone, Basil 127
Ray, Fred Olen 537
Raymond, Gary 373
Read, Jan 241, 367, 368
Re-Animator 74, 101, 182, 185, 261, 558, 597
Re-Animator 2 see *Bride of Re-Animator*
Reardon, Craig 199, 268, 270, 312, 549, 717
Reate, J. L. 283
Reed, Oliver 31
Reeves, Kynaston 239
Reference Guide to Fantastic Films (book) 426, 465
Reicher, Frank 392, 649
Reitman, Ivan 275
Rennie, Michael 550
Reptilicus 384
Return from Witch Mountain 573
Return of Godzilla see *Gojira no Gyakushu*
Return of the Jedi 8, 20, 22, 24, 26, 58, 192, 214, 228, 229, 234, 325, 332, 574–579, 583, 647, 664, 792, 797, 798, 799, 803, 808
Return to Oz 579–581, 804
Reubens, Paul *see* Pee-wee Herman
RFD 10,000 B.C.: A Mannikin Comedy 581–582, 797
Rhythm in the Ranks 745

Richards, Kim 573
Richardson, John 519, 521
Richardson, Ralph 188, 444
Ries, Irving 802
The Ring of the Nibelungen 37
Ritchie, Michael 283, 287
Rivas, Carlos 85–93
RKO Radio 11, 391–409, 410, 421, 465, 648, 654, 656
The RKO Story (book) 465
Robbins, Matthew 56, 188
Robbins, Tim 333–334
Roberts, Alan 177
Roberts, Julia 327
Robinson, David 26, 721
Robley, Les Paul 45
RoboCop 9, 25, 58, 165, 214, 324, 582–587, **583, 586**, 647, 676, 793, 795, 799, 800
RoboCop 2 19, 25, 587–595, 792, 795, 796, 797, 799, 800, 805; PLATE GG
RoboCop 3 595–596, 799, 800
Robot Jox 19, 25, 155, 214, 596–601, **598**, 664, 791, 795
Robot Monster 465
Robot Wars 601–602, 792, 793, 794, 796; PLATE KK
Robson, Flora 137
The Rocketeer 603–604, 798, 799
Rocketship X-M 421
Rocky 108
Rodine, Ralph 612
Rodriguez, Ismael 69
Rogan, Beth 476, 1–4
Rogers, Edward 10
Rogers, Will 787
Rohner, Clayton 313
Rojo, Gustavo 726
Rolfe, Guy 563
Romeow and Julicat 745
Romero, Cesar 421
Roop, J. L. 437
Rose, Ruth 655
Rosenman, Leonard 588
Rosenthal, Laurence 126, 140
Rossini 530
Rotha, Paul 750
Rothacker, Watterson R. 274, 427, 433
Roundtree, Richard 569, 571
Rovin, Jeff 40, 205, 274, 702, 753, 759
Rowe, Nicholas 786
Rozsa, Miklos 288, 295, 297
Ruben, Joseph 198
Ruggles, Wesley 465
Ruppell, Klaus-Ludwig 239
Rural Delivery, Ten Thousand B.C. see *RFD 10,000 B.C.*
Russell, Chuck 95
Ryder, Alfred 419

Sachs, Leonard 78
The Saga of the Phoenix see *Peacock King II*
Sahlin, Don 176, 356, 697, 779, 798
St. Amand, Tom 20, 21, 55–59, 165, 189, 204, 212, 215, 232, 282–287, 308, 320–326, 332, 340–341, 366, 386, 387, 502, 556, 572, 576, 577, 584, 589, 590, 603–604, 659, 770, 771, 773, 774, 784, 798, 809; PLATE GG
Salinger, Matt 106
Salkind, Alexander 604
Salkind, Ilya 604
Sam Lloyd's Famous Puzzles 552
Sands, Tommy 50
Sang d'un Poete, Le 695
Santa Claus 604–605, 796
Sarandon, Susan 338
Saturday the 14th 605, 795, 798
Saturday the 14th Strikes Back 606
Sawicki, Mark 668
Saxon, John 505
Sayles, John 535
Scherman, Tom 777
Scheuer, Steven H. 205
Schifrin, Lalo 108
Schnarre, Monica 424
Schneer, Charles 14, 15, 19, 206, 210, 242, 344, 352, 376, 471, 702, 715
Schoedsack, Ernest B. 392, 395, 406, 449, 451, 462, 465, 470
Schreck, Max 508–509
Schufftan, Eugen 447
Schwarzenegger, Arnold 418, 492, 677, 680–681
Science and Invention (magazine) 436
Science Fiction Film (book) 750
Science Fiction in the Cinema (book) 205
Scoggins, Tracy 171
Scott, Bruce 254
Scott, Ridley 338
Scott, Tony 338
Scream and Scream Again 288
Screamers 606–607, 670, 793
Screaming Mad George 29
Sears, Fred F. 206
Seawright, Roy 802
The Secret Adventures of Tom Thumb 607
Segall, Pamela 270
Sellers, Peter 695
Selznick, David O. 409
7 Faces of Dr Lao 16, 181, 355, 550, 551, 607–612, **609**, 693, 698, 759, 768, 793, 794, 796, 800, 802

Index

The 7th Voyage of Sinbad 4, 13, 45, 62, 69, 70, 73, 77, 111, 138, 189, 192, 194, 242, 259, 271, 284, 289, 354–357, 363, 375, 441, 442, 444, 472, 481, 504, 519, 520, 612–628, **613, 616, 621,** 688, 689, 690, 696, 702, 715, 796, 797, 805, 806, 807, 808, 809, 814; PLATES B, C

Seymour, Jane 629, 633

Shatner, William 658

Shay, Don 40, 85, 353, 386, 392

She (1935) 245, 304, 641

The She-Creature 177

Sheen, Charlie 47

Shelley, Barbara 303

Shelley, Mary 438

Sher, Jack 688

Shire, David 718

Shorr, Richard 778

Short, Bob 75

Shostrom, Mark 262

Sight and Sound (magazine) 510

Sims, Aaron 667

Simpson, Ivan 465

Sinbad and the Eye of the Tiger 5, 15, 16, 24, 127, 142, 243, 289, 298, 321, 367, 448, 456, 628–646, **630, 634, 638, 639, 644,** 704, 759, 796, 805, 807; PLATE I

Skaggs, Jimmie 559

Skeggs, Roy 761

Skelton, Red 786

Skotak, Dennis 47, 804

Skotak, Robert 47, 804

Skull Island see *The Most Dangerous Game*

The Sky Princess 745

Slapstick of Another Kind 795

Slave Girls from Beyond Infinity 646

The Sleeping Beauty 566, 745

The Sluggard 118

Small, Edward 354

Smith, Dick 338, 665

Smith, Kenneth F. 204, 803

Smith, Maggie 128, 130, 135

Smith, Thomas G. 321

Some Kind of a Nut 646–647, 793, 799, 800

Son of Blob see *Beware! The Blob*

The Son of Kong 11, 42, 49, 111, 122, 162, 427, 448, 454, 462, 647–656, **650, 654,** 732, 794, 797, 807, 808, 814

Sorvino, Paul 669

Sosalla, David 321, 576, 784, 799

Southsea Sweethearts 566

Spacehunter — Adventures in the Forbidden Zone 657, 796, 800

The Spaceman and King Arthur 658

Spartacus 48

Special Edition of Flesh Gordon see *Flesh Gordon*

Spellbound 288

SPFX (magazine) 359

Spielberg, Steven 23, 55, 151, 203, 247, 307, 326, 340, 380, 385–389, 488, 507, 548, 572, 716, 785

Spinell, Joe 663

Spivack, Murray 465

Sprott, Eoin 418

Stallone, Sylvester 530

Stanley and Livingstone 466

Star Trek (television series) 693

Star Trek III — The Search for Spock 658–659, 799

Star Wars 7, 8, 19, 20, 21, 22, 56, 84, 119, 126, 148, 188, 199, 211, 221, 228, 278, 321, 332, 412, 488, 497, 538, 572, 574, 633, 647, 657, 659, 659–661, 676, 689, 703, 716, 772, 791, 792, 797, 799, 803, 807

Starcrash 214, 661–664, **662, 663**

Starewicz, Ladislaw 10, 315

Starman 665

Starr, Ringo 54, 108–117; PLATE L

Steele, Barbara 536

Stein, Ronald 177

Steiner, Max 391–409, 449, 465, 470

Stephen King's It 666–667, 796, 800

Stetson, Mark 803

Stock, Nigel 783, 784, 785

Stoker, Bram 508

The Stolen Airship see *Ukradená Vzducholod*

The Stolen Dirigible see *Ukradená Vzducholod*

Stone, Lewis 427

Storke, Adam 319

The Story of King Midas 344

The Strangeness 667–668, 795

Strauss, Peter 657

Streep, Meryl 23

Stromberg, William R. 156–160, 499

Struss, Karl 411

Stuart, Alex Noel 288

Stuart, Alexander 288

The Stuff 669–670, 771, 791

The Stupids 670, 793

Subspecies 96, 97, 553, 671–673, 791, 794, 796; PLATE HH

Sullivan, Mark 96, 328, 329–331, 447, 799

Sullivan, Tom 222–224, 225, 799

Sundown — The Vampire in Retreat 317, 424, 499, 673–674

Superman (1978) 412, 604

Svankmajer, Jan 34–35, 237–238

Swift, Jonathan 14, 509, 688

The Sword and the Sorceror 503, 582

Szwarc, Jeannot 604

Taguchi, Tomoroh 682

Takacs, Tibor 268, 312

Tales from the Darkside: the Movie 674–675, 798

Tales from the Hood 675, 793

Tamblyn, Russ 50, 106, 696, 779

Tarantula 85, 92

Taste the Blood of Dracula 675–676

Taylor, Bill 777

Taylor, Dan 447

Taylor, Joan 207–210, 702, 705, 708

Taylor, Joyce 48

Taylor, Richard 103

Taylor, Rod 694

The Teddy Bears 10

The Ten Commandments 343

Terminal Force 676–677, 797

The Terminator 19, 24, 26, 102, 149, 156, 214, 264, 467, 492, 582, 664, 676, 677–679, 792, 796, 800; PLATE P

Terminator 2 — Judgment Day 8, 9, 23, 221, 257, 679–681, 795, 797, 800, 801, 804

Terry-Thomas 169, 352, 695, 780, 782

Tetsuo: The Iron Man 681–682

Tetsuo II: Body Hammer 682–683

Texas Chain Saw Massacre 307, 548

That Funny Feeling 683, 794

Thatcher, Torin 289, 354–365, 444, 612, 616

Theison, Rolf 668

Them! 85, 92, 322, 345, 465, 666

Thesiger, Ernest 444

They Live 99, 684–685, **684,** 794

The Thief of Bagdad (1924) 427, 428

The Thief of Bagdad (1940) 288, 695

The Thing (1951) 59

The Thing (1982) 20, 22, 95, 99, 149, 531, 539, 685–687, 693, 792, 794, 795; PLATE O

Things to Come 444

Thomerson, Tim 492, 493

Thompson, Lea 333–334

Thompson, Marshall 240, 256

Thonen, John 391

Thorburn, June 689, 695

Three Ages 687

The 3 Worlds of Gulliver 14,

39, 294, 304, 482, 529, 633, 688–692, 695, 704, 796, 814; PLATE C
Thunderball 494
Thunderbirds 1
Ticks 692–693, 793
Tilly, Jennifer 471
Time Bandits 31
The Time Machine 16, 17, **18**, 48, 86, 176, 338, 356, 551, 693–695, 698, 793, 794, 798, 802
Timegate 16, 769, 792, 794, 798, 799, 800; PLATE FF
Tippett, Phil 19–20, 25, **153**, 156–160, 187, 188–192, 228–230, 230–235, 279, 282–287, 312, 320–326, 328–331, 331, 335, 341, 385–389, 536, 556, 576, 577, 578, **583**, 584, 586, 587–595, 595–596, 601, 647, 660–661, 773, 774, 799, 803, 804, 807, 808, 809, 815, 816; PLATE AA
Tippett Studio vii, 153, 187, 211–218, 700
Tobey, Kenneth 345, 349, 351
Together in the Weather 566
Toho Studios 410, 534, 597
Tom Thumb 17, 50, 169, 176, 628, 695–698, **696**, 780, 793, 798, 800, 802, 809, 820
Took, Leigh 33
Topper 698
Topper Returns 699
Topper Takes a Trip 699, 802
The Tortoise and the Hare 344
Toxic Avenger 515
Trancers 558
Trcic, Mark 226
Tremors 700
Tremors II — Aftershocks 187, 699–700, 792, 799
Trevelyan, John 241
Trickel, Bart 387
A Trip to the Moon 9
Tripp, Louis 269
Trnka, Jiří 5, 807
Trog 40
Troll 700–701, 792
Troma 150
Tron 23
Trondeau, Bill 284
Troughton, Patrick 370, 371, 629
Tsuburaya, Eiji 411
Tsukamoto, Shinya 682
Tubby the Tuba 566
Tulips Shall Grow 566, 745
Tung, Ching Siu 124
Turner, George E. 392, 398, 426, 436, 465
Turner, Lana 777
Turner, Susan 686, 687

Tuttle, William 608
TV Movies (book) 205, 288, 426
20 Million Miles to Earth 13, 77, 167, 200, 206, 210, 235, 241, 294, 357, 448, 449, 626, 701–715, **705**, **710**, **714**, 796, 797, 805, 807, 808, 809, 814
20,000 Leagues Under the Sea 48, 471
20,000 Leagues Under the Sea (book) 748
Twilight of the Dogs 715, 793
Twilight Zone — The Movie 716–717, 791, 792, 794, 796
Two Musketeers see *Bláznova Kronika*
2001: A Space Odyssey 52, 151, 212, 490, 717–718, 802
2010 717, 718, 794, 803
The Two Year Holiday see *Ukradená Vzducholod*
Twohy, David 47
The Twonky 719, 800

Udenio, Fabiana 104
Ukradená Vzducholod 719–720, 800
Umbah 83
Unknown Island 282
Ustinov, Peter 94

Valcauda. Armando 661–664
Vallee, Rudy 342
The Valley of Gwangi vii, 5, 7, 15, 25, 64, 74, 247, 288, 289, 294, 301, 387, 448, 451, 472, 475, 495, 529, 542, 548, 688, 702, 704, 706, 720–744, **723**, **725**, **730**, **733**, **734**, **736**, **737**, **742**, 754, 758, 759, 761, 796, 806, 808, 809, 814; PLATE G
The Valley of Mist 85
Van Cleef, Lee 66
Van Damme, Jean-Claude 163
Van Dyke, Dick 646
Vargo, Mark 803
Variety Girl 745–747, **746**, 793, 800
Vaughn, Robert 381
VCE 279
Veevers, Wally 718
Vendetta de Ercole, La see *Goliath and the Dragon*
Vercoutere, Marcel 353
Verhoeven, Paul 582
Verne, Jules 14, 445, 471, 485, 748
Vetri, Victoria 760
Villemaire, James 269
Vinton, Will 6, 102, 467, 579–581, 803
A Visit to the Spiritualist 9

Vitagraph 9
Von Nordhoff, Baron Florenz 239
Von Sholly, Andrea 553
Vynález Zkázy 17, 51–53, 119, 486, 719, 720, 747–750, **748**, 800

Wake of the Red Witch 86
Walas, Chris 109, 116, 189, 308, 310, 330, 536, 572
Walken, Christopher 281
Wallace, Dee 337
Wallace, Tommy Lee 260
Wallace and Gromit 1
Waller, Don 589, 670
Waller, Fred 779
Walton, Harry vii, 20, 93, 193, 279, 283, 284, 320–326, 332, 342, 366, 419, 495, 502, 566, 584, 587, 589, 593, 594, 773, 774, 784, 799–800, 809; PLATES CC, EE
Wanamaker, Sam 629
Wang, Steve 311
War Eagles 11, 13
War in Toyland 10
The War of the Worlds 16, 58, 205, 207, 209, 608, 693, 695
Ward, Sophie 783, 786
Warner, David 99, 100
Warren, Gene vii, 17, **17**, **18**, 46, 48–49, 93, 163, 175–181, 256, 355, 384, 411, 419–420, 446, 466, 495, **550**, 549–551, 566, 609, 612, 647, 683, **696** , 697–698, 719, 745–747, **746**, 779, 800, 802
Warren, Gene, Jr. 29, 106–107, 257, 260, 308, 471, 492, 566, 657, 666, 678, 680, 800, 804
Wasson, Craig 505
Wathen, Stephen 464
Watkins, Karl 316
Wayne, John 86
Wayne, Patrick 289, 629
Waxwork 317, 424
Weapons of Destruction see *Vynález Zkázy*
Weaver, Sigourney 242, 275–278, 279
Webb, Roy 449
Welch, Raquel 515, 516, 518, 519, 520, 526, 758
Weller, Peter 32, 586
Wells, H.G. 14, 241, 444
The Werewolf 210
The Werewolf of London 343
West, Kit 803, 804
West of Kashmir: A Sherlock Holmes Adventure! 164, 750–751, **751**, 794; PLATE FF
Western Daze 745
The Westernettes 85

Index

When Dinosaurs Ruled the Earth 16, 19, 41, 109, 113, 117, 157, 312, 455, 485, 512, 519, 540, 554, 558, 751–769, **754**, **756**, **757**, **760**, **764**, **765**, **767**, 791, 794, 795, 803, 806, 808, 809, 814

When Worlds Collide 695

White, Brett 2–11

White, Frank 127

Whiting, Margaret 629

Whitlock, Albert 173, 339, 497

Who Framed Roger Rabbit 9, 255, 697, 769–771, **770**, 798, 799, 800, 804

The Wicked Stepmother 771

Widen, Gregory 281

Wilcox, Fred 257

Wilder, Gene 776

Williams, Clarence, III 675

Williams, Jason 248

Williams, JoBeth 549

Williams, John 126, 388, 412, 657, 659, 772

Williams, Richard 804

Williams, Robin 31, 326

Williamson, Nicol 579, 580

Willow 151, 771–776, **774**, 791, 795, 797, 799, 800

Willy Wonka and the Chocolate Factory 776–777, 791, 794, 797

Wilson, S. S. 39, 59, 181, 205, 288, 332, 419, 511, 692, 700, 724, 749, 766

Wing, Leslie 201

Wingrove, Ian 804

Winston, Stan 23, 385, 387, 665, 678, 681, 804

Winter, Alex 258

Winterbeast 777

Witchcraft Through the Ages see *Häxan*

Witches' Brew 777–778, 791

Wizard of Oz 169, 776

Wizards of the Demon Sword 537

Wonderful World of the Brothers Grimm 16, 17, 169, 181, 189, 355, 551, 698, 759, 778–783, **781**, 793, 794, 795, 796, 798, 800, 801, 809

Wong, Victor 649

Wood, Ed 211

Wood, Michael 803

Woods, Jack 217

Woodvine, John 195

Wray, Fay 179, 234, 391–409, 435, 449, 470, 522, 649, 652, 702, 760

Wright, Jenny 313

Wynn, Ed 50, 445

Wynn, Keenan 415, 536, 786

Yagher, Kevin 503, 504

Yates, George Worthing 206, 344

Yates, Peter 412, 413

Yeatman, Hoyt 29, 804

Yeaworth, Irving S. 175–181

Young, Aida 753, 766

Young, Alan 695

Young, Roland 444, 698, 699

Young Sherlock Holmes 19, 56, 279, 419, 558, 671, 697, 783–786, 797, 799, 800, 804; PLATE BB

Yuzna, Brian 103–105

Zappa, Frank 51

Zavitz, Lee 172, 802

Zeman, Karel 17, 51–54, 94–95, 117–124, 387, 485–488, 719–720, 747–750, 800

The Ziegfeld Follies 35, 786–787

Ziehm, Howard 248, 254

Ziff, Stuart 192, 803, 816

Zimbalist, Al 465

Zolotoi Klyuchik 787–789, 798

Zulu 472